THE
COMPLETE WORKS OF
WILLIAM SHAKESPEARE
VOLUME II

A NOTE TO THE READER

For each work in this set the editors have provided supplementary material that will help the reader better understand the work as both a play to be performed and a literary work.

In his general Foreword, Joseph Papp brings Shakespeare alive as he has for the audiences at his productions. The reader is also acquainted with the theater in which the plays were originally performed.

More detailed information precedes the text of each work: an Introduction places the work in context and discusses its structure and action, and performance notes give a director's view of the problems presented by the characters and themes of each work as interpreted in previous productions.

Each work is followed by a brief record of what is known about the original publication and performance and an attempt to date them; textual departures from the copy text; and an extensive essay on Shakespeare's sources. There are also suggestions for further reading on each work.

THE COMPLETE WORKS OF WILLIAM SHAKESPEARE

VOLUME II

THE TAMING OF THE SHREW

THE MERCHANT OF VENICE

ROMEO AND JULIET

KING JOHN

A MIDSUMMER NIGHT'S DREAM

RICHARD II

MUCH ADO ABOUT NOTHING

BANTAM BOOKS
Toronto • New York • London • Sydney • Auckland

THIS EDITION CREATED BY
QUALITY PAPERBACK BOOK CLUB

A Bantam Book / published by arrangement
with Scott, Foresman and Company

PRINTING HISTORY

Scott, Foresman edition published/January 1980
Bantam edition, with newly edited text and substantially
revised, edited, and amplified notes, introductions, and
other materials, published/February 1988
Valuable advice on staging matters has been
provided by Richard Hosley.
Collations checked by Eric Rasmussen.
Additional editorial assistance by Claire McEachern

Cover and display type designed by Charlotte Staub.

Bantam Books are published by Bantam Books,
a division of Bantam Doubleday Dell Publishing Group, Inc.
Its trademark, consisting of the words "Bantam Books"
and the portrayal of a rooster, is Registered in U.S. Patent
and Trademark Office and in other countries. Marca Registrada.
Bantam Books, 666 Fifth Avenue, New York, NY 10103.
Printed in the United States of America.

Foreword

It's hard to imagine, but Shakespeare wrote all of his plays with a quill pen, a goose feather whose hard end had to be sharpened frequently. How many times did he scrape the dull end to a point with his knife, dip it into the inkwell, and bring up, dripping wet, those wonderful words and ideas that are known all over the world?

In the age of word processors, typewriters, and ballpoint pens, we have almost forgotten the meaning of the word "blot." Yet when I went to school, in the 1930s, my classmates and I knew all too well what an inkblot from the metal-tipped pens we used would do to a nice clean page of a test paper, and we groaned whenever a splotch fell across the sheet. Most of us finished the school day with ink-stained fingers; those who were less careful also went home with ink-stained shirts, which were almost impossible to get clean.

When I think about how long it took me to write the simplest composition with a metal-tipped pen and ink, I can only marvel at how many plays Shakespeare scratched out with his goose-feather quill pen, year after year. Imagine him walking down one of the narrow cobblestoned streets of London, or perhaps drinking a pint of beer in his local alehouse. Suddenly his mind catches fire with an idea, or a sentence, or a previously elusive phrase. He is burning with impatience to write it down—but because he doesn't have a ballpoint pen or even a pencil in his pocket, he has to keep the idea in his head until he can get to his quill and parchment.

He rushes back to his lodgings on Silver Street, ignoring the vendors hawking brooms, the coaches clattering by, the piteous wails of beggars and prisoners. Bounding up the stairs, he snatches his quill and starts to write furiously, not even bothering to light a candle against the dusk. "To be, or not to be," he scrawls, "that is the—." But the quill point has gone dull, the letters have fattened out illegibly, and in the middle of writing one of the most famous passages in the history of dramatic literature, Shakespeare has to stop to sharpen his pen.

Taking a deep breath, he lights a candle now that it's dark, sits down, and begins again. By the time the candle has burned out and the noisy apprentices of his French Huguenot landlord have quieted down, Shakespeare has finished Act 3 of *Hamlet* with scarcely a blot.

Early the next morning, he hurries through the fog of a London summer morning to the rooms of his colleague Richard Burbage, the actor for whom the role of Hamlet is being written. He finds Burbage asleep and snoring loudly, sprawled across his straw mattress. Not only had the actor performed in *Henry V* the previous afternoon, but he had then gone out carousing all night with some friends who had come to the performance.

Shakespeare shakes his friend awake, until, bleary-eyed, Burbage sits up in his bed. "Dammit, Will," he grumbles, "can't you let an honest man sleep?" But the playwright, his eyes shining and the words tumbling out of his mouth, says, "Shut up and listen—tell me what you think of *this*!"

He begins to read to the still half-asleep Burbage, pacing around the room as he speaks. ". . . Whether 'tis nobler in the mind to suffer the slings and arrows of outrageous fortune—"

Burbage interrupts, suddenly wide awake, "That's excellent, very good, 'the slings and arrows of outrageous fortune,' yes, I think it will work quite well. . . ." He takes the parchment from Shakespeare and murmurs the lines to himself, slowly at first but with growing excitement.

The sun is just coming up, and the words of one of Shakespeare's most famous soliloquies are being uttered for the first time by the first actor ever to bring Hamlet to life. It must have been an exhilarating moment.

Shakespeare wrote most of his plays to be performed live by the actor Richard Burbage and the rest of the Lord Chamberlain's men (later the King's men). Today, however, our first encounter with the plays is usually in the form of the printed word. And there is no question that reading Shakespeare for the first time isn't easy. His plays aren't comic books or magazines or the dime-store detective novels I read when I was young. A lot of his sentences are complex. Many of his words are no longer used in our everyday speech. His profound thoughts are often condensed into poetry, which is not as straightforward as prose.

Yet when you hear the words spoken aloud, a lot of the language may strike you as unexpectedly modern. For Shakespeare's plays, like any dramatic work, weren't really meant to be read; they were meant to be spoken, seen, and performed. It's amazing how lines that are so troublesome in print can flow so naturally and easily when spoken.

I think it was precisely this music that first fascinated me. When I was growing up, Shakespeare was a stranger to me. I had no particular interest in him, for I was from a different cultural tradition. It never occurred to me that his plays might be more than just something to "get through" in school, like science or math or the physical education requirement we had to fulfill. My passions then were movies, radio, and vaudeville—certainly not Elizabethan drama.

I was, however, fascinated by words and language. Because I grew up in a home where Yiddish was spoken, and English was only a second language, I was acutely sensitive to the musical sounds of different languages and had an ear for lilt and cadence and rhythm in the spoken word. And so I loved reciting poems and speeches even as a very young child. In first grade I learned lots of short nature verses— "Who has seen the wind?," one of them began. My first foray into drama was playing the role of Scrooge in Charles Dickens's *A Christmas Carol* when I was eight years old. I liked summoning all the scorn and coldness I possessed and putting them into the words, "Bah, humbug!"

From there I moved on to longer and more famous poems and other works by writers of the 1930s. Then, in junior high school, I made my first acquaintance with Shakespeare through his play *Julius Caesar*. Our teacher, Miss McKay, assigned the class a passage to memorize from the opening scene of the play, the one that begins "Wherefore rejoice? What conquest brings he home?" The passage seemed so wonderfully theatrical and alive to me, and the experience of memorizing and reciting it was so much fun, that I went on to memorize another speech from the play on my own.

I chose Mark Antony's address to the crowd in Act 3,

scene 2, which struck me then as incredibly high drama. Even today, when I speak the words, I feel the same thrill I did that first time. There is the strong and athletic Antony descending from the raised pulpit where he has been speaking, right into the midst of a crowded Roman square. Holding the torn and bloody cloak of the murdered Julius Caesar in his hand, he begins to speak to the people of Rome:

> If you have tears, prepare to shed them now.
> You all do know this mantle. I remember
> The first time ever Caesar put it on;
> 'Twas on a summer's evening in his tent,
> That day he overcame the Nervii.
> Look, in this place ran Cassius' dagger through.
> See what a rent the envious Casca made.
> Through this the well-belovèd Brutus stabbed,
> And as he plucked his cursèd steel away,
> Mark how the blood of Caesar followed it,
> As rushing out of doors to be resolved
> If Brutus so unkindly knocked or no;
> For Brutus, as you know, was Caesar's angel.
> Judge, O you gods, how dearly Caesar loved him!
> This was the most unkindest cut of all . . .

I'm not sure now that I even knew Shakespeare had written a lot of other plays, or that he was considered "timeless," "universal," or "classic"—but I knew a good speech when I heard one, and I found the splendid rhythms of Antony's rhetoric as exciting as anything I'd ever come across.

Fifty years later, I still feel that way. Hearing good actors speak Shakespeare gracefully and naturally is a wonderful experience, unlike any other I know. There's a satisfying fullness to the spoken word that the printed page just can't convey. This is why seeing the plays of Shakespeare performed live in a theater is the best way to appreciate them. If you can't do that, listening to sound recordings or watching film versions of the plays is the next best thing.

But if you do start with the printed word, use the play as a script. Be an actor yourself and say the lines out loud. Don't worry too much at first about words you don't immediately understand. Look them up in the footnotes or a dictionary, but don't spend too much time on this. It is more profitable (and fun) to get the sense of a passage and sing it out. Speak naturally, almost as if you were talking to a friend, but be sure to enunciate the words properly. You'll be surprised at how much you understand simply by speaking the speech "trippingly on the tongue," as Hamlet advises the Players.

You might start, as I once did, with a speech from *Julius Caesar*, in which the tribune (city official) Marullus scolds the commoners for transferring their loyalties so quickly from the defeated and murdered general Pompey to the newly victorious Julius Caesar:

> Wherefore rejoice? What conquest brings he home?
> What tributaries follow him to Rome
> To grace in captive bonds his chariot wheels?
> You blocks, you stones, you worse than senseless
>   things!
> O you hard hearts, you cruel men of Rome,
> Knew you not Pompey? Many a time and oft
> Have you climbed up to walls and battlements,
> To towers and windows, yea, to chimney tops,
> Your infants in your arms, and there have sat
> The livelong day, with patient expectation,
> To see great Pompey pass the streets of Rome.

With the exception of one or two words like "wherefore" (which means "why," not "where"), "tributaries" (which means "captives"), and "patient expectation" (which means patient waiting), the meaning and emotions of this speech can be easily understood.

From here you can go on to dialogues or other more challenging scenes. Although you may stumble over unaccustomed phrases or unfamiliar words at first, and even fall flat when you're crossing some particularly rocky passages, pick yourself up and stay with it. Remember that it takes time to feel at home with anything new. Soon you'll come to recognize Shakespeare's unique sense of humor and way of saying things as easily as you recognize a friend's laughter.

And then it will just be a matter of choosing which one of Shakespeare's plays you want to tackle next. As a true fan of his, you'll find that you're constantly learning from his plays. It's a journey of discovery that you can continue for the rest of your life. For no matter how many times you read or see a particular play, there will always be something new there that you won't have noticed before.

Why do so many thousands of people get hooked on Shakespeare and develop a habit that lasts a lifetime? What can he really say to us today, in a world filled with inventions and problems he never could have imagined? And how do you get past his special language and difficult sentence structure to understand him?

The best way to answer these questions is to go see a live production. You might not know much about Shakespeare, or much about the theater, but when you watch actors performing one of his plays on the stage, it will soon become clear to you why people get so excited about a playwright who lived hundreds of years ago.

For the story—what's happening in the play—is the most accessible part of Shakespeare. In *A Midsummer Night's Dream*, for example, you can immediately understand the situation: a girl is chasing a guy who's chasing a girl who's chasing another guy. No wonder *A Midsummer Night's Dream* is one of the most popular of Shakespeare's plays: it's about one of the world's most popular pastimes— falling in love.

But the course of true love never did run smooth, as the young suitor Lysander says. Often in Shakespeare's comedies the girl whom the guy loves doesn't love him back, or she loves him but he loves someone else. In *The Two Gentlemen of Verona*, Julia loves Proteus, Proteus loves Sylvia, and Sylvia loves Valentine, who is Proteus's best friend. In the end, of course, true love prevails, but not without lots of complications along the way.

For in all of his plays—comedies, histories, and tragedies—Shakespeare is showing you human nature. His characters act and react in the most extraordinary ways—and sometimes in the most incomprehensible ways. People are always trying to find motivations for what a character does. They ask, "Why does Iago want to destroy Othello?"

The answer, to me, is very simple—because that's the way Iago is. That's just his nature. Shakespeare doesn't explain his characters; he sets them in motion—and away they go. He doesn't worry about whether they're likable or not. He's interested in interesting people, and his most fascinating characters are those who are unpredictable. If you lean back in your chair early on in one of his plays, thinking you've figured out what Iago or Shylock (in *The Merchant of Venice*) is up to, don't be too sure—because that great judge of human nature, Shakespeare, will surprise you every time.

He is just as wily in the way he structures a play. In *Macbeth*, a comic scene is suddenly introduced just after the bloodiest and most treacherous slaughter imaginable, of a guest and king by his host and subject, when in comes a drunk porter who has to go to the bathroom. Shakespeare is tickling your emotions by bringing a stand-up comic on-stage right on the heels of a savage murder.

It has taken me thirty years to understand even some of these things, and so I'm not suggesting that Shakespeare is immediately understandable. I've gotten to know him not through theory but through practice, the practice of the *living* Shakespeare—the playwright of the theater.

Of course the plays are a great achievement of dramatic literature, and they should be studied and analyzed in schools and universities. But you must always remember, when reading all the words *about* the playwright and his plays, that *Shakespeare's* words came first and that in the end there is nothing greater than a single actor on the stage speaking the lines of Shakespeare.

Everything important that I know about Shakespeare comes from the practical business of producing and directing his plays in the theater. The task of classifying, criticizing, and editing Shakespeare's printed works I happily leave to others. For me, his plays really do live on the stage, not on the page. That is what he wrote them for and that is how they are best appreciated.

Although Shakespeare lived and wrote hundreds of years ago, his name rolls off my tongue as if he were my brother. As a producer and director, I feel that there is a professional relationship between us that spans the centuries. As a human being, I feel that Shakespeare has enriched my understanding of life immeasurably. I hope you'll let him do the same for you.
Joseph Papp

Joseph Papp gratefully acknowledges the help of Elizabeth Kirkland in preparing this Foreword.

The Playhouse

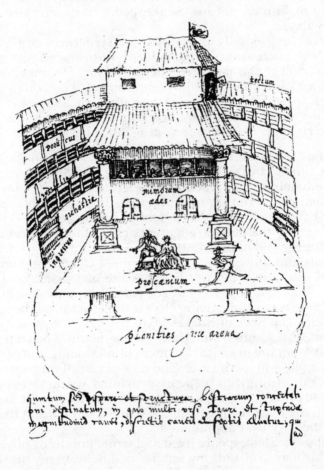

This early copy of a drawing by Johannes de Witt of the Swan Theatre in London (c. 1596), made by his friend Arend van Buchell, is the only surviving contemporary sketch of the interior of a public theater in the 1590s.

From other contemporary evidence, including the stage directions and dialogue of Elizabethan plays, we can surmise that the various public theaters where Shakespeare's plays were produced (the Theatre, the Curtain, the Globe) resembled the Swan in many important particulars, though there must have been some variations as well. The public playhouses were essentially round, or polygonal, and open to the sky, forming an acting arena approximately 70 feet in diameter; they did not have a large curtain with which to open and close a scene, such as we see today in opera and some traditional theater. A platform measuring approximately 43 feet across and 27 feet deep, referred to in the de Witt drawing as the *proscaenium*, projected into the yard, *planities sive arena*. The roof, *tectum*, above the stage and supported by two pillars, could contain machinery for ascents and descents, as were required in several of Shakespeare's late plays. Above this roof was a hut, shown in the drawing with a flag flying atop it and a trumpeter at its door announcing the performance of a play. The underside of the stage roof, called the heavens, was usually richly decorated with symbolic figures of the sun, the moon, and the constellations. The platform stage stood at a height of 5½ feet or so above the yard, providing room under the stage for underworldly effects. A trapdoor, which is not visible in this drawing, gave access to the space below.

The structure at the back of the platform (labeled *mimorum aedes*), known as the tiring-house because it was the actors' attiring (dressing) space, featured at least two doors, as shown here. Some theaters seem to have also had a discovery space, or curtained recessed alcove, perhaps between the two doors—in which Falstaff could have hidden from the sheriff (*1 Henry IV*, 2.4) or Polonius could have eavesdropped on Hamlet and his mother (*Hamlet*, 3.4). This discovery space probably gave the actors a means of access to and from the tiring-house. Curtains may also have been hung in front of the stage doors on occasion. The de Witt drawing shows a gallery above the doors that extends across the back and evidently contains spectators. On occasions when action "above" demanded the use of this space, as when Juliet appears at her "window" (*Romeo and Juliet*, 2.2 and 3.5), the gallery seems to have been used by the actors, but large scenes there were impractical.

The three-tiered auditorium is perhaps best described by Thomas Platter, a visitor to London in 1599 who saw on that occasion Shakespeare's *Julius Caesar* performed at the Globe:

> The playhouses are so constructed that they play on a raised platform, so that everyone has a good view. There are different galleries and places [*orchestra, sedilia, porticus*], however, where the seating is better and more comfortable and therefore more expensive. For whoever cares to stand below only pays one English penny, but if he wishes to sit, he enters by another door [*ingressus*] and pays another penny, while if he desires to sit in the most comfortable seats, which are cushioned, where he not only sees everything well but can also be seen, then he pays yet another English penny at another door. And during the performance food and drink are carried round the audience, so that for what one cares to pay one may also have refreshment.

Scenery was not used, though the theater building itself was handsome enough to invoke a feeling of order and hierarchy that lent itself to the splendor and pageantry onstage. Portable properties, such as thrones, stools, tables, and beds, could be carried or thrust on as needed. In the scene pictured here by de Witt, a lady on a bench, attended perhaps by her waiting-gentlewoman, receives the address of a male figure. If Shakespeare had written *Twelfth Night* by 1596 for performance at the Swan, we could imagine Malvolio appearing like this as he bows before the Countess Olivia and her gentlewoman, Maria.

From the 1978 New York Shakespeare Festival production of *The Taming of the Shrew,* with Meryl Streep as Katharina and Raul Julia as Petruchio, directed by Wilford Leach at the Delacorte Theater in Central Park.

THE
TAMING OF
THE SHREW

THE TAMING OF THE SHREW

Introductory Material
Foreword by Joseph Papp
Introduction
The Taming of the Shrew
in Performance

THE PLAY

Supplementary Material
Date and Text
Textual Notes
Shakespeare's Sources
Further Reading

Foreword

Does *The Taming of the Shrew* have anything to say to us today, or is it hopelessly outdated by its male chauvinism? After all, here's a guy, Petruchio, who starves his wife, Kate, half to death, mocks and embarrasses her publicly, calls her "my goods, my chattels . . . my house, My household stuff, my field, my barn, My horse, my ox, my ass, my anything," and hurls verbal abuse at her—all in the name of taming her, the shrew. After a play full of this kind of treatment from her husband, Kate does indeed seem chastened: in her last speech she advises the other "froward wives" to honor and obey their men and acknowledges her own submission by putting her hand beneath Petruchio's foot. "Such duty as the subject owes the prince," she says, "Even such a woman oweth to her husband."

This is certainly bound to raise the hackles of many women, and even some men, who feel that Kate has betrayed the principles of the women's movement. But if we approach the play unburdened by present-day politics, we will find that the last speech is the culmination of a hard-fought and hard-won love between Kate and Petruchio, and that the notion of one-upmanship isn't part of the picture.

Shakespeare says quite plainly that if two people are really in love, the issue of who does what for whom does not exist. It's taken for granted in *The Taming of the Shrew* that Kate's last speech is certainly not the basis for their relationship, but will serve to bring out the best in Petruchio. Remember—Kate isn't the only one who has learned a lesson. The teacher Petruchio has also been a student and beneficiary of the painful lessons both have undergone.

On the stage, the playing is the thing. For example, when Meryl Streep and Raul Julia played Kate and Petruchio at the Delacorte Theater in Central Park, it was quite clear that the two characters cared for each other intensely. These wonderful actors entered the spirit of the play so wholeheartedly that they brought the characters to life and made what happens in the play totally believable.

Kate is one of Shakespeare's intelligent women who will not be pushed around. She is dumbfounded when Petruchio attempts to do just that. But his intention, as she discovers, is not to dominate but to rid her of an intractable manner she herself dislikes; he alone has the chutzpah to tackle her.

Petruchio deserves a medal for understanding Kate so well;
instead, Shakespeare gave him a play!

JOSEPH PAPP

JOSEPH PAPP GRATEFULLY ACKNOWLEDGES THE HELP OF
ELIZABETH KIRKLAND IN PREPARING THIS FOREWORD.

Introduction

Like his other early comedies, *The Taming of the Shrew* (c. 1592–1594) looks forward to Shakespeare's mature comic drama in several ways. By skillfully juxtaposing two plots and an induction, or framing plot, it offers contrasting views on the battle of the sexes. This debate on the nature of the love relationship will continue through many later comedies. The play also adroitly manipulates the device of mistaken identity, as in *The Comedy of Errors*, inverting appearance and reality, dream and waking, and the master-servant relationship in order to create a transformed Saturnalian world anticipating that of *A Midsummer Night's Dream* and *Twelfth Night*.

The Induction sets up the theme of illusion, using an old motif known as "The Sleeper Awakened" (as found for example in *The Arabian Nights*). This device frames the main action of the play, giving to it an added perspective. *The Taming of the Shrew* purports in fact to be a play within a play, an entertainment devised by a witty nobleman as a practical joke on a drunken tinker, Christopher Sly. The jest is to convince Sly that he is not Sly at all, but an aristocrat suffering delusions. Outlandishly dressed in new finery, Sly is invited to witness a play from the gallery over the stage. In a rendition called *The Taming of a Shrew* (printed in 1594 and now generally thought to be taken from an earlier version of Shakespeare's play, employing a good deal of conscious originality along with some literary borrowing and even plagiarism), the framing plot concludes by actually putting Sly back out on the street in front of the alehouse where he was found. He awakes, recalls the play as a dream, and proposes to put the vision to good use by taming his own wife. Whether this ending reflects an epilogue now lost from the text of Shakespeare's play cannot be said, but it does reinforce the idea of the play as Sly's fantasy. Like Puck at the end of *A Midsummer Night's Dream*, urging us to dismiss what we have seen as the product of our own slumbering, Sly continually reminds us that the play is only an illusion or shadow.

With repeated daring, Shakespeare calls attention to the

contrived nature of his artifact, the play. When, for example, Sly is finally convinced that he is in fact a noble lord
recovering from madness and lustily proposes to hasten off
to bed with his long-neglected wife, we are comically aware
that the "wife" is an impostor, a young page in disguise. Yet
this counterfeiting of roles is no more unreal than the employment of Elizabethan boy-actors for the parts of Katharina and Bianca in the "real" play. As we watch Sly
watching a play, levels of meaning interplay in this evoca-
tive fashion. Again, the paintings offered to Sly by his new
attendants call attention to art's ability to confound illusion
and reality. In one painting, Cytherea is hidden by reeds
"Which seem to move and wanton with her breath / Even as
the waving sedges play wi' th' wind," and in another painting Io appears "As lively painted as the deed was done" (Induction. 2.50–56). Sly's function, then, is that of the naive
observer who inverts illusion and reality in his mind, concluding that his whole previous life of tinkers and alehouses and Cicely Hackets has been unreal. As his attendants explain to him, "These fifteen years you have been in
a dream, / Or when you waked, so waked as if you slept"
(79–80). We as audience laugh at Sly's naiveté, and yet we
too are moved and even transformed by an artistic vision
that we know to be illusory.

Like Sly, many characters in the main action of the play
are persuaded, or nearly persuaded, to be what they are
not. Lucentio and Tranio exchange roles of master and servant. Bianca's supposed tutors are in fact her wooers, using
their lessons to disguise messages of love. Katharina is prevailed upon by her husband, Petruchio, to declare that the
sun is the moon and that an old gentleman (Vincentio) is a
fair young maiden. Vincentio is publicly informed that he is
an impostor, and that the "real" Vincentio (the Pedant) is at
that very moment looking at him out of the window of his
son Lucentio's house. This last ruse does not fool the real
Vincentio, but it nearly succeeds in fooling everyone else.
Baptista Minola is about to commit Vincentio to jail for the
infamous slander of asserting that the supposed Lucentio
is only a servant in disguise. Vincentio, as the newly arrived
stranger, is able to see matters as they really are; but the
dwellers of Padua have grown so accustomed to the mad

and improbable fictions of their life that they are not easily
awakened to reality.

Shakespeare multiplies these devices of illusion by com-
bining two entirely distinct plots, each concerned at least in
part with the comic inversion of appearance and reality: the
shrew-taming plot involving Petruchio and Kate, and the
more conventional romantic plot involving Lucentio and
Bianca. The latter plot is derived from the *Supposes* of
George Gascoigne, a play first presented at Gray's Inn in
1566 as translated from Ariosto's neoclassical comedy *I
Suppositi*, 1509. (Ariosto's work in turn was based upon
Terence's *Eunuchus* and Plautus' *Captivi*.) The "Supposes"
are mistaken identities or misunderstandings, the kind of
hilarious farcical mix-ups Shakespeare had already experi-
mented with in *The Comedy of Errors*. Shakespeare has, as
usual, both romanticized his source and moralized it in a
characteristically English way. The heroine, who in the Roman comedy of Plautus and Terence would have been a
courtesan, and who in *Supposes* is made pregnant by her
clandestine lover, remains thoroughly chaste in Shakespeare's comedy. Consequently she has no need for a pan-
der, or go-between, such as the bawdy duenna, or nurse, of
Supposes. The satire directed at the heroine's unwelcome
old wooer is far less savage than in *Supposes*, where the
"pantaloon," Dr. Cleander, is a villainously corrupt lawyer
epitomizing the depravity of "respectable" society. Despite
Shakespeare's modifications, however, the basic plot remains an effort to foil parental authority. The young lovers,
choosing each other for romantic reasons, must fend off the
materialistic calculations of their parents.

In a stock situation of this sort, the character types are
also conventional. Gremio, the aged wealthy wooer, is actually labeled a "pantaloon" in the text (3.1.36–37) to stress
his neoclassical ancestry. (Lean and foolish old wooers of
this sort were customarily dressed in pantaloons, slippers,
and spectacles on the Italian stage.) Gremio is typically
"the graybeard," and Baptista Minola is "the narrow-
prying father" (3.2.145–146). Even though Shakespeare ren-
ders these characters far less unattractive than in
Supposes, their worldly behavior still invites reprisal from
the young. Since Baptista Minola insists on selling his

daughter Bianca to the highest bidder, it is fitting that her wealthiest suitor (the supposed Lucentio) should turn out in the end to be a penniless servant (Tranio) disguised as a man of affluence and position. In his traditional role as the clever servant of neoclassical comedy, Tranio skillfully apes the mannerisms of respectable society. He can deal in the mere surfaces, clothes or reputation, out of which a man's social importance is created, and can even furnish himself with a rich father. Gremio and Baptista deserve to be foiled because they accept the illusion of respectability as real.

Even the romantic lovers of this borrowed plot are largely conventional. To be sure, Shakespeare emphasizes their virtuous qualities and their sincerity. He adds Hortensio (not in *Supposes*) to provide Lucentio with a genuine, if foolish, rival and Bianca with two wooers closer to her age than old Gremio. Lucentio and Bianca deserve their romantic triumph; they are self-possessed, witty, and steadfast to each other. Yet we know very little about them, nor have they seen deeply into each other. Lucentio's love talk is laden with conventional images in praise of Bianca's dark eyes and scarlet lips. At the play's end, he discovers, to his surprise, that she can be willful, even disobedient. Has her appearance of virtue concealed something from him and from us? Because the relationship between these lovers is superficial, they are appropriately destined to a superficial marriage as well. The passive Bianca becomes the proud and defiant wife.

By contrast, Petruchio and Kate are the more interesting lovers, whose courtship involves mutual self-discovery. Admittedly, we must not overstate the case. Especially at first, these lovers are also stock types: the shrew tamer and his proverbially shrewish wife. Although Shakespeare seems not to have used any single source for this plot, he was well acquainted with crude misogynistic stories demonstrating the need for putting women in their place. In a ballad called *A Merry Jest of a Shrewd and Curst Wife Lapped in Morel's Skin* (printed c. 1550), for example, the husband tames his shrewish spouse by flaying her bloody with birch rods and then wrapping her in the freshly salted skin of a plow horse named Morel. (This shrewish wife, like Kate, has an obedient and gentle younger sister who is their father's favorite.)

Other features of Shakespeare's plot can be found in similar tales: the tailor scolded for devising a gown of outlandish fashion (Gerard Legh's *Accidence of Armory*, 1562), the wife obliged to agree with her husband's assertion of some patent falsehood (Don Juan Manuel's *El Conde Lucanor*, 1335), and the three husbands' wager on their wives' obedience (*The Book of the Knight of La Tour-Landry*, printed 1484). In the raw spirit of this sexist tradition, so unlike the refined Italianate sentiment of his other plot, Shakespeare introduces Petruchio as a man of reckless bravado who is ready to marry the ugliest or sharpest-tongued woman alive so long as she is rich. However much he may later be attracted by Kate's fiery spirit, his first attraction to her is crassly financial. Kate is, moreover, a thoroughly disagreeable young woman at first, described by those who know her as "intolerable curst / And shrewd, and froward" (1.2.88–89) and aggressive in her bullying of Bianca. She and Petruchio meet as grotesque comic counterparts. At the play's end, the traditional pattern of male dominance and female acquiescence is still prominent. Kate achieves peace only by yielding to a socially ordained patriarchal framework in which a husband is the princely ruler of his wife.

Within this male-oriented frame of reference, however, Petruchio and Kate are surprisingly like Benedick and Beatrice of *Much Ado about Nothing*. Petruchio, for all his rant, is increasingly drawn to Kate by her spirit. As wit-combatants they are worthy of each other's enmity—or love. No one else in the play is a fit match for either of them. Kate too is attracted to Petruchio, despite her war of words. Her guise of hostility is part defensive protection, part testing of his sincerity. If she is contemptuous of the wooers she has seen till now, she has good reason to be. We share her condescension toward the aged Gremio or the laughably inept Hortensio. She rightly fears that her father wishes to dispose of her so that he may auction off Bianca to the wealthiest competitor. Kate's jaded view of such marriage brokering is entirely defensible. Not surprisingly she first views Petruchio, whose professed intentions are far from reassuring, as another mere adventurer in love. She is impressed by his "line" in wooing her, but needs to test his constancy and sincerity. Possibly she is prepared to accept the prevailing Elizabethan view of marriage, with its dominant role for the husband, but only if she can choose a man deserving of her respect. She puts down most men with a shrewish manner that challenges their very masculinity; Petruchio is the first to be man enough to "board" her. Kate's rejection of men does not leave her very happy, however genuine her disdain is for most of those who come to woo. Petruchio's "schooling" is therefore curative. Having wooed and partly won her, he tests her with his late arrival at the marriage, his unconventional dress, and his crossing all her desires. In this display of willfulness, he shows her an ugly picture of what she herself is like. Most of all, however, he succeeds because he insists on what she too desires: a well-defined relationship tempered by mutual respect and love. Kate is visibly a more contented person at the play's end. Her closing speech, with its fine blend of irony and self-conscious hyperbole, together with its seriousness of concern, expresses beautifully the way in which Kate's independence of spirit and her newfound acceptance of a domestic role are successfully fused.

The Taming of the Shrew
in Performance

It is an odd kind of tribute to *The Taming of the Shrew* that it has inspired over the centuries so many adaptations and offshoots. Although Shakespeare's original play was popular in its own day and was kept in repertory seemingly through much of Shakespeare's lifetime, only in greatly altered forms did it enjoy stage success through much of the seventeenth, eighteenth, and early nineteenth centuries. These transformations were probably a response to the play's uncanny ability to make audiences of any era uncomfortable with its presentation of the war of the sexes.

Most adaptations seem to have had a twofold objective: to reinterpret the problematic taming and submission of Kate, and to do something with the unfinished Induction, or frame, of Christopher Sly. From the first, adapters of the play have felt a need to exaggerate, on both sides, the aggression between male and female. The anonymous *The Taming of a Shrew* (derived, sometime before 1594, from a now-lost early version of Shakespeare's play) specifies at one point that Ferando, the renamed Petruchio, is to enter *"with a piece of meat upon his dagger's point"*—presumably to terrorize Kate. Conversely, *The Woman's Prize, or The Tamer Tamed*, written by John Fletcher (Shakespeare's successor as chief dramatist to the acting company, the King's men) in 1611, provides a comic counterpart to the male victory in Shakespeare's play. In Fletcher's version Petruchio, remarried after Kate's death, meets his match in a woman who has nothing but scorn for tameness in wives. Petruchio has to learn to pacify his wife with gifts and is locked up and deceived by her, until a happy ending of sorts is worked out. Fletcher's premise, it would seem, is that the story of a husband's triumph in marriage ought to be answered by one in which the wife triumphs in her turn.

In subsequent adaptations, Shakespeare's portrayal of sexual warfare is pushed both toward further brutalizing the misogynistic elements (already present in Shakespeare's source, the ballad called *A Shrewd and Curst Wife*

Lapped in Morel's Skin) and toward giving the woman a chance to get back at her male tormentor. In *Sauny the Scot* by John Lacy, produced at the Drury Lane Theatre in 1667, Petruchio is indeed a brute. He threatens to whip Kate if she refuses him in marriage, insists she is suffering from a toothache so that he can summon a surgeon to pull one of her teeth, proclaims her dead and actually lashes her to her bier, and then complacently commends his wife when at last she submits to him. She is allowed only two lines to explain her views on the subject of obedience. The title of this adaptation comes from the name of Petruchio's comic servant (Grumio in Shakespeare), who speaks in such a broad Scottish dialect that Samuel Pepys, in 1667, had trouble understanding what was said. James Worsdale's *A Cure for a Scold* (Theatre Royal, Drury Lane, 1735, with Charles Macklin as Petruchio) retained much of Lacy's misogynistic humor, including the tooth-drawing episode. Lacy and Worsdale both provide their shrews with hints of reprisal: the women vow to tame their husbands if given a chance, and Worsdale's Peg Worthy (the renamed Kate, played by Kitty Clive) submits to her husband only after she has feigned death and thereby tricked him into demonstrating his affection for her. These versions by Lacy and Worsdale were immensely popular throughout the Restoration and the first half of the eighteenth century, eclipsing Shakespeare's original in the repertory.

Their popular successor, David Garrick's *Catharine and Petruchio*, held the stage without serious rival for nearly a century after its first performance in 1754 at Drury Lane. Like its predecessors, it at once brutalizes and intensifies the encounters of Kate and Petruchio. In order to focus on the warring lovers, Garrick eliminated both the Induction and the whole Bianca-Lucentio plot, and Kate's father, in this version, is unrelenting in his insistence that she marry or be disowned. It may have been Garrick who first gave Petruchio a whip; in any event, for decades afterward it was an obligatory prop. Yet Kate's speech after her wooing, in Act 1, includes a promise (or threat) of independence of spirit: "Sister Bianca now shall see / The poor abandoned Catharine, as she calls me, / Can hold her head as high, and be as proud, / And make her husband stoop unto her lure, / As she or e'er a wife in Padua." Garrick's instincts were sound in appraising the tastes of his day, for his shortened version (often part of a double bill) remained successful in England and America throughout the nineteenth century. In 1867, Henry Irving performed it with Ellen Terry at the Queen's Theatre, and in 1897 Herbert Beerbohm Tree presented Garrick's shortened version as an afterpiece for the opening night of Her Majesty's Theatre.

English audiences did not see a version close to Shakespeare's until 1844, when the play was produced by Benjamin Webster at the Haymarket Theatre with the Induction intact and with an attempt at Elizabethan costuming as conceived by J. R. Planché. The mise-en-scène was laid in a nobleman's hall as though for the entertainment of Christopher Sly, with no more scenery than could be supplied by two screens and a pair of curtains. Players in the Induction were made up to resemble playwrights Shakespeare and Ben Jonson and the actor Richard Tarlton. The dialogue of the play as a whole kept reasonably close to the original. In 1856 Samuel Phelps produced a slightly cut version of Shakespeare's text at the Sadler's Wells Theatre. He preserved the Induction (playing Sly himself), excised most of the play's bawdy, and softened Kate's character. The United States was provided with its first view of Shakespeare's play in 1887 by Augustin Daly at his theater in New York. The production featured handsome sets inspired by the painter Veronese and a commanding performance of Kate by Ada Rehan. In 1913 at the Prince of Wales Theatre, John Martin-Harvey, advised by William Poel, presented a robust, good-natured *Taming of the Shrew* that attempted to recreate the staging conventions of the Elizabethan theater.

Ever since being reestablished in its own right, *The Taming of the Shrew* has challenged actors and audiences alike to come to terms with its delicate balancing of misogyny and forbearance in marriage. Inevitably the critical point in a performance is the moment of Kate's final speech. How are we to take her gesture of submission? As early as 1908 in Melbourne, Australia, and then in 1914 in New York, Margaret Anglin delivered Kate's long speech on obedience with a mocking suggestion of a private understanding between her and her husband. Conversely, more conventional productions have succeeded with audiences that were still willing to enjoy a comedy of male triumph in the battle of the sexes. Oscillating between these poles of interpretation, the play has become something of a problem play. At the Shakespeare Festival performance in Ashland, Oregon, in 1977, when Petruchio refused to accept Kate's gesture of placing her hand beneath his foot and instead returned her cap to her, audiences were divided as to whether the belated gesture made up for all that Kate had undergone or was simply an attempt on the part of the acting company to be up-to-date.

The Royal Shakespeare Company, at Stratford-upon-Avon in 1978, confronted the potential offensiveness of Kate's submission by refusing to underplay the difficulty: Kate and the other women smouldered in resentment, while the men basked in complacency. One reviewer congratulated the director, Michael Bogdanov, on the honesty with which he tackled this "barbaric and disgusting" play. In 1975, at the Open Space Theatre in London, Charles Marowitz's adaptation called *The Shrew* had already taken this line of interpretation to its logical but frightening conclusion by playing the schooling of Kate as an illustration of the techniques of brainwashing. The ordeal ended in madness and rape for Katharina, and her final speech of submission was delivered as though by rote.

More temperately responsive to Shakespeare's text was the encounter of Meryl Streep and Raul Julia in Wilford Leach's production at the Delacorte Theatre in New York in 1978; Julia unabashedly called upon his own Latin American heritage of machismo to motivate Petruchio's way with women, while Streep, herself a modern woman, approached the role of Kate with the kind of ironic distance made possible by a self-aware and historical perspective. An ironic point of view gave to both actors a chance to enjoy role-playing and yet to preserve an essential part of their own integrity. In a 1960 production by the Royal Shakespeare Company, John Barton's direction of Peter O'Toole and Peggy Ashcroft, as Petruchio and Kate, stressed a good-natured playfulness between a man and a woman who obviously love each other from the start. Elizabeth Taylor and Richard Burton, in a very uneven film version by Franco Zeffirelli (1967), found in their best moments a modern idiom through which to explore the emotional nuances of an aggressive courtship; Taylor played Kate as a hot-tempered tomboy, understandably wary of male claims of prerogative, who has to decide how to respond to an attractive and virile man who seems to want her as a woman but whose motives are otherwise far from clear.

An entirely different strategy sometimes employed in modern productions is to downplay the complexities of the husband-wife issue and to focus instead on hilarity, as in the boisterous production at the Broadway Theatre in New York in 1935 starring Alfred Lunt and Lynn Fontaine, Clifford Williams's 1973 farce for the Royal Shakespeare Company, and a zany *commedia dell'arte* performance by the American Conservatory Theatre of San Francisco in 1976.

The Induction has required solutions as varied and ingenious as those for the wife-taming plot. The anonymous adaptation *The Taming of a Shrew* completed the framing plot of the Induction with an epilogue in which Sly awakens to find himself a beggar once again, ready to apply the lessons he has learned from the play to his own private life. In *Sauny the Scot* the Induction was simply left out. In 1716 Charles Johnson and Christopher Bullock went in the other direction in their nearly contemporaneous adaptations (both called *The Cobbler of Preston*) by making a whole short play out of the Induction. *A Cure for a Scold* and Garrick's *Catharine and Petruchio* also did without, so that the Induction was not often seen in conjunction with the rest of the play before Webster's revival of 1844. But even thereafter, Frank Benson omitted it in 1901 at the Comedy Theatre, as did William Bridges-Adams at Stratford-upon-Avon in 1919 and Dennis Carey, after opening night, at the Old Vic in 1954. Sir Barry Jackson, on the other hand, kept Sly and the Lord in view until the very end of the play, in one of the boxes, dressed in modern dress (Court Theatre, 1928). Ben Iden Payne at Stratford-upon-Avon in 1935 and Tyrone Guthrie at the Old Vic in 1939 similarly kept Sly onstage throughout.

The epilogue from *A Shrew* has been revived at times, as at the Old Vic in 1931 and at Stratford-upon-Avon in 1953. The Stratford Festival in Canada in the 1960s ended the play by having its performers, a band of strolling players, pack up and go off in search of another audience. The so-called Young Vic Company, on tour in the 1970s, conceived of Sly as a frustrated actor who eventually turns up in the play proper in the role of the Pedant, thus recalling a doubling effect used earlier at the New Theatre in 1937. Cole Porter's musical of 1948, *Kiss Me Kate*, converted the idea of a framing plot and a play-within-the-play into a story of actors whose tempestuous love life offstage reflects the difficulties of the wooers they portray.

Shakespeare's text calls for the second scene of the Induction to be played "aloft," that is, in the gallery at the back of the main stage, though the scene is longer, more elaborate, and more peopled with actors than is normal for action "above" in Shakespearean drama, and there is no interaction with persons below on the main stage as in most such scenes. If Sly were to continue to sit in the gallery throughout the play, his presence would complicate the staging of Act 5, scene 1, in which the gallery seems to be needed for a window in the house of Lucentio. In the anonymous *A Shrew*, where Sly does remain throughout, he appears to be situated at one side of the stage, not aloft. Shakespeare may have had to deal with varying theatrical conditions if the play was acted first in one theatre and then in another. We are not likely ever to know for certain how the Induction was staged in its original performances. In its own way, Shakespeare's Induction has remained as much a challenge to directors and actors of *The Taming of the Shrew* as has the battle for mastery between Petruchio and Kate.

THE
TAMING OF
THE SHREW

[*Dramatis Personae*

CHRISTOPHER SLY, *a tinker and beggar,*
HOSTESS *of an alehouse,*
A LORD,
A PAGE, SERVANTS, HUNTSMEN,
PLAYERS, } *Persons in the Induction*

BAPTISTA, *a rich gentleman of Padua*
KATHARINA, *the shrew, also called Katharine and Kate, Baptista's elder daughter*
BIANCA, *Baptista's younger daughter*

PETRUCHIO, *a gentleman of Verona, suitor to Katharina*
GRUMIO, *Petruchio's servant*
CURTIS, NATHANIEL, PHILIP, JOSEPH, NICHOLAS, PETER, *and other servants of Petruchio*

GREMIO, *elderly suitor to Bianca*
HORTENSIO, *suitor to Bianca*
LUCENTIO, *son of Vincentio, in love with Bianca*
TRANIO, *Lucentio's servant*
BIONDELLO, *Lucentio's servant*
VINCENTIO, *a gentleman of Pisa*
A PEDANT (*or Merchant*) *of Mantua*
A WIDOW, *courted by Hortensio*

A TAILOR
A HABERDASHER
AN OFFICER
Other Servants of Baptista and Lucentio

SCENE: *Padua, and Petruchio's country house in Italy; the Induction is located in the countryside and at a Lord's house in England*]

Induction 1

*Enter beggar (Christopher Sly)
and Hostess.*

SLY   I'll feeze you, in faith.   1
HOSTESS   A pair of stocks, you rogue!   2
SLY   You're a baggage. The Slys are no rogues. Look in   3
the chronicles; we came in with Richard Conqueror.   4
Therefore *paucas pallabris,* let the world slide. Sessa!   5
HOSTESS   You will not pay for the glasses you have
burst?
SLY   No, not a denier. Go by, Saint Jeronimy, go to thy   8
cold bed and warm thee.   9
HOSTESS   I know my remedy; I must go fetch the third-   10
borough.   [*Exit.*]   11
SLY   Third, or fourth, or fifth borough, I'll answer him   12
by law. I'll not budge an inch, boy. Let him come, and
kindly.   *Falls asleep.*   14

Wind horns [*within*]. *Enter a Lord from hunting,
with his train.*

LORD
Huntsman, I charge thee, tender well my hounds.   15
Breathe Merriman—the poor cur is embossed—   16
And couple Clowder with the deep-mouthed brach.   17
Sawst thou not, boy, how Silver made it good
At the hedge corner, in the coldest fault?   19
I would not lose the dog for twenty pound.
FIRST HUNTSMAN
Why, Bellman is as good as he, my lord.

Induction 1. Location: Before an alehouse, and subsequently before the
Lord's house nearby. (See ll. 75, 135.)
1 feeze you i.e., fix you, get even with you   **2 A . . . stocks** i.e., I'll have
you put in the stocks   **3 baggage** contemptible woman or prostitute
4 Richard (Sly's mistake for "William.")   **5 paucas pallabris** i.e., *pocas
palabras,* "few words." (Spanish.)   **Sessa** (Of doubtful meaning; perhaps
"be quiet," "cease," or "let it go.")   **8 denier** French copper coin of
little value.   **Go . . . Jeronimy** (Sly's variation of an often-quoted line
from Kyd's *The Spanish Tragedy,* expressing impatience.)   **8–9 go . . .
thee** (Perhaps a proverb; see *King Lear* 3.4.46–47.)   **10–11 thirdborough**
constable   **12 Third** (Sly shows his ignorance; the *third* in "thirdborough" derives from the Old English word *frith,* peace.)   **14 kindly**
welcome   **s.d. Wind** blow   **15 tender** care for   **16 embossed** foaming at
the mouth from exhaustion   **17 brach** bitch hound   **19 fault** loss of scent

He cried upon it at the merest loss,   22
And twice today picked out the dullest scent.
Trust me, I take him for the better dog.

LORD
Thou art a fool. If Echo were as fleet,
I would esteem him worth a dozen such.
But sup them well and look unto them all.
Tomorrow I intend to hunt again.

FIRST HUNTSMAN   I will, my lord.

LORD [*Seeing Sly*]
What's here? One dead, or drunk? See, doth he breathe?

SECOND HUNTSMAN [*Examining Sly*]
He breathes, my lord. Were he not warmed with ale,
This were a bed but cold to sleep so soundly.

LORD
O monstrous beast, how like a swine he lies!
Grim death, how foul and loathsome is thine image!   34
Sirs, I will practice on this drunken man.   35
What think you, if he were conveyed to bed,
Wrapped in sweet clothes, rings put upon his fingers,   37
A most delicious banquet by his bed,   38
And brave attendants near him when he wakes,   39
Would not the beggar then forget himself?

FIRST HUNTSMAN
Believe me, lord, I think he cannot choose.

SECOND HUNTSMAN
It would seem strange unto him when he waked.

LORD
Even as a flattering dream or worthless fancy.   43
Then take him up, and manage well the jest.
Carry him gently to my fairest chamber,
And hang it round with all my wanton pictures.
Balm his foul head in warm distilled waters,
And burn sweet wood to make the lodging sweet.
Procure me music ready when he wakes
To make a dulcet and a heavenly sound.
And if he chance to speak, be ready straight,   51

22 **cried . . . loss** bayed to signal recovery of the scent after it had been
completely lost   34 **image** likeness (since sleep was regarded as a
likeness of death)   35 **practice on** play a joke on   37 **sweet** perfumed
38 **banquet** light repast   39 **brave** finely arrayed   43 **fancy** flight of
imagination   51 **straight** at once

And with a low submissive reverence
Say, "What is it your honor will command?"
Let one attend him with a silver basin
Full of rosewater and bestrewed with flowers;
Another bear the ewer, the third a diaper,   56
And say, "Will 't please your lordship cool your hands?"
Someone be ready with a costly suit
And ask him what apparel he will wear;
Another tell him of his hounds and horse,
And that his lady mourns at his disease.
Persuade him that he hath been lunatic,
And when he says he is, say that he dreams,
For he is nothing but a mighty lord.
This do, and do it kindly, gentle sirs.   65
It will be pastime passing excellent,   66
If it be husbanded with modesty.   67

FIRST HUNTSMAN
My lord, I warrant you we will play our part
As he shall think by our true diligence   69
He is no less than what we say he is.

LORD
Take him up gently and to bed with him,
And each one to his office when he wakes.   72
       [*Some bear out Sly.*] *Sound trumpets* [*within*].
Sirrah, go see what trumpet 'tis that sounds.   73
                              [*Exit Servingman.*]
Belike some noble gentleman that means,   74
Traveling some journey, to repose him here.

       Enter Servingman.

How now? Who is it?
SERVINGMAN   An 't please your honor, players
That offer service to your lordship.

       Enter Players.

LORD
Bid them come near.—Now, fellows, you are welcome.

---

56 ewer jug, pitcher. **diaper** towel **65 kindly** naturally (and thus
persuasively) **66 passing** surpassingly **67 husbanded with modesty**
managed with decorum **69 As** so that **72 office** duty **73 Sirrah**
(Usual form of address to inferiors.) **74 Belike** perhaps

PLAYERS   We thank your honor.

LORD
Do you intend to stay with me tonight?

FIRST PLAYER
So please your lordship to accept our duty.   81

LORD
With all my heart. This fellow I remember
Since once he played a farmer's eldest son.—
'Twas where you wooed the gentlewoman so well.
I have forgot your name, but sure that part
Was aptly fitted and naturally performed.

SECOND PLAYER
I think 'twas Soto that your honor means.

LORD
'Tis very true. Thou didst it excellent.
Well, you are come to me in happy time,   89
The rather for I have some sport in hand   90
Wherein your cunning can assist me much.
There is a lord will hear you play tonight.
But I am doubtful of your modesties,   93
Lest, overeyeing of his odd behavior—   94
For yet his honor never heard a play—
You break into some merry passion   96
And so offend him; for I tell you, sirs,
If you should smile he grows impatient.

FIRST PLAYER
Fear not, my lord, we can contain ourselves
Were he the veriest antic in the world.   100

LORD [*To a Servingman*]
Go, sirrah, take them to the buttery,   101
And give them friendly welcome every one.
Let them want nothing that my house affords.   103
                              Exit one with the Players.
Sirrah, go you to Barthol'mew my page,   104
And see him dressed in all suits like a lady.   105

---

81 duty expression of respect   **89 happy** opportune   **90 The rather for**
the more so since   **93 doubtful** apprehensive.   **modesties** discretion,
self-control   **94 overeyeing of** witnessing   **96 merry passion** outburst of
laughter   **100 antic** buffoon or eccentric   **101 buttery** pantry, or a room
for storing liquor (in butts) and other provisions   **103 want** lack
104 Barthol'mew (Pronounced "Bartlemy.")   **105 in all suits** in every
detail

That done, conduct him to the drunkard's chamber,
And call him "madam," do him obeisance.
Tell him from me, as he will win my love,   108
He bear himself with honorable action,
Such as he hath observed in noble ladies
Unto their lords, by them accomplishèd.
Such duty to the drunkard let him do
With soft low tongue and lowly courtesy,
And say, "What is 't your honor will command,
Wherein your lady and your humble wife
May show her duty and make known her love?"
And then with kind embracements, tempting kisses,
And with declining head into his bosom,
Bid him shed tears, as being overjoyed
To see her noble lord restored to health,
Who for this seven years hath esteemèd him   121
No better than a poor and loathsome beggar.
And if the boy have not a woman's gift
To rain a shower of commanded tears,
An onion will do well for such a shift,   125
Which in a napkin being close conveyed   126
Shall in despite enforce a watery eye.
See this dispatched with all the haste thou canst.
Anon I'll give thee more instructions.   129

       Exit a Servingman.

I know the boy will well usurp the grace,   130
Voice, gait, and action of a gentlewoman.
I long to hear him call the drunkard husband,
And how my men will stay themselves from laughter
When they do homage to this simple peasant.
I'll in to counsel them. Haply my presence
May well abate the overmerry spleen   136
Which otherwise would grow into extremes.

         [*Exeunt.*]

     ❖

108 him i.e., the page Bartholomew   **121 him** himself   **125 shift** purpose   **126 napkin** handkerchief.   **close** secretly   **129 Anon** soon
130 usurp assume   **136 spleen** mood. (The spleen was the supposed seat of laughter and anger.)

Induction 2

Enter aloft the drunkard [Sly], with Attendants; some with apparel, basin, and ewer and other appurtenances; and Lord.

SLY For God's sake, a pot of small ale.   1

FIRST SERVANT
  Will 't please your lordship drink a cup of sack?   2

SECOND SERVANT
  Will 't please your honor taste of these conserves?   3

THIRD SERVANT
  What raiment will your honor wear today?

SLY I am Christophero Sly, call not me "honor" nor "lordship." I ne'er drank sack in my life; and if you give me any conserves, give me conserves of beef. 7 Ne'er ask me what raiment I'll wear, for I have no more doublets than backs, no more stockings than 9 legs, nor no more shoes than feet—nay, sometimes more feet than shoes, or such shoes as my toes look through the overleather.

LORD
  Heaven cease this idle humor in your honor!   13
  O, that a mighty man of such descent,
  Of such possessions and so high esteem,
  Should be infusèd with so foul a spirit!

SLY What, would you make me mad? Am not I Christopher Sly, old Sly's son of Burton-heath, by birth a 18 peddler, by education a cardmaker, by transmutation 19 a bearherd, and now by present profession a tinker? 20 Ask Marian Hacket, the fat alewife of Wincot, if she 21

Induction 2. Location: A bedchamber in the Lord's house.
s.d. aloft i.e., in the gallery over the rear facade of the stage **1 small** weak (and therefore cheap) **2 sack** sweet Spanish wine (suited for a gentleman to drink) **3 conserves** candied fruit **7 conserves of beef** preserved (salted) beef **9 doublets** men's jackets **13 idle** vain, foolish. **humor** whim, fancy **18 Burton-heath** (Perhaps Barton-on-the-Heath, about sixteen miles from Stratford, the home of Shakespeare's aunt.) **19 cardmaker** maker of cards or combs used to prepare wool for spinning **20 bearherd** keeper of a performing bear. **tinker** pot-mender **21 Wincot** small village about four miles from Stratford. (The parish register shows that there were Hackets living there in 1591.)

know me not. If she say I am not fourteen pence on   22
the score for sheer ale, score me up for the lyingest   23
knave in Christendom. What, I am not bestraught: 24
here's—

THIRD SERVANT
O, this it is that makes your lady mourn!

SECOND SERVANT
O, this is it that makes your servants droop!

LORD
Hence comes it that your kindred shuns your house,
As beaten hence by your strange lunacy.   29
O noble lord, bethink thee of thy birth,
Call home thy ancient thoughts from banishment,   31
And banish hence these abject lowly dreams.
Look how thy servants do attend on thee,
Each in his office ready at thy beck.
Wilt thou have music? Hark, Apollo plays,   *Music.* 35
And twenty cagèd nightingales do sing.
Or wilt thou sleep? We'll have thee to a couch,
Softer and sweeter than the lustful bed
On purpose trimmed up for Semiramis.   39
Say thou wilt walk; we will bestrew the ground.
Or wilt thou ride? Thy horses shall be trapped,   41
Their harness studded all with gold and pearl.
Dost thou love hawking? Thou hast hawks will soar
Above the morning lark. Or wilt thou hunt?
Thy hounds shall make the welkin answer them   45
And fetch shrill echoes from the hollow earth.

FIRST SERVANT
Say thou wilt course, thy greyhounds are as swift   47
As breathèd stags, ay, fleeter than the roe.   48

SECOND SERVANT
Dost thou love pictures? We will fetch thee straight
Adonis painted by a running brook,   50

22–23 **on the score** in debt (since such reckonings were originally
notched or scored on a stick)   23 **sheer** nothing but.   **score me up for**
reckon me to be   24 **bestraught** distracted   29 **As** as if   31 **ancient**
former   35 **Apollo** i.e., as god of music   39 **Semiramis** legendary queen
of Assyria famous for her voluptuousness   41 **trapped** adorned
45 **welkin** sky, heavens   47 **course** hunt the hare   48 **breathèd** in good
physical condition, with good wind.   **roe** small, swift deer   50 **Adonis** a
young huntsman with whom Venus is vainly in love. (See Shakespeare's
poem *Venus and Adonis*.)

And Cytherea all in sedges hid,   51
Which seem to move and wanton with her breath,   52
Even as the waving sedges play wi' th' wind.

LORD
We'll show thee Io as she was a maid,   54
And how she was beguilèd and surprised,
As lively painted as the deed was done.

THIRD SERVANT
Or Daphne roaming through a thorny wood,   57
Scratching her legs that one shall swear she bleeds,
And at that sight shall sad Apollo weep,
So workmanly the blood and tears are drawn.   60

LORD
Thou art a lord and nothing but a lord.
Thou hast a lady far more beautiful
Than any woman in this waning age.   63

FIRST SERVANT
And till the tears that she hath shed for thee
Like envious floods o'errun her lovely face,   65
She was the fairest creature in the world;
And yet she is inferior to none.   67

SLY
Am I a lord? And have I such a lady?
Or do I dream? Or have I dreamed till now?
I do not sleep: I see, I hear, I speak,
I smell sweet savors, and I feel soft things.
Upon my life, I am a lord indeed,
And not a tinker nor Christopher Sly.
Well, bring our lady hither to our sight,
And once again a pot o' the smallest ale.

SECOND SERVANT
Will 't please your mightiness to wash your hands?
O, how we joy to see your wit restored!   77
O, that once more you knew but what you are!

51 Cytherea one of the names for Venus (because of her association
with the island of Cythera). **sedges** grassy marsh plants **52 wanton**
play seductively **54 Io** one of Jupiter's lovers, transformed by him into
a heifer to conceal her from the envious Juno **57 Daphne** a wood
nymph beloved by Apollo, changed by Diana into a laurel tree to preserve her from Apollo's assault **60 workmanly** skillfully **63 waning**
degenerate **65 envious** spiteful **67 yet** even today **77 wit** mental
faculties, senses

These fifteen years you have been in a dream,
Or when you waked, so waked as if you slept.

SLY
    These fifteen years! By my fay, a goodly nap.   81
    But did I never speak of all that time?   82

FIRST SERVANT
    O, yes, my lord, but very idle words;
    For though you lay here in this goodly chamber,
    Yet would you say ye were beaten out of door,
    And rail upon the hostess of the house,   86
    And say you would present her at the leet,   87
    Because she brought stone jugs and no sealed quarts.   88
    Sometimes you would call out for Cicely Hacket.

SLY   Ay, the woman's maid of the house.

THIRD SERVANT
    Why, sir, you know no house nor no such maid,
    Nor no such men as you have reckoned up,
    As Stephen Sly, and old John Naps of Greece,   93
    And Peter Turf, and Henry Pimpernel,
    And twenty more such names and men as these,
    Which never were nor no man ever saw.

SLY
    Now Lord be thankèd for my good amends!   97

ALL
    Amen.

            Enter [the Page as a] lady, with Attendants.

SLY   I thank thee. Thou shalt not lose by it.

PAGE
    How fares my noble lord?

SLY   Marry, I fare well,   99
    For here is cheer enough. Where is my wife?

PAGE
    Here, noble lord. What is thy will with her?

81 fay faith   **82 of** during   **86 house** tavern   **87 present** bring accusation against.   **leet** manorial court   **88 sealed quarts** quart containers
officially stamped as a guarantee of that capacity   **93 Stephen . . .**
Greece (A Stephen Sly lived in Stratford during Shakespeare's day.
Greece is an apparent error for *Greet*, a Gloucestershire hamlet not far
from Stratford.)   **97 amends** recovery   **99 Marry** A mild oath, derived
from "by Mary."

SLY
  Are you my wife and will not call me husband?
  My men should call me "lord"; I am your goodman.   103
PAGE
  My husband and my lord, my lord and husband,
  I am your wife in all obedience.
SLY
  I know it well.—What must I call her?
                                          Madam.
LORD
SLY Al'ce madam, or Joan madam?
LORD
  Madam, and nothing else. So lords call ladies.
SLY
  Madam wife, they say that I have dreamed
  And slept above some fifteen year or more.
PAGE
  Ay, and the time seems thirty unto me,
  Being all this time abandoned from your bed.   112
SLY
  'Tis much. Servants, leave me and her alone.
  Madam, undress you and come now to bed.
PAGE
  Thrice-noble lord, let me entreat of you
  To pardon me yet for a night or two,
  Or, if not so, until the sun be set.
  For your physicians have expressly charged,
  In peril to incur your former malady,
  That I should yet absent me from your bed.
  I hope this reason stands for my excuse.
SLY Ay, it stands so that I may hardly tarry so long. But 122
  I would be loath to fall into my dreams again. I will
  therefore tarry in despite of the flesh and the blood.

      Enter a [Servant as] messenger.

SERVANT
  Your honor's players, hearing your amendment,
  Are come to play a pleasant comedy;
  For so your doctors hold it very meet,   127
  Seeing too much sadness hath congealed your blood,

103 goodman (A homely term for "husband.")   **112 abandoned** banished   **122 stands** is the case (with bawdy pun)   **127 meet** suitable

And melancholy is the nurse of frenzy.
Therefore they thought it good you hear a play
And frame your mind to mirth and merriment,
Which bars a thousand harms and lengthens life.
SLY Marry, I will, let them play it. Is not a comonty a   133
Christmas gambold or a tumbling-trick?   134
PAGE
No, my good lord, it is more pleasing stuff.
SLY What, household stuff?
PAGE It is a kind of history.   137
SLY Well, we'll see 't. Come, madam wife, sit by my
side and let the world slip; we shall ne'er be younger.
                    [*They sit over the stage.*] *Flourish.*

133, 134 comonty, gambold (Sly's words for *comedy* and *gambol*.)
137 history story

1.1 *Enter Lucentio and his man Tranio.*

LUCENTIO
  Tranio, since for the great desire I had
  To see fair Padua, nursery of arts,   2
  I am arrived for fruitful Lombardy,   3
  The pleasant garden of great Italy,
  And by my father's love and leave am armed
  With his good will and thy good company,
  My trusty servant, well approved in all,   7
  Here let us breathe and haply institute   8
  A course of learning and ingenious studies.   9
  Pisa, renownèd for grave citizens,
  Gave me my being, and my father first,   11
  A merchant of great traffic through the world,   12
  Vincentio, come of the Bentivolii.
  Vincentio's son, brought up in Florence,
  It shall become to serve all hopes conceived   15
  To deck his fortune with his virtuous deeds.   16
  And therefore, Tranio, for the time I study,
  Virtue and that part of philosophy
  Will I apply that treats of happiness   19
  By virtue specially to be achieved.
  Tell me thy mind, for I have Pisa left
  And am to Padua come, as he that leaves
  A shallow plash to plunge him in the deep   23
  And with satiety seeks to quench his thirst.

TRANIO
  Mi perdonate, gentle master mine.   25
  I am in all affected as yourself,   26
  Glad that you thus continue your resolve

1.1. Location: Padua. A street before Baptista's house.
2 Padua . . . arts (Padua's was one of the most renowned of universities
during Shakespeare's time.) **3 am arrived for** have arrived at. (Padua is
not in Lombardy, but imprecise maps may have allowed Shakespeare to
think of Lombardy as comprising all of northern Italy.) **7 approved**
tested and proved trustworthy **8 breathe** pause, remain. **institute**
begin **9 ingenious** i.e., "ingenuous," liberal, befitting a well-born
person **11 first** i.e., before me **12 of great traffic** involved in extensive
trade **15 It . . . conceived** i.e., it will befit me, Lucentio, to fulfill all the
hopes entertained for me by my friends and relatives **16 deck** adorn
19 apply study. **treats of** discusses, concerns **23 plash** pool **25 Mi
perdonate** pardon me **26 affected** disposed

To suck the sweets of sweet philosophy.
Only, good master, while we do admire
This virtue and this moral discipline,
Let's be no stoics nor no stocks, I pray,   31
Or so devote to Aristotle's checks   32
As Ovid be an outcast quite abjured.   33
Balk logic with acquaintance that you have,   34
And practice rhetoric in your common talk;
Music and poesy use to quicken you;   36
The mathematics and the metaphysics,
Fall to them as you find your stomach serves you.   38
No profit grows where is no pleasure ta'en.
In brief, sir, study what you most affect.   40
LUCENTIO
Gramercies, Tranio, well dost thou advise.   41
If, Biondello, thou wert come ashore,   42
We could at once put us in readiness,
And take a lodging fit to entertain
Such friends as time in Padua shall beget.
But stay awhile, what company is this?
TRANIO
Master, some show to welcome us to town.   47

Enter Baptista with his two daughters Katharina
and Bianca, Gremio a pantaloon, [and] Hortensio
suitor to Bianca. Lucentio [and] Tranio stand by.

BAPTISTA
Gentlemen, importune me no farther,
For how I firmly am resolved you know:
That is, not to bestow my youngest daughter
Before I have a husband for the elder.
If either of you both love Katharina,

---

31 stocks wooden posts, devoid of feeling (with a play on *stoics*)
32 devote devoted.   **checks** restraints   **33 As** so that.   **Ovid** Latin love
poet (used here to typify amorous light entertainment as contrasted
with the serious philosophic study of Aristotle)   **34 Balk logic** argue,
bandy words   **36 quicken** refresh   **38 stomach** inclination, appetite
40 affect find pleasant   **41 Gramercies** many thanks   **42 Biondello**
(Lucentio apostrophizes his absent servant.)   **come ashore** (Padua,
though inland, is given a harbor by Shakespeare, unless he is thinking
of the canals that crossed northern Italy in the sixteenth century.)
47 s.d. pantaloon foolish old man, a stock character in Italian comedy

Because I know you well and love you well,
Leave shall you have to court her at your pleasure.

GREMIO
To cart her rather; she's too rough for me.   55
There, there, Hortensio, will you any wife?

KATHARINA [*To Baptista*]
I pray you, sir, is it your will
To make a stale of me amongst these mates?   58

HORTENSIO
"Mates," maid? How mean you that? No mates for you,
Unless you were of gentler, milder mold.

KATHARINA
I' faith, sir, you shall never need to fear:
Iwis it is not halfway to her heart.   62
But if it were, doubt not her care should be
To comb your noddle with a three-legged stool,
And paint your face, and use you like a fool.   65

HORTENSIO
From all such devils, good Lord deliver us!

GREMIO   And me too, good Lord!

TRANIO [*Aside to Lucentio*]
Husht, master, here's some good pastime toward.   68
That wench is stark mad or wonderful froward.   69

LUCENTIO [*Aside to Tranio*]
But in the other's silence do I see
Maid's mild behavior and sobriety.
Peace, Tranio!

TRANIO [*Aside to Lucentio*]
Well said, master; mum, and gaze your fill.

BAPTISTA
Gentlemen, that I may soon make good
What I have said—Bianca, get you in,
And let it not displease thee, good Bianca,
For I will love thee ne'er the less, my girl.

55 cart carry in a cart through the streets by way of punishment or
public exposure (with a play on *court*)   **58 stale** laughingstock (with a
play on the meaning "harlot," since a harlot might well be carted).
mates rude fellows. (But Hortensio takes the word in the sense of
"husband.")   **62 Iwis** indeed.   **it** i.e., marriage.   **her** i.e., my, Kate's
65 paint i.e., make red with scratches   **68 toward** in prospect
69 froward perverse

KATHARINA   A pretty peat! It is best   78
  Put finger in the eye, an she knew why.   79
BIANCA
  Sister, content you in my discontent.—
  Sir, to your pleasure humbly I subscribe.
  My books and instruments shall be my company,
  On them to look and practice by myself.
LUCENTIO [*Aside to Tranio*]
  Hark, Tranio, thou mayst hear Minerva speak.   84
HORTENSIO
  Signor Baptista, will you be so strange?   85
  Sorry am I that our good will effects
  Bianca's grief.
GREMIO   Why will you mew her up,   87
  Signor Baptista, for this fiend of hell,
  And make her bear the penance of her tongue?   89
BAPTISTA
  Gentlemen, content ye; I am resolved.
  Go in, Bianca.   [*Exit Bianca.*]
  And for I know she taketh most delight   92
  In music, instruments, and poetry,
  Schoolmasters will I keep within my house
  Fit to instruct her youth. If you, Hortensio,
  Or Signor Gremio, you, know any such,
  Prefer them hither; for to cunning men   97
  I will be very kind, and liberal
  To mine own children in good bringing up.
  And so farewell.—Katharina, you may stay,
  For I have more to commune with Bianca.   *Exit.* 101
KATHARINA
  Why, and I trust I may go too, may I not?
  What, shall I be appointed hours,
  As though, belike, I knew not what to take,
  And what to leave? Ha!   *Exit.*
GREMIO   You may go to the devil's dam. Your gifts are 106
  so good, here's none will hold you.—Their love is not 107

78 peat darling, pet   **79 Put . . . eye** i.e., weep.   **an** if   **84 Minerva**
goddess of wisdom   **85 strange** distant, estranged   **87 mew** coop (as
one would a falcon)   **89 her . . . her** i.e., Bianca . . . Katharina's   **92 for**
because   **97 Prefer** recommend.   **cunning** skillful, learned   **101 commune** discuss   **106 dam** mother   **107 Their love** i.e., men's love of
women

so great, Hortensio, but we may blow our nails to- 108
gether, and fast it fairly out. Our cake's dough on both 109
sides. Farewell. Yet, for the love I bear my sweet
Bianca, if I can by any means light on a fit man to
teach her that wherein she delights, I will wish him to 112
her father.

HORTENSIO So will I, Signor Gremio. But a word, I
pray. Though the nature of our quarrel yet never
brooked parle, know now, upon advice, it toucheth us 116
both—that we may yet again have access to our fair
mistress and be happy rivals in Bianca's love—to labor
and effect one thing specially.

GREMIO What's that, I pray?

HORTENSIO Marry, sir, to get a husband for her sister.

GREMIO A husband? A devil.

HORTENSIO I say a husband.

GREMIO I say a devil. Think'st thou, Hortensio, though
her father be very rich, any man is so very a fool to be 125
married to hell?

HORTENSIO Tush, Gremio, though it pass your patience
and mine to endure her loud alarums, why, man, 128
there be good fellows in the world, an a man could
light on them, would take her with all faults, and
money enough.

GREMIO I cannot tell; but I had as lief take her dowry 132
with this condition, to be whipped at the high cross 133
every morning.

HORTENSIO Faith, as you say, there's small choice in
rotten apples. But come, since this bar in law makes 136
us friends, it shall be so far forth friendly maintained
till by helping Baptista's eldest daughter to a husband
we set his youngest free for a husband, and then have
to 't afresh. Sweet Bianca! Happy man be his dole! He 140

108–109 blow . . . together i.e., twiddle our thumbs, wait patiently
109 fast . . . out abstain as best we can. **Our cake's dough** i.e., we're
out of luck, getting nowhere **112 wish** commend **116 brooked parle**
tolerated conference. **advice** reflection. **toucheth** concerns **125 very**
utterly **128 alarums** i.e., loud, startling noises. (A military metaphor.)
132 had as lief would as willingly **133 high cross** cross set on a pedes-
tal in a marketplace or center of a town **136 bar in law** obstruction to
our (legal) cause **140 Happy . . . dole** i.e., may happiness be the reward
of him who wins. (Proverbial.)

that runs fastest gets the ring. How say you, Signor   141
Gremio?

GREMIO I am agreed, and would I had given him the
best horse in Padua to begin his wooing that would
thoroughly woo her, wed her, and bed her and rid the
house of her! Come on.   *Exeunt ambo.*   146
                        Manent Tranio and Lucentio.

TRANIO
I pray, sir, tell me, is it possible
That love should of a sudden take such hold?

LUCENTIO
O Tranio, till I found it to be true,
I never thought it possible or likely.
But see, while idly I stood looking on,
I found the effect of love in idleness,   152
And now in plainness do confess to thee,
That art to me as secret and as dear   154
As Anna to the Queen of Carthage was,   155
Tranio, I burn, I pine, I perish, Tranio,
If I achieve not this young modest girl.
Counsel me, Tranio, for I know thou canst;
Assist me, Tranio, for I know thou wilt.

TRANIO
Master, it is no time to chide you now.
Affection is not rated from the heart.   161
If love have touched you, naught remains but so,
"Redime te captum quam queas minimo."   163

LUCENTIO
Gramercies, lad. Go forward. This contents;
The rest will comfort, for thy counsel's sound.

TRANIO
Master, you looked so longly on the maid,   166
Perhaps you marked not what's the pith of all.   167

141 **the ring** (An allusion to the sport of riding at the ring, with quibble
on "wedding ring.") 146 **s.d. ambo** both. **Manent** they remain onstage 152 **love in idleness** the flower heartsease or pansy, to which was
attributed magical power in love. (See *A Midsummer Night's Dream*,
2.1.168.) 154 **secret** trusted, intimate 155 **Anna** confidante of her
sister Dido, Queen of Carthage, beloved of Aeneas 161 **rated** driven
away by chiding 163 **Redime . . . minimo** buy yourself out of bondage
for as little as you can. (From Terence's *Eunuchus* as quoted in Lily's
Latin Grammar.) 166 **so longly** for such a long time; perhaps, also, so
longingly 167 **pith** core, essence

LUCENTIO

O, yes, I saw sweet beauty in her face,

Such as the daughter of Agenor had,   169

That made great Jove to humble him to her hand,   170

When with his knees he kissed the Cretan strand.   171

TRANIO

Saw you no more? Marked you not how her sister

Began to scold and raise up such a storm

That mortal ears might hardly endure the din?

LUCENTIO

Tranio, I saw her coral lips to move,

And with her breath she did perfume the air.

Sacred and sweet was all I saw in her.

TRANIO [*Aside*]

Nay, then, 'tis time to stir him from his trance.—

I pray, awake, sir. If you love the maid,

Bend thoughts and wits to achieve her. Thus it stands:

Her elder sister is so curst and shrewd   181

That till the father rid his hands of her,

Master, your love must live a maid at home,

And therefore has he closely mewed her up,

Because she will not be annoyed with suitors.   185

LUCENTIO

Ah, Tranio, what a cruel father's he!

But art thou not advised he took some care   187

To get her cunning schoolmasters to instruct her?

TRANIO

Ay, marry, am I, sir; and now 'tis plotted.

LUCENTIO

I have it, Tranio.

TRANIO   Master, for my hand,   190

Both our inventions meet and jump in one.   191

LUCENTIO

Tell me thine first.

TRANIO   You will be schoolmaster,

And undertake the teaching of the maid:

That's your device.

---

169 daughter of Agenor Europa, beloved of Jupiter, who took the form
of a bull in order to abduct her   **170 him** himself   **171 kissed** i.e., knelt
on   **181 curst** shrewish. **shrewd** ill-natured   **185 Because** so that
187 advised aware   **190 for my hand** for my part, i.e., it's my guess
191 inventions plans. **jump** tally, agree

LUCENTIO   It is. May it be done?

TRANIO
Not possible; for who shall bear your part,
And be in Padua here Vincentio's son,
Keep house and ply his book, welcome his friends,
Visit his countrymen, and banquet them?

LUCENTIO
Basta, content thee, for I have it full.   199
We have not yet been seen in any house,
Nor can we be distinguished by our faces
For man or master. Then it follows thus:
Thou shalt be master, Tranio, in my stead,
Keep house, and port, and servants, as I should.   204
I will some other be, some Florentine,
Some Neapolitan, or meaner man of Pisa.   206
'Tis hatched and shall be so. Tranio, at once
Uncase thee. Take my colored hat and cloak.   208
When Biondello comes, he waits on thee,
But I will charm him first to keep his tongue.   210

TRANIO   So had you need.
In brief, sir, sith it your pleasure is,   212
And I am tied to be obedient—
For so your father charged me at our parting,
"Be serviceable to my son," quoth he,
Although I think 'twas in another sense—
I am content to be Lucentio,
Because so well I love Lucentio.
                         [*They exchange clothes.*]

LUCENTIO
Tranio, be so, because Lucentio loves.
And let me be a slave, t' achieve that maid
Whose sudden sight hath thralled my wounded eye.   221

     Enter Biondello.

Here comes the rogue.—Sirrah, where have you been?

BIONDELLO
Where have I been? Nay, how now, where are you?

---

199 **Basta** enough.   **full** i.e., fully thought out   **204 port** state, style of
living   **206 meaner** of a lower social class   **208 Uncase** i.e., remove hat
and cloak.   **colored** (as opposed to blue generally worn by servants; see
4.1.81)   **210 charm** i.e., persuade   **212 sith** since   **221 Whose sudden
sight** i.e., the sudden sight of whom

Master, has my fellow Tranio stol'n your clothes?
Or you stol'n his? Or both? Pray, what's the news?

LUCENTIO
Sirrah, come hither. 'Tis no time to jest,
And therefore frame your manners to the time.
Your fellow Tranio here, to save my life,
Puts my apparel and my countenance on,   229
And I for my escape have put on his;
For in a quarrel since I came ashore
I killed a man, and fear I was descried.   232
Wait you on him, I charge you, as becomes,   233
While I make way from hence to save my life.
You understand me?

BIONDELLO   I, sir?—Ne'er a whit.   235

LUCENTIO
And not a jot of Tranio in your mouth.
Tranio is changed into Lucentio.

BIONDELLO
The better for him. Would I were so too!

TRANIO
So could I, faith, boy, to have the next wish after,
That Lucentio indeed had Baptista's youngest daughter.
But, sirrah, not for my sake, but your master's, I advise
You use your manners discreetly in all kind of compa-
    nies.
When I am alone, why, then I am Tranio,
But in all places else your master Lucentio.

LUCENTIO   Tranio, let's go.
One thing more rests, that thyself execute: 246
To make one among these wooers. If thou ask me why,
Sufficeth my reasons are both good and weighty.   248
                                    Exeunt.

  The presenters above speak.

FIRST SERVANT
My lord, you nod. You do not mind the play.   249

229 **countenance** bearing, manner   232 **descried** observed   233 **as
becomes** as is suitable   235 **I, sir** (Lucentio may hear this as "Ay,
sir.")   246 **rests** remains to be done   248 **Sufficeth** it suffices that
s.d. presenters characters of the Induction, whose role it is to "present"
the play proper   249 **mind** attend to

SLY Yes, by Saint Anne, do I. A good matter, surely.
Comes there any more of it?
PAGE [*As Lady*] My lord, 'tis but begun.
SLY 'Tis a very excellent piece of work, madam lady;
would 'twere done!   *They sit and mark.* 254

1.2 *Enter Petruchio and his man Grumio.*

PETRUCHIO
Verona, for a while I take my leave
To see my friends in Padua, but of all
My best belovèd and approvèd friend,
Hortensio; and I trow this is his house.   4
Here, sirrah Grumio, knock, I say.
GRUMIO Knock, sir? Whom should I knock? Is there any
man has rebused your worship?   7
PETRUCHIO Villain, I say, knock me here soundly.   8
GRUMIO Knock you here, sir? Why, sir, what am I, sir,
that I should knock you here, sir?
PETRUCHIO
Villain, I say, knock me at this gate,   11
And rap me well, or I'll knock your knave's pate.
GRUMIO
My master is grown quarrelsome. I should knock you
first,
And then I know after who comes by the worst.
PETRUCHIO Will it not be?
Faith, sirrah, an you'll not knock, I'll ring it. 16
I'll try how you can *sol fa*, and sing it.   17
                    He wrings him by the ears.
GRUMIO
Help, masters, help! My master is mad.
PETRUCHIO
Now knock when I bid you, sirrah villain.

254 s.d. mark observe

1.2. Location: Padua. Before Hortensio's house.
4 trow believe **7 rebused** (A blunder for *abused*.) **8 me** i.e., for me.
(But Grumio, perhaps intentionally, misunderstands.) **11 gate** door
16 ring sound loudly, using a circular knocker (with a pun on *wring*)
17 I'll . . . sing it i.e., I'll make you cry out, howl

Enter Hortensio.

HORTENSIO   How now, what's the matter? My old friend
Grumio, and my good friend Petruchio? How do you
all at Verona?

PETRUCHIO
Signor Hortensio, come you to part the fray?
Con tutto il cuore, ben trovato, may I say.   24

HORTENSIO
Alla nostra casa ben venuto,   25
Molto onorato signor mio Petruchio.—   26
Rise, Grumio, rise. We will compound this quarrel.   27

GRUMIO   Nay, 'tis no matter, sir, what he 'leges in Latin.   28
If this be not a lawful cause for me to leave his service!
Look you, sir: he bid me knock him and rap him
soundly, sir. Well, was it fit for a servant to use his
master so, being perhaps, for aught I see, two-and-   32
thirty, a pip out?   33
Whom would to God I had well knocked at first,
Then had not Grumio come by the worst.

PETRUCHIO
A senseless villain! Good Hortensio,
I bade the rascal knock upon your gate,
And could not get him for my heart to do it.

GRUMIO   Knock at the gate? O heavens! Spake you not
these words plain, "Sirrah, knock me here, rap me
here, knock me well, and knock me soundly"? And
come you now with "knocking at the gate"?

PETRUCHIO
Sirrah, begone, or talk not, I advise you.

HORTENSIO
Petruchio, patience, I am Grumio's pledge.   44
Why, this's a heavy chance twixt him and you,   45
Your ancient, trusty, pleasant servant Grumio.   46
And tell me now, sweet friend, what happy gale
Blows you to Padua here from old Verona?

24 Con . . . trovato with all my heart, well met   **25–26 Alla . . . Petruchio** welcome to our house, my much honored Petruchio. (Italian.)
27 compound settle   **28 'leges** alleges   **32–33 two . . . out** i.e., drunk.
(Derived from the card game called *one-and-thirty*.)   **33 pip** a spot on a
playing card. (Hence *a pip out* means "off by one," or "one in excess of
thirty-one.")   **44 pledge** surety   **45 heavy chance** sad occurrence
46 ancient long-standing

PETRUCHIO
Such wind as scatters young men through the world
To seek their fortunes farther than at home,
Where small experience grows. But in a few,   51
Signor Hortensio, thus it stands with me:
Antonio, my father, is deceased,
And I have thrust myself into this maze,
Haply to wive and thrive as best I may.
Crowns in my purse I have, and goods at home,
And so am come abroad to see the world.
HORTENSIO
Petruchio, shall I then come roundly to thee   58
And wish thee to a shrewd ill-favored wife?
Thou'dst thank me but a little for my counsel.
And yet I'll promise thee she shall be rich,
And very rich. But thou'rt too much my friend,
And I'll not wish thee to her.
PETRUCHIO
Signor Hortensio, twixt such friends as we
Few words suffice. And therefore, if thou know
One rich enough to be Petruchio's wife—
As wealth is burden of my wooing dance—   67
Be she as foul as was Florentius' love,   68
As old as Sibyl, and as curst and shrewd   69
As Socrates' Xanthippe, or a worse,   70
She moves me not, or not removes, at least,
Affection's edge in me, were she as rough
As are the swelling Adriatic seas.
I come to wive it wealthily in Padua;
If wealthily, then happily in Padua.
GRUMIO   Nay, look you, sir, he tells you flatly what his
mind is. Why, give him gold enough and marry him 77

---

51 **in a few** in short   58 **come roundly** speak plainly   67 **burden** undersong, i.e., basis   68 **foul** ugly.   **Florentius' love** (An allusion to Gower's
version in *Confessio Amantis* of the fairy tale of the knight who promised to marry an ugly old woman if she solved the riddle he must
answer. After the fulfillment of all promises, she became young and
beautiful. Another version of this story is Chaucer's "Tale of the Wife of
Bath," from *The Canterbury Tales*.)   69 **Sibyl** prophetess of Cumae to
whom Apollo gave as many years of life as she held grains of sand in
her hand   70 **Xanthippe** the philosopher's notoriously shrewish wife
77 mind intention

to a puppet or an aglet-baby, or an old trot with ne'er 78
a tooth in her head, though she have as many diseases
as two-and-fifty horses. Why, nothing comes amiss, so
money comes withal.   81

HORTENSIO
Petruchio, since we are stepped thus far in,
I will continue that I broached in jest.   83
I can, Petruchio, help thee to a wife
With wealth enough, and young and beauteous,
Brought up as best becomes a gentlewoman.
Her only fault, and that is faults enough,
Is that she is intolerable curst
And shrewd, and froward, so beyond all measure
That, were my state far worser than it is,   90
I would not wed her for a mine of gold.

PETRUCHIO
Hortensio, peace! Thou know'st not gold's effect.
Tell me her father's name and 'tis enough;
For I will board her though she chide as loud   94
As thunder when the clouds in autumn crack.

HORTENSIO
Her father is Baptista Minola,
An affable and courteous gentleman.
Her name is Katharina Minola,
Renowned in Padua for her scolding tongue.

PETRUCHIO
I know her father, though I know not her,
And he knew my deceasèd father well.
I will not sleep, Hortensio, till I see her;
And therefore let me be thus bold with you
To give you over at this first encounter,   104
Unless you will accompany me thither.

GRUMIO [*To Hortensio*]   I pray you, sir, let him go while
the humor lasts. O' my word, an she knew him as well 107
as I do, she would think scolding would do little good
upon him. She may perhaps call him half a score

---

78 aglet-baby small figure carved on the tag of a lace.   **trot** old hag;
also, prostitute   **81 withal** with it   **83 that** what   **90 state** estate
94 board accost. (A metaphor from naval warfare.)   **104 give you over**
leave you   **107 humor** whim

knaves or so. Why, that's nothing; an he begin once,
he'll rail in his rope tricks. I'll tell you what, sir, an   111
she stand him but a little, he will throw a figure in her   112
face and so disfigure her with it that she shall have
no more eyes to see withal than a cat. You know him
not, sir.

HORTENSIO
Tarry, Petruchio, I must go with thee,
For in Baptista's keep my treasure is.   117
He hath the jewel of my life in hold,   118
His youngest daughter, beautiful Bianca,
And her withholds from me and other more,   120
Suitors to her and rivals in my love,
Supposing it a thing impossible,
For those defects I have before rehearsed,
That ever Katharina will be wooed.
Therefore this order hath Baptista ta'en,
That none shall have access unto Bianca
Till Katharine the curst have got a husband.
GRUMIO   Katharine the curst!
A title for a maid of all titles the worst.

HORTENSIO
Now shall my friend Petruchio do me grace,   130
And offer me disguised in sober robes
To old Baptista as a schoolmaster
Well seen in music, to instruct Bianca,   133
That so I may by this device at least
Have leave and leisure to make love to her,   135
And unsuspected court her by herself.

*Enter Gremio [with a paper], and Lucentio
disguised [as a schoolmaster].*

GRUMIO   Here's no knavery! See, to beguile the old
folks, how the young folks lay their heads together!
Master, master, look about you. Who goes there, ha?

---

111 rope tricks i.e., a blunder for "rhetricks," i.e., rhetoric (?) or tricks
worthy of hanging (?)   **112 stand** withstand.   **figure** figure of speech
117 keep keeping (with suggestion of "fortified place" where one would
store a treasure)   **118 hold** confinement (with a similar pun on "stronghold")   **120 other** others   **130 grace** a favor   **133 seen** skilled
135 make love to woo

HORTENSIO
    Peace, Grumio, it is the rival of my love.
    Petruchio, stand by awhile.   [*They stand aside.*]
GRUMIO [*Aside*]
    A proper stripling and an amorous!   142
GREMIO [*To Lucentio*]
    O, very well, I have perused the note.   143
    Hark you, sir, I'll have them very fairly bound—
    All books of love, see that at any hand—   145
    And see you read no other lectures to her.   146
    You understand me. Over and besides
    Signor Baptista's liberality,
    I'll mend it with a largess. Take your paper too,   149
                        [*Giving Lucentio the note*]
    And let me have them very well perfumed,   150
    For she is sweeter than perfume itself
    To whom they go to. What will you read to her?
LUCENTIO
    Whate'er I read to her, I'll plead for you
    As for my patron, stand you so assured,
    As firmly as yourself were still in place—   155
    Yea, and perhaps with more successful words
    Than you, unless you were a scholar, sir.
GREMIO
    O this learning, what a thing it is!
GRUMIO [*Aside*]
    O this woodcock, what an ass it is!   159
PETRUCHIO   Peace, sirrah!
HORTENSIO [*Coming forward*]
    Grumio, mum!—God save you, Signor Gremio.
GREMIO
    And you are well met, Signor Hortensio.
    Trow you whither I am going? To Baptista Minola.   163
    I promised to inquire carefully
    About a schoolmaster for the fair Bianca,
    And by good fortune I have lighted well

---

142 proper stripling handsome young fellow. (Said ironically, in reference to Gremio.)   **143 note** (Evidently, a list of books for Bianca's tutoring.)   **145 at any hand** in any case   **146 read . . . lectures** teach no other lessons   **149 mend** improve, increase.   **largess** gift of money   **150 them** i.e., the books   **155 as** as if.   **in place** present   **159 woodcock** (A bird easily caught; proverbially stupid.)   **163 Trow** know

On this young man—for learning and behavior
Fit for her turn, well read in poetry
And other books, good ones, I warrant ye.

HORTENSIO
'Tis well. And I have met a gentleman
Hath promised me to help me to another,   171
A fine musician to instruct our mistress.
So shall I no whit be behind in duty
To fair Bianca, so beloved of me.

GREMIO
Beloved of me, and that my deeds shall prove.

GRUMIO [*Aside*] And that his bags shall prove.   176

HORTENSIO
Gremio, 'tis now no time to vent our love.   177
Listen to me, and if you speak me fair,   178
I'll tell you news indifferent good for either.   179
Here is a gentleman whom by chance I met,
Upon agreement from us to his liking,   181
Will undertake to woo curst Katharine,
Yea, and to marry her, if her dowry please.

GREMIO So said, so done, is well.
Hortensio, have you told him all her faults?

PETRUCHIO
I know she is an irksome brawling scold.
If that be all, masters, I hear no harm.

GREMIO
No, sayst me so, friend? What countryman?

PETRUCHIO
Born in Verona, old Antonio's son.
My father dead, my fortune lives for me,
And I do hope good days and long to see.

GREMIO
O sir, such a life with such a wife were strange.
But if you have a stomach, to 't i' God's name.
You shall have me assisting you in all.
But will you woo this wildcat?

PETRUCHIO   Will I live?

171 **Hath** who has **176 bags** moneybags **177 vent** express **178 fair**
civilly, courteously **179 indifferent** equally **181 Upon . . . liking** who,
on terms agreeable to him. (In ll. 213–214 we learn that Bianca's suitors
will *bear his charge of wooing*.)

GRUMIO [*Aside*]
    Will he woo her? Ay, or I'll hang her.
PETRUCHIO
    Why came I hither but to that intent?
    Think you a little din can daunt mine ears?
    Have I not in my time heard lions roar?
    Have I not heard the sea, puffed up with winds,
    Rage like an angry boar chafèd with sweat?
    Have I not heard great ordnance in the field,   202
    And heaven's artillery thunder in the skies?
    Have I not in a pitchèd battle heard
    Loud 'larums, neighing steeds, and trumpets' clang?   205
    And do you tell me of a woman's tongue,
    That gives not half so great a blow to hear
    As will a chestnut in a farmer's fire?
    Tush, tush! Fear boys with bugs.
GRUMIO [*Aside*]   For he fears none.   209
GREMIO   Hortensio, hark.
    This gentleman is happily arrived,   211
    My mind presumes, for his own good and ours.
HORTENSIO
    I promised we would be contributors
    And bear his charge of wooing whatsoe'er.   214
GREMIO
    And so we will, provided that he win her.
GRUMIO [*Aside*]
    I would I were as sure of a good dinner.   216
        Enter Tranio brave [as Lucentio], and Biondello.
TRANIO
    Gentlemen, God save you. If I may be bold,
    Tell me, I beseech you, which is the readiest way
    To the house of Signor Baptista Minola?
BIONDELLO   He that has the two fair daughters, is 't he
    you mean?
TRANIO   Even he, Biondello.
GREMIO
    Hark you, sir, you mean not her to—

---

202 ordnance artillery   **205 'larums** calls to arms   **209 Fear . . . bugs**
frighten children with bugbears, bogeymen   **211 happily** fortunately,
just when needed   **214 charge** expense   **216 s.d. brave** elegantly
dressed

TRANIO
Perhaps him and her, sir. What have you to do?   224
PETRUCHIO
Not her that chides, sir, at any hand, I pray.
TRANIO
I love no chiders, sir. Biondello, let's away.
LUCENTIO [*Aside*]
Well begun, Tranio.
HORTENSIO   Sir, a word ere you go.
Are you a suitor to the maid you talk of, yea or no?
TRANIO
An if I be, sir, is it any offense?
GREMIO
No, if without more words you will get you hence.
TRANIO
Why, sir, I pray, are not the streets as free
For me as for you?
GREMIO   But so is not she.
TRANIO
For what reason, I beseech you?
GREMIO   For this reason, if you'll know,
That she's the choice love of Signor Gremio.
HORTENSIO
That she's the chosen of Signor Hortensio.
TRANIO
Softly, my masters! If you be gentlemen,
Do me this right: hear me with patience.
Baptista is a noble gentleman,
To whom my father is not all unknown;
And were his daughter fairer than she is,
She may more suitors have, and me for one.
Fair Leda's daughter had a thousand wooers;   242
Then well one more may fair Bianca have,
And so she shall. Lucentio shall make one,
Though Paris came in hope to speed alone.   245
GREMIO
What, this gentleman will outtalk us all.

---

224 him and her i.e., both Baptista Minola and his daughter.   **What . . .
do** what's that to you   **242 Leda's daughter** Helen of Troy   **245 Though**
even if.   **Paris** Trojan prince who abducted Helen from her husband,
Menelaus.   **speed** succeed

LUCENTIO
  Sir, give him head. I know he'll prove a jade.   247
PETRUCHIO
  Hortensio, to what end are all these words?
HORTENSIO [*To Tranio*]
  Sir, let me be so bold as ask you,
  Did you yet ever see Baptista's daughter?
TRANIO
  No, sir, but hear I do that he hath two,
  The one as famous for a scolding tongue
  As is the other for beauteous modesty.
PETRUCHIO
  Sir, sir, the first's for me. Let her go by.
GREMIO
  Yea, leave that labor to great Hercules,
  And let it be more than Alcides' twelve.   256
PETRUCHIO
  Sir, understand you this of me, in sooth: 257
  The youngest daughter, whom you hearken for,   258
  Her father keeps from all access of suitors,
  And will not promise her to any man
  Until the elder sister first be wed.
  The younger then is free, and not before.
TRANIO
  If it be so, sir, that you are the man
  Must stead us all, and me amongst the rest;   264
  And if you break the ice and do this feat,
  Achieve the elder, set the younger free
  For our access, whose hap shall be to have her   267
  Will not so graceless be to be ingrate.
HORTENSIO
  Sir, you say well, and well you do conceive.   269
  And since you do profess to be a suitor,
  You must, as we do, gratify this gentleman,   271
  To whom we all rest generally beholding.   272

---

247 prove a jade tire like an ill-conditioned horse   **256 Alcides'** descendant of Alcaeus (i.e., Hercules, who, noted for the achievement of the twelve great labors, is the only one capable of conquering Katharina) **257 sooth** truth   **258 hearken for** lie in wait for, seek to win   **264 Must stead** who must help   **267 whose hap** he whose good fortune   **269 conceive** understand   **271 gratify** reward, requite   **272 beholding** beholden, indebted

TRANIO
Sir, I shall not be slack, in sign whereof,
Please ye we may contrive this afternoon   274
And quaff carouses to our mistress' health,   275
And do as adversaries do in law,   276
Strive mightily, but eat and drink as friends.

GRUMIO, BIONDELLO
O excellent motion! Fellows, let's be gone.   278

HORTENSIO
The motion's good indeed, and be it so.
Petruchio, I shall be your *ben venuto*.   *Exeunt.* 280

✤

---

274 contrive spend, pass (time)   **275 quaff carouses** drink toasts
276 adversaries opposing lawyers   **278 motion** suggestion   **280 ben venuto** welcome, i.e., host

2.1 *Enter Katharina and Bianca [with her hands tied].*

BIANCA
Good sister, wrong me not, nor wrong yourself,
To make a bondmaid and a slave of me.
That I disdain. But for these other goods,   3
Unbind my hands, I'll pull them off myself,
Yea, all my raiment, to my petticoat,
Or what you will command me will I do,
So well I know my duty to my elders.

KATHARINA
Of all thy suitors, here I charge thee, tell
Whom thou lov'st best. See thou dissemble not.

BIANCA
Believe me, sister, of all the men alive
I never yet beheld that special face
Which I could fancy more than any other.

KATHARINA
Minion, thou liest. Is 't not Hortensio?   13

BIANCA
If you affect him, sister, here I swear   14
I'll plead for you myself but you shall have him.

KATHARINA
O, then belike you fancy riches more:
You will have Gremio to keep you fair.   17

BIANCA
Is it for him you do envy me so?
Nay, then, you jest, and now I well perceive
You have but jested with me all this while.
I prithee, sister Kate, untie my hands.

KATHARINA
If that be jest, then all the rest was so.
                                              Strikes her.

    Enter Baptista.

BAPTISTA
Why, how now, dame, whence grows this insolence?—

2.1. Location: Padua. Baptista's house.
3 **goods** possessions   13 **Minion** hussy   14 **affect** love   17 **fair** resplendent with finery

Bianca, stand aside. Poor girl, she weeps.
Go ply thy needle, meddle not with her.—
For shame, thou hilding of a devilish spirit,   26
Why dost thou wrong her that did ne'er wrong thee?
When did she cross thee with a bitter word?

KATHARINA
Her silence flouts me, and I'll be revenged.
           Flies after Bianca.

BAPTISTA
What, in my sight? Bianca, get thee in.
           Exit [Bianca].

KATHARINA
What, will you not suffer me? Nay, now I see
She is your treasure, she must have a husband;
I must dance barefoot on her wedding day,   33
And for your love to her lead apes in hell.   34
Talk not to me. I will go sit and weep
Till I can find occasion of revenge.   *[Exit.]*

BAPTISTA
Was ever gentleman thus grieved as I?
But who comes here?   38

*Enter Gremio, Lucentio [as a schoolmaster] in the
habit of a mean man, Petruchio, with [Hortensio
as a musician, and] Tranio [as Lucentio] with his
boy [Biondello] bearing a lute and books.*

GREMIO   Good morrow, neighbor Baptista.

BAPTISTA   Good morrow, neighbor Gremio. God save
you, gentlemen.

PETRUCHIO
And you, good sir. Pray, have you not a daughter
Called Katharina, fair and virtuous?

BAPTISTA
I have a daughter, sir, called Katharina.

GREMIO
You are too blunt. Go to it orderly.

PETRUCHIO
You wrong me, Signor Gremio; give me leave.—

---

26 hilding vicious (hence worthless) beast   **33, 34 dance . . . day, lead
. . . hell** (Popularly supposed to be the fate of old maids.)   **38 s.d. mean**
of low social station. (Said here of a schoolmaster.)

I am a gentleman of Verona, sir,
That, hearing of her beauty and her wit,
Her affability and bashful modesty,
Her wondrous qualities and mild behavior,
Am bold to show myself a forward guest
Within your house, to make mine eye the witness
Of that report which I so oft have heard.
And, for an entrance to my entertainment,   54
I do present you with a man of mine,
                          [*Presenting Hortensio*]
Cunning in music and the mathematics,
To instruct her fully in those sciences,   57
Whereof I know she is not ignorant.
Accept of him, or else you do me wrong.
His name is Litio, born in Mantua.

BAPTISTA
You're welcome, sir, and he, for your good sake.
But for my daughter Katharine, this I know,
She is not for your turn, the more my grief.

PETRUCHIO
I see you do not mean to part with her,
Or else you like not of my company.

BAPTISTA
Mistake me not, I speak but as I find.
Whence are you, sir? What may I call your name?

PETRUCHIO
Petruchio is my name, Antonio's son,
A man well known throughout all Italy.

BAPTISTA
I know him well. You are welcome for his sake.   70

GREMIO
Saving your tale, Petruchio, I pray,   71
Let us that are poor petitioners speak too.
Bacare! You are marvelous forward.   73

PETRUCHIO
O, pardon me, Signor Gremio, I would fain be doing. 74

---

54 entrance entrance fee. **entertainment** reception **57 sciences** subjects, branches of knowledge **70 know** know of (see also l. 105)
71 Saving with all due respect for **73 Bacare** stand back **74 fain**
gladly. **doing** getting on with the business (with sexual suggestion)

GREMIO

I doubt it not, sir, but you will curse your wooing.—
Neighbors, this is a gift very grateful, I am sure of it. [*To* 76
Baptista.] To express the like kindness, myself, that have
been more kindly beholding to you than any, freely give
unto you this young scholar [*Presenting Lucentio*],
that hath been long studying at Rheims, as cunning
in Greek, Latin, and other languages as the other in
music and mathematics. His name is Cambio. Pray, 82
accept his service.

BAPTISTA A thousand thanks, Signor Gremio. Welcome, good Cambio. [*To Tranio.*] But, gentle sir,
methinks you walk like a stranger. May I be so bold to 86
know the cause of your coming?

TRANIO

Pardon me, sir, the boldness is mine own,
That, being a stranger in this city here,
Do make myself a suitor to your daughter,
Unto Bianca, fair and virtuous.
Nor is your firm resolve unknown to me,
In the preferment of the eldest sister.
This liberty is all that I request,
That upon knowledge of my parentage
I may have welcome 'mongst the rest that woo,
And free access and favor as the rest.   97
And toward the education of your daughters
I here bestow a simple instrument,
And this small packet of Greek and Latin books.
If you accept them, then their worth is great.
       [*Biondello brings forward the lute and books.*]

BAPTISTA

Lucentio is your name? Of whence, I pray?   102

TRANIO

Of Pisa, sir, son to Vincentio.

BAPTISTA

A mighty man of Pisa. By report   104

---

76 grateful pleasing **82 Cambio** (In Italian, appropriately, the word
means "change" or "exchange.") **86 walk like a stranger** keep your
distance, stand apart **97 favor** leave, permission **102 Lucentio . . .
name** (Baptista may have learned this information from a note accom-
panying the books and lute.) **104 report** reputation

I know him well. You are very welcome, sir.
[*To Hortensio.*] Take you the lute, [*To Lucentio*] and you
  the set of books;
You shall go see your pupils presently.   107
Holla, within!
    Enter a Servant.

        Sirrah, lead these gentlemen
To my daughters, and tell them both
These are their tutors. Bid them use them well.
    [*Exit Servant, with Lucentio and Hortensio.*]
We will go walk a little in the orchard,   111
And then to dinner. You are passing welcome,   112
And so I pray you all to think yourselves.

PETRUCHIO
Signor Baptista, my business asketh haste,
And every day I cannot come to woo.
You knew my father well, and in him me,
Left solely heir to all his lands and goods,
Which I have bettered rather than decreased.
Then tell me, if I get your daughter's love,
What dowry shall I have with her to wife?

BAPTISTA
After my death the one half of my lands,
And in possession twenty thousand crowns.   122

PETRUCHIO
And, for that dowry, I'll assure her of
Her widowhood, be it that she survive me,   124
In all my lands and leases whatsoever.
Let specialties be therefore drawn between us,   126
That covenants may be kept on either hand.

BAPTISTA
Ay, when the special thing is well obtained,
That is, her love; for that is all in all.

PETRUCHIO
Why, that is nothing, for I tell you, Father,
I am as peremptory as she proud-minded;
And where two raging fires meet together,

107 presently immediately **111 orchard** garden **112 passing** exceedingly **122 in possession** i.e., in immediate possession **124 widowhood**
i.e., widow's share of the estate **126 specialties** terms of contract

They do consume the thing that feeds their fury.
Though little fire grows great with little wind,
Yet extreme gusts will blow out fire and all.
So I to her, and so she yields to me,
For I am rough and woo not like a babe.

BAPTISTA
Well mayst thou woo, and happy be thy speed!
But be thou armed for some unhappy words.

PETRUCHIO
Ay, to the proof, as mountains are for winds,   140
That shakes not, though they blow perpetually.   141

Enter Hortensio [as Litio], with his head broke.

BAPTISTA
How now, my friend, why dost thou look so pale?

HORTENSIO
For fear, I promise you, if I look pale.

BAPTISTA
What, will my daughter prove a good musician?

HORTENSIO
I think she'll sooner prove a soldier.
Iron may hold with her, but never lutes.   146

BAPTISTA
Why, then thou canst not break her to the lute?   147

HORTENSIO
Why, no, for she hath broke the lute to me.
I did but tell her she mistook her frets,   149
And bowed her hand to teach her fingering,
When, with a most impatient devilish spirit,
"Frets, call you these?" quoth she, "I'll fume with them."
And with that word she struck me on the head,
And through the instrument my pate made way;
And there I stood amazèd for a while,
As on a pillory, looking through the lute,   156

---

140 to the proof i.e., in armor, proof against her shrewishness
141 shakes shake. **s.d. broke** i.e., with a bleeding cut. (Hortensio
usually appears on stage with his head emerging through a broken
lute.) **146 hold with** hold out against **147 break** train (with pun in the
next line) **149 frets** ridges or bars on the fingerboard of the lute. (But
Kate puns on the sense of "fume," "be indignant.") **156 pillory**
wooden collar used as punishment

While she did call me rascal fiddler
And twangling Jack, with twenty such vile terms,   158
As had she studied to misuse me so.

PETRUCHIO
Now, by the world, it is a lusty wench!   160
I love her ten times more than e'er I did.
O, how I long to have some chat with her!

BAPTISTA [*To Hortensio*]
Well, go with me and be not so discomfited.
Proceed in practice with my younger daughter;   164
She's apt to learn and thankful for good turns.—
Signor Petruchio, will you go with us,
Or shall I send my daughter Kate to you?

PETRUCHIO
I pray you, do.   *Exeunt. Manet Petruchio.*
          I'll attend her here,   168
And woo her with some spirit when she comes.
Say that she rail, why then I'll tell her plain
She sings as sweetly as a nightingale.
Say that she frown, I'll say she looks as clear
As morning roses newly washed with dew.
Say she be mute and will not speak a word,
Then I'll commend her volubility
And say she uttereth piercing eloquence.
If she do bid me pack, I'll give her thanks,   177
As though she bid me stay by her a week.
If she deny to wed, I'll crave the day   179
When I shall ask the banns and when be married.   180
But here she comes; and now, Petruchio, speak.

          Enter Katharina.

Good morrow, Kate, for that's your name, I hear.

KATHARINA
Well have you heard, but something hard of hearing.   183
They call me Katharine that do talk of me.

PETRUCHIO
You lie, in faith, for you are called plain Kate,

---

158 Jack knave   **160 lusty** lively   **164 practice** instruction   **168 s.d.**
Manet he remains onstage   **177 pack** begone   **179 deny** refuse   **180 ask**
the banns have a reading of the required announcement in church of a
forthcoming marriage   **183 heard, hard** (Pronounced nearly alike.)

And bonny Kate and sometimes Kate the curst;
But Kate, the prettiest Kate in Christendom,
Kate of Kate Hall, my superdainty Kate,
For dainties are all Kates, and therefore, Kate,   189
Take this of me, Kate of my consolation: 190
Hearing thy mildness praised in every town,
Thy virtues spoke of, and thy beauty sounded,   192
Yet not so deeply as to thee belongs,
Myself am moved to woo thee for my wife.

KATHARINA
Moved? In good time! Let him that moved you hither   195
Remove you hence. I knew you at the first
You were a movable.

PETRUCHIO   Why, what's a movable?   197

KATHARINA
A joint stool.

PETRUCHIO   Thou hast hit it. Come, sit on me.   198

KATHARINA
Asses are made to bear, and so are you.   199

PETRUCHIO
Women are made to bear, and so are you.

KATHARINA
No such jade as you, if me you mean.   201

PETRUCHIO
Alas, good Kate, I will not burden thee,
For knowing thee to be but young and light.   203

KATHARINA
Too light for such a swain as you to catch,   204
And yet as heavy as my weight should be.

PETRUCHIO
Should be? Should—buzz!   206

189 all Kates (with a quibble on *cates*, confections, delicacies)   **190 of me** from me   **192 sounded** proclaimed (with a quibble on "plumbed," as indicated by *deeply* in the next line)   **195 In good time** forsooth, indeed   **197 movable** (1) one easily changed or dissuaded (2) an article of furniture   **198 joint stool** a well-fitted stool made by an expert craftsman   **199 bear** carry (with puns in the following lines suggesting "bear children" and "support a man during sexual intercourse")   **201 jade** an ill-conditioned horse   **203 light** (1) of delicate stature (2) lascivious (3) lacking a *burden* (see previous line) in the musical sense of lacking a bass undersong or accompaniment (4) elusive (in the following line)   **204 swain** young rustic in love   **206 buzz** i.e., a bee (punning on *be*) should make a buzzing sound; also, an interjection expressing impatience or contempt.

KATHARINA   Well ta'en, and like a buzzard. 206
PETRUCHIO
O slow-winged turtle, shall a buzzard take thee?
KATHARINA
Ay, for a turtle, as he takes a buzzard.
PETRUCHIO
Come, come, you wasp, i' faith, you are too angry.   209
KATHARINA
If I be waspish, best beware my sting.
PETRUCHIO
My remedy is then to pluck it out.
KATHARINA
Ay, if the fool could find it where it lies.
PETRUCHIO
Who knows not where a wasp does wear his sting?
In his tail.
KATHARINA   In his tongue.
PETRUCHIO   Whose tongue?
KATHARINA
Yours, if you talk of tails, and so farewell.   217
PETRUCHIO
What, with my tongue in your tail? Nay, come again.
Good Kate, I am a gentleman—
KATHARINA   That I'll try. *She strikes him.*
PETRUCHIO
I swear I'll cuff you, if you strike again.
KATHARINA   So may you lose your arms.
If you strike me, you are no gentleman,
And if no gentleman, why then no arms.   223
PETRUCHIO
A herald, Kate? O, put me in thy books!   224
KATHARINA   What is your crest, a coxcomb?   225

---

206 buzzard (1) figuratively, a fool (2) in the next line, an inferior kind of
hawk, fit only to overtake a slow-winged *turtle* or turtledove, as Petruchio might overtake Kate (3) a buzzing insect, caught by a turtle
209 wasp i.e., waspish, scolding woman (but suggested by *buzzard*,
buzzing insect)   **217 talk of tails** i.e., idly tells stories (with pun on *tale*,
tail)   **223 no arms** no coat of arms (with pun on *arms* as limbs of the
body)   **224 books** (1) books of heraldry, heraldic registers (2) grace,
favor   **225 crest** (1) armorial device (2) a rooster's comb, setting up the
joke on *coxcomb*, the cap of the court fool

PETRUCHIO
A combless cock, so Kate will be my hen.
KATHARINA
No cock of mine; you crow too like a craven.   227
PETRUCHIO
Nay, come, Kate, come, you must not look so sour.
KATHARINA
It is my fashion when I see a crab.   229
PETRUCHIO
Why, here's no crab, and therefore look not sour.
KATHARINA   There is, there is.
PETRUCHIO
Then show it me.
KATHARINA   Had I a glass, I would.
PETRUCHIO   What, you mean my face?
KATHARINA   Well aimed of such a young one.   234
PETRUCHIO
Now, by Saint George, I am too young for you.
KATHARINA
Yet you are withered.
PETRUCHIO   'Tis with cares.
KATHARINA   I care not.
PETRUCHIO
Nay, hear you, Kate. In sooth, you scape not so.
KATHARINA
I chafe you if I tarry. Let me go.
PETRUCHIO
No, not a whit. I find you passing gentle.
'Twas told me you were rough and coy and sullen,   240
And now I find report a very liar,
For thou art pleasant, gamesome, passing courteous,   242
But slow in speech, yet sweet as springtime flowers.   243
Thou canst not frown, thou canst not look askance,   244
Nor bite the lip, as angry wenches will,
Nor hast thou pleasure to be cross in talk;
But thou with mildness entertain'st thy wooers,
With gentle conference, soft and affable.

227 **craven** a cock that is not "game" or willing to fight   229 **crab** crab
apple   234 **aimed of** guessed for.   **young** i.e., inexperienced. (But
Petruchio picks up the word in the sense of "strong.")   240 **coy** disdainful   242 **gamesome** playful, spirited   243 **But slow** never anything but
slow   244 **askance** scornfully

Why does the world report that Kate doth limp?
O slanderous world! Kate like the hazel twig
Is straight and slender, and as brown in hue
As hazelnuts, and sweeter than the kernels.
O, let me see thee walk. Thou dost not halt.   253

KATHARINA
Go, fool, and whom thou keep'st command.   254

PETRUCHIO
Did ever Dian so become a grove   255
As Kate this chamber with her princely gait?
O, be thou Dian, and let her be Kate,
And then let Kate be chaste and Dian sportful!   258

KATHARINA
Where did you study all this goodly speech?

PETRUCHIO
It is extempore, from my mother wit.   260

KATHARINA
A witty mother! Witless else her son.   261

PETRUCHIO Am I not wise?   262

KATHARINA Yes, keep you warm.   263

PETRUCHIO
Marry, so I mean, sweet Katharine, in thy bed.
And therefore, setting all this chat aside,
Thus in plain terms: your father hath consented
That you shall be my wife; your dowry 'greed on;
And, will you, nill you, I will marry you.   268
Now, Kate, I am a husband for your turn,   269
For by this light, whereby I see thy beauty—
Thy beauty that doth make me like thee well—
Thou must be married to no man but me;

     Enter Baptista, Gremio, [and] Tranio [as
     Lucentio].

For I am he am born to tame you, Kate,

---

253 halt limp **254 whom thou keep'st** i.e., those whom you employ,
your servants **255 Dian** Diana, goddess of the hunt and of chastity.
become adorn **258 sportful** amorous **260 mother wit** native intelligence **261 Witless . . . son** i.e., without the intelligence inherited from
her, he would have none at all **262–263 wise . . . warm** (An allusion to
the proverbial phrase "enough wit to keep oneself warm.") **268 nill
you** will you not **269 for your turn** to suit you

And bring you from a wild Kate to a Kate   274
Conformable as other household Kates.
Here comes your father. Never make denial;
I must and will have Katharine to my wife.

BAPTISTA
Now, Signor Petruchio, how speed you with my
    daughter?

PETRUCHIO
How but well, sir, how but well?
It were impossible I should speed amiss.   280

BAPTISTA
Why, how now, daughter Katharine, in your dumps?

KATHARINA
Call you me daughter? Now, I promise you,   282
You have showed a tender fatherly regard,
To wish me wed to one half lunatic,
A madcap ruffian and a swearing Jack,
That thinks with oaths to face the matter out.   286

PETRUCHIO
Father, 'tis thus: yourself and all the world,
That talked of her, have talked amiss of her.
If she be curst, it is for policy,   289
For she's not froward, but modest as the dove.   290
She is not hot, but temperate as the morn.
For patience she will prove a second Grissel,   292
And Roman Lucrece for her chastity.   293
And to conclude, we have 'greed so well together
That upon Sunday is the wedding day.

KATHARINA
I'll see thee hanged on Sunday first.

GREMIO   Hark, Petruchio, she says she'll see thee hanged
    first.

TRANIO
Is this your speeding? Nay then, good night our part!

274 **wild Kate** (with a quibble on *wildcat*)   280 **speed** fare, get on
282 **promise** assure   286 **face** brazen   289 **policy** cunning, ulterior
motive   290 **froward** willful, perverse   292 **Grissel** patient Griselda, the
epitome of wifely patience and devotion (whose story was told by
Chaucer in "The Clerk's Tale" of *The Canterbury Tales* and earlier by
Boccaccio and Petrarch)   293 **Roman Lucrece** Lucretia, a Roman lady
who took her own life after her chastity had been violated by the Tar-
quin prince, Sextus. (Shakespeare told the story in *The Rape of Lucrece*.)

PETRUCHIO
Be patient, gentlemen, I choose her for myself.
If she and I be pleased, what's that to you?
'Tis bargained twixt us twain, being alone,
That she shall still be curst in company.
I tell you, 'tis incredible to believe
How much she loves me. O, the kindest Kate!
She hung about my neck, and kiss on kiss
She vied so fast, protesting oath on oath,   307
That in a twink she won me to her love.
O, you are novices! 'Tis a world to see   309
How tame, when men and women are alone,
A meacock wretch can make the curstest shrew.—   311
Give me thy hand, Kate. I will unto Venice
To buy apparel 'gainst the wedding day.—   313
Provide the feast, Father, and bid the guests;
I will be sure my Katharine shall be fine.   315
BAPTISTA
I know not what to say. But give me your hands.
God send you joy, Petruchio! 'Tis a match.
GREMIO, TRANIO
Amen, say we. We will be witnesses.
PETRUCHIO
Father, and wife, and gentlemen, adieu.
I will to Venice. Sunday comes apace.
We will have rings and things, and fine array;
And kiss me, Kate, we will be married o' Sunday.   322
            Exeunt Petruchio and Katharine [separately].
GREMIO
Was ever match clapped up so suddenly?   323
BAPTISTA
Faith, gentlemen, now I play a merchant's part,
And venture madly on a desperate mart.   325
TRANIO
'Twas a commodity lay fretting by you;   326
'Twill bring you gain, or perish on the seas.

---

307 vied went me one better, kiss for kiss   **309 a world** worth a whole
world   **311 meacock** cowardly   **313 'gainst** in anticipation of   **315 fine**
elegantly dressed   **322 kiss me** (Petruchio probably kisses her.)
323 clapped up settled (by a shaking of hands)   **325 desperate mart**
risky venture   **326 lay fretting** i.e., which lay in storage being destroyed
by moths, weevils, or spoilage (with a pun on "chafing")

BAPTISTA
The gain I seek is quiet in the match.
GREMIO
No doubt but he hath got a quiet catch.   329
But now, Baptista, to your younger daughter.
Now is the day we long have lookèd for.
I am your neighbor, and was suitor first.
TRANIO
And I am one that love Bianca more
Than words can witness or your thoughts can guess.
GREMIO
Youngling, thou canst not love so dear as I.
TRANIO
Graybeard, thy love doth freeze.
GREMIO   But thine doth fry.
Skipper, stand back. 'Tis age that nourisheth.   337
TRANIO
But youth in ladies' eyes that flourisheth.
BAPTISTA
Content you, gentlemen. I will compound this strife.   339
'Tis deeds must win the prize, and he of both   340
That can assure my daughter greatest dower
Shall have my Bianca's love.
Say, Signor Gremio, what can you assure her?
GREMIO
First, as you know, my house within the city
Is richly furnishèd with plate and gold,
Basins and ewers to lave her dainty hands;   346
My hangings all of Tyrian tapestry;   347
In ivory coffers I have stuffed my crowns;
In cypress chests my arras counterpoints,   349
Costly apparel, tents, and canopies,   350
Fine linen, Turkey cushions bossed with pearl,   351
Valance of Venice gold in needlework,   352
Pewter and brass, and all things that belongs
To house or housekeeping. Then at my farm

---

329 quiet catch (Said ironically; Gremio is sure that Kate will be anything but quiet.)   **337 Skipper** flighty fellow   **339 compound** settle
340 he of both i.e., the one of you two   **346 lave** wash   **347 Tyrian** dark
red or purple   **349 arras counterpoints** counterpanes of tapestry
350 tents bed-curtains   **351 Turkey** Turkish.   **bossed** embossed
352 Valance drapery around the canopy or bed frame

I have a hundred milch kine to the pail,   355
Sixscore fat oxen standing in my stalls,
And all things answerable to this portion.   357
Myself am struck in years, I must confess,   358
And if I die tomorrow, this is hers,
If whilst I live she will be only mine.

TRANIO
That "only" came well in. Sir, list to me:
I am my father's heir and only son.
If I may have your daughter to my wife,
I'll leave her houses three or four as good,
Within rich Pisa walls, as any one
Old Signor Gremio has in Padua,
Besides two thousand ducats by the year   367
Of fruitful land, all which shall be her jointure.   368
What, have I pinched you, Signor Gremio?

GREMIO
Two thousand ducats by the year of land!
[Aside.] My land amounts not to so much in all.—
That she shall have, besides an argosy   372
That now is lying in Marseilles' road.   373
[To Tranio.] What, have I choked you with an argosy?

TRANIO
Gremio, 'tis known my father hath no less
Than three great argosies, besides two galliases   376
And twelve tight galleys. These I will assure her,   377
And twice as much, whate'er thou offerest next.

GREMIO
Nay, I have offered all. I have no more,
And she can have no more than all I have.
[To Baptista.] If you like me, she shall have me and mine.

TRANIO
Why, then the maid is mine from all the world,
By your firm promise. Gremio is outvied.

BAPTISTA
I must confess your offer is the best;

355 **milch kine to the pail** dairy cattle   357 **answerable to** on the same
scale as   358 **struck** advanced   367 **ducats** gold coins   368 **Of** from.
jointure marriage settlement   372 **argosy** merchant vessel of the largest
size   373 **road** roadstead, harbor   376 **galliases** heavy, low-built vessels   377 **tight** watertight

And, let your father make her the assurance,   385
She is your own; else, you must pardon me.
If you should die before him, where's her dower?
TRANIO
That's but a cavil. He is old, I young.
GREMIO
And may not young men die as well as old?
BAPTISTA
Well, gentlemen, I am thus resolved:
On Sunday next, you know
My daughter Katharine is to be married.
Now on the Sunday following shall Bianca
Be bride [*To Tranio*] to you, if you make this assurance;
If not, to Signor Gremio.
And so I take my leave, and thank you both.   *Exit.*
GREMIO
Adieu, good neighbor.—Now I fear thee not.
Sirrah young gamester, your father were a fool
To give thee all, and in his waning age
Set foot under thy table. Tut, a toy!   400
An old Italian fox is not so kind, my boy.   *Exit.*
TRANIO
A vengeance on your crafty withered hide!
Yet I have faced it with a card of ten.   403
'Tis in my head to do my master good.
I see no reason but supposed Lucentio
Must get a father, called supposed Vincentio,
And that's a wonder. Fathers commonly
Do get their children; but in this case of wooing,   408
A child shall get a sire, if I fail not of my cunning.
                                               Exit.

❖

385 **let** provided   **400 Set . . . table** i.e., become a dependent in your
household.   **a toy** nonsense   **403 faced . . . ten** brazened it out with only
a ten-spot of cards   **408 get** beget (with a play on *get*, obtain, in l. 406)

3.1　*Enter Lucentio [as Cambio], Hortensio [as Litio], and Bianca.*

LUCENTIO
　Fiddler, forbear. You grow too forward, sir.
　Have you so soon forgot the entertainment
　Her sister Katharine welcomed you withal?

HORTENSIO
　But, wrangling pedant, this is
　The patroness of heavenly harmony.
　Then give me leave to have prerogative,　　　　　6
　And when in music we have spent an hour
　Your lecture shall have leisure for as much.　　　8

LUCENTIO
　Preposterous ass, that never read so far　　　　9
　To know the cause why music was ordained!
　Was it not to refresh the mind of man
　After his studies or his usual pain?　　　　　12
　Then give me leave to read philosophy,
　And, while I pause, serve in your harmony.　　　14

HORTENSIO
　Sirrah, I will not bear these braves of thine.　　15

BIANCA
　Why, gentlemen, you do me double wrong
　To strive for that which resteth in my choice.
　I am no breeching scholar in the schools;　　　18
　I'll not be tied to hours nor 'pointed times,
　But learn my lessons as I please myself.
　And, to cut off all strife, here sit we down.
　[*To Hortensio.*] Take you your instrument, play you the
　　　whiles;
　His lecture will be done ere you have tuned.

HORTENSIO
　You'll leave his lecture when I am in tune?

LUCENTIO
　That will be never. Tune your instrument.
　　　　　　　　[*Hortensio moves aside and tunes.*]

3.1. Location: The same.
6 prerogative precedence　**8 lecture** lesson　**9 Preposterous** inverting
the natural order of things, unreasonable　**12 pain** labor　**14 serve in**
present, serve up　**15 braves** insults　**18 breeching scholar** i.e., schoolboy liable to be whipped

BIANCA Where left we last?
LUCENTIO Here, madam. [*Reads.*]
"Hic ibat Simois; hic est Sigeia tellus;   28
Hic steterat Priami regia celsa senis."   29
BIANCA Conster them.   30
LUCENTIO *"Hic ibat,"* as I told you before, *"Simois,"* I
am Lucentio, *"hic est,"* son unto Vincentio of Pisa,
"Sigeia tellus," disguised thus to get your love; *"Hic
steterat,"* and that Lucentio that comes a-wooing,
"Priami," is my man Tranio, *"regia,"* bearing my port, 35
"celsa senis," that we might beguile the old panta- 36
loon.   37
HORTENSIO Madam, my instrument's in tune.
BIANCA Let's hear. [*He plays.*] O fie! The treble jars.
LUCENTIO Spit in the hole, man, and tune again.   40
                    [*Hortensio moves aside.*]
BIANCA Now let me see if I can conster it: *"Hic ibat Si-
mois,"* I know you not, *"hic est Sigeia tellus,"* I trust
you not; *"Hic steterat Priami,"* take heed he hear us
not, *"regia,"* presume not, *"celsa senis,"* despair not.
HORTENSIO
Madam, 'tis now in tune.   [*He plays again.*]
LUCENTIO   All but the bass.
HORTENSIO
The bass is right; 'tis the base knave that jars.
[*Aside.*] How fiery and forward our pedant is!
Now, for my life, the knave doth court my love.
Pedascule, I'll watch you better yet.   49
BIANCA [*To Lucentio*]
In time I may believe, yet I mistrust.
LUCENTIO
Mistrust it not, for, sure, Aeacides   51
Was Ajax, called so from his grandfather.

28–29 Hic . . . senis here flowed the river Simois; here is the Sigeian
land; here stood the lofty palace of old Priam. (Ovid, *Heroides*,
1.33–34.)   **30 Conster** construe   **35 port** social position, style of
living   **36–37 pantaloon** foolish old man, i.e., Gremio   **40 Spit in the
hole** i.e., to make the peg stick   **49 Pedascule** (A word contemptuously
coined by Hortensio, the vocative of *pedasculus*, little pedant.)
51 Aeacides descendant of Aeacus, King of Aegina, father of Telamon
and grandfather of Ajax. (Lucentio is pretending to go on with his
lesson.)

BIANCA
I must believe my master; else, I promise you,
I should be arguing still upon that doubt.
But let it rest.—Now, Litio, to you:
Good master, take it not unkindly, pray,
That I have been thus pleasant with you both.   57

HORTENSIO [*To Lucentio*]
You may go walk, and give me leave awhile.
My lessons make no music in three parts.

LUCENTIO
Are you so formal, sir? Well, I must wait,   60
[*Aside*] And watch withal; for, but I be deceived,   61
Our fine musician groweth amorous.
                                        [*He moves aside.*]

HORTENSIO
Madam, before you touch the instrument,
To learn the order of my fingering,   64
I must begin with rudiments of art,
To teach you gamut in a briefer sort,   66
More pleasant, pithy, and effectual
Than hath been taught by any of my trade.
And there it is in writing, fairly drawn.   69
                                        [*He gives her a paper.*]

BIANCA
Why, I am past my gamut long ago.

HORTENSIO
Yet read the gamut of Hortensio.

BIANCA [*Reads*]
"*Gamut* I am, the ground of all accord,   72
A re, to plead Hortensio's passion;
B mi, Bianca, take him for thy lord,
C fa ut, that loves with all affection.   75
D sol re, one clef, two notes have I;
E la mi, show pity, or I die."

57 pleasant merry   **60 formal** precise   **61 but** unless   **64 order**
method   **66 gamut** the scale, from the alphabet name (*gamma*) of the
first note plus *ut*, its syllable name, now commonly called *do*. (The
gamut of Hortensio begins on G instead of on C.)   **69 drawn** set out,
copied   **72 ground** bass note, foundation.   **accord** harmony   **75 fa ut**
(The note C is the fourth note, or *fa*, of a scale based on G, but is the
first note, *ut*, or *do*, of the more universal major scale based on C.
Similarly, D is fifth note or *sol* in the G scale but second or *re* in the C
scale; similarly with E as sixth and third.)

Call you this gamut? Tut, I like it not.
Old fashions please me best; I am not so nice   79
To change true rules for odd inventions.

Enter a [Servant as] messenger.

SERVANT
Mistress, your father prays you leave your books
And help to dress your sister's chamber up.
You know tomorrow is the wedding day.

BIANCA
Farewell, sweet masters both, I must be gone.

                    [Exeunt Bianca and Servant.]

LUCENTIO
Faith, mistress, then I have no cause to stay.   *[Exit.]*

HORTENSIO
But I have cause to pry into this pedant.
Methinks he looks as though he were in love.
Yet if thy thoughts, Bianca, be so humble
To cast thy wandering eyes on every stale,   89
Seize thee that list. If once I find thee ranging,   90
Hortensio will be quit with thee by changing.   *Exit.* 91

❖

3.2   *Enter Baptista, Gremio, Tranio [as Lucentio],*
Katharine, Bianca, [Lucentio as Cambio], and
others, attendants.

BAPTISTA *[To Tranio]*
Signor Lucentio, this is the 'pointed day
That Katharine and Petruchio should be married,
And yet we hear not of our son-in-law.
What will be said? What mockery will it be,
To want the bridegroom when the priest attends   5
To speak the ceremonial rites of marriage?
What says Lucentio to this shame of ours?

79 nice capricious   **89 stale** decoy, bait   **90 Seize . . . list** let him who
wants you have you.   **ranging** inconstant   **91 be quit** get even.   **changing** i.e., loving another

3.2. Location: Padua. Before Baptista's house.
5 want lack

KATHARINA
No shame but mine. I must, forsooth, be forced
To give my hand opposed against my heart
Unto a mad-brain rudesby full of spleen,   10
Who wooed in haste and means to wed at leisure.
I told you, I, he was a frantic fool,
Hiding his bitter jests in blunt behavior.
And, to be noted for a merry man,
He'll woo a thousand, 'point the day of marriage,
Make friends, invite, and proclaim the banns,
Yet never means to wed where he hath wooed.
Now must the world point at poor Katharine
And say, "Lo, there is mad Petruchio's wife,
If it would please him come and marry her!"

TRANIO
Patience, good Katharine, and Baptista too.
Upon my life, Petruchio means but well,
Whatever fortune stays him from his word.
Though he be blunt, I know him passing wise;
Though he be merry, yet withal he's honest.

KATHARINA
Would Katharine had never seen him though!
                              Exit weeping.

BAPTISTA
Go, girl, I cannot blame thee now to weep,
For such an injury would vex a very saint,
Much more a shrew of thy impatient humor.

        Enter Biondello.

BIONDELLO   Master, master! News, and such old news 30
as you never heard of!
BAPTISTA   Is it new and old too? How may that be?
BIONDELLO   Why, is it not news to hear of Petruchio's
coming?
BAPTISTA   Is he come?
BIONDELLO   Why, no, sir.
BAPTISTA   What, then?
BIONDELLO   He is coming.
BAPTISTA   When will he be here?

10 rudesby unmannerly fellow.   **spleen** i.e., changeable temper   **30 old**
rare; or perhaps referring to Petruchio's old clothes

BIONDELLO When he stands where I am and sees you there.

TRANIO But say, what to thine old news?   42

BIONDELLO Why, Petruchio is coming in a new hat and an old jerkin; a pair of old breeches thrice turned; a 44 pair of boots that have been candle-cases, one buck- 45 led, another laced; an old rusty sword ta'en out of the town armory, with a broken hilt, and chapeless; with 47 two broken points; his horse hipped, with an old 48 mothy saddle and stirrups of no kindred; besides, possessed with the glanders and like to mose in the 50 chine, troubled with the lampass, infected with the 51 fashions, full of windgalls, sped with spavins, rayed 52 with the yellows, past cure of the fives, stark spoiled 53 with the staggers, begnawn with the bots, swayed in 54 the back and shoulder-shotten; near-legged before, 55 and with a half-cheeked bit and a headstall of sheep's 56 leather which, being restrained to keep him from 57 stumbling, hath been often burst and now repaired with knots; one girth six times pieced, and a woman's 59

---

42 to about   **44 jerkin** man's jacket.   **turned** i.e., with the material reversed to get more wear   **45 candle-cases** i.e., discarded boots, used only as a receptacle for candle ends   **47 chapeless** without the chape, the metal plate or mounting of a scabbard, especially that which covers the point   **48 points** tagged laces for attaching hose to doublet.   **hipped** lamed in the hip. (Almost all the diseases here named are described in Gervase Markham's *How to Choose, Ride, Train, and Diet both Hunting Horses and Running Horses . . . Also a Discourse of Horsemanship*, probably first published in 1593.)   **50 glanders** contagious disease in horses causing swelling beneath the jaw and mucous discharge from the nostrils   **50–51 mose in the chine** suffer from glanders   **51 lampass** a thick spongy flesh growing over a horse's upper teeth and hindering his eating   **52 fashions** i.e., farcins, or farcy, a disease like glanders. **windgalls** soft tumors or swellings generally found on the fetlock joint, so called from having been supposed to contain air.   **sped** far gone. **spavins** a disease of the hock, marked by a small bony enlargement inside the leg.   **rayed** defiled   **53 yellows** jaundice.   **fives** avives, a glandular disease causing swelling behind the ear   **54 staggers** a disease causing palsylike staggering.   **bots** parasitic worms **55 shoulder-shotten** with sprained or dislocated shoulder.   **near-legged before** with knock-kneed forelegs   **56 half-cheeked bit** one to which the bridle is attached halfway up the cheek or sidepiece and thus not giving sufficient control over the horse.   **headstall** part of the bridle over the head   **56–57 sheep's leather** (i.e., of inferior quality; pigskin was used for strongest harness)   **57 restrained** drawn back   **59 pieced** mended

crupper of velour, which hath two letters for her name 60
fairly set down in studs, and here and there pieced
with packthread.

BAPTISTA Who comes with him?

BIONDELLO   O, sir, his lackey, for all the world capari- 64
soned like the horse; with a linen stock on one leg and 65
a kersey boot-hose on the other, gartered with a red 66
and blue list; an old hat, and the humor of forty fancies 67
pricked in 't for a feather—a monster, a very monster 68
in apparel, and not like a Christian footboy or a gentleman's lackey.

TRANIO
'Tis some odd humor pricks him to this fashion; 71
Yet oftentimes he goes but mean-appareled.

BAPTISTA   I am glad he's come, howsoe'er he comes.

BIONDELLO   Why, sir, he comes not.

BAPTISTA   Didst thou not say he comes?

BIONDELLO   Who? That Petruchio came?

BAPTISTA   Ay, that Petruchio came.

BIONDELLO   No, sir, I say his horse comes, with him on
his back.

BAPTISTA   Why, that's all one. 80

BIONDELLO
Nay, by Saint Jamy,
I hold you a penny, 82
A horse and a man
Is more than one,
And yet not many.

Enter Petruchio and Grumio.

PETRUCHIO
Come, where be these gallants? Who's at home?

BAPTISTA   You are welcome, sir.

PETRUCHIO   And yet I come not well.

BAPTISTA   And yet you halt not. 89

---

60 crupper leather loop passing under the horse's tail and fastened to
the saddle.   **velour** velvet   **64–65 caparisoned** outfitted   **65 stock**
stocking   **66 kersey boot-hose** overstocking of coarse material for
wearing under boots   **67 list** strip of cloth.   **the humor . . . fancies** i.e.,
with a caprice equal to some forty imaginings (?)   **68 pricked** pinned
71 humor pricks whim that spurs   **80 all one** the same thing   **82 hold**
wager   **89 halt** limp, move slowly

TRANIO
Not so well appareled as I wish you were.

PETRUCHIO
Were it better, I should rush in thus.   91
But where is Kate? Where is my lovely bride?
How does my father? Gentles, methinks you frown.
And wherefore gaze this goodly company
As if they saw some wondrous monument,   95
Some comet, or unusual prodigy?   96

BAPTISTA
Why, sir, you know this is your wedding day.
First were we sad, fearing you would not come,
Now sadder that you come so unprovided.   99
Fie, doff this habit, shame to your estate,   100
An eyesore to our solemn festival!

TRANIO
And tell us what occasion of import
Hath all so long detained you from your wife
And sent you hither so unlike yourself?

PETRUCHIO
Tedious it were to tell, and harsh to hear.
Sufficeth I am come to keep my word,
Though in some part enforcèd to digress,   107
Which at more leisure I will so excuse
As you shall well be satisfied withal.
But where is Kate? I stay too long from her.
The morning wears; 'tis time we were at church.

TRANIO
See not your bride in these unreverent robes.
Go to my chamber; put on clothes of mine.

PETRUCHIO
Not I, believe me. Thus I'll visit her.

BAPTISTA
But thus, I trust, you will not marry her.

PETRUCHIO
Good sooth, even thus. Therefore ha' done with words.
To me she's married, not unto my clothes.

---

91 Were it even if it (my apparel) were.   **rush** come quickly (referring to
halt not in l. 89)   **95 monument** portent   **96 prodigy** omen   **99 unprovided** ill equipped   **100 estate** position, station   **107 digress** i.e., deviate
from my promise

Could I repair what she will wear in me   118
As I can change these poor accoutrements,
'Twere well for Kate and better for myself.
But what a fool am I to chat with you,
When I should bid good morrow to my bride
And seal the title with a lovely kiss!   *Exit.* 123

TRANIO
He hath some meaning in his mad attire.
We will persuade him, be it possible,
To put on better ere he go to church.

BAPTISTA
I'll after him and see the event of this.   127
          Exit [with all but Tranio and Lucentio].

TRANIO
But, sir, love concerneth us to add   128
Her father's liking, which to bring to pass,   129
As I before imparted to your worship,
I am to get a man—whate'er he be
It skills not much, we'll fit him to our turn—   132
And he shall be Vincentio of Pisa,
And make assurance here in Padua
Of greater sums than I have promisèd.
So shall you quietly enjoy your hope
And marry sweet Bianca with consent.

LUCENTIO
Were it not that my fellow schoolmaster
Doth watch Bianca's steps so narrowly,
'Twere good, methinks, to steal our marriage,   140
Which once performed, let all the world say no,
I'll keep mine own, despite of all the world.

TRANIO
That by degrees we mean to look into,
And watch our vantage in this business.   144
We'll overreach the graybeard, Gremio,
The narrow-prying father, Minola,   146

118 Could . . . me if I could amend in my character what she'll have to
put up with   **123 lovely** loving   **127 event** outcome   **128–129 love . . .
liking** i.e., our love plot to secure Bianca makes it our business to
secure Baptista's approval of the feigned "Lucentio" as wooer
132 skills matters   **140 steal our marriage** i.e., elope   **144 vantage**
opportunity, advantage   **146 narrow-prying** suspicious, watchful

The quaint musician, amorous Litio,   147
All for my master's sake, Lucentio.
   Enter Gremio.
Signor Gremio, came you from the church?
GREMIO
As willingly as e'er I came from school.
TRANIO
And is the bride and bridegroom coming home?
GREMIO
A bridegroom, say you? 'Tis a groom indeed,   152
A grumbling groom, and that the girl shall find.
TRANIO
Curster than she? Why, 'tis impossible.
GREMIO
Why, he's a devil, a devil, a very fiend.
TRANIO
Why, she's a devil, a devil, the devil's dam.   156
GREMIO
Tut, she's a lamb, a dove, a fool to him.   157
I'll tell you, Sir Lucentio. When the priest
Should ask if Katharine should be his wife,
"Ay, by gogs wouns," quoth he, and swore so loud   160
That all amazed the priest let fall the book,
And as he stooped again to take it up
This mad-brained bridegroom took him such a cuff   163
That down fell priest and book, and book and priest.
"Now take them up," quoth he, "if any list."   165
TRANIO
What said the wench when he rose again?
GREMIO
Trembled and shook, forwhy he stamped and swore   167
As if the vicar meant to cozen him.   168
But after many ceremonies done,
He calls for wine. "A health!" quoth he, as if
He had been aboard, carousing to his mates   171

---

147 quaint skillful   **152 a groom indeed** i.e., a fine bridegroom he is.
(Said ironically, with pun on the sense of "servant," "rough fellow.")
156 dam mother   **157 a fool to** i.e., a pitiable weak creature compared
with   **160 gogs wouns** God's (Christ's) wounds   **163 took** gave, struck
165 list choose   **167 forwhy** because   **168 cozen** cheat   **171 aboard**
aboard ship

After a storm; quaffed off the muscatel
And threw the sops all in the sexton's face,   173
Having no other reason
But that his beard grew thin and hungerly   175
And seemed to ask him sops as he was drinking.
This done, he took the bride about the neck
And kissed her lips with such a clamorous smack
That at the parting all the church did echo.
And I seeing this came thence for very shame,
And after me, I know, the rout is coming.   181
Such a mad marriage never was before.
Hark, hark! I hear the minstrels play.   *Music plays.*

        Enter Petruchio, Kate, Bianca, Hortensio [as
        Litio], Baptista [with Grumio, and train].

PETRUCHIO
Gentlemen and friends, I thank you for your pains.
I know you think to dine with me today,
And have prepared great store of wedding cheer,
But so it is my haste doth call me hence,
And therefore here I mean to take my leave.

BAPTISTA
Is 't possible you will away tonight?

PETRUCHIO
I must away today, before night come.
Make it no wonder. If you knew my business,   191
You would entreat me rather go than stay.
And, honest company, I thank you all   193
That have beheld me give away myself
To this most patient, sweet, and virtuous wife.
Dine with my father, drink a health to me,
For I must hence; and farewell to you all.

TRANIO
Let us entreat you stay till after dinner.

PETRUCHIO
It may not be.

GREMIO   Let me entreat you.

PETRUCHIO
It cannot be.

---

173 sops cakes or bread soaked in the wine   **175 hungerly** hungry
looking, having a starved or famished look   **181 rout** crowd, wedding
party   **191 Make** consider   **193 honest** worthy, kind

KATHARINA   Let me entreat you.
PETRUCHIO
  I am content.
KATHARINA   Are you content to stay?
PETRUCHIO
  I am content you shall entreat me stay;
  But yet not stay, entreat me how you can.
KATHARINA
  Now, if you love me, stay.
PETRUCHIO   Grumio, my horse.   204
GRUMIO   Ay, sir, they be ready; the oats have eaten the   205
  horses.   206
KATHARINA   Nay, then,
  Do what thou canst, I will not go today,
  No, nor tomorrow, not till I please myself.
  The door is open, sir, there lies your way;
  You may be jogging whiles your boots are green.   211
  For me, I'll not be gone till I please myself.
  'Tis like you'll prove a jolly surly groom,   213
  That take it on you at the first so roundly.   214
PETRUCHIO
  O Kate, content thee; prithee, be not angry.
KATHARINA
  I will be angry. What hast thou to do?—   216
  Father, be quiet. He shall stay my leisure.   217
GREMIO
  Ay, marry, sir, now it begins to work.   218
KATHARINA
  Gentlemen, forward to the bridal dinner.
  I see a woman may be made a fool
  If she had not a spirit to resist.
PETRUCHIO
  They shall go forward, Kate, at thy command.—
  Obey the bride, you that attend on her.
  Go to the feast, revel and domineer,   224

---

204 horse horses   **205–206 oats . . . horses** (A comic inversion.)   **211 be
. . . green** (Proverbial for "getting an early start," with a sarcastic
allusion to his unseemly attire.)   **green** fresh, new   **213 like** likely.
jolly arrogant, overbearing   **214 take it on you** i.e., throw your weight
around.   **roundly** unceremoniously   **216 What . . . do** i.e., what business is it of yours   **217 stay my leisure** wait until I am ready   **218 it . . .
work** things are starting to happen   **224 domineer** feast riotously

Carouse full measure to her maidenhead,
Be mad and merry, or go hang yourselves.
But for my bonny Kate, she must with me.   227
Nay, look not big, nor stamp, nor stare, nor fret;   228
I will be master of what is mine own.
She is my goods, my chattels; she is my house,
My household stuff, my field, my barn,
My horse, my ox, my ass, my anything;   232
And here she stands, touch her whoever dare.
I'll bring mine action on the proudest he   234
That stops my way in Padua.—Grumio,
Draw forth thy weapon; we are beset with thieves.   236
Rescue thy mistress, if thou be a man.—
Fear not, sweet wench, they shall not touch thee, Kate!
I'll buckler thee against a million.   239
          Exeunt Petruchio, Katharina, [and Grumio].

BAPTISTA
Nay, let them go, a couple of quiet ones.

GREMIO
Went they not quickly, I should die with laughing.

TRANIO
Of all mad matches never was the like.

LUCENTIO
Mistress, what's your opinion of your sister?

BIANCA
That, being mad herself, she's madly mated.

GREMIO
I warrant him, Petruchio is Kated.   245

BAPTISTA
Neighbors and friends, though bride and bridegroom
   wants   246
For to supply the places at the table,   247
You know there wants no junkets at the feast.   248
Lucentio, you shall supply the bridegroom's place,
And let Bianca take her sister's room.

227 for as for **228 big** threatening **232 ox . . . anything** (This catalogue
of a man's possessions is from the Tenth Commandment.) **234 action**
(1) lawsuit (2) attack **236 Draw** (Perhaps Petruchio and Grumio actually
draw their swords.) **239 buckler** shield, defend **245 Kated** Gremio's
invention for "mated (and matched) with Kate" **246 wants** are lacking **246–247 wants For to supply** are not present to fill **248 junkets**
sweetmeats

TRANIO
  Shall sweet Bianca practice how to bride it?   251
BAPTISTA
  She shall, Lucentio. Come, gentlemen, let's go.

                                        Exeunt.

                              ❖

---

251 bride it play the bride

4.1 *Enter Grumio.*

GRUMIO Fie, fie on all tired jades, on all mad masters, 1
and all foul ways! Was ever man so beaten? Was ever 2
man so rayed? Was ever man so weary? I am sent be- 3
fore to make a fire, and they are coming after to warm
them. Now, were not I a little pot and soon hot, my 5
very lips might freeze to my teeth, my tongue to the
roof of my mouth, my heart in my belly, ere I should
come by a fire to thaw me. But I, with blowing the
fire, shall warm myself; for, considering the weather,
a taller man than I will take cold. Holla, ho! Curtis! 10

Enter Curtis.

CURTIS Who is that calls so coldly?
GRUMIO A piece of ice. If thou doubt it, thou mayst
slide from my shoulder to my heel with no greater a
run but my head and my neck. A fire, good Curtis.
CURTIS Is my master and his wife coming, Grumio?
GRUMIO O, ay, Curtis, ay, and therefore fire, fire; cast 16
on no water. 17
CURTIS Is she so hot a shrew as she's reported?
GRUMIO She was, good Curtis, before this frost. But,
thou know'st, winter tames man, woman, and beast;
for it hath tamed my old master and my new mistress
and myself, fellow Curtis.
CURTIS Away, you three-inch fool! I am no beast. 23
GRUMIO Am I but three inches? Why, thy horn is a foot, 24
and so long am I at the least. But wilt thou make a fire,
or shall I complain on thee to our mistress, whose
hand, she being now at hand, thou shalt soon feel, to
thy cold comfort, for being slow in thy hot office? 28

4.1. Location: Petruchio's country house. A table is set out, with seats.
1 jades ill-conditioned horses **2 ways** roads **3 rayed** dirtied **5 a little
. . . hot** (Proverbial expression for a person of small stature soon angered.) **10 taller** (with play on the meaning "better," "finer")
16–17 cast . . . water (Alludes to the round "Scotland's burning," in
which the phrase "Fire, fire!" is followed by "Pour on water, pour on
water.") **23 three-inch fool** (Another reference to Grumio's size.) **I am
no beast** (Curtis protests being called *fellow* by Grumio, since Grumio in
his previous speech has paralleled himself with *beast*.) **24 horn** i.e.,
cuckold's horn **28 hot office** i.e., duty of providing a fire

CURTIS   I prithee, good Grumio, tell me, how goes the world?

GRUMIO   A cold world, Curtis, in every office but thine, and therefore fire. Do thy duty, and have thy duty, for 32 my master and mistress are almost frozen to death.

CURTIS   There's fire ready, and therefore, good Grumio, the news.

GRUMIO   Why, "Jack boy, ho, boy!" and as much news 36 as wilt thou.

CURTIS   Come, you are so full of coney-catching!   38

GRUMIO   Why, therefore fire, for I have caught extreme cold. Where's the cook? Is supper ready, the house trimmed, rushes strewed, cobwebs swept, the serving- 41 men in their new fustian, their white stockings, and 42 every officer his wedding garment on? Be the jacks fair 43 within, the jills fair without, the carpets laid, and 44 everything in order?

CURTIS   All ready; and therefore, I pray thee, news.

GRUMIO   First know my horse is tired, my master and mistress fallen out.

CURTIS   How?

GRUMIO   Out of their saddles into the dirt—and thereby hangs a tale.

CURTIS   Let's ha 't, good Grumio.

GRUMIO   Lend thine ear.

CURTIS   Here.

GRUMIO   There.   [*He cuffs Curtis.*]

CURTIS   This 'tis to feel a tale, not to hear a tale.

GRUMIO   And therefore 'tis called a sensible tale, and this 57 cuff was but to knock at your ear and beseech listening. Now I begin: Imprimis, we came down a foul 59 hill, my master riding behind my mistress—

CURTIS   Both of one horse?   61

GRUMIO   What's that to thee?

---

32 have thy duty receive your reward   **36 Jack . . . boy** (The first line of another round or catch.)   **38 coney-catching** cheating, trickery (with a play on *catch*, round, in the previous line)   **41 rushes** (Used to cover the floor.)   **42 fustian** coarse cloth of cotton and flax **43 officer** household servant   **43, 44 jacks, jills** drinking measures of one-half and one-fourth pints (with quibble on "servingmen" and "maidservants")   **44 carpets** table covers   **57 sensible** (1) capable of being felt (2) showing good sense   **59 Imprimis** in the first place. **foul** muddy   **61 of** on

CURTIS Why, a horse.

GRUMIO Tell thou the tale. But hadst thou not crossed 64
me, thou shouldst have heard how her horse fell and
she under her horse; thou shouldst have heard in how
miry a place, how she was bemoiled, how he left her 67
with the horse upon her, how he beat me because her
horse stumbled, how she waded through the dirt to
pluck him off me, how he swore, how she prayed that
never prayed before, how I cried, how the horses ran
away, how her bridle was burst, how I lost my crupper, with many things of worthy memory, which now
shall die in oblivion and thou return unexperienced to
thy grave.

CURTIS By this reckoning he is more shrew than she.

GRUMIO Ay, and that thou and the proudest of you all
shall find when he comes home. But what talk I of 78
this? Call forth Nathaniel, Joseph, Nicholas, Philip,
Walter, Sugarsop, and the rest. Let their heads be
sleekly combed, their blue coats brushed, and their 81
garters of an indifferent knit; let them curtsy with their 82
left legs, and not presume to touch a hair of my master's horsetail till they kiss their hands. Are they all
ready?

CURTIS They are.

GRUMIO Call them forth.

CURTIS Do you hear, ho? You must meet my master to
countenance my mistress.   89

GRUMIO Why, she hath a face of her own.

CURTIS Who knows not that?

GRUMIO Thou, it seems, that calls for company to countenance her.

CURTIS I call them forth to credit her.   94

Enter four or five Servingmen.

GRUMIO Why, she comes to borrow nothing of them.

NATHANIEL Welcome home, Grumio!

64 crossed thwarted, interrupted   **67 bemoiled** befouled with mire
78 what why   **81 blue coats** (Usual dress for servingmen.)   **82 indifferent** i.e., well matched and not flamboyant   **89 countenance** pay
respects to (with a following pun on the meaning "face")   **94 credit**
pay respects to (with another pun following, on "extending financial
credit")

PHILIP How now, Grumio!
JOSEPH What, Grumio!
NICHOLAS Fellow Grumio!
NATHANIEL How now, old lad?
GRUMIO Welcome, you; how now, you; what, you; fel-
  low, you—and thus much for greeting. Now, my
  spruce companions, is all ready and all things neat?   103
NATHANIEL All things is ready. How near is our
  master?
GRUMIO E'en at hand, alighted by this; and therefore
  be not—Cock's passion, silence! I hear my master.   107

  Enter Petruchio and Kate.

PETRUCHIO
  Where be these knaves? What, no man at door
  To hold my stirrup, nor to take my horse?   109
  Where is Nathaniel, Gregory, Philip?
ALL SERVANTS Here, here, sir, here, sir.
PETRUCHIO
  Here, sir! Here, sir! Here, sir! Here, sir!
  You loggerheaded and unpolished grooms!
  What, no attendance? No regard? No duty?
  Where is the foolish knave I sent before?   115
GRUMIO
  Here, sir, as foolish as I was before.
PETRUCHIO
  You peasant swain, you whoreson malt-horse drudge!   117
  Did I not bid thee meet me in the park
  And bring along these rascal knaves with thee?
GRUMIO
  Nathaniel's coat, sir, was not fully made,
  And Gabriel's pumps were all unpinked i' the heel.   121
  There was no link to color Peter's hat,   122
  And Walter's dagger was not come from sheathing.   123

---

103 spruce lively **107 Cock's passion** by God's (Christ's) suffering
109 hold my stirrup i.e., help me dismount **115 before** ahead (with pun
in next line on "previously") **117 swain** rustic. **whoreson . . . drudge**
worthless plodding work animal, such as would be used on a treadmill
to grind malt **121 pumps** lowcut shoes. **unpinked** lacking in eyelets
or in ornamental tracing in the leather **122 link** torch, the smoke or
soot of which was used as blackening **123 sheathing** being fitted with
a sheath

There were none fine but Adam, Ralph, and Gregory;   124
The rest were ragged, old, and beggarly.
Yet, as they are, here are they come to meet you.

PETRUCHIO
Go, rascals, go, and fetch my supper in.

Exeunt Servants.

[*Sings.*] "Where is the life that late I led?
Where are those—" Sit down, Kate, and welcome.—

[*They sit at table.*]

Soud, soud, soud, soud!   130

Enter Servants with supper.

Why, when, I say?—Nay, good sweet Kate, be merry.—
Off with my boots, you rogues! You villains, when?

[*A Servant takes off Petruchio's boots.*]

[*Sings.*] "It was the friar of orders gray,   133
        As he forth walkèd on his way—"   134
Out, you rogue! You pluck my foot awry.   135

[*He kicks the Servant.*]

Take that, and mend the plucking off the other.
Be merry, Kate.—Some water, here; what, ho!

Enter one with water.

Where's my spaniel Troilus? Sirrah, get you hence,
And bid my cousin Ferdinand come hither—

[*Exit Servant.*]

One, Kate, that you must kiss and be acquainted with.
Where are my slippers? Shall I have some water?
Come, Kate, and wash, and welcome heartily.

[*Servant offers water, but spills some.*]

You whoreson villain, will you let it fall?

[*He strikes the Servant.*]

KATHARINA
Patience, I pray you, 'twas a fault unwilling.   144

PETRUCHIO
A whoreson, beetle-headed, flap-eared knave!—   145

124 fine well clothed   **130 Soud** (A nonsense song, or expression of
impatience, or perhaps "food!")   **133–134 "It . . . way"** (A fragment of a
bawdy ballad.)   **135 Out** (Exclamation of anger or reproach.)   **144 unwilling** accidental   **145 beetle-headed** i.e., blockheaded (since a *beetle* is
a pounding tool)

Come, Kate, sit down. I know you have a stomach.   146
Will you give thanks, sweet Kate, or else shall I?—   147
What's this? Mutton?
FIRST SERVANT   Ay.
PETRUCHIO   Who brought it?
PETER   I.
PETRUCHIO
'Tis burnt, and so is all the meat.
What dogs are these? Where is the rascal cook?
How durst you, villains, bring it from the dresser   151
And serve it thus to me that love it not?
There, take it to you, trenchers, cups, and all.   153
          [*He throws the meat, etc., at them.*]
You heedless joltheads and unmannered slaves!   154
What, do you grumble? I'll be with you straight.   155
          [*They run out.*]
KATHARINA
I pray you, husband, be not so disquiet.
The meat was well, if you were so contented.
PETRUCHIO
I tell thee, Kate, 'twas burnt and dried away,
And I expressly am forbid to touch it;
For it engenders choler, planteth anger,   160
And better 'twere that both of us did fast,
Since, of ourselves, ourselves are choleric,
Than feed it with such overroasted flesh.
Be patient. Tomorrow 't shall be mended,
And for this night we'll fast for company.
Come, I will bring thee to thy bridal chamber.
          Exeunt.

Enter Servants severally.

NATHANIEL   Peter, didst ever see the like?
PETER   He kills her in her own humor.   168

---

146 stomach appetite (with a suggestion also of "temper")   **147 give thanks** say grace   **151 dresser** sideboard   **153 trenchers** wooden dishes or plates   **154 joltheads** blockheads   **155 with you straight** after you at once (to get even for this)   **160 choler** the humor or bodily fluid, hot and dry in character, that supposedly produced ill temper and was thought to be aggravated by the eating of roast meat   **168 kills . . . humor** i.e., uses anger to subdue anger in her

Enter Curtis.

GRUMIO   Where is he?

CURTIS   In her chamber, making a sermon of continency   170
to her,
And rails, and swears, and rates, that she, poor soul,   172
Knows not which way to stand, to look, to speak,
And sits as one new risen from a dream.
Away, away! For he is coming hither.   [*Exeunt.*]

Enter Petruchio.

PETRUCHIO
Thus have I politicly begun my reign,
And 'tis my hope to end successfully.
My falcon now is sharp and passing empty,   178
And till she stoop she must not be full-gorged,   179
For then she never looks upon her lure.
Another way I have to man my haggard,   181
To make her come and know her keeper's call:
That is, to watch her, as we watch these kites   183
That bate and beat and will not be obedient.   184
She ate no meat today, nor none shall eat.
Last night she slept not, nor tonight she shall not.
As with the meat, some undeservèd fault
I'll find about the making of the bed,
And here I'll fling the pillow, there the bolster,
This way the coverlet, another way the sheets.
Ay, and amid this hurly I intend   191
That all is done in reverent care of her.
And in conclusion she shall watch all night,
And if she chance to nod I'll rail and brawl,
And with the clamor keep her still awake.
This is a way to kill a wife with kindness;
And thus I'll curb her mad and headstrong humor.   197

---

170 sermon of continency lecture on self-restraint   **172 rates** scolds
178 sharp hungry   **179 stoop** fly down to the lure   **181 man** tame (with
a pun on the sense of "assert masculine authority").   **haggard** wild
female hawk; hence, an intractable woman   **183 watch her** keep her
watching, i.e., awake.   **kites** a kind of hawk (with a pun on *Kate*)
184 bate and beat beat the wings impatiently and flutter away from the
hand or perch   **191 intend** pretend   **197 humor** disposition

He that knows better how to tame a shrew,
Now let him speak; 'tis charity to show.   *Exit.* 199

❖

4.2   *Enter Tranio [as Lucentio] and Hortensio [as Litio].*

TRANIO
Is 't possible, friend Litio, that Mistress Bianca
Doth fancy any other but Lucentio?
I tell you, sir, she bears me fair in hand.   3
HORTENSIO
Sir, to satisfy you in what I have said,
Stand by and mark the manner of his teaching.
                              [They stand aside.]
          Enter Bianca [and Lucentio as Cambio].

LUCENTIO
Now, mistress, profit you in what you read?   6
BIANCA
What, master, read you? First resolve me that.   7
LUCENTIO
I read that I profess, the Art to Love.   8
BIANCA
And may you prove, sir, master of your art!
LUCENTIO
While you, sweet dear, prove mistress of my heart!
          [They move aside and court each other.]
HORTENSIO [*To Tranio, coming forward*]
Quick proceeders, marry! Now tell me, I pray,   11
You that durst swear that your mistress Bianca
Loved none in the world so well as Lucentio.

---

199 'tis charity to show it's benevolent to share such wisdom. (On the rhyme with *shrew*, see also the play's final lines.)
4.2. Location: Padua. Before Baptista's house.
3 bears . . . hand gives me encouragement, leads me on   **6 read** (Evidently, both Bianca and "Cambio" carry books.)   **7 resolve** answer
8 that I profess what I practice.   **Art to Love** Ovid's *Ars Amandi*
11 proceeders (1) workers, doers (2) candidates for academic degrees (as suggested by the phrase *master of your art* in l. 9)

TRANIO
     O despiteful love! Unconstant womankind!   14
     I tell thee, Litio, this is wonderful.   15

HORTENSIO
     Mistake no more. I am not Litio,
     Nor a musician, as I seem to be,
     But one that scorn to live in this disguise   18
     For such a one as leaves a gentleman   19
     And makes a god of such a cullion.   20
     Know, sir, that I am called Hortensio.

TRANIO
     Signor Hortensio, I have often heard
     Of your entire affection to Bianca;   23
     And since mine eyes are witness of her lightness,   24
     I will with you, if you be so contented,
     Forswear Bianca and her love forever.

HORTENSIO
     See how they kiss and court! Signor Lucentio,
     Here is my hand, and here I firmly vow
                              [*Giving his hand*]
     Never to woo her more, but do forswear her
     As one unworthy all the former favors
     That I have fondly flattered her withal.   31

TRANIO
     And here I take the like unfeignèd oath,
     Never to marry with her though she would entreat.
     Fie on her, see how beastly she doth court him!

HORTENSIO
     Would all the world but he had quite forsworn!   35
     For me, that I may surely keep mine oath,
     I will be married to a wealthy widow,
     Ere three days pass, which hath as long loved me
     As I have loved this proud disdainful haggard.   39
     And so farewell, Signor Lucentio.
     Kindness in women, not their beauteous looks,

---

14 despiteful cruel   **15 wonderful** cause for wonder   **18 scorn** scorns
19 such a one i.e., Bianca   **20 cullion** base fellow (referring to "Cambio"; literally the word means "testicle")   **23 entire** sincere   **24 lightness** wantonness   **31 fondly** foolishly   **35 Would . . . forsworn** i.e., may
everyone in the world forsake her except the penniless "Cambio," and
may she thus get what she deserves   **39 haggard** wild hawk

Shall win my love. And so I take my leave,
In resolution as I swore before.   [*Exit.*] 43
TRANIO   [*As Lucentio and Bianca come forward again*]
Mistress Bianca, bless you with such grace
As 'longeth to a lover's blessèd case!   45
Nay, I have ta'en you napping, gentle love,   46
And have forsworn you with Hortensio.
BIANCA
Tranio, you jest. But have you both forsworn me?
TRANIO
Mistress, we have.
LUCENTIO   Then we are rid of Litio.
TRANIO
I' faith, he'll have a lusty widow now,   50
That shall be wooed and wedded in a day.
BIANCA   God give him joy!
TRANIO   Ay, and he'll tame her.
BIANCA   He says so, Tranio?
TRANIO
Faith, he is gone unto the taming school.
BIANCA
The taming school! What, is there such a place?
TRANIO
Ay, mistress, and Petruchio is the master,
That teacheth tricks eleven-and-twenty long,   58
To tame a shrew and charm her chattering tongue.

Enter Biondello.

BIONDELLO
O master, master, I have watched so long
That I am dog-weary, but at last I spied
An ancient angel coming down the hill   62
Will serve the turn.
TRANIO   What is he, Biondello?   63

43 In resolution determined   **45 'longeth** belongs   **46 ta'en you napping** i.e., surprised you   **50 lusty** merry, lively   **58 eleven . . . long** i.e.,
in sufficient number (alluding to the card game called "one-and-thirty"
referred to at 1.2.32–33)   **62 ancient angel** i.e., fellow of the good old
stamp. (Literally, an "angel" or gold coin bearing the stamp of the
archangel Michael and thus distinguishable from more recent debased
coinage.)   **63 Will . . . turn** who will serve our purposes

BIONDELLO
Master, a marcantant, or a pedant,   64
I know not what, but formal in apparel,
In gait and countenance surely like a father.

LUCENTIO And what of him, Tranio?

TRANIO
If he be credulous and trust my tale,
I'll make him glad to seem Vincentio
And give assurance to Baptista Minola
As if he were the right Vincentio.
Take in your love, and then let me alone.   72

[Exeunt Lucentio and Bianca.]

Enter a Pedant.

PEDANT
God save you, sir!

TRANIO   And you sir! You are welcome.
Travel you far on, or are you at the farthest?

PEDANT
Sir, at the farthest for a week or two,
But then up farther, and as far as Rome,
And so to Tripoli, if God lend me life.

TRANIO
What countryman, I pray?

PEDANT   Of Mantua.

TRANIO
Of Mantua, sir? Marry, God forbid!
And come to Padua, careless of your life?

PEDANT
My life, sir! How, I pray? For that goes hard.   81

TRANIO
'Tis death for anyone in Mantua
To come to Padua. Know you not the cause?
Your ships are stayed at Venice, and the Duke,   84
For private quarrel twixt your duke and him,
Hath published and proclaimed it openly.
'Tis marvel, but that you are but newly come,
You might have heard it else proclaimed about.

64 marcantant merchant. **pedant** schoolmaster (though at ll. 90–91 he
speaks more like a merchant) **72 let me alone** i.e., count on me
81 goes hard is serious indeed **84 stayed** detained

PEDANT
  Alas, sir, it is worse for me than so,
  For I have bills for money by exchange   90
  From Florence, and must here deliver them.
TRANIO
  Well, sir, to do you courtesy,
  This will I do, and this I will advise you—
  First, tell me, have you ever been at Pisa?
PEDANT
  Ay, sir, in Pisa have I often been,
  Pisa renownèd for grave citizens.
TRANIO
  Among them know you one Vincentio?
PEDANT
  I know him not, but I have heard of him;
  A merchant of incomparable wealth.
TRANIO
  He is my father, sir, and, sooth to say,
  In count'nance somewhat doth resemble you.
BIONDELLO [Aside]   As much as an apple doth an oyster,
  and all one.   103
TRANIO
  To save your life in this extremity,
  This favor will I do you for his sake;
  And think it not the worst of all your fortunes
  That you are like to Sir Vincentio.
  His name and credit shall you undertake,   108
  And in my house you shall be friendly lodged.
  Look that you take upon you as you should.   110
  You understand me, sir. So shall you stay
  Till you have done your business in the city.
  If this be courtesy, sir, accept of it.
PEDANT
  O sir, I do, and will repute you ever
  The patron of my life and liberty.
TRANIO
  Then go with me to make the matter good.   116
  This, by the way, I let you understand:

---

90 bills . . . exchange promissory notes   **103 all one** no matter
108 credit reputation   **110 take upon you** play your part   **116 make . . .
good** carry out the plan

My father is here looked for every day,
To pass assurance of a dower in marriage   119
Twixt me and one Baptista's daughter here.
In all these circumstances I'll instruct you.
Go with me to clothe you as becomes you.

                                              Exeunt.

❖

4.3   *Enter Katharina and Grumio.*

GRUMIO
No, no, forsooth, I dare not for my life.
KATHARINA
The more my wrong, the more his spite appears.   2
What, did he marry me to famish me?
Beggars that come unto my father's door
Upon entreaty have a present alms;   5
If not, elsewhere they meet with charity.
But I, who never knew how to entreat,
Nor never needed that I should entreat,
Am starved for meat, giddy for lack of sleep,   9
With oaths kept waking, and with brawling fed.
And that which spites me more than all these wants,
He does it under name of perfect love,
As who should say, if I should sleep or eat,   13
'Twere deadly sickness or else present death.
I prithee, go and get me some repast,
I care not what, so it be wholesome food.
GRUMIO   What say you to a neat's foot?   17
KATHARINA
'Tis passing good; I prithee, let me have it.
GRUMIO
I fear it is too choleric a meat.
How say you to a fat tripe finely broiled?
KATHARINA
I like it well, good Grumio, fetch it me.

119 pass assurance convey a legal guarantee

4.3. Location: Petruchio's house. A table is set out, with seats.
2 my wrong the wrong done to me   **5 present** immediate (as in l. 14)
9 meat food   **13 As who** as if one   **17 neat's** ox's

GRUMIO
  I cannot tell. I fear 'tis choleric.
  What say you to a piece of beef and mustard?
KATHARINA
  A dish that I do love to feed upon.
GRUMIO
  Ay, but the mustard is too hot a little.
KATHARINA
  Why then, the beef, and let the mustard rest.
GRUMIO
  Nay then, I will not; you shall have the mustard
  Or else you get no beef of Grumio.
KATHARINA
  Then both, or one, or anything thou wilt.
GRUMIO
  Why then, the mustard without the beef.
KATHARINA
  Go, get thee gone, thou false deluding slave,
                                        Beats him.
  That feed'st me with the very name of meat!
  Sorrow on thee and all the pack of you,
  That triumph thus upon my misery!
  Go, get thee gone, I say.

  Enter Petruchio and Hortensio with meat.

PETRUCHIO
  How fares my Kate? What, sweeting, all amort?   36
HORTENSIO
  Mistress, what cheer?
KATHARINA   Faith, as cold as can be.
PETRUCHIO
  Pluck up thy spirits; look cheerfully upon me.
  Here, love, thou see'st how diligent I am
  To dress thy meat myself and bring it thee.   40
  I am sure, sweet Kate, this kindness merits thanks.
  What, not a word? Nay, then thou lov'st it not,
  And all my pains is sorted to no proof.   43
  Here, take away this dish.
KATHARINA   I pray you, let it stand.

---

36 all amort dejected, dispirited   **40 dress** prepare   **43 sorted to no
proof** proved to be to no purpose

PETRUCHIO
  The poorest service is repaid with thanks,
  And so shall mine before you touch the meat.
KATHARINA   I thank you, sir.
HORTENSIO
  Signor Petruchio, fie, you are to blame.
  Come, Mistress Kate, I'll bear you company.
                            [*They sit at table*.]
PETRUCHIO [*Aside to Hortensio*]
  Eat it up all, Hortensio, if thou lovest me.—
  Much good do it unto thy gentle heart!
  Kate, eat apace. And now, my honey love,
  Will we return unto thy father's house
  And revel it as bravely as the best,   54
  With silken coats and caps and golden rings,
  With ruffs and cuffs and farthingales and things,   56
  With scarves and fans and double change of bravery,   57
  With amber bracelets, beads, and all this knavery.
  What, hast thou dined? The tailor stays thy leisure,
  To deck thy body with his ruffling treasure.   60

        Enter Tailor [with a gown].

  Come, tailor, let us see these ornaments.
  Lay forth the gown.

        Enter Haberdasher [with a cap].
                  What news with you, sir?
HABERDASHER
  Here is the cap your worship did bespeak.
PETRUCHIO
  Why, this was molded on a porringer—   64
  A velvet dish. Fie, fie, 'tis lewd and filthy.   65
  Why, 'tis a cockle or a walnut shell,   66
  A knack, a toy, a trick, a baby's cap.   67
  Away with it! Come, let me have a bigger.
KATHARINA
  I'll have no bigger. This doth fit the time,   69
  And gentlewomen wear such caps as these.

54 **bravely** splendidly dressed   56 **farthingales** hooped petticoats
57 **bravery** finery   60 **ruffling treasure** finery trimmed with ruffles
64 **porringer** porridge bowl   65 **lewd** vile   66 **cockle** cockleshell
67 **trick** trifle   69 **fit the time** suit the current fashion

PETRUCHIO
When you are gentle, you shall have one too,
And not till then.
HORTENSIO [*Aside*] That will not be in haste.
KATHARINA
Why, sir, I trust I may have leave to speak,
And speak I will. I am no child, no babe.
Your betters have endured me say my mind,
And if you cannot, best you stop your ears.
My tongue will tell the anger of my heart,
Or else my heart, concealing it, will break,
And rather than it shall, I will be free
Even to the uttermost, as I please, in words.
PETRUCHIO
Why, thou sayst true. It is a paltry cap,
A custard-coffin, a bauble, a silken pie.   82
I love thee well in that thou lik'st it not.
KATHARINA
Love me or love me not, I like the cap,
And it I will have, or I will have none.
                                        [*Exit Haberdasher.*]
PETRUCHIO
Thy gown? Why, ay. Come, tailor, let us see 't.
O, mercy, God, what masquing stuff is here?   87
What's this, a sleeve? 'Tis like a demi-cannon.   88
What, up and down carved like an apple tart?   89
Here's snip and nip and cut and slish and slash,
Like to a censer in a barber's shop.   91
Why, what i' devil's name, tailor, call'st thou this?   92
HORTENSIO [*Aside*]
I see she's like to have neither cap nor gown.
TAILOR
You bid me make it orderly and well,
According to the fashion and the time.
PETRUCHIO
Marry, and did. But if you be remembered,   96

---

82 custard-coffin pastry crust for a custard **87 masquing** i.e., suited
only for a masque **88 demi-cannon** large cannon **89 up and down** all
over, exactly. **like an apple tart** i.e., with slashing or slits like the slits
on the crust of fruit tarts, here revealing the brighter fabric underneath **91 censer** perfuming pan having an ornamental lid **92 i'** in
(the) **96 be remembered** recollect

I did not bid you mar it to the time.
Go, hop me over every kennel home,   98
For you shall hop without my custom, sir.
I'll none of it. Hence, make your best of it.

KATHARINA
I never saw a better-fashioned gown,
More quaint, more pleasing, nor more commendable.   102
Belike you mean to make a puppet of me.

PETRUCHIO
Why, true, he means to make a puppet of thee.

TAILOR
She says your worship means to make a puppet of her.

PETRUCHIO
O, monstrous arrogance! Thou liest, thou thread, thou
    thimble,
Thou yard, three-quarters, half-yard, quarter, nail!   107
Thou flea, thou nit, thou winter cricket thou!   108
Braved in mine own house with a skein of thread?   109
Away, thou rag, thou quantity, thou remnant,   110
Or I shall so be-mete thee with thy yard   111
As thou shalt think on prating whilst thou liv'st!   112
I tell thee, I, that thou hast marred her gown.

TAILOR
Your worship is deceived. The gown is made
Just as my master had direction.
Grumio gave order how it should be done.

GRUMIO   I gave him no order. I gave him the stuff.

TAILOR
But how did you desire it should be made?

GRUMIO   Marry, sir, with needle and thread.

TAILOR
But did you not request to have it cut?

GRUMIO   Thou hast faced many things.   121

TAILOR   I have.

GRUMIO   Face not me. Thou hast braved many men;   123

---

98 hop . . . home hop on home over every street gutter   102 quaint
elegant   107 nail a measure of length for cloth: 2¼ inches   108 nit
louse egg   109 Braved defied.   with by   110 quantity fragment
111 be-mete measure, i.e., thrash.   yard yardstick   112 think on prating
i.e., remember this thrashing and think twice before talking so again
121 faced trimmed. (But Grumio puns on the meaning "bullied.")
123 Face bully.   braved dressed finely

brave not me. I will neither be faced nor braved. I say   124
unto thee, I bid thy master cut out the gown, but I did
not bid him cut it to pieces. Ergo, thou liest.   126
TAILOR   Why, here is the note of the fashion to testify.
                              [*He displays his bill.*]
PETRUCHIO   Read it.
GRUMIO   The note lies in 's throat if he say I said so.
TAILOR [*Reads*]   "Imprimis, a loose-bodied gown—"
GRUMIO   Master, if ever I said loose-bodied gown,   131
sew me in the skirts of it and beat me to death with
a bottom of brown thread. I said a gown.   133
PETRUCHIO   Proceed.
TAILOR [*Reads*]   "With a small compassed cape—"   135
GRUMIO   I confess the cape.
TAILOR [*Reads*]   "With a trunk sleeve—"   137
GRUMIO   I confess two sleeves.
TAILOR [*Reads*]   "The sleeves curiously cut."   139
PETRUCHIO   Ay, there's the villainy.
GRUMIO   Error i' the bill, sir, error i' the bill. I com-
manded the sleeves should be cut out and sewed up
again, and that I'll prove upon thee, though thy little   143
finger be armed in a thimble.
TAILOR   This is true that I say. An I had thee in place   145
where, thou shouldst know it.   146
GRUMIO   I am for thee straight. Take thou the bill, give   147
me thy mete-yard, and spare not me.   148
HORTENSIO   God-a-mercy, Grumio, then he shall have
no odds.
PETRUCHIO   Well, sir, in brief, the gown is not for me.
GRUMIO   You are i' the right, sir, 'tis for my mistress.
PETRUCHIO   Go, take it up unto thy master's use.   153
GRUMIO   Villain, not for thy life! Take up my mistress'
gown for thy master's use!
PETRUCHIO   Why, sir, what's your conceit in that?   156

124 brave defy   **126 Ergo** therefore   **131 loose-bodied gown** (Grumio
plays on *loose*, wanton; a gown fit for a prostitute.)   **133 bottom** ball
wound from a skein. (A weaver's term.)   **135 compassed** with the edges
forming a semicircle   **137 trunk** full, wide   **139 curiously** elaborately
143 prove upon thee prove by fighting you   **145–146 in place where** in a
suitable place   **147 bill** (1) the note ordering the gown (2) a weapon, a
halberd   **148 mete-yard** measuring stick   **153 use** i.e., whatever use he
can make of it. (But Grumio deliberately misinterprets in a bawdy
sense.)   **156 conceit** idea

GRUMIO
  O, sir, the conceit is deeper than you think for:
  Take up my mistress' gown to his master's use!
  O, fie, fie, fie!
PETRUCHIO [*Aside to Hortensio*]
  Hortensio, say thou wilt see the tailor paid.—
  [*To Tailor.*] Go take it hence, begone, and say no more.
HORTENSIO [*Aside to Tailor*]
  Tailor, I'll pay thee for thy gown tomorrow.
  Take no unkindness of his hasty words.
  Away, I say. Commend me to thy master.

                                  Exit Tailor.

PETRUCHIO
  Well, come, my Kate. We will unto your father's
  Even in these honest mean habiliments.   166
  Our purses shall be proud, our garments poor,
  For 'tis the mind that makes the body rich;
  And as the sun breaks through the darkest clouds,
  So honor peereth in the meanest habit.   170
  What, is the jay more precious than the lark
  Because his feathers are more beautiful?
  Or is the adder better than the eel
  Because his painted skin contents the eye?   174
  O, no, good Kate; neither art thou the worse
  For this poor furniture and mean array.   176
  If thou account'st it shame, lay it on me.
  And therefore frolic; we will hence forthwith,
  To feast and sport us at thy father's house.
  [*To Grumio.*] Go call my men, and let us straight to him;
  And bring our horses unto Long Lane end.
  There will we mount, and thither walk on foot.
  Let's see, I think 'tis now some seven o'clock,
  And well we may come there by dinnertime.   184
KATHARINA
  I dare assure you, sir, 'tis almost two,
  And 'twill be suppertime ere you come there.
PETRUCHIO
  It shall be seven ere I go to horse.

166 honest mean habiliments respectable, plain clothes **170 peereth** is
seen. **habit** attire **174 painted** patterned **176 furniture** furnishings
of attire **184 dinnertime** i.e., about noon

Look what I speak, or do, or think to do,   188
You are still crossing it.—Sirs, let 't alone.   189
I will not go today, and ere I do
It shall be what o'clock I say it is.
HORTENSIO [*Aside*]
Why, so this gallant will command the sun.

                                              [*Exeunt.*]

                        ❖

4.4   *Enter Tranio [as Lucentio], and the Pedant
            dressed like Vincentio [booted].*

TRANIO
Sir, this is the house. Please it you that I call?
PEDANT
Ay, what else? And but I be deceived,   2
Signor Baptista may remember me,   3
Near twenty years ago, in Genoa,
Where we were lodgers at the Pegasus.   5
TRANIO
'Tis well; and hold your own in any case   6
With such austerity as 'longeth to a father.

        Enter Biondello.

PEDANT
I warrant you. But, sir, here comes your boy;
'Twere good he were schooled.   9
TRANIO
Fear you not him.—Sirrah Biondello,
Now do your duty throughly, I advise you.   11
Imagine 'twere the right Vincentio.
BIONDELLO   Tut, fear not me.

188 Look what whatever   **189 still crossing** always contradicting or
defying

4.4. Location: Padua. Before Baptista's house.
s.d. booted (signifying travel)   **2 but** unless   **3 may remember** (The
Pedant is rehearsing what he is to say.)   **5 the Pegasus** i.e., an inn, so
named after the famous winged horse of classical myth   **6 hold your
own** play your part   **9 schooled** i.e., rehearsed in his part   **11 throughly**
thoroughly

TRANIO
But hast thou done thy errand to Baptista?

BIONDELLO
I told him that your father was at Venice,
And that you looked for him this day in Padua.

TRANIO
Thou'rt a tall fellow. Hold thee that to drink.   17
                                        [*He gives money.*]
Here comes Baptista. Set your countenance, sir.

Enter Baptista and Lucentio [as Cambio]. [The]
Pedant [stands] bareheaded.

Signor Baptista, you are happily met.
[*To the Pedant.*] Sir, this is the gentleman I told you of.
I pray you, stand good father to me now;
Give me Bianca for my patrimony.

PEDANT   Soft, son!
Sir, by your leave, having come to Padua
To gather in some debts, my son Lucentio
Made me acquainted with a weighty cause
Of love between your daughter and himself;
And, for the good report I hear of you
And for the love he beareth to your daughter
And she to him, to stay him not too long,
I am content, in a good father's care,
To have him matched. And if you please to like
No worse than I, upon some agreement
Me shall you find ready and willing
With one consent to have her so bestowed;
For curious I cannot be with you,   36
Signor Baptista, of whom I hear so well.

BAPTISTA
Sir, pardon me in what I have to say;
Your plainness and your shortness please me well.
Right true it is your son Lucentio here
Doth love my daughter, and she loveth him,
Or both dissemble deeply their affections.
And therefore, if you say no more than this,
That like a father you will deal with him

17 tall fine. **Hold . . . drink** take that and buy a drink   **36 curious**
overly particular

And pass my daughter a sufficient dower,   45
The match is made and all is done.
Your son shall have my daughter with consent.

TRANIO
I thank you, sir. Where then do you know best
We be affied and such assurance ta'en   49
As shall with either part's agreement stand?

BAPTISTA
Not in my house, Lucentio, for you know
Pitchers have ears, and I have many servants.
Besides, old Gremio is hearkening still,   53
And happily we might be interrupted.   54

TRANIO
Then at my lodging, an it like you.   55
There doth my father lie, and there this night   56
We'll pass the business privately and well.   57
Send for your daughter by your servant here.
         [*He indicates Lucentio, and winks at him.*]
My boy shall fetch the scrivener presently.   59
The worst is this, that at so slender warning
You are like to have a thin and slender pittance.   61

BAPTISTA
It likes me well. Cambio, hie you home,
And bid Bianca make her ready straight.
And if you will, tell what hath happened:
Lucentio's father is arrived in Padua,
And how she's like to be Lucentio's wife.
                                    [*Exit Lucentio.*]

BIONDELLO
I pray the gods she may, with all my heart!

TRANIO
Dally not with the gods, but get thee gone.
                               Exit [*Biondello*].
Signor Baptista, shall I lead the way?
Welcome! One mess is like to be your cheer.   70
Come, sir, we will better it in Pisa.

---

45 pass settle on, give   **49 affied** betrothed   **53 hearkening still** continually listening   **54 happily** haply, perhaps   **55 an it like** if it please
56 lie lodge   **57 pass** transact   **59 scrivener** notary, one to draw up
contracts   **61 like** likely.   **slender pittance** i.e., scanty banquet
70 mess dish.   **cheer** entertainment

BAPTISTA I follow you.
                    Exeunt [Tranio, Pedant, and Baptista].

          Enter Lucentio [as Cambio] and Biondello.

BIONDELLO Cambio!
LUCENTIO What sayst thou, Biondello?
BIONDELLO You saw my master wink and laugh upon
you?
LUCENTIO Biondello, what of that?
BIONDELLO Faith, nothing; but he's left me here behind
to expound the meaning or moral of his signs and   79
tokens.
LUCENTIO I pray thee, moralize them.   81
BIONDELLO Then thus. Baptista is safe, talking with the 82
deceiving father of a deceitful son.
LUCENTIO And what of him?
BIONDELLO His daughter is to be brought by you to the
supper.
LUCENTIO And then?
BIONDELLO The old priest at Saint Luke's church is at
your command at all hours.
LUCENTIO And what of all this?
BIONDELLO I cannot tell, except they are busied about a 91
counterfeit assurance. Take you assurance of her,   92
cum privilegio ad imprimendum solum. To the   93
church take the priest, clerk, and some sufficient hon- 94
est witnesses.
If this be not that you look for, I have no more to say,
But bid Bianca farewell forever and a day.
                    [Biondello starts to leave.]
LUCENTIO Hear'st thou, Biondello?
BIONDELLO I cannot tarry. I knew a wench married in
an afternoon as she went to the garden for parsley to
stuff a rabbit, and so may you, sir. And so, adieu, sir.
My master hath appointed me to go to Saint Luke's, to

___

79 moral hidden meaning   **81 moralize** elucidate   **82 safe** i.e., safely
deceived   **91 except** unless   **92 counterfeit assurance** pretended be-
trothal agreement.   **Take . . . of her** legalize your claim to her (by
marriage)   **93 cum . . . solum** with exclusive printing rights. (A copy-
right formula often appearing on the title pages of books, here jokingly
applied to the marriage.)   **94 sufficient** financially competent, well-to-do

bid the priest be ready to come against you come with 103
your appendix.   *Exit.* 104
LUCENTIO
I may, and will, if she be so contented.
She will be pleased; then wherefore should I doubt?
Hap what hap may, I'll roundly go about her.   107
It shall go hard if Cambio go without her.   *Exit.* 108

❖

4.5 *Enter Petruchio, Kate, and Hortensio.*

PETRUCHIO
Come on, i' God's name, once more toward our father's. 1
Good Lord, how bright and goodly shines the moon!
KATHARINA
The moon? The sun. It is not moonlight now.
PETRUCHIO
I say it is the moon that shines so bright.
KATHARINA
I know it is the sun that shines so bright.
PETRUCHIO
Now, by my mother's son, and that's myself,
It shall be moon, or star, or what I list,   7
Or ere I journey to your father's house.—   8
Go on, and fetch our horses back again—
Evermore crossed and crossed, nothing but crossed!
HORTENSIO [*To Katharina*]
Say as he says, or we shall never go.
KATHARINA
Forward, I pray, since we have come so far,
And be it moon, or sun, or what you please;
An if you please to call it a rush candle,   14
Henceforth I vow it shall be so for me.

103 against you come in anticipation of your arrival   **104 appendix**
something appended, i.e., the bride (continuing the metaphor of printing)   **107 roundly . . . her** set about marrying her in no uncertain
terms   **108 go hard** be unfortunate (with bawdy pun)

4.5. Location: A road on the way to Padua.
1 our father's our father's house   **7 list** please   **8 Or ere** before
14 rush candle a rush dipped into tallow; hence a very feeble light

PETRUCHIO
  I say it is the moon.

KATHARINA   I know it is the moon.

PETRUCHIO
  Nay, then you lie. It is the blessèd sun.

KATHARINA
  Then, God be blest, it is the blessèd sun.
  But sun it is not when you say it is not,
  And the moon changes even as your mind.
  What you will have it named, even that it is,
  And so it shall be so for Katharine.

HORTENSIO
  Petruchio, go thy ways, the field is won.

PETRUCHIO
  Well, forward, forward, thus the bowl should run,
  And not unluckily against the bias.   25
  But, soft! Company is coming here.

  Enter Vincentio.

  [*To Vincentio.*] Good morrow, gentle mistress. Where
    away?—   27
  Tell me, sweet Kate, and tell me truly too,
  Hast thou beheld a fresher gentlewoman?
  Such war of white and red within her cheeks!
  What stars do spangle heaven with such beauty
  As those two eyes become that heavenly face?—
  Fair lovely maid, once more good day to thee.—
  Sweet Kate, embrace her for her beauty's sake.

HORTENSIO [*Aside*]
  'A will make the man mad, to make a woman of him.   35

KATHARINA [*Embracing Vincentio*]
  Young budding virgin, fair and fresh and sweet,
  Whither away, or where is thy abode?
  Happy the parents of so fair a child!
  Happier the man whom favorable stars
  Allots thee for his lovely bedfellow!

---

25 against the bias off its proper course. (The *bias* is an off-center
weight in a bowling ball enabling the bowler to roll the ball in an
oblique or curving path; it runs *unluckily*, that is, unsuccessfully,
against the bias when it encounters an obstacle.)   **27 Where away**
where are you going   **35 'A** he

PETRUCHIO
Why, how now, Kate? I hope thou art not mad.
This is a man, old, wrinkled, faded, withered,
And not a maiden, as thou sayst he is.

KATHARINA
Pardon, old father, my mistaking eyes,
That have been so bedazzled with the sun
That everything I look on seemeth green.   46
Now I perceive thou art a reverend father.
Pardon, I pray thee, for my mad mistaking.

PETRUCHIO
Do, good old grandsire, and withal make known
Which way thou travelest—if along with us,
We shall be joyful of thy company.

VINCENTIO
Fair sir, and you my merry mistress,
That with your strange encounter much amazed me,
My name is called Vincentio; my dwelling Pisa,
And bound I am to Padua, there to visit
A son of mine, which long I have not seen.

PETRUCHIO
What is his name?

VINCENTIO   Lucentio, gentle sir.

PETRUCHIO
Happily met, the happier for thy son.
And now by law, as well as reverend age,
I may entitle thee my loving father.
The sister to my wife, this gentlewoman,
Thy son by this hath married. Wonder not,   62
Nor be not grieved. She is of good esteem,   63
Her dowry wealthy, and of worthy birth;
Besides, so qualified as may beseem   65
The spouse of any noble gentleman.
Let me embrace with old Vincentio,
And wander we to see thy honest son,
Who will of thy arrival be full joyous.
                    [*He embraces Vincentio.*]

VINCENTIO
But is this true? Or is it else your pleasure,

---

46 green young and fresh   **62 by this** by this time   **63 esteem** reputation   **65 beseem** befit

Like pleasant travelers, to break a jest
Upon the company you overtake?

HORTENSIO
I do assure thee, father, so it is.

PETRUCHIO
Come, go along, and see the truth hereof,
For our first merriment hath made thee jealous.   75

Exeunt [all but Hortensio].

HORTENSIO
Well, Petruchio, this has put me in heart.
Have to my widow! And if she be froward,   77
Then hast thou taught Hortensio to be untoward.   78

Exit.

❧

75 jealous suspicious   **77 Have to** i.e., now for.   **froward** perverse
78 untoward unmannerly

5.1 *Enter Biondello, Lucentio [no longer*
disguised], and Bianca. Gremio is out before
[and stands aside].

BIONDELLO Softly and swiftly, sir, for the priest is
ready.
LUCENTIO I fly, Biondello. But they may chance to need
thee at home; therefore leave us.
BIONDELLO Nay, faith, I'll see the church a' your back,   5
and then come back to my master's as soon as I can.
          [Exeunt Lucentio, Bianca, and Biondello.]
GREMIO
I marvel Cambio comes not all this while.

          Enter Petruchio, Kate, Vincentio, Grumio, with
          attendants.

PETRUCHIO
Sir, here's the door; this is Lucentio's house.
My father's bears more toward the marketplace;   9
Thither must I, and here I leave you, sir.
VINCENTIO
You shall not choose but drink before you go.
I think I shall command your welcome here,
And, by all likelihood, some cheer is toward.   13
                                        Knock.
GREMIO *[Advancing]* They're busy within. You were
best knock louder.   15

          Pedant looks out of the window.

PEDANT What's he that knocks as he would beat down
the gate?
VINCENTIO Is Signor Lucentio within, sir?
PEDANT He's within, sir, but not to be spoken withal.

5.1. Location: Padua. Before Lucentio's house.
s.d. out before i.e., onstage first. (Gremio does not see Biondello, Lucentio, and Bianca as they steal to church, or else does not recognize
Lucentio in his own person.) **5 a' your back** at your back, behind you
(i.e., I'll see you in church and safely married) **9 father's** i.e., father-in-
law's, Baptista's. **bears** lies. (A nautical term.) **13 toward** in prospect **15 s.d. window** i.e., probably the gallery to the rear, over the
stage

VINCENTIO What if a man bring him a hundred pound or two, to make merry withal?

PEDANT Keep your hundred pounds to yourself. He shall need none, so long as I live.

PETRUCHIO [*To Vincentio*] Nay, I told you your son was well beloved in Padua.—Do you hear, sir? To leave frivolous circumstances, I pray you, tell Signor 26 Lucentio that his father is come from Pisa and is here at the door to speak with him.

PEDANT Thou liest. His father is come from Padua and here looking out at the window.

VINCENTIO Art thou his father?

PEDANT Ay, sir, so his mother says, if I may believe her.

PETRUCHIO [*To Vincentio*] Why, how now, gentleman! Why, this is flat knavery, to take upon you another 35 man's name.

PEDANT Lay hands on the villain. I believe 'a means to cozen somebody in this city under my countenance. 38

Enter Biondello.

BIONDELLO [*To himself*] I have seen them in the church together, God send 'em good shipping! But who is 40 here? Mine old master Vincentio! Now we are undone and brought to nothing.

VINCENTIO [*Seeing Biondello*] Come hither, crack-hemp. 43

BIONDELLO I hope I may choose, sir. 44

VINCENTIO Come hither, you rogue. What, have you forgot me?

BIONDELLO Forgot you? No, sir. I could not forget you, for I never saw you before in all my life.

VINCENTIO What, you notorious villain, didst thou never see thy master's father, Vincentio?

BIONDELLO What, my old worshipful old master? Yes, marry, sir, see where he looks out of the window.

VINCENTIO Is 't so, indeed?   *He beats Biondello.*

---

26 circumstances matters **35 flat** downright **38 cozen** cheat. **under my countenance** by pretending to be me **40 good shipping** bon voyage, good fortune **43 crack-hemp** i.e., rogue likely to end up being hanged **44 choose** do as I choose

BIONDELLO Help, help, help! Here's a madman will
murder me.   [Exit.]
PEDANT Help, son! Help, Signor Baptista!
                                [Exit from the window.]
PETRUCHIO Prithee, Kate, let's stand aside and see the
end of this controversy.   [They stand aside.]

Enter [below] Pedant with servants, Baptista,
[and] Tranio [as Lucentio].

TRANIO Sir, what are you that offer to beat my servant? 59
VINCENTIO What am I, sir? Nay, what are you, sir? O
immortal gods! O fine villain! A silken doublet, a vel-
vet hose, a scarlet cloak, and a copatain hat! O, I am 62
undone, I am undone! While I play the good husband 63
at home, my son and my servant spend all at the uni-
versity.
TRANIO How now, what's the matter?
BAPTISTA What, is the man lunatic?
TRANIO Sir, you seem a sober ancient gentleman by
your habit, but your words show you a madman. 69
Why, sir, what 'cerns it you if I wear pearl and gold? 70
I thank my good father, I am able to maintain it. 71
VINCENTIO Thy father! O villain, he is a sailmaker in
Bergamo.
BAPTISTA You mistake, sir, you mistake, sir. Pray, what
do you think is his name?
VINCENTIO His name! As if I knew not his name! I have
brought him up ever since he was three years old, and
his name is Tranio.
PEDANT Away, away, mad ass! His name is Lucentio,
and he is mine only son, and heir to the lands of me,
Signor Vincentio.
VINCENTIO Lucentio! O, he hath murdered his master!
Lay hold on him, I charge you, in the Duke's name.
O, my son, my son! Tell me, thou villain, where is my
son Lucentio?
TRANIO Call forth an officer.

---

59 offer dare, presume   **62 copatain** high-crowned, sugar-loaf shape
63 good husband careful provider, manager   **69 habit** clothing
70 'cerns concerns   **71 maintain** afford

[Enter an Officer.]

Carry this mad knave to the jail. Father Baptista, I
charge you see that he be forthcoming.   88
VINCENTIO   Carry me to the jail?
GREMIO   Stay, officer, he shall not go to prison.
BAPTISTA   Talk not, Signor Gremio, I say he shall go to
prison.
GREMIO   Take heed, Signor Baptista, lest you be coney-   93
catched in this business. I dare swear this is the right   94
Vincentio.
PEDANT   Swear, if thou dar'st.
GREMIO   Nay, I dare not swear it.
TRANIO   Then thou wert best say that I am not Lucentio.   98
GREMIO   Yes, I know thee to be Signor Lucentio.
BAPTISTA   Away with the dotard! To the jail with him!

Enter Biondello, Lucentio, and Bianca.

VINCENTIO   Thus strangers may be haled and abused.   101
—O monstrous villain!
BIONDELLO   O! We are spoiled and—yonder he is. Deny   103
him, forswear him, or else we are all undone.
            *Exeunt Biondello, Tranio, and Pedant, as fast
            as may be. [Lucentio and Bianca] kneel.*
LUCENTIO
Pardon, sweet Father.
VINCENTIO   Lives my sweet son?
BIANCA
Pardon, dear Father.
BAPTISTA   How hast thou offended?
Where is Lucentio?
LUCENTIO   Here's Lucentio,
Right son to the right Vincentio,
That have by marriage made thy daughter mine,
While counterfeit supposes bleared thine eyne.   110

---

88 forthcoming ready to stand trial when required   **93–94 coney-
catched** tricked   **98 wert best** might as well   **101 haled** hauled about,
maltreated   **103 spoiled** ruined   **110 supposes** suppositions, false
appearances (with an allusion to Gascoigne's *Supposes*, an adaptation of
I Suppositi by Ariosto, from which Shakespeare took the Lucentio-
Bianca plot of intrigue).   **eyne** eyes

GREMIO
Here's packing, with a witness, to deceive us all!   111
VINCENTIO
Where is that damnèd villain Tranio,
That faced and braved me in this matter so?   113
BAPTISTA
Why, tell me, is not this my Cambio?
BIANCA
Cambio is changed into Lucentio.   115
LUCENTIO
Love wrought these miracles. Bianca's love
Made me exchange my state with Tranio,   117
While he did bear my countenance in the town,   118
And happily I have arrivèd at the last
Unto the wishèd haven of my bliss.
What Tranio did, myself enforced him to;
Then pardon him, sweet Father, for my sake.
VINCENTIO I'll slit the villain's nose, that would have
sent me to the jail.
BAPTISTA [*To Lucentio*] But do you hear, sir? Have you
married my daughter without asking my good will?
VINCENTIO Fear not, Baptista, we will content you, go
to. But I will in, to be revenged for this villainy. *Exit.*
BAPTISTA And I, to sound the depth of this knavery.
                                                        Exit.
LUCENTIO Look not pale, Bianca; thy father will not
frown.   *Exeunt [Lucentio and Bianca].*
GREMIO
My cake is dough, but I'll in among the rest,   132
Out of hope of all but my share of the feast. [*Exit.*] 133
KATHARINA Husband, let's follow, to see the end of
this ado.
PETRUCHIO First kiss me, Kate, and we will.
KATHARINA What, in the midst of the street?
PETRUCHIO What, art thou ashamed of me?
KATHARINA No, sir, God forbid, but ashamed to kiss.

111 packing conspiracy   **113 faced and braved** bullied and defied
115 Cambio is changed (A pun; *Cambio* in Italian means "change" or
"exchange.")   **117 state** social station   **118 countenance** appearance
132 My . . . dough i.e., I'm out of luck   **133 Out . . . but** having hope for
nothing other than

PETRUCHIO
Why, then let's home again. [*To Grumio.*] Come, sirrah,
   let's away.

KATHARINA
Nay, I will give thee a kiss. [*She kisses him.*] Now pray
   thee, love, stay.

PETRUCHIO
Is not this well? Come, my sweet Kate.
Better once than never, for never too late.   *Exeunt.* 143

❖

5.2   *Enter Baptista, Vincentio, Gremio, the Pedant,
           Lucentio, and Bianca; [Petruchio, Kate,
           Hortensio,] Tranio, Biondello, Grumio, and
           Widow; the servingmen with Tranio bringing in
           a banquet.*

LUCENTIO
At last, though long, our jarring notes agree,
And time it is, when raging war is done,
To smile at scapes and perils overblown.   3
My fair Bianca, bid my father welcome,
While I with selfsame kindness welcome thine.
Brother Petruchio, sister Katharina,
And thou, Hortensio, with thy loving widow,
Feast with the best, and welcome to my house.
My banquet is to close our stomachs up   9
After our great good cheer. Pray you, sit down,   10
For now we sit to chat as well as eat.   [*They sit.*]

PETRUCHIO
Nothing but sit and sit, and eat and eat!

BAPTISTA
Padua affords this kindness, son Petruchio.

PETRUCHIO
Padua affords nothing but what is kind.

---

143 once at some time. (Cf. "better late than never.")

5.2. Location: Padua. Lucentio's house.
s.d. banquet i.e., dessert   **3 scapes** escapes, close calls   **9 stomachs**
appetites (with pun on "quarrels")   **10 our . . . cheer** i.e., the wedding
feast at Baptista's

HORTENSIO
  For both our sakes, I would that word were true.
PETRUCHIO
  Now, for my life, Hortensio fears his widow.   16
WIDOW
  Then never trust me if I be afeard.
PETRUCHIO
  You are very sensible, and yet you miss my sense:
  I mean Hortensio is afeard of you.   19
WIDOW
  He that is giddy thinks the world turns round.
PETRUCHIO
  Roundly replied.
KATHARINA   Mistress, how mean you that?   21
WIDOW   Thus I conceive by him.   22
PETRUCHIO
  Conceives by me! How likes Hortensio that?
HORTENSIO
  My widow says, thus she conceives her tale.   24
PETRUCHIO
  Very well mended. Kiss him for that, good widow.
KATHARINA
  "He that is giddy thinks the world turns round":
  I pray you, tell me what you meant by that.
WIDOW
  Your husband, being troubled with a shrew,
  Measures my husband's sorrow by his woe—   29
  And now you know my meaning.
KATHARINA
  A very mean meaning.
WIDOW   Right, I mean you.   31

---

16 fears is afraid of. (But the Widow takes the word in the sense of
"frightens"; she protests she is not at all *afeard*, frightened by Hortensio.) **19 afeard** (Petruchio takes up the Widow's word and uses it in the
sense of "suspicious," fearful she will be untrue.) **21 Roundly** boldly
22 Thus . . . him i.e., that's what I think of him, Petruchio. (But Petruchio takes up *conceives* in the sense of "is made pregnant.") **24 conceives** devises (with a possible pun on *tale, tail*) **29 Measures** judges
31 very mean contemptible. (But the Widow takes up *mean* in the sense
of "have in mind," and Kate replies in the sense of "moderate in shrewishness.")

KATHARINA
  And I am mean indeed, respecting you.   32
PETRUCHIO To her, Kate!
HORTENSIO To her, widow!
PETRUCHIO
  A hundred marks, my Kate does put her down.   35
HORTENSIO That's my office.
PETRUCHIO
  Spoke like an officer. Ha' to thee, lad!   37
                                    Drinks to Hortensio.

BAPTISTA
  How likes Gremio these quick-witted folks?
GREMIO
  Believe me, sir, they butt together well.   39
BIANCA
  Head, and butt! An hasty-witted body   40
  Would say your head and butt were head and horn.   41
VINCENTIO
  Ay, mistress bride, hath that awakened you?
BIANCA
  Ay, but not frighted me. Therefore I'll sleep again.
PETRUCHIO
  Nay, that you shall not; since you have begun,
  Have at you for a bitter jest or two!   45
BIANCA
  Am I your bird? I mean to shift my bush;   46
  And then pursue me as you draw your bow.
  You are welcome all.
                         Exit Bianca [with Kate and Widow].

PETRUCHIO
  She hath prevented me. Here, Signor Tranio,   49
  This bird you aimed at, though you hit her not.   50

32 respecting compared to   **35 marks** coins worth 13 shillings 4 pence.
put her down overcome her. (But Hortensio takes up the phrase
in a bawdy sense.)   **37 officer** (playing on Hortensio's speaking of his
office or function).   **Ha'** have, i.e., here's   **39 butt** butt heads   **40 butt**
tail, bottom   **41 head and horn** (alluding to the familiar joke about
cuckold's horns)   **45 Have at** I shall come at.   **bitter** sharp   **46 Am . . .
bush** i.e., if you mean to shoot your barbs at me, I intend to move out of
the way, as a bird would fly to another bush (with a possible bawdy
double meaning)   **49 prevented** forestalled   **50 This bird** i.e., Bianca,
whom Tranio courted (*aimed at*) in his disguise as Lucentio

Therefore a health to all that shot and missed.   51
                              [*He offers a toast.*]
TRANIO
   O, sir, Lucentio slipped me like his greyhound,   52
   Which runs himself and catches for his master.
PETRUCHIO
   A good swift simile, but something currish.   54
TRANIO
   'Tis well, sir, that you hunted for yourself;
   'Tis thought your deer does hold you at a bay.   56
BAPTISTA
   O ho, Petruchio! Tranio hits you now.
LUCENTIO
   I thank thee for that gird, good Tranio.   58
HORTENSIO
   Confess, confess, hath he not hit you here?
PETRUCHIO
   'A has a little galled me, I confess;
   And as the jest did glance away from me,   61
   'Tis ten to one it maimed you two outright.
BAPTISTA
   Now, in good sadness, son Petruchio,   63
   I think thou hast the veriest shrew of all.
PETRUCHIO
   Well, I say no. And therefore for assurance   65
   Let's each one send unto his wife;
   And he whose wife is most obedient
   To come at first when he doth send for her
   Shall win the wager which we will propose.
HORTENSIO
   Content. What's the wager?
LUCENTIO   Twenty crowns.
PETRUCHIO   Twenty crowns!
   I'll venture so much of my hawk or hound,   72
   But twenty times so much upon my wife.
LUCENTIO   A hundred, then.

---

51 a health a toast   **52 slipped** unleashed   **54 swift** (1) quick-witted
(2) concerning swiftness.   **currish** (1) ignoble (2) concerning dogs   **56 deer**
(punning on *dear*).   **does . . . bay** turns on you like a cornered animal
and holds you at a distance   **58 gird** sharp, biting jest   **61 glance away**
ricochet off   **63 sadness** seriousness   **65 assurance** proof   **72 of** on

HORTENSIO Content.
PETRUCHIO A match. 'Tis done.
HORTENSIO Who shall begin?
LUCENTIO That will I.
   Go, Biondello, bid your mistress come to me.
BIONDELLO I go.   *Exit.*
BAPTISTA
   Son, I'll be your half Bianca comes.   81
LUCENTIO
   I'll have no halves; I'll bear it all myself.

   Enter Biondello.

   How now, what news?
BIONDELLO
   Sir, my mistress sends you word
   That she is busy and she cannot come.
PETRUCHIO
   How? She's busy and she cannot come!
   Is that an answer?
GREMIO   Ay, and a kind one too.
   Pray God, sir, your wife send you not a worse.
PETRUCHIO I hope better.
HORTENSIO
   Sirrah Biondello, go and entreat my wife
   To come to me forthwith.   *Exit Biondello.*
PETRUCHIO   O ho, entreat her!
   Nay, then she must needs come.
HORTENSIO   I am afraid, sir,
   Do what you can, yours will not be entreated.

   Enter Biondello.

   Now, where's my wife?
BIONDELLO
   She says you have some goodly jest in hand.
   She will not come. She bids you come to her.
PETRUCHIO
   Worse and worse. She will not come!
   O, vile, intolerable, not to be endured!
   Sirrah Grumio, go to your mistress.
   Say I command her come to me.   *Exit [Grumio].*

81 be your half take half your bet

HORTENSIO
I know her answer.
PETRUCHIO   What?
HORTENSIO   She will not.
PETRUCHIO
The fouler fortune mine, and there an end.

Enter Katharina.

BAPTISTA
Now, by my halidom, here comes Katharina!   103
KATHARINA
What is your will, sir, that you send for me?
PETRUCHIO
Where is your sister, and Hortensio's wife?
KATHARINA
They sit conferring by the parlor fire.
PETRUCHIO
Go fetch them hither. If they deny to come,
Swinge me them soundly forth unto their husbands.   108
Away, I say, and bring them hither straight.
                                        [*Exit Katharina.*]
LUCENTIO
Here is a wonder, if you talk of a wonder.
HORTENSIO
And so it is. I wonder what it bodes.
PETRUCHIO
Marry, peace it bodes, and love, and quiet life,
An awful rule, and right supremacy,   113
And, to be short, what not that's sweet and happy.
BAPTISTA
Now, fair befall thee, good Petruchio!
The wager thou hast won, and I will add
Unto their losses twenty thousand crowns,
Another dowry to another daughter,
For she is changed as she had never been.   119
PETRUCHIO
Nay, I will win my wager better yet,

---

103 by my halidom (Originally an oath by the holy relics, but confused
with an oath to the Virgin Mary.)   **108 Swinge** thrash.   **me** i.e., at my
behest. (*Me* is used colloquially.)   **113 awful rule** authority commanding
awe or respect   **119 as . . . been** as if she had never existed, i.e., she is
totally changed

And show more sign of her obedience,
Her new-built virtue and obedience.

Enter Kate, Bianca, and Widow.

See where she comes, and brings your froward wives
As prisoners to her womanly persuasion.—
Katharine, that cap of yours becomes you not.
Off with that bauble. Throw it underfoot.

[*She obeys.*]

WIDOW
  Lord, let me never have a cause to sigh
  Till I be brought to such a silly pass!   128

BIANCA
  Fie, what a foolish duty call you this?

LUCENTIO
  I would your duty were as foolish too.
  The wisdom of your duty, fair Bianca,
  Hath cost me an hundred crowns since suppertime.

BIANCA
  The more fool you, for laying on my duty.   133

PETRUCHIO
  Katharine, I charge thee tell these headstrong women
  What duty they do owe their lords and husbands.

WIDOW
  Come, come, you're mocking; we will have no telling.

PETRUCHIO
  Come on, I say, and first begin with her.

WIDOW She shall not.

PETRUCHIO
  I say she shall—and first begin with her.

KATHARINA
  Fie, fie! Unknit that threatening unkind brow,
  And dart not scornful glances from those eyes,
  To wound thy lord, thy king, thy governor.
  It blots thy beauty as frosts do bite the meads,
  Confounds thy fame as whirlwinds shake fair buds,   144
  And in no sense is meet or amiable.
  A woman moved is like a fountain troubled,   146

128 pass state of affairs   **133 laying** wagering   **144 Confounds thy fame** ruins your reputation   **146 moved** angry

Muddy, ill-seeming, thick, bereft of beauty;
And while it is so, none so dry or thirsty
Will deign to sip or touch one drop of it.
Thy husband is thy lord, thy life, thy keeper,
Thy head, thy sovereign; one that cares for thee,
And for thy maintenance commits his body
To painful labor both by sea and land,
To watch the night in storms, the day in cold,
Whilst thou liest warm at home, secure and safe;
And craves no other tribute at thy hands
But love, fair looks, and true obedience—
Too little payment for so great a debt.
Such duty as the subject owes the prince,
Even such a woman oweth to her husband;
And when she is froward, peevish, sullen, sour,   161
And not obedient to his honest will,
What is she but a foul contending rebel
And graceless traitor to her loving lord?
I am ashamed that women are so simple   165
To offer war where they should kneel for peace,
Or seek for rule, supremacy, and sway
When they are bound to serve, love, and obey.
Why are our bodies soft and weak and smooth,
Unapt to toil and trouble in the world,   170
But that our soft conditions and our hearts   171
Should well agree with our external parts?
Come, come, you froward and unable worms!   173
My mind hath been as big as one of yours,   174
My heart as great, my reason haply more,
To bandy word for word and frown for frown;
But now I see our lances are but straws,
Our strength as weak, our weakness past compare,
That seeming to be most which we indeed least are.
Then vail your stomachs, for it is no boot,   180
And place your hands below your husband's foot,
In token of which duty, if he please,
My hand is ready; may it do him ease.   183

161 peevish obstinate **165 simple** foolish **170 Unapt** unfit **171 condi-**
tions qualities **173 unable worms** i.e., poor feeble creatures **174 big**
haughty **180 vail your stomachs** lower your pride. **boot** profit, use
183 do him ease give him pleasure

PETRUCHIO
  Why, there's a wench! Come on, and kiss me, Kate.
                                              [*They kiss.*]

LUCENTIO
  Well, go thy ways, old lad, for thou shalt ha 't.

VINCENTIO
  'Tis a good hearing when children are toward.   186

LUCENTIO
  But a harsh hearing when women are froward.

PETRUCHIO   Come, Kate, we'll to bed.
  We three are married, but you two are sped.   189
  [*To Lucentio.*] 'Twas I won the wager, though you hit the
    white,   190
  And, being a winner, God give you good night!
                            Exit Petruchio [*and Kate*].

HORTENSIO
  Now, go thy ways, thou hast tamed a curst shrew.   192

LUCENTIO
  'Tis a wonder, by your leave, she will be tamed so.
                                              [*Exeunt.*]

186 'Tis . . . toward i.e., one likes to hear when children are obedient
189 We . . . sped i.e., all we three men have taken wives, but you two are
done for (*sped*) through disobedient wives   **190 the white** the center of
the target (with quibble on the name of Bianca, which in Italian means
"white")   **192 shrew** pronounced "shrow" (and thus spelled in the
Folio). See also 4.1.198 and 5.2.28.

Date and Text

The Taming of the Shrew was not printed until the First Folio of 1623. Francis Meres does not mention the play in 1598 in his *Palladis Tamia: Wit's Treasury* (a slender volume on contemporary literature and art; valuable because it lists most of Shakespeare's plays that existed at that time), unless it is the mysterious *"Loue labours wonne"* on his list. (Meres is not totally accurate, for he omits *Henry VI* from the history plays.) The play must have existed prior to 1598, however, for its style is comparable with that of *The Two Gentlemen of Verona* and other early comedies. Moreover, a play called *The Taming of A Shrew* appeared in print in 1594 (Stationers' Register, May 1594). The relationship of that text to Shakespeare's play is problematic, and several theories prevail. One is that *A Shrew* represents a source for Shakespeare's play, or even an early version by Shakespeare. If, as seems more likely, *A Shrew* is later, then it may be an imitation by some rival dramatist, who relied chiefly on his memory and who changed characters' names and the location to make the play seem his. More probably, it is a somewhat uncharacteristic kind of reported or "bad" quarto, reconstructed and "improved" upon by a writer who also borrowed admiringly from Christopher Marlowe and other Elizabethan dramatists. In either case, Shakespeare's play would have to be dated earlier than May 1594.

The title page of *A Shrew* proclaims that "it was sundry times acted by the *Right honorable the Earle of* Pembrook his seruants.*"* Quite possibly this derivative version was merely trying to capitalize on the original's stage success and was in fact describing performances of Shakespeare's play. Theater owner and manager Philip Henslowe's record of a performance of *"the Tamynge of A Shrowe"* in 1594 at Newington Butts, a mile south of London Bridge, may also refer to Shakespeare's play; certainly the minute distinction between "A Shrew" and "The Shrew" is one that the official records of the time would overlook. The Admiral's men and the Lord Chamberlain's men, acting companies, were playing at Newington Butts at the time, either jointly or alternatingly. Since Shakespeare's company, the Chamberlain's, later owned *The Shrew*, they may well have owned and acted it on this occasion in 1594, having obtained it from the Earl of Pembroke's men when that company disbanded in 1593. Many of Pembroke's leading players joined the Chamberlain's, Shakespeare quite possibly among them. (The possibility that he came to the Chamberlain's from Lord Strange's men seems less certain today than it once did.) It is entirely possible, then, that *The Shrew* was acted by Pembroke's men in 1592–1593 and subsequently passed along to the Chamberlain's.

The Folio text of this play is now generally thought to have been printed from Shakespeare's working manuscript or possibly from a transcript incorporating some minor theatrical changes.

Textual Notes

These textual notes are not a historical collation, either of the early folios or of more recent editions; they are simply a record of departures in this edition from the copy text. The reading adopted in this edition appears in boldface, followed by the rejected reading from the copy text, i.e., the First Folio. Only major alterations in punctuation are noted. Changes in lineation are not indicated, nor are some minor and obvious typographical errors.

Abbreviations used:
F the First Folio
s.d. stage direction
s.p. speech prefix

Copy Text: The First Folio.

Ind.1. s.d. Christopher Sly [printed at the end of the s.d. in F] **1 s.p. [and elsewhere] Sly** Begger **10–11 thirdborough** Headborough **16 Breathe** Brach **21 s.p. [and elsewhere] First Huntsman** Hunts **81 s.p. First Player** 2. Player **87 s.p. Second Player** Sincklo **99 s.p. First Player** Plai **134 peasant.** peasant,

Ind.2. 2 lordship Lord **18 Sly's** Sies **26 s.p. [and elsewhere] Third Servant** 3 Man **27 s.p. [and elsewhere] Second Servant** 2 Man **47 s.p. [and elsewhere] First Servant** 1 Man **53 wi' th'** with **99 s.p. [and elsewhere] Page** Lady **125 s.p. Servant** Mes **133 it. Is** it is

1.1. 13 Vincentio Vincentio's **14 brought** brough **24 satiety** sacietie **25 Mi perdonate** Me Pardonato **47 s.d. suitor** sister **57 s.p. [and elsewhere] Katharina** Kate **146 s.d. Manent** Manet **163 captum** captam **208 colored** Conlord **227 time.** time **244 your** you **248 s.d. speak** speakes

1.2. 17 s.d. wrings rings **18 masters** mistris **24 Con . . . trovato** Contutti le core bene trobatto **25 ben** bene **26 Molto** multo **onorato** honorata **33 pip** peepe **45 this's** this **51 grows. But** growes but **72 she is** she is **120 me and other** me. Other **171 help me** helpe one **189 Antonio's** Butonios **212 ours** yours **265 feat** seeke **280 ben** Been

2.1. 8 thee, tell tel **79 unto you** vnto **104 Pisa. By** Pisa by **153 struck** stroke **157 rascal fiddler** Rascall, fidler **168 s.d. Exeunt** Exit **186 bonny** bony **244 askance** a sconce **322 s.d. Exeunt** Exit **328 in me** me **352 Valance** Vallens **355 pail** pale **373 Marseilles'** Marcellus

3.1. 28 Sigeia sigeria [also at ll. 33 and 42] **43 steterat** staterat **47 [Aside]** Luc **50 s.p. Bianca** [not in F] **51 s.p. Lucentio** Bian **53 s.p. Bianca** Hort **76 clef** Cliffe **80 change** charge **odd** old **81 s.p. Servant** Nicke

3.2. 29 of thy of **30 old news** newes **33 hear** heard **54 swayed** Waid **56 cheeked** chekt **130 As I** As **150 e'er** ere **199 s.p. Gremio** Gra

4.1. 23 s.p. Curtis Gru **42 their white** the white **81 sleekly** slickely **106 s.p. Grumio** Gre **136 off** of **168 s.d. Curtis** Curtis a Seruant [after l. 169 in F]

4.2. 4 s.p. Hortensio Luc **6 s.p. Lucentio** Hor [and at l. 8] **13 none** me
31 her them **72 Take . . . alone** [assigned to "Par." in F] **in** me

4.3. [F has "Actus Quartus. Scena Prima" here] **63 s.p. Haberdasher** Fel
81 is a is **88 like a** like **146 where,** where **177 account'st** accountedst

4.4. s.d. [booted] [appears at l. 18 in F] **1 Sir** Sirs **5 Where . . . Pegasus**
[assigned to Tranio in F] **68** [F adds a s.d.: "Enter Peter"] **91 except**
expect

4.5. 18 is in **35 make a** make the **37 where** whether **77 she be** she

5.1. 4. [F has "Exit" here] **6 master's** mistris **42 brought** brough
50 master's Mistris **104 s.d. Exeunt** Exit **139 No Mo** **143 than never**
then ueuer
5.2. [F has "Actus Quintus" here] **2 done** come **37 thee** the **45 bitter**
better **two** too **52 s.p. Tranio** Tri **57 ho** oh **62 two** too **65 for** sir
132 an fiue **136 you're** your

Shakespeare's Sources

Most recent critics agree that the play called *The Taming of a Shrew*, published in 1594, is derived from a now-lost earlier version of Shakespeare's play to which the compiler added original material and borrowed or even plagiarized from other literary sources as well. It does not, then, appear to be a source for Shakespeare's play as Geoffrey Bullough has argued in his *Narrative and Dramatic Sources of Shakespeare* (1966). Apart from this question, all critics agree that Shakespeare's play consists of three elements, each with its own source: the romantic love plot of Lucentio and Bianca, the wife-taming plot of Petruchio and Kate, and the framing plot or, induction, of Christopher Sly.

The romantic love plot is derived from George Gascoigne's *Supposes*, a neoclassical comedy performed at Gray's Inn (one of the Inns of Court, where young men studied law in London) in 1566. Gascoigne's play was a rather close translation of Lodovico Ariosto's *I Suppositi* (1509), which in turn was based on two classical plays, Terence's *Eunuchus* and Plautus' *Captivi*. The heroine of Gascoigne's version (as of Ariosto's) is Polynesta, the resourceful daughter of Damon, a widower of Ferrara. Two suitors vie for Polynesta's hand: Dr. Cleander, an aged and miserly lawyer, and Erostrato, a Sicilian gentleman who has purportedly come to Ferrara to study. In fact, however, this "Erostrato" is the servant Dulippo in disguise, having changed places with his master. (These disguisings are the "supposes" of the title.) As a servant in Damon's household, "Dulippo" has secretly become the lover of Polynesta and has made her pregnant. Balia, the nurse, or duenna, is their go-between. Meanwhile, "Erostrato" takes great delight in outwitting Dr. Cleander and his unattractive parasite, Pasiphilo. The counterfeit Erostrato's ruse is to produce a rich father who will guarantee a handsome dowry and thereby outbid Cleander in the contest for Polynesta's hand. The "father" he produces, however, is actually an old Sienese stranger, who is persuaded that he is in danger in Ferrara unless he cloaks his identity. Complications arise when Damon learns of his daughter's affair and throws the lover, "Dulippo," into a dungeon. The crafty Pasiphilo overhears this compromising information and resolves to cause mischief for all the principals. Moreover, when Erostrato's real father, Philogano, arrives in Ferrara, he is barred from his son's house by the counterfeit Philogano and resolves to get help. His clever servant, Litio, suggests employing the famous lawyer Cleander. All is happily resolved when the real Dulippo proves to be the son of Dr. Cleander, and the real Erostrato is revealed to be rich and socially eligible for Polynesta's hand in marriage. Cleander is even reconciled to his parasite, Pasiphilo.

Shakespeare, in his play, has almost entirely eliminated the satire of the law that is in his source. Gremio is aged and wealthy, but no shyster. The lover is not imprisoned in a dungeon. The parasite is gone, as also in *The Comedy of Errors*. Bianca does not consummate her affair with Lucentio as does Polynesta, and hence has no need for a go-between like Balia. Shakespeare adapts a sophisticated neoclassical comedy, racy and cosmopolitan, to the moral standards of his public theater. The witless Hortensio, the tutoring in Latin, and the music lesson are Shakespeare's invention.

The wife-taming plot of Petruchio and Kate reflects an ancient comic misogynistic tradition, still extant today in the Scottish folksong "The Cooper of Fife" or "The Wife Wrapped in Wether's Skin" (Francis James Child, *The English and Scottish Popular Ballads* [1888–1898], 5:104). Richard Hosley has argued (in *Huntington Library Quarterly* 27, 1964) that Shakespeare's likeliest source was *A Merry Jest of a Shrewd and Curst Wife Lapped in Morel's Skin, for her Good Behavior* (printed c. 1550). Excerpts of this ballad follow. In this version, the husband beats his shrewish wife with birch rods until she bleeds and faints, whereupon he wraps her in the raw salted skin of an old plow-horse named Morel. Like Kate, this shrewish wife has a gentle younger sister who is their father's favorite. This father warns the man who proposes to marry his older daughter that she is shrewish, but the suitor goes ahead and subsequently tames his wife with Morel's skin. Thereafter, at a celebratory dinner, everyone is impressed by the thoroughness of the taming.

Shakespeare avoids the misogynistic extremes of this story, despite the similarity of the narrative. Instead, he seems to have had in mind the more humanistic spirit of Erasmus's *A Merry Dialogue Declaring the Properties of Shrewd Shrews and Honest Wives* (translated 1557) and Juan Luis Vives's *The Office and Duty of an Husband* (translated 1555). Specific elements of the wife-taming plot have been traced to other possible sources. The scolding of a tailor occurs in Gerard Legh's *Accidence of Armory* (1562); a wife agrees with her husband's assertion of a patent falsehood in Don Juan Manuel's *El Conde Lucanor* (1335); and three husbands wager on the obedience of their wives in *The Book of the Knight of La Tour-Landry* (printed 1484).

The induction story, of the beggar duped into believing himself a rich lord, is an old tale occurring in the *Arabian Nights*. An interesting analogue occurs in P. Heuterus's *De Rebus Burgundicis* (1584), translated into the French of S. Goulart (1606?) and thence into the English of Edward Grimeston (1607). According to Heuterus, in 1440 Philip the Good of Burgundy actually entertained a drunken beggar in his palace "to make trial of the vanity of our life," plying him with fine clothes, bed, a feast, and the performance of "a pleasant comedy."

A Merry Jest
of a Shrewd and Curst Wife
Lapped in Morel's Skin

Listen, friends, and hold you still;
Abide awhile and dwell.
A merry jest tell you I will,
And how that it befell.
As I went walking upon a day
Among my friends to sport,
To an house I took the way
To rest me for my comfort.

A great feast was kept there then,
And many one was thereat,
With wives and maidens and many a good man
That made good game and chat.

Title: **Shrewd** shrewish

It befell then at that tide 13
An honest man was there;
A cursèd dame sat by his side
That often did him dere. 16

His wife she was, I tell you plain,
This dame, ye may me trow. 18
To play the master she would not lain 19
And make her husband bow.
At every word that she did speak
To be peace he was full fain, 22
Or else she would take him on the cheek 23
Or put him to other pain.

When she did wink, he durst not stir 25
Nor play wherever he went
With friend or neighbor to make good cheer,
When she her brows bent.
These folk had two maidens fair and free 29
Which were their daughters dear.
This is true, believe you me:
Of conditions was none their peer. 32

The youngest was meek and gentle, iwis; 33
Her father's condition she had.
The eldest her mother's, withouten miss: 35
Sometimes frantic and sometimes mad. 36
The father had his pleasure in the one alway,
And glad he was her to behold;
The mother in the other, this is no nay, 39
For in all her curstness she made her bold. 40

And at the last she was, in fay, 41
As curst as her mother in word and deed 42
Her mischievous pageants sometime to play, 43
Which caused her father's heart to bleed.

---

13 tide time   **16 dere** vex   **18 trow** believe   **19 lain** i.e., disguise her ambition   **22 be peace** be silent.   **full fain** very willing   **23 take him** give him a blow   **25 wink** close or avert her eye   **29 free** of good breeding   **32 conditions** quality, nature   **33 iwis** certainly   **35 withouten miss** without doubt   **36 frantic** ungovernable.   **mad** angry   **39 no nay** certain   **40 in all . . . bold** i.e., the mother encouraged her shrewishness in every way   **41 at the last** in sum.   **in fay** in good faith   **42 curst** shrewish   **43 Her . . . play** i.e., playing her mischievous tricks

For he was woe and nothing glad,   45
And of her would fain be rid.
He wished to God that some man her had,
But yet to marriage he dust her not bid.

Full many there came the youngest to have,
But her father was loath her to forgo.
None there came the eldest to crave
For fear it should turn them to woe.
The father was loath any man to beguile,
For he was true and just withal.   54
Yet there came one within a while
That her demanded in the hall.

[The meek and gentle younger daughter is quickly wooed
and wedded; the father grieves to lose her, but the mother is
only too glad to get rid of her. When a suitor to the shrewish
elder daughter shows up, much to the father's surprise, the
kind old man warns of the danger: this daughter has been
taught by her mother "to be master of her husband." The
young man persists nonetheless and wins the mother's consent to the match. The mother advises him to pay heed to
his wife's wishes if he wants to enjoy domestic harmony—
especially since the wife will bring with her a considerable
dowry. The young man is not wealthy but is a good craftsman and willing to work hard. The wife-to-be gives him
plain notice of her intention to rule the roost in marriage,
but he has his own plans about that; he knows he is marrying a woman with a "proud heart," but one who will in all
events bring with her "an heap of gold."
And so the wedding takes place, followed by a wedding
feast with much giving of gifts (including a hundred pounds
to set the bridegroom up in his chosen craft), and dancing.
The wedding night appears to be a success, the new husband playing with his wife "Even as the cat was wont with
the mouse." Their sparring begins on the very next morning, as husband and wife lie abed while the bride's mother
prepares them a caudle, a warm drink of gruel and wine.]

When that the mother departed was,

---

45 woe woeful. **nothing** not at all **54 withal** in addition

They dallied together and had good game.
He hit her awry. She cried, "Alas!
What do ye, man? Hold up, for shame!"   514
"I will, sweet wife," then gan he say,
"Fulfill your mind, both loud and still.   516
But ye be able, I swear in fay,   517
In all sports to abide my will."

And they wrestled so long beforn
That this they had for their great meed: 520
Both shirt and smock was all to-torne,   521
That their uprising had no speed.   522
But yet the mother came again
And said to her daughter, "How dost thou now?"
"Marry, mother, between us twain
Our shirts be torn, I make God a vow.

"By God's dear mother," she sware then,
"This order with us may not continue.   528
I will no more lie by this man,
For he doth me brast both vein and sinew.   530
Nay, nay, dear mother, this world goeth on wheels.   531
By sweet Saint George, ye may me trow:
He lieth kicking with his heels   533
That he is like to bear me a blow."   534

[The newlyweds get past this difficulty and join their
friends in the hall for the caudle and more celebration.
Even the father's apprehensions are quieted to a degree,
and parents and friends leave the happy couple to their new
household. The husband sets up his shop "with haberdash
ware," i.e., petty merchandise, and bestows great care on
his plows and livestock as well. Trouble next erupts when
the farm laborers who tend his cattle and sheep come in
from the field for their meal only to be greeted by a burst of
shrewish temper from their new mistress.]

514 Hold up stop 516 Fulfill satisfy the desire of 517 in fay in good
faith 520 meed reward 521 to-torne torn to bits 522 their . . . speed they
were in no hurry to get out of bed 528 order i.e., condition of matrimony 530 me brast . . . sinew i.e., bursts asunder my blood vessels and
tendons 531 goeth on wheels goes on its own way (i.e., this too will
pass) 533 kicking with his heels i.e., flat on his back 534 That . . .
bear me he that is likely to receive from me

With countenance grim and words smart   607
She gave them meat and bade them brast.   608
The poor folk that come from plow and cart
Of her lewd words they were aghast,   610
Saying each to other, "What dame is this?
The devil I trow hath brought us here.   612
Our master shall know it, by heaven's bliss,
That we will not serve him another year."

The goodman was forth in the town abroad   615
About other things, I you say.
When he came homeward, he met with a goad: 617
One of his carters was going away.
To whom he said, "Lob, whither goest thou?"
The carter spied his master then,
And said to him, "I make God a vow,
No longer with thy wife abide I can.

"Master," he said, "by God's blist,   623
Our dame is the devil, thou mayst me believe!
If thou have sought her, thou hast not missed   625
Of one that full often thee shall grieve.   626
By God, a man thou canst not have
To go to cart ne yet to plow,   628
Neither boy nor yet knave,
By God's dear mother, I make God a vow,

"That will bide with thee day or night.
Our dame is not for us, for she doth curse.
When we shall eat or drink with right,   633
She bans and frowns, that we be all the worse.   634
We be not used, wherever we wend,
To be sorely looked on for eating of our meat.   636
The devil I trow is to thee send.   637
God help us a better mistress to get!"

"Come on thy way, Lob, and turn again.
Go home with me and all shall be well.

607 **smart** stinging 608 **brast** stuff themselves until they burst 610 **lewd**
rude 612 **brought us** i.e., brought her to us 615 **goodman** yeoman, householder 617 **goad** i.e., sting, annoyance 623 **blist** bliss 625-626 **If . . .
grieve** i.e., if you chose her, you picked one that will grieve you very often
628 **ne** nor 633 **shall** wish to 634 **bans** curses 636 **sorely looked on**
harshly regarded 637 **is to thee send** has been sent to you

An ox for my meiny shall be slain 641
And the hide at the market I will sell."
Upon this together home they went.
The goodman was angry in his mind,
But yet to his wife with good intent
He said, "Sweetheart, ye be unkind.

"Entreat our meiny well alway, 647
And give them meat and drink enough,
For they get our living every day, 649
And theirs also, at cart and plough.
Therefore I would that they should have
Meat and drink to their behoof. 652
For, my sweet wife, so God me save,
Ye will do so, if ye me love."

"Give them what thou wilt! I do not care,
By day and night, man, believe thou me.
Whatever they have, or how they fare,
I pray God evil mote they thee. 658
And specially that whoreson that doth complain.
I will quit him once, if ever I live! 660
I will dash the knave upon the brain
That ever after it shall him grieve."

"What, my dear wife? For shame, be still.
This is a pain, such words to hear.
We cannot always have our will,
Though that we were a king's peer.
For, to shame a knave, what can they get? 667
Thou art as lewd, 'fore God, as they. 668
And therefore shalt thou serve them of meat
And drink also, from hence alway. 670

"What, wife? Ye be to blame
To speak to me thus in this wise.
If we should strive, folk would speak shame.
Therefore be still, in mine advice.
I am loath with you to strive,

641 meiny retinue, company **647 Entreat** treat **649 get** earn **652 behoof**
use, benefit **658 mote they thee** may they thrive **660 quit** repay **667 For
... get** i.e., what good does it do to scorn someone who is below you in
social station (?) or, you should be ashamed; what can they get on their
own **668 lewd** rude, ill-mannered **670 hence** henceforth. **alway** always

For aught that you shall do or say.
I swear to Christ, wife, by my life,
I had rather take Morel and ride my way

To seek mine adventure till your mood be past.
I say to you, these manners be not good.
Therefore, I pray you that this be the last
Of your furious anger that seemeth so wood.   682
What can it avail you me for to grieve
That loveth you so well as I do, mine heart?
By my troth, wife, you may me believe,
Such toys as these be would make us both smart."   686

"Smart, in the twenty feigning devils' name!
That list me once well for to see.   688
I pray God give thee evil shame.
What shouldest thou be, wert it not for me?   690
A rag on thine arse thou shouldst not have
Except my friends had given it thee.   692
Therefore I tell thee well, thou drunken knave,
Thou art not he that shall rule me."

"O good wife, cease and let this overpass,
For all your great anger and high words eke.   696
I am mine own self even as I was,
And to you will be loving and also meek.
But if ye should do thus as ye do begin,
It may not continue no time, iwis.
I would not let, for kith nor kin,   701
To make you mend all things that is amiss."

"Make me? Marry, out upon thee, drivel!   703
Sayest thou that, wilt thou begin?
I pray God and Our Lady that a foul evil
Lighten upon thee and all thy kin!   706
By God's dear blist, vex me no more,   707
For if thou do thou shalt repent.
I have yet something for thee in store."
And with that a staff in her hand she hent.   710

682 wood furious, mad   **686 toys** antics   **688 That** . . . **see** I'd really like to
see that   **690 What shouldest thou be** where would you be, what kind of
life would you have   **692 friends** relatives   **696 eke** also   **701 let** hesitate.
kith friends and neighbors   **703 drivel** drudge, imbecile   **706 Lighten**
alight   **707 blist** bliss   **710 hent** seized

At him full soon then she let flee,
And whirled about her as it had been a man.
Her husband then was fain, perdy,   713
To void her stroke and go his way then.   714
"By God's dear mother!" then gan she swear,
"From henceforth I will make thee bow.
For I will trim thee in thy gear,
Or else I would I were called a sow.

"Fie on all wretches that be like thee,
In word or work, both loud and still!
I swear by Him that made man free,
Of me thou shalt not have thy will,
Now nor never, I tell thee plain;
For I will have gold and riches enow
When thou shalt go jagged as a simple swain   725
With whip in hand at cart and plow."

"Of that, my dear wife, I take no scorn,
For many a goodman with mind and heart
Hath gone to plow and cart beforn
My time, iwis, with pain and smart,
Which now be rich and have good will,
Being at home, and make good cheer,
And there they intend to lead their life still
Till our Lord do send for them here.   734

"But now I must ride a little way,
Dear wife. I will come right soon again.
Appoint our dinner, I you pray,   737
For I do take on me great pain.
I do my best, I swear by my life,
To order you like a woman, iwis,
And yet it cannot be withouten strife,
Through your lewd tongue, by heaven's bliss."

"Ride to the devil and to his dame!
I would I should thee never see.
I pray God send thee mickle shame   745
In any place wherever thou be.
Thou wouldest fain the master play,

713 **fain, perdy** glad, by God   714 **void** avoid   725 **jagged** i.e., in jagged, tattered clothes   734 **here** i.e., on earth   737 **Appoint** prepare   745 **mickle** much

But thou shalt not, by God I make thee sure!
I swear I will thy petticoat pay,   749
That long with me thou shalt not endure."

[The husband rides away, musing on his misfortune and repenting that he ever married but blaming no one but himself. He vows to make his wife regret her behavior by
beating her until she is black and blue and groaning for
woe. Nothing will do, he perceives, except to wrap her in the
skin of Morel, a faithful horse that has long drawn the plow
and the cart but is now old and infirm. Having resolved on
this course of action, he returns home to see what kind of
welcome he will get.]

"Where art thou, wife? Shall I have any meat?
Or am I not so welcome unto thee
That at my commandment I shall aught get?
I pray thee heartily soon tell thou me.
If thou do not serve me, and that anon,   843
I shall thee show mine anger, iwis.
I swear by God and by Saint John
Thy bones will I swaddle, so have I bliss."   846

Forth she came, as breme as a boar,   847
And like a dog she rated him then,   848
Saying thus: "I set no store   849
By thee, thou wretch! Thou art no man.
Get thee hence out of my sight,
For meat nor drink thou gettest none here.
I swear to thee, by Mary bright,
Of me thou gettest here no good cheer."

"Well, wife," he said, "thou dost me compel
To do that thing that I were loath.
If I bereave Morel of his old fell   857
Thou shalt repent it, by the faith now goeth.   858

749 thy petticoat pay flog your waistcoat (with you in it); i.e., I will make
you pay for this

843 anon at once **846 straddle** beat soundly **847 breme** fierce **848 rated**
scolded **849–850 set no store By thee** esteem you of no value **857 fell**
skin **858 by the faith now goeth** by the faith of Christians nowadays;
i.e., that's for sure

For I see well that it will no better be 859
But in it thou must, after the new guise. 860
It had been better, so mote I thee, 861
That thou haddest not begun this enterprise.

"Now will I begin my wife to tame,
That all the world shall it know.
I would be loath her for to shame,
Though she do not care, ye may me trow. 866
Yet will I her honesty regard
And it preserve wherever ye may. 868
But Morel, that is in yonder yard,
His hide therefore he must leese, in fay." 870

And so he commanded anon
To slay old Morel, his great horse,
And flay him then the skin from the bone
To wrap it about his wife's white corse.
Also he commanded of a birchen tree 875
Rods to be made a good great heap,
And sware, by dear God in Trinity
His wife in his cellar should skip and leap.

"The hide must be salted," then he said eke, 879
"Because I would not have it stink.
I hope herewith she will be meek,
For this I trow will make her shrink
And bow at my pleasure when I her bed,
And obey my commandments both loud and still,
Or else I will make her body bleed
And with sharp rods beat her my fill."

Anon with that to her he gan to call.
She bid, "Abide, in the devil's name!
I will not come, whatso befall.
Sit still, with sorrow and mickle shame.
Thou shalt not rule me as pleaseth thee,
I will well thou know, by God's dear mother; 892
But thou shalt be ruled alway by me,

859–860 it will . . . must there is nothing else for it but that you must go into it 861 so mote I thee as I hope to prosper 866 Though even though. me trow believe me 868 wherever ye may wherever I may (?) 870 leese lose. in fay in good faith 875 birchen birch 879 eke also 892 I will I wish

And I will be master and none other."

"Wilt thou be master, dear wife? In fay,
Then must we wrestle for the best game.
If thou it win, then may I say
That I have done myself great shame.
But first I will make thee sweat, good Joan,   899
Red blood even to the heels a-down,
And lap thee in Morel's skin alone,   901
That the blood shall be seen even from the crown."

"Sayest thou me that, thou wretched knave?
It were better thou haddest me never seen!
I swear to thee, so God me save,
With my nails I will scratch out both thine eyen.   906
And therefore think not to touch me once,
For, by the Mass, if thou begin that,
Thou shalt be handled for the nonce   909
That all thy brains on the ground shall squat."

"Why, then, there is no remedy, I see,
But needs I must do even as I thought.
Seeing it will none otherwise be,
I will thee not spare, by God that me bought!   914
For now I am set thee for to charm   915
And make thee meek, by God's might,
Or else with rods, while thou art warm,
I shall thee scourge with reason and right.

"Now will I my sweet wife trim,
According as she deserveth to me.   920
I swear by God and by Saint Sim
With birchen rods well beat shall she be.
And after that, in Morel's salt skin
I will her lay and full fast bind,
That all her friends and eke her kin
Shall her long seek or they her find."   926

Then he her met, and to her gan say,
"How sayest thou, wife, wilt thou be master yet?"
She sware by God's body, and by that day,
And suddenly with her fist she did him hit,

899 sweat i.e., bleed   **901 lap** enwrap   **906 eyen** eyes   **909 for the
nonce** i.e., in such a way   **914 bought** redeemed   **915 charm** subdue
920 to me at my hands   **926 or** ere

And defied him, drivel, at every word,   931
Saying, "Precious whoreson, what dost thou think?   932
I set not by thee a stinking turd.   933
Thou shalt get of me neither meat nor drink."

"Sayest thou me that, wife?" quoth he then.
With that, in his arms he gan her catch.
Straight to the cellar with her he ran,
And fastened the door with lock and latch
And threw the key down him beside,
Asking her then if she would obey.
Then she said, "Nay, for all thy pride,"
But she was master and would abide alway.   942

"Then," quoth he, "we must make a fray."
And with that her clothes he gan to tear.
"Out upon thee, whoreson!" then she did say,
"Wilt thou rob me of all my gear?
It cost thee naught, thou arrant thief!"   947
And quickly she gat him by the head.
With that she said, "God give thee a mischief,
And them that fed thee first with bread!"   950

They wrestled together thus, they two,
So long that the clothes asunder went,
And to the ground he threw her tho,   953
That clean from the back her smock he rent.
In every hand a rod he gat   955
And laid upon her a right good pace,
Asking of her, "What game was that?"
And she cried out, "Whoreson! Alas! Alas!

"What wilt thou do? Wilt thou kill me?
I have made thee, a man of naught.   960
Thou shalt repent it, by God's pity,
That ever this deed thou hast y-wrought!"   962
"I care not for that, dame," he did say.

---

931 defied him, drivel scorned him as an imbecile (?) **932 Precious whore-son** i.e., worthless rogue **933 I set ... turd** i.e., I don't give a turd for you **942 But she** i.e., but said that she **947 It cost thee naught** i.e., you didn't pay for it (having had no money when you married me) **950 them ... bread** i.e., those who raised you **953 tho** then **955 every hand** both hands. **gat** got, held **960 I ... naught** i.e., I and my family made you what you are from a mere nobody **962 y-wrought** done

"Thou shalt give over, or we depart,   964
The mastership all, or all this day
I will not cease to make thee smart."

Ever he laid on, and ever she did cry,
"Alas! Alas, that ever I was born!
Out on thee, murderer, I thee defy!
Thou hast my white skin and my body all to-torne! 970
Leave off betime, I counsel thee."   971
"Nay, by God, dame, I say not so yet.
I swear to thee, by Mary so free,   973
We begin but now. This is the first fit.   974

"Once again we must dance about,
And then thou shalt rest in Morel's skin."
He gave her then so many a great clout   977
That on the ground the blood was seen.
Within a while he cried, "New rods, new!"
With that she cried full loud, "Alas!"
"Dance yet about, dame; thou came not where it grew." 981
And suddenly with that in a swoon she was.

He spied that, and up he her hent   983
And wrang her hard then by the nose.   984
With her to Morel's skin straight he went
And therein full fast he did her close.   986
Within a while she did revive,
Through the gross salt that did her smart.
She thought she should never have gone on live 989
Out of Morel's skin, so sore is her heart.

When she did spy that therein she lay,   991
Out of her wit she was full nigh,
And to her husband then did she say,
"How canst thou do this villainy?"
"Nay, how sayest thou, thou cursèd wife?
In this foul skin I will thee keep

---

964 or we depart ere we part, before we're done   **970 to-torne** torn to pieces
971 betime quickly   **973 free** excellent, magnanimous   **974 fit** section of a
poem or song (i.e., we've just begun)   **977 clout** blow   **981 thou came . . .
grew** i.e., you've just started, you've had only a taste of what I have in store
for you   **983 hent** seized   **984 wrang** wrung, pinched. (Wringing by the nose
is a procedure for bringing a person to consciousness.)   **986 fast** securely
989 on live alive   **991 that therein she lay** what she was lying in

During the time of all thy life,
Therein forever to wail and weep."

With that her mood began to sink,
And said, "Dear husband, for grace I call!
For I shall never sleep or wink   1001
Till I get your love, whatso befall;
And I will never to you offend,
In no manner of wise, of all my life,   1004
Nor to do nothing that may pretend   1005
To displease you with my wits five.

"For father, nor mother, whatsoever they say,
I will not anger you, by God in throne,
But glad will your commandments obey
In presence of people and eke alone."
"Well, on that condition thou shalt have
Grace, and fair bed to rest thy body in.
But if thou rage more, so God me save,
I will wrap thee again in Morel's skin."

Then he took her out in his arms twain
And beheld her so piteously with blood arrayed.
"How thinkest thou, wife, shall we again
Have such business more?" to her he said.
She answered, "Nay, my husband dear.
While I you know and you know me,
Your commandments I will, both far and near,
Fulfill alway in every degree."

"Well, then, I promise thee, by God, even now,
Between thee and me shall never be strife.
If thou to my commandments quickly bow
I will thee cherish all the days of my life."
In bed she was laid, and healed full soon
As fair and clear as she was beforn.
What he her bid was quickly done.
To be diligent, iwis, she took no scorn.   1030

Then was he glad and thought in his mind,
"Now have I done myself great good,
And her also, we shall it find,

1001 **wink** close the eyes   1004 **of** during   1005 **pretend** undertake, presume   1030 **To . . . scorn** she thought it no indignity to be diligent, certainly

Though I have shed part of her blood.
For, as methink she will be meek,
Therefore I will her father and mother
Bid to guest, now the next week,   1037
And of our neighbors many other."

Great pain he made his wife to take
Against the day that they should come.   1040
Of them was none that there did lack,
I dare well say unto my doom.   1042
Yea, father and mother and neighbors all
Did thither come to make good cheer.
Soon they were set in general,   1045
The wife was diligent, as did appear.

Father and mother was welcome then,
And so were they all, in good fay.
The husband sat there like a man;   1049
The wife did serve them all that day.
The goodman commanded what he would have;
The wife was quick at hand.
"What now?" thought the mother. "This arrant knave
Is master, I understand.

"What may this mean," then she gan think,
"That my daughter so diligent is?
Now can I neither eat nor drink
Till I it know, by heaven bliss."
When her daughter came again
To serve at the board as her husband bade,
The mother stared with her eyen twain   1061
Even as one that had been mad.

All the folk that at the board sat
Did her behold then, everychone.   1064
The mother from the board her gat,   1065
Following her daughter, and that anon,
And in the kitchen she her fand,   1067
Saying unto her in this wise:

1037 **Bid to guest** invite as guests   1040 **Against** in anticipation of
1042 **unto my doom** on pain of divine judgment   1045 **Soon** as soon
as   1049 **like a man** i.e., like the man of the household   1061 **eyen**
eyes   1064 **everychone** everyone   1065 **from the board her gat** got
herself up from the table   1067 **fand** found

"Daughter, thou shalt well understand
I did not teach thee after this guise."

"Ah, good mother, ye say full well.
All things with me is not as ye ween.   1072
If ye had been in Morel's fell
As well as I, it should be seen."   1074
"In Morel's fell! What devil is that?"   1075
"Marry, mother, I will it you show.
But beware that you come not thereat,   1077
Lest you yourself then do beshrew.   1078

"Come down now in this cellar so deep
And Morel's skin there shall you see,
With many a rod that hath made me to weep,
When the blood ran down fast by my knee."
The mother this beheld and cried out, "Alas!"
And ran out of the cellar as she had been wood.   1084
She came to the table where the company was
And said, "Out, whoreson! I will see thy heart blood."   1086

"Peace, good mother! Or, so have I bliss,   1087
Ye must dance else as did my wife,
And in Morel's skin lie, that well salted is,
Which you should repent all the days of your life."
All they that were there held with the young man   1091
And said he did well in every manner degree.
When dinner was done, they departed all then;
The mother no lenger durst there be.   1094

The father abode last and was full glad,
And gave his children his blessing, iwis,
Saying the young man full well done had,
And merrily departed withouten miss.   1098
This young man was glad, ye may be sure,
That he had brought his wife to this.
God give us all grace in rest to endure,
And hereafter to come unto his bliss!

1072 ween think   **1074 it should be seen** i.e., you would understand
1075 What devil i.e., what in the devil   **1077–1078 come not . . . beshrew**
i.e., be careful you don't get put in Morel's skin, lest you curse yourself then
1084 as as if.   **wood** mad   **1086 I will . . . blood** i.e., I'll have your life
1087 so have I bliss as I hope to be saved   **1091 held with** sided with
1094 lenger longer   **1098 withouten miss** undoubtedly, certainly

Thus was Morel flain out of his skin   1103
To charm a shrew, so have I bliss.   1104
Forgive the young man if he did sin,
But I think he did nothing amiss.
He did all thing even for the best,
As was well provèd then.
God save our wives from Morel's nest!
I pray you say all Amen.

Thus ending the jest of Morel's skin,
Where the curst wife was lappèd in.
Because she was of a shrewd leer,   1113
Thus was she served in this manner.

He that can charm a shrewd wife
    Better than thus,
Let him come to me, and fetch ten pound
    And a golden purse.

This ballad, *A Merry Jest of a Shrewd and Curst Wife Lapped in Morel's Skin*, was printed by Hugh Jackson without date, c. 1550–1560. A single damaged copy is located in the Bodleian Library, Oxford. It has been reprinted by, among others, *The Shakespeare Society (London) Publications*, vol. 4, no. 25, London, 1844.

1103 flain flayed **1104 charm** subdue. **so have I bliss** as I hope to be saved **1113 leer** disposition, countenance

Further Reading

Bean, John C. "Comic Structure and the Humanizing of Kate in *The Taming of the Shrew.*" In *The Woman's Part: Feminist Criticism of Shakespeare*, ed. Carolyn Ruth Swift Lenz, Gayle Greene, and Carol Thomas Neely. Urbana, Chicago, and London: Univ. of Illinois Press, 1980. Bean admires the romantic element of the play— the process by which Kate comes to understand herself "through her discovery first of play and then of love"— but finds the taming offensive. He defends Kate's final speech as the expression of a nontyrannical hierarchy in which partners have distinctive but cooperative roles, but he argues that the process that brings Kate to speak it (like "a trained bear") is evidence of a "depersonalizing farce unassimilated from the play's fabliau source."

Berry, Ralph. "The Rules of the Game." *Shakespeare's Comedies: Explorations in Form*. Princeton, N.J.: Princeton Univ. Press, 1972. Throughout the play, Berry argues, different patterns of wooing parallel and contrast with each other. Petruchio and Kate's emerges as the healthiest of the play's relationships, for the "taming" is in reality the process by which a well-matched pair of lovers together work out an agreement "upon the rules of its games."

Charlton, H. B. *"The Taming of the Shrew." Shakespearian Comedy*, 1938. Rpt. London: Methuen; New York: Barnes and Noble, 1966. Charlton examines the structure of Shakespeare's comedy against the background of Renaissance Italian comic models (which are echoed in the Bianca–Lucentio subplot). In the Petruchio–Kate plot, however, Shakespeare moves beyond familiar romantic conventions, focusing instead upon the lovers' "matter-of-fact recognition of the practical and expedient."

Daniell, David. "The Good Marriage of Katherine and Petruchio." *Shakespeare Survey* 37 (1984): 23–31. Daniell discovers in the Kate–Petruchio plot surprising affinities with the language and experience of Shakespeare's early history plays. Daniell uses this insight to explore the play's theatricality—the "special ability of acting to embrace and give form to violence"—which provides the terms in which Kate and Petruchio find the means "of being richly together with all their contradictions—and energies—very much alive and kicking."

Evans, Bertrand. *Shakespeare's Comedies*, pp. 24–32. Oxford: Clarendon Press, 1960. Evans focuses on the contrast between the play's two plots: the minor plot depends upon the dynamics of "false supposes and unperceived realities," while Kate and Petruchio's full awareness of each other's nature, a trait that is unique among Shakespeare's comic lovers, forms the basis of the major plot.

Garber, Marjorie B. "Dream and Structure: *The Taming of the Shrew*." *Dream in Shakespeare: From Metaphor to Metamorphosis*. New Haven and London: Yale Univ. Press, 1974. For Garber, the induction introduces the play's thematic concern with appearance and reality. Sly's dream "distances later action and insures lightness of tone"; his transformation also prefigures and parallels Kate's, allowing us to see her change as a metamorphosis rather than a taming.

Hibbard, G. R. "*The Taming of the Shrew*: A Social Comedy." In *Shakespearean Essays*, ed. Norman Sanders and Alwin Thaler. Knoxville, Tenn.: Univ. of Tennessee Press, 1964. Hibbard's discussion of the marital customs of Elizabethan England suggests that the play is not only a dramatic exploration of romantic attitudes but also "an incisive piece of social criticism." Kate's frustrations emerge from actual social and economic conditions. Bianca and Lucentio reveal the shallowness of the conventional values of romance, while Kate's and Petruchio's "realistic" approach to life and love gives their marriage an appeal absent from the subplot.

Huston, J. Dennis. "Enter the Hero: The Power of the Play in *The Taming of the Shrew*." *Shakespeare's Comedies of Play*. New York: Columbia Univ. Press, 1981. Arguing that both the Induction and the marriage in mid-play subvert traditional comic conventions, Huston finds that Shakespeare's handling of literary tradition is analogous to Petruchio's treatment of Kate: Shakespeare animates sterile romantic conventions in the same way as Petruchio summons Kate out of her unthinking and automatic shrewishness "into the human theatre of play."

Kahn, Coppélia. "*The Taming of the Shrew:* Shakespeare's Mirror of Marriage." *Modern Language Studies* 5 (1975): 88–102. Rpt. in "Coming of Age: Marriage and Manhood in *Romeo and Juliet* and *The Taming of the Shrew.*" *Man's Estate: Masculine Identity in Shakespeare.* Berkeley: Univ. of California Press, 1981. For Kahn, Kate's ironic submission liberates Petruchio from his stereotypic male dominance (reversing Huston's assessment; see above). The play satirizes not the shrewish female but the male desire to control women, and Kate's final speech not only "completes the fantasy of male domination but also mocks it as mere fantasy."

Leggatt, Alexander. "*The Taming of the Shrew.*" *Shakespeare's Comedy of Love.* London: Methuen; New York: Barnes and Noble, 1974. Leggatt discovers the relationship between the induction and the play world in their common interest in "sport, playacting, and education." The Lord, Petruchio, and Kate herself have the "power to manipulate convention, to create experience rather than have experience forced upon them."

Nevo, Ruth. "Kate of Kate Hall." *Comic Transformations in Shakespeare.* London and New York: Methuen, 1980. Nevo admires the unconventional Petruchio as "stage manager and chief actor" of the play's psychodrama. His taming of Kate is an "instructive, liberating, and therapeutic" activity, which rescues her from an unenviable family situation in which her only defense is "her insufferability."

Saccio, Peter. "Shrewd and Kindly Farce." *Shakespeare Survey* 37 (1984): 33–40. Defending the farcical quality of the play, Saccio praises the energy, determination, and cleverness of the characters in remedying the static social world of Padua. Kate, he finds, is a participant rather than a victim of the farce, and her growing abilities as a farceur mark the stages of her liberation from a compulsive shrewishness.

Shaw, George Bernard. "*The Taming of the Shrew.*" In *Shaw on Shakespeare,* ed. Edwin Wilson. New York: E. P. Dutton, 1961. Responding to a number of performances of the play, Shaw praises its "realistic" aspects. Petruchio rejects romantic affectation in favor of practical concerns for his own comfort. His taming of Kate is acceptable to an audience, since it is "good-humored and untainted by wanton cruelty." Nonetheless, Shaw is uncomfortable with Kate's final speech of submission: its "lord-of-creation moral," he asserts, is "disgusting to modern sensibility."

Tillyard, E. M. W. "The Fairy-Tale Element in *The Taming of the Shrew.*" In *Shakespeare 1564–1964: A Collection of Modern Essays by Various Hands,* ed. Edward A. Bloom. Providence, R.I.: Brown Univ. Press, 1964. Tillyard presents several versions of shrew-taming folktales that may have served Shakespeare as sources, singling out the story of King Thrushbeard as the most likely analogue to the Kate plot and as a model for the induction.

Photo © George Joseph

From the 1962 New York Shakespeare Festival production of *The Merchant of Venice*, with George C. Scott as Shylock, directed by Joseph Papp at the Delacorte Theater in Central Park.

THE MERCHANT OF VENICE

THE MERCHANT
OF VENICE

Introductory Material
Foreword by Joseph Papp
Introduction
The Merchant of Venice
in Performance

THE PLAY

Supplementary Material
Date and Text
Textual Notes
Shakespeare's Sources
Further Reading

Foreword

The Merchant of Venice has been one of Shakespeare's most popular—and controversial—plays wherever it has been performed. The controversy usually centers around the way Shylock the Jew is portrayed and treated. Many people think that Shakespeare himself was being anti-Semitic here. I personally don't believe this, judging from the humanity in all the works of this great writer, especially this one. It's difficult for me to label *The Merchant of Venice* as anti-Semitic when it has one of the most eloquent pleas to our sense of common humanity ever uttered on the stage:

> Hath not a Jew eyes? Hath not a Jew hands, organs, dimensions, senses, affections, passions? Fed with the same food, hurt with the same weapons, subject to the same diseases, healed by the same means, warmed and cooled by the same winter and summer, as a Christian is? If you prick us, do we not bleed? If you tickle us, do we not laugh? If you poison us, do we not die? And if you wrong us, shall we not revenge?

There is no indication that the romantic lead, Bassanio, and the woman he marries, Portia, are prejudiced against Shylock because he's a Jew. Portia's goal is to save Antonio's life in order to free her new husband from his obligations to the merchant. Bassanio wants to rescue a friend to whom he's heavily indebted. It would be difficult to prove that anything either of them says has an unusually anti-Semitic prejudice.

And yet there is anti-Semitism *within* the play. We find it most virulently in Antonio, the merchant of Venice, and his henchmen Salerio and Solanio, very strongly in Gratiano, somewhat in Lorenzo, and especially in the comedian Launcelot Gobbo, Shylock's former servant.

The Merchant of Venice was the first play we at the New York Shakespeare Festival produced at the Delacorte Theater in Central Park, with George C. Scott as Shylock. I can remember telling George not to play for sympathy, not to be nice, not to turn the other cheek, but to feel the righteous anger that belongs to him. After all, Shylock has been so kicked around and spat on just for trying to make a living that it would be unnatural for him *not* to want vengeance. He's taunted in the streets; his daughter runs away with a

Christian, taking his money and jewels with her; the ruling elite in Venice, personified by Antonio, are arrayed against him—who wouldn't press for his pound of flesh in those circumstances?

Shakespeare provides Shylock with a rationale—but not an excuse—for his behavior. But Antonio, unlike Shylock, has no real reason for his hatred and cruelty toward the Jewish man; nor can there ever be a rational explanation for anti-Semitism. Antonio treats Shylock abominably. In the early scenes of the play we learn that he has spurned and spat upon him, calling him a dog, and Antonio goes on to say, "I am as like to call thee so again, To spit on thee again, to spurn thee too." In the trial scene, Shylock is threatened with the confiscation of all of his remaining money and property. The compromise suggested by Antonio requires, among other things, that Shylock change his religion—the cruelest punishment that could be devised.

One of the most poignant moments Shakespeare gives Shylock occurs when Tubal tells him that Jessica, Shylock's daughter, who has run off with Lorenzo, has traded a family ring for a monkey. "It was my turquoise," says Shylock, "I had it of Leah when I was a bachelor. I would not have given it for a wilderness of monkeys." What makes me sad here is that Jessica seems to have completely disregarded the emotional value of the ring. There seems to be very little triumph in her act; instead, Jessica must suffer the consequences of her actions, as we perceive in the last scenes of the play, where she is unaccountably melancholic.

Because of Shylock, *The Merchant of Venice* can easily be called a tragedy. He will always remain a complex, fascinating character. No wonder so many actors want to play him, to understand him, and to enter into his tragedy—he is one of the greatest dramatic figures of all time.

Joseph Papp

Joseph Papp gratefully acknowledges the help of Elizabeth Kirkland in preparing this Foreword.

Introduction

Although Shylock is the most prominent character in *The Merchant of Venice*, he takes part in neither the beginning nor the ending of the play. Nor is he the "merchant" of the title, but a moneylender whose usury is portrayed as the very opposite of true commerce. His vengeful struggle to obtain a pound of flesh from Antonio contrasts with the various romantic episodes woven together in this play: Bassanio's choosing of Portia by means of the caskets, Gratiano's wooing of Nerissa, Jessica's elopement with Lorenzo, Launcelot Gobbo's changing of masters, and the episode of the rings. In all these stories, friendship and love triumph over faithlessness and hatred. However much we may come to sympathize with Shylock's misfortunes and question the motives of his enemies, however much we are made uncomfortable by the potential insularity of a Venetian ethic that has no genuine place for non-Christians or cultural outsiders, Shylock remains essentially the villain of a love comedy. His remorseless pursuit of Antonio darkens the mood of the play, and his overthrow signals the providential triumph of love and friendship, even though that triumph is not without its undercurrent of wry melancholy. Before we examine the undoubted ironies of his situation more closely, we need to establish the structural context of this love comedy as a whole.

Like many of Shakespeare's philosophical and festive comedies, *The Merchant of Venice* presents two contrasting worlds, one idealized and the other marked by conflict and anxiety. To an extent, these contrasting worlds can be identified with the locations of Belmont and Venice. Belmont, to which the various happy lovers and their friends eventually retire, is a place of magic and love. As its name implies, it is on a mountain, and it is reached by a journey across water. It is pure, serene, ethereal. As often happens in fairy stories, on this mountain dwells a princess who must be won by means of a riddling contest. We usually see Belmont at night. Music surrounds it, and women preside over it. Even its caskets, houses, and rings are essentially feminine symbols. Venice, on the other hand, is a place of bustle and economic competition, seen most characteristically in the heat of the day. It lies low and flat, at a point where rivers reach the sea. Men preside over its contentious marketplace and its haggling law courts. Actually, the opposition of Venice and Belmont is not quite so clear-cut: Venice contains much compassionate friendship, whereas Belmont is subject to the arbitrary command of Portia's dead father. (Portia somewhat resembles Jessica in being imprisoned by her father's will.) Even though Portia descends to Venice in the angelic role of mercy-giver, she also remains very human: sharp-tongued and even venomous in caricaturing her unwelcome wooers, crafty in her legal maneuvering, saucily prankish in her torturing of Bassanio about the rings. Nevertheless the polarity of two contrasting localities and two groups of characters is vividly real in this play.

The play's opening scene, from which Shylock is excluded, sets forth the interrelated themes of friendship, romantic love, and risk, or "hazard." The merchant of the title, Antonio, is the victim of a mysterious melancholy. He is wealthy enough and surrounded by friends, but something is missing from his life. He assures his solicitous companions that he has no financial worries, for he has been too careful to trust all his cargoes to one sea vessel. Antonio in fact has no idea why he is so sad. The question is haunting: what is the matter? Perhaps the answer is to be found in a paradox: those who strive to prosper in the world's terms are doomed to frustration, not because prosperity will necessarily elude them but because it will not satisfy the spirit. "You have too much respect upon the world," argues the carefree Gratiano. "They lose it that do buy it with much care" (1.1.74–75). Portia and Jessica too are at first afflicted by a melancholy that stems from the incompleteness of living isolated lives, with insufficient opportunities for love and sacrifice. They must learn, as Antonio learns with the help of his dear friend Bassanio, to seek happiness by daring to risk everything for friendship. Antonio's risk is most extreme: only when he has thrown away concern for his life can he discover what there is to live for.

At first, Bassanio's request for assistance seems just as materialistic as the worldliness from which Antonio suffers. Bassanio proposes to marry a rich young lady, Portia, in order to recoup his fortune lost through prodigality, and he needs money from Antonio so that he may woo Portia in proper fashion. She is "richly left," the heiress of a dead father, a golden fleece for whom this new Jason will make a quest. Bassanio's adventure is partly commercial. Yet his pilgrimage for Portia is magnanimous as well. The occasional modern practice of playing Bassanio and Portia as cynical antiheroes of a "black" comedy points up the problematic character of their materialism and calculation, but it inevitably distorts the play. Bassanio has lost his previous fortune through the amiable faults of reckless generosity and a lack of concern for financial prudence. The money he must now borrow, and the fortune he hopes to acquire, are to him no more than a means to carefree happiness. Although Portia's rich dowry is a strong consideration, he describes her also as "fair, and fairer than that word, / Of wondrous virtues" (1.1.162–163). Moreover, he enjoys the element of risk in wooing her. It is like shooting a second arrow in order to recover one that has been lost— double or nothing. This gamble, or "hazard," involves risk for Antonio as well as for Bassanio, and ultimately brings a double reward to them both, spiritual as well as financial. Unless one recognizes these aspects of Bassanio's quest, as well as the clear fairy-tale quality with which Shakespeare deliberately invests this part of the plot, one cannot properly assess Bassanio's role in this romantic comedy.

Bassanio's quest for Portia can in fact never succeed until he disavows the very financial considerations that brought him to Belmont in the first place. This is the paradox of the riddle of the three caskets, an ancient parable stressing the need for choosing by true substance rather than by outward show. To choose "what many men desire," as the Prince of Morocco does, is to pin one's hopes on worldly wealth; to believe that one "deserves" good fortune, as the Prince of Aragon does, is to reveal a fatal pride in one's own merit. Bassanio perceives that in order to win true love he must "give and hazard all he hath." He is not "deceived with ornament" (3.2.74). Just as Antonio must risk all for friendship, and just as Bassanio himself must later be willing to risk losing Portia for the higher cause of true friendship (in the episode of the rings), Bassanio must renounce worldly ambition and beauty before he can be rewarded with success. Paradoxically, only those who learn to subdue such worldly desires may then legitimately enjoy the world's pleasures. Only they have acknowledged the hierarchical subservience of the flesh to the spirit. These are the philosophical truisms of Renaissance Neoplatonism, depicting love as a chain or ladder from the basest carnality to the supreme love of God for man. On this ladder, perfect friendship and spiritual union are more sublimely Godlike than sexual fulfillment. This idealism may seem a strange doctrine for Bassanio the fortune hunter, but actually its conventional wisdom simply confirms his role as romantic hero. He and Portia are not denied worldly happiness or erotic pleasure; they are merely asked to give first thought to their Christian duty in marriage. The essentially Christian paradox of losing the world in order to gain the world lies at the center of their love relationship. This paradox illuminates not only the casket episode but the struggle for the pound of flesh, the elopement of Jessica, the ring episode, and even the comic foolery of Launcelot Gobbo.

Shylock, in his quest for the pound of flesh, represents a denial of all the paradoxical Christian truths just described. As a usurer he refuses to lend money interest-free in the name of friendship. Instead of taking risks, he insists on his bond. He spurns mercy and demands strict justice. By calculating all his chances too craftily, he appears to win at first but must eventually lose all. He has "too much respect upon the world" (1.1.74). His God is the Old Testament God of Moses, the God of wrath, the God of the Ten Commandments with their forbidding emphasis on "Thou shalt not." (This oversimplified contrast between Judaism and Christianity was commonplace in Shakespeare's time.) Shylock abhors stealing but admires equivocation as a means of outmaneuvering a competitor; he approvingly cites Jacob's ruse to deprive Laban of his sheep (1.3.69–88). Any tactic is permissible so long as it falls within the realm of legality and contract.

Shylock's ethical outlook, then, justifies both usury and the old dispensation of the Jewish law. The two are philosophically combined, just as usury and Judaism had become equated in the popular imagination of Renaissance Europe. Even though lending at interest was becoming increasingly necessary and common, old prejudices against it still persisted. Angry moralists pointed out that the New Testament had condemned usury and that Aristotle had described money as barren. To breed money was therefore regarded as unnatural. Usury was considered sinful because it did not involve the usual risks of commerce; the lender was assured against loss of his principal by the posting of collateral and, at the same time, was sure to earn a handsome interest. The usurer seemed to be getting something for nothing. For these reasons usury was sometimes declared illegal. Its practitioners were viewed as corrupt and grasping, hated as misers. In some European countries, Jews were permitted to practice this un-Christian living (and permitted to do very little else) and then, hypocritically, were detested for performing un-Christian deeds. Ironically, the moneylenders of England were Christians, and few Jews were to be found in any professions. Nominally excluded since Edward I's reign, the Jews had returned in small numbers to London but did not practice their Judaism openly. They attended Anglican services as required by law and then worshiped in private, relatively undisturbed by the authorities. Shylock is not based on observation from London life. He is derived from continental tradition and reflects a widespread conviction that Jews and usurers were alike in being non-Christian and sinister.

Shylock is unquestionably sinister. On the Elizabethan stage the actor portraying him apparently wore a red beard, as in traditional representations of Judas, and a hooked nose. He bears an "ancient grudge" against Antonio simply because Antonio is "a Christian." We recognize in Shylock the archetype of the supposed Jew who wishes to kill a Christian and obtain his flesh. In early medieval anti-Semitic legends of this sort, the flesh thus obtained was imagined to be eaten ritually during Passover. Because some Jews had once persecuted Christ, all were unfairly presumed to be implacable enemies of all Christians. These anti-Semitic superstitions were likely to erupt into hysteria at any time, as in 1594 when Dr. Roderigo Lopez, a Portuguese Jewish physician, was accused of having plotted against the life of Queen Elizabeth and of Don Antonio, pretender to the Portuguese throne. Marlowe's *The Jew of Malta* was revived for this occasion, enjoying an unusually successful run of fifteen performances, and scholars have often wondered if Shakespeare's play was not written under the same impetus. On this score the evidence is inconclusive, and the play might have been written any time between 1594 and 1598 (when it is mentioned by Francis Meres in his *Palladis Tamia*), but in any case Shakespeare has made no attempt to avoid the anti-Semitic nature of his story.

To offset the portrayal of Jewish villainy, however, the play also dramatizes the possibility of conversion to Christianity, suggesting that Judaism is more a matter of benighted faith than of ethnic origin. Converted Jews were not new on the stage: they had appeared in medieval cycle drama, in the Croxton *Play of the Sacrament* (late fifteenth century), and more recently in *The Jew of Malta*, in which Barabas's daughter Abigail falls in love with a Christian and eventually becomes a nun. Shylock's daughter Jessica similarly embraces Christianity as Lorenzo's wife and is received into the happy comradeship of Belmont. Shylock is forced to accept Christianity, presumably for the benefit of his eternal soul. Earlier in the play, Antonio repeatedly indicates his willingness to befriend Shylock if the latter will only give up usury, and is even cautiously hopeful when Shylock offers him an interest-free loan: "The Hebrew will turn Christian; he grows kind" (1.3.177). To be sure, Antonio's denunciation of Shylock's usurious Judaism has been vehement and personal; we learn that he has spat on Shylock's gaberdine and kicked him as one would kick a dog. This violent disapproval offers no opportunity for the toleration of cultural and religious differences that we expect today from persons of good will, but at least Antonio is prepared to accept Shylock if Shylock will embrace the Christian faith and its ethical responsibilities. Whether the play itself endorses Antonio's Christian point of view as normative, or insists on a darker reading by making us uneasy with intolerance, is a matter of unceasing critical debate. Quite possibly, the play's power to disturb emanates at least in part from the dramatic conflict of irreconcilable sets of values.

To Antonio, then, as well as to other Venetians, true Christianity is both an absolute good from which no deviation is possible without evil, and a state of faith to which aliens

may turn by abjuring the benighted creeds of their ancestors. By this token, the Prince of Morocco is condemned to
failure in his quest for Portia not so much because he is
black as because he is an infidel, one who worships "blind
fortune" and therefore chooses a worldly rather than a spiritual reward. Although Portia pertly dismisses him with
"Let all of his complexion choose me so" (2.7.79), she professes earlier to find him handsome and agrees that he
should not be judged by his complexion (2.1.13–22). Unless
she is merely being hypocritical, she means by her later remark that black-skinned men are generally infidels, just as
Jews are as a group non-Christian. Such pejorative thinking
about persons as types is no doubt distressing and suggests
at least to a modern audience the cultural limitation of Portia's view, but in any case it shows her to be no less well-
disposed toward blacks than toward others who are also
alien. She rejects the Prince of Aragon because he too lacks
proper faith, though nominally a Christian. All human beings, therefore, may aspire to truly virtuous conduct, and
those who choose virtue are equally blessed; but the terms
of defining that ideal are essentially Christian. Jews and
blacks may rise spiritually only by abandoning their pagan
creeds for the new dispensation of charity and forgiveness.

The superiority of Christian teaching to the older Jewish
dispensation was of course a widely accepted notion of
Shakespeare's time. After all, these were the years when
men fought and died to maintain their religious beliefs. Today the notion of a single true church is less widely held,
and we have difficulty understanding why anyone would
wish to force conversion on Shylock. Modern productions
find it tempting to portray Shylock as a victim of bigotry,
and to put great stress on his heartrending assertions of his
humanity: "Hath not a Jew eyes? . . . If you prick us, do we
not bleed?" (3.1.55–61). Shylock does indeed suffer from his
enemies, and his sufferings add a tortured complexity to
this play—even, one suspects, for an Elizabethan audience.
Those who profess Christianity must surely examine their
own motives and conduct. Is it right to steal treasure from
Shylock's house along with his eloped daughter? Is it considerate of Jessica and Lorenzo to squander Shylock's turquoise ring, the gift of his wife, Leah, on a monkey? Does
Shylock's vengeful insistence on law justify the quibbling

countermeasures devised by Portia even as she piously declaims about mercy? Do Shylock's misfortunes deserve the mirthful parodies of Solanio ("My daughter! O my ducats!") or the hostile jeering of Gratiano at the conclusion of the trial? Because he stands outside Christian faith, Shylock can provide a perspective whereby we see the hypocrisies of those who profess a higher ethical code. Nevertheless, Shylock's compulsive desire for vengeance according to an Old Testament code of an eye for an eye cannot be justified by the wrongdoings of any particular Christian. Such deeds condemn the doer rather than undermine the Christian standards of true virtue as ideally expressed. Shakespeare humanizes Shylock by portraying him as a believable and sensitive man, and shows much that is to be regretted in Shylock's Christian antagonists, but he also allows Shylock to place himself in the wrong by his refusal to forgive his enemies.

Shylock thus loses everything through his effort to win everything on his own terms. His daughter, Jessica, by her elopement, follows an opposite course. She characterizes her father's home as "hell," and she resents being locked up behind closed windows. Shylock detests music and the sounds of merriment; Jessica's new life in Belmont is immersed in music. He is old, suspicious, miserly; she is young, loving, adventurous. Most important, she seems to be at least part Christian when we first see her. As Launcelot jests half in earnest, "If a Christian did not play the knave and get thee, I am much deceived" (2.3.11–12). Her removal from Shylock's house involves theft, and her running from Venice is, she confesses, an "unthrift love." Paradoxically, however, she sees this recklessness as of more blessed effect than her father's legalistic caution. As she says, "I shall be saved by my husband. He hath made me a Christian" (3.5.17–18).

Launcelot Gobbo's clowning offers a similarly paradoxical comment on the tragedy of Shylock. Launcelot's debate with himself about whether or not to leave Shylock's service is put in terms of a soul struggle between his conscience and the devil (2.2.1–29). Conscience bids him stay, for service is a debt, a bond, an obligation, whereas abandonment of one's indenture is a kind of rebellion or stealing away. Yet Shylock's house is "hell" to Launcelot as to Jessica. Comparing his new master with his old, Launcelot observes to Bassanio, "you have the grace of God, sir, and he hath enough" (142–143). Service with Bassanio involves imprudent risks, since Bassanio is a spendthrift. The miserly Shylock rejoices to see the ever hungry Launcelot, this "huge feeder," wasting the substance of a hated Christian. Once again, however, Shylock will lose everything in his grasping quest for security. Another spiritual renewal occurs when Launcelot encounters his old and nearly blind father (2.2). In a scene echoing the biblical stories of the Prodigal Son and of Jacob and Esau, Launcelot teases the old man with false rumors of Launcelot's own death in order to make their reunion seem all the more unexpected and precious. The illusion of loss gives way to joy: Launcelot is, in language adapted from the liturgy, "your boy that was, your son that is, your child that shall be" (81–82).

In the episode of the rings we encounter a final playful variation on the paradox of winning through losing. Portia and Nerissa cleverly present their new husbands with a cruel choice: disguised as a doctor of laws and his clerk, who have just saved the life of Antonio from Shylock's wrath, the two wives ask nothing more for their services than the rings they see on the fingers of Bassanio and Gratiano. The two husbands, who have vowed never to part with these wedding rings, must therefore choose between love and friendship. The superior claim of friendship is clear, no matter what the cost, and Portia knows well enough that Bassanio's obedience to this Neoplatonic ideal is an essential part of his virtue. Just as he previously renounced beauty and riches before he could deserve Portia, he must now risk losing her for friendship's sake. The testing of the husbands' constancy does border at times on gratuitous harshness and exercise of power, for it deals with the oldest of masculine nightmares, cuckoldry. Wives are not without weapons in the struggle for control in marriage, and Portia and Nerissa enjoy trapping their new husbands in a no-win situation. Still, the threat is easily resolved by the dispelling of farcically mistaken identities. The young men have been tricked into bestowing their rings on their wives for a second time in the name of perfect friendship, thereby confirming a relationship that is both Platonic and fleshly. As Gratiano bawdily points out in the play's last line, the ring is both a spiritual and a sexual symbol of marriage. The resolution of this illusory quarrel also brings to an end the merry battle of the sexes between wives and husbands. Having hinted at the sorts of misunderstandings that afflict even the best of human relationships, and having proved themselves wittily able to torture and deceive their husbands, Portia and Nerissa submit at last to the authority of Bassanio and Gratiano.

All appears to be in harmony in Belmont. The disorders of Venice have been left far behind, however imperfectly they may have been resolved. Jessica and Lorenzo contrast their present happiness with the sufferings of less fortunate lovers of long ago: Troilus and Cressida, Pyramus and Thisbe, Aeneas and Dido, Jason and Medea. The tranquil joy found in Belmont is attuned to the music of the spheres, the singing of the "young-eyed cherubins" (5.1.62), although with a proper Christian humility the lovers also realize that the harmony of immortal souls is infinitely beyond their comprehension. Bound in by the grossness of the flesh, "this muddy vesture of decay" (5.1.64), they can only reach toward the bliss of eternity through music and the perfect friendship of true love. Even in their final joy, accordingly, the lovers find an incompleteness that lends a wistful and slightly melancholy reflective tone to the play's ending; but this Christian sense of the unavoidable incompleteness of all human life is of a very different order from that earlier melancholy of isolation and lack of commitment experienced by Portia, Jessica, Antonio, and others.

The Merchant of Venice
in Performance

"Shylock is a bloody-minded monster," confided Henry Irving in 1879, "but you mustn't play him so, if you wish to succeed; you must get some sympathy with him." The paradox that Irving described is central to the history of *The Merchant of Venice* in performance. Shylock is the play's villain, but he is also a towering presence onstage. Actors who have undertaken the role of Shylock have seldom been content (since the early eighteenth century, at any rate) to see him as simply a villain to be jeered at and cast out; instead, they have been drawn toward a tragic interpretation, sometimes so much so that the rest of the play has suffered.

In the first century and a half of its stage history, *The Merchant of Venice* was not often staged at all, possibly because audiences were not yet ready for a sympathetic Shylock. Shakespeare's acting company, the Lord Chamberlain's men, performed the play "divers times" before 1600 and (now called the King's men) twice at court in February of 1605, and they probably played it in a comic vein of acting (with Richard Burbage as Shylock in a red wig, according to a doubtful tradition), though one would like to think that the original performances also found room for a complex and even troubled response. For a long while thereafter, the play virtually disappeared from the stage. Thomas Betterton took the role not of Shylock but of Bassanio in an adaptation called *The Jew of Venice*, by George Granville, Lord Lansdowne, at the theater in Lincoln's Inn Fields, London, in 1701. Despite its title, this heavily rearranged version reduced the importance of Shylock in order both to ennoble the role of Bassanio and to provide the kind of masquelike spectacle demanded by Restoration audiences. The play opens on a banquet given by Bassanio, at which Antonio proposes a toast to eternal friendship; Bassanio, one to love; Gratiano, to women; and Shylock, sitting apart, to money. The banquet concludes with a long masque of Peleus and Thetis. In an added prison scene, Shylock protests to Antonio that he will have his bond. During the trial scene, Gratiano is given a number of interpolated lines to augment the comedy of his attack on Shylock. Shylock's rage against his daughter's elopement is toned down, and he is not forced to convert to Christianity. The Gobbos have disappeared. Thomas Doggett, the actor who played Shylock, was renowned as a comic actor and may have modeled his performance on disreputable moneylenders of his own day. Granville's version persisted well into the eighteenth century, though sometimes without the masque.

Charles Macklin not only restored Shakespeare's play in 1741 at the Theatre Royal, Drury Lane, reinstating the Gobbos, Morocco, and Aragon, but brought a passionate intensity to the role of Shylock that did much to establish the play as the moneylender's. Tubal also was returned, to heighten the effect of Shylock's scenes of outrage. A contemporary viewer reported that Shylock's calamities made "some tender impression on the audience," even though Shylock was at other times malevolent, cunning, and ferocious. He was, in other words, a complex figure, no longer a low comedy part as in Doggett's interpretation. Later eighteenth-century productions persisted in supplying various distractions—Morocco and Aragon were once again cut from the play, songs were supplied for Portia, Jessica, and Lorenzo by Thomas Arne and others, the casket scene was curtailed, and Kitty Clive amused audiences in her role of Portia by copying the mannerisms of certain well-known lawyers of the day—but the part of Shylock, even if not always conceived in a tragic vein, had proved a triumph for Macklin and was soon coveted by the leading actors of the eighteenth and nineteenth centuries.

George Frederick Cooke played Shylock in London first in 1800 and then, memorably, in 1803–1804, supported by John Philip Kemble, as Antonio, and Sarah Siddons, as Portia. Cooke's Shylock was, according to critic William Hazlitt, "bent with age and ugly with mental deformity, grinning with deadly malice, with the venom of his heart congealed in the expression of his countenance, sullen, morose, gloomy, inflexible." One version of the play, often performed during these years, featured an ending written by the Reverend Richard Valpy, with no fifth act at all but instead a recognition scene between Portia and Bassanio at the end of the trial; the play thus ended with the departure of its central figure, Shylock. Edmund Kean, at Drury Lane in 1814, the first actor to wear a black wig instead of the red wig of the stereotypical stage Jew, depicted Shylock with such scorn and energy that, to William Hazlitt at least, the Christians in the play were made to appear hypocrites by comparison. Romantic sympathies were turning in this direction, in any case; the older comedy of revenge and savagery seemed out of keeping with the play's love comedy and talk of mercy.

Victorian audiences were stirred not only by a sympathetic Shylock but by handsome sets calculated to enhance a mood of poetry, music, and romance. In 1841 at Drury Lane, William Charles Macready provided onstage a number of realistic scenes from Venice, including the cathedral and square of St. Mark's, Shylock's house facing on a canal with a distant view of the campanile, a court of justice reminiscent of the Roman Senate (as it had appeared before in Macready's revival of *Coriolanus*), and, most impressive of all, a moonlit garden in Act 5 that sparkled with soft light and melted away into poetic indistinctness toward the back of the set. Contemporary paintings of Act 5, such as those in John Boydell's Shakespeare gallery of art in Pall Mall, convey the kind of magical effect aimed at by Macready. At the Princess's Theatre in 1858 Charles Kean also began his production in St. Mark's Square, with milling crowds of noblemen and citizens, foreign visitors and flower girls, and the Doge in procession, all before the dialogue had begun. Edwin Booth's production of the play at the Winter Garden Theatre in New York in 1867 had magnificent scenery copied by Henry Hilliard and Charles Witham from famous paintings of well-known Venetian locales. In 1875 Sir Squire and Lady Bancroft, after a trip to Venice with their scene painter to select the sets, produced *The Merchant of Venice* at the Prince of Wales Theatre in Tottenham Court Road; because they could allow only one set to each act in their small theater, the play had to be rearranged considerably. The first tableau was located "under the arches of the Doge's palace," with a lovely view of the Church of Santa Maria della Salute. Merchants, sailors, beggars, and Jews passed and repassed in pantomimic action.

Henry Irving's lavish production at the Lyceum Theatre, London, in 1879 was thus only one, though perhaps the most famous, among a series of splendid visual evocations of Venice and Belmont. Continuing the tradition, begun by Charles Kean, of a usable bridge over the canals in the stage set, Irving employed this location for a memorable staging effect. He placed the elopement of Jessica in a season of carnival celebration: masked crowds walked about, gondolas arrived at waterside, merrymakers raced across the bridge. Shylock's return across the bridge alone to his dark and deserted house introduced a moment of supreme pathos that audiences, and a number of subsequent Shylocks, were quite unable to resist. At the trial scene a crowd of Jews followed the fate of Shylock with avid interest, listening intently to Portia's legal arguments and despairing of the outcome. Irving played Shylock as an aristocrat of his ancient religion, looking down with calm pride on the Europeans and then lashing out in rage and scorn. The nobility added to the pathos. Herbert Beerbohm Tree, in 1908, continued the tradition, and there have been numerous sympathetic Shylocks since.

More recent productions have tended to use sympathy for Shylock as a way of emphasizing the problematic morality of the entire play. George C. Scott, in Joseph Papp's production for the New York Shakespeare Festival in 1962, portrayed Shylock as neither a villain nor a victim but as a desperately defensive, paranoid, and persecuted man. In England, Laurence Olivier, in Jonathan Miller's National Theatre production of 1970 (subsequently televised), expressed through Shylock's long cry of pain as he left the courtroom the anguish of a bereaved and wronged man. The production, set in nineteenth-century Venice, took an unromantic look at the hypocrisy of the Christian community in that city, at its closed and bigoted world of privilege, at its complacent and mercantile ways. The playing of Jewish sacred music during the final scene reminded audiences that the feast of reconciliation at Belmont was achieved by excluding those who did not "belong."

A production at Stratford-upon-Avon in 1953 emphasized the friendship of Antonio and Bassanio in contrast to the solitariness of Michael Redgrave's wily and heavily accented Shylock, and other productions, such as Michael Kahn's at Stratford, Connecticut, in 1967, have gone so far as to see a homoerotic attraction between the Christian friends of this play.

Portia, in modern times, not infrequently becomes something of a calculating vixen, catty in her evaluation of her masculine wooers, insincere in her profession of hospitality to Morocco, ready to cheat by giving unfair hints to Bassanio in the casket scene (as in Theodore Komisarjevsky's production at Stratford-upon-Avon in 1932, in which Portia, singing "Tell me where is fancy bred," heavily stressed the words rhyming with "lead"), and adept at tormenting him in the episode of the rings. Jessica and Lorenzo can be portrayed as thoughtless in their frivolous dissipating of Shylock's wealth and keepsakes. As productions have returned to a full text, the earlier dominance of Shylock has made way for a ceaseless exploration of the play's provocative ambivalence, as, for example, in John Barton's 1978 production at London's Other Place, which sought to make both Shylock and the mercantile world of the Christians psychologically credible. *The Merchant of Venice* has increasingly been seen as one of Shakespeare's problem plays.

Shakespeare's original production had no scenery and so had to rely on costumed actors and on Shakespeare's language to conjure up a sense of place. The contrasts and similarities between Venice and Belmont built into the text must have called for an alternating rhythm of staging effects in the movement back and forth from largely male scenes of business and legal disputation in Venice to scenes of feminine wit, badinage, and the unveiling of caskets in Belmont. Shylock's house was visually invoked in the Elizabethan theater by Jessica's appearance "above" in the gallery, as at Shylock's window; from this vantage she could throw down money to the maskers below in the street before exiting above and then joining them on the main stage for the elopement (2.6). The trial scene (4.1) was visualized presumably by means of robed justices in their seats, by Portia in disguise as a doctor of laws, by Shylock with his bond and his knife, and by an atmosphere of confrontation. The actors established the mood of Belmont in Act 5 chiefly by their talk about the starry night and by their recollection of old tales about the tribulations of love. Twentieth-century theater has attempted, by and large, to find new theatrical ways of suggesting these effects in place of the heavy representational sets of the nineteenth century, recognizing that theater should not mechanically replicate what Shakespeare calls for in the image-laden language of his characters. Above all, staging today seems intent on capturing the dark ambivalences that are so integrally a part of the play's stage history.

—THE—
MERCHANT OF VENICE

1.1   *Enter Antonio, Salerio, and Solanio.*

ANTONIO
In sooth, I know not why I am so sad.
It wearies me, you say it wearies you;
But how I caught it, found it, or came by it,
What stuff 'tis made of, whereof it is born,
I am to learn;   5
And such a want-wit sadness makes of me   6
That I have much ado to know myself.

SALERIO
Your mind is tossing on the ocean,
There where your argosies with portly sail,   9
Like signors and rich burghers on the flood,   10
Or as it were the pageants of the sea,   11
Do overpeer the petty traffickers   12
That curtsy to them, do them reverence   13
As they fly by them with their woven wings.

SOLANIO
Believe me, sir, had I such venture forth,   15
The better part of my affections would
Be with my hopes abroad. I should be still   17
Plucking the grass to know where sits the wind,
Peering in maps for ports and piers and roads;   19
And every object that might make me fear
Misfortune to my ventures, out of doubt
Would make me sad.

SALERIO   My wind cooling my broth
Would blow me to an ague when I thought
What harm a wind too great might do at sea.
I should not see the sandy hourglass run
But I should think of shallows and of flats,   26
And see my wealthy *Andrew* docked in sand,   27

1.1. Location: A street in Venice.
5 am to learn have yet to learn   **6 want-wit** one lacking in good sense
9 argosies large merchant ships. (So named from *Ragusa*, the modern
city of Dubrovnik.)   **portly** majestic   **10 signors** gentlemen
11 pageants mobile stages used in plays or processions   **12 overpeer**
look down upon   **13 curtsy** i.e., bob up and down   **15 venture forth**
investment risked   **17 still** continually   **19 roads** anchorages, open
harbors   **26 But** without it happening that.   **flats** shoals   **27 Andrew**
name of a ship (perhaps after the *St. Andrew*, a Spanish galleon captured at Cadiz in 1596)

Vailing her high-top lower than her ribs   28
To kiss her burial. Should I go to church   29
And see the holy edifice of stone,
And not bethink me straight of dangerous rocks,   31
Which touching but my gentle vessel's side
Would scatter all her spices on the stream,
Enrobe the roaring waters with my silks,
And, in a word, but even now worth this,   35
And now worth nothing? Shall I have the thought
To think on this, and shall I lack the thought
That such a thing bechanced would make me sad?   38
But tell not me; I know Antonio
Is sad to think upon his merchandise.

ANTONIO
Believe me, no. I thank my fortune for it,
My ventures are not in one bottom trusted,   42
Nor to one place; nor is my whole estate
Upon the fortune of this present year.   44
Therefore my merchandise makes me not sad.

SOLANIO
Why, then you are in love.

ANTONIO   Fie, fie!

SOLANIO
Not in love neither? Then let us say you are sad
Because you are not merry; and 'twere as easy
For you to laugh and leap, and say you are merry
Because you are not sad. Now, by two-headed Janus,   50
Nature hath framed strange fellows in her time:
Some that will evermore peep through their eyes
And laugh like parrots at a bagpiper,   53
And other of such vinegar aspect   54
That they'll not show their teeth in way of smile
Though Nestor swear the jest be laughable.   56

28 Vailing lowering (usually as a sign of submission). **high-top** top-
mast   **29 burial** burial place   **31 bethink me straight** be put in mind
immediately   **35 this** i.e., all this concern   **38 bechanced** having happened   **42 bottom** ship's hold   **44 Upon . . . year** i.e., risked upon the
chance of the present   **50 two-headed Janus** a Roman god of all beginnings, represented by a figure with two faces   **53 at a bagpiper** i.e.,
even at a bagpiper, whose music was regarded as melancholic
54 vinegar sour, sullen   **56 Nestor** venerable senior officer in the *Iliad*,
noted for gravity

Enter Bassanio, Lorenzo, and Gratiano.

Here comes Bassanio, your most noble kinsman,
Gratiano, and Lorenzo. Fare ye well.
We leave you now with better company.

SALERIO
I would have stayed till I had made you merry,
If worthier friends had not prevented me.   61

ANTONIO
Your worth is very dear in my regard.
I take it your own business calls on you,
And you embrace th' occasion to depart.   64

SALERIO   Good morrow, my good lords.

BASSANIO
Good signors both, when shall we laugh? Say, when?   66
You grow exceeding strange. Must it be so?   67

SALERIO
We'll make our leisures to attend on yours.   68
                              Exeunt Salerio and Solanio.

LORENZO
My lord Bassanio, since you have found Antonio,
We two will leave you, but at dinnertime,
I pray you, have in mind where we must meet.

BASSANIO   I will not fail you.

GRATIANO
You look not well, Signor Antonio.
You have too much respect upon the world;   74
They lose it that do buy it with much care.
Believe me, you are marvelously changed.

ANTONIO
I hold the world but as the world, Gratiano,
A stage where every man must play a part,
And mine a sad one.

GRATIANO   Let me play the fool!
With mirth and laughter let old wrinkles come,
And let my liver rather heat with wine   81

61 prevented forestalled   **64 occasion** opportunity   **66 laugh** i.e., be
merry together   **67 strange** distant.   **Must it be so** must you go; or,
must you show reserve   **68 attend on** wait upon, i.e., suit   **74 respect**
. . . world concern for worldly affairs of business   **81 heat with wine**
(The liver was regarded as the seat of the passions and wine as an
agency for inflaming them.)

Than my heart cool with mortifying groans.   82
Why should a man whose blood is warm within
Sit like his grandsire cut in alabaster?   84
Sleep when he wakes, and creep into the jaundice   85
By being peevish? I tell thee what, Antonio—
I love thee, and 'tis my love that speaks—
There are a sort of men whose visages
Do cream and mantle like a standing pond,   89
And do a willful stillness entertain   90
With purpose to be dressed in an opinion   91
Of wisdom, gravity, profound conceit,   92
As who should say, "I am Sir Oracle,   93
And when I ope my lips let no dog bark!"   94
O my Antonio, I do know of these
That therefore only are reputed wise
For saying nothing, when, I am very sure,
If they should speak, would almost damn those ears
Which, hearing them, would call their brothers fools.   99
I'll tell thee more of this another time.
But fish not with this melancholy bait   101
For this fool gudgeon, this opinion.   102
Come, good Lorenzo. Fare ye well awhile;
I'll end my exhortation after dinner.

LORENZO
Well, we will leave you then till dinnertime.
I must be one of these same dumb wise men,   106
For Gratiano never lets me speak.

GRATIANO
Well, keep me company but two years more,
Thou shalt not know the sound of thine own tongue.

---

82 mortifying deadly   **84 in alabaster** i.e., in a stone effigy upon a
tomb   **85 jaundice** (Regarded as arising from the effects of too much
choler or yellow bile, one of the four humors, in the blood.)   **89 cream
and mantle** become covered with scum, i.e., acquire a lifeless, stiff
expression.   **standing** stagnant   **90 And . . . entertain** and who maintain
or assume a self-imposed, obstinate silence   **91 opinion** reputation
92 profound conceit deep thought   **93 As . . . say** as if to say   **94 And
. . . bark** i.e., and I am worthy of great respect   **99 fools** (Cf. Matthew
5:22, in which anyone calling another fool is threatened with damnation.)   **101 melancholy bait** i.e., your own melancholy   **102 fool . . .
opinion** i.e., reputation, which is merely gained through others' credulity. (*Gudgeon*, a small fish, was used to mean a gullible person.)
106 dumb mute, speechless

ANTONIO
Fare you well; I'll grow a talker for this gear.   110
GRATIANO
Thanks, i' faith, for silence is only commendable
In a neat's tongue dried and a maid not vendible.   112
            Exeunt [Gratiano and Lorenzo].
ANTONIO   Is that anything now?   113
BASSANIO   Gratiano speaks an infinite deal of nothing,
more than any man in all Venice. His reasons are as
two grains of wheat hid in two bushels of chaff; you
shall seek all day ere you find them, and when you
have them they are not worth the search.

ANTONIO
Well, tell me now what lady is the same   119
To whom you swore a secret pilgrimage,
That you today promised to tell me of.

BASSANIO
'Tis not unknown to you, Antonio,
How much I have disabled mine estate
By something showing a more swelling port   124
Than my faint means would grant continuance.   125
Nor do I now make moan to be abridged   126
From such a noble rate; but my chief care   127
Is to come fairly off from the great debts   128
Wherein my time, something too prodigal,
Hath left me gaged. To you, Antonio,   130
I owe the most, in money and in love,
And from your love I have a warranty   132
To unburden all my plots and purposes
How to get clear of all the debts I owe.

ANTONIO
I pray you, good Bassanio, let me know it;
And if it stand, as you yourself still do,
Within the eye of honor, be assured

---

110 for this gear as a result of this business, i.e., your talk   **112 neat's**
ox's.   **vendible** salable, i.e., in the marriage market   **113 Is . . . now** i.e.,
was all that talk about anything?   **119 the same** i.e., the one   **124 By**
. . . port by showing a somewhat more lavish style of living   **125 grant**
continuance allow to continue   **126–127 make . . . rate** complain at
being cut back from such a high style of living   **128 to . . . off** honorably to extricate myself   **130 gaged** pledged   **132 warranty** authorization

My purse, my person, my extremest means,
Lie all unlocked to your occasions.

BASSANIO
In my schooldays, when I had lost one shaft,   140
I shot his fellow of the selfsame flight   141
The selfsame way with more advisèd watch   142
To find the other forth, and by adventuring both   143
I oft found both. I urge this childhood proof
Because what follows is pure innocence.   145
I owe you much, and, like a willful youth,
That which I owe is lost; but if you please
To shoot another arrow that self way   148
Which you did shoot the first, I do not doubt,
As I will watch the aim, or to find both   150
Or bring your latter hazard back again   151
And thankfully rest debtor for the first.

ANTONIO
You know me well, and herein spend but time   153
To wind about my love with circumstance;   154
And out of doubt you do me now more wrong   155
In making question of my uttermost   156
Than if you had made waste of all I have.
Then do but say to me what I should do
That in your knowledge may by me be done,
And I am prest unto it. Therefore speak.   160

BASSANIO
In Belmont is a lady richly left;   161
And she is fair and, fairer than that word,
Of wondrous virtues. Sometime from her eyes   163
I did receive fair speechless messages.
Her name is Portia, nothing undervalued   165
To Cato's daughter, Brutus' Portia.   166

140 shaft arrow   141 his its.   selfsame flight same kind and range
142 advisèd careful   143 forth out.   adventuring risking   145 innocence ingenuousness, sincerity   148 self same   150 or either   151 hazard that which was risked   153 spend but time only waste time   154 To
. . . circumstance i.e., in not asking plainly what you want. (Circumstance here means "circumlocution.")   155 out of beyond   156 In . . .
uttermost in showing any doubt of my intention to do all I can
160 prest ready   161 richly left left a large fortune (by her father's
will)   163 Sometime once   165–166 nothing undervalued To of no less
worth than   166 Portia (The same Portia as in Shakespeare's Julius
Caesar.)

Nor is the wide world ignorant of her worth,
For the four winds blow in from every coast
Renownèd suitors, and her sunny locks
Hang on her temples like a golden fleece,
Which makes her seat of Belmont Colchis' strand,   171
And many Jasons come in quest of her.
O my Antonio, had I but the means
To hold a rival place with one of them,
I have a mind presages me such thrift   175
That I should questionless be fortunate.

ANTONIO
Thou know'st that all my fortunes are at sea;
Neither have I money nor commodity   178
To raise a present sum. Therefore go forth.
Try what my credit can in Venice do;
That shall be racked, even to the uttermost,   181
To furnish thee to Belmont, to fair Portia.
Go presently inquire, and so will I,   183
Where money is, and I no question make   184
To have it of my trust or for my sake.   *Exeunt.* 185

❖

1.2   *Enter Portia with her waiting-woman, Nerissa.*

PORTIA   By my troth, Nerissa, my little body is aweary
of this great world.
NERISSA   You would be, sweet madam, if your miseries
were in the same abundance as your good fortunes
are; and yet, for aught I see, they are as sick that surfeit   5
with too much as they that starve with nothing. It is
no mean happiness, therefore, to be seated in the   7
mean; superfluity comes sooner by white hairs, but   8
competency lives longer.   9

---

171 Colchis' (Jason adventured for the golden fleece in the land of
Colchis, on the Black Sea.) **strand** shore **175 presages** i.e., which
presages. **thrift** profit and good fortune **178 commodity** merchandise **181 racked** stretched **183 presently** immediately **184 no question make** have no doubt **185 of my trust** on the basis of my credit as
a merchant. **sake** i.e., personal sake

1.2. Location: Belmont. Portia's house.
5 surfeit overindulge **7–8 in the mean** having neither too much nor too
little **8 comes sooner by** acquires sooner **9 competency** modest means

PORTIA Good sentences, and well pronounced.   10
NERISSA They would be better if well followed.
PORTIA If to do were as easy as to know what were
good to do, chapels had been churches and poor
men's cottages princes' palaces. It is a good divine that 14
follows his own instructions. I can easier teach twenty
what were good to be done than to be one of the
twenty to follow mine own teaching. The brain may
devise laws for the blood, but a hot temper leaps o'er 18
a cold decree—such a hare is madness the youth, to
skip o'er the meshes of good counsel the cripple. But 20
this reasoning is not in the fashion to choose me a 21
husband. O, me, the word "choose"! I may neither 22
choose who I would nor refuse who I dislike; so is the
will of a living daughter curbed by the will of a dead 24
father. Is it not hard, Nerissa, that I cannot choose one
nor refuse none?
NERISSA Your father was ever virtuous, and holy men
at their death have good inspirations; therefore the
lottery that he hath devised in these three chests of
gold, silver, and lead, whereof who chooses his mean- 30
ing chooses you, will no doubt never be chosen by
any rightly but one who you shall rightly love. But
what warmth is there in your affection towards any of
these princely suitors that are already come?
PORTIA I pray thee, overname them, and as thou nam- 35
est them I will describe them, and according to my
description level at my affection.   37
NERISSA First, there is the Neapolitan prince.
PORTIA Ay, that's a colt indeed, for he doth nothing but 39
talk of his horse, and he makes it a great appropriation 40
to his own good parts that he can shoe him him- 41

10 sentences maxims. **pronounced** delivered **14 divine** clergyman
18 blood (Thought of as a chief agent of the passions, which in turn
were regarded as the enemies of reason.) **20 meshes** nets (used here for
hunting hares). **good counsel the cripple** (Wisdom is portrayed as old
and no longer agile.) **20–22 But . . . husband** but this talk is not the
way to help me choose a husband **24 will . . . will** volition . . . testament **30 who** whoever. **his** i.e., the father's **35 overname them** name
them over **37 level** aim, guess **39 colt** i.e., wanton and foolish young
man (with a punning appropriateness to his interest in horses)
40 appropriation addition **41 good parts** accomplishments

self. I am much afeard my lady his mother played false
with a smith.

NERISSA Then is there the County Palatine.   44

PORTIA He doth nothing but frown, as who should say,   45
"An you will not have me, choose." He hears merry   46
tales and smiles not. I fear he will prove the weeping   47
philosopher when he grows old, being so full of un-   48
mannerly sadness in his youth. I had rather be married to a death's-head with a bone in his mouth than
to either of these. God defend me from these two!

NERISSA How say you by the French lord, Monsieur   52
Le Bon?

PORTIA God made him, and therefore let him pass for
a man. In truth, I know it is a sin to be a mocker, but
he! Why, he hath a horse better than the Neapolitan's,
a better bad habit of frowning than the Count Palatine; he is every man in no man. If a throstle sing, he   58
falls straight a-capering. He will fence with his own
shadow. If I should marry him, I should marry twenty
husbands. If he would despise me, I would forgive
him, for if he love me to madness, I shall never requite him.

NERISSA What say you, then, to Falconbridge, the
young baron of England?

PORTIA You know I say nothing to him, for he understands not me, nor I him. He hath neither Latin,
French, nor Italian, and you will come into the court
and swear that I have a poor pennyworth in the English. He is a proper man's picture, but alas, who can   70
converse with a dumb show? How oddly he is suited!   71
I think he bought his doublet in Italy, his round hose   72
in France, his bonnet in Germany, and his behavior   73
everywhere.

---

44 County count. **Palatine** one possessing royal privileges   **45 who
should say** one might say   **46 An** if.   **choose** i.e., do as you please
47–48 weeping philosopher i.e., Heraclitus of Ephesus, a melancholic
and retiring philosopher of about 500 B.C., often contrasted with Demo-
critus, the "laughing philosopher"   **52 by** about   **58 throstle** thrush
70 He . . . picture i.e., he looks handsome   **71 dumb show** panto-
mime.   **suited** dressed   **72 doublet** upper garment corresponding to a
jacket.   **round hose** short, puffed-out breeches   **73 bonnet** hat

NERISSA What think you of the Scottish lord, his neighbor?

PORTIA That he hath a neighborly charity in him, for he borrowed a box of the ear of the Englishman and swore he would pay him again when he was able. I think the Frenchman became his surety and sealed under for another.   80
                                                                                                       81

NERISSA How like you the young German, the Duke of Saxony's nephew?

PORTIA Very vilely in the morning, when he is sober, and most vilely in the afternoon, when he is drunk. When he is best he is a little worse than a man, and when he is worst he is little better than a beast. An the worst fall that ever fell, I hope I shall make shift to   88
go without him.

NERISSA If he should offer to choose, and choose the right casket, you should refuse to perform your father's will if you should refuse to accept him.

PORTIA Therefore, for fear of the worst, I pray thee, set a deep glass of Rhenish wine on the contrary casket,   94
for if the devil be within and that temptation without, I know he will choose it. I will do anything, Nerissa, ere I will be married to a sponge.

NERISSA You need not fear, lady, the having any of these lords. They have acquainted me with their determinations, which is indeed to return to their home and to trouble you with no more suit, unless you may be won by some other sort than your father's imposi-   102
tion depending on the caskets.   103

PORTIA If I live to be as old as Sibylla, I will die as chaste   104
as Diana, unless I be obtained by the manner of my father's will. I am glad this parcel of wooers are so rea-   106
sonable, for there is not one among them but I dote on

80–81 became . . . another guaranteed the Scot's payment (of a box on the ear) and put himself under obligation to give the Englishman yet another on his own behalf. (An allusion to the age-old alliance of the French and the Scots against the English.) **88 fall** befall. **make shift** manage **94 Rhenish wine** a German white wine from the Rhine Valley. **contrary** i.e., wrong **102 sort** way, manner (with perhaps a suggestion too of "casting" or "drawing of lots") **102–103 imposition** conditions imposed **104 Sibylla** the Cumaean Sibyl, to whom Apollo gave as many years as there were grains in her handful of sand **106 parcel** assembly, group

his very absence, and I pray God grant them a fair departure.

NERISSA Do you not remember, lady, in your father's time, a Venetian, a scholar and a soldier, that came hither in company of the Marquess of Montferrat?

PORTIA Yes, yes, it was Bassanio, as I think, so was he called.

NERISSA True, madam. He, of all the men that ever my foolish eyes looked upon, was the best deserving a fair lady.

PORTIA I remember him well, and I remember him worthy of thy praise.

Enter a Servingman.

How now, what news?

SERVINGMAN The four strangers seek for you, madam, to take their leave; and there is a forerunner come from a fifth, the Prince of Morocco, who brings word the Prince his master will be here tonight.   121 122

PORTIA If I could bid the fifth welcome with so good heart as I can bid the other four farewell, I should be glad of his approach. If he have the condition of a saint and the complexion of a devil, I had rather he should shrive me than wive me.   127 128 129

Come, Nerissa. [*To Servingman.*] Sirrah, go before. Whiles we shut the gate upon one wooer, another knocks at the door.   *Exeunt.*   130

❖

1.3 *Enter Bassanio with Shylock the Jew.*

SHYLOCK Three thousand ducats, well.   1
BASSANIO Ay, sir, for three months.
SHYLOCK For three months, well.

121 four (Nerissa actually names six suitors; possibly a sign of revision.) **122 forerunner** herald **127 condition** disposition, character **128 complexion of a devil** (Devils were thought to be black; but *complexion* can also mean "temperament," "disposition.") **129 shrive me** act as my confessor **130 Sirrah** (Form of address to social inferior.)

1.3. Location: Venice. A public place.
1 ducats gold coins

BASSANIO   For the which, as I told you, Antonio shall be bound.

SHYLOCK   Antonio shall become bound, well.

BASSANIO   May you stead me? Will you pleasure me? 7 Shall I know your answer?

SHYLOCK   Three thousand ducats for three months and Antonio bound.

BASSANIO   Your answer to that.

SHYLOCK   Antonio is a good man.   12

BASSANIO   Have you heard any imputation to the contrary?

SHYLOCK   Ho, no, no, no, no! My meaning in saying he is a good man is to have you understand me that he is sufficient. Yet his means are in supposition: he hath an 17 argosy bound to Tripolis, another to the Indies; I understand, moreover, upon the Rialto, he hath a 19 third at Mexico, a fourth for England, and other ventures he hath squandered abroad. But ships are but 21 boards, sailors but men; there be land rats and water rats, water thieves and land thieves—I mean pirates— and then there is the peril of waters, winds, and rocks. The man is, notwithstanding, sufficient. Three thousand ducats; I think I may take his bond.

BASSANIO   Be assured you may.   27

SHYLOCK   I will be assured I may; and that I may be 28 assured, I will bethink me. May I speak with Antonio?

BASSANIO   If it please you to dine with us.

SHYLOCK   Yes, to smell pork, to eat of the habitation which your prophet the Nazarite conjured the devil 32 into. I will buy with you, sell with you, talk with you, walk with you, and so following, but I will not eat with you, drink with you, nor pray with you. What news on the Rialto? Who is he comes here?

---

7 stead supply, assist   **12 good** (Shylock means "solvent," a good credit risk; Bassanio interprets in the moral sense.)   **17 sufficient** i.e., a good security.   **in supposition** doubtful, uncertain   **19 Rialto** the merchants' exchange in Venice and the center of commercial activity   **21 squandered** scattered, spread   **27, 28 assured** (Bassanio means that Shylock may trust Antonio, whereas Shylock means that he will provide legal assurances.)   **32 Nazarite** Nazarene. (For the reference to Christ's casting evil spirits into a herd of swine, see Matthew 8:30–32, Mark 5:1–13, and Luke 8:32–33.)

Enter Antonio.

BASSANIO This is Signor Antonio.

SHYLOCK [*Aside*]

How like a fawning publican he looks!   38
I hate him for he is a Christian,   39
But more for that in low simplicity
He lends out money gratis and brings down
The rate of usance here with us in Venice.   42
If I can catch him once upon the hip,   43
I will feed fat the ancient grudge I bear him.
He hates our sacred nation, and he rails,
Even there where merchants most do congregate,
On me, my bargains, and my well-won thrift,   47
Which he calls interest. Cursèd be my tribe
If I forgive him!

BASSANIO   Shylock, do you hear?

SHYLOCK

I am debating of my present store,   50
And, by the near guess of my memory,
I cannot instantly raise up the gross   52
Of full three thousand ducats. What of that?
Tubal, a wealthy Hebrew of my tribe,
Will furnish me. But soft, how many months   55
Do you desire? [*To Antonio.*] Rest you fair, good signor!
Your worship was the last man in our mouths.   57

ANTONIO

Shylock, albeit I neither lend nor borrow
By taking nor by giving of excess,   59
Yet, to supply the ripe wants of my friend,   60
I'll break a custom. [*To Bassanio.*] Is he yet possessed 61
How much ye would?

SHYLOCK Ay, ay, three thousand ducats.

ANTONIO And for three months.

SHYLOCK

I had forgot—three months, you told me so.

38 publican Roman tax gatherer (a term of opprobrium); or, innkeeper
39 for because **42 usance** usury, interest **43 upon the hip** i.e., at my
mercy. (A figure of speech from wrestling; see Genesis 32:24–29.)
47 thrift thriving **50 store** supply (of money) **52 gross** total **55 soft**
i.e., wait a minute **57 Your . . . mouths** i.e., we were just speaking of
you **59 excess** interest **60 ripe wants** pressing needs **61 possessed**
informed

Well then, your bond. And let me see—but hear you,
Methought you said you neither lend nor borrow
Upon advantage.
ANTONIO   I do never use it.   68
SHYLOCK
When Jacob grazed his uncle Laban's sheep—   69
This Jacob from our holy Abram was,   70
As his wise mother wrought in his behalf,
The third possessor; ay, he was the third—   72
ANTONIO
And what of him? Did he take interest?
SHYLOCK
No, not take interest, not as you would say
Directly interest. Mark what Jacob did.
When Laban and himself were compromised   76
That all the eanlings which were streaked and pied   77
Should fall as Jacob's hire, the ewes, being rank,   78
In end of autumn turnèd to the rams,
And when the work of generation was
Between these woolly breeders in the act,
The skillful shepherd peeled me certain wands,   82
And in the doing of the deed of kind   83
He stuck them up before the fulsome ewes,
Who then conceiving did in eaning time   85
Fall parti-colored lambs, and those were Jacob's.   86
This was a way to thrive, and he was blest;
And thrift is blessing, if men steal it not.
ANTONIO
This was a venture, sir, that Jacob served for,   89
A thing not in his power to bring to pass,
But swayed and fashioned by the hand of heaven.
Was this inserted to make interest good?   92
Or is your gold and silver ewes and rams?

68 advantage interest   **69 Jacob** (See Genesis 27, 30:25–43.)   **70 Abram**
Abraham   **72 third** i.e., after Abraham and Isaac.   **possessor** i.e., of the
birthright of which, with the help of Rebecca, he was able to cheat
Esau, his elder brother   **76 compromised** agreed   **77 eanlings** young
lambs or kids.   **pied** spotted   **78 hire** wages, share.   **rank** in heat
82 me (*Me* is used colloquially.)   **83 deed of kind** i.e., copulation
85 eaning lambing   **86 Fall** give birth to   **89 venture . . . for** uncertain
commercial venture on which Jacob risked his wages   **92 inserted . . .**
good brought in to justify the practice of usury

SHYLOCK
I cannot tell; I make it breed as fast.
But note me, signor—
ANTONIO   Mark you this, Bassanio,
The devil can cite Scripture for his purpose.   96
An evil soul producing holy witness
Is like a villain with a smiling cheek,
A goodly apple rotten at the heart.
O, what a goodly outside falsehood hath!
SHYLOCK
Three thousand ducats. 'Tis a good round sum.
Three months from twelve, then let me see, the rate—
ANTONIO
Well, Shylock, shall we be beholding to you?   103
SHYLOCK
Signor Antonio, many a time and oft
In the Rialto you have rated me   105
About my moneys and my usances.
Still have I borne it with a patient shrug,
For sufferance is the badge of all our tribe.   108
You call me misbeliever, cutthroat dog,
And spit upon my Jewish gaberdine,   110
And all for use of that which is mine own.
Well then, it now appears you need my help.
Go to, then. You come to me and you say,   113
"Shylock, we would have moneys"—you say so,
You, that did void your rheum upon my beard   115
And foot me as you spurn a stranger cur   116
Over your threshold! Moneys is your suit.
What should I say to you? Should I not say,
"Hath a dog money? Is it possible
A cur can lend three thousand ducats?" Or
Shall I bend low and in a bondman's key,   121
With bated breath and whispering humbleness,   122
Say this:
"Fair sir, you spit on me on Wednesday last,
You spurned me such a day, another time

---

96 devil . . . Scripture (See Matthew 4:6.) **103 beholding** beholden,
indebted **105 rated** berated, rebuked **108 sufferance** endurance
110 gaberdine loose upper garment like a cape or mantle **113 Go to**
(An exclamation of impatience or annoyance.) **115 rheum** spittle
116 spurn kick **121 bondman's** serf's **122 bated** subdued, reduced

You called me dog, and for these courtesies
I'll lend you thus much moneys"?

ANTONIO
I am as like to call thee so again,   128
To spit on thee again, to spurn thee too.
If thou wilt lend this money, lend it not
As to thy friends, for when did friendship take
A breed for barren metal of his friend?   132
But lend it rather to thine enemy,
Who, if he break, thou mayst with better face   134
Exact the penalty.

SHYLOCK   Why, look you how you storm!
I would be friends with you and have your love,
Forget the shames that you have stained me with,
Supply your present wants, and take no doit   138
Of usance for my moneys, and you'll not hear me.
This is kind I offer.

BASSANIO   This were kindness.   141

SHYLOCK   This kindness will I show.
Go with me to a notary. Seal me there
Your single bond; and, in a merry sport,   144
If you repay me not on such a day,
In such a place, such sum or sums as are
Expressed in the condition, let the forfeit
Be nominated for an equal pound   148
Of your fair flesh, to be cut off and taken
In what part of your body pleaseth me.

ANTONIO
Content, in faith. I'll seal to such a bond
And say there is much kindness in the Jew.

BASSANIO
You shall not seal to such a bond for me!
I'll rather dwell in my necessity.   154

ANTONIO
Why, fear not, man, I will not forfeit it.

---

128 like likely   **132 breed . . . metal** offspring from money, which
cannot naturally breed. (One of the oldest arguments against usury was
that it was thereby "unnatural.")   **134 Who** from whom.   **break** fail to
pay on time   **138 doit** a Dutch coin of very small value   **141 were**
would be (if seriously offered)   **144 single bond** bond signed alone
without other security   **148 nominated** named, specified.   **equal**
exact   **154 dwell** remain

Within these two months—that's a month before
This bond expires—I do expect return
Of thrice three times the value of this bond.

SHYLOCK
O father Abram, what these Christians are,
Whose own hard dealings teaches them suspect
The thoughts of others! Pray you, tell me this:
If he should break his day, what should I gain
By the exaction of the forfeiture?
A pound of man's flesh taken from a man
Is not so estimable, profitable neither,   165
As flesh of muttons, beefs, or goats. I say
To buy his favor I extend this friendship.
If he will take it, so; if not, adieu.
And for my love, I pray you, wrong me not.   169

ANTONIO
Yes, Shylock, I will seal unto this bond.

SHYLOCK
Then meet me forthwith at the notary's;
Give him direction for this merry bond,
And I will go and purse the ducats straight,
See to my house, left in the fearful guard   174
Of an unthrifty knave, and presently
I'll be with you.   *Exit.*

ANTONIO   Hie thee, gentle Jew.
The Hebrew will turn Christian; he grows kind.

BASSANIO
I like not fair terms and a villain's mind.

ANTONIO
Come on. In this there can be no dismay;
My ships come home a month before the day.
                                            Exeunt.

❖

165 **estimable** valuable   169 **wrong me not** do not think evil of me
174 **fearful** to be mistrusted

2.1 [*Flourish of cornets.*] *Enter* [*the Prince of*] *Morocco, a tawny Moor all in white, and three or four followers accordingly, with Portia, Nerissa, and their train.*

MOROCCO
Mislike me not for my complexion,
The shadowed livery of the burnished sun,   2
To whom I am a neighbor and near bred.   3
Bring me the fairest creature northward born,
Where Phoebus' fire scarce thaws the icicles,   5
And let us make incision for your love
To prove whose blood is reddest, his or mine.   7
I tell thee, lady, this aspect of mine   8
Hath feared the valiant. By my love I swear,   9
The best-regarded virgins of our clime
Have loved it too. I would not change this hue,
Except to steal your thoughts, my gentle queen.

PORTIA
In terms of choice I am not solely led
By nice direction of a maiden's eyes;   14
Besides, the lottery of my destiny
Bars me the right of voluntary choosing.
But if my father had not scanted me,   17
And hedged me by his wit to yield myself   18
His wife who wins me by that means I told you,
Yourself, renownèd Prince, then stood as fair
As any comer I have looked on yet
For my affection.

MOROCCO   Even for that I thank you.
Therefore, I pray you, lead me to the caskets
To try my fortune. By this scimitar
That slew the Sophy and a Persian prince,   25
That won three fields of Sultan Solyman,   26

2.1. Location: Belmont. Portia's house.
s.d. accordingly similarly (i.e., dressed in white and dark-skinned like Morocco) 2 shadowed livery i.e., dark complexion, worn as though it were a costume of the sun's servants 3 near bred closely related 5 Phoebus' i.e., the sun's 7 reddest (Red blood was regarded as a sign of courage.) 8 aspect visage 9 feared frightened 14 nice direction careful guidance 17 scanted limited 18 wit wisdom 25 Sophy Shah of Persia 26 fields battles. Solyman a Turkish sultan ruling 1520–1566

I would o'erstare the sternest eyes that look,   27
Outbrave the heart most daring on the earth,
Pluck the young sucking cubs from the she-bear,
Yea, mock the lion when 'a roars for prey,   30
To win thee, lady. But alas the while!
If Hercules and Lichas play at dice   32
Which is the better man, the greater throw
May turn by fortune from the weaker hand.
So is Alcides beaten by his page,
And so may I, blind Fortune leading me,
Miss that which one unworthier may attain,
And die with grieving.
PORTIA   You must take your chance,
And either not attempt to choose at all
Or swear before you choose, if you choose wrong
Never to speak to lady afterward
In way of marriage. Therefore be advised.
MOROCCO
Nor will not. Come, bring me unto my chance.   43
PORTIA
First, forward to the temple. After dinner   44
Your hazard shall be made.
MOROCCO   Good fortune then!
To make me blest or cursed'st among men.
                                   [*Cornets, and*] *exeunt.*

❖

2.2   *Enter [Launcelot] the Clown, alone.*

LAUNCELOT   Certainly my conscience will serve me to 1
run from this Jew my master. The fiend is at mine
elbow and tempts me, saying to me, "Gobbo, Launcelot
Gobbo, good Launcelot," or "Good Gobbo," or "Good
Launcelot Gobbo, use your legs, take the start, run
away." My conscience says, "No, take heed, honest
Launcelot, take heed, honest Gobbo," or, as aforesaid,

27 o'erstare outstare   **30 'a** he   **32 Lichas** a page of Hercules (Alcides)
43 Nor will not i.e., nor indeed will I violate the oath   **44 to the
temple** i.e., in order to take the oaths

2.2. Location: Venice. A street.
1 serve permit

"honest Launcelot Gobbo, do not run; scorn running
with thy heels." Well, the most courageous fiend bids 9
me pack. "Fia!" says the fiend; "Away!" says the fiend. 10
"For the heavens, rouse up a brave mind," says the 11
fiend, "and run." Well, my conscience, hanging about 12
the neck of my heart, says very wisely to me, "My hon- 13
est friend Launcelot, being an honest man's son," or
rather an honest woman's son—for indeed my father
did something smack, something grow to, he had a 16
kind of taste—well, my conscience says, "Launcelot, 17
budge not." "Budge," says the fiend. "Budge not," says
my conscience. "Conscience," say I, "you counsel
well." "Fiend," say I, "you counsel well." To be ruled by
my conscience, I should stay with the Jew my master,
who, God bless the mark, is a kind of devil; and to run 22
away from the Jew, I should be ruled by the fiend, who,
saving your reverence, is the devil himself. Certainly
the Jew is the very devil incarnation; and, in my con- 25
science, my conscience is but a kind of hard conscience,
to offer to counsel me to stay with the Jew. The fiend
gives the more friendly counsel. I will run, fiend; my
heels are at your commandment; I will run.

Enter Old Gobbo, with a basket.

GOBBO Master young man, you, I pray you, which is 30
the way to master Jew's?
LAUNCELOT [*Aside*] O heavens, this is my true-
begotten father, who, being more than sand-blind, 33
high-gravel-blind, knows me not. I will try confusions 34
with him.
GOBBO Master young gentleman, I pray you, which is
the way to master Jew's?

9 with thy heels i.e., emphatically (with a pun on the literal sense)
10 pack begone. **Fia** i.e., via, away **11 For the heavens** i.e., in heaven's
name **12–13 hanging . . . heart** i.e., timidly **16–17 something . . . taste**
i.e., had a tendency to lechery **22 God . . . mark** (An expression by way
of apology for introducing something potentially offensive, as also in
saving your reverence.) **25 incarnation** (Launcelot means "incarnate.")
30 you (Gobbo uses the formal *you* but switches to the familiar
thou, l. 88, when he accepts Launcelot as his son.) **33 sand-blind** dim-
sighted **34 high-gravel-blind** blinder than sand-blind. (A term seemingly
invented by Launcelot.) **try confusions** (Launcelot's blunder for *try
conclusions*, i.e., experiment, though his error is comically apt.)

LAUNCELOT Turn up on your right hand at the next
turning, but at the next turning of all on your left;
marry, at the very next turning, turn of no hand, but 40
turn down indirectly to the Jew's house.
GOBBO By God's sonties, 'twill be a hard way to hit. 42
Can you tell me whether one Launcelot, that dwells
with him, dwell with him or no?
LAUNCELOT Talk you of young Master Launcelot?
[*Aside.*] Mark me now; now will I raise the waters.— 46
Talk you of young Master Launcelot?
GOBBO No master, sir, but a poor man's son. His father, 48
though I say 't, is an honest exceeding poor man and,
God be thanked, well to live.   50
LAUNCELOT Well, let his father be what 'a will, we talk 51
of young Master Launcelot.
GOBBO Your worship's friend, and Launcelot, sir.   53
LAUNCELOT But I pray you, ergo, old man, ergo, I be- 54
seech you, talk you of young Master Launcelot?
GOBBO Of Launcelot, an 't please your mastership.
LAUNCELOT Ergo, Master Launcelot. Talk not of Master
Launcelot, Father, for the young gentleman, according 58
to Fates and Destinies and such odd sayings, the Sis- 59
ters Three and such branches of learning, is indeed 60
deceased, or, as you would say in plain terms, gone to
heaven.
GOBBO Marry, God forbid! The boy was the very staff
of my age, my very prop.
LAUNCELOT Do I look like a cudgel or a hovel post, a 65
staff, or a prop? Do you know me, Father?
GOBBO Alack the day, I know you not, young gentleman. But I pray you, tell me, is my boy, God rest his
soul, alive or dead?
LAUNCELOT Do you not know me, Father?
GOBBO Alack, sir, I am sand-blind. I know you not.

40 marry i.e., by the Virgin Mary, indeed. (A mild interjection.)
42 sonties saints   **46 raise the waters** start tears   **48 master** (The title
was applied to gentlefolk only.)   **50 well to live** enjoying a good livelihood. (Perhaps Old Gobbo intends the phrase to mean "in good health,"
since he protests that he is poor.)   **51 'a** he   **53 Your . . . Launcelot**
(Again, Old Gobbo denies that Launcelot is entitled to be called "Master.")   **54 ergo** therefore (if it means anything)   **58 Father** (1) old man
(2) Father   **59–60 the Sisters Three** the three Fates   **65 hovel post** support for a hovel or open shed

LAUNCELOT Nay, indeed, if you had your eyes you
might fail of the knowing me; it is a wise father that 73
knows his own child. Well, old man, I will tell you 74
news of your son. [*He kneels.*] Give me your blessing;
truth will come to light; murder cannot be hid long; a
man's son may, but in the end truth will out.

GOBBO Pray you, sir, stand up. I am sure you are not
Launcelot, my boy.

LAUNCELOT Pray you, let's have no more fooling about
it, but give me your blessing. I am Launcelot, your 81
boy that was, your son that is, your child that shall be. 82

GOBBO I cannot think you are my son.

LAUNCELOT I know not what I shall think of that; but I
am Launcelot, the Jew's man, and I am sure Margery
your wife is my mother.

GOBBO Her name is Margery, indeed. I'll be sworn, if
thou be Launcelot, thou art mine own flesh and blood.
Lord worshiped might he be, what a beard hast thou 89
got! Thou hast got more hair on thy chin than Dobbin
my fill horse has on his tail.   91

LAUNCELOT [*Rising*] It should seem, then, that Dobbin's tail grows backward. I am sure he had more hair 93
of his tail than I have of my face when I last saw him. 94

GOBBO Lord, how art thou changed! How dost thou and
thy master agree? I have brought him a present. How
'gree you now?

LAUNCELOT Well, well; but for mine own part, as I
have set up my rest to run away, so I will not rest till 99
I have run some ground. My master's a very Jew. Give 100
him a present? Give him a halter! I am famished in his 101
service; you may tell every finger I have with my ribs. 102
Father, I am glad you are come. Give me your present 103

73–74 it is . . . child (Reverses the proverb "It is a wise child that knows
his own father.")   **81–82 your . . . shall be** (Echoes the *Gloria* from the
Book of Common Prayer: "As it was in the beginning, is now, and ever
shall be.")   **89 beard** (Stage tradition has Old Gobbo mistake Launcelot's long hair for a beard.)   **91 fill horse** cart horse   **93 grows backward** (1) grows inward, shorter (2) grows at the wrong end   **94 of** in, on
99 set up my rest determined, risked all. (A metaphor from the card
game *primero*, in which a final wager is made.)   **100 very** veritable
101 halter hangman's noose   **102 tell** count.   **tell . . . ribs** (Comically
reverses the usual saying of counting one's ribs with one's fingers.)
103 Give me give. (*Me* is used colloquially.)

to one Master Bassanio, who indeed gives rare new
liveries. If I serve not him, I will run as far as God has   105
any ground. O rare fortune, here comes the man! To
him, Father, for I am a Jew if I serve the Jew any longer.

*Enter Bassanio, with [Leonardo and] a follower
or two.*

BASSANIO   You may do so, but let it be so hasted that   108
supper be ready at the farthest by five of the clock. See   109
these letters delivered, put the liveries to making, and
desire Gratiano to come anon to my lodging.

                                        [*Exit a Servant.*]

LAUNCELOT   To him, Father.

GOBBO [*Advancing*]   God bless your worship!

BASSANIO   Gramercy. Wouldst thou aught with me?   114

GOBBO   Here's my son, sir, a poor boy—

LAUNCELOT   Not a poor boy, sir, but the rich Jew's man,
that would, sir, as my father shall specify—

GOBBO   He hath a great infection, sir, as one would say,   118
to serve—

LAUNCELOT   Indeed, the short and the long is, I serve
the Jew, and have a desire, as my father shall specify—

GOBBO   His master and he, saving your worship's reverence, are scarce cater-cousins—   123

LAUNCELOT   To be brief, the very truth is that the Jew,
having done me wrong, doth cause me, as my father,
being, I hope, an old man, shall frutify unto you—   126

GOBBO   I have here a dish of doves that I would bestow
upon your worship, and my suit is—

LAUNCELOT   In very brief, the suit is impertinent to my-   129
self, as your worship shall know by this honest old
man, and, though I say it, though old man, yet poor
man, my father.

BASSANIO   One speak for both. What would you?

LAUNCELOT   Serve you, sir.

GOBBO   That is the very defect of the matter, sir.   135

---

105 liveries uniforms or costumes for servants   **108 hasted** hastened,
hurried   **109 farthest** latest   **114 Gramercy** many thanks.   **aught**
anything   **118 infection** (Blunder for *affection* or *inclination*.)
123 cater-cousins good friends   **126 frutify** (Launcelot may be trying to
say "fructify," but he means "certify" or "notify.")   **129 impertinent**
(Blunder for *pertinent*.)   **135 defect** (Blunder for *effect*, i.e., "purport.")

BASSANIO

I know thee well; thou hast obtained thy suit.
Shylock thy master spoke with me this day,
And hath preferred thee, if it be preferment   138
To leave a rich Jew's service to become
The follower of so poor a gentleman.

LAUNCELOT   The old proverb is very well parted be-   141
tween my master Shylock and you, sir: you have the
grace of God, sir, and he hath enough.

BASSANIO

Thou speak'st it well. Go, father, with thy son.
Take leave of thy old master, and inquire
My lodging out. [*To a Servant.*] Give him a livery
More guarded than his fellows'. See it done.   147

LAUNCELOT   Father, in. I cannot get a service, no! I have
ne'er a tongue in my head, well! [*Looks at his palm.*] If
any man in Italy have a fairer table which doth offer to   150
swear upon a book, I shall have good fortune. Go to,
here's a simple line of life. Here's a small trifle of
wives! Alas, fifteen wives is nothing. Eleven widows
and nine maids is a simple coming-in for one man.   154
And then to scape drowning thrice, and to be in peril
of my life with the edge of a feather bed! Here are   156
simple scapes. Well, if Fortune be a woman, she's a   157
good wench for this gear. Father, come, I'll take my   158
leave of the Jew in the twinkling.

                              Exit Clown [with Old Gobbo].

BASSANIO

I pray thee, good Leonardo, think on this:
                              [*Giving him a list*]
These things being bought and orderly bestowed,
Return in haste, for I do feast tonight   162
My best-esteemed acquaintance. Hie thee, go.

LEONARDO

My best endeavors shall be done herein.
                              [*He starts to leave.*]

---

138 preferred recommended   **141 proverb** i.e., "He who has the grace
of God has enough"   **147 guarded** trimmed with braided ornament
150 table palm of the hand. (Launcelot now reads the lines of his
palm.)   **154 simple coming-in** modest income (with sexual suggestion)
156 feather bed (suggesting marriage bed or love bed; Launcelot sees
sexual adventure in his palm reading)   **157 Fortune . . . woman** (Fortune
was personified as a goddess.)   **158 gear** matter   **162 feast** give a feast for

Enter Gratiano.

GRATIANO
Where's your master?

LEONARDO   Yonder, sir, he walks.

                                              Exit Leonardo.

GRATIANO   Signor Bassanio!

BASSANIO   Gratiano!

GRATIANO
I have a suit to you.

BASSANIO   You have obtained it.

GRATIANO   You must not deny me. I must go with you
to Belmont.

BASSANIO
Why, then you must. But hear thee, Gratiano;
Thou art too wild, too rude and bold of voice—
Parts that become thee happily enough,   173
And in such eyes as ours appear not faults,
But where thou art not known, why, there they show
Something too liberal. Pray thee, take pain   176
To allay with some cold drops of modesty   177
Thy skipping spirit, lest through thy wild behavior
I be misconstered in the place I go to   179
And lose my hopes.

GRATIANO   Signor Bassanio, hear me:
If I do not put on a sober habit,
Talk with respect and swear but now and then,
Wear prayer books in my pocket, look demurely,
Nay more, while grace is saying, hood mine eyes   184
Thus with my hat, and sigh and say "amen,"
Use all the observance of civility,
Like one well studied in a sad ostent   187
To please his grandam, never trust me more.

BASSANIO   Well, we shall see your bearing.

GRATIANO
Nay, but I bar tonight. You shall not gauge me
By what we do tonight.

BASSANIO   No, that were pity.
I would entreat you rather to put on

173 **Parts** qualities   176 **liberal** free of manner (often with sexual connotation)   177 **allay** temper, moderate   179 **misconstered** misconstrued
184 **saying** being said   187 **sad ostent** grave appearance

Your boldest suit of mirth, for we have friends
That purpose merriment. But fare you well;
I have some business.

GRATIANO
And I must to Lorenzo and the rest,
But we will visit you at suppertime.   *Exeunt.*

2.3   *Enter Jessica and [Launcelot] the Clown.*

JESSICA
I am sorry thou wilt leave my father so.
Our house is hell, and thou, a merry devil,
Didst rob it of some taste of tediousness.
But fare thee well; there is a ducat for thee.
                                    [*Giving money.*]
And, Launcelot, soon at supper shalt thou see
Lorenzo, who is thy new master's guest.
Give him this letter; do it secretly.   [*Giving a letter.*]
And so farewell; I would not have my father
See me in talk with thee.

LAUNCELOT Adieu! Tears exhibit my tongue. Most 10
beautiful pagan, most sweet Jew! If a Christian did not
play the knave and get thee, I am much deceived. But, 12
adieu! These foolish drops do something drown my
manly spirit. Adieu!

JESSICA Farewell, good Launcelot.   [*Exit Launcelot.*]
Alack, what heinous sin is it in me
To be ashamed to be my father's child!
But though I am a daughter to his blood,
I am not to his manners. O Lorenzo,
If thou keep promise, I shall end this strife,
Become a Christian and thy loving wife.   *Exit.*

2.3. Location: Venice. Shylock's house.
10 exhibit (Blunder for *inhibit*, "restrain.")   12 get beget

2.4   *Enter Gratiano, Lorenzo, Salerio, and Solanio.*

LORENZO
Nay, we will slink away in suppertime,   1
Disguise us at my lodging, and return
All in an hour.
GRATIANO
We have not made good preparation.
SALERIO
We have not spoke us yet of torchbearers.   5
SOLANIO
'Tis vile, unless it may be quaintly ordered,   6
And better in my mind not undertook.
LORENZO
'Tis now but four o'clock. We have two hours
To furnish us.
         Enter Launcelot [with a letter].

              Friend Launcelot, what's the news?
LAUNCELOT An it shall please you to break up this, it 10
shall seem to signify.   *[Giving the letter.]*
LORENZO
I know the hand. In faith, 'tis a fair hand,
And whiter than the paper it writ on
Is the fair hand that writ.
GRATIANO   Love news, in faith.
LAUNCELOT By your leave, sir.   *[He starts to leave.]*
LORENZO Whither goest thou?
LAUNCELOT Marry, sir, to bid my old master the Jew to
sup tonight with my new master the Christian.
LORENZO
Hold here, take this. *[He gives money.]* Tell gentle Jessica
I will not fail her; speak it privately.
                        Exit Clown [Launcelot].
Go, gentlemen,
Will you prepare you for this masque tonight?
I am provided of a torchbearer.

2.4. Location: Venice. A street.
1 in during **5 spoke . . . of** yet bespoken, ordered **6 quaintly ordered**
skillfully and tastefully managed **10 An** if. **break up** i.e., open the
seal. (Literally, a term from carving.)

SALERIO
  Ay, marry, I'll be gone about it straight.
SOLANIO
  And so will I.
LORENZO   Meet me and Gratiano
  At Gratiano's lodging some hour hence.
SALERIO 'Tis good we do so.   *Exit [with Solanio].*
GRATIANO
  Was not that letter from fair Jessica?
LORENZO
  I must needs tell thee all. She hath directed
  How I shall take her from her father's house,
  What gold and jewels she is furnished with,
  What page's suit she hath in readiness.
  If e'er the Jew her father come to heaven,
  It will be for his gentle daughter's sake;   34
  And never dare Misfortune cross her foot,   35
  Unless she do it under this excuse,   36
  That she is issue to a faithless Jew.   37
  Come, go with me; peruse this as thou goest.
                    [He gives Gratiano the letter.]
  Fair Jessica shall be my torchbearer.   *Exeunt.*

✣

2.5   *Enter [Shylock the] Jew and [Launcelot,] his
          man that was, the Clown.*

SHYLOCK
  Well, thou shalt see, thy eyes shall be thy judge,
  The difference of old Shylock and Bassanio.—   2
  What, Jessica!—Thou shalt not gormandize,   3
  As thou hast done with me—What, Jessica!—
  And sleep and snore, and rend apparel out—   5
  Why, Jessica, I say!
LAUNCELOT Why, Jessica!

34 gentle (with pun on *gentile*?)   **35 foot** footpath   **36 she**
i.e., Misfortune   **37 she is issue** i.e., Jessica is child.   **faithless**
pagan

2.5. Location: Venice. Before Shylock's house.
2 of between   **3 gormandize** eat gluttonously   **5 rend apparel out** i.e.,
wear out your clothes

SHYLOCK
Who bids thee call? I do not bid thee call.
LAUNCELOT   Your worship was wont to tell me I could
do nothing without bidding.

Enter Jessica.

JESSICA   Call you? What is your will?
SHYLOCK
I am bid forth to supper, Jessica.
There are my keys. But wherefore should I go?
I am not bid for love—they flatter me—
But yet I'll go in hate, to feed upon
The prodigal Christian. Jessica, my girl,
Look to my house. I am right loath to go.   17
There is some ill a-brewing towards my rest,
For I did dream of moneybags tonight.   19
LAUNCELOT   I beseech you, sir, go. My young master
doth expect your reproach.   21
SHYLOCK   So do I his.
LAUNCELOT   And they have conspired together. I will
not say you shall see a masque, but if you do, then it
was not for nothing that my nose fell a-bleeding on
Black Monday last at six o'clock i' the morning, falling   26
out that year on Ash Wednesday was four year in th'
afternoon.
SHYLOCK
What, are there masques? Hear you me, Jessica:
Lock up my doors, and when you hear the drum
And the vile squealing of the wry-necked fife,   31
Clamber not you up to the casements then,
Nor thrust your head into the public street
To gaze on Christian fools with varnished faces,   34
But stop my house's ears, I mean my casements.
Let not the sound of shallow foppery enter
My sober house. By Jacob's staff I swear   37

17 right loath reluctant   **19 tonight** last night   **21 reproach** (Launcelot's blunder for *approach*. Shylock takes it in grim humor.)   **26 Black
Monday** Easter Monday. (So called, according to Stow, because of a cold
and stormy Easter Monday when Edward III was besieging Paris. Launcelot's talk of omens is perhaps intentional gibberish, a parody of Shylock's fears.)   **31 wry-necked** i.e., played with the musician's head awry;
or, on an instrument with the head twisted awry   **34 varnished faces** i.e.,
painted masks   **37 Jacob's staff** (See Genesis 32:10 and Hebrews 11:21.)

I have no mind of feasting forth tonight.
But I will go. Go you before me, sirrah;
Say I will come.
LAUNCELOT   I will go before, sir. [*To Jessica.*] Mistress,
   look out at window, for all this;
      There will come a Christian by,
      Will be worth a Jewess' eye.   [*Exit.*]
SHYLOCK
   What says that fool of Hagar's offspring, ha?   45
JESSICA
   His words were "Farewell, mistress," nothing else.
SHYLOCK
   The patch is kind enough, but a huge feeder,   47
   Snail-slow in profit, and he sleeps by day   48
   More than the wildcat. Drones hive not with me;
   Therefore I part with him, and part with him
   To one that I would have him help to waste
   His borrowed purse. Well, Jessica, go in.
   Perhaps I will return immediately.
   Do as I bid you; shut doors after you.
   Fast bind, fast find—   55
   A proverb never stale in thrifty mind.   *Exit.*
JESSICA
   Farewell, and if my fortune be not crossed,
   I have a father, you a daughter, lost.   *Exit.*

❖

2.6   *Enter the maskers, Gratiano and Salerio.*

GRATIANO
   This is the penthouse under which Lorenzo   1
   Desired us to make stand.
SALERIO   His hour is almost past.
GRATIANO
   And it is marvel he outdwells his hour,   4

45 Hagar's offspring (Hagar, a gentile and Abraham's servant, gave
birth to Ishmael; both mother and son were cast out after the birth of
Isaac.)   **47 patch** fool   **48 profit** profitable labor   **55 Fast . . . find** i.e.,
something firmly secured or bound will always be easily located

2.6. Location: Before Shylock's house, as in scene 5.
1 penthouse projecting roof from a house   **4 it . . . hour** i.e., it is surprising that he is late

For lovers ever run before the clock.

SALERIO
O, ten times faster Venus' pigeons fly   6
To seal love's bonds new-made than they are wont
To keep obligèd faith unforfeited!   8

GRATIANO
That ever holds. Who riseth from a feast
With that keen appetite that he sits down?
Where is the horse that doth untread again   11
His tedious measures with the unbated fire
That he did pace them first? All things that are,
Are with more spirit chasèd than enjoyed.
How like a younger or a prodigal   15
The scarfèd bark puts from her native bay,   16
Hugged and embracèd by the strumpet wind!   17
How like the prodigal doth she return,
With overweathered ribs and ragged sails,   19
Lean, rent, and beggared by the strumpet wind!   20

        Enter Lorenzo, [masked].

SALERIO
Here comes Lorenzo. More of this hereafter.

LORENZO
Sweet friends, your patience for my long abode;   22
Not I, but my affairs, have made you wait.
When you shall please to play the thieves for wives,
I'll watch as long for you then. Approach;
Here dwells my father Jew. Ho! Who's within?   26

        [Enter] Jessica, above [in boy's clothes].

JESSICA
Who are you? Tell me for more certainty,
Albeit I'll swear that I do know your tongue.
LORENZO   Lorenzo, and thy love.

6 **Venus' pigeons** the doves that drew Venus' chariot   8 **obligèd** bound
by marriage or engagement.   **unforfeited** unbroken   11 **untread** retrace   15 **younger** i.e., younger son, as in the parable of the Prodigal
Son (Luke 15). (Often emended to *younker*, youth.)   16 **scarfèd** decorated
with flags or streamers   17 **strumpet** i.e., inconsistent, variable. (Refers
metaphorically to the harlots with whom the Prodigal Son wasted his
fortune.)   19 **overweathered** weatherbeaten   20 **rent** torn   22 **your patience** i.e., I beg your patience.   **abode** delay   26 **father** i.e., father-in-law

JESSICA
Lorenzo, certain, and my love indeed,
For who love I so much? And now who knows
But you, Lorenzo, whether I am yours?

LORENZO
Heaven and thy thoughts are witness that thou art.

JESSICA [*Throwing down a casket*]
Here, catch this casket; it is worth the pains.
I am glad 'tis night, you do not look on me,
For I am much ashamed of my exchange.   36
But love is blind, and lovers cannot see
The pretty follies that themselves commit,   38
For if they could, Cupid himself would blush
To see me thus transformèd to a boy.

LORENZO
Descend, for you must be my torchbearer.

JESSICA
What, must I hold a candle to my shames?   42
They in themselves, good sooth, are too too light.   43
Why, 'tis an office of discovery, love,   44
And I should be obscured.   So are you, sweet,
Even in the lovely garnish of a boy.   46
But come at once,
For the close night doth play the runaway,   48
And we are stayed for at Bassanio's feast.   49

JESSICA
I will make fast the doors, and gild myself   50
With some more ducats, and be with you straight.
                                    [*Exit above.*]

GRATIANO
Now, by my hood, a gentle and no Jew.   52

LORENZO
Beshrew me but I love her heartily,   53
For she is wise, if I can judge of her,

36 exchange change of clothes **38 pretty** ingenious, artful **42 hold a candle** stand by and witness (with a play on the idea of acting as torchbearer) **43 light** immodest (with pun on literal meaning) **44 'tis . . . discovery** i.e., torchbearing is intended to shed light on matters **46 garnish** outfit, trimmings **48 close** dark. **doth . . . runaway** i.e., is quickly passing **49 stayed** waited **50 gild** adorn. (Literally, cover with gold.) **52 gentle** (with pun on *gentile*, as at 2.4.34) **53 Beshrew** i.e., a mischief on. (A mild oath.)

And fair she is, if that mine eyes be true,
And true she is, as she hath proved herself;
And therefore, like herself—wise, fair, and true—
Shall she be placèd in my constant soul.

Enter Jessica [below].

What, art thou come? On, gentlemen, away!
Our masking mates by this time for us stay.

Exit [with Jessica and Salerio;
Gratiano is about to follow them].

Enter Antonio.

ANTONIO   Who's there?
GRATIANO   Signor Antonio?
ANTONIO
Fie, fie, Gratiano! Where are all the rest?
'Tis nine o'clock; our friends all stay for you.
No masque tonight. The wind is come about;
Bassanio presently will go aboard.
I have sent twenty out to seek for you.
GRATIANO
I am glad on 't. I desire no more delight
Than to be under sail and gone tonight.   *Exeunt.*

❖

2.7   *[Flourish of cornets.] Enter Portia, with [the*
Prince of] Morocco, and both their trains.

PORTIA
Go draw aside the curtains and discover   1
The several caskets to this noble prince.
                    [The curtains are drawn.]
Now make your choice.
MOROCCO
The first, of gold, who this inscription bears,
"Who chooseth me shall gain what many men desire";
The second, silver, which this promise carries,
"Who chooseth me shall get as much as he deserves";
This third, dull lead, with warning all as blunt,

2.7. Location: Belmont. Portia's house.
1 discover reveal

"Who chooseth me must give and hazard all he hath."
How shall I know if I do choose the right?

PORTIA

The one of them contains my picture, Prince.
If you choose that, then I am yours withal.

MOROCCO

Some god direct my judgment! Let me see.
I will survey th' inscriptions back again.
What says this leaden casket?
"Who chooseth me must give and hazard all he hath."
Must give—for what? For lead? Hazard for lead?
This casket threatens. Men that hazard all
Do it in hope of fair advantages.
A golden mind stoops not to shows of dross;   20
I'll then nor give nor hazard aught for lead.   21
What says the silver with her virgin hue?
"Who chooseth me shall get as much as he deserves."
As much as he deserves! Pause there, Morocco,
And weigh thy value with an even hand.
If thou be'st rated by thy estimation,   26
Thou dost deserve enough; and yet enough
May not extend so far as to the lady;
And yet to be afeard of my deserving
Were but a weak disabling of myself.   30
As much as I deserve? Why, that's the lady.
I do in birth deserve her, and in fortunes,
In graces, and in qualities of breeding;
But more than these, in love I do deserve.
What if I strayed no farther, but chose here?
Let's see once more this saying graved in gold:
"Who chooseth me shall gain what many men desire."
Why, that's the lady; all the world desires her.
From the four corners of the earth they come
To kiss this shrine, this mortal breathing saint.
The Hyrcanian deserts and the vasty wilds   41
Of wide Arabia are as throughfares now

---

20 dross worthless matter. (Literally, the impurities cast off in the
melting down of metals.)   **21 nor give** neither give   **26 estimation**
valuation   **30 disabling** underrating   **41 Hyrcanian** (Hyrcania was the
country south of the Caspian Sea celebrated for its wildness.)

For princes to come view fair Portia.
The watery kingdom, whose ambitious head
Spits in the face of heaven, is no bar
To stop the foreign spirits, but they come,
As o'er a brook, to see fair Portia.
One of these three contains her heavenly picture.
Is 't like that lead contains her? 'Twere damnation
To think so base a thought; it were too gross
To rib her cerecloth in the obscure grave.   51
Or shall I think in silver she's immured,   52
Being ten times undervalued to tried gold?   53
O, sinful thought! Never so rich a gem
Was set in worse than gold. They have in England
A coin that bears the figure of an angel   56
Stamped in gold, but that's insculped upon;   57
But here an angel in a golden bed
Lies all within. Deliver me the key.
Here do I choose, and thrive I as I may!
PORTIA
There, take it, Prince; and if my form lie there,
Then I am yours.   [*He unlocks the golden casket.*]
MOROCCO   O hell! What have we here?
A carrion Death, within whose empty eye   63
There is a written scroll! I'll read the writing.
[*Reads.*] "All that glisters is not gold;
          Often have you heard that told.
          Many a man his life hath sold
          But my outside to behold.
          Gilded tombs do worms infold.
          Had you been as wise as bold,
          Young in limbs, in judgment old,
          Your answer had not been enscrolled.   72
          Fare you well; your suit is cold."
Cold, indeed, and labor lost.
Then, farewell, heat, and welcome, frost!

---

51 rib i.e., enclose. **cerecloth** wax cloth used in wrapping for burial
52 immured enclosed, confined **53 Being . . . to** which has only one
tenth of the value of **56 coin** i.e., the gold coin known as the *angel*,
which bore the device of the archangel Michael treading on the
dragon **57 insculped upon** merely engraved upon the surface
63 carrion Death death's-head **72 enscrolled** i.e., written on this scroll

Portia, adieu. I have too grieved a heart
To take a tedious leave. Thus losers part.
                    Exit [with his train. Flourish of cornets].
PORTIA
A gentle riddance. Draw the curtains, go.
Let all of his complexion choose me so.   79
                    [The curtains are closed, and] Exeunt.

✣

2.8   *Enter Salerio and Solanio.*

SALERIO
Why, man, I saw Bassanio under sail.
With him is Gratiano gone along,
And in their ship I am sure Lorenzo is not.
SOLANIO
The villain Jew with outcries raised the Duke,
Who went with him to search Bassanio's ship.
SALERIO
He came too late; the ship was under sail.
But there the Duke was given to understand
That in a gondola were seen together
Lorenzo and his amorous Jessica.
Besides, Antonio certified the Duke
They were not with Bassanio in his ship.
SOLANIO
I never heard a passion so confused,
So strange, outrageous, and so variable
As the dog Jew did utter in the streets:
"My daughter! O, my ducats! O, my daughter!
Fled with a Christian! O, my Christian ducats!
Justice! The law! My ducats, and my daughter!
A sealèd bag, two sealèd bags of ducats,
Of double ducats, stol'n from me by my daughter!
And jewels, two stones, two rich and precious stones,
Stol'n by my daughter! Justice! Find the girl!
She hath the stones upon her, and the ducats."

79 complexion temperament (not merely skin color)
2.8. Location: Venice. A street.

SALERIO
  Why, all the boys in Venice follow him,
  Crying, his stones, his daughter, and his ducats.
SOLANIO
  Let good Antonio look he keep his day,   25
  Or he shall pay for this.
SALERIO   Marry, well remembered.
  I reasoned with a Frenchman yesterday,   27
  Who told me, in the narrow seas that part   28
  The French and English, there miscarried
  A vessel of our country richly fraught.   30
  I thought upon Antonio when he told me,
  And wished in silence that it were not his.
SOLANIO
  You were best to tell Antonio what you hear.
  Yet do not suddenly, for it may grieve him.
SALERIO
  A kinder gentleman treads not the earth.
  I saw Bassanio and Antonio part.
  Bassanio told him he would make some speed
  Of his return; he answered, "Do not so.
  Slubber not business for my sake, Bassanio,   39
  But stay the very riping of the time;   40
  And for the Jew's bond which he hath of me,   41
  Let it not enter in your mind of love.
  Be merry, and employ your chiefest thoughts
  To courtship and such fair ostents of love   44
  As shall conveniently become you there."
  And even there, his eye being big with tears,   46
  Turning his face, he put his hand behind him,
  And with affection wondrous sensible   48
  He wrung Bassanio's hand; and so they parted.
SOLANIO
  I think he only loves the world for him.
  I pray thee, let us go and find him out

---

25 look . . . day see to it that he repays his loan on time   **27 reasoned**
talked   **28 narrow seas** English Channel   **30 fraught** freighted
39 Slubber do hastily and badly   **40 But . . . time** i.e., pursue your
business at Belmont until it is brought to completion   **41 for** as for
44 ostents expressions, shows   **46 there** thereupon, then   **48 sensible**
strongly evident

And quicken his embracèd heaviness   52
With some delight or other.
SALERIO   Do we so.   *Exeunt.*

❖

2.9   *Enter Nerissa and a Servitor.*

NERISSA
Quick, quick, I pray thee, draw the curtain straight.   1
                    [*The curtains are drawn.*]
The Prince of Aragon hath ta'en his oath,
And comes to his election presently.   3

        [*Flourish of cornets.*] *Enter* [*the Prince of*]
        Aragon, his train, and Portia.

PORTIA
Behold, there stand the caskets, noble Prince.
If you choose that wherein I am contained,
Straight shall our nuptial rites be solemnized;
But if you fail, without more speech, my lord,
You must be gone from hence immediately.
ARAGON
I am enjoined by oath to observe three things:
First, never to unfold to anyone
Which casket 'twas I chose; next, if I fail
Of the right casket, never in my life
To woo a maid in way of marriage;
Lastly,
If I do fail in fortune of my choice,
Immediately to leave you and be gone.
PORTIA
To these injunctions everyone doth swear
That comes to hazard for my worthless self.
ARAGON
And so have I addressed me. Fortune now   19
To my heart's hope! Gold, silver, and base lead.

52 quicken . . . heaviness lighten the sorrow he has embraced

2.9. Location: Belmont. Portia's house.
s.d. Servitor servant   **1 straight** at once   **3 election** choice.   **presently**
immediately   **19 addressed me** prepared myself (by this swearing)

"Who chooseth me must give and hazard all he hath."
You shall look fairer ere I give or hazard.
What says the golden chest? Ha, let me see:
"Who chooseth me shall gain what many men desire."
What many men desire! That "many" may be meant   25
By the fool multitude that choose by show,
Not learning more than the fond eye doth teach,   27
Which pries not to th' interior, but like the martlet   28
Builds in the weather on the outward wall,   29
Even in the force and road of casualty.   30
I will not choose what many men desire,
Because I will not jump with common spirits   32
And rank me with the barbarous multitudes.
Why then, to thee, thou silver treasure-house!
Tell me once more what title thou dost bear:
"Who chooseth me shall get as much as he deserves."
And well said too; for who shall go about
To cozen fortune and be honorable   38
Without the stamp of merit? Let none presume   39
To wear an undeservèd dignity.
O, that estates, degrees, and offices   41
Were not derived corruptly, and that clear honor
Were purchased by the merit of the wearer!
How many then should cover that stand bare?   44
How many be commanded that command?   45
How much low peasantry would then be gleaned   46
From the true seed of honor, and how much honor   47
Picked from the chaff and ruin of the times
To be new-varnished? Well, but to my choice: 49
"Who chooseth me shall get as much as he deserves."
I will assume desert. Give me a key for this,
And instantly unlock my fortunes here.

                    [*He opens the silver casket.*]

---

25 meant interpreted   **27 fond** foolish   **28 martlet** swift   **29 in** exposed
to   **30 force . . . casualty** power and path of mischance   **32 jump**
agree   **38 cozen** cheat   **39 stamp** seal of approval   **41 estates, degrees**
status, social rank   **44 cover . . . bare** i.e., wear hats (of authority) who
now stand bareheaded   **45 How . . . command** how many then should
be servants that are now masters   **46 gleaned** culled out   **47 the true
seed of honor** i.e., persons of noble descent   **49 new-varnished** i.e.,
having the luster of their true nobility restored to them

PORTIA
Too long a pause for that which you find there.

ARAGON
What's here? The portrait of a blinking idiot,
Presenting me a schedule! I will read it.   55
How much unlike art thou to Portia!
How much unlike my hopes and my deservings!
"Who chooseth me shall have as much as he deserves."
Did I deserve no more than a fool's head?
Is that my prize? Are my deserts no better?

PORTIA
To offend and judge are distinct offices   61
And of opposèd natures.

ARAGON   What is here?   62
[*Reads*.] "The fire seven times tried this;   63
Seven times tried that judgment is
That did never choose amiss.
Some there be that shadows kiss;
Such have but a shadow's bliss.
There be fools alive, iwis,   68
Silvered o'er, and so was this.   69
Take what wife you will to bed,
I will ever be your head.   71
So begone; you are sped."   72

Still more fool I shall appear   73
By the time I linger here.   74
With one fool's head I came to woo,
But I go away with two.
Sweet, adieu. I'll keep my oath,
Patiently to bear my wroth.   78
          [*Exeunt Aragon and train.*]

PORTIA
Thus hath the candle singed the moth.

55 **schedule** written paper   61–62 **To offend . . . natures** i.e., you have
no right, having submitted your case to judgment, to attempt to judge
your own case   63 **tried** tested, purified (?)   **this** i.e., the wise sayings on
the scroll (that have often been proved right by hard experience)
68 **iwis** certainly   69 **Silvered o'er** i.e., with silver hair and so apparently wise   71 **I . . . head** i.e., you will always have a fool's head
72 **sped** done for   73–74 **Still . . . here** i.e., I shall seem all the greater
fool for wasting any more time here   78 **wroth** sorrow, unhappy lot. (A
variant of *ruth*.)

O, these deliberate fools! When they do choose,   80
They have the wisdom by their wit to lose.
NERISSA
The ancient saying is no heresy:
Hanging and wiving goes by destiny.
PORTIA   Come, draw the curtain, Nerissa.
                              [*The curtains are closed.*]
   Enter Messenger.

MESSENGER
Where is my lady?
PORTIA   Here. What would my lord?   85
MESSENGER
Madam, there is alighted at your gate
A young Venetian, one that comes before
To signify th' approaching of his lord,
From whom he bringeth sensible regreets,   89
To wit, besides commends and courteous breath,   90
Gifts of rich value. Yet I have not seen   91
So likely an ambassador of love.   92
A day in April never came so sweet
To show how costly summer was at hand   94
As this fore-spurrer comes before his lord.   95
PORTIA
No more, I pray thee. I am half afeard
Thou wilt say anon he is some kin to thee,
Thou spend'st such high-day wit in praising him.   98
Come, come, Nerissa, for I long to see
Quick Cupid's post that comes so mannerly.   100
NERISSA
Bassanio, Lord Love, if thy will it be!   *Exeunt.*

❖

80 **deliberate** reasoning, calculating   85 **my lord** (A jesting response to
"my lady.")   89 **sensible regreets** tangible gifts, greetings   90 **commends** greetings.   **breath** speech   91 **Yet** heretofore   92 **likely**
promising   94 **costly** lavish, rich   95 **fore-spurrer** herald, harbinger
98 **high-day** holiday (i.e., extravagant)   100 **post** messenger

3.1   [*Enter*] *Solanio and Salerio.*

SOLANIO   Now, what news on the Rialto?

SALERIO   Why, yet it lives there unchecked that Antonio 2
hath a ship of rich lading wrecked on the narrow 3
seas—the Goodwins, I think they call the place, a very 4
dangerous flat, and fatal, where the carcasses of many 5
a tall ship lie buried, as they say, if my gossip Report 6
be an honest woman of her word.

SOLANIO   I would she were as lying a gossip in that as
ever knapped ginger or made her neighbors believe 9
she wept for the death of a third husband. But it is
true, without any slips of prolixity or crossing the 11
plain highway of talk, that the good Antonio, the hon- 12
est Antonio—O, that I had a title good enough to keep
his name company!—

SALERIO   Come, the full stop.   15

SOLANIO   Ha, what sayest thou? Why, the end is, he
hath lost a ship.

SALERIO   I would it might prove the end of his losses.

SOLANIO   Let me say "amen" betimes, lest the devil 19
cross my prayer, for here he comes in the likeness of 20
a Jew.

Enter Shylock.

How now, Shylock, what news among the merchants?

SHYLOCK   You knew, none so well, none so well as you,
of my daughter's flight.

SALERIO   That's certain. I for my part knew the tailor
that made the wings she flew withal.   26

SOLANIO   And Shylock for his own part knew the bird

3.1. Location: Venice. A street.
2 unchecked undenied   **3–4 the narrow seas** the English Channel, as at
2.8.28.   **4 Goodwins** Goodwin Sands, off the Kentish coast near the
Thames estuary   **5 flat** shoal, sandbank   **6 gossip Report** i.e., Dame
Rumor   **9 knapped** nibbled   **11 slips of prolixity** lapses into long-
windedness; or, longwinded lies   **11–12 crossing . . . talk** deviating
from honest plain speech   **15 Come . . . stop** finish your story   **19 betimes** while there is yet time   **20 cross** thwart   **26 wings** i.e., the
boy's clothes in which she fled. Jessica's flight is compared to a bird's
(cf. ll. 27–28), but *wings* is also a tailor's word to describe an ornamental flap near the shoulder of a garment.

was fledge, and then it is the complexion of them all 28
to leave the dam. 29

SHYLOCK She is damned for it.

SALERIO That's certain, if the devil may be her judge.

SHYLOCK My own flesh and blood to rebel!

SOLANIO Out upon it, old carrion! Rebels it at these 33
years? 34

SHYLOCK I say, my daughter is my flesh and my blood.

SALERIO There is more difference between thy flesh and
hers than between jet and ivory, more between your 37
bloods than there is between red wine and Rhenish. 38
But tell us, do you hear whether Antonio have had
any loss at sea or no?

SHYLOCK There I have another bad match! A bankrupt, 41
a prodigal, who dare scarce show his head on the
Rialto; a beggar, that was used to come so smug upon
the mart! Let him look to his bond. He was wont to
call me usurer. Let him look to his bond. He was wont
to lend money for a Christian courtesy. Let him look to
his bond.

SALERIO Why, I am sure, if he forfeit, thou wilt not take
his flesh. What's that good for?

SHYLOCK To bait fish withal. If it will feed nothing else, 50
it will feed my revenge. He hath disgraced me, and
hindered me half a million, laughed at my losses,
mocked at my gains, scorned my nation, thwarted my
bargains, cooled my friends, heated mine enemies;
and what's his reason? I am a Jew. Hath not a Jew
eyes? Hath not a Jew hands, organs, dimensions,
senses, affections, passions? Fed with the same food,
hurt with the same weapons, subject to the same diseases, healed by the same means, warmed and cooled
by the same winter and summer, as a Christian is? If
you prick us, do we not bleed? If you tickle us, do we
not laugh? If you poison us, do we not die? And if you
wrong us, shall we not revenge? If we are like you in

---

28 fledge ready to fly. **complexion** natural disposition **29 dam**
mother **33–34 Rebels . . . years** (Solanio pretends to interpret Shylock's
cry about the rebellion of his own flesh and blood as referring to his
own carnal desires.) **37 jet** a hard form of coal capable of taking a
brilliant polish **38 Rhenish** i.e., a German white wine from the Rhine
valley **41 match** bargain **50 To bait** to lure, to act as bait for

the rest, we will resemble you in that. If a Jew wrong
a Christian, what is his humility? Revenge. If a Chris- 65
tian wrong a Jew, what should his sufferance be by 66
Christian example? Why, revenge. The villainy you
teach me I will execute, and it shall go hard but I will
better the instruction.

Enter a Man from Antonio.

MAN   Gentlemen, my master Antonio is at his house
and desires to speak with you both.

SALERIO   We have been up and down to seek him.

Enter Tubal.

SOLANIO   Here comes another of the tribe. A third cannot be matched, unless the devil himself turn Jew. 74

Exeunt gentlemen [Solanio, Salerio, with Man].

SHYLOCK   How now, Tubal, what news from Genoa?
Hast thou found my daughter?

TUBAL   I often came where I did hear of her, but cannot
find her.

SHYLOCK   Why, there, there, there, there! A diamond
gone, cost me two thousand ducats in Frankfort! The
curse never fell upon our nation till now; I never felt it
till now. Two thousand ducats in that, and other precious, precious jewels. I would my daughter were
dead at my foot, and the jewels in her ear! Would she
were hearsed at my foot, and the ducats in her coffin! 85
No news of them? Why, so—and I know not what's
spent in the search. Why, thou loss upon loss! The
thief gone with so much, and so much to find the
thief, and no satisfaction, no revenge! Nor no ill luck
stirring but what lights o' my shoulders, no sighs but
o' my breathing, no tears but o' my shedding.

TUBAL   Yes, other men have ill luck too. Antonio, as I
heard in Genoa—

SHYLOCK   What, what, what? Ill luck, ill luck?

TUBAL   —hath an argosy cast away, coming from Tripolis.

SHYLOCK   I thank God, I thank God. Is it true, is it true?

TUBAL   I spoke with some of the sailors that escaped the
wreck.

65–66 his ... his the Christian's ... the Jew's   **74 matched** i.e., found to
match them   **85 hearsed** coffined

SHYLOCK   I thank thee, good Tubal. Good news, good news! Ha, ha! Heard in Genoa?

TUBAL   Your daughter spent in Genoa, as I heard, one night fourscore ducats.

SHYLOCK   Thou stick'st a dagger in me. I shall never see my gold again. Fourscore ducats at a sitting, fourscore ducats!

TUBAL   There came divers of Antonio's creditors in my company to Venice that swear he cannot choose but break.   108

SHYLOCK   I am very glad of it. I'll plague him, I'll torture him. I am glad of it.

TUBAL   One of them showed me a ring that he had of your daughter for a monkey.

SHYLOCK   Out upon her! Thou torturest me, Tubal. It was my turquoise; I had it of Leah when I was a bach- 114 elor. I would not have given it for a wilderness of monkeys.

TUBAL   But Antonio is certainly undone.

SHYLOCK   Nay, that's true, that's very true. Go, Tubal, fee me an officer; bespeak him a fortnight before. I will 119 have the heart of him if he forfeit, for were he out of Venice I can make what merchandise I will. Go, 121 Tubal, and meet me at our synagogue; go, good Tubal; at our synagogue, Tubal.   *Exeunt.*

3.2   *Enter Bassanio, Portia, Gratiano, [Nerissa,] and all their trains.*

PORTIA

I pray you, tarry. Pause a day or two
Before you hazard, for in choosing wrong   2
I lose your company. Therefore forbear awhile.
There's something tells me, but it is not love,
I would not lose you; and you know yourself,

---

108 break go bankrupt   **114 Leah** Shylock's wife   **119 fee** hire.   **officer** bailiff.   **bespeak** engage   **121 make . . . I will** drive whatever bargains I please

3.2. Location: Belmont. Portia's house.
2 in choosing in your choosing

Hate counsels not in such a quality. 6
But lest you should not understand me well—
And yet a maiden hath no tongue but thought—
I would detain you here some month or two
Before you venture for me. I could teach you
How to choose right, but then I am forsworn.
So will I never be. So may you miss me. 12
But if you do, you'll make me wish a sin,
That I had been forsworn. Beshrew your eyes,
They have o'erlooked me and divided me! 15
One half of me is yours, the other half yours—
Mine own, I would say; but if mine, then yours,
And so all yours. O, these naughty times 18
Puts bars between the owners and their rights! 19
And so, though yours, not yours. Prove it so, 20
Let Fortune go to hell for it, not I.
I speak too long, but 'tis to peise the time, 22
To eke it and to draw it out in length, 23
To stay you from election.

BASSANIO   Let me choose,
For as I am, I live upon the rack.

PORTIA
Upon the rack, Bassanio? Then confess 26
What treason there is mingled with your love. 27

BASSANIO
None but that ugly treason of mistrust, 28
Which makes me fear th' enjoying of my love. 29
There may as well be amity and life
'Tween snow and fire, as treason and my love.

PORTIA
Ay, but I fear you speak upon the rack,
Where men enforcèd do speak anything.

BASSANIO
Promise me life, and I'll confess the truth.

6 quality way, manner   12 So ... So that ... therefore.   miss
i.e., fail to win   15 o'erlooked bewitched   18 naughty worthless, wicked   19 bars barriers   20 Prove it so if it prove so
22 peise retard (by hanging on of weights)   23 eke eke out, augment   26–27 confess What treason (The rack was used to force
traitors to confess.)   28 mistrust misapprehension   29 fear fearful
about

PORTIA
Well then, confess and live.

BASSANIO   "Confess and love"
Had been the very sum of my confession.
O happy torment, when my torturer
Doth teach me answers for deliverance!
But let me to my fortune and the caskets.   39

PORTIA
Away, then! I am locked in one of them.
If you do love me, you will find me out.
Nerissa and the rest, stand all aloof.   42
Let music sound while he doth make his choice;
Then, if he lose, he makes a swanlike end,   44
Fading in music. That the comparison
May stand more proper, my eye shall be the stream
And watery deathbed for him. He may win;
And what is music then? Then music is
Even as the flourish when true subjects bow   49
To a new-crownèd monarch. Such it is
As are those dulcet sounds in break of day
That creep into the dreaming bridegroom's ear
And summon him to marriage. Now he goes,
With no less presence, but with much more love,
Than young Alcides, when he did redeem   55
The virgin tribute paid by howling Troy   56
To the sea monster. I stand for sacrifice;   57
The rest aloof are the Dardanian wives,   58
With blearèd visages, come forth to view   59
The issue of th' exploit. Go, Hercules!   60
Live thou, I live. With much, much more dismay   61
I view the fight than thou that mak'st the fray.

39 **fortune . . . caskets** (Presumably the curtains are drawn at about
this point, as in the previous "casket" scenes, revealing the three
caskets.)   42 **aloof** apart, at a distance   44 **swanlike** (Swans were
believed to sing when they came to die.)   49 **flourish** sounding of
trumpets   55 **Alcides** (Hercules rescued Hesione, daughter of the Trojan king Laomedon, from a monster to which, by command of Neptune,
she was about to be sacrificed. Hercules was rewarded, however, not
with the lady's love, but with a famous pair of horses.)   56 **howling**
lamenting   57 **stand for sacrifice** represent the sacrificial victim
58 **Dardanian** Trojan   59 **blearèd** weeping   60 **issue** outcome   61 **Live
thou** if you live

*A song, [sung by one of Portia's train,] the whilst
Bassanio comments on the caskets to himself.*

[*Song.*]

Tell me where is fancy bred,   63
Or in the heart or in the head?   64
How begot, how nourishèd?
   Reply, reply.
It is engenderèd in the eyes,   67
With gazing fed, and fancy dies
In the cradle where it lies.   69
   Let us all ring fancy's knell.
   I'll begin it—Ding, dong, bell.
ALL   Ding, dong, bell.

BASSANIO
So may the outward shows be least themselves;   73
The world is still deceived with ornament.   74
In law, what plea so tainted and corrupt
But, being seasoned with a gracious voice,
Obscures the show of evil? In religion,
What damnèd error but some sober brow
Will bless it and approve it with a text,   79
Hiding the grossness with fair ornament?
There is no vice so simple but assumes   81
Some mark of virtue on his outward parts.   82
How many cowards, whose hearts are all as false
As stairs of sand, wear yet upon their chins   84
The beards of Hercules and frowning Mars,
Who, inward searched, have livers white as milk!   86
And these assume but valor's excrement   87
To render them redoubted. Look on beauty,   88
And you shall see 'tis purchased by the weight,
Which therein works a miracle in nature,

63 fancy love   **64 Or** either   **67 eyes** (Love entered the heart especially
through the eyes.)   **69 In the cradle** i.e., in its infancy, in the eyes
73 be least themselves least represent the inner reality   **74 still** ever
79 approve confirm   **81 simple** unadulterated   **82 his** its   **84 stairs**
steps   **86 livers** (The liver was thought to be the seat of courage; for it
to be deserted by the blood would be the condition of cowardice.)
87 excrement outgrowth, such as a beard (as in this case) or finger-
nails   **88 redoubted** feared

Making them lightest that wear most of it. 91
So are those crispèd snaky golden locks, 92
Which maketh such wanton gambols with the wind
Upon supposèd fairness, often known 94
To be the dowry of a second head, 95
The skull that bred them in the sepulcher. 96
Thus ornament is but the guilèd shore 97
To a most dangerous sea, the beauteous scarf
Veiling an Indian beauty; in a word, 99
The seeming truth which cunning times put on
To entrap the wisest. Therefore, thou gaudy gold,
Hard food for Midas, I will none of thee; 102
Nor none of thee, thou pale and common drudge 103
'Tween man and man. But thou, thou meager lead, 104
Which rather threaten'st than dost promise aught,
Thy paleness moves me more than eloquence;
And here choose I. Joy be the consequence!
PORTIA [*Aside*]
How all the other passions fleet to air,
As doubtful thoughts, and rash-embraced despair, 109
And shuddering fear, and green-eyed jealousy!
O love, be moderate, allay thy ecstasy,
In measure rain thy joy, scant this excess! 112
I feel too much thy blessing. Make it less,
For fear I surfeit.
BASSANIO [*Opening the leaden casket*]
               What find I here?
Fair Portia's counterfeit! What demigod 115
Hath come so near creation? Move these eyes?
Or whether, riding on the balls of mine,
Seem they in motion? Here are severed lips,
Parted with sugar breath; so sweet a bar 119
Should sunder such sweet friends. Here in her hairs 120

91 **lightest** most lascivious (with pun on the sense of "least heavy")
92 **crispèd** curly 94 **Upon supposèd fairness** i.e., on a woman supposed
beautiful and fairhaired 95–96 **To . . . sepulcher** i.e., to be a wig of hair
taken from a woman now dead 97 **guilèd** treacherous 99 **Indian** i.e.,
swarthy, not fair 102 **Midas** the Phrygian king whose touch turned
everything to gold, including his food 103–104 **pale . . . man** i.e., silver,
used in commerce 109 **As** such as 112 **rain** rain down, or perhaps
rein. **scant** lessen 115 **counterfeit** portrait. **demigod** i.e., the painter
as creator 119 **so sweet a bar** i.e., Portia's breath 120 **sweet friends**
i.e., her lips

The painter plays the spider, and hath woven
A golden mesh t' entrap the hearts of men
Faster than gnats in cobwebs. But her eyes—   123
How could he see to do them? Having made one,
Methinks it should have power to steal both his
And leave itself unfurnished. Yet look how far   126
The substance of my praise doth wrong this shadow   127
In underprizing it, so far this shadow
Doth limp behind the substance. Here's the scroll,   129
The continent and summary of my fortune.   130
　　[*Reads.*] "You that choose not by the view,
　　Chance as fair, and choose as true!   132
　　Since this fortune falls to you,
　　Be content and seek no new.
　　If you be well pleased with this,
　　And hold your fortune for your bliss,
　　Turn you where your lady is
　　And claim her with a loving kiss."
A gentle scroll. Fair lady, by your leave,
I come by note, to give and to receive.   140
Like one of two contending in a prize,   141
That thinks he hath done well in people's eyes,
Hearing applause and universal shout,
Giddy in spirit, still gazing in a doubt
Whether those peals of praise be his or no,   145
So, thrice-fair lady, stand I even so,
As doubtful whether what I see be true,
Until confirmed, signed, ratified by you.
PORTIA
You see me, Lord Bassanio, where I stand,
Such as I am. Though for myself alone
I would not be ambitious in my wish
To wish myself much better, yet for you
I would be trebled twenty times myself,
A thousand times more fair, ten thousand times more
　　rich,
That only to stand high in your account   155

123 **Faster** more tightly   126 **unfurnished** i.e., without a companion.
look how far however far   127 **shadow** painting   129 **the substance** the
subject, i.e., Portia   130 **continent** container   132 **Chance as fair** hazard
as fortunately   140 **by note** as indicated (i.e., as directed by the scroll)
141 **prize** competition   145 **his** for him   155 **account** estimation

I might in virtues, beauties, livings, friends,   156
Exceed account. But the full sum of me   157
Is sum of something, which, to term in gross,   158
Is an unlessoned girl, unschooled, unpracticèd;
Happy in this, she is not yet so old
But she may learn; happier than this,
She is not bred so dull but she can learn;
Happiest of all is that her gentle spirit
Commits itself to yours to be directed,
As from her lord, her governor, her king.
Myself and what is mine to you and yours
Is now converted. But now I was the lord   167
Of this fair mansion, master of my servants,
Queen o'er myself; and even now, but now,
This house, these servants, and this same myself
Are yours, my lord's. I give them with this ring,
Which when you part from, lose, or give away,
Let it presage the ruin of your love
And be my vantage to exclaim on you.   174
                    [*She puts a ring on his finger.*]
BASSANIO
Madam, you have bereft me of all words.
Only my blood speaks to you in my veins,
And there is such confusion in my powers   177
As, after some oration fairly spoke
By a belovèd prince, there doth appear
Among the buzzing pleasèd multitude,
Where every something being blent together   181
Turns to a wild of nothing save of joy   182
Expressed and not expressed. But when this ring   183
Parts from this finger, then parts life from hence.
O, then be bold to say Bassanio's dead!
NERISSA
My lord and lady, it is now our time,
That have stood by and seen our wishes prosper,   187
To cry, good joy. Good joy, my lord and lady!

156 livings possessions   **157 account** calculation   **158 something** i.e., at
least something.   **term in gross** relate in full   **167 But now** a moment
ago   **174 exclaim on** reproach   **177 powers** faculties   **181–183 Where
. . . expressed** i.e., in which every individual utterance, being blended
and confused, turns into a hubbub of joy that speaks and yet in no
understood tongue   **187 That** we who

GRATIANO

My lord Bassanio and my gentle lady,
I wish you all the joy that you can wish—
For I am sure you can wish none from me.   191
And when your honors mean to solemnize
The bargain of your faith, I do beseech you,
Even at that time I may be married too.

BASSANIO

With all my heart, so thou canst get a wife.   195

GRATIANO

I thank your lordship, you have got me one.
My eyes, my lord, can look as swift as yours.
You saw the mistress, I beheld the maid;   198
You loved, I loved; for intermission   199
No more pertains to me, my lord, than you.
Your fortune stood upon the caskets there,
And so did mine too, as the matter falls;
For wooing here until I sweat again,   203
And swearing till my very roof was dry   204
With oaths of love, at last, if promise last,   205
I got a promise of this fair one here
To have her love, provided that your fortune
Achieved her mistress.

PORTIA   Is this true, Nerissa?

NERISSA

Madam, it is, so you stand pleased withal.   209

BASSANIO

And do you, Gratiano, mean good faith?

GRATIANO   Yes, faith, my lord.

BASSANIO

Our feast shall be much honored in your marriage.

GRATIANO   We'll play with them the first boy for a thou-   213
sand ducats.

NERISSA   What, and stake down?   215

---

191 For . . . me i.e., I'm sure I can't wish you any more joy than you
could wish for yourselves   **195 so** provided   **198 maid** (Nerissa is a
lady-in-waiting, not a house servant.)   **199 intermission** delay (in loving)   **203 sweat again** sweated repeatedly   **204 roof** roof of my mouth
205 if promise last i.e., if Nerissa's promise should last, hold out
209 so provided   **213 play** wager   **215 stake down** cash placed in
advance. (But Gratiano, in his reply, turns the phrase into a bawdy joke;
stake down to him suggests a nonerect phallus.)

GRATIANO No, we shall ne'er win at that sport, and
stake down.
But who comes here? Lorenzo and his infidel?
What, and my old Venetian friend Salerio?

*Enter Lorenzo, Jessica, and Salerio, a messenger
from Venice.*

BASSANIO
Lorenzo and Salerio, welcome hither,
If that the youth of my new interest here   221
Have power to bid you welcome.—By your leave,
I bid my very friends and countrymen,   223
Sweet Portia, welcome.
PORTIA   So do I, my lord.
They are entirely welcome.
LORENZO
I thank your honor. For my part, my lord,
My purpose was not to have seen you here,
But meeting with Salerio by the way,
He did intreat me, past all saying nay,
To come with him along.
SALERIO   I did, my lord,
And I have reason for it. Signor Antonio
Commends him to you.   [*He gives Bassanio a letter.*]
BASSANIO   Ere I ope his letter,   232
I pray you tell me how my good friend doth.
SALERIO
Not sick, my lord, unless it be in mind,
Nor well, unless in mind. His letter there
Will show you his estate. [*Bassanio*] *open*[*s*] *the letter.* 236
GRATIANO
Nerissa, cheer yond stranger, bid her welcome.   237
Your hand, Salerio. What's the news from Venice?
How doth that royal merchant, good Antonio?   239
I know he will be glad of our success;
We are the Jasons, we have won the fleece.   241

---

221 youth . . . interest i.e., newness of my household authority
223 very true   **232 Commends him** desires to be remembered   **236 estate** condition   **237 stranger** i.e., Jessica   **239 royal merchant** i.e., chief
among merchants   **241 Jasons . . . fleece** (Cf. 1.1.170–172.)

SALERIO
I would you had won the fleece that he hath lost.

PORTIA
There are some shrewd contents in yond same paper   243
That steals the color from Bassanio's cheek—
Some dear friend dead, else nothing in the world
Could turn so much the constitution
Of any constant man. What, worse and worse?   247
With leave, Bassanio; I am half yourself,
And I must freely have the half of anything
That this same paper brings you.

BASSANIO   O sweet Portia,
Here are a few of the unpleasant'st words
That ever blotted paper! Gentle lady,
When I did first impart my love to you,
I freely told you all the wealth I had
Ran in my veins, I was a gentleman;
And then I told you true. And yet, dear lady,
Rating myself at nothing, you shall see
How much I was a braggart. When I told you
My state was nothing, I should then have told you   259
That I was worse than nothing; for indeed
I have engaged myself to a dear friend,
Engaged my friend to his mere enemy,   262
To feed my means. Here is a letter, lady,
The paper as the body of my friend,
And every word in it a gaping wound
Issuing lifeblood. But is it true, Salerio?
Hath all his ventures failed? What, not one hit?   267
From Tripolis, from Mexico, and England,
From Lisbon, Barbary, and India,
And not one vessel scape the dreadful touch
Of merchant-marring rocks?

SALERIO   Not one, my lord.   271
Besides, it should appear that if he had
The present money to discharge the Jew,   273
He would not take it. Never did I know   274
A creature that did bear the shape of man

243 **shrewd** cursed, grievous   247 **constant** settled, not swayed by
passion   259 **state** estate   262 **mere** absolute   267 **hit** success
271 **merchant** merchant ship   273 **present** available.   **discharge** pay
off   274 **He** i.e., Shylock

So keen and greedy to confound a man.   276
He plies the Duke at morning and at night,
And doth impeach the freedom of the state   278
If they deny him justice. Twenty merchants,
The Duke himself, and the magnificoes   280
Of greatest port have all persuaded with him,   281
But none can drive him from the envious plea
Of forfeiture, of justice, and his bond.

JESSICA
When I was with him I have heard him swear
To Tubal and to Chus, his countrymen,
That he would rather have Antonio's flesh
Than twenty times the value of the sum
That he did owe him; and I know, my lord,
If law, authority, and power deny not,
It will go hard with poor Antonio.

PORTIA
Is it your dear friend that is thus in trouble?

BASSANIO
The dearest friend to me, the kindest man,
The best-conditioned and unwearied spirit   293
In doing courtesies, and one in whom
The ancient Roman honor more appears
Than any that draws breath in Italy.

PORTIA   What sum owes he the Jew?

BASSANIO
For me, three thousand ducats.

PORTIA   What, no more?
Pay him six thousand, and deface the bond;   299
Double six thousand, and then treble that,
Before a friend of this description
Shall lose a hair through Bassanio's fault.
First go with me to church and call me wife,
And then away to Venice to your friend;
For never shall you lie by Portia's side
With an unquiet soul. You shall have gold
To pay the petty debt twenty times over.
When it is paid, bring your true friend along.

---

276 keen cruel. **confound** destroy **278 impeach . . . state** i.e., call in question the ability of Venice to defend legally the freedom of commerce of its citizens **280 magnificoes** chief men of Venice **281 port** dignity. **persuaded** argued **293 best-conditioned** best natured **299 deface** erase

My maid Nerissa and myself meantime
Will live as maids and widows. Come, away!
For you shall hence upon your wedding day.
Bid your friends welcome, show a merry cheer;   312
Since you are dear bought, I will love you dear.
But let me hear the letter of your friend.

BASSANIO [*Reads*] "Sweet Bassanio, my ships have all
miscarried, my creditors grow cruel, my estate is very
low, my bond to the Jew is forfeit; and since in paying
it, it is impossible I should live, all debts are cleared
between you and I, if I might but see you at my death.
Notwithstanding, use your pleasure; if your love do
not persuade you to come, let not my letter."

PORTIA
O love, dispatch all business, and begone!

BASSANIO
Since I have your good leave to go away,
I will make haste; but till I come again,
No bed shall e'er be guilty of my stay,
Nor rest be interposer twixt us twain.   *Exeunt.*

❖

3.3   *Enter [Shylock] the Jew and Solanio and*
     Antonio and the Jailer.

SHYLOCK
Jailer, look to him. Tell not me of mercy.
This is the fool that lent out money gratis.
Jailer, look to him.

ANTONIO   Hear me yet, good Shylock.

SHYLOCK
I'll have my bond. Speak not against my bond!
I have sworn an oath that I will have my bond.
Thou calledst me dog before thou hadst a cause,
But since I am a dog, beware my fangs.
The Duke shall grant me justice. I do wonder,
Thou naughty jailer, that thou art so fond   9

312 cheer countenance

3.3. Location: Venice. A street.
9 naughty worthless.   **fond** foolish

To come abroad with him at his request.   10
ANTONIO   I pray thee, hear me speak.
SHYLOCK
I'll have my bond. I will not hear thee speak.
I'll have my bond, and therefore speak no more.
I'll not be made a soft and dull-eyed fool,
To shake the head, relent, and sigh, and yield
To Christian intercessors. Follow not;
I'll have no speaking. I will have my bond.   *Exit Jew.*
SOLANIO
It is the most impenetrable cur
That ever kept with men.
ANTONIO   Let him alone.   19
I'll follow him no more with bootless prayers.   20
He seeks my life. His reason well I know:
I oft delivered from his forfeitures
Many that have at times made moan to me;
Therefore he hates me.
SOLANIO   I am sure the Duke
Will never grant this forfeiture to hold.
ANTONIO
The Duke cannot deny the course of law;
For the commodity that strangers have   27
With us in Venice, if it be denied,
Will much impeach the justice of the state,
Since that the trade and profit of the city   30
Consisteth of all nations. Therefore go.
These griefs and losses have so bated me   32
That I shall hardly spare a pound of flesh
Tomorrow to my bloody creditor.
Well, jailer, on. Pray God Bassanio come
To see me pay his debt, and then I care not.   *Exeunt.*

❖

3.4   *Enter Portia, Nerissa, Lorenzo, Jessica, and*
            [Balthasar,] a man of Portia's.

10 abroad outside   **19 kept** associated, dwelt   **20 bootless** unavailing
27 commodity facilities or privileges for trading.   **strangers** nonciti-
zens, including Jews   **30 Since that** since   **32 bated** reduced

3.4. Location: Belmont. Portia's house.

LORENZO
Madam, although I speak it in your presence,
You have a noble and a true conceit   2
Of godlike amity, which appears most strongly
In bearing thus the absence of your lord.
But if you knew to whom you show this honor,
How true a gentleman you send relief,
How dear a lover of my lord your husband,
I know you would be prouder of the work
Than customary bounty can enforce you.   9

PORTIA
I never did repent for doing good,
Nor shall not now; for in companions
That do converse and waste the time together,   12
Whose souls do bear an equal yoke of love,
There must be needs a like proportion   14
Of lineaments, of manners, and of spirit;   15
Which makes me think that this Antonio,
Being the bosom lover of my lord,
Must needs be like my lord. If it be so,
How little is the cost I have bestowed
In purchasing the semblance of my soul   20
From out the state of hellish cruelty!
This comes too near the praising of myself;
Therefore no more of it. Hear other things:
Lorenzo, I commit into your hands
The husbandry and manage of my house   25
Until my lord's return. For mine own part,
I have toward heaven breathed a secret vow
To live in prayer and contemplation,
Only attended by Nerissa here,
Until her husband and my lord's return.
There is a monastery two miles off,
And there we will abide. I do desire you
Not to deny this imposition,   33
The which my love and some necessity
Now lays upon you.

2 conceit understanding   9 Than . . . you than ordinary benevolence
can make you   12 waste spend   14 must be needs must be   15 lineaments physical features   20 the semblance of my soul i.e., Antonio, so
like my Bassanio   25 husbandry and manage care of the household
33 deny this imposition refuse this charge imposed

LORENZO   Madam, with all my heart.
I shall obey you in all fair commands.

PORTIA
My people do already know my mind,
And will acknowledge you and Jessica
In place of Lord Bassanio and myself.
So fare you well till we shall meet again.

LORENZO
Fair thoughts and happy hours attend on you!

JESSICA
I wish your ladyship all heart's content.

PORTIA
I thank you for your wish and am well pleased
To wish it back on you. Fare you well, Jessica.
                              Exeunt [Jessica and Lorenzo].
Now, Balthasar,
As I have ever found thee honest-true,
So let me find thee still. Take this same letter,
                              [Giving a letter]
And use thou all th' endeavor of a man
In speed to Padua. See thou render this
Into my cousin's hands, Doctor Bellario;
And look what notes and garments he doth give thee,   51
Bring them, I pray thee, with imagined speed   52
Unto the traject, to the common ferry   53
Which trades to Venice. Waste no time in words,   54
But get thee gone. I shall be there before thee.

BALTHASAR
Madam, I go with all convenient speed.   *[Exit.]* 56

PORTIA
Come on, Nerissa, I have work in hand
That you yet know not of. We'll see our husbands
Before they think of us.

NERISSA   Shall they see us?

PORTIA
They shall, Nerissa, but in such a habit   60
That they shall think we are accomplishèd   61

---

51 look what whatever   **52 imagined** imaginable   **53 traject** ferry.
(Italian *traghetto*.)   **54 trades** plies back and forth   **56 convenient** due,
proper   **60 habit** apparel, garb   **61 accomplishèd** supplied

With that we lack. I'll hold thee any wager,   62
When we are both accoutred like young men,
I'll prove the prettier fellow of the two,
And wear my dagger with the braver grace,
And speak between the change of man and boy
With a reed voice, and turn two mincing steps
Into a manly stride, and speak of frays
Like a fine bragging youth, and tell quaint lies,   69
How honorable ladies sought my love,
Which I denying, they fell sick and died—
I could not do withal! Then I'll repent,   72
And wish, for all that, that I had not killed them;
And twenty of these puny lies I'll tell,   74
That men shall swear I have discontinued school   75
Above a twelvemonth. I have within my mind   76
A thousand raw tricks of these bragging Jacks,   77
Which I will practice.
NERISSA   Why, shall we turn to men?   78
PORTIA   Fie, what a question's that,
If thou wert near a lewd interpreter!
But come, I'll tell thee all my whole device
When I am in my coach, which stays for us
At the park gate; and therefore haste away,
For we must measure twenty miles today.   *Exeunt.*

❖

3.5   *Enter [Launcelot the] Clown and Jessica.*

LAUNCELOT   Yes truly, for look you, the sins of the father are to be laid upon the children; therefore, I promise you, I fear you. I was always plain with you, and   3
so now I speak my agitation of the matter. Therefore   4
be o' good cheer, for truly I think you are damned.

62 **that** that which (with a bawdy suggestion)   69 **quaint** elaborate,
clever   72 **do withal** help it   74 **puny** childish   75–76 **I . . . twelvemonth** i.e., that I am no mere schoolboy   76 **Above** more than
77 **Jacks** fellows   78 **turn to** turn into. (But Portia sees the occasion
for a bawdy quibble on the idea of "turning toward, lying next to.")

3.5. Location: Belmont. Outside Portia's house.
3 fear you fear for you   **4 agitation** consideration

There is but one hope in it that can do you any good, and that is but a kind of bastard hope neither.   7

JESSICA   And what hope is that, I pray thee?

LAUNCELOT   Marry, you may partly hope that your father got you not, that you are not the Jew's daughter.   10

JESSICA   That were a kind of bastard hope indeed! So the sins of my mother should be visited upon me.

LAUNCELOT   Truly then I fear you are damned both by father and mother. Thus when I shun Scylla, your father, I fall into Charybdis, your mother. Well, you are   14
gone both ways.   15
                                                                16

JESSICA   I shall be saved by my husband. He hath made   17
me a Christian.

LAUNCELOT   Truly, the more to blame he! We were Christians enough before, e'en as many as could well   20
live one by another. This making of Christians will   21
raise the price of hogs. If we grow all to be pork eaters, we shall not shortly have a rasher on the coals for   23
money.   24

   Enter Lorenzo.

JESSICA   I'll tell my husband, Launcelot, what you say. Here he comes.

LORENZO   I shall grow jealous of you shortly, Launcelot, if you thus get my wife into corners.

JESSICA   Nay, you need not fear us, Lorenzo. Launcelot and I are out. He tells me flatly there's no mercy for me   30
in heaven because I am a Jew's daughter; and he says you are no good member of the commonwealth, for in converting Jews to Christians you raise the price of pork.

LORENZO   I shall answer that better to the commonwealth than you can the getting up of the Negro's belly. The Moor is with child by you, Launcelot.

---

7 neither i.e., to be sure   **10 got** begot   **14, 15 Scylla, Charybdis** twin dangers of the *Odyssey*, 12.255, a monster and a whirlpool guarding the straits presumably between Italy and Sicily   **16 gone** done for   **17 I . . . husband** (Cf. 1 Corinthians 7:14: "the unbelieving wife is sanctified by the husband.")   **20 enough** i.e., there were enough of us   **21 one by another** together   **23 rasher** i.e., of bacon   **23–24 for money** even for ready money, at any price   **30 are out** have fallen out

LAUNCELOT It is much that the Moor should be more 38
than reason; but if she be less than an honest woman, 39
she is indeed more than I took her for.

LORENZO How every fool can play upon the word! I
think the best grace of wit will shortly turn into si- 42
lence, and discourse grow commendable in none only
but parrots. Go in, sirrah, bid them prepare for
dinner.

LAUNCELOT That is done, sir. They have all stomachs. 46

LORENZO Goodly Lord, what a wit-snapper are you!
Then bid them prepare dinner.

LAUNCELOT That is done too, sir, only "cover" is the 49
word.

LORENZO Will you cover then, sir? 51

LAUNCELOT Not so, sir, neither. I know my duty.

LORENZO Yet more quarreling with occasion! Wilt thou 53
show the whole wealth of thy wit in an instant? I pray
thee, understand a plain man in his plain meaning: go
to thy fellows, bid them cover the table, serve in the
meat, and we will come in to dinner. 57

LAUNCELOT For the table, sir, it shall be served in; for 58
the meat, sir, it shall be covered; for your coming in to 59
dinner, sir, why, let it be as humors and conceits shall 60
govern.   *Exit Clown.*

LORENZO

O dear discretion, how his words are suited! 62
The fool hath planted in his memory
An army of good words; and I do know
A many fools, that stand in better place, 65
Garnished like him, that for a tricksy word 66
Defy the matter. How cheer'st thou, Jessica? 67

38–39 more than reason larger than is reasonable (with wordplay on
Moor, more, continued in l. 40) **39 honest** chaste **42 best grace** highest quality **46 stomachs** appetites **49, 51 cover** spread the table for
the meal. (But in his next speech Launcelot uses the word to mean "put
on one's hat.") **53 Yet . . . occasion** i.e., still quibbling at every opportunity **57 meat** food **58 table** (Here Launcelot quibblingly uses the word
to mean the food itself.) **59 covered** (Here used in the sense of providing a cover for each separate dish.) **60 humors and conceits** whims and
fancies **62 discretion** discrimination. **suited** suited to the occasion
65 A many many. **better place** higher social station **66 Garnished** i.e.,
furnished with words. **tricksy** playful **66–67 that . . . matter** who for
the sake of ingenious wordplay do violence to common sense **67 How
cheer'st thou** i.e., what cheer

And now, good sweet, say thy opinion,
How dost thou like the Lord Bassanio's wife?
JESSICA
Past all expressing. It is very meet   70
The Lord Bassanio live an upright life,
For, having such a blessing in his lady,
He finds the joys of heaven here on earth;
And if on earth he do not merit it,
In reason he should never come to heaven.   75
Why, if two gods should play some heavenly match
And on the wager lay two earthly women,   77
And Portia one, there must be something else   78
Pawned with the other, for the poor rude world   79
Hath not her fellow.
LORENZO   Even such a husband
Hast thou of me as she is for a wife.
JESSICA
Nay, but ask my opinion too of that!
LORENZO
I will anon. First let us go to dinner.
JESSICA
Nay, let me praise you while I have a stomach.   84
LORENZO
No, pray thee, let it serve for table talk;
Then, howsoe'er thou speak'st, 'mong other things
I shall digest it.
JESSICA   Well, I'll set you forth.   *Exeunt.*   87

❖

70 **meet** fitting   75 **In reason** it stands to reason. (Jessica jokes that for
Bassanio to receive unmerited bliss on earth—unmerited because no
person can earn bliss through his or her own deserving—is to run the
risk of eternal damnation.)   77 **lay** stake   78 **else** more   79 **Pawned**
staked, wagered   84 **stomach** (1) appetite (2) inclination   87 **digest**
(1) ponder, analyze (2) "swallow," put up with (with a play also on the
gastronomic sense).   **set you forth** (1) serve you up, as at a feast (2) set
forth your praises

4.1 *Enter the Duke, the Magnificoes, Antonio,*
Bassanio, [Salerio,] and Gratiano [with others.
The judges take their places.]

DUKE What, is Antonio here?
ANTONIO Ready, so please Your Grace.
DUKE
I am sorry for thee. Thou art come to answer   3
A stony adversary, an inhuman wretch
Uncapable of pity, void and empty
From any dram of mercy.
ANTONIO   I have heard   6
Your Grace hath ta'en great pains to qualify   7
His rigorous course; but since he stands obdurate
And that no lawful means can carry me
Out of his envy's reach, I do oppose   10
My patience to his fury and am armed
To suffer with a quietness of spirit
The very tyranny and rage of his.   13
DUKE
Go one, and call the Jew into the court.
SALERIO
He is ready at the door; he comes, my lord.

        Enter Shylock.

DUKE
Make room, and let him stand before our face.   16
Shylock, the world thinks, and I think so too,
That thou but leadest this fashion of thy malice   18
To the last hour of act, and then 'tis thought   19
Thou'lt show thy mercy and remorse more strange   20
Than is thy strange apparent cruelty;   21
And where thou now exacts the penalty,
Which is a pound of this poor merchant's flesh,

**4.1. Location: Venice. A court of justice. Benches, etc., are provided for
the justices.**
3 answer defend yourself against. (A legal term.)   **6 dram** 60 grains
apothecaries' weight, a tiny quantity   **7 qualify** moderate   **10 envy's**
malice's   **13 tyranny** cruelty   **16 our** (The royal plural.)   **18 thou . . .
fashion** you only maintain this pretense or form   **19 act** action, performance   **20 remorse** pity. **strange** remarkable   **21 apparent** conspicuous, overt

Thou wilt not only loose the forfeiture,   24
But, touched with human gentleness and love,
Forgive a moiety of the principal,   26
Glancing an eye of pity on his losses
That have of late so huddled on his back—
Enough to press a royal merchant down
And pluck commiseration of his state
From brassy bosoms and rough hearts of flint,   31
From stubborn Turks and Tartars never trained
To offices of tender courtesy.
We all expect a gentle answer, Jew.

SHYLOCK
I have possessed Your Grace of what I purpose,   35
And by our holy Sabbath have I sworn
To have the due and forfeit of my bond.
If you deny it, let the danger light   38
Upon your charter and your city's freedom!   39
You'll ask me why I rather choose to have
A weight of carrion flesh than to receive
Three thousand ducats. I'll not answer that,
But say it is my humor. Is it answered?   43
What if my house be troubled with a rat
And I be pleased to give ten thousand ducats
To have it baned? What, are you answered yet?   46
Some men there are love not a gaping pig,   47
Some that are mad if they behold a cat,
And others, when the bagpipe sings i' the nose,
Cannot contain their urine; for affection,   50
Mistress of passion, sways it to the mood
Of what it likes or loathes. Now, for your answer:
As there is no firm reason to be rendered
Why he cannot abide a gaping pig,   54
Why he a harmless necessary cat,   55
Why he a woolen bagpipe, but of force   56
Must yield to such inevitable shame

---

24 loose release, waive   **26 moiety** part, portion   **31 brassy** unfeeling,
i.e., hard like brass   **35 possessed** informed   **38 danger** injury
39 Upon . . . freedom (See 3.2.278.)   **43 humor** whim   **46 baned** killed,
especially by poison or ratsbane   **47 love** who love.   **gaping pig** pig
roasted whole with its mouth open   **50 affection** feeling, inclination
54, 55, 56 he, he, he one person, another, yet another   **56 woolen** i.e.,
with flannel-covered bag

As to offend, himself being offended;
So can I give no reason, nor I will not,
More than a lodged hate and a certain loathing   60
I bear Antonio, that I follow thus
A losing suit against him. Are you answered?   62

BASSANIO
This is no answer, thou unfeeling man,
To excuse the current of thy cruelty.   64

SHYLOCK
I am not bound to please thee with my answers.

BASSANIO
Do all men kill the things they do not love?

SHYLOCK
Hates any man the thing he would not kill?

BASSANIO
Every offense is not a hate at first.

SHYLOCK
What, wouldst thou have a serpent sting thee twice?

ANTONIO
I pray you, think you question with the Jew.   70
You may as well go stand upon the beach
And bid the main flood bate his usual height;   72
You may as well use question with the wolf   73
Why he hath made the ewe bleat for the lamb;
You may as well forbid the mountain pines
To wag their high tops and to make no noise
When they are fretten with the gusts of heaven;   77
You may as well do anything most hard
As seek to soften that—than which what's harder?—
His Jewish heart. Therefore I do beseech you
Make no more offers, use no farther means,
But with all brief and plain conveniency   82
Let me have judgment, and the Jew his will.

BASSANIO
For thy three thousand ducats here is six.

SHYLOCK
If every ducat in six thousand ducats

60 lodged settled, steadfast.   **certain** unwavering, fixed   **62 losing**
unprofitable   **64 current** flow, tendency   **70 think** bear in mind.
question argue   **72 main flood** sea at high tide.   **bate** abate   **73 use**
question with interrogate   **77 fretten** fretted, i.e., disturbed, ruffled
82 conveniency propriety

Were in six parts, and every part a ducat,
I would not draw them. I would have my bond.   87
DUKE
How shalt thou hope for mercy, rendering none?
SHYLOCK
What judgment shall I dread, doing no wrong?
You have among you many a purchased slave,
Which, like your asses and your dogs and mules,
You use in abject and in slavish parts,   92
Because you bought them. Shall I say to you,
"Let them be free, marry them to your heirs!
Why sweat they under burdens? Let their beds
Be made as soft as yours, and let their palates
Be seasoned with such viands"? You will answer,   97
"The slaves are ours." So do I answer you:
The pound of flesh which I demand of him
Is dearly bought, is mine, and I will have it.
If you deny me, fie upon your law!
There is no force in the decrees of Venice.
I stand for judgment. Answer: shall I have it?
DUKE
Upon my power I may dismiss this court,   104
Unless Bellario, a learnèd doctor,
Whom I have sent for to determine this,
Come here today.
SALERIO   My lord, here stays without   107
A messenger with letters from the doctor,
New come from Padua.
DUKE
Bring us the letters. Call the messenger.
BASSANIO
Good cheer, Antonio! What, man, courage yet!
The Jew shall have my flesh, blood, bones, and all,
Ere thou shalt lose for me one drop of blood.
ANTONIO
I am a tainted wether of the flock,   114
Meetest for death. The weakest kind of fruit   115
Drops earliest to the ground, and so let me.

---

87 draw receive **92 parts** duties, capacities **97 viands** food **104 Upon** in accordance with **107 stays without** waits outside **114 tainted wether** old and diseased ram **115 Meetest** fittest

You cannot better be employed, Bassanio,
Than to live still and write mine epitaph.

Enter Nerissa [dressed like a lawyer's clerk].

DUKE
Came you from Padua, from Bellario?
NERISSA
From both, my lord. Bellario greets Your Grace.
[*She presents a letter. Shylock whets his knife
on his shoe.*]
BASSANIO
Why dost thou whet thy knife so earnestly?
SHYLOCK
To cut the forfeiture from that bankrupt there.
GRATIANO
Not on thy sole, but on thy soul, harsh Jew,
Thou mak'st thy knife keen; but no metal can,
No, not the hangman's ax, bear half the keenness   125
Of thy sharp envy. Can no prayers pierce thee?   126
SHYLOCK
No, none that thou hast wit enough to make.
GRATIANO
O, be thou damned, inexecrable dog!   128
And for thy life let justice be accused.   129
Thou almost mak'st me waver in my faith
To hold opinion with Pythagoras,   131
That souls of animals infuse themselves
Into the trunks of men. Thy currish spirit
Governed a wolf who, hanged for human slaughter,   134
Even from the gallows did his fell soul fleet,   135
And, whilst thou layest in thy unhallowed dam,   136
Infused itself in thee; for thy desires
Are wolvish, bloody, starved, and ravenous.

125 hangman's executioner's.   **keenness** (1) sharpness (2) savagery
126 envy malice   **128 inexecrable** that cannot be overly execrated or
detested   **129 for thy life** i.e., because you are allowed to live
131 Pythagoras ancient Greek philosopher who argued for the transmi-
gration of souls   **134 hanged for human slaughter** (A possible allusion
to the ancient practice of trying and punishing animals for various
crimes.)   **135 fell** fierce, cruel.   **fleet** flit, i.e., pass from the body
136 dam mother (usually used of animals)

SHYLOCK
  Till thou canst rail the seal from off my bond,   139
  Thou but offend'st thy lungs to speak so loud.   140
  Repair thy wit, good youth, or it will fall
  To cureless ruin. I stand here for law.   142
DUKE
  This letter from Bellario doth commend
  A young and learnèd doctor to our court.
  Where is he?
NERISSA   He attendeth here hard by
  To know your answer, whether you'll admit him.
DUKE
  With all my heart. Some three or four of you
  Go give him courteous conduct to this place.
                              [*Exeunt some.*]
  Meantime the court shall hear Bellario's letter.
  [*Reads.*] "Your Grace shall understand that at the   150
  receipt of your letter I am very sick; but in the instant
  that your messenger came, in loving visitation was
  with me a young doctor of Rome. His name is Balthasar. I acquainted him with the cause in controversy
  between the Jew and Antonio the merchant. We
  turned o'er many books together. He is furnished with
  my opinion, which, bettered with his own learning,
  the greatness whereof I cannot enough commend,
  comes with him, at my importunity, to fill up Your   159
  Grace's request in my stead. I beseech you, let his lack
  of years be no impediment to let him lack a reverend   161
  estimation, for I never knew so young a body with so
  old a head. I leave him to your gracious acceptance,
  whose trial shall better publish his commendation."   164

  *Enter Portia for Balthasar [dressed like a doctor
  of laws, escorted].*

  You hear the learned Bellario, what he writes;

139 rail revile, use abusive language   **140 offend'st** injurest   **142 cureless** incurable   **150 [Reads.]** (In many modern editions, the reading of
the letter is assigned to a clerk, but the original text gives no such indication.)   **159 comes with him** i.e., my opinion is brought by him.   **importunity** insistence   **161 to let him lack** such as would deprive him of   **164 trial**
testing, performance.   **publish** make known   **s.d., for** i.e., disguised as

And here, I take it, is the doctor come.
Give me your hand. Come you from old Bellario?

PORTIA
I did, my lord.

DUKE   You are welcome. Take your place.
                     [*Portia takes her place.*]
Are you acquainted with the difference   169
That holds this present question in the court?

PORTIA
I am informèd throughly of the cause.   171
Which is the merchant here, and which the Jew?

DUKE
Antonio and old Shylock, both stand forth.

PORTIA
Is your name Shylock?

SHYLOCK   Shylock is my name.

PORTIA
Of a strange nature is the suit you follow,
Yet in such rule that the Venetian law   176
Cannot impugn you as you do proceed.—   177
You stand within his danger, do you not?   178

ANTONIO
Ay, so he says.

PORTIA   Do you confess the bond?

ANTONIO
I do.

PORTIA   Then must the Jew be merciful.

SHYLOCK
On what compulsion must I? Tell me that.

PORTIA
The quality of mercy is not strained.   182
It droppeth as the gentle rain from heaven
Upon the place beneath. It is twice blest: 184
It blesseth him that gives and him that takes.
'Tis mightiest in the mightiest; it becomes
The thronèd monarch better than his crown.
His scepter shows the force of temporal power,

---

169 difference argument   **171 throughly** thoroughly.   **cause** case
176 rule order   **177 impugn** find fault with   **178 danger** power to do
harm   **182 strained** forced, constrained   **184 is twice blest** grants a
double blessing

The attribute to awe and majesty,   189
Wherein doth sit the dread and fear of kings.
But mercy is above this sceptered sway;
It is enthronèd in the hearts of kings;
It is an attribute to God himself;
And earthly power doth then show likest God's
When mercy seasons justice. Therefore, Jew,
Though justice be thy plea, consider this,
That in the course of justice none of us
Should see salvation. We do pray for mercy,
And that same prayer doth teach us all to render
The deeds of mercy. I have spoke thus much
To mitigate the justice of thy plea,   201
Which if thou follow, this strict court of Venice
Must needs give sentence 'gainst the merchant there.

SHYLOCK
My deeds upon my head! I crave the law,   204
The penalty and forfeit of my bond.

PORTIA
Is he not able to discharge the money?

BASSANIO
Yes, here I tender it for him in the court,
Yea, twice the sum. If that will not suffice,
I will be bound to pay it ten times o'er,
On forfeit of my hands, my head, my heart.
If this will not suffice, it must appear
That malice bears down truth. And I beseech you,   212
Wrest once the law to your authority.   213
To do a great right, do a little wrong,
And curb this cruel devil of his will.

PORTIA
It must not be. There is no power in Venice
Can alter a decree establishèd.
'Twill be recorded for a precedent,
And many an error by the same example
Will rush into the state. It cannot be.

189 **attribute to** symbol of   201 **To . . . plea** i.e., to moderate your plea
for strict justice   204 **My . . . head** i.e., I am prepared to be judged,
as well as live, by a code of strict justice   212 **bears down truth** overwhelms righteousness   213 **Wrest once** for once, forcibly subject

SHYLOCK
    A Daniel come to judgment! Yea, a Daniel!   221
    O wise young judge, how I do honor thee!
PORTIA
    I pray you, let me look upon the bond.
SHYLOCK [*Giving the bond*]
    Here 'tis, most reverend doctor, here it is.
PORTIA
    Shylock, there's thrice thy money offered thee.
SHYLOCK
    An oath, an oath, I have an oath in heaven!
    Shall I lay perjury upon my soul?
    No, not for Venice.   Why, this bond is forfeit,
PORTIA
    And lawfully by this the Jew may claim
    A pound of flesh, to be by him cut off
    Nearest the merchant's heart. Be merciful.
    Take thrice thy money; bid me tear the bond.
SHYLOCK
    When it is paid according to the tenor.   233
    It doth appear you are a worthy judge;
    You know the law, your exposition
    Hath been most sound. I charge you by the law,
    Whereof you are a well-deserving pillar,
    Proceed to judgment. By my soul I swear
    There is no power in the tongue of man
    To alter me. I stay here on my bond.   240
ANTONIO
    Most heartily I do beseech the court
    To give the judgment.   Why then, thus it is:
PORTIA
    You must prepare your bosom for his knife.
SHYLOCK
    O noble judge! O excellent young man!
PORTIA
    For the intent and purpose of the law
    Hath full relation to the penalty   246
    Which here appeareth due upon the bond.

221 **Daniel** (In the apocryphal Book of Susannah, Daniel is the young
judge who rescues Susannah from her false accusers.)   233 **tenor**
conditions   240 **stay here on** remain committed to, insist upon
246 **Hath . . . to** is fully in accord with

SHYLOCK
'Tis very true. O wise and upright judge!
How much more elder art thou than thy looks!

PORTIA
Therefore lay bare your bosom.

SHYLOCK   Ay, his breast;
So says the bond, doth it not, noble judge?
"Nearest his heart," those are the very words.

PORTIA
It is so. Are there balance here   253
To weigh the flesh?

SHYLOCK   I have them ready.

PORTIA
Have by some surgeon, Shylock, on your charge,   255
To stop his wounds, lest he do bleed to death.

SHYLOCK
Is it so nominated in the bond?

PORTIA
It is not so expressed, but what of that?
'Twere good you do so much for charity.

SHYLOCK
I cannot find it; 'tis not in the bond.

PORTIA
You, merchant, have you anything to say?

ANTONIO
But little. I am armed and well prepared.   262
Give me your hand, Bassanio; fare you well!
Grieve not that I am fall'n to this for you,
For herein Fortune shows herself more kind
Than is her custom. It is still her use   266
To let the wretched man outlive his wealth,
To view with hollow eye and wrinkled brow
An age of poverty; from which lingering penance
Of such misery doth she cut me off.
Commend me to your honorable wife.
Tell her the process of Antonio's end.   272
Say how I loved you, speak me fair in death;   273
And, when the tale is told, bid her be judge
Whether Bassanio had not once a love.   275

253 **balance** scales   255 **on your charge** at your personal expense   262 **armed**
ready   266 **still her use** i.e., commonly Fortune's practice   272 **process**
story   273 **speak me fair** speak well of me   275 **a love** a friend's love

Repent but you that you shall lose your friend,   276
And he repents not that he pays your debt.
For if the Jew do cut but deep enough,
I'll pay it instantly with all my heart.

BASSANIO
Antonio, I am married to a wife
Which is as dear to me as life itself;
But life itself, my wife, and all the world
Are not with me esteemed above thy life.
I would lose all, ay, sacrifice them all
Here to this devil, to deliver you.

PORTIA
Your wife would give you little thanks for that,
If she were by to hear you make the offer.   287

GRATIANO
I have a wife who I protest I love;
I would she were in heaven, so she could
Entreat some power to change this currish Jew.

NERISSA
'Tis well you offer it behind her back;
The wish would make else an unquiet house.

SHYLOCK
These be the Christian husbands. I have a daughter;
Would any of the stock of Barabbas   294
Had been her husband rather than a Christian!—
We trifle time. I pray thee, pursue sentence.   296

PORTIA
A pound of that same merchant's flesh is thine.
The court awards it, and the law doth give it.

SHYLOCK   Most rightful judge!

PORTIA
And you must cut this flesh from off his breast.
The law allows it, and the court awards it.

SHYLOCK
Most learnèd judge! A sentence! Come, prepare.

PORTIA
Tarry a little; there is something else.

---

276 Repent but you grieve only   **287 by** nearby   **294 Barabbas** a thief
whom Pontius Pilate set free instead of Christ in response to the people's demand (see Mark 15); also, the villainous protagonist of
Marlowe's *The Jew of Malta*   **296 trifle** waste.   **pursue** proceed with

This bond doth give thee here no jot of blood;
The words expressly are "a pound of flesh."
Take then thy bond, take thou thy pound of flesh;
But in the cutting it if thou dost shed
One drop of Christian blood, thy lands and goods
Are by the laws of Venice confiscate
Unto the state of Venice.

GRATIANO
O upright judge! Mark, Jew. O learnèd judge!

SHYLOCK
Is that the law?

PORTIA   Thyself shalt see the act;
For, as thou urgest justice, be assured
Thou shalt have justice, more than thou desir'st.

GRATIANO
O learnèd judge! Mark, Jew, a learnèd judge!

SHYLOCK
I take this offer, then. Pay the bond thrice
And let the Christian go.

BASSANIO   Here is the money.

PORTIA   Soft!   318
The Jew shall have all justice. Soft, no haste.   319
He shall have nothing but the penalty.

GRATIANO
O Jew! An upright judge, a learnèd judge!

PORTIA
Therefore prepare thee to cut off the flesh.
Shed thou no blood, nor cut thou less nor more
But just a pound of flesh. If thou tak'st more
Or less than a just pound, be it but so much
As makes it light or heavy in the substance   326
Or the division of the twentieth part   327
Of one poor scruple, nay, if the scale do turn   328
But in the estimation of a hair,
Thou diest, and all thy goods are confiscate.

GRATIANO
A second Daniel, a Daniel, Jew!
Now, infidel, I have you on the hip.   332

318 Soft i.e., not so fast   **319 all** nothing but   **326 substance** mass or
gross weight   **327 division** fraction   **328 scruple** 20 grains apothecaries' weight, a small quantity   **332 on the hip** i.e., at a disadvantage (a
phrase from wrestling)

PORTIA
Why doth the Jew pause? Take thy forfeiture.

SHYLOCK
Give me my principal, and let me go.

BASSANIO
I have it ready for thee; here it is.

PORTIA
He hath refused it in the open court.
He shall have merely justice and his bond.

GRATIANO
A Daniel, still say I, a second Daniel!
I thank thee, Jew, for teaching me that word.

SHYLOCK
Shall I not have barely my principal?

PORTIA
Thou shalt have nothing but the forfeiture,
To be so taken at thy peril, Jew.

SHYLOCK
Why, then the devil give him good of it!
I'll stay no longer question.   [*He starts to go.*]

PORTIA   Tarry, Jew!   344
The law hath yet another hold on you.
It is enacted in the laws of Venice,
If it be proved against an alien
That by direct or indirect attempts
He seek the life of any citizen,
The party 'gainst the which he doth contrive
Shall seize one half his goods; the other half
Comes to the privy coffer of the state,   352
And the offender's life lies in the mercy   353
Of the Duke only, 'gainst all other voice.
In which predicament, I say, thou stand'st;
For it appears, by manifest proceeding,
That indirectly and directly too
Thou hast contrived against the very life
Of the defendant; and thou hast incurred
The danger formerly by me rehearsed.   360
Down therefore, and beg mercy of the Duke.

344 I'll . . . question I'll stay no further pursuing of the case **352 privy coffer** private treasury **353 lies in** lies at **360 danger . . . rehearsed** penalty already cited by me

GRATIANO
Beg that thou mayst have leave to hang thyself!
And yet, thy wealth being forfeit to the state,
Thou hast not left the value of a cord;
Therefore thou must be hanged at the state's charge.   365
DUKE
That thou shalt see the difference of our spirit,
I pardon thee thy life before thou ask it.
For half thy wealth, it is Antonio's;   368
The other half comes to the general state,
Which humbleness may drive unto a fine.   370
PORTIA
Ay, for the state, not for Antonio.   371
SHYLOCK
Nay, take my life and all! Pardon not that!
You take my house when you do take the prop
That doth sustain my house. You take my life
When you do take the means whereby I live.
PORTIA
What mercy can you render him, Antonio?
GRATIANO
A halter gratis! Nothing else, for God's sake.   377
ANTONIO
So please my lord the Duke and all the court
To quit the fine for one half of his goods,   379
I am content, so he will let me have   380
The other half in use, to render it,   381
Upon his death, unto the gentleman
That lately stole his daughter.
Two things provided more: that for this favor
He presently become a Christian;   385
The other, that he do record a gift
Here in the court of all he dies possessed   387
Unto his son Lorenzo and his daughter.

365 charge expense   368 For as for   370 Which . . . fine i.e., which
penitence on your part may persuade me to reduce to a fine   371 Ay
. . . Antonio i.e., yes, the state's half may be reduced to a fine, but not
Antonio's half   377 halter hangman's noose   379 quit remit, relinquish,
or perhaps settle for. (That is, Antonio may ask the court to forgive even
the fine imposed in lieu of a heavier penalty.)   380 so provided that
381 in use in trust, or possibly, to be used as a source of income   385 presently at once   387 of . . . possessed i.e., what remains of the portion not
placed under Antonio's trust (which will also go to Lorenzo and Jessica)

DUKE
He shall do this, or else I do recant
The pardon that I late pronouncèd here.

PORTIA
Art thou contented, Jew? What dost thou say?

SHYLOCK
I am content.

PORTIA   Clerk, draw a deed of gift.

SHYLOCK
I pray you, give me leave to go from hence;
I am not well. Send the deed after me,
And I will sign it.

DUKE   Get thee gone, but do it.

GRATIANO
In christening shalt thou have two godfathers.
Had I been judge, thou shouldst have had ten more,   397
To bring thee to the gallows, not to the font.
                              Exit [Shylock].

DUKE
Sir, I entreat you home with me to dinner.

PORTIA
I humbly do desire Your Grace of pardon.
I must away this night toward Padua,
And it is meet I presently set forth.

DUKE
I am sorry that your leisure serves you not.
Antonio, gratify this gentleman,   404
For in my mind you are much bound to him.
                Exeunt Duke and his train.

BASSANIO
Most worthy gentleman, I and my friend
Have by your wisdom been this day acquitted
Of grievous penalties, in lieu whereof,   408
Three thousand ducats due unto the Jew
We freely cope your courteous pains withal.   410
                        [He offers money.]

ANTONIO
And stand indebted over and above
In love and service to you evermore.

397 ten more i.e., to make up a jury of twelve. (Jurors were colloquially
termed *godfathers*.)   **404 gratify** reward   **408 in lieu whereof** in return
for which   **410 cope** requite

PORTIA

He is well paid that is well satisfied,
And I, delivering you, am satisfied
And therein do account myself well paid.
My mind was never yet more mercenary.
I pray you, know me when we meet again.
I wish you well, and so I take my leave.

[*She starts to leave.*]

BASSANIO

Dear sir, of force I must attempt you further.   419
Take some remembrance of us as a tribute,
Not as fee. Grant me two things, I pray you:
Not to deny me, and to pardon me.

PORTIA

You press me far, and therefore I will yield.
Give me your gloves; I'll wear them for your sake.   424
And, for your love, I'll take this ring from you.
Do not draw back your hand; I'll take no more,
And you in love shall not deny me this.

BASSANIO

This ring, good sir? Alas, it is a trifle!
I will not shame myself to give you this.

PORTIA

I will have nothing else but only this;
And now methinks I have a mind to it.

BASSANIO

There's more depends on this than on the value.
The dearest ring in Venice will I give you,   433
And find it out by proclamation.
Only for this, I pray you, pardon me.

PORTIA

I see, sir, you are liberal in offers.   436
You taught me first to beg, and now, methinks,
You teach me how a beggar should be answered.

BASSANIO

Good sir, this ring was given me by my wife,
And when she put it on, she made me vow
That I should neither sell nor give nor lose it.

---

419 attempt urge   **424 gloves** (Perhaps Bassanio removes his gloves,
thereby revealing the ring that "Balthasar" asks of him.)   **433 dearest**
most expensive   **436 liberal** generous

PORTIA
That 'scuse serves many men to save their gifts.
An if your wife be not a madwoman,
And know how well I have deserved this ring,
She would not hold out enemy forever   445
For giving it to me. Well, peace be with you!
                    Exeunt [Portia and Nerissa].

ANTONIO
My lord Bassanio, let him have the ring.
Let his deservings and my love withal
Be valued 'gainst your wife's commandement.   449

BASSANIO
Go, Gratiano, run and overtake him;
Give him the ring, and bring him, if thou canst,
Unto Antonio's house. Away, make haste!
                    Exit Gratiano [with the ring].
Come, you and I will thither presently,
And in the morning early will we both
Fly toward Belmont. Come, Antonio.   *Exeunt.*

❖

4.2   *Enter [Portia and] Nerissa [still disguised].*

PORTIA *[Giving a deed to Nerissa]*
Inquire the Jew's house out; give him this deed   1
And let him sign it. We'll away tonight
And be a day before our husbands home.
This deed will be well welcome to Lorenzo.

        Enter Gratiano.

GRATIANO   Fair sir, you are well o'erta'en.
My lord Bassanio upon more advice   6
Hath sent you here this ring and doth entreat
Your company at dinner.   *[He gives a ring.]*
PORTIA   That cannot be.
His ring I do accept most thankfully,

---

445 would . . . out i.e., would not remain   **449 commandement** (Pronounced in four syllables.)

4.2. Location: Venice. A street.
1 deed i.e., the deed of gift   **6 advice** consideration

And so, I pray you, tell him. Furthermore,
I pray you, show my youth old Shylock's house.
GRATIANO
That will I do.
NERISSA   Sir, I would speak with you.
[*Aside to Portia.*] I'll see if I can get my husband's ring,
Which I did make him swear to keep forever.
PORTIA [*Aside to Nerissa*]
Thou mayst, I warrant. We shall have old swearing   15
That they did give the rings away to men;
But we'll outface them, and outswear them too.—   17
Away, make haste! Thou know'st where I will tarry.
NERISSA
Come, good sir, will you show me to this house?
                    [*Exeunt, Nerissa and Gratiano together,*
                    Portia another way.]

❖

---

15 old plenty of   **17 outface** boldly contradict

5.1 *Enter Lorenzo and Jessica.*

LORENZO
The moon shines bright. In such a night as this,
When the sweet wind did gently kiss the trees
And they did make no noise, in such a night
Troilus methinks mounted the Trojan walls   4
And sighed his soul toward the Grecian tents
Where Cressid lay that night.
JESSICA   In such a night
Did Thisbe fearfully o'ertrip the dew,   7
And saw the lion's shadow ere himself,
And ran dismayed away.
LORENZO   In such a night
Stood Dido with a willow in her hand   10
Upon the wild sea banks, and waft her love   11
To come again to Carthage.
JESSICA   In such a night
Medea gathered the enchanted herbs   13
That did renew old Aeson.
LORENZO   In such a night
Did Jessica steal from the wealthy Jew   15
And with an unthrift love did run from Venice   16
As far as Belmont.
JESSICA   In such a night
Did young Lorenzo swear he loved her well,
Stealing her soul with many vows of faith,
And ne'er a true one.
LORENZO   In such a night
Did pretty Jessica, like a little shrew,
Slander her love, and he forgave it her.

5.1. Location: Belmont. Outside Portia's house.
4 Troilus Trojan prince deserted by his beloved, Cressida, after she had
been transferred to the Greek camp   **7 Thisbe** beloved of Pyramus who,
arranging to meet him by night, was frightened by a lion. (See *A Midsummer Night's Dream*, Act 5.)   **10 Dido** Queen of Carthage, deserted by
Aeneas.   **willow** (A symbol of forsaken love.)   **11 waft** wafted, beck-
oned   **13 Medea** famous sorceress of Colchis who, after falling in love
with Jason and helping him to gain the Golden Fleece, used her magic
to restore youth to Aeson, Jason's father   **15 steal** (1) escape (2) rob
16 unthrift prodigal

JESSICA
    I would out-night you, did nobody come;   23
    But hark, I hear the footing of a man.   24

        Enter [Stephano,] a messenger.

LORENZO
    Who comes so fast in silence of the night?
STEPHANO   A friend.
LORENZO
    A friend? What friend? Your name, I pray you, friend?
STEPHANO
    Stephano is my name, and I bring word
    My mistress will before the break of day
    Be here at Belmont. She doth stray about
    By holy crosses, where she kneels and prays   31
    For happy wedlock hours.
LORENZO   Who comes with her?
STEPHANO
    None but a holy hermit and her maid.
    I pray you, is my master yet returned?
LORENZO
    He is not, nor we have not heard from him.
    But go we in, I pray thee, Jessica,
    And ceremoniously let us prepare
    Some welcome for the mistress of the house.

        Enter [Launcelot, the] Clown.

LAUNCELOT   Sola, sola! Wo ha, ho! Sola, sola!   39
LORENZO   Who calls?
LAUNCELOT   Sola! Did you see Master Lorenzo? Master
    Lorenzo, sola, sola!
LORENZO   Leave holloing, man! Here.
LAUNCELOT   Sola! Where, where?
LORENZO   Here.
LAUNCELOT   Tell him there's a post come from my mas-
    ter, with his horn full of good news: my master will be
    here ere morning.   [*Exit.*]
LORENZO
    Sweet soul, let's in, and there expect their coming.   49

23 **out-night** i.e., outdo in the verbal games we've been playing   24 **footing** footsteps   31 **holy crosses** wayside shrines   39 **Sola** (Imitation of a
posthorn.)   49 **expect** await

And yet no matter. Why should we go in?
My friend Stephano, signify, I pray you,   51
Within the house, your mistress is at hand,
And bring your music forth into the air.
                              [*Exit Stephano.*]
How sweet the moonlight sleeps upon this bank!
Here will we sit and let the sounds of music
Creep in our ears. Soft stillness and the night
Become the touches of sweet harmony.   57
Sit, Jessica. [*They sit.*] Look how the floor of heaven
Is thick inlaid with patens of bright gold.   59
There's not the smallest orb which thou behold'st
But in his motion like an angel sings,
Still choiring to the young-eyed cherubins;   62
Such harmony is in immortal souls,
But whilst this muddy vesture of decay   64
Doth grossly close it in, we cannot hear it.   65

          [*Enter Musicians.*]

Come, ho, and wake Diana with a hymn!   66
With sweetest touches pierce your mistress' ear
And draw her home with music.   *Play music.*
JESSICA
I am never merry when I hear sweet music.
LORENZO
The reason is, your spirits are attentive.   70
For do but note a wild and wanton herd
Or race of youthful and unhandled colts   72
Fetching mad bounds, bellowing and neighing loud,
Which is the hot condition of their blood;
If they but hear perchance a trumpet sound,
Or any air of music touch their ears,
You shall perceive them make a mutual stand,   77
Their savage eyes turned to a modest gaze

---

51 signify make known **57 Become** suit. **touches** notes (produced by
the fingering of an instrument) **59 patens** thin, circular plates of
metal **62 choiring** singing. **young-eyed** eternally clear-sighted
64 muddy . . . decay i.e., mortal flesh **65 close it in** i.e., enclose the
soul. **hear it** i.e., hear the music of the spheres **66 Diana** (Here,
goddess of the moon; cf. 1.2.105.) **70 spirits are attentive** (The spirits
would be in motion within the body in merriment, whereas in sadness
they would be drawn to the heart and, as it were, busy listening.)
72 race herd **77 mutual** common or simultaneous

By the sweet power of music. Therefore the poet   79
Did feign that Orpheus drew trees, stones, and floods,   80
Since naught so stockish, hard, and full of rage   81
But music for the time doth change his nature.
The man that hath no music in himself,
Nor is not moved with concord of sweet sounds,
Is fit for treasons, stratagems, and spoils;   85
The motions of his spirit are dull as night
And his affections dark as Erebus.   87
Let no such man be trusted. Mark the music.

Enter Portia and Nerissa.

PORTIA
That light we see is burning in my hall.
How far that little candle throws his beams!
So shines a good deed in a naughty world.   91
NERISSA
When the moon shone, we did not see the candle.
PORTIA
So doth the greater glory dim the less.
A substitute shines brightly as a king
Until a king be by, and then his state   95
Empties itself, as doth an inland brook
Into the main of waters. Music! Hark!   97
NERISSA
It is your music, madam, of the house.
PORTIA
Nothing is good, I see, without respect.   99
Methinks it sounds much sweeter than by day.
NERISSA
Silence bestows that virtue on it, madam.
PORTIA
The crow doth sing as sweetly as the lark
When neither is attended; and I think   103
The nightingale, if she should sing by day,
When every goose is cackling, would be thought

79 poet possibly Ovid, with whom the story of Orpheus was a favorite
theme   **80 Orpheus** legendary musician.   **drew** attracted, charmed
81 stockish unfeeling   **85 spoils** acts of pillage   **87 Erebus** a place of
primeval darkness on the way to Hades   **91 naughty** wicked   **95 his**
i.e., the substitute's   **97 main of waters** sea   **99 respect** comparison,
context   **103 neither is attended** i.e., either is alone

No better a musician than the wren.
How many things by season seasoned are   107
To their right praise and true perfection!
Peace, ho! The moon sleeps with Endymion   109
And would not be awaked.   [*The music ceases.*]

LORENZO   That is the voice,
Or I am much deceived, of Portia.

PORTIA
He knows me as the blind man knows the cuckoo,
By the bad voice.

LORENZO   Dear lady, welcome home.

PORTIA
We have been praying for our husbands' welfare,
Which speed, we hope, the better for our words.
Are they returned?

LORENZO   Madam, they are not yet;
But there is come a messenger before,
To signify their coming.

PORTIA   Go in, Nerissa.
Give order to my servants that they take
No note at all of our being absent hence;
Nor you, Lorenzo; Jessica, nor you. [*A tucket sounds.*]   121

LORENZO
Your husband is at hand. I hear his trumpet.
We are no telltales, madam, fear you not.

PORTIA
This night methinks is but the daylight sick;
It looks a little paler. 'Tis a day
Such as the day is when the sun is hid.

*Enter Bassanio, Antonio, Gratiano, and their
followers.*

BASSANIO
We should hold day with the Antipodes,   127
If you would walk in absence of the sun.   128

---

107 season favorable occasion   **109 Endymion** a shepherd loved by the
moon goddess, who caused him to sleep a perennial sleep in a cave on
Mount Latmos where she could visit him   **121 s.d. tucket** flourish on a
trumpet   **127–128 We . . . sun** i.e., if you, Portia, like a second sun,
would always walk about during the sun's absence, we should never
have night, but would enjoy daylight even when the Antipodes, those
who dwell on the opposite side of the globe, enjoy daylight

PORTIA

Let me give light, but let me not be light;   129
For a light wife doth make a heavy husband,   130
And never be Bassanio so for me.
But God sort all! You are welcome home, my lord.   132

BASSANIO

I thank you, madam. Give welcome to my friend.
This is the man, this is Antonio,
To whom I am so infinitely bound.

PORTIA

You should in all sense be much bound to him,   136
For, as I hear, he was much bound for you.

ANTONIO

No more than I am well acquitted of.   138

PORTIA

Sir, you are very welcome to our house.
It must appear in other ways than words;
Therefore I scant this breathing courtesy.   141

GRATIANO [To Nerissa]

By yonder moon I swear you do me wrong!
In faith, I gave it to the judge's clerk.
Would he were gelt that had it, for my part,   144
Since you do take it, love, so much at heart.

PORTIA

A quarrel, ho, already? What's the matter?

GRATIANO

About a hoop of gold, a paltry ring
That she did give me, whose posy was   148
For all the world like cutler's poetry
Upon a knife, "Love me, and leave me not."

NERISSA

What talk you of the posy or the value?
You swore to me, when I did give it you,
That you would wear it till your hour of death
And that it should lie with you in your grave.
Though not for me, yet for your vehement oaths,
You should have been respective and have kept it.   156

---

129 be light be wanton, unchaste   **130 heavy** sad   **132 sort** decide,
dispose   **136 in all sense** in every way, with every reason   **138 acquitted of** repaid for   **141 scant . . . courtesy** make brief this empty (i.e.,
merely verbal) courtesy   **144 gelt** gelded.   **for my part** as far as I'm
concerned   **148 posy** a motto on a ring   **156 respective** mindful

Gave it a judge's clerk! No, God's my judge,
The clerk will ne'er wear hair on 's face that had it.
GRATIANO
He will, an if he live to be a man.   159
NERISSA
Ay, if a woman live to be a man.
GRATIANO
Now, by this hand, I gave it to a youth,
A kind of boy, a little scrubbèd boy,   162
No higher than thyself, the judge's clerk,
A prating boy, that begged it as a fee.   164
I could not for my heart deny it him.
PORTIA
You were to blame—I must be plain with you—
To part so slightly with your wife's first gift,
A thing stuck on with oaths upon your finger,
And so riveted with faith unto your flesh.
I gave my love a ring and made him swear
Never to part with it; and here he stands.
I dare be sworn for him he would not leave it,
Nor pluck it from his finger, for the wealth
That the world masters. Now, in faith, Gratiano,   174
You give your wife too unkind a cause of grief.
An 'twere to me, I should be mad at it.   176
BASSANIO [*Aside*]
Why, I were best to cut my left hand off
And swear I lost the ring defending it.
GRATIANO
My lord Bassanio gave his ring away
Unto the judge that begged it and indeed
Deserved it too; and then the boy, his clerk,
That took some pains in writing, he begged mine;
And neither man nor master would take aught   183
But the two rings.
PORTIA   What ring gave you, my lord?
Not that, I hope, which you received of me.
BASSANIO
If I could add a lie unto a fault,
I would deny it; but you see my finger

159 an if if   **162 scrubbèd** stunted   **164 prating** chattering
174 masters owns   **176 An** if.   **mad** beside myself   **183 aught** anything

Hath not the ring upon it. It is gone.

PORTIA
Even so void is your false heart of truth.
By heaven, I will ne'er come in your bed
Until I see the ring!

NERISSA   Nor I in yours
Till I again see mine.

BASSANIO   Sweet Portia,
If you did know to whom I gave the ring,
If you did know for whom I gave the ring,
And would conceive for what I gave the ring,
And how unwillingly I left the ring,
When naught would be accepted but the ring,
You would abate the strength of your displeasure.

PORTIA
If you had known the virtue of the ring,   199
Or half her worthiness that gave the ring,
Or your own honor to contain the ring,   201
You would not then have parted with the ring.
What man is there so much unreasonable,
If you had pleased to have defended it
With any terms of zeal, wanted the modesty   205
To urge the thing held as a ceremony?   206
Nerissa teaches me what to believe:
I'll die for 't but some woman had the ring.

BASSANIO
No, by my honor, madam! By my soul,
No woman had it, but a civil doctor,   210
Which did refuse three thousand ducats of me
And begged the ring, the which I did deny him
And suffered him to go displeased away—
Even he that had held up the very life
Of my dear friend. What should I say, sweet lady?
I was enforced to send it after him.
I was beset with shame and courtesy.
My honor would not let ingratitude
So much besmear it. Pardon me, good lady!
For by these blessèd candles of the night,   220

199 virtue power   **201 contain** retain   **205 wanted the modesty** who
would have been so lacking in consideration as   **206 urge** insist upon
receiving.   **ceremony** something sacred   **210 civil doctor** i.e., doctor of
civil law   **220 blessèd . . . night** i.e., stars

Had you been there, I think you would have begged
The ring of me to give the worthy doctor.

PORTIA
Let not that doctor e'er come near my house.
Since he hath got the jewel that I loved,
And that which you did swear to keep for me,
I will become as liberal as you: 226
I'll not deny him anything I have,
No, not my body nor my husband's bed.
Know him I shall, I am well sure of it.
Lie not a night from home. Watch me like Argus;   230
If you do not, if I be left alone,
Now, by mine honor, which is yet mine own,
I'll have that doctor for my bedfellow.

NERISSA
And I his clerk; therefore be well advised
How you do leave me to mine own protection.

GRATIANO
Well, do you so. Let not me take him, then!   236
For if I do, I'll mar the young clerk's pen.   237

ANTONIO
I am th' unhappy subject of these quarrels.

PORTIA
Sir, grieve not you; you are welcome notwithstanding.

BASSANIO
Portia, forgive me this enforcèd wrong,
And in the hearing of these many friends
I swear to thee, even by thine own fair eyes
Wherein I see myself—

PORTIA   Mark you but that!
In both my eyes he doubly sees himself;
In each eye, one. Swear by your double self,   245
And there's an oath of credit.

BASSANIO   Nay, but hear me.   246
Pardon this fault, and by my soul I swear
I never more will break an oath with thee.

ANTONIO
I once did lend my body for his wealth,   249

226 **liberal** generous (sexually as well as otherwise)   230 **from** away
from.   **Argus** mythological monster with a hundred eyes   236 **take**
apprehend   237 **pen** (with sexual double meaning)   245 **double** i.e.,
deceitful   246 **of credit** worthy to be believed   249 **wealth** welfare

Which, but for him that had your husband's ring,
Had quite miscarried. I dare be bound again,
My soul upon the forfeit, that your lord
Will never more break faith advisedly.   253

PORTIA
Then you shall be his surety. Give him this,   254
And bid him keep it better than the other.
                    [*She gives the ring to Antonio, who*
                              gives it to Bassanio.]

ANTONIO
Here, Lord Bassanio. Swear to keep this ring.

BASSANIO
By heaven, it is the same I gave the doctor!

PORTIA
I had it of him. Pardon me, Bassanio,
For by this ring the doctor lay with me.

NERISSA
And pardon me, my gentle Gratiano,
For that same scrubbèd boy, the doctor's clerk,
In lieu of this last night did lie with me.   262
                    [*Presenting her ring.*]

GRATIANO
Why, this is like the mending of highways
In summer, where the ways are fair enough.   264
What, are we cuckolds ere we have deserved it?   265

PORTIA
Speak not so grossly. You are all amazed.   266
Here is a letter; read it at your leisure.[*She gives a letter.*]
It comes from Padua, from Bellario.
There you shall find that Portia was the doctor,
Nerissa there her clerk. Lorenzo here
Shall witness I set forth as soon as you,
And even but now returned; I have not yet
Entered my house. Antonio, you are welcome,
And I have better news in store for you
Than you expect. Unseal this letter soon.
                    [*She gives him a letter.*]
There you shall find three of your argosies

253 **advisedly** intentionally 254 **surety** guarantor 262 **In lieu of** in
return for 264 **In . . . enough** i.e., before repair is necessary
265 **cuckolds** husbands whose wives are unfaithful 266 **grossly** stu-
pidly, licentiously. **amazed** bewildered

Are richly come to harbor suddenly.
You shall not know by what strange accident
I chancèd on this letter.

ANTONIO   I am dumb.

BASSANIO
Were you the doctor and I knew you not?

GRATIANO
Were you the clerk that is to make me cuckold?

NERISSA
Ay, but the clerk that never means to do it,
Unless he live until he be a man.

BASSANIO
Sweet doctor, you shall be my bedfellow.
When I am absent, then lie with my wife.

ANTONIO
Sweet lady, you have given me life and living;
For here I read for certain that my ships
Are safely come to road.

PORTIA   How now, Lorenzo?   288
My clerk hath some good comforts too for you.

NERISSA
Ay, and I'll give them him without a fee.
                              [*She gives a deed.*]
There do I give to you and Jessica,
From the rich Jew, a special deed of gift,
After his death, of all he dies possessed of.

LORENZO
Fair ladies, you drop manna in the way   294
Of starvèd people.

PORTIA   It is almost morning,
And yet I am sure you are not satisfied
Of these events at full. Let us go in;
And charge us there upon inter'gatories,   298
And we will answer all things faithfully.

GRATIANO
Let it be so. The first inter'gatory
That my Nerissa shall be sworn on is,

288 road anchorage **294 manna** the food miraculously supplied to the
Israelites in the wilderness (Exodus 16) **298 charge . . . inter'gatories**
require ourselves to answer all things under oath

Whether till the next night she had rather stay   302
Or go to bed now, being two hours to day.
But were the day come, I should wish it dark
Till I were couching with the doctor's clerk.
Well, while I live I'll fear no other thing
So sore as keeping safe Nerissa's ring.   *Exeunt.* 307

302 stay wait   **307 ring** (with sexual suggestion)

Date and Text

The Stationers' Register, the official record book of the London Company of Stationers (booksellers and printers), for July 22, 1598, contains an entry on behalf of the printer James Roberts for "a booke of the Marchaunt of Venyce, or otherwise called the Jewe of Venyce, Prouided, that yt bee not prynted by the said James Robertes or anye other whatsoeuer without lycence first had from the Right honorable the lord Chamberlen." Roberts evidently enjoyed a close connection with the Chamberlain's men (Shakespeare's acting company) and seemingly was granted the special favor of registering the play at this time even though the company did not wish to see the play published until later. In 1600, at any rate, Roberts transferred his rights as publisher to Thomas Heyes and printed the volume for him with the following title:

> The most excellent Historie of the *Merchant of Venice*. VVith the extreame crueltie of *Shylocke* the Iewe towards the sayd Merchant, in cutting a iust pound of his flesh: and the obtayning of *Portia* by the choyse of three chests. *As it hath beene diuers times acted by the Lord Chamberlaine his Seruants*. Written by William Shakespeare. AT LONDON, Printed by *I. R.* [James Roberts] for Thomas Heyes, and are to be sold in Paules Church-yard, at the signe of the Greene Dragon. 1600.

The text of this 1600 quarto is generally a good one, based seemingly on the author's papers. It served as copy for the second quarto of 1619 (printed by William Jaggard for Thomas Pavier, and fraudulently dated 1600) and for the First Folio of 1623. The Folio stage directions may represent some authoritative consultation of a theatrical document.

Francis Meres mentions the play in 1598 in his *Palladis Tamia: Wit's Treasury* (a slender volume on contemporary literature and art; valuable because it lists most of Shakespeare's plays that existed at that time). Establishing an earlier limit for dating has proven not so easy. Many scholars have urged a connection with the Roderigo Lopez affair of 1594 (see the Introduction to the play). The supposed allusion to Lopez in the lines about "a wolf, who, hanged for human slaughter" (4.1.134) may simply indicate, however, that wolves were actually hanged for attacking men in Shakespeare's day (as dogs were for killing sheep). Besides, the Lopez case remained so notorious throughout the 1590s that even a proven allusion to it in *The Merchant* would not limit the play to 1594 or 1595. Christopher Marlowe's play *The Jew of Malta* was revived in 1594 to exploit anti-Lopez sentiment but was also revived in 1596. There may, on the other hand, be an allusion in 1.1.27 to the *St. Andrew,* a Spanish ship captured at Cadiz in 1596. Any date between 1594 and early 1598 is possible, though the latter half of this period is more likely.

Textual Notes

These textual notes are not a historical collation, either of the early quartos and the early folios or of more recent editions; they are simply a record of departures in this edition from the copy text. The reading adopted in this edition appears in boldface, followed by the rejected reading from the copy text, i.e., the quarto of 1600. Only major alterations in punctuation are noted. Changes in lineation are not indicated, nor are some minor and obvious typographical errors.

Abbreviations used:
Q quarto
s.d. stage direction
s.p. speech prefix

Copy text: the first quarto of 1600 [Q1].

1.1. s.d. [and elsewhere] Salerio, and Solanio Salaryno, and Salanio **19 Peering** Piring **27 docked** docks **85 jaundice** Iaundies **112 tongue** togue **113 Is** It is **128 off** of **151 back** bake

1.2. 44 Palatine Palentine [and at ll. 57–58] **53 Bon** Boune **58 throstle** Trassell **119 s.d. Enter a Servingman** [after l. 120 in Q1]

1.3. 28 s.p. [and elsewhere] Shylock Jew **76 compromised** compremyzd **110 spit** spet [also at ll. 124 and 129]

2.1. s.d. Morocco Morochus **25 Sophy . . . prince,** Sophy, and a Persian Prince **31 thee** the **35 page** rage

2.2. 1 s.p. [and elsewhere] Launcelot Clowne **3 [and elsewhere in this scene] Gobbo** Iobbe **42 By** Be **76 murder** muder **94 last** lost **165 s.d. Exit Leonardo** [after l. 164 in Q1] **168 a suit** sute

2.3. 11 did doe

2.4. 39 s.d. Exeunt Exit

2.6. 26 Who's whose [also at l. 61] **35 night, you** night you **59 gentlemen** gentleman

2.7. 18 threatens. Men threatens men **45 Spits** Spets **69 tombs** timber

2.8. 8 gondola Gondylo **39 Slubber** slumber

2.9. 64 judgment iudement

3.1. 21 s.d. Enter Shylock [after l. 22 in Q1] **70 s.p. Man** [not in Q1] **74 s.d.** [Q1 repeats the s.d. "Enter Tuball"] **100 Heard** heere **114 turquoise** Turkies

3.2. 61 live. With liue with **67 eyes** eye **81 vice** voyce **84 stairs** stayers **199 loved; for intermission** lou'd for intermission, **204 roof** rough **315 s.p. Bassanio** [not in Q1]

3.3 s.d. Solanio Salerio **24 s.p. Solanio** Sal

3.4. 49 Padua Mantua **50 cousin's** cosin **53 traject** Tranect **80 near** nere **81 my** my my

3.5. 20 e'en in **26 comes** come **74 merit it** meane it, it **81 a wife** wife **87 s.d. Exeunt** Exit

4.1. 30 his state this states **31 flint** flints **35 s.p. [and elsewhere in this scene] Shylock** Jew **50 urine; for affection,** vrine for affection. **51 Mistress** Maisters **73 You may as well** well **74 Why he hath made the** the **bleat** bleake **75 pines** of Pines **100 is** as **113 lose** loose **136 whilst** whilest **228 No, not** Not not **270 off** of **322 off** of **396 s.p. Gratiano** Shy **405 s.d. Exeunt** Exit

5.1. 26 s.p. Stephano Messen [also at ll. 28 and 33] **41 Lorenzo** Lorenzo, **& 49 Sweet soul** [assigned in Q1 to Launcelot] **51 Stephano** Stephen **87 Erebus** Terebus **109 ho** how **152 give it** giue **233 my** mine

Shakespeare's Sources

Shakespeare's probable chief source for *The Merchant of Venice* was the first story of the fourth day of *Il Pecorone* (The Dunce), by Ser Giovanni Fiorentino. This collection of tales dates from the late fourteenth century but was first published in 1558 at Milan and was not published in English translation in Shakespeare's time. If Shakespeare was unable to read it in Italian, he may conceivably have consulted a translation in some now-lost manuscript; such translations did sometimes circulate. Behind Ser Giovanni's story lies an old tradition of a bond given for human flesh, as found in Persia, India, and the Twelve Tables of Roman Law. This legend first appears in English in the thirteenth-century *Cursor Mundi* (a long verse history of the world from creation to doomsday), with a Jew as the creditor. A thirteenth-century version of the *Gesta Romanorum* (a popular collection of stories in Latin) adds a romantic love plot; the evil moneylender in this story is not Jewish. The hero pawns his own flesh to a merchant in order to win a lady. He succeeds on his third attempt, having learned to avoid a magic spell that had previously put him to sleep and cost him a large number of florins. When he goes to pay his forfeit, the lady follows him disguised as a knight and foils the evil merchant by pointing out a quibbling distinction between flesh and blood.

Il Pecorone, presented here in a new and complete translation, provided Shakespeare with a number of essential elements, although not all that he included in his play. Ser Giovanni's story tells of Giannetto, the adventurous youngest son of a Florentine merchant, who goes to live with his father's dearest friend, Ansaldo, in Venice. This worthy merchant gives him money to seek his fortune at sea. Unbeknownst to Ansaldo, Giannetto twice risks everything to woo the lady of Belmont: if he can succeed in sleeping with her, he will win her and her country, but if he fails, he loses all his wealth. Twice Giannetto is given a sleeping medicine in his wine and has to forfeit everything. Returning destitute to Venice twice, he is reunited each time with Ansaldo and given the means to seek his fortune again. For the third such voyage, however, Ansaldo is driven to borrow ten thousand florins from a Jew, using the forfeiture of a pound of flesh as a guarantee. This time, one of the lady's maids warns Giannetto not to drink his wine, and he finally possesses the lady as his wife. Sometime later, remembering that the day of Ansaldo's forfeiture has arrived, Giannetto explains the predicament to his wife and is sent by her to Venice with a hundred thousand florins, but he arrives after the forfeiture has fallen due. The lady, however, following after him in the disguise of a doctor of laws, decrees that the Jew may have no blood and must take no more or no less than one pound of flesh. The Jew is jeered at and receives no money. The "doctor of laws" refuses any payment other than the ring Giannetto was given by his lady. Yielding it up unwillingly, he returns to Belmont, where his lady vexes him about the ring but finally relents and tells him all. Shakespeare could thus have found in one source the wooing, the borrowing from a Jewish moneylender, the pound of flesh, the trial, and the business of the rings. The story provides no casket episode, courtship of Nerissa by Gratiano, elopement of Jessica, or clowning of Launcelot Gobbo. The Jew's motive is not prompted by the way he has been treated.

Shakespeare may also have known "The Ballad of Gernutus," a popular English work that seems to be older than the play. It has no love plot but dwells on the unnatural cruelty of a Jewish Venetian usurer who takes a bond of flesh for "a merry jest." Anthony Munday's prose *Zelauto* (1580), though its villain is a Christian rather than a Jewish moneylender, also features a bond of this sort, taken purportedly as a mere sport but with hidden malice. Truculento, the villain, takes the bond of two young men, Rodolfo and his friend Strabino, as surety for a loan. If they forfeit the loan, the young men are to lose their lands and their right eyes as well. The villain has a daughter, Brisana, whom he permits to marry Rodolfo since Truculento expects to marry Rodolfo's sister Cornelia himself. When Cornelia instead marries Strabino, Truculento angrily takes the young men to court to demand his bond. The two brides disguise themselves as scholars and go to court, where they appeal for mercy and then foil Truculento by means of the legal quibble about blood.

Another possible source for the courtroom scene is *The Orator*, translated into English in 1596 from the French of Alexandre Sylvain. An oration, entitled "Of a Jew, who would for his debt have a pound of the flesh of a Christian," uses many specious arguments also employed by Shylock, and is forthrightly confuted in "The Christian's Answer."

Shylock's relationship to his daughter finds obvious earlier parallels in *Zelauto* and in Christopher Marlowe's play *The Jew of Malta* (c. 1589), in which Barabas's daughter Abigail loves a Christian and ultimately renounces her faith. The actual elopement, however, is closer to the fourteenth story in Masuccio of Salerno's fifteenth-century *Il Novellino* (not published in English translation in Shakespeare's day).

The casket-choosing episode, not found in *Il Pecorone*, was a widespread legend, occurring for example in the story of *Barlaam and Josophat* (ninth-century Greek, translated into Latin by the thirteenth century), in Vincent of Beauvais's *Speculum Historiale*, in the *Legenda Aurea*, in Giovanni Boccaccio's *Decameron* (Day 10, Story 1), in John Gower's *Confessio Amantis*, and—closest to Shakespeare— in the *Gesta Romanorum* (translated into English in 1577 by Richard Robinson and "bettered" by him in 1595). In this last account, the choice is between a gold, silver, and lead casket, each with its own inscription. The first two inscriptions are like Shakespeare's; the third reads, "They that choose me, shall find [in] me that God hath disposed." The chooser, however, is a maiden, and she is not preceded by other contestants.

An old play called *The Jew* is referred to by Stephen Gosson in 1579 as containing "the greediness of worldly choosers, and bloody minds of usurers." Scholars have speculated that this was a source play for Shakespeare, but actually we have too little to go on to make a reliable judgment. Gosson was surely not referring to Robert Wilson's *The Three Ladies of London* (c. 1581) in any case, even though it is sometimes suggested as an analogue to *The Merchant of Venice*, for its Jewish figure named Gerontus (compare Gernutus in the ballad) is an exemplary person. Besides, the probable date of this play is later than Gosson's remark.

Il Pecorone
By Ser Giovanni Fiorentino
Translated by David Bevington and Kate Bevington

FOURTH DAY, FIRST STORY: GIANNETTO
AND THE LADY OF BELMONT

There once was in Florence, in the house of the Scali, a merchant named Bindo, who had been to Tana and to Alexandria many times, and on all the usual long voyages that are made for the sake of merchandise. This Bindo was very rich, and he had three strapping sons. As he was approaching death, he summoned the eldest and the middle son and, in their presence, made his last will and testament, designating the two of them heirs of all he had in the world, and making no mention of his youngest son.

When he had made his will, his youngest son, named Giannetto, hearing of this, went to him in his bed and said, "Father, I am much amazed at what you have done, not to have remembered me in your will."

"Giannetto," his father answered, "there is no creature in the world whom I hold dearer than you. And for that reason I do not want you to stay here after my death, but wish instead that you go to Venice when I am dead, to your godfather, Signor Ansaldo, who has no son of his own and who has many times written me to send you to him. I can tell you that he is the richest merchant today in all Christendom. So I want you, when I am dead, to go to him and take this letter; if you behave wisely, you will become a rich man."

"Father," the young man said, "I am ready to do what you command me."

Then the father gave him his blessing, and a few days later he died. All the sons lamented bitterly and gave to the body the ceremonies that were its due.

A few days later the two brothers summoned Giannetto and said, "Brother, it is true that our father made his will and left us his heirs, and did not mention you; nonetheless, you are our brother, and whatever we have is also yours as long as it lasts."

"Brothers," answered Giannetto, "I thank you for your

offer, but, as for me, I intend to seek my fortune elsewhere. My mind is made up on this, so let the inheritance be yours by right of law and with our father's blessing."

The brothers, seeing that his mind was made up, gave him a horse and money for expenses. Giannetto took leave of them and went to Venice, and, arriving at the counting-house of Signor Ansaldo, presented him with the letter his father had given him before his death. Signor Ansaldo, as he read the letter, realized that this was the son of his dearest friend, Bindo; and when he had finished the letter, he at once embraced the young man, saying, "Welcome, my son, whom I have so much desired to see." And immediately he asked about Bindo, to which Giannetto replied that he was dead. With many tears Signor Ansaldo embraced and kissed Giannetto, and said, "I am very grieved at the death of Bindo, for it was he who helped me earn a great part of what I have; but the happiness that I have in seeing you is so great that it takes away some of my sorrow." And he had him conducted to his house, and told his clerks and attendants and servants and grooms and whoever else belonged to the household that Giannetto was to be obeyed and served more than his own self. He consigned to him the keys to all his ready money and said, "My son, whatever there is is yours; spend it on clothes today as you please; keep a table for the important people of the city, and become known. For I leave this thought with you: The more you win others' good will, the more I will love you."

And so Giannetto began to enter into Venetian society, to dine out and give dinner parties, to make gifts, to keep liveried servants, to buy fine horses, and to take part in jousts and tournaments, for he was expert and well versed in such matters and magnanimous and gracious in all things, knowing well how to show respect and courtesy as was fitting; and always he honored Signor Ansaldo more than if he had been a hundred times his father. So sensible was his behavior toward persons of all conditions that virtually everyone in Venice liked him, seeing him to be so wise and pleasing in manner and courteous beyond measure. Women and men alike were quite taken with him, and Signor Ansaldo had eyes for no one but him, so pleasing were his behavior and his manners. Scarcely a party went by to which Giannetto was not invited, so well was he liked by one and all.

Now, it happened that two dear friends of his planned to make a voyage to Alexandria with their two ships and their merchandise, as they did each year. They spoke of this to Giannetto and asked if he wished to enjoy himself by going with them to see the world, especially Damascus and the region where it lies.

"In good faith," answered Giannetto, "I would very much like to go, if my father Signor Ansaldo gives me his permission."

"We'll see to it that he does," they said, "and that he will be content."

And so right away they went to Signor Ansaldo and said, "We want to ask you please to give your permission for Giannetto to go next spring with us to Alexandria, and to furnish him with some kind of ship so that he can see a little of the world."

"I am content," said Signor Ansaldo, "if he wants to."

"Sir," said they, "he does."

So Signor Ansaldo at once had him furnished with a splendid ship and arranged for it to be loaded with a great deal of merchandise and decked out with flags and provided with whatever arms were needed. And when all was ready, Signor Ansaldo ordered the captain and those others who served on board that they were to do what Giannetto commanded them and that his safety was in their hands. "For," said Signor Ansaldo, "I am not sending him out for any profits that I want him to make, but rather for him to enjoy himself and see something of the world."

When Giannetto was about to leave, all Venice gathered to see, for not in a long while had so magnificent and well equipped a vessel sailed from Venice. Everyone was sorry at his departure. He took leave of Signor Ansaldo and of all his friends, then put out to sea, hoisted sail, and set his course for Alexandria in the name of God and good fortune.

As the three friends in their three ships were sailing along day after day, early one morning, before it was broad daylight, Giannetto looked out and saw a most splendid harbor in a gulf of the sea, and asked the captain what it was called.

"Sir," the captain answered, "that harbor belongs to a widowed lady, one who has meant trouble for a lot of gentlemen."

"How?" said Giannetto.

"Sir," said the other, "the truth is that she is a beautiful woman, and enchanting too, and she has established this law: Whatever man arrives there must sleep with her, and if he succeeds in enjoying her, he is to take her as his wife and be lord of the whole country, but if he does not succeed in enjoying her, he loses everything that he has in the world."

Giannetto thought about that for a bit, and then said, "Devise any means you can to bring me into that harbor."

"Sir," the captain said, "take care what you say, for many gentlemen have gone there only to lose all their goods and their lives in the bargain."

"Don't interfere," said Giannetto. "Do what I tell you."

And so it was done. Quickly they changed the ship's course and brought her to berth in that harbor, without his friends in the other ships seeing a thing. Now, when morning came, the news spread that this splendid ship had arrived in the harbor; everybody gathered to see it, and the news was brought to the lady, who sent for Giannetto. He went to her at once, and greeted her with great respect. She took him by the hand and asked who he was and where he was from, and if he knew the custom of the country.

Giannetto replied that he did, and that he had come for no other reason.

"You are a hundred times welcome," she said.

She paid him great honor all that day, and had many barons, counts, and knights who were her subjects invited to attend on him. The manners of this young man delighted all the barons, so well educated was he, so pleasing of person, and so well spoken, and nearly everybody was taken with him. All that day there was dancing and singing and festivity at the court as an expression of affection for him, and everyone would have been well content to have him as lord.

Now, as evening approached, the lady took him by the hand and led him into her room, and said, "It seems to me that it's time to go to bed."

"My lady," said Giannetto, "I am at your service."

Immediately two damsels came into the room, one with wine and the other with sweetmeats.

"You must be thirsty," said the lady. "Have something to drink."

Giannetto took some of the sweetmeats and drank some

wine, which had been drugged to make him sleep, though he didn't know this, and so he drank half a glass, since it seemed good to him. Immediately he undressed and went to lie down. And as soon as he reached the bed, he fell sound asleep. The lady lay down at his side, but he was out for the rest of the night, until nine o'clock. The lady, as soon as it was day, arose and gave orders to unload the ship, and found it full of rich and worthy merchandise. When it was nine o'clock, the lady's maidservants went to the bed, roused Giannetto, and told him to begone with God's blessing, for he had lost his ship and all that was in it. He was ashamed and realized he had done badly. The lady gave him money for expenses and a horse, which he mounted, and, sad and gloomy, he made his way toward Venice. Arriving there, he was too ashamed to want to go home to Signor Ansaldo, and so by night he went to the house of a friend.

This friend marveled at him and said, "Giannetto, what happened?"

"My ship struck a rock one night," he answered, "and split apart and scattered every which way. I lashed myself to a timber that cast me ashore, and so I have come home on dry land, and here I am."

He remained several days hidden in the house of his friend.

One day this friend paid a visit to Signor Ansaldo and found him very melancholy. "What's wrong," he said, "that you are so downhearted?"

"I'm greatly afraid," said Signor Ansaldo, "that my son is dead, or that the sea has brought him misfortune. I can find no peace of mind or happiness until I see him again, so great is the love I bear him."

"Sir," said the young man, "I can tell you news of him, which is that he was shipwrecked and lost everything, but saved himself."

"Praised be God!" said Signor Ansaldo. "If he is saved, I am happy. As to what he lost, I don't care at all." And immediately he got up and went off to see Giannetto. And when he saw him, immediately he ran to embrace him, and said, "My son, there is no need for you to be ashamed as far as I am concerned. Shipwrecks happen all the time. So, my son, don't be downcast. As long as no harm has come to you, I am happy." And he led him home, comforting him all the while. The news spread through all Venice, and everyone felt sorry for the loss that Giannetto had suffered.

Now, it happened that a short time later the two friends of Giannetto came back from Alexandria, very wealthy. And when they arrived, they inquired after Giannetto and were told the whole business. At once they ran to greet him, saying, "How did you get separated, or where did you go, that we were unable to get any news of you? We doubled back on our track all day long, but could never see you or find out where you had gone. And we were so sorry about this that all our journey we could not succeed in cheering ourselves up, thinking you were dead."

"A wind came up in a gulf of the sea," Giannetto answered, "and drove my ship against a rock close to the shore. I hardly was able to save myself, and everything was scattered."

Such was the excuse that Giannetto gave in order not to reveal his error. Together they made a great feast, thanking God that he had been saved, saying, "Next spring, God willing, we will make enough profit to recover what you have lost this time, but now let's give ourselves a good time without any gloominess." And so they devoted themselves to pleasure and enjoyment, as they used to do.

But Giannetto did nothing but think about how he might return to that lady, dreaming of this and saying to himself, "Certainly I must have her for my wife, or I will die," and for the most part he could not be merry.

Signor Ansaldo said to him many times, "My son, don't give yourself up to melancholy. We have goods enough to live very well."

"My lord," answered Giannetto, "I can never be content unless I make that journey again."

Seeing that his mind was made up, Signor Ansaldo, when it was time, fitted out another ship for him with much more merchandise and of better value than before. And he began so early that, when the time finally came, the ship was well furnished and adorned. He gave for it the greater part of all that he had in the world. The friends, when they had fitted out their ships with what they needed, put out to sea, hoisted sail, and set forth on their voyage.

They sailed along for several days, and Giannetto constantly kept a lookout, to see once more the harbor of that lady, which was called the Harbor of the Lady of Belmont. Arriving one night at the mouth of the harbor, which was in a gulf of the sea, Giannetto recognized it at once, had the sails and the rudder brought about, and berthed within the harbor.

The lady, when she arose in the morning, looked down to the harbor and saw the flags of that ship flying. At once she recognized it, and summoned a maidservant and said, "Do you recognize those flags?"

"My lady," said the maidservant, "it seems to me they are the insignia of the young man who arrived here a year ago and who brought such an abundance of riches with his merchandise."

"Certainly what you say is true," said the lady, "and truly this is no ordinary matter; truly he must be in love with me, for I never saw anyone come back a second time."

"I never saw a more courteous and graceful man than he," said the maidservant.

The lady sent many damsels and squires for him, who greeted him with great festivity; and he treated all of them with cheerfulness and joy. And so he came into the presence of the lady. When she saw him, she embraced him with joy and delight, and he embraced her with reverential courtesy. They passed all that day in revelry and pleasure, for the lady sent invitations to many barons and ladies, who came to her court to celebrate in Giannetto's honor. Almost all the barons were full of regret and gladly would have had him for their lord, because of his amiability and liberality, and almost all the ladies were in love with him, seeing with what skill he led the dancing and that he held his countenance always cheerful, so that everyone believed him to be the son of some great nobleman.

When it came time for sleep, the lady took Giannetto by the hand and said, "Let us go and lie down." They went to her room and sat down, and behold, two damsels came with wine and sweetmeats, and the couple drank and ate, and then they went to bed. And as soon as Giannetto was in bed, he fell sound asleep. The lady undressed and lay down beside him, and—to be brief—he was out for the whole night. And when morning came, the lady arose and immediately ordered the unloading of the ship. When it was nine o'clock,

Giannetto came to his senses and looked about for the lady but could not find her. He lifted up his head and saw that it was broad daylight, and so got up and began to feel ashamed. He was given a horse and money for expenses and quickly departed, sad and gloomy, and he did not rest until he was at Venice. By night he went to the house of his friend, who, on seeing him, was the most astonished person in the world, saying, "What happened?"

"Things are bad with me," said Giannetto. "Accursed be the fortune that ever brought me to this country!"

"Certainly you have reason to curse your fortune," said his friend, "for you have ruined Signor Ansaldo, who was the greatest and richest merchant in Christendom, and the shame of that is worse than the loss."

For several days Giannetto remained hidden in his friend's house, not knowing what to do or to say. He almost decided to go back to Florence without saying a word to Signor Ansaldo, but in the end he made up his mind to go to him, and so he did.

When Signor Ansaldo saw him, he got up and ran and embraced him, saying, "Welcome, my dear son." And Giannetto, weeping, embraced him. Signor Ansaldo said, "Do you know what? Do not give yourself the slightest grief. Since I have you once again, I am happy. There is still enough remaining for us to be able to live simply."

The news of what had happened went all over Venice, and everyone talked of Signor Ansaldo, wishing him well and grieving for what he had suffered. And it was necessary for him to sell many of his possessions to pay his creditors who had provided him with the lost merchandise.

Now, it happened that Giannetto's two friends returned, rich from their journey, and arrived in Venice, where they were told that Giannetto had come back having been shipwrecked and having lost everything. They marveled at this, saying, "This is the most amazing thing ever seen." And they went to Signor Ansaldo and Giannetto in a jovial mood, saying, "Signors, don't be downcast, for we intend to go this coming year and make a profit on your behalf. After all, we are partly responsible for your loss, since we are the ones who induced Giannetto to come with us in the first place. Don't worry. As long as we have any goods ourselves, treat them as your own."

Signor Ansaldo thanked them and said that he still had enough to get by on.

Now, it happened that Giannetto, thinking day and night on what had taken place, could not bring himself to be cheerful. Signor Ansaldo asked him what was the matter.

"I shall never be content," he said, "until I have gotten back what I lost."

"My son," said Signor Ansaldo, "I don't want you to go away any more, for it is better that we live here simply, with what little we have, than that you again undertake such a risky journey."

"I am firmly resolved to do what I've said," said Giannetto, "for I would consider myself in a shameful state if I left things as they are."

Signor Ansaldo, seeing that his mind was made up, made arrangements to sell everything he had in the world and fit out another ship for him. And he did this, so that he had nothing left, and fitted out a magnificent ship with merchandise. Because he still needed ten thousand florins, he went to a Jew at Mestre and borrowed the money on these terms and conditions: If he had not repaid him by St. John's Day in the following June, the said Jew should have the right to take a pound of his flesh from whatever part of the body he pleased. Signor Ansaldo was content with this, and so the Jew had a deed drawn up for the purpose, authenticated by witnesses and with those forms and ceremonies pertaining in such a case; and then he counted out ten thousand gold florins. With this money Signor Ansaldo supplied what was still lacking for the ship; and if the other two were fine, this one was much richer and better equipped. And so the friends did the same for their two ships, having it in mind that whatever profit they made would be for Giannetto. When it came time for departure, Signor Ansaldo said to Giannetto, "My son, you are going away, and you know how things stand with me. One favor I ask of you: If you come to grief, please come see me, so that I can see you again before I die, and I will depart content." Giannetto promised him this, and Signor Ansaldo gave him his blessing. And so the three took their leave and set off on their voyage.

The two friends kept a constant eye on Giannetto's ship. Giannetto meanwhile was always watching to see how he might drop into the harbor of Belmont. And so he made a deal with one of the sailors that one night the man would pilot the ship into the harbor of that lady. When the morning light grew clear, his friends in the other two ships looked about them, but nowhere did they see Giannetto's ship. They said to each other, "Bad luck again, for sure!" And they decided to keep on their way, wondering greatly all the while.

Now, it happened that when the ship came into the harbor, the whole city drew near to see, realizing that Giannetto had returned. They marveled greatly at this, saying, "Certainly this must be the son of some very important man, seeing how he comes here each year with so much merchandise and so beautiful a ship. Would to God he were our lord!" And so he was waited on by all the dignitaries, barons, and knights of that city.

Word was brought to the lady that Giannetto had come. She placed herself at a window and saw the handsome ship and recognized the flags. Whereupon she made the sign of the cross, saying, "Certainly this is the same man who brought such riches into this country," and she sent for him. Giannetto came to her, and with many embraces they greeted each other and offered their respects. And the whole day was spent amid joy and festivity. For love of Giannetto a splendid joust was held, and many barons and knights jousted that day. Giannetto wanted to joust also, and that day he performed many miraculous feats himself, so skillful was he in arms and horsemanship. So much did his conduct please all the barons that everyone wanted him to be their lord.

Now, when evening came and it was time for bed, the lady took Giannetto by the hand and said, "Let us go and rest."

And as he was about to leave the room, one of the maidservants, feeling sorry for Giannetto, whispered in his ear in a soft voice, "Pretend to drink, but don't drink tonight." Giannetto understood her words, and went into the bedchamber.

"You must be thirsty," said the lady, "and I want you to drink before you go to sleep."

And right away two damsels came in, looking like angels, with wine and sweetmeats according to the usual custom, and offered him drink.

"Who could refuse drink," said Giannetto, "seeing two such beautiful damsels?"

The lady laughed at that. And Giannetto took the cup and pretended to drink, but instead poured the wine into his bosom. The lady, believing him to have drunk, said to herself, "You will have to bring another ship, since you've just lost this one." Giannetto went to bed, feeling wide awake and in good spirits, and it seemed to him to take a thousand years for the lady to come to bed, and he said to himself, "For certain I've caught her this time; turnabout is fair play." To make the lady come to bed sooner, he began to snore and to feign sleep. "Everything is going fine," 'said the lady, and she quickly undressed and lay down by Giannetto. He lost no time: as soon as the lady was under the sheets, he turned toward her and embraced her and said, "Now I have what I have so much desired." And with these words he gave her the blissful peace that comes with holy matrimony, and all night long she did not leave his arms, so content was she. And next morning she arose before daylight and sent for all the barons and knights and other worthy citizens and said to them: "Giannetto is your lord; therefore make ready to celebrate." With that, a shout went up through all the land, "Long live our lord!" while bells and trumpets sounded. And she sent for many barons and counts from the surrounding countryside to come and see their lord. Then began a huge and splendid celebration. When Giannetto came out of the bedchamber, he was knighted and placed on the throne, and the scepter was put in his hand, and he was named lord with great ceremony and splendor. And as soon as all the barons and lords and ladies had come to court, he married the lady with such festivity and joy as can scarcely be told or imagined. All the lords and barons of the country came to the city to celebrate with jousts, trials of arms, dances, singing, the playing of instruments, and all that belongs to such a celebration. Signor Giannetto, like the generous and noble youth that he was, commenced to make gifts of silken materials and other rich things that he had brought with him. And he showed himself to be a strong ruler, one to be respected and feared, one who maintained right and justice on behalf of all sorts and conditions of men. And so he continued in joy and happiness, and took no thought or remembrance of poor Signor Ansaldo, who had pledged himself for ten thousand florins to the Jew.

One day it happened that Signor Giannetto was at a window with his lady and saw pass through the square a company of men with torches in their hands who were going to make an offering.

"What does that mean?" asked Signor Giannetto.

His lady answered, "That is a company of craftsmen, who are going to make an offering at the Church of St. John, whose festival is today."

At this Signor Giannetto remembered Signor Ansaldo. He left the window, sighing deeply, his countenance changed, and paced up and down the room several times thinking the matter over. His wife asked him what was the matter.

"Nothing," he answered.

His wife began to question him, saying, "Something certainly is the matter with you, but you don't want to tell me." And she kept asking so insistently that Signor Giannetto told her the whole story, how Signor Ansaldo had pledged himself for ten thousand florins, how the time for repayment had expired this very day, and how Signor Ansaldo would have to lose a pound of his flesh. His lady said to him, "Quick, to horse, and take whatever company seems best to you and a hundred thousand florins, and don't rest until you are at Venice; and if he isn't dead yet, bring him back here."

And so he at once ordered a trumpet to be sounded, and mounted on horseback, with more than a hundred companions, and carrying enough money with him, he took his leave and journeyed without delay toward Venice.

Now, it happened that with the arrival of the due date, the Jew had Signor Ansaldo arrested and made clear his intention of taking a pound of flesh. Signor Ansaldo begged him please to delay his death several days, so that if his Giannetto were to come, he would be able to see him.

"I am content to do what you wish as far as the delay is concerned," said the Jew, "but even if he were to come a hundred times, I intend to take a pound of flesh as specified in the bond."

Signor Ansaldo answered that he was satisfied with this. All Venice buzzed with this matter, and everyone was sorry for Signor Ansaldo, and many merchants got together with a view to paying the money, but the Jew would not agree to that, wishing instead to carry out the homicide so that he might say that he had put to death the greatest merchant in Christendom.

Now, it happened that when Signor Giannetto had set forth eagerly on his way, his lady had quickly followed after him, clad as a doctor of laws and taking two servants with her. Arriving in Venice, Signor Giannetto went to the house of the Jew, joyfully embraced Signor Ansaldo, and then said to the Jew that he was ready to pay him his money and as much more as he cared to demand. The Jew answered that he didn't want the money, since he had not received it on the date it was due, but that he wanted to take a pound of Signor Ansaldo's flesh. Over this matter there arose a great debate, and everyone blamed the Jew, but since Venice was a city that respected the rule of law and the Jew had his legal rights fully set forth and in the proper form, no one could find arguments to deny him; all they could do was plead with him. And so all the merchants of Venice came there to entreat the Jew, but he grew harder than ever. Signor Giannetto was willing to give him twenty thousand, and he refused that. He advanced his offer to thirty thousand, then forty, then fifty, and finally a hundred thousand florins.

The Jew said to him, "Do you want to know something? If you were to give me more than this whole city is worth, it would not satisfy me. I would rather have what the bond says is mine."

And that is where things stood in this dispute when, behold, the lady arrived in Venice, dressed like a doctor of laws, and alighted at an inn. The innkeeper asked one of the servants, "Who is this gentleman?"

The servant answered, "This gentleman is a doctor of laws coming from his studies at Bologna and returning home."

The innkeeper, hearing this, treated him with great respect. And while he was at the dinner table the doctor of laws said to the innkeeper, "How is this city of yours governed?"

"Sir," the innkeeper answered, "we make too much of justice here."

"How can that be?" said the doctor of laws.

"Sir," said the innkeeper, "I will tell you. Once there came here from Florence a young man called Giannetto, and he came here to his godfather, called Signor Ansaldo. He was so gracious and pleasing in his behavior that all the women, and the men too, were quite taken with him. Never before has there come to this city anyone so engaging as he. Now, this godfather of his fitted out for him, on three different occasions, three ships, all of the greatest value, and every time disaster struck. Signor Ansaldo didn't have enough money for the last ship, and so he borrowed ten thousand florins of a certain Jew on the condition that if he didn't repay what was due by St. John's Day in the following June, the said Jew would be authorized to take a pound of flesh from whatever part of him he pleased. Now this fortunate young man has come back and has offered to give, in place of those ten thousand florins, a hundred thousand, but the wicked Jew won't accept them. And all the good people of this place have been to him to plead with him, but to no avail."

"This is an easy question to settle," answered the doctor of laws.

"If you will only take the trouble to settle it," said the host, "so that this good man won't have to die, you will win the thanks and love of the worthiest young man that ever was born and of all the citizens of this land."

And so this doctor of laws had it proclaimed throughout the city that whoever had any legal question to settle should come to him. This was told to Signor Giannetto, that a doctor of laws had come from Bologna who was ready to settle any legal dispute.

Said Signor Giannetto to the Jew, "Let us go to this doctor of laws who I hear has arrived."

"All right, let us go," said the Jew.

When they came into the presence of the doctor of laws and offered him the respect that was his due, the doctor of laws at once recognized Signor Giannetto, but Signor Giannetto did not recognize him, because he had disguised his face with certain herbs. Signor Giannetto and the Jew stated their cases, each in turn and in proper order, before the doctor of laws.

The doctor of laws took the Jew's bond and read it, and

then said to the Jew, "I would rather you took the hundred thousand florins and freed this good man, who will always be obliged to you."

"Nothing doing," said the Jew.

"It's your best course," said the doctor of laws.

The Jew said he absolutely refused.

"Now, come forward then," said the doctor of laws, "and take a pound of flesh from wherever you choose."

With that the Jew called for Signor Ansaldo. And when he had arrived, the doctor of laws said to the Jew, "Do your business." And so the Jew had him stripped naked and took in his hand a razor that he had prepared for the purpose and approached him from behind to seize him.

Signor Giannetto turned to the doctor of laws and said, "Sir, this is not what I asked you to do."

"Don't interfere," said the doctor of laws. "Let me handle this." And seeing that the Jew was about to start, the doctor of laws said, "Take care what you do. For if you take more or less than one pound, I will have your head struck off. And let me tell you, moreover, that if you shed a single drop of blood, I will have you put to death. Your bond makes no mention of the shedding of blood, but says only that you are to take a pound of flesh, neither more nor less. Now, if you are wise, you will think carefully what is the best way to do this." And then he at once had the executioner sent for and had him bring his block and ax, and said, "When I see a drop of blood flow, I will have your head struck off."

The Jew began to be afraid, and Signor Giannetto began to take heart. And after much argument, the Jew said, "Master Doctor, you are wiser than I am in these matters; let me be given those hundred thousand florins and I am content."

"I agree to your taking a pound of flesh," said the doctor of laws, "as your bond specifies; otherwise, I will not give you a penny. You should have taken it when I was willing to give it to you."

The Jew came down to ninety thousand, then eighty, but the doctor of laws held firm.

"Give him what he wants," said Signor Giannetto to the doctor of laws, "as long as he releases Signor Ansaldo."

"Let me handle this, I tell you," said the doctor of laws.

"Give me fifty thousand," said the Jew.

"I wouldn't give you the most miserable coin you've ever had," said the doctor of laws.

"Give me at least my ten thousand," said the Jew, "and a curse be on the air you breathe and the place where you live!"

"Didn't you hear what I said?" said the doctor of laws. "I won't give you a thing. If you want to take your forfeit from him, take it. If not, I will declare a nonperformance and void your bond."

Everyone present rejoiced greatly at this, and they all jeered at the Jew, saying, "He who thought to lay a trap has fallen into it himself." And so, seeing that he could not have his will, the Jew took his bond and tore it to pieces in a fury. Then Signor Ansaldo was freed and, with great rejoicing, was led home, and Signor Giannetto took those hundred thousand florins and went to the doctor of laws, finding him in his chambers making ready to depart.

Signor Giannetto went to him and said, "Sir, you have done me the greatest possible service, and for that reason I would like you to take home this money; you have well earned it."

"My dear Signor Giannetto," said the doctor of laws, "I thank you very much, but I have no need of it; take it yourself so that your lady won't be saying that you have spent it recklessly."

"By my faith," answered Signor Giannetto, "she is so generous and kind and good that even if I were to spend four times this, she would not mind; she asked if I wanted to bring much more than this."

"Are you happy with her?" said the doctor of laws.

"There is no creature in the world whom I love so dearly," answered Signor Giannetto, "for she is wise and beautiful, so much so that nature could do nothing more. And if you would do me the great favor of coming home to see her, you would marvel at the honorable reception she would give you, and you would see if she is all that I tell you."

"See to it, when you see her," said the doctor of laws, "that you greet her on my behalf."

"I shall do so," said Signor Giannetto, "but I wish you would take this money."

While he was saying this, the doctor of laws saw on his finger a ring, and so he said, "I would like that ring. I don't want any money."

"It shall be as you wish," said Signor Giannetto, "but I give it most unwillingly, since my wife gave it to me and said that I should wear it always for love of her; and if she sees me without it, she will think that I have given it to some woman and so be angry with me and believe that I am unfaithful; and the truth is that I love her more than I love myself."

"I am certain," answered the doctor of laws, "that she must love you well enough to believe you when you tell her that you have given it to me. But perhaps you want to give it to some former mistress of yours?"

"Such is the love and faith that I bear her," answered Signor Giannetto, "that there is no woman in the whole wide world for whom I would exchange her, so utterly beautiful is she in every way."

And thereupon he took the ring from his finger and gave it to the doctor of laws. Then they embraced and respectfully saluted each other and took their leave.

"Do me one favor," said the doctor of laws.

"You have only to ask," answered Signor Giannetto.

"Do not remain here," said the doctor of laws. "Go home quickly to see your wife."

"It seems to me a hundred thousand years," answered Signor Giannetto, "until I see her again."

And so they took their leave. The doctor of laws put out to sea, and with God's grace went on his journey. For his part Signor Giannetto gave banquets and made presents of horses and money to his friends, and thus made merry and kept open house, and then took his leave of all the Venetians, taking Signor Ansaldo with him; and many of his old friends went with them. And almost all the men and women of Venice were tearful at his departure, so graciously had he borne himself toward one and all the whole time that he had been in Venice. And so he left and returned to Belmont.

Now, it happened that his lady arrived some time before him and pretended she had been to the baths. She dressed herself as a woman, made festive preparations, had the streets hung in silk, and ordered many companies of soldiers to array themselves. When Signor Giannetto and

Signor Ansaldo arrived, all the barons and the court went to greet them, shouting, "Long live our lord! Long live our lord!" And when they arrived at the city, the lady ran to embrace Signor Ansaldo but pretended to be a little angry with Signor Giannetto, even though she loved him better than herself. A great celebration was made, with jousting, feats of arms, and dancing and singing by all the barons and ladies and damsels who were there. But Signor Giannetto, seeing that his wife did not receive him with her accustomed kindness, went to their room and called her, and said, "What's wrong?" and tried to embrace her.

"There's no need here for these embraces," said the lady, "for I know only too well that you have been meeting your former mistresses."

Signor Giannetto started to deny this.

"Where is the ring I gave you?" said his lady.

"What I thought would happen has indeed happened," said Signor Giannetto. "I said you would think badly of me. But I swear by the faith I bear to God and to you that I gave that ring to the doctor of laws who brought me victory in the case."   .

"And I swear by the faith I bear to God and to you," said his lady, "that you gave it to a woman. I know it, and aren't you ashamed to swear as you have sworn?"

"May God wipe me from the face of the earth," said Signor Giannetto, "if I am not speaking true, and if I did not say to that doctor of laws as I have told you, when he asked for the ring."

"You should have stayed in Venice," said his lady, "and sent Signor Ansaldo here while you enjoyed yourself with your mistresses, who, I hear, were all in tears when you left."

Then Signor Giannetto began to weep and to give himself over to grief, saying, "You are swearing what isn't true and couldn't possibly be true."

When his lady saw him weeping, it seemed to her like a knife wound to the heart, and at once she ran and embraced him, laughing heartily; and she showed him the ring and told him everything—what he had said to the doctor of laws, how she herself was that doctor of laws. Signor Giannetto was greatly astonished at this and, seeing that it was all true, was immensely amused. He went out of the room and told the story to some of his barons and friends. And this adventure increased and multiplied the love between the couple. Then Signor Giannetto summoned the maidservant who had warned him that evening not to drink, and gave her in marriage to Signor Ansaldo. And so they lived ever after in happiness and pleasure, and enjoyed good things and good fortune.

Il Pecorone by Ser Giovanni Fiorentino was first published in Milan in 1558. This new translation is based on the critical edition prepared under the supervision of Enzo Esposito, Longo Editore, Ravenna, 1974, which was based in turn on manuscript sources as well as the early printed texts.

Further Reading

Auden, W. H. "Brothers and Others." *"The Dyer's Hand" and Other Essays*. New York: Random House, 1948. In a casual but seminal essay on the play, Auden calls *The Merchant of Venice* one of Shakespeare's "Unpleasant Plays." The presence of Antonio and Shylock disrupts the unambiguous fairy-tale world of romantic comedy, reminding us that the utopian qualities of Belmont are illusory: "in the real world, no hatred is totally without justification, no love totally innocent."

Barber, C. L. "The Merchants and the Jew of Venice: Wealth's Communion and an Intruder." *Shakespeare's Festive Comedy*. Princeton, N.J.: Princeton Univ. Press, 1959. Barber acknowledges that while *"on reflection"* Shakespeare's handling of the use of wealth and his depiction of Shylock are disturbing, in the theater the play's insistent festive design works to affirm "its concern for the grace of community." As a threat to the social harmony that the comedy celebrates, Shylock, "who embodies the evil side of the power of money," must be removed.

Barnet, Sylvan, ed. *Twentieth Century Interpretations of "The Merchant of Venice."* Englewood Cliffs, N.J.: Prentice-Hall, 1970. To help modern students see the play as Elizabethans would have, Barnet provides a useful collection of interpretive and historical essays, including studies by Auden, Barber, Granville-Barker, Kermode, and Moody that are discussed here.

Brown, John Russell. "The Realization of Shylock: A Theatrical Criticism." In *Early Shakespeare*, ed. John Russell Brown and Bernard Harris. Stratford-upon-Avon Studies 3. London: Edward Arnold, 1961. Brown argues that Shylock dominates the stage and that the meaning of the character can fully be discovered only in performance. He examines the "opportunities given to the actor by Shakespeare" and the acting traditions established by Charles Macklin, Edmund Kean, Henry Irving, and Sir John Gielgud.

Burckhardt, Sigurd. *"The Merchant of Venice:* The Gentle Bond." *ELH* 29 (1962): 239–262. Rpt. in *Shakespearean Meanings.* Princeton, N.J.: Princeton Univ. Press, 1968. Burckhardt identifies "the bond" as the play's controlling metaphor and explores the way attention to it reveals the play's exacting structure. The comic design of the play, Burckhardt argues, emerges when "the vicious circle of the bond's law" is "transformed into the ring of love."

Cohen, D. M. "The Jew and Shylock." *Shakespeare Quarterly* 31 (1980): 53–63. In spite of its many defenders, the play, for Cohen, remains profoundly anti-Semitic. Shylock's humanity is effaced and his Jewishness used to alienate him from the world of the play and the audience. "It is as though," Cohen writes, "*The Merchant of Venice* is an anti-Semitic play written by an author who is not an anti-Semite—but an author who has been willing to use the cruel stereotypes of that ideology for mercenary and artistic purposes."

Danson, Lawrence. *The Harmonies of "The Merchant of Venice."* New Haven, Conn.: Yale Univ. Press, 1978. As his title reveals, Danson is concerned with the play's "harmonies" rather than the discordant notes heard by many modern critics. He sensitively explores a series of dramatic oppositions that are posed but finally resolved by the play: law/freedom, justice/mercy, feuding/marriage, Jew/Christian, Venice/Belmont.

Evans, Bertrand. *Shakespeare's Comedies.* Esp. pp. 46–67. Oxford: Clarendon Press, 1960. The comic design of *The Merchant of Venice,* Evans finds, is determined by the manipulation of discrepancies of awareness between characters and the audience of the play. Only when these discrepancies dissolve in the trial scene, with the revelation of Portia's remarkable control of events, can we be confident that "the world of *The Merchant of Venice* is one in which goodness and mirth prevail," and only then can we experience any sympathy for Shylock.

Girard, René. " 'To Entrap the Wisest': A Reading of *The Merchant of Venice.*" In *Literature and Society: Selected Papers from the English Institute, 1978,* ed. Edward W. Said. Baltimore and London: The Johns Hopkins Univ. Press, 1980. Girard explores the disturbing symmetries that the play establishes between Jew and Christian.

Their mutual hatred, according to Girard, turns Shylock and Antonio into "doubles of each other," creating a moral burden for an audience confronted with action that simultaneously produces and undermines the scapegoating of Shylock.

Granville-Barker, Harley. *"The Merchant of Venice."* In *Prefaces to Shakespeare*, vol. 4, 1946. Rpt. Princeton, N.J.: Princeton Univ. Press, 1966. With his characteristic sensitivity to the demands of performance, Granville-Barker examines the play's form and temper. For him, *"The Merchant of Venice* is the simplest of plays, so long as we do not bedevil it with sophistries": the "unlikelihood" of its fairy-tale plot is "redeemed by veracity of character."

Kermode, Frank. "The Mature Comedies." In *Early Shakespeare*, ed. John Russell Brown and Bernard Harris. Stratford-upon-Avon Studies 3. London: Edward Arnold, 1961. In his account of Shakespeare's mature comic vision, Kermode finds *The Merchant of Venice* designed around a contrast between "gentleness" and "its opposite, for which Shylock stands." The comedy, Kermode says, confirms Christian values and patterns: it begins with "usury and corrupt love" and moves purposefully toward "harmony and perfect love."

Leggatt, Alexander. *"The Merchant of Venice." Shakespeare's Comedy of Love.* New York: Barnes and Noble, 1974. Leggatt explores the tension the play generates between its formalized and conventional plot and its characters' "human reality, naturalistically conceived." The formal design moves toward harmony and happiness but can have, Leggatt argues, "only a limited success in bringing order out of an intractable world."

Moody, A. D. *Shakespeare: "The Merchant of Venice."* London: Edward Arnold, 1964. In this short book (64 pages), Moody argues that the play presents a deeply ironic portrait of the Christian community. It reveals the essential "likeness" of Shylock and his accusers and "does not celebrate the Christian virtues so much as expose their absence."

Nevo, Ruth. "Jessica's Monkey; or, the Goodwins." *Comic Transformations in Shakespeare.* London and New York: Methuen, 1980. Nevo explores "the rupture of comic form" in the play, which never fully credits either the idealizations of Belmont or the scapegoating of Venice. The play, Nevo finds, takes its power precisely from this refusal to resolve the dichotomies it poses.

Palmer, D. J. *"The Merchant of Venice,* or the Importance of Being Earnest." In *Shakespearian Comedy,* ed. Malcolm Bradbury and D. J. Palmer. Stratford-upon-Avon Studies 14. London: Edward Arnold, 1972. Palmer recognizes the powerful discords of the play and its prevailing seriousness. Antonio's sadness at the opening of the play, Palmer finds, "sets in motion the forces of division and disharmony which will take the play to the brink of tragedy before it is retrieved as a comedy."

Rabkin, Norman. "Meaning and *The Merchant of Venice." Shakespeare and the Problem of Meaning.* Chicago: Univ. of Chicago Press, 1981. As part of an argument about the limitation of "meaning as the principle of unity in a work," Rabkin explores the tensions, contradictions, and ambivalent signals that the play generates. The structure of the play, Rabkin finds, demands from an audience a constant reassessment of what it has seen, presenting it with elements "provocative of inconsistent responses."

Stoll, E. E. "Shylock." *Journal of English and Germanic Philology* 10 (1911): 236–279. Rpt. in *Shakespeare Studies: Historical and Comparative in Method.* New York: Macmillan, 1927. Stoll denies that Shylock is presented sympathetically; rather, he is a conventional, comic stage villain who exists to be foiled. From an analysis of the literary and cultural traditions underlying the character, Stoll concludes that our "notions of justice and social responsibility" distort the play's "intention."

Photo © George Joseph

From the 1968 New York Shakespeare Festival production of *Romeo and Juliet*, with Martin
Sheen and Susan McArthur, directed by Joseph Papp at the Delacorte Theater
in Central Park.

ROMEO
— AND —
JULIET

ROMEO AND JULIET

Introductory Material
Foreword by Joseph Papp
Introduction
Romeo and Juliet in
Performance

THE PLAY

Supplementary Material
Date and Text
Textual Notes
Shakespeare's Sources
Further Reading

Foreword

The real tragedy in *Romeo and Juliet* is the lack of a telephone. Throughout the play slow communications cause hairline misses, and silences are tragically misinterpreted. Juliet's cry over the dead body of Romeo—"Thy lips are warm"—gets right to the heart of the tragedy. If only she had awakened seconds earlier, he would still be alive; if only he had waited seconds longer, she would have awakened. Indeed, "if only" is so often in our thoughts as we watch or read the play that it becomes a sad refrain. The prominent role that time plays makes the tragedy seem that much more senseless and unnecessary.

Romeo and Juliet is really Juliet's play, just as *Antony and Cleopatra* belongs to Cleopatra—and both are marvelous roles for talented actresses. It is amazing that in a period of theatrical history when only men and boys occupied the stage, many of Shakespeare's greatest roles were written for women. Juliet has many of the best speeches in the play, verses rich in imagery and filled with the passion of adolescent yearning. Of course other characters have good lines; there is Mercutio's zesty "O, then, I see Queen Mab hath been with you" speech (1.4), or Romeo's distracted "Death, that hath sucked the honey of thy breath, / Hath had not power yet upon thy beauty" and "Thus with a kiss I die."

But Juliet really has the lion's share of show-stopping speeches. Waiting for word from Romeo, she says impatiently, "The clock struck nine when I did send the Nurse; / In half an hour she promised to return" (2.5). Later, she calls for night (and Romeo) to come, with verse that is absolutely exquisite—"Gallop apace, you fiery-footed steeds, / Towards Phoebus' lodging!" (3.2). And then, before she drinks the sleeping potion—"I have a faint cold fear thrills through my veins / That almost freezes up the heat of life." But the best lines that Juliet has in the entire play—certainly *my* favorites—are those she says to Romeo as he departs, in Act 2, scene 2:

> My bounty is as boundless as the sea,
> My love as deep; the more I give to thee,
> The more I have, for both are infinite.

Though they sum up the deep love that Romeo and Juliet have just vowed to each other, these lines also go beyond the

immediate context to the great world outside, expressing
what to me is the quintessence of love.

In the past, productions of the play have been dominated
by superstar actresses who insisted that the play end with
Juliet's dying words: "O happy dagger! / This is thy sheath.
There rust, and let me die." Happily, this way of ending the
play has gone out of fashion, and modern productions preserve the play as Shakespeare wrote it, with the final scene
of reconciliation between the two warring families, a scene
that is essential to rounding out the tragedy. Here we have
the gathering of the Capulets and Montagues, stricken by
the loss of their children, a loss that forcefully brings home
the futility of their hatred.

Such endings are essential to the integrity of Shakespeare's plays; he is giving the audience time to absorb the
meaning of the tragedy. The ending of *Hamlet* is a case in
point. Shakespeare has Fortinbras march into the midst of
the horrific chaos of death to observe Hamlet's passing
with appropriate ceremony and remind us that life goes on.

Even *King Lear* does not end abruptly with this old man's
tragic death, which would produce a feeling of emptiness in
the audience. This is not Shakespeare's objective. Instead
he knows that we need a chance to breathe and to wonder,
along with loyal Kent, that Lear "hath endured so long." As
Nym remarks philosophically to Bardolph in *Henry V,*
"There must be conclusions."

JOSEPH PAPP

JOSEPH PAPP GRATEFULLY ACKNOWLEDGES THE HELP OF
ELIZABETH KIRKLAND IN PREPARING THIS FOREWORD.

Introduction

Though a tragedy, *Romeo and Juliet* is in some ways more closely comparable to Shakespeare's romantic comedies than to his other tragedies. Stylistically belonging to the years 1594–1596, it is in the lyric vein of the sonnets, *A Midsummer Night's Dream*, and *The Merchant of Venice*, all from the mid 1590s. Like those plays, it uses a variety of rhyme schemes (couplets, quatrains, octets, even sonnets) and revels in punning, metaphor, and wit combat. It is separated in tone and in time from the earliest of the great tragedies, *Julius Caesar* and *Hamlet*, by almost half a decade, and, except for the experimental *Titus Andronicus*, it is the only tragedy (that is not also a history) that Shakespeare wrote in the first decade of his career—a period devoted otherwise to romantic comedy and English history.

Like many comedies, *Romeo and Juliet* is a love story, celebrating the exquisite brief joy of youthful passion. Even its tragic ending stresses the poignancy of that brief beauty, not the bitter futility of love, as in *Troilus and Cressida* or *Othello*. The tragic ending of *Romeo and Juliet* underscores the observation made by a vexed lover in *A Midsummer Night's Dream* that "The course of true love never did run smooth" (1.1.134). True love in *Romeo and Juliet*, as in *A Midsummer Night's Dream*, is destined to be crossed by differences in blood or family background, differences in age, arbitrary choices of family or friends, or uncontrollable catastrophes such as war, death, and sickness. Love is thus, as in *A Midsummer Night's Dream*, "momentary as a sound, / Swift as a shadow, short as any dream," swallowed up by darkness; "So quick bright things come to confusion" (1.1.143–149). A dominant pattern of imagery in *Romeo and Juliet* evokes a corresponding sense of suddenness and violence: fire, gunpowder, hot blood, lightning, the inconstant wind, the storm-tossed or shipwrecked vessel. Love so threatened and fragile is beautiful because it is brief. A tragic outcome therefore affirms the uniqueness and pristine quality of youthful ecstasy. The flowering and fading of a joy "too rich for use, for earth too dear" (1.5.48), does not so much condemn the unfeeling world as welcome the martyrdom of literally dying for love.

As protagonists, Romeo and Juliet lack tragic stature by any classical definition or in terms of the medieval convention of the Fall of Princes. The lovers are not extraordinary except in their passionate attachment to each other. They belong to respectable families rather than to the nobility. They are very young, more so than most tragic protagonists (and indeed younger than most couples marrying in England at the time the play was written; the average age for women was between twenty-one and twenty-four, for men between twenty-four and twenty-seven). Romeo and Juliet's dilemma of parental opposition is of the domestic sort often found in comedy. In fact, several characters in the play partly resemble the conventional character types of the Latin comic playwright Plautus or of Italian neoclassical comedy: the domineering father who insists that his daughter marry according to his choice, the unwelcome rival wooer, the garrulous and bawdy nurse, and, of course, the lovers. The Italian novella, to which Shakespeare often turned for his plots, made use of these same types and paid little attention to the classical precept that protagonists in a tragic story ought to be persons of lofty station who are humbled through some inner flaw, or hamartia.

The story of Romeo and Juliet goes back ultimately to the fifth-century A.D. Greek romance of *Ephesiaca*, in which we find the motif of the sleeping potion as a means of escaping an unwelcome marriage. Masuccio of Salerno, in his *Il Novellino*, in 1476, combined the narrative of the heroine's deathlike trance and seeming burial alive with that of the hero's tragic failure to receive news from the friar that she is still alive. Luigi da Porto, in his *Historia* (c. 1530), set the scene at Verona, provided the names of Romeo and Giulietta for the hero and heroine, added the account of their feuding families, the Montecchi and Cappelletti, introduced the killing of Tybalt (Theobaldo), and provided other important details. Luigi's version was followed by Matteo Bandello's famous *Novelle* of 1554, which was translated into French by Pierre Boaistuau (1559). The French version became the source for Arthur Brooke's long narrative poem in English, *The Tragical History of Romeus and Juliet* (1562). Brooke mentions having seen a play on the subject, but it is doubtful that Shakespeare either knew or made use of this old play. Brooke's poem was his chief and probably only source. Shakespeare has condensed Brooke's action from nine months to less than a week, greatly expanded the role of Mercutio, and given to the Nurse a warmth and humorous richness not found in the usual Italian duenna, or *balia*. He has also tidied up the Friar's immorality and deleted the antipapal tone. Throughout all these changes, Shakespeare retains the romantic (rather than classically tragic) conception of love overwhelmed by external obstacles.

Like the romantic comedies, *Romeo and Juliet* is often funny and bawdy. Samson and Gregory in the first scene are slapstick cowards, hiding behind the law and daring to quarrel only when reinforcements arrive. The Nurse delights us with her earthy recollections of the day she weaned Juliet: the child tasting "the wormwood on the nipple / Of my dug" (1.3.31–32), the warm Italian sun, an earthquake, the Nurse's husband telling his lame but often-repeated bawdy joke about women falling on their backs. Mercutio employs his inventive and sardonic humor to twit Romeo for lovesickness and the Nurse for her pomposity. She in turn scolds Peter and plagues Juliet (who is breathlessly awaiting news from Romeo) with a history of her back ailments. Mercutio and the Nurse are among Shakespeare's bawdiest characters. Their wry and salacious view of love contrasts with the nobly innocent and yet physically passionate love of Romeo and Juliet. Mercutio and the Nurse cannot take part in the play's denouement; one dies, misinterpreting Romeo's appeasement of Tybalt, and the other proves insensitive to Juliet's depth of feeling. Yet the play loses much of its funniness and vitality with the disappearance of these engaging companions.

The lovers, too, are at first well suited to Shakespearean romantic comedy. When we meet Romeo, he is not in love with Juliet at all, despite the play's title, but is mooning over a "hardhearted wench" (in Mercutio's words) named Rosaline. This "goddess" appropriately never appears in the play; she is almost a disembodied idea in Romeo's mind, a scornful beauty like Phoebe in *As You Like It*. Romeo's love for her is tedious and self-pitying, like that of the conventional wooer in a sonnet sequence by Francesco Petrarch or one of his imitators. Juliet, although not yet fourteen, must change all this by teaching him the nature of true love. She will have none of his shopworn clichés learned in the service of Rosaline, his flowery protestations and swearing by the moon, lest they prove to be love's perjuries. With her innocent candor she insists (like many heroines of the romantic comedies) on dispelling the mask of pretense that lovers too often show each other. "Capulet" and "Montague" are mere labels, not the inner self. Although Juliet would have been more coy, she confesses, had she known that Romeo was overhearing her, she will now "prove more true / Than those that have more coying to be strange" (2.2.100–101). She is more practical than he in assessing danger and making plans. Later she also proves herself remarkably able to bear misfortune.

The comedy of the play's first half is, of course, overshadowed by the certainty of disaster. The opening chorus plainly warns us that the lovers will die. They are "star-crossed," and speak of themselves as such. Romeo fears "Some consequence yet hanging in the stars" when he reluctantly goes to the Capulets' feast (1.4.107); after he has slain Tybalt, he cries "O, I am fortune's fool!" (3.1.135); and at the news of Juliet's supposed death he proclaims "Then I defy you, stars!" (5.1.24). Yet in what sense are Romeo and Juliet "star-crossed"? The concept is deliberately broad in this play, encompassing many factors such as hatred, bumbling, bad luck, and simple lack of awareness.

The first scene presents feuding as a major cause in the tragedy. The quarrel between the two families is so ancient that the original motives are no longer even discussed. Inspired by the "fiery" Tybalt, factionalism pursues its mindless course despite the efforts of the Prince to end it. Although the elders of both families talk of peace, they call for their swords quickly enough when a fray begins. Still, this senseless hatred does not lead to tragedy until its effects are fatally complicated through misunderstanding. With poignant irony, good intentions are repeatedly undermined by lack of knowledge. We can see why Juliet does not tell her family of her secret marriage with a presumably hated Montague, but in fact Capulet has accepted Romeo as a guest in his house, praising him as a "virtuous and well governed youth" (1.5.69). For all his dictatorial ways, and the manifest advantages he sees in marrying his daughter to an aristocrat, Capulet would never knowingly force his daughter into bigamy. Not knowing of Juliet's marriage, he and his wife can only interpret her refusal to marry Paris as caprice. Count Paris himself is a victim of this tragedy of unawareness. He is an eminently suitable wooer for Juliet, rich and nobly born, yet considerate, peace-loving, and deeply fond of Juliet (as he shows by his private and sincere grief at her tomb). Certainly he would never intentionally woo a married woman. Not knowing, he plays the unattractive role of the rival wooer and dies for it. Similarly, Mercutio cannot understand Romeo's seemingly craven behavior toward Tybalt, and so begins the duel that leads to Romeo's banishment. The final scene, with Friar Laurence's retelling of the story, allows us to see the survivors confronted with what they have all unknowingly done.

Chance, or accident, plays a role of importance equal to that of hatred and unawareness. An outbreak of the plague prevents Friar John from conveying Friar Laurence's letter to Romeo at Mantua. Friar Laurence, going hurriedly to the Capulets' tomb, arrives in time for Juliet's awakening but some minutes after Romeo has killed Paris and taken poison. Juliet awakens only moments later. The Watch comes just too late to prevent her suicide. As Friar Laurence laments, "what an unkind hour / Is guilty of this lamentable chance!" (5.3.145–146). Earlier, Capulet's decision to move the wedding date up one day has crucially affected the timing. Human miscalculation contributes also to the catastrophe: Mercutio is killed under Romeo's arm, and Friar Laurence wonders unhappily if any of his complicated plans "Miscarried by my fault" (l. 267). Character and human decision play a part in this tragedy, for Romeo should not have dueled with Tybalt no matter what the provocation. In choosing to kill Tybalt, he deliberately casts aside as "effeminate" the gentle and forgiving qualities he has learned from his love of Juliet (3.1.113), and thus is guilty of a rash and self-destructive action. To ascribe the cause of the tragedy in Aristotelian fashion to his and Juliet's impulsiveness is, however, to ignore much of the rest of the play.

Instead, the ending of the play brings a pattern out of the seeming welter of mistakes and animosities. "A greater power than we can contradict / Hath thwarted our intents," says Friar Laurence, suggesting that the seeming bad luck of the delayed letter was in fact the intent of a mysterious higher intelligence (5.3.153–154). Prince Escalus, too, finds a necessary meaning in tragic event. "See what a scourge is laid upon your hate," he admonishes the Montagues and Capulets, "That heaven finds means to kill your joys with love." Romeo and Juliet are "Poor sacrifices of our enmity" (5.3.292–304). As the Prologue had foretold, their deaths will "bury their parents' strife"; the families' feud is a stubborn evil force "Which, but their children's end, naught could remove." Order is preciously restored; the price is great, but the sacrifice nonetheless confirms a sense of a larger intention in what had appeared to be simply hatred and misfortune. Throughout the play, love and hate are interrelated opposites, yoked through the rhetorical device of oxymoron or inherent contradiction. Romeo apostrophizes "O brawling love, O loving hate" (1.1.176), and Juliet later echoes his words: "My only love sprung from my only hate" (1.5.139). This paradox expresses a conflict in humankind as in the universe itself. "Two such opposèd kings encamp them still / In man as well as herbs," says Friar Laurence, "—grace and rude will" (2.3.27–28). Hatred is a condition of our corrupted wills, of our fall from grace, and it attempts to destroy what is gracious in human beings. In this cosmic strife, love must pay the sacrifice, as Romeo and Juliet do with their lives; but because their deaths are finally perceived as the cost of so much hatred, the two families come to terms with their collective guilt and resolve henceforth to be worthy of the sacrifice.

Structurally, *Romeo and Juliet* gives considerable prominence to the feuding of the two families. Public scenes occur at key points, at beginning, middle, and end (1.1, 3.1, and 5.3), and each such scene concerns violence and its consequences. The play begins with a brawl. Tybalt is a baleful presence in Act 1, scene 1, and Act 3, scene 1, implacably bent on vengeance. The three public scenes are alike too, in that they bring into confrontation the entire families of Capulets and Montagues, who call for swords and demand reprisal from the state for what they themselves have set in motion. Prince Escalus dominates these three public scenes. He must offer judgment in each, giving the families fair warning, then exiling Romeo for Tybalt's death, and finally counseling the families on the meaning of their collective tragedy. He is a spokesman for public order ("Mercy but murders, pardoning those that kill," 3.1.196) and is indeed something of a voice of reason for the play as a whole; being a Prince, he is above the family conflict though affected by it. Onstage, his role is sometimes doubled with that of the Chorus. To him is given the final speech promising both punishment and pardon, and it is he who sums up the paradoxical interdependence of love and hate. Although the morning after the catastrophe brings with it sorrow, it also brings peace, however "glooming." Escalus is spokesman for the restored order through which the families and we are reconciled to what has occurred.

In good part, the public scenes of the play serve to frame the love plot and the increasing isolation of the separated lovers, but these public scenes have a function of their own to the extent that the tragedy has touched and altered everyone. The final tableau is not the kiss of the dying lovers but the handclasp of the reconciled fathers. The long last public ceremonial is important because, although the private catastrophe of the lovers is unalterably complete, recognition occurs only when the whole story is known by all. This recognition is not that of the protagonists, as in the Aristotelian conception of recognition, nor does it accompany a reversal of the love tragedy; that reversal has already taken place in Romeo's banishment and the lovers' deaths. This lack of correspondence with an Aristotelian definition of tragedy is not a structural flaw, but rather a manifestation of the dual focus of the tragedy on the lovers and all Verona. The city itself is a kind of protagonist, suffering through its own violence and coming at last to the sad comfort that wisdom brings.

Romeo and Juliet
in Performance

Romeo and Juliet made full and imaginative use of the Elizabethan stage for which it was written, whether at the Theatre in Moorfields, at the Curtain, or in revival (after 1599) at the Globe Theatre. The play has an unusual number of scenes that begin in one location and then shift to another before the audience's eyes, providing continuous action where more traditional staging would call for a curtain or a change of sets. For example, at the end of Act 1, scene 4, during which the stage has represented a street in Verona near Capulet's house, Mercutio and his fellow maskers (including Romeo) do not exit to end the scene, but instead *"march about the stage"* to indicate that they are proceeding to Capulet's house, and then stand to one side. Servants immediately *"come forth with napkins,"* suggesting by these props and their servants' attire, as well as by their conversation, that the scene has now shifted inside to the hall at Capulet's house. There is talk of joint stools and the "plate"; Capulet, his family, and the guests come forward to greet the maskers, and the action proceeds swiftly to the meeting of Romeo and Juliet.

After the dancing, as well, the scene moves forward almost without interruption. The stage is briefly cleared at the start of Act 2, with the departure of the evening's guests, but at once Romeo returns onstage, refusing to go home and insistent on trying to see Juliet again. When he hears his friends Mercutio and Benvolio looking for him, he hides, perhaps behind a pillar on the open Elizabethan stage, until they have left. The "orchard wall" they suspect he has leapt over certainly need not have been supplied onstage; the actor's gestures of concealment are enough to convey the idea. Once his friends have departed, Romeo comes forward, now within the "orchard" or garden; although he has not left the stage, the scene has shifted to a new location. (The conventional marking of a new scene, 2.2, is in this sense misleading.) He beholds a light in "yonder window" and then Juliet herself; she is in the gallery above and to the rear of the stage, as though at her window. The entire stage facade in the Elizabethan theater, without scenery, provides a plausible visual impression of a house and window, while Romeo, below, is clearly understood to be in the garden adjoining the house. The vertical relationship between window and garden is spatially unmistakable and theatrically significant: the lovers are separated, and Juliet is high above Romeo's head like a "bright angel" or "winged messenger of heaven." Scenery is not only unnecessary for the visual transformations of this scene, but would render them theatrically meaningless.

When Romeo bids farewell to Juliet on his way to exile (3.5), Shakespeare uses another kind of scenic flexibility permitted him by his theater. The lovers begin the scene at Juliet's window, at daybreak. Romeo descends from Juliet's window by means of a rope ladder, in full view of the audience, and is once again in Capulet's garden, once more below Juliet and separated from her by an impossible distance. After he has made his exit, however, the concluding action of Act 3, scene 5, does not remain "aloft." Juliet's mother enters to tell Juliet of her father's intention that she marry Paris. Juliet, rather than receiving her mother in what heretofore has been her chamber, that is, the upper acting area, or gallery, *"goeth down"* from her window. (This stage direction is from the so-called "bad" quarto of 1597, which is unreliable in most ways but often informative on staging, since the "reporter" who stole the text was at a performance and tells what he saw.) After a brief pause, Juliet reenters on the main stage platform, now understood to represent her chambers, and goes through the stormy scene with her father. This remainder of Act 3, scene 5, simply has too many participants and too much action to be confined in the gallery above the stage.

Later, when Juliet has taken the sleeping potion given her by the Friar, Juliet's bed provides continuity throughout a dramatic sequence conventionally broken down into three separate scenes (4.3–5). As Juliet takes the potion, the "bad" quarto tells us, she *"falls upon her bed, within the curtains,"* drawing the bed curtains in such a way as to conceal herself from the audience. The bed has either been thrust onstage, as happens not infrequently in Elizabethan plays, or is located in the "discovery space," the curtained alcove at the rear of the stage. Here Juliet lies while members of the Capulet household bustle about, noisily preparing for the wedding that will never take place. The ironic discrepancy between their happy preparations and Juliet's extremity is continually reinforced for the audience by the mute presence of the bed. When the Nurse goes to the bed curtains and finds Juliet seemingly dead, a scene of mourning follows that is once again marked by ironic discrepancy, since the audience knows that she is still alive. Conventional stage divisions would deprive this sequence of much of its ironic effect.

The play's final scene at the tomb calls for an impressively metaphorical use of the stage. The discovery space or a similar location was probably used on Shakespeare's stage to represent the Capulets' burial vault, while a trapdoor in front of it served as a symbolic rather than a practical entrance to the tomb. Any such arrangement would have the effect of reinforcing thematic repetitions visually. The tomb would recall Juliet's bed, the scene of her first apparent death; as Capulet grievingly observes, "Death is my son-in-law, Death is my heir," since Death has deflowered Juliet in her bed (4.5.37–38). The tomb's grim presence backstage would also recall Juliet's lament, as she looked down from her window and saw Romeo below her, "Methinks I see thee, now thou art so low, / As one dead in the bottom of a tomb" (3.5.55–56). The strongly vertical element in these stage images connects them with the idea of tragic fall.

Throughout most of its history onstage, producers of *Romeo and Juliet* have generally taken little advantage of Shakespeare's swift, presentational mode of staging. William Davenant presented the play at the theater in Lincoln's Inn Fields in 1662, with Thomas Betterton as Mercutio, in a production that Samuel Pepys called "the worst that ever I heard." Soon afterward the text underwent significant changes. A tragicomic version, in which Romeo and Juliet do not die after all, was sometimes substituted for Shakespeare's play. John Downes reports that the two versions alternated onstage, "tragical one day and tragic-comical another." Thomas Otway's adaptation of 1679, *Caius Marius,* imposed a neoclassic structure on the play and relocated the story of star-crossed lovers to ancient Rome. This relocation made possible a timely political commentary as well, since the ceaseless faction of Rome could be made to illustrate, in Otway's Tory pro-monarchist view, the folly of both Rome's republican agitators and Restoration England's parliamentary advocates of constitutional restraints and the exclusion of James Stuart from the throne. Otway's talent for knowing what audiences wanted in his neoclassical age was evidently acute; his version displaced Shakespeare's text for more than sixty years. Perhaps Otway's most noteworthy contribution was to allow his dying hero to live until the heroine awakens in the tomb, so that the two can share their final moments on earth. This idea appealed so greatly that it was adopted in Theophilus Cibber's revival of *Romeo and Juliet* at the Little Theatre in the Haymarket, London (1744), in David Garrick's vastly influential production at the Theatre Royal, Drury Lane, in 1748, and in Charles Gounod's opera *Romeo et Juliette* (1867).

Garrick's version, which had run for over 450 performances by 1800 and gave *Romeo and Juliet* the distinction of being Shakespeare's most often performed play in that era, omitted Romeo's love for Rosaline as too great a blemish on his character, increased Juliet's age to eighteen, excised some language that was considered indecorous, and rearranged scenes to accommodate the set. As the successful run proceeded, Garrick added a splendid masquerade dance for the meeting of the lovers in Act 1, scene 5, and a funeral procession for the burial of Juliet at the opening of Act 5. Like other actor-managers of his day, Garrick presumably used painted scenery mounted on movable screens to indicate a street, a ballroom, or a bedchamber; these sets could be shifted without great delay, but they did fix the visual setting for any segment of action in one place and required a curtained interval before the action could move on to another location. The Capulets' monument in Act 5 was, to judge from a contemporary (1753) engraving by R. S. Ravenet, an enclosed vault surrounded by trees with the moon visible in the sky. Another contemporary illustration of Spranger Barry and Maria Isabella Nossiter as Romeo and Juliet at the Theatre Royal, Covent Garden, in 1753, pictures Juliet on a balcony. The misnaming of the "balcony scene" (Shakespeare mentions only a window) originates in staging conventions of this period.

The late eighteenth and early nineteenth centuries were not particularly auspicious times for *Romeo and Juliet*. John Philip Kemble acted the play in 1788, 1789 (with his sister Sarah Siddons, in her only London appearance as Juliet), and again in 1796, but never with great success. His biographer, James Boaden, wrote that "the thoughtful strength of his features was at variance with juvenile passion." Kemble, nevertheless, admired *Romeo and Juliet* and chose it as the first play to be performed at Covent Garden after he took over its management in 1803. He cast his brother Charles and Harriet Siddons as Romeo and Juliet. Charles Kemble's debut in this successful production initiated a role he continued to play until 1828. In 1829 Charles Kemble undertook the role of Mercutio and soon became a great favorite in this part. He acted it again in 1836, with Helen Faucit making her first appearance as Juliet, and for a final time in 1840 at Covent Garden as one of four command performances for the Queen. In 1838 William Charles Macready, whose first appearance onstage was as Romeo in 1810 at Birmingham, elegantly produced the play at Covent Garden, playing Friar Laurence and leaving the title roles to James Anderson and Helen Faucit. Yet Macready, who had heralded the return of Shakespeare's text to the stage with other plays, still depended on the Garrick-Kemble version of *Romeo and Juliet* that had effectively replaced Shakespeare's play onstage. In 1841 he began work on a new production that might well have restored Shakespeare's text and for which he intended to replace the usual eighteenth- or early nineteenth-century dress employed up until his time with costumes and sets that would accurately represent the style of thirteenth-century Verona. Unfortunately, he never was able to bring these plans to fruition.

The success of many lavish Shakespearean productions in the nineteenth century created a continuing expectation for verisimilar sets, ones that could be shifted only with difficulty and necessitated a rearrangement of scenes in the play. Shakespeare's text had to be substantially cut as well, but at least what remained of it was Shakespeare's language rather than the Garrick-Kemble version that had so long prevailed in the theater. When the American actress Charlotte Cushman toured England in her "breeches" role as Romeo opposite her sister Susan's Juliet, she used authentic Renaissance dress and a cut version of Shakespeare's play. The following year Samuel Phelps produced the play at the Sadler's Wells Theatre, also with Shakespeare's text restored, and revived the play four more times during his management of the theater. (In 1859 Phelps performed his *Romeo* for Queen Victoria at Windsor Castle.) Henry Irving's revival at the Lyceum Theatre in 1882 was especially illustrative of the trend toward using a cut Shakespearean text while reveling in the spectacular elements of production. "Every line suggests a picture," he said, and Irving's production was indeed elaborately pictorial, depending on some insights for the staging of crowd scenes and other matters gleaned from Helena Modjeska's production of the previous year at the Court Theatre. Irving paid special attention to horticultural and arboricultural displays, and ended with a grand tableau of the two stricken families at the tomb. Vaulted arches, stone staircases leading down into the tomb, and ironwork grill gates created a gloomy atmosphere of death into which the moon shone with poignant effect. Mary Anderson, in 1884 at the Lyceum Theatre, gave an impression of the Piazza Dante in Verona through the use of realistic masonry, delicate architectural detail, handsome gardens, flowing Renaissance gowns, satin and brocade in profusion, and elaborate machinery by means of which houses could be transformed into gardens and cloisters into tombs. Both the Friar's cell and Juliet's chamber were, according to a contemporary account, "turned inside out in full view of the house." The love scene in Capulet's garden revealed terrace after terrace descending and receding into a distant moonlit haze.

Twentieth-century staging, beginning with a production by William Poel in 1905, in the last performance by his Elizabethan Stage Society as an organized group, has helped to free the play from the restricting requirements of nineteenth-century realistic illusion. A single permanent set for the entire performance, introduced by John Gielgud at the New Theatre in 1935 (with Laurence Olivier and Gielgud exchanging the roles of Romeo and Mercutio, Peggy Ashcroft as Juliet, and Edith Evans as the Nurse), provided something like the unlocalized stage used for Shakespeare's original performance. Peter Brook, remarking that *Romeo and Juliet* is "a play of wide spaces in which all scenery and decoration can easily become an irrelevance," gave his 1947 production at Stratford-upon-Avon a stylized set of crenellated walls with which to focus and contain the play's violent passion. At Stratford-upon-Avon in 1954, Glen Byam Shaw used a partly abstract and geometrical single set, with steps in concentric circles and a curved walkway or gallery above at the back flanked by houses on either side; the decor, including the costumes, suggested Renaissance Italy. Thrust stages in many new theaters have encouraged flexibility and presentational staging methods, as in Joseph Papp's 1968 production at New York's Delacorte Theater, featuring a set of intricate scaffolds and a runway extending into the seating area on which the scene of Juliet's window and orchard (2.2) was located.

The temptation to use gorgeous scenery (and gorgeous actresses) is understandably irresistible in film, and Franco Zeffirelli's well-known film version (1968, based on an earlier stage production at the Old Vic in 1960) makes no effort to resist. In order to achieve sensuous and intimate delight in the love scenes between Leonard Whiting and Olivia Hussey, Zeffirelli has to sacrifice the sense of distance that so separated the lovers on Shakespeare's stage; Zeffirelli's lovers show us what physical passion is like, whereas Shakespeare's lovers (Juliet played by a boy actor) were required to evoke feeling through language and eloquent delivery. Zeffirelli sought in other ways to make the play readily available to modern audiences, by conceiving of Romeo not as a sensitive Renaissance courtier but as a self-absorbed teenager in love, and by suggesting Mercutio's attachment to Romeo. Terry Hands's 1973 production at Stratford-upon-Avon carried this latter idea still further, with Mercutio a "flamboyant pervert," as one reviewer called him, angry and often drunk, whose only emotional commitment is to Romeo. The musical *West Side Story* (1957), Jerome Robbins, Stephen Sondheim, and Leonard Bernstein's adaptation of the play into the milieu of New York's Spanish Harlem, unabashedly translated Shakespeare's play into terms of modern relevance. In a similar spirit, director Ron Daniels, in a production at Stratford-upon-Avon in 1980, turned the play into a study of urban violence played out on an almost bare stage with dirty plaster walls. Two years later, seeking even more baldly to make the play's social tensions relevant, the Young Vic company, in a production at Birmingham, cast black actors as Montagues and white actors as Capulets. Michael Bogdanov's production at Stratford-upon-Avon in 1986 set the play in postwar mafioso Italy. If some of these recent experiments have at times oversimplified and sensationalized rather than clarified the tensions of Shakespeare's play, they have nonetheless revealed the continuing appeal of *Romeo and Juliet* and have offered, in many cases, theatrical realizations not far removed in spirit from the Shakespearean script.

ROMEO
— AND —
JULIET

Citizens, Maskers, Torchbearers, Guards, Servants, and Attendants

SCENE: *Verona: Mantua*]

The Prologue [*Enter Chorus.*]

CHORUS

Two households, both alike in dignity, 1
 In fair Verona, where we lay our scene,
From ancient grudge break to new mutiny, 3
 Where civil blood makes civil hands unclean. 4
From forth the fatal loins of these two foes
 A pair of star-crossed lovers take their life; 6
Whose misadventured piteous overthrows 7
 Doth with their death bury their parents' strife.
The fearful passage of their death-marked love, 9
 And the continuance of their parents' rage
Which, but their children's end, naught could remove,
 Is now the two hours' traffic of our stage; 12
The which if you with patient ears attend,
What here shall miss, our toil shall strive to mend. 14

[*Exit.*]

❖

Prologue.
1 dignity rank, status **3 mutiny** strife, discord **4 civil . . . civil** of civil
strife . . . citizens' (with a suggestion of "civility") **6 star-crossed**
thwarted by destiny, by adverse stars **7 misadventured** unlucky
9 passage progress **12 traffic** business **14 miss** i.e., miss the mark (in
this performance).   **our toil** the actors' efforts

1.1 *Enter Samson and Gregory, with swords and bucklers, of the house of Capulet.*

SAMSON   Gregory, on my word, we'll not carry coals.   1

GREGORY   No, for then we should be colliers.   2

SAMSON   I mean, an we be in choler, we'll draw.   3

GREGORY   Ay, while you live, draw your neck out of collar.   5

SAMSON   I strike quickly, being moved.   6

GREGORY   But thou art not quickly moved to strike.

SAMSON   A dog of the house of Montague moves me.   8

GREGORY   To move is to stir, and to be valiant is to stand. Therefore, if thou art moved, thou runn'st away.   10

SAMSON   A dog of that house shall move me to stand. I will take the wall of any man or maid of Montague's.   12

GREGORY   That shows thee a weak slave, for the weakest   13
goes to the wall.   14

SAMSON   'Tis true, and therefore women, being the weaker vessels, are ever thrust to the wall. Therefore I   16
will push Montague's men from the wall and thrust his maids to the wall.

GREGORY   The quarrel is between our masters and us   19
their men.   20

SAMSON   'Tis all one. I will show myself a tyrant: when   21
I have fought with the men, I will be civil with the maids—I will cut off their heads.

GREGORY   The heads of the maids?

SAMSON   Ay, the heads of the maids, or their maiden-heads. Take it in what sense thou wilt.   26

1.1. Location: Verona. A public place.
s.d. bucklers small shields   **1 carry coals** i.e., endure insults   **2 colliers** (Coal carriers were regarded as dirty and of evil repute.)   **3 an** if. **choler** anger (produced by one of the four humors).   **draw** draw swords   **5 collar** i.e., hangman's noose (with pun on *colliers* and *choler*)   **6 moved** i.e., to anger (with pun in next line)   **8 moves** incites **10 stand** i.e., stand one's ground   **12 take the wall** i.e., take the cleaner side of the walk nearest the wall, thus forcing others out into the gutter   **13–14 the weakest . . . wall** (A proverb expressing the idea that the weakest are always forced to give way.)   **16 thrust to the wall** (with bawdy suggestion)   **19–20 between . . . men** i.e., between the males of one household and the males of the other household; the women would not fight   **21 one** the same   **26 what sense** whatever meaning

GREGORY   They must take it in sense that feel it.   27
SAMSON   Me they shall feel while I am able to stand, and   28
'tis known I am a pretty piece of flesh.   29
GREGORY   'Tis well thou art not fish; if thou hadst, thou   30
hadst been Poor John. Draw thy tool. Here comes of   31
the house of Montagues.

Enter two other servingmen [Abraham and
another].

SAMSON   My naked weapon is out. Quarrel. I will back
thee.
GREGORY   How, turn thy back and run?
SAMSON   Fear me not.   36
GREGORY   No, marry. I fear thee!
SAMSON   Let us take the law of our sides. Let them   38
begin.
GREGORY   I will frown as I pass by, and let them take it
as they list.   41
SAMSON   Nay, as they dare. I will bite my thumb at   42
them, which is disgrace to them if they bear it.
[Samson makes taunting gestures.]
ABRAHAM   Do you bite your thumb at us, sir?
SAMSON   I do bite my thumb, sir.
ABRAHAM   Do you bite your thumb at us, sir?
SAMSON *[Aside to Gregory]*   Is the law of our side if I
say ay?
GREGORY *[Aside to Samson]*   No.
SAMSON *[To Abraham]*   No, sir, I do not bite my thumb at
you, sir, but I bite my thumb, sir.
GREGORY   Do you quarrel, sir?
ABRAHAM   Quarrel, sir? No, sir.

27 They . . . feel it i.e., it is the maids who must receive by way of
physical sensation (*sense*) what I have to offer, because they are the ones
who can feel it   **28 stand** (With bawdy suggestion, continued in the next
few lines in *draw thy tool* and *my naked weapon is out.*)   **29–30 flesh
. . . fish** (Refers to the proverbial phrase, "neither fish nor flesh.")
31 Poor John hake salted and dried—a poor Lenten kind of food (probably with a bawdy suggestion of sexual insufficiency).   **comes of** i.e.,
come members of   **36 Fear** mistrust. (But Gregory deliberately misunderstands in the next line, saying in effect, No indeed, do you think I'd
be afraid of you?)   **38 take the law of** have the law on   **41 list** please
42 bite my thumb i.e., make an insulting gesture

SAMSON   But if you do, sir, I am for you. I serve as good
a man as you.
ABRAHAM   No better.
SAMSON   Well, sir.

Enter Benvolio.

GREGORY [*To Samson*]   Say "better." Here comes one of
my master's kinsmen.
SAMSON [*To Abraham*]   Yes, better, sir.
ABRAHAM   You lie.
SAMSON   Draw, if you be men. Gregory, remember thy
washing blow.   *They fight.* 63
BENVOLIO   Part, fools!
Put up your swords. You know not what you do.

Enter Tybalt [with sword drawn].

TYBALT
What, art thou drawn among these heartless hinds?   66
Turn thee, Benvolio. Look upon thy death.
BENVOLIO
I do but keep the peace. Put up thy sword,
Or manage it to part these men with me.   69
TYBALT
What, drawn and talk of peace? I hate the word
As I hate hell, all Montagues, and thee.
Have at thee, coward!   [*They fight.*] 72

*Enter three or four Citizens with clubs or
partisans.*

CITIZENS
Clubs, bills, and partisans! Strike! Beat them down!   73
Down with the Capulets! Down with the Montagues!   74

Enter old Capulet in his gown, and his Wife.

CAPULET
What noise is this? Give me my long sword, ho!   75

---

63 washing slashing with great force   **66 heartless hinds** cowardly
menials   **69 manage** use   **72 Have at thee** i.e., on guard, here I come
73 Clubs rallying cry, summoning apprentices with their clubs.   **bills**
long-handled spears with hooked blades.   **partisans** long-handled
spears   **74 s.d. gown** nightgown, dressing gown   **75 long sword** heavy,
old-fashioned sword

CAPULET'S WIFE
A crutch, a crutch! Why call you for a sword?

CAPULET
My sword, I say! Old Montague is come
And flourishes his blade in spite of me.   78

Enter old Montague and his Wife.

MONTAGUE
Thou villain Capulet!—Hold me not; let me go.

MONTAGUE'S WIFE
Thou shalt not stir one foot to seek a foe.

Enter Prince Escalus, with his train.

PRINCE
Rebellious subjects, enemies to peace,
Profaners of this neighbor-stainèd steel—   82
Will they not hear? What, ho! You men, you beasts,
That quench the fire of your pernicious rage
With purple fountains issuing from your veins,   85
On pain of torture, from those bloody hands
Throw your mistempered weapons to the ground   87
And hear the sentence of your movèd prince.   88
Three civil brawls, bred of an airy word,   89
By thee, old Capulet, and Montague,
Have thrice disturbed the quiet of our streets
And made Verona's ancient citizens
Cast by their grave-beseeming ornaments   93
To wield old partisans, in hands as old,
Cankered with peace, to part your cankered hate.   95
If ever you disturb our streets again
Your lives shall pay the forfeit of the peace.   97
For this time all the rest depart away.
You, Capulet, shall go along with me,

---

78 spite defiance, despite   **82 Profaners . . . steel** i.e., you who profane
your weapons by staining them with neighbors' blood   **85 purple** i.e.,
bloody, dark red   **87 mistempered** (1) having been tempered, or hardened, to a wrong use (2) malignant, angry   **88 movèd** angry   **89 airy**
i.e., merely a breath, trivial   **93 grave-beseeming ornaments** i.e., staffs
and other appurtenances suited to wise old age   **95 Cankered . . .
cankered** corroded . . . malignant   **97 Your . . . peace** i.e., death will be
the penalty for breaking the peace

And, Montague, come you this afternoon,
To know our farther pleasure in this case,
To old Freetown, our common judgment-place.   102
Once more, on pain of death, all men depart.
    Exeunt [all but Montague, Montague's Wife,
                              and Benvolio].
MONTAGUE
Who set this ancient quarrel new abroach?   104
Speak, nephew, were you by when it began?   105
BENVOLIO
Here were the servants of your adversary,
And yours, close fighting ere I did approach.
I drew to part them. In the instant came
The fiery Tybalt with his sword prepared,   109
Which, as he breathed defiance to my ears,
He swung about his head and cut the winds
Who, nothing hurt withal, hissed him in scorn.   112
While we were interchanging thrusts and blows,
Came more and more, and fought on part and part   114
Till the Prince came, who parted either part.   115
MONTAGUE'S WIFE
O, where is Romeo? Saw you him today?
Right glad I am he was not at this fray.
BENVOLIO
Madam, an hour before the worshiped sun
Peered forth the golden window of the east,   119
A troubled mind drave me to walk abroad,   120
Where, underneath the grove of sycamore
That westward rooteth from this city's side,   122
So early walking did I see your son.
Towards him I made, but he was ware of me   124
And stole into the covert of the wood.   125

---

102 Freetown (Brooke's translation, in his poem *Romeus and Juliet*, of
Villa Franca, as found in the Italian story.) **common** public **104 set**
. . . abroach reopened this old quarrel, set it flowing **105 by** near
109 prepared drawn, ready **112 Who, nothing** which not at all. **withal**
therewith. **hissed** hissed at **114 on part and part** on one side and the
other **115 either part** both parties **119 forth** from forth **120 drave**
drove. **abroad** outside **122 That . . . side** that grows on the west side
of this city **124 made** moved. **ware** wary, aware **125 covert** cover,
hiding place

I, measuring his affections by my own,   126
Which then most sought where most might not be
    found,   127
Being one too many by my weary self,
Pursued my humor, not pursuing his,   129
And gladly shunned who gladly fled from me.   130

MONTAGUE
Many a morning hath he there been seen,
With tears augmenting the fresh morning's dew,
Adding to clouds more clouds with his deep sighs;
But all so soon as the all-cheering sun
Should in the farthest east begin to draw
The shady curtains from Aurora's bed,   136
Away from light steals home my heavy son   137
And private in his chamber pens himself,
Shuts up his windows, locks fair daylight out,
And makes himself an artificial night.
Black and portentous must this humor prove
Unless good counsel may the cause remove.

BENVOLIO
My noble uncle, do you know the cause?

MONTAGUE
I neither know it nor can learn of him.

BENVOLIO
Have you importuned him by any means?

MONTAGUE
Both by myself and many other friends.
But he, his own affections' counselor,
Is to himself—I will not say how true,   148
But to himself so secret and so close,   149
So far from sounding and discovery,   150
As is the bud bit with an envious worm   151
Ere he can spread his sweet leaves to the air
Or dedicate his beauty to the sun.
Could we but learn from whence his sorrows grow,
We would as willingly give cure as know.

---

126 affections wishes, inclination   **127 Which . . . found** i.e., I who then
chiefly desired a place where I might be alone   **129 humor** mood,
whim   **130 who** him who   **136 Aurora** goddess of dawn   **137 heavy**
(1) sad (2) the opposite of *light*. **son** (punning on *sun*, l. 134)   **148 true**
trustworthy   **149 close** concealed   **150 sounding** being fathomed (to
discover deep or inner secrets) **151 envious** malicious

Enter Romeo.

BENVOLIO
See where he comes. So please you, step aside.   156
I'll know his grievance or be much denied.

MONTAGUE
I would thou wert so happy by thy stay   158
To hear true shrift. Come, madam, let's away.   159
                    Exeunt [Montague and his Wife].

BENVOLIO
Good morrow, cousin.

ROMEO   Is the day so young?   160

BENVOLIO
But new struck nine.

ROMEO   Ay me! Sad hours seem long.
Was that my father that went hence so fast?

BENVOLIO
It was. What sadness lengthens Romeo's hours?

ROMEO
Not having that which, having, makes them short.

BENVOLIO   In love?

ROMEO   Out—

BENVOLIO   Of love?

ROMEO
Out of her favor where I am in love.

BENVOLIO
Alas, that Love, so gentle in his view,   169
Should be so tyrannous and rough in proof!   170

ROMEO
Alas, that Love, whose view is muffled still,   171
Should without eyes see pathways to his will!   172
Where shall we dine?—O me! What fray was here?
Yet tell me not, for I have heard it all.
Here's much to do with hate, but more with love.
Why, then, O brawling love, O loving hate,
O anything of nothing first create,   177
O heavy lightness, serious vanity,
Misshapen chaos of well-seeming forms,

156 **So please you** if you please   158 **happy** fortunate, successful
159 **shrift** confession   160 **cousin** kinsman   169 **his view** its appearance   170 **in proof** in reality, in experience   171 **view ... still** sight is
blindfolded always   172 **to his will** to what he wants   177 **create** created

Feather of lead, bright smoke, cold fire, sick health,
Still-waking sleep, that is not what it is!   181
This love feel I, that feel no love in this.
Dost thou not laugh?
BENVOLIO   No, coz, I rather weep.   183
ROMEO
Good heart, at what?
BENVOLIO   At thy good heart's oppression.
ROMEO
Why, such is love's transgression.
Griefs of mine own lie heavy in my breast,
Which thou wilt propagate, to have it pressed   187
With more of thine. This love that thou hast shown   188
Doth add more grief to too much of mine own.
Love is a smoke made with the fume of sighs;
Being purged, a fire sparkling in lovers' eyes;   191
Being vexed, a sea nourished with lovers' tears.
What is it else? A madness most discreet,   193
A choking gall, and a preserving sweet.
Farewell, my coz.
BENVOLIO   Soft! I will go along.   195
An if you leave me so, you do me wrong.   196
ROMEO
Tut, I have lost myself. I am not here.
This is not Romeo; he's some other where.
BENVOLIO
Tell me in sadness, who is that you love?   199
ROMEO   What, shall I groan and tell thee?
BENVOLIO
Groan? Why, no, but sadly tell me who.   201
ROMEO
Bid a sick man in sadness make his will—
A word ill urged to one that is so ill!   203
In sadness, cousin, I do love a woman.

---

181 **Still-waking** continually awake   183 **coz** cousin, kinsman
187–188 **propagate . . . thine** increase by having it, i.e., my own grief,
oppressed or made still heavier with your grief on my account
191 **purged** i.e., of smoke   193 **discreet** judicious, prudent   195 **Soft**
i.e., wait a moment   196 **An if** if   199 **sadness** seriousness. **is that** is it
whom   201 **sadly** seriously. (But Romeo plays on the word, and on *in
sadness*, in the sense of "sorrowfully.")   203 **A word** i.e., *sadly* or *in
sadness*—too sad a word, says Romeo, for a melancholy lover

BENVOLIO
  I aimed so near when I supposed you loved.
ROMEO
  A right good markman! And she's fair I love.   206
BENVOLIO
  A right fair mark, fair coz, is soonest hit.   207
ROMEO
  Well, in that hit you miss. She'll not be hit
  With Cupid's arrow. She hath Dian's wit,   209
  And, in strong proof of chastity well armed,   210
  From love's weak childish bow she lives unharmed.
  She will not stay the siege of loving terms,   212
  Nor bide th' encounter of assailing eyes,   213
  Nor ope her lap to saint-seducing gold.
  O, she is rich in beauty, only poor
  That when she dies, with beauty dies her store.   216
BENVOLIO
  Then she hath sworn that she will still live chaste?   217
ROMEO
  She hath, and in that sparing makes huge waste,   218
  For beauty starved with her severity   219
  Cuts beauty off from all posterity.
  She is too fair, too wise, wisely too fair,
  To merit bliss by making me despair.   222
  She hath forsworn to love, and in that vow   223
  Do I live dead that live to tell it now.
BENVOLIO
  Be ruled by me. Forget to think of her.
ROMEO
  O, teach me how I should forget to think!
BENVOLIO
  By giving liberty unto thine eyes:
  Examine other beauties.
ROMEO   'Tis the way

---

206 fair beautiful   **207 fair mark** clear, distinct target   **209 Dian** Diana,
huntress and goddess of chastity   **210 proof** armor   **212 stay** submit
to   **213 bide** abide, endure   **216 store** wealth. (She will die without
children and therefore her beauty will die with her.)   **217 still** always
218 sparing miserliness   **219 starved with** killed by   **222 To . . . despair**
i.e., earning her own salvation through chaste living while driving me to
the spiritually dangerous state of despair   **223 forsworn to** renounced,
repudiated

To call hers, exquisite, in question more.   229
These happy masks that kiss fair ladies' brows,
Being black, puts us in mind they hide the fair.
He that is strucken blind cannot forget
The precious treasure of his eyesight lost.
Show me a mistress that is passing fair: 234
What doth her beauty serve but as a note
Where I may read who passed that passing fair?   236
Farewell. Thou canst not teach me to forget.

BENVOLIO
I'll pay that doctrine, or else die in debt.   *Exeunt.* 238

❖

1.2   *Enter Capulet, County Paris, and the Clown*
            [a Servingman].

CAPULET
But Montague is bound as well as I,   1
In penalty alike, and 'tis not hard, I think,
For men so old as we to keep the peace.

PARIS
Of honorable reckoning are you both,   4
And pity 'tis you lived at odds so long.
But now, my lord, what say you to my suit?

CAPULET
But saying o'er what I have said before: 7
My child is yet a stranger in the world;
She hath not seen the change of fourteen years.
Let two more summers wither in their pride
Ere we may think her ripe to be a bride.

PARIS
Younger than she are happy mothers made.

---

229 **in question more** even more keenly to mind, into consideration
234 **passing** surpassingly   **236 passed** surpassed   **238 pay that doctrine**
i.e., give that instruction.   **die in debt** i.e., feel I've failed as a friend

1.2. Location: Verona. A street.
s.d. County Count   **1 bound** legally obligated (to keep the peace)
4 reckoning estimation, repute   **7 o'er** again

CAPULET
And too soon marred are those so early made.
The earth hath swallowed all my hopes but she;
She's the hopeful lady of my earth.   15
But woo her, gentle Paris, get her heart;
My will to her consent is but a part;
And, she agreed, within her scope of choice   18
Lies my consent and fair according voice.   19
This night I hold an old accustomed feast,   20
Whereto I have invited many a guest
Such as I love; and you among the store,   22
One more, most welcome, makes my number more.
At my poor house look to behold this night
Earth-treading stars that make dark heaven light.
Such comfort as do lusty young men feel   26
When well-appareled April on the heel   27
Of limping winter treads, even such delight
Among fresh fennel buds shall you this night   29
Inherit at my house. Hear all, all see,   30
And like her most whose merit most shall be;
Which on more view of many, mine, being one,   32
May stand in number, though in reckoning none.   33
Come, go with me. [*To the Servingman, giving a paper.*]
   Go, sirrah, trudge about   34
Through fair Verona; find those persons out
Whose names are written there, and to them say,
My house and welcome on their pleasure stay.   37
                              Exit [*with Paris*].
SERVINGMAN   Find them out whose names are written
here! It is written that the shoemaker should meddle 39

15 the hopeful . . . earth i.e., my heir and hope for posterity. (*Earth*
includes property and lands.)   18 she if she be   19 according agreeing   20 old accustomed traditional   22 store group   26 lusty lively
27 well-appareled newly clothed in green   29 fennel flowering herb
thought to have the power of awakening passion   30 Inherit possess
32–33 Which . . . none i.e., when you have looked over many ladies, my
daughter, being one of them, may be numerically counted among the lot
but will count for little in your *reckoning* or estimation. (Capulet puns
on *reckoning* in the sense of arithmetical calculating, and also on the
proverbial saying "one is no number.")   34 sirrah (Customary form of
address to servants.)   37 on . . . stay wait to serve their pleasure
39 meddle (The bawdy suggestion of sexual activity is continued in *yard*
and *pencil*, slang terms for the male sexual organ.)

with his yard and the tailor with his last, the fisher with 40
his pencil, and the painter with his nets; but I am sent 41
to find those persons whose names are here writ, 42
and can never find what names the writing person 43
hath here writ. I must to the learned.—In good time! 44

Enter Benvolio and Romeo.

BENVOLIO
Tut, man, one fire burns out another's burning,
   One pain is lessened by another's anguish; 46
Turn giddy, and be holp by backward turning; 47
   One desperate grief cures with another's languish. 48
Take thou some new infection to thy eye,
And the rank poison of the old will die. 50
ROMEO
Your plantain leaf is excellent for that. 51
BENVOLIO
For what, I pray thee?
ROMEO   For your broken shin.
BENVOLIO   Why, Romeo, art thou mad?
ROMEO
Not mad, but bound more than a madman is; 54
Shut up in prison, kept without my food,
Whipped and tormented and—Good e'en, good fellow. 56
SERVINGMAN   God gi' good e'en. I pray, sir, can you read? 57
ROMEO
Ay, mine own fortune in my misery.

40–41 yard, last, pencil, nets (The servingman humorously assigns
these tools of a trade to the wrong person, to suggest how useless it
is for him, an illiterate servant, to be given a written instruction.)
yard yardstick.   **last** a shoemaker's form.   **pencil** paint brush
42–43 find . . . find locate . . . learn   **44 In good time** i.e., here comes
help   **46 another's anguish** the anguish of another pain   **47 holp**
helped.   **backward** i.e., reverse   **48 cures . . . languish** is cured by the
suffering of a second *grief* or pain   **50 rank** foul   **51 Your** i.e., the kind
of thing people talk about.   **plantain leaf** herb used for cuts and abra-
sions, such as a *broken* or bleeding shin. (Romeo undercuts Benvolio's
sententiousness by taking his medical metaphor literally, as if curing
love were like curing a minor cut.)   **54 bound** (The usual treatment for
madness.)   **56 Good e'en** good evening. (Used after noon.)   **57 gi'**
give you

SERVINGMAN   Perhaps you have learned it without book.   59
But, I pray, can you read anything you see?
ROMEO
Ay, if I know the letters and the language.
SERVINGMAN   Ye say honestly. Rest you merry! [*Going.*]   62
ROMEO   Stay, fellow, I can read.   *He reads the letter.*

"Signor Martino and his wife and daughters,
County Anselme and his beauteous sisters,
The lady widow of Vitruvio,
Signor Placentio and his lovely nieces,
Mercutio and his brother Valentine,
Mine uncle Capulet, his wife, and daughters,
My fair niece Rosaline, and Livia,
Signor Valentio and his cousin Tybalt,
Lucio and the lively Helena."
A fair assembly. Whither should they come?   73
SERVINGMAN   Up.
ROMEO   Whither? To supper?
SERVINGMAN   To our house.
ROMEO   Whose house?
SERVINGMAN   My master's.
ROMEO
Indeed, I should have asked thee that before.
SERVINGMAN   Now I'll tell you without asking. My master
is the great rich Capulet; and if you be not of the
house of Montagues, I pray, come and crush a cup of   82
wine. Rest you merry!   [*Exit.*]
BENVOLIO
At this same ancient feast of Capulet's   84
Sups the fair Rosaline whom thou so loves,
With all the admirèd beauties of Verona.
Go thither, and with unattainted eye   87
Compare her face with some that I shall show,
And I will make thee think thy swan a crow.

59 without book by memory. (The servingman takes Romeo's flowery response to his simple question as though it were the title of a
literary work; his comment also suggests that one can learn misery
without knowing how to read.)   **62 Rest you merry** i.e., farewell. (The
servingman can see he is getting nowhere.)   **73 Whither** where
82 crush i.e., drink   **84 ancient** customary   **87 unattainted** unbiased

ROMEO

When the devout religion of mine eye
   Maintains such falsehood, then turn tears to fires;   91
And these who, often drowned, could never die,   92
   Transparent heretics, be burnt for liars!   93
One fairer than my love? The all-seeing sun
Ne'er saw her match since first the world begun.

BENVOLIO

Tut, you saw her fair, none else being by,
Herself poised with herself in either eye;   97
But in that crystal scales let there be weighed   98
Your lady's love against some other maid
That I will show you shining at this feast,
And she shall scant show well that now seems best.   101

ROMEO

I'll go along, no such sight to be shown,
But to rejoice in splendor of mine own.   [*Exeunt.*] 103

❖

1.3   *Enter Capulet's Wife and Nurse.*

WIFE

Nurse, where's my daughter? Call her forth to me.

NURSE

Now, by my maidenhead at twelve year old,
I bade her come. What, lamb! What, ladybird!   3
God forbid. Where's this girl? What, Juliet!

    Enter Juliet.

JULIET   How now? Who calls?

NURSE   Your mother.

JULIET

Madam, I am here. What is your will?

---

91 Maintains upholds   **92 these** i.e., these my eyes.   **drowned** i.e., in
tears   **93 Transparent** (1) self-evident (2) clear   **97 poised** weighed,
balanced   **98 crystal scales** i.e., Romeo's eyes, in which the ladies are to
be balanced and compared   **101 scant** scarcely   **103 mine own** i.e., the
sight of my own Rosaline

1.3. Location: Verona. Capulet's house.
3 What (An expression of impatience.)   **ladybird** i.e., sweetheart; also,
loose woman (used endearingly, though perhaps also with the immediate apology, "God forbid")

WIFE

  This is the matter.—Nurse, give leave awhile,   8
  We must talk in secret.—Nurse, come back again;
  I have remembered me, thou's hear our counsel.   10
  Thou knowest my daughter's of a pretty age.

NURSE

  Faith, I can tell her age unto an hour.

WIFE

  She's not fourteen.

NURSE   I'll lay fourteen of my teeth—
  And yet, to my teen be it spoken, I have but four—   14
  She's not fourteen. How long is it now
  To Lammastide?

WIFE   A fortnight and odd days.   16

NURSE

  Even or odd, of all days in the year,
  Come Lammas Eve at night shall she be fourteen.
  Susan and she—God rest all Christian souls!—   19
  Were of an age. Well, Susan is with God;
  She was too good for me. But, as I said,
  On Lammas Eve at night shall she be fourteen,
  That shall she, marry, I remember it well.   23
  'Tis since the earthquake now eleven years,
  And she was weaned—I never shall forget it—
  Of all the days of the year, upon that day;
  For I had then laid wormwood to my dug,   27
  Sitting in the sun under the dovehouse wall.
  My lord and you were then at Mantua—
  Nay, I do bear a brain! But, as I said,   30
  When it did taste the wormwood on the nipple
  Of my dug and felt it bitter, pretty fool,   32
  To see it tetchy and fall out wi' th' dug!   33
  "Shake," quoth the dovehouse. 'Twas no need, I trow,   34
  To bid me trudge!   35

---

8 **give leave** leave us   10 **thou's** thou shalt   14 **teen** sorrow (playing on
teen and *four* in *fourteen*)   16 **Lammastide** the days near August 1
19 **Susan** i.e., the Nurse's own child who has evidently died   23 **marry**
i.e., by the Virgin Mary. (A mild oath.)   27 **wormwood** (A bitter-tasting
plant used to wean the child from the *dug* or teat.)   30 **bear a brain**
maintain a keen memory   32 **fool** (A term of endearment here.)
33 **tetchy** fretful   34 **"Shake" . . . dovehouse** i.e., the dovehouse
shook. **trow** believe, assure you   35 **trudge** i.e., be off quickly

And since that time it is eleven years,
For then she could stand high-lone; nay, by the rood,   37
She could have run and waddled all about.
For even the day before, she broke her brow,   39
And then my husband—God be with his soul!
'A was a merry man—took up the child.   41
"Yea," quoth he, "dost thou fall upon thy face?
Thou wilt fall backward when thou hast more wit,   43
Wilt thou not, Jule?" and, by my halidom,   44
The pretty wretch left crying and said "Ay."
To see now how a jest shall come about!   46
I warrant, an I should live a thousand years,
I never should forget it. "Wilt thou not, Jule?" quoth he,
And, pretty fool, it stinted and said "Ay."   49

WIFE
Enough of this. I pray thee, hold thy peace.

NURSE
Yes, madam. Yet I cannot choose but laugh
To think it should leave crying and say "Ay."
And yet, I warrant, it had upon its brow
A bump as big as a young cockerel's stone—   54
A perilous knock—and it cried bitterly.
"Yea," quoth my husband. "Fall'st upon thy face?
Thou wilt fall backward when thou comest to age,
Wilt thou not, Jule?" It stinted and said "Ay."

JULIET
And stint thou too, I pray thee, Nurse, say I.   59

NURSE
Peace, I have done. God mark thee to his grace!
Thou wast the prettiest babe that e'er I nursed.
An I might live to see thee married once,   62
I have my wish.

WIFE
Marry, that "marry" is the very theme
I came to talk of. Tell me, daughter Juliet,
How stands your disposition to be married?   66

---

37 high-lone on her feet, without help.   **rood** cross   **39 broke her brow** bruised her forehead (by falling)   **41 'A** he   **43 wit** understanding **44 halidom** a relic or holy thing   **46 come about** come true   **49 stinted** ceased   **54 cockerel's stone** young rooster's testicle   **59 say I** (with a pun on *said "Ay"* of previous line)   **62 once** someday   **66 disposition** inclination

JULIET
 It is an honor that I dream not of.
NURSE
 An honor? Were not I thine only nurse,
 I would say thou hadst sucked wisdom from thy teat.   69
WIFE
 Well, think of marriage now. Younger than you
 Here in Verona, ladies of esteem   71
 Are made already mothers. By my count
 I was your mother much upon these years   73
 That you are now a maid. Thus then in brief:
 The valiant Paris seeks you for his love.
NURSE
 A man, young lady! Lady, such a man
 As all the world—why, he's a man of wax.   77
WIFE
 Verona's summer hath not such a flower.
NURSE
 Nay, he's a flower, in faith, a very flower.   79
WIFE
 What say you? Can you love the gentleman?
 This night you shall behold him at our feast.
 Read o'er the volume of young Paris' face
 And find delight writ there with beauty's pen;
 Examine every married lineament   84
 And see how one another lends content,   85
 And what obscured in this fair volume lies
 Find written in the margent of his eyes.   87
 This precious book of love, this unbound lover,   88
 To beautify him, only lacks a cover.   89
 The fish lives in the sea, and 'tis much pride   90
 For fair without the fair within to hide.   91

69 thy teat i.e., the teat that nourished you   **71 esteem** worth, nobility
73 much . . . years at much the same age   **77 a man of wax** such as one
would picture in wax, i.e., handsome   **79 Nay** i.e., indeed   **84 married**
harmonized.   **lineament** facial feature   **85 content** (1) satisfaction
(2) substance   **87 margent** commentary or marginal gloss   **88 unbound**
i.e., because not bound in marriage (with a double meaning in the
continuing metaphor of an unbound book)   **89 a cover** i.e., marriage, a
wife   **90–91 The fish . . . hide** i.e., the fish has its own suitable environment, and similarly in marriage the fair Juliet (here imagined as a
beautiful book cover "binding" Paris) would suitably embrace Paris's
worth

That book in many's eyes doth share the glory   92
That in gold clasps locks in the golden story;   93
So shall you share all that he doth possess,
By having him, making yourself no less.

NURSE
No less? Nay, bigger. Women grow by men.   96

WIFE
Speak briefly: can you like of Paris' love?   97

JULIET
I'll look to like, if looking liking move,   98
But no more deep will I endart mine eye   99
Than your consent gives strength to make it fly.

Enter Servingman.

SERVINGMAN Madam, the guests are come, supper
served up, you called, my young lady asked for, the
Nurse cursed in the pantry, and everything in extremity.   103
I must hence to wait. I beseech you, follow straight.   104

WIFE
We follow thee. [*Exit Servingman.*] Juliet, the County
stays.   105

NURSE
Go, girl, seek happy nights to happy days.   *Exeunt.*

❖

1.4   *Enter Romeo, Mercutio, Benvolio, with five or*
        six other maskers; torchbearers.

ROMEO
What, shall this speech be spoke for our excuse?   1
Or shall we on without apology?   2

92–93 That book . . . story i.e., in many persons' eyes a good story is all
the more admirable for being handsomely bound.   **clasps** (1) book
fastenings (2) embraces   **96 bigger** i.e., by pregnancy   **97 like of** be
pleased with   **98 liking move** may provoke affection   **99 endart mine
eye** i.e., let my eyes shoot Love's darts   **103 cursed** i.e., for not helping
with the preparations   **104 straight** at once   **105 County stays** Count
(Paris) waits for you

1.4. Location: Verona. A street in the vicinity of Capulet's house.
1 speech (Maskers were customarily preceded by a messenger or "presenter" with a set speech of compliment.)   **2 on** go on, approach

BENVOLIO
  The date is out of such prolixity.   3
  We'll have no Cupid hoodwinked with a scarf,   4
  Bearing a Tartar's painted bow of lath,   5
  Scaring the ladies like a crowkeeper;   6
  Nor no without-book prologue, faintly spoke   7
  After the prompter, for our entrance;
  But, let them measure us by what they will,
  We'll measure them a measure, and be gone.   10
ROMEO
  Give me a torch. I am not for this ambling.
  Being but heavy, I will bear the light.   12
MERCUTIO
  Nay, gentle Romeo, we must have you dance.
ROMEO
  Not I, believe me. You have dancing shoes
  With nimble soles; I have a soul of lead
  So stakes me to the ground I cannot move.
MERCUTIO
  You are a lover; borrow Cupid's wings
  And soar with them above a common bound.   18
ROMEO
  I am too sore enpiercèd with his shaft   19
  To soar with his light feathers, and so bound 20
  I cannot bound a pitch above dull woe.   21
  Under love's heavy burden do I sink.
MERCUTIO
  And, to sink in it, should you burden love—   23
  Too great oppression for a tender thing.

3 The date . . . prolixity such windy rhetoric is out of fashion. (Directors
sometimes assign this speech to Mercutio.) **4 Cupid** i.e., messenger or
"presenter," probably a boy, disguised as Cupid. **hoodwinked** blindfolded **5 Tartar's . . . bow** (Tartar's bows, shorter and more curved
than the English longbow, were thought to have resembled the old
Roman bow with which Cupid was pictured.) **lath** flimsy wood
6 crowkeeper scarecrow **7 without-book** memorized **10 measure . . .
measure** perform for them a dance **12 heavy** (1) sad (2) the opposite of
light (as at 1.1.137) **18 common** ordinary. **bound** (1) leap in the dance
(2) limit **19 sore** sorely (with pun on *soar;* see also pun on *soles* and
soul in l. 15) **20 bound** confined (with play in l. 21 on the sense of
"leap") **21 pitch** height. (A term from falconry for the highest point of
a hawk's flight.) **23 to sink . . . love** i.e., if you should sink in love, you
would prove a burden to it

ROMEO
  Is love a tender thing? It is too rough,
  Too rude, too boisterous, and it pricks like thorn.

MERCUTIO
  If love be rough with you, be rough with love;
  Prick love for pricking, and you beat love down.   28
  Give me a case to put my visage in.   29
                         [*He puts on a mask.*]
  A visor for a visor! What care I   30
  What curious eye doth quote deformities?   31
  Here are the beetle brows shall blush for me.

BENVOLIO
  Come knock and enter, and no sooner in
  But every man betake him to his legs.   34

ROMEO
  A torch for me. Let wantons light of heart
  Tickle the senseless rushes with their heels,   36
  For I am proverbed with a grandsire phrase: 37
  I'll be a candle holder and look on.   38
  The game was ne'er so fair, and I am done.   39

MERCUTIO
  Tut, dun's the mouse, the constable's own word.   40
  If thou art dun, we'll draw thee from the mire
  Of—save your reverence—love, wherein thou stickest   42
  Up to the ears. Come, we burn daylight, ho!   43

28 Prick . . . down i.e., if love gets rough, fight back (but with bawdy suggestion of *pricking* as a way to satisfy desire and cause it to subside) **29 case** mask **30 A visor . . . visor** i.e., a mask for an ugly mask-like face **31 quote** take notice of **34 to his legs** i.e., to dancing **36 senseless** lacking sensation. **rushes** (used for floor covering) **37 proverbed . . . phrase** furnished with an old proverb **38 candle holder** i.e., onlooker. (Alludes to the proverb, "A good candle holder is a good gamester," i.e., he who merely looks on can't get in trouble.) **39 The game . . . done** (Another proverbial notion, that it is wisest to quit when the gambling is at its best.) **40 dun's the mouse** (A common phrase usually taken to mean "keep still." *Dun*, gray-brown color, plays on *done*, done for. *Dun* also alludes to a Christmas game, "Dun [the gray-brown horse] is in the mire," in which a heavy log representing a horse was hauled out of an imaginary mire by the players.) **constable's own word** (A constable might caution one to keep still; Mercutio mocks Romeo's caution as lovesickness.) **42 save your reverence** (An apology for an improper expression, which Mercutio supposes "love" to be.) **43 burn daylight** i.e., waste time. (But Romeo quibbles, protesting that it is not literally daytime.)

ROMEO
   Nay, that's not so.
MERCUTIO   I mean, sir, in delay
   We waste our lights in vain, like lamps by day.
   Take our good meaning, for our judgment sits   46
   Five times in that ere once in our five wits.   47
ROMEO
   And we mean well in going to this masque,
   But 'tis no wit to go.
MERCUTIO   Why, may one ask?   49
ROMEO
   I dreamt a dream tonight.
MERCUTIO   And so did I.   50
ROMEO
   Well, what was yours?
MERCUTIO   That dreamers often lie.
ROMEO
   In bed asleep, while they do dream things true.
MERCUTIO
   O, then, I see Queen Mab hath been with you.   53
   She is the fairies' midwife, and she comes
   In shape no bigger than an agate stone   55
   On the forefinger of an alderman,   56
   Drawn with a team of little atomi   57
   Over men's noses as they lie asleep.
   Her chariot is an empty hazelnut,
   Made by the joiner squirrel or old grub,   60
   Time out o' mind the fairies' coachmakers.
   Her wagon spokes made of long spinners' legs,   62
   The cover of the wings of grasshoppers,
   Her traces of the smallest spider web,
   Her collars of the moonshine's watery beams,

46–47 Take . . . wits i.e., try to understand what I intend to say, relying
on common sense rather than on the exercise of wit. (The five "wits" or
faculties were common sense, imagination, fantasy, judgment, and
reason.)   **49 wit** wisdom (playing on *wits* in l. 47; *mean* in l. 48 plays on
meaning in l. 46)   **50 tonight** last night   **53 Queen Mab** (Possibly a
name of Celtic origin for the Fairy Queen.)   **55 agate stone** (Precious
stone often carved with diminutive figures and set in a ring.)
56 alderman member of the municipal council   **57 atomi** tiny creatures
(atoms)   **60 joiner** furniture maker.   **grub** insect larva (which bores
holes in nuts)   **62 spinners'** spiders'

Her whip of cricket's bone, the lash of film,   66
Her wagoner a small gray-coated gnat,   67
Not half so big as a round little worm   68
Pricked from the lazy finger of a maid.
And in this state she gallops night by night   70
Through lovers' brains, and then they dream of love;
O'er courtiers' knees, that dream on curtsies straight;   72
O'er lawyers' fingers, who straight dream on fees;
O'er ladies' lips, who straight on kisses dream,
Which oft the angry Mab with blisters plagues
Because their breaths with sweetmeats tainted are.   76
Sometimes she gallops o'er a courtier's nose,
And then dreams he of smelling out a suit.   78
And sometimes comes she with a tithe-pig's tail   79
Tickling a parson's nose as 'a lies asleep;
Then dreams he of another benefice.   81
Sometimes she driveth o'er a soldier's neck,
And then dreams he of cutting foreign throats,
Of breaches, ambuscadoes, Spanish blades,   84
Of healths five fathom deep, and then anon   85
Drums in his ear, at which he starts and wakes,
And being thus frighted swears a prayer or two
And sleeps again. This is that very Mab
That plats the manes of horses in the night,   89
And bakes the elflocks in foul sluttish hairs,   90
Which once untangled much misfortune bodes.
This is the hag, when maids lie on their backs,
That presses them and learns them first to bear,   93

66 film gossamer thread   **67 wagoner** chariot driver   **68 worm** (Alludes to an ancient superstition that "worms breed in the fingers of the idle.")   **70 state** pomp, dignity   **72 curtsies** i.e., bows, obeisances. **straight** immediately   **76 sweetmeats** candies or candied preserves **78 smelling . . . suit** i.e., finding a petitioner who will pay for the use of his influence at court   **79 tithe-pig** pig given to the parson in lieu of money as the parishioner's tithing, or granting of a tenth   **81 benefice** ecclesiastical living   **84 breaches** opening of gaps in fortifications. **ambuscadoes** ambushes.   **Spanish blades** i.e., swords from Toledo, where the best swords were made   **85 healths** toasts.   **five fathom deep** a very deep or tall drink   **89 plats . . . horses** (Alludes to the familiar superstition of "witches' stirrups," tangles in the manes of horses.) **90 elflocks** tangles. (Thought superstitiously to be the work of elves, who would seek revenge if the elflocks were untangled.)   **93 learns** teaches

Making them women of good carriage.   94
This is she—
ROMEO   Peace, peace, Mercutio, peace!
Thou talk'st of nothing.
MERCUTIO   True, I talk of dreams,
Which are the children of an idle brain,
Begot of nothing but vain fantasy,   98
Which is as thin of substance as the air,
And more inconstant than the wind, who woos
Even now the frozen bosom of the north,
And being angered, puffs away from thence,
Turning his side to the dew-dropping south.
BENVOLIO
This wind you talk of blows us from ourselves.   104
Supper is done, and we shall come too late.
ROMEO
I fear, too early; for my mind misgives   106
Some consequence yet hanging in the stars
Shall bitterly begin his fearful date   108
With this night's revels, and expire the term   109
Of a despisèd life closed in my breast
By some vile forfeit of untimely death.
But He that hath the steerage of my course
Direct my suit! On, lusty gentlemen.   113
BENVOLIO   Strike, drum.   114
                    They march about the stage,
                    and [retire to one side].

1.5   *Servingmen come forth with napkins.*

FIRST SERVINGMAN   Where's Potpan, that he helps not to
take away? He shift a trencher? He scrape a trencher? 2

---

94 good carriage (1) commendable deportment (2) skill in bearing the
weight of men in sexual intercourse (3) able subsequently to carry a
child   **98 vain fantasy** empty imagination   **104 from ourselves** i.e.,
from our plans   **106 misgives** fears   **108 date** appointed time
109 expire bring to an end   **113 lusty** lively   **114 drum** drummer

**1.5. Location: The action, continuous from the previous scene, is now
imaginatively transferred to a hall in Capulet's house.**
2 take away clear the table.   **trencher** wooden dish or plate

SECOND SERVINGMAN When good manners shall lie all
in one or two men's hands, and they unwashed too,
'tis a foul thing.

FIRST SERVINGMAN Away with the joint stools, remove 6
the court cupboard, look to the plate. Good thou, save 7
me a piece of marchpane, and, as thou loves me, let 8
the porter let in Susan Grindstone and Nell. [*Exit
Second Servingman.*] Anthony and Potpan!

[*Enter two more Servingmen.*]

THIRD SERVINGMAN Ay, boy, ready.

FIRST SERVINGMAN You are looked for and called for,
asked for and sought for, in the great chamber.

FOURTH SERVINGMAN We cannot be here and there
too. Cheerly, boys! Be brisk awhile, and the longer 15
liver take all.   *Exeunt.* 16

Enter [*Capulet and family and*] all the guests and
gentlewomen to the maskers.

CAPULET [*To the maskers*]
Welcome, gentlemen! Ladies that have their toes
Unplagued with corns will walk a bout with you.   18
Ah, my mistresses, which of you all
Will now deny to dance? She that makes dainty,   20
She, I'll swear, hath corns. Am I come near ye now? 21
Welcome, gentlemen! I have seen the day
That I have worn a visor and could tell
A whispering tale in a fair lady's ear
Such as would please. 'Tis gone, 'tis gone, 'tis gone.
You are welcome, gentlemen! Come, musicians, play.
                  Music plays, and they dance.
A hall, a hall! Give room! And foot it, girls.   27

---

6 joint stools stools with joined corners made by a joiner or furniture
maker **7 court cupboard** sideboard. **plate** silverware **8 marchpane** cake made from sugar and almonds, marzipan **15–16 the longer
. . . all** (A proverb, "the survivor takes all," here used to advocate
seizing the moment of pleasure.) **18 walk a bout** dance a turn
20 makes dainty seems coyly reluctant (to dance) **21 Am . . . now** i.e.,
have I hit a sensitive point, struck home **27 A hall** i.e., clear the hall
for dancing

[*To Servingmen.*] More light, you knaves, and turn the
   tables up,   28
And quench the fire; the room is grown too hot.
[*To his cousin.*] Ah, sirrah, this unlooked-for sport comes
   well.   30
Nay, sit, nay, sit, good cousin Capulet,   31
For you and I are past our dancing days.
How long is 't now since last yourself and I
   Were in a mask?
SECOND CAPULET   By 'r Lady, thirty years.
CAPULET
What, man? 'Tis not so much, 'tis not so much;
'Tis since the nuptial of Lucentio,
Come Pentecost as quickly as it will,   37
Some five-and-twenty years, and then we masked.
SECOND CAPULET
'Tis more, 'tis more. His son is elder, sir;
His son is thirty.
CAPULET   Will you tell me that?
His son was but a ward two years ago.   41
ROMEO [*To a Servingman*]
What lady's that which doth enrich the hand
Of yonder knight?
SERVINGMAN   I know not, sir.
ROMEO
O, she doth teach the torches to burn bright!
It seems she hangs upon the cheek of night
As a rich jewel in an Ethiop's ear—
Beauty too rich for use, for earth too dear!   48
So shows a snowy dove trooping with crows   49
As yonder lady o'er her fellows shows.
The measure done, I'll watch her place of stand,   51
And, touching hers, make blessèd my rude hand.   52

---

28 turn the tables up (Tables were probably made of hinged leaves and
placed on trestles. They were put aside for dancing.)   **30 unlooked-for
sport** i.e., arrival of the maskers, making a dance possible   **31 cousin**
kinsman   **37 Pentecost** seventh Sunday after Easter (and never as late
as mid-July, two weeks before Lammas or August 1 when, according to
1.3.16, the play takes place; a seeming inconsistency)   **41 a ward** a
minor under guardianship   **48 dear** precious   **49 shows** appears
51 The measure done when this dance is over. **her place of stand**
where she stands   **52 hers** i.e., her hand. **rude** rough

Did my heart love till now? Forswear it, sight!   53
For I ne'er saw true beauty till this night.

TYBALT
This, by his voice, should be a Montague.
Fetch me my rapier, boy. What dares the slave   56
Come hither, covered with an antic face,   57
To fleer and scorn at our solemnity?   58
Now, by the stock and honor of my kin,
To strike him dead I hold it not a sin.

CAPULET
Why, how now, kinsman? Wherefore storm you so?

TYBALT
Uncle, this is a Montague, our foe,
A villain that is hither come in spite   63
To scorn at our solemnity this night.

CAPULET
Young Romeo is it?

TYBALT   'Tis he, that villain Romeo.

CAPULET
Content thee, gentle coz, let him alone.
'A bears him like a portly gentleman,   67
And, to say truth, Verona brags of him
To be a virtuous and well governed youth.
I would not for the wealth of all this town
Here in my house do him disparagement.
Therefore be patient; take no note of him.
It is my will, the which if thou respect,
Show a fair presence and put off these frowns,
An ill-beseeming semblance for a feast.   75

TYBALT
It fits when such a villain is a guest.
I'll not endure him.

CAPULET   He shall be endured.
What, goodman boy? I say he shall. Go to!   78
Am I the master here, or you? Go to.

53 **Forswear it** deny any previous oath   56 **What** how   57 **antic face**
grotesque mask   58 **fleer** look mockingly.   **solemnity** time-honored
festivity   63 **spite** malice   67 **portly** of good deportment   75 **semblance**
facial expression   78 **goodman boy** (A belittling term for Tybalt; "Goodman" applied to one below the rank of gentleman, but still of some
substance, like a wealthy farmer.)   **Go to** (An expression of irritation.)

You'll not endure him! God shall mend my soul,
You'll make a mutiny among my guests!   81
You will set cock-a-hoop! You'll be the man!   82

TYBALT
Why, uncle, 'tis a shame.

CAPULET   Go to, go to,
You are a saucy boy. Is 't so, indeed?
This trick may chance to scathe you. I know what.   85
You must contrary me! Marry, 'tis time.—   86
Well said, my hearts!—You are a princox, go.   87
Be quiet, or—More light, more light! —For shame!
I'll make you quiet, what!—Cheerly, my hearts!

TYBALT
Patience perforce with willful choler meeting   90
Makes my flesh tremble in their different greeting.   91
I will withdraw. But this intrusion shall,
Now seeming sweet, convert to bitterest gall.   *Exit.*

ROMEO [*To Juliet*]
If I profane with my unworthiest hand   94
    This holy shrine, the gentle sin is this: 95
My lips, two blushing pilgrims, ready stand
    To smooth that rough touch with a tender kiss.

JULIET
Good pilgrim, you do wrong your hand too much,
    Which mannerly devotion shows in this;   99
For saints have hands that pilgrims' hands do touch,
    And palm to palm is holy palmers' kiss.   101

ROMEO
Have not saints lips, and holy palmers too?

JULIET
Ay, pilgrim, lips that they must use in prayer.

---

81 mutiny disturbance   **82 You . . . cock-a-hoop** i.e., you will behave
recklessly, abandon all restraint.   **be the man** play the big man
85 scathe harm.   **what** what I'm doing, or what I'll do   **86 contrary**
oppose, thwart.   **'tis time** i.e., it's time you were taught a lesson
87 Well said well done. (Said to the dancers.)   **princox** saucy boy
90 Patience perforce patience upon compulsion.   **willful choler** i.e.,
passionate anger   **91 different greeting** antagonistic opposition
94–107 (These lines are in the form of a Shakespearean sonnet; they are
followed by a quatrain.)   **95 shrine** i.e., Juliet's hand   **99 mannerly**
proper   **101 palmers** pilgrims who have been to the Holy Land and
brought back a palm (with a pun on the palm of the hand)

ROMEO
O, then, dear saint, let lips do what hands do.
They pray; grant thou, lest faith turn to despair.   105
JULIET
Saints do not move, though grant for prayers' sake.   106
ROMEO
Then move not, while my prayer's effect I take.   107
                                      [*He kisses her.*]
Thus from my lips, by thine, my sin is purged.
JULIET
Then have my lips the sin that they have took.
ROMEO
Sin from my lips? O trespass sweetly urged!
Give me my sin again.   [*He kisses her.*]
JULIET   You kiss by th' book.   111
NURSE [*Approaching*]
Madam, your mother craves a word with you.
                                      [*Juliet retires.*]
ROMEO
What is her mother?
NURSE   Marry, bachelor,   113
Her mother is the lady of the house,
And a good lady, and a wise and virtuous.
I nursed her daughter that you talked withal.   116
I tell you, he that can lay hold of her
Shall have the chinks.
ROMEO   Is she a Capulet?   118
O dear account! My life is my foe's debt.   119
BENVOLIO [*Approaching*]
Away, begone! The sport is at the best.   120
ROMEO
Ay, so I fear; the more is my unrest.
                            [*The maskers prepare to leave.*]

---

105 grant thou i.e., you must answer their prayers   **106 move** take
the initiative.   **grant** they grant (through intercession with God)
107 move (Romeo quibbles on Juliet's word in the common sense of
"change place or position.")   **111 again** back again.   **by th' book** i.e.,
by the rule, expertly   **113 What** who.   **Marry** i.e., by the Virgin Mary.
bachelor young man   **116 withal** with   **118 the chinks** i.e., plenty of
money   **119 dear account** heavy reckoning.   **my foe's debt** due to my
foe, at his mercy   **120 The sport . . . best** i.e., it is time to leave. (Refers
to the proverb, "When play is at the best, it is time to leave," as at 1.4.39.)

CAPULET
  Nay, gentlemen, prepare not to be gone.
  We have a trifling foolish banquet towards.   123
              [*One whispers in his ear.*]
  Is it e'en so? Why, then, I thank you all.
  I thank you, honest gentlemen. Good night.   125
  More torches here! Come on then, let's to bed.
  [*To his cousin.*] Ah, sirrah, by my fay, it waxes late.   127
  I'll to my rest.
      [*All proceed to leave but Juliet and the Nurse.*]
JULIET
  Come hither, Nurse. What is yond gentleman?
NURSE
  The son and heir of old Tiberio.
JULIET
  What's he that now is going out of door?
NURSE
  Marry, that, I think, be young Petruchio.
JULIET
  What's he that follows here, that would not dance?
NURSE   I know not.
JULIET
  Go ask his name. [*The Nurse goes.*] If he be marrièd,
  My grave is like to be my wedding bed.   136
NURSE [*Returning*]
  His name is Romeo, and a Montague,
  The only son of your great enemy.
JULIET
  My only love sprung from my only hate!
  Too early seen unknown, and known too late!
  Prodigious birth of love it is to me   141
  That I must love a loathèd enemy.
NURSE
  What's tis? What's tis?
JULIET   A rhyme I learned even now   143
  Of one I danced withal.   *One calls within* "Juliet."
NURSE   Anon, anon!   144
  Come, let's away. The strangers all are gone.   *Exeunt.*

❖

123 **foolish banquet towards** insignificant light refreshment in preparation   125 **honest** honorable   127 **fay** faith   136 **like** likely   141 **Prodigious** ominous   143 **tis** this. (Dialect pronunciation.)   144 **Anon** i.e., we're coming

2.0   [*Enter*] *Chorus.*

CHORUS
Now old desire doth in his deathbed lie,
   And young affection gapes to be his heir;   2
That fair for which love groaned for and would die,   3
   With tender Juliet matched, is now not fair.   4
Now Romeo is beloved and loves again,
   Alike bewitchèd by the charm of looks;   6
But to his foe supposed he must complain,   7
   And she steal love's sweet bait from fearful hooks.
Being held a foe, he may not have access
   To breathe such vows as lovers use to swear;   10
And she as much in love, her means much less
   To meet her new-belovèd anywhere.
But passion lends them power, time means, to meet,   13
Tempering extremities with extreme sweet.   [*Exit.*]   14

❖

2.1   *Enter Romeo alone.*

ROMEO
Can I go forward when my heart is here?   1
Turn back, dull earth, and find thy center out.   2
                                        [*Romeo retires.*]

   Enter Benvolio with Mercutio.

BENVOLIO
Romeo! My cousin Romeo! Romeo!
MERCUTIO He is wise
And, on my life, hath stolen him home to bed.

2.0. Chorus.
2 gapes yearns, clamors   **3 fair** beauty, i.e., Rosaline   **4 matched**
compared   **6 Alike** i.e., equally with Juliet   **7 foe supposed** i.e., Juliet, a
Capulet; also, his opposite number in the war of love.   **complain** offer
his love plaint   **10 use** are accustomed   **13 time means** time lends them
means   **14 Tempering extremities** reducing the hardships.   **sweet**
sweetness, pleasure

2.1. Location: Verona. Outside of Capulet's walled orchard.
1 forward i.e., away   **2 dull earth** i.e., Romeo's body.   **center** i.e., Juliet.
(The figure of speech is that of humankind as a microcosm or little world.)

BENVOLIO

He ran this way and leapt this orchard wall.
Call, good Mercutio.

MERCUTIO   Nay, I'll conjure too.   7
Romeo! Humors! Madman! Passion! Lover!   8
Appear thou in the likeness of a sigh.
Speak but one rhyme, and I am satisfied;
Cry but "Ay me!" Pronounce but "love" and "dove."
Speak to my gossip Venus one fair word,   12
One nickname for her purblind son and heir,   13
Young Abraham Cupid, he that shot so trim   14
When King Cophetua loved the beggar maid.—   15
He heareth not, he stirreth not, he moveth not;
The ape is dead, and I must conjure him.—   17
I conjure thee by Rosaline's bright eyes,
By her high forehead and her scarlet lip,
By her fine foot, straight leg, and quivering thigh,
And the demesnes that there adjacent lie,   21
That in thy likeness thou appear to us!

BENVOLIO

An if he hear thee, thou wilt anger him.   23

MERCUTIO

This cannot anger him. 'Twould anger him
To raise a spirit in his mistress' circle   25
Of some strange nature, letting it there stand   26
Till she had laid it and conjured it down;   27
That were some spite. My invocation   28
Is fair and honest; in his mistress' name
I conjure only but to raise up him.

BENVOLIO

Come, he hath hid himself among these trees

---

7 conjure raise him with magical incantation   **8 Humors** moods
12 gossip crony   **13 purblind** dim-sighted   **14 Young Abraham** i.e., one
who is young and yet old, like the Biblical Abraham; Cupid was paradoxically the youngest and oldest of the gods   **15 King Cophetua** (In an
old ballad, the King falls in love with a beggar maid and makes her his
queen.)   **17 ape** (Used as a term of endearment.)   **21 demesnes** regions
(with bawdy suggestion as to what is adjacent to the thighs; bawdy
puns on terms of conjuration continue in *raise, spirit,* i.e., phallus or
semen, *circle, stand, laid it, raise up*)   **23 An if** if   **25 circle** (1) conjuring
circle (2) vagina   **26 strange** belonging to another person (with suggestion of a rival possessing Rosaline sexually)   **27 laid it** (1) laid the spirit
to rest (2) provided sexual satisfaction leading to cessation of erection
28 were would be.   **spite** injury, vexation

To be consorted with the humorous night.   32
Blind is his love, and best befits the dark.
MERCUTIO
If love be blind, love cannot hit the mark.
Now will he sit under a medlar tree   35
And wish his mistress were that kind of fruit
As maids call medlars when they laugh alone.
O, Romeo, that she were, O, that she were
An open-arse, and thou a poppering pear!   39
Romeo, good night. I'll to my truckle bed;   40
This field bed is too cold for me to sleep.
Come, shall we go?
BENVOLIO   Go, then, for 'tis in vain
To seek him here that means not to be found.
                              Exit [*with Mercutio*].

2.2

ROMEO [*Coming forward*]
He jests at scars that never felt a wound.   1
        [*A light appears above, as at Juliet's window.*]
But soft, what light through yonder window breaks?
It is the east, and Juliet is the sun.
Arise, fair sun, and kill the envious moon,
Who is already sick and pale with grief
That thou her maid art far more fair than she.   6

32 **consorted** associated.   **humorous** moist; also, influenced by humor
or mood   **35, 39 medlar, poppering** (Fruits used as slang terms for the
sexual organs, female and male respectively. The medlar was edible
only when partly decayed; the poppering pear, taking its name from
Poperinghe in Flanders, had a phallic shape; the sound of its name is
also suggestive.)   **39 open-arse** (A name for the *medlar* making explicit
the sexual metaphor.)   **40 truckle bed** a bed on casters to be rolled
under a standing bed

**2.2. Location: The action, continuous from the previous scene, is now
imaginatively transferred to inside Capulet's orchard. A rhymed couplet
links the two scenes. Romeo has been hiding from his friends as though
concealed by the orchard wall. He speaks at once, then turns to observe
Juliet's window, which is probably in the gallery above, rearstage.**
1 s.d. A light appears (Some editors assume that Juliet is visible at l. 1.)
6 maid i.e., votary of Diana, goddess of the moon and patroness of
virgins

Be not her maid, since she is envious;
Her vestal livery is but sick and green   8
And none but fools do wear it. Cast it off.
                          [*Juliet is visible at her window.*]
It is my lady, O, it is my love!
O, that she knew she were!
She speaks, yet she says nothing. What of that?
Her eye discourses; I will answer it.
I am too bold. 'Tis not to me she speaks.
Two of the fairest stars in all the heaven,
Having some business, do entreat her eyes
To twinkle in their spheres till they return.   17
What if her eyes were there, they in her head?
The brightness of her cheek would shame those stars
As daylight doth a lamp; her eyes in heaven
Would through the airy region stream so bright   21
That birds would sing and think it were not night.
See how she leans her cheek upon her hand!
O, that I were a glove upon that hand,
That I might touch that cheek!
JULIET   Ay me!
ROMEO   She speaks!
O, speak again, bright angel, for thou art
As glorious to this night, being o'er my head,
As is a wingèd messenger of heaven
Unto the white-upturnèd wondering eyes   29
Of mortals that fall back to gaze on him
When he bestrides the lazy puffing clouds
And sails upon the bosom of the air.
JULIET
O Romeo, Romeo, wherefore art thou Romeo?   33
Deny thy father and refuse thy name!

---

8 **Her vestal livery** the uniform of Diana's chaste votaries. **sick and
green** (Suggesting the pallor of moonlight as well as anemia or *greensickness* [see 3.5.156] to which teenage girls were susceptible.)
17 **spheres** transparent concentric shells supported to carry the heavenly bodies with them in their revolution around the earth   21 **stream**
shine   29 **white-upturnèd** looking upward so that the whites of the eyes
are visible   33 **wherefore** why

Or, if thou wilt not, be but sworn my love,
And I'll no longer be a Capulet.
ROMEO [*Aside*]
Shall I hear more, or shall I speak at this?
JULIET
'Tis but thy name that is my enemy;
Thou art thyself, though not a Montague.   39
What's Montague? It is nor hand, nor foot,   40
Nor arm, nor face, nor any other part
Belonging to a man. O, be some other name!
What's in a name? That which we call a rose
By any other word would smell as sweet;
So Romeo would, were he not Romeo called,
Retain that dear perfection which he owes   46
Without that title. Romeo, doff thy name,   47
And for thy name, which is no part of thee,   48
Take all myself.
ROMEO   I take thee at thy word!
Call me but love, and I'll be new baptized;
Henceforth I never will be Romeo.
JULIET
What man art thou that, thus bescreened in night,   52
So stumblest on my counsel?
ROMEO   By a name   53
I know not how to tell thee who I am.
My name, dear saint, is hateful to myself,
Because it is an enemy to thee;
Had I it written, I would tear the word.
JULIET
My ears have not yet drunk a hundred words
Of thy tongue's uttering, yet I know the sound:
Art thou not Romeo and a Montague?
ROMEO
Neither, fair maid, if either thee dislike.   61
JULIET
How camest thou hither, tell me, and wherefore?
The orchard walls are high and hard to climb,

---

39 though not a Montague i.e., even if you were not a Montague **40 nor
hand** neither hand **46 owes** owns **47 doff** cast off **48 for** in exchange
for **52 bescreened** concealed **53 counsel** secret thought **61 thee dislike**
displease you

And the place death, considering who thou art,
If any of my kinsmen find thee here.

ROMEO
With love's light wings did I o'erperch these walls,   66
For stony limits cannot hold love out,
And what love can do, that dares love attempt;
Therefore thy kinsmen are no stop to me.

JULIET
If they do see thee, they will murder thee.

ROMEO
Alack, there lies more peril in thine eye
Than twenty of their swords. Look thou but sweet,
And I am proof against their enmity.   73

JULIET
I would not for the world they saw thee here.

ROMEO
I have night's cloak to hide me from their eyes;
And but thou love me, let them find me here.   76
My life were better ended by their hate
Than death proroguèd, wanting of thy love.   78

JULIET
By whose direction foundst thou out this place?

ROMEO
By love, that first did prompt me to inquire.
He lent me counsel, and I lent him eyes.
I am no pilot; yet, wert thou as far
As that vast shore washed with the farthest sea,
I should adventure for such merchandise.

JULIET
Thou knowest the mask of night is on my face,
Else would a maiden blush bepaint my cheek
For that which thou hast heard me speak tonight.
Fain would I dwell on form—fain, fain deny   88
What I have spoke; but farewell compliment!   89
Dost thou love me? I know thou wilt say "Ay,"
And I will take thy word. Yet if thou swear'st
Thou mayst prove false. At lovers' perjuries,
They say, Jove laughs. O gentle Romeo,

---

66 o'erperch fly over   **73 proof** protected   **76 but** unless   **78 proroguèd**
postponed.   **wanting of** lacking   **88 Fain** gladly.   **dwell on form** preserve
the proper formalities   **89 compliment** etiquette, convention

If thou dost love, pronounce it faithfully.
Or if thou thinkest I am too quickly won,
I'll frown and be perverse and say thee nay,
So thou wilt woo, but else not for the world.   97
In truth, fair Montague, I am too fond,   98
And therefore thou mayst think my havior light.   99
But trust me, gentleman, I'll prove more true
Than those that have more coying to be strange.   101
I should have been more strange, I must confess,
But that thou overheardst, ere I was ware,   103
My true-love passion. Therefore pardon me,
And not impute this yielding to light love,
Which the dark night hath so discoverèd.   106

ROMEO
Lady, by yonder blessèd moon I vow,
That tips with silver all these fruit-tree tops—

JULIET
O, swear not by the moon, th' inconstant moon,
That monthly changes in her circled orb,   110
Lest that thy love prove likewise variable.

ROMEO
What shall I swear by?

JULIET   Do not swear at all;
Or, if thou wilt, swear by thy gracious self,
Which is the god of my idolatry,
And I'll believe thee.

ROMEO   If my heart's dear love—

JULIET
Well, do not swear. Although I joy in thee,
I have no joy of this contract tonight.   117
It is too rash, too unadvised, too sudden,   118
Too like the lightning, which doth cease to be
Ere one can say "It lightens." Sweet, good night!
This bud of love, by summer's ripening breath,
May prove a beauteous flower when next we meet.
Good night, good night! As sweet repose and rest   123
Come to thy heart as that within my breast!

97 So as long as, if only.   **else** otherwise   **98 fond** infatuated   **99 havior light** behavior frivolous   **101 coying** coyness.   **strange** reserved, aloof, modest   **103 ware** aware   **106 Which** i.e., which yielding.   **discoverèd** revealed   **110 orb** i.e., sphere; see above, l. 17   **117 contract** exchanging of vows   **118 unadvised** unconsidered   **123 As** may just as

ROMEO
  O, wilt thou leave me so unsatisfied?
JULIET
  What satisfaction canst thou have tonight?
ROMEO
  Th' exchange of thy love's faithful vow for mine.
JULIET
  I gave thee mine before thou didst request it;
  And yet I would it were to give again.   129
ROMEO
  Wouldst thou withdraw it? For what purpose, love?
JULIET
  But to be frank and give it thee again.   131
  And yet I wish but for the thing I have.
  My bounty is as boundless as the sea,
  My love as deep; the more I give to thee,
  The more I have, for both are infinite.
                              [*The Nurse calls within.*]
  I hear some noise within; dear love, adieu!—
  Anon, good Nurse!—Sweet Montague, be true.
  Stay but a little, I will come again.   [*Exit, above.*]
ROMEO
  O blessèd, blessèd night! I am afeard,
  Being in night, all this is but a dream,
  Too flattering-sweet to be substantial.

        [*Enter Juliet, above.*]

JULIET
  Three words, dear Romeo, and good night indeed.
  If that thy bent of love be honorable,   143
  Thy purpose marriage, send me word tomorrow,
  By one that I'll procure to come to thee,
  Where and what time thou wilt perform the rite;
  And all my fortunes at thy foot I'll lay
  And follow thee my lord throughout the world.
NURSE [*Within*]   Madam!
JULIET
  I come, anon.—But if thou meanest not well,
  I do beseech thee—
NURSE [*Within*]   Madam!

129 were were available   **131 frank** liberal, bounteous   **143 bent** purpose

JULIET   By and by, I come—   151
  To cease thy strife and leave me to my grief.   152
  Tomorrow will I send.
ROMEO   So thrive my soul—
JULIET   A thousand times good night!   [*Exit, above.*]
ROMEO
  A thousand times the worse, to want thy light.
  Love goes toward love as schoolboys from their books,
  But love from love, toward school with heavy looks.
                              [*He starts to leave.*]
        Enter Juliet [above] again.
JULIET
  Hist! Romeo, hist! O, for a falconer's voice,
  To lure this tassel-gentle back again!   160
  Bondage is hoarse and may not speak aloud,   161
  Else would I tear the cave where Echo lies   162
  And make her airy tongue more hoarse than mine
  With repetition of "My Romeo!"
ROMEO
  It is my soul that calls upon my name.
  How silver-sweet sound lovers' tongues by night,
  Like softest music to attending ears!
JULIET
  Romeo!
ROMEO   My nyas?
JULIET   What o'clock tomorrow   168
  Shall I send to thee?
ROMEO   By the hour of nine.
JULIET
  I will not fail. 'Tis twenty years till then.—
  I have forgot why I did call thee back.
ROMEO
  Let me stand here till thou remember it.
JULIET
  I shall forget, to have thee still stand there,   173
  Remembering how I love thy company.

151 By and by immediately   **152 strife** striving   **160 tassel-gentle** tercel
gentle, the male of the goshawk   **161 Bondage is hoarse** i.e., in confinement one can speak only in a loud whisper   **162 tear** pierce (with
noise).   **Echo** (In Book 3 of Ovid's *Metamorphoses*, Echo, rejected by
Narcissus, pines away in lonely caves until only her voice is left.)
168 nyas eyas, fledgling   **173 still** always

ROMEO
  And I'll still stay, to have thee still forget,
  Forgetting any other home but this.
JULIET
  'Tis almost morning. I would have thee gone—
  And yet no farther than a wanton's bird,   178
  That lets it hop a little from his hand,
  Like a poor prisoner in his twisted gyves,   180
  And with a silken thread plucks it back again,
  So loving-jealous of his liberty.   182
ROMEO
  I would I were thy bird.
JULIET   Sweet, so would I.
  Yet I should kill thee with much cherishing.
  Good night, good night! Parting is such sweet sorrow
  That I shall say good night till it be morrow.
                        [Exit, above.]
ROMEO
  Sleep dwell upon thine eyes, peace in thy breast!
  Would I were sleep and peace, so sweet to rest!
  Hence will I to my ghostly friar's close cell,   189
  His help to crave, and my dear hap to tell.   *Exit.* 190

2.3   *Enter Friar [Laurence] alone, with a basket.*

FRIAR LAURENCE
  The gray-eyed morn smiles on the frowning night,
  Check'ring the eastern clouds with streaks of light,
  And fleckled darkness like a drunkard reels   3
  From forth day's path and Titan's fiery wheels.   4
  Now, ere the sun advance his burning eye,   5
  The day to cheer and night's dank dew to dry,
  I must up-fill this osier cage of ours   7

178 **wanton's** spoiled child's   180 **gyves** fetters   182 **his** its   189 **ghostly**
spiritual.   **close** narrow   190 **dear hap** good fortune

2.3. Location: Verona. Near Friar Laurence's cell, perhaps in the monastery garden.
3 **fleckled** dappled   4 **From forth** out of the way of.   **Titan's** (Helios,
the sun god, was a descendant of the race of Titans.)   5 **advance** raise
7 **osier cage** willow basket

With baleful weeds and precious-juicèd flowers.   8
The earth that's nature's mother is her tomb;
What is her burying grave, that is her womb;
And from her womb children of divers kind
We sucking on her natural bosom find,
Many for many virtues excellent,
None but for some, and yet all different.   14
O, mickle is the powerful grace that lies   15
In plants, herbs, stones, and their true qualities.   16
For naught so vile that on the earth doth live   17
But to the earth some special good doth give;
Nor aught so good but, strained from that fair use,   19
Revolts from true birth, stumbling on abuse.
Virtue itself turns vice, being misapplied,
And vice sometime's by action dignified.

    Enter Romeo.

Within the infant rind of this weak flower
Poison hath residence and medicine power:
For this, being smelt, with that part cheers each part;   25
Being tasted, stays all senses with the heart.   26
Two such opposèd kings encamp them still   27
In man as well as herbs—grace and rude will;
And where the worser is predominant,
Full soon the canker death eats up that plant.   30
ROMEO
Good morrow, Father.
FRIAR LAURENCE   Benedicite!   31
What early tongue so sweet saluteth me?
Young son, it argues a distempered head   33
So soon to bid good morrow to thy bed.
Care keeps his watch in every old man's eye,
And where care lodges sleep will never lie;
But where unbruisèd youth with unstuffed brain   37
Doth couch his limbs, there golden sleep doth reign.

8 baleful harmful   **14 None but for some** there are none that are not
useful for something   **15 mickle** great.   **grace** beneficent virtue
16 true proper, inherent   **17 For naught so vile** for there is nothing so
vile   **19 strained** forced, perverted   **25 that part** i.e., the odor   **26 stays**
halts   **27 still** always   **30 canker** cankerworm   **31 Benedicite** a blessing on you   **33 argues** demonstrates, provides evidence of.   **distem-**
pered disturbed, disordered   **37 unstuffed** not overcharged, carefree

Therefore thy earliness doth me assure
Thou art uproused with some distemp'rature;
Or if not so, then here I hit it right:
Our Romeo hath not been in bed tonight.

ROMEO
That last is true. The sweeter rest was mine.

FRIAR LAURENCE
God pardon sin! Wast thou with Rosaline?

ROMEO
With Rosaline, my ghostly father? No.
I have forgot that name, and that name's woe.

FRIAR LAURENCE
That's my good son. But where hast thou been, then?

ROMEO
I'll tell thee ere thou ask it me again.
I have been feasting with mine enemy,
Where on a sudden one hath wounded me
That's by me wounded. Both our remedies   51
Within thy help and holy physic lies.   52
I bear no hatred, blessèd man, for, lo,
My intercession likewise steads my foe.   54

FRIAR LAURENCE
Be plain, good son, and homely in thy drift.   55
Riddling confession finds but riddling shrift.   56

ROMEO
Then plainly know my heart's dear love is set
On the fair daughter of rich Capulet.
As mine on hers, so hers is set on mine,
And all combined, save what thou must combine
By holy marriage. When and where and how
We met, we wooed, and made exchange of vow
I'll tell thee as we pass; but this I pray,
That thou consent to marry us today.

FRIAR LAURENCE
Holy Saint Francis, what a change is here!
Is Rosaline, that thou didst love so dear,
So soon forsaken? Young men's love then lies
Not truly in their hearts, but in their eyes.

51 Both our remedies i.e., the remedy for both of us **52 physic** medicine, healing property **54 intercession** petition. **steads** helps
55 homely simple **56 shrift** absolution

Jesu Maria, what a deal of brine
Hath washed thy sallow cheeks for Rosaline!   70
How much salt water thrown away in waste
To season love, that of it doth not taste!
The sun not yet thy sighs from heaven clears,
Thy old groans yet ringing in mine ancient ears.
Lo, here upon thy cheek the stain doth sit
Of an old tear that is not washed off yet.
If e'er thou wast thyself and these woes thine,   77
Thou and these woes were all for Rosaline.
And art thou changed? Pronounce this sentence then: 79
Women may fall, when there's no strength in men.

ROMEO
Thou chidst me oft for loving Rosaline.   81

FRIAR LAURENCE
For doting, not for loving, pupil mine.

ROMEO
And badst me bury love.

FRIAR LAURENCE   Not in a grave   83
To lay one in, another out to have.

ROMEO
I pray thee, chide not. She whom I love now
Doth grace for grace and love for love allow.   86
The other did not so.

FRIAR LAURENCE   O, she knew well
Thy love did read by rote, that could not spell.   88
But come, young waverer, come, go with me.
In one respect I'll thy assistant be;   90
For this alliance may so happy prove
To turn your households' rancor to pure love.   92

ROMEO
O, let us hence! I stand on sudden haste.   93

FRIAR LAURENCE
Wisely and slow. They stumble that run fast.

Exeunt.

❖

70 **sallow** sickly yellow   77 **wast thyself** i.e., were sincere   79 **sentence**
sententious conclusion   81 **chidst** rebuked   83 **badst** bade   86 **grace**
favor, graciousness   88 **did read by rote** i.e., repeated conventional
expressions without understanding them   90 **In one respect** for one
reason (at least)   92 **To** as to   93 **stand on** am in need of, insist on

2.4 *Enter Benvolio and Mercutio.*

MERCUTIO
Where the devil should this Romeo be?   1
Came he not home tonight?   2
BENVOLIO
Not to his father's. I spoke with his man.
MERCUTIO
Why, that same pale hardhearted wench, that Rosaline,
Torments him so that he will sure run mad.
BENVOLIO
Tybalt, the kinsman to old Capulet,
Hath sent a letter to his father's house.
MERCUTIO   A challenge, on my life.
BENVOLIO   Romeo will answer it.   9
MERCUTIO   Any man that can write may answer a letter.
BENVOLIO   Nay, he will answer the letter's master, how
he dares, being dared.
MERCUTIO   Alas poor Romeo! He is already dead,
stabbed with a white wench's black eye, run through
the ear with a love song, the very pin of his heart cleft 15
with the blind bow-boy's butt shaft. And is he a man   16
to encounter Tybalt?
BENVOLIO   Why, what is Tybalt?
MERCUTIO   More than prince of cats. O, he's the   19
courageous captain of compliments. He fights as you   20
sing prick song, keeps time, distance, and pro-   21
portion; he rests his minim rests, one, two, and the   22
third in your bosom. The very butcher of a silk button,   23
a duellist, a duellist, a gentleman of the very first   24
house, of the first and second cause. Ah, the immortal   25

2.4. Location: Verona. A street.
1 should can   **2 tonight** last night   **9 answer it** accept the challenge
15 pin peg in the center of a target   **16 butt shaft** unbarbed arrow,
allotted to children and thus to Cupid   **19 prince of cats** (The name of
the king of cats in *Reynard the Fox* was Tybalt or Tybert.)   **20 captain of
compliments** master of ceremony and dueling etiquette   **21 prick song**
music written out   **21–22 proportion** rhythm   **22 minim rests** short
rests in musical notation   **23 butcher . . . button** i.e., one able to strike a
specific button on his adversary's person   **24–25 first house** best school
of fencing   **25 first and second cause** causes according to the code of
dueling that would oblige one to seek the satisfaction of one's honor

passado! The *punto reverso*! The *hay*!   26
BENVOLIO   The what?
MERCUTIO   The pox of such antic, lisping, affecting phan-   28
tasimes, these new tuners of accent! "By Jesu, a very   29
good blade! A very tall man! A very good whore!"   30
Why, is not this a lamentable thing, grandsire, that we   31
should be thus afflicted with these strange flies, these   32
fashionmongers, these pardon-me's, who stand so   33
much on the new form that they cannot sit at ease on   34
the old bench? O, their bones, their bones!   35

   Enter Romeo.

BENVOLIO   Here comes Romeo, here comes Romeo.
MERCUTIO   Without his roe, like a dried herring. O   37
flesh, flesh, how art thou fishified! Now is he for the
numbers that Petrarch flowed in. Laura to his lady was   39
but a kitchen wench—marry, she had a better love to
berhyme her—Dido a dowdy, Cleopatra a gypsy, Helen   41
and Hero hildings and harlots, Thisbe a gray eye   42
or so, but not to the purpose. Signor Romeo, *bon-*   43
jour! There's a French salutation to your French slop.   44
You gave us the counterfeit fairly last night.   45
ROMEO   Good morrow to you both. What counterfeit
did I give you?

26 passado forward thrust.   **punto reverso** backhanded stroke.   **hay** thrust
through. (From the Italian *hai*, meaning "you have [it].")   **28 The pox of**
plague take.   **antic** grotesque   **28–29 phantasimes** coxcombs, fantastically
dressed or mannered   **29 new tuners of accent** those who introduce new
foreign words and slang phrases into their speech   **30 tall** valiant
31 grandsire i.e., one who disapproves the new fashion and prefers old
custom   **32 flies** parasites   **33 pardon-me's** i.e., those who affect overly
polite manners.   **stand** (1) insist (2) the opposite of *sit*, l. 34   **34–35 form**
. . . bench (*Form* means both "fashion" or "code of manners" and
"bench.")   **35 bones** French *bon*, good (with play on English *bone*)
37 Without his roe i.e., looking thin and emaciated, sexually spent. (With a
pun on the first syllable of Romeo's name; the remaining syllables, *me-oh*,
sound like the expression of a melancholy lover. *Roe* also suggests a female
deer or "dear.")   **39 numbers** verses.   **Laura** the lady to whom the Italian
Renaissance poet Petrarch addressed his love poems. (Other romantic
heroines are named in the following passage: Dido, Queen of Carthage;
Cleopatra; Helen of Troy; Hero, beloved of Leander; and Thisbe, beloved of
Pyramus.)   **to** in comparison to   **41 dowdy** homely woman.   **gypsy** Egyp-
tian; whore   **42 hildings** good-for-nothings   **43 not** i.e., that is not
44 French slop loose trousers of French fashion   **45 fairly** handsomely,
effectively

MERCUTIO   The slip, sir, the slip. Can you not conceive?   48
ROMEO   Pardon, good Mercutio, my business was great,
  and in such a case as mine a man may strain courtesy.
MERCUTIO   That's as much as to say, such a case as yours   51
  constrains a man to bow in the hams.   52
ROMEO   Meaning, to curtsy.   53
MERCUTIO   Thou hast most kindly hit it.   54
ROMEO   A most courteous exposition.
MERCUTIO   Nay, I am the very pink of courtesy.
ROMEO   Pink for flower.
MERCUTIO   Right.
ROMEO   Why then is my pump well flowered.   59
MERCUTIO   Sure wit, follow me this jest now till thou
  hast worn out thy pump, that when the single sole of
  it is worn, the jest may remain, after the wearing, solely   62
  singular.   63
ROMEO   O single-soled jest, solely singular for the single-   64
  ness!   65
MERCUTIO   Come between us, good Benvolio. My wits
  faints.
ROMEO   Switch and spurs, switch and spurs! Or I'll cry a   68
  match.   69
MERCUTIO   Nay, if our wits run the wild-goose chase, I   70
  am done, for thou hast more of the wild goose in one
  of thy wits than, I am sure, I have in my whole five.
  Was I with you there for the goose?   73
ROMEO   Thou wast never with me for anything when
  thou wast not there for the goose.   75
MERCUTIO   I will bite thee by the ear for that jest.   76

---

48 slip (Counterfeit coins were called "slips.")   **conceive** i.e., get the joke
51 case (1) situation (2) physical condition. (Mercutio also bawdily suggests
that Romeo has been in a *case*, i.e., the female genitalia.)   **52 bow in the
hams** (1) kneel, curtsy (2) show the effects of venereal disease   **53 curtsy**
make obeisance   **54 kindly** naturally; politely   **59 pump** shoe.   **well
flowered** expertly pinked or perforated in ornamental figures   **62–63 solely
singular** unique   **64 single-soled** i.e., thin, contemptible   **64–65 singleness**
feebleness   **68 Switch and spurs** i.e., keep up the rapid pace of the hunt (in
the game of wits)   **68–69 cry a match** claim the victory   **70 wild-goose
chase** a horse race in which the leading rider dares his competitors to
follow him wherever he goes   **73 Was . . . goose** did I score a point in
calling you a goose   **75 for the goose** (1) behaving like a goose (2) looking
for a prostitute   **76 bite . . . ear** i.e., give you an affectionate nibble on the
ear. (Said ironically, however, and Romeo parries.)

ROMEO   Nay, good goose, bite not.

MERCUTIO   Thy wit is a very bitter sweeting; it is a most 78
sharp sauce. 79

ROMEO   And is it not, then, well served in to a sweet
goose?

MERCUTIO   O, here's a wit of cheveril, that stretches 82
from an inch narrow to an ell broad! 83

ROMEO   I stretch it out for that word "broad," which,
added to the goose, proves thee far and wide a broad 85
goose.

MERCUTIO   Why, is not this better now than groaning
for love? Now art thou sociable, now art thou Romeo;
now art thou what thou art, by art as well as by nature.
For this driveling love is like a great natural that runs 90
lolling up and down to hide his bauble in a hole. 91

BENVOLIO   Stop there, stop there.

MERCUTIO   Thou desirest me to stop in my tale against 93
the hair. 94

BENVOLIO   Thou wouldst else have made thy tale large.

MERCUTIO   O, thou art deceived; I would have made it
short, for I was come to the whole depth of my tale
and meant indeed to occupy the argument no longer.

ROMEO   Here's goodly gear! 99

Enter Nurse and her man [Peter].

A sail, a sail!

MERCUTIO   Two, two: a shirt and a smock. 101

NURSE   Peter!

PETER   Anon!

NURSE   My fan, Peter.

MERCUTIO   Good Peter, to hide her face, for her fan's the
fairer face.

---

78 sweeting sweet-flavored variety of apple   **79 sharp sauce** (1) "biting"
retort (2) tart sauce, of the sort that should be served with cooked goose
(as Romeo points out)   **82 cheveril** kid leather, easily stretched   **83 ell**
(forty-five inches)   **85 broad** large, complete; perhaps also wanton
90 natural idiot   **91 lolling** with his tongue (or bauble) hanging out.
bauble (1) jester's wand (2) phallus   **93–94 against the hair** against the
grain, against my wish (with a bawdy play on *tale, tail;* continued with
large, short, depth, occupy, etc.)   **99 gear** substance, stuff (with sexual
innuendo)   **101 a shirt . . . smock** i.e., a man and a woman

NURSE   God gi' good morrow, gentlemen.

MERCUTIO   God gi' good e'en, fair gentlewoman.

NURSE   Is it good e'en?   109

MERCUTIO   'Tis no less, I tell ye, for the bawdy hand of
the dial is now upon the prick of noon.   111

NURSE   Out upon you! What a man are you?   112

ROMEO   One, gentlewoman, that God hath made for
himself to mar.   114

NURSE   By my troth, it is well said. "For himself to mar,"   115
quoth 'a? Gentlemen, can any of you tell me where I   116
may find the young Romeo?

ROMEO   I can tell you; but young Romeo will be older
when you have found him than he was when you
sought him. I am the youngest of that name, for fault   120
of a worse.

NURSE   You say well.

MERCUTIO   Yea, is the worst well? Very well took, i'   123
faith, wisely, wisely.

NURSE   If you be he, sir, I desire some confidence   125
with you.

BENVOLIO   She will indite him to some supper.   127

MERCUTIO   A bawd, a bawd, a bawd! So ho!   128

ROMEO   What hast thou found?

MERCUTIO   No hare, sir, unless a hare, sir, in a lenten   130
pie, that is something stale and hoar ere it be spent.   131

[*He sings.*]

An old hare hoar,
And an old hare hoar,
Is very good meat in Lent.
But a hare that is hoar

---

109 Is it good e'en is it afternoon already   **111 prick** point on the dial
of a clock (with bawdy suggestion)   **112 Out upon you** (Expression of
indignation.)   **What** what kind of   **114 mar** i.e., disfigure morally
through sin. (Man, made in God's image, mars that image sinfully.)
115 troth faith   **116 quoth 'a** said he. (A sarcastic interjection, meaning
"forsooth" or "indeed.")   **120 fault** lack   **123 took** understood
125 confidence (The Nurse's mistake for *conference*.)   **127 indite** (Benvolio's deliberate malapropism for *invite*.)   **128 So ho** (Cry of hunter
sighting game.)   **130 hare** (Slang word for "prostitute"; similarly with
stale and *meat* in the following lines.)   **130–131 a lenten pie** a pie that
should contain no meat, in observance of Lent   **131 hoar** moldy (with
pun on *whore*).   **spent** consumed

Is too much for a score,   136
When it hoars ere it be spent.
Romeo, will you come to your father's? We'll to dinner
thither.
ROMEO   I will follow you.
MERCUTIO   Farewell, ancient lady. Farewell, [*Singing*]
"Lady, lady, lady."   *Exeunt [Mercutio and Benvolio].*   142
NURSE   I pray you, sir, what saucy merchant was this   143
that was so full of his ropery?   144
ROMEO   A gentleman, Nurse, that loves to hear himself
talk, and will speak more in a minute than he will
stand to in a month.   147
NURSE   An 'a speak anything against me, I'll take him   148
down, an 'a were lustier than he is, and twenty such   149
Jacks; and if I cannot, I'll find those that shall. Scurvy 150
knave! I am none of his flirt-gills. I am none of his   151
skains-mates. [*To Peter.*] And thou must stand by, too,   152
and suffer every knave to use me at his pleasure!
PETER   I saw no man use you at his pleasure. If I had,
my weapon should quickly have been out; I warrant   155
you, I dare draw as soon as another man, if I see occasion in a good quarrel, and the law on my side.
NURSE   Now, afore God, I am so vexed that every part   158
about me quivers. Scurvy knave! Pray you, sir, a   159
word; and as I told you, my young lady bid me inquire you out. What she bid me say, I will keep to
myself. But first let me tell ye, if ye should lead her in
a fool's paradise, as they say, it were a very gross kind
of behavior, as they say. For the gentlewoman is
young; and therefore if you should deal double with
her, truly it were an ill thing to be offered to any gentlewoman, and very weak dealing.   167

136 for a score for a reckoning, to pay good money for   **142 "Lady,
lady, lady"** (Refrain from the ballad *Chaste Susanna.*)   **143 merchant**
i.e., fellow   **144 ropery** vulgar humor, knavery   **147 stand to** perform,
abide by   **148–149 take him down** i.e., cut him down to size (with
unintended bawdy suggestion)   **150 Jacks** (used as a term of disparagement)   **151 flirt-gills** loose women   **152 skains-mates** (Perhaps dagger-
mates, outlaws, or gangster molls.)   **155 weapon** (with bawdy
suggestion, perhaps unrecognized by the speaker, as also in *at his
pleasure*)   **158–159 every part . . . quivers** (More bawdy suggestion,
unrecognized by the Nurse.)   **167 weak** contemptible

ROMEO   Nurse, commend me to thy lady and mistress.
I protest unto thee—   169
NURSE   Good heart, and i' faith I will tell her as much.
Lord, Lord, she will be a joyful woman.
ROMEO   What wilt thou tell her, Nurse? Thou dost not
mark me.   173
NURSE   I will tell her, sir, that you do protest, which, as
I take it, is a gentlemanlike offer.
ROMEO   Bid her devise
Some means to come to shrift this afternoon,   177
And there she shall at Friar Laurence' cell
Be shrived and married. Here is for thy pains.   179
                                            [*He offers money.*]
NURSE   No, truly, sir, not a penny.
ROMEO   Go to, I say you shall.
NURSE
This afternoon, sir? Well, she shall be there.
ROMEO
And stay, good Nurse, behind the abbey wall.
Within this hour my man shall be with thee
And bring thee cords made like a tackled stair,   185
Which to the high topgallant of my joy   186
Must be my convoy in the secret night.   187
Farewell. Be trusty, and I'll quit thy pains.   188
Farewell. Commend me to thy mistress.
                                    [*Romeo starts to leave.*]
NURSE
Now God in heaven bless thee! Hark you, sir.
ROMEO   What sayst thou, my dear Nurse?
NURSE
Is your man secret? Did you ne'er hear say,   192
"Two may keep counsel, putting one away"?   193
ROMEO
'Warrant thee, my man's as true as steel.

---

169 protest vow. (Romeo may intend only to protest his good intentions,
but the Nurse seemingly takes the word to signify a *gentlemanlike offer*
[l. 175] of marriage that would ensure against Juliet's being led into a
fool's paradise [l. 163]—i.e., being seduced.)   **173 mark** attend to
177 shrift confession and absolution   **179 shrived** absolved   **185 tackled
stair** rope ladder   **186 topgallant** highest mast and sail of a ship, the
summit   **187 convoy** conveyance, means of passage   **188 quit** reward,
requite   **192 secret** trustworthy   **193 keep counsel** keep a secret

NURSE Well, sir, my mistress is the sweetest lady—
Lord, Lord! When 'twas a little prating thing—O,
there is a nobleman in town, one Paris, that would
fain lay knife aboard; but she, good soul, had as lief 198
see a toad, a very toad, as see him. I anger her sometimes and tell her that Paris is the properer man, but 200
I'll warrant you, when I say so, she looks as pale as
any clout in the versal world. Doth not rosemary and 202
Romeo begin both with a letter? 203
ROMEO Ay, Nurse, what of that? Both with an R.
NURSE Ah, mocker! That's the dog's name; R is for 205
the—No; I know it begins with some other letter; 206
and she hath the prettiest sententious of it, of you and 207
rosemary, that it would do you good to hear it.
ROMEO Commend me to thy lady.
NURSE Ay, a thousand times. [*Exit Romeo.*] Peter!
PETER Anon!
NURSE Before, and apace.   *Exeunt.* 212

❖

2.5   *Enter Juliet.*

JULIET
The clock struck nine when I did send the Nurse;
In half an hour she promised to return.
Perchance she cannot meet him. That's not so.
O, she is lame! Love's heralds should be thoughts,
Which ten times faster glide than the sun's beams
Driving back shadows over louring hills.   6

198 fain gladly.   **lay knife aboard** i.e., assert his claim (just as a guest
did by bringing his knife to the dinner table; with sexual suggestion
also).   **lief** willingly   **200 properer** handsomer   **202 clout** rag, cloth.
versal universal   **203 a letter** one and the same letter   **205 the dog's
name** (The letter *R* was thought to resemble the dog's growl.)   **206 No
. . . other letter** (The Nurse perhaps thinks that the letter means "arse"
and repudiates the association.)   **207 sententious** (The Nurse probably
means *sentences*, pithy sayings.)   **212 Before, and apace** go before me
quickly

**2.5. Location: Verona. Outside Capulet's house, perhaps in the orchard
or garden.**
6 louring threatening

Therefore do nimble-pinioned doves draw Love,   7
And therefore hath the wind-swift Cupid wings.
Now is the sun upon the highmost hill
Of this day's journey, and from nine till twelve
Is three long hours, yet she is not come.
Had she affections and warm youthful blood,
She would be as swift in motion as a ball;
My words would bandy her to my sweet love,   14
And his to me.
But old folks, many feign as they were dead—   16
Unwieldy, slow, heavy, and pale as lead.

    Enter Nurse [and Peter].

O God, she comes!—O honey Nurse, what news?
Hast thou met with him? Send thy man away.
NURSE   Peter, stay at the gate.   [*Exit Peter*.]
JULIET
Now, good sweet Nurse—O Lord, why lookest thou sad?
Though news be sad, yet tell them merrily;
If good, thou shamest the music of sweet news
By playing it to me with so sour a face.
NURSE
I am aweary. Give me leave awhile.   25
Fie, how my bones ache! What a jaunce have I had!   26
JULIET
I would thou hadst my bones, and I thy news.
Nay, come, I pray thee, speak. Good, good Nurse, speak.
NURSE
Jesu, what haste! Can you not stay awhile?   29
Do you not see that I am out of breath?
JULIET
How art thou out of breath, when thou hast breath
To say to me that thou art out of breath?
The excuse that thou dost make in this delay
Is longer than the tale thou dost excuse.
Is thy news good or bad? Answer to that;
Say either, and I'll stay the circumstance.   36
Let me be satisfied; is 't good or bad?

7 Love i.e., Venus, whose chariot was drawn by swift-winged doves
14 bandy toss to and fro, as in tennis   **16 feign as** act as though
25 Give me leave let me alone   **26 jaunce** jouncing, jolting   **29 stay**
wait   **36 stay the circumstance** await the details

NURSE Well, you have made a simple choice. You know 38
not how to choose a man. Romeo? No, not he. Though
his face be better than any man's, yet his leg excels all
men's; and for a hand, and a foot, and a body, though
they be not to be talked on, yet they are past compare. 42
He is not the flower of courtesy, but, I'll warrant him,
as gentle as a lamb. Go thy ways, wench. Serve God.
What, have you dined at home?
JULIET
No, no; but all this did I know before.
What says he of our marriage? What of that?
NURSE
Lord, how my head aches! What a head have I!
It beats as it would fall in twenty pieces.
My back o' t'other side—ah, my back, my back!   50
Beshrew your heart for sending me about   51
To catch my death with jauncing up and down!
JULIET
I' faith, I am sorry that thou art not well.
Sweet, sweet, sweet Nurse, tell me, what says my love?
NURSE
Your love says, like an honest gentleman,
And a courteous, and a kind, and a handsome,
And, I warrant, a virtuous—Where is your mother?
JULIET
Where is my mother? Why, she is within,
Where should she be? How oddly thou repliest!
"Your love says, like an honest gentleman,
'Where is your mother?'"
NURSE   O God's Lady dear!
Are you so hot? Marry, come up, I trow.   62
Is this the poultice for my aching bones?
Henceforward do your messages yourself.
JULIET
Here's such a coil! Come, what says Romeo?   65
NURSE
Have you got leave to go to shrift today?

38 simple foolish **42 be not to be talked on** are not worth discussing
(perhaps with a suggestion of being unmentionable in refined ladylike
company) **50 o' t'other** on the other **51 Beshrew** a curse on (used as a
mild oath) **62 hot** impatient. **Marry, come up** (An expression of
impatient reproof.) **65 coil** turmoil, fuss

JULIET I have.

NURSE
    Then hie you hence to Friar Laurence' cell;   68
    There stays a husband to make you a wife.
    Now comes the wanton blood up in your cheeks;
    They'll be in scarlet straight at any news.   71
    Hie you to church. I must another way,
    To fetch a ladder, by the which your love
    Must climb a bird's nest soon when it is dark.   74
    I am the drudge, and toil in your delight,
    But you shall bear the burden soon at night.
    Go. I'll to dinner. Hie you to the cell.
JULIET
    Hie to high fortune! Honest Nurse, farewell.
                     Exeunt [*separately*].

                     ❖

2.6   *Enter Friar* [*Laurence*] *and Romeo.*

FRIAR LAURENCE
    So smile the heavens upon this holy act   1
    That after-hours with sorrow chide us not!
ROMEO
    Amen, amen! But come what sorrow can,
    It cannot countervail the exchange of joy   4
    That one short minute gives me in her sight.
    Do thou but close our hands with holy words,   6
    Then love-devouring death do what he dare;
    It is enough I may but call her mine.
FRIAR LAURENCE
    These violent delights have violent ends
    And in their triumph die, like fire and powder,   10
    Which as they kiss consume. The sweetest honey
    Is loathsome in his own deliciousness,   12

---

68 hie hasten   **71 in scarlet straight** i.e., blushing immediately
74 bird's nest i.e., Juliet's room (with suggestion of pubic hair; the
bawdry is continued in *bear the burden* two lines later)

2.6. Location: Verona. Friar Laurence's cell.
1 So . . . heavens may the heavens so smile   **4 countervail** outweigh,
counterbalance   **6 close** join   **10 powder** gunpowder   **12 his** its

And in the taste confounds the appetite.   13
Therefore love moderately. Long love doth so;
Too swift arrives as tardy as too slow.
 Enter Juliet.
Here comes the lady. O, so light a foot
Will ne'er wear out the everlasting flint.
A lover may bestride the gossamer   18
That idles in the wanton summer air,   19
And yet not fall; so light is vanity.   20

JULIET
Good even to my ghostly confessor.   21

FRIAR LAURENCE
Romeo shall thank thee, daughter, for us both.   22

JULIET
As much to him, else is his thanks too much.   23

ROMEO
Ah, Juliet, if the measure of thy joy
Be heaped like mine, and that thy skill be more   25
To blazon it, then sweeten with thy breath   26
This neighbor air, and let rich music's tongue
Unfold the imagined happiness that both   28
Receive in either by this dear encounter.   29

JULIET
Conceit, more rich in matter than in words,   30
Brags of his substance, not of ornament.   31
They are but beggars that can count their worth.
But my true love is grown to such excess
I cannot sum up sum of half my wealth.   34

FRIAR LAURENCE
Come, come with me, and we will make short work;
For, by your leaves, you shall not stay alone
Till Holy Church incorporate two in one.   [*Exeunt.*]

13 confounds destroys   **18 gossamer** spider's thread   **19 wanton**
playful   **20 vanity** transitory human love   **21 ghostly** spiritual
22 thank thee i.e., give a kiss in thanks for your greeting   **23 As . . .**
much i.e., then I greet him with a kiss in repayment, lest I be overpaid
25 that if   **26 blazon** describe set forth. (A heraldic term.)   **28 Unfold**
make known.   **imagined** i.e., unexpressed   **29 in either** from each
other   **30–31 Conceit . . . ornament** true understanding, more enriched
by the actual reality (of love) than by mere words, finds more worth in
the substance of that reality than in outward show   **34 sum up sum**
add up the total

3.1   *Enter Mercutio, Benvolio, and men.*

BENVOLIO
I pray thee, good Mercutio, let's retire.
The day is hot, the Capels are abroad,   2
And if we meet we shall not scape a brawl,
For now, these hot days, is the mad blood stirring.
MERCUTIO   Thou art like one of these fellows that when
he enters the confines of a tavern, claps me his sword
upon the table and says, "God send me no need of
thee!" and by the operation of the second cup draws   8
him on the drawer, when indeed there is no need.   9
BENVOLIO   Am I like such a fellow?
MERCUTIO   Come, come, thou art as hot a Jack in thy 11
mood as any in Italy, and as soon moved to be moody, 12
and as soon moody to be moved.   13
BENVOLIO   And what to?
MERCUTIO   Nay, an there were two such, we should   15
have none shortly, for one would kill the other. Thou!
Why, thou wilt quarrel with a man that hath a hair
more or a hair less in his beard than thou hast. Thou
wilt quarrel with a man for cracking nuts, having no
other reason but because thou hast hazel eyes. What
eye but such an eye would spy out such a quarrel? Thy
head is as full of quarrels as an egg is full of meat, and 22
yet thy head hath been beaten as addle as an egg for 23
quarreling. Thou hast quarreled with a man for cough-
ing in the street, because he hath wakened thy dog that
hath lain asleep in the sun. Didst thou not fall out with
a tailor for wearing his new doublet before Easter?   27
With another, for tying his new shoes with old rib-
bon? And yet thou wilt tutor me from quarreling!
BENVOLIO   An I were so apt to quarrel as thou art, any
man should buy the fee simple of my life for an hour   31
and a quarter.   32

3.1. Location: Verona. A public place.
2 Capels Capulets   **8–9 draws . . . drawer** draws his sword against the
tapster or waiter   **9 there is no need** i.e., of his sword   **11 as hot a Jack** as
hot-tempered a fellow   **12 moody** angry   **13 to be moved** at being provoked   **15 an** if   **22 meat** i.e., edible matter   **23 addle** addled, confused
27 doublet man's jacket   **31 fee simple** outright possession   **31–32 an hour
. . . quarter** i.e., my life would last no longer in such circumstances

MERCUTIO   The fee simple! O simple!   33

Enter Tybalt, Petruchio, and others.

BENVOLIO   By my head, here comes the Capulets.

MERCUTIO   By my heel, I care not.

TYBALT [*To his companions*]
Follow me close, for I will speak to them.—
Gentlemen, good e'en. A word with one of you.

MERCUTIO   And but one word with one of us? Couple it
with something: make it a word and a blow.

TYBALT   You shall find me apt enough to that, sir, an
you will give me occasion.

MERCUTIO   Could you not take some occasion without
giving?

TYBALT   Mercutio, thou consortest with Romeo.   44

MERCUTIO   "Consort"? What, dost thou make us minstrels? An thou make minstrels of us, look to hear
nothing but discords. Here's my fiddlestick; here's   47
that shall make you dance. Zounds, "consort"!   48

BENVOLIO
We talk here in the public haunt of men.
Either withdraw unto some private place,
Or reason coldly of your grievances,   51
Or else depart; here all eyes gaze on us.   52

MERCUTIO
Men's eyes were made to look, and let them gaze.
I will not budge for no man's pleasure, I.

Enter Romeo.

TYBALT
Well, peace be with you, sir. Here comes my man.

MERCUTIO
But I'll be hanged, sir, if he wear your livery.   56
Marry, go before to field, he'll be your follower;   57
Your worship in that sense may call him "man."   58

---

33 simple stupid   **44 consortest** keep company with. (But Mercutio
quibbles on its musical sense of "accompany" or "play together.")
47 fiddlestick (Mercutio means his sword.)   **48 that** that which.
Zounds i.e., by God's (Christ's) wounds   **51 coldly** calmly   **52 depart** go
away separately   **56 livery** servant's costume. (Mercutio deliberately
mistakes Tybalt's phrase *my man* to mean "my servant.")   **57 field** field
where a duel might occur   **58 Your worship** (A title of honor used here
with mock politeness.)

TYBALT

Romeo, the love I bear thee can afford
No better term than this: thou art a villain.

ROMEO

Tybalt, the reason that I have to love thee
Doth much excuse the appertaining rage   62
To such a greeting. Villain am I none.
Therefore, farewell. I see thou knowest me not.

TYBALT

Boy, this shall not excuse the injuries
That thou hast done me. Therefore turn and draw.

ROMEO

I do protest I never injured thee,
But love thee better than thou canst devise   68
Till thou shalt know the reason of my love.
And so, good Capulet—which name I tender   70
As dearly as mine own—be satisfied.

MERCUTIO

O calm, dishonorable, vile submission!
Alla stoccata carries it away.   [*He draws.*] 73
Tybalt, you ratcatcher, will you walk?   74

TYBALT   What wouldst thou have with me?

MERCUTIO   Good king of cats, nothing but one of your
nine lives; that I mean to make bold withal, and, as   77
you shall use me hereafter, dry-beat the rest of the   78
eight. Will you pluck your sword out of his pilcher by   79
the ears? Make haste, lest mine be about your ears ere
it be out.

TYBALT   I am for you.   [*He draws.*]

ROMEO

Gentle Mercutio, put thy rapier up.

MERCUTIO   Come, sir, your *passado.*   [*They fight.*] 84

ROMEO

Draw, Benvolio, beat down their weapons.
Gentlemen, for shame, forbear this outrage!

---

62 excuse . . . rage mollify the angry reaction appropriate   **68 devise**
understand   **70 tender** value   **73 Alla stoccata** at the thrust (Italian);
i.e., Tybalt, with his fine fencing phrases, *carries it away,* wins the day
74 ratcatcher (An allusion to Tybalt as king of cats; see 2.4.19.)
77 make bold withal make free with   **78 dry-beat** beat soundly (without
drawing blood)   **79 his pilcher** its scabbard   **84 passado** forward
thrust. (Said derisively.)

Tybalt, Mercutio, the Prince expressly hath
Forbid this bandying in Verona streets.
Hold, Tybalt! Good Mercutio!
      [Tybalt under Romeo's arm stabs Mercutio.]
          Away Tybalt [with his followers].

MERCUTIO   I am hurt.   89
A plague o' both your houses! I am sped.   90
Is he gone, and hath nothing?
BENVOLIO   What, art thou hurt?
MERCUTIO
Ay, ay, a scratch, a scratch; marry, 'tis enough.
Where is my page? Go, villain, fetch a surgeon.
                          [Exit Page.]
ROMEO
Courage, man, the hurt cannot be much.
MERCUTIO   No, 'tis not so deep as a well, nor so wide as
a church door, but 'tis enough, 'twill serve. Ask for me
tomorrow, and you shall find me a grave man. I am 97
peppered, I warrant, for this world. A plague o' both 98
your houses! Zounds, a dog, a rat, a mouse, a cat, to
scratch a man to death! A braggart, a rogue, a villain,
that fights by the book of arithmetic! Why the devil 101
came you between us? I was hurt under your arm.
ROMEO   I thought all for the best.
MERCUTIO
Help me into some house, Benvolio,
Or I shall faint. A plague o' both your houses!
They have made worm's meat of me. I have it,
And soundly too. Your houses!
                  Exit [supported by Benvolio].
ROMEO
This gentleman, the Prince's near ally,   108
My very friend, hath got this mortal hurt   109
In my behalf; my reputation stained
With Tybalt's slander—Tybalt, that an hour
Hath been my cousin! O sweet Juliet,   112

---

89 s.d. Away Tybalt (Some editors assign this as a speech to Petruchio.) **90 sped** done for **97 grave** (Mercutio thus puns with his last
breath.) **98 peppered** finished, done for **101 by . . . arithmetic** by the
numbers, as in a textbook on fencing **108 ally** kinsman **109 very**
true **112 cousin** kinsman

Thy beauty hath made me effeminate,   113
And in my temper softened valor's steel!   114
   Enter Benvolio.

BENVOLIO
O Romeo, Romeo, brave Mercutio is dead!
That gallant spirit hath aspired the clouds,   116
Which too untimely here did scorn the earth.

ROMEO
This day's black fate on more days doth depend;   118
This but begins the woe others must end.   119
   [*Enter Tybalt.*]

BENVOLIO
Here comes the furious Tybalt back again.

ROMEO
Alive in triumph, and Mercutio slain!
Away to heaven, respective lenity,   122
And fire-eyed fury be my conduct now!   123
Now, Tybalt, take the "villain" back again
That late thou gavest me, for Mercutio's soul
Is but a little way above our heads,
Staying for thine to keep him company.
Either thou or I, or both, must go with him.

TYBALT
Thou, wretched boy, that didst consort him here,
Shalt with him hence.

ROMEO   This shall determine that.
            They fight. Tybalt falls.

BENVOLIO   Romeo, away, begone!
The citizens are up, and Tybalt slain.
Stand not amazed. The Prince will doom thee death   133
If thou art taken. Hence, begone, away!

ROMEO
O, I am fortune's fool!

BENVOLIO   Why dost thou stay?   135
              Exit Romeo.

---

113 effeminate weak   **114 temper** disposition (but with a play on the
tempering of a steel sword)   **116 aspired** ascended to   **118 depend** hang
over threateningly   **119 others** other days to come   **122 respective**
lenity considerate gentleness   **123 conduct** guide   **133 amazed** dazed.
doom thee death sentence you to death   **135 fool** dupe

Enter Citizens.

FIRST CITIZEN
Which way ran he that killed Mercutio?
Tybalt, that murderer, which way ran he?
BENVOLIO
There lies that Tybalt.
FIRST CITIZEN   Up, sir, go with me.
I charge thee in the Prince's name, obey.

*Enter Prince [attended], old Montague, Capulet,
their Wives, and all.*

PRINCE
Where are the vile beginners of this fray?
BENVOLIO
O noble Prince, I can discover all   141
The unlucky manage of this fatal brawl.   142
There lies the man, slain by young Romeo,
That slew thy kinsman, brave Mercutio.
CAPULET'S WIFE
Tybalt, my cousin! O my brother's child!
O Prince! O cousin! Husband! O, the blood is spilled
Of my dear kinsman! Prince, as thou art true,
For blood of ours shed blood of Montague.
O cousin, cousin!
PRINCE
Benvolio, who began this bloody fray?
BENVOLIO
Tybalt, here slain, whom Romeo's hand did slay.
Romeo, that spoke him fair, bid him bethink   152
How nice the quarrel was, and urged withal   153
Your high displeasure. All this—utterèd
With gentle breath, calm look, knees humbly bowed—
Could not take truce with the unruly spleen   156
Of Tybalt deaf to peace, but that he tilts
With piercing steel at bold Mercutio's breast,
Who, all as hot, turns deadly point to point,
And, with a martial scorn, with one hand beats
Cold death aside and with the other sends
It back to Tybalt, whose dexterity

141 discover reveal   **142 manage** conduct   **152 fair** civilly.   **bethink**
consider   **153 nice** trivial.   **withal** besides   **156 take truce** make peace

Retorts it. Romeo he cries aloud,   163
"Hold, friends! Friends, part!" and swifter than his
    tongue
His agile arm beats down their fatal points,
And twixt them rushes; underneath whose arm
An envious thrust from Tybalt hit the life   167
Of stout Mercutio, and then Tybalt fled;   168
But by and by comes back to Romeo,
Who had but newly entertained revenge,   170
And to 't they go like lightning, for, ere I
Could draw to part them was stout Tybalt slain,
And, as he fell, did Romeo turn and fly.
This is the truth, or let Benvolio die.
CAPULET'S WIFE
He is a kinsman to the Montague.
Affection makes him false; he speaks not true.   176
Some twenty of them fought in this black strife,
And all those twenty could but kill one life.
I beg for justice, which thou, Prince, must give.   *
Romeo slew Tybalt; Romeo must not live.
PRINCE
Romeo slew him, he slew Mercutio.
Who now the price of his dear blood doth owe?
MONTAGUE
Not Romeo, Prince, he was Mercutio's friend;
His fault concludes but what the law should end,   184
The life of Tybalt.
PRINCE   And for that offense
Immediately we do exile him hence.
I have an interest in your heart's proceeding;
My blood for your rude brawls doth lie a-bleeding;   188
But I'll amerce you with so strong a fine   189
That you shall all repent the loss of mine.
I will be deaf to pleading and excuses;
Nor tears nor prayers shall purchase out abuses.   192
Therefore use none. Let Romeo hence in haste,   193
Else, when he is found, that hour is his last.   194

163 Retorts returns   **167 envious** malicious   **168 stout** brave   **170 entertained** harbored thoughts of   **176 Affection** partiality   **184 concludes but** only finishes   **188 My blood** i.e., blood of my kinsman   **189 amerce** punish by a fine   **192 Nor tears** neither tears.   **purchase out abuses** redeem misdeeds   **193 hence** depart   **194 Else** otherwise

Bear hence this body and attend our will.   195
Mercy but murders, pardoning those that kill.
            Exeunt, [some carrying Tybalt's body].

❖

3.2   *Enter Juliet alone.*

JULIET
Gallop apace, you fiery-footed steeds,   1
Towards Phoebus' lodging! Such a wagoner   2
As Phaëthon would whip you to the west   3
And bring in cloudy night immediately.
Spread thy close curtain, love-performing night,   5
That runaways' eyes may wink, and Romeo   6
Leap to these arms, untalked of and unseen.
Lovers can see to do their amorous rites
By their own beauties; or, if love be blind,
It best agrees with night. Come, civil night,   10
Thou sober-suited matron all in black,
And learn me how to lose a winning match   12
Played for a pair of stainless maidenhoods.
Hood my unmanned blood, bating in my cheeks,   14
With thy black mantle till strange love grow bold,   15
Think true love acted simple modesty.   16
Come, night. Come, Romeo. Come, thou day in night;
For thou wilt lie upon the wings of night
Whiter than new snow upon a raven's back.
Come, gentle night, come, loving, black-browed night,

---

195 attend our will be on hand to hear further judgment
3.2. Location: Verona. Capulet's house.
1 apace quickly.   **steeds** i.e., the horses of the sun god's chariot
2 Phoebus (Often equated with Helios, the sun god.)   **lodging** i.e., in the
west, below the horizon   **2–3 Such . . . Phaëthon** i.e., a rash charioteer
like Phaëthon, who would quickly bring the day to an end. (Phaëthon
was son of the sun god, and was allowed to assume the reins of the sun
for a day; not being able to restrain the steeds, he had to be slain by the
thunderbolt of Zeus.)   **5 close** enclosing   **6 runaways'** (Refers to the
horses of the sun chariot that ran away with Phaëthon?)   **wink** shut,
close   **10 civil** circumspect, somberly attired   **12 learn** teach   **14 Hood**
cover. (A term in falconry; the hawk's eyes were covered so that it would
not *bate* or beat its wings.)   **unmanned** untamed (in falconry; with a
pun on "unmarried")   **15 strange** diffident   **16 Think** i.e., and think

Give me my Romeo, and when I shall die　　　　21
Take him and cut him out in little stars,
And he will make the face of heaven so fine
That all the world will be in love with night
And pay no worship to the garish sun.　　　　25
O, I have bought the mansion of a love　　　　26
But not possessed it, and though I am sold,
Not yet enjoyed. So tedious is this day
As is the night before some festival
To an impatient child that hath new robes
And may not wear them. O, here comes my nurse,　　31

Enter Nurse, with cords.

And she brings news, and every tongue that speaks
But Romeo's name speaks heavenly eloquence.
Now, Nurse, what news? What hast thou there? The
　　cords
That Romeo bid thee fetch?
NURSE　　　　　　　　　　Ay, ay, the cords.
　　　　　　　　　　　　　[She throws them down.]
JULIET
Ay me, what news? Why dost thou wring thy hands?
NURSE
Ah, weraday! He's dead, he's dead, he's dead!　　37
We are undone, lady, we are undone!
Alack the day, he's gone, he's killed, he's dead!
JULIET
Can heaven be so envious?
NURSE　　　　　　　　　　Romeo can,　　　　40
Though heaven cannot. O Romeo, Romeo!
Whoever would have thought it? Romeo!
JULIET
What devil art thou, that dost torment me thus?
This torture should be roared in dismal hell.
Hath Romeo slain himself? Say thou but "Ay,"
And that bare vowel "I" shall poison more　　46

21 I (Often emended to *he,* following Quarto 4, but Juliet may mean that
when she is dead she will share Romeo's beauty with the world. Dying
may also hint at sexual climax.)　**25 garish** dazzling　**26 mansion** dwelling　**31 s.d. cords** ropes (for the ladder)　**37 weraday** i.e., wellaway,
alas　**40 envious** malicious　**46 "I"** (Pronounced identically with *ay.*)

Than the death-darting eye of cockatrice.   47
I am not I, if there be such an "Ay,"
Or those eyes shut, that makes thee answer "Ay."   49
If he be slain, say "Ay," or if not, "No."
Brief sounds determine of my weal or woe.   51

NURSE
I saw the wound. I saw it with mine eyes—
God save the mark!—here on his manly breast.   53
A piteous corpse, a bloody piteous corpse;
Pale, pale as ashes, all bedaubed in blood,
All in gore-blood. I swoonèd at the sight.   56

JULIET
O, break, my heart! Poor bankrupt, break at once!
To prison, eyes; ne'er look on liberty!
Vile earth, to earth resign; end motion here,   59
And thou and Romeo press one heavy bier!   60

NURSE
O Tybalt, Tybalt, the best friend I had!
O courteous Tybalt! Honest gentleman!
That ever I should live to see thee dead!

JULIET
What storm is this that blows so contrary?
Is Romeo slaughtered, and is Tybalt dead?
My dearest cousin, and my dearer lord?
Then, dreadful trumpet, sound the general doom!   67
For who is living, if those two are gone?

NURSE
Tybalt is gone, and Romeo banishèd;
Romeo that killed him, he is banishèd.

JULIET
O God! Did Romeo's hand shed Tybalt's blood?

NURSE
It did, it did. Alas the day it did!

JULIET
O serpent heart, hid with a flowering face!   73

47 **cockatrice** i.e., basilisk, a mythical serpent that could kill by its
look   49 **those eyes shut** i.e., if Romeo's eyes are shut (in death)
51 **weal** welfare, happiness   53 **God save the mark** (A familiar oath
originally intended to avert ill omen.)   56 **gore-blood** clotted blood
59 **Vile earth** i.e., my body.   **resign** surrender, return   60 **press** weigh
down.   **bier** litter for carrying corpses   67 **trumpet** i.e., the last trumpet.   **general doom** Day of Judgment   73 **hid with** hidden by.   **flowering** i.e., fair, like that of the serpent in the Garden of Eden

Did ever dragon keep so fair a cave?   74
Beautiful tyrant! Fiend angelical!
Dove-feathered raven! Wolvish-ravening lamb!
Despisèd substance of divinest show!   77
Just opposite to what thou justly seem'st,   78
A damnèd saint, an honorable villain!
O nature, what hadst thou to do in hell
When thou didst bower the spirit of a fiend   81
In mortal paradise of such sweet flesh?
Was ever book containing such vile matter
So fairly bound? O, that deceit should dwell
In such a gorgeous palace!
NURSE   There's no trust,
No faith, no honesty in men; all perjured,
All forsworn, all naught, all dissemblers.   87
Ah, where's my man? Give me some aqua vitae.   88
These griefs, these woes, these sorrows make me old.
Shame come to Romeo!
JULIET   Blistered be thy tongue
For such a wish! He was not born to shame.
Upon his brow shame is ashamed to sit;
For 'tis a throne where honor may be crowned
Sole monarch of the universal earth.
O, what a beast was I to chide at him!
NURSE
Will you speak well of him that killed your cousin?
JULIET
Shall I speak ill of him that is my husband?
Ah, poor my lord, what tongue shall smooth thy name   98
When I, thy three-hours wife, have mangled it?
But wherefore, villain, didst thou kill my cousin?
That villain cousin would have killed my husband.
Back, foolish tears, back to your native spring!
Your tributary drops belong to woe,   103
Which you, mistaking, offer up to joy.

---

74 keep occupy, guard.   **cave** i.e., one with treasure in it   **77 show**
appearance   **78 Just** precisely (with a play on *justly*, truly)   **81 bower**
give lodging to   **87 naught** worthless, evil   **88 aqua vitae** alcoholic
spirits   **98 poor my lord** my poor lord.   **smooth** speak kindly of
103 Your . . . woe i.e., you should be shed, offered as a tribute, on some
occasion of real woe

My husband lives, that Tybalt would have slain,   105
And Tybalt's dead, that would have slain my husband.
All this is comfort. Wherefore weep I then?
Some word there was, worser than Tybalt's death,
That murdered me. I would forget it fain,   109
But O, it presses to my memory
Like damnèd guilty deeds to sinners' minds:
"Tybalt is dead, and Romeo—banishèd."
That "banishèd," that one word "banishèd,"
Hath slain ten thousand Tybalts. Tybalt's death
Was woe enough, if it had ended there;
Or, if sour woe delights in fellowship
And needly will be ranked with other griefs,   117
Why followed not, when she said "Tybalt's dead,"
"Thy father," or "thy mother," nay, or both,
Which modern lamentation might have moved?   120
But with a rearward following Tybalt's death,   121
"Romeo is banishèd"—to speak that word
Is father, mother, Tybalt, Romeo, Juliet,
All slain, all dead. "Romeo is banishèd!"
There is no end, no limit, measure, bound,
In that word's death; no words can that woe sound.   126
Where is my father and my mother, Nurse?

NURSE
Weeping and wailing over Tybalt's corpse.
Will you go to them? I will bring you thither.

JULIET
Wash they his wounds with tears? Mine shall be spent,
When theirs are dry, for Romeo's banishment.
Take up those cords. Poor ropes, you are beguiled,
Both you and I, for Romeo is exiled.
He made you for a highway to my bed;
But I, a maid, die maiden-widowèd.
Come, cords, come, Nurse. I'll to my wedding bed,
And death, not Romeo, take my maidenhead!

NURSE [*Taking up the cords*]
Hie to your chamber. I'll find Romeo
To comfort you. I wot well where he is.   139

---

105 that whom   **109 fain** gladly   **117 needly** of necessity.   **ranked with**
accompanied by   **120 modern** ordinary   **121 rearward** rearguard
126 sound (1) fathom (2) express   **139 wot** know

Hark ye, your Romeo will be here at night.
I'll to him. He is hid at Laurence' cell.
JULIET
  O, find him! Give this ring to my true knight,
                    [*Giving a ring*]
  And bid him come to take his last farewell.
                  Exeunt [*separately*].

✣

3.3   *Enter Friar* [*Laurence*].

FRIAR LAURENCE
  Romeo, come forth; come forth, thou fearful man.   1
  Affliction is enamored of thy parts,   2
  And thou art wedded to calamity.

    [*Enter*] *Romeo.*

ROMEO
  Father, what news? What is the Prince's doom?   4
  What sorrow craves acquaintance at my hand
  That I yet know not?
FRIAR LAURENCE   Too familiar
  Is my dear son with such sour company.
  I bring thee tidings of the Prince's doom.
ROMEO
  What less than doomsday is the Prince's doom?   9
FRIAR LAURENCE
  A gentler judgment vanished from his lips: 10
  Not body's death, but body's banishment.
ROMEO
  Ha, banishment? Be merciful, say "death";
  For exile hath more terror in his look,
  Much more than death. Do not say "banishment."
FRIAR LAURENCE
  Here from Verona art thou banishèd.
  Be patient, for the world is broad and wide.

3.3. Location: Verona. Friar Laurence's cell.
1 fearful full of fear (but also inspiring fear as a tragic figure)   **2 parts**
qualities   **4 doom** judgment   **9 doomsday** the Day of Judgment, i.e.,
death   **10 vanished** issued (into air)

ROMEO
  There is no world without Verona walls   17
  But purgatory, torture, hell itself.
  Hence "banishèd" is banished from the world,
  And world's exile is death. Then "banishèd"   20
  Is death mistermed. Calling death "banishèd,"
  Thou cutt'st my head off with a golden ax
  And smilest upon the stroke that murders me.
FRIAR LAURENCE
  O deadly sin! O rude unthankfulness!
  Thy fault our law calls death, but the kind Prince,   25
  Taking thy part, hath rushed aside the law   26
  And turned that black word "death" to "banishment."
  This is dear mercy, and thou seest it not.
ROMEO
  'Tis torture, and not mercy. Heaven is here
  Where Juliet lives, and every cat and dog
  And little mouse, every unworthy thing,
  Live here in heaven and may look on her,
  But Romeo may not. More validity,   33
  More honorable state, more courtship lives   34
  In carrion flies than Romeo. They may seize
  On the white wonder of dear Juliet's hand
  And steal immortal blessing from her lips,
  Who even in pure and vestal modesty   38
  Still blush, as thinking their own kisses sin;   39
  But Romeo may not, he is banishèd.
  Flies may do this, but I from this must fly.
  They are free men, but I am banishèd.
  And sayest thou yet that exile is not death?
  Hadst thou no poison mixed, no sharp-ground knife,
  No sudden mean of death, though ne'er so mean,   45
  But "banishèd" to kill me? "Banishèd"?
  O Friar, the damnèd use that word in hell;
  Howling attends it. How hast thou the heart,
  Being a divine, a ghostly confessor,

---

17 **without** outside of   **20 world's exile** exile from the world   **25 Thy fault . . . death** for your crime the law demands a death sentence **26 rushed** thrust (aside)   **33 validity** value   **34 courtship** (1) courtliness (2) occasion for wooing   **38 vestal** maidenly   **39 their own kisses** i.e., their touching one another   **45 mean . . . mean** means . . . base

A sin absolver, and my friend professed,
To mangle me with that word "banishèd"?

FRIAR LAURENCE
Thou fond mad man, hear me a little speak.   52

ROMEO
O, thou wilt speak again of banishment.

FRIAR LAURENCE
I'll give thee armor to keep off that word,
Adversity's sweet milk, philosophy,
To comfort thee, though thou art banishèd.

ROMEO
Yet "banishèd"? Hang up philosophy!   57
Unless philosophy can make a Juliet,
Displant a town, reverse a prince's doom,   59
It helps not, it prevails not. Talk no more.

FRIAR LAURENCE
O, then I see that madmen have no ears.

ROMEO
How should they, when that wise men have no eyes?

FRIAR LAURENCE
Let me dispute with thee of thy estate.   63

ROMEO
Thou canst not speak of that thou dost not feel.   64
Wert thou as young as I, Juliet thy love,
An hour but married, Tybalt murderèd,
Doting like me and like me banishèd,
Then mightst thou speak, then mightst thou tear thy
          hair,
And fall upon the ground, as I do now,
Taking the measure of an unmade grave.
                    [He falls upon the ground.]
                              Knock [within].

FRIAR LAURENCE
Arise. One knocks. Good Romeo, hide thyself.

ROMEO
Not I, unless the breath of heartsick groans,
Mistlike, infold me from the search of eyes.   Knock.

FRIAR LAURENCE
Hark, how they knock!—Who's there?—Romeo, arise.

52 fond foolish   **57 Yet** still   **59 Displant** uproot   **63 dispute** reason.
estate situation   **64 that** that which

Thou wilt be taken.—Stay awhile!—Stand up.
                                        Knock.
Run to my study.—By and by!—God's will,
What simpleness is this?—I come, I come!   *Knock.* 77
Who knocks so hard? Whence come you? What's your
   will?   [*Going to the door.*]
NURSE [*Within*]
Let me come in, and you shall know my errand.
I come from Lady Juliet.
FRIAR LAURENCE   Welcome, then.
                              [*He opens the door.*]

   Enter Nurse.

NURSE
   O holy Friar, O, tell me, holy Friar,
   Where's my lady's lord, where's Romeo?
FRIAR LAURENCE
   There on the ground, with his own tears made drunk.
NURSE
   O, he is even in my mistress' case,   84
   Just in her case! O woeful sympathy!   85
   Piteous predicament! Even so lies she,
   Blubbering and weeping, weeping and blubbering.—
   Stand up, stand up! Stand, an you be a man.   88
   For Juliet's sake, for her sake, rise and stand!
   Why should you fall into so deep an O?   90
ROMEO   Nurse!   [*He rises.*]
NURSE
   Ah, sir, ah, sir! Death's the end of all.
ROMEO
   Spakest thou of Juliet? How is it with her?
   Doth not she think me an old murderer,   94
   Now I have stained the childhood of our joy
   With blood removed but little from her own?
   Where is she? And how doth she? And what says
   My concealed lady to our canceled love?   98

---

77 simpleness foolishness **84 even** exactly. **case** situation **85 woeful
sympathy** mutuality of grief **88 an** if **90 an O** a fit of groaning
94 old hardened **98 concealed** secret. **canceled** nullified (by the
impending exile)

NURSE
  O, she says nothing, sir, but weeps and weeps,
  And now falls on her bed, and then starts up,
  And "Tybalt" calls, and then on Romeo cries,   101
  And then down falls again.
ROMEO   As if that name,
  Shot from the deadly level of a gun,   103
  Did murder her, as that name's cursèd hand
  Murdered her kinsman. O, tell me, Friar, tell me,
  In what vile part of this anatomy
  Doth my name lodge? Tell me, that I may sack   107
  The hateful mansion.
              [*He draws a weapon, but is restrained.*]
FRIAR LAURENCE   Hold thy desperate hand!
  Art thou a man? Thy form cries out thou art;
  Thy tears are womanish, thy wild acts denote
  The unreasonable fury of a beast.
  Unseemly woman in a seeming man,
  And ill-beseeming beast in seeming both!
  Thou hast amazed me. By my holy order,
  I thought thy disposition better tempered.   115
  Hast thou slain Tybalt? Wilt thou slay thyself,
  And slay thy lady, that in thy life lives,
  By doing damnèd hate upon thyself?
  Why railest thou on thy birth, the heaven, and earth,
  Since birth, and heaven, and earth, all three do meet   120
  In thee at once, which thou at once wouldst lose?
  Fie, fie, thou shamest thy shape, thy love, thy wit,   122
  Which, like a usurer, abound'st in all,   123
  And usest none in that true use indeed   124
  Which should bedeck thy shape, thy love, thy wit.
  Thy noble shape is but a form of wax,   126
  Digressing from the valor of a man;   127
  Thy dear love sworn but hollow perjury,
  Killing that love which thou hast vowed to cherish;   129

---

101 on Romeo cries exclaims against Romeo, calls his name   **103 level**
aim   **107 sack** destroy   **115 tempered** harmonized, balanced
120 heaven, and earth i.e., soul and body   **122 wit** intellect   **123 Which**
(you) who.   **all** all capabilities   **124 true use** i.e., proper use of your
resources, not usury   **126 form of wax** waxwork, mere outer form
127 Digressing if it deviates   **129 Killing** if it kills

Thy wit, that ornament to shape and love,
Misshapen in the conduct of them both,   131
Like powder in a skilless soldier's flask   132
Is set afire by thine own ignorance,
And thou dismembered with thine own defense.   134
What, rouse thee, man! Thy Juliet is alive,
For whose dear sake thou wast but lately dead;   136
There art thou happy. Tybalt would kill thee,   137
But thou slewest Tybalt; there art thou happy.
The law that threatened death becomes thy friend
And turns it to exile; there art thou happy.
A pack of blessings light upon thy back,
Happiness courts thee in her best array,
But like a mishavèd and sullen wench   143
Thou pouts upon thy fortune and thy love.
Take heed, take heed, for such die miserable.
Go, get thee to thy love, as was decreed;
Ascend her chamber; hence and comfort her.
But look thou stay not till the watch be set,   148
For then thou canst not pass to Mantua,
Where thou shalt live till we can find a time
To blaze your marriage, reconcile your friends,   151
Beg pardon of the Prince, and call thee back
With twenty hundred thousand times more joy
Than thou went'st forth in lamentation.
Go before, Nurse. Commend me to thy lady,
And bid her hasten all the house to bed,
Which heavy sorrow makes them apt unto.
Romeo is coming.

NURSE
O Lord, I could have stayed here all the night
To hear good counsel. O, what learning is!—
My lord, I'll tell my lady you will come.

ROMEO
Do so, and bid my sweet prepare to chide.

131 **conduct** guidance   132 **powder** gunpowder.   **flask** powder horn
134 **dismembered with** blown to pieces by.   **thine own defense** that which
should defend you, i.e., your *wit* or intellect   136 **wast . . . dead** i.e., only
recently were wishing yourself dead (see l. 70)   137 **happy** fortunate
143 **mishavèd** misbehaved   148 **the watch be set** guards be posted (at the
city gates)   151 **blaze** publish, divulge.   **friends** relations

NURSE [*Giving a ring*]
  Here, sir, a ring she bid me give you, sir.
  Hie you, make haste, for it grows very late.   [*Exit.*]
ROMEO
  How well my comfort is revived by this!   165
FRIAR LAURENCE
  Go hence. Good night. And here stands all your state: 166
  Either be gone before the watch be set,
  Or by the break of day disguised from hence.
  Sojourn in Mantua. I'll find out your man,
  And he shall signify from time to time
  Every good hap to you that chances here.   171
  Give me thy hand. 'Tis late. Farewell, good night.
ROMEO
  But that a joy past joy calls out on me,
  It were a grief so brief to part with thee.   174
  Farewell.   *Exeunt [separately].*

❖

3.4   *Enter old Capulet, his Wife, and Paris.*

CAPULET
  Things have fallen out, sir, so unluckily   1
  That we have had no time to move our daughter.   2
  Look you, she loved her kinsman Tybalt dearly,
  And so did I. Well, we were born to die.
  'Tis very late. She'll not come down tonight.
  I promise you, but for your company   6
  I would have been abed an hour ago.
PARIS
  These times of woe afford no times to woo.
  Madam, good night. Commend me to your daughter.
WIFE
  I will, and know her mind early tomorrow.
  Tonight she's mewed up to her heaviness.   11

---

165 comfort happiness   **166 here . . . state** your fortune depends on
what follows   **171 good hap** fortunate event   **174 brief** quickly

3.4. Location: Verona. Capulet's house.
1 fallen out happened   **2 move** persuade   **6 promise** assure   **11 mewed
up to** cooped up with. (A falconry term.)   **heaviness** sorrow

CAPULET

Sir Paris, I will make a desperate tender   12
Of my child's love. I think she will be ruled
In all respects by me; nay, more, I doubt it not.
Wife, go you to her ere you go to bed.
Acquaint her here of my son Paris' love,
And bid her, mark you me, on Wednesday next—   17
But soft, what day is this?

PARIS   Monday, my lord.

CAPULET

Monday! Ha, ha! Well, Wednesday is too soon;
O' Thursday let it be. O' Thursday, tell her,
She shall be married to this noble earl.
Will you be ready? Do you like this haste?
We'll keep no great ado—a friend or two;
For hark you, Tybalt being slain so late,   24
It may be thought we held him carelessly,   25
Being our kinsman, if we revel much.
Therefore we'll have some half a dozen friends,
And there an end. But what say you to Thursday?

PARIS

My lord, I would that Thursday were tomorrow.

CAPULET

Well, get you gone. O' Thursday be it, then.
[*To his Wife.*] Go you to Juliet ere you go to bed;
Prepare her, wife, against this wedding day.—   32
Farewell, my lord.—Light to my chamber, ho!—
Afore me, it is so very late   34
That we may call it early by and by.
Good night.   *Exeunt.*

❖

12 **desperate tender** bold offer   17 **mark you me** are you paying attention   24 **late** recently   25 **held him carelessly** did not regard him
highly   32 **against** in anticipation of   34 **Afore me** i.e., by my life.
(A mild oath.)

3.5   *Enter Romeo and Juliet aloft [at the window].*

JULIET
  Wilt thou be gone? It is not yet near day.
  It was the nightingale, and not the lark,
  That pierced the fearful hollow of thine ear;   3
  Nightly she sings on yond pomegranate tree.
  Believe me, love, it was the nightingale.

ROMEO
  It was the lark, the herald of the morn,
  No nightingale. Look, love, what envious streaks
  Do lace the severing clouds in yonder east.   8
  Night's candles are burnt out, and jocund day   9
  Stands tiptoe on the misty mountain tops.
  I must be gone and live, or stay and die.

JULIET
  Yond light is not daylight, I know it, I.
  It is some meteor that the sun exhaled   13
  To be to thee this night a torchbearer
  And light thee on thy way to Mantua.
  Therefore stay yet. Thou need'st not to be gone.

ROMEO
  Let me be ta'en; let me be put to death.
  I am content, so thou wilt have it so.   18
  I'll say yon gray is not the morning's eye;
  'Tis but the pale reflex of Cynthia's brow.   20
  Nor that is not the lark whose notes do beat
  The vaulty heaven so high above our heads.
  I have more care to stay than will to go.   23
  Come, death, and welcome! Juliet wills it so.
  How is 't, my soul? Let's talk. It is not day.

JULIET
  It is, it is. Hie hence, begone, away!   26

**3.5. Location: Verona. Capulet's orchard with Juliet's chamber window
above, and subsequently (l. 68) the interior of Juliet's chamber.**

3 fearful apprehensive, anxious   **8 severing** separating   **9 jocund**
cheerful   **13 exhaled** i.e., has drawn out of the ground. (Meteors were
thought to be vapors of luminous gas drawn up by the sun.)   **18 so thou**
if you   **20 reflex** reflection.   **Cynthia's** the moon's   **23 care** desire,
concern   **26 Hie hence** hasten away

It is the lark that sings so out of tune,
Straining harsh discords and unpleasing sharps.   28
Some say the lark makes sweet division;   29
This doth not so, for she divideth us.
Some say the lark and loathèd toad changed eyes;   31
O, now I would they had changed voices too,
Since arm from arm that voice doth us affray,   33
Hunting thee hence with hunt's-up to the day.   34
O, now begone! More light and light it grows.

ROMEO
More light and light, more dark and dark our woes!

    Enter Nurse [hastily].

NURSE Madam!
JULIET Nurse?
NURSE
Your lady mother is coming to your chamber.
The day is broke; be wary, look about.   [*Exit.*]
JULIET
Then window, let day in, and let life out.
ROMEO
Farewell, farewell! One kiss, and I'll descend.
    [*They kiss. He climbs down from the window.*]
JULIET
Art thou gone so? Love, lord, ay, husband, friend!   43
I must hear from thee every day in the hour,
For in a minute there are many days.
O, by this count I shall be much in years   46
Ere I again behold my Romeo!
ROMEO [*From below her window*]   Farewell!
I will omit no opportunity
That may convey my greetings, love, to thee.
JULIET
O, think'st thou we shall ever meet again?

28 sharps notes relatively high in pitch and hence discordant
29 division variations on a melody, made by dividing each note into
notes of briefer duration   **31 changed** exchanged. (A popular saying, to
account for the observation that the lark has very ordinary eyes and the
toad remarkable ones.)   **33 arm from arm** from one another's arms.
affray frighten   **34 hunt's-up** a song or tune to awaken huntsmen and,
later, a newly married couple   **43 friend** lover   **46 count** method of
calculation.   **much in years** very old

ROMEO
   I doubt it not, and all these woes shall serve
   For sweet discourses in our times to come.
JULIET
   O God, I have an ill-divining soul!   54
   Methinks I see thee, now thou art so low,
   As one dead in the bottom of a tomb.
   Either my eyesight fails or thou lookest pale.
ROMEO
   And trust me, love, in my eye so do you.
   Dry sorrow drinks our blood. Adieu, adieu!   *Exit.* 59
JULIET
   O Fortune, Fortune! All men call thee fickle.
   If thou art fickle, what dost thou with him
   That is renowned for faith? Be fickle, Fortune.
   For then, I hope, thou wilt not keep him long,
   But send him back.

       Enter Mother [Capulet's Wife].

WIFE   Ho, daughter, are you up?
JULIET
   Who is 't that calls? It is my lady mother.
   Is she not down so late, or up so early?   66
   What unaccustomed cause procures her hither?   67
         [She goeth down from the window.]
WIFE
   Why, how now, Juliet?
JULIET   Madam, I am not well.
WIFE
   Evermore weeping for your cousin's death?
   What, wilt thou wash him from his grave with tears?

---

54 ill-divining prophesying of evil   **59 Dry sorrow** (The heat of the body
in sorrow and despair was thought to descend into the bowels and dry
up the blood.)   **66 down** in bed   **67 procures** induces to come. (As indicated by the bracketed stage direction, which is from the first quarto,
Juliet, who has appeared until now at her "window" above the stage,
evidently descends quickly to the main stage and joins her mother for
the remainder of the scene. The stage, which before was to have been
imagined as Capulet's orchard, is now Juliet's chamber. Juliet's mother
has entered onto the main stage four lines earlier.)

An if thou couldst, thou couldst not make him live;   71
Therefore, have done. Some grief shows much of love,
But much of grief shows still some want of wit.   73
JULIET
Yet let me weep for such a feeling loss.   74
WIFE
So shall you feel the loss, but not the friend
Which you weep for.
JULIET   Feeling so the loss,
I cannot choose but ever weep the friend.
WIFE
Well, girl, thou weep'st not so much for his death
As that the villain lives which slaughtered him.
JULIET
What villain, madam?
WIFE   That same villain, Romeo.
JULIET [*Aside*]
Villain and he be many miles asunder.—
God pardon him! I do, with all my heart;
And yet no man like he doth grieve my heart.   83
WIFE
That is because the traitor murderer lives.
JULIET
Ay, madam, from the reach of these my hands.
Would none but I might venge my cousin's death!
WIFE
We will have vengeance for it, fear thou not.
Then weep no more. I'll send to one in Mantua,
Where that same banished runagate doth live,   89
Shall give him such an unaccustomed dram   90
That he shall soon keep Tybalt company.
And then, I hope, thou wilt be satisfied.
JULIET
Indeed, I never shall be satisfied
With Romeo till I behold him—dead—
Is my poor heart so for a kinsman vexed.

71 An if if   **73 wit** intellect   **74 feeling** deeply felt   **83 no man like he**
no man so much as he.   **grieve** (1) anger (2) grieve with longing. (Juliet
speaks to her mother throughout in intentional ambiguities, at ll. 86, 99,
100–102, etc.)   **89 runagate** renegade, fugitive   **90 Shall** who shall.
dram dose. (Literally, one-eighth of a fluid ounce.)

Madam, if you could find out but a man
To bear a poison, I would temper it,   97
That Romeo should, upon receipt thereof,
Soon sleep in quiet. O, how my heart abhors
To hear him named, and cannot come to him
To wreak the love I bore my cousin   101
Upon his body that hath slaughtered him!   102

WIFE
Find thou the means, and I'll find such a man.
But now I'll tell thee joyful tidings, girl.

JULIET
And joy comes well in such a needy time.
What are they, beseech your ladyship?

WIFE
Well, well, thou hast a careful father, child,   107
One who, to put thee from thy heaviness,   108
Hath sorted out a sudden day of joy   109
That thou expects not, nor I looked not for.

JULIET
Madam, in happy time, what day is that?

WIFE
Marry, my child, early next Thursday morn,   112
The gallant, young, and noble gentleman,
The County Paris, at Saint Peter's Church
Shall happily make thee there a joyful bride.

JULIET
Now, by Saint Peter's Church, and Peter too,
He shall not make me there a joyful bride!
I wonder at this haste, that I must wed
Ere he that should be husband comes to woo.
I pray you, tell my lord and father, madam,
I will not marry yet, and when I do I swear
It shall be Romeo, whom you know I hate,
Rather than Paris. These are news indeed!

WIFE
Here comes your father. Tell him so yourself,
And see how he will take it at your hands.

97 temper (1) mix, concoct (2) alloy, dilute **101 wreak** (1) avenge
(2) bestow **102 his body that** the body of him who **107 careful** full of
care (for you) **108 heaviness** sorrow **109 sorted** chosen **112 Marry**
i.e., by the Virgin Mary

Enter Capulet and Nurse.

CAPULET
When the sun sets, the earth doth drizzle dew,
But for the sunset of my brother's son
It rains downright.
How now, a conduit, girl? What, still in tears?   129
Evermore showering? In one little body
Thou counterfeits a bark, a sea, a wind;   131
For still thy eyes, which I may call the sea,
Do ebb and flow with tears; the bark thy body is,
Sailing in this salt flood; the winds, thy sighs,
Who, raging with thy tears, and they with them,
Without a sudden calm, will overset   136
Thy tempest-tossèd body.—How now, wife?
Have you delivered to her our decree?

WIFE
Ay, sir, but she will none, she gives you thanks.   139
I would the fool were married to her grave!

CAPULET
Soft, take me with you, take me with you, wife.   141
How? Will she none? Doth she not give us thanks?
Is she not proud? Doth she not count her blest,   143
Unworthy as she is, that we have wrought   144
So worthy a gentleman to be her bride?   145

JULIET
Not proud you have, but thankful that you have.
Proud can I never be of what I hate,
But thankful even for hate that is meant love.   148

CAPULET
How, how, how, how, chopped logic? What is this?   149
"Proud," and "I thank you," and "I thank you not,"
And yet "not proud"? Mistress minion, you,   151
Thank me no thankings, nor proud me no prouds,

---

129 conduit water pipe, fountain   **131 bark** sailing vessel   **136 Without
. . . calm** unless they quickly calm themselves   **139 will . . . thanks** says
"no thank you," she'll have none, no part of it   **141 take . . . you** let me
understand you   **143 count her** consider herself   **144 wrought** pro-
cured   **145 bride** bridegroom   **148 hate . . . love** i.e., that which is
hateful but which was meant lovingly   **149 chopped logic** a shallow and
sophistical argument, or arguer   **151 minion** spoiled darling, minx

But fettle your fine joints 'gainst Thursday next   153
To go with Paris to Saint Peter's Church,
Or I will drag thee on a hurdle thither.   155
Out, you greensickness carrion! Out, you baggage!   156
You tallow-face!
WIFE [*To Capulet*] Fie, fie! What, are you mad?   157
JULIET [*Kneeling*]
Good father, I beseech you on my knees,
Hear me with patience but to speak a word.
CAPULET
Hang thee, young baggage, disobedient wretch!
I tell thee what: get thee to church o' Thursday
Or never after look me in the face.
Speak not, reply not, do not answer me!
My fingers itch. Wife, we scarce thought us blest
That God had lent us but this only child;
But now I see this one is one too much,
And that we have a curse in having her.
Out on her, hilding!
NURSE   God in heaven bless her!   168
You are to blame, my lord, to rate her so.   169
CAPULET
And why, my Lady Wisdom? Hold your tongue,
Good Prudence. Smatter with your gossips, go.   171
NURSE
I speak no treason.
CAPULET   O, God-i'-good-e'en!   172
NURSE
May not one speak?
CAPULET   Peace, you mumbling fool!
Utter your gravity o'er a gossip's bowl,   174
For here we need it not.
WIFE   You are too hot.

---

153 fettle make ready.   **'gainst** in anticipation of   **155 a hurdle** a conveyance on which criminals were dragged to execution   **156 greensickness**
(An anemic ailment of young unmarried women; it suggests Juliet's
paleness.)   **baggage** good-for-nothing   **157 tallow-face** pale-face
168 hilding worthless person   **169 rate** berate, scold   **171 Smatter** chat-
ter   **172 God-i'-good-e'en** i.e., for God's sake. (Literally, God give you good
evening.)   **174 gravity** wisdom. (Said contemptuously.)

CAPULET   God's bread, it makes me mad!   177
   Day, night, hour, tide, time, work, play,   178
   Alone, in company, still my care hath been
   To have her matched. And having now provided
   A gentleman of noble parentage,
   Of fair demesnes, youthful, and nobly liened,   182
   Stuffed, as they say, with honorable parts,   183
   Proportioned as one's thought would wish a man—
   And then to have a wretched puling fool,   185
   A whining mammet, in her fortune's tender,   186
   To answer, "I'll not wed, I cannot love,
   I am too young; I pray you, pardon me."
   But, an you will not wed, I'll pardon you.   189
   Graze where you will, you shall not house with me.
   Look to 't, think on 't. I do not use to jest.   191
   Thursday is near. Lay hand on heart; advise.   192
   An you be mine, I'll give you to my friend;
   An you be not, hang, beg, starve, die in the streets,
   For, by my soul, I'll ne'er acknowledge thee,
   Nor what is mine shall never do thee good.
   Trust to 't, bethink you. I'll not be forsworn.   *Exit.* 197
JULIET
   Is there no pity sitting in the clouds
   That sees into the bottom of my grief?
   O sweet my Mother, cast me not away!
   Delay this marriage for a month, a week;
   Or if you do not, make the bridal bed
   In that dim monument where Tybalt lies.
WIFE
   Talk not to me, for I'll not speak a word.
   Do as thou wilt, for I have done with thee.   *Exit.*
JULIET
   O God!—O Nurse, how shall this be prevented?
   My husband is on earth, my faith in heaven.   207

---

177 God's bread i.e., by God's (Christ's) Sacrament   **178 tide** season
182 demesnes estates.   **liened** descended   **183 parts** qualities
185 puling whining   **186 mammet** doll.   **in . . . tender** when an offer of
good fortune is made to her   **189 pardon you** i.e., allow you to depart.
(Said caustically.)   **191 do not use** am not accustomed   **192 advise**
consider carefully   **197 be forsworn** i.e., go back on my word   **207 my
faith in heaven** (Juliet refers to her marriage vows.)

How shall that faith return again to earth,   208
Unless that husband send it me from heaven   209
By leaving earth? Comfort me, counsel me.   210
Alack, alack, that heaven should practice stratagems   211
Upon so soft a subject as myself!
What sayst thou? Hast thou not a word of joy?
Some comfort, Nurse.
NURSE   Faith, here it is.
Romeo is banished, and all the world to nothing   215
That he dares ne'er come back to challenge you,   216
Or if he do, it needs must be by stealth.
Then, since the case so stands as now it doth,
I think it best you married with the County.
O, he's a lovely gentleman!
Romeo's a dishclout to him. An eagle, madam,   221
Hath not so green, so quick, so fair an eye   222
As Paris hath. Beshrew my very heart,   223
I think you are happy in this second match,
For it excels your first; or if it did not,
Your first is dead—or 'twere as good he were,
As living here and you no use of him.   227
JULIET   Speak'st thou from thy heart?
NURSE
And from my soul too. Else beshrew them both.
JULIET   Amen!   230
NURSE   What?
JULIET
Well, thou hast comforted me marvelous much.
Go in, and tell my lady I am gone,
Having displeased my father, to Laurence' cell
To make confession and to be absolved.
NURSE
Marry, I will; and this is wisely done.   [*Exit.*]
JULIET
Ancient damnation! O most wicked fiend!   237

208–210 How . . . leaving earth i.e., how can I remarry unless Romeo
dies   211 practice scheme, contrive   215 all . . . nothing the odds are
overwhelming   216 challenge lay claim to   221 dishclout dishrag
222 quick keen   223 Beshrew i.e., cursed be (also at l. 229)   227 here
i.e., on earth   230 Amen i.e., yes, indeed, *beshrew* (cursed be) your heart
and soul. (But Juliet does not explain this private meaning to the
Nurse.)   237 Ancient damnation damnable old woman

Is it more sin to wish me thus forsworn,   238
Or to dispraise my lord with that same tongue
Which she hath praised him with above compare
So many thousand times? Go, counselor,
Thou and my bosom henceforth shall be twain.   242
I'll to the Friar to know his remedy.
If all else fail, myself have power to die.   *Exit.*

❖

238 forsworn i.e., false to my marriage vows   **242 bosom** secret
thoughts.   **twain** separated

4.1   *Enter Friar [Laurence] and County Paris.*

FRIAR LAURENCE
  On Thursday, sir? The time is very short.
PARIS
  My father Capulet will have it so,
  And I am nothing slow to slack his haste.   3
FRIAR LAURENCE
  You say you do not know the lady's mind?
  Uneven is the course. I like it not.
PARIS
  Immoderately she weeps for Tybalt's death,
  And therefore have I little talked of love,
  For Venus smiles not in a house of tears.   8
  Now, sir, her father counts it dangerous
  That she do give her sorrow so much sway,
  And in his wisdom hastes our marriage   11
  To stop the inundation of her tears,
  Which, too much minded by herself alone,   13
  May be put from her by society.   14
  Now do you know the reason of this haste.
FRIAR LAURENCE [*Aside*]
  I would I knew not why it should be slowed.—
  Look, sir, here comes the lady toward my cell.

        Enter Juliet.

PARIS
  Happily met, my lady and my wife!
JULIET
  That may be, sir, when I may be a wife.
PARIS
  That "may be" must be, love, on Thursday next.
JULIET
  What must be shall be.
FRIAR LAURENCE   That's a certain text.

4.1. Location: Verona. Friar Laurence's cell.
3 nothing . . . haste not at all reluctant in a way that might slacken his
haste   **8 Venus . . . tears** (1) amorousness isn't appropriate in a house of
mourning (2) the planet Venus does not exert a favorable influence when
it is in an inauspicious *house* or portion of the zodiac   **11 hastes** hurries   **13 minded** thought about   **14 society** companionship

PARIS
Come you to make confession to this father?
JULIET
To answer that, I should confess to you.
PARIS
Do not deny to him that you love me.
JULIET
I will confess to you that I love him.
PARIS
So will ye, I am sure, that you love me.
JULIET
If I do so, it will be of more price,   27
Being spoke behind your back, than to your face.
PARIS
Poor soul, thy face is much abused with tears.
JULIET
The tears have got small victory by that,
For it was bad enough before their spite.   31
PARIS
Thou wrong'st it more than tears with that report.
JULIET
That is no slander, sir, which is a truth;
And what I spake, I spake it to my face.   34
PARIS
Thy face is mine, and thou hast slandered it.
JULIET
It may be so, for it is not mine own.—
Are you at leisure, holy Father, now,
Or shall I come to you at evening Mass?
FRIAR LAURENCE
My leisure serves me, pensive daughter, now.   39
My lord, we must entreat the time alone.   40
PARIS
God shield I should disturb devotion!   41
Juliet, on Thursday early will I rouse ye.
Till then, adieu, and keep this holy kiss.   *Exit.*
JULIET
O, shut the door! And when thou hast done so,
Come weep with me—past hope, past cure, past help!

27 more price greater worth   **31 spite** malice   **34 to my face** (1) openly
(2) about my face   **39 pensive** sorrowful   **40 entreat . . . alone** i.e., ask
you to leave us alone   **41 shield** prevent (that)

FRIAR LAURENCE
   Ah, Juliet, I already know thy grief;
   It strains me past the compass of my wits.   47
   I hear thou must, and nothing may prorogue it,   48
   On Thursday next be married to this county.
JULIET
   Tell me not, Friar, that thou hearest of this,
   Unless thou tell me how I may prevent it.
   If in thy wisdom thou canst give no help,
   Do thou but call my resolution wise
   And with this knife I'll help it presently.   54
                         [*She shows a knife.*]
   God joined my heart and Romeo's, thou our hands;
   And ere this hand, by thee to Romeo's sealed,
   Shall be the label to another deed,   57
   Or my true heart with treacherous revolt
   Turn to another, this shall slay them both.   59
   Therefore, out of thy long-experienced time,   60
   Give me some present counsel, or, behold,
   Twixt my extremes and me this bloody knife   62
   Shall play the umpire, arbitrating that
   Which the commission of thy years and art   64
   Could to no issue of true honor bring.
   Be not so long to speak; I long to die   66
   If what thou speak'st speak not of remedy.
FRIAR LAURENCE
   Hold, daughter. I do spy a kind of hope,
   Which craves as desperate an execution
   As that is desperate which we would prevent.
   If, rather than to marry County Paris,
   Thou hast the strength of will to slay thyself,
   Then is it likely thou wilt undertake
   A thing like death to chide away this shame,
   That cop'st with Death himself to scape from it;   75
   And if thou darest, I'll give thee remedy.

---

47 strains forces.   **compass** bounds   **48 may prorogue** can delay
54 presently at once   **57 label** strip attached to a deed to carry the seal;
hence, confirmation, seal   **59 both** i.e., hand and heart   **60 time** age
62 extremes extreme difficulties   **64 commission** authority.   **art** skill
66 so long so slow   **75 That cop'st** you who would encounter or negotiate with; or, a thing that would cope.   **it** i.e., shame

JULIET
O, bid me leap, rather than marry Paris,
From off the battlements of any tower,
Or walk in thievish ways, or bid me lurk   79
Where serpents are; chain me with roaring bears,
Or hide me nightly in a charnel house,   81
O'ercovered quite with dead men's rattling bones,
With reeky shanks and yellow chopless skulls;   83
Or bid me go into a new-made grave
And hide me with a dead man in his tomb—
Things that, to hear them told, have made me tremble—
And I will do it without fear or doubt,
To live an unstained wife to my sweet love.
FRIAR LAURENCE
Hold, then. Go home, be merry, give consent
To marry Paris. Wednesday is tomorrow.
Tomorrow night look that thou lie alone;
Let not the Nurse lie with thee in thy chamber.
Take thou this vial, being then in bed,
                          [*Showing her a vial*]
And this distilling liquor drink thou off,   94
When presently through all thy veins shall run
A cold and drowsy humor; for no pulse   96
Shall keep his native progress, but surcease;   97
No warmth, no breath shall testify thou livest;
The roses in thy lips and cheeks shall fade
To wanny ashes, thy eyes' windows fall   100
Like death when he shuts up the day of life;
Each part, deprived of supple government,   102
Shall, stiff and stark and cold, appear like death.
And in this borrowed likeness of shrunk death
Thou shalt continue two-and-forty hours,
And then awake as from a pleasant sleep.
Now, when the bridegroom in the morning comes
To rouse thee from thy bed, there art thou dead.
Then, as the manner of our country is,

---

79 thievish ways roads frequented by thieves   **81 charnel house** vault
for human bones   **83 reeky** reeking, malodorous.   **chopless** without the
lower jaw   **94 distilling** infusing   **96 humor** fluid, moisture   **97 his
native** its natural.   **surcease** cease   **100 wanny** wan, pale   **102 supple
government** control of motion

In thy best robes uncovered on the bier
Thou shalt be borne to that same ancient vault
Where all the kindred of the Capulets lie.
In the meantime, against thou shalt awake,   113
Shall Romeo by my letters know our drift,   114
And hither shall he come; and he and I
Will watch thy waking, and that very night
Shall Romeo bear thee hence to Mantua.
And this shall free thee from this present shame,
If no inconstant toy nor womanish fear   119
Abate thy valor in the acting it.
JULIET [*Taking the vial*]
Give me, give me! O, tell not me of fear!
FRIAR LAURENCE
Hold, get you gone. Be strong and prosperous   122
In this resolve. I'll send a friar with speed
To Mantua, with my letters to thy lord.
JULIET
Love give me strength, and strength shall help afford. 125
Farewell, dear Father!   *Exeunt [separately].*

❖

4.2   *Enter Father Capulet, Mother [Capulet's Wife],*
        Nurse, and Servingmen, two or three.

CAPULET
So many guests invite as here are writ.
                    [*Exit one or two Servingmen.*]
Sirrah, go hire me twenty cunning cooks.   2
SERVINGMAN   You shall have none ill, sir, for I'll try 3
if they can lick their fingers.
CAPULET   How canst thou try them so?
SERVINGMAN   Marry, sir, 'tis an ill cook that cannot
lick his own fingers; therefore he that cannot lick his
fingers goes not with me.
CAPULET   Go, begone.   [*Exit Servingman.*]

---

113 against anticipating when   **114 drift** plan   **119 toy** idle fancy
122 prosperous successful   **125 help afford** provide help

4.2. Location: Verona. Capulet's house.
2 cunning skilled   **3 none ill** no bad ones.   **try** test

We shall be much unfurnished for this time.   10
What, is my daughter gone to Friar Laurence?
NURSE   Ay, forsooth.
CAPULET
Well, he may chance to do some good on her.
A peevish self-willed harlotry it is.   14

    Enter Juliet.

NURSE
See where she comes from shrift with merry look.
CAPULET
How now, my headstrong, where have you been
    gadding?   16
JULIET
Where I have learned me to repent the sin
Of disobedient opposition
To you and your behests, and am enjoined   19
By holy Laurence to fall prostrate here,   [*Kneeling*]
To beg your pardon. Pardon, I beseech you!
Henceforward I am ever ruled by you.
CAPULET
Send for the County! Go tell him of this.
I'll have this knot knit up tomorrow morning.
JULIET
I met the youthful lord at Laurence' cell
And gave him what becomèd love I might,   26
Not stepping o'er the bounds of modesty.
CAPULET
Why, I am glad on 't. This is well. Stand up.
                        [*Juliet rises.*]
This is as 't should be. Let me see the County;
Ay, marry, go, I say, and fetch him hither.
Now, afore God, this reverend holy friar,
All our whole city is much bound to him.   32
JULIET
Nurse, will you go with me into my closet   33
To help me sort such needful ornaments   34
As you think fit to furnish me tomorrow?

___

10 unfurnished unprovided **14 A peevish . . . is** i.e., she's a silly good-for-nothing **16 gadding** wandering **19 behests** commands **26 becomèd** befitting **32 bound** indebted **33 closet** chamber **34 sort** choose

WIFE
No, not till Thursday. There is time enough.
CAPULET
Go, Nurse, go with her. We'll to church tomorrow.
                              Exeunt [Juliet and Nurse].
WIFE
We shall be short in our provision.
'Tis now near night.
CAPULET   Tush, I will stir about,
And all things shall be well, I warrant thee, wife.
Go thou to Juliet, help to deck up her.   41
I'll not to bed tonight. Let me alone.
I'll play the huswife for this once.—What ho!—   43
They are all forth. Well, I will walk myself
To County Paris, to prepare up him
Against tomorrow. My heart is wondrous light,
Since this same wayward girl is so reclaimed.
                              Exeunt.

❖

4.3   *Enter Juliet and Nurse.*

JULIET
Ay, those attires are best. But, gentle Nurse,
I pray thee, leave me to myself tonight;
For I have need of many orisons   3
To move the heavens to smile upon my state,
Which, well thou knowest, is cross and full of sin.   5

        Enter Mother [Capulet's Wife].

WIFE
What, are you busy, ho? Need you my help?
JULIET
No, madam, we have culled such necessaries   7
As are behooveful for our state tomorrow.   8
So please you, let me now be left alone,

41 **deck up** dress, adorn   43 **huswife** housewife
4.3. Location: Verona. Capulet's house; Juliet's bed, enclosed by bedcur-
tains, is thrust out or is otherwise visible.
3 **orisons** prayers   5 **cross** contrary, perverse   7 **culled** picked out
8 **behooveful** needful.   **state** ceremony

And let the Nurse this night sit up with you,
For I am sure you have your hands full all
In this so sudden business.
WIFE   Good night.
Get thee to bed and rest, for thou hast need.
                         Exeunt [Capulet's Wife and Nurse].
JULIET
Farewell! God knows when we shall meet again.
I have a faint cold fear thrills through my veins   15
That almost freezes up the heat of life.
I'll call them back again to comfort me.
Nurse!—What should she do here?
My dismal scene I needs must act alone.
Come, vial.   *[She takes out the vial.]*
What if this mixture do not work at all?
Shall I be married then tomorrow morning?
No, no, this shall forbid it. Lie thou there.
                         [She lays down a dagger.]
What if it be a poison which the Friar
Subtly hath ministered to have me dead,
Lest in this marriage he should be dishonored
Because he married me before to Romeo?
I fear it is; and yet methinks it should not,
For he hath still been tried a holy man.   29
How if, when I am laid into the tomb,
I wake before the time that Romeo
Come to redeem me? There's a fearful point!
Shall I not then be stifled in the vault,
To whose foul mouth no healthsome air breathes in,
And there die strangled ere my Romeo comes?
Or, if I live, is it not very like,   36
The horrible conceit of death and night,   37
Together with the terror of the place—
As in a vault, an ancient receptacle,   39
Where for this many hundred years the bones
Of all my buried ancestors are packed;
Where bloody Tybalt, yet but green in earth,   42

---

15 faint producing faintness. **thrills** pierces, shivers **29 still** always.
tried proved **36 like** likely (also at l. 45) **37 conceit** idea **39 As**
namely **42 green** new, freshly

Lies festering in his shroud; where, as they say,
At some hours in the night spirits resort—
Alack, alack, is it not like that I,
So early waking, what with loathsome smells,
And shrieks like mandrakes torn out of the earth,   47
That living mortals, hearing them, run mad—   48
O, if I wake, shall I not be distraught,
Environèd with all these hideous fears,   50
And madly play with my forefathers' joints,
And pluck the mangled Tybalt from his shroud,
And in this rage, with some great kinsman's bone   53
As with a club dash out my desperate brains?
O, look! Methinks I see my cousin's ghost
Seeking out Romeo, that did spit his body   56
Upon a rapier's point. Stay, Tybalt, stay!   57
Romeo, Romeo, Romeo! Here's drink—I drink to thee.
      [*She drinks and falls upon her bed,*
                  within the curtains.]

4.4   *Enter Lady of the House [Capulet's Wife] and*
          Nurse.

WIFE
   Hold, take these keys, and fetch more spices, Nurse.
NURSE
   They call for dates and quinces in the pastry.   2

      Enter old Capulet.

CAPULET
   Come, stir, stir, stir! The second cock hath crowed.
   The curfew bell hath rung; 'tis three o'clock.
   Look to the baked meats, good Angelica.   5
   Spare not for cost.

---

47 mandrakes (The root of the mandragora or mandrake resembled the
human form; the plant was fabled to utter a shriek when torn from the
ground.)   **48 That** so that   **50 fears** objects of fear   **53 rage** madness.
great i.e., of an earlier generation, as in *great*-grandfather   **56 spit**
impale   **57 Stay** stop

4.4. Location: Scene continues. Juliet's bed remains visible.
2 pastry room in which pastry was made   **5 baked meats** pies, pastry

NURSE   Go, you cotquean, go,   6
Get you to bed. Faith, you'll be sick tomorrow
For this night's watching.   8

CAPULET
No, not a whit. What, I have watched ere now
All night for lesser cause, and ne'er been sick.

WIFE
Ay, you have been a mouse-hunt in your time,   11
But I will watch you from such watching now.   12
                              Exeunt Lady and Nurse.

CAPULET   A jealous hood, a jealous hood!   13

*Enter three or four [Servingmen] with spits and
logs, and baskets.*

Now, fellow, what is there?

FIRST SERVINGMAN
Things for the cook, sir, but I know not what.

CAPULET
Make haste, make haste. [*Exit First Servingman.*] Sir-
rah, fetch drier logs.
Call Peter. He will show thee where they are.

SECOND SERVINGMAN
I have a head, sir, that will find out logs
And never trouble Peter for the matter.

CAPULET
Mass, and well said. A merry whoreson, ha!   20
Thou shalt be loggerhead. [*Exit Servingman.*] Good
faith, 'tis day.   21
The County will be here with music straight,   22
For so he said he would. I hear him near.
                              Play music [within].
Nurse! Wife! What ho! What, Nurse, I say!

Enter Nurse.

Go waken Juliet, go and trim her up.   25

---

6 cotquean i.e., a man who acts the housewife. (Literally, a cottage
housewife.)   **8 watching** being awake   **11 mouse-hunt** i.e., hunter of
women   **12 watch . . . watching** i.e., keep an eye on you to prevent such
nighttime activity   **13 A jealous hood** i.e., you wear the cap of jealousy   **20 Mass** by the Mass.   **whoreson** i.e., fellow. (An abusive term
used familiarly.)   **21 loggerhead** (1) put in charge of getting logs (2) a
blockhead   **22 straight** straightway, immediately   **25 trim** dress

I'll go and chat with Paris. Hie, make haste,
Make haste. The bridegroom he is come already.
Make haste, I say.   [*Exit Capulet.*]

4.5   [*The Nurse goes to the bed.*]

NURSE
Mistress! What, mistress! Juliet! Fast, I warrant her,
    she.   1
Why, lamb, why, lady! Fie, you slugabed!
Why, love, I say! Madam! Sweetheart! Why, bride!
What, not a word? You take your pennyworths now.   4
Sleep for a week; for the next night, I warrant,
The County Paris hath set up his rest   6
That you shall rest but little. God forgive me,
Marry, and amen! How sound is she asleep!
I needs must wake her. Madam, madam, madam!
Ay, let the County take you in your bed;
He'll fright you up, i' faith. Will it not be?
                        [*She opens the bedcurtains.*]
What, dressed, and in your clothes, and down again?
I must needs wake you. Lady, lady, lady!
Alas, alas! Help, help! My lady's dead!
O, weraday, that ever I was born!   15
Some aqua vitae, ho! My lord! My lady!   16

        [*Enter Capulet's Wife.*]

WIFE
    What noise is here?
NURSE   O lamentable day!
WIFE
    What is the matter?
NURSE   Look, look! O heavy day!   18
WIFE
    O me, O me! My child, my only life!

4.5. Location: Scene continues. Juliet's bed remains visible.
1 Fast fast asleep   **4 pennyworths** small portions (of sleep)   **6 set up his
rest** firmly resolved. (From primero, a card game, where it means "staked
his reserve." The Nurse speaks bawdily.)   **15 weraday** wellaway, alas
16 aqua vitae strong alcoholic spirits   **18 heavy** sorrowful

Revive, look up, or I will die with thee!
Help, help! Call help.

    Enter Father [Capulet].

CAPULET
For shame, bring Juliet forth. Her lord is come.
NURSE
She's dead, deceased. She's dead, alack the day!
WIFE
Alack the day, she's dead, she's dead, she's dead!
CAPULET
Ha! Let me see her. Out, alas! She's cold.
Her blood is settled, and her joints are stiff;   26
Life and these lips have long been separated.
Death lies on her like an untimely frost
Upon the sweetest flower of all the field.
NURSE
O lamentable day!
WIFE   O woeful time!
CAPULET
Death, that hath ta'en her hence to make me wail,
Ties up my tongue and will not let me speak.

    Enter Friar [Laurence] and the County [Paris,
    with Musicians].

FRIAR LAURENCE
Come, is the bride ready to go to church?
CAPULET
Ready to go, but never to return.
O son, the night before thy wedding day
Hath Death lain with thy wife. There she lies,
Flower as she was, deflowered by him.
Death is my son-in-law, Death is my heir;
My daughter he hath wedded. I will die
And leave him all; life, living, all is Death's.   40
PARIS
Have I thought long to see this morning's face,   41
And doth it give me such a sight as this?

26 settled congealed   **40 living** means of living, property   **41 thought
long** looked forward to

WIFE
Accurst, unhappy, wretched, hateful day!   43
Most miserable hour that e'er time saw
In lasting labor of his pilgrimage!   45
But one, poor one, one poor and loving child,
But one thing to rejoice and solace in,
And cruel Death hath catched it from my sight!   48

NURSE
O woe! O woeful, woeful, woeful day!
Most lamentable day, most woeful day
That ever, ever I did yet behold!
O day, O day, O day! O hateful day!
Never was seen so black a day as this.
O woeful day, O woeful day!

PARIS
Beguiled, divorcèd, wrongèd, spited, slain!   55
Most detestable Death, by thee beguiled,
By cruel, cruel thee quite overthrown!
O love! O life! Not life, but love in death!

CAPULET
Despisèd, distressèd, hated, martyred, killed!
Uncomfortable time, why cam'st thou now   60
To murder, murder our solemnity?   61
O child! O child! My soul, and not my child!
Dead art thou! Alack, my child is dead,
And with my child my joys are burièd.

FRIAR LAURENCE
Peace, ho, for shame! Confusion's cure lives not   65
In these confusions. Heaven and yourself
Had part in this fair maid; now heaven hath all,
And all the better is it for the maid.
Your part in her you could not keep from death,   69
But heaven keeps his part in eternal life.
The most you sought was her promotion,   71
For 'twas your heaven she should be advanced;   72
And weep ye now, seeing she is advanced
Above the clouds, as high as heaven itself?

43 unhappy fatal   **45 lasting** unceasing   **48 catched** snatched
55 Beguiled cheated   **60 Uncomfortable** comfortless   **61 solemnity**
ceremony, festivity   **65 Confusion's** calamity's   **69 Your part** i.e., the
mortal part   **71 promotion** social advancement   **72 your heaven** i.e.,
your idea of the greatest good

O, in this love you love your child so ill
That you run mad, seeing that she is well.
She's not well married that lives married long,
But she's best married that dies married young.
Dry up your tears, and stick your rosemary   79
On this fair corpse, and, as the custom is,
And in her best array, bear her to church;
For though fond nature bids us all lament,   82
Yet nature's tears are reason's merriment.   83

CAPULET
All things that we ordainèd festival   84
Turn from their office to black funeral: 85
Our instruments to melancholy bells,
Our wedding cheer to a sad burial feast,
Our solemn hymns to sullen dirges change,   88
Our bridal flowers serve for a buried corpse,
And all things change them to the contrary.   90

FRIAR LAURENCE
Sir, go you in, and, madam, go with him,
And go, Sir Paris. Everyone prepare
To follow this fair corpse unto her grave.
The heavens do lour upon you for some ill;   94
Move them no more by crossing their high will.   95

                    Exeunt. Manet [Nurse with Musicians].

FIRST MUSICIAN
Faith, we may put up our pipes and be gone.

NURSE
Honest good fellows, ah, put up, put up!
For well you know this is a pitiful case.   [*Exit.*]

FIRST MUSICIAN
Ay, by my troth, the case may be amended.   99

---

79 rosemary symbol of immortality and enduring love; therefore used at
both funerals and weddings   **82 fond nature** foolish human nature
83 nature's . . . merriment that which causes human nature to weep is
an occasion of joy to reason   **84 ordainèd festival** intended to be festive   **85 office** function   **88 sullen** mournful   **90 them** themselves
94 lour threaten.   **for some ill** on account of some sin   **95 Move** i.e.,
anger   **s.d. Manet** she remains onstage   **99 case . . . amended**
(1) things generally could be much better (2) the instrument case could
be repaired

Enter Peter.

PETER Musicians, O, musicians, "Heart's ease," 100
"Heart's ease." O, an you will have me live, play
"Heart's ease."
FIRST MUSICIAN Why "Heart's ease"?
PETER O, musicians, because my heart itself plays "My 104
heart is full." O, play me some merry dump to comfort 105
me.
FIRST MUSICIAN Not a dump we! 'Tis no time to play
now.
PETER You will not, then?
FIRST MUSICIAN No.
PETER I will then give it you soundly.
FIRST MUSICIAN What will you give us?
PETER No money, on my faith, but the gleek; I will give 113
you the minstrel. 114
FIRST MUSICIAN Then will I give you the serving-crea-
ture.
PETER Then will I lay the serving-creature's dagger on
your pate. I will carry no crotchets. I'll re you, I'll fa you. 118
Do you note me? 119
FIRST MUSICIAN An you re us and fa us, you note us.
SECOND MUSICIAN Pray you, put up your dagger and
put out your wit. 122
PETER Then have at you with my wit! I will dry-beat 123
you with an iron wit, and put up my iron dagger. Answer me like men:
    "When griping griefs the heart doth wound, 126
      And doleful dumps the mind oppress,
    Then music with her silver sound"— 128

s.d. Enter Peter (The second quarto has *Enter Will Kemp*, well-known comic
actor and member of Shakespeare's company, for whom Shakespeare evidently intended this role and so named him in the manuscript.)
100, 104–105 "Heart's ease," "My heart is full" (Popular ballads.)
105 dump mournful tune or dance 113 gleek jest, gibe 113–114 give
you the minstrel insultingly term you a minstrel, i.e., vagabond
118 carry no crotchets (1) endure no whims (2) sing no quarter notes.
re, fa musical notes 119 note (1) heed (2) set to music 122 put out
display 123 dry-beat thrash (without drawing blood) 126–128 "When
. . . sound" (From Richard Edwards's song "In Commendation of Music," published in *The Paradise of Dainty Devices*, 1576.)

Why "silver sound"? Why "music with her silver
sound"? What say you, Simon Catling?   130
FIRST MUSICIAN   Marry, sir, because silver hath a sweet
sound.
PETER   Pretty! What say you, Hugh Rebeck?   133
SECOND MUSICIAN   I say "silver sound" because musi-
cians sound for silver.   135
PETER   Pretty too! What say you, James Soundpost?   136
THIRD MUSICIAN   Faith, I know not what to say.
PETER   O, I cry you mercy, you are the singer. I will say 138
for you. It is "music with her silver sound" because
musicians have no gold for sounding: 140
        "Then music with her silver sound
        With speedy help doth lend redress."   *Exit.*
FIRST MUSICIAN   What a pestilent knave is this same!
SECOND MUSICIAN   Hang him, Jack! Come, we'll in here,
tarry for the mourners, and stay dinner.   *Exeunt.*   145

❖

130 **Catling** (A catling was a small lutestring made of catgut.)
133 **Rebeck** (A rebeck was a fiddle with three strings.)   135 **sound** make
music   136 **Soundpost** (A soundpost is the pillar or peg that supports
the sounding board of a stringed instrument.)   138 **cry you mercy** beg
your pardon   140 **have . . . sounding** i.e., are paid only silver for playing   145 **stay** await

5.1 *Enter Romeo.*

ROMEO
If I may trust the flattering truth of sleep,   1
My dreams presage some joyful news at hand.
My bosom's lord sits lightly in his throne,   3
And all this day an unaccustomed spirit
Lifts me above the ground with cheerful thoughts.
I dreamt my lady came and found me dead—
Strange dream that gives a dead man leave to think!—
And breathed such life with kisses in my lips
That I revived and was an emperor.
Ah me, how sweet is love itself possessed   10
When but love's shadows are so rich in joy!   11

Enter Romeo's man [Balthasar, booted].

News from Verona! How now, Balthasar,
Dost thou not bring me letters from the Friar?
How doth my lady? Is my father well?
How fares my Juliet? That I ask again,
For nothing can be ill if she be well.
BALTHASAR
Then she is well, and nothing can be ill.
Her body sleeps in Capels' monument,
And her immortal part with angels lives.
I saw her laid low in her kindred's vault
And presently took post to tell it you.   21
O, pardon me for bringing these ill news,
Since you did leave it for my office, sir.   23
ROMEO
Is it e'en so? Then I defy you, stars!
Thou knowest my lodging. Get me ink and paper,
And hire post-horses. I will hence tonight.
BALTHASAR
I do beseech you, sir, have patience.

5.1. Location: Mantua. A street.
1 flattering favorable (but potentially illusory)   **3 bosom's lord** i.e.,
heart   **10 itself possessed** actually enjoyed   **11 shadows** dreams
s.d. booted wearing riding boots—a conventional stage sign of traveling
21 presently took post at once started off in haste; or, with post-
horses   **23 office** duty

Your looks are pale and wild, and do import   28
Some misadventure.
ROMEO   Tush, thou art deceived.
Leave me, and do the thing I bid thee do.
Hast thou no letters to me from the Friar?
BALTHASAR
No, my good lord.
ROMEO   No matter. Get thee gone,
And hire those horses. I'll be with thee straight.

                              Exit [Balthasar].

Well, Juliet, I will lie with thee tonight.
Let's see for means. O mischief, thou art swift   35
To enter in the thoughts of desperate men!
I do remember an apothecary—   37
And hereabouts 'a dwells—which late I noted   38
In tattered weeds, with overwhelming brows,   39
Culling of simples. Meager were his looks;   40
Sharp misery had worn him to the bones;
And in his needy shop a tortoise hung,
An alligator stuffed, and other skins
Of ill-shaped fishes; and about his shelves
A beggarly account of empty boxes,   45
Green earthen pots, bladders, and musty seeds,
Remnants of packthread, and old cakes of roses   47
Were thinly scattered to make up a show.
Noting this penury, to myself I said,
"An if a man did need a poison now,   50
Whose sale is present death in Mantua,   51
Here lives a caitiff wretch would sell it him."   52
O, this same thought did but forerun my need,
And this same needy man must sell it me.
As I remember, this should be the house.
Being holiday, the beggar's shop is shut.
What, ho! Apothecary!

    [*Enter Apothecary.*]

28 import signify   **35 for means** by what means   **37 apothecary** drug-
gist   **38 which . . . noted** whom lately I noticed   **39 weeds** garments.
overwhelming brows eyebrows jutting out over his eyes   **40 simples**
medicinal herbs.   **Meager** impoverished   **45 beggarly account** poor
array   **47 cakes of roses** petals pressed into cakes to be used as perfume   **50 An if** if   **51 present** immediate   **52 caitiff** miserable.   **would**
who would

APOTHECARY   Who calls so loud?
ROMEO
    Come hither, man. I see that thou art poor.
    Hold, there is forty ducats. [*He shows gold.*] Let me have 59
    A dram of poison, such soon-speeding gear 60
    As will disperse itself through all the veins
    That the life-weary taker may fall dead,
    And that the trunk may be discharged of breath 63
    As violently as hasty powder fired
    Doth hurry from the fatal cannon's womb.
APOTHECARY
    Such mortal drugs I have, but Mantua's law 66
    Is death to any he that utters them. 67
ROMEO
    Art thou so bare and full of wretchedness,
    And fearest to die? Famine is in thy cheeks,
    Need and oppression starveth in thy eyes, 70
    Contempt and beggary hangs upon thy back.
    The world is not thy friend, nor the world's law;
    The world affords no law to make thee rich.
    Then be not poor, but break it, and take this.
APOTHECARY
    My poverty but not my will consents.
ROMEO
    I pay thy poverty and not thy will.
APOTHECARY
    Put this in any liquid thing you will
    And drink it off, and if you had the strength
    Of twenty men it would dispatch you straight.
              [*He gives poison, and takes the gold.*]
ROMEO
    There is thy gold—worse poison to men's souls,
    Doing more murder in this loathsome world
    Than these poor compounds that thou mayst not sell.
    I sell thee poison; thou hast sold me none.
    Farewell. Buy food, and get thyself in flesh.—
    Come, cordial and not poison, go with me 85

---

59 ducats gold coins **60 soon-speeding gear** quickly effective stuff
63 trunk body **66 mortal** deadly **67 any he** anyone. **utters** issues,
gives out **70 starveth** are revealed by the starving look **85 cordial**
restorative for the heart

To Juliet's grave, for there must I use thee.
                              Exeunt [separately].

❖

5.2   *Enter Friar John to Friar Laurence.*

FRIAR JOHN
  Holy Franciscan friar! Brother, ho!

      Enter [Friar] Laurence.

FRIAR LAURENCE
  This same should be the voice of Friar John.
  Welcome from Mantua! What says Romeo?
  Or if his mind be writ, give me his letter.   4
FRIAR JOHN
  Going to find a barefoot brother out—
  One of our order—to associate me   6
  Here in this city visiting the sick,
  And finding him, the searchers of the town,   8
  Suspecting that we both were in a house
  Where the infectious pestilence did reign,
  Sealed up the doors and would not let us forth,
  So that my speed to Mantua there was stayed.   12
FRIAR LAURENCE
  Who bare my letter, then, to Romeo?
FRIAR JOHN
  I could not send it—here it is again—
  Nor get a messenger to bring it thee,
  So fearful were they of infection.   [*He gives a letter.*]
FRIAR LAURENCE
  Unhappy fortune! By my brotherhood,
  The letter was not nice but full of charge,   18
  Of dear import, and the neglecting it   19

5.2. Location: Verona. Friar Laurence's cell.
4 mind thoughts **6 associate** accompany **8 searchers of the town**
town officials charged with public health (and especially concerned
about the *pestilence* or plague) **12 speed** successful journey,
progress. **stayed** prevented **18 nice** trivial. **charge** importance
19 dear precious, urgent

May do much danger. Friar John, go hence.
Get me an iron crow and bring it straight　　　21
Unto my cell.

FRIAR JOHN　Brother, I'll go and bring it thee.　　*Exit.*

FRIAR LAURENCE
Now must I to the monument alone.
Within this three hours will fair Juliet wake.
She will beshrew me much that Romeo　　　26
Hath had no notice of these accidents;　　　27
But I will write again to Mantua,
And keep her at my cell till Romeo come—
Poor living corpse, closed in a dead man's tomb! *Exit.*

❖

5.3　　*Enter Paris, and his Page [bearing flowers,
perfumed water, and a torch].*

PARIS
Give me thy torch, boy. Hence, and stand aloof.　　　1
Yet put it out, for I would not be seen.
Under yond yew trees lay thee all along,　　　3
Holding thy ear close to the hollow ground.
So shall no foot upon the churchyard tread,
Being loose, unfirm, with digging up of graves,　　　6
But thou shalt hear it. Whistle then to me
As signal that thou hearest something approach.
Give me those flowers. Do as I bid thee. Go.

PAGE [*Aside*]
I am almost afraid to stand alone
Here in the churchyard, yet I will adventure.
　　　　　　　　　　　　　　　　[*He retires.*]

PARIS [*Strewing flowers and perfumed water*]
Sweet flower, with flowers thy bridal bed I strew—
　O woe! Thy canopy is dust and stones—　　　13

---

21 crow crowbar　**26 beshrew** i.e., reprove　**27 accidents** events

**5.3. Location: Verona. A churchyard and the vault or tomb belonging to
the Capulets.**
1 aloof to one side, at a distance　**3 all along** at full length　**6 Being** i.e.,
the soil being　**13 canopy** covering

Which with sweet water nightly I will dew,   14
  Or wanting that, with tears distilled by moans.   15
The obsequies that I for thee will keep   16
Nightly shall be to strew thy grave and weep.
                                  Whistle Boy.
The boy gives warning something doth approach.
What cursèd foot wanders this way tonight,
To cross my obsequies and true love's rite?   20
What, with a torch? Muffle me, night, awhile.   21
                                   [He retires.]

    Enter Romeo and [Balthasar, with a torch, a
    mattock, and a crowbar].

ROMEO
Give me that mattock and the wrenching iron.   22
                          [He takes the tools.]
Hold, take this letter. Early in the morning
See thou deliver it to my lord and father.
               [He gives a letter and takes a torch.]
Give me the light. Upon thy life I charge thee,
Whate'er thou hearest or seest, stand all aloof
And do not interrupt me in my course.   27
Why I descend into this bed of death
Is partly to behold my lady's face,
But chiefly to take thence from her dead finger
A precious ring—a ring that I must use
In dear employment. Therefore hence, begone.   32
But if thou, jealous, dost return to pry   33
In what I farther shall intend to do,
By heaven, I will tear thee joint by joint
And strew this hungry churchyard with thy limbs.
The time and my intents are savage-wild,
More fierce and more inexorable far
Than empty tigers or the roaring sea.   39
BALTHASAR
I will be gone, sir, and not trouble ye.

14 **dew** moisten   15 **wanting** lacking   16 **obsequies** ceremonies in
memory of the dead   20 **cross** interrupt   21 **Muffle** conceal
s.d. mattock pickax   22 **wrenching iron** crowbar   27 **course** intended
action   32 **dear employment** important business   33 **jealous** suspicious   39 **empty** hungry

ROMEO
  So shalt thou show me friendship. Take thou that.
                            [*He gives him money.*]
  Live, and be prosperous; and farewell, good fellow.
BALTHASAR [*Aside*]
  For all this same, I'll hide me hereabout.   43
  His looks I fear, and his intents I doubt.   [*He retires.*] 44
ROMEO
  Thou detestable maw, thou womb of death,   45
  Gorged with the dearest morsel of the earth,
  Thus I enforce thy rotten jaws to open,
  And in despite I'll cram thee with more food.   48
                [*He begins to open the tomb.*]
PARIS
  This is that banished haughty Montague
  That murdered my love's cousin, with which grief
  It is supposèd the fair creature died,
  And here is come to do some villainous shame
  To the dead bodies. I will apprehend him.
                [*He comes forward.*]
  Stop thy unhallowed toil, vile Montague!
  Can vengeance be pursued further than death?
  Condemnèd villain, I do apprehend thee.
  Obey and go with me, for thou must die.
ROMEO
  I must indeed, and therefore came I hither.
  Good gentle youth, tempt not a desperate man.
  Fly hence and leave me. Think upon these gone;   60
  Let them affright thee. I beseech thee, youth,
  Put not another sin upon my head
  By urging me to fury. O, begone!
  By heaven, I love thee better than myself,
  For I come hither armed against myself.
  Stay not, begone. Live, and hereafter say
  A madman's mercy bid thee run away.
PARIS
  I do defy thy conjuration,
  And apprehend thee for a felon here.

43 For all this same all the same **44 doubt** suspect **45 womb** belly
48 in despite defiantly **60 gone** dead

ROMEO
Wilt thou provoke me? Then have at thee, boy!
                                    [*They fight.*]
PAGE
O Lord, they fight! I will go call the watch.   [*Exit.*]
PARIS
O, I am slain! [*He falls.*] If thou be merciful,
Open the tomb, lay me with Juliet.   [*He dies.*]
ROMEO
In faith, I will. Let me peruse this face.
Mercutio's kinsman, noble County Paris!
What said my man when my betossèd soul
Did not attend him as we rode? I think
He told me Paris should have married Juliet.
Said he not so? Or did I dream it so?
Or am I mad, hearing him talk of Juliet,
To think it was so? O, give me thy hand,
One writ with me in sour misfortune's book.
I'll bury thee in a triumphant grave.
                          [*He opens the tomb.*]
A grave? O, no! A lantern, slaughtered youth,   84
For here lies Juliet, and her beauty makes
This vault a feasting presence full of light.   86
Death, lie thou there, by a dead man interred.
                    [*He lays Paris in the tomb.*]
How oft when men are at the point of death
Have they been merry, which their keepers call   89
A lightening before death! O, how may I   90
Call this a lightening? O my love, my wife!
Death, that hath sucked the honey of thy breath,
Hath had no power yet upon thy beauty.
Thou art not conquered; beauty's ensign yet   94
Is crimson in thy lips and in thy cheeks,
And death's pale flag is not advancèd there.   96
Tybalt, liest thou there in thy bloody sheet?   97
O, what more favor can I do to thee
Than with that hand that cut thy youth in twain

---

84 lantern turret room full of windows   **86 feasting presence** reception
chamber for feasting   **89 keepers** attendants   **90 lightening** exhilara-
tion (supposed to occur just before death)   **94 ensign** banner
96 advancèd raised   **97 sheet** shroud

To sunder his that was thine enemy?   100
Forgive me, cousin! Ah, dear Juliet,
Why art thou yet so fair? Shall I believe
That unsubstantial Death is amorous,   103
And that the lean abhorrèd monster keeps
Thee here in dark to be his paramour?
For fear of that I still will stay with thee   106
And never from this palace of dim night
Depart again. Here, here will I remain
With worms that are thy chambermaids. O, here
Will I set up my everlasting rest   110
And shake the yoke of inauspicious stars
From this world-wearied flesh. Eyes, look your last!
Arms, take your last embrace! And, lips, O you
The doors of breath, seal with a righteous kiss
A dateless bargain to engrossing death!   115
                              [*He kisses Juliet.*]
Come, bitter conduct, come, unsavory guide,   116
Thou desperate pilot, now at once run on   117
The dashing rocks thy seasick weary bark!
Here's to my love. [*He drinks.*] O true apothecary!
Thy drugs are quick. Thus with a kiss I die. [*He dies.*]

        Enter [*at the other end of the churchyard*] *Friar*
        [*Laurence*] *with lantern, crow, and spade.*

FRIAR LAURENCE
Saint Francis be my speed! How oft tonight   121
Have my old feet stumbled at graves! Who's there?
BALTHASAR
Here's one, a friend, and one that knows you well.
FRIAR LAURENCE
Bliss be upon you. Tell me, good my friend,
What torch is yond that vainly lends his light   125
To grubs and eyeless skulls? As I discern,   126
It burneth in the Capels' monument.

---

100 his i.e., my (Romeo's) own   **103 unsubstantial** lacking material existence   **106 still** always   **110 set . . . rest** (See 4.5.6. The meaning is,
"make my final determination," with allusion to the idea of repose.)
115 dateless bargain everlasting contract.   **engrossing** monopolizing,
taking all; also, drawing up the contract   **116 conduct** guide (i.e., the
poison)   **117 desperate** reckless, despairing   **121 be my speed** prosper
me   **125 vainly** uselessly   **126 grubs** insect larvae

BALTHASAR
  It doth so, holy sir, and there's my master,
  One that you love.
FRIAR LAURENCE   Who is it?
BALTHASAR   Romeo.
FRIAR LAURENCE
  How long hath he been there?
BALTHASAR   Full half an hour.
FRIAR LAURENCE
  Go with me to the vault.
BALTHASAR   I dare not, sir.
  My master knows not but I am gone hence,
  And fearfully did menace me with death
  If I did stay to look on his intents.
FRIAR LAURENCE
  Stay, then, I'll go alone. Fear comes upon me.
  O, much I fear some ill unthrifty thing.   136
BALTHASAR
  As I did sleep under this yew tree here
  I dreamt my master and another fought,
  And that my master slew him.
FRIAR LAURENCE [*Advancing to the tomb*]   Romeo!
  Alack, alack, what blood is this which stains
  The stony entrance of this sepulcher?
  What mean these masterless and gory swords
  To lie discolored by this place of peace?
                              [*He enters the tomb.*]
  Romeo! O, pale! Who else? What, Paris too?
  And steeped in blood? Ah, what an unkind hour   145
  Is guilty of this lamentable chance!
  The lady stirs.   [*Juliet wakes.*]
JULIET
  O comfortable Friar, where is my lord?   148
  I do remember well where I should be,
  And there I am. Where is my Romeo? [*A noise within.*]
FRIAR LAURENCE
  I hear some noise. Lady, come from that nest
  Of death, contagion, and unnatural sleep.
  A greater power than we can contradict

136 unthrifty unfortunate   **145 unkind** unnatural   **148 comfortable**
comforting

Hath thwarted our intents. Come, come away.
Thy husband in thy bosom there lies dead,
And Paris, too. Come, I'll dispose of thee
Among a sisterhood of holy nuns.
Stay not to question, for the watch is coming.
Come, go, good Juliet. [*A noise again.*] I dare no longer
    stay.   *Exit* [*Friar Laurence*].
JULIET
Go, get thee hence, for I will not away.
What's here? A cup, closed in my true love's hand?
Poison, I see, hath been his timeless end.   162
O churl, drunk all, and left no friendly drop   163
To help me after? I will kiss thy lips;
Haply some poison yet doth hang on them,   165
To make me die with a restorative.   [*She kisses him.*]
Thy lips are warm.

> *Enter* [*Paris's*] *Boy and Watch* [*at the other end of*
> *the churchyard*].

FIRST WATCH   Lead, boy. Which way?
JULIET
Yea, noise? Then I'll be brief. O happy dagger!   169
                    [*She takes Romeo's dagger.*]
This is thy sheath. There rust, and let me die.
                    [*She stabs herself and falls.*]
PAGE
This is the place, there where the torch doth burn.
FIRST WATCH
The ground is bloody. Search about the churchyard.
Go, some of you, whoe'er you find attach.   173
                          [*Exeunt some.*]
Pitiful sight! Here lies the County slain,
And Juliet bleeding, warm, and newly dead,
Who here hath lain this two days burièd.
Go tell the Prince. Run to the Capulets.
Raise up the Montagues. Some others search.
                          [*Exeunt others.*]
We see the ground whereon these woes do lie,

162 timeless (1) untimely (2) everlasting   **163 churl** miser   **165 Haply**
perhaps   **169 happy** opportune   **173 attach** arrest, detain

But the true ground of all these piteous woes   180
We cannot without circumstance descry.   181

> *Enter [some of the Watch, with] Romeo's man*
> *[Balthasar].*

SECOND WATCH
Here's Romeo's man. We found him in the churchyard.
FIRST WATCH
Hold him in safety till the Prince come hither.   183

> *Enter Friar [Laurence], and another Watchman*
> *[with tools].*

THIRD WATCH
Here is a friar, that trembles, sighs, and weeps.
We took this mattock and this spade from him
As he was coming from this churchyard's side.
FIRST WATCH
A great suspicion. Stay the Friar too.   187

> *Enter the Prince [and attendants].*

PRINCE
What misadventure is so early up
That calls our person from our morning rest?

> *Enter Capels [Capulet and his Wife].*

CAPULET
What should it be that is so shrieked abroad?
CAPULET'S WIFE
O, the people in the street cry "Romeo,"
Some "Juliet," and some "Paris," and all run
With open outcry toward our monument.
PRINCE
What fear is this which startles in our ears?   194
FIRST WATCH
Sovereign, here lies the County Paris slain,
And Romeo dead, and Juliet, dead before,
Warm and new killed.

---

180 ground basis (playing on the literal meaning in l. 179)
181 circumstance details   **183 in safety** under guard   **187 Stay** detain   **194 startles** cries alarmingly

PRINCE
   Search, seek, and know how this foul murder comes.   198
FIRST WATCH
   Here is a friar, and slaughtered Romeo's man,
   With instruments upon them fit to open   200
   These dead men's tombs.
CAPULET
   O heavens! O wife, look how our daughter bleeds!
   This dagger hath mista'en, for lo, his house   203
   Is empty on the back of Montague,
   And it mis-sheathèd in my daughter's bosom!
CAPULET'S WIFE
   O me! This sight of death is as a bell
   That warns my old age to a sepulcher.

     Enter Montague.

PRINCE
   Come, Montague, for thou art early up
   To see thy son and heir now early down.
MONTAGUE
   Alas, my liege, my wife is dead tonight;
   Grief of my son's exile hath stopped her breath.
   What further woe conspires against mine age?
PRINCE   Look, and thou shalt see.
MONTAGUE [*Seeing Romeo's body*]
   O thou untaught! What manners is in this,   214
   To press before thy father to a grave?   215
PRINCE
   Seal up the mouth of outrage for a while,   216
   Till we can clear these ambiguities
   And know their spring, their head, their true descent;   218
   And then will I be general of your woes   219
   And lead you even to death. Meantime forbear,   220
   And let mischance be slave to patience.   221
   Bring forth the parties of suspicion.   222

---

198 know learn   **200 instruments** tools   **203 his house** its scabbard
214 untaught ill-mannered youth. (Said with affectionate irony.)   **215 press**
hasten, go   **216 outrage** outcry   **218 spring, head** source   **219 be . . . woes**
be leader in lamentation   **220 to death** i.e., (1) as far as the dead bodies
(2) so far in lamentation that we shall seem dead   **221 let . . . patience**
i.e., submit patiently to our misfortune   **222 of** under

FRIAR LAURENCE
I am the greatest, able to do least,
Yet most suspected, as the time and place
Doth make against me, of this direful murder;   225
And here I stand, both to impeach and purge   226
Myself condemnèd and myself excused.   227

PRINCE
Then say at once what thou dost know in this.

FRIAR LAURENCE
I will be brief, for my short date of breath   229
Is not so long as is a tedious tale.
Romeo, there dead, was husband to that Juliet,
And she, there dead, that Romeo's faithful wife.
I married them, and their stol'n marriage day
Was Tybalt's doomsday, whose untimely death
Banished the new-made bridegroom from this city,
For whom, and not for Tybalt, Juliet pined.
You, to remove that siege of grief from her,
Betrothed and would have married her perforce   238
To County Paris. Then comes she to me,
And with wild looks bid me devise some means
To rid her from this second marriage,
Or in my cell there would she kill herself.
Then gave I her—so tutored by my art—
A sleeping potion, which so took effect
As I intended, for it wrought on her   245
The form of death. Meantime I writ to Romeo   246
That he should hither come as this dire night   247
To help to take her from her borrowed grave,
Being the time the potion's force should cease.
But he which bore my letter, Friar John,
Was stayed by accident, and yesternight   251
Returned my letter back. Then all alone
At the prefixèd hour of her waking
Came I to take her from her kindred's vault,
Meaning to keep her closely at my cell   255

225 make conspire, tell   **226–227 to . . . excused** to accuse myself of
what is to be condemned in me, and to exonerate myself where I ought
to be excused   **229 date of breath** time left to live   **238 perforce** by
compulsion   **245 wrought** fashioned   **246 form** appearance   **247 as
this** this very   **251 stayed** stopped   **255 closely** secretly

Till I conveniently could send to Romeo.
But when I came, some minute ere the time
Of her awakening, here untimely lay
The noble Paris and true Romeo dead.
She wakes, and I entreated her come forth
And bear this work of heaven with patience.
But then a noise did scare me from the tomb,
And she, too desperate, would not go with me,
But, as it seems, did violence on herself.
All this I know, and to the marriage
Her nurse is privy; and if aught in this   266
Miscarried by my fault, let my old life
Be sacrificed some hour before his time   268
Unto the rigor of severest law.

PRINCE
We still have known thee for a holy man.   270
Where's Romeo's man? What can he say to this?

BALTHASAR
I brought my master news of Juliet's death,
And then in post he came from Mantua   273
To this same place, to this same monument.
This letter he early bid me give his father,   275
                              [*Showing a letter*]
And threatened me with death, going in the vault,
If I departed not and left him there.

PRINCE [*Taking the letter*]
Give me the letter. I will look on it.
Where is the County's page, that raised the watch?
Sirrah, what made your master in this place?   280

PAGE
He came with flowers to strew his lady's grave,
And bid me stand aloof, and so I did.
Anon comes one with light to ope the tomb,
And by and by my master drew on him,
And then I ran away to call the watch.

PRINCE
This letter doth make good the Friar's words,
Their course of love, the tidings of her death;
And here he writes that he did buy a poison

266 privy in on the secret   **268 his** its   **270 still** always   **273 post**
haste   **275 early** early in the morning   **280 made** did

Of a poor 'pothecary, and therewithal   289
Came to this vault to die, and lie with Juliet.
Where be these enemies? Capulet, Montague,
See what a scourge is laid upon your hate,
That heaven finds means to kill your joys with love.   293
And I, for winking at your discords, too   294
Have lost a brace of kinsmen. All are punished.   295

CAPULET
O brother Montague, give me thy hand.
This is my daughter's jointure, for no more   297
Can I demand.

MONTAGUE   But I can give thee more,
For I will raise her statue in pure gold,   299
That whiles Verona by that name is known
There shall no figure at such rate be set   301
As that of true and faithful Juliet.

CAPULET
As rich shall Romeo's by his lady's lie;
Poor sacrifices of our enmity!

PRINCE
A glooming peace this morning with it brings;
    The sun, for sorrow, will not show his head.
Go hence to have more talk of these sad things.
    Some shall be pardoned, and some punishèd;
For never was a story of more woe
Than this of Juliet and her Romeo.   [*Exeunt.*]

289 therewithal i.e., with the poison   **293 kill your joys** (1) destroy your
happiness (2) kill your children. **with** by means of   **294 winking at**
shutting my eyes to   **295 a brace of** two   **297 jointure** marriage portion   **299 raise** (The Quarto 2 reading, *raie*, is defended by some editors
in the sense of "array," make ready.)   **301 rate** value

Date and Text

A corrupt and unregistered quarto of *Romeo and Juliet* appeared in 1597 with the following title:

> AN EXCELLENT conceited Tragedie OF Romeo and Iuliet, As it hath been often (with great applause) plaid publiquely, by the right Honourable the L. of *Hunsdon* his Seruants. LONDON, Printed by Iohn Danter. 1597.

This was a pirated edition issued by an unscrupulous publisher, no doubt to capitalize on the play's great popularity. It seems to have been memorially reconstructed by two or more actors (probably those playing Romeo and Paris), and possibly thereafter used as a promptbook. Its appearance seems to have caused the issuance two years later of a clearly authoritative version:

> THE MOST EXcellent and lamentable Tragedie, of Romeo and *Iuliet. Newly corrected, augmented, and amended:* As it hath bene sundry times publiquely acted, by the right Honourable the Lord Chamberlaine his Seruants. LONDON Printed by Thomas Creede, for Cuthbert Burby, and are to be sold at his shop neare the Exchange. 1599.

This text is some 800 lines longer than the first, and corrects errors in that earlier version. It seems at one point, however, to have been contaminated by the first quarto, as though the manuscript source for the second quarto (probably the author's foul papers) was defective at some point. A passage from 1.2.53 to 1.3.34 was apparently set directly from the first quarto. (On this matter, see George W. Williams's old-spelling edition of the play, Duke Univ. Press, 1964). The first quarto may also have influenced the second quarto in some other isolated instances. Despite this contamination, however, the second quarto is the authoritative text except for the passage of direct indebtedness to the first quarto. The second quarto served as the basis for the third quarto (1609) which in turn served as copy for the fourth quarto (undated, but placed in 1622) and the First Folio of 1623. A fifth quarto appeared in 1637. The Folio text may embody a few authoritative readings of its own, perhaps by way of reference to a theatrical manuscript.

Francis Meres, in his *Palladis Tamia: Wit's Treasury* (a slender volume on contemporary literature and art; valuable because it lists most of the plays of Shakespeare that existed at that time), assigns the play to Shakespeare in 1598. So does John Weever in his *Epigrams* of 1599. Internal evidence on dating is not reliable. The Nurse observes that " 'Tis since the earthquake now eleven years" (1.3.24); but suitable earthquakes have been discovered in 1580, 1583, 1584, and 1585, giving us a wide choice of dates even if we accept the dubious proposition that the Nurse is speaking accurately. Astronomical reckoning of the position of the moon at the time the play purportedly takes place ("A fortnight and odd days" before Lammastide, August 1, 1.3.16) indicates the year 1596; again, however, we have no reason to assume Shakespeare cared about this sort of internal accuracy. More suggestive perhaps is the argument that Danter's unauthorized publication in 1597 was seeking to exploit a popular new play, one the acting company certainly did not yet wish to see published, since it was a money-maker. Danter assigns the play to Lord Hunsdon's servants, a name that Shakespeare's company could have used only from July 22, 1596 (when the old Lord Chamberlain, Henry Carey, first Lord Hunsdon, died) to April 17, 1597 (when George Carey, second Lord Hunsdon, was appointed to his father's erstwhile position as Lord Chamberlain). Danter could simply have been using the name of the company at the time he pirated the play, but he may also indicate performance in late 1596. Stylistically, the play is clearly of the "lyric" period of *A Midsummer Night's Dream* and *Richard II*. There are also stylistic affinities to the sonnets and to the narrative poems of 1593–1594. A date between 1594 and 1596 is likely, especially toward the latter end of this period. Whether the play comes before or after *A Midsummer Night's Dream* is, however, a matter of conjecture.

Textual Notes

These textual notes are not a historical collation, either of the early quartos and the early folios or of more recent editions; they are simply a record of departures in this edition from the copy text. The reading adopted in this edition appears in boldface, followed by the rejected reading from the copy text, i.e., the second quarto of 1599. Only major alterations in punctuation are noted. Changes in lineation are not indicated, nor are some minor and obvious typographical errors.

Abbreviations used:
Q1 the first quarto of 1597
Q2 the second quarto of 1599
s.d. stage direction
s.p. speech prefix

Copy text: the second quarto of 1599, except for 1.2.53–1.3.34, for which Q1 is the prior authority.

1.1. 27 it in [Q1] it   **73 s.p. Citizens** Offi   **76 s.p. Capulet's Wife** Wife
92 Verona's Neronas   **120 drave** drive   **147 his** is   **153 sun** same
177 create [Q1] created   **179 well-seeming** [Q1] welseeing   **189 grief to** [Q1]
grief, too   **192 lovers'** [Q1] loving   **202 Bid a** [Q1] A   **make** [Q1] makes
206 markman mark man   **211 unharmed** [Q1] vncharmd   **218 makes** make

1.2. 14 The earth Earth   **32 on** one   **38–39 written here** written. Here
46 One [Q1] on   **70 and Livia** [Q1] Liuia [Q2]   **79 thee** [Q1] you [Q2]
91 fires fier

1.3. 12 an [Q2] a [Q1]   **18 shall** [Q1] stal [Q2]   **33 wi' th'** [Q1: with] with the
[Q2]   **50 s.p. [and elsewhere] Wife** Old La   **66 disposition** [F] dispositions
67, 68 honor [Q1] houre   **100 it fly** [Q1] flie   **105 s.p. [and elsewhere] Wife**
Mo

1.4. 7–8 [Q1; not in Q2]   **23 s.p. Mercutio** Horatio   **39 done** [Q1] dum   **42 Of**
Or   **45 like lamps** [Q1] lights lights   **47 five** fine   **57 atomi** [Q1] ottamie
59–61 [these lines follow l. 69 in Q2]   **66 film** Philome   **69 maid** [Q1] man
72 O'er [Q1] On   **74 on** one   **76 breaths** [Q1] breath   **80 parson's** Persons
81 dreams he [Q1] he dreams   **90 elflocks** Elklocks   **111 fofreit** [Q1] fofreit

1.5. s.d. [Q2 adds: "Enter Romeo"]   **1 s.p. First Servingman** Ser [also at ll. 6
and 12]   **3 s.p. Second Servingman** 1   **11 s.p. Third Servingman** 2
14 s.p. Fourth Servingman 3   **17 s.p. Capulet** 1. Capu [also at ll. 35 and 40]
18 a bout about   **96 ready** [Q1] did readie

2.0 Chorus   1 s.p. Chorus [not in Q2]   **4 matched** match

2.1. 7 Nay . . . too [assigned in Q2 to Benvolio]   **10 one** [Q1] on
11 Pronounce [Q1] prouaunt   **dove** [Q1] day   **13 heir** [Q1] her   **14 trim** [Q1]
true   **39 open-arse, and** open, or

2.2. 16 do [Q1] to   **20 eyes** [Q1] eye   **41–42 nor any . . . name** ô be some
other name / Belonging to a man   **45 were** [Q1] wene   **58 not yet** yet not
82 pilot Pylat   **83 washed** [Q1] washeth   **92–93 false . . . They** false at louers

periuries. / They   **101 more coying** [Q1] coying   **110 circled** [Q1] circle
149, 151 s.p. Nurse [not in Q2]   **150, 151 s.p. Juliet** [not in Q2]   **163 than
mine** then   **170 years** [Q1] yeare   **180 gyves** giues   **187 Sleep . . . breast** [Q1;
assigned in Q2 to Juliet]   **189–190** [preceded in Q2 by an earlier version of
ll. 1–4 of the next scene, in which "fleckled darkness" reads "darknesse
fleckted" and "and Titan's fiery wheels" reads "made by *Tytans* wheeles"]

2.3. 2 Check'ring [Q1] Checking   **4 fiery** [Q1] burning   **51 wounded. Both
our** wounded both, our   **85 not. She whom** [Q1] me not, her

2.4. 18 s.p. Benvolio [Q1] Ro.   **28–29 phantasimes** phantacies   **33 pardon-
me's** pardons mees   **40 but a** a   **113–114 for himself** [Q1] himself
205 dog's dog   **212 s.d. Exeunt** Exit

2.5. 5 glide glides   **11 three** there   **15 And M.** And   **26 I had** [Q1] I

2.6. 18 gossamer gossamours   **27 music's** musicke

3.1. 2 Capels are Capels   **67 injured** iniuried   **73 stoccata** stucatho   **90 your
houses** houses   **107 soundly too. Your** soundly, to your   **121 Alive** He gan
123 fire-eyed [Q1] fier end   **136, 138 s.d. First Citizen** Citti   **165 agile** [Q1]
aged   **183 s.p. Montague** Capu   **191 I** [Q1] It   **196 s.d. Exeunt** Exit

3.2. 1 s.p. Juliet [not in Q2]   **9 By** And by   **47 darting** arting   **49 shut** shot
51 of my my   **60 one** on   **72 It . . . did** [assigned in Q2 to Juliet]   **73 O . . .
face** [assigned in Q2 to Nurse]   **76 Dove-feathered** Rauenous douefeatherd
79 damnèd dimme   **143 s.d. Exeunt** Exit

3.3. s.d. [Q2 has "Enter Friar and Romeo"]   **39** [Q2 follows with a line:
"This may flyes do, when I from this must flie"]   **43** [printed in Q2 before
l. 40]   **52 Thou** [Q1] Then   **61 madmen** [Q1] mad man   **70 s.d. Knock** Enter
Nurse, and knocke   **73 s.d. Knock** They knocke   **75 s.d. Knock** Slud knock
80 s.d. Enter Nurse [at l. 78 in Q2]   **110 denote** [Q1] deuote   **117 lives** [Q1]
lies   **144 pouts upon** puts vp   **168 disguised** disguise

3.4. 10 s.d. [and elsewhere] **Wife** La   **13 be** me

3.5. 13 exhaled exhale   **19 the** the the   **31 changed** change   **36 s.d. Enter
Nurse** Enter Madame and Nurse   **54 s.p. Juliet** Ro   **67 s.d.** [bracketed s.d.
from Q1]   **82 pardon him** padon   **130–131 body . . . a bark** body? / Thou
counterfeits. A bark   **139 gives** giue   **142 How? Will** How will
151–152 proud . . . Thank proud mistresse minion you? / Thanke
160 s.p. [and elsewhere] **Capulet** Fa   **172 s.p. and text Capulet** O, God-i'-
good-e'en Father, ô Godigeden   **173 s.p. Nurse** [not in Q2]   **182 liened** liand

4.1. 7 talked [Q1] talke   **45 cure** [Q1] care   **46 Ah** [Q1] O   **72 slay** [Q1] stay
78 off [Q1] of   **83 chopless** [Q1] chapels   **85 his tomb** his   **98 breath** [Q1]
breast   **100 wanny** many   **110 In** Is [Q2 follows with a line: "Be borne to
buriall in thy kindreds graue"]   **111 shalt** shall   **115 and he** an he
116 waking walking   **126 s.d. Exeunt** Exit

4.2. 3, 6 s.p. Servingman Ser   **14 willed** wield   **38 s.p.** [and elsewhere] **Wife**
Mo   **47 s.d. Exeunt** Exit

4.3. 49 wake walke

4.4. 1 s.p. [and elsewhere] **Wife** La   **12 s.d. Exeunt** Exit   **15 s.p. First Servingman** Fel   **18 s.p. Second Servingman** Fel   **21 Thou** Twou   **faith** father
23 s.d. [at l. 21 in Q2]

4.5. 41 long [Q1] loue   **51 behold** bedold   **65 cure** care   **65–66 not . . . Heaven** not, / In these confusions heauen   **82 fond** some   **96 s.p. First Musician** Musi   **99, 103 s.p. First Musician** Fid   **99 by** [Q1] my. [Q2 has s.d. here: "Exit omnes"]   **s.d. Enter Peter** Enter Will Kemp   **107 s.p. First Musician** Minstrels [and subsequently in this scene indicated by *Minst* or *Minstrel*]   **123 Then . . . wit** [assigned in Q2 to 2 M]   **127 And . . . oppress** [Q1; not in Q2]   **133, 136 Pretty** [Q1] Prates   **145 s.d. Exeunt** Exit

5.1. 15 fares my [Q1] doth my Lady   **17, 27, 32 s.p. Balthasar** Man   **24 e'en** in   **defy** [Q1] denie   **33 s.d.** [at l. 32 in Q2]   **76 pay** [Q1] pray

5.3. 3 yew [Q1] young   **21 s.d. [Balthasar]** [Q1] Peter   **40, 43 s.p. Balthasar** Pet   **68 conjuration** commiration   **71 s.p. Page** Boy [Q1; s.p. missing in Q2 and line treated as a s.d.]   **102 fair** faire? I will beleeue   **107 palace** pallat   **108** [Q2 has four undeleted lines here: "Depart againe, come lye thou in my arme, / Heer's to thy health, where ere thou tumblest in. / O true Appothecarie! / Thy drugs are quicke. Thus with a kisse I die."]   **123 s.p. [and elsewhere] Balthasar** Man   **137 yew** yong   **168 s.p. First Watch** Watch [also at ll. 172, 195, 199]   **171 s.p. Page** Watch boy   **182 s.p. Second Watch** Watch   **183, 187 s.p. First Watch** Chief. watch   **187 too** too too   **190 shrieked** shrike   **194 our** your   **199 slaughtered** Slaughter   **201** [Q2 has a s.d. here: "Enter Capulet and his wife"]   **209 early** [Q1] earling   **232 that** thats   **274–275 place . . . This** place. To this same monument / This   **281 s.p. Page** Boy   **299 raise** raie

Shakespeare's Sources

Shakespeare's chief source for *Romeo and Juliet* was a long narrative poem (a selection of which follows) by Arthur Brooke called *The Tragical History of Romeus and Juliet, written first in Italian by Bandell and now in English by Ar. Br.* (1562). Other English versions of this popular legend were available to Shakespeare, in particular in William Painter's *The Palace of Pleasure* (1566), but Shakespeare shows only a passing indebtedness to it. Brooke mentions having seen (prior to 1562) a play about the two lovers, but such an old play is not likely to have been of much service to Shakespeare. Nor does he appear to have extensively consulted the various continental versions that lay behind Brooke's poem. Still, these versions help explain the genesis of the story.

The use of a sleeping potion to escape an unwelcome marriage goes back at least to the *Ephesiaca* of Xenophon of Ephesus (by the fifth century A.D.). Masuccio of Salerno, in his *Il Novellino* (1476), seems to have been the first to combine this sleeping potion story with an ironic aftermath of misunderstanding and suicide (as found in the Pyramus and Thisbe story of Ovid's *Metamorphoses*). In Masuccio's account, the lovers Mariotto and Giannozza of Siena are secretly married by a friar. When Mariotto kills a prominent citizen of Siena in a quarrel, he is banished to Alexandria. Giannozza, to avoid marriage with a suitor of her father's choosing, takes a sleeping potion given her by the friar and is buried as though dead. She is thereupon taken from the tomb by the friar and sent on her way to Alexandria. Mariotto, however, having failed to hear from her because the messenger is intercepted by pirates, returns in disguise to her tomb where he is discovered and executed. Giannozza, hearing this sad news, retires to a Sienese convent and dies of a broken heart.

In Luigi da Porto's *Historia novellamente ritrovata di due Nobili Amanti* (published c. 1530), based on Masuccio's account, the scene shifts to Verona. Despite the feuding of their two families, the Montecchi and the Cappelletti, Romeo and Guilietta meet and fall in love at a carnival ball. Romeo at once forgets his unrequited passion for a scornful lady. Friar Lorenzo, an experimenter in magic, secretly marries the lovers. Romeo tries to avoid brawling with the Cappelletti, but when some of his own kinsmen suffer defeat, he kills Theobaldo Cappelletti. After Romeo's departure for Mantua, Guilietta's family arranges a match for her with the Count of Lodrone. Friar Lorenzo gives Guilietta a sleeping potion and sends a letter to Romeo by a fellow friar, but this messenger is unable to find Romeo in Mantua. Romeo, hearing of Guilietta's supposed death from her servant Peter, returns to Verona with a poison he already possesses. Guilietta awakens in time to converse with Romeo before he dies. Then, refusing the Friar's advice to retire to a convent, she dies by stopping her own breath. This story provides no equivalents for Mercutio and the Nurse, although a young man named Marcuccio appears briefly at the Cappelletti's ball.

Da Porto's version inspired that of Matteo Bandello in his *Novelle* of 1554. Some details are added: Romeo goes to the ball in a vizard (mask), he has a servant named Pietro, a rope ladder is given to the Nurse enabling Romeo to visit Julietta's chamber before their marriage, Romeo obtains a poison from one Spolentino, etc. The young man at the ball, Marcuccio, is now named Mercutio but is still a minor figure. This Bandello version was translated into French by Pierre Boaistuau in his *Histoires Tragiques* (1559); Boaistuau adds the Apothecary (who is racked and hanged for his part in the tragedy), and has Romeo die before Juliet awakens and slays herself with Romeo's dagger.

Despite Arthur Brooke's implication on the title page that his version is based on Bandello, the narrative poem *Romeus and Juliet* is taken from Boaistuau. As can be seen in the following selection, Brooke's is a severely pious work written in "Poulter's Measure," couplets with alternating lines of six and seven feet. Brooke openly disapproves of the lovers' carnality and haste, although fortunately the story itself remains sympathetic to Romeus and Juliet. Brooke stresses star-crossed fortune and the antithesis of love and hate. He reduces Juliet's age from eighteen (as in Bandello) to sixteen. (Shakespeare further reduced her age to less than fourteen.) Brooke's narrative is generally close to Shakespeare's, though with important exceptions. Shakespeare compresses time from some nine months to a few days. In

Brooke, for example, some two weeks elapse between the masked ball and Romeus's encounter with Juliet in her garden, and about two months elapse between the marriage and Tybalt's death. In Shakespeare, Capulet moves the wedding up from Thursday to Wednesday, thereby complicating the time schedule for the lovers. Shakespeare also unifies his play by such devices as introducing Tybalt and Paris early in the story; in Brooke, Tybalt appears only at the time he is slain, and Juliet's proposed marriage to Count Paris emerges as a threat only after Romeus's banishment. Shakespeare's greatest transformation is of the characters. Brooke's Juliet is scheming. His Mercutio remains a shadowy figure as in Bandello et al. Brooke's Nurse is unattractive, although she does occasionally hint at comic greatness: for example, she garrulously confides to Romeus the details of Juliet's infancy and then keeps Juliet on tenterhooks while she prates about Romeus's fine qualities (ll. 631–714). Even if Shakespeare's play is incomparably superior to Brooke's drably versified poem, the indebtedness is extensive.

The Tragical History of Romeus and Juliet
By Arthur Brooke

There is beyond the Alps a town of ancient fame
Whose bright renown yet shineth clear. Verona men it
    name,
Built in an happy time, built on a fertile soil,
Maintainèd by the heavenly fates and by the townish
    toil.
. . . .

There were two ancient stocks, which Fortune high
    did place
Above the rest, endued with wealth and nobler of
    their race,
Loved of the common sort, loved of the Prince alike—
And like unhappy were they both when Fortune list
    to strike—   28
Whose praise with equal blast Fame in her trumpet
    blew.
The one was clepèd Capilet and th'other Montague.   30
  A wonted use it is that men of likely sort—   31
I wot not by what fury forced—envy each others'
    port.   32
So these, whose equal state bred envy pale of hue;
And then of grudging envy's root, black hate and
    rancor grew.
As of a little spark oft riseth mighty fire,
So, of a kindled spark of grudge, in flames flash out
    their ire.   36
And then their deadly food, first hatched of trifling
    strife,
Did bathe in blood of smarting wounds; it reavèd
    breath and life.   38
No legend lie I tell; scarce yet their eyes be dry   39
That did behold this grisly sight with wet and
    weeping eye.

28 like alike. **list** pleased   **30 clepèd** named   **31 wonted use** customary behavior. **likely sort** equal rank   **32 wot** know. **port** style of
living **36 grudge** resentment **38 reavèd** robbed, took away **39 legend**
unauthentic

But when the prudent Prince who there the scepter
    held
So great a new disorder in his commonweal beheld,
By gentle means he sought their choler to assuage   43
And by persuasion to appease their blameful furious
    rage.
But both his words and time the Prince hath spent in
    vain;
So rooted was the inward hate, he lost his busy pain.
When friendly sage advice ne gentle words avail,   47
By thundering threats and princely power their
    courage gan he quail,   48
In hope that when he had the wasting flame
    suppressed,
In time he should quite quench the sparks that
    burned within their breast.
    Now whilst these kindreds do remain in this estate
And each with outward friendly show doth hide his
    inward hate,
One Romeus, who was of race a Montague,
Upon whose tender chin as yet no manlike beard
    there grew,
Whose beauty and whose shape so far the rest did
    stain   55
That from the chief of Veron youth he greatest fame
    did gain,
Hath found a maid so fair (he found so foul his hap),   57
Whose beauty, shape, and comely grace did so his
    heart entrap
That from his own affairs his thought she did
    remove.
Only he sought to honor her, to serve her, and to love. 60
To her he writeth oft; oft messengers are sent.
At length, in hope of better speed, himself the lover
    went   62
Present to plead for grace which, absent, was not
    found,   63
And to discover to her eye his new-receivèd wound.   64

43 choler anger   **47 ne** nor   **48 gan he quail** he tried to end, suppress
55 stain eclipse   **57 so foul his hap** so miserable his fortune   **60 Only
he** he only   **62 speed** success   **63 Present** in person, or presently
64 discover reveal, present

But she, that from her youth was fostered evermore
With virtue's food and taught in school of wisdom's
    skillful lore,
By answer did cut off th' affections of his love,
That he no more occasion had so vain a suit to move. 68

[After many months of this hopeless wooing, Romeus is
ready to leave Verona, but is instead persuaded by a friend
to cure his lovesickness by finding some other place to bestow his "witless wandering heart." Romeus agrees to frequent every place where ladies are accustomed to gather.]

    The weary winter nights restore the Christmas
      games,
And now the season doth invite to banquet townish
    dames.
And first, in Capel's house, the chief of all the kin
Spar'th for no cost the wonted use of banquets to
    begin.
No lady fair or foul was in Verona town,
No knight or gentleman of high or low renown
But Capilet himself hath bid unto his feast,
Or, by his name in paper sent, appointed as a guest.
Young damsels thither flock, of bachelors a rout, 163
Not so much for the banquet's sake as beauties to
    search out.
But not a Montague would enter at his gate—
For, as you heard, the Capilets and they were at
    debate—
Save Romeus; and he, in mask with hidden face,
The supper done, with other five did press into the
    place.
When they had masked awhile with dames in courtly
    wise,
All did unmask. The rest did show them to their
    ladies' eyes,
But bashful Romeus with shamefast face forsook
The open press, and him withdrew into the
    chamber's nook. 172

68 vain hopeless

163 rout large assemblage **172 press** crowd. **him** himself

But brighter than the sun the waxen torches shone,
That, maugre what he could, he was espied of
    everyone,   174
But of the women chief, their gazing eyes that threw
To wonder at his sightly shape and beauty's spotless
    hew
With which the heavens him had and nature so
    bedecked
That ladies thought the fairest dames were foul in his
    respect.
And in their head besides another wonder rose:
How he durst put himself in throng among so many
    foes.
Of courage stout they thought his coming to
    proceed—
And women love an hardy heart, as I in stories read.
  The Capilets disdain the presence of their foe,
Yet they suppress their stirrèd ire—the cause I do not
    know.
Perhaps t' offend their guests the courteous knights
    are loath.
Perhaps they stay from sharp revenge, dreading the
    Prince's wroth.   186
Perhaps for that they shamed to exercise their rage
Within their house 'gainst one alone, and him of
    tender age.
They use no taunting talk, ne harm him by their deed;
They neither say "What mak'st thou here?" ne yet
    they say "God speed."
So that he freely might the ladies view at ease,
And they also, beholding him, their change of fancies
    please;
Which nature had him taught to do with such a grace
That there was none but joyèd at his being there in
    place.
With upright beam he weighed the beauty of each
    dame,   195
And judged who best, and who next her, was wrought
    in nature's frame.

---

174 maugre in spite of **186 stay** abstain. **wroth** wrath **195 upright
beam** i.e., the scales of judgment

At length he saw a maid right fair, of perfect shape,
Which Theseus or Paris would have chosen to their
    rape.   198
Whom erst he never saw, of all she pleased him most.   199
Within himself he said to her, "Thou justly mayst
    thee boast
Of perfect shape's renown and beauty's sounding
    praise,
Whose like ne hath ne shall be seen, ne liveth in our
    days!"   202
And whilst he fixed on her his partial piercèd eye,   203
His former love, for which of late he ready was to
    die,
Is now as quite forgot as it had never been.
The proverb saith, "Unminded oft are they that are
    unseen."   206
And as out of a plank a nail a nail doth drive,
So novel love out of the mind the ancient love doth
    rive.   208
This sudden-kindled fire in time is wox so great   209
That only death and both their bloods might quench
    the fiery heat.
  When Romeus saw himself in this new tempest
    tossed,
Where both was hope of pleasant sport and danger to
    be lost,
He, doubtful, scarcely knew what countenance to
    keep.   213
In Lethe's flood his wonted flames were quenched
    and drenchèd deep.   214
Yea, he forgets himself, ne is the wretch so bold
To ask her name that without force hath him in
    bondage fold.   216

---

198 to their rape for seizing and carrying off   **199 Whom . . . saw** she
whom he had never seen before   **202 ne hath ne shall be** has never been
and never will be   **203 partial piercèd** favorably disposed and pierced
(by her beauty)   **206 Unminded . . . unseen** out of sight, out of mind
208 novel new. **ancient** former, old. **rive** pull, tear   **209 wox** waxed,
grown   **213 doubtful** full of doubts and fears   **214 Lethe's flood** the
river of forgetfulness. **wonted** accustomed, former. **drenchèd**
drowned   **216 fold** enfolded, confined

Ne how t' unloose his bonds doth the poor fool
    devise,
But only seeketh by her sight to feed his hungry eyes.
Through them he swalloweth down love's sweet
    empoisoned bait.
How surely are the wareless rapt by those that lie in
    wait? 220
So is the poison spread throughout his bones and
    veins
That in a while—alas the while!—it hasteth deadly
    pains.
    Whilst Juliet—for so this gentle damsel hight— 223
From side to side on everyone did cast about her
    sight.
At last her floating eyes were anchored fast on him
Who for her sake did banish health and freedom from
    each limb.
He in her sight did seem to pass the rest as far
As Phoebus' shining beams do pass the brightness of
    a star.
In wait lay warlike Love with golden bow and shaft, 229
And to his ear with steady hand the bowstring up he
    raft. 230
Till now she had escaped his sharp inflaming dart;
Till now he listed not assault her young and tender
    heart. 232
His whetted arrow, loosed, so touched her to the
    quick
That through the eye it strake the heart, and there the
    head did stick.
It booted not to strive, forwhy she wanted strength; 235
The weaker aye unto the strong of force must yield at
    length. 236
The pomps now of the feast her heart gins to despise,
And only joyeth when her eyen meet with her lover's
    eyes.

---

220 wareless unwary. **rapt** seized **223 Whilst** meanwhile. **hight** was
named **229 Love** Cupid **230 raft** pulled **232 he listed not** he (Cupid)
chose not to **235 booted** availed. **forwhy** because. **wanted** was
lacking in **236 aye** ever, always. **of force** necessarily

When their new-smitten hearts had fed on loving
    gleams,
Whilst passing to and fro their eyes ymingled were
    their beams,   240
Each of these lovers gan by other's looks to know
That friendship in their breast had root, and both
    would have it grow.
   When thus in both their hearts had Cupid made his
    breach,
And each of them had sought the mean to end the
    war by speech,   244
Dame Fortune did assent their purpose to advance:
With torch in hand, a comely knight did fetch her
    forth to dance.
She quit herself so well, and with so trim a grace,   247
That she the chief praise wan that night from all
    Verona race;   248
The whilst our Romeus a place had warily won   249
Nigh to the seat where she must sit, the dance once
    being done.
   Fair Juliet turnèd to her chair with pleasant cheer,   251
And glad she was her Romeus approachèd was so
    near.
At th' one side of her chair, her lover Romeo;
And on the other side there sat one called Mercutio,
A courtier that eachwhere was highly had in price,   255
For he was courteous of his speech and pleasant of
    device.
Even as a lion would among the lambs be bold,
Such was, among the bashful maids, Mercutio to
    behold.
With friendly grip he seized fair Juliet's snowish
    hand.
A gift he had, that nature gave him in his swaddling
    band,   260
That frozen mountain ice was never half so cold

---

240 their eyes . . . beams their eyebeams intertwined   **244 mean** means
247 quit acquitted   **248 wan** won   **249 The whilst** meanwhile.   **warily**
discreetly   **251 turnèd** returned.   **cheer** countenance   **255 eachwhere**
everywhere.   **highly . . . price** highly regarded   **260 in . . . band** i.e., in
his cradle, from birth

As were his hands, though ne'er so near the fire he
   did them hold.
As soon as had the knight the virgin's right hand
   raught,   263
Within his trembling hand her left hath loving
   Romeus caught;
For he wist well himself for her abode most pain,   265
And well he wist she loved him best, unless she list to
   feign.   266
  Then she with tender hand his tender palm hath
   pressed.
What joy trow you was grafted so in Romeus' cloven
   breast?   268
The sudden sweet delight hath stoppèd quite his
   tongue,
Ne can he claim of her his right, ne crave redress of
   wrong.   270
But she espied straightway, by changing of his hue
From pale to red, from red to pale, and so from pale
   anew,
That vehement love was cause why so his tongue did
   stay,   273
And so much more she longed to hear what love
   could teach him say.
  When she had longèd long, and he long held his
   peace,
And her desire of hearing him by silence did
   increase,
At last, with trembling voice and shamefast cheer, the
   maid   277
Unto her Romeus turned herself and thus to him she
   said:
"O, blessèd be the time of thy arrival here!"
But, ere she could speak forth the rest, to her Love
   drew so near   280

263 raught grasped   **265 For . . . pain** i.e., for Romeus well knew that he suffered more than anyone out of lovesickness for Juliet   **266 she list to feign** she was feigning   **268 trow you** do you think   **270 Ne . . . wrong** i.e., he can neither claim his right of love in her nor beg redress for the injuries he suffers in love. (A legal metaphor.)   **273 stay** cease, remain silent   **277 shamefast cheer** bashful countenance   **280 Love** Cupid

And so within her mouth her tongue he gluèd fast   281
That not one word could scape her more than what
    already passed.
In great contented ease the young man straight is
    wrapped.
"What chance," quoth he, "unware to me, O lady
    mine, is happed,
That gives you worthy cause my coming here to
    bliss?"   285
Fair Juliet was come again unto herself by this.
First ruthfully she looked, then said, with smiling
    cheer,   287
"Marvel no whit, my heart's delight, my only knight
    and fere.   288
Mercutio's icy hand had all to-frozen mine,   289
And of thy goodness thou again hast warmèd it with
    thine."
Whereto with staid brow gan Romeus to reply: 291
"If so the gods have granted me such favor from the
    sky
That by my being here some service I have done
That pleaseth you, I am as glad as I a realm had won.   294
O well-bestowèd time, that hath the happy hire,   295
Which I would wish if I might have my wishèd
    heart's desire!
For I of God would crave, as price of pains forepast,   297
To serve, obey, and honor you, so long as life shall
    last—
As proof shall teach you plain, if that you like to try
His faultless truth that nill for aught unto his lady
    lie.   300
But if my touchèd hand have warmèd yours
    somedeal,   301
Assure yourself the heat is cold which in your hand
    you feel
Compared to such quick sparks and glowing furious
    gleed   303

281 **he** i.e., Cupid   285 **bliss** bless, give thanks for   287 **ruthfully** com-
passionately   288 **fere** mate, companion   289 **to-frozen** completely
frozen   291 **staid** fixed, set   294 **as I** as if I   295 **hire** recompense,
reward   297 **forepast** past   300 **truth** troth, faith.   **nill** will not
301 **somedeal** somewhat   303 **gleed** fire, ember

As from your beauty's pleasant eyne Love causèd to
   proceed!   304
Which have so set on fire each feeling part of mine
That, lo, my mind doth melt away; my outward parts
   do pine,
And, but you help, all whole to ashes shall I turn.   307
Wherefore, alas! have ruth on him whom you do
   force to burn.''   308
  Even with his ended tale the torches' dance had
   end,
And Juliet of force must part from her new-chosen
   friend.   310
His hand she claspèd hard, and all her parts did
   shake,
When, leisureless, with whispering voice thus did she
   answer make: 312
"You are no more your own, dear friend, than I am
   yours—
My honor saved—prest t' obey your will while life
   endures."   314
  Lo, here the lucky lot that seld true lovers find.   315
Each takes away the other's heart and leaves the own
   behind.   316
A happy life is love, if God grant from above
That heart with heart by even weight do make
   exchange of love.
  But Romeus, gone from her, his heart for care is
   cold.
He hath forgot to ask her name that hath his heart in
   hold!
With forgèd careless cheer, of one he seeks to know   321
Both how she hight and whence she came, that him
   enchanted so.   322
So hath he learned her name, and knoweth she is no
   guest;
Her father was a Capilet and master of the feast!

---

304 eyne eyes   **307 but** unless.   **all whole** wholly   **308 ruth** pity
310 of force of necessity   **312 leisureless** i.e., in haste   **314 My honor
saved** so long as my chastity is not violated.   **prest** ready, eager
315 seld seldom   **316 the own** i.e., his or her own   **321 forgèd careless
cheer** a look of pretended nonchalance   **322 hight** was named

Thus hath his foe in choice to give him life or death, 325
That scarcely can his woeful breast keep in the lively
    breath.
Wherefore with piteous plaint fierce Fortune doth he
    blame,
That in his ruth and wretched plight doth seek her
    laughing game. 328
And he reproveth Love, chief cause of his unrest,
Who ease and freedom hath exiled out of his youthful
    breast.
Twice hath he made him serve, hopeless of his
    reward. 331
Of both the ills, to choose the less I ween the choice
    were hard. 332
First to a ruthless one he made him sue for grace,
And now with spur he forceth him to run an endless
    race.
Amid these stormy seas one anchor doth him hold:
He serveth not a cruel one, as he had done of old,
And therefore is content, and chooseth still to serve,
Though hap should swear that guerdonless the
    wretched wight should starve. 338
The lot of Tantalus is, Romeus, like to thine:
For want of food amid his food the miser still doth
    pine.
  As careful was the maid what way were best devise
To learn his name that entertained her in so gentle
    wise,
Of whom her heart received so deep, so wide a
    wound.
An ancient dame she called to her and in her ear gan
    round. 344
This old dame in her youth had nursed her with her
    milk,
With slender needle taught her sew, and how to spin
  · with silk.

---

325 in choice i.e., in her power **328 doth seek . . . game** plays to amuse
herself **331 hath . . . serve** i.e., has Cupid made Romeo obey the god of
love **332 ween** think, suppose **338 Though . . . starve** i.e., even though
Fate should swear an oath that the wretched Romeo must perish without reward **344 round** whisper

"What twain are those," quoth she, "which press
  unto the door,
Whose pages in their hands do bear two torches light
  before?"   348
And then, as each of them had of his household
  name,   349
So she him named yet once again, the young and wily
  dame.   350
"And tell me who is he, with visor in his hand,
That yonder doth in masking weed beside the
  window stand?"   352
"His name is Romeus," said she, "a Montague,
Whose father's pride first stirred the strife which
  both your households rue."
  The word of "Montague" her joys did overthrow,
And straight, instead of happy hope, despair began to
  grow.   356
"What hap have I," quoth she, "to love my father's
  foe?
What, am I weary of my weal? What, do I wish my
  woe?"   358
But though her grievous pains distrained her tender
  heart,   359
Yet with an outward show of joy she cloakèd inward
  smart,
And of the courtlike dames her leave so courtly took
That none did guess the sudden change by changing
  of her look.

[Unable to sleep, Juliet ponders her predicament, "ycaught
in subtle snare," and wonders if, like Dido, she is being deceived by her lover's attractive outside. She decides in Romeus's favor, since, as Brooke editorializes, we can
persuade ourselves "to what we like" when the mind is captured by the fancy of love. Romeus meanwhile is likewise
driven "to forsake his weary bed" by restless thoughts.
Walking by Juliet's house, he catches a glimpse of her and

---

348 **light** lighted   349 **had . . . name** was named according to his family   350 **she . . . again** Juliet repeated each name aloud   352 **weed**
garments   356 **straight** at once   358 **weal** well-being   359 **distrained**
afflicted

soon discovers a garden plot that faces on her window, but, fearful of detection by her kinsmen, he is unable to speak with her for a week or two. Juliet meanwhile has been distracted by worry. At last they are able to converse in the secrecy of night.]

Now, whilst with bitter tears her eyes as fountains
    run,
With whispering voice ybroke with sobs thus is her
    tale begun:
"O Romeus, of your life too lavish sure you are
That in this place and at this time to hazard it you
    dare!
What if your deadly foes, my kinsmen, saw you here?
Like lions wild your tender parts asunder would they
    tear.
In ruth and in disdain I, weary of my life,
With cruel hand by mourning heart would pierce
    with bloody knife.
For you, mine own, once dead, what joy should I have
    here?
And eke my honor stained, which I than life do hold
    more dear."   498
  "Fair lady mine, dame Juliet, my life," quod he,   499
"Even from my birth committed was to fatal sisters
    three.   500
They may, in spite of foes, draw forth my lively
    thread,   501
And they also—whoso saith nay—asunder may it
    shred.   502
But who to reave my life his rage and force would
    bend   503
Perhaps should try unto his pain how I it could
    defend.   504
Ne yet I love it so but always for your sake   505

---

498 eke also   **499–500 my life . . . three** i.e., from the time of my birth my life has been in the hands of the three Fates (Clotho, Lachesis, and Atropos)   **501 draw forth** extend, lengthen   **502 whoso saith nay** no matter who wishes to deny it   **503 who to reave** whoever to bereave me of.   **bend** aim, intend   **504 unto his pain** to his cost   **505 it** i.e., life

A sacrifice to death I would my wounded corpse
    betake.   506
If my mishap were such that here, before your sight,
I should restore again to death of life my borrowed
    light,   508
This one thing and no more my parting sprite would
    rue: 509
That part he should before that you by certain trial
    knew   510
The love I owe to you, the thrall I languish in,   511
And how I dread to lose the gain which I do hope to
    win,
And how I wish for life, not for my proper ease,   513
But that in it you might I love, you honor, serve, and
    please   514
Till deadly pangs the sprite out of the corpse shall
    send."
And thereupon he sware an oath, and so his tale had
    end.
    Now love and pity boil in Juliet's ruthful breast.
In window on her leaning arm her weary head doth
    rest,
Her bosom bathed in tears to witness inward pain.
With dreary cheer to Romeus thus answered she
    again:
    "Ah, my dear Romeus, keep in these words!" quod
    she.   521
"For lo, the thought of such mischance already
    maketh me
For pity and for dread wellnigh to yield up breath.
In even balance peisèd are my life and eke my death,   524
For so my heart is knit, yea, made one self with yours
That sure there is no grief so small by which your
    mind endures
But, as you suffer pain, so I do bear in part—

506 A . . . betake I would deliver over my wounded body to death as a
sacrifice (for your sake)   508 I . . . light i.e., I should give back to death
the borrowed light of my life   509 sprite spirit, soul   510 That . . . that
i.e., that my soul should depart before   511 thrall thralldom, bondage
513 proper own   514 you might I love I might love you   521 keep in do
not utter   524 peisèd weighed.   eke also

Although it lessens not your grief—the half of all
    your smart.
But these things overpast, if of your health and mine
You have respect, or pity aught my teary weeping
    eyen,   530
In few unfeignèd words your hidden mind unfold,
That, as I see your pleasant face your heart I may
    behold.
For if you do intend my honor to defile,
In error shall you wander still, as you have done this
    while.
But if your thought be chaste and have on virtue
    ground,
If wedlock be the end and mark which your desire
    hath found,
Obedience set aside unto my parents due,   537
The quarrel eke that long ago between our
    households grew,   538
Both me and mine I will all whole to you betake   539
And, following you whereso you go, my father's
    house forsake.
But if by wanton love and by unlawful suit
You think in ripest years to pluck my maidenhood's
    dainty fruit,   542
You are beguiled, and now your Juliet you beseeks 543
To cease your suit and suffer her to live among her
    likes."   544
    Then Romeus, whose thought was free from foul
    desire,
And to the top of virtue's height did worthily aspire,
Was filled with greater joy than can my pen
    express—
Or, till they have enjoyed the like, the hearer's heart
    can guess.
And then with joinèd hands heaved up into the skies,

530 teary tear-filled. **eyen** eyes **537–538 Obedience . . . grew** setting
aside the obedience due my parents and also the allegiances of the
ancient quarrel between our two families **539 all whole** wholly. **betake** give **542 ripest years** i.e., the years when beauty is most in flower
543 you beseeks beseeches you **544 likes** equals, i.e., family and friends

He thanks the gods, and from the heavens for
    vengeance down he cries
If he have other thought but as his lady spake.
And then his look he turned to her and thus did
    answer make:
  "Since, lady, that you like to honor me so much
As to accept me for your spouse, I yield myself for
    such.
In true witness whereof, because I must depart,
Till that my deed do prove my word, I leave in pawn
    my heart.
Tomorrow eke betimes, before the sun arise,   557
To Friar Laurence will I wend, to learn his sage
    advice.
He is my ghostly sire, and oft he hath me taught   559
What I should do in things of weight when I his aid
    have sought.
And at this selfsame hour, I plight you here my faith,   561
I will be here, if you think good, and tell you what he
    saith."
She was contented well, else favor found he none   563
That night, at Lady Juliet's hand, save pleasant words
    alone.
   This barefoot friar girt with cord his grayish weed,
For he of Francis' order was, a friar, as I rede.   566
Not as the most was he, a gross unlearned fool,   567
But doctor of divinity proceeded he in school.   568
The secrets eke he knew in nature's works that lurk;   569
By magic's art most men supposed that he could
    wonders work.
Ne doth it ill beseem divines those skills to know
If on no harmful deed they do such skillfulness
    bestow.
For justly of no art can men condemn the use;
But right and reason's lore cry out against the lewd
    abuse.   574

---

557 betimes early   **559 ghostly** spiritual   **561 plight** pledge   **563 else**
otherwise   **566 rede** advise (or possibly *read*)   **567 Not . . . fool** he was
not, like most of his kind, a grossly unlearned fool   **568 proceeded**
advanced to the higher degree of   **569 eke** also   **574 lewd** wicked

The bounty of the Friar and wisdom hath so won
The townsfolks' hearts that wellnigh all to Friar
  Laurence run
To shrive themself—the old, the young, the great and
  small.   577
Of all he is belovèd well and honored much of all.
And, for he did the rest in wisdom far exceed, 579
The Prince by him, his counsel craved, was holp at
  time of need.   580
Betwixt the Capilets and him great friendship grew;
A secret and assurèd friend unto the Montague.
Loved of this young man more than any other guest,
The Friar eke of Verone youth aye likèd Romeus best,
For whom he ever hath, in time of his distress,
As erst you heard, by skillful lore found out his
  harm's redress.
 To him is Romeus gone, ne stayeth he till the
  morrow.
To him he painteth all his case: his passèd joy and
  sorrow,
How he hath her espied with other dames in dance,
And how that first to talk with her himself he did
  advance.
Their talk and change of looks he gan to him declare,
And how so fast by faith and troth they both
  ycoupled are,   592
That neither hope of life nor dread of cruel death
Shall make him false his faith to her while life shall
  lend him breath.   594
And then with weeping eyes he prays his ghostly sire
To further and accomplish all their honest heart's
  desire.
 A thousand doubts and more in th' old man's head
  arose;
A thousand dangers like to come the old man doth
  disclose.   598
And from the spousal rites he redeth him refrain; 599

---

577 **shrive themself** make their confessions 579 **for** because 580 **his counsel craved** the Friar's advice being sought. **holp** helped 592 **fast** firmly 594 **false** falsify 598 **like** likely 599 **redeth** advises

Perhaps he shall be bet advised within a week or
    twain.   600
  Advice is banished quite from those that follow
    love,
Except advice to what they like their bending mind
    do move.
As well the father might have counseled him to stay   603
That from a mountain's top thrown down is falling
    half the way   604
As warn his friend to stop, amid his race begun,
Whom Cupid with his smarting whip enforceth forth
    to run.   606
Part won by earnest suit, the Friar doth grant at last,
And part because he thinks the storms so lately
    overpast
Of both the households' wrath this marriage might
    appease,
So that they should not rage again, but quite forever
    cease.
The respite of a day he asketh to devise
What way were best, unknown, to end so great an
    enterprise.   612
The wounded man, that now doth deadly pains
    endure,   613
Scarce patient tarryeth whilst his leech doth make
    the salve to cure;   614
So Romeus hardly grants a short day and a night.   615
Yet needs he must, else must he want his only heart's
    delight.   616
  You see that Romeus no time or pain doth spare;
Think that the whilst fair Juliet is not devoid of care!   618
Young Romeus poureth forth his hap and his mishap
Into the Friar's breast, but where shall Juliet unwrap
The secrets of her heart? To whom shall she unfold
Her hidden burning love and eke her thought and
    cares so cold?

600 he . . . advised he will think better of it, be better advised
603 father i.e., friar **603–604 stay That** stop an object that **606 Whom**
him whom **612 end** accomplish **613 The wounded man** i.e., one who,
like Romeus, is wounded with love's arrow **614 Scarce** scarcely. **leech**
doctor (i.e., the Friar) **615 hardly grants** reluctantly agrees to a delay
of **616 want** lack **618 the whilst** meanwhile

The Nurse, of whom I spake, within the chamber
    lay.
Upon the maid she waiteth still. To her she doth
    bewray   624
Her new-receivèd wound, and then her aid doth
    crave.
In her she saith it lies to spill, in her her life to save. 626
Not easily she made the froward Nurse to bow, 627
But, won at length, with promised hire she made a
    solemn vow   628
To do what she commands, as handmaid of her hest. 629
Her mistress' secrets hide she will within her covert
    breast.
    To Romeus she goes. Of him she doth desire
To know the mean of marriage, by counsel of the
    Friar.   632
"On Saturday," quod he, "if Juliet come to shrift, 633
She shall be shrived and married. How like you,
    Nurse, this drift?"   634
"Now, by my truth," quod she, "God's blessing have
    your heart!
For yet in all my life I have not heard of such a part. 636
Lord, how you young men can such crafty wiles
    devise,
If that you love the daughter well, to blear the
    mother's eyes!
An easy thing it is with cloak of holiness
To mock the silly mother that suspecteth nothing
    less.   640
But that it pleasèd you tell me of the case, 641
For all my many years, perhaps, I should have found
    it scarce.   642
Now, for the rest, let me and Juliet alone.
To get her leave, some feat excuse I will devise anon, 644

---

624 still always. **bewray** reveal **626 spill** kill, destroy **627 froward**
perverse, refractory. **bow** yield **628 hire** monetary reward **629 hest**
command **632 mean** means **633 shrift** confession **634 She . . . shrived**
her confession will be heard **636 part** thing **640 silly** innocent, unsuspecting. **nothing less** i.e., nothing at all **641 But that** were it not that
642 found it scarce i.e., scarcely believed it **644 feat** suitable

For that her golden locks by sloth have been
    unkempt,   645
Or for unwares some wanton dream the youthful
    damsel dreamt,
Or for in thoughts of love her idle time she spent,
Or otherwise within her heart deservèd to be shent.   648
I know her mother will in no case say her nay;
I warrant you she shall not fail to come on
    Saturday."
  And then she swears to him the mother loves her
    well;
And how she gave her suck in youth she leaveth not
    to tell.   652
"A pretty babe," quod she, "it was when it was
    young.
Lord, how it could full prettily have prated with it
    tongue!   654
A thousand times and more I laid her on my lap,
And clapped her on the buttock soft and kissed
    where I did clap.
And gladder then was I of such a kiss, forsooth,
Than I had been to have a kiss of some old lecher's
    mouth."
  And thus of Juliet's youth began this prating nurse,
And of her present state to make a tedious long
    discourse.
For, though he pleasure took in hearing of his love,
The message answer seemèd him to be of more
    behoof.   662
But when these beldams sit at ease upon their tail, 663
The day and eke the candlelight before their talk
    shall fail.
And part they say is true, and part they do devise;
Yet boldly do they chat of both when no man checks
    their lies.   666
  Then he six crowns of gold out of his pocket drew

645 **For . . . unkempt** i.e., that her hair is uncombed. (This is one of the excuses that the Nurse will use to cover Juliet's absence.) **648 shent** blamed **652 leaveth not** does not omit **654 it** its **662 behoof** benefit **663 beldams** old women **666 no man** no one

And gave them her. "A slight reward," quod he, "and
   so, adieu."
In seven years twice told she had not bowed so low   669
Her crooked knees as now they bow. She swears she
   will bestow
Her crafty wit, her time, and all her busy pain
To help him to his hopèd bliss, and, cowering down
   again,
She takes her leave and home she hies with speedy
   pace.
  The chamber door she shuts, and then she saith,
   with smiling face,
"Good news for thee, my girl, good tidings I thee
   bring!
Leave off thy wonted song of care, and now of
   pleasure sing.
For thou mayst hold thyself the happiest under sun,
That in so little while so well so worthy a knight hast
   won.
The best yshaped is he and hath the fairest face
Of all this town, and there is none hath half so good a
   grace,
So gentle of his speech, and of his counsel wise."
And still with many praises more she heaved him to
   the skies.   682
  "Tell me else what," quod she. "This evermore I
   thought.   683
But of our marriage, say at once, what answer have
   you brought?"
"Nay, soft," quoth she, "I fear your hurt by sudden
   joy."
"I list not play," quoth Juliet, "although thou list to
   toy."   686
How glad, trow you, was she when she had heard her
   say
No farther off than Saturday deferrèd was the day!
Again the ancient nurse doth speak of Romeus.

669 told counted   **682 still . . . skies** i.e., she continually praised him to
the skies   **683 Tell . . . thought** i.e., tell me something new, said Juliet; I
knew all this before. (Compare *Romeo and Juliet*, 2.5.46.)   **686 I list not
play** i.e., I'm not in a mood for jesting.   **toy** trifle

"And then," said she, "he spake to me, and then I
  spake him thus."
Nothing was done or said that she hath left untold
Save only one, that she forgot the taking of the gold.   692
  "There is no loss," quod she, "sweet wench, to loss
    of time,   693
Ne in thine age shalt thou repent so much of any
    crime.   694
For when I call to mind my former passèd youth,
One thing there is which most of all doth cause my
    endless ruth.   696
At sixteen years I first did choose my loving fere,   697
And I was fully ripe before, I dare well say, a year.   698
The pleasure that I lost that year so overpast
A thousand times I have bewept, and shall while life
    doth last.
In faith, it were a shame, yea, sin it were, iwis,   701
When thou mayst live in happy joy to set light by thy
    bliss."   702
She that this morning could her mistress' mind
    dissuade   703
Is now become an oratoress her lady to persuade.

[The "wily" Juliet gets permission to go with the Nurse to
shrift at Friar Lawrence's cell, where she and Romeus are
married. The Nurse provides a ladder of cords by which Romeus climbs to her window and consummates his marriage
to Juliet. Shortly after, the feud between the Capilets and
Montagues flares up again, and Tybalt, Juliet's cousin (mentioned now for the first time), challenges Romeus in the
streets, attacking so relentlessly that Romeus is forced to
lay aside his scruples and his secret loyalty to Juliet. Mercutio and Benvolio take no part in this scene. Romeus's banishment follows as a consequence of his killing Tybalt, and
the story proceeds much as in Shakespeare except that the
proposed marriage to Paris is not mentioned until after
Romeus's exile. When Romeus, having heard of Juliet's

692 forgot i.e., neglected to mention   **693 to** compared to   **694 in thine
age** in all your life   **696 ruth** regret   **697 fere** mate   **698 before . . . a
year** a year earlier, I dare say   **701 iwis** certainly   **702 set light by** set
little value on   **703 could** would have

supposed death and having sought out poison from an apothecary, returns from Mantua to Verona, he proceeds at once with lantern and digging instruments to Juliet's tomb.]

And then our Romeus, the vault stone set upright,
Descended down, and in his hand he bare the
    candlelight.   2630
And then with piteous eye the body of his wife
He gan behold, who surely was the organ of his life,
For whom unhappy now he is, but erst was blist.
He watered her with tears, and then an hundred
    times her kissed,
And in his folded arms full straitly he her plight,   2635
But no way could his greedy eyes be fillèd with her
    sight.
His fearful hands he laid upon her stomach cold,
And them on divers parts beside the woeful wight did
    hold.   2638
But when he could not find the signs of life he
    sought,
Out of his cursèd box he drew the poison that he
    bought.
Whereof he greedily devoured the greater part,
And then he cried with deadly sigh, fetched from his
    mourning heart:
"O Juliet, of whom the world unworthy was,
From which, for world's unworthiness, thy worthy
    ghost did pass,
What death more pleasant could my heart wish to
    abide
Than that which here it suffereth now, so near thy
    friendly side?
Or else so glorious tomb how could my youth have
    craved
As in one selfsame vault with thee haply to be
    engraved?
What epitaph more worth, or half so excellent,
To consecrate my memory could any man invent

2630 bare bore   **2635 straitly** tightly.   **plight** folded, embraced
2638 wight person

As this our mutual and our piteous sacrifice
Of life, set light for love?" But while he talketh in
   this wise,
And thought as yet awhile his dolors to enforce,   2653
His tender heart began to faint, pressed with the
   venom's force,
Which little and little gan to overcome his heart.
  And whilst his busy eyne he threw about to every
   part,
He saw hard by the corpse of sleeping Juliet
Bold Tybalt's carcass dead, which was not all
   consumèd yet,
To whom, as having life, in this sort speaketh he: 2659
"Ah, cousin, dear Tybalt, whereso thy restless sprite
   now be,
With stretchèd hands to thee for mercy now I cry,
For that before thy kindly hour I forcèd thee to die.   2662
But if with quenchèd life not quenchèd be thine ire,
But with revenging lust as yet thy heart be set on
   fire,
What more amends or cruel wreak desirest thou   2665
To see on me than this which here is showed forth to
   thee now?
Who reft by force of arms from thee thy living breath,   2667
The same with his own hand, thou seest, doth poison
   himself to death.
And, for he causèd thee in tomb too soon to lie,
Too soon also, younger than thou, himself he layeth
   by."
  These said, when he gan feel the poison's force
   prevail,
And little and little mastered life for aye began to fail,   2672
Kneeling upon his knees, he said with voice full low,
"Lord Christ, that so to ransom me descendedst long
   ago
Out of thy Father's bosom, and in the Virgin's womb
Didst put on flesh, O, let my plaint out of this hollow
   tomb

2653 **his dolors to enforce** to emphasize his griefs   2659 **as having life**
as if he (Tybalt) were still alive   2662 **kindly hour** natural time
2665 **wreak** vengeance   2667 **Who** he who   2672 **mastered life** the life
he tamed or defeated.   **for aye** forever

Pierce through the air, and grant my suit may favor
    find!
Take pity on my sinful and my poor afflicted mind.
For well enough I know this body is but clay,
Naught but a mass of sin, too frail and subject to
    decay."
Then, pressed with extreme grief, he threw with so
    great force
His overpressèd parts upon his lady's wailèd corse   2682
That now his weakened heart, weakened with
    torments past,
Unable to abide this pang, the sharpest and the last,
Remainèd quite deprived of sense and kindly
    strength;   2685
And so the long-imprisoned soul hath freedom won at
    length.

[The Friar finds Juliet awakening and tries to persuade her
to take up a life of religious seclusion, but flees, leaving her
alone.]

When Juliet saw herself left in the vault alone
That freely she might work her will—for let or stay
    was none—   2766
Then once for all she took the cause of all her harms,
The body dead of Romeus, and clasped it in her
    arms.
Then she, with earnest kiss, sufficiently did prove
That more than by the fear of death she was attaint
    by love.   2770
And then, past deadly fear—for life ne had she care—   2771
With hasty hand she did draw out the dagger that he
    ware.   2772
"O, welcome, Death," quoth she, "end of
    unhappiness,
That also art beginning of assurèd happiness!

2682 His overpressèd parts his afflicted body. (He falls upon her body.)
wailèd bewailed   **2685 kindly** natural

2766 let or stay hindrance   **2770 attaint** infected, affected   **2771 ne had
she** she had no   **2772 ware** wore

Fear not to dart me now; thy stripe no longer stay.　2775
Prolong no longer now my life; I hate this long delay.
For straight my parting sprite, out of this carcass
    fled,　2777
At ease shall find my Romeus' sprite among so many
    dead.
And thou, my loving lord, Romeus, my trusty fere,　2779
If knowledge yet do rest in thee, if thou these words
    dost hear,
Receive thou her whom thou didst love so lawfully,
That caused, alas, thy violent death, although
    unwillingly,
And therefore willingly offers to thee her ghost
To th' end that no wight else but thou might have just
    cause to boast
Th' enjoying of my love which aye I have reserved
Free from the rest, bound unto thee that hast it well
    deserved;
That so our parted sprites, from light that we see
    here,　2787
In place of endless light and bliss may ever live
    yfere!"　2788
This said, her ruthless hand through girt her valiant
    heart.　2789
Ah, ladies, help with tears to wail the lady's deadly
    smart!

[The poem's final scene centers, as in Shakespeare's play, on the Friar's narrative of events and the reconciliation of the two grieving families.]

Text based on *The Tragical History of Romeus and Juliet, written First in Italian by Bandell and Now in English by Ar. Br. . . .* [1562].

2775 dart pierce with a dart.　**stripe** blow.　**stay** hold back
2777 straight straightway, at once　**2779 fere** mate　**2787 parted** departed.　**from** departed from　**2788 yfere** together　**2789 ruthless** unsparing.　**through girt** thrust through

In the following, departures from the original text appear in boldface; original readings are in roman.

30 Capilet Capelet   **192 beholding** behelding   **212 sport** port   **213 scarcely** skasely
220 rapt wrapt   **260 swaddling** swathing   **268 grafted** graffed   **282 not** no
283 wrapped rapt   **306 outward** vtwerd   **312 leisureless** lay sureles   **348 hands** hand
666 chat that   **2682 corse** corpse

Further Reading

Auden, W. H. "Introduction." *Romeo and Juliet*. The Laurel Shakespeare, gen. ed. Francis Fergusson, with a modern commentary by W. H. Auden. New York: Dell, 1958. Auden views *Romeo and Juliet* as a tragedy of "Fate, Choice, and Chance," though his discussion of the play emphasizes the culpability of both the lovers and the community of Verona. The feuding families create an atmosphere that encourages the lovers' self-absorption, and the lovers' decision to take their own lives is, for Auden, "in the profoundest sense, a failure of love, a proof of selfishness."

Brooke, Nicholas. *"Romeo and Juliet." Shakespeare's Early Tragedies*. London: Methuen, 1968. For Brooke, *Romeo and Juliet* is not an immature play but, in large part, a play about immaturity. The lovers' emotional attitudes, familiar from the Renaissance sonnet tradition, are qualified by the play's language and structure.

Calderwood, James L. *"Romeo and Juliet:* A Formal Dwelling." *Shakespearean Metadrama*. Minneapolis: Univ. of Minnesota Press, 1971. Calderwood explores through his metadramatic perspective an analogy between the lovers' search for an authentic language of feeling and Shakespeare's search for an authentic dramatic style. Ultimately, Calderwood argues, the lovers are unable to find a language that can do any more than leave them isolated in the purity and privacy of their love; Shakespeare, however, discovers in the formal organization of his play a means of reconciling the public and private dimensions of language.

Charlton, H. B. "Experiment and Interregnum." *Shakespearian Tragedy*. Cambridge: Cambridge Univ. Press, 1948. Charlton's influential essay argues that *Romeo and Juliet* was experimental both in its subject matter—its focus on fictional, unheroic young lovers rather than on public figures drawn from history—and in its emphasis upon fate as the driving force of the tragic action. Fate, working through the agency of the feud, movingly brings the lovers to their doom. Nonetheless, Charlton argues,

Shakespeare does not repeat this experiment with a tragedy of fate, seeking in his later tragedies less arbitrary motives for the tragic action.

Coleridge, Samuel Taylor. *"Romeo and Juliet." Coleridge's Writings on Shakespeare,* ed. Terence Hawkes. New York: G. P. Putnam's Sons, 1959. Though an early play, *Romeo and Juliet,* for Coleridge, gives evidence of both the organic structure and the strong sense of character found fully developed in Shakespeare's mature art. Coleridge admires the play's presentation of the passion of love, as it develops from its origin in Romeo's sense of insufficiency, demanding the completion of a beloved, to his discovery of Juliet and a love that, though violent, is true and pure.

Dickey, Franklin M. *Not Wisely but Too Well: Shakespeare's Love Tragedies,* pp. 63–117. San Marino, Calif.: Huntington Library, 1957. Examining *Romeo and Juliet* against the background of its sources and Elizabethan literary and philosophical treatments of fate and love, Dickey discovers moral patterns that qualify the attractiveness of the lovers. For Dickey, the play is a tragedy of character, as the lovers, in their inability to control their passionate love and grief, become subject to a fate that operates as the agent of the moral order that they transgress.

Evans, Bertrand. "Fate as Practicer: *Romeo and Juliet." Shakespeare's Tragic Practice.* Oxford: Clarendon Press; New York: Oxford Univ. Press, 1979. Evans is concerned with the differences established between an audience's understanding of the events of a play and the characters' own perceptions. In *Romeo and Juliet,* these differences are established from the beginning by the Chorus: we are immediately given an awareness of the play's logic that is denied to the characters, allowing us to see the play's incidents not in isolation but as stages in the progress of fate toward ending the feud.

Evans, Robert O. *The Osier Cage.* Lexington, Ky.: Univ. of Kentucky Press, 1966. Evans's short book examines the rhetorical style of *Romeo and Juliet,* focusing especially upon the use of oxymoron that, as a figure yoking disjointed elements, seems particularly suited to the play's concerns. Evans considers how rhetorical patterns relate to and reveal both character and action, suggesting that finally what is tragic in the play is neither character nor fate, but life itself, with its inevitable hostility to youth and to love.

Granville-Barker, Harley. *"Romeo and Juliet." Prefaces to Shakespeare,* 1946. Rpt. Princeton, N.J.: Princeton Univ. Press, 1963. Granville-Barker's sensitivity to the theatrical possibilities of *Romeo and Juliet* leads him to admire its strengths and also to note its immaturity. Unlike the mature tragedies, it is a play shaped by circumstance rather than by character, though he sees how, in the portrayal of the lovers, Shakespeare succeeds in making their fate seem inevitable rather than merely the result of ill luck.

Hazlitt, William. "Romeo and Juliet." *Characters of Shakespear's Plays,* 1817. London: Oxford Univ. Press, 1966. Hazlitt enthusiastically praises the play for its accurate portrayal of youthful passion. The love of Romeo and Juliet becomes, for Hazlitt, evidence of the truth and power of the imagination. The lovers are led to their exuberant delight not by what they have experienced of love but by what they hope for, and they die when they are unwilling to live without the vibrant hope that has made their lives valuable.

Kahn, Coppélia. "Coming of Age in Verona." In *The Woman's Part: Feminist Criticism of Shakespeare,* ed. Carolyn Ruth Swift Lenz, Gayle Greene, and Carol Thomas Neely. Urbana, Ill.: Univ. of Illinois Press, 1980. Kahn focuses on the feud as the primary tragic force within the play. Polarizing all social relations in Verona and demanding that masculinity find expression only in aggression, the feud insists that the lovers' union can be achieved only in death. The lovers' deaths, Kahn finds, are not fated but willed, acts of assertion over the destructive codes of patriarchal Verona that would keep them apart.

Lawlor, John. *"Romeo and Juliet."* In *Early Shakespeare,* ed. John Russell Brown and Bernard Harris, Stratford-upon-Avon Studies 3. London: Edward Arnold, 1961; New York: Schocken, 1966. Lawlor considers *Romeo and Juliet* in the tradition of medieval rather than classical tragedy to explore and explain the play's emphasis upon transcendent love. Like its medieval forebears, the play moves beyond the spectacle of suffering to an awareness of a happiness beyond time's reach. The play, Lawlor argues, thus both acknowledges and resists time's power, as the lovers in death at last find themselves together beyond the world of challenge and change.

Levin, Harry. "Form and Formality in *Romeo and Juliet*." *Shakespeare Quarterly* 11 (1960): 3–11. Rpt. in *Shakespeare and the Revolution of the Times*. New York: Oxford Univ. Press, 1976. Levin explores the tension between the immature and unrealistic emotional attitudes expressed by the play's elaborate formal patterning and the authentic dimension of feeling discovered by the lovers as they repudiate the artificial language and emotional codes they have inherited. In the tragedy, as Levin finds, the lovers are unable to sustain their private world: the patterns that the lovers seek to break through break them in the end.

Mahood, M. M. "*Romeo and Juliet*." *Shakespeare's Wordplay*. London: Methuen, 1957. As the title of her book suggests, Mahood examines the wordplay of *Romeo and Juliet* as it articulates and organizes the play's tragic concerns. The ambiguities, tensions, and contradictions of the play's puns express the equilibrium achieved between the value of the lovers' experience and the awareness that it cannot be either permanent or perfect.

Nevo, Ruth. "*Romeo and Juliet*." *Tragic Form in Shakespeare*. Princeton, N.J.: Princeton Univ. Press, 1972. In tracing the play's five-act structure, Nevo finds that *Romeo and Juliet* displays a continuous unfolding action, based on classical models of tragic form. With the reversal of their fortunes, the lovers move through the stages of tragic awareness to an acceptance of death as an assertion of their freedom and fidelity.

Peterson, Douglas L. "*Romeo and Juliet* and the Art of Moral Navigation." In *Pacific Coast Studies in Shakespeare*, ed. Thelma N. Greenfield and Waldo F. McNeir. Eugene, Oreg.: Univ. of Oregon Books, 1966. Arguing against a romantic view of the play, Peterson discovers the lovers' responsibility for their tragic fate in their repudiation of divine and rational guidance. Peterson examines the play's images of navigation and finds that they reveal the lovers' impatient commitment to a course guided only by blind passion and ending on the rocks of despair.

Rabkin, Norman. "Eros and Death." *Shakespeare and the Common Understanding.* New York: Free Press, 1967. Rabkin explores the play's paradoxical vision: the tragic action confirms the destructive irrationality of the lovers' passion, but at the same time the conventional logic of restraint and rationality seems impoverished next to the lovers' intensity. The play, Rabkin finds, articulates the tragic paradox of love itself: a yearning for completion and perfection that can be fully satisfied only by death.

Ribner, Irving. "Then I Denie You Starres: A Reading of *Romeo and Juliet.*" In *Studies in English Renaissance Drama: In Memory of Karl Julius Holzknecht,* ed. Josephine W. Bennett, Oscar Cargill, and Vernon Hall, Jr. New York: New York Univ. Press, 1959. Rpt. and rev. in *Patterns in Shakespearean Tragedy.* New York: Barnes and Noble, 1960. For Ribner, *Romeo and Juliet* affirms a Christian view of man's position in an ultimately benevolent and harmonious universe. The lovers are born into a world tainted by an evil for which they are not responsible and from which they are unable to escape. The play, Ribner argues, traces their growth toward an acceptance of death as a necessary means to the perfection they seek.

Snow, Edward. "Language and Sexual Difference in *Romeo and Juliet.*" In *Shakespeare's "Rough Magic": Renaissance Essays in Honor of C. L. Barber,* ed. Peter Erickson and Coppélia Kahn. Newark, Del.: Univ. of Delaware Press, 1985. Examining the lovers' language of emotion, Snow finds that it reveals the linking of their imaginations in "the same idiom," but it also reveals significant differences in their emotional responses. They inhabit, he finds, "separate worlds of desire": the universe generated by Romeo's desire is dominated by sight and is subject to greater rational control than is Juliet's world, which reflects a greater unity of feeling.

Snyder, Susan. "*Romeo and Juliet:* Comedy into Tragedy." *Essays in Criticism* 20 (1970): 391–402. Rpt. and rev. in *The Comic Matrix of Shakespeare's Tragedies.* Princeton, N.J.: Princeton Univ. Press, 1979. Snyder attends sensitively to the structure of the play and finds it unique among the tragedies in that it *becomes* rather than *is* tragic. Until Mercutio dies in Act 3, Snyder argues, the play is essentially comic, but with his death the play reverses its comic movement and the lovers find themselves in a new world of tragic responsibility.

Spurgeon, Caroline F. E. *Shakespeare's Imagery, and What It Tells Us,* pp. 310–316. Cambridge: Cambridge Univ. Press, 1935. Spurgeon traces the dominant imagery in *Romeo and Juliet* of light in its various forms: sun, moon, stars, lightning, fires, etc. The recurring images transform what might be obvious and conventional similes into a significant pattern of imagery that articulates the tragic action, as the brightness of Romeo and Juliet's love is suddenly extinguished.

Wells, Stanley. "Juliet's Nurse: The Uses of Inconsequentiality." In *Shakespeare's Styles,* ed. Philip Edwards, Inga-Stina Ewbank, and G. K. Hunter. Cambridge: Cambridge Univ. Press, 1980. Wells examines the play's rich stylistic diversity, especially the ways in which verbal style serves as a guide to character. The clearest example of this, Wells finds, is the Nurse's speech in Act 1, scene 3, where Shakespeare's skill at conveying her mental processes through rhythm and diction marks an important step in his artistic development.

From the 1967 New York Shakespeare Festival production of *King John*, with Harris Yulin as King John and Clarence Williams III as Hubert de Burgh, directed by Joseph Papp at the Delacorte Theater in Central Park.

Photo © George Joseph

—KING JOHN—

KING JOHN

Introductory Material
Foreword by Joseph Papp
Introduction
King John in Performance

THE PLAY

Supplementary Material
Date and Text
Textual Notes
Shakespeare's Sources
Further Reading

Foreword

The two scenes in *King John* that I like best concern the planned murder of young Arthur, the claimant to the throne, by Hubert de Burgh. In the first, Act 3, scene 3, King John is trying to *suggest* to Hubert that the boy be murdered, without actually coming out and saying the incriminating words. It's a gorgeous piece of writing; as the King tosses the issue noncommittally up in the air, Hubert takes it and runs with it:

KING JOHN
Good Hubert, Hubert, Hubert, throw thine eye
On yon young boy. I'll tell thee what, my friend,
He is a very serpent in my way,
And wheresoe'er this foot of mine doth tread
He lies before me. Dost thou understand me?
Thou art his keeper.
HUBERT   And I'll keep him so
That he shall not offend Your Majesty.
KING JOHN   Death.
HUBERT
My lord?
KING JOHN   A grave.
HUBERT   He shall not live.
KING JOHN   Enough.
I could be merry now. Hubert, I love thee.

Throughout the scene, of which this is the latter part, the King is marvelously subtle and suggestive as he carefully communicates his wishes. And Hubert is quick to pick up on the cue, unlike Buckingham in *Richard III*, who pretends not to understand Richard's hints and forces the King to say, "Cousin, thou wast not wont to be so dull / Shall I be plain? I wish the bastards dead."

Another favorite scene is Act 4, scene 1, when Hubert is preparing to carry out the murder, and the boy tries to dissuade him. To me this is the most moving scene of the play. Young Arthur is sensitive, and precocious, and extremely eloquent as he pleads for his life. Indeed, the little fellow is so endearing that Hubert starts to worry that he won't be able to go through with the murder: "If I talk to him, with his innocent prate / He will awake my mercy, which lies dead. / Therefore I will be sudden, and dispatch."

The tension between the murderous plan in Hubert's mind and the innocence of the young boy who asks, "Must you with hot irons burn out both mine eyes?" builds throughout the scene, as Hubert tries to begin the binding and blinding of Arthur while struggling to master the pity welling up in his heart. He's undergoing a wrenching psychological struggle, but finally his better self wins, and, letting go of the irons, he says, "I'll fill these dogged spies with false reports. / And, pretty child, sleep doubtless and secure / That Hubert, for the wealth of all the world, / Will not offend thee." The lines are so moving, especially when read aloud, that I practically get tears in my eyes every time I hear them.

Joseph Papp

Joseph Papp gratefully acknowledges the help of Elizabeth Kirkland in preparing this Foreword.

Introduction

King John is usually dated on grounds of style between Shakespeare's two historical tetralogies, perhaps shortly before *Richard II* in 1594 or 1595. In structure and characterization it is also transitional from the episodic first series (*Henry VI* through *Richard III*) to the more tightly organized second series (*Richard II* through *Henry V*). It stands alone among Shakespeare's history plays of the 1590s in choosing the early thirteenth century for its subject rather than the fifteenth. Yet the political problems are familiar.

Foremost is the uncertainty of John's claim to the English throne. He occupies that throne by "strong possession" and also seemingly by the last will and testament of his deceased eldest brother, King Richard I. But could such a will disinherit Arthur, the son of John's older brother Geoffrey? English primogeniture specified that property must descend to the eldest son; after Richard's death without direct heirs, his next brother Geoffrey would inherit, and then Geoffrey's son Arthur. Significantly, even John's mother, Queen Eleanor, who publicly supports John's claim, privately admits that "strong possession" is much more on their side than "right" (1.1.39–40). All parties concede, then, that young Arthur's claim is legally superior.

Yet such a claim raises serious practical questions, because it challenges the status quo. John is de facto king, and Arthur a child. To make the dilemma complete, Arthur has no ambitions to rule and seemingly no talent for leadership. Without the unremitting zeal of his widowed mother, Constance, Arthur would retire into the private world of kindness and love where his virtues shine. Moreover, Constance's uncompromising defense of her son's true claim requires her to seek alliance with the French for an invasion of England. Such an appalling prospect of invasion and civil war inevitably poses the question: Is the replacement of John by Arthur worth the price? Which is better, an ongoing regime flawed by uncertain claim and political compromises, or restitution of the "right" by violent and potentially self-destructive means?

Shakespeare refuses to simplify the issues. John is neither a monstrous tyrant nor a martyred hero, although both interpretations were available to Shakespeare in sixteenth-century historical writings. Catholic historians of the late Middle Ages such as Polydore Vergil had uniformly condemned John, partly at least because of his interference with the Church. The English Reformation brought about a conscious rewriting of history, and in John Bale's play of *King Johan* (1538, with later revisions) the protagonist is unassailably virtuous. Centuries ahead of his time, this King John comprehends the true interests of the state in fending off the encroachments of the international Church. He fails only because his people are superstitious and his aristocrats are the dupes of Catholic meddling. Bale's play is transparently a warning to Tudor England. This portrait of John as a martyr continues unabated in John Foxe's *Acts and Monuments,* and in the chronicles of Richard Grafton and Raphael Holinshed that were based on Foxe. Most virulent of all is the play called *The Troublesome Reign of King John* (c. 1587–1591), once thought to be by Shakespeare and analyzed by one recent editor as a bad quarto of Shakespeare's text, but now almost universally regarded as the work of some more chauvinistic playwright such as George Peele. Although generally close to Shakespeare's play in its narrative of events, it also contains scenes of the most degraded anti-Catholic humor, featuring gross abbots who conceal nuns in their private rooms, and the like. Against such a corrupt institution, the Bastard's plundering is wholly justifiable. John and the Bastard would be invincible, were it not for the base Catholic loyalties of the nobility.

Shakespeare consciously declines to endorse either the Catholic or the Protestant interpretation of King John. (Interestingly, neither side showed any interest in Magna Carta; not until the seventeenth century was that event interpreted as a famous precedent for constitutional restraints imposed on the monarchy.) To be sure, some anticlericalism still remains in the play. John grandly proclaims that "no Italian priest / Shall tithe or toll in our dominions." John is "supreme head" of church and state (the actual title claimed by Henry VIII), defending his people against "this meddling priest" with his "juggling witchcraft" (3.1.153–169). Yet Shakespeare's King John is not vindictive against the Church. He seizes some of its wealth not as a reprisal but to support his costly military campaigns; and, when he is poisoned by a monk, neither John nor anyone else assumes that a Catholic conspiracy is responsible —as it is in *Troublesome Reign*. Similarly, the baronial opposition to John is motivated not by secret leanings toward Rome but by understandable revulsion at the apparent murder of Arthur.

Shakespeare's balanced treatment need not merely reflect his own political allegiances, whatever they were. Artistically, *King John* is a study of impasse, of tortured political dilemmas to which there can be no clear answer. How do people behave under such trying circumstances? Shakespeare's play is remarkable for its sensitivity and compassion toward all sides. His most completely sympathetic characters are those innocently caught in the political crossfire, such as Arthur and the Lady Blanche. Among the major contenders for power, all except the ruthless Dauphin Lewis are guided by worthy intentions and yet are forced to make unfortunate and self-contradictory compromises. Constance, for all her virtuous singleness of mind, must seek a French invasion of England. King Philip of France, bound to Constance's cause by all the holy vows of heaven, changes his purpose when England offers a profitable marriage alliance, and then shifts quickly back again when the papacy demands in the name of the Church that Philip punish King John for heresy. Philip's conscience is troubled about both decisions, but what is a king to do when faced with practical choices affecting his people's welfare and his own political safety?

Even Pandulph, the papal legate, can be viewed as a well-intentioned statesman caught in the web of political compromise. Presumably he is sincere in his belief that King John's heresy—in particular, his refusal to accept the Pope's choice, Stephen Langton, as Archbishop of Canterbury—represents a grave threat to Catholic Christendom. Yet Pandulph reveals an unprincipled cunning when he teaches King Philip how to equivocate a sacred vow, or instructs the apt young Lewis in Machiavellian intrigue. As Pandulph explains, the French can exploit King John's capture of Arthur by invading England in Arthur's name, thereby forcing John to murder his nephew in order to terminate the rival claim to the throne. Arthur's death will in turn drive the English nobility over to the French side. By this stratagem, the seemingly bad luck of Arthur's capture can neatly be turned to the advantage of France and the international Church (3.4.126–181). Lewis learns his lesson only too well. What Pandulph has failed to take into account is the insincerity of Lewis's alliance with papal power. When the legate has achieved through the invasion what he wants—the submission of John—and then tries to call off Lewis's army, Pandulph discovers too late that the young Frenchman cares only for war on his own terms. Pandulph's cunning becomes a weapon turned against himself.

John is, like his enemies, a talented man justly punished by his own perjuries. His failings are serious, but they are also understandable. Given the fact that he is king, his desire to maintain rule serves both his own interests and those of political order generally. The deal by which John bargains away his French territories of Angiers, Touraine, Maine, Poitiers, and the rest, in order to win peace with France, is prudent under the circumstances but a blow to those English dreams of greatness that John professes to uphold. When France immediately repudiates this treaty, John merely gets what he deserves for entering such a deal. His surrender of the crown to the papacy is again the canny result of yielding to the least dangerous of the alternatives available but diminishes John's already shaky authority nonetheless.

Most heinous is John's determination to be rid of Arthur. He has compelling reasons, to be sure. As Pandulph predicts, the French invasion of England using Arthur's claim as its pretext forces John to consider Arthur as an immediate threat to himself. (Queen Elizabeth had long agonized over a similar problem with her captive, Mary, Queen of Scots; so long as Mary lived, a Catholic and claimant to the throne, English Catholics had a perennial rallying point.) What is a ruling king to do with a rival claimant in his captivity? As Henry IV also discovers once he has captured Richard II, the logic demanding death is inexorable. Yet such a deed is not only murder, but murder of one's close kinsman and murder of the Lord's anointed in the eyes of those believing the captive, in this case Arthur, to be rightful king. Furthermore, it is sure to backfire and punish the doer by arousing national resentment and rebellion. John quickly regrets Arthur's death, but we suspect that the regret is in part motivated by fear of the consequences. The same unseen power that protects John against his own worst instincts, momentarily saving the boy from Hubert's instruments of torture, also justly prevents John from obtaining any political benefit from this brief reprieve; Hubert is too late, Arthur dies in a fall, the lords are convinced of John's guilt. With fitting irony, John is punished for his crime after he has decided not to do it and after the murder itself has failed to take place.

The word used to sum up the universal political scheming and oath-breaking in this play is "commodity," or self-interest (2.1.574). The word is introduced by the Bastard, the fascinating choric figure of *King John* whose reactions to the events of the play are so important in shaping our own. The Bastard is an outsider from birth and so not beholden to society for its usual tawdry benefits. As the natural son of the great King Richard Coeur de Lion, the Bastard is a kind of folk hero: he is instinctively royal and yet a commoner, a projection of the audience's sentimental fondness for monarchy and at the same time a hero representing all of society. He is a fictional character in a largely historical world. His quarrel with his effete brother Robert over the inheritance of their father's property comically underscores the futility of the dynastic quarrel between King John and Arthur. In both contentions a will left by the deceased confuses the issue of genealogical priority. Thus John, who defends the Bastard's unconventional claim to his inheritance, discovers a natural ally.

The Bastard is strangely drawn to commodity at first. He finds it exhilarating to trust his fortune to war and the King's favor, rather than to the easy comfort of a landed estate. The wars enable him to pursue a quest for self-identity. After learning from his reluctant mother who his real father was, the Bastard must venge himself upon the Duke of Austria, who killed his father. When the Bastard is first confronted with the moral ambiguity of the war, his response is mischievous, almost Vice-like. He makes the cunning suggestion, for example, that France and England join against the city of Angiers until it surrenders, after which they may resume fighting each other. Clearly this

Machiavellian proposal embodies, even satirizes, the spirit of commodity. Yet the Bastard is not motivated by self-interest or a cynical delight in duping men, as is the bastard Edmund in *King Lear*. This Bastard's illegitimacy has no such ominous cosmic import. Instead he is at first the detached witty observer, wryly amused at the seemingly inherent absurdity of politics. Although he does protest also that he will worship commodity for his own gain, we never see him doing so. Despite his philosophic detachment, he remains loyal to England and to John. In fact he is the play's greatest patriot.

The supreme test for the Bastard, as for all well-meaning characters and for the audience as well, is the death of Arthur. The Bastard must experience disaffection and even revulsion if he is to retain our sympathy as choric interpreter. Yet his chief function is to triumph over that revulsion, and in so doing to act as counterpart to the more rash English lords. They have come hastily to the conclusion that John is guilty of Arthur's death. This is of course true in the main, but they do not know all the circumstances, and truth, as always, is more complicated than they suppose. Only the Bastard consistently phrases his condemnation in qualified terms: "It is a damnéd and a bloody work . . . If that it be the work of any hand" (4.3.57–59). Moreover, the lords have concluded that John's guilt justifies their rebellion. Yet they stoop to commodity of the very sort they condemn. They fight for the supposed good of England by allying themselves with Lewis of France. Once again, the ironies of cosmic justice demand that such commodity be repaid by treachery. The lords are luckily saved just in time by Lord Melun's revelation of Lewis's plan, just as John had been saved from his own headstrong folly by the kindness of Hubert. The Bastard's decision to remain loyal to John thus proves not only prudent but virtuous. He has led our sympathies through disaffection to acceptance. Rebellion only worsens matters by playing into the hands of opportunists. Loyalty to John is still, in a sense, a kind of commodity, for it involves compromise and acceptance of politics as morally a world unto itself. Nevertheless, loyalty is a conscientious choice and is rewarded finally by the accession of young Henry III, who at last combines political legitimacy and the will to act.

The ending of *King John* is not without its ironies. England, having suffered through the dynastic uncertainties of a child claimant to the throne (as also in the *Henry VI* plays, *Richard III*, *Richard II*, and Christopher Marlowe's *Edward II*), must now face a new destiny under the young and unproven Henry III. The irony is often underscored, in modern productions at least, by doubling the parts of Arthur and Henry III for the same juvenile actor. Is there sufficient reason to suppose that the problem will not recur? The Bastard's role in seeking affirmation is a crucial one, and yet he does so from his vantage point as the play's most visibly unhistorical personage. As a fictional character, the Bastard is free to invent fictions around him, to instruct King John in the playing of a part that will benefit England, and to fashion a concluding speech in which there can be hope for the future. What sort of consolation does this fiction provide? To dwell on the conflict between history and fiction is not to subvert all hope by labeling fiction as mere fantasy, but it does call attention to the fruitfully ambiguous relation between Shakespeare's stubbornly historical subject matter and his function as creative artist.

King John
in Performance

Like *Henry VIII*, *King John* is seldom seen onstage today but was a great favorite of the nineteenth century. The key to the former popularity of both plays no doubt lies in the manner in which they were staged. Both plays invited opulent and detailed historical sets of the sort nineteenth-century audiences loved, and both provided big emotional speeches that lent themselves to oratorical and even melodramatic delivery. Productions of *Henry VIII* centered on the piteous falls of Buckingham, Queen Katharine, and Wolsey; productions of *King John* focused on John's defiance of the French King at Angiers, Constance's speech about her absent young son Arthur, Arthur's persuading Hubert not to put out his eyes, Arthur's escape attempt and death, John's encounter with the papal legate, and the last moments of the life of King John. As with other historical subjects, that of *King John* also gave actor-managers the opportunity to stage spectacular tableaux, including scenes that do not appear in Shakespeare's script.

The nineteenth century inherited from the eighteenth a play that had been rearranged with a view to unifying its action and sharpening its thrust at the international political intriguing of the Catholic Church. Only occasionally performed after a long hiatus in the late seventeenth and early eighteenth centuries, *King John* enjoyed its first successful reintroduction to the theater in a version by Colley Cibber called *Papal Tyranny in the Reign of King John* (1745). Cibber's adaptation strove for unity by eliminating Shakespeare's first act and by locating its own first two acts at a camp near Angiers. Other cuts and interpolations followed. Cibber's animus against the meddling of the Catholic Church in English politics is evident in his title and in his avowed purpose to "paint the intoxicated tyranny of Rome in its proper colors," with obvious application to current agitation in 1745 over attempts to place the Catholic pretender Charles Edward on the English throne. Adjustment of the text also made possible considerable scenic display, with individual sets for Angiers, the French court, the Castle of Rouen, the Dauphin's camp at St. Edmundsbury, Swinstead Abbey, and so on. Cibber gave particular attention to two splendid processions, one in which Cardinal Pandulph entered in state to receive and then tread on the robe and crown of English royalty before returning them to a submissive John, and another bit of pageantry (not called for in Shakespeare's text) in which a funeral ceremony for Arthur moved toward Swinstead Abbey in a dead march.

Not to be outdone by Cibber, David Garrick brought forth a more avowedly Shakespearean version of the play at the Theatre Royal, Drury Lane, only five days after Cibber's version opened at the Theatre Royal, Covent Garden. Garrick played John; Susannah Cibber, Theophilus Cibber's wife, played Constance; and Charles Macklin acted the part of Pandulph. The playbill claimed, with an obviously scornful glance at Cibber's play at the rival theater, that *King John* was "not acted 50 years," though in fact there had been a revival—indeed, the first certain production of the play—in February of 1737 at Covent Garden, and in March of that year the Haymarket Theatre saw another production of the play claiming to be "as originally written by Shakespeare. Supervised, read over, revised, and unaltered." Garrick's text also was essentially Shakespeare's, though it interpolated two speeches from the anonymous *The Troublesome Reign of King John*.

In 1751 Shakespeare's *King John* replaced Cibber's version at Covent Garden. Susannah Cibber had now joined that company and acted Constance opposite James Quin as the King. When Mrs. Cibber took ill at the end of February, Peg Woffington replaced her in the four remaining performances of the year. In 1754 Garrick again produced the play at Drury Lane, now taking the part of the Bastard and leaving John to Henry Mossop. The production advertised its characters as "new dressed," apparently initiating the move away from contemporary attire and toward period costume that would become a virtual obsession on the nineteenth-century stage.

After Garrick it was John Philip Kemble who brought the greatest distinction to productions of the play. In December of 1783 Kemble and his sister, Sarah Siddons, first performed *King John* at Drury Lane, and he revived the play in five of the next seventeen years. Kemble produced a version in 1800 at Drury Lane that, although not lavish, was carefully attentive to spectacle, and he was much praised for the production's "mimic art" and for its fidelity to Shakespeare's text. At Covent Garden, meanwhile, *King John* was still a victim of adaptation. Richard Valpy, who had revised the play in 1800 for his students at Reading School, introduced his version on the Covent Garden stage in 1803 with the candid avowal that it had been "altered from Shakespeare." The production starred George Frederick Cooke as King John. Working from both Shakespeare's *King John* and Cibber's *Papal Tyranny*, Valpy followed Cibber in cutting away Shakespeare's first act while ameliorating the sharp anti-Catholic tone of Cibber's play. Later that year, Kemble left Drury Lane to become manager of Covent Garden, bringing his Shakespearean version with him and ensuring its place in the Covent Garden repertory until his retirement in 1817.

Building on the emerging traditions of scenic rearrangement and visual splendor, and no longer restricted to the Catholic issue after the subsiding of the Jacobite challenge of 1745, the nineteenth-century theater managers had great success in bringing a spectacular realism to *King John*. Charles Kemble's revival at Covent Garden in 1823 made use of design innovations proposed mainly by the antiquary and theatrical consultant, J. R. Planché. The opening scene showed John in a costume derived from the effigy of the historical King John in Worcester Cathedral, surrounded, as Planché wrote, "by his barons sheathed in mail, with cylindrical helmets and correct armorial shields, and his courtiers in the long tunics and mantles of the thirteenth century." Other sources for the authentic costuming included Queen Eleanor's effigy at the Abbey of Fonteveraud, the effigy of the Earl of Salisbury in Salisbury Cathedral, and medieval illuminated manuscripts. The designers had done careful research; the playbill boasted of their "attention to costume never equalled on the English stage." To audiences accustomed to actors in wigs and long waistcoats, the historical reconstruction was a revelation and the production a great success.

William Charles Macready, who had first acted the play

in 1823, produced in 1842 a spectacle that was perhaps the most financially lavish of his tenure at Drury Lane. His aim was to bring to the stage; as *The Times* of October 25 put it, an "animated picture of those Gothic times" in which the play was set. Costumes were designed with scrupulous attention to historical accuracy, and, with upwards of two hundred supernumeraries moving against the elaborate medieval backgrounds painted by William Telbin, the stage was "thronged with the stalwart forms of the middle ages." Macready played John and Helen Faucit played Constance; Samuel Phelps was, in the estimation of *The Times*, "an admirable Hubert."

Phelps produced his own *King John* in 1844, his first season at the Sadler's Wells Theatre. With Phelps himself in the role of the King, the play was enthusiastically received. The costumes and sets were favorably compared with Macready's, and Phelps's acting was also highly praised; *The Critic* claimed, for example, that "he has more real genius in him than any actor of our time." Phelps's *King John* was revived in six of the eighteen seasons that he was at Sadler's Wells.

Though Macready and Phelps repeatedly demonstrated how actor-managers could succeed with elaborate visual representations of Shakespeare's locales, other actor-managers before them, such as Cibber and Kemble, had shown that the most promising subjects for stage pictures were not always to be found in Shakespeare's text. Charles Kean, undeterred by *King John*'s virtual ignoring of Magna Carta, interpolated a splendid dumb show of its signing in his 1852 production at the Princess's Theatre. Like Kemble and Macready before him, Kean insisted on historical accuracy in matters of scenery, costumes, and accoutrements, even if his fidelity to Shakespeare's text was something less than scrupulous. From seals, tapestries, illustrated manuscripts, effigies on tombs, and medieval ruins, Kean made authentic copies in his stage design of the Norman architecture appropriate to John's reign. The room of state in Act 1 was an exact replica of the hall in Rochester Castle. In fact, every succeeding location was copied from a specific historical ruin of the twelfth and thirteenth centuries. Kean also had success acting the play, appearing as King John for the first time at the Park Theatre in New York in 1846, and making his London debut in his splendid production of 1852.

Herbert Beerbohm Tree, at Her Majesty's Theatre in 1899, retained Kean's tableau of the granting of Magna Carta, along with striking verisimilar effects. Percy Anderson's costumes impressively reproduced twelfth-century dress, armor, and heraldic devices. The sets were equally elaborate. The walls of Angiers in Act 2 were replete with Norman archways, a moat, battlements, crenellated parapet walls, corbels, and, in the distance, the towers of the medieval castle. A contemporary reviewer praised the "fresh and delicate beauty" of the orchard at Swinstead where John dies. The extensive cuts needed to accommodate the massive scenes and interpolated tableaux of this production fitted well into the actor-manager's wishes to concentrate on moments of intense emotion and high seriousness. The play was performed in a three-act version, each act ending with a scene of pathos: the first with Arthur's capture, the second with his death, and the third with the miserable end of King John.

The twentieth century, by contrast, has witnessed a return to something apparently closer to the staging principles of Shakespeare's own theater. Increasingly, directors have opted for what they perceive to be Shakespeare's rather than the set designer's artistry and are no longer willing to rearrange the text to accommodate massive sets like those of Kean or Tree. Frank Benson's company energetically performed the play in a virtually uncut text at Stratford-upon-Avon in 1901 as part of a season that included five other history plays. Although Benson appeared only in the minor role of the second executioner in Act 4, scene 1, he entered to tumultuous applause. Robert Atkins directed the play in 1920 at the Old Vic in a production whose swift pacing and simplified staging revealed Atkins's training with William Poel, the initiator of the movement away from realistic illusion in producing Shakespeare. In 1926 Andrew Leigh opened the season at the Old Vic with a modest production of *King John*, focused on Baliol Holloway's truculent Bastard, that played to capacity houses. Five years later at the Old Vic, Harcourt Williams directed Robert Speaight as John and Ralph Richardson as the Bastard in a successful production that also demonstrated the new simplicity of staging, though it is unclear whether the sparseness was because of Williams's aesthetic belief or because all of England, which had just gone off the gold standard, was in a deep financial crisis.

During World War II, no doubt in part because of its patriotic rhetoric, the play continued to find eager audiences. Ben Iden Payne and Andrew Leigh directed a lively *King John* at Stratford-upon-Avon in 1940 as "a bright medieval pageant," according to *The Times*. In the following year, the Old Vic Company's production at London's New Theatre, directed by Tyrone Guthrie and Lewis Casson and with Sybil Thorndike as Constance, effectively used curtains, banners, and creative lighting effects to suggest the battlefields, pavilions, courts, and castles called for in the play script. Four years later, a twenty-one-year-old Peter Brook directed *King John*, his first Shakespeare play, at the Birmingham Repertory in a production that centered upon Paul Scofield's portrayal of the Bastard as the play world's harshest critic and ablest champion. The production became notorious for Brook's emendation in the Bastard's soliloquy in Act 2, scene 1: "That smooth-faced gentleman, expediency, / Or, as they say, commodity."

After the war, it became possible to play *King John* with a darker sense of its political vision. Michael Benthall's production at Stratford-upon-Avon in 1948 featured Robert Helpmann as a calculating King John, one who was haunted by the production's most striking visual effect: the menacing shadow of a cross that towered over the stage during the entrance of the papal legation. In 1960 at Stratford, Ontario, Douglas Seale emphasized the vicious opportunism of all but Christopher Plummer's Bastard. Joseph Papp's production of the play in 1967 for the New York Shakespeare Festival established provocative tensions between the bright promise of the colorful pageantry and the deep cynicism of most of the action. At Stratford, Ontario, in 1974, Peter Dews directed Edward Atienza as a paranoid John destroyed by the power he proved unfit to wield. That same year, at Stratford-upon-Avon, John Barton further explored the play's dispiriting political vision in a restructured text incorporating lines that he himself wrote, as well as material from John Bale's *King Johan* and from the anonymous *The Troublesome Reign of King John*.

Though recently there have been significant European productions of the play, for example, in Weimar in 1980 at the Deutsches Nationaltheater and in Berlin in 1985 at the Theater im Palast, the 1980s have not offered the English-speaking world many opportunities to see *King John*. In 1982 Randall Duk Kim acted John with an unusual sensitivity to the complex political situation in which he is caught, in a colorful production of the play by the American Players Theatre on the outdoor stage in Spring Green, Wisconsin. When the Jean Cocteau Repertory company performed the play at New York's Bouwerie Lane Theater in 1983, halfway through the performance the dull tunics that served for medieval costume were rolled up, turning into modern battle fatigues. More traditionally, if somewhat ponderously, the BBC television production in 1984 starred Leonard Rossiter as a desperate John and Claire Bloom as a passionate Constance whose deeply felt grief provided some balance to the inhumanity of the surrounding world of courtly sophistication. In 1985 the play was performed at the Oregon Shakespeare Festival in Ashland, where, in the open-air theater, director Pat Patton used richly colored costumes and a simple set to produce an absorbing historical pageant punctuated by the cynicism of John David Castellanos's Bastard.

Although recent productions such as Patton's have repudiated the cumbersome visual elaboration of Kemble, Macready, Kean, and Tree, the impulse toward pageantlike display is actually a valid response to Shakespeare's text. The scene at Angiers in Act 2, so dear to actor-managers of the eighteenth and nineteenth centuries (at times, indeed, the production's crowning scene), calls for impressive visual effects on the unadorned Elizabethan stage for which it was devised. As King Philip of France and King John of England meet before the walls of Angiers, accompanied by numerous followers, an element of symmetrical opposition organizes the exchange of thrust and counterthrust in the parley before the battle. When Hubert and other citizens of Angiers appear *"upon the walls,"* that is, in the gallery above at the rear of the stage, we are shown in spatially symbolic form the dilemma of the town itself, caught between two powerful nations, willing to offer submission to the victor but not knowing who will win.

Throughout the battle of Angiers, the walls and the citizens upon them remain as vivid reminders of the occasion of the quarrel between France and England. Personal loyalties are divided by the conflict as well: the Lady Blanche, John's niece, is offered to the French Dauphin as his prize if he will make accommodation, and so she, like the town, must see her fate determined by the uncertain outcome of battle.

Later (4.3), the gallery above the stage is imaginatively transformed into castle walls in England, from which young Arthur, disguised as a shipboy, attempts escape and leaps to his death—that is, onto the main stage. No scenery was used in Shakespeare's theater to create the effects of castle walls, but the theater building itself, with its impressive architecture, its pillars, its colorful decoration, and above all its vertical differentiation between gallery and main stage, offered a plausible space in which the actors' words and gestures could conjure up a stage picture of political conflict. Rich costuming and a throne of state, quickly brought onstage when needed, lent to scenes of interview between John and his irate barons or the papal legate an aura of ceremonial magnificence that contrasted ironically with the realities of John's dubious claim to the throne, his underhanded way of dealing with the stronger claim of his nephew, young Arthur, and his craven capitulation to the papacy. The most visually impressive scenes of his sitting in royal state are fatally marred, as his nobles point out to him, by the "superfluous" nature of the double ritual through which his crown, already bestowed on him by English law and custom, is rendered him again by Cardinal Pandulph (4.2, 5.1). A theatrical language of ceremony is vital to any production of *King John*, not for the sake of pageantry or for any attempt to recapture the flavor of medieval life, but because of what it implies through contrast about John's failures.

—KING JOHN—

[*Dramatis Personae*

KING JOHN
QUEEN ELEANOR, *his mother*
PRINCE HENRY, *his son, afterward King Henry III*
ARTHUR, *Duke of Brittaine (Brittany), King John's nephew*
CONSTANCE, *Arthur's mother, widow of King John's elder
    brother, Geoffrey*
BLANCHE *of Spain, niece of King John*

LADY FAULCONBRIDGE, *widow of Sir Robert Faulconbridge*
Philip the BASTARD, *afterward knighted as Sir Richard
    Plantagenet, her illegitimate son by Richard I (Richard Coeur
    de Lion)*
ROBERT FAULCONBRIDGE, *her legitimate son*
JAMES GURNEY, *her attendant*

EARL OF PEMBROKE
EARL OF ESSEX
EARL OF SALISBURY
LORD BIGOT
HUBERT DE BURGH, *a citizen of Angiers and afterward in the
    service of King John*
PETER OF POMFRET, *a prophet*
An English HERALD
Two MESSENGERS *to King John*
FIRST EXECUTIONER

KING PHILIP *of France (Philip II)*
LEWIS, *the Dauphin*
DUKE OF AUSTRIA *(Limoges)*
MELUN, *a French lord·*
CHATILLON, *ambassador from France to King John*
A French HERALD
A MESSENGER *to the Dauphin*

CARDINAL PANDULPH, *the Pope's legate*

*Lords, a Sheriff, Soldiers, Citizens of Angiers, Executioners,
    and Attendants*

SCENE: *Partly in England and partly in France*]

1.1 *Enter King John, Queen Eleanor, Pembroke,*
Essex, and Salisbury, with the Chatillon of
France.

KING JOHN
Now, say, Chatillon, what would France with us?   1
CHATILLON
Thus, after greeting, speaks the King of France
In my behavior to the majesty—   3
The borrowed majesty—of England here.   4
ELEANOR
A strange beginning: "borrowed majesty"!
KING JOHN
Silence, good Mother. Hear the embassy.   6
CHATILLON
Philip of France, in right and true behalf
Of thy deceasèd brother Geoffrey's son,
Arthur Plantagenet, lays most lawful claim
To this fair island and the territories,
To Ireland, Poitiers, Anjou, Touraine, Maine,
Desiring thee to lay aside the sword
Which sways usurpingly these several titles,   13
And put the same into young Arthur's hand,
Thy nephew and right royal sovereign.
KING JOHN
What follows if we disallow of this?   16
CHATILLON
The proud control of fierce and bloody war,   17
To enforce these rights so forcibly withheld.
KING JOHN
Here have we war for war and blood for blood,
Controlment for controlment. So answer France.
CHATILLON
Then take my king's defiance from my mouth,
The farthest limit of my embassy.

1.1. Location: England. The court of King John.
1 what . . . us what does the King of France want with us   **3 In my**
behavior in my person and conduct, through me   **4 borrowed** i.e., not
belonging by true right   **6 embassy** message   **13 sways** manages,
directs.   **several titles** distinct possessions   **16 disallow of** reject
17 control compulsion

KING JOHN
　　Bear mine to him, and so depart in peace.
　　Be thou as lightning in the eyes of France;
　　For ere thou canst report I will be there,   25
　　The thunder of my cannon shall be heard.   26
　　So, hence! Be thou the trumpet of our wrath
　　And sullen presage of your own decay.—   28
　　An honorable conduct let him have.   29
　　Pembroke, look to 't.—Farewell, Chatillon.
　　　　　　　　　　Exeunt Chatillon and Pembroke.

ELEANOR
　　What now, my son? Have I not ever said
　　How that ambitious Constance would not cease   32
　　Till she had kindled France and all the world
　　Upon the right and party of her son?   34
　　This might have been prevented and made whole   35
　　With very easy arguments of love,   36
　　Which now the manage of two kingdoms must   37
　　With fearful bloody issue arbitrate.   38

KING JOHN
　　Our strong possession and our right for us.

ELEANOR [*Aside to King John*]
　　Your strong possession much more than your right,
　　Or else it must go wrong with you and me—
　　So much my conscience whispers in your ear,
　　Which none but heaven and you and I shall hear.

　　　　Enter a Sheriff, [who whispers to Essex].

ESSEX
　　My liege, here is the strangest controversy,
　　Come from the country to be judged by you,
　　That e'er I heard. Shall I produce the men?
KING JOHN   Let them approach.
　　　　　　　　[The Sheriff goes to summon the men.]

---

25 report (1) deliver your message (2) sound like thunder   **26 cannon**
(An anachronism, since gunpowder was not employed in Europe until
the fourteenth century.)   **28 sullen presage** dismal portent, omen.
decay ruin   **29 conduct** escort, guard   **32 How that** how   **34 Upon** in
behalf of.   **party** cause   **35 prevented** foreseen.   **made whole** set
right   **36 arguments of love** amicable negotiation   **37 manage** government   **38 issue** consequence

Our abbeys and our priories shall pay
This expeditious charge.

    Enter Robert Faulconbridge and Philip, [his
    bastard brother].

                      What men are you?   49

BASTARD
Your faithful subject I, a gentleman,
Born in Northamptonshire, and eldest son,
As I suppose, to Robert Faulconbridge,
A soldier, by the honor-giving hand
Of Coeur de Lion knighted in the field.   54

KING JOHN   What art thou?

ROBERT
The son and heir to that same Faulconbridge.

KING JOHN
Is that the elder, and art thou the heir?
You came not of one mother then, it seems.

BASTARD
Most certain of one mother, mighty King—
That is well known—and, as I think, one father.
But for the certain knowledge of that truth
I put you o'er to heaven and to my mother.   62
Of that I doubt, as all men's children may.

ELEANOR
Out on thee, rude man! Thou dost shame thy mother,
And wound her honor, with this diffidence.   65

BASTARD
I, madam? No, I have no reason for it.
That is my brother's plea and none of mine—
The which if he can prove, 'a pops me out   68
At least from fair five hundred pound a year.
Heaven guard my mother's honor and my land!

KING JOHN
A good blunt fellow.—Why, being younger born,
Doth he lay claim to thine inheritance?

---

49 expeditious charge sudden expense   **54 Coeur de Lion** Lion-heart,
i.e., Richard I   **62 put you o'er** refer you   **65 diffidence** distrust, suspicion   **68 'a** he

BASTARD

I know not why, except to get the land.

But once he slandered me with bastardy.   74

But whe'er I be as true begot or no,   75

That still I lay upon my mother's head;   76

But that I am as well begot, my liege—

Fair fall the bones that took the pains for me!—   78

Compare our faces and be judge yourself.

If old Sir Robert did beget us both

And were our father, and this son like him,

O old Sir Robert, Father, on my knee

I give heaven thanks I was not like to thee!

KING JOHN

Why, what a madcap hath heaven lent us here!

ELEANOR

He hath a trick of Coeur de Lion's face;   85

The accent of his tongue affecteth him.   86

Do you not read some tokens of my son

In the large composition of this man?   88

KING JOHN

Mine eye hath well examinèd his parts

And finds them perfect Richard. [*To Robert.*] Sirrah,

speak.   90

What doth move you to claim your brother's land?

BASTARD

Because he hath a half-face like my father.   92

With half that face would he have all my land—   93

A half-faced groat five hundred pound a year!   94

ROBERT

My gracious liege, when that my father lived,   95

Your brother did employ my father much—   96

---

74 once in short   **75 whe'er** whether   **76 lay . . . head** leave to my
mother to give account   **78 Fair fall** may good fortune befall.   **the
bones** i.e., the man, now dead   **85 trick** characteristic look   **86 affecteth** resembles   **88 large composition** (1) general constitution (2) big
build   **90 Sirrah** (Customary form of address to inferiors.)   **92 half-face**
(1) profile (2) defective, scant face   **93 With half that face** i.e., with only
half his father's thin face (but with plenty of cheek)   **94 half-faced groat**
i.e., coin bearing the sovereign's profile, and perhaps also clipped and
devalued. (The groat, worth four pence, is a figure for Robert's insig-
nificance, in antithesis to his fortune, five hundred pounds a year.)
95 when that when   **96 Your brother** i.e., Richard Coeur de Lion

BASTARD
Well, sir, by this you cannot get my land.
Your tale must be how he employed my mother.
ROBERT
—And once dispatched him in an embassy
To Germany, there with the Emperor
To treat of high affairs touching that time.   101
Th' advantage of his absence took the King
And in the meantime sojourned at my father's;
Where how he did prevail I shame to speak,
But truth is truth. Large lengths of seas and shores
Between my father and my mother lay,
As I have heard my father speak himself,
When this same lusty gentleman was got.   108
Upon his deathbed he by will bequeathed
His lands to me, and took it on his death   110
That this my mother's son was none of his;
And if he were, he came into the world
Full fourteen weeks before the course of time.
Then, good my liege, let me have what is mine,
My father's land, as was my father's will.
KING JOHN
Sirrah, your brother is legitimate.
Your father's wife did after wedlock bear him,
And if she did play false, the fault was hers—
Which fault lies on the hazards of all husbands   119
That marry wives. Tell me, how if my brother,
Who, as you say, took pains to get this son,
Had of your father claimed this son for his?
In sooth, good friend, your father might have kept
This calf, bred from his cow, from all the world;
In sooth he might. Then, if he were my brother's,   125
My brother might not claim him, nor your father,
Being none of his, refuse him. This concludes: 127
My mother's son did get your father's heir;
Your father's heir must have your father's land.

101 To . . . time to discuss matters that were currently of first importance   108 lusty merry.   got begotten   110 took . . . death i.e., swore
solemnly (the most solemn oath being a deathbed oath)   119 lies on the
hazards is one of the risks   125 if even if   127 Being . . . his i.e., even if
the Bastard were not sired by him.   refuse disclaim.   concludes settles
the problem

ROBERT
> Shall then my father's will be of no force
> To dispossess that child which is not his?

BASTARD
> Of no more force to dispossess me, sir,
> Than was his will to get me, as I think.

ELEANOR [*To the Bastard*]
> Whether hadst thou rather be: a Faulconbridge   134
> And, like thy brother, to enjoy thy land,
> Or the reputed son of Coeur de Lion,
> Lord of thy presence, and no land besides?   137

BASTARD
> Madam, an if my brother had my shape   138
> And I had his, Sir Robert's his, like him,   139
> And if my legs were two such riding-rods,   140
> My arms such eel skins stuffed, my face so thin
> That in mine ear I durst not stick a rose   142
> Lest men should say "Look, where three-farthings
>   goes!"
> And, to his shape, were heir to all this land,   144
> Would I might never stir from off this place,   145
> I would give it every foot to have this face;   146
> I would not be Sir Nob in any case.   147

ELEANOR
> I like thee well. Wilt thou forsake thy fortune,
> Bequeath thy land to him, and follow me?
> I am a soldier and now bound to France.

BASTARD
> Brother, take you my land. I'll take my chance.
> Your face hath got five hundred pound a year,

---

134 Whether which of two choices   **137 Lord of thy presence** i.e.,
master of your own person   **138 an if** if   **139 I had . . . him** i.e., I had
Sir Robert's shape as my brother now has. (*Sir Robert's his* means "Sir
Robert's.")   **140 riding-rods** switches (probably with a suggestion of
sexual emaciation and insufficiency, as also in *eel skins stuffed*, l. 141,
and *Sir Nob in any case*, l. 147)   **142 stick a rose** (The Queen's likeness
on the three-farthing coin was distinguished from that on the three-
halfpence by a rose behind her head. The Bastard's taunt is based on
the thinness of the coin.)   **144 to his shape** in addition to (inheriting) his
physical characteristics   **145 Would . . . place** i.e., may I never stir from
this spot if I am not speaking the truth   **146 it every foot** every foot of
it   **147 Nob** (Diminutive of *Robert*; with a possible play on *head* in a
sexual sense and as head of the family.)

Yet sell your face for five pence and 'tis dear.—
Madam, I'll follow you unto the death.

ELEANOR
Nay, I would have you go before me thither.

BASTARD
Our country manners give our betters way.   156

KING JOHN   What is thy name?

BASTARD
Philip, my liege, so is my name begun;
Philip, good old Sir Robert's wife's eldest son.

KING JOHN
From henceforth bear his name whose form thou
    bearest.
Kneel thou down Philip, but rise more great:
                [*The Bastard kneels and is knighted*]
Arise Sir Richard, and Plantagenet. [*The Bastard rises.*]

BASTARD
Brother by th' mother's side, give me your hand.
My father gave me honor; yours gave land.
Now blessèd be the hour, by night or day,   165
When I was got, Sir Robert was away!   166

ELEANOR
The very spirit of Plantagenet!
I am thy grandam, Richard. Call me so.

BASTARD
Madam, by chance but not by truth; what though?   169
Something about, a little from the right,   170
    In at the window, or else o'er the hatch.   171
Who dares not stir by day must walk by night,
    And have is have, however men do catch.   173
Near or far off, well won is still well shot,   174
And I am I, howe'er I was begot.

156 give . . . way yield precedence to our superiors. (The Bastard jokes
that he will not upset social precedence to rush before Queen Eleanor
to death.) **165–166 Now . . . away** i.e., I thank God that, at the blessed
time when I was conceived, whether by night or day, Sir Robert was
absent **169 not by truth** not honorably, not chastely. **what though**
what of that **170 Something about** somewhat roundabout, clandestinely **171 hatch** lower half door. (*O'er the hatch* means clandestinely,
out of wedlock.) **173 have is . . . catch** possession is what matters,
however it is achieved **174 Near . . . shot** i.e., in archery, hitting the
target is what matters, whatever the distance. (With sexual suggestion.)

KING JOHN
Go, Faulconbridge. Now hast thou thy desire;
A landless knight makes thee a landed squire.   177
Come, madam, and come, Richard, we must speed
For France, for France, for it is more than need.
BASTARD
Brother, adieu. Good fortune come to thee!
For thou wast got i' the way of honesty.
                              Exeunt all but Bastard.
A foot of honor better than I was,   182
But many a many foot of land the worse!
Well, now can I make any Joan a lady.   184
"Good e'en, Sir Richard!"—"God-a-mercy, fellow!"—   185
And if his name be George, I'll call him Peter,
For new-made honor doth forget men's names;
'Tis too respective and too sociable   188
For your conversion. Now your traveler,   189
He and his toothpick at my worship's mess,   190
And when my knightly stomach is sufficed,
Why then I suck my teeth and catechize   192
My pickèd man of countries: "My dear sir,"   193
Thus, leaning on mine elbow, I begin,
"I shall beseech you"—that is Question now;
And then comes Answer like an Absey book: 196
"O sir," says Answer, "at your best command;
At your employment; at your service, sir."
"No sir," says Question, "I, sweet sir, at yours";
And so, ere Answer knows what Question would,   200
Saving in dialogue of compliment,   201

177 A landless knight i.e., the Bastard, who is willing to trade his inheritance for a knighthood   **182 foot** degree   **184 Joan** (Frequently used to designate any girl, usually of the lower class.)   **185 Good e'en** good evening, good afternoon. (The Bastard imagines himself, in his new title, encountering a lower-class person.)   **God-a-mercy** God reward you   **188 respective** considerate   **189 conversion** change of status, acquisition of *new-made honor*. (The Bastard wryly jokes that remembering names is too considerate a thing for a newly made knight to bother about.)   **190 toothpick** (An affectation associated with foreign travel and the latest courtly fashion.)   **my worship's mess** i.e., my dinner table. (A knight was formally addressed as "your worship.")   **192 suck my teeth** (i.e., in contrast to the use of toothpick by the *traveler*)   **193 pickèd** (1) refined (2) having picked his teeth   **196 Absey** ABC, primer   **200 would** intends, asks   **201 Saving . . . compliment** except in polite but inane conversation

And talking of the Alps and Apennines,
The Pyrenean and the river Po,
It draws toward supper in conclusion so.
But this is worshipful society
And fits the mounting spirit like myself,
For he is but a bastard to the time   207
That doth not smack of observation.   208
And so am I—whether I smack or no,   209
And not alone in habit and device,   210
Exterior form, outward accoutrement,
But from the inward motion—to deliver   212
Sweet, sweet, sweet poison for the age's tooth;   213
Which, though I will not practice to deceive,   214
Yet, to avoid deceit, I mean to learn;   215
For it shall strew the footsteps of my rising.   216
But who comes in such haste in riding robes?
What woman-post is this? Hath she no husband   218
That will take pains to blow a horn before her?   219

Enter Lady Faulconbridge and James Gurney.

O me! 'Tis my mother.—How now, good lady?
What brings you here to court so hastily?

LADY FAULCONBRIDGE
Where is that slave, thy brother? Where is he,
That holds in chase mine honor up and down?   223

BASTARD
My brother Robert, old Sir Robert's son?
Colbrand the Giant, that same mighty man?   225
Is it Sir Robert's son that you seek so?

207–208 but a bastard . . . observation i.e., not a true son of the times
unless he observes and practices courtly obsequiousness   **209 And
so . . . no** and so I intend, whether or not I have a true smack of obsequiousness   **210 habit and device** attire and outward appearance (with
a suggestion too of "coat of arms")   **212 from . . . motion** from my own
inclination. (The Bastard is partly attracted to the use of flattery for
self-advancement, even though he also laughs at it.)   **213 Sweet . . .
poison** flattery.   **tooth** i.e., sweet tooth, appetite   **214 practice to deceive** deliberately plan to deceive others   **215 deceit** being deceived
216 it . . . rising i.e., deceitful flattery will inevitably make easy my rise
in importance, just as rushes are strewn on the floors of great men
218 woman-post female messenger   **219 blow a horn** (The ordinary
signal of approach; with a punning reference to the horn of cuckoldry.)   **223 holds in chase** pursues   **225 Colbrand the Giant** legendary
Danish giant slain by Guy of Warwick in a popular romance named
after its hero

LADY FAULCONBRIDGE
  Sir Robert's son! Ay, thou unreverent boy,
  Sir Robert's son. Why scorn'st thou at Sir Robert?
  He is Sir Robert's son, and so art thou.
BASTARD
  James Gurney, wilt thou give us leave awhile?   230
GURNEY
  Good leave, good Philip.
BASTARD   Philip? Sparrow! James,   231
  There's toys abroad; anon I'll tell thee more.   232
                                        Exit James.
  Madam, I was not old Sir Robert's son;
  Sir Robert might have eat his part in me   234
  Upon Good Friday and ne'er broke his fast.
  Sir Robert could do well—marry, to confess—   236
  Could he get me! Sir Robert could not do it;   237
  We know his handiwork. Therefore, good Mother,
  To whom am I beholding for these limbs?   239
  Sir Robert never holp to make this leg.   240
LADY FAULCONBRIDGE
  Hast thou conspirèd with thy brother too,
  That for thine own gain shouldst defend mine honor?
  What means this scorn, thou most untoward knave?   243
BASTARD
  Knight, knight, good Mother, Basilisco-like.   244
  What! I am dubbed; I have it on my shoulder.   245
  But, Mother, I am not Sir Robert's son.
  I have disclaimed Sir Robert and my land;
  Legitimation, name, and all is gone.
  Then, good my Mother, let me know my father;
  Some proper man, I hope. Who was it, Mother?   250

---

230 give us leave leave us alone   **231 Philip? Sparrow** i.e., call me Philip
no more, a name commonly used for sparrows (because of their "Phip"-
like chirp), since I'm now Sir Richard   **232 toys** rumors, follies, interesting events   **234 eat** eaten. (Pronounced "et.")   **236 do** (With sexual
suggestion.)   **marry, to confess** indeed, to speak truly. (*Marry* was
originally an oath "by the Virgin Mary.")   **237 Could he get** if he could
beget   **239 beholding** beholden   **240 holp** helped   **243 untoward** unmannerly   **244 Basilisco-like** (The character Basilisco in the play
Solyman and Perseda, presumably by Thomas Kyd, insists braggartlike
on his knighthood but nevertheless is called "Knave" by his servant.)
245 dubbed made a knight by a touch of the sword on the shoulder
250 proper handsome, fine

LADY FAULCONBRIDGE
  Hast thou denied thyself a Faulconbridge?
BASTARD
  As faithfully as I deny the devil.
LADY FAULCONBRIDGE
  King Richard Coeur de Lion was thy father.
  By long and vehement suit I was seduced
  To make room for him in my husband's bed.
  Heaven lay not my transgression to my charge!
  Thou art the issue of my dear offense,   257
  Which was so strongly urged past my defense.
BASTARD
  Now, by this light, were I to get again,   259
  Madam, I would not wish a better father.
  Some sins do bear their privilege on earth,   261
  And so doth yours. Your fault was not your folly.
  Needs must you lay your heart at his dispose,   263
  Subjected tribute to commanding love,
  Against whose fury and unmatchèd force
  The aweless lion could not wage the fight,   266
  Nor keep his princely heart from Richard's hand.
  He that perforce robs lions of their hearts   268
  May easily win a woman's. Ay, my Mother,
  With all my heart I thank thee for my father!
  Who lives and dares but say thou didst not well
  When I was got, I'll send his soul to hell.
  Come, lady, I will show thee to my kin;
    And they shall say, when Richard me begot,
  If thou hadst said him nay, it had been sin.
  Who says it was, he lies; I say 'twas not.   *Exeunt.*

❖

257 **dear** (1) precious, costly (2) loving   **259 get** be conceived
261 **do . . . earth** i.e., are excusable, venial   **263 dispose** disposal
266 **aweless lion** (During his imprisonment by the Duke of Austria,
according to legend, Coeur de Lion slew the Duke's son and as punishment was given to a hungry lion. When the lion attacked him, he slew it
by thrusting his hand down its throat and tearing out its heart, which
he is supposed to have eaten.)   **268 perforce** forcibly

2.1   *Enter, before Angiers, Philip King of France,*
Lewis [the] Dauphine, Austria, Constance,
Arthur, [and soldiers].

KING PHILIP
Before Angiers well met, brave Austria.—
Arthur, that great forerunner of thy blood,   2
Richard, that robbed the lion of his heart
And fought the holy wars in Palestine,
By this brave duke came early to his grave;   5
And for amends to his posterity,
At our importance hither is he come   7
To spread his colors, boy, in thy behalf,   8
And to rebuke the usurpation   9
Of thy unnatural uncle, English John.
Embrace him, love him, give him welcome hither.
ARTHUR [*To Austria*]
God shall forgive you Coeur de Lion's death
The rather that you give his offspring life,
Shadowing their right under your wings of war.   14
I give you welcome with a powerless hand,
But with a heart full of unstainèd love.
Welcome before the gates of Angiers, Duke.
KING PHILIP
A noble boy! Who would not do thee right?
AUSTRIA [*Kissing Arthur*]
Upon thy cheek lay I this zealous kiss,
As seal to this indenture of my love: 20
That to my home I will no more return
Till Angiers and the right thou hast in France,

**2.1. Location: France. Before Angiers. (The French and Austrian forces
enter from opposite sides before the "gates" of Angiers seen backstage.)
s.d. Austria** (The Duke of Austria wears a lion skin that he supposedly
took from Coeur de Lion; see note 5 and l. 292.)   **2 forerunner** ancestor.
(Richard was actually not a direct ancestor of Arthur, but his uncle.)
5 By . . . duke (A confusion of the Duke of Austria with Viscount Limoges, before whose castle Richard was mortally wounded. The roles of
the two were combined in *The Troublesome Reign of King John* as they
are in this play.)   **7 importance** importunity   **8 spread his colors** display his military colors, his battle ensigns   **9 rebuke** put down
14 Shadowing sheltering   **20 indenture** contract

Together with that pale, that white-faced shore,   23
Whose foot spurns back the ocean's roaring tides
And coops from other lands her islanders,   25
Even till that England, hedged in with the main,   26
That water-wallèd bulwark, still secure   27
And confident from foreign purposes,
Even till that utmost corner of the west
Salute thee for her king. Till then, fair boy,
Will I not think of home, but follow arms.

CONSTANCE
O, take his mother's thanks, a widow's thanks,
Till your strong hand shall help to give him strength
To make a more requital to your love!   34

AUSTRIA
The peace of heaven is theirs that lift their swords
In such a just and charitable war.

KING PHILIP
Well then, to work. Our cannon shall be bent   37
Against the brows of this resisting town.
Call for our chiefest men of discipline,   39
To cull the plots of best advantages.   40
We'll lay before this town our royal bones,
Wade to the marketplace in Frenchmen's blood,
But we will make it subject to this boy.   43

CONSTANCE
Stay for an answer to your embassy,
Lest unadvised you stain your swords with blood.   45
My Lord Chatillon may from England bring
That right in peace which here we urge in war,
And then we shall repent each drop of blood
That hot rash haste so indirectly shed.   49

     Enter Chatillon.

KING PHILIP
A wonder, lady! Lo, upon thy wish,
Our messenger Chatillon is arrived.—

---

23 pale . . . shore i.e., the chalk cliffs at Dover   **25 coops** encloses for
defense   **26 main** ocean   **27 still** perpetually   **34 more** greater
37 bent directed   **39 men of discipline** men trained in military strategy   **40 To . . . advantages** to select positions that are most favorable for
attack   **43 But** unless   **45 unadvised** rashly   **49 indirectly** wrongfully,
misdirectedly

What England says, say briefly, gentle lord;   52
We coldly pause for thee. Chatillon, speak.   53
CHATILLON
Then turn your forces from this paltry siege
And stir them up against a mightier task.
England, impatient of your just demands,
Hath put himself in arms. The adverse winds,
Whose leisure I have stayed, have given him time   58
To land his legions all as soon as I.
His marches are expedient to this town,   60
His forces strong, his soldiers confident.
With him along is come the Mother-Queen,
An Ate, stirring him to blood and strife;   63
With her her niece, the Lady Blanche of Spain;   64
With them a bastard of the King's deceased.   65
And all th' unsettled humors of the land—   66
Rash, inconsiderate, fiery voluntaries,   67
With ladies' faces and fierce dragons' spleens—   68
Have sold their fortunes at their native homes,
Bearing their birthrights proudly on their backs,   70
To make a hazard of new fortunes here.
In brief, a braver choice of dauntless spirits   72
Than now the English bottoms have waft o'er   73
Did never float upon the swelling tide
To do offense and scathe in Christendom. *Drum beats.* 75
The interruption of their churlish drums   76
Cuts off more circumstance. They are at hand,   77
To parley or to fight. Therefore prepare.
KING PHILIP
How much unlooked-for is this expedition!   79

---

52 England the King of England (also in l. 56 and perhaps l. 46).
gentle noble   **53 coldly** calmly   **58 leisure** convenience.   **stayed** waited
for   **60 expedient** speedy   **63 Ate** Greek goddess of discord   **64 niece**
i.e., granddaughter   **65 of . . . deceased** of the deceased King, i.e.,
Richard   **66 unsettled humors** i.e., disgruntled individuals   **67 inconsiderate** reckless, heedless.   **voluntaries** volunteers   **68 With ladies'
faces** i.e., beardless.   **fierce dragons' spleens** i.e., utmost fierceness.
(The spleen was thought to be the seat of the passions.)   **70 Bearing . . .
backs** i.e., having sold everything to obtain armor   **72 choice** picked
company   **73 bottoms** i.e., ships.   **waft** wafted   **75 scathe** harm
76 churlish uncouth, rude   **77 circumstance** detailed reporting
79 expedition speed

AUSTRIA
By how much unexpected, by so much
We must awake endeavor for defense,
For courage mounteth with occasion.   82
Let them be welcome, then. We are prepared.

Enter King [John] of England, Bastard, Queen
[Eleanor], Blanche, Pembroke, and others.

KING JOHN
Peace be to France, if France in peace permit
Our just and lineal entrance to our own.   85
If not, bleed France, and peace ascend to heaven,
Whiles we, God's wrathful agent, do correct   87
Their proud contempt that beats His peace to heaven.

KING PHILIP
Peace be to England, if that war return
From France to England, there to live in peace.
England we love, and for that England's sake   91
With burden of our armor here we sweat.
This toil of ours should be a work of thine;   93
But thou from loving England art so far
That thou hast underwrought his lawful king,   95
Cut off the sequence of posterity,   96
Outfacèd infant state, and done a rape   97
Upon the maiden virtue of the crown.
Look here upon thy brother Geoffrey's face:
These eyes, these brows, were molded out of his;
This little abstract doth contain that large   101
Which died in Geoffrey, and the hand of time   102
Shall draw this brief into as huge a volume.   103
That Geoffrey was thy elder brother born,
And this his son. England was Geoffrey's right,
And this is Geoffrey's. In the name of God,   106

82 **occasion** emergency   85 **lineal** by right of birth   87 **correct** chastise   91 **England's** i.e., Arthur's, whose claim to England the French
King is supporting   93 **This . . . thine** i.e., you should be supporting our
cause also, since it is your duty   95 **underwrought his** undermined
its   96 **sequence of posterity** lawful succession   97 **Outfacèd infant
state** defied the majesty of a boy king   101 **little abstract** abridgment or
epitome   101–102 **doth . . . Geoffrey** contains that which, in its complete form, died in Geoffrey   103 **draw this brief** enlarge this epitome
106 **this** i.e., Arthur himself, or Angiers, or the English crown

How comes it then that thou art called a king,
When living blood doth in these temples beat
Which owe the crown that thou o'ermasterest?   109

KING JOHN
From whom hast thou this great commission, France,
To draw my answer from thy articles?   111

KING PHILIP
From that supernal judge that stirs good thoughts   112
In any breast of strong authority
To look into the blots and stains of right.
That judge hath made me guardian to this boy,
Under whose warrant I impeach thy wrong   116
And by whose help I mean to chastise it.

KING JOHN
Alack, thou dost usurp authority.

KING PHILIP
Excuse it is to beat usurping down.   119

ELEANOR
Who is it thou dost call usurper, France?

CONSTANCE
Let me make answer: thy usurping son.

ELEANOR
Out, insolent! Thy bastard shall be king,   122
That thou mayst be a queen and check the world!   123

CONSTANCE
My bed was ever to thy son as true
As thine was to thy husband, and this boy
Liker in feature to his father Geoffrey
Than thou and John in manners—being as like
As rain to water, or devil to his dam.   128
My boy a bastard? By my soul, I think

109 owe own   **111 draw . . . articles** i.e., claim the right to demand of
me an answer to the items in your indictment   **112 supernal** celestial,
supreme   **116 whose** i.e., the supreme judge's, God's.   **impeach** accuse   **119 Excuse . . . down** i.e., the excuse for what you call my usurping of authority is that I am in fact resisting and defeating usurpation
122 Out (An exclamation of remonstrance.)   **123 check** control
128 dam mother. (Constance says that Arthur is more like his father,
and therefore no bastard, than John is like his mother—a resemblance
that would not rule out bastardy, especially when the two are as alike
as the devil and his mother. Constance goes on to wonder if John's
brother Geoffrey might also be a bastard.)

His father never was so true begot.
It cannot be, an if thou wert his mother.   131

ELEANOR [*To Arthur*]
There's a good mother, boy, that blots thy father.   132

CONSTANCE [*To Arthur*]
There's a good grandam, boy, that would blot thee.   133

AUSTRIA
Peace!

BASTARD   Hear the crier!

AUSTRIA   What the devil art thou?   134

BASTARD
One that will play the devil, sir, with you,
An 'a may catch your hide and you alone.   136
You are the hare of whom the proverb goes,   137
Whose valor plucks dead lions by the beard.
I'll smoke your skin coat an I catch you right.   139
Sirrah, look to 't. I' faith I will, i' faith.

BLANCHE
O, well did he become that lion's robe   141
That did disrobe the lion of that robe!

BASTARD
It lies as sightly on the back of him   143
As great Alcides' shows upon an ass.   144
But, ass, I'll take that burden from your back,
Or lay on that shall make your shoulders crack.   146

AUSTRIA
What cracker is this same that deafs our ears   147
With this abundance of superfluous breath?
King Philip, determine what we shall do straight.   149

KING PHILIP
Women and fools, break off your conference.   150

---

131 an if if   **132 blots** slanders   **133 blot** (with a pun on "obliterate, efface")   **134 Hear the crier** (A mocking suggestion by the Bastard that Austria's call for silence likens him to the town crier.)   **136 An 'a** if he.   **hide** i.e., the lion's skin Austria wears in celebration of his triumph over Richard Coeur de Lion   **137 the proverb** i.e., "even hares may insult the dead lion." (This proverb occurs in Erasmus's *Adages*.)   **139 smoke** thrash, beat.   **your skin coat** your own skin   **141 he** i.e., Richard Coeur de Lion   **143 sightly** suitably. (Said ironically.)   **him** i.e., the Duke of Austria   **144 Alcides** Hercules, who slew the Nemean lion as one of his twelve labors and thereafter wore its pelt   **146 lay on that** i.e., beat you with a club that   **147 cracker** i.e., boaster (with a play on *crack*, l. 146)   **149 straight** at once   **150 fools** children

King John, this is the very sum of all:
England and Ireland, Anjou, Touraine, Maine,
In right of Arthur do I claim of thee.
Wilt thou resign them and lay down thy arms?

KING JOHN
My life as soon. I do defy thee, France.
Arthur of Brittaine, yield thee to my hand,   156
And out of my dear love I'll give thee more
Than e'er the coward hand of France can win.
Submit thee, boy.

ELEANOR   Come to thy grandam, child.

CONSTANCE
Do, child, go to it grandam, child;   160
Give grandam kingdom, and it grandam will
Give it a plum, a cherry, and a fig.
There's a good grandam.

ARTHUR   Good my Mother, peace!
I would that I were low laid in my grave.
I am not worth this coil that's made for me.   165

[*He weeps.*]

ELEANOR
His mother shames him so, poor boy, he weeps.

CONSTANCE
Now shame upon you, whe'er she does or no!   167
His grandam's wrongs, and not his mother's shames,   168
Draws those heaven-moving pearls from his poor eyes,
Which heaven shall take in nature of a fee.   170
Ay, with these crystal beads heaven shall be bribed   171
To do him justice and revenge on you.

ELEANOR
Thou monstrous slanderer of heaven and earth!

CONSTANCE
Thou monstrous injurer of heaven and earth!
Call not me slanderer. Thou and thine usurp
The dominations, royalties, and rights   176

---

156 Brittaine Brittany   **160 Do . . . grandam** (Contemptuous baby
talk.)   **it** its (also in l. 161)   **165 coil** disturbance, fuss   **167 whe'er**
whether   **168 wrongs** wrongdoings.   **shames** insults   **170 a fee** i.e.,
the fee paid to heaven in return for pleading as Arthur's advocate
171 beads i.e., tears, here as gifts used to curry favor, or prayer beads
176 dominations dominions, sovereignties.   **royalties** royal prerogatives

Of this oppressèd boy. This is thy eldest son's son,   177
Infortunate in nothing but in thee.   178
Thy sins are visited in this poor child;   179
The canon of the law is laid on him,   180
Being but the second generation
Removèd from thy sin-conceiving womb.
KING JOHN
Bedlam, have done.
CONSTANCE   I have but this to say,   183
That he is not only plaguèd for her sin,   184
But God hath made her sin and her the plague   185
On this removèd issue, plagued for her   186
And with her plague; her sin his injury,   187
Her injury the beadle to her sin,   188
All punished in the person of this child,
And all for her. A plague upon her!
ELEANOR
Thou unadvisèd scold, I can produce   191
A will that bars the title of thy son.   192
CONSTANCE
Ay, who doubts that? A will, a wicked will,
A woman's will, a cankered grandam's will!
KING PHILIP
Peace, lady! Pause, or be more temperate.
It ill beseems this presence to cry aim   196
To these ill-tunèd repetitions.   197
Some trumpet summon hither to the walls   198

177 **eldest son's son** i.e., eldest grandchild, not son of the eldest son
178 **Infortunate** unfortunate   179 **visited** punished   180 **canon . . . law**
i.e., that the sins of parents shall be visited upon their children to the
third and fourth generation; see Exodus 20:5   183 **Bedlam** lunatic
184 **he** i.e., Arthur.   **her sin** i.e., Eleanor's alleged adultery when she
conceived John. (See ll. 124 ff.)   185 **her sin** i.e., John, the issue of her
sin   186 **removèd issue** distant descendant, i.e., Arthur.   **for her** on her
account   187 **with her plague** i.e., by the offspring, John, with whom
she was cursed.   **his injury** i.e., the wrong done to Arthur   188 **Her
injury** Eleanor's wrong deeds, which act as the officer (*beadle*) to incite
her son John (*her sin*) on to further wrongs   191 **unadvisèd** rash   192 **A
will** i.e., according to Holinshed and other chroniclers, the final testament of Richard Coeur de Lion naming John as his heir and disinherit-
ing Arthur who had been named heir in a previous will. (But Constance
deliberately takes *will* to mean "willfulness.")   196 **ill . . . presence** is
not proper in the presence of royalty   196–197 **cry aim To** encourage.
(An archery term.)   198 **trumpet** trumpeter

These men of Angiers. Let us hear them speak
Whose title they admit, Arthur's or John's.   200

> *Trumpet sounds. Enter citizens [one of them*
> *Hubert] upon the walls.*

HUBERT
Who is it that hath warned us to the walls?   201
KING PHILIP
'Tis France, for England.
KING JOHN   England, for itself.   202
You men of Angiers, and my loving subjects—
KING PHILIP
You loving men of Angiers, Arthur's subjects,
Our trumpet called you to this gentle parle—   205
KING JOHN
For our advantage; therefore hear us first.
These flags of France, that are advancèd here   207
Before the eye and prospect of your town,
Have hither marched to your endamagement.
The cannons have their bowels full of wrath,
And ready mounted are they to spit forth
Their iron indignation 'gainst your walls.
All preparation for a bloody siege
And merciless proceeding by these French
Confronts your city's eyes, your winking gates;   215
And but for our approach those sleeping stones,
That as a waist doth girdle you about,
By the compulsion of their ordinance   218
By this time from their fixèd beds of lime
Had been dishabited, and wide havoc made   220
For bloody power to rush upon your peace.
But on the sight of us your lawful king,
Who painfully, with much expedient march,   223
Have brought a countercheck before your gates

---

200 s.d. upon the walls i.e., in the upper gallery rearstage. (Throughout
this scene, the tiring house facade is visualized as the walls of Angiers.) **201 warned** summoned **202 'Tis France, for England** i.e., it is
the French King, on behalf of Arthur, true King of England **205 parle**
parley **207 advancèd** raised **215 winking** closed **218 their** i.e., *these
French* (l. 214). **ordinance** ordnance, artillery **220 dishabited** dis-
lodged **223 painfully** having taken great pains or care. **expedient**
swift

To save unscratched your city's threatened cheeks,
Behold, the French, amazed, vouchsafe a parle;   226
And now, instead of bullets wrapped in fire,   227
To make a shaking fever in your walls,
They shoot but calm words folded up in smoke   229
To make a faithless error in your ears.   230
Which trust accordingly, kind citizens,   231
And let us in, your king, whose labored spirits,   232
Forwearied in this action of swift speed,   233
Craves harborage within your city walls.

KING PHILIP
When I have said, make answer to us both.   235
Lo, in this right hand, whose protection   236
Is most divinely vowed upon the right   237
Of him it holds, stands young Plantagenet,   238
Son to the elder brother of this man,
And king o'er him and all that he enjoys.   240
For this downtrodden equity we tread   241
In warlike march these greens before your town,
Being no further enemy to you
Than the constraint of hospitable zeal   244
In the relief of this oppressèd child
Religiously provokes. Be pleasèd then
To pay that duty which you truly owe
To him that owes it, namely this young prince;   248
And then our arms, like to a muzzled bear,
Save in aspect, hath all offense sealed up.   250
Our cannons' malice vainly shall be spent
Against th' invulnerable clouds of heaven;
And with a blessèd and unvexed retire,   253
With unhacked swords and helmets all unbruised,
We will bear home that lusty blood again

226 **amazed** stunned   227 **bullets** cannonballs   229 **folded up in smoke**
i.e., deceptively concealed in rhetoric   230 **faithless error** perfidious
lie   231 **trust accordingly** trust as such lies deserve, i.e., not at all
232 **labored** oppressed with labor   233 **Forwearied in** exhausted by
235 **said** finished speaking   236–238 **in . . . holds** i.e., led by my right
hand, which hand is most sacredly committed to defend the right of the
person whose hand it now holds   240 **enjoys** possesses, rules over
241 **For** on behalf of.   **equity** justice, right   244 **constraint** necessity
248 **owes** owns, has a right to   250 **Save in aspect** except in appearance.   **hath . . . up** will see to it that all capacity for injury to you is
sealed up   253 **unvexed retire** unhindered withdrawal

Which here we came to spout against your town,
And leave your children, wives, and you in peace.
But if you fondly pass our proffered offer,   258
'Tis not the roundure of your old-faced walls   259
Can hide you from our messengers of war,   260
Though all these English and their discipline   261
Were harbored in their rude circumference.   262
Then tell us, shall your city call us lord
In that behalf which we have challenged it,   264
Or shall we give the signal to our rage
And stalk in blood to our possession?

HUBERT
In brief, we are the King of England's subjects.
For him, and in his right, we hold this town.

KING JOHN
Acknowledge then the King and let me in.

HUBERT
That can we not. But he that proves the King,   270
To him will we prove loyal. Till that time
Have we rammed up our gates against the world.

KING JOHN
Doth not the crown of England prove the King?
And if not that, I bring you witnesses,
Twice fifteen thousand hearts of England's breed—

BASTARD   Bastards, and else.   276

KING JOHN
To verify our title with their lives.

KING PHILIP
As many and as wellborn bloods as those—   278

BASTARD   Some bastards too.

KING PHILIP
Stand in his face to contradict his claim.   280

HUBERT
Till you compound whose right is worthiest,   281
We for the worthiest hold the right from both.   282

---

258 fondly pass foolishly pass up **259 roundure** roundness, enclosure,
circumference **260 messengers** i.e., cannonballs **261 discipline** military skill **262 rude** rough **264 In . . . which** on behalf of him for
whom **270 proves** i.e., proves himself, proves to be **276 else** others,
suchlike **278 bloods** men of mettle and of good breeding **280 in his
face** opposite to him **281 compound** settle, agree **282 for** in the
interests of. **hold** withhold

KING JOHN
  Then God forgive the sin of all those souls
  That to their everlasting residence,
  Before the dew of evening fall, shall fleet,   285
  In dreadful trial of our kingdom's king!   286
KING PHILIP
  Amen, amen! Mount, chevaliers! To arms!
BASTARD
  Saint George, that swinged the dragon, and e'er since   288
  Sits on 's horseback at mine hostess' door,   289
  Teach us some fence! [*To Austria*.] Sirrah, were I at
    home,   290
  At your den, sirrah, with your lioness,   291
  I would set an ox head to your lion's hide,   292
  And make a monster of you.
AUSTRIA   Peace! No more.
BASTARD
  O, tremble, for you hear the lion roar.
KING JOHN
  Up higher to the plain, where we'll set forth
  In best appointment all our regiments.   296
BASTARD
  Speed then, to take advantage of the field.   297
KING PHILIP
  It shall be so; and at the other hill
  Command the rest to stand. God and our right!   299
                  Exeunt [*separately. The citizens remain
                                above, on the walls.*]

       *Here after excursions, enter the Herald of France,
       with trumpets, to the gates.*

FRENCH HERALD
  You men of Angiers, open wide your gates,

285 fleet fly, leave (their bodies)   **286 dreadful trial** fearful encounter,
contest (with a suggestion too of the soul's *dreadful trial* before God).
of . . . king to determine who is king of our kingdom   **288 swinged**
whipped, thrashed   **289 Sits . . . door** (One of the most common signs at
tavern doors was that of Saint George and the dragon.)   **290 fence** skill
in swordsmanship   **291 lioness** (with a suggestion of "whore")   **292 set
an ox head** i.e., give you the horns of a cuckold   **296 appointment** order,
readiness   **297 take . . . field** gain tactical position   **299 the rest** i.e.,
our reserve forces.   **s.d. excursions** skirmishes, sorties

And let young Arthur, Duke of Brittaine, in,
Who by the hand of France this day hath made   302
Much work for tears in many an English mother,   303
Whose sons lie scattered on the bleeding ground.
Many a widow's husband groveling lies,
Coldly embracing the discolored earth,
And victory, with little loss, doth play
Upon the dancing banners of the French,
Who are at hand, triumphantly displayed,   309
To enter conquerors and to proclaim
Arthur of Brittaine England's king and yours.   311

    Enter English Herald, with trumpet.

ENGLISH HERALD
Rejoice, you men of Angiers, ring your bells!
King John, your king and England's, doth approach,
Commander of this hot malicious day.   314
Their armors, that marched hence so silver bright,
Hither return all gilt with Frenchmen's blood.   316
There stuck no plume in any English crest   317
That is removèd by a staff of France.   318
Our colors do return in those same hands   319
That did display them when we first marched forth;   320
And like a jolly troop of huntsmen come
Our lusty English, all with purpled hands   322
Dyed in the dying slaughter of their foes.   323
Open your gates and give the victors way.

HUBERT
Heralds, from off our towers we might behold,
From first to last, the onset and retire   326

302 by . . . France with the aid of the French King   **303 work** cause
309 triumphantly displayed deployed or arranged for a triumphal
celebration   **311 s.d. trumpet** trumpeter   **314 Commander** victor.   **hot
malicious day** a day hotly and violently contested   **316 gilt** gilded in
red   **317–318 There . . . France** i.e., no English helmet was so dishonored as to have the plume of its crest struck off by a French spear.
staff spear   **319–320 Our . . . forth** i.e., we have not been obliged to
strike our colors   **322 lusty** vigorous   **323 Dyed . . . foes** (Huntsmen
dipped their hands in the blood of a slain deer to celebrate the slaughter.)   **326 onset and retire** attack and retreat

Of both your armies, whose equality   327
By our best eyes cannot be censurèd.   328
Blood hath bought blood, and blows have answered
    blows,
Strength matched with strength, and power confronted
    power.
Both are alike, and both alike we like.
One must prove greatest. While they weigh so even,
We hold our town for neither, yet for both.   333

> *Enter the two Kings, with their powers, at several*
> *doors: [King John with Queen Eleanor, Blanche,*
> *the Bastard, and forces at one door, King Philip*
> *with Lewis, Austria, and forces at the other.]*

KING JOHN
France, hast thou yet more blood to cast away?
Say, shall the current of our right run on,
Whose passage, vexed with thy impediment,
Shall leave his native channel and o'erswell   337
With course disturbed even thy confining shores,   338
Unless thou let his silver water keep
A peaceful progress to the ocean?
KING PHILIP
England, thou hast not saved one drop of blood
In this hot trial more than we of France;
Rather, lost more. And by this hand I swear,
That sways the earth this climate overlooks,   344
Before we will lay down our just-borne arms,
We'll put thee down, 'gainst whom these arms we bear,
Or add a royal number to the dead,   347
Gracing the scroll that tells of this war's loss
With slaughter coupled to the name of kings.

327–328 whose . . . censurèd whose equality is such that our keenest
observations cannot determine any difference   **333 s.d. powers** armies. **several** separate   **337 his native** its normal   **338 even . . . shores**
(John hints that his might, fully roused in defense of what he claims for
his own right, will spill over into French territory.)   **344 climate** portion
of the sky   **347 a royal number** i.e., a king's name. (King Philip will win
or die in the attempt, and perhaps take other kings with him.)

BASTARD
　Ha, majesty! How high thy glory towers   350
　When the rich blood of kings is set on fire!
　O, now doth Death line his dead chaps with steel;   352
　The swords of soldiers are his teeth, his fangs;
　And now he feasts, mousing the flesh of men   354
　In undetermined differences of kings.   355
　Why stand these royal fronts amazèd thus?   356
　Cry havoc, Kings! Back to the stainèd field,   357
　You equal potents, fiery-kindled spirits!   358
　Then let confusion of one part confirm   359
　The other's peace. Till then, blows, blood, and death!

KING JOHN
　Whose party do the townsmen yet admit?   361

KING PHILIP
　Speak, citizens, for England. Who's your king?

HUBERT
　The King of England, when we know the king.

KING PHILIP
　Know him in us, that here hold up his right.

KING JOHN
　In us, that are our own great deputy
　And bear possession of our person here,   366
　Lord of our presence, Angiers, and of you.   367

HUBERT
　A greater power than we denies all this,
　And, till it be undoubted, we do lock
　Our former scruple in our strong-barred gates,
　Kinged of our fear, until our fears, resolved,   371
　Be by some certain king purged and deposed.

BASTARD
　By heaven, these scroyles of Angiers flout you, Kings,   373
　And stand securely on their battlements
　As in a theater, whence they gape and point

350 **How . . . towers** to what height the glory-seeking spirit of majesty
soars. (An image from hawking.) **352 chaps** jaws **354 mousing** tearing,
gnawing **355 undetermined differences** unsettled quarrels **356 royal
fronts** i.e., faces of kings **357 Cry havoc** proclaim a general slaughter
with no taking of prisoners **358 potents** potentates **359 confusion**
destruction, overthrow. **part** faction, party **361 yet** now **366 bear . . .
person** embody the claims of sovereignty in my own person, needing no
deputy **367 Lord of our presence** my own master **371 Kinged of** ruled
by **373 scroyles** scoundrels

At your industrious scenes and acts of death.
Your royal presences be ruled by me: 377
Do like the mutines of Jerusalem,   378
Be friends awhile, and both conjointly bend   379
Your sharpest deeds of malice on this town.
By east and west let France and England mount
Their battering cannon chargèd to the mouths,   382
Till their soul-fearing clamors have brawled down   383
The flinty ribs of this contemptuous city.
I'd play incessantly upon these jades,   385
Even till unfencèd desolation   386
Leave them as naked as the vulgar air.   387
That done, dissever your united strengths
And part your mingled colors once again;
Turn face to face and bloody point to point.
Then, in a moment, Fortune shall cull forth
Out of one side her happy minion,   392
To whom in favor she shall give the day   393
And kiss him with a glorious victory.
How like you this wild counsel, mighty states?   395
Smacks it not something of the policy?   396
KING JOHN
Now, by the sky that hangs above our heads,
I like it well. France, shall we knit our powers
And lay this Angiers even with the ground,
Then after fight who shall be king of it?
BASTARD [*To King Philip*]
An if thou hast the mettle of a king,
Being wronged as we are by this peevish town,   402
Turn thou the mouth of thy artillery,
As we will ours, against these saucy walls;
And when that we have dashed them to the ground,   405

377 Your royal presences may Your Majesties   **378 mutines** muti-
neers.   **Jerusalem** (During the siege of Jerusalem by Titus, A.D. 70, two
rival Jewish factions united to resist the Romans.)   **379 conjointly bend**
together aim   **382 chargèd to the mouths** filled to the brim with shot
383 soul-fearing inspiring fear in the soul.   **brawled down** i.e., noisily
leveled   **385 play . . . jades** i.e., (1) fire cannon repeatedly upon these
wretches (2) torment these nags. (*Jades* are ill-conditioned horses.)
386 unfencèd defenseless   **387 vulgar** common   **392 minion** favorite
393 give the day award the victory   **395 states** kings   **396 something**
somewhat.   **the policy** the art of politics, a canny maneuver
402 peevish stubborn   **405 when that** when

Why, then defy each other, and pell-mell   406
Make work upon ourselves, for heaven or hell.

KING PHILIP
Let it be so. Say, where will you assault?

KING JOHN
We from the west will send destruction
Into this city's bosom.

AUSTRIA   I from the north.

KING PHILIP   Our thunder from the south
Shall rain their drift of bullets on this town.   413

BASTARD
O prudent discipline! From north to south   414
Austria and France shoot in each other's mouth.
I'll stir them to it.—Come, away, away!
                    [*The armies start to move.*]

HUBERT
Hear us, great kings! Vouchsafe awhile to stay,
And I shall show you peace and fair-faced league,
Win you this city without stroke or wound,
Rescue those breathing lives to die in beds
That here come sacrifices for the field.
Persever not, but hear me, mighty kings.   422

KING JOHN
Speak on with favor. We are bent to hear.   423

HUBERT
That daughter there of Spain, the Lady Blanche,
Is near to England. Look upon the years   425
Of Lewis the Dauphin and that lovely maid.
If lusty love should go in quest of beauty,
Where should he find it fairer than in Blanche?
If zealous love should go in search of virtue,   429
Where should he find it purer than in Blanche?
If love ambitious sought a match of birth,   431
Whose veins bound richer blood than Lady Blanche?   432
Such as she is, in beauty, virtue, birth,
Is the young Dauphin every way complete.   434

406 pell-mell headlong   **413 drift** shower.   **bullets** cannonballs
414 prudent discipline fine military skill. (Said sarcastically.)   **422 Persever** persevere   **423 favor** permission.   **bent** inclined   **425 near to
England** a near relative of King John, i.e., his niece   **429 zealous** virtue-
seeking   **431 of birth** i.e., of equal royal rank   **432 bound** contain
434 complete accomplished, perfect in

If not complete of, say he is not she,	435
And she again wants nothing, to name want,	436
If want it be not that she is not he.	437

He is the half part of a blessèd man,
Left to be finishèd by such as she,
And she a fair divided excellence,
Whose fullness of perfection lies in him.
O, two such silver currents, when they join,
Do glorify the banks that bound them in;
And two such shores to two such streams made one,
Two such controlling bounds, shall you be, Kings,
To these two princes, if you marry them.

This union shall do more than battery can	447
To our fast-closèd gates; for at this match,	448
With swifter spleen than powder can enforce,	449

The mouth of passage shall we fling wide ope
And give you entrance. But without this match,
The sea enragèd is not half so deaf,
Lions more confident, mountains and rocks
More free from motion, no, not Death himself

In mortal fury half so peremptory,	455
As we to keep this city.	
BASTARD Here's a stay	456
That shakes the rotten carcass of old Death	457
Out of his rags! Here's a large mouth, indeed,	458

That spits forth Death and mountains, rocks and seas,
Talks as familiarly of roaring lions
As maids of thirteen do of puppy dogs.

What cannoneer begot this lusty blood?	462
He speaks plain cannon: fire and smoke and bounce.	463
He gives the bastinado with his tongue.	464

Our ears are cudgeled; not a word of his

435–437 **If . . . he** (The idea here appears to be that the two young people lack only each other to be perfect in themselves.) **436 wants** lacks   **437 If . . . he** unless it is called a lack that she is not he   **447 battery** artillery   **448 match** (1) marriage (2) fire used to ignite gunpowder   **449 spleen** i.e., eager violent energy   **455 peremptory** determined   **456–458 Here's . . . rags** i.e., here's a pause for consideration, one that shakes things up so that the skeleton of Death itself is shaken out of its rags and tatters.   **stay** hindrance, obstacle   **458 mouth** i.e., like the mouth of a cannon, but spewing forth rhetoric   **462 lusty blood** hot-blooded chap. (Said sardonically.)   **463 bounce** i.e., the noise of the cannon   **464 bastinado** beating with a cudgel

But buffets better than a fist of France.
Zounds! I was never so bethumped with words   467
Since I first called my brother's father Dad.   468
                    [*The French confer apart.*]
ELEANOR [*To King John*]
Son, list to this conjunction; make this match.   469
Give with our niece a dowry large enough,
For by this knot thou shalt so surely tie
Thy now unsured assurance to the crown
That yon green boy shall have no sun to ripe   473
The bloom that promiseth a mighty fruit.
I see a yielding in the looks of France;
Mark how they whisper. Urge them while their souls
Are capable of this ambition,   477
Lest zeal, now melted by the windy breath   478
Of soft petitions, pity, and remorse,   479
Cool and congeal again to what it was.

HUBERT
Why answer not the double majesties
This friendly treaty of our threatened town?   482

KING PHILIP
Speak England first, that hath been forward first
To speak unto this city. What say you?

KING JOHN
If that the Dauphin there, thy princely son,   485
Can in this book of beauty read "I love,"   486
Her dowry shall weigh equal with a queen;
For Anjou and fair Touraine, Maine, Poitiers,
And all that we upon this side the sea—
Except this city now by us besieged—
Find liable to our crown and dignity,   491
Shall gild her bridal bed and make her rich

---

467 Zounds by God's (Christ's) wounds   **468 Since . . . Dad** i.e., since I
learned to speak. (Colloquial, but here with particular fitness to the
Bastard's illegitimacy.)   **469 list** listen   **473 green** youthful, hence
unripe.   **boy** i.e., Arthur   **477 capable of** susceptible to.   **ambition** i.e.,
scheme that might seem to their advantage   **478 zeal** i.e., the French
King's zeal in Arthur's behalf. (The metaphor is one of melting and
hardening wax.)   **479 remorse** compassion   **482 treaty** proposal   **485 If
that** if   **486 book . . . "I love"** (An allusion to William Lilly's famous
Latin grammar, in which the verb *amo*, "I love," was used as a para-
digm.)   **491 Find liable** regard as subject

In titles, honors, and promotions,   493
As she in beauty, education, blood,
Holds hand with any princess of the world.   495

KING PHILIP
What sayst thou, boy? Look in the lady's face.

LEWIS
I do, my lord, and in her eye I find
A wonder, or a wondrous miracle,
The shadow of myself formed in her eye,   499
Which, being but the shadow of your son,   500
Becomes a sun and makes your son a shadow.   501
I do protest I never loved myself
Till now infixèd I beheld myself
Drawn in the flattering table of her eye.   504
                              Whispers with Blanche.

BASTARD
Drawn in the flattering table of her eye!   505
   Hanged in the frowning wrinkle of her brow
And quartered in her heart! He doth espy   507
   Himself love's traitor. This is pity now,
That, hanged and drawn and quartered, there should be
In such a love so vile a lout as he.   510

BLANCHE [*To Lewis*]
My uncle's will in this respect is mine.
If he see aught in you that makes him like,
That anything he sees which moves his liking   513
I can with ease translate it to my will;   514
Or if you will, to speak more properly,   515
I will enforce it easily to my love.

493 **promotions** elevations, advancements in courtly degree   495 **Holds
hand with** equals   499 **shadow** image, reflection   500 **being** from
being.   **shadow** pale and substanceless imitation   501 **a shadow** i.e., a
mere shaded area contrasted with the sun's brightness. (The Dauphin
poetically describes a *miracle* in which his new self, formed in
Blanche's eye, casts into the shade his former self.)   504 **Drawn** pictured.   **table** tablet or flat surface on which the picture is painted
505 **Drawn** (with a pun on the meaning "disemboweled." The pun is
continued in the next two lines in *Hanged* and *quartered;* Elizabethan
punishment for traitors specified that they be *hanged,* taken down while
still alive, *drawn,* or disemboweled, and *quartered,* or cut up.)
507 **quartered** (with a pun on the meaning "lodged," and, in heraldry,
"placed quarterly on a shield or coat of arms")   510 **love** (1) profession
of love (2) lover   513 **That anything** whatever   514 **will** desire
515 **properly** exactly

Further I will not flatter you, my lord,
That all I see in you is worthy love,
Than this: that nothing do I see in you,
Though churlish thoughts themselves should be your
    judge,   520
That I can find should merit any hate.

KING JOHN
What say these young ones? What say you, my niece?

BLANCHE
That she is bound in honor still to do   523
What you in wisdom still vouchsafe to say.   524

KING JOHN
Speak then, Prince Dauphin. Can you love this lady?

LEWIS
Nay, ask me if I can refrain from love,
For I do love her most unfeignedly.

KING JOHN
Then do I give Volquessen, Touraine, Maine,
Poitiers, and Anjou, these five provinces,
With her to thee, and this addition more,
Full thirty thousand marks of English coin.   531
Philip of France, if thou be pleased withal,   532
Command thy son and daughter to join hands.   533

KING PHILIP
It likes us well. Young princes, close your hands.   534
    [*Lewis and Blanche exchange pledges of love.*]

AUSTRIA
And your lips too, for I am well assured
That I did so when I was first assured.   [*They kiss.*] 536

KING PHILIP
Now, citizens of Angiers, ope your gates.
Let in that amity which you have made,
For at Saint Mary's chapel presently   539
The rites of marriage shall be solemnized.
Is not the Lady Constance in this troop?
I know she is not, for this match made up   542

---

520 churlish sparing of praise   **523, 524 still** always   **531 marks** (A mark was the equivalent of 13 shillings 4 pence.)   **532 withal** with this   **533 daughter** i.e., future daughter-in-law   **534 likes** pleases. **close** clasp   **536 assured** betrothed (with a play on *assured*, "certain," in l. 535)   **539 presently** at once   **542 made up** arranged, concluded

Her presence would have interrupted much.
Where is she and her son? Tell me, who knows.   544
LEWIS
She is sad and passionate at Your Highness' tent.   545
KING PHILIP
And, by my faith, this league that we have made
Will give her sadness very little cure.
Brother of England, how may we content
This widow lady? In her right we came,
Which we, God knows, have turned another way,
To our own vantage.
KING JOHN   We will heal up all,
For we'll create young Arthur Duke of Brittaine
And Earl of Richmond, and this rich, fair town
We make him lord of. Call the Lady Constance.
Some speedy messenger bid her repair   555
To our solemnity. I trust we shall,   556
If not fill up the measure of her will,   557
Yet in some measure satisfy her so   558
That we shall stop her exclamation.   559
Go we, as well as haste will suffer us,   560
To this unlooked-for, unpreparèd pomp.
                    Exeunt [all but the Bastard].
BASTARD
Mad world, mad kings, mad composition!   562
John, to stop Arthur's title in the whole,
Hath willingly departed with a part;   564
And France, whose armor conscience buckled on,
Whom zeal and charity brought to the field
As God's own soldier, rounded in the ear   567
With that same purpose-changer, that sly devil,   568
That broker that still breaks the pate of faith,   569
That daily break-vow, he that wins of all,   570
Of kings, of beggars, old men, young men, maids—
Who, having no external thing to lose   572

544 who whoever 545 passionate filled with passionate sorrow
555 repair come 556 our solemnity i.e., the wedding 557 the measure
the full measure and extent 558 so in such a way 559 exclamation
complaint 560 suffer allow 562 composition agreement, compromise 564 departed with given up 567 rounded whispered to
568 With by 569 broker go-between (with a pun on "one who
breaks"). still . . . faith continually knocks loyalty and truth over the
head 570 wins of gets the better of 572 Who i.e., the maids

But the word "maid," cheats the poor maid of that—   573
That smooth-faced gentleman, tickling Commodity,   574
Commodity, the bias of the world—   575
The world, who of itself is peisèd well,   576
Made to run even upon even ground,
Till this advantage, this vile-drawing bias,   578
This sway of motion, this Commodity,   579
Makes it take head from all indifferency,   580
From all direction, purpose, course, intent.
And this same bias, this Commodity,
This bawd, this broker, this all-changing word,   583
Clapped on the outward eye of fickle France,   584
Hath drawn him from his own determined aid,   585
From a resolved and honorable war,   586
To a most base and vile-concluded peace.
And why rail I on this Commodity?
But for because he hath not wooed me yet.   589
Not that I have the power to clutch my hand   590
When his fair angels would salute my palm,   591
But for my hand, as unattempted yet,   592
Like a poor beggar, raileth on the rich.
Well, whiles I am a beggar, I will rail
And say there is no sin but to be rich;
And being rich, my virtue then shall be
To say there is no vice but beggary.
Since kings break faith upon commodity,   598
Gain, be my lord, for I will worship thee.   *Exit.*

❖

573 cheats i.e., he, Commodity, cheats   **574 smooth-faced** bland, plausible.   **tickling Commodity** flattering self-interest   **575 bias** swaying influence. (From the game of bowls, in which a weight in the side of a bowl caused it to curve.)   **576 peisèd** balanced, in equilibrium   **578 advantage** advantage-seeking Commodity.   **vile-drawing** attracting to evil   **579 sway of motion** swaying or controlling of motion from its intended course   **580 take . . . indifferency** rush away from all balanced, equal motion   **583 all-changing** causing change in everything   **584 Clapped on** stuck on, presented to.   **outward eye** (1) eyeball (2) hole in the bowling ball where the lead creating the "bias" was inserted.   **France** i.e., the King of France. (Commodity, presented to King Philip's eye in the guise of the marriage treaty, has acted like the bias in a bowling ball to divert him from his former intention.)   **585 his . . . aid** the aid he had determined to give Arthur   **586 resolved** resolved upon   **589 But for** merely   **590 clutch** clench (in a gesture of refusal)   **591 angels** coins bearing the figure of an angel, worth 10 shillings.   **salute** kiss (with a pun on the idea of an angelic salutation)   **592 unattempted** untempted   **598 upon** because of

3.1 *Enter Constance, Arthur, and Salisbury.*

CONSTANCE
  Gone to be married? Gone to swear a peace?
  False blood to false blood joined! Gone to be friends?
  Shall Lewis have Blanche, and Blanche those provinces?
  It is not so; thou hast misspoke, misheard.
  Be well advised; tell o'er thy tale again.   5
  It cannot be; thou dost but say 'tis so.
  I trust I may not trust thee, for thy word
  Is but the vain breath of a common man.   8
  Believe me, I do not believe thee, man;
  I have a king's oath to the contrary.
  Thou shalt be punished for thus frighting me,
  For I am sick and capable of fears,   12
  Oppressed with wrongs, and therefore full of fears,
  A widow, husbandless, subject to fears,
  A woman, naturally born to fears;
  And though thou now confess thou didst but jest,
  With my vexed spirits I cannot take a truce,   17
  But they will quake and tremble all this day.
  What dost thou mean by shaking of thy head?
  Why dost thou look so sadly on my son?
  What means that hand upon that breast of thine?
  Why holds thine eye that lamentable rheum,   22
  Like a proud river peering o'er his bounds?   23
  Be these sad signs confirmers of thy words?
  Then speak again—not all thy former tale,
  But this one word, whether thy tale be true.
SALISBURY
  As true as I believe you think them false   27
  That give you cause to prove my saying true.
CONSTANCE
  O, if thou teach me to believe this sorrow,
  Teach thou this sorrow how to make me die!
  And let belief and life encounter so
  As doth the fury of two desperate men

3.1. Location: France. The French King's quarters.
5 Be well advised be sure of what you are saying **8 a common man** i.e.,
a subject, not a king **12 capable of** susceptible to **17 take a truce**
make peace **22 lamentable rheum** sad moisture, i.e., tears **23 peering
o'er his** i.e., overflowing its **27 them** i.e., the French

Which in the very meeting fall and die.
Lewis marry Blanche? O boy, then where art thou?
France friend with England, what becomes of me?
[*To Salisbury*.] Fellow, begone! I cannot brook thy sight. 36
This news hath made thee a most ugly man.
SALISBURY
What other harm have I, good lady, done,
But spoke the harm that is by others done?
CONSTANCE
Which harm within itself so heinous is
As it makes harmful all that speak of it.
ARTHUR
I do beseech you, madam, be content.   42
CONSTANCE
If thou that bidd'st me be content wert grim,
Ugly, and slanderous to thy mother's womb,   44
Full of unpleasing blots and sightless stains,   45
Lame, foolish, crooked, swart, prodigious,   46
Patched with foul moles and eye-offending marks, 47
I would not care, I then would be content,
For then I should not love thee, no, nor thou
Become thy great birth nor deserve a crown.   50
But thou art fair, and at thy birth, dear boy,
Nature and Fortune joined to make thee great.
Of Nature's gifts thou mayst with lilies boast,
And with the half-blown rose. But Fortune, O,   54
She is corrupted, changed, and won from thee.
Sh' adulterates hourly with thine uncle John,   56
And with her golden hand hath plucked on France   57
To tread down fair respect of sovereignty,   58
And made his majesty the bawd to theirs.   59
France is a bawd to Fortune and King John,
That strumpet Fortune, that usurping John!

36 brook endure **42 content** calm **44 slanderous** disgraceful
45 sightless unsightly **46 swart** swarthy. **prodigious** monstrous, an
evil omen **47 Patched** blotched **50 Become** befit **54 half-blown** only
partly opened, still young **56 adulterates** commits adultery **57 golden**
i.e., offering gold **57–59 hath plucked on . . . theirs** i.e., she, Fortune,
has induced the King of France to tread underfoot Arthur's rights of
sovereignty, and has made the King of France the bawd between Fortune and King John

[*To Salisbury.*] Tell me, thou fellow, is not France
  forsworn?   62
Envenom him with words, or get thee gone   63
And leave those woes alone which I alone   64
Am bound to underbear.
SALISBURY   Pardon me, madam,   65
I may not go without you to the kings.
CONSTANCE
Thou mayst, thou shalt. I will not go with thee.
I will instruct my sorrows to be proud,
For grief is proud and makes his owner stoop.
                      [*She sits on the ground.*]
To me and to the state of my great grief   70
Let kings assemble, for my grief's so great
That no supporter but the huge, firm earth
Can hold it up. Here I and sorrows sit.
Here is my throne; bid kings come bow to it.

    Enter King John, [King Philip of] France, [Lewis
    the] Dauphin, Blanche, Eleanor, Philip [the
    Bastard], Austria, [and attendants]. [The two
    kings are arm in arm.]

KING PHILIP
'Tis true, fair daughter, and this blessèd day
Ever in France shall be kept festival.
To solemnize this day the glorious sun
Stays in his course and plays the alchemist,   78
Turning with splendor of his precious eye
The meager cloddy earth to glittering gold.
The yearly course that brings this day about
Shall never see it but a holy day.
CONSTANCE [*Rising*]
A wicked day, and not a holy day!
What hath this day deserved? What hath it done,
That it in golden letters should be set   85

---

62 is not France forsworn hasn't the French King broken his oath
63 Envenom . . . words i.e., curse him for being forsworn, as I do.
Envenom poison   **64 leave those woes alone** leave behind only those
woes   **65 underbear** endure   **70 state** majesty, as in a chair of state
78 Stays in his course stands still   **85 golden** i.e., red

Among the high tides in the calendar?   86
Nay, rather turn this day out of the week,
This day of shame, oppression, perjury.
Or if it must stand still, let wives with child   89
Pray that their burdens may not fall this day,
Lest that their hopes prodigiously be crossed.   91
But on this day let seamen fear no wreck;   92
No bargains break that are not this day made.   93
This day, all things begun come to ill end,
Yea, faith itself to hollow falsehood change!

KING PHILIP
By heaven, lady, you shall have no cause
To curse the fair proceedings of this day.
Have I not pawned to you my majesty?   98

CONSTANCE
You have beguiled me with a counterfeit
Resembling majesty, which, being touched and tried,   100
Proves valueless. You are forsworn, forsworn!
You came in arms to spill mine enemies' blood,   102
But now in arms you strengthen it with yours.   103
The grappling vigor and rough frown of war
Is cold in amity and painted peace,   105
And our oppression hath made up this league.   106
Arm, arm, you heavens, against these perjured kings!
A widow cries; be husband to me, heavens!   108
Let not the hours of this ungodly day
Wear out the day in peace, but ere sunset
Set armèd discord twixt these perjured kings!
Hear me, O, hear me!

AUSTRIA   Lady Constance, peace!

CONSTANCE
War, war, no peace! Peace is to me a war.
O Limoges, O Austria, thou dost shame   114

86 high tides i.e., great festivals   89 stand still remain   91 prodigiously
be crossed be thwarted by some monstrous birth defect   92 But except,
other than (since this is the most evil of days).   wreck shipwreck
93 No . . . made break only agreements made on this day   98 pawned
pledged.   my majesty i.e., my kingly word   100 touched tested (as one
tests gold by rubbing it on a touchstone)   102 in arms in armor   103 in
arms embracing.   with yours i.e., by uniting your enemies to your royal
house in marriage   105 painted specious, unreal   106 our oppression
our being oppressed   108 A widow cries it is a widow that cries
114 Limoges (Cf 2.1.5 note.)

3.1 *Enter Constance, Arthur, and Salisbury.*

CONSTANCE
 Gone to be married? Gone to swear a peace?
 False blood to false blood joined! Gone to be friends?
 Shall Lewis have Blanche, and Blanche those provinces?
 It is not so; thou hast misspoke, misheard.
 Be well advised; tell o'er thy tale again.   5
 It cannot be; thou dost but say 'tis so.
 I trust I may not trust thee, for thy word
 Is but the vain breath of a common man.   8
 Believe me, I do not believe thee, man;
 I have a king's oath to the contrary.
 Thou shalt be punished for thus frighting me,
 For I am sick and capable of fears,   12
 Oppressed with wrongs, and therefore full of fears,
 A widow, husbandless, subject to fears,
 A woman, naturally born to fears;
 And though thou now confess thou didst but jest,
 With my vexed spirits I cannot take a truce,   17
 But they will quake and tremble all this day.
 What dost thou mean by shaking of thy head?
 Why dost thou look so sadly on my son?
 What means that hand upon that breast of thine?
 Why holds thine eye that lamentable rheum,   22
 Like a proud river peering o'er his bounds?   23
 Be these sad signs confirmers of thy words?
 Then speak again—not all thy former tale,
 But this one word, whether thy tale be true.
SALISBURY
 As true as I believe you think them false   27
 That give you cause to prove my saying true.
CONSTANCE
 O, if thou teach me to believe this sorrow,
 Teach thou this sorrow how to make me die!
 And let belief and life encounter so
 As doth the fury of two desperate men

3.1. Location: France. The French King's quarters.
5 Be well advised be sure of what you are saying **8 a common man** i.e.,
a subject, not a king **12 capable of** susceptible to **17 take a truce**
make peace **22 lamentable rheum** sad moisture, i.e., tears **23 peering**
o'er his i.e., overflowing its **27 them** i.e., the French

Which in the very meeting fall and die.
Lewis marry Blanche? O boy, then where art thou?
France friend with England, what becomes of me?
[*To Salisbury.*] Fellow, begone! I cannot brook thy sight. 36
This news hath made thee a most ugly man.
SALISBURY
What other harm have I, good lady, done,
But spoke the harm that is by others done?
CONSTANCE
Which harm within itself so heinous is
As it makes harmful all that speak of it.
ARTHUR
I do beseech you, madam, be content.   42
CONSTANCE
If thou that bidd'st me be content wert grim,
Ugly, and slanderous to thy mother's womb,   44
Full of unpleasing blots and sightless stains,   45
Lame, foolish, crooked, swart, prodigious,   46
Patched with foul moles and eye-offending marks,   47
I would not care, I then would be content,
For then I should not love thee, no, nor thou
Become thy great birth nor deserve a crown.   50
But thou art fair, and at thy birth, dear boy,
Nature and Fortune joined to make thee great.
Of Nature's gifts thou mayst with lilies boast,
And with the half-blown rose. But Fortune, O,   54
She is corrupted, changed, and won from thee.
Sh' adulterates hourly with thine uncle John,   56
And with her golden hand hath plucked on France   57
To tread down fair respect of sovereignty,   58
And made his majesty the bawd to theirs.   59
France is a bawd to Fortune and King John,
That strumpet Fortune, that usurping John!

36 brook endure   **42 content** calm   **44 slanderous** disgraceful
45 sightless unsightly   **46 swart** swarthy.   **prodigious** monstrous, an
evil omen   **47 Patched** blotched   **50 Become** befit   **54 half-blown** only
partly opened, still young   **56 adulterates** commits adultery   **57 golden**
i.e., offering gold   **57–59 hath plucked on . . . theirs** i.e., she, Fortune,
has induced the King of France to tread underfoot Arthur's rights of
sovereignty, and has made the King of France the bawd between Fortune and King John

That bloody spoil. Thou slave, thou wretch, thou
   coward!   115
Thou little valiant, great in villainy!
Thou ever strong upon the stronger side!
Thou Fortune's champion, that dost never fight
But when her humorous ladyship is by   119
To teach thee safety! Thou art perjured too,   120
And sooth'st up greatness. What a fool art thou,   121
A ramping fool, to brag and stamp and swear   122
Upon my party! Thou cold-blooded slave,   123
Hast thou not spoke like thunder on my side,
Been sworn my soldier, bidding me depend
Upon thy stars, thy fortune, and thy strength?
And dost thou now fall over to my foes?   127
Thou wear a lion's hide! Doff it for shame,
And hang a calfskin on those recreant limbs.   129

AUSTRIA
  O, that a man should speak those words to me!

BASTARD
  And hang a calfskin on those recreant limbs.

AUSTRIA
  Thou dar'st not say so, villain, for thy life.

BASTARD
  And hang a calfskin on those recreant limbs.

KING JOHN [*To Bastard*]
  We like not this. Thou dost forget thyself.

    Enter Pandulph.

KING PHILIP
  Here comes the holy legate of the Pope.

PANDULPH
  Hail, you anointed deputies of heaven!
  To thee, King John, my holy errand is.
  I, Pandulph, of fair Milan cardinal,
  And from Pope Innocent the legate here,
  Do in his name religiously demand

---

115 spoil booty, i.e., the lion's pelt that Austria wears   **119 humorous**
capricious   **120 safety** i.e., how to choose the safe side   **121 sooth'st up
greatness** flatter the influential   **122 ramping** making a fierce show
123 Upon my party in my behalf   **127 fall over** go over, desert
129 calfskin (Customarily used to make coats for the fools kept to
amuse great families.)   **recreant** cowardly, having deserted his cause

Why thou against the Church, our holy mother,
So willfully dost spurn, and force perforce   142
Keep Stephen Langton, chosen Archbishop   143
Of Canterbury, from that Holy See.
This, in our foresaid Holy Father's name,
Pope Innocent, I do demand of thee.

KING JOHN
What earthy name to interrogatories   147
Can taste the free breath of a sacred king?   148
Thou canst not, Cardinal, devise a name
So slight, unworthy, and ridiculous,
To charge me to an answer, as the Pope.   151
Tell him this tale, and from the mouth of England
Add thus much more: that no Italian priest
Shall tithe or toll in our dominions;   154
But as we, under God, are supreme head,   155
So, under Him, that great supremacy
Where we do reign we will alone uphold
Without th' assistance of a mortal hand.
So tell the Pope, all reverence set apart
To him and his usurped authority.

KING PHILIP
Brother of England, you blaspheme in this.

KING JOHN
Though you and all the kings of Christendom
Are led so grossly by this meddling priest,   163
Dreading the curse that money may buy out,   164
And by the merit of vile gold, dross, dust,
Purchase corrupted pardon of a man

142 spurn oppose scornfully. (Literally, "kick.") **force perforce** violently **143 Stephen Langton** Pope Innocent's choice to be Archbishop of Canterbury, whose rejection by King John led to a papal bull of deposition and eventual resolution only after John had been forced to pay tribute and acknowledge England to be a papal fiefdom **147–148 What . . . king** what secular official can put the free breath of a sacred king to the test by asking it so submit to formal questioning. **taste** test. (Many editors emend to *task*.) **151 charge . . . answer** command me to answer **154 tithe** impose tithes, a tenth of one's income given to the Church. **toll** collect taxes **155 supreme head** (The title assumed by Henry VIII at the time of the Reformation.) **163 led** led astray. **this meddling priest** i.e., the Pope **164 the curse . . . out** i.e., excommunication, which a bribe to Rome can fix

Who in that sale sells pardon from himself,   167
Though you and all the rest, so grossly led,
This juggling witchcraft with revenue cherish,   169
Yet I alone, alone do me oppose
Against the Pope, and count his friends my foes.

PANDULPH
Then, by the lawful power that I have,
Thou shalt stand cursed and excommunicate;
And blessèd shall he be that doth revolt
From his allegiance to an heretic;
And meritorious shall that hand be called,
Canonizèd and worshiped as a saint,
That takes away by any secret course
Thy hateful life.

CONSTANCE   O, lawful let it be
That I have room with Rome to curse awhile!   180
Good father Cardinal, cry thou "Amen"
To my keen curses, for without my wrong   182
There is no tongue hath power to curse him right.

PANDULPH
There's law and warrant, lady, for my curse.

CONSTANCE
And for mine too. When law can do no right,   185
Let it be lawful that law bar no wrong.   186
Law cannot give my child his kingdom here,
For he that holds his kingdom holds the law;   188
Therefore, since law itself is perfect wrong,
How can the law forbid my tongue to curse?

PANDULPH
Philip of France, on peril of a curse,   191
Let go the hand of that arch-heretic,

---

167 Who . . . himself i.e., who, in selling indulgences, incurs his own
damnation. (*From himself* may also suggest that the pardon stems only
from him, not from God, and is therefore invalid.)   **169 juggling** cheating, deceiving.   **cherish** maintain   **180 room, Rome** (An obvious pun,
pronounced alike in Elizabethan England.)   **182 without my wrong** i.e.,
(1) without recognition of the wrong done to me (2) without the motive
of suffering wrongs as I have suffered   **185–186 When . . . wrong** i.e.,
when the law itself is powerless to remedy evils, people must be free to
pursue wrongful remedies (such as cursing)   **188 holds the law** i.e.,
holds the law hostage   **191 a curse** excommunication

And raise the power of France upon his head
Unless he do submit himself to Rome.

ELEANOR
Look'st thou pale, France? Do not let go thy hand.

CONSTANCE [*To Eleanor*]
Look to it, devil, lest that France repent,   196
And by disjoining hands, hell lose a soul.

AUSTRIA
King Philip, listen to the Cardinal.

BASTARD
And hang a calfskin on his recreant limbs.

AUSTRIA
Well, ruffian, I must pocket up these wrongs,   200
Because—

BASTARD   Your breeches best may carry them.

KING JOHN
Philip, what sayst thou to the Cardinal?

CONSTANCE
What should he say, but as the Cardinal?   203

LEWIS
Bethink you, Father, for the difference   204
Is purchase of a heavy curse from Rome
Or the light loss of England for a friend.
Forgo the easier.

BLANCHE   That's the curse of Rome.

CONSTANCE
O Lewis, stand fast! The devil tempts thee here
In likeness of a new, untrimmèd bride.   209

BLANCHE
The Lady Constance speaks not from her faith
But from her need.

CONSTANCE [*To King Philip*]   O, if thou grant my need,

196 Look to it see to it, take care.   **devil** i.e., Eleanor, or the devil
himself.   **lest that** lest   **200 pocket up** submit to. (But the Bastard
plays on the literal sense of putting in one's breeches pocket, perhaps
suggesting further that Austria will get a swift kick in the breeches.)
203 but as the Cardinal except what the Cardinal has already spoken
and as he would be expected to speak   **204 difference** choice   **209 untrimmèd** i.e., freshly married, unshorn (suggesting she is still a virgin).
(Alludes to the temptation of Saint Anthony by the devil in the form of a
naked woman.)

Which only lives but by the death of faith,   212
That need must needs infer this principle: 213
That faith would live again by death of need.   214
O, then tread down my need, and faith mounts up;   215
Keep my need up, and faith is trodden down!
KING JOHN
The King is moved, and answers not to this.
CONSTANCE [*To King Philip*]
O, be removed from him, and answer well!   218
AUSTRIA
Do so, King Philip. Hang no more in doubt.
BASTARD
Hang nothing but a calfskin, most sweet lout.   220
KING PHILIP
I am perplexed and know not what to say.
PANDULPH
What canst thou say but will perplex thee more,
If thou stand excommunicate and cursed?
KING PHILIP
Good Reverend Father, make my person yours,   224
And tell me how you would bestow yourself.   225
This royal hand and mine are newly knit,
And the conjunction of our inward souls
Married in league, coupled and linked together
With all religious strength of sacred vows.
The latest breath that gave the sound of words   230
Was deep-sworn faith, peace, amity, true love
Between our kingdoms and our royal selves;
And even before this truce, but new before,   233
No longer than we well could wash our hands
To clap this royal bargain up of peace,   235

212 **Which . . . faith** i.e., which need is so strong that I must put it ahead of matters of faith and promise-keeping   213 **needs infer** necessarily imply   214 **That . . . need** i.e., my faith will be rekindled once my prior and compelling necessity, Arthur's claim, has been satisfied   215 **tread down** i.e., put down by satisfying, subdue   218 **removed** separated (playing on *moved* in l. 217)   220 **Hang** i.e., wear (playing on *Hang*, hesitate, in l. 219)   224 **make . . . yours** put yourself in my place   225 **bestow** conduct   230 **latest** most recent   233 **even before** just before. **but new** immediately   235 **clap . . . up** i.e., conclude with a grasping of hands

Heaven knows, they were besmeared and overstained
With slaughter's pencil, where revenge did paint   237
The fearful difference of incensèd kings.   238
And shall these hands, so lately purged of blood,
So newly joined in love, so strong in both,   240
Unyoke this seizure and this kind regreet?   241
Play fast and loose with faith? So jest with heaven,
Make such unconstant children of ourselves,
As now again to snatch our palm from palm,
Unswear faith sworn, and on the marriage bed
Of smiling peace to march a bloody host
And make a riot on the gentle brow
Of true sincerity? O holy sir,
My Reverend Father, let it not be so!
Out of your grace, devise, ordain, impose
Some gentle order; and then we shall be blest
To do your pleasure and continue friends.

PANDULPH
All form is formless, order orderless,
Save what is opposite to England's love.
Therefore to arms! Be champion of our Church,
Or let the Church, our mother, breathe her curse,
A mother's curse, on her revolting son.   257
France, thou mayst hold a serpent by the tongue,
A chafèd lion by the mortal paw,   259
A fasting tiger safer by the tooth,
Than keep in peace that hand which thou dost hold.

KING PHILIP
I may disjoin my hand, but not my faith.

PANDULPH
So mak'st thou faith an enemy to faith,   263
And like a civil war sett'st oath to oath,
Thy tongue against thy tongue. O, let thy vow,
First made to heaven, first be to heaven performed,
That is, to be the champion of our Church!
What since thou swor'st is sworn against thyself   268

---

237 pencil paintbrush   **238 difference** dissension   **240 both** i.e., blood
and love   **241 Unyoke this seizure** disjoin this handclasp.   **regreet**
returned salutation, counterclasp   **257 revolting** rebellious   **259 mortal**
deadly   **263 So . . . to faith** i.e., you are trying to set your promise to
John against your religious vow to the Church   **268 since** since then

And may not be performèd by thyself,
For that which thou hast sworn to do amiss
Is not amiss when it is truly done;   271
And being not done where doing tends to ill,
The truth is then most done not doing it.
The better act of purposes mistook   274
Is to mistake again; though indirect,   275
Yet indirection thereby grows direct,
And falsehood falsehood cures, as fire cools fire   277
Within the scorchèd veins of one new-burned.   278
It is religion that doth make vows kept,
But thou hast sworn against religion;
By what thou swear'st against the thing thou swear'st, 281
And mak'st an oath the surety for thy truth
Against an oath. The truth thou art unsure   283
To swear, swears only not to be forsworn,   284
Else what a mockery should it be to swear!
But thou dost swear only to be forsworn,   286
And most forsworn to keep what thou dost swear.
Therefore thy later vows against thy first
Is in thyself rebellion to thyself;
And better conquest never canst thou make
Than arm thy constant and thy nobler parts
Against these giddy loose suggestions,   292
Upon which better part our prayers come in,   293
If thou vouchsafe them. But if not, then know   294
The peril of our curses light on thee
So heavy as thou shalt not shake them off,   296

271 truly done i.e., not done at all (since, as Pandulph explains two lines
later, an ill-considered vow is best performed by not performing it. This
is an example of equivocation, much deplored by many Elizabethans
and regarded as typical of Catholic duplicity.)   **274–275 The better . . .
again** i.e., the best thing to do when one has made a wrong turn is to
turn again   **277–278 as fire . . . new-burned** (Burns were commonly
treated with heat on the proverbial theory that one fire drives out
another.)   **281 By . . . thing thou swearest** you swear against the very
thing by which you swear, i.e., by your oath of allegiance to John you
directly violate your prior vows given to the Church   **283–284 The
truth . . . forsworn** i.e., your oath of allegiance to the true faith, which
you are now hesitant to affirm, is above all a promise not to break your
oath   **286 But . . . forsworn** i.e., but you are now proposing an oath to
John in which you will indeed break your prior oath   **292 suggestions**
temptations   **293 Upon . . . part** in support of which better side
294 vouchsafe accept, agree to   **296 as** that

But in despair die under their black weight.
AUSTRIA
Rebellion, flat rebellion!
BASTARD   Will 't not be?   298
Will not a calfskin stop that mouth of thine?
LEWIS
Father, to arms!
BLANCHE   Upon thy wedding day?
Against the blood that thou hast marrièd?   301
What, shall our feast be kept with slaughtered men?
Shall braying trumpets and loud churlish drums,
Clamors of hell, be measures to our pomp?   304
[Kneeling.] O husband, hear me! Ay, alack, how new
Is "husband" in my mouth! Even for that name,
Which till this time my tongue did ne'er pronounce,
Upon my knee I beg, go not to arms
Against mine uncle.
CONSTANCE [Kneeling]   O, upon my knee,
Made hard with kneeling, I do pray to thee,
Thou virtuous Dauphin, alter not the doom
Forethought by heaven!   312
BLANCHE [To Lewis]
Now shall I see thy love. What motive may
Be stronger with thee than the name of wife?
CONSTANCE
That which upholdeth him that thee upholds:
His honor. O, thine honor, Lewis, thine honor!
LEWIS
I muse Your Majesty doth seem so cold,   317
When such profound respects do pull you on.   318
PANDULPH
I will denounce a curse upon his head.   319
KING PHILIP [Letting go of King John's hand]
Thou shalt not need. England, I will fall from thee.
CONSTANCE [Rising]
O, fair return of banished majesty!

298 Will 't not be i.e., will nothing serve (to keep you quiet)   **301 blood**
(Blanche is related by blood to King John.)   **304 measures** musical
accompaniment.   **pomp** i.e., wedding ceremony   **312 Forethought**
destined   **317 muse** wonder   **318 respects** considerations
319 denounce proclaim, call down

ELEANOR
  O, foul revolt of French inconstancy!
KING JOHN
  France, thou shalt rue this hour within this hour.
BASTARD
  Old Time the clock setter, that bald sexton Time,
  Is it as he will? Well then, France shall rue.   325
BLANCHE [*Rising*]
  The sun's o'ercast with blood. Fair day, adieu!
  Which is the side that I must go withal?   327
  I am with both: each army hath a hand,
  And in their rage, I having hold of both,
  They whirl asunder and dismember me.
  Husband, I cannot pray that thou mayst win;
  Uncle, I needs must pray that thou mayst lose;
  Father, I may not wish the fortune thine;   333
  Grandam, I will not wish thy wishes thrive.
  Whoever wins, on that side shall I lose;
  Assurèd loss before the match be played.
LEWIS
  Lady, with me, with me thy fortune lies.
BLANCHE
  There where my fortune lives, there my life dies.
KING JOHN [*To the Bastard*]
  Cousin, go draw our puissance together.   339
                              [*Exit the Bastard.*]
  France, I am burned up with inflaming wrath,
  A rage whose heat hath this condition,
  That nothing can allay, nothing but blood—
  The blood, and dearest-valued blood, of France.
KING PHILIP
  Thy rage shall burn thee up, and thou shalt turn
  To ashes, ere our blood shall quench that fire.
  Look to thyself. Thou art in jeopardy.
KING JOHN
  No more than he that threats. To arms let's hie!   347
                              Exeunt [*separately*].

---

325 France shall rue i.e., if Time is to decide, France will rue sooner or
later   **327 withal** with   **333 Father** i.e., father-in-law, King Philip
339 Cousin kinsman.   **puissance** armed force   **347 hie** hasten

3.2   *Alarums, excursions. Enter [the] Bastard, with Austria's head.*

BASTARD
Now, by my life, this day grows wondrous hot.
Some airy devil hovers in the sky   2
And pours down mischief. Austria's head lie there,
While Philip breathes.   [*He puts down the head.*] 4

   Enter [King] John, Arthur, [and] Hubert.

KING JOHN
Hubert, keep this boy. Philip, make up.   5
My mother is assailèd in our tent,
And ta'en, I fear.
BASTARD   My lord, I rescued her;
Her Highness is in safety, fear you not.
But on, my liege! For very little pains
Will bring this labor to an happy end.
                  Exeunt [with Austria's head].

3.3   *Alarums, excursions, retreat. Enter [King] John, Eleanor, Arthur, [the] Bastard, Hubert, [and] lords.*

KING JOHN [*To Eleanor*]
So shall it be; Your Grace shall stay behind
So strongly guarded. [*To Arthur.*] Cousin, look not sad. 2
Thy grandam loves thee, and thy uncle will
As dear be to thee as thy father was.
ARTHUR
O, this will make my mother die with grief!

3.2. Location: France. Plains near Angiers. The battle is seen as following immediately upon the previous scene.
s.d. **Alarums** calls to arms.   **excursions** sorties   **2 airy devil** (Aerial spirits or devils were thought to be the cause of tempests, thunder, lightning, etc.)   **4 breathes** i.e., gets his breath   **5 make up** advance, press on

3.3. Location: Scene continues on the plains near Angiers.
s.d. **retreat** signal for withdrawal of forces   **2 So** thus

KING JOHN [*To the Bastard*]
  Cousin, away for England! Haste before,
  And, ere our coming, see thou shake the bags
  Of hoarding abbots; imprisoned angels   8
  Set at liberty. The fat ribs of peace   9
  Must by the hungry now be fed upon.
  Use our commission in his utmost force.   11
BASTARD
  Bell, book, and candle shall not drive me back   12
  When gold and silver becks me to come on.   13
  I leave Your Highness.—Grandam, I will pray,
  If ever I remember to be holy,
  For your fair safety. So I kiss your hand.
ELEANOR
  Farewell, gentle cousin.
KING JOHN   Coz, farewell.   17

                    [*Exit the Bastard.*]

ELEANOR
  Come hither, little kinsman. Hark, a word.
                [*She takes Arthur aside.*]
KING JOHN
  Come hither, Hubert. O my gentle Hubert,
  We owe thee much! Within this wall of flesh   20
  There is a soul counts thee her creditor   21
  And with advantage means to pay thy love;   22
  And, my good friend, thy voluntary oath   23
  Lives in this bosom, dearly cherishèd.   24
  Give me thy hand. I had a thing to say,
  But I will fit it with some better tune.   26
  By heaven, Hubert, I am almost ashamed
  To say what good respect I have of thee.   28
HUBERT
  I am much bounden to Your Majesty.   29

---

8 angels gold coins (with a common pun) **9 fat ribs of peace** (i.e., in contrast to the skeleton of war, the *bare-ribbed Death* of 5.2.177) **11 his** its **12 Bell, book, and candle** (Articles used in the office of excommunication.) **13 becks** beckon **17 Coz** cousin, i.e., kinsman **20 Within . . . flesh** i.e., within me **21 counts** that counts **22 advantage** interest **23 thy voluntary oath** your freely given allegiance **24 Lives in this bosom** is vividly felt in my heart **26 some better tune** i.e., better words, and some better reward **28 respect** opinion **29 bounden** obligated

KING JOHN
Good friend, thou hast no cause to say so yet,
But thou shalt have; and, creep time ne'er so slow,
Yet it shall come for me to do thee good.
I had a thing to say—but let it go.
The sun is in the heaven, and the proud day,
Attended with the pleasures of the world,
Is all too wanton and too full of gauds   36
To give me audience. If the midnight bell   37
Did with his iron tongue and brazen mouth
Sound on into the drowsy race of night;   39
If this same were a churchyard where we stand,
And thou possessèd with a thousand wrongs;   41
Or if that surly spirit, melancholy,
Had baked thy blood and made it heavy, thick,
Which else runs tickling up and down the veins,
Making that idiot, laughter, keep men's eyes   45
And strain their cheeks to idle merriment,   46
A passion hateful to my purposes;   47
Or if that thou couldst see me without eyes,
Hear me without thine ears, and make reply
Without a tongue, using conceit alone,   50
Without eyes, ears, and harmful sound of words—   51
Then, in despite of brooded watchful day,   52
I would into thy bosom pour my thoughts.
But, ah, I will not! Yet I love thee well,
And, by my troth, I think thou lov'st me well.
HUBERT
So well that what you bid me undertake,   56
Though that my death were adjunct to my act,   57
By heaven, I would do it.
KING JOHN   Do not I know thou wouldst?
Good Hubert, Hubert, Hubert, throw thine eye
On yon young boy. I'll tell thee what, my friend,

36 gauds showy ornaments, trifles   **37 To give me audience** i.e., for you
to hearken to my words   **39 race** running, course. (*Face* and *ear* have
been suggested as emendations.)   **41 possessèd with** obsessed by
45 idiot jester   **46 strain** stretch (in laughter)   **47 passion** emotion
50 conceit the mental faculty   **51 harmful** (because it is dangerous to
speak of such matters)   **52 brooded** brooding (and hence vigilant in
defense of its young)   **56 what** whatever   **57 adjunct to** consequent
upon

He is a very serpent in my way,
And wheresoe'er this foot of mine doth tread
He lies before me. Dost thou understand me?
Thou art his keeper.
HUBERT   And I'll keep him so
That he shall not offend Your Majesty.
KING JOHN   Death.
HUBERT
  My lord?
KING JOHN A grave.
HUBERT   He shall not live.
KING JOHN   Enough.
  I could be merry now. Hubert, I love thee.
  Well, I'll not say what I intend for thee.
  Remember.—Madam, fare you well.
  I'll send those powers o'er to Your Majesty.   70
ELEANOR
  My blessing go with thee!
KING JOHN   For England, cousin, go.   71
  Hubert shall be your man, attend on you
  With all true duty.—On toward Calais, ho!   *Exeunt.*

❖

3.4   *Enter [King Philip of] France, [Lewis the]*
           Dauphin, Pandulph, [and] attendants.

KING PHILIP
  So, by a roaring tempest on the flood,   1
  A whole armada of convicted sail   2
  Is scattered and disjoined from fellowship.
PANDULPH
  Courage and comfort! All shall yet go well.
KING PHILIP
  What can go well when we have run so ill?
  Are we not beaten? Is not Angiers lost?
  Arthur ta'en prisoner? Divers dear friends slain?

70 powers troops   **71 cousin** i.e., Arthur

3.4. Location: France. The French King's quarters.
1 flood seas   **2 convicted** doomed

And bloody England into England gone,	8
O'erbearing interruption, spite of France?	9

LEWIS
What he hath won, that hath he fortified.	
So hot a speed, with such advice disposed,	11
Such temperate order in so fierce a cause,	
Doth want example. Who hath read or heard	13
Of any kindred action like to this?	14

KING PHILIP
Well could I bear that England had this praise,	
So we could find some pattern of our shame.	16

Enter Constance, [with her hair about her ears].

Look who comes here! A grave unto a soul,	17
Holding th' eternal spirit, against her will,	
In the vile prison of afflicted breath.—	19
I prithee, lady, go away with me.	

CONSTANCE
Lo, now! Now see the issue of your peace.	21

KING PHILIP
Patience, good lady. Comfort, gentle Constance.	

CONSTANCE
No, I defy all counsel, all redress,	23
But that which ends all counsel, true redress:	
Death. Death, O amiable, lovely Death!	
Thou odoriferous stench! Sound rottenness!	26
Arise forth from the couch of lasting night,	
Thou hate and terror to prosperity,	
And I will kiss thy detestable bones,	
And put my eyeballs in thy vaulty brows,	30
And ring these fingers with thy household worms,	31
And stop this gap of breath with fulsome dust,	32

8 bloody England the bloodstained King of England   **9 O'erbearing interruption** overcoming all resistance.   **spite** in spite   **11 with . . . disposed** directed with such judgment   **13 Doth want example** lacks parallel instance   **14 kindred** comparable   **16 So** provided.   **pattern** precedent   **17 A grave . . . soul** i.e., a mere shell of a body without the will to live   **19 prison . . . breath** (The soul was thought to leave the body from the mouth with the last expiring breath.)   **21 issue** outcome   **23 defy** reject.   **redress** comfort   **26 odoriferous** sweet-smelling.   **Sound** wholesome   **30 vaulty** arched and hollow   **31 thy household worms** the worms of your retinue   **32 this gap of breath** i.e., my mouth.   **fulsome** loathsome

And be a carrion monster like thyself.
Come, grin on me, and I will think thou smil'st,
And buss thee as thy wife. Misery's love,   35
O, come to me!
KING PHILIP   O fair affliction, peace!   36
CONSTANCE
No, no, I will not, having breath to cry.   37
O, that my tongue were in the thunder's mouth!
Then with a passion would I shake the world,
And rouse from sleep that fell anatomy   40
Which cannot hear a lady's feeble voice,
Which scorns a modern invocation.   42
PANDULPH
Lady, you utter madness, and not sorrow.
CONSTANCE
Thou art not holy to belie me so.
I am not mad. This hair I tear is mine;
My name is Constance; I was Geoffrey's wife;
Young Arthur is my son, and he is lost.
I am not mad; I would to heaven I were,
For then 'tis like I should forget myself!   49
O, if I could, what grief should I forget?
Preach some philosophy to make me mad,
And thou shalt be canonized, Cardinal;
For, being not mad but sensible of grief,   53
My reasonable part produces reason   54
How I may be delivered of these woes,   55
And teaches me to kill or hang myself.
If I were mad, I should forget my son,
Or madly think a babe of clouts were he.   58
I am not mad. Too well, too well I feel
The different plague of each calamity.   60
KING PHILIP
Bind up those tresses. O, what love I note

---

35 buss kiss. **Misery's love** you whom those in misery love (as a way of
ending their misery) **36 affliction** afflicted one **37 having** as long as I
have **40 fell anatomy** cruel skeleton (the usual figure of Death in pictorial representations) **42 modern** everyday, commonplace. **invocation**
entreaty **49 like** likely **53 sensible of** capable of feeling **54 reasonable
part** i.e., brain **55 delivered of** (1) freed from (2) delivered of, as in childbirth **58 babe of clouts** rag doll **60 different plague** distinct affliction

In the fair multitude of those her hairs!
Where but by chance a silver drop hath fallen,   63
Even to that drop ten thousand wiry friends   64
Do glue themselves in sociable grief,   65
Like true, inseparable, faithful loves,
Sticking together in calamity.
CONSTANCE
To England, if you will.
KING PHILIP   Bind up your hairs.   68
CONSTANCE
Yes, that I will. And wherefore will I do it?
I tore them from their bonds and cried aloud,
"O, that these hands could so redeem my son,   71
As they have given these hairs their liberty!"
But now I envy at their liberty,
And will again commit them to their bonds,
Because my poor child is a prisoner.
                              [*She binds up her hair.*]
And, father Cardinal, I have heard you say
That we shall see and know our friends in heaven.
If that be true, I shall see my boy again;
For since the birth of Cain, the first male child,
To him that did but yesterday suspire,   80
There was not such a gracious creature born.
But now will canker sorrow eat my bud   82
And chase the native beauty from his cheek,   83
And he will look as hollow as a ghost,
As dim and meager as an ague's fit,
And so he'll die; and, rising so again,   86
When I shall meet him in the court of heaven
I shall not know him. Therefore never, never
Must I behold my pretty Arthur more.
PANDULPH
You hold too heinous a respect of grief.   90

63 **silver drop** i.e., tear 64 **wiry friends** i.e., hairs 65 **Do . . . grief** i.e.,
cling together in sympathy of grief, bound to one another by the tears
falling on them 68 **To England** (Perhaps an answer to Philip's invitation at l. 20; perhaps evidence of textual revision.) 71 **redeem** free from
imprisonment 80 **suspire** breathe his first breath 82 **canker** like a
cankerworm, feeding on buds 83 **native** natural 86 **so . . . so** thus . . .
thus 90 **heinous a respect** terrible an opinion

CONSTANCE
He talks to me that never had a son.
KING PHILIP
You are as fond of grief as of your child.   92
CONSTANCE
Grief fills the room up of my absent child,   93
Lies in his bed, walks up and down with me,
Puts on his pretty looks, repeats his words,
Remembers me of all his gracious parts,   96
Stuffs out his vacant garments with his form;
Then, have I reason to be fond of grief?
Fare you well! Had you such a loss as I,
I could give better comfort than you do.
                         [*She unbinds her hair again.*]
I will not keep this form upon my head   101
When there is such disorder in my wit.   102
O Lord! My boy, my Arthur, my fair son!
My life, my joy, my food, my all the world!
My widow-comfort, and my sorrows' cure!   *Exit.*
KING PHILIP
I fear some outrage, and I'll follow her. *Exit* [*attended*]. 106
LEWIS
There's nothing in this world can make me joy.
Life is as tedious as a twice-told tale
Vexing the dull ear of a drowsy man;   109
And bitter shame hath spoiled the sweet world's taste,
That it yields naught but shame and bitterness.   111
PANDULPH
Before the curing of a strong disease,
Even in the instant of repair and health,
The fit is strongest. Evils that take leave,   114
On their departure most of all show evil.
What have you lost by losing of this day?   116
LEWIS
All days of glory, joy, and happiness.

92 fond of foolishly doting on   **93 room** place   **96 Remembers** reminds   **101 form** coiffure (with idea of order, contrasted with *disorder* in l. 102)   **102 wit** i.e., brain   **106 outrage** i.e., outrage upon herself, suicide   **109 dull** inattentive   **111 That** so that   **114 fit** bout of illness **116 this day** this day's battle. (But the Dauphin replies bitterly, using *day* in the more common meaning.)

PANDULPH
> If you had won it, certainly you had.
> No, no. When Fortune means to men most good,   119
> She looks upon them with a threatening eye.
> 'Tis strange to think how much King John hath lost
> In this which he accounts so clearly won.
> Are not you grieved that Arthur is his prisoner?

LEWIS
> As heartily as he is glad he hath him.

PANDULPH
> Your mind is all as youthful as your blood.
> Now hear me speak with a prophetic spirit;
> For even the breath of what I mean to speak
> Shall blow each dust, each straw, each little rub,   128
> Out of the path which shall directly lead
> Thy foot to England's throne. And therefore mark.
> John hath seized Arthur, and it cannot be
> That, whiles warm life plays in that infant's veins,   132
> The misplaced John should entertain an hour,   133
> One minute, nay, one quiet breath of rest.
> A scepter snatched with an unruly hand   135
> Must be as boisterously maintained as gained;   136
> And he that stands upon a slippery place
> Makes nice of no vile hold to stay him up.   138
> That John may stand, then Arthur needs must fall;
> So be it, for it cannot be but so.

LEWIS
> But what shall I gain by young Arthur's fall?

PANDULPH
> You, in the right of Lady Blanche your wife,
> May then make all the claim that Arthur did.

LEWIS
> And lose it, life and all, as Arthur did.

PANDULPH
> How green you are and fresh in this old world!
> John lays you plots; the times conspire with you,   146

---

119 means intends   **128 rub** obstacle. (From the game of bowls.)
132 whiles while.   **warm life** i.e., blood   **133 misplaced** i.e., usurping
135 unruly violating proper rule   **136 boisterously** violently
138 Makes nice of no is not scrupulous about any   **146 lays you plots**
i.e., makes plots by which you may profit

For he that steeps his safety in true blood 147
Shall find but bloody safety, and untrue. 148
This act so evilly borne shall cool the hearts 149
Of all his people and freeze up their zeal,
That none so small advantage shall step forth 151
To check his reign but they will cherish it;
No natural exhalation in the sky, 153
No scope of nature, no distempered day, 154
No common wind, no customèd event, 155
But they will pluck away his natural cause 156
And call them meteors, prodigies, and signs,
Abortives, presages, and tongues of heaven, 158
Plainly denouncing vengeance upon John. 159

LEWIS
Maybe he will not touch young Arthur's life,
But hold himself safe in his prisonment. 161

PANDULPH
O, sir, when he shall hear of your approach,
If that young Arthur be not gone already,
Even at that news he dies; and then the hearts
Of all his people shall revolt from him, 165
And kiss the lips of unacquainted change, 166
And pick strong matter of revolt and wrath 167
Out of the bloody fingers' ends of John. 168
Methinks I see this hurly all on foot; 169
And, O, what better matter breeds for you 170
Than I have named! The bastard Faulconbridge
Is now in England, ransacking the Church,
Offending charity. If but a dozen French
Were there in arms, they would be as a call 174

---

147 **true blood** blood of a true prince　148 **untrue** uncertain, insecure
149 **borne** carried out　151 **none . . . advantage** no opportunity, however
small　153 **exhalation** meteor　154 **scope of nature** i.e., one of those
prodigious phenomena within nature's power. **distempered** stormy
155 **customèd** customary　156 **pluck away his** discard its. **cause**
explanation　158 **Abortives** untimely or monstrous births
159 **denouncing** calling down　161 **But . . . prisonment** but regard
himself as safe so long as Arthur is imprisoned　165 **him** i.e., John
166 **kiss . . . change** i.e., welcome any change. **unacquainted** unfamiliar　167 **pick strong matter of** find compelling reason for　168 **Out . . .**
John i.e., out of John's bloody-handed deeds　169 **hurly** commotion.
on foot in motion　170 **breeds** is ripening　174 **call** (1) decoy (2) call to
arms

To train ten thousand English to their side,   175
Or as a little snow, tumbled about,
Anon becomes a mountain. O noble Dauphin,
Go with me to the King. 'Tis wonderful
What may be wrought out of their discontent,
Now that their souls are topful of offense.   180
For England go. I will whet on the King.

LEWIS
Strong reasons make strange actions. Let us go.
If you say ay, the King will not say no.   *Exeunt.*

❖

175 train attract **180 topful of offense** brimful of grievance and sated
with John's offenses

4.1　　*Enter Hubert and Executioners [with irons and rope].*

HUBERT
Heat me these irons hot, and look thou stand　　　1
Within the arras. When I strike my foot　　　2
Upon the bosom of the ground, rush forth
And bind the boy which you shall find with me
Fast to the chair. Be heedful. Hence, and watch.

FIRST EXECUTIONER
I hope your warrant will bear out the deed.　　　6

HUBERT
Uncleanly scruples! Fear not you. Look to 't.　　　7
　　　　　　　　　[The Executioners withdraw.]
Young lad, come forth. I have to say with you.　　　8

　　　Enter Arthur.

ARTHUR
Good morrow, Hubert.

HUBERT　　　　　　　　　Good morrow, little prince.

ARTHUR
As little prince, having so great a title　　　10
To be more prince, as may be. You are sad.　　　11

HUBERT
Indeed, I have been merrier.

ARTHUR　　　　　　　　　Mercy on me!
Methinks nobody should be sad but I.
Yet I remember, when I was in France,
Young gentlemen would be as sad as night,
Only for wantonness. By my christendom,　　　16
So I were out of prison and kept sheep,　　　17
I should be as merry as the day is long;

4.1. Location: England. A room in a castle. A chair is provided.
1 look take care　**2 Within the arras** behind the wall hangings. (Evidently the Executioners go out as though to heat their irons and then conceal themselves behind the arras, ready at l. 71 to come forth.)
6 bear out provide sufficient authority for　**7 Uncleanly** improper, unbecoming　**8 to say** something to speak about　**10–11 As . . . be** i.e., I am as little a prince, despite my being entitled to be greater, as is possible　**16 for wantonness** out of affected behavior.　**By my christendom** as I am a Christian　**17 So** provided

And so I would be here, but that I doubt   19
My uncle practices more harm to me.   20
He is afraid of me and I of him.
Is it my fault that I was Geoffrey's son?
No, indeed, is 't not; and I would to heaven
I were your son, so you would love me, Hubert.   24
HUBERT [*Aside*]
Is it my fault that I was Geoffrey's son?
If I talk to him, with his innocent prate   25
He will awake my mercy, which lies dead.
Therefore I will be sudden, and dispatch.
ARTHUR
Are you sick, Hubert? You look pale today.
In sooth, I would you were a little sick,   29
That I might sit all night and watch with you.   30
I warrant I love you more than you do me.
HUBERT [*Aside*]
His words do take possession of my bosom.—
Read here, young Arthur.   [*Showing a paper.*]
                        [*Aside*.] How now, foolish rheum? 33
Turning dispiteous torture out of door?   34
I must be brief, lest resolution drop
Out at mine eyes in tender womanish tears.—
Can you not read it? Is it not fair writ?   37
ARTHUR
Too fairly, Hubert, for so foul effect.   38
Must you with hot irons burn out both mine eyes?
HUBERT
Young boy, I must.
ARTHUR   And will you?
HUBERT   And I will.
ARTHUR
Have you the heart? When your head did but ache,
I knit my handkerchief about your brows—   42
The best I had, a princess wrought it me—   43
And I did never ask it you again;   44

19 **would be** would like to be. **but** except. **doubt** fear   **20 practices**
plots   **24 so** provided   **25 prate** prattle   **29 sooth** truth   **30 watch with**
stay awake tending to   **33 rheum** i.e., tears. (Literally, a fluid discharge.)   **34 Turning . . . door** i.e., banishing pitiless torture   **37 fair**
handsomely, legibly   **38 effect** purpose, meaning   **42 knit** bound
43 wrought i.e., embroidered.   **me** for me   **44 did . . . you** never asked
for it back from you

And with my hand at midnight held your head,
And like the watchful minutes to the hour   46
Still and anon cheered up the heavy time,   47
Saying, "What lack you?" and "Where lies your grief?"
Or "What good love may I perform for you?"   49
Many a poor man's son would have lain still
And ne'er have spoke a loving word to you,
But you at your sick service had a prince.   52
Nay, you may think my love was crafty love,
And call it cunning. Do, an if you will.
If heaven be pleased that you must use me ill,
Why then you must. Will you put out mine eyes?
These eyes that never did nor never shall
So much as frown on you?
HUBERT   I have sworn to do it,
And with hot irons must I burn them out.
ARTHUR
Ah, none but in this iron age would do it!   60
The iron of itself, though heat red-hot,   61
Approaching near these eyes, would drink my tears
And quench his fiery indignation   63
Even in the matter of mine innocence;   64
Nay, after that, consume away in rust,
But for containing fire to harm mine eye.   66
Are you more stubborn-hard than hammered iron?
An if an angel should have come to me   68
And told me Hubert should put out mine eyes,
I would not have believed him—no tongue but Hubert's.
HUBERT   Come forth!   [*He stamps his foot.*
        Executioners come forth, with a cord, irons, etc.]
              Do as I bid you do.
ARTHUR
O, save me, Hubert, save me! My eyes are out
Even with the fierce looks of these bloody men.

---

46 watchful . . . hour minutes that mark the progress of the hour
47 Still and anon continually   **49 love** loving assistance   **52 at your
sick service** to serve you in your sickness   **60 iron age** degenerate time
(with play on *hot irons*)   **61 heat** heated   **63 his** its   **64 matter . . .
innocence** substance betokening my innocence, i.e., my tears   **66 But
for containing** merely because it had contained   **68 An if** if.   **should
have** had

HUBERT
  Give me the iron, I say, and bind him here.
                    [*They start to bind Arthur to a chair.*]
ARTHUR
  Alas, what need you be so boisterous-rough?   75
  I will not struggle; I will stand stone-still.
  For heaven's sake, Hubert, let me not be bound!
  Nay, hear me, Hubert: drive these men away,
  And I will sit as quiet as a lamb;
  I will not stir, nor wince, nor speak a word,
  Nor look upon the iron angerly.   81
  Thrust but these men away, and I'll forgive you,
  Whatever torment you do put me to.
HUBERT
  Go stand within. Let me alone with him.
FIRST EXECUTIONER
  I am best pleased to be from such a deed.   85
                            [*Exeunt Executioners.*]
ARTHUR
  Alas, I then have chid away my friend!
  He hath a stern look, but a gentle heart.
  Let him come back, that his compassion may
  Give life to yours.
HUBERT   Come, boy, prepare yourself.
ARTHUR
  Is there no remedy?
HUBERT   None but to lose your eyes.
ARTHUR
  O heaven, that there were but a mote in yours,   91
  A grain, a dust, a gnat, a wandering hair,
  Any annoyance in that precious sense!   93
  Then feeling what small things are boisterous there,   94
  Your vile intent must needs seem horrible.
HUBERT
  Is this your promise? Go to, hold your tongue.   96
ARTHUR
  Hubert, the utterance of a brace of tongues   97

75 what why   **81 angerly** angrily, complainingly   **85 from** away from
91 mote minute particle of anything   **93 precious sense** i.e., sight
94 boisterous painful, irritating   **96 Go to** (An exclamation of remonstrance.)   **97 of a brace** of even a pair

Must needs want pleading for a pair of eyes.   98
Let me not hold my tongue. Let me not, Hubert!   99
Or, Hubert, if you will, cut out my tongue,
So I may keep mine eyes. O, spare mine eyes,   101
Though to no use but still to look on you!   102
Lo, by my troth, the instrument is cold   103
And would not harm me.
HUBERT   I can heat it, boy.
ARTHUR
No, in good sooth. The fire is dead with grief,   105
Being create for comfort, to be used   106
In undeserved extremes. See else yourself.   107
There is no malice in this burning coal;
The breath of heaven hath blown his spirit out
And strewed repentant ashes on his head.   110
HUBERT
But with my breath I can revive it, boy.
ARTHUR
An if you do, you will but make it blush
And glow with shame of your proceedings, Hubert.
Nay, it perchance will sparkle in your eyes,   114
And, like a dog that is compelled to fight,
Snatch at his master that doth tarre him on.   116
All things that you should use to do me wrong
Deny their office. Only you do lack   118
That mercy which fierce fire and iron extends,   119
Creatures of note for mercy-lacking uses.   120
HUBERT
Well, see to live. I will not touch thine eye   121
For all the treasure that thine uncle owes.   122
Yet am I sworn, and I did purpose, boy,
With this same very iron to burn them out.

98 Must . . . pleading must be inadequate to plead sufficiently   **99 Let
me not** don't make me, don't hold me to my promise to   **101 So** provided, if thereby   **102 still** always   **103 troth** faith   **105 in good sooth**
certainly   **106 create** created   **107 extremes** i.e., extreme cruelties.
See else yourself see for yourself if it isn't true   **110 on his head** i.e.,
like a penitent sinner heaping ashes on his head   **114 sparkle in** scatter
sparks into   **116 Snatch** snap.   **tarre** provoke, incite   **118 Deny** refuse
to do.   **office** function   **119 extends** proffer   **120 Creatures . . . uses**
things (i.e., fire and iron) noted as instruments of torture   **121 see to
live** i.e., live, and continue to see   **122 owes** owns

ARTHUR
    O, now you look like Hubert! All this while
    You were disguisèd.
HUBERT   Peace! No more. Adieu.
    Your uncle must not know but you are dead.   127
    I'll fill these doggèd spies with false reports.   128
    And, pretty child, sleep doubtless and secure   129
    That Hubert, for the wealth of all the world,
    Will not offend thee.
ARTHUR   O heaven! I thank you, Hubert.   131
HUBERT
    Silence! No more. Go closely in with me.   132
    Much danger do I undergo for thee.   *Exeunt.*

❖

4.2   *Enter [King] John, Pembroke, Salisbury, and*
           other lords. [The King sits on his throne.]

KING JOHN
    Here once again we sit, once again crowned,
    And looked upon, I hope, with cheerful eyes.
PEMBROKE
    This "once again," but that Your Highness pleased,
    Was once superfluous. You were crowned before,
    And that high royalty was ne'er plucked off,
    The faiths of men ne'er stainèd with revolt.
    Fresh expectation troubled not the land
    With any longed-for change or better state.
SALISBURY
    Therefore, to be possessed with double pomp,   9
    To guard a title that was rich before,   10
    To gild refinèd gold, to paint the lily,
    To throw a perfume on the violet,
    To smooth the ice, or add another hue
    Unto the rainbow, or with taper light

127 but other than that   **128 doggèd** fierce, malicious   **129 doubtless**
fearless   **131 offend** harm   **132 closely** secretly

4.2. Location: England. The court of King John.
9 be possessed with have possession of (the crown)   **10 guard** trim,
ornament; also, protect

To seek the beauteous eye of heaven to garnish,   15
Is wasteful and ridiculous excess.

PEMBROKE
But that your royal pleasure must be done,
This act is as an ancient tale new told,
And in the last repeating troublesome,
Being urgèd at a time unseasonable.

SALISBURY
In this the antique and well-noted face   21
Of plain old form is much disfigurèd;   22
And, like a shifted wind unto a sail,   23
It makes the course of thoughts to fetch about,   24
Startles and frights consideration,   25
Makes sound opinion sick and truth suspected,   26
For putting on so new a fashioned robe.   27

PEMBROKE
When workmen strive to do better than well,
They do confound their skill in covetousness;   29
And oftentimes excusing of a fault
Doth make the fault the worse by th' excuse,
As patches set upon a little breach   32
Discredit more in hiding of the fault
Than did the fault before it was so patched.

SALISBURY
To this effect, before you were new-crowned,
We breathed our counsel. But it pleased Your Highness   36
To overbear it, and we are all well pleased,   37
Since all and every part of what we would
Doth make a stand at what Your Highness will.   39

KING JOHN
Some reasons of this double coronation

---

15 eye of heaven i.e., the sun (much too fair and bright to be enhanced by a *taper light* or candle)   **21 well-noted** familiar   **22 form** custom   **23 a shifted wind** a wind that shifts direction   **24 fetch about** change direction, tack   **25 frights consideration** i.e., frightens everyone into anxious reflection   **26–27 Makes . . . robe** i.e., leads to the weakening of sound loyalty and to suspicions about the truth of John's dynastic claims, in that the English throne has dressed itself in this strange new ceremony   **29 confound** destroy, disrupt.   **in covetousness** i.e., by their greedy desire to do better   **32 breach** hole   **36 breathed** spoke   **37 overbear** overrule   **39 Doth . . . will** may go no further than what Your Highness desires

I have possessed you with, and think them strong;   41
And more, more strong, when lesser is my fear   42
I shall endue you with. Meantime but ask   43
What you would have reformed that is not well,
And well shall you perceive how willingly
I will both hear and grant you your requests.

PEMBROKE
Then I, as one that am the tongue of these   47
To sound the purposes of all their hearts,   48
Both for myself and them—but chief of all
Your safety, for the which myself and them   50
Bend their best studies—heartily request   51
Th' enfranchisement of Arthur, whose restraint   52
Doth move the murmuring lips of discontent
To break into this dangerous argument:
If what in rest you have in right you hold,   55
Why then your fears—which, as they say, attend   56
The steps of wrong—should move you to mew up   57
Your tender kinsman, and to choke his days
With barbarous ignorance and deny his youth
The rich advantage of good exercise.   60
That the time's enemies may not have this   61
To grace occasions, let it be our suit   62
That you have bid us ask his liberty,   63
Which for our goods we do no further ask   64
Than whereupon our weal, on you depending,   65
Counts it your weal he have his liberty.   66

41 possessed you with informed you of   **42–43 And . . . with** i.e., and I
shall provide you with even more and stronger reasons, strong in proportion as my fear (in Arthur) grows less   **47 tongue** spokesman   **48 sound**
express   **50 them** i.e., they   **51 Bend** direct.   **studies** efforts   **52 enfranchisement** freeing from imprisonment   **55 If . . . hold** if in fact you hold by
right of law what you now possess in peace.   **in rest** in security, peaceably,
or, possibly, in arrest (referring to Arthur)   **56 Why then** i.e., why is it,
then, that   **56–57 attend . . . wrong** i.e., are evidence of wrongdoing, follow
in the train of wrongdoing   **57 mew up** shut up. (A falconing term.)
60 exercise i.e., exercise in arms and other gentlemanly accomplishments
61 the time's enemies enemies of the present state of affairs   **62 grace
occasions** i.e., suit their purposes, lend credence to their criticisms
62–63 let . . . liberty let the petition that you invited us to present (ll. 43–46)
be Arthur's liberty   **64 our goods** our personal benefit   **65 whereupon** to
the extent that.   **weal** welfare   **66 Counts . . . liberty** i.e., considers that it
will be good for your welfare to have Arthur at liberty, and therefore for
ours too, since we depend on you

Enter Hubert.

KING JOHN
Let it be so. I do commit his youth
To your direction.—Hubert, what news with you?
                              [*He takes Hubert aside.*]

PEMBROKE
This is the man should do the bloody deed;
He showed his warrant to a friend of mine.
The image of a wicked heinous fault
Lives in his eye; that close aspect of his   72
Doth show the mood of a much troubled breast,
And I do fearfully believe 'tis done,
What we so feared he had a charge to do.   75

SALISBURY
The color of the King doth come and go
Between his purpose and his conscience,
Like heralds twixt two dreadful battles set.   78
His passion is so ripe it needs must break.   79

PEMBROKE
And when it breaks, I fear will issue thence
The foul corruption of a sweet child's death.

KING JOHN [*Coming forward*]
We cannot hold mortality's strong hand.
Good lords, although my will to give is living,
The suit which you demand is gone and dead.
He tells us Arthur is deceased tonight.   85

SALISBURY
Indeed we feared his sickness was past cure.

PEMBROKE
Indeed we heard how near his death he was
Before the child himself felt he was sick.
This must be answered, either here or hence.   89

KING JOHN
Why do you bend such solemn brows on me?
Think you I bear the shears of destiny?
Have I commandment on the pulse of life?

---

72 close aspect furtive appearance   **75 charge** commission   **78 battles**
armies in battle order   **79 ripe** (like a boil full of pus, the *foul corrup-*
tion of l. 81)   **85 tonight** last night   **89 answered** atoned for.   **hence** i.e.,
in heaven, or perhaps on the field of battle

SALISBURY
It is apparent foul play, and 'tis shame   93
That greatness should so grossly offer it.   94
So thrive it in your game! And so, farewell.   95
PEMBROKE
Stay yet, Lord Salisbury. I'll go with thee,
And find th' inheritance of this poor child,
His little kingdom of a forcèd grave.   98
That blood which owed the breadth of all this isle,   99
Three foot of it doth hold; bad world the while!   100
This must not be thus borne. This will break out
To all our sorrows, and ere long, I doubt.   102
                                      Exeunt [*lords*].

KING JOHN
They burn in indignation. I repent.
There is no sure foundation set on blood,
No certain life achieved by others' death.

    Enter Messenger.

A fearful eye thou hast. Where is that blood   106
That I have seen inhabit in those cheeks?
So foul a sky clears not without a storm.
Pour down thy weather: how goes all in France?   109
MESSENGER
From France to England. Never such a power
For any foreign preparation   111
Was levied in the body of a land.   112
The copy of your speed is learned by them;   113
For when you should be told they do prepare,
The tidings comes that they are all arrived.
KING JOHN
O, where hath our intelligence been drunk?   116

93 apparent evident, blatant   **94 That . . . it** i.e., that a king should
flaunt foul play so flagrantly   **95 So . . . game** may your schemes lead
to the same (bad) end   **98 forcèd** imposed by violence   **99 owed**
owned   **100 the while** while such things occur   **102 doubt** fear
106 fearful full of fear, and prompting fear in others   **109 weather**
storm, tempest.   **goes all** is it all going. (But the Messenger replies
literally in the sense that everything is physically going from France to
England in an invasion.)   **111 preparation** expedition   **112 body** i.e.,
length and breadth   **113 copy** example.   **your speed** (as when John
proceeded to Angiers; see 2.1.56 ff.)   **116 our intelligence** our spies, spy
network

Where hath it slept? Where is my mother's care,
That such an army could be drawn in France   118
And she not hear of it?
MESSENGER   My liege, her ear
Is stopped with dust. The first of April died
Your noble mother; and, as I hear, my lord,
The Lady Constance in a frenzy died
Three days before. But this from rumor's tongue
I idly heard; if true or false I know not.   124
KING JOHN
Withhold thy speed, dreadful Occasion!   125
O, make a league with me till I have pleased
My discontented peers! What, Mother dead?
How wildly then walks my estate in France!   128
Under whose conduct came those powers of France   129
That thou for truth giv'st out are landed here?   130
MESSENGER
Under the Dauphin.

Enter [the] Bastard and Peter of Pomfret.

KING JOHN   Thou hast made me giddy
With these ill tidings. [*To the Bastard.*] Now, what
   says the world
To your proceedings? Do not seek to stuff   133
My head with more ill news, for it is full.
BASTARD
But if you be afeard to hear the worst,   135
Then let the worst unheard fall on your head.   136
KING JOHN
Bear with me, cousin, for I was amazed   137
Under the tide; but now I breathe again
Aloft the flood, and can give audience   139
To any tongue, speak it of what it will.
BASTARD
How I have sped among the clergymen,   141

118 drawn mustered, assembled **124 idly** by chance **125 Occasion**
course of events **128 estate** power **129 conduct** command **130 for
truth giv'st out** claim to be true **133 proceedings** i.e., mission against
the monasteries; see 3.3.6 ff. **135–136 But . . . head** but if you are
afraid to listen to bad news, misfortune will come upon you unawares
(and be much more dangerous) **137 amazed** bewildered **139 Aloft the
flood** riding on the sea's surface (continuing the metaphor of *tide*,
l. 138) **141 sped** succeeded

The sums I have collected shall express.
But as I traveled hither through the land,
I find the people strangely fantasied,   144
Possessed with rumors, full of idle dreams,
Not knowing what they fear, but full of fear.
And here's a prophet that I brought with me
From forth the streets of Pomfret, whom I found   148
With many hundreds treading on his heels,
To whom he sung, in rude harsh-sounding rhymes,
That ere the next Ascension Day at noon   151
Your Highness should deliver up your crown.
KING JOHN
Thou idle dreamer, wherefore didst thou so?
PETER
Foreknowing that the truth will fall out so.
KING JOHN
Hubert, away with him! Imprison him,
And on that day at noon, whereon he says
I shall yield up my crown, let him be hanged.
Deliver him to safety and return,   158
For I must use thee. [*Exit Hubert with Peter of Pomfret.*]
    O my gentle cousin,   159
Hear'st thou the news abroad, who are arrived?
BASTARD
The French, my lord. Men's mouths are full of it.
Besides, I met Lord Bigot and Lord Salisbury,
With eyes as red as new-enkindled fire,
And others more, going to seek the grave
Of Arthur, whom they say is killed tonight   165
On your suggestion.
KING JOHN   Gentle kinsman, go,   166
And thrust thyself into their companies.
I have a way to win their loves again.
Bring them before me.
BASTARD   I will seek them out.
KING JOHN
Nay, but make haste, the better foot before.   170

144 **strangely fantasied** full of strange fancies   148 **Pomfret** Pontefract,
in Yorkshire   151 **Ascension Day** the Thursday forty days after Easter
celebrating the ascent of Christ into heaven   158 **safety** safekeeping
159 **gentle** noble   165 **is killed tonight** was killed last night   166 **suggestion** instigation   170 **the better foot before** i.e., as quickly as you can

O, let me have no subject enemies
When adverse foreigners affright my towns   172
With dreadful pomp of stout invasion!   173
Be Mercury, set feathers to thy heels,   174
And fly like thought from them to me again.   175
BASTARD
The spirit of the time shall teach me speed.   *Exit.*
KING JOHN
Spoke like a sprightful noble gentleman!   177
[*To the Messenger.*] Go after him, for he perhaps shall
    need
Some messenger betwixt me and the peers;
And be thou he.
MESSENGER   With all my heart, my liege.   [*Exit.*]
KING JOHN   My mother dead!

Enter Hubert.

HUBERT
My lord, they say five moons were seen tonight:
Four fixèd, and the fifth did whirl about
The other four in wondrous motion.
KING JOHN
Five moons!
HUBERT   Old men and beldams in the streets   186
Do prophesy upon it dangerously.   187
Young Arthur's death is common in their mouths,
And, when they talk of him, they shake their heads
And whisper one another in the ear;
And he that speaks doth grip the hearer's wrist,
Whilst he that hears makes fearful action,   192
With wrinkled brows, with nods, with rolling eyes.
I saw a smith stand with his hammer, thus,
The whilst his iron did on the anvil cool,
With open mouth swallowing a tailor's news;
Who, with his shears and measure in his hand,
Standing on slippers, which his nimble haste

172 adverse hostile   **173 stout** bold   **174 feathers** (Mercury, messenger
of the gods, had winged sandals.)   **175 like thought** as swift as thought
177 sprightful spirited   **186 beldams** old women   **187 prophesy upon it**
make predictions from it, expound its meaning for the future.   **dangerously** in terms of future danger, or threateningly to public order
192 action gestures

Had falsely thrust upon contrary feet,   199
Told of a many thousand warlike French   200
That were embattlèd and ranked in Kent.   201
Another lean unwashed artificer   202
Cuts off his tale and talks of Arthur's death.

KING JOHN
Why seek'st thou to possess me with these fears?   204
Why urgest thou so oft young Arthur's death?
Thy hand hath murdered him. I had a mighty cause
To wish him dead, but thou hadst none to kill him.

HUBERT
No had, my lord? Why, did you not provoke me?   208

KING JOHN
It is the curse of kings to be attended
By slaves that take their humors for a warrant   210
To break within the bloody house of life,   211
And on the winking of authority   212
To understand a law, to know the meaning   213
Of dangerous majesty, when perchance it frowns
More upon humor than advised respect.   215

HUBERT [*Showing his warrant*]
Here is your hand and seal for what I did.

KING JOHN
O, when the last account twixt heaven and earth
Is to be made, then shall this hand and seal
Witness against us to damnation!
How oft the sight of means to do ill deeds   220
Make deeds ill done! Hadst not thou been by,   221
A fellow by the hand of nature marked,
Quoted, and signed to do a deed of shame,   223
This murder had not come into my mind.

199 upon contrary feet the left slipper on the right foot and vice versa
200 a many thousand many thousands of   **201 embattlèd** drawn up in
battle array   **202 artificer** artisan   **204 possess . . . fears** give me these
fearful tidings   **208 No had** had I not.   **provoke** incite   **210 humors**
whims   **211 the bloody . . . life** the body, animated by life blood and
made bloody by murder   **212 winking** closing the eyes (i.e., when the
person in authority closes his eyes to the law, or gives the merest hint of
approving illegality)   **213 understand a law** i.e., infer what is being
commanded   **215 upon humor** through whim.   **advised respect** careful
consideration   **220–221 How . . . done** how often seeing a way to do ill
deeds prompts us to go ahead   **223 Quoted, and signed** particularly
designated and marked out

But, taking note of thy abhorred aspect,
Finding thee fit for bloody villainy,
Apt, liable to be employed in danger,   227
I faintly broke with thee of Arthur's death,   228
And thou, to be endearèd to a king,
Made it no conscience to destroy a prince.   230

HUBERT   My lord—

KING JOHN
Hadst thou but shook thy head or made a pause
When I spake darkly what I purposèd,   233
Or turned an eye of doubt upon my face,
As bid me tell my tale in express words,   235
Deep shame had struck me dumb, made me break off,
And those thy fears might have wrought fears in me.
But thou didst understand me by my signs
And didst in signs again parley with sin,
Yea, without stop didst let thy heart consent,
And consequently thy rude hand to act
The deed which both our tongues held vile to name.
Out of my sight, and never see me more!
My nobles leave me, and my state is braved,   244
Even at my gates, with ranks of foreign powers.
Nay, in the body of this fleshly land,   246
This kingdom, this confine of blood and breath,   247
Hostility and civil tumult reigns
Between my conscience and my cousin's death.

HUBERT
Arm you against your other enemies;
I'll make a peace between your soul and you.
Young Arthur is alive. This hand of mine
Is yet a maiden and an innocent hand,
Not painted with the crimson spots of blood.
Within this bosom never entered yet
The dreadful motion of a murderous thought;   256

---

227 liable suitable.   **danger** something dangerous to the victim
228 faintly broke with hesitatingly broached the subject with   **230 conscience** matter of conscience   **233 darkly** indirectly   **235 As** as though
to.   **express** explicit   **244 my state is braved** my authority is challenged   **246 body . . . land** i.e., John's own body. (Uses the figure of
the microcosm, in which man is conceived as the epitome of the universe.)   **247 confine** (1) territorial limit (2) prison   **256 motion** impulse

And you have slandered nature in my form,   257
Which, howsoever rude exteriorly,   258
Is yet the cover of a fairer mind
Than to be butcher of an innocent child.

KING JOHN
Doth Arthur live? O, haste thee to the peers!
Throw this report on their incensèd rage,   262
And make them tame to their obedience.
Forgive the comment that my passion made
Upon thy feature, for my rage was blind,   265
And foul imaginary eyes of blood   266
Presented thee more hideous than thou art.
O, answer not, but to my closet bring   268
The angry lords with all expedient haste.
I conjure thee but slowly; run more fast!   270

Exeunt [separately].

❖

4.3   *Enter Arthur, on the walls, [disguised as a shipboy].*

ARTHUR
The wall is high, and yet will I leap down.
Good ground, be pitiful and hurt me not!
There's few or none do know me; if they did,
This shipboy's semblance hath disguised me quite.   4
I am afraid, and yet I'll venture it.
If I get down, and do not break my limbs,
I'll find a thousand shifts to get away.   7
As good to die and go as die and stay. [*He leaps down.*]

---

257 slandered . . . form i.e., slandered my nature by judging me harshly in terms of my unattractive appearance; or, slandered human nature in my person   **258 rude** rough   **262 Throw . . . rage** i.e., tell them this news as though throwing water on their burning rage   **265 feature** outward appearance   **266 imaginary . . . blood** your eyes, which I imagined to be bloody in thought, or, more probably, my eyes made bloodshot with rage at imagined wrong   **268 closet** private chamber   **270 conjure** adjure, urge

4.3. Location: England. Before the walls of a castle.
s.d. on the walls in the gallery rearstage, above the doors   **4 semblance** disguise   **7 shifts** (1) stratagems (2) changes of costume

O me! My uncle's spirit is in these stones.
Heaven take my soul, and England keep my bones!

Dies.

*Enter Pembroke, Salisbury [with a letter], and
Bigot.*

SALISBURY
Lords, I will meet him at Saint Edmundsbury.   11
It is our safety, and we must embrace   12
This gentle offer of the perilous time.

PEMBROKE
Who brought that letter from the Cardinal?

SALISBURY
The Count Melun, a noble lord of France,
Whose private with me of the Dauphin's love   16
Is much more general than these lines import.   17

BIGOT
Tomorrow morning let us meet him, then.

SALISBURY
Or rather then set forward, for 'twill be
Two long days' journey, lords, or ere we meet.   20

Enter [the] Bastard.

BASTARD
Once more today well met, distempered lords!   21
The King by me requests your presence straight.   22

SALISBURY
The King hath dispossessed himself of us.
We will not line his thin bestainèd cloak
With our pure honors, nor attend the foot   25
That leaves the print of blood where'er it walks.
Return and tell him so. We know the worst.

BASTARD
Whate'er you think, good words, I think, were best.

SALISBURY
Our griefs, and not our manners, reason now.   29

---

11 him i.e., the Dauphin. **Saint Edmundsbury** Bury St. Edmunds, in
Suffolk   **12 our safety** our only means of safety   **16 private** private
communication   **17 general** all-embracing   **20 or ere** before   **21 distempered** disaffected   **22 straight** at once   **25 attend the foot** follow in
the footsteps of one, serve one   **29 griefs** grievances.   **reason** speak.
(But the Bastard answers in the sense of "rationality," l. 30, and "common sense," l. 31.)

BASTARD
   But there is little reason in your grief.
   Therefore 'twere reason you had manners now.
PEMBROKE
   Sir, sir, impatience hath his privilege.   32
BASTARD
   'Tis true—to hurt his master, no man else.   33
SALISBURY
   This is the prison. [*He sees Arthur's body.*] What is he lies
   here?
PEMBROKE
   O death, made proud with pure and princely beauty!
   The earth had not a hole to hide this deed.
SALISBURY
   Murder, as hating what himself hath done,   37
   Doth lay it open to urge on revenge.
BIGOT
   Or, when he doomed this beauty to a grave,   39
   Found it too precious-princely for a grave.
SALISBURY [*To the Bastard*]
   Sir Richard, what think you? You have beheld.   41
   Or have you read or heard, or could you think,   42
   Or do you almost think, although you see,   43
   That you do see? Could thought, without this object, 44
   Form such another? This is the very top,   45
   The height, the crest, or crest unto the crest,
   Of murder's arms. This is the bloodiest shame,   47
   The wildest savagery, the vilest stroke
   That ever walleyed wrath or staring rage   49
   Presented to the tears of soft remorse.   50
PEMBROKE
   All murders past do stand excused in this;   51
   And this, so sole and so unmatchable,   52

32, 33 his its   **33 'Tis . . . else** i.e., perhaps anger must be allowed to
speak, as you say, but it is apt to hurt the speaker more than his listen-
ers. You'll be sorry for what you say.   **37 as** as if   **39 he** i.e., murder
41 Sir Richard i.e., the Bastard   **42 Or . . . think** have you either read
or heard (of anything like this) or could you believe   **43 almost** even
44 That that which   **44–45 Could . . . another** could you possibly imagine another sight like this without its actually being set before you
47 arms coat of arms. (This deed is the crest on top of the crest of
murder's coat of arms.)   **49 walleyed** glaring fiercely   **50 remorse**
pity   **51 in this** in comparison to this   **52 sole** unique

Shall give a holiness, a purity,
To the yet unbegotten sin of times,   54
And prove a deadly bloodshed but a jest,   55
Exampled by this heinous spectacle.   56

BASTARD
It is a damnèd and a bloody work,
The graceless action of a heavy hand—   58
If that it be the work of any hand.

SALISBURY
If that it be the work of any hand?
We had a kind of light what would ensue.   61
It is the shameful work of Hubert's hand,
The practice and the purpose of the King,   63
From whose obedience I forbid my soul,
Kneeling before this ruin of sweet life,   [*He kneels*]
And breathing to his breathless excellence
The incense of a vow, a holy vow,   67
Never to taste the pleasures of the world,
Never to be infected with delight,   69
Nor conversant with ease and idleness,
Till I have set a glory to this hand   71
By giving it the worship of revenge.   72

PEMBROKE, BIGOT [*Kneeling*]
Our souls religiously confirm thy words.   [*All rise.*]

        Enter Hubert.

HUBERT
Lords, I am hot with haste in seeking you.
Arthur doth live. The King hath sent for you.

SALISBURY
O, he is bold and blushes not at death.
Avaunt, thou hateful villain! Get thee gone!   77

HUBERT
I am no villain.

SALISBURY [*Drawing his sword*]   Must I rob the law?   78

54 times i.e., future times   **55 but** to be only   **56 Exampled by** compared with   **58 graceless** unholy.   **heavy** wicked   **61 light** premonition   **63 practice** plot, treachery   **67 The incense of a vow** i.e., a vow that ascends to heaven, like incense   **69 infected** tainted, imbued   **71 this hand** i.e., either Arthur's hand, or Salisbury's own hand, which he raises in taking an oath   **72 worship** honor   **77 Avaunt** begone   **78 Must . . . law** must I deprive the law of its intended victim by killing you myself

BASTARD
Your sword is bright, sir. Put it up again.   79
SALISBURY
Not till I sheathe it in a murderer's skin.
HUBERT [*Drawing*]
Stand back, Lord Salisbury, stand back, I say!
By heaven, I think my sword's as sharp as yours.
I would not have you, lord, forget yourself,
Nor tempt the danger of my true defense,   84
Lest I, by marking of your rage, forget   85
Your worth, your greatness, and nobility.
BIGOT
Out, dunghill! Dar'st thou brave a nobleman?   87
HUBERT
Not for my life. But yet I dare defend
My innocent life against an emperor.
SALISBURY
Thou art a murderer.
HUBERT   Do not prove me so;   90
Yet I am none. Whose tongue soe'er speaks false,
Not truly speaks; who speaks not truly, lies.
PEMBROKE
Cut him to pieces!
BASTARD [*Drawing*]   Keep the peace, I say!
SALISBURY
Stand by, or I shall gall you, Faulconbridge.   94
BASTARD
Thou wert better gall the devil, Salisbury.
If thou but frown on me, or stir thy foot,
Or teach thy hasty spleen to do me shame,   97
I'll strike thee dead. Put up thy sword betimes,   98
Or I'll so maul you and your toasting iron   99
That you shall think the devil is come from hell.
BIGOT
What wilt thou do, renownèd Faulconbridge?
Second a villain and a murderer?

---

79 bright i.e., unused   **84 tempt** risk, test   **85 by marking of your rage**
paying attention only to your wrath   **87 brave** insult   **90 prove me so**
i.e., make me a murderer by tempting me to kill you   **94 Stand by** stand
aside.   **gall** wound   **97 spleen** i.e., wrath   **98 betimes** promptly
99 toasting iron sword. (Used contemptuously.)

HUBERT
Lord Bigot, I am none.
BIGOT   Who killed this prince?
HUBERT
'Tis not an hour since I left him well.
I honored him, I loved him, and will weep
My date of life out for his sweet life's loss. [*He weeps.*] 106
SALISBURY
Trust not those cunning waters of his eyes,
For villainy is not without such rheum,   108
And he, long traded in it, makes it seem   109
Like rivers of remorse and innocency.
Away with me, all you whose souls abhor
Th' uncleanly savors of a slaughterhouse!   112
For I am stifled with this smell of sin.
BIGOT
Away toward Bury, to the Dauphin there!
PEMBROKE
There, tell the King, he may inquire us out.
                                        Exeunt lords.
BASTARD
Here's a good world! Knew you of this fair work?
Beyond the infinite and boundless reach
Of mercy, if thou didst this deed of death,
Art thou damned, Hubert.
HUBERT   Do but hear me, sir.
BASTARD   Ha! I'll tell thee what;
Thou'rt damned as black—nay, nothing is so black;
Thou art more deep damned than Prince Lucifer.
There is not yet so ugly a fiend of hell
As thou shalt be, if thou didst kill this child.
HUBERT
Upon my soul—
BASTARD   If thou didst but consent
To this most cruel act, do but despair;
And if thou want'st a cord, the smallest thread
That ever spider twisted from her womb
Will serve to strangle thee; a rush will be a beam   129
To hang thee on; or wouldst thou drown thyself,

106 date duration   **108 rheum** watery discharge, i.e., tears   **109 traded**
experienced   **112 savors** odors   **129 rush** reed

Put but a little water in a spoon
And it shall be as all the ocean,
Enough to stifle such a villain up.
I do suspect thee very grievously.

HUBERT
If I in act, consent, or sin of thought
Be guilty of the stealing that sweet breath
Which was embounded in this beauteous clay,   137
Let hell want pains enough to torture me.   138
I left him well.

BASTARD   Go, bear him in thine arms.
I am amazed, methinks, and lose my way   140
Among the thorns and dangers of this world.
                        [*Hubert picks up Arthur.*]
How easy dost thou take all England up!
From forth this morsel of dead royalty,
The life, the right, and truth of all this realm
Is fled to heaven; and England now is left
To tug and scamble and to part by th' teeth   146
The unowed interest of proud-swelling state.   147
Now for the bare-picked bone of majesty
Doth doggèd war bristle his angry crest,   149
And snarleth in the gentle eyes of peace.
Now powers from home and discontents at home   151
Meet in one line; and vast confusion waits,   152
As doth a raven on a sick-fall'n beast,
The imminent decay of wrested pomp.   154
Now happy he whose cloak and cincture can   155
Hold out this tempest! Bear away that child
And follow me with speed. I'll to the King.
A thousand businesses are brief in hand,   158
And heaven itself doth frown upon the land.

                                        Exeunt.

137 clay i.e., Arthur's body   **138 want** lack   **140 amazed** stunned
146 scamble scramble.   **part by th' teeth** tear apart by the teeth, as a
ravenous animal would do   **147 unowed interest** disputed ownership or
control   **149 doggèd** fierce. (War is viewed as a pack of dogs fighting
over a bone and bristling their hackles, continuing the metaphor of
l. 146.)   **151 powers from home** foreign armies   **152 in one line** in
united purpose.   **vast confusion waits** limitless chaos awaits
154 wrested pomp usurped majesty   **155 cincture** belt   **158 are brief in
hand** demand immediate action

5.1   *Enter King John and Pandulph, [with]*
attendants.

KING JOHN [*Giving Pandulph the crown*]
  Thus have I yielded up into your hand
  The circle of my glory.
PANDULPH [*Giving back the crown*]   Take again
  From this my hand, as holding of the Pope,
  Your sovereign greatness and authority.
KING JOHN
  Now keep your holy word. Go meet the French,
  And from His Holiness use all your power
  To stop their marches 'fore we are inflamed.
  Our discontented counties do revolt;   8
  Our people quarrel with obedience,
  Swearing allegiance and the love of soul   10
  To stranger blood, to foreign royalty.   11
  This inundation of mistempered humor   12
  Rests by you only to be qualified.   13
  Then pause not, for the present time's so sick
  That present med'cine must be ministered,   15
  Or overthrow incurable ensues.
PANDULPH
  It was my breath that blew this tempest up,
  Upon your stubborn usage of the Pope;   18
  But since you are a gentle convertite,   19
  My tongue shall hush again this storm of war
  And make fair weather in your blustering land.
  On this Ascension Day, remember well,
  Upon your oath of service to the Pope,
  Go I to make the French lay down their arms.
                              Exit [with attendants].
KING JOHN
  Is this Ascension Day? Did not the prophet
  Say that before Ascension Day at noon

5.1. Location: England. The court of King John.
8 counties shires; possibly, nobles   **10 love of soul** most sincere love
11 stranger foreign   **12–13 This . . . qualified** this erratic behavior
(thought to be caused by the excess of one of the bodily humors) can be
reduced to its right proportion only by you   **15 present** prompt
18 Upon following   **19 convertite** convert

My crown I should give off? Even so I have.
I did suppose it should be on constraint;
But, heaven be thanked, it is but voluntary.

    Enter [the] Bastard.

BASTARD
All Kent hath yielded. Nothing there holds out
But Dover Castle. London hath received,
Like a kind host, the Dauphin and his powers.   32
Your nobles will not hear you, but are gone
To offer service to your enemy,
And wild amazement hurries up and down
The little number of your doubtful friends.   36
KING JOHN
Would not my lords return to me again
After they heard young Arthur was alive?
BASTARD
They found him dead and cast into the streets,
An empty casket, where the jewel of life
By some damned hand was robbed and ta'en away.
KING JOHN
That villain Hubert told me he did live.
BASTARD
So, on my soul, he did, for aught he knew.
But wherefore do you droop? Why look you sad?
Be great in act, as you have been in thought.
Let not the world see fear and sad distrust   46
Govern the motion of a kingly eye.
Be stirring as the time; be fire with fire;   48
Threaten the threatener, and outface the brow
Of bragging horror. So shall inferior eyes,
That borrow their behaviors from the great,
Grow great by your example and put on
The dauntless spirit of resolution.
Away, and glister like the god of war
When he intendeth to become the field!   55
Show boldness and aspiring confidence.

32 powers army   **36 doubtful** not to be relied on; fearful   **46 distrust**
lack of confidence, fainting courage   **48 as the time** as the state of
affairs demands   **55 become** grace, adorn

What, shall they seek the lion in his den,
And fright him there? And make him tremble there?
O, let it not be said! Forage, and run   59
To meet displeasure farther from the doors,
And grapple with him ere he come so nigh.

KING JOHN
The legate of the Pope hath been with me,
And I have made a happy peace with him;
And he hath promised to dismiss the powers
Led by the Dauphin.

BASTARD   O inglorious league!
Shall we, upon the footing of our land,   66
Send fair-play orders and make compromise,   67
Insinuation, parley, and base truce
To arms invasive? Shall a beardless boy,   69
A cockered silken wanton, brave our fields   70
And flesh his spirit in a warlike soil,   71
Mocking the air with colors idly spread,   72
And find no check? Let us, my liege, to arms!   73
Perchance the Cardinal cannot make your peace;
Or if he do, let it at least be said
They saw we had a purpose of defense.   76

KING JOHN
Have thou the ordering of this present time.

BASTARD
Away, then, with good courage! Yet, I know,   78
Our party may well meet a prouder foe.   *Exeunt.* 79

---

59 Forage seek out the enemy as prey   **66 upon . . . land** standing on
our native soil   **67 fair-play orders** chivalric conditions   **69 invasive**
invading   **70 cockered . . . wanton** spoiled, dandified youngster.   **brave**
(1) arrogantly display his splendor in (2) defy   **71 flesh** initiate in bloodshed or inure to bloodshed   **72 idly** carelessly, insolently   **73 check**
restraint   **76 of defense** to defend ourselves   **78–79 Yet . . . foe** i.e., yet
this call for courage is scarcely necessary, since our side is ready to
take on a more spirited and fierce foe than this one. (Or he could mean,
to himself, that he fears the enemy will prove too much for them.)

5.2   *Enter, in arms, [Lewis the] Dauphin, Salisbury, Melun, Pembroke, Bigot, soldiers.*

LEWIS
My Lord Melun, let this be copied out,   1
And keep it safe for our remembrance.
                              [He gives a document.]
Return the precedent to these lords again,   3
That, having our fair order written down,   4
Both they and we, perusing o'er these notes,
May know wherefore we took the Sacrament,   6
And keep our faiths firm and inviolable.

SALISBURY
Upon our sides it never shall be broken.
And, noble Dauphin, albeit we swear
A voluntary zeal and an unurged faith   10
To your proceedings, yet believe me, Prince,
I am not glad that such a sore of time   12
Should seek a plaster by contemnèd revolt,   13
And heal the inveterate canker of one wound   14
By making many. O, it grieves my soul
That I must draw this metal from my side   16
To be a widow maker! O, and there
Where honorable rescue and defense
Cries out upon the name of Salisbury!   19
But such is the infection of the time
That, for the health and physic of our right,   21
We cannot deal but with the very hand   22
Of stern injustice and confusèd wrong.
And is 't not pity, O my grievèd friends,

5.2. Location: England. The Dauphin's camp at St. Edmundsbury.
1 this i.e., the agreement with the English lords. (See ll. 33–34 of the preceding scene.)   3 precedent original document, first draft   4 order proposal   6 took the Sacrament i.e., received communion to confirm the sacredness of our vows   10 unurged uncompelled   12–13 that . . . revolt i.e., that the ills of this troublesome time should seek out the despised remedy of rebellion.   plaster dressing for a wound.   contemned reviled   14 inveterate canker chronic and deep-seated ulcer   16 metal i.e., sword   19 Cries out upon appeal to, or, exclaim against   21 physic medical cure   22 We . . . hand i.e., we are obliged to use the very means (which we otherwise deplore). The nobles must fight fire with fire.

That we, the sons and children of this isle,
Were born to see so sad an hour as this,
Wherein we step after a stranger, march   27
Upon her gentle bosom, and fill up
Her enemies' ranks—I must withdraw and weep
Upon the spot of this enforcèd cause—   30
To grace the gentry of a land remote,   31
And follow unacquainted colors here?   [*He weeps.*]   32
What, here? O nation, that thou couldst remove!   33
That Neptune's arms, who clippeth thee about,   34
Would bear thee from the knowledge of thyself,
And grapple thee unto a pagan shore,
Where these two Christian armies might combine   37
The blood of malice in a vein of league,   38
And not to spend it so unneighborly!

LEWIS
A noble temper dost thou show in this,
And great affections wrestling in thy bosom   41
Doth make an earthquake of nobility.   42
O, what a noble combat hast thou fought
Between compulsion and a brave respect!   44
Let me wipe off this honorable dew,
That silverly doth progress on thy cheeks.
                          [*He wipes Salisbury's eyes.*]
My heart hath melted at a lady's tears,
Being an ordinary inundation;
But this effusion of such manly drops,
This shower, blown up by tempest of the soul,
Startles mine eyes, and makes me more amazed
Than had I seen the vaulty top of heaven   52
Figured quite o'er with burning meteors.   53

27 step after follow (as in a march).   **stranger** foreign (leader)   **30 spot**
(1) stain (2) place.   **enforcèd cause** i.e., cause into which I am forced
31 grace honor   **32 unacquainted colors** i.e., the banners of a foreign
power   **33 remove** depart, change location, i.e., go from this scene of
civil carnage to a crusade against pagan enemies   **34 clippeth** embraces   **37–38 combine . . . league** i.e., unite the malice they now ex-
pend on one another in a league of hostility, a crusade, against a pagan
foe   **41 affections** passions   **42 Doth . . . nobility** i.e., produces tumult
in your noble nature   **44 compulsion** what you are compelled to do (by
the hard necessities of the times).   **brave respect** gallant consideration
(of your country's need)   **52 had I seen** if I had seen   **53 Figured**
adorned

Lift up thy brow, renownèd Salisbury,
And with a great heart heave away this storm.
Commend these waters to those baby eyes   56
That never saw the giant world enraged,
Nor met with fortune other than at feasts,
Full warm of blood, of mirth, of gossiping.
Come, come, for thou shalt thrust thy hand as deep
Into the purse of rich prosperity
As Lewis himself. So, nobles, shall you all,
That knit your sinews to the strength of mine.

    Enter Pandulph.

And even there, methinks, an angel spake.   64
Look where the holy legate comes apace,
To give us warrant from the hand of heaven,
And on our actions set the name of right
With holy breath.
PANDULPH   Hail, noble prince of France!
The next is this: King John hath reconciled
Himself to Rome. His spirit is come in   70
That so stood out against the holy Church,
The great metropolis and See of Rome.
Therefore thy threatening colors now wind up,   73
And tame the savage spirit of wild war,
That, like a lion fostered up at hand,   75
It may lie gently at the foot of peace
And be no further harmful than in show.
LEWIS
Your Grace shall pardon me; I will not back.   78
I am too highborn to be propertied,   79
To be a secondary at control,   80
Or useful servingman and instrument
To any sovereign state throughout the world.
Your breath first kindled the dead coal of wars

56 Commend entrust, bequeath. (Leave tears to babies, says the Dauphin, that have never known the fury of the world at large and have had no worse fortune than to be well fed and entertained.) **64 an angel spake** (1) i.e., Pandulph comes with warrant from "the hand of heaven" (2) a pun on *angel* meaning a coin, in "the purse of rich prosperity." A trumpet may sound at this point. **70 is come in** has submitted **73 wind up** furl **75 at hand** by hand (and hence tame) **78 shall** must. **back** go back **79 propertied** made a tool of **80 secondary at control** subordinate under someone else's command

Between this chastised kingdom and myself,
And brought in matter that should feed this fire;   85
And now 'tis far too huge to be blown out
With that same weak wind which enkindled it.
You taught me how to know the face of right,   88
Acquainted me with interest to this land,   89
Yea, thrust this enterprise into my heart.
And come ye now to tell me John hath made
His peace with Rome? What is that peace to me?
I, by the honor of my marriage bed,   93
After young Arthur, claim this land for mine;
And, now it is half conquered, must I back
Because that John hath made his peace with Rome?
Am I Rome's slave? What penny hath Rome borne,
What men provided, what munition sent,
To underprop this action? Is 't not I   99
That undergo this charge? Who else but I,   100
And such as to my claim are liable,   101
Sweat in this business and maintain this war?
Have I not heard these islanders shout out
"*Vive le roi!*" as I have banked their towns?   104
Have I not here the best cards for the game
To win this easy match played for a crown?   106
And shall I now give o'er the yielded set?   107
No, no, on my soul, it never shall be said.

PANDULPH
You look but on the outside of this work.

LEWIS
Outside or inside, I will not return
Till my attempt so much be glorified
As to my ample hope was promisèd
Before I drew this gallant head of war,   113
And culled these fiery spirits from the world

---

85 matter i.e., fuel   **88 right** my true claim   **89 interest** title, right
93 by the . . . bed i.e., in the name of Blanche, my wife   **99 underprop**
support   **100 charge** expense   **101 liable** subject   **104 Vive le roi** long
live the king. (Also a term in card playing; the metaphor continues in
banked, won by putting in the bank, *game, match, crown*, a five-shilling
stake, *set*, round in a game, etc.)   **banked** coasted, skirted   **106 crown**
(1) symbol of monarchy (2) stake in a game   **107 give o'er** abandon.
the yielded set the round or rubber already won   **113 drew** assembled.   **head of war** army

To outlook conquest and to win renown   115
Even in the jaws of danger and of death.

> [*A trumpet sounds.*]

What lusty trumpet thus doth summon us?   117

> *Enter [the] Bastard.*

BASTARD
According to the fair play of the world,   118
Let me have audience. I am sent to speak.
My holy lord of Milan, from the King
I come, to learn how you have dealt for him;
And, as you answer, I do know the scope
And warrant limited unto my tongue.

PANDULPH
The Dauphin is too willful-opposite,   124
And will not temporize with my entreaties.   125
He flatly says he'll not lay down his arms.

BASTARD
By all the blood that ever fury breathed,   127
The youth says well. Now hear our English king,
For thus his royalty doth speak in me.
He is prepared, and reason too he should.   130
This apish and unmannerly approach,
This harnessed masque and unadvisèd revel,   132
This unhaired sauciness and boyish troops,   133
The King doth smile at, and is well prepared
To whip this dwarfish war, these pygmy arms,
From out the circle of his territories.
That hand which had the strength, even at your door,
To cudgel you and make you take the hatch,   138
To dive like buckets in concealèd wells,   139
To crouch in litter of your stable planks,   140
To lie like pawns locked up in chests and trunks,   141

115 outlook stare down   **117 lusty** vigorous   **118 fair play** i.e., rules of
chivalry   **124 willful-opposite** stubbornly opposed   **125 temporize**
come to an agreement   **127 blood** bold warriors   **130 reason . . . should**
with good reason   **132 harnessed** in armor.   **unadvisèd revel** ill-
considered entertainment   **133 unhaired** beardless, youthful   **138 take
the hatch** leap over the lower half door; i.e., make a hasty and undignified retreat   **139 concealèd wells** wells offering a place to hide
140 crouch i.e., hide.   **litter** straw bedding for animals.   **planks**
floors   **141 pawns** articles in pawn

To hug with swine, to seek sweet safety out   142
In vaults and prisons, and to thrill and shake   143
Even at the crying of your nation's crow,   144
Thinking his voice an armèd Englishman—
Shall that victorious hand be feebled here
That in your chambers gave you chastisement?   147
No! Know the gallant monarch is in arms,
And like an eagle o'er his aerie towers,   149
To souse annoyance that comes near his nest.   150
And you degenerate, you ingrate revolts,   151
You bloody Neroes, ripping up the womb   152
Of your dear mother England, blush for shame!
For your own ladies and pale-visaged maids
Like Amazons come tripping after drums;   155
Their thimbles into armèd gauntlets change,   156
Their needles to lances, and their gentle hearts
To fierce and bloody inclination.

LEWIS
There end thy brave, and turn thy face in peace.   159
We grant thou canst outscold us. Fare thee well.
We hold our time too precious to be spent
With such a brabbler.

PANDULPH   Give me leave to speak.   162

BASTARD
No, I will speak.

LEWIS   We will attend to neither.   163
Strike up the drums, and let the tongue of war
Plead for our interest and our being here.

BASTARD
Indeed, your drums, being beaten, will cry out;
And so shall you, being beaten. Do but start
An echo with the clamor of thy drum,

---

142 hug i.e., bed down   **143 thrill** shiver   **144 crying . . . crow** i.e.,
crowing of the rooster, a French national symbol   **147 your chambers**
i.e., your own terrain   **149 aerie** nest.   **towers** soars   **150 souse** swoop
down upon   **151 revolts** rebels   **152 Neroes** (The Roman emperor Nero
allegedly ripped open the womb of his mother after having murdered
her.)   **155 Amazons** female warriors of ancient mythology   **156 armèd
gauntlets** steel-plated gloves worn as part of the armor   **159 brave**
defiant boast.   **turn thy face** go back where you came from
162 brabbler noisy, quarrelsome person   **163 attend to** (1) listen to
(2) wait for

And even at hand a drum is ready braced   169
That shall reverberate all as loud as thine.
Sound but another, and another shall,
As loud as thine, rattle the welkin's ear   172
And mock the deep-mouthed thunder. For at hand—
Not trusting to this halting legate here,
Whom he hath used rather for sport than need—
Is warlike John; and in his forehead sits
A bare-ribbed Death, whose office is this day   177
To feast upon whole thousands of the French.

LEWIS
Strike up our drums, to find this danger out.

BASTARD
And thou shalt find it, Dauphin, do not doubt.
                    [*Drums beat.*] *Exeunt* [*separately*].

5.3   *Alarums. Enter* [*King*] *John and Hubert.*

KING JOHN
How goes the day with us? O, tell me, Hubert.

HUBERT
Badly, I fear. How fares Your Majesty?

KING JOHN
This fever that hath troubled me so long
Lies heavy on me. O, my heart is sick!

        Enter a Messenger.

MESSENGER
My lord, your valiant kinsman, Faulconbridge,
Desires Your Majesty to leave the field
And send him word by me which way you go.

KING JOHN
Tell him, toward Swinestead, to the abbey there.   8

MESSENGER
Be of good comfort, for the great supply   9

---

169 **ready braced** i.e., tightened, ready to be struck   172 **welkin's**
heaven's, sky's   177 **bare-ribbed Death** i.e., Death envisaged as a skeleton.   **office** function

5.3. Location: England. The field of battle.
8 **Swinestead** (in Lincolnshire)   9 **supply** reinforcement

That was expected by the Dauphin here
Are wrecked three nights ago on Goodwin Sands.   11
This news was brought to Richard but even now.   12
The French fight coldly, and retire themselves.   13
KING JOHN
Ay me, this tyrant fever burns me up,
And will not let me welcome this good news.
Set on toward Swinestead. To my litter straight;
Weakness possesseth me, and I am faint.   *Exeunt.*

5.4   *Enter Salisbury, Pembroke, and Bigot.*

SALISBURY
I did not think the King so stored with friends.
PEMBROKE
Up once again! Put spirit in the French.
If they miscarry, we miscarry too.
SALISBURY
That misbegotten devil, Faulconbridge,
In spite of spite, alone upholds the day.   5
PEMBROKE
They say King John, sore sick, hath left the field.

     Enter Melun, wounded, [led by a soldier].

MELUN
Lead me to the revolts of England here.   7
SALISBURY
When we were happy we had other names.
PEMBROKE
It is the Count Melun.
SALISBURY   Wounded to death.
MELUN
Fly, noble English, you are bought and sold!   10
Unthread the rude eye of rebellion   11

---

11 Goodwin Sands dangerous shoals off Kent   **12 Richard** i.e., the
Bastard   **13 retire themselves** retreat

5.4. Location: The field of battle, as before.
5 In spite of spite i.e., despite anything we do   **7 revolts** rebels
10 bought and sold i.e., betrayed   **11 Unthread . . . eye** i.e., withdraw
from the hazardous undertaking in which you are engaged, just as you
would withdraw thread from a needle's eye

And welcome home again discarded faith.
Seek out King John and fall before his feet;
For if the French be lords of this loud day,
He means to recompense the pains you take   15
By cutting off your heads. Thus hath he sworn,
And I with him, and many more with me,
Upon the altar at Saint Edmundsbury,
Even on that altar where we swore to you
Dear amity and everlasting love.

SALISBURY
May this be possible? May this be true?

MELUN
Have I not hideous death within my view,
Retaining but a quantity of life,   23
Which bleeds away, even as a form of wax
Resolveth from his figure 'gainst the fire?   25
What in the world should make me now deceive,
Since I must lose the use of all deceit?   27
Why should I then be false, since it is true
That I must die here and live hence by truth?   29
I say again, if Lewis do win the day,
He is forsworn if e'er those eyes of yours
Behold another daybreak in the east.
But even this night, whose black contagious breath 33
Already smokes about the burning crest   34
Of the old, feeble, and day-wearied sun,
Even this ill night, your breathing shall expire,
Paying the fine of rated treachery   37
Even with a treacherous fine of all your lives,   38
If Lewis by your assistance win the day.
Commend me to one Hubert with your king;
The love of him, and this respect besides,   41
For that my grandsire was an Englishman,   42
Awakes my conscience to confess all this.
In lieu whereof, I pray you, bear me hence   44

15 **He** i.e., the French Dauphin   **23 quantity** small quantity
25 Resolveth from his figure melts and loses its shape   **27 use** profit
29 hence i.e., in heaven   **33 contagious** (Night air was thought to be
noxious.)   **34 smokes** becomes misty   **37 fine** penalty.   **rated**
(1) assessed, evaluated (2) rebuked, chided   **38 fine** end (with a pun on
fine of the previous line)   **41 respect** consideration   **42 For that** because, in that   **44 In lieu whereof** in payment for which (information)

From forth the noise and rumor of the field,   45
Where I may think the remnant of my thoughts
In peace, and part this body and my soul
With contemplation and devout desires.

SALISBURY
We do believe thee, and beshrew my soul   49
But I do love the favor and the form   50
Of this most fair occasion, by the which
We will untread the steps of damnèd flight,   52
And like a bated and retirèd flood,   53
Leaving our rankness and irregular course,   54
Stoop low within those bounds we have o'erlooked   55
And calmly run on in obedience
Even to our ocean, to our great King John.
My arm shall give thee help to bear thee hence,
For I do see the cruel pangs of death
Right in thine eye. Away, my friends! New flight,   60
And happy newness, that intends old right!   61
             Exeunt [leading off Melun].

❖

5.5   *Enter [Lewis the] Dauphin and his train.*

LEWIS
The sun of heaven, methought, was loath to set,
But stayed and made the western welkin blush,
When English measure backward their own ground   3
In faint retire. O, bravely came we off,   4
When with a volley of our needless shot,   5

45 rumor noise   **49 beshrew** curse   **50 But** unless. **favor . . . form** i.e.,
outward appearance   **52 untread** retrace. **damnèd flight** cursed
breaking away from proper obedience   **53 bated** checked, abated.
retirèd having receded. **flood** river   **54 rankness** overgrowth, i.e.,
flooding, exceeding of proper bounds   **55 Stoop low** (1) subside, like a
river (2) kneel. **o'erlooked** (1) overflowed (2) disregarded   **60 Right**
unmistakably. **New flight** i.e., another breaking away (see l. 52)
61 happy newness a change for the better. **intends old right** intends to
reestablish an ancient right or just cause

5.5. Location: England. The French camp.
3 measure traverse   **4 faint retire** fainthearted retreat. **bravely . . . off**
we left the field of battle in fine fettle   **5 needless** i.e., fired toward a
disappearing enemy that needed no encouragement to flee

After such bloody toil, we bid good night,
And wound our tattering colors clearly up,   7
Last in the field, and almost lords of it!

    Enter a Messenger.

MESSENGER
Where is my prince, the Dauphin?
LEWIS   Here. What news?
MESSENGER
The Count Melun is slain. The English lords
By his persuasion are again fall'n off,   11
And your supply, which you have wished so long,
Are cast away and sunk on Goodwin Sands.
LEWIS
Ah, foul shrewd news! Beshrew thy very heart!   14
I did not think to be so sad tonight
As this hath made me. Who was he that said
King John did fly an hour or two before
The stumbling night did part our weary powers?   18
MESSENGER
Whoever spoke it, it is true, my lord.
LEWIS
Well, keep good quarter and good care tonight.   20
The day shall not be up so soon as I,
To try the fair adventure of tomorrow.   *Exeunt.*

                     ❖

5.6   *Enter [the] Bastard and Hubert, severally.*

HUBERT
Who's there? Speak, ho! Speak quickly, or I shoot.
BASTARD
A friend. What art thou?
HUBERT   Of the part of England.   2

7 tattering flying in tatters (because of the day's fierce engagement).
clearly free from entanglement, without enemy interference   **11 are
again fall'n off** have withdrawn allegiance once again   **14 shrewd** of
evil import   **18 stumbling** causing to stumble   **20 quarter** watch

**5.6. Location: England. An open place in the neighborhood of Swine-
stead Abbey.**
s.d. severally at separate doors   **2 Of the part** on the side

BASTARD
  Whither dost thou go?
HUBERT   What's that to thee?
  Why may not I demand of thine affairs
  As well as thou of mine?
BASTARD   Hubert, I think?
HUBERT   Thou hast a perfect thought.   7
  I will upon all hazards well believe   8
  Thou art my friend, that know'st my tongue so well.
  Who art thou?
BASTARD   Who thou wilt. And if thou please,
  Thou mayst befriend me so much as to think
  I come one way of the Plantagenets.
HUBERT
  Unkind remembrance! Thou and eyeless night   13
  Have done me shame. Brave soldier, pardon me,
  That any accent breaking from thy tongue   15
  Should scape the true acquaintance of mine ear.
BASTARD
  Come, come; sans compliment, what news abroad?   17
HUBERT
  Why, here walk I in the black brow of night,
  To find you out.
BASTARD   Brief, then; and what's the news?
HUBERT
  O, my sweet sir, news fitting to the night,
  Black, fearful, comfortless, and horrible.
BASTARD
  Show me the very wound of this ill news.
  I am no woman; I'll not swoon at it.
HUBERT
  The King, I fear, is poisoned by a monk.
  I left him almost speechless, and broke out   25
  To acquaint you with this evil, that you might
  The better arm you to the sudden time   27
  Than if you had at leisure known of this.   28

7 **perfect** correct   8 **upon all hazards** against any odds   13 **Unkind remembrance** (Hubert chides his own faulty memory.)   **Thou** i.e., my memory   15 **accent** speech   17 **sans compliment** without the usual civilities   25 **out** away   27 **to the sudden time** for this emergency   28 **at leisure** i.e., later, because of a leisurely report

BASTARD
  How did he take it? Who did taste to him?   29
HUBERT
  A monk, I tell you, a resolvèd villain,
  Whose bowels suddenly burst out. The King
  Yet speaks, and peradventure may recover.
BASTARD
  Who didst thou leave to tend His Majesty?
HUBERT
  Why, know you not? The lords are all come back,
  And brought Prince Henry in their company,   35
  At whose request the King hath pardoned them,
  And they are all about His Majesty.
BASTARD
  Withhold thine indignation, mighty heaven,
  And tempt us not to bear above our power!   39
  I'll tell thee, Hubert, half my power this night,   40
  Passing these flats, are taken by the tide;   41
  These Lincoln Washes have devourèd them.
  Myself, well mounted, hardly have escaped.
  Away before! Conduct me to the King.
  I doubt he will be dead or ere I come.   *Exeunt.* 45

❖

5.7   *Enter Prince Henry, Salisbury, and Bigot.*

PRINCE HENRY
  It is too late. The life of all his blood   1
  Is touched corruptibly, and his pure brain,   2

---

29 it i.e., the poison. **Who did taste to him** (A "taster" was supposed to eat a portion of everything the King was to eat in order to protect him from poisoning. The monk who did so here took the poison knowingly—as a *resolvèd villain*—to ensure the King's death.) **35 Prince Henry** i.e., John's son, the future Henry III **39 tempt . . . power** don't try us beyond our power of endurance **40 power** army **41 Passing** traversing. **flats** tidal flatlands in the large inlet called the Wash, between Lincolnshire and Norfolk **45 doubt** fear. **or ere** before

5.7. Location: England. The orchard of Swinestead Abbey.
1 life essence **2 touched** infected. **corruptibly** leading to corruption and death. **pure** clear

Which some suppose the soul's frail dwelling-house,
Doth by the idle comments that it makes　　　　4
Foretell the ending of mortality.　　　　　　　5

　　　Enter Pembroke.

PEMBROKE
His Highness yet doth speak, and holds belief
That, being brought into the open air,
It would allay the burning quality
Of that fell poison which assaileth him.　　　　9
PRINCE HENRY
Let him be brought into the orchard here.
　　　　　　　　　　　　　[Exit Bigot.]
Doth he still rage?
PEMBROKE　　　　　　He is more patient
Than when you left him. Even now he sung.
PRINCE HENRY
O vanity of sickness! Fierce extremes　　　　13
In their continuance will not feel themselves.　　14
Death, having preyed upon the outward parts,
Leaves them invisible, and his siege is now　　　16
Against the mind, the which he pricks and wounds
With many legions of strange fantasies,　　　　18
Which, in their throng and press to that last hold,　19
Confound themselves. 'Tis strange that Death should
　　sing.　　　　　　　　　　　　　　　20
I am the cygnet to this pale faint swan,　　　　21
Who chants a doleful hymn to his own death,
And from the organ pipe of frailty sings
His soul and body to their lasting rest.
SALISBURY
Be of good comfort, Prince, for you are born

---

4 idle comments babble　**5 mortality** life　**9 fell** cruel　**13 vanity**
absurdity　**14 In . . . themselves** i.e., by the very intensity of their
continuation produce a loss of sensation　**16 invisible** imperceptibly (?),
insensate (?)　**his** its, Death's　**18 legions** (1) vast numbers (2) armies
19 hold stronghold (the mind)　**20 Confound** destroy, i.e., make incoher-
ent and senseless　**21 cygnet** young swan. (It was a popular belief
that the swan sang only once in its life, just before it died, as its spirit
attempted to pass through its long neck, the *organ pipe of frailty*
of l. 23.)

To set a form upon that indigest   26
Which he hath left so shapeless and so rude.   27

> [King] John brought in [in a chair, attended by
> Bigot].

KING JOHN
Ay, marry, now my soul hath elbowroom;
It would not out at windows nor at doors.
There is so hot a summer in my bosom
That all my bowels crumble up to dust.
I am a scribbled form, drawn with a pen
Upon a parchment, and against this fire
Do I shrink up.
PRINCE HENRY   How fares Your Majesty?
KING JOHN
Poisoned—ill fare! Dead, forsook, cast off;   35
And none of you will bid the winter come
To thrust his icy fingers in my maw,
Nor let my kingdom's rivers take their course
Through my burned bosom, nor entreat the north
To make his bleak winds kiss my parchèd lips
And comfort me with cold. I do not ask you much—
I beg cold comfort; and you are so strait   42
And so ingrateful, you deny me that.
PRINCE HENRY
O, that there were some virtue in my tears   44
That might relieve you!
KING JOHN   The salt in them is hot.
Within me is a hell, and there the poison
Is as a fiend confined to tyrannize
On unreprievable condemnèd blood.

> Enter [the] Bastard.

BASTARD
O, I am scalded with my violent motion
And spleen of speed to see Your Majesty!   50

26 **indigest** shapeless mass, i.e., the confused state   27 **rude** shapeless,
crude   35 **fare** (1) food (2) fortune   42 **cold comfort** (1) the comfort of
cold to my burning (2) empty consolation (since real consolation is no
longer possible).   **strait** niggardly   44 **virtue** power   50 **spleen** i.e.,
eagerness

KING JOHN
O cousin, thou art come to set mine eye.   51
The tackle of my heart is cracked and burnt,   52
And all the shrouds wherewith my life should sail   53
Are turnèd to one thread, one little hair.
My heart hath one poor string to stay it by,   55
Which holds but till thy news be utterèd,
And then all this thou seest is but a clod
And module of confounded royalty.   58
BASTARD
The Dauphin is preparing hitherward,   59
Where God He knows how we shall answer him!   60
For in a night the best part of my power,   61
As I upon advantage did remove,   62
Were in the Washes all unwarily
Devourèd by the unexpected flood.   [*The King dies.*] 64
SALISBURY
You breathe these dead news in as dead an ear.—
My liege! My lord!—But now a king, now thus.
PRINCE HENRY
Even so must I run on, and even so stop.
What surety of the world, what hope, what stay,   68
When this was now a king and now is clay?
BASTARD [*To the King*]
Art thou gone so? I do but stay behind
To do the office for thee of revenge,
And then my soul shall wait on thee to heaven,   72
As it on earth hath been thy servant still.—   73
Now, now, you stars that move in your right spheres,   74
Where be your powers? Show now your mended faiths,   75
And instantly return with me again
To push destruction and perpetual shame

51 **set mine eye** close my eyes (in death)   52 **tackle** rigging of a ship
53 **shrouds** ropes giving support to masts (with a suggestion also of
burial garments)   55 **string** (1) heartstring (2) rope, as in ll. 53–54.   **stay
it** support itself   58 **module** counterfeit, mere image.   **confounded**
destroyed   59 **preparing** repairing, coming   60 **answer** encounter
61 **in a night** during the night.   **power** army   62 **upon advantage** to
gain, or taking, favorable opportunity.   **remove** shift position   64 **flood**
i.e., tide   68 **stay** support   72 **wait on** attend   73 **still** always   74 **stars**
i.e., nobles.   **right spheres** proper orbits (around the throne, like heavenly bodies around the earth)   75 **faiths** loyalties (to the crown)

Out of the weak door of our fainting land.
Straight let us seek, or straight we shall be sought;   79
The Dauphin rages at our very heels.
SALISBURY
It seems you know not, then, so much as we.
The Cardinal Pandulph is within at rest,
Who half an hour since came from the Dauphin,
And brings from him such offers of our peace
As we with honor and respect may take,   85
With purpose presently to leave this war.
BASTARD
He will the rather do it when he sees
Ourselves well sinewèd to our defense.   88
SALISBURY
Nay, 'tis in a manner done already,
For many carriages he hath dispatched   90
To the seaside, and put his cause and quarrel
To the disposing of the Cardinal,
With whom yourself, myself, and other lords,
If you think meet, this afternoon will post   94
To consummate this business happily.
BASTARD
Let it be so. And you, my noble Prince,
With other princes that may best be spared,
Shall wait upon your father's funeral.   98
PRINCE HENRY
At Worcester must his body be interred,
For so he willed it.
BASTARD   Thither shall it, then.
And happily may your sweet self put on   101
The lineal state and glory of the land,   102
To whom, with all submission, on my knee
I do bequeath my faithful services   104
And true subjection everlastingly.   [*He kneels.*]
SALISBURY
And the like tender of our love we make,   106

79 **Straight** at once   85 **respect** self-respect   88 **well sinewèd to our**
well strengthened in our own   90 **carriages** baggage vehicles   94 **post**
hasten   98 **wait upon** act as escorts and pallbearers in   101 **happily**
propitiously   102 **lineal state** crown by right of succession
104 **bequeath** give   106 **tender** offer

To rest without a spot for evermore.   107
      [*All kneel to Prince Henry, and then rise.*]

PRINCE HENRY
I have a kind soul that would give you thanks
And knows not how to do it but with tears.

BASTARD
O, let us pay the time but needful woe,   110
Since it hath been beforehand with our griefs.
This England never did, nor never shall,
Lie at the proud foot of a conqueror
But when it first did help to wound itself.
Now these her princes are come home again,   115
Come the three corners of the world in arms   116
And we shall shock them. Naught shall make us rue,   117
If England to itself do rest but true.
          Exeunt [*with the King's body*].

---

107 rest remain. **spot** stain   **110 but needful woe** no more weeping
than necessary   **115 home** i.e., back to true faith and allegiance
116 three . . . world i.e., all the world except England, the fourth corner   **117 shock** meet with force

Date and Text

The Life and Death of King John, as it is called in the original text, first appeared in the First Folio of 1623. That text appears to have been set up from Shakespeare's foul papers as copied by two scribes with a view to future theatrical use, although the manuscript does not show signs of having been actually employed as a promptbook. Apart from Francis Meres's listing of the play (in his *Palladis Tamia: Wit's Treasury,* 1598, a slender volume on contemporary literature and art, valuable because it lists most of Shakespeare's plays that existed at that time), dating clues are scarce. Editors have suggested dates ranging from 1590 to 1598, and have proposed topical allusions to bolster their various arguments. The consensus today is that *King John* was probably written shortly before or after *Richard II* in about 1594–1595, or 1596. Many editors assume that Shakespeare would have preferred to write this historically independent play in the interim between his two four-play series (*Henry VI* through *Richard III* and *Richard II* through *Henry V*), rather than interrupt the flow of composition on either of those series. This suggestion is scarcely provable, however. In any case, the link between *Richard II* and *1 Henry IV* is not so close as to preclude interruption.

A major critic of the consensus view is E. A. J. Honigmann, editor of the Arden *King John* (1954), who argues for a date in 1590 preceding the publication in 1591 of *The Troublesome Reign of King John* (which he regards as a bad quarto). Honigmann is joined by Robert Smallwood in his New Penguin edition of *King John* (1974). This argument has aroused controversy but little acceptance.

Textual Notes

These textual notes are not a historical collation, either of the early folios or of more recent editions; they are simply a record of departures in this edition from the copy text. The reading adopted in this edition appears in boldface, followed by the rejected reading from the copy text, i.e., the First Folio. Only major alterations in punctuation are noted. Changes in lineation are not indicated, nor are some minor and obvious typographical errors.

Abbreviations used:
F the First Folio
s.d. stage direction
s.p. speech prefix

Copy text: the First Folio.

1.1. 30 s.d. Exeunt Exit   **49 s.d. Enter . . . Philip** [after "What men are you?" in F]   **50 s.p. [and elsewhere] Bastard** Philip   **75 whe'er** where [also at 2.1.167]   **147 I** It   **188 too** two   **189 conversion. Now** conuersion, now   **208 smack** smoake   **219 s.d.** [at l. 221 in F]   **237 he get** get   **me! Sir** me sir   **257 Thou** That

2.1 [here F reads "Scaena Secunda"]   **1 s.p. King Philip** Lewis [also at l. 18]   **63 Ate** Ace   **75 s.d. Drum beats** [at l. 77 in F]   **89 s.p. [and elsewhere] King Philip** Fran   **106 Geoffrey's. In** Geffreyes in   **113 breast** beast   **120 s.p. [and elsewhere] Eleanor** Queen   **144 shows** shooes   **149 Philip** Lewis   **150 s.p. King Philip** Lew   **152 Anjou** Angiers   **166 s.p. Eleanor** Qu. Mo   **187 plague; her sin** plague her sinne,   **200 s.d. citizens** a Citizen   **201 s.p. Hubert** Cit [and so until l. 325]   **215 Confronts your** Comfort yours   **252 invulnerable** involuerable   **259 roundure** rounder   **335 run** rome   **368 s.p. Hubert** Fra   **371 Kinged** Kings   **463 cannon: fire** Cannon fire,   **469 s.p. Eleanor** Old Qu   **488 Anjou** Angiers   **497 s.p. [and elsewhere] Lewis** Dol

3.1 [here F reads "Actus Secundus"]   **74** [following this line, F reads "Actus Tertius, Scaena prima"]   **s.d. Austria** Austria, Constance   **110 day** daies   **155 God** heauen   **196 it** that   **259 chafèd** cased   **283 oath. The** oath the   **317 s.p. [and elsewhere] Lewis** Dolph   **323 s.p. King John** Eng

3.2. 4 s.d. Enter . . . Hubert [at l. 3 in F]   **10 s.d. Exeunt** Exit

3.4 [here F reads "Scaena Tertia"]   **2 armada** Armado   **44 not holy** holy   **64 friends** fiends   **110 world's** words   **182 make** makes

4.1. 6 s.p. First Executioner Exec [also at l. 85]   **50 lain** lyen   **63 his** this   **80 wince** winch   **91 mote** moth   **120 mercy-lacking** mercy, lacking

4.2. 1 again crowned against crown'd   **42 when** then   **73 Doth** Do   **105 s.d. Enter Messenger** [at l. 103 in F]   **143 traveled** trauail'd   **247 blood and breath,** blood, and breathe   **261 haste** hast [also at l. 269]

4.3. 33 man mans   **155 cincture** center   **159 s.d. Exeunt** Exit

5.2. 16 metal mettle   **26 Were** Was   **36 grapple** cripple   **43 hast thou** hast   **133 unhaired** vn-heard   **135 these** this   **145 his** this

5.4. 27 lose loose
5.5. 7 wound woon'd
5.6. 13 eyeless endles
5.7. 17 mind winde **21 cygnet** Symet **60 God** heauen **108 give you** giue

Shakespeare's Sources

To understand Shakespeare's use of sources in *King John*, we must first understand the play's relationship to the anonymous play *The Troublesome Reign of King John*, published in 1591. According to E.A.J. Honigmann (in his Arden edition of *King John*, 1954), *Troublesome Reign* is a bad quarto pirated from Shakespeare's text rather than a source for it. *Troublesome Reign* does indeed show features of a bad quarto. Moreover, a 1611 reprint of this play is attributed to "W. Sh.," and another in 1622 to "W. Shakespeare." The Folio editors did not register *King John* for publication in 1623, as though assuming it had already been published in some form. Nevertheless, most scholars still hold to the view that *Troublesome Reign* is a source. Its early date, by 1591, would mean a still earlier date for a play on which it was based. Honingmann's argument for dating *King John* in 1590 has not won acceptance.

If, on the other hand, we accept the argument that Shakespeare was substantially rewriting an earlier play on King John, the pattern of his indebtedness becomes clear on two points: (1) *Troublesome Reign* was his main though not his only source, and (2) Shakespeare consciously toned down the earlier play's anti-Catholic excesses and scurrilous humor. His characters are more thoughtful and complex, the paradoxes of kingship more disturbing. Shakespeare's alteration of a crude and chauvinistic source play into a subtle exploration of political rule anticipates his similar transformation of the irrepressible *Famous Victories of Henry V* (c. 1586–1587) into the *Henry IV* plays and *Henry V*.

Briefly, some differences between *Troublesome Reign* and *King John* are as follows. In *Troublesome Reign*, as the following excerpt suggests, John is a hero and a martyr for his defiance of Rome. His claim to the English throne is unquestioned. The barons who rise against him are loyal to Rome. Vice is rampant in monasteries and other ecclesiastical institutions. An abbot is discovered to be hiding a nun in his treasure chest. John is poisoned by a monk who is in league with the abbot and who receives absolution for his deed. The Bastard, John's loyal supporter, is an invincible foe of ecclesiastical corruption and treason against the state. In Shakespeare, on the other hand, John's claim to the throne is dynastically questionable, and his treatment of his nephew Arthur is reprehensible. The barons' opposition to him is prompted by a genuine moral revulsion. Although they learn belatedly that rebellion is more destructive than the evil it seeks to correct, since rebellion provides a fatal opportunity for foreign opportunists such as the French Dauphin, the barons are not simply tools of the Papacy. The Bastard struggles too with his conscience over John's treatment of Arthur. The Church is often guilty of political duplicity, as are virtually all the kings and political leaders in the play, but the Church shows no signs of moral decadence. John is poisoned by a monk, but without evidence of conspiracy.

These contrasting estimates of King John reflect the two views of him held concurrently in Tudor England. One, the older and more critical, is that of medieval historians generally and Polydore Vergil in particular. The other, a more favorable estimate, is essentially a Protestant defense of John, a rewriting of history in order to view him (despite his failures) as a martyr of Catholic oppression and hence a forerunner of the Reformation. William Tyndale began this revisionist view of John in his *The Obedience of a Christian Man* (1528). The case was vividly expounded by John Bale in his *King Johan,* a play begun before 1536 and rewritten in 1538 and 1561. Whether the author of *Troublesome Reign,* or Shakespeare, consulted Bale is uncertain, but the author of *Troublesome Reign* was certainly heir to the Protestant tradition. A major repository of the Protestant view, in any event, was John Foxe's *Acts and Monuments* (1583 edition), known as the *Book of Martyrs;* more copies of this work were to be found in English households than of any other book except the Bible, and its influence on Shakespeare must have been considerable. (A brief selection follows.) Richard Grafton and Raphael Holinshed took the Protestant line in their chronicles, and thus passed on the tradition to *Troublesome Reign.*

Shakespeare's play, though based primarily for its materials on *Troublesome Reign,* allows for expression of the more critical attitude toward John of the older non-Protestant line. Honigmann argues that Shakespeare also consulted the *Historia Maior* of Matthew Paris (published 1571) and perhaps the Latin manuscript *Wakefield Chronicle*, but scholarly opinion on this point is divided.

The Troublesome Reign of King John

[The historical narrative in *Troublesome Reign* is generally close to that of Shakespeare's *King John*. This selection begins with King John receiving his crown again from the Pope's Legate, and corresponds to the whole of Act 5 in Shakespeare's play.]

PART 2

2.4   *Enter King John, Bastard, Pandulph, and a*
        many priests with them.

PANDULPH [*Returning the crown to John*]
    Thus, John, thou art absolved from all thy sins
    And freed by order from our father's curse.   2
    Receive thy crown again with this proviso:
    That thou remain true liegeman to the Pope
    And carry arms in right of holy Rome.
JOHN
    I hold the same as tenant to the Pope,
    And thank Your Holiness for your kindness shown.
BASTARD
    A proper jest, when kings must stoop to friars!   8
    Need hath no law when friars must be kings.   9

        Enter a Messenger.

MESSENGER
    Please it Your Majesty, the Prince of France,
    With all the nobles of Your Grace's land,
    Are marching hitherward in good array.
    Where'er they set their foot, all places yield.

2.4. Location: The royal court of England.
s.d. a many many   **2 our father's** i.e., the Pope's   **8 proper** fine. (Said ironically.)   **9 Need hath no law** i.e., law bows to sheer political might

Thy land is theirs, and not a foot holds out
But Dover Castle, which is hard besieged.

PANDULPH
Fear not, King John. Thy kingdom is the Pope's,
And they shall know His Holiness hath power
To beat them soon from whence he hath to do.   18

> *Drums and trumpets. Enter Lewis, Melun,*
> *Salisbury, Essex, Pembroke, and all the nobles*
> *from France and England.*

LEWIS
Pandulph, as gave His Holiness in charge,   19
So hath the Dauphin mustered up his troops
And won the greatest part of all this land.
But ill becomes Your Grace, Lord Cardinal,
Thus to converse with John, that is accurst.   23

PANDULPH
Lewis of France, victorious conqueror,
Whose sword hath made this island quake for fear,
Thy forwardness to fight for holy Rome   26
Shall be remunerated to the full.
But know, my lord, King John is now absolved.
The Pope is pleased, the land is blest again,
And thou hast brought each thing to good effect.
It resteth then that thou withdraw thy powers   31
And quietly return to France again,
For all is done the Pope would wish thee do.

LEWIS
But all's not done that Lewis came to do.
Why Pandulph, hath King Philip sent his son
And been at such excessive charge in wars   36
To be dismissed with words? King John shall know
England is mine, and he usurps my right.

PANDULPH
Lewis, I charge thee and thy complices,   39
Upon the pain of Pandulph's holy curse,

---

18 from whence . . . do from wherever his authority extends   **19 as . . .
in charge** as His Holiness commanded   **23 accurst** excommunicated
26 forwardness eagerness   **31 It resteth** it remains only   **36 And . . .
charge** and been put to such considerable expense   **39 complices**
accomplices

That thou withdraw thy powers to France again
And yield up London and the neighbor towns
That thou hast ta'en in England by the sword.

MELUN
Lord Cardinal, by Lewis' princely leave, 44
It can be naught but usurpation
In thee, the Pope, and all the Church of Rome
Thus to insult on kings of Christendom— 47
Now with a word to make them carry arms,
Then with a word to make them leave their arms.
This must not be. Prince Lewis, keep thine own!
Let Pope and popelings curse their bellies full.

BASTARD
My lord of Melun, what title had the Prince
To England and the crown of Albion 53
But such a title as the Pope confirmed?
The prelate now lets fall his feignèd claim;
Lewis is but the agent for the Pope;
Then must the Dauphin cease, sith he hath ceased. 57
But cease or no it greatly matters not,
If you, my lords and barons of the land,
Will leave the French and cleave unto your King.
For shame, ye peers of England! Suffer not
Yourselves, your honors, and your land to fall,
But with resolvèd thoughts beat back the French
And free the land from yoke of servitude.

SALISBURY
Philip, not so. Lord Lewis is our king 65
And we will follow him unto the death.

PANDULPH
Then in the name of Innocent the Pope
I curse the Prince and all that take his part,
And excommunicate the rebel peers
As traitors to the King and to the Pope.

LEWIS
Pandulph, our swords shall bless ourselves again. 71

---

44 by . . . leave if Prince Lewis will allow me to speak   47 insult on
triumph contemptuously over   53 Albion England   57 sith he i.e., since
Pandulph (representing the Pope)   65 Philip i.e., the Bastard   71 bless
ourselves i.e., undo the excommunication

Prepare thee, John! Lords, follow me your king.

Exeunt [Lewis and the English lords].

JOHN

Accursèd John! The devil owes thee shame.   73

Resisting Rome or yielding to the Pope, all's one.   74

The devil take the Pope, the peers, and France!

Shame be my share for yielding to the priest.

PANDULPH

Comfort thyself, King John. The Cardinal goes

Upon his curse to make them leave their arms.   *Exit.* 78

BASTARD

Comfort, my lord, and curse the Cardinal!

Betake yourself to arms. My troops are prest   80

To answer Lewis with a lusty shock.   81

The English archers have their quivers full;

Their bows are bent, the pikes are prest to push.

Good cheer, my lord! King Richard's fortune hangs   84

Upon the plume of warlike Philip's helm.

Then let them know his brother and his son

Are leaders of the Englishmen in arms.

JOHN

Philip, I know not how to answer thee.

But let us hence to answer Lewis' pride.   [*Exeunt.*]

2.5   *Excursions. Enter Melun with English lords.*

MELUN

O, I am slain! Nobles, Salisbury, Pembroke,

My soul is charged. Here me, for what I say   2

Concerns the peers of England and their state.

---

73 owes thee shame is ashamed of you   **74 Resisting . . . one** (John
bitterly complains that he is caught between the supporters of the hated
Papacy and those who would take away his kingdom by force, both of
them intolerable.)   **78 Upon his curse** on pain of excommunication
80 prest ready   **81 lusty** vigorous   **84 Richard** i.e., Richard I, Coeur de
Lion, father of the Bastard and brother of John

**2.5. Location: The field of battle. The scene is essentially continuous
with the previous; excursions would start onstage as the actors of
scene 4 leave.**
2 charged burdened with sin

Listen, brave lords, a fearful mourning tale
To be delivered by a man of death.
Behold these scars, the dole of bloody Mars,
Are harbingers from nature's common foe, 7
Citing this trunk to Tellus' prison house. 8
Life's charter, lordings, lasteth not an hour,
And fearful thoughts, forerunners of my end,
Bids me give physic to a sickly soul. 11
O peers of England, know you what you do?
There's but a hair that sunders you from harm. 13
The hook is baited and the train is made, 14
And simply you run doting to your deaths. 15
But, lest I die and leave my tale untold,
With silence slaughtering so brave a crew,
This I aver: if Lewis win the day,
There's not an Englishman that lifts his hand
Against King John to plant the heir of France 20
But is already damned to cruel death.
I heard it vowed! Myself amongst the rest
Swore on the later aid to this edict.
Two causes, lords, makes me display this drift:
The greatest for the freedom of my soul,
That longs to leave this mansion free from guilt; 26
The other on a natural instinct,
For that my grandsire was an Englishman. 28
Misdoubt not, lords, the truth of my discourse.
No frenzy, nor no brainsick idle fit,
But well advised and wotting what I say 31
Pronounce I here before the face of heaven
That nothing is discovered but a truth.
'Tis time to fly. Submit yourselves to John.
The smiles of France shade in the frowns of death. 35
Lift up your swords! Turn face against the French;
Expel the yoke that's framèd for your necks.
Back, war-men, back! Imbowel not the clime, 38

---

7 **nature's common foe** i.e., death   8 **Citing** summoning.   **trunk** body.
Tellus' earth's   11 **physic** medicine   13 **sunders** separates   14 **train**
trap   15 **doting** foolishly, infatuatedly   20 **plant** i.e., plant as king in
England   26 **mansion** i.e., body   28 **For that** because   31 **wotting**
knowing   35 **shade in** conceal as in a shadow   38 **Imbowel not the
clime** do not disembowel your realm

Your seat, your nurse, your birthday's breathing place, 39
That bred you, bears you, brought you up in arms.
Ah, be not so ingrate to dig your mother's grave!
Preserve your lambs and beat away the wolf.
My soul hath said. Contrition's penitence 43
Lays hold on man's redemption for my sin.
Farewell, my lords!
Witness my faith when we are met in heaven,
And, for my kindness, give me grave room here. 47
My soul doth fleet. World's vanities, farewell! [*He dies.*]

SALISBURY
Now, joy betide thy soul, well-meaning man!
How now, my lords, what cooling card is this? 50
A greater grief grows now than erst hath been. 51
What counsel give you? Shall we stay and die,
Or shall we home and kneel unto the King?

PEMBROKE
My heart misgave this sad accursèd news. 54
What have we done? Fie, lords, what frenzy moved
Our hearts to yield unto the pride of France?
If we persever, we are sure to die;
If we desist, small hope again of life.

SALISBURY
Bear hence the body of this wretched man,
That made us wretched with his dying tale,
And stand not wailing on our present harms,
As women wont, but seek our harm's redress. 62
As for myself, I will in haste be gone
And kneel for pardon to our sovereign John.

PEMBROKE
Ay, there's the way. Let's rather kneel to him
Than to the French, that would confound us all.

Exeunt.

---

39 Your . . . place the place where you were born and first drew breath
43 said spoken   **47 give me grave room** provide me a grave, bury me
50 cooling card something that cools one's enthusiasm. (A metaphor
from card playing.)   **51 erst** formerly   **54 misgave** had a foreboding of
62 wont are accustomed to do

2.6 *Enter King John, carried between two lords.*

JOHN
  Set down, set down the load not worth your pain,
  For done I am with deadly wounding grief,
  Sickly and succorless, hopeless of any good.
  The world hath wearied me, and I have wearied it.
  It loaths I live; I live and loath myself.
  Who pities me? To whom have I been kind?
  But to a few; a few will pity me.
  Why die I not? Death scorns so vile a prey.
  Why live I not? Life hates so sad a prize.
  I sue to both to be retained of either,
  But both are deaf; I can be heard of neither.
  Nor death nor life, yet life and ne'er the near,   12
  Ymixed with death, biding I wot not where.

      [*Enter the Bastard.*]

BASTARD
  How fares my lord, that he is carried thus?
  Not all the awkward fortunes yet befall'n
  Made such impression of lament in me.
  Nor ever did my eye attaint my heart   17
  With any object moving more remorse
  Than now beholding of a mighty king
  Borne by his lords in such distressèd state.
JOHN
  What news with thee? If bad, report it straight;
  If good, be mute. It doth but flatter me.   22
BASTARD
  Such as it is, and heavy though it be   23
  To glut the world with tragic elegies,
  Once will I breathe, to aggravate the rest,   25
  Another moan to make the measure full.   26
  The bravest bowman had not yet sent forth
  Two arrows from the quiver at his side

2.6. Location: Near Swinestead Abbey.
12 ne'er the near never the nearer (to life or death)   **17 attaint** strike,
affect   **22 flatter me** i.e., beguile me with a false sense of hope
23 heavy sad   **25–26 Once . . . full** (The Bastard will punctuate his
gloomy report with sighs.)

But that a rumor went throughout our camp
That John was fled, the King had left the field.
At last the rumor scaled these ears of mine, 31
Who rather chose as sacrifice for Mars 32
Than ignominious scandal by retire. 33
I cheered the troops as did the Prince of Troy 34
His weary followers 'gainst the Myrmidons, 35
Crying aloud, "Saint George! The day is ours!"
But fear had captivated courage quite,
And, like the lamb before the greedy wolf,
So, heartless, fled our war-men from the field. 39
Short tale to make, myself amongst the rest
Was fain to fly before the eager foe. 41
By this time night had shadowed all the earth
With sable curtains of the blackest hue,
And fenced us from the fury of the French,
As Io from the jealous Juno's eye. 45
When in the morning our troops did gather head, 46
Passing the Washes with our carriages, 47
The impartial tide, deadly and inexorable,
Came raging in with billows threatening death
And swallowed up the most of all our men.
Myself upon a Galloway right free, well paced, 51
Outstripped the floods that followed, wave by wave.
I so escaped to tell this tragic tale.

JOHN

Grief upon grief, yet none so great a grief
To end this life and thereby rid my grief.
Was ever any so infortunate,
The right idea of a cursèd man, 57
As I, poor I, a triumph for despite? 58
My fever grows. What ague shakes me so?

---

31 scaled attacked, as if scaling a fortified wall   **32–33 Who . . . retire**
i.e., I who chose defeat and death if necessary rather than retreat
34 Prince of Troy i.e., Hector   **35 Myrmidons** followers of Achilles
39 heartless dispirited, having lost courage   **41 eager** fierce   **45 Io**
beloved of Jove and transformed into a heifer to conceal her from the
jealous eyes of Juno   **46 gather head** assemble in strength   **47 the
Washes** the Wash, a low area by the sea in Lincolnshire and Norfolk,
often flooded   **51 a Galloway . . . paced** a small-sized riding horse,
easily managed and of good gait   **57 right idea** exact portrait, epitome
58 a triumph for despite an object of scorn

How far to Swinestead, tell me, do you know?
Present unto the Abbot word of my repair.   61
My sickness rages, to tyrannize upon me.
I cannot live unless this fever leave me.

BASTARD
Good cheer, my lord. The abbey is at hand.
Behold, my lord, the churchmen come to meet you.

Enter the Abbot and certain Monks.

ABBOT
All health and happiness to our sovereign lord the King!

JOHN
Nor health nor happiness hath John at all.
Say, Abbot, am I welcome to thy house?

ABBOT
Such welcome as our abbey can afford
Your Majesty shall be assurèd of.

BASTARD
The King, thou seest, is weak and very faint.
What victuals hast thou to refresh His Grace?

ABBOT
Good store, my lord. Of that you need not fear,
For Lincolnshire and these our abbey grounds
Were never fatter nor in better plight.   75

JOHN
Philip, thou never need'st to doubt of cates.   76
Nor king nor lord is seated half so well
As are the abbeys throughout all the land.
If any plot of ground do pass another,   79
The friars fasten on it straight.   80
But let us in, to taste of their repast.
It goes against my heart to feed with them,
Or be beholding to such abbey grooms.   83
                          Exeunt. Manet the Monk.

MONK
Is this the King that never loved a friar?
Is this the man that doth contemn the Pope?   85

---

61 my repair my imminent arrival **75 plight** condition **76 doubt of cates** fear lack of delicacies **79 pass another** surpass others (in fertility) **80 straight** straightway **83 beholding** beholden. **grooms** i.e., rascals **s.d. Manet** he remains onstage **85 contemn** scorn

Is this the man that robbed the holy Church
And yet will fly unto a friary?
Is this the King that aims at abbey's lands?
Is this the man whom all the world abhors
And yet will fly unto a friary?
Accurst be Swinestead Abbey, abbot, friars,
Monks, nuns, and clerks, and all that dwells therein,   92
If wicked John escape alive away!
Now, if that thou wilt look to merit heaven
And be canonized for a holy saint,
To please the world with a deserving work
Be thou the man to set thy country free
And murder him that seeks to murder thee.

    Enter the Abbot.

ABBOT
Why are not you within to cheer the King?
He now begins to mend, and will to meat.   100
MONK [*To himself, not seeing the Abbot*]
What if I 'say to strangle him in his sleep?   101
ABBOT
What, at thy *mumpsimus*? Away,   102
And seek some means for to pastime the King.   103
MONK [*To himself*]
I'll set a dudgeon dagger at his heart   104
And with a mallet knock him on the head.
ABBOT
Alas, what means this monk, to murder me?
Dare lay my life he'll kill me for my place.   107
MONK [*To himself*]
I'll poison him, and it shall ne'er be known,
And then I'll be the chiefest of my house.
ABBOT
If I were dead, indeed he is the next.   110
But I'll away, forwhy the monk is mad,   111
And in his madness he will murder me.

92 **clerk** clerics   100 **meat** food   101 **'say** essay   102 **mumpsimus**
(Literally, bigoted opposition to reform; here, a vague term of contempt,
ironically appropriate to the speech of an abbot.)   103 **for to pastime** to
entertain   104 **dudgeon dagger** dagger with a hilt made of dudgeon, a
special kind of wood   107 **Dare lay** I dare wager   110 **the next** i.e., next
in line to be abbot   111 **forwhy** because

MONK
My lord, I cry your lordship mercy! I saw you not.   113
ABBOT
Alas, good Thomas, do not murder me!
And thou shalt have my place with thousand thanks.
MONK
I murder you? God shield from such a thought!
ABBOT
If thou wilt needs, yet let me say my prayers.   117
MONK
I will not hurt your lordship, good my lord.
But, if you please, I will impart a thing
That shall be beneficial to us all.
ABBOT
Wilt thou not hurt me, holy monk, say on.   121
MONK
You know, my lord, the King is in our house.
ABBOT   True.
MONK
You know likewise the King abhors a friar.
ABBOT   True.
MONK
And he that loves not a friar is our enemy.
ABBOT   Thou say'st true.
MONK   Then the King is our enemy.
ABBOT   True.
MONK
Why then should we not kill our enemy?
And, the King being our enemy,
Why then should we not kill the King?
ABBOT
O blessèd monk! I see God moves thy mind
To free this land from tyrant's slavery.
But who dare venture for to do this deed?   135
MONK
Who dare? Why I, my lord, dare do the deed.
I'll free my country and the Church from foes
And merit heaven by killing of a king.

---

113 I cry . . . mercy I beg your lordship's pardon   **117 wilt needs** must
121 Wilt thou not if you won't   **135 for to do** to do

ABBOT

Thomas, kneel down. [*The Monk kneels.*] And if thou
    art resolved,
I will absolve thee here from all thy sins,
Forwhy the deed is meritorious.   141
Forward! And fear not, man, for every month
Our friars shall sing a Mass for Thomas' soul.

MONK

God and Saint Francis prosper my attempt!
For now, my lord, I go about my work.   *Exeunt.*

2.7   *Enter Lewis and his army.*

LEWIS

Thus victory, in bloody laurel clad,
Follows the fortune of young Lodowick.   2
The Englishmen, as daunted at our sight,   3
Fall as the fowl before the eagle's eyes.
Only two crosses of contrary change   5
Do nip my heart and vex me with unrest:
Lord Melun's death, the one part of my soul;
A braver man did never live in France.
The other grief—ay, that's a gall indeed—   9
To think that Dover Castle should hold out
'Gainst all assaults, and rest impregnable.   11
Ye warlike race of Francus, Hector's son,   12
Triumph in conquest of that tyrant John!
The better half of England is our own,
And towards the conquest of the other part
We have the face of all the English lords.   16
What then remains but overrun the land?

---

141 Forwhy because

2.7. Location: With Lewis the Dauphin in the field, in the east of England.
2 Lodowick i.e., Lewis the Dauphin. (See also l. 44.)   **3 at our sight** at
the sight of us   **5 crosses of contrary change** thwartings, changes for
the worse   **9 gall** irritation   **11 rest** remain   **12 race of Francus, Hector's son** i.e., the Franci, the Franks or French, mythologically regarded
as descended from Hector of Troy   **16 face** countenance, support

Be resolute, my warlike followers,
And, if good fortune serve as she begins,
The poorest peasant of the realm of France
Shall be a master o'er an English lord.

Enter a Messenger.

Fellow, what news?

FIRST MESSENGER
Pleaseth Your Grace, the Earl of Salisbury,
Pembroke, Essex, Clare, and Arundel,
With all the barons that did fight for thee,
Are on a sudden fled with all their powers
To join with John, to drive thee back again.

Enter another Messenger.

SECOND MESSENGER
Lewis, my lord, why standst thou in a maze?   28
Gather thy troops; hope not of help from France!
For all thy forces, being fifty sail,
Containing twenty thousand soldiers,
With victual and munition for the war,
Putting from Calais in unlucky time,   33
Did cross the seas, and on the Goodwin Sands   34
The men, munition, and the ships are lost.

Enter another Messenger.

LEWIS More news? Say on.

THIRD MESSENGER
John, my lord, with all his scattered troops,
Flying the fury of your conquering sword,
As Pharaoh erst within the bloody sea,   39
So he and his, environed with the tide,
On Lincoln Washes all were overwhelmed;
The barons fled, our forces cast away.   42

28 maze state of bewilderment   **33 Putting** putting forth   **34 Goodwin
Sands** a treacherous place for ships off Kent   **39 Pharaoh** (when crossing the Red Sea, Exodus 14).   **erst** formerly, of yore   **42 The barons . . .
away** (The Messenger reports, along with the good news of John's army
being drowned in the Wash, the bad news that the English barons have
deserted Lewis and that the French reinforcements have been *cast away*
or lost as already reported at ll. 30–35; see also l. 47.)

LEWIS
  Was ever heard such unexpected news?
THIRD MESSENGER
  Yet, Lodowick, revive thy dying heart.
  King John and all his forces are consumed;
  The less thou needst the aid of English earls,
  The less thou needst to grieve thy navy's wreck,
  And follow time's advantage with success.   48
LEWIS
  Brave Frenchmen, armed with magnanimity,   49
  March after Lewis, who will lead you on
  To chase the barons' power that wants a head!   51
  For John is drowned, and I am England's king.
  Though our munition and our men be lost,
  Philip of France will send us fresh supplies.   *Exeunt.*

2.8   *Enter two Friars, laying a cloth.*

FIRST FRIAR   Dispatch, dispatch! The King desires to eat.
  Would 'a might eat his last, for the love he bears to   2
  churchmen.
SECOND FRIAR   I am of thy mind, too, and so it should be,
  an we might be our own carvers. I marvel why they dine   5
  here in the orchard.
FIRST FRIAR   I know not, nor I care not. The King comes.

  [*Enter King John, the Bastard, the Abbot, and
  the Monk.*]

JOHN   Come on, Lord Abbot, shall we sit together?
ABBOT   Pleaseth Your Grace, sit down.   [*The King sits.*]
JOHN   Take your places, sirs. No pomp in penury; all beg-

---

48 **And . . . success** i.e., and so it is time to follow up your advantages
with further successes   49 **magnanimity** lofty courage and fortitude
51 **wants a head** lacks an army

2.8. Location: Swinestead Abbey.
2 **'a** he   5 **an** if

gars and friends may come. Where necessity keeps the house, courtesy is barred the table. Sit down, Philip.

BASTARD   My lord, I am loath to allude so much to the proverb, "Honors change manners." A king is a king, 14 though fortune do her worst, and we as dutiful, in despite of her frown, as if Your Highness were now in the highest type of dignity. 17

JOHN   Come, no more ado. An you tell me much of dignity, 18 you'll mar my appetite in a surfeit of sorrow. What cheer, Lord Abbot? Methinks you frown like an host that knows his guest hath no money to pay the reckoning.

ABBOT   No, my liege, if I frown at all it is for I fear this cheer too homely to entertain so mighty a guest as Your Majesty.

BASTARD   I think rather, my Lord Abbot, you remember my last being here, when I went in progress for pouches; [To John] and the rancor of his heart breaks out 27 in his countenance to show he hath not forgot me.

ABBOT   Not so, my lord. You, and the meanest follower of 29 His Majesty, are heartily welcome to me.

MONK   Wassail, my liege! And, as a poor monk may say, welcome to Swinestead.

JOHN   Begin, monk, and report hereafter thou was taster to a king.

MONK As much health to Your Highness as to my own heart! 35
               [The Monk drinks to the King.]

JOHN [Drinking]   I pledge thee, kind monk.

MONK   The merriest draft that ever was drunk in England! Am I not too bold with Your Highness?

JOHN   Not a whit. All friends and fellows for a time.

MONK [Aside]   If the inwards of a toad be a compound of 40 any proof, why, so, it works!   Exit. 41

---

14 Honors change manners i.e., a change in station or fortune will lead to a change in the way people behave toward one; here, a king lowered in fortune might expect to be less ceremoniously treated   **17 type** image, epitome   **18 An** if   **27 pouches** money pouches   **29 meanest** most humble   **35 As much . . . heart** (With ironic hidden meaning: may you be as healthy as I am, I who have just poisoned us both.)   **40 toad** (Thought to be poisonous.)   **41 proof** potency

JOHN
Stay, Philip! Where's the monk?
BASTARD   He is dead, my lord.   42
JOHN
Then drink not, Philip, for a world of wealth!
BASTARD
What cheer, my liege? Your color 'gins to change.
JOHN
So doth my life. O Philip, I am poisoned!
The monk? The devil! The poison 'gins to rage.
It will depose myself, a king, from reign.
BASTARD
This abbot hath an interest in this act.
At all adventures, take thou that from me!   49
                              [*He kills the Abbot.*]
There lie the Abbot, abbey, lubber, devil!
March with the monk unto the gates of hell.
How fares my lord?
JOHN
Philip, some drink! O, for the frozen Alps
To tumble on and cool this inward heat
That rageth as the furnace, sevenfold hot,
To burn the holy three in Babylon!   56
Power after power forsake their proper power;   57
Only the heart impugns with faint resist   58
The fierce invade of him that conquers kings.   59
Help, God! O, pain! Die, John! O plague
Inflicted on thee for thy grievous sins!
Philip, a chair, and by and by a grave.   62
My legs disdain the carriage of a king.   63
                    [*The King is helped into a chair.*]

---

42 Where's the monk (In John Foxe's *Acts and Monuments*, the monk,
once he has drunk the poison drink and has seen John do so also, goes
out to the farmery, or farm area, of the abbey and there dies; probably
he leaves the stage in this scene, although somehow the Bastard must
know immediately that he is dead.)   **49 At all adventures** in any event
56 the holy three in Babylon i.e., Shadrach, Meshach, and Abednego,
delivered from the burning fiery furnace by Daniel. (See Daniel 3.)
57 Power ... power i.e., my faculties, one by one, forsake their strength
58 impugns fights against.   **resist** resistance   **59 invade** invasion.   **him**
i.e., death   **62 a chair** i.e., get me a sick chair or litter   **63 the carriage
of** to uphold or sustain

BASTARD
Ah, good my liege, with patience conquer grief
And bear this pain with kingly fortitude.
JOHN
Methinks I see a catalogue of sin,
Wrote by a fiend in marble characters—   67
The least enough to lose my part in heaven.
Methinks the devil whispers in mine ears
And tells me 'tis in vain to hope for grace;
I must be damned for Arthur's sudden death.
I see, I see a thousand thousand men
Come to accuse me for my wrong on earth,
And there is none so merciful a God
That will forgive the number of my sins.
How have I lived but by another's loss?
What have I loved but wrack of others' weal?   77
When have I vowed and not infringed mine oath?
Where have I done a deed deserving well?
How, what, when, and where have I bestowed a day
That tended not to some notorious ill?
My life, replete with rage and tyranny,
Craves little pity for so strange a death.
Or who will say that John deceased too soon?
Who will not say he rather lived too long?
Dishonor did attaint me in my life
And shame attendeth John unto his death.
Why did I scape the fury of the French
And died not by the temper of their swords?
Shameless my life, and shamefully it ends,
Scorned by my foes, disdainèd of my friends.
BASTARD
Forgive the world and all your earthly foes
And call on Christ, who is your latest friend.   93
JOHN
My tongue doth falter. Philip, I tell thee, man,
Since John did yield unto the priest of Rome,
Nor he nor his have prospered on the earth.
Curst are his blessings, and his curse is bliss.   97

_____

67 in marble characters i.e., carved in stone   **77 wrack . . . weal** the
destruction of others' well-being   **93 latest** last   **97 Curst . . . bliss** i.e.,
those he blesses are cursed, and those he curses are blessed

But in the spirit I cry unto my God,
As did the kingly prophet David cry,
Whose hands, as mine, with murder were attaint.   100
I am not he shall build the Lord a house,
Or root these locusts from the face of earth;   102
But, if my dying heart deceive me not,
From out these loins shall spring a kingly branch   104
Whose arms shall reach unto the gates of Rome,
And with his feet tread down the strumpet's pride   106
That sits upon the chair of Babylon.
Philip, my heartstrings break. The poison's flame
Hath overcome in me weak nature's power,
And, in the faith of Jesu, John doth die.

BASTARD
See how he strives for life, unhappy lord,
Whose bowels are divided in themselves!   112
This is the fruit of popery, when true kings
Are slain and shouldered out by monks and friars.

     Enter a Messenger.

MESSENGER
Please it Your Grace, the barons of the land,
Which all this while bare arms against the King,
Conducted by the Legate of the Pope,   117
Together with the Prince His Highness' son,   118
Do crave to be admitted to the presence of the King.

BASTARD
Your son, my lord, young Henry, craves to see   120
Your Majesty, and brings with him besides
The barons that revolted from Your Grace.—   122
O, piercing sight! He fumbleth in the mouth.   123

---

100 attaint attainted, convicted   **102 these locusts** i.e., the Catholic
prelates   **104 kingly branch** i.e., Henry VIII, father of Queen Elizabeth
106 the strumpet's i.e., the Whore of Babylon's, the Pope's   **112 bowels
are divided** (John Foxe reports in his *Acts and Monuments* that a monk
named Simon prepared a poisoned cup of wine from "a most venomous
toad" with which he toasted the King and was toasted in return, whereupon the monk died, "his guts gushing out of his belly," and thereafter
"had continually from thenceforth three monks to sing Mass for his
soul.")   **117 Conducted** led here.   **Legate** i.e., Pandulph   **118 Prince . . .
son** i.e., Prince Henry, John's son   **120–122 Your . . . Grace** (The Bastard repeats the Messenger's news in the ears of the King, who is
rapidly failing.)   **123 fumbleth** mumbles

His speech doth fail.—Lift up yourself, my lord,
And see the Prince to comfort you in death.

Enter Pandulph, young Henry, [and] Barons with
daggers in their hands, [and kneel].

PRINCE
O, let me see my Father ere he die!
O uncle, were you here and suffered him   127
To be thus poisoned by a damnèd monk?
Ah, he is dead! Father, sweet Father, speak!
BASTARD
His speech doth fail. He hasteth to his end.
PANDULPH
Lords, give me leave to joy the dying king
With sight of these his nobles kneeling here
With daggers in their hands, who offer up
Their lives for ransom of their foul offense.
Then, good my lord, if you forgive them all,
Lift up your hand in token you forgive.
                                   [*The King makes a sign.*]
SALISBURY
We humbly thank Your royal Majesty,
And vow to fight for England and her King.
And, in the sight of John, our sovereign lord,
In spite of Lewis and the power of France,
Who hitherward are marching in all haste,
We crown young Henry in his father's stead.
PRINCE
Help, help, he dies! Ah, Father, look on me!
PANDULPH
King John, farewell. In token of thy faith,
And sign thou diest the servant of the Lord,
Lift up thy hand, that we may witness here
Thou diest the servant of our Savior Christ.
                         [*The King makes a sign, and dies.*]
Now, joy betide thy soul! [*A noise within.*] What noise is
this?

Enter a Messenger.

127 uncle i.e., the Bastard

MESSENGER
   Help, lords! The Dauphin maketh hitherward
   With ensigns of defiance in the wind,
   And all our army standeth at a gaze,   151
   Expecting what their leaders will command.   152
BASTARD
   Let's arm ourselves in young King Henry's right,
   And beat the power of France to sea again.
PANDULPH
   Philip, not so. But I will to the Prince   155
   And bring him face to face to parle with you. 156
BASTARD
   Lord Salisbury, yourself shall march with me;
   So shall we bring these troubles to an end.
KING HENRY
   Sweet uncle, if thou love thy sovereign,
   Let not a stone of Swinestead Abbey stand,
   But pull the house about the friars' ears,
   For they have killed my father and my king.
               Exeunt [with the Abbot's body. King
               Henry III and the dead body of King
               John remain onstage.]

2.9   *A parle sounded. [Enter] Lewis, Pandulph,
Salisbury, etc., [to young King Henry III and the
body of the dead King John].*

PANDULPH
   Lewis of France, young Henry, England's king,
   Requires to know the reason of the claim
   That thou canst make to anything of his.
   King John, that did offend, is dead and gone.

151 at a gaze bewildered **152 Expecting** awaiting **155 the Prince** i.e.,
Lewis **156 parle** parley, negotiate
**2.9. Location: Near Swinestead Abbey. The scene appears to occur soon
after 2.8 and to be essentially continuous; Pandulph must go meet the
Dauphin while the Bastard and Salisbury prepare to fight, but
Henry III and the dead King John may remain onstage.**
s.d. parle trumpet call for a parley, negotiation under a truce

See where his breathless trunk in presence lies,
And he as heir apparent to the crown
Is now succeeded to his father's room.

KING HENRY
Lewis, what law of arms doth lead thee thus
To keep possession of my lawful right?
Answer in fine if thou wilt take a peace   10
And make surrender of my right again,
Or try thy title with the dint of sword.
I tell thee, Dauphin, Henry fears thee not.
For now the barons cleave unto their king,
And, what thou hast in England, they did get.

LEWIS
Henry of England, now that John is dead,
That was the chiefest enemy to France,
I may the rather be induced to peace.
But Salisbury, and you barons of the realm,
This strange revolt agrees not with the oath
That you on Bury altar lately sware.   21

SALISBURY
Nor did the oath Your Highness there did take
Agree with honor of the Prince of France.

BASTARD
My lord, what answer make you to the King?

LEWIS
Faith, Philip, this I say: It boots not me   25
Nor any prince nor power of Christendom
To seek to win this island Albion
Unless he have a party in the realm   28
By treason for to help him in his wars.
The peers which were the party on my side
Are fled from me. Then boots me not to fight.
But on conditions, as mine honor wills,
I am contented to depart the realm.

KING HENRY
On what conditions will Your Highness yield?

LEWIS
That shall we think upon by more advice.   35

10 in fine in conclusion   **21 Bury** Bury St. Edmunds   **25 boots** avails
28 party faction   **35 by more advice** on more consideration

BASTARD

    Then, kings and princes, let these broils have end,   36
    And at more leisure talk upon the league.   37
    Meanwhile, to Worcester let us bear the King
    And there inter his body, as beseems.   39
    But first, in sight of Lewis, heir of France,
    Lords, take the crown and set it on his head
    That by succession is our lawful king.

                     They crown young Henry.

    Thus England's peace begins in Henry's reign,
    And bloody wars are closed with happy league.
    Let England live but true within itself
    And all the world can never wrong her state.
    Lewis, thou shalt be bravely shipped to France,
    For never Frenchman got of English ground
    The twentieth part that thou hast conquerèd.
    Dauphin, thy hand. To Worcester we will march.
    Lords, all lay hands to bear your sovereign
    With obsequies of honor to his grave.
    If England's peers and people join in one,
    Nor pope, nor France, nor Spain can do them wrong.

          [Exeunt, ceremoniously bearing off the body
                       of King John.]

Text based on *The Troublesome Reign of John, King of England, with the Discovery of King Richard Coeur de Lion's Base Son, Vulgarly Named the Bastard Faulconbridge; Also the Death of King John at Swinestead Abbey...* *1591.* On dating, see Sources headnote. Speech prefixes have been silently regularized.

2.4.84 Good God   **2.7.29 not** out   **2.8.56 three** tree   **106 tread** treads

---

36 broils conflicts, squabbles   **37 talk upon the league** discuss terms of peace   **39 beseems** is fitting

Acts and Monuments of Martyrs (1583 edition)
By John Foxe

Any departures from the original text are noted with an asterisk and appear at the bottom of the page in boldface; original readings are in roman.

[Among the events of King John's reign providing material for Foxe's anti-Catholic polemicism is that of Peter the false prophet. The year is 1212.]

The next year, the French King began his attempt in hope of the crown of England, being well manned with the bishops, monks, prelates, and priests, and their servants to maintain the same, bragging of the letters which they had received from the great men there. But behold the work of God: the English navy took three hundred of the French King's ships, well loaden[1] with wheat, wine, meal, flesh,[2] armor, and such other like meet[3] for the war, and an hundred they brent[4] within the haven, taking the spoil[5] with them. In the meantime, the priests within England had provided them a certain false counterfeit prophet called Peter Wakefield of Poiz, who was an idle gadder-about and a prattling merchant.[6] This Peter they made to prophesy lies, rumoring his prophecies abroad[7] to bring the King out of all credit with his people. . . .

This counterfeit soothsayer prophecied of King John that he should reign no longer than Ascension Day[8] within the year of Our Lord 1213, which was the fourteenth year from his coronation, and this, he said, he had by revelation. Then was it of him demanded whether he[9] should be slain or be expelled, or should of himself[10] give over the crown. He answered that he could not tell. But of this he was sure, he said: that neither he[11] nor any of his stock or lineage should reign, that day once finished.

The King, hearing of this, laughed much at it and made but a scoff thereof. "Tush," saith he, "it is but an idiot knave and such a one as lacketh his right wits." But when

---

1 **loaden** laden   2 **flesh** meat   3 **meet** suitable   4 **brent** burned   5 **spoil** plunder   6 **prattling merchant** i.e., dealer in gossip   7 **abroad** far and wide   8 **Ascension Day** the day of Christ's ascension into heaven, forty days after his resurrection   9 **demanded whether he** asked whether he, i.e., King John   10 **of himself** of his own initiative   11 **he** i.e., King John

this foolish prophet had so escaped the danger of the King's displeasure and that he made no more of it, he gat him abroad[12] and prated thereof at large (as he was a very idle vagabond) and used to tattle and talk more than enough. So that they which loved the King caused him anon after[13] to be apprehended as a malefactor and to be thrown in prison, the King not yet knowing thereof.

Anon after, the fame of this fantastical prophet went all the realm over, and his name was known everywhere—as foolishness is much regarded of[14] people where wisdom is not in place. Specially because he was then imprisoned for the matter, the rumor was the larger, their wonderings[15] were the wantoner,[16] their practicing[17] the foolisher, their busy talks and other idle occupying[18] the greater. Continually from thence, as the rude manner of people is, old gossips' tales went abroad, new tales were invented, fables were added to fables, and lies grew upon lies. So that every day new slanders were raised on[19] the King, and not one of them true. Rumors arose, blasphemies were spread, the enemies rejoiced, and treasons by the priests were maintained, and what[20] likewise was surmised or other subtlety practiced, all was then fathered upon this foolish prophet. As, "thus saith Peter Wakefield," "thus hath he prophesied," and "this shall come to pass"—yea, many times when he thought nothing less.

When the Ascension Day was come which was prophesied of afore,[21] King John commanded his regal tent to be spread abroad in the open field, passing that day with his noble Council and men of honor in the greatest solemnity[22] that ever he did afore, solacing himself with musical instruments and songs, most in sight amongst his trusty friends. When that day was past in all prosperity and mirth, his enemies, being confused, turned all to an allegorical understanding to make the prophecy good, and said: "He is no longer king, for the Pope reigneth and not he." Yet reigned he still, and his son after him, to prove that prophet a liar.

---

12 gat him abroad went about   **13 anon after** soon afterward   **14 of** by **15 wonderings** speculations   **16 wantoner** more ungoverned, irresponsible   **17 practicing** devising (of speculations)   **18 occupying** passing of the time   **19 on** about   **20 what** whatever   **21 prophesied of afore** prophesied earlier   **22 solemnity** ceremonial magnificence

Then was the King by his Council persuaded that this false prophet had troubled all the realm, perverted the hearts of the people, and raised the commons against him. For his words went over the sea by the help of his prelates and came to the French King's ear and gave unto him a great encouragement to invade the land; he had not else[23] done it so suddenly.[24] But he was most foully deceived, as all they are and shall be that put their trust in such dark drowsy dreams of hypocrites. The King therefore commanded that he[25] should be drawn[26] and hanged like a traitor.

[Foxe's account of the submission of King John to the Pope dwells in detail on the horrors of such a betrayal of English interests and rights to the Papacy.]

Then sent the Pope again into England his legate, Pandulph, with other ambassadors; the King, also at Canterbury (by letters, as it should seem, certified from[27] his own ambassadors), waited their coming. Where, the thirteenth day of May, the King received them, making unto them an oath that, of and for all things wherein he stood accursed,[28] he would make ample restitution and satisfaction. Unto whom also all the lords and barons of England—so many as there were with the King attending the legate's coming—sware[29] in like manner, and that, if the King would not accomplish in everything the oath which he had taken, that then they would cause him to hold and confirm the same whether that he would or not. . . .

Then submitted the King himself unto the court of Rome and to the Pope, and, resigning, gave up his dominions and realms of England and Ireland from him and from his heirs for evermore that should come of him,[30] with this condition: that the King and his heirs should take again these two dominions[31] of the Pope to farm,[32]* paying yearly therefor to

*farm forme

23 else otherwise 24 suddenly quickly 25 he i.e., Peter 26 drawn disemboweled 27 as it should seem, certified from as it appears, informed by 28 accursed excommunicated 29 sware swore 30 come of him be descended from him 31 these two dominions i.e., England and Ireland 32 to farm on terms of rental. (The Pope remains the feudal landlord.) Or perhaps to ferm, to establish or make firm.

the court of Rome a thousand marks of silver. Then took the King the crown from his head, kneeling upon his knees in the presence of all his lords and barons of England to Pandulph, the Pope's chief legate, saying in this wise: "Here I resign up the crown of the realm of England to the Pope's hands, Innocent the Third, and put me wholly in his mercy and ordinance." Then took Pandulph the crown of King John and kept it five days as a possession and seisin,[33] taking of these two realms of England and Ireland. Confirming also all things promised by his charter obligatory. . . .

Upon this obligation, the King was discharged the second day of July from that tyrannical interdiction under which he continued[34] six years and three months.

[Foxe's account of the death of King John leaves no doubt as to the murderous perfidy of the assassin at Swinestead Abbey: the King was "most traitorously poisoned by a monk of that abbey, of the sect of the Cistercians or Saint Bernard's brethren, called Simon of Swinestead." Foxe's chief source is the *Chronicle* of William Caxton, Book 7.]

The foresaid monk Simon, being much offended with certain talk that the King had at his table concerning Lodowick, the French King's son, which then had entered and usurped upon him,[35] did cast in his wicked heart how he most speedily might bring him to his end. And first of all he counseled with his abbot, showing[36] him the whole matter and what he was minded to do. He alleged for himself the prophecy of Caiaphas, John 11, saying, "It is better that one man die than all the people should perish. I am well contented," saith he, "to lose my life and so become a martyr, that I may utterly destroy this tyrant." With that the abbot did weep for gladness and much commended his fervent zeal, as he took it.

The monk, then being absolved of his abbot for doing this act aforehand,[37] went secretly into a garden upon the back side and, finding there a most venomous toad, he so pricked

---

33 **seisin** possession as of a freehold   34 **continued** had continued
35 **which . . . upon him** who had at that time invaded England and usurped power. (*Lodowick*, i.e., Lewis the Dauphin; see *Troublesome Reign*, 2.7, note 2.)   36 **showing** revealing   37 **absolved . . . aforehand** absolved ahead of time by the abbot for doing this deed

him and pressed him with his penknife that he made him vomit all the poison that was within him. This done, he conveyed it into a cup of wine and, with a smiling and flattering countenance, he said thus to the King: "If it shall like Your princely Majesty, here is such a cup of wine as ye never drunk a better before in all your lifetime. I trust this wassail shall make all England glad." And with that he drank a great draft thereof, the King pledging[38] him. The monk anon after went to the farmery[39] and there died, his guts gushing out of his belly, and had continually from thenceforth three monks to sing Mass for his soul, confirmed by their general chapter.[40] What became after that of King John ye shall know right well in the process[41] following. I would ye did mark well the wholesome proceedings of these holy votaries, how virtuously they obey their kings whom God hath appointed, and how religiously they bestow their confessions, absolutions, and Masses.

The King, within a short space after feeling great grief in his body, asked for Simon the monk, and answer was made that he was departed this life. "Then God have mercy upon me," said he, "I suspected as much after he had said that all England should thereof be glad; he meant now, I perceive then, of his own generation."[42] With that he commanded his chariot to be prepared, for he was not able to ride. So went he from thence to Slaford Castle and from thence to Newark upon Trent, and there, within less than three days, he died.

Text based on John Foxe, *Acts and Monuments of Matters Most Special and Memorable Happening in the Church . . . against the True Martyrs of Christ. . . . Newly revised and recognized, partly also augmented, and now the fourth time again published . . . by . . . John Foxe. . . . An. 1583. . . . Printed by John Day . . . 1583*, pp. 252–256. The first edition of this work appeared in 1563.

38 pledging toasting   **39 farmery** buildings and yards belonging to the abbey farm   **40 chapter** assembly of members of the monastic order   **41 process** narrative   **42 generation** sect

Further Reading

Blanpied, John W. "Stalking 'Strong Possession' in *King John*." *Time and the Artist in Shakespeare's English Histories*. Newark, Del.: Univ. of Delaware Press, 1983. Blanpied focuses on Shakespeare's treatment of the political struggles in his nine history plays, exploring the dramatist's effort to impose form upon the intransigent materials of history. In *King John*, Blanpied argues, the formlessness of history ultimately overwhelms the desire to order it; political power in the play is split between John's de facto authority and the Bastard's theatrical energy, which John needs in order to transform his possession into effective rule.

Bonjour, Adrien. "The Road to Swinstead Abbey: A Study of the Sense and Structure of *King John*." *ELH* 18 (1951): 253–274. Bonjour is perhaps the first critic to argue for the play's artistic unity. The play, he finds, articulates the falling curve of John's career and the rising curve of the Bastard's. Their linked, unfolding destinies determine the fate of the nation and demonstrate the necessity of personal integrity for the maintenance of England's strength.

Burckhardt, Sigurd. "*King John:* The Ordering of this Present Time." *ELH* 33 (1966): 133–153. Rpt. in *Shakespearean Meanings*. Princeton, N.J.: Princeton Univ. Press, 1968. Beginning with the single line *King John* shares with its source, the anonymous *The Troublesome Reign of King John*, Burckhardt shows how Shakespeare's play refuses the orthodox moral and political logic of the earlier play. Shakespeare's *King John*, in Burckhardt's suggestive account, reveals the inadequacy of the Tudor doctrines of obedience, demonstrating that the bonds of community rather than the operations of providence solve the problems of authority posed by the play.

Calderwood, James L. "Commodity and Honour in *King John*." *University of Toronto Quarterly* 29 (1960): 341–356. Rpt. in *Shakespeare, The Histories: A Collection of Critical Essays*, ed. Eugene M. Waith. Englewood Cliffs,

N.J.: Prentice Hall, 1965. For Calderwood, *King John* is structured around two opposing value systems: one based on commodity and the other on honor. Characters are continually presented with choices that pit self-interest against more public, generous loyalties; in their decisions Calderwood discovers the play's political implications and its unity.

Campbell, Lily B. "The Troublesome Reign of King John." *Shakespeare's "Histories": Mirrors of Elizabethan Policy.* San Marino, Calif.: Huntington Library, 1947. Campbell explores how Shakespeare shapes the play's presentation of the conflicts between John and the Catholic Church to mirror political issues of Elizabeth's reign raised by the imprisonment and death of Mary Stuart: the monarch's right to the throne, the relationship of papal and civil authority, the duty of obedience, and the accountability of royalty.

Champion, Larry S. "The Maturity of Perspective: *King John, 1, 2 Henry IV, Henry V.*" *Perspective in Shakespeare's English Histories.* Athens, Ga.: Univ. of Georgia Press, 1980. Champion's book examines how Shakespeare's dramaturgy manipulates and modifies his audience's responses to the characters and events of the history plays. In *King John* Champion finds that the organization and arrangement of scenes require the audience to view characters from divergent public and private angles, provoking the play's complex ambiguity and shifting sympathies.

Elliott, John R., Jr. "Shakespeare and the Double Image of King John." *Shakespeare Studies* 1 (1965): 64–84. Elliott discovers two antithetical images of King John in Shakespeare's sources: one, a villainous usurper; the other, a proto-Protestant martyr. In *King John*, he argues, Shakespeare draws material from both traditions, producing a play sensitive to the ironies of history, resisting the simplifications of Tudor political doctrine.

Hibbard, G. R. "From Dialectical Rhetoric to Metaphorical Thinking: *King John.*" *The Making of Shakespeare's Dramatic Poetry.* Toronto: Univ. of Toronto Press, 1981. Hibbard finds in *King John*'s variety of rhetorical styles evidence of Shakespeare's interest in reassessing old techniques and testing new ones. The familiar rhetoric of argument, well-suited to the claims and counterclaims of the combatants, gives way at moments to a more dramatic rhetorical mode that anticipates the achievement of the great tragedies, where language is not merely the medium of speech but a way of apprehending reality.

Jones, Emrys. "*King John:* The Self and the World." *The Origins of Shakespeare.* Oxford: Clarendon Press, 1977. Emphasizing the uniqueness of *King John*'s tone and vision, Jones sees its theme as the encounter of innocence with worldliness. The play's political action is dominated by self-interest and self-deception, and reveals the insufficiency of human will to control events. In the Bastard, Jones contends, Shakespeare creates a character initiated into full moral awareness, who registers both his skepticism about, and his hope for, a loyal and unified England.

Jones, Robert C. "Truth in *King John*." *Studies in English Literature, 1500–1900* 25 (1985): 397–417. Focusing primarily on the Bastard as a fictional character in the midst of historical action, Jones explores *King John*'s relation to the truth it putatively claims to represent. History, as Jones finds it dramatized, continually reveals disturbing gaps between the realities of power and the orthodox notions of legitimate rule, resisting the discovery of the "right and true" except in the construction of clarifying fictions.

Matchett, William H. "Richard's Divided Heritage in *King John*." *Essays in Criticism* 12 (1962): 231–253. Rpt. in *Shakespeare's Histories: An Anthology of Modern Criticism*, ed. William A. Armstrong. Baltimore: Penguin, 1972. Finding the play's central concern to be the question of who should rule England, Matchett explores the respective claims of John, Arthur, and the Bastard, who divide the necessities for rule between them: possession, right, and character. Matchett finds that the play's thematic focus deepens in the final scene to consider the question of true honor, embodied in the Bastard as he kneels to Henry III and relinquishes personal ambition for his loyalty to England.

Pierce, Robert B. "*King John*." *Shakespeare's History Plays: The Family and the State.* Columbus, Ohio: Ohio State Univ. Press, 1971. *King John*, for Pierce, represents

Shakespeare's movement beyond the rigid pattern of retribution and moral polarities in his first tetralogy of history plays. Pierce sees John as a villain-king finally defeated and replaced by a monarch who reestablishes order and right, but he argues that the moral urgency of the conflict is subordinated in the play to a sense of the flawed humanity of the characters.

Reese, M. M. "King John." The Cease of Majesty: A Study of Shakespeare's History Plays. New York: St. Martin's Press, 1961. Seeing King John as a bridge between Shakespeare's two historical tetralogies, Reese argues that the play marks a significant transition in Shakespeare's understanding of political morality. The play's sober patriotism affirms the duty of obedience to a de facto king, but it reveals also that the public good may best be served by commitments to principles at odds with the ethics of private life.

Saccio, Peter. "John: The Legitimacy of the King." Shakespeare's English Kings: History, Chronicle, and Drama. New York: Oxford Univ. Press, 1977. Saccio examines the difference between the historians' accounts of John's reign and Shakespeare's dramatic version of it. Shakespeare compresses the events of John's seventeen-year rule so that the ecclesiastical and baronial conflicts appear related to the dynastic struggle between John and Arthur, and unlike his sources, he presents John unequivocally as a usurper, as part of the play's thematic exploration of illegitimacy.

Sprague, Arthur Colby. "King John." Shakespeare's Histories: Plays for the Stage. London: The Society for Theatre Research, 1964. Tracing the history of King John on the stage, Sprague considers what performance reveals about the play's thematic concerns and dramatic appeal.

Tillyard, E. M. W. "King John." Shakespeare's History Plays, 1944. Rpt., New York: Barnes and Noble, 1964. For Tillyard, King John marks a new direction for Shakespeare's histories with its innovations of language and character. Turning away from the retributive pattern of history discovered in the first tetralogy and the metaphysical language that expressed it, Shakespeare moves toward a new realism and vitality, especially in his creation of the Bastard, who serves to focus the play's two main concerns: the ethics of rebellion and the character of the true king.

Waith, Eugene M. *"King John* and the Drama of History." *Shakespeare Quarterly* 29 (1978): 192–211. Examining the traditions of acting, costuming, and set design during the period of the play's great theatrical popularity from 1745 to the end of the nineteenth century, Waith claims that the principal interest of the play lay not in its political concerns but in its emotional effects, and that the play's insistence upon its own historicity was viewed primarily as a means of encouraging an audience's emotional response through the intensified impression of reality.

From the 1961 New York Shakespeare Festival production of *A Midsummer Night's Dream*, with Kathleen Widdoes as Titania, Albert Quinton as Nick Bottom, and Ralph Hoffman, Herman Dalkieth Howell, Jan Mickens, and Basil Thompson as fairies, directed by Joel J. Friedman at the Wollman Memorial Rink in Central Park.

-A MIDSUMMER-
NIGHT'S DREAM

A MIDSUMMER NIGHT'S DREAM

Introductory Material
Foreword by Joseph Papp
Introduction
A Midsummer Night's Dream
in Performance

THE PLAY

Supplementary Material
Date and Text
Textual Notes
Shakespeare's Sources
Further Reading

Foreword

You may be a corporate executive or a plain everyday wage slave, a brilliant student or a high-school dropout, eight years old or eighty-plus—but dollars to doughnuts you'll laugh your head off at the antics of Nick Bottom and company in *A Midsummer Night's Dream.*

A group of workingmen meet in a wood (that is also, unbeknownst to them, an enchanted fairyland) and set out to rehearse a play. All of them are shy and modest, with one large exception: Nick Bottom. He is an arrogant, pushy, pompous bully, an egotistical know-it-all—in plain words, a big ass.

But he gets his comeuppance. First we see him actually transformed into an ass through a spell cast by a mischievous wood sprite called Puck; then we see him adored by the beautiful and sexy Queen of the Fairies, Titania, who has been bewitched by her jealous lover, Oberon; and finally we see him awakened from his midsummer night's dream. Typically, in calling it "Bottom's Dream," he takes the credit away from his creator, William Shakespeare.

Two sets of desperate lovers chase each other through the forest, while two magical monarchs, Titania and Oberon, contend for supremacy of the leafy kingdom. To add to the magic, tiny wood creatures abound, with such names as Peaseblossom, Cobweb, Moth, and Mustardseed. Along the way we light upon some of Shakespeare's loveliest poetry—such as Oberon's description of a white blossom turning "purple with love's wound."

And, in the midst of all this enchantment of love and passion, Nick Bottom and his "hempen homespuns"—Quince, Snug, Flute, and Starveling—press on with their hilarious efforts to make a play. The mingling of all these is what makes *A Midsummer Night's Dream* Shakespeare's most captivating comedy.

Joseph Papp

Joseph Papp gratefully acknowledges the help of Elizabeth Kirkland in preparing this Foreword.

Introduction

A Midsummer Night's Dream (c. 1594–1595) belongs to the
period of transition from Shakespeare's experimental, imitative comedy to his mature, romantic, philosophical, festive vein. In its lighthearted presentation of love's
tribulations, the play resembles Shakespeare's earlier comedies. The two sets of young lovers (Lysander and Hermia,
Demetrius and Helena), scarcely distinguishable one from
the other, are conventional figures. In them we find
scarcely a hint of the profound self-discovery experienced
by Beatrice and Benedick *(Much Ado about Nothing)* or Ro-
salind and Orlando *(As You Like It)*. At the same time, this
play develops the motif of love as an imaginative journey
from reality into a fantasy world created by the artist, ending in a return to a reality that has itself been partly transformed by the experience of the journey. (Shakespeare gives
us an earlier hint of such an imaginary sylvan landscape in
The Two Gentlemen of Verona.) This motif, with its contrasting worlds of social order and imaginative escape, remained an enduring vision for Shakespeare to the very last.

In construction, *A Midsummer Night's Dream* is a skillful
interweaving of four plots involving four groups of characters: the court party of Theseus, the four young lovers, the
fairies, and the "rude mechanicals" or would-be actors. Felix Mendelssohn's incidental music for the play evokes the
contrasting textures of the various groups: Theseus' hunting horns and ceremonial wedding marches, the lovers'
soaring and throbbing melodies, the fairies' pianissimo
staccato, the tradesmen's clownish bassoon. Moreover,
each plot is derived from its own set of source materials.
The action involving Theseus and Hippolyta, for example,
owes several details to Thomas North's translation (1579) of
Plutarch's *Lives of the Noble Grecians and Romans*, to
Chaucer's "Knight's Tale" and perhaps to his *Legend of Good
Women*, and to Ovid's *Metamorphoses* (in the Latin text or
in William Golding's popular Elizabethan translation). The
lovers' story, meanwhile, is Italianate and Ovidian in tone,
and also in the broadest sense follows the conventions of
plot in Plautus' and Terence's Roman comedies, although

no particular source is known. Shakespeare's rich fairy lore, by contrast, is part folk tradition and part learned. Although he certainly needed no books to tell him about mischievous spirits that could prevent churned milk from turning to butter, for instance, Shakespeare might have borrowed Oberon's name either from the French romance *Huon of Bordeaux* (translated into English by 1540), or from Robert Greene's play *James IV* (c. 1591), or from Edmund Spenser's *The Faerie Queen*, 2.10.75–76 (1590). Similarly, he may have taken Titania's name from the *Metamorphoses*, where it is used as an epithet for both Diana and Circe. Finally, for Bottom the weaver and company, Shakespeare's primary inspiration was doubtless his own theatrical experience, although even here he is indebted to Ovid for the story of Pyramus and Thisbe, and probably to Apuleius' *Golden Ass* (translated by William Adlington, 1566) for Bottom's transformation.

Each of the four main plots in *A Midsummer Night's Dream* contains one or more pairs of lovers whose happiness has been frustrated by misunderstanding or parental opposition. Theseus and Hippolyta, once enemies in battle, become husband and wife; and their court marriage, constituting the overplot of the play, provides a framework for other dramatic actions that similarly oscillate between conflict and harmony. In fact, Theseus' actions are instrumental in setting in motion and finally resolving the tribulations of the other characters. In the beginning of the play, for example, the lovers flee from Theseus' Athenian law; at the end, they are awakened by him from their dream. The king and queen of fairies come to Athens to celebrate Theseus' wedding, but quarrel with each other because Oberon has long been partial to Hippolyta, and Titania partial to Theseus. The Athenian tradesmen go off into the forest to rehearse their performance of "Pyramus and Thisbe" in anticipation of the wedding festivities.

The tragic love story of Pyramus and Thisbe, although it seems absurdly ill-suited for a wedding, simply reinforces by contrast the universal accord reuniting the other couples. This accord is, to be sure, stated in terms of male conquest of the female. Theseus, who originally won the Amazonian Hippolyta with his sword, doing her injuries, finally becomes the devoted husband. Hippolyta, legendary figure of woman's self-assertive longing to dominate the male, emerges as the happily married wife. The reconciliation of Oberon and Titania, meanwhile, reinforces this hierarchy of male over female. Having taught Titania a lesson for trying to keep a changeling boy from him, Oberon relents and eventually frees Titania from her enchantment. Thus, the occasion of Theseus' wedding both initiates and brings to an end the difficulties that have beset the drama's various couples.

Despite Theseus' cheerful preoccupation with marriage, his court embodies at first a stern attitude toward young love. As administrator of the law, Theseus must accede to the remorseless demands of Hermia's father, Egeus. The inflexible Athenian law sides with parentage, age, male dominance, wealth, and position against youth and romantic choice in love. The penalties are harsh: death or perpetual virginity—and virginity is presented in this comedy (despite the nobly chaste examples of Christ, Saint Paul, and Queen Elizabeth) as a fate worse than death. Egeus is a familiar type, the interfering parent found in the Roman comedy of Plautus and Terence (and in Shakespeare's *Romeo and Juliet*). Indeed, the lovers' story is distantly derived from Roman comedy, which conventionally celebrated the triumph of young love over the machinations of age and wealth. Lysander reminds us that "the course of true love never did run smooth," and he sees its enemies as being chiefly external: the conflicting interests of parents or friends; mismating with respect to years and blood; war; death; sickness (1.1.134–142). This description clearly applies to "Pyramus and Thisbe," and it is tested by the action of *A Midsummer Night's Dream* as a whole (as well as by other early Shakespearean plays, such as *Romeo and Juliet*). The archetypal story, whether ending happily or sadly, is an evocation of love's difficulties in the face of social hostility and indifference.

While Shakespeare uses several elements of Roman comedy in setting up the basic conflicts of his drama, he also introduces important modifications from the beginning. For example, he discards one conventional confrontation of classical and neoclassical comedy in which the heroine must choose between an old, wealthy suitor supported by her family and the young but impecunious darling of her heart. Lysander is equal to his rival in social position, income, and attractiveness. Egeus' demand, therefore—that Hermia marry Demetrius rather than Lysander—seems simply arbitrary and unjust. Shakespeare emphasizes in this way the irrationality of Egeus' harsh insistence on being obeyed and Theseus' rather complacent acceptance of the law's inequity. Spurned by an unfeeling social order, Lysander and Hermia are compelled to elope. To be sure, in the end Egeus proves to be no formidable threat; even he must admit the logic of permitting the lovers to couple as they ultimately desire. Thus, the obstacles to love are from the start seen as fundamentally superficial and indeed almost whimsical. Egeus is as heavy a villain as we are likely to find in this jeu d'esprit. Moreover, the very irrationality of his position prepares the way for an ultimate resolution of the conflict. Nevertheless, by the end of the first act the supposedly rational world of conformity and duty, by its customary insensitivity to youthful happiness, has set in motion a temporary escape to a fantasy world where the law cannot reach.

In the forest, all the lovers—including Titania and Bottom—undergo a transforming experience engineered by the mischievous Puck. This experience demonstrates the universal power of love, which can overcome the queen of fairies as readily as the lowliest of men. It also suggests the irrational nature of love and its affinity to enchantment, witchcraft, and even madness. Love is seen as an affliction taken in through the frail senses, particularly the eyes. When it strikes, the victim cannot choose but to embrace the object of his infatuation. By his amusing miscalculations, Puck shuffles the four lovers through various permutations with mathematical predictability. First, two gentlemen compete for one lady, leaving the second lady sadly unrequited in love; then everything is at cross-purposes, with each gentleman pursuing the lady who is in love with the other man; then the two gentlemen compete for the lady they both previously ignored. Finally, of course, Jack shall have his Jill—whom else should he have? The couples are properly united, as they evidently were at some time prior to the commencement of the play, when Demetrius had been in love with Helena, and Lysander and Hermia had courted each other.

We sense that Puck is by no means unhappy about his knavish errors. "Lord, what fools these mortals be!" Along with the other fairies in this play, Puck takes his being and his complex motivation from many denizens of the invisible world. As the agent of all-powerful love, Puck compares himself to Cupid. The love juice he administers comes from Cupid's flower, "love-in-idleness." Like Cupid, Puck acts at the behest of the gods, and yet he wields a power that the chiefest gods themselves cannot resist. Essentially, however, Puck is less a classical love deity than a prankish folk spirit, such as we find in every folklore: gremlin, leprechaun, hobgoblin, and the like. Titania's fairies recognize Puck as one who, for example, can deprive a beer barrel of its yeast so that it spoils rather than ferments. Puck characterizes himself as a practical joker, pulling stools out from under old ladies.

Folk wisdom imagines the inexplicable and unaccountable events in life to be caused by invisible forces who laugh at man's discomfiture and mock him for mere sport. Puck is related to these mysterious forces dwelling in nature who must be placated with gifts and ceremonies. Although Shakespeare restricts Puck to a benign sportive role in dealing with the lovers or with Titania, the actual folk legends about Puck mentioned in this play are frequently disquieting. Puck is known to "mislead night-wanderers, laughing at their harm"; indeed, he demonstrates as much with Demetrius and Lysander, engineering a confrontation that greatly oppresses the lovers even though we perceive the sportful intent. At the play's end, Puck links himself and his fellows with the ghoulish apparitions of death and night: wolves howling at the moon, screech owls, shrouds, gaping graves. Associations of this sort go beyond mere sportiveness to witchcraft and demonology involving spirits rising from the dead. Even Oberon's assurance that the fairies will bless all the marriages of this play, shielding their progeny against mole, harelip, or other birth defects, carries the implication that such misfortunes can be caused by offended spirits. The magic of this play is thus explicitly related to deep irrational powers and forces capable of doing great harm, although of course the spirit of comedy keeps such veiled threats safely at a distance in *A Midsummer Night's Dream*.

Oberon and Titania, in their view of the relationship between gods and men, reflect yet another aspect of the fairies' spiritual ancestry—one more nearly related to the gods and goddesses of the world of Greek mythology. The king and queen of fairies assert that, because they are immortal, their regal quarrels in love must inevitably have dire consequences on earth, either in the love relationship of Theseus and Hippolyta or in the management of the weather. Floods, storms, diseases, and sterility abound, "And this same progeny of evils comes / From our debate, from our dissension; / We are their parents and original" (2.1.115–117). Even though this motif of the gods' quarreling over human affairs is Homeric or Virgilian in conception, the motif in this lighthearted play is more nearly mock-epic than truly epic. The consequences of the gods' anger are simply mirth-provoking, most of all in Titania's love affair with Bottom the weaver.

The story of Bottom and Titania is recognizably a metamorphosis in a playfully classical mode, a love affair between a god and an earthly creature, underscoring man's dual nature. Bottom himself becomes half man and half beast, although he is ludicrously unlike the centaurs, mermaids, and other half-human beings of classical mythology. Whereas the head should be the aspiring part of him and his body the bestial part, Bottom wears an ass's head on his shoulders. His very name suggests the solid nature of his fleshly being (*bottom* is appropriately also a weaving term). He and Titania represent the opposites of flesh and spirit, miraculously yoked for a time in a twofold vision of man's absurd and ethereal nature.

A play bringing together fairies and mortals inevitably raises questions of illusion and reality. These questions reach their greatest intensity in the presentation of "Pyramus and Thisbe." This play within a play focuses our attention on the familiarly Shakespearean metaphor of art as illusion, and of the world itself as a stage on which men and women are merely players. As Theseus observes, apologizing for the ineptness of the tradesmen's performance, "The best in this kind are but shadows" (5.1.210). That is, Shakespeare's own play is of the same order of reality as Bottom's play. Puck too, in his epilogue, invites any spectator offended by Shakespeare's play to dismiss it as a mere dream—as, indeed, the play's very title suggests. Theseus goes even further, linking dream to the essence of imaginative art, although he does so in a clearly critical and rather patronizing way. The artist, he says, is like the madman or the lover in his frenzy of inspiration, giving "to airy nothing / A local habitation and a name" (5.1.16–17). Artistic achievements are too unsubstantial for Theseus; from his point of view they are the products of mere fantasy and irrationality, mere myths or fairy stories or old wives' tales. Behind this critical persona defending the "real" world of his court, however, we can hear Shakespeare's characteristically self-effacing defense of "dreaming."

"Pyramus and Thisbe," like the larger play surrounding it, attempts to body forth "the forms of things unknown." The play within the play gives us personified moonshine, a speaking wall, and an apologetic lion. Of course it is an absurdly bad play, full of lame epithets, bombastic alliteration, and bathos. In part Shakespeare is here satirizing the abuses of a theater he had helped reform. The players' chosen method of portraying imaginative matters is ridiculous, and calls forth deliciously wry comments from the courtly spectators onstage: "Would you desire lime and hair to speak better?" (5.1.164–165). At the same time, those spectators onstage are actors in our play. Their sarcasms render them less sympathetic in our eyes; we see that their kind of sophistication is as restrictive as it is illuminating. Bottom and his friends have conceived moonshine and lion as they did because these simple men are so responsive to the terrifying power of art. A lion might frighten the ladies and get the men hanged. Theirs is a primitive faith, naive but strong, and in this sense it contrasts favorably with the jaded rationality of the court party. Theseus' valuable reminder, that all art is only "illusion," is thus juxtaposed with Bottom's insistence that imaginative art has a reality of its own.

Theseus above all embodies the sophistication of the court in his description of art as a frenzy of seething brains. Genially scoffing at "These antique fables" and "these fairy toys" (5.1.3), he is unmoved by the lovers' account of their dreamlike experience. Limited by his own skepticism, Theseus has never experienced the enchantment of the forest. Even Bottom can claim more than that, for he has been the lover of the queen of fairies; and although his language cannot adequately describe the experience, Bottom will see it made into a ballad called "Bottom's Dream." Shakespeare leaves the status of his fantasy world deliberately complex; Theseus' lofty denial of dreaming is too abrupt. Even if the Athenian forest world can be made only momentarily substantial in the artifact of Shakespeare's play, we as audience respond to its tantalizing vision. We emerge back into our lives wondering if the fairies were "real"; that is, we are puzzled by the relationship of these artistic symbols to the tangible concreteness of our daily existence. Unless our perceptions have been thus enlarged by sharing in the author's dream, we have not surrendered to the imaginative experience.

A *Midsummer Night's Dream*
in Performance

Two rival staging traditions vie for attention in the performance history of *A Midsummer Night's Dream*. One
stresses the musical and magical qualities of the play, the
fairy enchantment, the gossamer illusion, the romance. The
other, more disenchanting tradition stresses the dark side
of the forest, the degrading aspect of erotic love, the conflict between the sexes, and the breaking of theatrical illusion. The first tradition, although it reigned virtually
supreme for three centuries and remains important in the
twentieth century, has had to contend in recent years with a
more radical vision of disillusionment. In today's theater
we are able to respond to both and to see in their marked
differences a debate about the play's dramatic qualities.

During the seventeenth-century civil wars in England and
the closing of its theaters, *A Midsummer Night's Dream* was
kept alive in the form of a farcical skit, or droll, called *The
Merry Conceited Humours of Bottom the Weaver*, which emphasized the clownish antics of the Athenian tradesmen.
The full play itself did not make much of an impression in
the Restoration era until Thomas Betterton hit on the idea
of a spectacular operatic version with music by Henry Pur-
cell. Under the title of *The Fairy Queen*, it appeared in 1692
and was billed as "an opera represented at the Queen's Theatre." Shakespeare's text was rearranged and cut to make
room for elaborate entries at the end of each act in the style
of Italian *intermedii*. At the end of Act 2, for example, the
woodland scene was transformed into a prospect of grot-
toes, arches, and walks adorned with flowers in order to
provide an elaborate setting for songs, a masque, and a
dance by the followers of Night. After Act 3 two great dragons, part of the movable scenery, made themselves into a
bridge over a river, forming an arch through which the audience could see swimming in the distance, to symphonic
accompaniment, two swans who then transformed themselves into dancing fairies. "Pyramus and Thisbe" was
moved to Act 3, just before the transformation of Bottom, to

make room for an unusually gorgeous entry near the end of Act 5 that featured Juno in a machine drawn by peacocks with spreading tails, a Chinese garden, six monkeys coming from among the trees, and six moving pedestals, all of which was followed by a grand dance for the finale. The then recent consolidation of England's only two licensed acting companies into one made possible the large cast and resources needed to mount so lavish a display.

David Garrick's *The Fairies*, at the Theatre Royal, Drury Lane, in 1755, continued the musical tradition, its prologue self-consciously attributing the play to "Signor Shakespearelli." It disposed of the Athenian tradesmen entirely, along with their performance of "Pyramus and Thisbe," and dealt with only the fairies and the four young lovers, providing some twenty-eight songs with lyrics by John Dryden, Edmund Waller, John Milton (from his *L'Allegro*), and even Shakespeare. When Garrick tried a more fully operatic version of *A Midsummer Night's Dream* in 1763, this time with thirty-three songs, it lasted exactly one night, though an attempt to salvage some parts of it under the title of *A Fairy Tale* did better. This adaptation included Bottom and his fellows together with their play, but left out the young lovers as well as Theseus and Hippolyta. Frederic Reynolds, in his production at the Theatre Royal, Covent Garden, in 1816, provided music by Thomas Arne and others for its sixteen songs, eliminated the scene with Helena in Act 1, transposed "Pyramus and Thisbe" to the forest as Betterton had done, and concluded with a grand pageant of Theseus' legendary triumphs: his defeat of the Amazons, his finding his way through the labyrinth with Ariadne's help, his killing the Minotaur, his sailing with the Argonauts in search of the Golden Fleece, and still more.

Felix Mendelssohn's well-known musical score for Shakespeare's play, then, follows a long tradition of musical elaboration. Mendelssohn's complete score was first used by Ludwig Tieck in a production at the Neues Palais in Potsdam in 1843 (the overture having been written in 1826 and used first in England by Alfred Bunn in a production at Drury Lane in 1833). It soon became standard fare, since it expressed so well, in nineteenth-century terms, the contrast between the playful fairies, the bumptious tradesmen, the stately Theseus and Hippolyta, and the romantic lovers.

Along with musical elaboration, an increasing tendency in nineteenth-century performances was toward lavishness and verisimilitude in set designs and costumes. The production of Madame Lucia Vestris and Charles Matthews at Covent Garden in 1840, though it restored much of the play that had been cut in earlier musical versions, indulged in numerous songs (fourteen this time, as well as Mendelssohn's overture, "Wedding March," and other incidental music), and spared no expense in creating stage spectacle. During Act 3 the moon sank gradually, its rays disappearing from the tops of the trees until daylight arrived. Act 5 featured staircases, a hall of statues, a gallery along the back of the stage, and Parisian lanterns of various colors for the fairies to carry. The fairies were clad in virgin white, with immaculate silk stockings. Nothing threatening was to be found in this wholesome vision. Madame Vestris herself took the part of Oberon and seems thus to have initiated a tradition of contralto fairy kings.

Samuel Phelps's production at the Sadler's Wells Theatre in 1853, with Phelps himself as Bottom, again gave prominence to the moon, first in the forest and then as it shone upon Theseus' palace in Act 5. Charles Kean, at the Princess's Theatre in 1856, gave Puck's opening speech to a nameless fairy in order that the audience might then see Puck (Ellen Terry, aged eight) rising on a mushroom. Kean's set invoked ancient Athens (admittedly not that of Theseus' era) by showing the Acropolis surrounded by marble temples and the theater of Bacchus. A dummy Puck flew through the air to the accompaniment of Mendelssohn's music, and one evening, when the dummy happened to fall to the stage, Ellen Terry got a laugh by going out in view of the audience to pick it up.

The fairies in Augustin Daly's New York production of 1888 flickered like fireflies through the shadowy mists. Frank Benson at the Globe Theatre in London in 1889 similarly had scampering fairies and glittering lights as well as a fight between a spider and a wasp. In 1900, at Her Majesty's Theatre, Herbert Beerbohm Tree provided a carpet of thyme and wildflowers along with the (by now) usual twinkling lights and floating shapes. In 1911 Tree populated his enchanted forest with live rabbits scurrying across the stage of His Majesty's Theatre. In more recent times, Tyrone Guthrie at the Old Vic in London in 1937–1938 concocted a handsome spectacle of dance and moonlit forest, with Vivien Leigh as Titania, Robert Helpmann as Oberon, and Ralph Richardson as Bottom. The tradition of innocent and lavish musical entertainment was fixed on film in Warner Brothers' 1935 *A Midsummer Night's Dream*, directed by Max Reinhardt with a cast that included Dick Powell (Lysander), Olivia de Havilland (Hermia), James Cagney (Bottom), and Mickey Rooney (Puck). The romantic spectacular even included a miniature orchestra of dwarfs performing in the forest. The Shakespeare Memorial Theatre production of 1949, in Stratford-upon-Avon, directed by Michael Benthall, continued the romantic tradition with graceful women in gauze dresses as Titania's fairies.

The other, disillusioning approach to the play dates seemingly from Harley Granville-Barker's interpretation at the Savoy Theatre in London in 1914 on an apron stage in a swift-paced continuous performance, with three symbolic locations (court, forest, town) and a minimum of realistic effects. The costumes suggested something remote, oriental, exotic. Puck made it plain that he was the theatrical manager of affairs onstage; he consciously broke the dramatic illusion, reminding spectators that they were in the theater. From the first, this awareness of the contrivance of theater was an essential part of this new perspective. Harcourt Williams's production at the Old Vic in 1929 (with John Gielgud as Oberon) was a Jacobean masque, its fairies not the gauzy sprites of the Victorians but elemental figures, based on sketches by Inigo Jones, with green faces and costumes of seaweed. George Devine, at the Shakespeare Memorial Theatre in 1954, gave a strange, birdlike aspect to his fairies and an ominous tone to the whole production. Peter Hall, in 1959, directed his young lovers to be foolish and clumsy, devoted to horseplay. Benjamin Britten's striking opera, performed at the Aldeburgh Festival in Suffolk in 1960, invoked a forest full of eerie sounds and disturbing dreamlike effects.

The most influential production in this disillusioning vein is Peter Brook's with the Royal Shakespeare Company in 1970, which was subsequently taken on tour. Plainly acknowledging the influence of Bertolt Brecht, Samuel Beckett, Antonin Artaud, and *Shakespeare Our Contemporary*, by Jan Kott, which argues in an intemperate but insightful way for the darker sexual side of the play, Brook created an intensely self-aware theatrical world within a three-sided brilliantly lit white box. The actors, often on trapezes, were circus performers, athletes, tumblers; Bottom, with his button nose and clumsy shoes, was both ass and circus clown. A fisted arm thrust between his legs as he was carried offstage from his rendezvous with the Fairy Queen suggested a triumphant phallus. The fairies were adult male actors. The production reveled in exposing its stage devices. The actors of Oberon and Titania not only doubled as Theseus and Hippolyta in order to explore a sense in which the fairy king and queen act out the aggressions of their human counterparts, but this doubling was flaunted in the final scene. Oberon and Titania, with a swift change of garments, transformed themselves onstage into Theseus and Hippolyta and were thus able to join the courtly audience of "Pyramus and Thisbe."

Since the time of Brook's pace-setting production, it has not been unusual to see athletic lovers who are unceasingly aggressive toward each other, or fairies who are spaced out on drugs. In 1985, on a bloodred set at the Guthrie Threatre in Minneapolis, Liviu Ciulei produced the play as a dark comedy of sexual strife and patriarchal abuse. The hallmark of modern productions throughout has been the constant use of theatrical illusion as a plaything: Puck and Oberon walk among the mortals, nearly touching them, separated only by the audience's understanding that they are invisible.

Fed by these two acting traditions, Shakespeare's text offers itself for endless speculation and experiment. Certainly the text's own indications for performance encourage the self-conscious methods of presentation that have become so popular in recent productions. Juxtapositions of the seen and unseen run through the play, as when, in Act 2, scene 2, and Act 3, scene 1, Titania sleeps in her bower while first the lovers and then Bottom and company wrestle with love's difficulties or with the problems of rehearsing a play. Possibly her bower was intended for some curtained space backstage in the Elizabethan playhouse, but the full visual contrast is present if she sleeps in view of the audience until she is at length awakened by Bottom's singing. Certainly at the end of Act 4 the four lovers are to remain asleep onstage while Titania first sports with her lover Bottom, then sleeps, and finally is awakened by Oberon; the four lovers are still there when Theseus and his train arrive.

Shakespeare's theater provides ample means, too, of dramatizing the contrasts between court and forest, not (in the original production) through scenery, but by means of costumed actors and their gestures and blocking: Theseus is a figure of noble splendor, richly dressed, accompanied by followers and surrounded by ceremony, while the creatures of the forest visibly come from another world, one of dreams, nighttime, and magic. Whether the fairies are presented benignly, in the romantic tradition of staging, or darkly, through the eyes of disenchantment, the imaginative world they create onstage is one that thrives on tricks of illusion and theatrical self-awareness.

-A MIDSUMMER-
NIGHT'S DREAM

[*Dramatis Personae*

THESEUS, *Duke of Athens*
HIPPOLYTA, *Queen of the Amazons, betrothed to Theseus*
PHILOSTRATE, *Master of the Revels*
EGEUS, *father of Hermia*

HERMIA, *daughter of Egeus, in love with Lysander*
LYSANDER, *in love with Hermia*
DEMETRIUS, *in love with Hermia and favored by Egeus*
HELENA, *in love with Demetrius*

OBERON, *King of the Fairies*
TITANIA, *Queen of the Fairies*
PUCK, *or* ROBIN GOODFELLOW
PEASEBLOSSOM,
COBWEB, *fairies attending*
MOTE, *Titania*
MUSTARDSEED,
Other FAIRIES *attending*

PETER QUINCE, *a carpenter,*   PROLOGUE
NICK BOTTOM, *a weaver,*   PYRAMUS
FRANCIS FLUTE, *a bellows mender,*   THISBE
TOM SNOUT, *a tinker,*   *representing* WALL
SNUG, *a joiner,*   LION
ROBIN STARVELING, *a tailor,*   MOONSHINE

Lords and Attendants on Theseus and Hippolyta

SCENE: *Athens, and a wood near it*]

1.1 *Enter Theseus, Hippolyta, [and Philostrate,] with others*

THESEUS
Now, fair Hippolyta, our nuptial hour
Draws on apace. Four happy days bring in
Another moon; but, O, methinks, how slow
This old moon wanes! She lingers my desires,⁣   4
Like to a stepdame or a dowager   5
Long withering out a young man's revenue.   6

HIPPOLYTA
Four days will quickly steep themselves in night,
Four nights will quickly dream away the time;
And then the moon, like to a silver bow
New bent in heaven, shall behold the night
Of our solemnities.

THESEUS   Go, Philostrate,
Stir up the Athenian youth to merriments,
Awake the pert and nimble spirit of mirth,
Turn melancholy forth to funerals;
The pale companion is not for our pomp.   15

[Exit Philostrate.]

Hippolyta, I wooed thee with my sword   16
And won thy love doing thee injuries;
But I will wed thee in another key,
With pomp, with triumph, and with reveling.   19

Enter Egeus and his daughter Hermia, and Lysander, and Demetrius.

EGEUS
Happy be Theseus, our renownèd duke!

THESEUS
Thanks, good Egeus. What's the news with thee?

EGEUS
Full of vexation come I, with complaint
Against my child, my daughter Hermia.

1.1. Location: Athens. Theseus' court.
4 lingers postpones, delays the fulfillment of   **5 stepdame** step-mother.   **dowager** i.e., a widow (whose right of inheritance from her dead husband is eating into her son's estate)   **6 withering out** causing to dwindle   **15 companion** fellow.   **pomp** ceremonial magnificence **16 with my sword** i.e., in a military engagement against the Amazons, when Hippolyta was taken captive   **19 triumph** public festivity

Stand forth, Demetrius. My noble lord,
This man hath my consent to marry her.
Stand forth, Lysander. And, my gracious Duke,
This man hath bewitched the bosom of my child.
Thou, thou, Lysander, thou hast given her rhymes
And interchanged love tokens with my child.
Thou hast by moonlight at her window sung
With feigning voice verses of feigning love,   31
And stol'n the impression of her fantasy   32
With bracelets of thy hair, rings, gauds, conceits,   33
Knacks, trifles, nosegays, sweetmeats—messengers   34
Of strong prevailment in unhardened youth.   35
With cunning hast thou filched my daughter's heart,
Turned her obedience, which is due to me,
To stubborn harshness. And, my gracious Duke,
Be it so she will not here before Your Grace   39
Consent to marry with Demetrius,
I beg the ancient privilege of Athens:
As she is mine, I may dispose of her,
Which shall be either to this gentleman
Or to her death, according to our law
Immediately provided in that case.   45

THESEUS
What say you, Hermia? Be advised, fair maid.
To you your father should be as a god—
One that composed your beauties, yea, and one
To whom you are but as a form in wax
By him imprinted, and within his power
To leave the figure or disfigure it.   51
Demetrius is a worthy gentleman.

HERMIA
So is Lysander.

THESEUS   In himself he is;
But in this kind, wanting your father's voice,   54
The other must be held the worthier.

31 **feigning** (1) counterfeiting (2) faining, desirous **32 And . . . fantasy**
and made her fall in love with you (imprinting your image on her
imagination) by stealthy and dishonest means **33 gauds** playthings.
conceits fanciful trifles **34 Knacks** knickknacks **35 prevailment in**
influence on **39 Be it so** if **45 Immediately** directly, with nothing
intervening **51 leave** i.e., leave unaltered. **disfigure** obliterate
54 kind respect. **wanting** lacking. **voice** approval

HERMIA
I would my father looked but with my eyes.
THESEUS
Rather your eyes must with his judgment look.
HERMIA
I do entreat Your Grace to pardon me.
I know not by what power I am made bold,
Nor how it may concern my modesty   60
In such a presence here to plead my thoughts;
But I beseech Your Grace that I may know
The worst that may befall me in this case
If I refuse to wed Demetrius.
THESEUS
Either to die the death or to abjure
Forever the society of men.
Therefore, fair Hermia, question your desires,
Know of your youth, examine well your blood,   68
Whether, if you yield not to your father's choice,
You can endure the livery of a nun,   70
For aye to be in shady cloister mewed,   71
To live a barren sister all your life,
Chanting faint hymns to the cold fruitless moon.
Thrice blessèd they that master so their blood
To undergo such maiden pilgrimage;
But earthlier happy is the rose distilled   76
Than that which, withering on the virgin thorn,
Grows, lives, and dies in single blessedness.
HERMIA
So will I grow, so live, so die, my lord,
Ere I will yield my virgin patent up   80
Unto his lordship, whose unwishèd yoke
My soul consents not to give sovereignty.
THESEUS
Take time to pause, and by the next new moon—
The sealing day betwixt my love and me
For everlasting bond of fellowship—
Upon that day either prepare to die
For disobedience to your father's will,
Or else to wed Demetrius, as he would,   88

60 concern befit   **68 blood** passions   **70 livery** habit   **71 aye** ever.
mewed shut in. (Said of a hawk, poultry, etc.)   **76 earthlier happy**
happier as respects this world   **80 patent** privilege   **88 Or** either

Or on Diana's altar to protest   89
For aye austerity and single life.

DEMETRIUS
Relent, sweet Hermia, and, Lysander, yield
Thy crazèd title to my certain right.   92

LYSANDER
You have her father's love, Demetrius;
Let me have Hermia's. Do you marry him.

EGEUS
Scornful Lysander! True, he hath my love,
And what is mine my love shall render him.
And she is mine, and all my right of her
I do estate unto Demetrius.   98

LYSANDER
I am, my lord, as well derived as he,   99
As well possessed; my love is more than his;   100
My fortunes every way as fairly ranked,   101
If not with vantage, as Demetrius';   102
And, which is more than all these boasts can be,
I am beloved of beauteous Hermia.
Why should not I then prosecute my right?
Demetrius, I'll avouch it to his head,   106
Made love to Nedar's daughter, Helena,
And won her soul; and she, sweet lady, dotes,
Devoutly dotes, dotes in idolatry,
Upon this spotted and inconstant man.   110

THESEUS
I must confess that I have heard so much,
And with Demetrius thought to have spoke thereof;
But, being overfull of self-affairs,   113
My mind did lose it. But, Demetrius, come,
And come, Egeus, you shall go with me;
I have some private schooling for you both.   116
For you, fair Hermia, look you arm yourself   117
To fit your fancies to your father's will;   118

89 protest vow   **92 crazèd** cracked, unsound   **98 estate unto** settle or
bestow upon   **99 derived** descended, i.e., as well born   **100 possessed**
endowed with wealth   **101 fairly** handsomely   **102 vantage** superiority   **106 head** i.e., face   **110 spotted** i.e., morally stained   **113 self-
affairs** my own concerns   **116 schooling** admonition   **117 look you arm**
take care you prepare   **118 fancies** likings, thoughts of love

Or else the law of Athens yields you up—
Which by no means we may extenuate—   120
To death or to a vow of single life.
Come, my Hippolyta. What cheer, my love?
Demetrius and Egeus, go along.   123
I must employ you in some business
Against our nuptial and confer with you   125
Of something nearly that concerns yourselves.   126

EGEUS
With duty and desire we follow you.
                    Exeunt [all but Lysander and Hermia].

LYSANDER
How now, my love, why is your cheek so pale?
How chance the roses there do fade so fast?

HERMIA
Belike for want of rain, which I could well   130
Beteem them from the tempest of my eyes.   131

LYSANDER
Ay me! For aught that I could ever read,
Could ever hear by tale or history,
The course of true love never did run smooth;
But either it was different in blood—   135

HERMIA
O cross! Too high to be enthralled to low.   136

LYSANDER
Or else misgrafted in respect of years—   137

HERMIA
O spite! Too old to be engaged to young.

LYSANDER
Or else it stood upon the choice of friends—   139

HERMIA
O hell, to choose love by another's eyes!

LYSANDER
Or if there were a sympathy in choice,   141
War, death, or sickness did lay siege to it,
Making it momentany as a sound,   143

120 extenuate mitigate   **123 go** i.e., come   **125 Against** in preparation
for   **126 nearly that** that closely   **130 Belike** very likely   **131 Beteem**
grant, afford   **135 blood** hereditary station   **136 cross** vexation
137 misgrafted ill grafted, badly matched   **139 friends** relatives
141 sympathy agreement   **143 momentany** lasting but a moment

Swift as a shadow, short as any dream,
Brief as the lightning in the collied night,   145
That in a spleen unfolds both heaven and earth,   146
And ere a man hath power to say "Behold!"
The jaws of darkness do devour it up.
So quick bright things come to confusion.   149

HERMIA
If then true lovers have been ever crossed,   150
It stands as an edict in destiny.
Then let us teach our trial patience,   152
Because it is a customary cross,
As due to love as thoughts and dreams and sighs,
Wishes and tears, poor fancy's followers.   155

LYSANDER
A good persuasion. Therefore, hear me, Hermia: 156
I have a widow aunt, a dowager
Of great revenue, and she hath no child.
From Athens is her house remote seven leagues;
And she respects me as her only son.   160
There, gentle Hermia, may I marry thee,
And to that place the sharp Athenian law
Cannot pursue us. If thou lovest me, then,
Steal forth thy father's house tomorrow night;
And in the wood, a league without the town,
Where I did meet thee once with Helena
To do observance to a morn of May,   167
There will I stay for thee.

HERMIA   My good Lysander!
I swear to thee by Cupid's strongest bow,
By his best arrow with the golden head,   170
By the simplicity of Venus' doves,   171
By that which knitteth souls and prospers loves,

---

145 **collied** blackened (as with coal dust), darkened   146 **in a spleen** in a
swift impulse, in a violent flash.   **unfolds** discloses   149 **quick** quickly;
or, perhaps, living, alive.   **confusion** ruin   150 **ever crossed** always
thwarted   152 **teach . . . patience** i.e., teach ourselves patience in this
trial   155 **fancy's** amorous passion's   156 **persuasion** conviction
160 **respects** regards   167 **do . . . May** perform the ceremonies of May
Day   170 **best arrow** (Cupid's best gold-pointed arrows were supposed
to induce love, his blunt leaden arrows, aversion.)   171 **simplicity** innocence.   **doves** i.e., those that drew Venus' chariot

And by that fire which burned the Carthage queen   173
When the false Trojan under sail was seen,   174
By all the vows that ever men have broke,
In number more than ever women spoke,
In that same place thou hast appointed me
Tomorrow truly will I meet with thee.

LYSANDER
Keep promise, love. Look, here comes Helena.

Enter Helena.

HERMIA
God speed, fair Helena! Whither away?   180

HELENA
Call you me fair? That "fair" again unsay.
Demetrius loves your fair. O happy fair!   182
Your eyes are lodestars, and your tongue's sweet air   183
More tunable than lark to shepherd's ear   184
When wheat is green, when hawthorn buds appear.
Sickness is catching. O, were favor so!   186
Yours would I catch, fair Hermia, ere I go;
My ear should catch your voice, my eye your eye,
My tongue should catch your tongue's sweet melody.
Were the world mine, Demetrius being bated,   190
The rest I'd give to be to you translated.   191
O, teach me how you look and with what art
You sway the motion of Demetrius' heart.   193

HERMIA
I frown upon him, yet he loves me still.

HELENA
O, that your frowns would teach my smiles such skill!

HERMIA
I give him curses, yet he gives me love.

HELENA
O, that my prayers could such affection move!   197

173, 174 **Carthage queen, false Trojan** (Dido, Queen of Carthage, immo-
lated herself on a funeral pyre after having been deserted by the Trojan
hero Aeneas.)   180 **fair** fair-complexioned (generally regarded by the
Elizabethans as more beautiful than dark complexion)   182 **your fair**
your beauty (even though Hermia is dark-complexioned).   **happy fair**
lucky fair one   183 **lodestars** guiding stars.   **air** music   184 **tunable**
tuneful, melodious   186 **favor** appearance, looks   190 **bated** excepted
191 **translated** transformed   193 **motion** impulse   197 **affection** passion.   **move** arouse

HERMIA
The more I hate, the more he follows me.
HELENA
The more I love, the more he hateth me.
HERMIA
His folly, Helena, is no fault of mine.
HELENA
None but your beauty. Would that fault were mine!
HERMIA
Take comfort. He no more shall see my face.
Lysander and myself will fly this place.
Before the time I did Lysander see
Seemed Athens as a paradise to me.
O, then, what graces in my love do dwell
That he hath turned a heaven unto a hell!
LYSANDER
Helen, to you our minds we will unfold.
Tomorrow night, when Phoebe doth behold   209
Her silver visage in the watery glass,   210
Decking with liquid pearl the bladed grass,
A time that lovers' flights doth still conceal,   212
Through Athens' gates have we devised to steal.
HERMIA
And in the wood, where often you and I
Upon faint primrose beds were wont to lie,   215
Emptying our bosoms of their counsel sweet,   216
There my Lysander and myself shall meet;
And thence from Athens turn away our eyes,
To seek new friends and stranger companies.
Farewell, sweet playfellow. Pray thou for us,
And good luck grant thee thy Demetrius!
Keep word, Lysander. We must starve our sight
From lovers' food till morrow deep midnight.
LYSANDER
I will, my Hermia.   *Exit Hermia.*
          Helena, adieu.
As you on him, Demetrius dote on you!
          Exit Lysander.

209 **Phoebe** Diana, the moon   210 **glass** mirror   212 **still** always
215 **faint** pale   216 **counsel** secret thought

HELENA
How happy some o'er other some can be!   226
Through Athens I am thought as fair as she.
But what of that? Demetrius thinks not so;
He will not know what all but he do know.
And as he errs, doting on Hermia's eyes,
So I, admiring of his qualities.   231
Things base and vile, holding no quantity,   232
Love can transpose to form and dignity.
Love looks not with the eyes, but with the mind,
And therefore is winged Cupid painted blind.
Nor hath Love's mind of any judgment taste;   236
Wings, and no eyes, figure unheedy haste.   237
And therefore is Love said to be a child,
Because in choice he is so oft beguiled.
As waggish boys in game themselves forswear,   240
So the boy Love is perjured everywhere.
For ere Demetrius looked on Hermia's eyne,   242
He hailed down oaths that he was only mine;
And when this hail some heat from Hermia felt,
So he dissolved, and showers of oaths did melt.
I will go tell him of fair Hermia's flight.
Then to the wood will he tomorrow night
Pursue her; and for this intelligence   248
If I have thanks, it is a dear expense.   249
But herein mean I to enrich my pain,
To have his sight thither and back again.   *Exit.*

❖

1.2   *Enter Quince the carpenter, and Snug the*
joiner, and Bottom the weaver, and Flute the
bellows mender, and Snout the tinker, and
Starveling the tailor.

226 o'er . . . can be can be in comparison to some others   231 admiring
of wondering at   232 holding no quantity i.e., unsubstantial, unshapely
236 Nor . . . taste i.e., nor has Love, which dwells in the fancy or
imagination, any *taste* or least bit of judgment or reason   237 figure
are a symbol of   240 waggish playful, mischievous.   game sport, jest
242 eyne eyes. (Old form of plural.)   248 intelligence information   249 a
dear expense i.e., a trouble worth taking.   dear costly

1.2. Location: Athens.

QUINCE   Is all our company here?

BOTTOM   You were best to call them generally, man by 2
man, according to the scrip. 3

QUINCE   Here is the scroll of every man's name which is
thought fit, through all Athens, to play in our interlude
before the Duke and the Duchess on his wedding day
at night.

BOTTOM   First, good Peter Quince, say what the play
treats on, then read the names of the actors, and so
grow to a point. 10

QUINCE   Marry, our play is "The most lamentable com- 11
edy and most cruel death of Pyramus and Thisbe."

BOTTOM   A very good piece of work, I assure you, and
a merry. Now, good Peter Quince, call forth your actors by the scroll. Masters, spread yourselves.

QUINCE   Answer as I call you. Nick Bottom, the weaver. 16

BOTTOM   Ready. Name what part I am for, and proceed.

QUINCE   You, Nick Bottom, are set down for Pyramus.

BOTTOM   What is Pyramus? A lover or a tyrant?

QUINCE   A lover, that kills himself most gallant for love.

BOTTOM   That will ask some tears in the true performing
of it. If I do it, let the audience look to their eyes. I will
move storms; I will condole in some measure. To the 23
rest—yet my chief humor is for a tyrant. I could play 24
Ercles rarely, or a part to tear a cat in, to make all split. 25

  "The raging rocks
And shivering shocks
Shall break the locks
  Of prison gates;
And Phibbus' car 30
Shall shine from far
And make and mar
  The foolish Fates."

This was lofty! Now name the rest of the players. This is

---

2 generally (Bottom's blunder for *individually*.)   **3 scrip** scrap. (Bottom's error for *script*.)   **10 grow to** come to   **11 Marry** (A mild oath,
originally the name of the Virgin Mary.)   **16 Bottom** (As a weaver's
term, a *bottom* was an object around which thread was wound.)
23 condole lament, arouse pity   **24 humor** inclination, whim   **25 Ercles**
Hercules. (The tradition of ranting came from Seneca's *Hercules
Furens*.)   **tear a cat** i.e., rant.   **make all split** i.e., cause a stir, bring the
house down   **30 Phibbus' car** Phoebus', the sun-god's, chariot

Ercles' vein, a tyrant's vein. A lover is more condoling.

QUINCE   Francis Flute, the bellows mender.

FLUTE   Here, Peter Quince.

QUINCE   Flute, you must take Thisbe on you.

FLUTE   What is Thisbe? A wandering knight?

QUINCE   It is the lady that Pyramus must love.

FLUTE   Nay, faith, let not me play a woman. I have a
beard coming.

QUINCE   That's all one. You shall play it in a mask, and ⁴³
you may speak as small as you will.   ⁴⁴

BOTTOM   An I may hide my face, let me play Thisbe too. ⁴⁵
I'll speak in a monstrous little voice, "Thisne, Thisne!"
"Ah Pyramus, my lover dear! Thy Thisbe dear, and
lady dear!"

QUINCE   No, no, you must play Pyramus, and, Flute,
you Thisbe.

BOTTOM   Well, proceed.

QUINCE   Robin Starveling, the tailor.

STARVELING   Here, Peter Quince.

QUINCE   Robin Starveling, you must play Thisbe's
mother. Tom Snout, the tinker.

SNOUT   Here, Peter Quince.

QUINCE   You, Pyramus' father; myself, Thisbe's father;
Snug, the joiner, you, the lion's part; and I hope here
is a play fitted.

SNUG   Have you the lion's part written? Pray you, if it
be, give it me, for I am slow of study.

QUINCE   You may do it extempore, for it is nothing but
roaring.

BOTTOM   Let me play the lion too. I will roar that I will
do any man's heart good to hear me. I will roar that I
will make the Duke say, "Let him roar again, let him
roar again."

QUINCE   An you should do it too terribly, you would
fright the Duchess and the ladies, that they would
shriek; and that were enough to hang us all.

ALL   That would hang us, every mother's son.

BOTTOM   I grant you, friends, if you should fright the

---

43 That's all one it makes no difference   **44 small** high-pitched   **45 An**
if (also at l. 68)

ladies out of their wits, they would have no more discretion but to hang us; but I will aggravate my voice 74
so that I will roar you as gently as any sucking dove; I 75
will roar you an 'twere any nightingale.

QUINCE   You can play no part but Pyramus; for Pyramus
is a sweet-faced man, a proper man as one shall see in 78
a summer's day, a most lovely gentlemanlike man.
Therefore you must needs play Pyramus.

BOTTOM   Well, I will undertake it. What beard were I
best to play it in?

QUINCE   Why, what you will.

BOTTOM   I will discharge it in either your straw-color 84
beard, your orange-tawny beard, your purple-in-grain 85
beard, or your French-crown-color beard, your perfect 86
yellow.

QUINCE   Some of your French crowns have no hair at all, 88
and then you will play barefaced. But, masters, here
are your parts. [*He distributes parts.*] And I am to entreat you, request you, and desire you to con them by 91
tomorrow night; and meet me in the palace wood, a
mile without the town, by moonlight. There will we
rehearse; for if we meet in the city, we shall be dogged
with company, and our devices known. In the mean- 95
time I will draw a bill of properties, such as our play 96
wants. I pray you, fail me not.

BOTTOM   We will meet, and there we may rehearse most
obscenely and courageously. Take pains, be perfect; 99
adieu.

QUINCE   At the Duke's oak we meet.

BOTTOM   Enough. Hold, or cut bowstrings.   *Exeunt.* 102

❖

74 aggravate (Bottom's blunder for *moderate*.)   **75 roar you** i.e., roar for
you.   **sucking dove** (Bottom conflates *sitting dove* and *sucking lamb*,
two proverbial images of innocence.)   **78 proper** handsome   **84 discharge** perform.   **your** i.e., you know the kind I mean   **85 purple-in-
grain** dyed a very deep red. (From *grain*, the name applied to the dried
insect used to make the dye.)   **86 French-crown-color** i.e., color of a
French crown, a gold coin   **88 crowns** heads bald from syphilis, the
"French disease"   **91 con** learn by heart   **95 devices** plans   **96 bill**
list   **99 obscenely** (An unintentionally funny blunder, whatever Bottom
meant to say.)   **perfect** i.e., letter-perfect in memorizing your parts
102 Hold . . . bowstrings (An archers' expression not definitely explained,
but probably meaning here "keep your promises, or give up the play.")

2.1

Enter a Fairy at one door, and Robin Goodfellow [Puck] at another.

PUCK

How now, spirit, whither wander you?

FAIRY

Over hill, over dale,
   Thorough bush, thorough brier,   3
Over park, over pale,   4
   Thorough flood, thorough fire,
I do wander everywhere,
Swifter than the moon's sphere;   7
And I serve the Fairy Queen,
To dew her orbs upon the green.   9
The cowslips tall her pensioners be.   10
In their gold coats spots you see:
Those be rubies, fairy favors;   12
In those freckles live their savors.   13
I must go seek some dewdrops here
And hang a pearl in every cowslip's ear.
Farewell, thou lob of spirits; I'll be gone.   16
Our Queen and all her elves come here anon.   17

PUCK

The King doth keep his revels here tonight.
Take heed the Queen come not within his sight.
For Oberon is passing fell and wrath,   20
Because that she as her attendant hath
A lovely boy, stolen from an Indian king;
She never had so sweet a changeling.   23
And jealous Oberon would have the child
Knight of his train, to trace the forests wild.   25
But she perforce withholds the lovèd boy,   26
Crowns him with flowers, and makes him all her joy.

2.1. Location: A wood near Athens.
3 Thorough through **4 pale** enclosure **7 sphere** orbit **9 orbs** circles, i.e., fairy rings (circular bands of grass, darker than the surrounding area, caused by fungi enriching the soil) **10 pensioners** retainers, members of the royal bodyguard **12 favors** love tokens **13 savors** sweet smells **16 lob** country bumpkin **17 anon** at once **20 passing fell** exceedingly angry. **wrath** wrathful **23 changeling** child exchanged for another by the fairies **25 trace** range through **26 perforce** forcibly

And now they never meet in grove or green,
By fountain clear, or spangled starlight sheen,   29
But they do square, that all their elves for fear   30
Creep into acorn cups and hide them there.

FAIRY
Either I mistake your shape and making quite,
Or else you are that shrewd and knavish sprite   33
Called Robin Goodfellow. Are not you he
That frights the maidens of the villagery,   35
Skim milk, and sometimes labor in the quern,   36
And bootless make the breathless huswife churn,   37
And sometimes make the drink to bear no barm,   38
Mislead night wanderers, laughing at their harm?
Those that "Hobgoblin" call you, and "Sweet Puck,"
You do their work, and they shall have good luck.
Are you not he?

PUCK   Thou speakest aright;
I am that merry wanderer of the night.
I jest to Oberon and make him smile
When I a fat and bean-fed horse beguile,
Neighing in likeness of a filly foal;
And sometimes lurk I in a gossip's bowl,   47
In very likeness of a roasted crab,   48
And when she drinks, against her lips I bob
And on her withered dewlap pour the ale.   50
The wisest aunt, telling the saddest tale,   51
Sometimes for three-foot stool mistaketh me;
Then slip I from her bum, down topples she,
And "Tailor" cries, and falls into a cough;   54
And then the whole choir hold their hips and laugh,   55
And waxen in their mirth, and neeze, and swear   56
A merrier hour was never wasted there.
But, room, fairy! Here comes Oberon.   58

FAIRY
And here my mistress. Would that he were gone!

29 **fountain** spring. **starlight sheen** shining starlight   30 **square** quarrel   33 **shrewd** mischievous. **sprite** spirit   35 **villagery** village population   36 **quern** handmill   37 **bootless** in vain. **huswife** housewife   38 **barm** yeast, head on the ale   47 **gossip's** old woman's   48 **crab** crab apple   50 **dewlap** loose skin on neck   51 **aunt** old woman. **saddest** most serious   54 **Tailor** (Possibly because she ends up sitting cross-legged on the floor, looking like a tailor.)   55 **choir** company   56 **waxen** increase. **neeze** sneeze   58 **room** stand aside, make room

Enter [Oberon] the King of Fairies at one door,
with his train; and [Titania] the Queen at
another, with hers.

OBERON
Ill met by moonlight, proud Titania.

TITANIA
What, jealous Oberon? Fairies, skip hence.
I have forsworn his bed and company.

OBERON
Tarry, rash wanton. Am not I thy lord?   63

TITANIA
Then I must be thy lady; but I know
When thou hast stolen away from Fairyland
And in the shape of Corin sat all day,   66
Playing on pipes of corn and versing love   67
To amorous Phillida. Why art thou here   68
Come from the farthest step of India   69
But that, forsooth, the bouncing Amazon,
Your buskined mistress and your warrior love,   71
To Theseus must be wedded, and you come
To give their bed joy and prosperity.

OBERON
How canst thou thus for shame, Titania,
Glance at my credit with Hippolyta,   75
Knowing I know thy love to Theseus?
Didst not thou lead him through the glimmering night
From Perigenia, whom he ravishèd?   78
And make him with fair Aegles break his faith,   79
With Ariadne and Antiopa?   80

63 **wanton** headstrong creature   **66, 68 Corin, Phillida** (Conventional names of pastoral lovers.)   **67 corn** (Here, oat stalks.)
69 step farthest limit of travel, or, perhaps, *steep*, mountain range
71 buskined wearing half-boots called buskins   **75 Glance . . .
Hippolyta** make insinuations about my favored relationship with
Hippolyta   **78 Perigenia** i.e., Perigouna, one of Theseus' conquests.
(This and the following women are named in Thomas North's translation
of Plutarch's "Life of Theseus.")   **79 Aegles** i.e., Aegle, for whom
Theseus deserted Ariadne according to some accounts   **80 Ariadne**
the daughter of Minos, King of Crete, who helped Theseus to escape
the labyrinth after killing the Minotaur; later she was abandoned
by Theseus.   **Antiopa** Queen of the Amazons and wife of Theseus;
elsewhere identified with Hippolyta, but here thought of as a separate
woman

TITANIA
These are the forgeries of jealousy;
And never, since the middle summer's spring,   82
Met we on hill, in dale, forest, or mead,
By pavèd fountain or by rushy brook,   84
Or in the beachèd margent of the sea,   85
To dance our ringlets to the whistling wind,   86
But with thy brawls thou hast disturbed our sport.
Therefore the winds, piping to us in vain,
As in revenge, have sucked up from the sea
Contagious fogs; which, falling in the land,   90
Hath every pelting river made so proud   91
That they have overborne their continents.   92
The ox hath therefore stretched his yoke in vain,
The plowman lost his sweat, and the green corn   94
Hath rotted ere his youth attained a beard;
The fold stands empty in the drownèd field,   96
And crows are fatted with the murrain flock;   97
The nine-men's-morris is filled up with mud,   98
And the quaint mazes in the wanton green   99
For lack of tread are undistinguishable.
The human mortals want their winter here;   101
No night is now with hymn or carol blessed.
Therefore the moon, the governess of floods,   103
Pale in her anger, washes all the air,
That rheumatic diseases do abound.   105
And thorough this distemperature we see   106
The seasons alter: hoary-headed frosts
Fall in the fresh lap of the crimson rose,
And on old Hiems' thin and icy crown   109

82 **middle summer's spring** beginning of midsummer   84 **pavèd** with
pebbled bottom.   **rushy** bordered with rushes   85 **in** on.   **margent**
edge, border   86 **ringlets** dances in a ring. (See *orbs* in l. 9.)   90 **Contagious** noxious   91 **pelting** paltry   92 **continents** banks that contain
them   94 **corn** grain of any kind   96 **fold** pen for sheep or cattle
97 **murrain** having died of the plague   98 **nine-men's-morris** i.e., portion of the village green marked out in a square for a game played with
nine pebbles or pegs   99 **quaint mazes** i.e., intricate paths marked out
on the village green to be followed rapidly on foot as a kind of contest.   **wanton** luxuriant   101 **want** lack.   **winter** i.e., regular winter
season; or, proper observances of winter, such as the *hymn or carol* in
the next line (?)   103 **Therefore** i.e., as a result of our quarrel
105 **rheumatic diseases** colds, flu, and other respiratory infections
106 **distemperature** disturbance in nature   109 **Hiems'** the winter god's

An odorous chaplet of sweet summer buds
Is, as in mockery, set. The spring, the summer,
The childing autumn, angry winter, change   112
Their wonted liveries, and the mazèd world   113
By their increase now knows not which is which.   114
And this same progeny of evils comes
From our debate, from our dissension;   116
We are their parents and original.   117

OBERON
Do you amend it, then; it lies in you.
Why should Titania cross her Oberon?
I do but beg a little changeling boy
To be my henchman.

TITANIA   Set your heart at rest. 121
The fairy land buys not the child of me.
His mother was a vot'ress of my order,
And in the spicèd Indian air by night
Full often hath she gossiped by my side
And sat with me on Neptune's yellow sands,
Marking th' embarkèd traders on the flood,   127
When we have laughed to see the sails conceive
And grow big-bellied with the wanton wind;   129
Which she, with pretty and with swimming gait,   130
Following—her womb then rich with my young squire—
Would imitate, and sail upon the land
To fetch me trifles, and return again
As from a voyage, rich with merchandise.
But she, being mortal, of that boy did die;
And for her sake do I rear up her boy,
And for her sake I will not part with him.

OBERON
How long within this wood intend you stay?

TITANIA
Perchance till after Theseus' wedding day.
If you will patiently dance in our round   140
And see our moonlight revels, go with us;

112 **childing** fruitful, pregnant   113 **wonted liveries** usual apparel.
mazèd bewildered   114 **their increase** their yield, what they produce
116 **debate** quarrel   117 **original** origin   121 **henchman** attendant,
page   127 **traders** trading vessels.   **flood** flood tide   129 **wanton**
sportive   130 **swimming** smooth, gliding   140 **round** circular
dance

If not, shun me, and I will spare your haunts.   142

OBERON
Give me that boy and I will go with thee.

TITANIA
Not for thy fairy kingdom. Fairies, away!
We shall chide downright if I longer stay.
                    Exeunt [*Titania with her train*].

OBERON
Well, go thy way. Thou shalt not from this grove   146
Till I torment thee for this injury.
My gentle Puck, come hither. Thou rememb'rest
Since once I sat upon a promontory,   149
And heard a mermaid on a dolphin's back
Uttering such dulcet and harmonious breath   151
That the rude sea grew civil at her song,   152
And certain stars shot madly from their spheres
To hear the sea-maid's music.

PUCK   I remember.

OBERON
That very time I saw, but thou couldst not,
Flying between the cold moon and the earth,
Cupid all armed. A certain aim he took   157
At a fair vestal thronèd by the west,   158
And loosed his love shaft smartly from his bow   159
As it should pierce a hundred thousand hearts;   160
But I might see young Cupid's fiery shaft   161
Quenched in the chaste beams of the watery moon,
And the imperial vot'ress passèd on
In maiden meditation, fancy-free.   164
Yet marked I where the bolt of Cupid fell: 165
It fell upon a little western flower,
Before milk-white, now purple with love's wound,
And maidens call it "love-in-idleness."   168
Fetch me that flower; the herb I showed thee once.
The juice of it on sleeping eyelids laid

---

142 spare shun   **146 from** go from   **149 Since** when   **151 breath** voice,
song   **152 rude** rough   **157 all** fully   **158 vestal** vestal virgin. (Contains
a complimentary allusion to Queen Elizabeth as a votaress of Diana and
probably refers to an actual entertainment in her honor at Elvetham in
1591.)   **159 loosed** released   **160 As** as if   **161 might** could   **164 fancy-
free** free of love's spell   **165 bolt** arrow   **168 love-in-idleness** pansy,
heartsease

Will make or man or woman madly dote   171
Upon the next live creature that it sees.
Fetch me this herb, and be thou here again
Ere the leviathan can swim a league.   174

PUCK
I'll put a girdle round about the earth
In forty minutes.   [*Exit.*]

OBERON   Having once this juice,   176
I'll watch Titania when she is asleep
And drop the liquor of it in her eyes.
The next thing then she waking looks upon,
Be it on lion, bear, or wolf, or bull,
On meddling monkey, or on busy ape,
She shall pursue it with the soul of love.
And ere I take this charm from off her sight,
As I can take it with another herb,
I'll make her render up her page to me.
But who comes here? I am invisible,
And I will overhear their conference.

Enter Demetrius, Helena following him.

DEMETRIUS
I love thee not; therefore pursue me not.
Where is Lysander and fair Hermia?
The one I'll slay; the other slayeth me.
Thou toldst me they were stol'n unto this wood;
And here am I, and wode within this wood,   192
Because I cannot meet my Hermia.
Hence, get thee gone, and follow me no more.

HELENA
You draw me, you hardhearted adamant!   195
But yet you draw not iron, for my heart
Is true as steel. Leave you your power to draw,   197
And I shall have no power to follow you.

DEMETRIUS
Do I entice you? Do I speak you fair?   199

---

171 **or . . . or** either . . . or   174 **leviathan** sea monster, whale   176 **forty**
(Used indefinitely.)   192 **wode** mad. (Pronounced "wood" and often
spelled so.)   195 **adamant** lodestone, magnet (with pun on *hardhearted*,
since adamant was also thought to be the hardest of all stones and was
confused with the diamond)   197 **Leave** give up   199 **fair** courteously

Or rather do I not in plainest truth
Tell you I do not nor I cannot love you?

HELENA
And even for that do I love you the more.
I am your spaniel; and, Demetrius,
The more you beat me, I will fawn on you.
Use me but as your spaniel, spurn me, strike me,
Neglect me, lose me; only give me leave,
Unworthy as I am, to follow you.
What worser place can I beg in your love—
And yet a place of high respect with me—
Than to be usèd as you use your dog?

DEMETRIUS
Tempt not too much the hatred of my spirit,
For I am sick when I do look on thee.

HELENA
And I am sick when I look not on you.

DEMETRIUS
You do impeach your modesty too much   214
To leave the city and commit yourself
Into the hands of one that loves you not,
To trust the opportunity of night
And the ill counsel of a desert place   218
With the rich worth of your virginity.

HELENA
Your virtue is my privilege. For that   220
It is not night when I do see your face,
Therefore I think I am not in the night;
Nor doth this wood lack worlds of company,
For you, in my respect, are all the world.   224
Then how can it be said I am alone
When all the world is here to look on me?

DEMETRIUS
I'll run from thee and hide me in the brakes,   227
And leave thee to the mercy of wild beasts.

HELENA
The wildest hath not such a heart as you.
Run when you will, the story shall be changed:

214 **impeach** call into question   218 **desert** deserted   220 **virtue** goodness or power to attract.   **privilege** safeguard, warrant.   **For that**
because   224 **in my respect** as far as I am concerned   227 **brakes**
thickets

Apollo flies and Daphne holds the chase,   231
The dove pursues the griffin, the mild hind   232
Makes speed to catch the tiger—bootless speed,   233
When cowardice pursues and valor flies!

DEMETRIUS
I will not stay thy questions. Let me go!   235
Or if thou follow me, do not believe
But I shall do thee mischief in the wood.

HELENA
Ay, in the temple, in the town, the field,
You do me mischief. Fie, Demetrius!
Your wrongs do set a scandal on my sex.   240
We cannot fight for love, as men may do;
We should be wooed and were not made to woo.
                              [*Exit Demetrius.*]
I'll follow thee and make a heaven of hell,
To die upon the hand I love so well.   [*Exit.*] 244

OBERON
Fare thee well, nymph. Ere he do leave this grove,
Thou shalt fly him and he shall seek thy love.

   Enter Puck.

Hast thou the flower there? Welcome, wanderer.

PUCK
Ay, there it is.   [*He offers the flower.*]
OBERON   I pray thee, give it me.
I know a bank where the wild thyme blows,   249
Where oxlips and the nodding violet grows,   250
Quite overcanopied with luscious woodbine,   251
With sweet muskroses and with eglantine.   252
There sleeps Titania sometimes of the night,
Lulled in these flowers with dances and delight;

---

231 Apollo . . . chase (In the ancient myth, Daphne fled from Apollo and
was saved from rape by being transformed into a laurel tree; here it is
the female who *holds the chase*, or pursues, instead of the male.)
232 griffin a fabulous monster with the head of an eagle and the body
of a lion. **hind** female deer **233 bootless** fruitless **235 stay** wait
for. **questions** talk or argument **240 Your . . . sex** i.e., the wrongs
that you do me cause me to act in a manner that disgraces my sex
244 upon by **249 blows** blooms **250 oxlips** flowers resembling cowslip
and primrose **251 woodbine** honeysuckle **252 muskroses** a kind of
large, sweet-scented rose. **eglantine** sweetbrier, another kind of rose

And there the snake throws her enameled skin,   255
Weed wide enough to wrap a fairy in.   256
And with the juice of this I'll streak her eyes   257
And make her full of hateful fantasies.
Take thou some of it, and seek through this grove.
                    [*He gives some love juice.*]
A sweet Athenian lady is in love
With a disdainful youth. Anoint his eyes,
But do it when the next thing he espies
May be the lady. Thou shalt know the man
By the Athenian garments he hath on.
Effect it with some care, that he may prove
More fond on her than she upon her love;   266
And look thou meet me ere the first cock crow.

PUCK
Fear not, my lord, your servant shall do so.
                              Exeunt.

❖

2.2   *Enter Titania, Queen of Fairies, with her train.*

TITANIA
Come, now a roundel and a fairy song;   1
Then, for the third part of a minute, hence—
Some to kill cankers in the muskrose buds,   3
Some war with reremice for their leathern wings   4
To make my small elves coats, and some keep back
The clamorous owl, that nightly hoots and wonders
At our quaint spirits. Sing me now asleep.   7
Then to your offices, and let me rest.

        Fairies sing.

FIRST FAIRY
        You spotted snakes with double tongue,   9
            Thorny hedgehogs, be not seen;

---

255 throws sloughs off, sheds   **256 Weed** garment   **257 streak** anoint,
touch gently   **266 fond on** doting on

2.2. Location: The wood.
1 roundel dance in a ring   **3 cankers** cankerworms (i.e., caterpillars or
grubs)   **4 reremice** bats   **7 quaint** dainty   **9 double** forked

Newts and blindworms, do no wrong,   11
Come not near our Fairy Queen.

CHORUS
Philomel, with melody   13
Sing in our sweet lullaby;
Lulla, lulla, lullaby, lulla, lulla, lullaby.
    Never harm
    Nor spell nor charm
Come our lovely lady nigh.
So good night, with lullaby.

FIRST FAIRY
Weaving spiders, come not here;
Hence, you long-legged spinners, hence!
Beetles black, approach not near;
Worm nor snail, do no offense.

CHORUS
Philomel, with melody
Sing in our sweet lullaby;
Lulla, lulla, lullaby, lulla, lulla, lullaby.
    Never harm
    Nor spell nor charm
Come our lovely lady nigh.
So good night, with lullaby.

                                    [*Titania sleeps.*]

SECOND FAIRY
Hence, away! Now all is well.
One aloof stand sentinel.

                                    [*Exeunt Fairies.*]

*Enter Oberon [and squeezes the flower on
Titania's eyelids*].

OBERON
What thou seest when thou dost wake,
Do it for thy true love take;
Love and languish for his sake.

---

11 Newts water lizards (considered poisonous, as were *blindworms*—
small snakes with tiny eyes—and spiders)   **13 Philomel** the nightingale.
(Philomela, daughter of King Pandion, was transformed into a nightingale, according to Ovid's *Metamorphoses* 6, after she had been raped by
her sister Procne's husband, Tereus.)

Be it ounce, or cat, or bear,   36
Pard, or boar with bristled hair,   37
In thy eye that shall appear
When thou wak'st, it is thy dear.
Wake when some vile thing is near.   [*Exit.*]

Enter Lysander and Hermia.

LYSANDER
Fair love, you faint with wandering in the wood;
    And to speak truth, I have forgot our way.
We'll rest us, Hermia, if you think it good,
    And tarry for the comfort of the day.
HERMIA
Be it so, Lysander. Find you out a bed,
For I upon this bank will rest my head.
LYSANDER
One turf shall serve as pillow for us both;
One heart, one bed, two bosoms, and one troth.   48
HERMIA
Nay, good Lysander, for my sake, my dear,
Lie further off yet; do not lie so near.
LYSANDER
O, take the sense, sweet, of my innocence!   51
Love takes the meaning in love's conference.   52
I mean that my heart unto yours is knit
So that but one heart we can make of it;
Two bosoms interchainèd with an oath—
So then two bosoms and a single troth.
Then by your side no bed-room me deny,
For lying so, Hermia, I do not lie.   58
HERMIA
Lysander riddles very prettily.
Now much beshrew my manners and my pride   60
If Hermia meant to say Lysander lied.
But, gentle friend, for love and courtesy
Lie further off, in human modesty;   63

36 **ounce** lynx   37 **Pard** leopard   48 **troth** faith, trothplight   51 **take . . .
innocence** i.e., interpret my intention as innocent   52 **Love . . . conference** i.e., when lovers confer, love teaches each lover to interpret the
other's meaning lovingly   58 **lie** tell a falsehood (with a riddling pun on
lie, recline)   60 **beshrew** curse. (But mildly meant.)   63 **human**
courteous

Such separation as may well be said
Becomes a virtuous bachelor and a maid,
So far be distant; and good night, sweet friend.
Thy love ne'er alter till thy sweet life end!

LYSANDER
Amen, amen, to that fair prayer, say I,
And then end life when I end loyalty!
Here is my bed. Sleep give thee all his rest!

HERMIA
With half that wish the wisher's eyes be pressed!   71
         [*They sleep, separated by a short distance.*]

         Enter Puck.

PUCK
         Through the forest have I gone,
         But Athenian found I none
         On whose eyes I might approve   74
         This flower's force in stirring love.
         Night and silence.—Who is here?
         Weeds of Athens he doth wear.
         This is he, my master said,
         Despisèd the Athenian maid;
         And here the maiden, sleeping sound,
         On the dank and dirty ground.
         Pretty soul, she durst not lie
         Near this lack-love, this kill-courtesy.
         Churl, upon thy eyes I throw
         All the power this charm doth owe.   85
                   [*He applies the love juice.*]
         When thou wak'st, let love forbid
         Sleep his seat on thy eyelid.
         So awake when I am gone,
         For I must now to Oberon.   *Exit.*

         Enter Demetrius and Helena, running.

HELENA
         Stay, though thou kill me, sweet Demetrius!
DEMETRIUS
         I charge thee, hence, and do not haunt me thus.

71 With . . . pressed i.e., may we share your wish, so that your eyes too
are *pressed*, closed, in sleep **74 approve** test **85 owe** own

HELENA

O, wilt thou darkling leave me? Do not so.   92

DEMETRIUS

Stay, on thy peril! I alone will go.   [*Exit.*] 93

HELENA

O, I am out of breath in this fond chase!   94
The more my prayer, the lesser is my grace.   95
Happy is Hermia, wheresoe'er she lies,   96
For she hath blessèd and attractive eyes.
How came her eyes so bright? Not with salt tears;
If so, my eyes are oftener washed than hers.
No, no, I am as ugly as a bear;
For beasts that meet me run away for fear.
Therefore no marvel though Demetrius   102
Do, as a monster, fly my presence thus.   103
What wicked and dissembling glass of mine
Made me compare with Hermia's sphery eyne?   105
But who is here? Lysander, on the ground?
Dead, or asleep? I see no blood, no wound.
Lysander, if you live, good sir, awake.

LYSANDER [*Awaking*]

And run through fire I will for thy sweet sake.
Transparent Helena! Nature shows art,   110
That through thy bosom makes me see thy heart.
Where is Demetrius? O, how fit a word
Is that vile name to perish on my sword!

HELENA

Do not say so, Lysander, say not so.
What though he love your Hermia? Lord, what though?
Yet Hermia still loves you. Then be content.

LYSANDER

Content with Hermia? No! I do repent
The tedious minutes I with her have spent.
Not Hermia but Helena I love.
Who will not change a raven for a dove?
The will of man is by his reason swayed,

92 **darkling** in the dark   93 **on thy peril** i.e., on pain of danger to you if
you don't obey me and stay   94 **fond** doting   95 **my grace** the favor I
obtain   96 **lies** dwells   102–103 **no marvel . . . thus** i.e., no wonder that
Demetrius flies from me as from a monster   105 **compare** vie.   **sphery
eyne** eyes as bright as stars in their spheres   110 **Transparent** (1) radiant (2) able to be seen through

And reason says you are the worthier maid.
Things growing are not ripe until their season;
So I, being young, till now ripe not to reason.   124
And touching now the point of human skill,   125
Reason becomes the marshal to my will
And leads me to your eyes, where I o'erlook   127
Love's stories written in love's richest book.

HELENA
Wherefore was I to this keen mockery born?   129
When at your hands did I deserve this scorn?
Is 't not enough, is 't not enough, young man,
That I did never, no, nor never can,
Deserve a sweet look from Demetrius' eye,
But you must flout my insufficiency?
Good troth, you do me wrong, good sooth, you do,   135
In such disdainful manner me to woo.
But fare you well. Perforce I must confess
I thought you lord of more true gentleness.   138
O, that a lady, of one man refused,   139
Should of another therefore be abused!   *Exit.* 140

LYSANDER
She sees not Hermia. Hermia, sleep thou there,
And never mayst thou come Lysander near!
For as a surfeit of the sweetest things
The deepest loathing to the stomach brings,
Or as the heresies that men do leave   145
Are hated most of those they did deceive,   146
So thou, my surfeit and my heresy,
Of all be hated, but the most of me!
And, all my powers, address your love and might   149
To honor Helen and to be her knight!   *Exit.*

HERMIA [*Awaking*]
Help me, Lysander, help me! Do thy best
To pluck this crawling serpent from my breast!
Ay me, for pity! What a dream was here!
Lysander, look how I do quake with fear.

---

124 ripe not (am) not ripened   **125 touching** reaching.   **point** summit.
skill judgment   **127 o'erlook** read   **129 Wherefore** why   **135 Good
troth, good sooth** i.e., indeed, truly   **138 lord of** i.e., possessor of.
gentleness courtesy   **139 of** by   **140 abused** ill treated   **145–146 as . . .
deceive** as renounced heresies are hated most by those persons who
formerly were deceived by them   **149 address** direct, apply

Methought a serpent ate my heart away,
And you sat smiling at his cruel prey.   156
Lysander! What, removed? Lysander! Lord!
What, out of hearing? Gone? No sound, no word?
Alack, where are you? Speak, an if you hear;   159
Speak, of all loves! I swoon almost with fear.   160
No? Then I well perceive you are not nigh.
Either death, or you, I'll find immediately.

Exit. [*The sleeping Titania remains.*]

156 prey act of preying   **159 an if** if   **160 of loves** for all love's sake

3.1 *Enter the clowns [Quince, Snug, Bottom, Flute,
Snout, and Starveling].*

BOTTOM Are we all met?

QUINCE Pat, pat; and here's a marvelous convenient 2
place for our rehearsal. This green plot shall be our
stage, this hawthorn brake our tiring-house, and we 4
will do it in action as we will do it before the Duke.

BOTTOM Peter Quince?

QUINCE What sayest thou, bully Bottom? 7

BOTTOM There are things in this comedy of Pyramus
and Thisbe that will never please. First, Pyramus must
draw a sword to kill himself, which the ladies cannot
abide. How answer you that?

SNOUT By 'r lakin, a parlous fear. 12

STARVELING I believe we must leave the killing out,
when all is done. 14

BOTTOM Not a whit. I have a device to make all well.
Write me a prologue, and let the prologue seem to say 16
we will do no harm with our swords, and that Pyramus
is not killed indeed; and for the more better assurance,
tell them that I, Pyramus, am not Pyramus but Bottom
the weaver. This will put them out of fear.

QUINCE Well, we will have such a prologue, and it shall
be written in eight and six. 22

BOTTOM No, make it two more; let it be written in eight
and eight.

SNOUT Will not the ladies be afeard of the lion?

STARVELING I fear it, I promise you.

BOTTOM Masters, you ought to consider with yourselves, to bring in—God shield us!—a lion among la- 28
dies is a most dreadful thing. For there is not a more 29

3.1. Location: The action is continuous.
2 Pat on the dot, punctually   **4 brake** thicket.   **tiring-house** attiring
area, hence backstage   **7 bully** i.e., worthy, jolly, fine fellow   **12 By 'r
lakin** by our ladykin, i.e., the Virgin Mary.   **parlous** alarming   **14 when
all is done** i.e., when all is said and done   **16 Write me** i.e., write at my
suggestion. (*Me* is used colloquially.)   **22 eight and six** alternate lines of
eight and six syllables, a common ballad measure   **28–29 lion among
ladies** (A contemporary pamphlet tells how at the christening in 1594 of
Prince Henry, eldest son of King James VI of Scotland, later James I of
England, a "blackamoor" instead of a lion drew the triumphal chariot,
since the lion's presence might have "brought some fear to the nearest.")

fearful wildfowl than your lion living; and we ought 30
to look to 't.

SNOUT Therefore another prologue must tell he is not a
lion.

BOTTOM Nay, you must name his name, and half his
face must be seen through the lion's neck, and he himself must speak through, saying thus, or to the same
defect: "Ladies"—or "Fair ladies—I would wish 37
you"—or "I would request you"—or "I would entreat
you—not to fear, not to tremble; my life for yours. If 39
you think I come hither as a lion, it were pity of my 40
life. No, I am no such thing; I am a man as other men 41
are." And there indeed let him name his name and
tell them plainly he is Snug the joiner.

QUINCE Well, it shall be so. But there is two hard things:
that is, to bring the moonlight into a chamber; for, you
know, Pyramus and Thisbe meet by moonlight.

SNOUT Doth the moon shine that night we play our
play?

BOTTOM A calendar, a calendar! Look in the almanac.
Find out moonshine, find out moonshine.

                    [*They consult an almanac.*]

QUINCE Yes, it doth shine that night.

BOTTOM Why, then, may you leave a casement of the
great chamber window, where we play, open, and the
moon may shine in at the casement.

QUINCE Ay; or else one must come in with a bush of 55
thorns and a lantern and say he comes to disfigure, or 56
to present, the person of Moonshine. Then there is 57
another thing: we must have a wall in the great chamber; for Pyramus and Thisbe, says the story, did talk
through the chink of a wall.

SNOUT You can never bring in a wall. What say you,
Bottom?

BOTTOM Some man or other must present Wall. And let

30 fearful fear-inspiring   **37 defect** (Bottom's blunder for *effect*.)
39 my life for yours i.e., I pledge my life to make your lives safe
40–41 it were . . . life my life would be endangered   **55–56 bush of
thorns** bundle of thornbush faggots (part of the accoutrements of the
man in the moon, according to the popular notions of the time, along
with his lantern and his dog)   **56 disfigure** (Quince's blunder for *figure*.)   **57 present** represent

him have some plaster, or some loam, or some rough- 64
cast about him, to signify wall; or let him hold his 65
fingers thus, and through that cranny shall Pyramus
and Thisbe whisper.

QUINCE   If that may be, then all is well. Come, sit down,
every mother's son, and rehearse your parts. Pyramus,
you begin. When you have spoken your speech, enter
into that brake, and so everyone according to his cue.

    Enter Robin [Puck].

PUCK
What hempen homespuns have we swaggering here 72
So near the cradle of the Fairy Queen? 73
What, a play toward? I'll be an auditor; 74
An actor too perhaps, if I see cause.

QUINCE   Speak, Pyramus. Thisbe, stand forth.

BOTTOM [*As Pyramus*]
"Thisbe, the flowers of odious savors sweet—"

QUINCE   Odors, odors.

BOTTOM   "—Odors savors sweet;
So hath thy breath, my dearest Thisbe dear.
But hark, a voice! Stay thou but here awhile,
And by and by I will to thee appear."   *Exit.*

PUCK
A stranger Pyramus than e'er played here.   [*Exit.*] 83

FLUTE   Must I speak now?

QUINCE   Ay, marry, must you; for you must understand
he goes but to see a noise that he heard, and is to come
again.

FLUTE [*As Thisbe*]
"Most radiant Pyramus, most lily-white of hue,
Of color like the red rose on triumphant brier, 89
Most brisky juvenal and eke most lovely Jew, 90

64–65 roughcast a mixture of lime and gravel used to plaster the outside of buildings   **72 hempen homespuns** i.e., rustics dressed in clothes
woven of coarse, homespun fabric made from hemp   **73 cradle** i.e.,
Titania's bower   **74 toward** about to take place   **83 A stranger . . . here**
(Puck indicates that he has conceived of his plan to present a "stranger"
Pyramus than ever seen before, and so Puck exits to put his plan into
effect.)   **89 triumphant** magnificent   **90 brisky juvenal** lively youth.
eke also.   **Jew** (Probably an absurd repetition of the first syllable of
juvenal, or Flute's error for *jewel.*)

As true as truest horse, that yet would never tire.
I'll meet thee, Pyramus, at Ninny's tomb."
QUINCE "Ninus' tomb," man. Why, you must not 93
speak that yet. That you answer to Pyramus. You
speak all your part at once, cues and all. Pyramus, en- 95
ter. Your cue is past; it is "never tire."
FLUTE
O—"As true as truest horse, that yet would never
tire."   97

          [*Enter Puck, and Bottom as Pyramus with the ass
          head.*]

BOTTOM
"If I were fair, Thisbe, I were only thine."   98
QUINCE O, monstrous! O, strange! We are haunted.
Pray, masters! Fly, masters! Help!
                              [*Exeunt Quince, Snug, Flute,
                                   Snout, and Starveling.*]
PUCK
I'll follow you, I'll lead you about a round,   101
    Through bog, through bush, through brake, through
        brier.
Sometimes a horse I'll be, sometimes a hound,
    A hog, a headless bear, sometimes a fire;   104
And neigh, and bark, and grunt, and roar, and burn,
Like horse, hound, hog, bear, fire, at every turn. *Exit.*
BOTTOM Why do they run away? This is a knavery of
them to make me afeard.

          Enter Snout.

SNOUT O Bottom, thou art changed! What do I see on
thee?
BOTTOM What do you see? You see an ass head of your
own, do you?   [*Exit Snout.*]

_____

93 Ninus mythical founder of Nineveh (whose wife, Semiramis, was
supposed to have built the walls of Babylon where the story of Pyramus
and Thisbe takes place)   **95 part** (An actor's *part* was a script consisting
only of his speeches and their cues.)   **97 s.d. with the ass head** (This
stage direction, taken from the Folio, presumably refers to a standard
stage property.)   **98 fair** handsome.   **were** would be   **101 about a
round** roundabout   **104 fire** will-o'-the-wisp

Enter Quince.

QUINCE   Bless thee, Bottom, bless thee! Thou art trans-   113
lated.   *Exit.*   114
BOTTOM   I see their knavery. This is to make an ass of
me, to fright me, if they could. But I will not stir from
this place, do what they can. I will walk up and down
here, and will sing, that they shall hear I am not
afraid.   [*Sings.*]
         The ouzel cock so black of hue,   120
             With orange-tawny bill,
         The throstle with his note so true,   122
         The wren with little quill—   123
TITANIA [*Awaking*]
   What angel wakes me from my flowery bed?
BOTTOM [*Sings*]
         The finch, the sparrow, and the lark,
         The plainsong cuckoo gray,   126
         Whose note full many a man doth mark,   ·
             And dares not answer nay—   128
   For, indeed, who would set his wit to so foolish a
   bird? Who would give a bird the lie, though he cry   130
   "cuckoo" never so?   131
TITANIA
   I pray thee, gentle mortal, sing again.
   Mine ear is much enamored of thy note;
   So is mine eye enthrallèd to thy shape;
   And thy fair virtue's force perforce doth move me   135
   On the first view to say, to swear, I love thee.
BOTTOM   Methinks, mistress, you should have little rea-
   son for that. And yet, to say the truth, reason and love
   keep little company together nowadays. The more the
   pity that some honest neighbors will not make them
   friends. Nay, I can gleek upon occasion.   141
TITANIA
   Thou art as wise as thou art beautiful.

113-114 translated transformed   **120 ouzel cock** male blackbird
122 throstle song thrush   **123 quill** (Literally, a reed pipe; hence, the
bird's piping song.)   **126 plainsong** singing a melody without variations   **128 dares . . . nay** i.e., cannot deny that he is a cuckold   **130 give
. . . lie** call the bird a liar   **131 never so** ever so much   **135 thy . . . force**
the power of your beauty   **141 gleek** scoff, jest

BOTTOM Not so, neither. But if I had wit enough to get
out of this wood, I have enough to serve mine own 144
turn.   145

TITANIA
Out of this wood do not desire to go.
Thou shalt remain here, whether thou wilt or no.
I am a spirit of no common rate.   148
The summer still doth tend upon my state,   149
And I do love thee. Therefore go with me.
I'll give thee fairies to attend on thee,
And they shall fetch thee jewels from the deep,
And sing while thou on pressèd flowers dost sleep.
And I will purge thy mortal grossness so   154
That thou shalt like an airy spirit go.
Peaseblossom, Cobweb, Mote, and Mustardseed! 156

*Enter four Fairies [Peaseblossom, Cobweb, Mote,
and Mustardseed].*

PEASEBLOSSOM Ready.
COBWEB
And I.
MOTE And I.
MUSTARDSEED And I.
ALL   Where shall we go?
TITANIA
Be kind and courteous to this gentleman.
Hop in his walks and gambol in his eyes;   160
Feed him with apricots and dewberries,   161
With purple grapes, green figs, and mulberries;
The honey bags steal from the humble-bees,
And for night tapers crop their waxen thighs
And light them at the fiery glowworms' eyes,
To have my love to bed and to arise;
And pluck the wings from painted butterflies
To fan the moonbeams from his sleeping eyes.
Nod to him, elves, and do him courtesies.

144–145 serve . . . turn answer my purpose   **148 rate** rank, value
149 still ever, always.   **doth . . . state** waits upon me as a part of my
royal retinue   **154 mortal grossness** materiality (i.e., the corporal nature
of a mortal being)   **156 Mote** i.e., speck. (The two words *moth* and *mote*
were pronounced alike, and both meanings may be present.)   **160 in his
eyes** in his sight (i.e., before him)   **161 dewberries** blackberries

PEASEBLOSSOM Hail, mortal!
COBWEB Hail!
MOTE Hail!
MUSTARDSEED Hail!
BOTTOM I cry your worships mercy, heartily. I beseech
your worship's name.
COBWEB Cobweb.
BOTTOM I shall desire you of more acquaintance, good
Master Cobweb. If I cut my finger, I shall make bold   178
with you.—Your name, honest gentleman?   179
PEASEBLOSSOM Peaseblossom.
BOTTOM I pray you, commend me to Mistress Squash,   181
your mother, and to Master Peascod, your father.   182
Good Master Peaseblossom, I shall desire you of more
acquaintance too.—Your name, I beseech you, sir?
MUSTARDSEED Mustardseed.
BOTTOM Good Master Mustardseed, I know your pa-   186
tience well. That same cowardly, giantlike ox-beef   187
hath devoured many a gentleman of your house. I
promise you, your kindred hath made my eyes water   189
ere now. I desire you of more acquaintance, good
Master Mustardseed.
TITANIA
Come, wait upon him; lead him to my bower.
The moon methinks looks with a watery eye;
And when she weeps, weeps every little flower,   194
Lamenting some enforcèd chastity.   195
Tie up my lover's tongue, bring him silently.   196
                                          Exeunt.

❖

3.2 *Enter [Oberon,] King of Fairies.*

OBERON
I wonder if Titania be awaked;

178–179 If . . . you (Cobwebs were used to stanch bleeding.) 181 Squash
unripe pea pod 182 Peascod ripe pea pod 186–187 your patience what
you have endured 189 water (1) weep for sympathy (2) smart, sting
194 she weeps i.e., she causes dew 195 enforcèd forced, violated; or, possibly, constrained (since Titania at this moment is hardly concerned about
chastity) 196 Tie . . . tongue (Presumably Bottom is braying like an ass.)
3.2. Location: The wood.

Then what it was that next came in her eye,
Which she must dote on in extremity.

[*Enter*] *Robin Goodfellow* [*Puck*].

Here comes my messenger. How now, mad spirit?
What night-rule now about this haunted grove?   5
PUCK
My mistress with a monster is in love.
Near to her close and consecrated bower,   7
While she was in her dull and sleeping hour,   8
A crew of patches, rude mechanicals,   9
That work for bread upon Athenian stalls,   10
Were met together to rehearse a play
Intended for great Theseus' nuptial day.
The shallowest thick-skin of that barren sort,   13
Who Pyramus presented in their sport,   14
Forsook his scene and entered in a brake.   15
When I did him at this advantage take,
An ass's noll I fixèd on his head.   17
Anon his Thisbe must be answerèd,
And forth my mimic comes. When they him spy,   19
As wild geese that the creeping fowler eye,   20
Or russet-pated choughs, many in sort,   21
Rising and cawing at the gun's report,
Sever themselves and madly sweep the sky,   23
So, at his sight, away his fellows fly;
And, at our stamp, here o'er and o'er one falls;
He "Murder!" cries and help from Athens calls.
Their sense thus weak, lost with their fears thus strong,
Made senseless things begin to do them wrong,
For briers and thorns at their apparel snatch;
Some, sleeves—some, hats; from yielders all things
     catch.   30

5 **night-rule** diversion for the night.   **haunted** much frequented   **7 close**
secret, private   **8 dull** drowsy   **9 patches** clowns, fools.   **rude mechani-**
cals ignorant artisans   **10 stalls** market booths   **13 barren sort** stupid
company or crew   **14 presented** acted   **15 scene** playing area   **17 noll**
noddle, head   **19 mimic** burlesque actor   **20 fowler** hunter of game
birds   **21 russet-pated choughs** reddish brown or gray-headed jack-
daws.   **in sort** in a flock   **23 Sever** i.e., scatter   **30 from . . . catch** i.e.,
everything preys on those who yield to fear

I led them on in this distracted fear
And left sweet Pyramus translated there,
When in that moment, so it came to pass,
Titania waked and straightway loved an ass.

OBERON
This falls out better than I could devise.
But hast thou yet latched the Athenian's eyes   36
With the love juice, as I did bid thee do?

PUCK
I took him sleeping—that is finished too—
And the Athenian woman by his side,
That, when he waked, of force she must be eyed.   40

Enter Demetrius and Hermia.

OBERON
Stand close. This is the same Athenian.

PUCK
This is the woman, but not this the man.
                              [*They stand aside.*]

DEMETRIUS
O, why rebuke you him that loves you so?
Lay breath so bitter on your bitter foe.

HERMIA
Now I but chide; but I should use thee worse,
For thou, I fear, hast given me cause to curse.
If thou hast slain Lysander in his sleep,
Being o'er shoes in blood, plunge in the deep,   48
And kill me too.
The sun was not so true unto the day
As he to me. Would he have stolen away
From sleeping Hermia? I'll believe as soon
This whole earth may be bored, and that the moon   53
May through the center creep, and so displease
 . Her brother's noontide with th' Antipodes.   55
It cannot be but thou hast murdered him;
So should a murderer look, so dead, so grim.   57

---

36 latched fastened, snared   **40 of force** perforce   **48 o'er shoes** i.e., so
far gone   **53 whole** solid   **55 Her brother's** i.e., the sun's.   **th' Antipodes** the people on the opposite side of the earth (where the moon is
imagined bringing night to noontime)   **57 dead** deadly, or deathly pale

DEMETRIUS

So should the murdered look, and so should I,
Pierced through the heart with your stern cruelty.
Yet you, the murderer, look as bright, as clear,
As yonder Venus in her glimmering sphere.

HERMIA

What's this to my Lysander? Where is he?   62
Ah, good Demetrius, wilt thou give him me?

DEMETRIUS

I had rather give his carcass to my hounds.

HERMIA

Out, dog! Out, cur! Thou driv'st me past the bounds
Of maiden's patience. Hast thou slain him, then?
Henceforth be never numbered among men.
O, once tell true, tell true, even for my sake:
Durst thou have looked upon him being awake?
And hast thou killed him sleeping? O brave touch!   70
Could not a worm, an adder, do so much?   71
An adder did it; for with doubler tongue
Than thine, thou serpent, never adder stung.

DEMETRIUS

You spend your passion on a misprised mood.   74
I am not guilty of Lysander's blood,
Nor is he dead, for aught that I can tell.

HERMIA

I pray thee, tell me then that he is well.

DEMETRIUS

An if I could, what should I get therefor?

HERMIA

A privilege never to see me more.
And from thy hated presence part I so.
See me no more, whether he be dead or no.   *Exit.*

DEMETRIUS

There is no following her in this fierce vein.
Here therefore for a while I will remain.
So sorrow's heaviness doth heavier grow   84
For debt that bankrupt sleep doth sorrow owe;   85

---

62 to to do with   **70 brave touch** noble exploit. (Said ironically.)   **71 worm**
serpent   **74 passion** violent feelings.   **misprised mood** anger based on mis-
conception   **84 heavier** (1) harder to bear (2) more drowsy   **85 bankrupt** (Demetrius is saying that his sleepiness adds to the weariness caused by sorrow.)

Which now in some slight measure it will pay,   86
If for his tender here I make some stay.   87
                    Lie[s] down [and sleeps].

OBERON
What hast thou done? Thou hast mistaken quite
And laid the love juice on some true love's sight.
Of thy misprision must perforce ensue   90
Some true love turned, and not a false turned true.

PUCK
Then fate o'errules, that, one man holding troth,   92
A million fail, confounding oath on oath.   93

OBERON
About the wood go swifter than the wind,
And Helena of Athens look thou find.   95
All fancy-sick she is and pale of cheer   96
With sighs of love, that cost the fresh blood dear.   97
By some illusion see thou bring her here.
I'll charm his eyes against she do appear.   99

PUCK
I go, I go, look how I go,
Swifter than arrow from the Tartar's bow.   101
                              [Exit.]

OBERON [*Applying love juice to Demetrius' eyes*]
          Flower of this purple dye,
          Hit with Cupid's archery,
          Sink in apple of his eye.
          When his love he doth espy,
          Let her shine as gloriously
          As the Venus of the sky.
          When thou wak'st, if she be by,
          Beg of her for remedy.

     Enter Puck.

86–87 **Which . . . stay** i.e., to a small extent I will be able to
"pay back" and hence find some relief from sorrow, if I pause here
awhile *(make some stay)* while sleep "tenders" or offers itself by
way of paying the debt owed to sorrow   90 **misprision** mistake   92 **troth** faith   93 **confounding . . . oath** i.e., invalidating
one oath with another   95 **look** i.e., be sure   96 **fancy-sick** love-
sick.   **cheer** face   97 **sighs . . . blood** (An allusion to the physio-
logical theory that each sigh costs the heart a drop of blood.)
99 **against . . . appear** in anticipation of her coming   101 **Tartar's
bow** (Tartars were famed for their skill with the bow.)

PUCK

 Captain of our fairy band,
 Helena is here at hand,
 And the youth, mistook by me,
 Pleading for a lover's fee.   113
 Shall we their fond pageant see?   114
 Lord, what fools these mortals be!

OBERON

 Stand aside. The noise they make
 Will cause Demetrius to awake.

PUCK

 Then will two at once woo one;
 That must needs be sport alone.   119
 And those things do best please me
 That befall preposterously.   121

         [They stand aside.]

 Enter Lysander and Helena.

LYSANDER

Why should you think that I should woo in scorn?
 Scorn and derision never come in tears.
Look when I vow, I weep; and vows so born, 124
 In their nativity all truth appears.   125
How can these things in me seem scorn to you,
Bearing the badge of faith to prove them true? 127

HELENA

You do advance your cunning more and more. 128
 When truth kills truth, O, devilish-holy fray! 129
These vows are Hermia's. Will you give her o'er?
 Weigh oath with oath, and you will nothing weigh.
Your vows to her and me, put in two scales,
Will even weigh, and both as light as tales. 133

LYSANDER

I had no judgment when to her I swore.

---

113 fee privilege, reward **114 fond pageant** foolish exhibition
119 alone unequaled **121 preposterously** out of the natural order
124 Look when whenever **124–125 vows . . . appears** i.e., vows made by
one who is weeping give evidence thereby of their sincerity **127 badge**
identifying device such as that worn on servants' livery (here, his
tears) **128 advance** carry forward, display **129 truth kills truth** i.e.,
one of Lysander's vows must invalidate the other **133 tales** lies

HELENA
  Nor none, in my mind, now you give her o'er.
LYSANDER
  Demetrius loves her, and he loves not you.
DEMETRIUS [*Awaking*]
  O Helen, goddess, nymph, perfect, divine!
  To what, my love, shall I compare thine eyne?
  Crystal is muddy. O, how ripe in show   139
  Thy lips, those kissing cherries, tempting grow!
  That pure congealèd white, high Taurus' snow,   141
  Fanned with the eastern wind, turns to a crow   142
  When thou hold'st up thy hand. O, let me kiss
  This princess of pure white, this seal of bliss!   144
HELENA
  O spite! O hell! I see you all are bent
  To set against me for your merriment.   146
  If you were civil and knew courtesy,
  You would not do me thus much injury.
  Can you not hate me, as I know you do,
  But you must join in souls to mock me too?
  If you were men, as men you are in show,
  You would not use a gentle lady so—
  To vow, and swear, and superpraise my parts,   153
  When I am sure you hate me with your hearts.
  You both are rivals, and love Hermia;
  And now both rivals, to mock Helena.
  A trim exploit, a manly enterprise,   157
  To conjure tears up in a poor maid's eyes
  With your derision! None of noble sort   159
  Would so offend a virgin and extort   160
  A poor soul's patience, all to make you sport.
LYSANDER
  You are unkind, Demetrius. Be not so;
  For you love Hermia; this you know I know.
  And here, with all good will, with all my heart,
  In Hermia's love I yield you up my part;

---

139 show appearance   **141 Taurus** a lofty mountain range in Asia
Minor   **142 turns to a crow** i.e., seems black by contrast   **144 seal**
pledge   **146 set against** attack   **153 superpraise** overpraise.   **parts**
qualities   **157 trim** pretty, fine. (Said ironically.)   **159 sort** character,
quality   **160 extort** twist, torture

And yours of Helena to me bequeath,
Whom I do love and will do till my death.

HELENA
Never did mockers waste more idle breath.

DEMETRIUS
Lysander, keep thy Hermia; I will none.   169
If e'er I loved her, all that love is gone.
My heart to her but as guest-wise sojourned,   171
And now to Helen is it home returned,
There to remain.

LYSANDER   Helen, it is not so.

DEMETRIUS
Disparage not the faith thou dost not know,
Lest, to thy peril, thou aby it dear.   175
Look where thy love comes; yonder is thy dear.

Enter Hermia.

HERMIA
Dark night, that from the eye his function takes,   177
The ear more quick of apprehension makes;
Wherein it doth impair the seeing sense,
It pays the hearing double recompense.
Thou art not by mine eye, Lysander, found;
Mine ear, I thank it, brought me to thy sound.
But why unkindly didst thou leave me so?

LYSANDER
Why should he stay whom love doth press to go?

HERMIA
What love could press Lysander from my side?

LYSANDER
Lysander's love, that would not let him bide—
Fair Helena, who more engilds the night   187
Than all yon fiery oes and eyes of light.   188
Why seek'st thou me? Could not this make thee know,
The hate I bear thee made me leave thee so?

HERMIA
You speak not as you think. It cannot be.

HELENA
Lo, she is one of this confederacy!

169 will none i.e., want no part of her   **171 to ... sojourned** only visited
with her   **175 aby** pay for   **177 his** its   **187 engilds** brightens with a
golden light   **188 oes** spangles (here, stars)

Now I perceive they have conjoined all three
To fashion this false sport in spite of me.   194
Injurious Hermia, most ungrateful maid!
Have you conspired, have you with these contrived   196
To bait me with this foul derision?   197
Is all the counsel that we two have shared,   198
The sisters' vows, the hours that we have spent,
When we have chid the hasty-footed time
For parting us—O, is all forgot?
All schooldays' friendship, childhood innocence?
We, Hermia, like two artificial gods,   203
Have with our needles created both one flower,
Both on one sampler, sitting on one cushion,
Both warbling of one song, both in one key,
As if our hands, our sides, voices, and minds
Had been incorporate. So we grew together   208
Like to a double cherry, seeming parted
But yet an union in partition,
Two lovely berries molded on one stem;   211
So with two seeming bodies but one heart,
Two of the first, like coats in heraldry,   213
Due but to one and crownèd with one crest.   214
And will you rend our ancient love asunder
To join with men in scorning your poor friend?
It is not friendly, 'tis not maidenly.
Our sex, as well as I, may chide you for it,
Though I alone do feel the injury.

HERMIA
I am amazèd at your passionate words.
I scorn you not. It seems that you scorn me.

HELENA
Have you not set Lysander, as in scorn,
To follow me and praise my eyes and face?
And made your other love, Demetrius,
Who even but now did spurn me with his foot,
To call me goddess, nymph, divine and rare,

194 **in spite of me** to vex me   196 **contrived** plotted   197 **bait** torment,
as one sets on dogs to bait a bear   198 **counsel** confidential talk
203 **artificial** skilled in art or creation   208 **incorporate** of one body
211 **lovely** loving   213–214 **Two . . . crest** i.e., we have two separate
bodies, just as a coat of arms in heraldry can be represented twice on a
shield but surmounted by a single crest

Precious, celestial? Wherefore speaks he this
To her he hates? And wherefore doth Lysander
Deny your love, so rich within his soul,
And tender me, forsooth, affection,   230
But by your setting on, by your consent?
What though I be not so in grace as you,   232
So hung upon with love, so fortunate,
But miserable most, to love unloved?
This you should pity rather than despise.

HERMIA
I understand not what you mean by this.

HELENA
Ay, do! Persever, counterfeit sad looks,   237
Make mouths upon me when I turn my back,   238
Wink each at other, hold the sweet jest up.   239
This sport, well carried, shall be chronicled.   240
If you have any pity, grace, or manners,
You would not make me such an argument.   242
But fare ye well. 'Tis partly my own fault,
Which death, or absence, soon shall remedy.

LYSANDER
Stay, gentle Helena; hear my excuse,
My love, my life, my soul, fair Helena!

HELENA
O excellent!

HERMIA [*To Lysander*]   Sweet, do not scorn her so.

DEMETRIUS
If she cannot entreat, I can compel.   248

LYSANDER
Thou canst compel no more than she entreat.
Thy threats have no more strength than her weak
    prayers.
Helen, I love thee, by my life, I do!
I swear by that which I will lose for thee,
To prove him false that says I love thee not.

DEMETRIUS
I say I love thee more than he can do.

230 tender offer   **232 grace** favor   **237 sad** grave, serious   **238 mouths**
i.e., mows, faces, grimaces.   **upon** at   **239 hold ... up** keep up the
joke   **240 carried** managed   **242 argument** subject for a jest   **248 entreat** i.e., succeed by entreaty

LYSANDER
If thou say so, withdraw, and prove it too.

DEMETRIUS
Quick, come!

HERMIA   Lysander, whereto tends all this?

LYSANDER
Away, you Ethiop!

[He tries to break away from Hermia.]

DEMETRIUS   No, no; he'll   257
Seem to break loose; take on as you would follow,   258
But yet come not. You are a tame man, go!

LYSANDER
Hang off, thou cat, thou burr! Vile thing, let loose,   260
Or I will shake thee from me like a serpent!

HERMIA
Why are you grown so rude? What change is this,
Sweet love?

LYSANDER   Thy love? Out, tawny Tartar, out! ·
Out, loathèd med'cine! O hated potion, hence!   264

HERMIA
Do you not jest?

HELENA   Yes, sooth, and so do you.   265

LYSANDER
Demetrius, I will keep my word with thee.

DEMETRIUS
I would I had your bond, for I perceive
A weak bond holds you. I'll not trust your word.   268

LYSANDER
What, should I hurt her, strike her, kill her dead?
Although I hate her, I'll not harm her so.

HERMIA
What, can you do me greater harm than hate?
Hate me? Wherefore? O me, what news, my love?   272
Am not I Hermia? Are not you Lysander?
I am as fair now as I was erewhile.   274
Since night you loved me; yet since night you left me.

---

257 Ethiop (Referring to Hermia's relatively dark hair and complexion;
see also *tawny Tartar* six lines later.)   **258 take on as** act as if   **260 Hang
off** let go   **264 med'cine** i.e., poison   **265 sooth** truly   **268 weak bond**
i.e., Hermia's arm (with a pun on *bond*, oath, in the previous line)
272 what news what is the matter   **274 erewhile** just now

Why, then you left me—O, the gods forbid!—
In earnest, shall I say?
LYSANDER   Ay, by my life!
And never did desire to see thee more.
Therefore be out of hope, of question, of doubt;
Be certain, nothing truer. 'Tis no jest
That I do hate thee and love Helena.
HERMIA [*To Helena*]
O me! You juggler! You cankerblossom!   282
You thief of love! What, have you come by night
And stol'n my love's heart from him?
HELENA   Fine, i' faith!
Have you no modesty, no maiden shame,
No touch of bashfulness? What, will you tear
Impatient answers from my gentle tongue?
Fie, fie! You counterfeit, you puppet, you!   288
HERMIA
"Puppet"? Why, so! Ay, that way goes the game.   289
Now I perceive that she hath made compare
Between our statures; she hath urged her height,
And with her personage, her tall personage,
Her height, forsooth, she hath prevailed with him.
And are you grown so high in his esteem
Because I am so dwarfish and so low?
How low am I, thou painted maypole? Speak!
How low am I? I am not yet so low
But that my nails can reach unto thine eyes.
            [*She flails at Helena but is restrained.*]
HELENA
I pray you, though you mock me, gentlemen,
Let her not hurt me. I was never curst;   300
I have no gift at all in shrewishness;
I am a right maid for my cowardice.   302
Let her not strike me. You perhaps may think,
Because she is something lower than myself,   304
That I can match her.
HERMIA   Lower? Hark, again!

---

282 cankerblossom worm that destroys the flower bud (?)   **288 puppet**
(1) counterfeit (2) dwarfish woman (in reference to Hermia's smaller
stature)   **289 Why, so** i.e., Oh, so that's how it is   **300 curst** shrewish
302 right true   **304 something** somewhat

HELENA
  Good Hermia, do not be so bitter with me.
  I evermore did love you, Hermia,
  Did ever keep your counsels, never wronged you;
  Save that, in love unto Demetrius,
  I told him of your stealth unto this wood.   310
  He followed you; for love I followed him.
  But he hath chid me hence and threatened me   312
  To strike me, spurn me, nay, to kill me too.
  And now, so you will let me quiet go,   314
  To Athens will I bear my folly back
  And follow you no further. Let me go.
  You see how simple and how fond I am.   317
HERMIA
  Why, get you gone. Who is 't that hinders you?
HELENA
  A foolish heart, that I leave here behind.
HERMIA
  What, with Lysander?
HELENA   With Demetrius.
LYSANDER
  Be not afraid; she shall not harm thee, Helena.
DEMETRIUS
  No, sir, she shall not, though you take her part.
HELENA
  O, when she is angry, she is keen and shrewd.   323
  She was a vixen when she went to school,
  And though she be but little, she is fierce.
HERMIA
  "Little" again? Nothing but "low" and "little"?
  Why will you suffer her to flout me thus?
  Let me come to her.
LYSANDER   Get you gone, you dwarf!
  You minimus, of hindering knotgrass made!   329
  You bead, you acorn!
DEMETRIUS   You are too officious
  In her behalf that scorns your services.
  Let her alone. Speak not of Helena;

310 stealth stealing away 312 chid me hence driven me away with his
scolding 314 so if only 317 fond foolish 323 keen fierce, cruel.
shrewd shrewish 329 minimus diminutive creature. knotgrass a
weed, an infusion of which was thought to stunt the growth

Take not her part. For, if thou dost intend   333
Never so little show of love to her,
Thou shalt aby it.

LYSANDER   Now she holds me not;   335
Now follow, if thou dar'st, to try whose right,
Of thine or mine, is most in Helena.   [*Exit.*]

DEMETRIUS
Follow? Nay, I'll go with thee, cheek by jowl.   338
        [*Exit, following Lysander.*]

HERMIA
You, mistress, all this coil is 'long of you.   339
Nay, go not back.

HELENA   I will not trust you, I,   340
Nor longer stay in your curst company.
Your hands than mine are quicker for a fray;
My legs are longer, though, to run away.   [*Exit.*]

HERMIA
I am amazed and know not what to say.   *Exit.*

        [*Oberon and Puck come forward.*]

OBERON
This is thy negligence. Still thou mistak'st,
Or else committ'st thy knaveries willfully.

PUCK
Believe me, king of shadows, I mistook.
Did not you tell me I should know the man
By the Athenian garments he had on?
And so far blameless proves my enterprise
That I have 'nointed an Athenian's eyes;
And so far am I glad it so did sort,   352
As this their jangling I esteem a sport.   353

OBERON
Thou seest these lovers seek a place to fight.
Hie therefore, Robin, overcast the night;   355
The starry welkin cover thou anon   356
With drooping fog as black as Acheron,   357
And lead these testy rivals so astray

---

333 **intend** give sign of   335 **aby** pay for   338 **cheek by jowl** i.e., side by
side   339 **coil** turmoil, dissension.   **'long of** on account of   340 **go not
back** i.e., don't retreat. (Hermia is again proposing a fight.)   352 **sort**
turn out   353 **As** that (also at l. 359)   355 **Hie** hasten   356 **welkin** sky
357 **Acheron** river of Hades (here representing Hades itself)

As one come not within another's way.
Like to Lysander sometimes frame thy tongue,
Then stir Demetrius up with bitter wrong;   361
And sometimes rail thou like Demetrius.
And from each other look thou lead them thus,
Till o'er their brows death-counterfeiting sleep
With leaden legs and batty wings doth creep.   365
Then crush this herb into Lysander's eye,   366
                    [*Giving herb*]
Whose liquor hath this virtuous property,   367
To take from thence all error with his might   368
And make his eyeballs roll with wonted sight.   369
When they next wake, all this derision   370
Shall seem a dream and fruitless vision,
And back to Athens shall the lovers wend
With league whose date till death shall never end.   373
Whiles I in this affair do thee employ,
I'll to my queen and beg her Indian boy;
And then I will her charmèd eye release
From monster's view, and all things shall be peace.

PUCK
My fairy lord, this must be done with haste,
For night's swift dragons cut the clouds full fast,   379
And yonder shines Aurora's harbinger,   380
At whose approach, ghosts, wand'ring here and there,
Troop home to churchyards. Damnèd spirits all,
That in crossways and floods have burial,   383
Already to their wormy beds are gone.
For fear lest day should look their shames upon,
They willfully themselves exile from light
And must for aye consort with black-browed night.   387

OBERON
But we are spirits of another sort.

361 wrong insults   **365 batty** batlike   **366 this herb** i.e., the antidote
(mentioned in 2.1.184) to love-in-idleness   **367 virtuous** efficacious
368 his its   **369 wonted** accustomed   **370 derision** laughable business
373 date term of existence   **379 dragons** (Supposed by Shakespeare to
be yoked to the car of the goddess of night.)   **380 Aurora's harbinger**
the morning star, precursor of dawn   **383 crossways ... burial** (Those
who had committed suicide were buried at crossways, with a stake
driven through them; those drowned, i.e., buried in floods or great
waters, would be condemned to wander disconsolate for want of burial
rites.)   **387 for aye** forever

I with the Morning's love have oft made sport,   389
And, like a forester, the groves may tread   390
Even till the eastern gate, all fiery red,
Opening on Neptune with fair blessèd beams,
Turns into yellow gold his salt green streams.
But notwithstanding, haste, make no delay.
We may effect this business yet ere day.   [*Exit.*]

PUCK
    Up and down, up and down,
    I will lead them up and down.
    I am feared in field and town.
    Goblin, lead them up and down.
Here comes one.

    Enter Lysander.

LYSANDER
    Where art thou, proud Demetrius? Speak thou now.
PUCK [*Mimicking Demetrius*]
    Here, villain, drawn and ready. Where art thou?   402
LYSANDER
    I will be with thee straight.
PUCK   Follow me, then,   403
    To plainer ground.
        [*Lysander wanders about, following the voice.*]

    Enter Demetrius.

DEMETRIUS   Lysander! Speak again!   404
    Thou runaway, thou coward, art thou fled?
    Speak! In some bush? Where dost thou hide thy head?
PUCK [*Mimicking Lysander*]
    Thou coward, art thou bragging to the stars,
    Telling the bushes that thou look'st for wars,
    And wilt not come? Come, recreant; come, thou child,   409
    I'll whip thee with a rod. He is defiled
    That draws a sword on thee.
DEMETRIUS   Yea, art thou there?

---

389 Morning's love Cephalus, a beautiful youth beloved by Aurora; or
perhaps the goddess of the dawn herself   **390 forester** keeper of a royal
forest   **402 drawn** with drawn sword   **403 straight** immediately
404 plainer more open   **s.d. Lysander wanders about** (It is not
clearly necessary that Lysander exit at this point; neither exit nor
reentrance is indicated in the early texts.)   **409 recreant** cowardly wretch

PUCK
Follow my voice. We'll try no manhood here.   412

Exeunt.

[*Lysander returns.*]

LYSANDER
He goes before me and still dares me on.
When I come where he calls, then he is gone.
The villain is much lighter-heeled than I.
I followed fast, but faster he did fly,
That fallen am I in dark uneven way,
And here will rest me. [*He lies down.*] Come, thou gentle
    day!
For if but once thou show me thy gray light,
I'll find Demetrius and revenge this spite. [*He sleeps.*]

[*Enter*] *Robin* [*Puck*] *and Demetrius.*

PUCK
Ho, ho, ho! Coward, why com'st thou not?

DEMETRIUS
Abide me, if thou dar'st; for well I wot   422
Thou runn'st before me, shifting every place,
And dar'st not stand nor look me in the face.
Where art thou now?

PUCK   Come hither. I am here.

DEMETRIUS
Nay, then, thou mock'st me. Thou shalt buy this dear, 426
If ever I thy face by daylight see.
Now, go thy way. Faintness constraineth me
To measure out my length on this cold bed.
By day's approach look to be visited.

[*He lies down and sleeps.*]

Enter Helena.

HELENA
O weary night, O long and tedious night,
    Abate thy hours! Shine comforts from the east,   432
That I may back to Athens by daylight,
    From these that my poor company detest;

412 **try** test   422 **Abide** confront, face.   **wot** know   426 **buy** aby, pay
for.   **dear** dearly   432 **Abate** lessen, shorten

And sleep, that sometimes shuts up sorrow's eye,
Steal me awhile from mine own company.
                    [*She lies down and*] *sleep*[*s*].

PUCK
        Yet but three? Come one more;
        Two of both kinds makes up four.
        Here she comes, curst and sad.   439
        Cupid is a knavish lad,
        Thus to make poor females mad.

        [*Enter Hermia.*]

HERMIA
Never so weary, never so in woe,
    Bedabbled with the dew and torn with briers,
I can no further crawl, no further go;
    My legs can keep no pace with my desires.
Here will I rest me till the break of day.
Heavens shield Lysander, if they mean a fray!
                    [*She lies down and sleeps.*]

PUCK
        On the ground
        Sleep sound.
        I'll apply
        To your eye,
        Gentle lover, remedy.
                [*Squeezing the juice on Lysander's eyes.*]
        When thou wak'st,
        Thou tak'st
        True delight
        In the sight
        Of thy former lady's eye;
        And the country proverb known,
        That every man should take his own,
        In your waking shall be shown:
            Jack shall have Jill;   461
            Naught shall go ill;
        The man shall have his mare again, and all shall be
            well.   [*Exit. The four sleeping lovers remain.*]

---

439 curst ill-tempered   **461 Jack shall have Jill** (Proverbial for "boy gets
girl.")

4.1   *Enter [Titania,] Queen of Fairies, and [Bottom the] clown, and Fairies; and [Oberon,] the King, behind them.*

TITANIA
Come, sit thee down upon this flowery bed,
  While I thy amiable cheeks do coy,   2
And stick muskroses in thy sleek smooth head,
  And kiss thy fair large ears, my gentle joy.
                           [They recline.]

BOTTOM   Where's Peaseblossom?

PEASEBLOSSOM   Ready.

BOTTOM   Scratch my head, Peaseblossom. Where's Monsieur Cobweb?

COBWEB   Ready.

BOTTOM   Monsieur Cobweb, good monsieur, get you your weapons in your hand, and kill me a red-hipped humble-bee on the top of a thistle; and, good monsieur, bring me the honey bag. Do not fret yourself too much in the action, monsieur; and, good monsieur, have a care the honey bag break not; I would be loath to have you overflown with a honey bag, signor. *[Exit Cobweb.]* Where's Monsieur Mustardseed?

MUSTARDSEED   Ready.

BOTTOM   Give me your neaf, Monsieur Mustardseed. 19
Pray you, leave your courtesy, good monsieur. 20

MUSTARDSEED   What's your will?

BOTTOM   Nothing, good monsieur, but to help Caval- 22
ery Cobweb to scratch. I must to the barber's, mon- 23
sieur, for methinks I am marvelous hairy about the face; and I am such a tender ass, if my hair do but tickle me, I must scratch.

TITANIA
What, wilt thou hear some music, my sweet love?

4.1. Location: The action is continuous. The four lovers are still asleep onstage.
2 amiable lovely.   **coy** caress   **19 neaf** fist   **20 leave your courtesy** i.e., stop bowing, or put on your hat   **22–23 Cavalery** cavalier. (Form of address for a gentleman.)   **23 Cobweb** (Seemingly an error, since Cobweb has been sent to bring honey while Peaseblossom has been asked to scratch.)

BOTTOM I have a reasonable good ear in music. Let's
have the tongs and the bones.   29

[*Music: tongs, rural music.*]

TITANIA
Or say, sweet love, what thou desirest to eat.

BOTTOM Truly, a peck of provender. I could munch 31
your good dry oats. Methinks I have a great desire to
a bottle of hay. Good hay, sweet hay, hath no fellow.   33

TITANIA
I have a venturous fairy that shall seek
The squirrel's hoard, and fetch thee new nuts.

BOTTOM I had rather have a handful or two of dried
peas. But, I pray you, let none of your people stir me. 37
I have an exposition of sleep come upon me.   38

TITANIA
Sleep thou, and I will wind thee in my arms.
Fairies, begone, and be all ways away.   40

[*Exeunt Fairies.*]

So doth the woodbine the sweet honeysuckle
Gently entwist; the female ivy so
Enrings the barky fingers of the elm.
O, how I love thee! How I dote on thee!

[*They sleep.*]

Enter Robin Goodfellow [Puck].

OBERON [*Coming forward*]
Welcome, good Robin. Seest thou this sweet sight?
Her dotage now I do begin to pity.
For, meeting her of late behind the wood,
Seeking sweet favors for this hateful fool,   48
I did upbraid her and fall out with her.
For she his hairy temples then had rounded
With coronet of fresh and fragrant flowers;
And that same dew, which sometime on the buds   52

---

29 tongs . . . bones instruments for rustic music. (The tongs were played
like a triangle, whereas the bones were held between the fingers and
used as clappers.)   **s.d. Music . . . music** (This stage direction is
added from the Folio.)   **31 peck of provender** one-quarter bushel of
grain   **33 bottle** bundle. **fellow** equal   **37 stir** disturb **38 exposition**
(Bottom's word for *disposition*.)   **40 all ways** in all directions **48 favors**
i.e., gifts of flowers   **52 sometime** formerly

Was wont to swell like round and orient pearls,   53
Stood now within the pretty flowerets' eyes
Like tears that did their own disgrace bewail.
When I had at my pleasure taunted her,
And she in mild terms begged my patience,
I then did ask of her her changeling child,
Which straight she gave me, and her fairy sent
To bear him to my bower in Fairyland.
And, now I have the boy, I will undo
This hateful imperfection of her eyes.
And, gentle Puck, take this transformèd scalp
From off the head of this Athenian swain,
That he, awaking when the other do,   65
May all to Athens back again repair,   66
And think no more of this night's accidents
But as the fierce vexation of a dream.
But first I will release the Fairy Queen.
                    [*He squeezes a herb on her eyes.*]
       Be as thou wast wont to be;
       See as thou wast wont to see.
       Dian's bud o'er Cupid's flower   72
       Hath such force and blessèd power.
    Now, my Titania, wake you, my sweet queen.
TITANIA [*Waking*]
    My Oberon! What visions have I seen!
    Methought I was enamored of an ass.
OBERON
    There lies your love.
TITANIA   How came these things to pass?
    O, how mine eyes do loathe his visage now!
OBERON
    Silence awhile. Robin, take off this head.
    Titania, music call, and strike more dead
    Than common sleep of all these five the sense.   81

---

53 orient pearls i.e., the most beautiful of all pearls, those coming
from the Orient   **65 other** others   **66 repair** return   **72 Dian's bud**
(Perhaps the flower of the *agnus castus* or chaste-tree, supposed to
preserve chastity; or perhaps referring simply to Oberon's herb by
which he can undo the effects of "Cupid's flower," the love-in-
idleness of 2.1.166–168.)   **81 these five** i.e., the four lovers and
Bottom

TITANIA

Music, ho! Music, such as charmeth sleep!   82

[*Music.*]

PUCK [*Removing the ass head*]

Now, when thou wak'st, with thine own fool's eyes peep.

OBERON

Sound, music! Come, my queen, take hands with me,

And rock the ground whereon these sleepers be.

[*They dance.*]

Now thou and I are new in amity,

And will tomorrow midnight solemnly   87

Dance in Duke Theseus' house triumphantly,

And bless it to all fair prosperity.

There shall the pairs of faithful lovers be

Wedded, with Theseus, all in jollity.

PUCK

Fairy King, attend, and mark:

I do hear the morning lark.

OBERON

Then, my queen, in silence sad,   94

Trip we after night's shade.

We the globe can compass soon,

Swifter than the wandering moon.

TITANIA

Come, my lord, and in our flight

Tell me how it came this night

That I sleeping here was found

With these mortals on the ground.   *Exeunt.*

Wind horn [*within*].

Enter Theseus and all his train; [*Hippolyta,
Egeus*].

THESEUS

Go, one of you, find out the forester,

For now our observation is performed;   103

And since we have the vaward of the day,   104

My love shall hear the music of my hounds.

---

82 charmeth brings about, as though by a charm   **87 solemnly** ceremoniously   **94 sad** sober   **103 observation** i.e., observance to a morn of
May (1.1.167)   **104 vaward** vanguard, i.e., earliest part

Uncouple in the western valley, let them go.   106
Dispatch, I say, and find the forester.
                              [*Exit an Attendant.*]
We will, fair queen, up to the mountain's top
And mark the musical confusion
Of hounds and echo in conjunction.

HIPPOLYTA
I was with Hercules and Cadmus once,   111
When in a wood of Crete they bayed the bear   112
With hounds of Sparta. Never did I hear   113
Such gallant chiding; for, besides the groves,   114
The skies, the fountains, every region near
Seemed all one mutual cry. I never heard
So musical a discord, such sweet thunder.

THESEUS
My hounds are bred out of the Spartan kind,   118
So flewed, so sanded; and their heads are hung   119
With ears that sweep away the morning dew;
Crook-kneed, and dewlapped like Thessalian bulls;   121
Slow in pursuit, but matched in mouth like bells,   122
Each under each. A cry more tunable   123
Was never holloed to, nor cheered with horn,   124
In Crete, in Sparta, nor in Thessaly.
Judge when you hear. [*He sees the sleepers.*] But, soft!
  What nymphs are these?

EGEUS
My lord, this is my daughter here asleep,
And this Lysander; this Demetrius is,
This Helena, old Nedar's Helena.
I wonder of their being here together.   130

THESEUS
No doubt they rose up early to observe

---

106 Uncouple set free for the hunt   **111 Cadmus** mythical founder of
Thebes. (This story about him is unknown.)   **112 bayed** brought to
bay   **113 hounds of Sparta** (A breed famous in antiquity for their
hunting skill.)   **114 chiding** i.e., yelping   **118 kind** strain, breed   **119 So
flewed** similarly having large hanging chaps or fleshy covering of the
jaw.   **sanded** of sandy color   **121 dewlapped** having pendulous folds of
skin under the neck   **122–123 matched ... each** i.e., harmoniously
matched in their various cries like a set of bells, from treble down to
bass   **123 cry** pack of hounds.   **tunable** well tuned, melodious
124 cheered encouraged   **130 wonder of** wonder at

The rite of May, and hearing our intent,
Came here in grace of our solemnity.   133
But speak, Egeus. Is not this the day
That Hermia should give answer of her choice?
EGEUS It is, my lord.
THESEUS
Go, bid the huntsmen wake them with their horns.
                              [*Exit an Attendant.*]

Shout within. Wind horns. They all start up.

Good morrow, friends. Saint Valentine is past.   138
Begin these woodbirds but to couple now?
LYSANDER
Pardon, my lord.   [*They kneel.*]
THESEUS   I pray you all, stand up.
I know you two are rival enemies;
How comes this gentle concord in the world,
That hatred is so far from jealousy   143
To sleep by hate and fear no enmity?
LYSANDER
My lord, I shall reply amazedly,
Half sleep, half waking; but as yet, I swear,
I cannot truly say how I came here.
But, as I think—for truly would I speak,
And now I do bethink me, so it is—
I came with Hermia hither. Our intent
Was to be gone from Athens, where we might,   151
Without the peril of the Athenian law—   152
EGEUS
Enough, enough, my lord; you have enough.
I beg the law, the law, upon his head.
They would have stol'n away; they would, Demetrius,
Thereby to have defeated you and me,   156
You of your wife and me of my consent,
Of my consent that she should be your wife.
DEMETRIUS
My lord, fair Helen told me of their stealth,

133 in . . . solemnity in honor of our wedding   138 Saint Valentine
(Birds were supposed to choose their mates on Saint Valentine's Day.)
143 jealousy suspicion   151 where wherever; or, to where   152 Without
outside of, beyond   156 defeated defrauded

Of this their purpose hither to this wood,   160
And I in fury hither followed them,
Fair Helena in fancy following me.
But, my good lord, I wot not by what power—
But by some power it is—my love to Hermia,
Melted as the snow, seems to me now
As the remembrance of an idle gaud   166
Which in my childhood I did dote upon;
And all the faith, the virtue of my heart,
The object and the pleasure of mine eye,
Is only Helena. To her, my lord,
Was I betrothed ere I saw Hermia,
But like a sickness did I loathe this food;
But, as in health, come to my natural taste,
Now I do wish it, love it, long for it,
And will for evermore be true to it.

THESEUS
Fair lovers, you are fortunately met.
Of this discourse we more will hear anon.
Egeus, I will overbear your will;
For in the temple, by and by, with us
These couples shall eternally be knit.
And, for the morning now is something worn,   181
Our purposed hunting shall be set aside.
Away with us to Athens. Three and three,
We'll hold a feast in great solemnity.
Come, Hippolyta.
          [*Exeunt Theseus, Hippolyta, Egeus, and train.*]

DEMETRIUS
These things seem small and undistinguishable,
Like far-off mountains turnèd into clouds.

HERMIA
Methinks I see these things with parted eye,   188
When everything seems double.

HELENA   So methinks;
And I have found Demetrius like a jewel,   190
Mine own, and not mine own.

DEMETRIUS   Are you sure   191

160 **hither** in coming hither   166 **idle gaud** worthless trinket   181 **for**
since.   **something** somewhat   188 **parted** improperly focused
190–191 **like . . . mine own** i.e., like a jewel that one finds by chance and
therefore possesses but cannot certainly consider one's own property

That we are awake? It seems to me
That yet we sleep, we dream. Do not you think
The Duke was here, and bid us follow him?

HERMIA
Yea, and my father.

HELENA   And Hippolyta.

LYSANDER
And he did bid us follow to the temple.

DEMETRIUS
Why, then, we are awake. Let's follow him,
And by the way let us recount our dreams.   [*Exeunt.*]

BOTTOM [*Awaking*] When my cue comes, call me, and
I will answer. My next is, "Most fair Pyramus." Heigh-
ho! Peter Quince! Flute, the bellows mender! Snout,
the tinker! Starveling! God's my life, stolen hence and   202
left me asleep! I have had a most rare vision. I have
had a dream, past the wit of man to say what dream it
was. Man is but an ass if he go about to expound this   205
dream. Methought I was—there is no man can tell
what. Methought I was—and methought I had—but
man is but a patched fool if he will offer to say what   208
methought I had. The eye of man hath not heard, the   209
ear of man hath not seen, man's hand is not able to
taste, his tongue to conceive, nor his heart to report,   211
what my dream was. I will get Peter Quince to write
a ballad of this dream. It shall be called "Bottom's
Dream," because it hath no bottom; and I will sing it
in the latter end of a play, before the Duke. Peradventure, to make it the more gracious, I shall sing it at her   216
death.   [*Exit.*]

✤

4.2   *Enter Quince, Flute, [Snout, and Starveling].*

QUINCE   Have you sent to Bottom's house? Is he come
home yet?

202 **God's** may God save   205 **go about** attempt   208 **patched** wearing
motley, i.e., a dress of various colors.   **offer** venture   209–211 **The eye
. . . report** (Bottom garbles the terms of 1 Corinthians 2:9.)   216 **her**
Thisbe's (?)

4.2. Location: Athens.

STARVELING   He cannot be heard of. Out of doubt he is
  transported.   4
FLUTE   If he come not, then the play is marred. It goes
  not forward, doth it?
QUINCE   It is not possible. You have not a man in all
  Athens able to discharge Pyramus but he.   8
FLUTE   No, he hath simply the best wit of any handicraft 9
  man in Athens.
QUINCE   Yea, and the best person too, and he is a very 11
  paramour for a sweet voice.
FLUTE   You must say "paragon." A paramour is, God
  bless us, a thing of naught.   14

> *Enter Snug the joiner.*

SNUG   Masters, the Duke is coming from the temple,
  and there is two or three lords and ladies more married. If our sport had gone forward, we had all been 17
  made men.   18
FLUTE   O sweet bully Bottom! Thus hath he lost six- 19
  pence a day during his life; he could not have scaped 20
  sixpence a day. An the Duke had not given him sixpence a day for playing Pyramus, I'll be hanged. He
  would have deserved it. Sixpence a day in Pyramus, or
  nothing.

> *Enter Bottom.*

BOTTOM   Where are these lads? Where are these hearts? 25
QUINCE   Bottom! O most courageous day! O most
  happy hour!
BOTTOM   Masters, I am to discourse wonders. But ask 28
  me not what; for if I tell you, I am no true Athenian. I
  will tell you everything, right as it fell out.
QUINCE   Let us hear, sweet Bottom.
BOTTOM   Not a word of me. All that I will tell you is— 32
  that the Duke hath dined. Get your apparel together,

---

4 transported carried off by fairies; or, possibly, transformed
8 discharge perform   **9 wit** intellect   **11 person** appearance   **14 a . . .**
naught a shameful thing   **17–18 we . . . men** i.e., we would have had our
fortunes made   **19–20 sixpence a day** i.e., as a royal pension   **25 hearts**
good fellows   **28 am . . . wonders** have wonders to relate   **32 of** out of

good strings to your beards, new ribbons to your 34
pumps; meet presently at the palace; every man look 35
o'er his part; for the short and the long is, our play is
preferred. In any case, let Thisbe have clean linen; and 37
let not him that plays the lion pare his nails, for they
shall hang out for the lion's claws. And, most dear actors, eat no onions nor garlic, for we are to utter sweet
breath; and I do not doubt but to hear them say it is
a sweet comedy. No more words. Away! Go, away!
                                        [*Exeunt.*]

❖

---

34 strings (to attach the beards)   **35 pumps** light shoes or slippers.
presently immediately   **37 preferred** selected for consideration

5.1　*Enter Theseus, Hippolyta, and Philostrate,*
　　　[lords, and attendants].

HIPPOLYTA
　'Tis strange, my Theseus, that these lovers speak of.　1
THESEUS
　More strange than true. I never may believe　2
　These antique fables nor these fairy toys.　3
　Lovers and madmen have such seething brains,
　Such shaping fantasies, that apprehend　5
　More than cool reason ever comprehends.　6
　The lunatic, the lover, and the poet
　Are of imagination all compact.　8
　One sees more devils than vast hell can hold;
　That is the madman. The lover, all as frantic,
　Sees Helen's beauty in a brow of Egypt.　11
　The poet's eye, in a fine frenzy rolling,
　Doth glance from heaven to earth, from earth to heaven;
　And as imagination bodies forth
　The forms of things unknown, the poet's pen
　Turns them to shapes and gives to airy nothing
　A local habitation and a name.
　Such tricks hath strong imagination
　That, if it would but apprehend some joy,
　It comprehends some bringer of that joy;　20
　Or in the night, imagining some fear,　21
　How easy is a bush supposed a bear!
HIPPOLYTA
　But all the story of the night told over,
　And all their minds transfigured so together,
　More witnesseth than fancy's images　25
　And grows to something of great constancy;　26
　But, howsoever, strange and admirable.　27

5.1. Location: Athens. The palace of Theseus.
1 that that which　**2 may** can　**3 antique** old-fashioned (punning too on
antic, strange, grotesque).　**fairy toys** trifling stories about fairies
5 fantasies imaginations.　**apprehend** conceive, imagine　**6 comprehends** understands　**8 compact** formed, composed　**11 Helen's** i.e., of
Helen of Troy, pattern of beauty.　**brow of Egypt** i.e., face of a gypsy
20 bringer i.e., source　**21 fear** object of fear　**25 More . . . images** testifies to something more substantial than mere imaginings　**26 constancy**
certainty　**27 howsoever** in any case.　**admirable** a source of wonder

*Enter lovers: Lysander, Demetrius, Hermia, and
Helena.*

THESEUS
　Here come the lovers, full of joy and mirth.
　Joy, gentle friends! Joy and fresh days of love
　Accompany your hearts!
LYSANDER　　　　　　　　More than to us
　Wait in your royal walks, your board, your bed!
THESEUS
　Come now, what masques, what dances shall we have　32
　To wear away this long age of three hours
　Between our after-supper and bedtime?
　Where is our usual manager of mirth?
　What revels are in hand? Is there no play
　To ease the anguish of a torturing hour?
　Call Philostrate.
PHILOSTRATE　　　　Here, mighty Theseus.
THESEUS
　Say what abridgment have you for this evening?　　39
　What masque? What music? How shall we beguile
　The lazy time, if not with some delight?
PHILOSTRATE [*Giving him a paper*]
　There is a brief how many sports are ripe.　　　　42
　Make choice of which Your Highness will see first.
THESEUS [*Reads*]
　"The battle with the Centaurs, to be sung　　　　44
　By an Athenian eunuch to the harp"?
　We'll none of that. That have I told my love,
　In glory of my kinsman Hercules.　　　　　　47
　[*Reads*.] "The riot of the tipsy Bacchanals,　　48
　Tearing the Thracian singer in their rage"?　　49
　That is an old device; and it was played　　　　50

---

32 masques courtly entertainments　**39 abridgment** pastime (to abridge
or shorten the evening)　**42 brief** short written statement, summary
44 battle . . . Centaurs (Probably refers to the battle of the Centaurs and
the Lapithae, when the Centaurs attempted to carry off Hippodamia,
bride of Theseus' friend Pirothous.)　**47 kinsman** (Plutarch's "Life of
Theseus" states that Hercules and Theseus were near kinsmen. Theseus
is referring to a version of the battle of the Centaurs in which Hercules
was said to be present.)　**48–49 The riot . . . rage** (This was the story of
the death of Orpheus, as told in *Metamorphoses* 9.)　**50 device** show,
performance

When I from Thebes came last a conqueror.
[*Reads.*] "The thrice three Muses mourning for the
   death   52
Of Learning, late deceased in beggary"?   53
That is some satire, keen and critical,
Not sorting with a nuptial ceremony.   55
[*Reads.*] "A tedious brief scene of young Pyramus
And his love Thisbe; very tragical mirth"?
Merry and tragical? Tedious and brief?
That is hot ice and wondrous strange snow.   59
How shall we find the concord of this discord?

PHILOSTRATE
A play there is, my lord, some ten words long,
Which is as brief as I have known a play;
But by ten words, my lord, it is too long,
Which makes it tedious. For in all the play
There is not one word apt, one player fitted.
And tragical, my noble lord, it is,
For Pyramus therein doth kill himself.
Which, when I saw rehearsed, I must confess,
Made mine eyes water; but more merry tears
The passion of loud laughter never shed.

THESEUS   What are they that do play it?

PHILOSTRATE
Hard-handed men that work in Athens here,
Which never labored in their minds till now,
And now have toiled their unbreathed memories   74
With this same play, against your nuptial.   75

THESEUS   And we will hear it.

PHILOSTRATE   No, my noble lord,
It is not for you. I have heard it over,
And it is nothing, nothing in the world;
Unless you can find sport in their intents,
Extremely stretched and conned with cruel pain   80
To do you service.

THESEUS   I will hear that play;

52–53 The thrice . . . beggary (Possibly an allusion to Spenser's *Teares of the Muses*, 1591, though "satires" deploring the neglect of learning and the creative arts were commonplace.) **55 sorting with** befitting **59 strange** (Sometimes emended to an adjective that would contrast with *snow*, just as *hot* contrasts with *ice*.) **74 toiled** taxed. **unbreathed** unexercised **75 against** in preparation for **80 stretched** strained. **conned** memorized

For never anything can be amiss
When simpleness and duty tender it.   83
Go bring them in; and take your places, ladies.
                   [*Philostrate goes to summon the players.*]
HIPPOLYTA
I love not to see wretchedness o'ercharged,   85
And duty in his service perishing.   86
THESEUS
Why, gentle sweet, you shall see no such thing.
HIPPOLYTA
He says they can do nothing in this kind.   88
THESEUS
The kinder we, to give them thanks for nothing.
Our sport shall be to take what they mistake;
And what poor duty cannot do, noble respect   91
Takes it in might, not merit.   92
Where I have come, great clerks have purposèd   93
To greet me with premeditated welcomes;
Where I have seen them shiver and look pale,
Make periods in the midst of sentences,
Throttle their practiced accent in their fears,   97
And in conclusion dumbly have broke off,
Not paying me a welcome. Trust me, sweet,
Out of this silence yet I picked a welcome;
And in the modesty of fearful duty
I read as much as from the rattling tongue
Of saucy and audacious eloquence.
Love, therefore, and tongue-tied simplicity
In least speak most, to my capacity.   105

        [*Philostrate returns.*]

PHILOSTRATE
So please Your Grace, the Prologue is addressed.   106
THESEUS Let him approach.   [*A flourish of trumpets.*]

83 **simpleness** simplicity   85 **wretchedness o'ercharged** incompetence
overburdened   86 **his service** its attempt to serve   88 **kind** kind of thing
91 **respect** evaluation, consideration   92 **Takes . . . merit** values it
for the effort made rather than for the excellence achieved   93 **clerks**
learned men   97 **practiced accent** i.e., rehearsed speech; or, usual way of
speaking   105 **least** i.e., saying least.   **to my capacity** in my judgment
and understanding   106 **Prologue** speaker of the prologue.   **addressed**
ready

Enter the Prologue [Quince].

PROLOGUE
If we offend, it is with our good will.
 That you should think, we come not to offend,
But with good will. To show our simple skill,
 That is the true beginning of our end.
Consider then, we come but in despite.
 We do not come, as minding to content you,   113
Our true intent is. All for your delight
 We are not here. That you should here repent you,
The actors are at hand; and, by their show,
You shall know all that you are like to know.
THESEUS   This fellow doth not stand upon points.   118
LYSANDER   He hath rid his prologue like a rough colt; 119
he knows not the stop. A good moral, my lord: it is not 120
enough to speak, but to speak true.
HIPPOLYTA   Indeed he hath played on his prologue like
a child on a recorder; a sound, but not in government. 123
THESEUS   His speech was like a tangled chain: nothing 124
impaired, but all disordered. Who is next?

Enter Pyramus [Bottom] and Thisbe [Flute], and
Wall [Snout], and Moonshine [Starveling], and
Lion [Snug].

PROLOGUE
Gentles, perchance you wonder at this show;
 But wonder on, till truth make all things plain.
This man is Pyramus, if you would know;
 This beauteous lady Thisbe is certain.
This man with lime and roughcast doth present
 Wall, that vile Wall which did these lovers sunder;
And through Wall's chink, poor souls, they are content
 To whisper. At the which let no man wonder.
This man, with lantern, dog, and bush of thorn,
 Presenteth Moonshine; for, if you will know,

---

113 minding intending   **118 stand upon points** (1) heed niceties or small
points (2) pay attention to punctuation in his reading. (The humor of
Quince's speech is in the blunders of its punctuation.)   **119 rid** ridden.
rough unbroken   **120 stop** (1) the stopping of a colt by reining it in
(2) punctuation mark   **123 recorder** a wind instrument like a flute or fla-
geolet.   **government** control   **124 nothing** not at all

By moonshine did these lovers think no scorn   136
   To meet at Ninus' tomb, there, there to woo.
This grisly beast, which Lion hight by name,   138
The trusty Thisbe coming first by night
Did scare away, or rather did affright;
And as she fled, her mantle she did fall,   141
   Which Lion vile with bloody mouth did stain.
Anon comes Pyramus, sweet youth and tall,   143
   And finds his trusty Thisbe's mantle slain;
Whereat, with blade, with bloody blameful blade,
   He bravely broached his boiling bloody breast.   146
And Thisbe, tarrying in mulberry shade,
   His dagger drew, and died. For all the rest,
Let Lion, Moonshine, Wall, and lovers twain
At large discourse while here they do remain.   150
        Exeunt Lion, Thisbe, and Moonshine.

THESEUS   I wonder if the lion be to speak.
DEMETRIUS   No wonder, my lord. One lion may, when
many asses do.

WALL
In this same interlude it doth befall   154
That I, one Snout by name, present a wall;
And such a wall as I would have you think
That had in it a crannied hole or chink,
Through which the lovers, Pyramus and Thisbe,
Did whisper often, very secretly.
This loam, this roughcast, and this stone doth show
That I am that same wall; the truth is so.
And this the cranny is, right and sinister,   162
Through which the fearful lovers are to whisper.
THESEUS   Would you desire lime and hair to speak
better?
DEMETRIUS   It is the wittiest partition that ever I heard   166
discourse, my lord.

    [Pyramus comes forward.]

---

136 think no scorn think it no disgraceful matter   **138 hight** is called
141 fall let fall   **143 tall** courageous   **146 broached** stabbed   **150 At large**
in full, at length   **154 interlude** play   **162 right and sinister** i.e., the right
side of it and the left; or, running from right to left, horizontally   **166 partition** (1) wall (2) section of a learned treatise or oration

THESEUS   Pyramus draws near the wall. Silence!

PYRAMUS
　　O grim-looked night! O night with hue so black!   169
　　　O night, which ever art when day is not!
　　O night, O night! Alack, alack, alack,
　　　I fear my Thisbe's promise is forgot.
　　And thou, O wall, O sweet, O lovely wall,
　　　That stand'st between her father's ground and mine,
　　Thou wall, O wall, O sweet and lovely wall,
　　　Show me thy chink, to blink through with mine eyne!
　　　　　[*Wall makes a chink with his fingers.*]
　　Thanks, courteous wall. Jove shield thee well for this.
　　But what see I? No Thisbe do I see.
　　O wicked wall, through whom I see no bliss!
　　Cursed be thy stones for thus deceiving me!

THESEUS   The wall, methinks, being sensible, should   181
curse again.

PYRAMUS   No, in truth, sir, he should not. "Deceiving
me" is Thisbe's cue: she is to enter now, and I am to
spy her through the wall. You shall see, it will fall pat   185
as I told you. Yonder she comes.

　　　Enter Thisbe.

THISBE
　　O wall, full often hast thou heard my moans,
　　　For parting my fair Pyramus and me.
　　My cherry lips have often kissed thy stones,
　　　Thy stones with lime and hair knit up in thee.

PYRAMUS
　　I see a voice. Now will I to the chink,
　　　To spy an I can hear my Thisbe's face.   192
　　Thisbe!

THISBE   My love! Thou art my love, I think.

PYRAMUS
　　Think what thou wilt, I am thy lover's grace,   194
　　And like Limander am I trusty still.   195

THISBE
　　And I like Helen, till the Fates me kill.   196

---

169 grim-looked grim-looking   **181 sensible** capable of feeling   **185 pat**
exactly   **192 an** if   **194 lover's grace** i.e., gracious lover   **195, 196 Limander, Helen** (Blunders for *Leander* and *Hero*.)

PYRAMUS
  Not Shafalus to Procrus was so true.   197
THISBE
  As Shafalus to Procrus, I to you.
PYRAMUS
  O, kiss me through the hole of this vile wall!
THISBE
  I kiss the wall's hole, not your lips at all.
PYRAMUS
  Wilt thou at Ninny's tomb meet me straightway?
THISBE
  'Tide life, 'tide death, I come without delay.   202
                    [*Exeunt Pyramus and Thisbe.*]
WALL
  Thus have I, Wall, my part dischargèd so;
  And, being done, thus Wall away doth go.   [*Exit.*]
THESEUS Now is the mural down between the two
  neighbors.
DEMETRIUS No remedy, my lord, when walls are so
  willful to hear without warning.   208
HIPPOLYTA This is the silliest stuff that ever I heard.
THESEUS The best in this kind are but shadows; and the 210
  worst are no worse, if imagination amend them.
HIPPOLYTA It must be your imagination then, and not
  theirs.
THESEUS If we imagine no worse of them than they of
  themselves, they may pass for excellent men. Here
  come two noble beasts in, a man and a lion.

        Enter Lion and Moonshine.

LION
  You, ladies, you whose gentle hearts do fear
    The smallest monstrous mouse that creeps on floor,
  May now perchance both quake and tremble here,
    When lion rough in wildest rage doth roar.
  Then know that I, as Snug the joiner, am

---

197 Shafalus, Procrus (Blunders for *Cephalus* and *Procris*, also famous
lovers.)   **202 'Tide** betide, come   **208 willful** willing.   **without warning**
i.e., without warning the parents. (Demetrius makes a joke on the proverb
"Walls have ears.")   **210 in this kind** of this sort.   **shadows** likenesses,
representations

A lion fell, nor else no lion's dam;   222
For, if I should as lion come in strife
Into this place, 'twere pity on my life.

THESEUS   A very gentle beast, and of a good conscience.

DEMETRIUS   The very best at a beast, my lord, that e'er
I saw.

LYSANDER   This lion is a very fox for his valor.   228

THESEUS   True; and a goose for his discretion.   229

DEMETRIUS   Not so, my lord; for his valor cannot carry
his discretion; and the fox carries the goose.

THESEUS   His discretion, I am sure, cannot carry his
valor; for the goose carries not the fox. It is well. Leave
it to his discretion, and let us listen to the moon.

MOON
This lanthorn doth the hornèd moon present—   235

DEMETRIUS   He should have worn the horns on his   236
head.   237

THESEUS   He is no crescent, and his horns are invisible
within the circumference.

MOON
This lanthorn doth the hornèd moon present;
Myself the man i' the moon do seem to be.

THESEUS   This is the greatest error of all the rest. The
man should be put into the lanthorn. How is it else
the man i' the moon?

DEMETRIUS   He dares not come there for the candle, for 245
you see, it is already in snuff.   246

HIPPOLYTA   I am aweary of this moon. Would he would
change!

THESEUS   It appears, by his small light of discretion, that
he is in the wane; but yet, in courtesy, in all reason,
we must stay the time.

---

222 lion fell fierce lion (with a play on the idea of "lion skin")   **228 is . . .
valor** i.e., his valor consists of craftiness and discretion   **229 goose . . .
discretion** i.e., as discreet as a goose, that is, more foolish than discreet
235 lanthorn (This original spelling, *lanthorn*, may suggest a play on the
horn of which lanterns were made, and also on a cuckold's horns; but the
spelling *lanthorn* is not used consistently for comic effect in this play or
elsewhere. At 5.1.134, for example, the word is *lantern* in the original.)
236–237 on his head (as a sign of cuckoldry)   **245 for the** because of the
246 in snuff (1) offended (2) in need of snuffing or trimming

LYSANDER   Proceed, Moon.

MOON   All that I have to say is to tell you that the lanthorn is the moon, I, the man i' the moon, this thornbush my thornbush, and this dog my dog.

DEMETRIUS   Why, all these should be in the lanthorn,
for all these are in the moon. But silence! Here comes
Thisbe.

  Enter Thisbe.

THISBE
This is old Ninny's tomb. Where is my love?

LION [*Roaring*]   O!

DEMETRIUS   Well roared, Lion.
                [*Thisbe runs off, dropping her mantle.*]

THESEUS   Well run, Thisbe.

HIPPOLYTA   Well shone, Moon. Truly, the moon shines
with a good grace.
                [*The Lion worries Thisbe's mantle.*]

THESEUS   Well moused, Lion.   265

  Enter Pyramus.   [*Exit Lion.*]

DEMETRIUS   And then came Pyramus.

LYSANDER   And so the lion vanished.

PYRAMUS
Sweet Moon, I thank thee for thy sunny beams;
  I thank thee, Moon, for shining now so bright;
For, by thy gracious, golden, glittering gleams,
  I trust to take of truest Thisbe sight.
      But stay, O spite!
      But mark, poor knight,
  What dreadful dole is here?   274
      Eyes, do you see?
      How can it be?
  O dainty duck! O dear!
      Thy mantle good,
      What, stained with blood!
  Approach, ye Furies fell!   280
      O Fates, come, come,   281

265 **moused** shaken, torn, bitten   274 **dole** grievous event   280 **Furies**
avenging goddesses of Greek myth.   **fell** fierce   281 **Fates** the three
goddesses (Clotho, Lachesis, Atropos) of Greek myth who drew and cut
the thread of human life

Cut thread and thrum;   282
Quail, crush, conclude, and quell!   283
THESEUS This passion, and the death of a dear friend,   284
would go near to make a man look sad.   285
HIPPOLYTA Beshrew my heart, but I pity the man.

PYRAMUS
O, wherefore, Nature, didst thou lions frame?
Since lion vile hath here deflowered my dear,
Which is—no, no, which was—the fairest dame
That lived, that loved, that liked, that looked with cheer. 290
    Come, tears, confound,
    Out, sword, and wound
    The pap of Pyramus;   293
    Ay, that left pap,
    Where heart doth hop.   [*He stabs himself.*]
Thus die I, thus, thus, thus.
    Now am I dead,
    Now am I fled;
    My soul is in the sky.
    Tongue, lose thy light;
    Moon, take thy flight.   [*Exit Moonshine.*]
    Now die, die, die, die, die.   [*Pyramus dies.*]
DEMETRIUS No die, but an ace, for him; for he is   303
but one.   304
LYSANDER Less than an ace, man; for he is dead, he is
nothing.
THESEUS With the help of a surgeon he might yet re-
cover, and yet prove an ass.   308
HIPPOLYTA How chance Moonshine is gone before
Thisbe comes back and finds her lover?
THESEUS She will find him by starlight.

[*Enter Thisbe.*]

Here she comes, and her passion ends the play.

282 thread and thrum the warp in weaving and the loose end of the
warp   **283 Quail** overpower. **quell** kill, destroy   **284–285 This . . . sad**
i.e., if one had other reason to grieve, one might be sad, but not from this
absurd portrayal of passion   **290 cheer** countenance   **293 pap** breast
303 ace the side of the die featuring the single pip, or spot. (The pun is on
die as a singular of *dice;* Bottom's performance is not worth a whole *die*
but rather one single face of it, one small portion.)   **304 one** (1) an individual person (2) unique   **308 ass** (with a pun on *ace*)

HIPPOLYTA   Methinks she should not use a long one for
such a Pyramus. I hope she will be brief.

DEMETRIUS   A mote will turn the balance, which Pyra- 315
mus, which Thisbe, is the better: he for a man, God 316
warrant us; she for a woman, God bless us.

LYSANDER   She hath spied him already with those sweet
eyes.

DEMETRIUS   And thus she means, videlicet: 320

THISBE
      Asleep, my love?
      What, dead, my dove?
   O Pyramus, arise!
      Speak, speak. Quite dumb?
      Dead, dead? A tomb
   Must cover thy sweet eyes.
      These lily lips,
      This cherry nose,
   These yellow cowslip cheeks,
      Are gone, are gone!
   Lovers, make moan.
   His eyes were green as leeks.
      O Sisters Three,   333
      Come, come to me,
   With hands as pale as milk;
      Lay them in gore,
      Since you have shore   337
   With shears his thread of silk.
      Tongue, not a word.
      Come, trusty sword,
   Come, blade, my breast imbrue! [*Stabs herself.*]   341
      And farewell, friends.
      Thus Thisbe ends.
   Adieu, adieu, adieu.   [*She dies.*]

THESEUS   Moonshine and Lion are left to bury the dead.

DEMETRIUS   Ay, and Wall too.

BOTTOM [*Starting up, as Flute does also*]   No, I assure you,
   the wall is down that parted their fathers. Will it

---

315 mote small particle   **315–316 which . . . which** whether . . . or
320 means moans, laments.   **videlicet** to wit   **333 Sisters Three** the
Fates   **337 shore** shorn   **341 imbrue** stain with blood

please you to see the epilogue, or to hear a Bergomask 349
dance between two of our company?   350
                          [*The other players enter.*]
THESEUS   No epilogue, I pray you; for your play needs
no excuse. Never excuse; for when the players are all
dead, there need none to be blamed. Marry, if he that
writ it had played Pyramus and hanged himself in
Thisbe's garter, it would have been a fine tragedy; and
so it is, truly, and very notably discharged. But, come,
your Bergomask. Let your epilogue alone.   [*A dance.*]
The iron tongue of midnight hath told twelve.   358
Lovers, to bed, 'tis almost fairy time.
I fear we shall outsleep the coming morn
As much as we this night have overwatched.   361
This palpable-gross play hath well beguiled   362
The heavy gait of night. Sweet friends, to bed.   363
A fortnight hold we this solemnity,
In nightly revels and new jollity.   *Exeunt.*

    Enter Puck [*carrying a broom*].

PUCK
        Now the hungry lion roars,
          And the wolf behowls the moon;
        Whilst the heavy plowman snores,   368
          All with weary task fordone.   369
        Now the wasted brands do glow,   370
          Whilst the screech owl, screeching loud,
        Puts the wretch that lies in woe
          In remembrance of a shroud.
        Now it is the time of night
          That the graves, all gaping wide,
        Every one lets forth his sprite,   376
          In the church-way paths to glide.
        And we fairies, that do run

349-350 Bergomask dance a rustic dance named from Bergamo, a prov-
ince in the state of Venice   **358 iron tongue** i.e., of a bell.   **told** counted,
struck ("tolled")   **361 overwatched** stayed up too late   **362 palpable-gross**
palpably gross, obviously crude   **363 heavy** drowsy, dull   **368 heavy**
tired   **369 fordone** exhausted   **370 wasted brands** burned-out logs
376 Every . . . sprite every grave lets forth its ghost

By the triple Hecate's team   379
From the presence of the sun,
    Following darkness like a dream,
Now are frolic. Not a mouse   382
Shall disturb this hallowed house.
I am sent with broom before,
To sweep the dust behind the door.   385

*Enter [Oberon and Titania,] King and Queen of
Fairies, with all their train.*

OBERON

Through the house give glimmering light,
    By the dead and drowsy fire;
Every elf and fairy sprite
    Hop as light as bird from brier;
And this ditty, after me,
Sing, and dance it trippingly.

TITANIA

First, rehearse your song by rote,
To each word a warbling note.
Hand in hand, with fairy grace,
Will we sing, and bless this place.
                        [Song and dance.]

OBERON

Now, until the break of day,
Through this house each fairy stray.
To the best bride-bed will we,
Which by us shall blessèd be;
And the issue there create   400
Ever shall be fortunate.
So shall all the couples three
Ever true in loving be;
And the blots of Nature's hand
Shall not in their issue stand;
Never mole, harelip, nor scar,
Nor mark prodigious, such as are   407
Despisèd in nativity,

379 triple Hecate's (Hecate ruled in three capacities: as Luna or Cynthia
in heaven, as Diana on earth, and as Proserpina in hell.) **382 frolic**
merry **385 behind** from behind. (Robin Goodfellow was a household
spirit who helped good housemaids and punished lazy ones.) **400 create**
created **407 prodigious** monstrous, unnatural

Shall upon their children be.
With this field dew consecrate   410
Every fairy take his gait,   411
And each several chamber bless,   412
Through this palace, with sweet peace;
And the owner of it blest
Ever shall in safety rest.
Trip away; make no stay;
Meet me all by break of day.
                    Exeunt [*Oberon, Titania, and train*].

PUCK [*To the audience*]
If we shadows have offended,
Think but this, and all is mended,
That you have but slumbered here   420
While these visions did appear.
And this weak and idle theme,
No more yielding but a dream,   423
Gentles, do not reprehend.
If you pardon, we will mend.   425
And, as I am an honest Puck,
If we have unearnèd luck
Now to scape the serpent's tongue,   428
We will make amends ere long;
Else the Puck a liar call.
So, good night unto you all.
Give me your hands, if we be friends,   432
And Robin shall restore amends.   [*Exit*.] 433

---

410 **consecrate** consecrated   411 **take his gait** go his way   412 **several**
separate   420 **That . . . here** i.e., that it is a "midsummer night's
dream"   423 **No . . . but** yielding no more than   425 **mend** improve
428 **serpent's tongue** i.e., hissing   432 **Give . . . hands** applaud
433 **restore amends** give satisfaction in return

Date and Text

A Midsummer Night's Dream was entered on the Stationers' Register, the official record book of the London Company of Stationers (booksellers and printers), by Thomas Fisher on October 8, 1600, and printed by him that same year in quarto:

> A Midsommer nights dreame. As it hath beene sundry times pub*lickely acted, by the Right honour*able, the Lord Chamberlaine his *seruants. Written by William Shakespeare.* Imprinted at London, for *Thomas Fisher,* and are to be soulde at his shoppe, at the Signe of the White Hart, in *Fleetestreete.* 1600.

This text appears to have been set from Shakespeare's working manuscript. Its inconsistencies in time scheme and other irregularities may reflect some revision, although the inconsistencies are not noticeable in performance. A second quarto appeared in 1619, though falsely dated 1600; it was a reprint of the first quarto, with some minor corrections and many new errors. A copy of this second quarto, evidently with some added stage directions and other minor changes from a theatrical manuscript in the company's possession, served as the basis for the First Folio text of 1623. Essentially, the first quarto remains the authoritative text.

Other than Francis Meres's listing of the play in 1598 in his *Palladis Tamia: Wit's Treasury* (a slender volume on contemporary literature and art; valuable because it lists most of the plays of Shakespeare's that existed at that time), external clues as to date are elusive. The description of unruly weather (2.1.88–114) has been related to the bad summer of 1594, but complaints about the weather are perennial. On the assumption that the play celebrates some noble wedding of the period, scholars have come up with a number of suitable marriages. Chief are those of Sir Thomas Heneage to Mary, Countess of Southampton, in 1594; of William Stanley, Earl of Derby, to Elizabeth Vere, daughter of the Earl of Oxford, in 1595; and of Thomas, son of Lord Berkeley, to Elizabeth, daughter of Lord Carey, in 1596. The Countess of Southampton was the widowed mother of the young Earl of Southampton, to whom Shakespeare had dedicated his *Venus and Adonis* and *The Rape of Lucrece.* No one has ever proved convincingly, however, that the play was written for any occasion other than commercial public performance. The play makes sense for a general audience and does not need to depend on references to a private marriage. Shakespeare was, after all, in the business of writing plays for his fellow actors, who earned their livelihood chiefly by public acting before large paying audiences. In any event the search for a court marriage is a circular argument in terms of dating; suitable court marriages can be found for any year of the decade. In the last analysis, the play has to be dated on the basis of its stylistic affinity to plays like *Romeo and Juliet* and *Richard II,* works of the "lyric" mid 1590s. The "Pyramus and Thisbe" performance in *A Midsummer Night's Dream* would seem to bear an obvious relation to *Romeo and Juliet,* although no one can say for sure which came first.

Textual Notes

These textual notes are not a historical collation, either of the early quartos and the early folios or of more recent editions; they are simply a record of departures in this edition from the copy text. The reading adopted in this edition appears in boldface, followed by the rejected reading from the copy text, i.e., the quarto of 1600. Only major alterations in punctuation are noted. Changes in lineation are not indicated, nor are some minor and obvious typographical errors.

Abbreviations used:
Q the first quarto of 1600
s.d. stage direction
s.p. speech prefix

Copy text: the first quarto of 1600.

1.1. 4 wanes waues **10 New bent** Now bent **19 s.d. Lysander** Lysander and Helena **24 Stand forth, Demetrius** [printed as s.d. in Q] **26 Stand forth, Lysander** [printed as s.d. in Q] **74 their** there **132 Ay** Eigh **136 low** loue **187 Yours would** Your words **191 I'd** ile **216 sweet** sweld **219 stranger companies** strange companions

2.1. 1 s.p. [and elsewhere] **Puck** Robin **61 s.p.** [and elsewhere] **Titania** Qu **61 Fairies** Fairy **69 step** steppe **79 Aegles** Eagles **109 thin** chinne **158 the west** west **190 slay** stay. **slayeth** stayeth **194 thee** the **201 not nor** not not **246 s.d.** [at l. 247 in Q]

2.2. 9 s.p. First Fairy [not in Q; also at l. 20] **13 s.p. Chorus** [not in Q; also at l. 24] **45 Be it** Bet it **49 good** god **53 is** it

3.1. 27–28 yourselves your selfe **52 s.p. Bottom** Cet **72 s.p. Puck** Ro **77 s.p. Bottom** Pyra [also at ll. 79 and 98] **78 Odors, odors** Odours, odorous **83 s.p. Puck** Quin **84 s.p. Flute** Thys [also at ll. 88 and 97] **144 own** owe **157–158 Ready . . . go** [assigned to **Fairies** in Q] **170 s.p. Peaseblossom** 1. Fai **171 Hail** [assigned in Q to 1. Fai] **172 s.p. Mote** 2. Fair **173 s.p. Mustardseed** 3. Fai **190 you of** you **196 s.d. Exeunt** Exit

3.2. s.d. [Q: Enter King of Fairies, and Robin goodfellow] **19 mimic** Minnick **38 s.p.** [and elsewhere] **Puck** Rob **80 I so** I **85 sleep** slippe **213 like** life **220 passionate words** words **250 prayers** praise **260 off** of **299 gentlemen** gentleman **344 s.d. Exit** Exeunt **406 Speak! In** Speake in **426 shalt** shat **451 To your** your

4.1. 5 s.p. [and elsewhere] **Bottom** Clown **64 off** of **72 o'er** or **81 five fine** 82 **ho** howe **116 Seemed** Seeme **127 this is** this **137 s.d. Wind . . . up** they all start vp. Winde hornes **171 saw** see **190 found** fonnd **198 let us** lets **205 to expound** expound **208 a patched** patcht a

4.2. s.d. [Snout, and Starveling] Thisby and the rabble **3 s.p. Starveling** Flut **5 s.p. Flute** Thys [and at ll. 9, 13, 19] **29 no** not

5.1. 34 our Or **107 s.p.** [and elsewhere] **Theseus** Duke **122 his** this **150 s.d. Exeunt** Exit [and at l. 153 in Q] **155 Snout** Flute **190 up in thee**

now againe   **205 mural down** Moon vsed   **209 s.p. [and elsewhere] Hippo-lyta** Dutch   **270 gleams** beames   **309 before** before?   **317 warrant** warnd   **347 s.p. Bottom** Lyon   **366 lion** Lyons   **367 behowls** beholds   **415–416 And . . . rest** [these lines are transposed in Q]

Shakespeare's Sources

No single source has been discovered that unites the various elements we find in *A Midsummer Night's Dream,* but the four main strands of action can be individually discussed in terms of sources. The four strands are: (1) the marriage of Duke Theseus and Queen Hippolyta, (2) the romantic tribulations and triumphs of the four young lovers, (3) the quarrel of King Oberon and Queen Titania, together with the fairies' manipulations of human affairs, and (4) the "rude mechanicals" and their play of "Pyramus and Thisbe."

For his conception of Theseus, Shakespeare went chiefly to Geoffrey Chaucer's "The Knight's Tale," of which a brief excerpt follows, and to Thomas North's 1579 translation of "The Life of Theseus" in Plutarch's *Lives of the Noble Grecians and Romans.* Chaucer's Theseus is a duke of "wisdom" and "chivalrye," renowned for his conquest of the Amazons and his marriage to Hippolyta. Plutarch provides information concerning Theseus' other conquests (to which Oberon alludes in 2.1.77 ff.), including that of Antiopa. Shakespeare could have learned more about Theseus from Chaucer's *The Legend of Good Women* and from Ovid's *Metamorphoses.* He seems to have blended all or some of these impressions together with his own notion of a noble yet popular Renaissance ruler.

The romantic narrative of the four lovers appears to be original with Shakespeare, although one can find many analogous situations of misunderstanding and rivalry in love. Chaucer's "The Knight's Tale" tells of two friends battling over one woman. Shakespeare's own *The Two Gentlemen of Verona* gives us four lovers, properly matched at first until one of the men shifts his attentions to his friend's ladylove; eventually all is righted when the false lover recovers his senses. Parallel situations arise in Sir Philip Sidney's *Arcadia* (1590) and in Jorge de Montemayor's *Diana* (c. 1559), a source for *The Two Gentlemen.* What Shakespeare adds in *A Midsummer* is the intervention of the fairies in human love affairs.

Shakespeare's knowledge of fairy lore must have been extensive and is hard to trace exactly. Doubtless much of it was from oral traditions about leprechauns, gremlins, and elves, who were thought to cause such mischief as spoiling fermentation or preventing milk from churning into butter; Puck's tricks mentioned in 2.1.34 ff. are derived from such lore. Yet Shakespeare seems to have consulted literary sources as well. In Chaucer's "The Merchant's Tale," Pluto and Proserpina as king and queen of the fairies intervene in the affairs of old January, his young wife May, and her lover Damyan. Fairies appear onstage in John Lyly's *Endymion* (1588), protecting true lovers and tormenting those who are morally tainted. Shakespeare later reflects this tradition in *The Merry Wives of Windsor* (1597–1601). The name Oberon probably comes from the French romance *Huon of Bordeaux* (translated by Lord Berners by about 1540), where Oberon is a dwarfish fairy king from the mysterious East who practices enchantment in a haunted wood. In Edmund Spenser's *The Faerie Queene*, Oberon is the Elfin father of Queen Gloriana (2.10.75–76). Robert Greene's *James IV* (c. 1591) also features Oberon as the fairy king, and a lost play called *Huon of Bordeaux* was performed by Sussex's men, an acting company, at about this same time. The name Titania comes from Ovid's *Metamorphoses*, where it is used as a synonym for both the enchantress Circe and the chaste goddess Diana. The name Titania does not appear in Arthur Golding's translation (1567), suggesting that Shakespeare found it in the original. Puck, or Robin Goodfellow, is essentially the product of oral tradition, although Reginald Scot's *The Discovery of Witchcraft* (1584) discusses Robin in pejorative terms as an incubus or hobgoblin in whom intelligent people no longer believe.

Scot also reports the story of a man who finds an ass's head placed on his shoulders by enchantment. Similar legends of transformation occur in Apuleius' *The Golden Ass* (translated by William Adlington, 1566) and in the well-known story of the ass's ears bestowed by Phoebus Apollo on King Midas for his presumption. Perhaps the most suggestive possible source for Shakespeare's clownish actors, however, is Anthony Munday's play *John a Kent and John a Cumber* (c. 1587–1590). In it a group of rude artisans, led by the intrepid Turnop, stage a ludicrous interlude written by their churchwarden in praise of his millhorse. Turnop's prologue is a medley of lofty comparisons. The entertainment is presented before noble spectators, who are graciously amused. *John a Kent* also features a lot of magic trickery, a boy named Shrimp whose role is comparable to that of Puck, and a multiple love plot.

"Pyramus and Thisbe" itself is based on the *Metamorphoses* (4.55 ff.), as can be seen from the following selection. Other versions Shakespeare may have known include Chaucer's *The Legend of Good Women*, William Griffith's poem *Pyramus and Thisbe* (1562), George Pettie's *A Petite Palace of Pettie His Pleasure* (1576), *A Gorgeous Gallery of Gallant Inventions* (1578), and "A New Sonnet of Pyramus and Thisbe" from Clement Robinson's *A Handful of Pleasant Delights* (1584). Several of these, especially the last three, are bad enough to have given Shakespeare materials to lampoon, though the sweep of his parody goes beyond the particular story of Pyramus and Thisbe. The occasionally stilted phraseology of Golding's translation of *The Metamorphoses* contributed to the fun. According to Kenneth Muir (*Shakespeare's Sources,* 1957), Shakespeare must also have known Thomas Mouffet's *Of the Silkworms and Their Flies* (published 1599, but possibly circulated earlier in manuscript), which contains perhaps the most ridiculous of all versions of the Pyramus and Thisbe story. Shakespeare also appears to be spoofing the inept dramatic style and lame verse of English dramas of the 1560s, 1570s, and 1580s, especially in their treatment of tragic sentiment and high emotion; *Cambises, Damon and Pythias,* and *Appius and Virginia* are examples.

The Canterbury Tales
By Geoffrey Chaucer

HERE BEGINNETH THE KNIGHTES TALE

Whilom, as olde stories tellen us,	859
There was a duke that highte Theseus.	860
Of Athens he was lord and governor,	
And in his time swich a conqueror	862
That greater was there none under the sonne.	
Full many a rich country had he wonne;	
What with his wisdom and his chivalrye	
He conquered all the reign of Feminye,	866
That whilom was ycleped Scythia,	867
And weddede the queen Hippolyta	
And brought her home with him in his country	
With muchel glory and great solemnity,	870
And eke her faire suster Emily.	871
And thus with victory and with melody	
Let I this noble duke to Athens ride,	
And all his host in armes him beside.	874
And certes, if it nere too long to hear,	875
I would han told you fully the manner	876
How wonnen was the reign of Feminye	
By Theseus and by his chivalrye,	
And of the greate bataille for the nones	879
Bitwixen Athenes and Amazones,	
And how asseged was Hippolyta,	881
The faire, hardy queen of Scythia,	882
And of the feast that was at hir weddinge,	883
And of the tempest at hir home-cominge;	884
But all that thing I moot as now forbeare.	885
I have, God wot, a large field to eare,	886

859 **Whilom** once upon a time   860 **highte** was called   862 **swich** such
866 **reign of Feminye** country of the Amazons   867 **ycleped** called
870 **muchel** much.   **solemnity** ceremony   871 **eke** also.   **suster** sister
874 **him beside** beside him   875 **nere too** were not too   876 **would han**
would have   879 **for the nones** in particular   881 **asseged** besieged
882 **hardy** brave   883 **hir** their (also in l. 884)   884 **tempest** tumult
885 **moot** must   886 **eare** ear, plow

And weake been the oxen in my plough.
The remnant of the tale is long enough;
I woll nat letten eke none of this route.   889
Let every fellow tell his tale aboute,   890
And let see now who shall the supper winne;   891
And there I left I will again beginne.   892
   This duke, of whom I make mencioun,   893
When he was come almost unto the toun,
In all his weal and in his moste pride,   895
He was war, as he cast his eye aside,   896
Where that there kneeled in the highe waye   897
A company of ladies, tweye and tweye,   898
Each after other, clad in clothes blacke;
But swich a cry and swich a woe they make
That in this world nys creature livinge   901
That hearde swich another waymentinge.   902
And of this cry they nolde nevere stinten   903
Till they the reines of his bridle henten.   904
   "What folk been ye, that at mine home-cominge
Perturben so my feaste with crynge?"   906
Quod Theseus. "Have ye so great envye   907
Of mine honor, that thus complain and crye?   908
Or who hath you misboden or offended?   909
And telleth me if it may been amended,   910
And why that ye been clothed thus in black?"
   The eldest lady of hem alle spak,   912
When she had swooned with a deadly cheere   913
That it was routhe for to seen and heare,   914
And saide, "Lord, to whom fortune hath given
Victory, and as a conqueror to liven,
Nat grieveth us your glory and your honor,   917
But we beseeken mercy and succor.   918
Have mercy on our woe and our distresse!

889 **woll nat letten** will not hinder.   **route** assembly (the Canterbury pilgrims)   **890 aboute** in succession   **891 let see** let it be seen   **892 there** there
where   **893 mencioun** mention   **895 weal** splendor   **896 war** aware.   **aside**
to one side   **897 highe waye** highway   **898 tweye and tweye** two by two
901 nys is not   **902 waymentinge** lamenting   **903 nolde** would not.   **stinten**
stint, cease   **904 reines** reins.   **henten** seized, grasped   **906 feaste** feast,
festival celebration   **907–908 envye Of** ill will toward   **909 misboden**
harmed   **910 telleth** tell.   **been** be   **912 hem** them   **913 deadly cheere**
deathlike appearance   **914 routhe** pity   **917 Nat ... glory** your glory doesn't
grieve us   **918 beseeken** beseech, beg

Some drop of pity, through thy gentillesse,	920
Upon us wretched women let thou falle!	
For certes, lord, there is none of us alle	922
That she ne hath been a duchess or a queene.	923
Now be we caitives, as it is well seene.	924
Thanked be Fortune and her false wheel	
That none estate assureth to be weel.	926
And certes, lord, to abiden your presence,	927
Here in the temple of the goddess Clemence	
We han been waiting all this fourteennight;	929
Now help us, lord, sith it is in thy might . . .	930

[The story of rivalry between Palamon and Arcite bears only a general resemblance to that of the young lovers in *A Midsummer Night's Dream*, but when Chaucer and the Knight return to an account of revels and tournaments in honor of the wedding of Theseus and Hippolyta, the splendor of the Athenian court is not unlike that in Act 5 of Shakespeare's play.]

The Canterbury Tales of Chaucer date from 1387–1400. This sparingly modernized selection from "The Knight's Tale" is based on the Ellesmere manuscript, Ellesmere 26 c. 12, now in the Huntington Library, San Marino, California. Group A, ll. 859–930.

In the following, departures from the original text appear in boldface; the original readings follow in roman:

868 weddede wedded   **876 han told you** yow haue toold   **897 highe waye** weye

920 gentillesse courtesy, good breeding   **922 certes** certainly   **923 ne hath** has not   **924 caitives** caitiffs, wretches   **926 none . . . weel** i.e., no human prosperity can assure itself of long felicity   **927 abiden** await   **929 fourteennight** fortnight   **930 sith** since

Metamorphoses
By Ovid
Translated by Arthur Golding

BOOK 4

Within the town (of whose huge walls so monstrous
  high and thick
The fame is given Semiramis for making them of
  brick)   68
Dwelt hard together two young folk, in houses joined
  so near   69
That under all one roof well nigh both twain con-
  veyèd were.   70
The name of him was Pyramus, and Thisbe called
  was she.
So fair a man in all the East was none alive as he,
Nor ne'er a woman, maid, nor wife in beauty like to
  her.
This neighborhood bred acquaintance first; this
  neighborhood first did stir   74
The secret sparks; this neighborhood first an en-
  trance in did show
For love to come to that to which it afterward did
  grow.
  And if that right had taken place, they had been
    man and wife;
But still their parents went about to let which, for
  their life,   78
They could not let. For both their hearts with equal
  flame did burn.
No man was privy to their thoughts; and, for to serve
  their turn,
Instead of talk, they usèd signs. The closelier they
  suppressed

---

68 Semiramis the Queen of Assyria, 810–806 B.C., who was reputed to have
ordered the building of the walls of Babylon   **69 hard together** hard by
70 conveyèd taken, led, placed   **74 neighborhood** friendly relations between
neighbors   **78 still** always. **let which** hinder that which. **for their life** even
if their lives depended on it

The fire of love, the fiercer still it ragèd in their
    breast.
  The wall that parted house from house had riven
    therein a cranny,
Which shrunk at making of the wall. This fault, not
    marked of any   84
Of many hundred years before—what doth not love
    espy?—
These lovers first of all found out and made a way
    whereby
To talk together secretly; and through the same did
    go
Their loving whisperings, very light and safely, to and
    fro.
  Now, as at one side Pyramus, and Thisbe on the
    tother,
Stood often drawing one of them the pleasant breath
    from other,
  "O thou envious wall!" they said. "Why lett'st thou
    lovers thus?   91
What matter were it if that thou permitted both of us
In arms each other to embrace? Or if thou think that
    this
Were overmuch, yet mightest thou at least make
    room to kiss.
And yet thou shalt not find us churls; we think our-
    selves in debt
For the same piece of courtesy, in vouching safe to let 96
Our sayings to our friendly ears thus freely come and
    go."
Thus having, where they stood in vain, complainèd of
    their woe,
When night drew near they bade adieu, and each
    gave kisses sweet
Unto the parget on their side, the which did never
    meet.   100
  Next morning with her cheerful light had driven
    the stars aside,

---

84 shrunk i.e., resulted from shrinkage   **91 lett'st thou** do you hinder
96 vouching safe vouchsafing, permitting   **100 parget** roughcast, plaster
usually made of lime and cow-dung.   **the which** i.e., which kisses

And Phoebus with his burning beams the dewy grass
    had dried.
These lovers at their wonted place by foreappoint-
    ment met;
Where, after much complaint and moan, they cove-
    nanted to get
Away from such as watchèd them, and in the evening
    late
To steal out of their fathers' house and eke the city
    gate.   106
And to th' intent that in the fields they strayed not
    up and down,   107
They did agree at Ninus' tomb to meet without the
    town   108
And tarry underneath a tree that by the same did
    grow,
Which was a fair high mulberry with fruit as white
    as snow,
Hard by a cool and trickling spring. This bargain
    pleased them both,
And so daylight, which to their thought away but
    slowly go'th,
Did in the ocean fall to rest, and night from thence
    doth rise.
    As soon as darkness once was come, straight
        Thisbe did devise
A shift to wind her out of doors, that none that were
    within   115
Perceivèd her, and muffling her with clothes about
    her chin
That no man might discern her face, to Ninus' tomb
    she came
Unto the tree, and sat her down there underneath the
    same.
    Love made her bold. But see the chance! There
        comes, besmeared with blood
About the chaps, a lioness, all foaming, from the
    wood,

106 eke also   **107 strayed not** would not stray   **108 Ninus** husband of
Semiramis, mythical founder of Nineveh. (Nineveh and Babylon appear to
have been confused.)   **without** outside   **115 shift** device.   **wind her** move by
sinuous course

From slaughter lately made of kine, to stanch her
    bloody thirst   121
With water of the foresaid spring. Whom Thisbe,
    spying first
Afar by moonlight, thereupon with fearful steps gan
    fly,
And in a dark and irksome cave did hide herself
    thereby.
And as she fled away for haste she let her mantle fall,
The which for fear she left behind, not looking back
    at all.
    Now, when the cruel lioness her thirst had
       stanchèd well,
In going to the wood she found the slender weed that
    fell   128
From Thisbe, which with bloody teeth in pieces she
    did tear.
    The night was somewhat further spent ere Pyramus
       came there,
Who, seeing in this subtle sand the print of lion's
    paw,   131
Waxed pale for fear. But when also the bloody cloak
    he saw
All rent and torn, "One night," he said, "shall lovers
    two confound!   133
Of which long life deservèd she of all that live on
    ground.   134
My soul deserves of this mischance the peril for to
    bear.
I, wretch, have been the death of thee, which to this
    place of fear
Did cause thee in the night to come, and came not
    here before.
My wicked limbs and wretched guts with cruel teeth
    therefore
Devour ye, O ye lions all that in this rock do dwell!

---

121 kine cattle. **stanch** slake **128 weed** garment **131 subtle** i.e., capable
of preserving an indistinct impression **133 confound** destroy **134 Of . . .
ground** one of whom (Thisbe) deserved long life more than any other person
on earth

But cowards use to wish for death." The slender
   weed that fell   140

From Thisbe up he takes and straight doth bear it to
   the tree   141

Which was appointed erst the place of meeting for to
   be.   142

And when he had bewept and kissed the garment
   which he knew,

"Receive thou my blood too!" quoth he, and therewithal he drew

His sword, the which among his guts he thrust, and
   by and by

Did draw it from the bleeding wound, beginning for
   to die,

And cast himself upon his back. The blood did spin
   on high;

As when a conduit pipe is cracked, the water bursting
   out

Doth shoot itself a great way off and pierce the air
   about.

The leaves that were upon the tree, besprinkled with
   his blood,

Were dyèd black. The root also, bestainèd as it stood,

A deep dark purple color straight upon the berries
   cast.

   Anon, scarce ridded of her fear with which she was
      aghast,

For doubt of disappointing him comes Thisbe forth
   in haste   154

And for her lover looks about, rejoicing for to tell

How hardly she had scaped that night the danger
   that befell.   156

And as she knew right well the place and fashion of
   the tree,

As which she saw so late before, even so, when she
   did see   158

---

140 use to make it a practice to. (Cowards only pretend to be ready to die; brave persons act.) **141 straight** straightway, at once **142 erst** at an earlier time **154 doubt** fear **156 hardly** scarcely **158 As . . . before** which she had seen so recently

The color of the berries turned, she was uncertain
   whether
It were the tree at which they both agreed to meet
   together.
  While in this doubtful stound she stood, she cast
   her eye aside,   161
And there, beweltered in his blood, her lover she
   espied
Lie sprawling with his dying limbs; at which she
   started back
And lookèd pale as any box. A shuddering through
   her strack,   164
Even like the sea which suddenly with whizzing noise
   doth move
When with a little blast of wind it is but touched
   above.
But, when approaching nearer him, she knew it was
   her love,
She beat her breast, she shriekèd out, she tare her
   golden hairs,   168
And, taking him between her arms, did wash his
   wounds with tears.
  She meynt her weeping with his blood, and kissing
   all his face,   170
Which now became as cold as ice, she cried in woeful
   case,
"Alas! What chance, my Pyramus, hath parted thee
   and me?
Make answer, O my Pyramus. It is thy Thisb, even she
Whom thou dost love most heartily, that speaketh
   unto thee.
Give ear, and raise thy heavy head!" He, hearing
   Thisbe's name,
Lift up his dying eyes and, having seen her, closed
   the same.   176
  But when she knew her mantle there and saw his
   scabbard lie

161 stound pang, shock; difficult time   **164 pale as any box** i.e., ashen,
pallid, like the color of boxwood.   **strack** struck   **168 tare** tore   **170 meynt**
(past tense of *meng*), mingled   **176 Lift** lifted

Without the sword: "Unhappy man! Thy love hath
    made thee die.
Thy love," she said, "hath made thee slay thyself.
    This hand of mine
Is strong enough to do the like. My love no less than
    thine
Shall give me force to work my wound. I will pursue
    thee dead,   181
And, wretched woman as I am, it shall of me be said
That, like as of thy death I was the only cause and
    blame,   183
So am I thy companion eke and partner in the same.   184
For death, which only could, alas! asunder part us
    twain,   185
Shall never so dissever us but we will meet again.
    "And you the parents of us both, most wretched
        folk alive,
Let this request that I shall make in both our names
    belive   188
Entreat you to permit that we, whom chaste and
    steadfast love
And whom even death hath joined in one, may, as it
    doth behoove,
In one grave be together laid. And thou, unhappy
    tree,
Which shroudest now the corpse of one, and shalt
    anon through me
Shroud two, of this same slaughter hold the sicker
    signs for aye.   193
Black be the color of thy fruit, and mourning-like
    alway,
Such as the murder of us twain may evermore
    bewray."   195
    This said, she took the sword, yet warm with
        slaughter of her love,
And setting it beneath her breast, did to her heart it
    shove.

181 work inflict   **183 like as** just as   **184 eke** also   **185 only** alone
188 belive urgently   **193 sicker** sure.   **aye** ever   **195 bewray** reveal

Her prayer with the gods and with their parents took
    effect.
For when the fruit is throughly ripe, the berry is
    bespecked,   199
With color tending to a black. And that which after
    fire   200
Remainèd, rested in one tomb, as Thisbe did desire.

The text is based on *The XV Books of P. Ovidius Naso, Entitled Metamorphosis. Translated out of Latin into English meter by Arthur Golding.* London, 1567. This is the first edition of Golding's translation.

199 throughly thoroughly   **200 fire** i.e., cremation

Further Reading

Barber, C. L. "May Games and Metamorphoses on a Midsummer Night." *Shakespeare's Festive Comedy*. Princeton, N.J.: Princeton Univ. Press, 1959. Barber explores how the social forms of Elizabethan holiday and celebration contribute to the dramatic form of Shakespeare's comedy. *A Midsummer Night's Dream* uses folk customs and aristocratic pageantry to organize its contrasts between reason and feeling, waking and dreaming, enabling the play to acknowledge the creative power of the human imagination while simultaneously recognizing that its creations are often "more strange than true."

Bevington, David. " 'But We Are Spirits of Another Sort': The Dark Side of Love and Magic in *A Midsummer Night's Dream*." *Medieval and Renaissance Studies* 7 (1975): 80–92. Bevington draws attention to the tension in the play "between comic reassurance and the suggestion of something dark and threatening." In pointing to the play's disturbing currents of libidinous sexuality, Bevington recognizes but distances himself from the position of Jan Kott (see below), arguing that the play successfully effects a reconciliation between the dark and affirmative sides of love—reconciliation that finds its symbol in the image of Titania and the ass's head.

Calderwood, James L. "*A Midsummer Night's Dream:* Art's Illusory Sacrifice." *Shakespearean Metadrama*. Minneapolis: Univ. of Minnesota Press, 1971. In Calderwood's metadramatic perspective, *A Midsummer Night's Dream* is the comedy that most fully participates in Shakespeare's ongoing dramatic exploration of the nature, function, and value of art. The characters' experience *in* the play mirrors the audience's experience *of* the play, as each is challenged to discover reality through illusions. Dream thereby becomes an analogue of the drama itself, a drama "in which man sees his dreams."

Dent, R. W. "Imagination in *A Midsummer Night's Dream*." *Shakespeare Quarterly* 15, no. 2 (1964), 115–129. Although Theseus indiscriminately lumps together lunatics, lovers, and poets, Shakespeare, Dent argues, carefully distinguishes between the role of imagination in love and in art. This distinction, demonstrated in Shakespeare's handling of the mechanicals' play, confirms *A Midsummer Night's Dream*'s unity of design, while offering us Shakespeare's own "Defense of Dramatic Poesy."

Evans, Bertrand. "All Shall Be Well: The Way Found." *Shakespeare's Comedies*. Oxford: Clarendon Press, 1960. Evans explores Shakespeare's handling of the different levels of awareness and understanding that characters display in the play. Oberon comes closest to the audience's privileged vantage point, while Bottom, who seems to have a wonderful resistance to understanding, is most distant. *A Midsummer Night's Dream* departs from the usual pattern of Shakespeare's comedies in that the denouement does not raise the characters to a level of awareness equal to that of the audience.

Fender, Stephen. *Shakespeare: "A Midsummer Night's Dream."* London: Edward Arnold, 1968. In a brief (64 pages), engaging book, Fender argues that provocative moral ambiguities emerge from the play's unusual structural complexity. We are constantly made aware of tensions and contradictions in the depiction of characters and settings, even in blind love itself. The play demands of us what Keats called Negative Capability: the ability to accept multiplicity, mystery, and doubt without reaching out for the illusory comforts of certainty and fact.

Garber, Marjorie B. "Spirits of Another Sort: *A Midsummer Night's Dream*." *Dream in Shakespeare: From Metaphor to Metamorphosis*. New Haven and London: Yale Univ. Press, 1974. The dreams in *A Midsummer Night's Dream*, according to Garber, function both to articulate the central theme of the play—imaginative transformation—and to provide a model for the play's construction. Dreams become emblems of the visionary experience itself, forcing characters as well as the audience out of familiar habits of mind into new modes of perception and understanding.

Girard, René. "Myth and Ritual in Shakespeare: *A Midsummer Night's Dream*." In *Textual Strategies: Perspectives in Post-Structuralist Criticism*, ed. Josué V. Harari. Ithaca, N.Y.: Cornell Univ. Press, 1979. Girard argues that in the confusions of the forest the lovers lose their identities because of their insistence on loving "through another's eyes." In the destructiveness of this mimetic desire Girard finds not only the theme of this play but also the "basic Shakespearean relationship" of all the comedies and tragedies.

Granville-Barker, Harley. *"A Midsummer Night's Dream."* In *More Prefaces to Shakespeare,* ed. Edward M. Moore. Princeton, N.J.: Princeton Univ. Press, 1974. Granville-Barker, writing as both critic and director, addresses the special problems raised in producing *A Midsummer Night's Dream* in a world accustomed to the realistic conventions of the modern theater. His analysis focuses on how the clowns, fairies, dance, and music could be handled effectively and convincingly, and he urges that the stage business be subordinated to Shakespeare's overriding emphasis on the play's language.

Kermode, Frank. "The Mature Comedies." In *Early Shakespeare,* ed. John Russell Brown and Bernard Harris. Stratford-upon-Avon Studies 3. London: Edward Arnold, 1961. For Kermode, the play, rich in intellectual content and sophisticated in design, is Shakespeare's "best comedy." His essay examines how Shakespeare's thematic preoccupation with blind love draws upon the philosophical treatment of this idea in the works of Macrobius, Apuleius, and Bruno. The result, Kermode argues, is a complex and serious work of art, intellectually and theatrically satisfying in its comic achievement.

Kott, Jan. "Titania and the Ass's Head." *Shakespeare Our Contemporary,* trans. Boleslaw Taborski. New York: Doubleday, 1964. In Kott's dark vision of love and human relations in *A Midsummer Night's Dream,* the night in the forest releases an "erotic madness" of perversity and obsession that is abruptly censured by the coming of day. Love is revealed as undignified and degrading, denying the lovers even their individuality in their compulsive behavior.

Leggatt, Alexander. *"A Midsummer Night's Dream." Shakespeare's Comedy of Love.* London: Methuen, 1974. In a sensitive essay, Leggatt explores Shakespeare's skillful arrangement of characters and perspectives. The play, he argues, achieves its imaginative power through a series of comic contrasts that confirms both the folly and the integrity of each group of characters.

Merchant, W. Moelwyn. *"A Midsummer Night's Dream:* A Visual Recreation." In *Early Shakespeare,* ed. John Russell Brown and Bernard Harris. Stratford-upon-Avon Studies 3. London: Edward Arnold, 1961. The play, which demanded the full range of the theatrical possibilities of the Elizabethan stage, in the ensuing centuries has received treatments that have tended to oversimplify the play to achieve certain desired theatrical effects. Merchant, surveying this stage history, concludes that directors have generally failed to integrate the undeniable charm of the fairy world with the more unsettling side of the play.

Montrose, Louis Adrian. " 'Shaping Fantasies': Figurations of Gender and Power in Elizabethan Culture." *Representations* 1, no. 2 (1983): 61–94. Montrose is interested in the relationship of Elizabethan drama to the culture that produced it, especially in how Shakespeare's plays reproduce and challenge existing social structures. His discussion of how the world of Queen Elizabeth's England and the world of *A Midsummer Night's Dream* are mutually illuminating focuses on questions of power, patriarchy, and sexual politics, concluding that in a double sense the play is a *"creation* of Elizabethan culture."

Olson, Paul A. *"A Midsummer Night's Dream* and the Meaning of Court Marriage." *ELH* 24 (1957): 95–119. Rpt. in *Shakespeare's Comedies: An Anthology of Modern Criticism,* ed. Laurence Lerner. Baltimore: Penguin, 1967. Olson calls attention to one possible occasion of the play's first performance (the celebration of a courtly marriage) as a sign of its seriousness and sophistication. He surveys Renaissance ideas about love and art to discover the principles that organize the play's elaborate formal contrasts, examining how the language and structure of the play "work together to make luminous a traditional understanding of marriage" that mirrors and reinforces the social order.

Selbourne, David. *The Making of "A Midsummer Night's Dream."* London: Methuen, 1982. Selbourne's account of the development of Peter Brook's Royal Shakespeare

Company production of *A Midsummer Night's Dream* (1970) offers insight into the creative interplay of director, cast, and text that resulted in this remarkable and influential production.

Young, David P. *Something of Great Constancy: The Art of "A Midsummer Night's Dream."* New Haven, Conn.: Yale Univ. Press, 1966. In this book-length study of the carefully constructed and interlocking harmonies of the play, Young examines Shakespeare's fusion of the courtly and popular material of his sources, his integration of stylistic and structural elements, and his manipulation of audience response. For Young, the transforming power of the imagination allows the play's apparently discordant elements to grow into "something of great constancy."

From the 1987 New York Shakespeare Festival production of *Richard II*, with Peter MacNicol as Richard II, directed by Joseph Papp at the Delacorte Theater in Central Park.

—RICHARD II—

RICHARD II

Foreword

After more than thirty years of reading and producing Shakespeare, I learned something new about *Richard II* when I directed it recently, something about the central relationship between King Richard and his cousin Bolingbroke, who displaces Richard and becomes king. I had always thought of Bolingbroke as a villain and a treacherous usurper. He's often interpreted as a kind of embryonic Richard III, a crook scheming to wrench the crown away from the rightful king and put it on his own head.

But when I began to look at the speeches and work on the scenes, I realized that Bolingbroke is not at all the scheming politician he's made out to be. He *worships* Richard, and he feels totally in awe of him as a king ordained by God. I found something very innocent about Bolingbroke; he is halfway toward deposing England's king before he realizes what is happening. As he marches through England to claim the hereditary land that Richard has unjustly taken from him, he is amazed that all the people are flocking to his side. He's not the villain of the piece; for that role we should look to Northumberland, the king-maker, who sets everything in motion while Bolingbroke offers no resistance.

Richard himself has often been regarded by some directors and critics as a Christ-like figure who suffers the taunts and insults of rebellious subjects, patiently awaiting the death he knows must come to him—for he is aware that when his kingship is challenged, his life is challenged. A deposed king will only breed dissatisfied factions who will try to capture and reinstate him; Richard knows that his only engagement after he loses his crown will be a meeting with death.

But if Bolingbroke isn't a villain, Richard isn't necessarily a martyr. Indeed, he is always the master of Bolingbroke because he's so good with words, and his cousin isn't. In the deposition scene, for example, when Richard is surrendering his crown, Bolingbroke remains extremely quiet. It's clear that the doomed Richard is verbally in control of the situation. With his quick sarcasm, he traps and tangles his cousin in sticky nets of language. Richard says, "Mark, silent king, the moral of this sport: / How soon my sorrow hath destroyed my face." When Bolingbroke replies, "The shadow of your sorrow hath destroyed / The shadow of your face," Richard cries, "Say that again. / The shadow of my sorrow? Ha! Let's see." He then proceeds to demolish Bolingbroke with his clever, bitter irony, thanking his cousin "that not only giv'st / Me cause to wail, but teachest me the way / How to lament the cause."

It's this verbal dexterity that allows Richard to dominate the play so thoroughly. Although he may lose in politics, he unquestionably wins in the theater—for in Shakespeare the character who controls language is the character who controls the play. On any stage, and particularly on the Shakespearean stage, language *is* power, and language is life.

JOSEPH PAPP

JOSEPH PAPP GRATEFULLY ACKNOWLEDGES THE HELP OF ELIZABETH KIRKLAND IN PREPARING THIS FOREWORD.

Introduction

Richard II (c. 1595–1596) is the first play in Shakespeare's great four-play historical saga, or tetralogy, that continues with the two parts of *Henry IV* (c. 1596–1598) and concludes with *Henry V* (1599). In this, his second, tetralogy, Shakespeare dramatizes the beginnings of the great conflict called the Wars of the Roses, having already dramatized the conclusion of that civil war in his earlier tetralogy on Henry VI and Richard III (c. 1589–1594). Both sequences move from an outbreak of civil faction to the eventual triumph of political stability. Together, they comprise the story of England's long century of political turmoil from the 1390s until Henry Tudor's victory over Richard III in 1485. Yet Shakespeare chose to tell the two halves of this chronicle in reverse order. His crowning statement about kingship in *Henry V* focuses on the earlier historical period, on the education and kingly success of Prince Hal.

With *Richard II*, then, Shakespeare turns to the events that had launched England's century of crisis. These events were still fresh and relevant to Elizabethan minds. Richard and Bolingbroke's contest for the English crown provided a sobering example of political wrongdoing and, at least by implication, a rule for political right conduct. One prominent reason for studying history, to an Elizabethan, was to avoid the errors of the past. The relevance of such historical analogy was in fact vividly underscored some six years after Shakespeare wrote the play: in 1601, followers of the Earl of Essex commissioned Shakespeare's acting company to perform a revived play about Richard II on the eve of what was to be an abortive rebellion, evidently with the intention of inciting a riot. Whether the play was Shakespeare's is not certain, but it seems likely. The acting company was ultimately exonerated, but not before Queen Elizabeth concluded that she was being compared to Richard II. Shakespeare presumably did not know when he wrote the play that it would be used for such a purpose, but he must have known that the overthrow of Richard II was in any case a controversial subject because of its potential use as a precedent for rebellion. The scene of Richard's deposition (4.1) was considered so provocative by Elizabeth's government that it was censored in the printed quartos of Shakespeare's play during the Queen's lifetime.

In view of the startling relevance of this piece of history to Shakespeare's own times, then, what are the rights and wrongs of Richard's deposition, and to what extent can political lessons be drawn from Shakespeare's presentation?

To begin with, we should not underestimate Richard's attractive qualities, as a man and even as a king. Throughout the play, Richard is consistently more impressive and majestic in appearance than his rival Bolingbroke. Richard fascinates us with his verbal sensitivity, his poetic insight, and his dramatic self-consciousness. He eloquently expounds a sacramental view of kingship, according to which "Not all the water in the rough rude sea / Can wash the balm off from an anointed king" (3.2.54–55). Bolingbroke can depose Richard but can never capture the aura of majesty Richard possesses; Bolingbroke may succeed politically, but only at the expense of desecrating an idea. Richard is much more interesting to us as a man than Bolingbroke, more capable of grief, more tender in his personal relationships, more in need of being understood. Indeed, a major factor in Richard's tragedy is the conflict between his public role (wherein he sees himself as divinely appointed, almost superhuman) and his private role (wherein he is emotionally dependent and easily hurt). He confuses what the medieval and Renaissance world knew as the king's "two bodies," the sacramental body of kingship, which is eternal, and the human body of a single occupant of the throne, whose frail mortal condition is subject to time and fortune. Richard's failure to perceive and act wisely on this difference is part of his tragic predicament, but his increasing insight, through suffering, into the truth of the distinction is also part of his spiritual growth. His dilemma, however poignantly individual, lies at the heart of kingship. Richard is thus very much a king. Although he sometimes indulges in childish sentimentality, at his best he is superbly refined, perceptive, and poetic.

These qualities notwithstanding, Richard is an incompetent ruler compared with the man who supplants him. Richard himself confesses to the prodigal expense of "too great a court." In order to raise funds, he has been obliged to "farm our royal realm": that is, sell for ready cash the right of collecting taxes to individual courtiers, who are then free to extort what the market will bear (1.4.43–45). Similarly, Richard proposes to issue "blank charters" (l. 48) to his minions, who will then be authorized to fill in the amount of tax to be paid by any hapless subject. These abuses were infamous to Elizabethan audiences as symbols of autocratic misgovernment. No less heinous is Richard's seizure of the dukedom of Lancaster from his cousin Bolingbroke. Although Richard does receive the consent of his Council to banish Bolingbroke, he violates the very idea of inheritance of property when he takes away Bolingbroke's title and lands. And, as his uncle the Duke of York remonstrates, Richard's own right to the throne depends on that idea of due inheritance. By offending against the most sacred concepts of order and degree, he teaches others to rebel.

Richard's behavior even prior to the commencement of the play arouses suspicion. The nature of his complicity in the death of his uncle Thomas of Woodstock, Duke of Gloucester, is perhaps never entirely clear, and Gloucester may have given provocation. Indeed, one can sympathize with the predicament of a young ruler prematurely thrust into the center of power by the untimely death of his father, the crown prince, now having to cope with an array of worldly-wise, advice-giving uncles. Nevertheless, Richard is unambiguously guilty of murder in the eyes of Gloucester's widow and of her brother-in-law John of Gaunt, Duke of Lancaster. Apparently, too, Gaunt's son Bolingbroke believes Richard to be a murderer, and he brings accusation against Thomas Mowbray, Duke of Norfolk, partly as a means of embarrassing the King, whom he cannot accuse directly. Mowbray's lot is an unenviable one: he was in command at Calais when Gloucester was executed there, and he hints that Richard ordered the execution (even though Mowbray alleges that he himself did not carry out the order). For his part, Richard is only too glad to banish the man suspected of having been his agent in murder. Mowbray is a convenient scapegoat.

The polished, ceremonial tone of the play's opening is vitiated, then, by our growing awareness of dirty politics going on behind the display. Our first impression of Richard is of a king devoted to the public display of conciliatory evenhandedness. He listens to the rival claims of Bolingbroke and Mowbray, and when he cannot reconcile them peacefully he orders a trial by combat. This trial (1.3) is replete with ceremonial repetition and ritual. The combatants are duly sworn in the justice of their cause, and God is to decide the quarrel by awarding victory to the champion who speaks the truth. Richard, the presiding officer, is God's anointed deputy on earth. Yet it becomes evident in due course that Richard is a major perpetrator of injustice rather than an impartial judge, that Bolingbroke is after greater objectives than he acknowledges even to himself, and that Richard's refusal to let the trial by combat take place and his banishment of the two contenders are his desperate way of burying a problem he cannot deal with forthrightly. His uncles reluctantly consent to the banishment only because they too see that disaffection has reached alarming proportions.

Bolingbroke's motivation in these opening scenes is perhaps even more obscure than Richard's. Our first impression of Bolingbroke is of forthrightness, moral indignation, and patriotic zeal. In fact we never really question the earnestness of his outrage at Richard's misgovernance, his longing to avenge a family murder (for Gloucester was his uncle, too), or his bitter disappointment at being banished. Yet we are prompted to ask further: what is the essential cause of the enmity between Bolingbroke and Richard? If Mowbray is only a stalking-horse, is not Gloucester's death also the excuse for pursuing a preexistent animosity? Richard, for one, appears to think so. His portrayal of Bolingbroke as a scheming politician, one who curries favor with the populace in order to build a widely based alliance against the King himself, is telling and prophetic. Bolingbroke, says Richard, acts "As were our England in reversion his, / And he our subjects' next degree in hope" (1.4.35–36). This unflattering appraisal might be ascribed to malicious envy on Richard's part, were it not proved by subsequent events to be wholly accurate.

Paradoxically, Richard is far the more prescient of the two contenders for the English throne. It is he, in fact, who perceives from the start that the conflict between them is irreconcilable. He banishes Bolingbroke as his chief rival and does not doubt what motives will call Bolingbroke home again. Meanwhile, Bolingbroke disclaims any motive for his deed other than love of country and hatred of injustice. Although born with a political canniness that Richard lacks, Bolingbroke does not reflect upon the consequences of his own acts. As a man of action he lives in the present. Richard, conversely, a person of exquisite contemplative powers and poetic imagination, does not deign to cope with the practical. He both envies and despises Bolingbroke's easy way with the commoners. Richard cherishes kingship for the majesty and the royal prerogative it confers, not for the power to govern wisely. Thus it is that, despite his perception of what will follow, Richard habitually indulges his worst instincts, buying a moment of giddy pleasure at the expense of future disaster.

Granted Richard's incompetence as a ruler, is Bolingbroke justified in armed rebellion against him? According to Bolingbroke's own father, John of Gaunt, to his uncle the Duke of York (who later, to be sure, shifts his allegiance), and to the Bishop of Carlisle, Bolingbroke is not justified in the rebellion. The attitude of these men can be summed up by the phrase "passive obedience." As Gaunt expresses the concept, "God's is the quarrel" (1.2.37). Because Richard is God's anointed deputy on earth, only God may punish the King's wrongdoing. Gaunt does not question Richard's guilt, but neither does he question God's ability to avenge. Gaunt sees human intervention in God's affair as blasphemous: "for I may never lift / An angry arm against His minister" (1.2.40–41). To be sure, Gaunt does acknowledge a solemn duty to offer frank advice to extremists of both sides, and he does so unsparingly. He consents to the banishment of his son, and he rebukes Richard with his dying breath.

This doctrine of passive obedience was familiar to Elizabethans, for they heard it in church periodically in official homilies against rebellion. It was the Tudor state's answer to those who asserted a right to overthrow reputedly evil kings. The argument was logically ingenious. Why are evil rulers permitted to govern from time to time? Presumably because God wishes to test a people or punish them for waywardness. Any king performing such chastisement is a divine scourge. Accordingly, the worst thing a people can do is to rebel against God's scourge, thereby manifesting more waywardness. Instead, they must attempt to remedy the insolence in their hearts, advise the King to mend his ways, and patiently await God's pardon. If they do so they will not long be disappointed. The doctrine is essentially conservative, defending the status quo. Nevertheless, in *Richard II* it is a moderate position between the extremes of tyranny and rebellion, and is expressed by thoughtful, self-less men. We might be tempted to label it Shakespeare's view if we did not also perceive that the doctrine is continually placed in ironic conflict with harsh political realities. The character who most reflects the ironies and even ludicrous incongruities of the position is the Duke of York.

York is to an extent a choric character—that is, one who helps direct our viewpoint—because his transfer of loyalties from Richard to Bolingbroke structurally delineates the decline of Richard's fortunes and the concurrent rise of Bolingbroke's. At first York shares with his brother Gaunt a dismay at Richard's willfulness, together with a reluctance to act. It is only when Richard seizes the dukedom of Lancaster that York can no longer hold his tongue. His condemnation is as bitter as that of Gaunt, hinting even at loss of allegiance (2.1.200–208). Still, he accepts the responsibility, so cavalierly bestowed by Richard, of governing England in the King's absence. He musters what force he can to oppose Bolingbroke's advance and lectures against this rebellion with the same vehemence he had used against Richard's despotism. Yet when faced with Bolingbroke's overwhelming military superiority, he accedes rather than fight in behalf of a lost cause. However much this may resemble cowardice or mere expediency, it also displays a pragmatic logic. Once Bolingbroke has become de facto king, in York's view he must be acknowledged and obeyed. By a kind of analogy to the doctrine of passive obedience (which more rigorous theorists would never allow), York accepts the status quo as inevitable. He is vigorously ready to defend the new regime, just as he earlier defended Richard's rule.

When, however, this conclusion brings York to the point of turning in his own son, Aumerle, for a traitor, and quarreling with his wife as to whether their son shall live, the ironic absurdity is apparent. Bolingbroke, now King Henry, himself is amused, in one of the play's rare lighthearted moments (5.3.79–80). When a family and a kingdom are divided against one another, there can be no really satisfactory resolution.

We are never entirely convinced that all the fine old medieval theories surrounding kingship—divine right, passive obedience, trial by combat, and the like—can ever wholly explain or remedy the complex and nasty political situation afflicting England. The one man capable of decisive action, in fact, is he who never theorizes at all: Bolingbroke. As we have seen, his avowed motive for opposing Mowbray—simple patriotic indignation—is uttered with such earnestness that we wonder if indeed Bolingbroke has examined those political ambitions in himself so plainly visible to Richard and others. This same discrepancy between surface and depth applies to Bolingbroke's motives in returning to England. We cannot be sure at what time he begins to plot that return; the conspiracy announced by Northumberland (2.1.224–300) follows so closely after Richard's violation of Bolingbroke's hereditary rights and is already so well advanced that we gain the impression of an already-existing plot, though some of this impression may be simply owing to Shakespeare's characteristic compression of historic time. When Bolingbroke arrives in England, in any case, he protests to York with seemingly passionate sincerity that he comes only for his dukedom of Lancaster (2.3.113–136). If so, why does he set about executing Richard's followers without legal authority and otherwise establishing his own claim to power? Does Bolingbroke seriously think he can reclaim his dukedom by force and then yield to Richard without either maintaining Richard as a puppet king or placing himself in intolerable jeopardy? And can he suppose that his allies, Northumberland and the rest, who have now openly defied the King, will countenance the return to power of one who would never trust them again? It is in this context that York protests, "Well, well, I see the issue of these arms" (l. 152). The deposition of Richard, and then Richard's death, are unavoidable conclusions once Bolingbroke has succeeded in an armed rebellion. There can be no turning back. Yet Bolingbroke simply will not think in these terms. He repeatedly admonishes Northumberland for treating Richard harshly, even though Northumberland is only taking upon himself the unpleasant but unavoidable duty of arresting and impeaching a king. When the new King Henry discovers—to his surprise, evidently—that Richard's life is now a burden to the state, he ponders aloud, "Have I no friend will rid me of this living fear?" (5.4.2) and then rebukes Exton for proceeding on cue.

Bolingbroke's pragmatic spirit and new mode of governing are the embodiment of de facto rule. Ultimately, the justification for his authority is the very fact of its existence, its functioning. Bolingbroke is the man of the hour. In William Butler Yeats's fine maxim, Bolingbroke is the vessel of clay, Richard the vessel of porcelain. One is durable and utilitarian, yet unattractive; the other is exquisite, fragile, impractical. The comparison does not force us to prefer one to the other, even though Yeats himself characteristically sided with beauty against politics. Rather, Shakespeare gives us our choice, allowing us to see in ourselves an inclination toward political and social stability or toward artistic temperament.

The paradox may suggest that the qualities of a good administrator are not those of a sensitive, thoughtful man. However hopeless as a king, Richard stands before us increasingly as an introspective and fascinating person. When his power crumbles, his spirit is enhanced, as though loss of power and royal identity were necessary for the discovery of true values.

In this there is a faint anticipation of King Lear's self-learning, fearfully and preciously bought. The trace is only slight here, because in good part *Richard II* is a political history play rather than a tragedy, and because Richard's self-realization is imperfect. Nevertheless, when Richard faces deposition and separation from his queen, and especially when he is alone in prison expecting to die, he strives to understand his life and through it the general condition of humanity. He perceives a contradiction in heaven's assurances about salvation: Christ promises to receive all God's children, and yet He also warns that it is as hard for a rich man to enter heaven as for a camel to be threaded through a needle's eye (5.5.16–17). The paradox echoes the Beatitudes: the last shall be first, the meek shall inherit the earth. Richard, now one of the downtrodden, gropes for an understanding of the vanity of human achievement whereby he can aspire to the victory Christ promised. At his death, that victory seems to him assured: his soul will mount to its seat on high "Whilst my gross flesh sinks downward, here to die" (l. 112).

In this triumph of spirit over flesh, the long downward motion of Richard's worldly fortune is crucially reversed. By the same token, the worldly success of Bolingbroke is shown to be no more than that: worldly success. His archetype is Cain, the primal murderer of a brother. To the extent that the play is a history, Bolingbroke's de facto success is still a matter of political relevance; but in the belated movement toward Richard's personal tragedy, we experience a profound countermovement that partly achieves a purgative sense of atonement and reassurance. Whatever Richard may have lost, his gain is also great.

Balance and symmetry are unusually important in *Richard II*. The play begins and ends with elaborate ritual obeisance to the concept of social and monarchic order, and yet in both cases a note of personal disorder refuses to be subdued by the public ceremonial. Shakespeare keeps our response to both Richard and Bolingbroke ambivalent by clouding their respective responsibilities for murder. Just as Richard's role in Gloucester's death remains unclear, so Bolingbroke's role in the assassination of Richard remains equally unclear. Mowbray and Exton, as scapegoats, are in some respects parallel. Because Richard and Bolingbroke are both implicated in the deaths of near kinsmen, both are associated with Cain's murder of Abel. As Bolingbroke rises in worldly fortune, Richard falls; as Richard finds insight and release through suffering, Bolingbroke finds guilt and remorse through distasteful political necessity. Again and again, the ritual effects of staging and style draw our attention to the balanced conflicts between the two men and within Richard. Symmetry helps to focus these conflicts in visual and aural ways. In particular, the deposition scene with its spectacle of a coronation in reverse brings the sacramental and human sides of the central figure into poignant dramatic relationship.

The imagery of *Richard II* reinforces structure and meaning. The play is unlike the history plays that follow in its extensive use of blank verse and rhyme, and in its interwoven sets of recurring images; *Richard II* is in this respect more typical of the so-called lyric period (c. 1594–1596) that also produced *Romeo and Juliet* and *A Midsummer Night's Dream*. Image patterns locate the play in our imaginations as a kind of lost Eden. England is a garden mismanaged by her royal gardener, so that weeds and caterpillars (e.g., Bushy, Bagot, and Green) flourish. The "garden" scene (3.4), located at the center of the play, offering a momentary haven of allegorical reflection on the play's hectic events, is central in the development of the garden metaphor. England is also a sick body ill-tended by her royal physician, and a family divided against itself yielding abortive and sterile progeny. Her political ills are attested to by disorders in the cosmos: comets, shooting stars, withered bay trees, weeping rains. Night owls, associated with death, prevail over the larks of morning. The sun, royally associated at first with Richard, deserts him for Bolingbroke and leaves Richard as the Phaëthon who has mishandled the sun god's chariot and so scorched the earth. Linked to the sun image is the prevalent leitmotif of ascent and descent. And, touching upon all these, a cluster of Biblical images sees England as a despoiled garden of Eden witnessing a second fall of man. Richard repeatedly brands his enemies and deserters as Judases and Pilates, not always fairly; nonetheless, in his last agony he finds genuine consolation in Christ's example. For a man so self-absorbed in the drama of his existence, this poetic method is intensely suitable. Language and stage action have combined perfectly to express the conflict between a sensitive but flawed king and his efficient but unlovable successor.

Richard II
in Performance

Richard II was popular with Shakespeare's audience, retaining its appeal well beyond the year of its first performance (probably 1596). The politically ambitious Earl of Essex was "often present at the playing thereof," according to evidence given at the trial of John Hayward in 1600, and it is clear that one reason for the play's continuing presence in the repertory was its political relevance. The fact that Shakespeare's company was commissioned to perform a revival on the eve of Essex's abortive rebellion in 1601 (see the play's Introduction) testifies to the immediacy of the controversy about Richard's unhappy reign and its potential applicability to Elizabethan politics.

Richard II must have been first performed at the Theatre in Shoredich, north of London, and then at the Globe Theatre. The play admirably demonstrates how these theaters, essentially devoid of scenery, featuring a large bare platform with two or more stage doors and a gallery above and to the rear of the stage, could be used to invoke a world of impressive pageantry and political conflict. One key to its staging is the use of symmetry. In the first scene and then again in scene 3, Bolingbroke and Mowbray meet as antagonists from opposite sides of the stage. The elaborate ceremony of trial by combat in scene 3 is conducted in symmetrically antiphonal movements: trumpet signals answer one another, the appellants each enter accompanied by a herald, and the Lord Marshal asks them in turn to state their names and causes, according to prescribed ritual. King Richard, meantime, is enthroned in a raised location, no doubt center stage, symbolically above the level of the combatants. When it is time to bid them farewell, he literally condescends to them—that is, descends to their level. The canopied and resplendent throne, carried onstage for this scene, provides a commanding stage property. Richard dominates the scene with his theatrical gestures. The whole effect is one of royal magnificence and ceremonial occasion; the playhouse visually embodies, and seems to celebrate, the institution of kingship. Yet it does so ironically in this play, for Richard's royal splendor only masks the prodigality and irresponsibility of his rule.

The encounter of King Richard and Bolingbroke at Flint Castle in Act 3, scene 3, uses this same theatrical environment to express in visual terms the taut and delicate negotiations for control taking place between these two contenders. Bolingbroke, illegally back from exile, finds Richard at Flint Castle in Wales and lays siege to that fortress. The presence of the castle is established on the Elizabethan stage not by scenery but by gesture and verbal invocation of "the limits of yon lime and stone" and "the rude ribs of that ancient castle" (ll. 26–32). The Elizabethan theater building needs no scenic assistance to answer this description, for it presents to the spectators an imposing facade with a gallery above, betokening the walls of Flint Castle, and a bare stage representing the ground in front of the castle where the besieging army of Bolingbroke is gathered. Shakespeare's use of the spatial dimensions of this arena seems carefully planned. Bolingbroke resolves on a parley before laying active siege, and so he dispatches his chief supporter, Northumberland, to go with a trumpeter to the walls and demand audience. Bolingbroke and his forces will meantime march "here," "Upon the grassy carpet of this plain"—that is, the front of the stage, which we understand to represent the ground lying at some distance from the castle. Northumberland advances to the castle, a trumpet sounds, and Richard appears *"on the walls"*—that is, in the gallery above the stage, looking down on those who surround him. Richard should be impressively attired on this momentous occasion (as indeed he was, for example, in Brian Bedford's performance at Stratford, Ontario, in 1983). He icily condemns the affront to his royal authority but knows he can do nothing. Northumberland, trafficking back and forth from King to challenger, proposes in due course the terms of a face-saving surrender: Richard must come down into the "base court" of the castle, to its outer or lower court, where he will receive Bolingbroke's homage. Richard's descent is metaphorical, like the setting of the sun or the fall of Phaëthon to which he alludes, but it is also a literal action in the theater. So is Bolingbroke's kneeling to Richard; it betokens formal obedience, but an obedience that is rendered only after Bolingbroke has obtained the crucial right of his return to England. Once again an impressively ceremonial scene expresses through visual irony the contrast between ritual order and the political reality of conflict and overthrow.

The climactic instance of this kind of inverted or interrupted ceremony in *Richard II* is the trial and deposition of Richard (4.1)—a coronation in reverse. Since no precedents are to be found for such a ritual, Richard invents the form of his own undoing; he commands the scene, though he must lose all. The scene is filled with abortive ritual. Bolingbroke undertakes to mount the throne as King Henry IV but is interrupted by the Bishop of Carlisle; instead, the throne remains vacant for the entire sequence as an eloquent stage symbol of disputed royal authority. Richard offers the crown to Bolingbroke ("Here, cousin, seize the crown") and then holds on to it, refusing to relinquish his last vestige of power without an unseemly struggle, and so the two men grapple unceremoniously for the symbolic object that Bolingbroke had hoped to attain through a more dignified proceeding. At every turn, this play explores visually the tension between ceremony and the realities of power.

Onstage in the Restoration and eighteenth century, *Richard II* was regarded chiefly as a political play in which the dilemmas of royal misrule and illegal deposition remained highly controversial. Indeed, as long as English viewers were concerned about the political consequences of the seventeenth-century civil war and subsequent struggles to achieve a balance between monarchy and constitutionalism, *Richard II* seemed as timely as it had for the followers of the Earl of Essex. Dismay at the misgovernance of the Stuart monarchs gave topical significance to Nahum Tate's adaptation in 1680. Fears of renewed rebellion, of forced abdication, and of mob violence were as painfully timely in 1680 as they appeared to have been in Richard II's reign. In spite of Tate's efforts to make the character of Richard personally attractive, the play was banned before it could be performed. By January of 1681, Tate had produced a suggestively titled revision, *The Sicilian Usurper*, sometimes referred to as *The Tyrant of Sicily*, but this, too, attracted the censor's attention with its updated portrayal of an irresponsible royal martyr and was "silenced on the third day," with the Theatre Royal, Drury Lane, itself closed for ten days as punishment. Lewis Theobald took an opposite tack in his adaptation of 1719, making "some innovations upon history and Shakespeare," as he said, in an attempt to blunt any antimonarchical application. His solution was to sentimentalize the story, in part, by adding a love plot between Aumerle and a Lady Piercy newly introduced into the action. John Rich returned to a more critical view of government in his production of *Richard II* at the Theatre Royal, Covent Garden, in 1738, by seeing Shakespeare's play as an indictment of governmental oppression and mismanagement and hence a timely commentary on stage licensing laws recently introduced by Robert Walpole.

Once the issue of monarchical authority had been largely resolved, on the other hand, the emphasis of productions became increasingly sentimental, usually focusing on Richard's tragic role as a sensitively poetic man destroyed by his own political willfulness. Nineteenth-century actors in the grand oratorical style, such as Edmund Kean and Edwin Booth, found the cadences of Richard's speech well suited to tragically moving delivery. Kean produced the play in 1815 in an adaptation by Richard Wroughton that emphasized scenes of high emotion, including an invented one between the Queen and Bolingbroke in which she pleads to be allowed to visit Richard and moves Bolingbroke with such eloquence that he resolves to return the crown, only to be defeated in his virtuous resolve by Exton's precipitate murder of Richard. The Queen, equally defeated by the swift-moving action, arrives too late to see Richard before he dies.

The nineteenth-century actor-managers also did everything they could through the use of magnificent sets and visual effects to intensify the awe and majesty of Richard's fall and Bolingbroke's rise to power. Charles Kean's spectacular production at the Princess's Theatre in 1857 featured a series of splendid Gothic architectural locations: St. Stephen's chapel, Pembroke Castle, Flint Castle, Milford Harbor, Westminster Hall, the Traitors' Gate of the Tower, the dungeon in Pomfret Castle, and still others. These effects reached their visual climax in the scene of Richard's entry into London in the custody of Bolingbroke—a scene that in Shakespeare's play is described by the Duke of York to his wife (5.2) rather than being staged. Kean not only put the event onstage but added a huge cast of extras: dancing itinerant fools, observers crowding the streets and house-tops, and a procession of craft guilds, minstrels, and flower girls. Bolingbroke entered in armor and on horseback; Richard's entrance brought a moment of stunned silence, then murmurs from the mob and increasingly loud calls for vengeance. The visual splendor was devised not only to pro-vide an impressive display but to enhance the pity of Rich-ard's overthrow. Herbert Beerbohm Tree, in one of his most opulently mounted historical revivals (at His Majesty's The-atre, 1903), managed to outdo Kean. Not only did Tree's Richard and Bolingbroke, like Kean's, enter on horseback in Act 5, scene 2, but also Mowbray and Bolingbroke rode into the lists at Coventry in Act 1, scene 3; and Tree provided other spectacular effects, including a lavish coronation scene for Bolingbroke to contrast with the pathos of Rich-ard's solitude and victimization.

Such opulence and scenic inflexibility could not continue indefinitely. Encouraged by the example of William Poel and his efforts with the Elizabethan Stage Society (1899, with a then unknown amateur named Harley Granville-Barker as Richard) to recover the pacing and nonillu-sionistic staging practices of Shakespeare's theater, twentieth-century directors have generally brought an end to cumbersome sets and operatic grand emotions, eschew-ing Victorian sentimentality to explore the deeper psycho-logical roots of an action generally conceived as Rich-ard's tragedy. Harcourt Williams, at London's Old Vic in 1929, strove for a fast-paced, naturalistic performance that would, he said, do away with "the absurd convention of the Shakespearean voice." As portrayed by John Gielgud, the Richard of Williams's production failed politically be-cause of his excessive self-pity and his willingness to retreat into fantasy. Gielgud returned to the part in 1937 at the Queen's Theatre, himself directing a production that em-phasized Richard's self-indulgent extravagance. Gielgud once again directed the play, in 1952 at the Lyric Theatre, Hammersmith, this time with Paul Scofield as a tragically isolated Richard. At New York's St. James Theater in 1937, Margaret Webster's production starred Maurice Evans as a flighty and frivolous king who turns away from the world and into himself as his political fortunes decline. Ralph Richardson directed the play in 1947 at London's New Theatre, with Alec Guinness in the title role as "a proud weakling" who, in J. C. Trewin's phrase, "uses irony as a defense." In 1951 Michael Redgrave starred in Anthony Quayle's production at Stratford-upon-Avon as a sensitive and self-absorbed Richard, infatuated with failure, ill-suited to the political world into which he was born.

Recent productions have been more attuned to a skeptical vision of the world of political struggle, ironically bringing the stage history of *Richard II* full circle, returning to it the political focus, though one less narrowly topical, that determined much of its early popularity. In 1964, at Stratford-upon-Avon, Peter Hall, John Barton, and Clifford Williams directed *Richard II* and both parts of *Henry IV* in an extended dramatic exploration of the triumph of realpolitik. David Warner's peremptory and petulant Richard was no match for Eric Porter's purposefully Machiavellian Bolingbroke. John Barton's version of 1973 at Stratford-upon-Avon used the devices of the modern theater to call attention to the means by which theatrical illusion is made, thereby suggesting the illusions that politics depends upon and even the illusory character of life itself. Bolingbroke and Mowbray in the lists at Coventry were mounted on hobbyhorses, in order to underscore the hollow nature of the ritual. The figure of Death was repeatedly present: in the Duchess of Gloucester's last scene on earth (1.2), in the garden scene when the gardeners were habited as monks (3.4), and as the presiding figure in the final scene. The groom visiting Richard in prison turned out to be Bolingbroke in disguise. Richard's coffin in Act 5, scene 6, was only large enough for a child. Richard Pasco and Ian Richardson alternated as Richard and Bolingbroke in different performances to stress a sense of interchangeability in the protagonists. However different from one another in style and character, the capricious king and his usurping cousin were seen as finally alike in their vulnerability to the ironies of history, both of them playing games of state without fully comprehending or controlling their destinies.

Still more recent productions have similarly acknowledged the grim necessity of history itself. Terry Hands, at

Stratford-upon-Avon in 1980, directed Alan Howard as an energetic and intelligent Richard, one who improvised strategies of survival while realizing nonetheless that he must inevitably fall before the quiet strength of David Suchet's pragmatic Bolingbroke. Howard movingly shifted from the feverish arrogance of the early scenes to a contemplative and ironic vision of a world he no longer could or even wished to control. Hands's production, like Barton's, showed the play's power on the stage to articulate a vision of history shockingly modern in its disillusioned sense of the political process. Bolingbroke inherited a throne that could no longer be propped up with the traditional myths of authority, and the mourning of the final scene was as much for England's troubled future as for Richard's tragic past. Joseph Papp, in his 1987 production for the New York Shakespeare Festival in the Delacorte Theater, Central Park, saw the play as a psychological conflict between a Richard (Peter MacNicol) who was sometimes bored with the affairs of state and his intimidating rival Bolingbroke (John Bedford Lloyd). MacNicol's Richard was sensitive, complex, funny at times, born to be a martyr, a fiasco as a ruler but ennobled by his ruin. Papp strove for a quintessentially "American" *Richard II*, one that did not take the play too seriously or echo the solemnities of Gielgud's influential tragic interpretation (as also in Jeremy Irons's portrayal of Richard in Barry Kyle's production at Stratford-upon-Avon in 1986). The ironies of Hands's and Papp's productions illustrate again the timeless pertinence of this historical drama that Shakespeare's first audience immediately saw as a comment on the politics of its own generation.

—RICHARD II—

[*Dramatis Personae*

KING RICHARD THE SECOND
QUEEN, *Richard's wife*
JOHN OF GAUNT, *Duke of Lancaster, King Richard's uncle*
HENRY BOLINGBROKE, *John of Gaunt's son, Duke of Hereford and
    claimant to his father's dukedom of Lancaster, later King
    Henry IV*
DUKE OF YORK, *Edmund of Langley, King Richard's uncle*
DUCHESS OF YORK
DUKE OF AUMERLE, *York's son and the Earl of Rutland*
DUCHESS OF GLOUCESTER, *widow of Thomas of Woodstock, Duke
    of Gloucester (King Richard's uncle)*

THOMAS MOWBRAY, *Duke of Norfolk,*
EARL OF SALISBURY,
LORD BERKELEY,
DUKE OF SURREY,
BISHOP OF CARLISLE,   *supporters
SIR STEPHEN SCROOP,   of King
ABBOT OF WESTMINSTER,   Richard*
BUSHY,
BAGOT,   }*favorites of King Richard,*
GREEN,
CAPTAIN *of the Welsh Army,*

EARL OF NORTHUMBERLAND,
HARRY PERCY, *Northumberland's son,*
LORD ROSS,
LORD WILLOUGHBY,   *supporters
LORD FITZWATER,   of Bolingbroke*
SIR PIERCE OF EXTON,
Another LORD,

LORD MARSHAL
Two HERALDS
GARDENER
GARDENER'S MAN
LADY *attending the Queen*
KEEPER *of the prison*
A MAN *attending Exton*

SERVINGMAN *to York*
GROOM *of the stable*

Lords, Officers, Soldiers, Attendants, Ladies attending the Queen

SCENE: *England and Wales*]

1.1   *Enter King Richard, John of Gaunt, with other nobles and attendants.*

KING RICHARD
Old John of Gaunt, time-honored Lancaster,   1
Hast thou according to thy oath and bond
Brought hither Henry Hereford, thy bold son,
Here to make good the boisterous late appeal,   4
Which then our leisure would not let us hear,   5
Against the Duke of Norfolk, Thomas Mowbray?
GAUNT   I have, my liege.   7
KING RICHARD
Tell me, moreover, hast thou sounded him   8
If he appeal the Duke on ancient malice,   9
Or worthily, as a good subject should,
On some known ground of treachery in him?
GAUNT
As near as I could sift him on that argument,   12
On some apparent danger seen in him   13
Aimed at Your Highness, no inveterate malice.
KING RICHARD
Then call them to our presence. [*Exit Attendant.*] Face
   to face,
And frowning brow to brow, ourselves will hear
The accuser and the accusèd freely speak.
High-stomached are they both, and full of ire;   18
In rage, deaf as the sea, hasty as fire.

    Enter Bolingbroke and Mowbray.

BOLINGBROKE
Many years of happy days befall
My gracious sovereign, my most loving liege!

1.1. Location: A room of state. (Holinshed's *Chronicles* places this scene at Windsor, in 1398.)
1 Old John of Gaunt (Born in 1340 at Ghent; hence the surname *Gaunt*. In 1398 he was fifty-eight years old.)   **4 late** recent.   **appeal** accusation, formal challenge or impeachment that the accuser was obliged to maintain in combat   **5 our, us** (The royal plural.)   **leisure** i.e., lack of leisure   **7 liege** i.e., sovereign   **8 sounded** inquired of   **9 appeal** accuse.   **on . . . malice** on the grounds of a long-standing enmity   **12 sift** discover true motives by indirect questioning.   **argument** subject   **13 apparent** obvious, manifest   **18 High-stomached** haughty

MOWBRAY

Each day still better other's happiness,   22
Until the heavens, envying earth's good hap,   23
Add an immortal title to your crown!

KING RICHARD

We thank you both. Yet one but flatters us,
As well appeareth by the cause you come: 26
Namely, to appeal each other of high treason.
Cousin of Hereford, what dost thou object   28
Against the Duke of Norfolk, Thomas Mowbray?

BOLINGBROKE

First—heaven be the record to my speech!—
In the devotion of a subject's love,
Tend'ring the precious safety of my prince,   32
And free from other misbegotten hate,
Come I appellant to this princely presence.   34
Now, Thomas Mowbray, do I turn to thee;
And mark my greeting well, for what I speak
My body shall make good upon this earth
Or my divine soul answer it in heaven.
Thou art a traitor and a miscreant,   39
Too good to be so, and too bad to live,   40
Since the more fair and crystal is the sky,   41
The uglier seem the clouds that in it fly.
Once more, the more to aggravate the note,   43
With a foul traitor's name stuff I thy throat,
And wish, so please my sovereign, ere I move,
What my tongue speaks my right-drawn sword may
  prove.   46

MOWBRAY

Let not my cold words here accuse my zeal.   47
'Tis not the trial of a woman's war,   48
The bitter clamor of two eager tongues,   49

22 **Each day** may each day   23 **hap** fortune   26 **you come** i.e., about
which you come   28 **what . . . object** what accusation do you bring
32 **Tend'ring** holding dear   34 **appellant** as the accuser   39 **miscreant**
irreligious villain   40 **good** i.e., noble, high-born   41 **crystal** clear. (The
image alludes to the crystal spheres in which, according to the Ptole-
maic conception of the universe, the heavenly bodies were fixed.)
43 **aggravate** emphasize.   **note** reproach, stigma, i.e., charge of treason   46 **right-drawn** justly or rightly drawn   47 **accuse my zeal** cast
doubt on my zeal or loyalty   48 **woman's war** i.e., war of words
49 **eager** sharp, biting

Can arbitrate this cause betwixt us twain;   50
The blood is hot that must be cooled for this.
Yet can I not of such tame patience boast
As to be hushed and naught at all to say.
First, the fair reverence of Your Highness curbs me
From giving reins and spurs to my free speech,
Which else would post until it had returned   56
These terms of treason doubled down his throat.
Setting aside his high blood's royalty,   58
And let him be no kinsman to my liege,   59
I do defy him and I spit at him,
Call him a slanderous coward and a villain;
Which to maintain I would allow him odds   62
And meet him, were I tied to run afoot   63
Even to the frozen ridges of the Alps,
Or any other ground inhabitable   65
Wherever Englishman durst set his foot.
Meantime let this defend my loyalty:
By all my hopes, most falsely doth he lie.
BOLINGBROKE [*Throwing down his gage*]
Pale trembling coward, there I throw my gage,   69
Disclaiming here the kindred of the King,   70
And lay aside my high blood's royalty,
Which fear, not reverence, makes thee to except.   72
If guilty dread have left thee so much strength
As to take up mine honor's pawn, then stoop.   74
By that, and all the rites of knighthood else,
Will I make good against thee, arm to arm,
What I have spoke, or thou canst worse devise.   77
MOWBRAY [*Taking up the gage*]
I take it up; and by that sword I swear
Which gently laid my knighthood on my shoulder,
I'll answer thee in any fair degree
Or chivalrous design of knightly trial;

50 Can that can   **56 post** ride at high speed (by means of relays of
horses)   **58 Setting . . . royalty** disregarding Bolingbroke's royal blood
(as grandson of Edward III)   **59 let him be** suppose him to be
62 Which i.e., which charges.   **odds** advantage   **63 tied** obliged   **65 inhabitable** uninhabitable   **69 gage** a pledge to combat (usually a glove or
gauntlet)   **70 Disclaiming** relinquishing.   **kindred** kinship   **72 except**
exempt, make an exception of   **74 pawn** i.e., the gage   **77 or . . . devise**
or anything worse you can imagine me to have said about you

And when I mount, alive may I not light,   82
If I be traitor or unjustly fight!   83

KING RICHARD

What doth our cousin lay to Mowbray's charge?   84
It must be great that can inherit us   85
So much as of a thought of ill in him.

BOLINGBROKE

Look what I speak, my life shall prove it true: 87
That Mowbray hath received eight thousand nobles   88
In name of lendings for Your Highness' soldiers,   89
The which he hath detained for lewd employments,   90
Like a false traitor and injurious villain.
Besides I say, and will in battle prove
Or here or elsewhere to the furthest verge   93
That ever was surveyed by English eye,
That all the treasons for these eighteen years   95
Complotted and contrivèd in this land   96
Fetch from false Mowbray their first head and spring. 97
Further I say, and further will maintain
Upon his bad life to make all this good,
That he did plot the Duke of Gloucester's death,   100
Suggest his soon-believing adversaries,   101
And consequently, like a traitor coward,   102
Sluiced out his innocent soul through streams of
   blood—   103
Which blood, like sacrificing Abel's, cries   104
Even from the tongueless caverns of the earth   105
To me for justice and rough chastisement.

82 light alight, dismount   **83 unjustly** in an unjust cause   **84 lay to** offer
in response to   **85 inherit us** put us in possession of, make us have
87 Look what whatever   **88 nobles** gold coins worth 6 shillings 8 pence
89 lendings money advanced to soldiers when the regular pay cannot be
given   **90 lewd** vile, base   **93 Or** either.   **verge** limit, reach   **95 these
eighteen years** i.e., ever since the Peasants' Revolt of 1381   **96 Complotted**
conspired   **97 Fetch** derive.   **head and spring** (Synonymous words meaning "origin.")   **100 Duke of Gloucester's death** (Thomas of Woodstock,
Duke of Gloucester, a younger son of Edward III and brother of John of
Gaunt, was murdered at Calais in September 1397, while under Mowbray's
custody.)   **101 Suggest** prompt, incite.   **soon-believing** easily persuaded,
overcredulous   **102 consequently** afterwards   **103 Sluiced out** let flow (as
by the opening of a sluice, or valve)   **104 Abel's** (For the story of Cain's
murder of his brother Abel, the first such murder on earth and the archetype of the killing of a kinsman, see Genesis 4:3–12.)   **105 tongueless**
resonant but without articulate speech, echoing

And, by the glorious worth of my descent,
This arm shall do it or this life be spent.

KING RICHARD
How high a pitch his resolution soars!   109
Thomas of Norfolk, what sayst thou to this?

MOWBRAY
O, let my sovereign turn away his face
And bid his ears a little while be deaf,
Till I have told this slander of his blood   113
How God and good men hate so foul a liar!

KING RICHARD
Mowbray, impartial are our eyes and ears.
Were he my brother, nay, my kingdom's heir,
As he is but my father's brother's son,
Now by my scepter's awe I make a vow,   118
Such neighbor nearness to our sacred blood
Should nothing privilege him nor partialize   120
The unstooping firmness of my upright soul.
He is our subject, Mowbray; so art thou.
Free speech and fearless I to thee allow.

MOWBRAY
Then, Bolingbroke, as low as to thy heart
Through the false passage of thy throat thou liest!
Three parts of that receipt I had for Calais   126
Disbursed I duly to His Highness' soldiers;
The other part reserved I by consent,
For that my sovereign liege was in my debt   129
Upon remainder of a dear account   130
Since last I went to France to fetch his queen.   131
Now swallow down that lie. For Gloucester's death,   132
I slew him not, but to my own disgrace   133
Neglected my sworn duty in that case.   134
[*To Gaunt.*] For you, my noble lord of Lancaster,

109 pitch highest reach of a falcon's flight   **113 slander of** disgrace or
reproach to   **118 my scepter's awe** the reverence due my scepter
120 nothing not at all.   **partialize** make partial, bias   **126 receipt**
money received   **129 For that** because   **130 Upon . . . account** for the
balance of a heavy debt   **131 Since . . . queen** i.e., since my most recent
voyage to France to negotiate the King's marriage (1396) with Isabella,
daughter of the French King Charles VI   **132 For** as for   **132–134 For
. . . case** (Mowbray speaks guardedly but seems to imply that he postponed the execution of Gloucester that he was ordered by Richard to
carry out.)

The honorable father to my foe,
Once did I lay an ambush for your life,
A trespass that doth vex my grievèd soul;
But ere I last received the Sacrament
I did confess it, and exactly begged   140
Your Grace's pardon, and I hope I had it.
This is my fault. As for the rest appealed,   142
It issues from the rancor of a villain,
A recreant and most degenerate traitor,   144
Which in myself I boldly will defend,   145
And interchangeably hurl down my gage   146
Upon this overweening traitor's foot,   147
To prove myself a loyal gentleman
Even in the best blood chambered in his bosom.   149
[*He throws down his gage. Bolingbroke picks it up.*]
In haste whereof most heartily I pray   150
Your Highness to assign our trial day.
KING RICHARD
Wrath-kindled gentlemen, be ruled by me;
Let's purge this choler without letting blood.   153
This we prescribe, though no physician;
Deep malice makes too deep incision.
Forget, forgive; conclude and be agreed;   156
Our doctors say this is no month to bleed.—   157
Good uncle, let this end where it begun;
We'll calm the Duke of Norfolk, you your son.
GAUNT
To be a make-peace shall become my age.
Throw down, my son, the Duke of Norfolk's gage.
KING RICHARD
And Norfolk, throw down his.
GAUNT   When, Harry, when?
Obedience bids I should not bid again.

140 exactly (1) explicitly (2) fully   **142 appealed** of which I am
charged   **144 recreant** cowardly; or, coward (used as a noun)
145 Which which charge   **146 interchangeably** in exchange, in turn
147 overweening arrogant, proud   **149 Even in** equal to   **150 In haste
whereof** to hasten which proof of my innocence   **153 Let's . . . blood**
let's treat this wrath (caused by an excess of bile or choler) by purga-
tion rather than by medical bloodletting (with a play on "bloodshed in
combat")   **156 conclude** come to a final agreement   **157 no month to
bleed** (Spring and autumn were regarded as the proper times to bleed
patients.)

KING RICHARD
  Norfolk, throw down, we bid; there is no boot.   164
MOWBRAY [*Kneeling*]
  Myself I throw, dread sovereign, at thy foot.   165
  My life thou shalt command, but not my shame.
  The one my duty owes; but my fair name,
  Despite of death that lives upon my grave,   168
  To dark dishonor's use thou shalt not have.
  I am disgraced, impeached, and baffled here,   170
  Pierced to the soul with slander's venomed spear,
  The which no balm can cure but his heart-blood
  Which breathed this poison.
KING RICHARD   Rage must be withstood.   173
  Give me his gage. Lions make leopards tame.   174
MOWBRAY
  Yea, but not change his spots. Take but my shame,
  And I resign my gage. My dear dear lord,
  The purest treasure mortal times afford   177
  Is spotless reputation; that away,
  Men are but gilded loam or painted clay.
  A jewel in a ten-times-barred-up chest
  Is a bold spirit in a loyal breast.
  Mine honor is my life; both grow in one;
  Take honor from me, and my life is done.
  Then, dear my liege, mine honor let me try;   184
  In that I live, and for that will I die.
KING RICHARD [*To Bolingbroke*]
  Cousin, throw up your gage; do you begin.   186
BOLINGBROKE
  O, God defend my soul from such deep sin!
  Shall I seem crestfallen in my father's sight?
  Or with pale beggar-fear impeach my height   189
  Before this out-dared dastard? Ere my tongue   190

164 boot remedy   **165 Myself I throw** i.e., I throw myself, instead of my
gage   **168 Despite . . . lives** that will live in spite of death   **170 impeached** accused.   **baffled** publicly dishonored   **173 Which breathed** of
him who uttered   **174 Lions . . . tame** (The royal arms showed a lion
rampant; Mowbray's emblem was a leopard.)   **177 mortal times** our
earthly lives   **184 try** put to the test   **186 throw . . . gage** i.e., throw
your gage up to me, thereby ending the quarrel. (Richard is probably
seated in an elevated position, as in scene 3.)   **189 impeach my height**
discredit my high rank   **190 out-dared** dared down, cowed.   **dastard**
coward

Shall wound my honor with such feeble wrong,   191
Or sound so base a parle, my teeth shall tear   192
The slavish motive of recanting fear   193
And spit it bleeding in his high disgrace,   194
Where shame doth harbor, even in Mowbray's face.   195
                          [*Exit Gaunt.*]
KING RICHARD
  We were not born to sue but to command;
  Which since we cannot do to make you friends,
  Be ready, as your lives shall answer it
  At Coventry upon Saint Lambert's day.   199
  There shall your swords and lances arbitrate
  The swelling difference of your settled hate.
  Since we cannot atone you, we shall see   202
  Justice design the victor's chivalry.   203
  Lord Marshal, command our officers at arms
  Be ready to direct these home alarms.   205
                          Exit [*with others*].

❖

1.2   *Enter John of Gaunt with the Duchess of*
          Gloucester.

GAUNT
  Alas, the part I had in Woodstock's blood   1
  Doth more solicit me than your exclaims   2

191 feeble wrong dishonorable submission   **192 sound . . . parle** trumpet so shameful a negotiation, i.e., consent to such a truce   **193 motive** instrument, i.e., the tongue.   **recanting fear** i.e., fear that makes one recant, or renounce one's vows   **194 in his** to its, the tongue's   **195 s.d. Exit Gaunt** (A stage direction from the Folio, adopted by most editors so that Gaunt will not be required to exit at the end of scene 1 and then immediately reenter.)   **199 Saint Lambert's day** September 17
202 atone reconcile   **203 design** designate, point out.   **chivalry** true knightly qualities (as demonstrated by victory in trial by combat)
205 home alarms domestic conflicts

1.2. Location: John of Gaunt's house (? No place is specified, and the scene is not in Holinshed.)
1 part . . . blood my kinship with Thomas of Woodstock, the Duke of Gloucester (i.e., as his older brother)   **2 exclaims** exclamations

To stir against the butchers of his life! 3
But since correction lieth in those hands 4
Which made the fault that we cannot correct,
Put we our quarrel to the will of heaven,
Who, when they see the hours ripe on earth,
Will rain hot vengeance on offenders' heads.

DUCHESS
Finds brotherhood in thee no sharper spur?
Hath love in thy old blood no living fire?
Edward's seven sons, whereof thyself art one, 11
Were as seven vials of his sacred blood
Or seven fair branches springing from one root.
Some of those seven are dried by nature's course,
Some of those branches by the Destinies cut;
But Thomas, my dear lord, my life, my Gloucester,
One vial full of Edward's sacred blood,
One flourishing branch of his most royal root,
Is cracked, and all the precious liquor spilt,
Is hacked down, and his summer leaves all faded,
By envy's hand and murder's bloody ax. 21
Ah, Gaunt, his blood was thine! That bed, that womb,
That metal, that self mold, that fashioned thee 23
Made him a man; and though thou livest and breathest,
Yet art thou slain in him. Thou dost consent 25
In some large measure to thy father's death,
In that thou seest thy wretched brother die,
Who was the model of thy father's life. 28
Call it not patience, Gaunt; it is despair.
In suffering thus thy brother to be slaughtered,
Thou showest the naked pathway to thy life, 31
Teaching stern murder how to butcher thee.
That which in mean men we entitle patience 33
Is pale cold cowardice in noble breasts.
What shall I say? To safeguard thine own life,
The best way is to venge my Gloucester's death. 36

---

3 stir take action   **4 those hands** i.e., Richard's (whom Gaunt charges
with responsibility for Gloucester's death)   **11 Edward's** Edward III's
21 envy's malice's   **23 metal** substance out of which a person or a
thing is made (with a sense too of *mettle*, temperament, disposition).
self selfsame   **25 consent** acquiesce   **28 model** likeness, copy
31 naked i.e., undefended   **33 mean** lowly   **36 venge** avenge

GAUNT

God's is the quarrel; for God's substitute,   37
His deputy anointed in His sight,
Hath caused his death; the which if wrongfully   39
Let heaven revenge, for I may never lift
An angry arm against His minister.

DUCHESS

Where then, alas, may I complain myself?   42

GAUNT

To God, the widow's champion and defense.

DUCHESS

Why, then, I will. Farewell, old Gaunt.
Thou goest to Coventry, there to behold
Our cousin Hereford and fell Mowbray fight.   46
O, sit my husband's wrongs on Hereford's spear,   47
That it may enter butcher Mowbray's breast!
Or if misfortune miss the first career,   49
Be Mowbray's sins so heavy in his bosom
That they may break his foaming courser's back
And throw the rider headlong in the lists,
A caitiff recreant to my cousin Hereford!   53
Farewell, old Gaunt. Thy sometime brother's wife   54
With her companion, Grief, must end her life.

GAUNT

Sister, farewell. I must to Coventry.
As much good stay with thee as go with me!

DUCHESS

Yet one word more. Grief boundeth where it falls,   58
Not with the empty hollowness, but weight.   59
I take my leave before I have begun,   60
For sorrow ends not when it seemeth done.
Commend me to thy brother, Edmund York.   62
Lo, this is all. Nay, yet depart not so!

---

37 God's substitute i.e., the King, God's deputy on earth   **39 his** i.e.,
Gloucester's   **42 complain myself** lodge a complaint on my own behalf   **46 cousin** kinsman.   **fell** fierce   **47 sit . . . wrongs** may my husband's wrongs sit   **49 misfortune** i.e., Mowbray's downfall.   **career**
charge of the horse in a tourney or combat   **53 caitiff** base, cowardly
54 sometime late   **58 boundeth** bounces, rebounds, returns. (Grief
continues on and on, like a bouncing tennis ball.)   **59 Not . . . weight**
(Grief is not hollow, like a tennis ball, but continues to move because of
its heaviness.)   **60 begun** i.e., begun to grieve   **62 Edmund York**
Edmund of Langley, fifth son of Edward III

Though this be all, do not so quickly go;
I shall remember more. Bid him—ah, what?—
With all good speed at Pleshey visit me.   66
Alack, and what shall good old York there see
But empty lodgings and unfurnished walls,   68
Unpeopled offices, untrodden stones,   69
And what hear there for welcome but my groans?
Therefore commend me; let him not come there
To seek out sorrow that dwells everywhere.
Desolate, desolate, will I hence and die.
The last leave of thee takes my weeping eye.   *Exeunt.*

❖

1.3   *Enter Lord Marshal and the Duke [of] Aumerle.*

MARSHAL
My lord Aumerle, is Harry Hereford armed?
AUMERLE
Yea, at all points, and longs to enter in.   2
MARSHAL
The Duke of Norfolk, sprightfully and bold,   3
Stays but the summons of the appellant's trumpet.   4
AUMERLE
Why then, the champions are prepared, and stay
For nothing but His Majesty's approach.

> *The trumpets sound, and the King enters with*
> *his nobles [Gaunt, Bushy, Bagot, Green, and*
> *others]. When they are set, enter [Mowbray] the*
> *Duke of Norfolk in arms, defendant [with a*
> *Herald].*

KING RICHARD
Marshal, demand of yonder champion
The cause of his arrival here in arms.

66 Pleshey Gloucester's country seat, in Essex   **68 unfurnished** bare
69 offices service quarters, workrooms

**1.3. Location: The lists at Coventry. Scaffolds or raised seats are pro-
vided for the King and his nobles, and chairs for the combatants.**
2 at all points completely.   **in** i.e., into the lists, the space designed for
combat   **3 sprightfully** with high spirit   **4 Stays** awaits

Ask him his name, and orderly proceed
To swear him in the justice of his cause.
MARSHAL
In God's name and the King's, say who thou art
And why thou comest thus knightly clad in arms,
Against what man thou com'st, and what thy quarrel. 13
Speak truly on thy knighthood and thy oath,
As so defend thee heaven and thy valor!
MOWBRAY
My name is Thomas Mowbray, Duke of Norfolk,
Who hither come engagèd by my oath—
Which God defend a knight should violate!—   18
Both to defend my loyalty and truth
To God, my king, and my succeeding issue
Against the Duke of Hereford that appeals me,
And by the grace of God and this mine arm
To prove him, in defending of myself,
A traitor to my God, my king, and me;
And as I truly fight, defend me heaven!

*The trumpets sound. Enter [Bolingbroke,] Duke
of Hereford, appellant, in armor [with a Herald].*

KING RICHARD
Marshal, ask yonder knight in arms
Both who he is and why he cometh hither
Thus plated in habiliments of war;   28
And formally, according to our law,
Depose him in the justice of his cause.   30
MARSHAL
What is thy name? And wherefore com'st thou hither,
Before King Richard in his royal lists?
Against whom comest thou? And what's thy quarrel?
Speak like a true knight, so defend thee heaven!
BOLINGBROKE
Harry of Hereford, Lancaster, and Derby
Am I, who ready here do stand in arms
To prove, by God's grace and my body's valor,
In lists, on Thomas Mowbray, Duke of Norfolk,

13 quarrel complaint **18 defend** forbid **28 plated** armored.
habiliments the attire **30 Depose him** take his sworn deposition

That he is a traitor foul and dangerous
To God of heaven, King Richard, and to me;
And as I truly fight, defend me heaven!

MARSHAL
On pain of death, no person be so bold
Or daring-hardy as to touch the lists,   43
Except the Marshal and such officers
Appointed to direct these fair designs.

BOLINGBROKE
Lord Marshal, let me kiss my sovereign's hand
And bow my knee before His Majesty;   47
For Mowbray and myself are like two men
That vow a long and weary pilgrimage.
Then let us take a ceremonious leave
And loving farewell of our several friends.

MARSHAL [*To King Richard*]
The appellant in all duty greets Your Highness
And craves to kiss your hand and take his leave.

KING RICHARD [*Coming down*]
We will descend and fold him in our arms.
                              [*He embraces Bolingbroke.*]
Cousin of Hereford, as thy cause is right,
So be thy fortune in this royal fight!   56
Farewell, my blood—which if today thou shed,
Lament we may, but not revenge thee dead.

BOLINGBROKE
O, let no noble eye profane a tear   59
For me, if I be gored with Mowbray's spear.   60
As confident as is the falcon's flight
Against a bird do I with Mowbray fight.
[*To the Lord Marshal.*] My loving lord, I take my leave of
    you;
[*To Aumerle*] Of you, my noble cousin, Lord Aumerle;
Not sick, although I have to do with death,
But lusty, young, and cheerly drawing breath.   66
Lo, as at English feasts, so I regreet   67

---

43 daring-hardy daringly bold, reckless. **touch** i.e., interfere in
47 bow my knee (Presumably Bolingbroke kneels to Richard and, at
about l. 69, to Gaunt.) **56 royal fight** i.e., a fight taking place in the
presence of the King **59–60 profane . . . For me** misuse tears by weeping for me **66 lusty** full of vigor. **cheerly** cheerfully **67 regreet** greet,
salute

The daintiest last, to make the end most sweet.   68
[*To Gaunt*.] O thou, the earthly author of my blood,
Whose youthful spirit, in me regenerate,   70
Doth with a twofold vigor lift me up   71
To reach at victory above my head,
Add proof unto mine armor with thy prayers,   73
And with thy blessings steel my lance's point
That it may enter Mowbray's waxen coat   75
And furbish new the name of John o' Gaunt   76
Even in the lusty havior of his son.   77

GAUNT
God in thy good cause make thee prosperous!
Be swift like lightning in the execution,
And let thy blows, doubly redoubled,
Fall like amazing thunder on the casque   81
Of thy adverse pernicious enemy.
Rouse up thy youthful blood, be valiant, and live.

BOLINGBROKE
Mine innocence and Saint George to thrive!   84

MOWBRAY
However God or fortune cast my lot,
There lives or dies, true to King Richard's throne,
A loyal, just, and upright gentleman.
Never did captive with a freer heart
Cast off his chains of bondage and embrace
His golden uncontrolled enfranchisement   90
More than my dancing soul doth celebrate
This feast of battle with mine adversary.
Most mighty liege, and my companion peers,
Take from my mouth the wish of happy years.   94
As gentle and as jocund as to jest   95
Go I to fight. Truth hath a quiet breast.   96

68 The daintiest i.e., the most tasty, the finest. (Bolingbroke refers to the custom of ending banquets with a sweet dessert.)   **70 regenerate** born anew   **71 twofold** i.e., of father and son   **73 proof** invulnerability   **75 enter ... coat** pierce Mowbray's armor as though it were made of wax   **76 furbish** polish   **77 lusty havior** vigorous behavior, deportment   **81 amazing** bewildering.   **casque** helmet   **84 to thrive** i.e., I rely on for my thriving   **90 enfranchisement** freedom   **94 Take ... years** i.e., take from me the wish that you may enjoy many happy years   **95 gentle** unperturbed in spirit.   **to jest** i.e., to a play or entertainment   **96 quiet** calm

KING RICHARD
Farewell, my lord. Securely I espy   97
Virtue with valor couchèd in thine eye.   98
Order the trial, Marshal, and begin.
MARSHAL
Harry of Hereford, Lancaster, and Derby,
Receive thy lance; and God defend the right!
                    [*A lance is given to Bolingbroke.*]
BOLINGBROKE
Strong as a tower in hope, I cry "Amen!"   102
MARSHAL [*To an officer*]
Go bear this lance to Thomas, Duke of Norfolk.
                    [*A lance is given to Norfolk.*]
FIRST HERALD
Harry of Hereford, Lancaster, and Derby
Stands here for God, his sovereign, and himself,
On pain to be found false and recreant,
To prove the Duke of Norfolk, Thomas Mowbray,
A traitor to his God, his king, and him,   108
And dares him to set forward to the fight.
SECOND HERALD
Here standeth Thomas Mowbray, Duke of Norfolk,
On pain to be found false and recreant,
Both to defend himself and to approve   112
Henry of Hereford, Lancaster, and Derby,
To God, his sovereign, and to him disloyal,
Courageously and with a free desire
Attending but the signal to begin.   116
MARSHAL
Sound, trumpets, and set forward, combatants!
                    [*A charge is sounded. Richard throws
                              down his baton.*]
Stay! The King hath thrown his warder down.   118
KING RICHARD
Let them lay by their helmets and their spears,

---

97 Securely confidently   **98 couchèd** lodged, expressed, leveled in
readiness (as with a lance)   **102 Strong . . . hope** (Alludes to Psalm 61:3:
"for thou hast been my hope, and a strong tower for me against the
face of the enemy.")   **108 him** himself   **112 approve** prove   **116 Attending** awaiting   **118 warder** staff or truncheon borne by the King when
presiding over a trial by combat

And both return back to their chairs again.
[*To his counselors.*] Withdraw with us, and let the
    trumpets sound
While we return these dukes what we decree.   122
                [*A long flourish. Richard consults apart
                        with Gaunt and others.*]
Draw near,
And list what with our council we have done.   124
For that our kingdom's earth should not be soiled   125
With that dear blood which it hath fosterèd;
And for our eyes do hate the dire aspect   127
Of civil wounds plowed up with neighbors' sword;
And for we think the eagle-wingèd pride
Of sky-aspiring and ambitious thoughts,
With rival-hating envy, set on you   131
To wake our peace, which in our country's cradle
Draws the sweet infant breath of gentle sleep,
Which, so roused up with boisterous untuned drums,   134
With harsh-resounding trumpets' dreadful bray
And grating shock of wrathful iron arms,
Might from our quiet confines fright fair peace
And make us wade even in our kindred's blood:
Therefore we banish you our territories.
You, cousin Hereford, upon pain of life,   140
Till twice five summers have enriched our fields,
Shall not regreet our fair dominions,
But tread the stranger paths of banishment.   143
BOLINGBROKE
    Your will be done. This must my comfort be:
    That sun that warms you here shall shine on me,
    And those his golden beams to you here lent
    Shall point on me and gild my banishment.
KING RICHARD
    Norfolk, for thee remains a heavier doom,
    Which I with some unwillingness pronounce:
    The sly slow hours shall not determinate   150

122 **While we return** until I inform   **s.d. flourish** fanfare   **124 list**
hear   **125 For that** in order that   **127 for** because (also in l. 129)
131 envy enmity. **set on you** set you on   **134 Which** i.e., which enmity,
disturbance of the peace. (Although in literal terms the antecedent of
Which is *peace* in l. 132.)   **140 life** i.e., loss of life   **143 stranger** alien
150 determinate put to an end

The dateless limit of thy dear exile.   151
The hopeless word of "never to return"
Breathe I against thee, upon pain of life.
MOWBRAY
A heavy sentence, my most sovereign liege,
And all unlooked-for from Your Highness' mouth.
A dearer merit, not so deep a maim   156
As to be cast forth in the common air,
Have I deservèd at Your Highness' hands.
The language I have learned these forty years,
My native English, now I must forgo;
And now my tongue's use is to me no more
Than an unstringèd viol or a harp,   162
Or like a cunning instrument cased up,   163
Or, being open, put into his hands   164
That knows no touch to tune the harmony.
Within my mouth you have enjailed my tongue,
Doubly portcullised with my teeth and lips,   167
And dull unfeeling barren ignorance
Is made my jailer to attend on me.
I am too old to fawn upon a nurse,
Too far in years to be a pupil now.
What is thy sentence then but speechless death,
Which robs my tongue from breathing native breath?
KING RICHARD
It boots thee not to be compassionate.   174
After our sentence plaining comes too late.   175
MOWBRAY
Then thus I turn me from my country's light,
To dwell in solemn shades of endless night.
                                        [*He starts to leave.*]
KING RICHARD
Return again, and take an oath with thee.
Lay on our royal sword your banished hands.
                        [*They place their hands on Richard's sword.*]

---

151 dateless limit unlimited term.   **dear** grievous   **156 dearer merit**
more valued reward.   **maim** injury   **162 viol** a six-stringed instrument,
related to the modern violin, played with a curved bow   **163 cunning**
skillfully made   **164 open** taken from its case   **167 portcullised** shut in
by a portcullis, an iron grating over a gateway that can be raised and
lowered   **174 boots** avails.   **compassionate** full of laments   **175 plaining** complaining

Swear by the duty that you owe to God—
Our part therein we banish with yourselves—   181
To keep the oath that we administer:
You never shall, so help you truth and God,
Embrace each other's love in banishment,
Nor never look upon each other's face,
Nor never write, regreet, nor reconcile
This louring tempest of your homebred hate;   187
Nor never by advisèd purpose meet   188
To plot, contrive, or complot any ill   189
'Gainst us, our state, our subjects, or our land.

BOLINGBROKE   I swear.

MOWBRAY   And I, to keep all this.

BOLINGBROKE
Norfolk, so far as to mine enemy: 193
By this time, had the King permitted us,
One of our souls had wandered in the air,
Banished this frail sepulcher of our flesh,   196
As now our flesh is banished from this land.
Confess thy treasons ere thou fly the realm.
Since thou hast far to go, bear not along
The clogging burden of a guilty soul.   200

MOWBRAY
No, Bolingbroke. If ever I were traitor,
My name be blotted from the book of life,
And I from heaven banished as from hence!
But what thou art, God, thou, and I do know,
And all too soon, I fear, the King shall rue.
Farewell, my liege. Now no way can I stray;   206
Save back to England, all the world's my way.   *Exit.*

KING RICHARD [*To Gaunt*]
Uncle, even in the glasses of thine eyes   208
I see thy grievèd heart. Thy sad aspect
Hath from the number of his banished years
Plucked four away. [*To Bolingbroke.*] Six frozen winters
   spent,

---

181 Our part therein i.e., the duty you owe me as king   **187 louring**
threatening, scowling   **188 advisèd** deliberate, premeditated   **189 complot** conspire   **193 so . . . enemy** so far as I would speak to or wish
success to my sworn enemy   **196 sepulcher** tomb   **200 clogging** (A clog
was a wooden block attached to the leg to hinder movement.)   **206 stray**
take the wrong road   **208 glasses** mirrors (here glistening with tears)

Return with welcome home from banishment.

BOLINGBROKE
How long a time lies in one little word!
Four lagging winters and four wanton springs   214
End in a word; such is the breath of kings.

GAUNT
I thank my liege that in regard of me
He shortens four years of my son's exile.
But little vantage shall I reap thereby;
For, ere the six years that he hath to spend
Can change their moons and bring their times about,
My oil-dried lamp and time-bewasted light   221
Shall be extinct with age and endless night;
My inch of taper will be burnt and done,   223
And blindfold Death not let me see my son.   224

KING RICHARD
Why, uncle, thou hast many years to live.

GAUNT
But not a minute, King, that thou canst give.
Shorten my days thou canst with sullen sorrow,
And pluck nights from me, but not lend a morrow;
Thou canst help Time to furrow me with age,
But stop no wrinkle in his pilgrimage;   230
Thy word is current with him for my death,   231
But dead, thy kingdom cannot buy my breath.   232

KING RICHARD
Thy son is banished upon good advice,
Whereto thy tongue a party verdict gave.   234
Why at our justice seem'st thou then to lour?

GAUNT
Things sweet to taste prove in digestion sour.
You urged me as a judge, but I had rather
You would have bid me argue like a father.
O, had it been a stranger, not my child,

---

214 **wanton** luxuriant   221 **oil-dried** empty of oil   223 **taper** candle
224 **blindfold Death** i.e., *blindfold* because *Death* deprives its victims of
their sight and because it is often pictured as an eyeless skull   230 **stop**
. . . **pilgrimage** prevent no wrinkle that comes with time   231 **current**
i.e., as good as current coin, valid   232 **dead** i.e., once I am dead.   **buy**
i.e., restore with a payment   234 **a party verdict** one person's share in a
joint verdict

To smooth his fault I should have been more mild.   240
A partial slander sought I to avoid   241
And in the sentence my own life destroyed.
Alas, I looked when some of you should say   243
I was too strict, to make mine own away;   244
But you gave leave to my unwilling tongue
Against my will to do myself this wrong.

KING RICHARD
Cousin, farewell; and, uncle, bid him so.
Six years we banish him, and he shall go.
          [*Flourish. Exit King Richard with his train.*]

AUMERLE [*To Bolingbroke*]
Cousin, farewell. What presence must not know,   249
From where you do remain let paper show.

MARSHAL [*To Bolingbroke*]
My lord, no leave take I, for I will ride,   251
As far as land will let me, by your side.
          [*Bolingbroke makes no answer. Aumerle and*
                    the Lord Marshal retire.]

GAUNT
O, to what purpose dost thou hoard thy words,
That thou returnest no greeting to thy friends?

BOLINGBROKE
I have too few to take my leave of you,
When the tongue's office should be prodigal   256
To breathe the abundant dolor of the heart.   257

GAUNT
Thy grief is but thy absence for a time.   258

BOLINGBROKE
Joy absent, grief is present for that time.   259

GAUNT
What is six winters? They are quickly gone.

BOLINGBROKE
To men in joy; but grief makes one hour ten.

---

240 smooth extenuate **241 partial slander** accusation of partiality (on
behalf of my son) **243 looked when** expected that, awaited the point at
which **244 to . . . away** in making away with my own (son) **249 What
. . . know** what I cannot learn from you in person **251 no leave take I**
i.e., I will not take my leave of you, my lord; I will not say good-bye
256 office function. **prodigal** lavish **257 To breathe** in breathing
258 grief grievance **259 grief** unhappiness

GAUNT
  Call it a travel that thou tak'st for pleasure.   262

BOLINGBROKE
  My heart will sigh when I miscall it so,
  Which finds it an enforcèd pilgrimage.

GAUNT
  The sullen passage of thy weary steps   265
  Esteem as foil wherein thou art to set   266
  The precious jewel of thy home return.

BOLINGBROKE
  Nay, rather every tedious stride I make
  Will but remember me what a deal of world   269
  I wander from the jewels that I love.
  Must I not serve a long apprenticehood
  To foreign passages, and in the end,   272
  Having my freedom, boast of nothing else
  But that I was a journeyman to grief?   274

GAUNT
  All places that the eye of heaven visits
  Are to a wise man ports and happy havens.
  Teach thy necessity to reason thus:
  There is no virtue like necessity.
  Think not the King did banish thee,
  But thou the King. Woe doth the heavier sit
  Where it perceives it is but faintly borne.   281
  Go, say I sent thee forth to purchase honor,   282
  And not the King exiled thee; or suppose
  Devouring pestilence hangs in our air
  And thou art flying to a fresher clime.
  Look what thy soul holds dear, imagine it   286
  To lie that way thou goest, not whence thou com'st.
  Suppose the singing birds musicians,
  The grass whereon thou tread'st the presence strewed,   289

262 travel (The Quarto spelling, *travaile*, suggests an interchangeable meaning of "labor.")   **265 sullen** (1) melancholy (2) dull   **266 foil** thin metal leaf set behind gems to show off their luster; hence, that which sets something off to advantage   **269 remember** remind.   **a deal of world** a great distance   **272 passages** wanderings, experiences **274 journeyman** one who labors for daily wages (with a hint also of "one who makes a journey")   **281 faintly** faintheartedly   **282 purchase** acquire   **286 Look what** whatever   **289 the presence strewed** the royal presence chamber strewn with rushes

The flowers fair ladies, and thy steps no more
Than a delightful measure or a dance;   291
For gnarling sorrow hath less power to bite   292
The man that mocks at it and sets it light.   293
BOLINGBROKE
O, who can hold a fire in his hand
By thinking on the frosty Caucasus?   295
Or cloy the hungry edge of appetite
By bare imagination of a feast?
Or wallow naked in December snow
By thinking on fantastic summer's heat?   299
O, no, the apprehension of the good
Gives but the greater feeling to the worse.
Fell Sorrow's tooth doth never rankle more   302
Than when he bites but lanceth not the sore.   303
GAUNT
Come, come, my son, I'll bring thee on thy way.   304
Had I thy youth and cause, I would not stay.   305
BOLINGBROKE
Then, England's ground, farewell; sweet soil, adieu,
My mother and my nurse that bears me yet!
Where'er I wander, boast of this I can,
Though banished, yet a trueborn Englishman.   309
Exeunt.

❖

1.4   *Enter the King, with Bagot, [Green,] etc., at one
door, and the Lord Aumerle at another.*

KING RICHARD
We did observe. Cousin Aumerle,   1
How far brought you high Hereford on his way?

291 measure stately, formal dance   **292 gnarling** snarling, growling
293 sets it light regards it as trivial   **295 Caucasus** mountain range now
located in the Soviet Union between the Black and Caspian seas
299 fantastic imaginary   **302 Fell** fierce.   **rankle** cause irritation and
festering   **303 lanceth not** does not open the wound (to permit the
release of the infection; Bolingbroke's point is that sorrow should be
openly confronted, not rationalized or covered over and thus allowed to
fester)   **304 bring** escort   **305 stay** linger   **309 trueborn** loyal

1.4. Location: The court.
1 We did observe (The scene begins in the midst of a conversation.)

AUMERLE
I brought high Hereford, if you call him so,
But to the next highway, and there I left him.   4
KING RICHARD
And say, what store of parting tears were shed?
AUMERLE
Faith, none for me, except the northeast wind,   6
Which then blew bitterly against our faces,
Awaked the sleeping rheum and so by chance   8
Did grace our hollow parting with a tear.   9
KING RICHARD
What said our cousin when you parted with him?
AUMERLE   "Farewell!"
And, for my heart disdainèd that my tongue   12
Should so profane the word, that taught me craft   13
To counterfeit oppression of such grief
That words seemed buried in my sorrow's grave.
Marry, would the word "farewell" have lengthened
    hours   16
And added years to his short banishment,
He should have had a volume of farewells;
But since it would not, he had none of me.   19
KING RICHARD
He is our cousin, cousin; but 'tis doubt,
When time shall call him home from banishment,
Whether our kinsman come to see his friends.   22
Ourself and Bushy, Bagot here, and Green
Observed his courtship to the common people,
How he did seem to dive into their hearts
With humble and familiar courtesy,
What reverence he did throw away on slaves,
Wooing poor craftsmen with the craft of smiles
And patient underbearing of his fortune,   29
As 'twere to banish their affects with him.   30
Off goes his bonnet to an oyster wench;

---

4 next nearest   **6 for me** for my part   **8 rheum** watery discharge (i.e.,
tears)   **9 hollow** insincere   **12 for** because   **13 that** i.e., my disdain.
(Aumerle says he pretended to be overcome by grief in order to avoid
saying an insincere "Farewell" to Bolingbroke.)   **16 Marry** indeed.
(From the oath "by the Virgin Mary.")   **19 of** from   **22 friends** kinsmen, i.e., us, his cousins   **29 underbearing** bearing, endurance
30 banish their affects take their affections with him into banishment

A brace of draymen bid God speed him well 32
And had the tribute of his supple knee,
With "Thanks, my countrymen, my loving friends,"
As were our England in reversion his, 35
And he our subjects' next degree in hope. 36

GREEN
Well, he is gone, and with him go these thoughts. 37
Now, for the rebels which stand out in Ireland, 38
Expedient manage must be made, my liege, 39
Ere further leisure yield them further means
For their advantage and Your Highness' loss.

KING RICHARD
We will ourself in person to this war.
And, for our coffers with too great a court 43
And liberal largess are grown somewhat light,
We are enforced to farm our royal realm, 45
The revenue whereof shall furnish us
For our affairs in hand. If that come short,
Our substitutes at home shall have blank charters, 48
Whereto, when they shall know what men are rich,
They shall subscribe them for large sums of gold 50
And send them after to supply our wants;
For we will make for Ireland presently. 52

    Enter Bushy.

Bushy, what news?

BUSHY
Old John of Gaunt is grievous sick, my lord,
Suddenly taken, and hath sent posthaste
To entreat Your Majesty to visit him.

KING RICHARD Where lies he?

BUSHY At Ely House. 58

---

32 draymen cart drivers **35 in reversion** by right of future succession **36 our . . . hope** i.e., the heir presumptive to the throne **37 go** let go **38 stand out** rise in rebellion **39 Expedient manage** expeditious management **43 for** because. **too great a court** i.e., too great an extravagance at court **45 farm** lease the right of collecting taxes, for a present cash payment, to the highest bidder **48 substitutes** deputies. **blank charters** writs authorizing the collection of revenues or forced loans to the crown, blank spaces being left for the names of the parties and the sums they were to provide **50 subscribe them** put down their names **52 presently** at once **58 Ely House** (Palace of the Bishop of Ely in Holborn, a London district.)

KING RICHARD
  Now put it, God, in the physician's mind
  To help him to his grave immediately!
  The lining of his coffers shall make coats   61
  To deck our soldiers for these Irish wars.
  Come, gentlemen, let's all go visit him.
  Pray God we may make haste, and come too late!
ALL Amen.   *Exeunt.*

❖

61 lining contents (with pun on lining for coats).   **coats** coats of mail,
armor

2.1 *Enter John of Gaunt sick, with the Duke of York, etc.*

GAUNT
  Will the King come, that I may breathe my last
  In wholesome counsel to his unstaid youth?   2
YORK
  Vex not yourself, nor strive not with your breath,   3
  For all in vain comes counsel to his ear.
GAUNT
  O, but they say the tongues of dying men
  Enforce attention like deep harmony.
  Where words are scarce, they are seldom spent in vain,
  For they breathe truth that breathe their words in pain.   8
  He that no more must say is listened more   9
    Than they whom youth and ease have taught to glose.   10
  More are men's ends marked than their lives before.   11
    The setting sun, and music at the close,
  As the last taste of sweets, is sweetest last,
  Writ in remembrance more than things long past.
  Though Richard my life's counsel would not hear,   15
  My death's sad tale may yet undeaf his ear.   16
YORK
  No, it is stopped with other, flattering sounds,
  As praises, of whose taste the wise are fond;   18
  Lascivious meters, to whose venom sound   19
  The open ear of youth doth always listen;
  Report of fashions in proud Italy,   21
  Whose manners still our tardy-apish nation   22
  Limps after in base imitation.
  Where doth the world thrust forth a vanity—
  So it be new, there's no respect how vile—   25

2.1. Location: Ely House.
s.d. Enter John of Gaunt sick (Presumably he is carried in by servants
in a chair.) **2 unstaid** uncontrolled **3 strive . . . breath** i.e., don't waste
your breath **8 they** those persons **9 listened** listened to **10 glose**
flatter, deceive in speech **11 marked** noticed **15 my life's counsel** my
advice while I lived **16 My . . . tale** my grave dying speech **18 As . . .
fond** such as praises, which even wise men are foolishly inclined to
hear **19 venom** poisonous **21 proud Italy** (Ascham, Lyly, and other
sixteenth-century writers complained of the growing influence of Italian
luxury.) **22 still** always. **tardy-apish** imitative but behind the times
25 So so long as. **there's no respect** it makes no difference

That is not quickly buzzed into his ears?
Then all too late comes counsel to be heard
Where will doth mutiny with wit's regard.   28
Direct not him whose way himself will choose.
'Tis breath thou lack'st, and that breath wilt thou lose.

GAUNT
Methinks I am a prophet new inspired,
And thus expiring do foretell of him:
His rash fierce blaze of riot cannot last,   33
For violent fires soon burn out themselves;
Small showers last long, but sudden storms are short;
He tires betimes that spurs too fast betimes;   36
With eager feeding food doth choke the feeder;
Light vanity, insatiate cormorant,   38
Consuming means, soon preys upon itself.   39
This royal throne of kings, this sceptered isle,
This earth of majesty, this seat of Mars,   41
This other Eden, demi-paradise,
This fortress built by Nature for herself
Against infection and the hand of war,   44
This happy breed of men, this little world,   45
This precious stone set in the silver sea,
Which serves it in the office of a wall,   47
Or as a moat defensive to a house,
Against the envy of less happier lands,
This blessed plot, this earth, this realm, this England,
This nurse, this teeming womb of royal kings,   51
Feared by their breed and famous by their birth,   52
Renownèd for their deeds as far from home
For Christian service and true chivalry
As is the sepulcher in stubborn Jewry   55
Of the world's ransom, blessed Mary's Son,
This land of such dear souls, this dear dear land,
Dear for her reputation through the world,

---

28 will . . . regard natural inclination rebels against what reason es-
teems   **33 riot** profligacy   **36 betimes** soon, early   **38 Light vanity**
frivolous dissipation.   **cormorant** glutton. (Literally, a voracious sea-
bird.)   **39 means** i.e., means of sustenance   **41 earth** land   **44 infection**
(1) plague (2) moral pollution   **45 breed** race   **47 office** function
51 teeming fruitful   **52 by their breed** for their ancestral reputation for
prowess   **55 stubborn Jewry** i.e., Judea, called stubborn because it
resisted Christianity

Is now leased out—I die pronouncing it—
Like to a tenement or pelting farm.   60
England, bound in with the triumphant sea,   61
Whose rocky shore beats back the envious siege   62
Of watery Neptune, is now bound in with shame,   63
With inky blots and rotten parchment bonds.   64
That England that was wont to conquer others
Hath made a shameful conquest of itself.
Ah, would the scandal vanish with my life,
How happy then were my ensuing death!

> *Enter King [Richard] and Queen, [Aumerle,*
> *Bushy, Green, Bagot, Ross, and Willoughby,] etc.*

YORK
The King is come. Deal mildly with his youth,
For young hot colts being reined do rage the more.
QUEEN
How fares our noble uncle, Lancaster?
KING RICHARD
What comfort, man? How is 't with agèd Gaunt?
GAUNT
O, how that name befits my composition!   73
Old Gaunt indeed, and gaunt in being old.
Within me grief hath kept a tedious fast,
And who abstains from meat that is not gaunt?   76
For sleeping England long time have I watched;   77
Watching breeds leanness, leanness is all gaunt.
The pleasure that some fathers feed upon
Is my strict fast—I mean, my children's looks—
And, therein fasting, hast thou made me gaunt.   81
Gaunt am I for the grave, gaunt as a grave,
Whose hollow womb inherits naught but bones.   83
KING RICHARD
Can sick men play so nicely with their names?   84

60 tenement land or property held by a tenant.   **pelting** paltry
61 bound in bordered, surrounded   **62 envious** hostile   **63 bound in**
legally constrained   **64 blots . . . bonds** i.e., the blank charters   **73 com-**
position constitution   **76 meat** food   **77 watched** kept watch at night,
been vigilant   **81 therein fasting** i.e., since I am starved of the pleasure
some fathers have, in seeing happy looks in the next generation. (Because of Richard's banishment of Bolingbroke, Gaunt will lack his son's
company.)   **83 inherits** possesses, will receive   **84 nicely** (1) ingeniously
(2) trivially

GAUNT
No, misery makes sport to mock itself.   85
Since thou dost seek to kill my name in me,   86
I mock my name, great King, to flatter thee.   87

KING RICHARD
Should dying men flatter with those that live?   88

GAUNT
No, no, men living flatter those that die.   89

KING RICHARD
Thou, now a-dying, sayest thou flatterest me.

GAUNT
O, no, thou diest, though I the sicker be.

KING RICHARD
I am in health, I breathe, and see thee ill.

GAUNT
Now He that made me knows I see thee ill;
Ill in myself to see, and in thee seeing ill.   94
Thy deathbed is no lesser than thy land,
Wherein thou liest in reputation sick;
And thou, too careless patient as thou art,
Commit'st thy anointed body to the cure
Of those physicians that first wounded thee.   99
A thousand flatterers sit within thy crown,
Whose compass is no bigger than thy head;   101
And yet, encagèd in so small a verge,   102
The waste is no whit lesser than thy land.   103
O, had thy grandsire with a prophet's eye   104
Seen how his son's son should destroy his sons,   105
From forth thy reach he would have laid thy shame,   106
Deposing thee before thou wert possessed,   107

85 to mock of mocking **86 kill . . . me** i.e., by banishing my son **87 I
. . . thee** i.e., I disparage what you seek to overcome in order to flatter
your greatness **88 flatter with** try to please **89 flatter** i.e., are attentive to, offer comfort to **94 Ill . . . ill** poorly, by virtue of my failing
sight, and seeing the evil in you **99 physicians** i.e., the King's favorites **101 compass** circle, circumference **102 verge** (1) circle, ring
(2) the compass about the King's court, which extended for twelve
miles **103 waste** that which is destroyed (with a quibble on the legal
meaning of *waste*, "damage done to property by a tenant"). **whit** bit,
speck **104 grandsire** i.e., Edward III **105 destroy his sons** (1) destroy
Edward III's sons, Richard's uncles (2) destroy Richard's own heritage **106 From . . . shame** he would have put the matter you have
shamefully handled out of your reach **107 Deposing** dispossessing.
possessed put in possession of the crown

Which art possessed now to depose thyself.   108
Why, cousin, wert thou regent of the world,   109
It were a shame to let this land by lease;
But, for thy world enjoying but this land,   111
Is it not more than shame to shame it so?
Landlord of England art thou now, not king.   113
Thy state of law is bondslave to the law,   114
And thou—
KING RICHARD A lunatic lean-witted fool,
Presuming on an ague's privilege,   116
Darest with thy frozen admonition   117
Make pale our cheek, chasing the royal blood
With fury from his native residence.   119
Now, by my seat's right royal majesty,   120
Wert thou not brother to great Edward's son,
This tongue that runs so roundly in thy head   122
Should run thy head from thy unreverent shoulders.   123
GAUNT
O, spare me not, my brother Edward's son,
For that I was his father Edward's son!   125
That blood already, like the pelican,   126
Hast thou tapped out and drunkenly caroused.   127
My brother Gloucester, plain well-meaning soul—
Whom fair befall in heaven 'mongst happy souls!—   129
May be a precedent and witness good
That thou respect'st not spilling Edward's blood.   131
Join with the present sickness that I have,
And thy unkindness be like crooked age   133
To crop at once a too-long-withered flower.   134

108 possessed seized by a diabolical spirit, an obsession **109 cousin**
kinsman. **regent** ruler **111 But . . . land** i.e., but since you enjoy as
your domain only this land of England (rather than the whole world)
113 Landlord i.e., one who leases out a property **114 Thy . . . the law**
i.e., your legal status as King is now subservient to and at the mercy of
the law governing contracts, such as blank charters **116 an ague's
privilege** i.e., a sick person's right to be testy **117 frozen** (1) chilly
(2) caused by a chill **119 his** its **120 seat's** throne's **122–123 runs . . .
run** runs on, talks . . . drive, chase **122 roundly** unceremoniously,
bluntly **123 unreverent** irreverent, disrespectful **125 For that** because **126 pelican** (The pelican was thought to feed its ingrateful and
murderous young with its own blood.) **127 tapped out** drawn as from a
tapped barrel. **caroused** gulped, quaffed **129 Whom fair befall** to
whom may good come **131 thou respect'st not** you care nothing
about **133 unkindness** unnatural behavior **134 crop** cut

Live in thy shame, but die not shame with thee!   135
These words hereafter thy tormentors be!
Convey me to my bed, then to my grave.
Love they to live that love and honor have.   138
                   Exit [borne off by his attendants].

KING RICHARD
And let them die that age and sullens have,   139
For both hast thou, and both become the grave.   140

YORK
I do beseech Your Majesty, impute his words
To wayward sickliness and age in him.
He loves you, on my life, and holds you dear
As Harry Duke of Hereford, were he here.

KING RICHARD
Right, you say true. As Hereford's love, so his;   145
As theirs, so mine; and all be as it is.

        [*Enter Northumberland.*]

NORTHUMBERLAND
My liege, old Gaunt commends him to Your Majesty.

KING RICHARD
What says he?

NORTHUMBERLAND   Nay, nothing, all is said.
His tongue is now a stringless instrument;
Words, life, and all, old Lancaster hath spent.

YORK
Be York the next that must be bankrupt so!
Though death be poor, it ends a mortal woe.

KING RICHARD
The ripest fruit first falls, and so doth he;
His time is spent, our pilgrimage must be.   154
So much for that. Now for our Irish wars:
We must supplant those rough rug-headed kerns,   156

135 die . . . thee i.e., may your shame live after you   **138 Love they** let
them desire   **139 sullens** sullenness, melancholy   **140 become** suit
145 Right . . . his (Richard deliberately takes the opposite of what York
had intended to say; Richard jibes that Gaunt is as little fond of the
King as is Hereford.)   **154 our . . . be** i.e., our journey through life is yet
to be completed   **156 supplant** expel (from the English territories of
Ireland).   **rug-headed** shaggy-haired.   **kerns** light-armed Irish foot
soldiers

Which live like venom where no venom else   157
But only they have privilege to live.   158
And, for these great affairs do ask some charge,   159
Towards our assistance we do seize to us
The plate, coin, revenues, and movables   161
Whereof our uncle Gaunt did stand possessed.

YORK
How long shall I be patient? Ah, how long
Shall tender duty make me suffer wrong?
Not Gloucester's death, nor Hereford's banishment,
Not Gaunt's rebukes, nor England's private wrongs,   166
Nor the prevention of poor Bolingbroke   167
About his marriage, nor my own disgrace,   168
Have ever made me sour my patient cheek
Or bend one wrinkle on my sovereign's face.   170
I am the last of noble Edward's sons,
Of whom thy father, Prince of Wales, was first.
In war was never lion raged more fierce,   173
In peace was never gentle lamb more mild,
Than was that young and princely gentleman.
His face thou hast, for even so looked he,
Accomplished with the number of thy hours;   177
But when he frowned, it was against the French
And not against his friends. His noble hand
Did win what he did spend, and spent not that
Which his triumphant father's hand had won.
His hands were guilty of no kindred blood,   182
But bloody with the enemies of his kin.
O Richard! York is too far gone with grief,
Or else he never would compare between.   185

KING RICHARD
Why, uncle, what's the matter?
YORK   O my liege,

157–158 where . . . live (Allusion to the freedom of Ireland from snakes,
traditionally ascribed to Saint Patrick.)   no venom no poisonous
snakes   159 for because.   charge expense   161 movables personal
property   166 Gaunt's rebukes i.e., the rebukes given to Gaunt
167–168 prevention . . . marriage (The chronicles report that Richard
had forestalled Bolingbroke's intended marriage with the Duke de
Berri's daughter.)   170 bend . . . on once frown at   173 was . . . fierce
never was there a lion more fiercely enraged   177 Accomplished . . .
hours i.e., when he was your age   182 kindred blood blood of one's
relatives   185 compare between draw comparisons

Pardon me, if you please; if not, I, pleased
Not to be pardoned, am content withal.   188
Seek you to seize and grip into your hands
The royalties and rights of banished Hereford?   190
Is not Gaunt dead? And doth not Hereford live?
Was not Gaunt just? And is not Harry true?
Did not the one deserve to have an heir?
Is not his heir a well-deserving son?
Take Hereford's rights away, and take from Time   195
His charters and his customary rights;   196
Let not tomorrow then ensue today;   197
Be not thyself; for how art thou a king
But by fair sequence and succession?
Now, afore God—God forbid I say true!—
If you do wrongfully seize Hereford's rights,
Call in the letters patents that he hath   202
By his attorneys general to sue   203
His livery, and deny his offered homage,   204
You pluck a thousand dangers on your head,
You lose a thousand well-disposèd hearts,
And prick my tender patience to those thoughts   207
Which honor and allegiance cannot think.

KING RICHARD
Think what you will, we seize into our hands
His plate, his goods, his money, and his lands.

YORK
I'll not be by the while. My liege, farewell.   211
What will ensue hereof there's none can tell;
But by bad courses may be understood
That their events can never fall out good.   *Exit.* 214

KING RICHARD
Go, Bushy, to the Earl of Wiltshire straight.   215

188 withal with that, nonetheless   **190 royalties** privileges granted
through the King, and belonging in this case to a member of the royal
family   **195 Take . . . and take** i.e., if you take . . . you take   **196 his
customary rights** i.e., the right of due inheritance by an heir, a long-
established custom   **197 ensue** follow   **202–204 Call . . . livery** i.e.,
revoke the royal grant giving him the privilege to sue through his attorneys for possession of his inheritance   **204 deny** refuse.   **homage**
avowal of allegiance (by which ceremony he would be able legally to
secure his inheritance)   **207 prick** i.e., incite   **211 by** nearby, present
214 events outcomes   **215 Earl of Wiltshire** (The King's Lord Treasurer
and one of his notorious favorites.)

Bid him repair to us to Ely House 216
To see this business. Tomorrow next 217
We will for Ireland, and 'tis time, I trow. 218
And we create, in absence of ourself,
Our uncle York Lord Governor of England,
For he is just and always loved us well.
Come on, our queen. Tomorrow must we part.
Be merry, for our time of stay is short. 223

                    [*Flourish.*] *Exeunt King and Queen*
            [*with attendants*]. *Manet Northumberland*
                    [*with Willoughby and Ross*].

NORTHUMBERLAND
Well, lords, the Duke of Lancaster is dead.

ROSS
And living too, for now his son is duke.

WILLOUGHBY
Barely in title, not in revenues.

NORTHUMBERLAND
Richly in both, if justice had her right.

ROSS
My heart is great, but it must break with silence, 228
Ere 't be disburdened with a liberal tongue. 229

NORTHUMBERLAND
Nay, speak thy mind; and let him ne'er speak more
That speaks thy words again to do thee harm!

WILLOUGHBY
Tends that thou wouldst speak to the Duke of Hereford? 232
If it be so, out with it boldly, man.
Quick is mine ear to hear of good towards him.

ROSS
No good at all that I can do for him,
Unless you call it good to pity him,
Bereft and gelded of his patrimony. 237

NORTHUMBERLAND
Now, afore God, 'tis shame such wrongs are borne
In him, a royal prince, and many more
Of noble blood in this declining land.
The King is not himself, but basely led

216 repair go **217 see** see to. **Tomorrow next** tomorrow **218 trow** believe **223 s.d. Manet** remains onstage **228 great** i.e., great with sorrow **229 liberal** unrestrained, freely speaking **232 Tends . . . to** does what you wish to say concern **237 gelded** i.e., deprived. (Literally, castrated.)

By flatterers; and what they will inform   242
Merely in hate 'gainst any of us all,   243
That will the King severely prosecute
'Gainst us, our lives, our children, and our heirs.

ROSS
The commons hath he pilled with grievous taxes,   246
And quite lost their hearts; the nobles hath he fined
For ancient quarrels, and quite lost their hearts.

WILLOUGHBY
And daily new exactions are devised,   249
As blanks, benevolences, and I wot not what.   250
But what i' God's name doth become of this?

NORTHUMBERLAND
Wars hath not wasted it, for warred he hath not,
But basely yielded upon compromise
That which his noble ancestors achieved with blows.
More hath he spent in peace than they in wars.

ROSS
The Earl of Wiltshire hath the realm in farm.   256

WILLOUGHBY
The King's grown bankrupt, like a broken man.   257

NORTHUMBERLAND
Reproach and dissolution hangeth over him.

ROSS
He hath not money for these Irish wars,
His burdenous taxations notwithstanding,
But by the robbing of the banished Duke.

NORTHUMBERLAND
His noble kinsman. Most degenerate king!
But, lords, we hear this fearful tempest sing,
Yet seek no shelter to avoid the storm;
We see the wind sit sore upon our sails,   265
And yet we strike not, but securely perish.   266

ROSS
We see the very wrack that we must suffer,   267

242 inform charge, report as spies   **243 Merely in hate** out of pure
hatred   **246 pilled** peeled, skinned, plundered   **249 exactions** enforced
payments   **250 blanks** blank charters.   **benevolences** forced loans to
the crown (not actually employed until considerably later, in 1473).   **wot**
know   **256 in farm** on lease   **257 broken** financially ruined   **265 sore**
sorely, grievously   **266 strike** (1) furl the sails (2) strike blows.   **securely**
heedlessly, overconfidently   **267 wrack** ruin

And unavoided is the danger now   268
For suffering so the causes of our wrack.   269

NORTHUMBERLAND
Not so. Even through the hollow eyes of death
I spy life peering; but I dare not say
How near the tidings of our comfort is.

WILLOUGHBY
Nay, let us share thy thoughts, as thou dost ours.

ROSS
Be confident to speak, Northumberland.
We three are but thyself, and speaking so
Thy words are but as thoughts. Therefore be bold.

NORTHUMBERLAND
Then thus: I have from Le Port Blanc,
A bay in Brittany, received intelligence
That Harry Duke of Hereford, Rainold Lord Cobham,
. . . . 280
That late broke from the Duke of Exeter,   281
His brother, Archbishop late of Canterbury,   282
Sir Thomas Erpingham, Sir John Ramston,
Sir John Norbery, Sir Robert Waterton, and Francis
   Coint,
All these well furnished by the Duke of Brittany
With eight tall ships, three thousand men of war,   286
Are making hither with all due expedience   287
And shortly mean to touch our northern shore.
Perhaps they had ere this, but that they stay   289
The first departing of the King for Ireland.   290
If then we shall shake off our slavish yoke,
Imp out our drooping country's broken wing,   292

268 **unavoided** unavoidable   269 **suffering** permitting   280 . . . (A line is
probably missing here, perhaps because of censorship. From information contained in Holinshed, it may have read something like "Thomas,
son and heir to the Earl of Arundel" or "The son of Richard, Earl of
Arundel.")   281 **late broke from** lately escaped from the custody of.
(Holinshed records that "the Earl of Arundel's son, named Thomas,
which was kept in the Duke of Exeter's house, escaped out of the realm
. . . and went to his uncle Thomas Arundel, late Archbishop of Canterbury.")   282 **His** i.e., the Earl of Arundel's.   **late** until recently
286 **tall** stately.   **men of war** troops   287 **expedience** expedition,
speed   289–290 **stay . . . King** wait until the King departs   292 **Imp out**
piece out. (A term from falconry meaning to attach new feathers to a
disabled wing of a bird.)

Redeem from broking pawn the blemished crown,   293
Wipe off the dust that hides our scepter's gilt,   294
And make high majesty look like itself,
Away with me in post to Ravenspurgh;   296
But if you faint, as fearing to do so,   297
Stay and be secret, and myself will go.
ROSS
To horse, to horse! Urge doubts to them that fear.
WILLOUGHBY
Hold out my horse, and I will first be there.   *Exeunt.* 300

❖

2.2   *Enter the Queen, Bushy, [and] Bagot.*

BUSHY
Madam, Your Majesty is too much sad.
You promised, when you parted with the King,   2
To lay aside life-harming heaviness   3
And entertain a cheerful disposition.   4
QUEEN
To please the King I did; to please myself
I cannot do it. Yet I know no cause
Why I should welcome such a guest as grief,
Save bidding farewell to so sweet a guest
As my sweet Richard. Yet again methinks
Some unborn sorrow ripe in Fortune's womb
Is coming towards me, and my inward soul
With nothing trembles. At some thing it grieves
More than with parting from my lord the King.
BUSHY
Each substance of a grief hath twenty shadows,   14
Which shows like grief itself but is not so;
For sorrow's eyes, glazèd with blinding tears,

293 **broking pawn** the security held by a pawnbroker   294 **gilt** gold
(with pun on *guilt*)   296 **post** haste.   **Ravenspurgh** a busy seaport in
Yorkshire on the Humber River, destroyed since by the sea   297 **faint**
are fainthearted   300 **Hold ... and** if my horse holds out

2.2. **Location: The court. According to Holinshed, the Queen remained
at Windsor Castle when Richard left for Ireland.**
2 **with** from   3 **heaviness** melancholy   4 **entertain** put on   14 **Each ...
shadows** i.e., for every real grief there exist twenty imagined ones

Divides one thing entire to many objects,   17
Like perspectives, which rightly gazed upon   18
Show nothing but confusion, eyed awry   19
Distinguish form. So your sweet Majesty,   20
Looking awry upon your lord's departure,   21
Find shapes of grief more than himself to wail,   22
Which, looked on as it is, is naught but shadows
Of what it is not. Then, thrice-gracious Queen,
More than your lord's departure weep not. More is not
   seen,
Or if it be, 'tis with false sorrow's eye,
Which for things true weeps things imaginary.   27

QUEEN
It may be so, but yet my inward soul
Persuades me it is otherwise. Howe'er it be,
I cannot but be sad—so heavy sad
As, though on thinking on no thought I think,   31
Makes me with heavy nothing faint and shrink.   32

BUSHY
'Tis nothing but conceit, my gracious lady.   33

QUEEN
'Tis nothing less. Conceit is still derived   34
From some forefather grief. Mine is not so,
For nothing hath begot my something grief,   36
Or something hath the nothing that I grieve.   37
'Tis in reversion that I do possess;   38
But what it is, that is not yet known what,   39
I cannot name. 'Tis nameless woe, I wot.   40

   [*Enter Green.*]

17 thing entire to complete thing into   **18 perspectives** (In ll. 16–17,
Bushy seems to have in mind a glass with a multifaceted lens, multiply-
ing images of the object being viewed; in ll. 18–20, *perspectives* are
pictures of figures made to appear distorted or confused except when
viewed obliquely, *eyed awry*.)   **rightly** directly, straight   **19 awry**
obliquely   **20 Distinguish form** make the form distinct and normal
21 awry i.e., mistakenly, distortedly   **22 himself** i.e., the grief itself
27 for in place of   **31–32 As . . . shrink** that, though I seem to be thinking of nothing, my "nothing" is so *heavy* or saddening that I faint and
fall back under the weight   **33 conceit** fancy   **34 'Tis nothing less** i.e.,
it is anything but that.   **still** always   **36 something** i.e., substantial
37 something . . . grieve the unsubstantial grief, the nothing, that I
grieve about has something to it, some substance   **38–40 'Tis . . . name**
i.e., my grief is like a legacy that will come to me at some future time,
but I cannot tell its nature yet   **40 wot** know, assume

GREEN
  God save Your Majesty! And well met, gentlemen.
  I hope the King is not yet shipped for Ireland.
QUEEN
  Why hopest thou so? 'Tis better hope he is,
  For his designs crave haste, his haste good hope.
  Then wherefore dost thou hope he is not shipped?
GREEN
  That he, our hope, might have retired his power,   46
  And driven into despair an enemy's hope,
  Who strongly hath set footing in this land.
  The banished Bolingbroke repeals himself   49
  And with uplifted arms is safe arrived   50
  At Ravenspurgh.
QUEEN   Now God in heaven forbid!
GREEN
  Ah, madam, 'tis too true; and that is worse,   52
  The lord Northumberland, his son young Harry Percy,
  The lords of Ross, Beaumont, and Willoughby,
  With all their powerful friends, are fled to him.
BUSHY
  Why have you not proclaimed Northumberland
  And all the rest revolted faction traitors?   57
GREEN
  We have, whereupon the Earl of Worcester
  Hath broken his staff, resigned his stewardship,   59
  And all the household servants fled with him
  To Bolingbroke.
QUEEN
  So, Green, thou art the midwife to my woe,
  And Bolingbroke my sorrow's dismal heir.   63
  Now hath my soul brought forth her prodigy,   64
  And I, a gasping new-delivered mother,
  Have woe to woe, sorrow to sorrow joined.
BUSHY
  Despair not, madam.
QUEEN   Who shall hinder me?

46 retired drawn back.   **power** army   **49 repeals** recalls (from exile)
50 uplifted arms brandished weapons   **52 that** what   **57 rest** rest of the
59 broken his staff broken his badge of office (in token of resignation as
Lord High Steward. Worcester is brother of the Earl of Northumberland.)
63 dismal heir ill-omened offspring   **64 prodigy** monstrous birth

I will despair, and be at enmity
With cozening hope. He is a flatterer,   69
A parasite, a keeper-back of death
Who gently would dissolve the bonds of life   71
Which false hope lingers in extremity.   72

    [Enter York.]

GREEN   Here comes the Duke of York.

QUEEN
With signs of war about his agèd neck.   74
O, full of careful business are his looks!   75
Uncle, for God's sake, speak comfortable words.   76

YORK
Should I do so, I should belie my thoughts.
Comfort's in heaven, and we are on the earth,
Where nothing lives but crosses, cares, and grief.   79
Your husband, he is gone to save far off,   80
Whilst others come to make him lose at home.
Here am I left to underprop his land,   82
Who, weak with age, cannot support myself.
Now comes the sick hour that his surfeit made;
Now shall he try his friends that flattered him.   85

    [Enter a Servingman.]

SERVINGMAN
My lord, your son was gone before I came.   86

YORK
He was? Why, so. Go all which way it will!
The nobles they are fled, the commons they are cold,
And will, I fear, revolt on Hereford's side.
Sirrah, get thee to Pleshey, to my sister Gloucester;   90
Bid her send me presently a thousand pound.   91
Hold, take my ring.

SERVINGMAN
My lord, I had forgot to tell your lordship:

69 cozening cheating. **He** i.e., false hope   **71 Who** i.e., death
72 lingers causes to linger   **74 signs of war** i.e., a piece of armor called
the gorget, an iron collar that could be worn with ordinary clothes
75 careful business worried preoccupation   **76 comfortable** affording
comfort   **79 crosses** obstacles, obstructions   **80 save far off** i.e., defend
his rule in Ireland   **82 underprop** prop up, support   **85 try** test
86 your son i.e., the Duke of Aumerle   **90 sister** i.e., sister-in-law
91 presently immediately

Today, as I came by, I callèd there—
But I shall grieve you to report the rest.
YORK   What is 't, knave?   96
SERVINGMAN
An hour before I came, the Duchess died.
YORK
God for his mercy, what a tide of woes
Comes rushing on this woeful land at once!
I know not what to do. I would to God,
So my untruth had not provoked him to it,   101
The King had cut off my head with my brother's.   102
What, are there no posts dispatched for Ireland?
How shall we do for money for these wars?
Come, sister—cousin, I would say—pray pardon me.
Go, fellow, get thee home, provide some carts
And bring away the armor that is there.
                              [*Exit Servingman.*]
Gentlemen, will you go muster men?   108
If I know how or which way to order these affairs
Thus disorderly thrust into my hands,
Never believe me. Both are my kinsmen:
Th' one is my sovereign, whom both my oath
And duty bids defend; t'other again
Is my kinsman, whom the King hath wronged,
Whom conscience and my kindred bids to right.   115
Well, somewhat we must do. Come, cousin,   116
I'll dispose of you. Gentlemen,   117
Go muster up your men, and meet me presently
At Berkeley. I should to Pleshey too,   119
But time will not permit. All is uneven,
And everything is left at six and seven.   121
                  Exeunt Duke [*of York*], *Queen. Manent*
                         Bushy, [*Bagot,*] *Green.*
BUSHY
The wind sits fair for news to go for Ireland,
But none returns. For us to levy power

96 knave i.e., fellow   **101 So** providing that.   **untruth** disloyalty
102 brother's i.e., the Duke of Gloucester's   **108 muster** assemble
115 my . . . right my kinship to him bids me right his wrong
116 somewhat something   **117 dispose of** make arrangements for
119 Berkeley a castle near Bristol   **121 at six and seven** i.e., in
confusion   **s.d. Manent** they remain onstage

Proportionable to the enemy
Is all unpossible.

GREEN

Besides, our nearness to the King in love
Is near the hate of those love not the King.   127

BAGOT

And that is the wavering commons, for their love
Lies in their purses, and whoso empties them
By so much fills their hearts with deadly hate.

BUSHY

Wherein the King stands generally condemned.   131

BAGOT

If judgment lie in them, then so do we,   132
Because we ever have been near the King.   133

GREEN

Well, I will for refuge straight to Bristol Castle.
The Earl of Wiltshire is already there.

BUSHY

Thither will I with you, for little office   136
Will the hateful commons perform for us,   137
Except like curs to tear us all to pieces.
Will you go along with us?

BAGOT

No, I will to Ireland to His Majesty.
Farewell. If heart's presages be not vain,
We three here part that ne'er shall meet again.

BUSHY

That's as York thrives to beat back Bolingbroke.   143

GREEN

Alas, poor duke! The task he undertakes
Is numbering sands and drinking oceans dry.
Where one on his side fights, thousands will fly.
Farewell at once, for once, for all, and ever.

BUSHY

Well, we may meet again.

BAGOT   I fear me, never.

[Exeunt.]

---

127 those love those who love   **131 Wherein** on which account   **132 If
... we** i.e., if the power to pass judgment is given to the wavering
commons, then we too stand condemned   **133 ever** always   **136 office**
service   **137 hateful** full of hate, angry   **143 That's ... thrives** i.e., that
depends upon York's efforts and success

2.3   *Enter [Bolingbroke, Duke of] Hereford, [and]*
           Northumberland [with forces].

BOLINGBROKE
  How far is it, my lord, to Berkeley now?
NORTHUMBERLAND   Believe me, noble lord,
  I am a stranger here in Gloucestershire.
  These high wild hills and rough uneven ways
  Draws out our miles and makes them wearisome;
  And yet your fair discourse hath been as sugar,
  Making the hard way sweet and delectable.
  But I bethink me what a weary way
  From Ravenspurgh to Cotswold will be found   9
  In Ross and Willoughby, wanting your company,   10
  Which, I protest, hath very much beguiled
  The tediousness and process of my travel.   12
  But theirs is sweetened with the hope to have
  The present benefit which I possess;
  And hope to joy is little less in joy
  Than hope enjoyed. By this the weary lords   16
  Shall make their way seem short, as mine hath done
  By sight of what I have, your noble company.
BOLINGBROKE
  Of much less value is my company
  Than your good words. But who comes here?

       Enter Harry Percy.

NORTHUMBERLAND
  It is my son, young Harry Percy,
  Sent from my brother Worcester whencesoever.   22
  Harry, how fares your uncle?   23
PERCY
  I had thought, my lord, to have learned his health of you.
NORTHUMBERLAND   Why, is he not with the Queen?
PERCY
  No, my good lord. He hath forsook the court,

2.3. Location: In Gloucestershire, near Berkeley Castle.
9 Cotswold hilly district in Gloucestershire   **10 In** by.   **wanting** lacking   **12 tediousness and process** tedious process   **16 this** this expectation   **22 whencesoever** from wherever he is   **23 your uncle** i.e., the Earl
of Worcester

Broken his staff of office, and dispersed
The household of the King.

NORTHUMBERLAND   What was his reason?
He was not so resolved when last we spake together.

PERCY
Because your lordship was proclaimèd traitor.
But he, my lord, is gone to Ravenspurgh
To offer service to the Duke of Hereford,
And sent me over by Berkeley to discover
What power the Duke of York had levied there,
Then with directions to repair to Ravenspurgh.   35

NORTHUMBERLAND
Have you forgot the Duke of Hereford, boy?   36

PERCY
No, my good lord, for that is not forgot
Which ne'er I did remember. To my knowledge
I never in my life did look on him.

NORTHUMBERLAND
Then learn to know him now. This is the Duke.

PERCY
My gracious lord, I tender you my service,   41
Such as it is, being tender, raw, and young,
Which elder days shall ripen and confirm
To more approvèd service and desert.   44

BOLINGBROKE
I thank thee, gentle Percy, and be sure
I count myself in nothing else so happy
As in a soul remembering my good friends;
And as my fortune ripens with thy love,
It shall be still thy true love's recompense.   49
My heart this covenant makes, my hand thus seals it.
                        [*He offers Percy his hand.*]

NORTHUMBERLAND
How far is it to Berkeley? And what stir   51
Keeps good old York there with his men of war?

PERCY
There stands the castle by yon tuft of trees,

35 **directions** instructions. **repair** go   36 **boy** (A rebuke for not respectfully greeting Bolingbroke, though historically Percy was two years
Bolingbroke's senior.)   41 **my service** (Presumably Percy kneels to
Bolingbroke, and so do Ross and Willoughby when they enter.)
44 **approved** proven, demonstrated   49 **still** always   51 **stir** action

Manned with three hundred men, as I have heard,
And in it are the lords of York, Berkeley, and Seymour,
None else of name and noble estimate.   56

[*Enter Ross and Willoughby.*]

NORTHUMBERLAND
Here come the lords of Ross and Willoughby,
Bloody with spurring, fiery red with haste.   58

BOLINGBROKE
Welcome, my lords. I wot your love pursues   59
A banished traitor. All my treasury
Is yet but unfelt thanks, which, more enriched,   61
Shall be your love and labor's recompense.

ROSS
Your presence makes us rich, most noble lord.

WILLOUGHBY
And far surmounts our labor to attain it.

BOLINGBROKE
Evermore thank's the exchequer of the poor,   65
Which, till my infant fortune comes to years,   66
Stands for my bounty. But who comes here?   67

[*Enter Berkeley.*]

NORTHUMBERLAND
It is my lord of Berkeley, as I guess.

BERKELEY
My lord of Hereford, my message is to you.

BOLINGBROKE
My lord, my answer is—to "Lancaster";   70
And I am come to seek that name in England,
And I must find that title in your tongue
Before I make reply to aught you say.

BERKELEY
Mistake me not, my lord, 'tis not my meaning

56 estimate rank   **58 spurring** i.e., hard riding   **59 wot** know   **61 unfelt**
impalpable, expressed in words, not gifts.   **more enriched** i.e., with still
more thanks added; or, with substantial gifts at a later date   **65 Evermore . . . poor** "thank you" is always the exchequer of the poor, i.e., the
only means they have to repay favors   **66 comes to years** reaches
maturity   **67 Stands for** serves in place of   **70 "Lancaster"** (Bolingbroke will enter into no negotiations unless his proper title is given
him, the title taken away by Richard.)

To rase one title of your honor out.   75
To you, my lord, I come, what lord you will,
From the most gracious regent of this land,
The Duke of York, to know what pricks you on   78
To take advantage of the absent time   79
And fright our native peace with self-borne arms.   80

    [*Enter York.*]

BOLINGBROKE
I shall not need transport my words by you;
Here comes His Grace in person. My noble uncle!
                          [*He kneels.*]
YORK
Show me thy humble heart, and not thy knee,
Whose duty is deceivable and false.   84
BOLINGBROKE   My gracious uncle—
YORK   Tut, tut!
Grace me no grace, nor uncle me no uncle.
I am no traitor's uncle; and that word "grace"
In an ungracious mouth is but profane.
Why have those banished and forbidden legs
Dared once to touch a dust of England's ground?   91
But then more "why?" Why have they dared to march
So many miles upon her peaceful bosom,
Frighting her pale-faced villages with war
And ostentation of despisèd arms?   95
Com'st thou because the anointed King is hence?
Why, foolish boy, the King is left behind,
And in my loyal bosom lies his power.
Were I but now the lord of such hot youth
As when brave Gaunt, thy father, and myself
Rescued the Black Prince, that young Mars of men,   101
From forth the ranks of many thousand French,
O, then how quickly should this arm of mine,
Now prisoner to the palsy, chastise thee
And minister correction to thy fault!

---

75 rase erase (or perhaps *raze*, scrape)   **78 pricks you on** incites you
79 the absent time i.e., the time of the King's absence   **80 self-borne**
i.e., borne for oneself, not for the King (also *self-born*, originating in the
self)   **84 deceivable** deceitful, deceptive   **91 dust** particle of dust
95 ostentation display.   **despisèd** despicable   **101 the Black Prince** i.e.,
Edward, the eldest son of Edward III and King Richard's father

BOLINGBROKE
My gracious uncle, let me know my fault.
On what condition stands it and wherein?   107
YORK
Even in condition of the worst degree,
In gross rebellion and detested treason.
Thou art a banished man, and here art come
Before the expiration of thy time
In braving arms against thy sovereign.   112
BOLINGBROKE
As I was banished, I was banished Hereford;
But as I come, I come for Lancaster.   114
And, noble uncle, I beseech Your Grace
Look on my wrongs with an indifferent eye.   116
You are my father, for methinks in you
I see old Gaunt alive. O, then, my father,
Will you permit that I shall stand condemned   119
A wandering vagabond, my rights and royalties   120
Plucked from my arms perforce and given away
To upstart unthrifts? Wherefore was I born?   122
If that my cousin king be King of England,
It must be granted I am Duke of Lancaster.
You have a son, Aumerle, my noble cousin;
Had you first died, and he been thus trod down,   126
He should have found his uncle Gaunt a father
To rouse his wrongs and chase them to the bay.   128
I am denied to sue my livery here,   129
And yet my letters patents give me leave.   130
My father's goods are all distrained and sold,   131
And these, and all, are all amiss employed.
What would you have me do? I am a subject,
And I challenge law. Attorneys are denied me,   134

107 condition i.e., defect in me.   **wherein** in what does it consist
112 braving defiant (also in l. 143)   **114 for Lancaster** i.e., under the
title of Lancaster, and in order to claim it   **116 indifferent** impartial
119 condemned condemned as   **120 royalties** privileges granted by the
King   **122 unthrifts** spendthrifts   **126 first** i.e., before Gaunt
128 rouse chase from cover, expose.   **the bay** the extremity where the
hunted animal turns on its pursuers   **129 denied** denied the right.   **sue
my livery** sue for possession of hereditary rights. (See 2.1.202–204 and
note.)   **130 letters patents** i.e., letters from the King indicating
Bolingbroke's legal rights   **131 distrained** seized by legal process
134 challenge law claim my legal rights

And therefore personally I lay my claim
To my inheritance of free descent.   136

NORTHUMBERLAND
The noble Duke hath been too much abused.

ROSS
It stands Your Grace upon to do him right.   138

WILLOUGHBY
Base men by his endowments are made great.   139

YORK
My lords of England, let me tell you this:
I have had feeling of my cousin's wrongs
And labored all I could to do him right;
But in this kind to come, in braving arms,   143
Be his own carver, and cut out his way   144
To find out right with wrong—it may not be;
And you that do abet him in this kind
Cherish rebellion and are rebels all.

NORTHUMBERLAND
The noble Duke hath sworn his coming is
But for his own, and for the right of that
We all have strongly sworn to give him aid;
And let him never see joy that breaks that oath!

YORK
Well, well, I see the issue of these arms.   152
I cannot mend it, I must needs confess,
Because my power is weak and all ill-left;   154
But if I could, by Him that gave me life,
I would attach you all and make you stoop   156
Unto the sovereign mercy of the King.
But since I cannot, be it known unto you
I do remain as neuter. So fare you well—   159
Unless you please to enter in the castle
And there repose you for this night.

BOLINGBROKE
An offer, uncle, that we will accept;
But we must win Your Grace to go with us   163

136 of free descent by legal succession   **138 stands . . . upon** is incumbent upon Your Grace   **139 his endowments** i.e., his properties that they have seized   **143 kind** fashion   **144 Be . . . carver** i.e., act on his own authority   **152 issue** outcome   **154 power** army.   **ill-left** left with inadequate means   **156 attach** arrest   **159 as neuter** neutral   **163 win** persuade

To Bristol Castle, which they say is held
By Bushy, Bagot, and their complices,   165
The caterpillars of the commonwealth,
Which I have sworn to weed and pluck away.

YORK
It may be I will go with you; but yet I'll pause,
For I am loath to break our country's laws.
Nor friends nor foes, to me welcome you are.   170
Things past redress are now with me past care.
                                          Exeunt.

❖

2.4   *Enter Earl of Salisbury and a Welsh Captain.*

WELSH CAPTAIN
My lord of Salisbury, we have stayed ten days   1
And hardly kept our countrymen together,   2
And yet we hear no tidings from the King.   3
Therefore we will disperse ourselves. Farewell.

SALISBURY
Stay yet another day, thou trusty Welshman.
The King reposeth all his confidence in thee.

WELSH CAPTAIN
'Tis thought the King is dead. We will not stay.
The bay trees in our country are all withered,
And meteors fright the fixèd stars of heaven;
The pale-faced moon looks bloody on the earth,
And lean-looked prophets whisper fearful change;   11
Rich men look sad, and ruffians dance and leap,
The one in fear to lose what they enjoy,
The other to enjoy by rage and war.   14
These signs forerun the death or fall of kings.   15
Farewell. Our countrymen are gone and fled,
As well assured Richard their king is dead.   [*Exit.*] 17

---

165 Bagot (According to 2.2.140, Bagot had gone to Ireland.)   **170 Nor**
neither as

2.4. Location: A camp in Wales.
1 stayed waited   **2 hardly** with difficulty   **3 yet** still   **11 lean-looked**
lean-looking   **14 to . . . rage** in hopes of enjoying by violence
15 forerun anticipate   **17 As** as being

SALISBURY
    Ah, Richard! With the eyes of heavy mind
    I see thy glory like a shooting star
    Fall to the base earth from the firmament.
    Thy sun sets weeping in the lowly west,
    Witnessing storms to come, woe, and unrest.   22
    Thy friends are fled to wait upon thy foes,   23
    And crossly to thy good all fortune goes.   [*Exit.*] 24

22 Witnessing betokening   **23 wait upon** attend, offer allegiance to
24 crossly adversely

3.1   *Enter [Bolingbroke,] Duke of Hereford, York,*
Northumberland, [with] Bushy and Green,
prisoners.

BOLINGBROKE   Bring forth these men.
Bushy and Green, I will not vex your souls—
Since presently your souls must part your bodies—   3
With too much urging your pernicious lives,   4
For 'twere no charity; yet, to wash your blood
From off my hands, here in the view of men
I will unfold some causes of your deaths.
You have misled a prince, a royal king,
A happy gentleman in blood and lineaments,   9
By you unhappied and disfigured clean.   10
You have in manner with your sinful hours   11
Made a divorce betwixt his queen and him,
Broke the possession of a royal bed,
And stained the beauty of a fair queen's cheeks
With tears drawn from her eyes by your foul wrongs.
Myself, a prince by fortune of my birth,
Near to the King in blood, and near in love
Till you did make him misinterpret me,
Have stooped my neck under your injuries
And sighed my English breath in foreign clouds,   20
Eating the bitter bread of banishment,
Whilst you have fed upon my signories,   22
Disparked my parks and felled my forest woods,   23
From my own windows torn my household coat,   24
Razed out my imprese, leaving me no sign,   25
Save men's opinions and my living blood,
To show the world I am a gentleman.
This and much more, much more than twice all this,

3.1. Location: Bristol. The castle.
3 presently immediately   **4 urging** emphasizing as reasons (for your
executions)   **9 happy** fortunate.   **blood and lineaments** birth and
natural characteristics   **10 unhappied** made wretched, ruined. **clean**
completely   **11 in manner** as it were   **20 foreign clouds** i.e., the air of
foreign lands (and adding to the clouds with his sighs)   **22 signories**
estates   **23 Disparked** thrown open to uses other than hunting and
forestry   **24 household coat** coat of arms (frequently emblazoned on
stained or painted windows)   **25 Razed** scraped (or perhaps *rased,*
erased).   **imprese** heraldic device, emblematic design

Condemns you to the death.—See them delivered over
To execution and the hand of death.
BUSHY
More welcome is the stroke of death to me
Than Bolingbroke to England. Lords, farewell.
GREEN
My comfort is that heaven will take our souls
And plague injustice with the pains of hell.
BOLINGBROKE
My lord Northumberland, see them dispatched.
      [*Exeunt Northumberland with the prisoners.*]
Uncle, you say the Queen is at your house.
For God's sake, fairly let her be entreated.   37
Tell her I send to her my kind commends;   38
Take special care my greetings be delivered.
YORK
A gentleman of mine I have dispatched
With letters of your love to her at large.   41
BOLINGBROKE
Thanks, gentle uncle. Come, lords, away,
To fight with Glendower and his complices.   43
Awhile to work, and after holiday.   *Exeunt.* 44

❖

3.2   [*Drums. Flourish and colors.*] *Enter the King,*
Aumerle, [*the Bishop of*] *Carlisle, etc.* [*with*
soldiers].

KING RICHARD
Barkloughly Castle call they this at hand?   1
AUMERLE
Yea, my lord. How brooks Your Grace the air   2
After your late tossing on the breaking seas?   3

---

37 entreated treated   **38 commends** regards, commendations   **41 at
large** conveyed in full   **43 Glendower** (Owen Glendower was not, according to Holinshed's *Chronicles*, at this time in arms against Bolingbroke. Possibly he is to be identified here with the Welsh captain of
the preceding scene.)   **44 after** afterwards

3.2. Location: The coast of Wales, near Barkloughly Castle.
1 Barkloughly i.e., Harlech   **2 brooks** enjoys   **3 late** recent

KING RICHARD
Needs must I like it well. I weep for joy   4
To stand upon my kingdom once again.
Dear earth, I do salute thee with my hand,
          [*He bends and touches the ground*]
Though rebels wound thee with their horses' hoofs.
As a long-parted mother with her child   8
Plays fondly with her tears and smiles in meeting,
So, weeping, smiling, greet I thee, my earth,
And do thee favors with my royal hands.
Feed not thy sovereign's foe, my gentle earth,
Nor with thy sweets comfort his ravenous sense,   13
But let thy spiders, that suck up thy venom,   14
And heavy-gaited toads lie in their way,
Doing annoyance to the treacherous feet
Which with usurping steps do trample thee.
Yield stinging nettles to mine enemies;
And when they from thy bosom pluck a flower,
Guard it, I pray thee, with a lurking adder   20
Whose double tongue may with a mortal touch   21
Throw death upon thy sovereign's enemies.
Mock not my senseless conjuration, lords.   23
This earth shall have a feeling, and these stones
Prove armèd soldiers, ere her native king   25
Shall falter under foul rebellion's arms.
CARLISLE
Fear not, my lord. That Power that made you king
Hath power to keep you king in spite of all.
The means that heavens yield must be embraced
And not neglected; else heaven would,   30
And we will not. Heaven's offer we refuse,   31
The proffered means of succor and redress.   32
AUMERLE
He means, my lord, that we are too remiss,

---

4 Needs must necessarily   **8 a long-parted mother with** a mother long
parted from   **13 sweets** i.e., bounty.   **sense** appetite   **14 suck . . . venom**
(Alludes to the belief that spiders drew their poison from the earth.)
20 Guard (1) watch over (2) trim, decorate with braid   **21 double** forked.
mortal deadly   **23 senseless conjuration** solemn entreaty of senseless
things   **25 native** entitled (to the crown) by birth, rightful. (Richard was
born at Bordeaux.)   **30–31 else . . . not** i.e., otherwise we spurn heaven's
will   **32 succor and redress** help and remedy

Whilst Bolingbroke through our security   34
Grows strong and great in substance and in power.
KING RICHARD
Discomfortable cousin, know'st thou not   36
That when the searching eye of heaven is hid
Behind the globe, that lights the lower world,   38
Then thieves and robbers range abroad unseen
In murders and in outrage boldly here;
But when from under this terrestrial ball
He fires the proud tops of the eastern pines   42
And darts his light through every guilty hole,
Then murders, treasons, and detested sins,
The cloak of night being plucked from off their backs,
Stand bare and naked, trembling at themselves?
So when this thief, this traitor, Bolingbroke,
Who all this while hath reveled in the night
Whilst we were wand'ring with the Antipodes,   49
Shall see us rising in our throne, the east,
His treasons will sit blushing in his face,
Not able to endure the sight of day,
But self-affrighted tremble at his sin.
Not all the water in the rough rude sea
Can wash the balm off from an anointed king;   55
The breath of worldly men cannot depose   56
The deputy elected by the Lord.
For every man that Bolingbroke hath pressed   58
To lift shrewd steel against our golden crown,   59
God for his Richard hath in heavenly pay
A glorious angel. Then, if angels fight,
Weak men must fall, for heaven still guards the right. 62

Enter Salisbury.

Welcome, my lord. How far off lies your power?
SALISBURY
Nor near nor farther off, my gracious lord,   64

34 security overconfidence **36 Discomfortable** uncomforting, discour-
aging **38 globe** earth. **that** i.e., the *eye of heaven*, the sun **42 fires**
i.e., lights up. (Literally, "sets on fire.") **49 Antipodes** people on the
other side of the world; here, the Irish **55 balm** consecrated oil used in
anointing a king **56 worldly** earthly **58 pressed** impressed, forced into
the ranks **59 shrewd** keen, biting **62 still** always **64 Nor near** neither
nearer

Than this weak arm. Discomfort guides my tongue   65
And bids me speak of nothing but despair.
One day too late, I fear me, noble lord,
Hath clouded all thy happy days on earth.
O, call back yesterday, bid time return,
And thou shalt have twelve thousand fighting men!
Today, today, unhappy day too late,
O'erthrows thy joys, friends, fortune, and thy state;   72
For all the Welshmen, hearing thou wert dead,
Are gone to Bolingbroke, dispersed, and fled.

AUMERLE
Comfort, my liege. Why looks Your Grace so pale?

KING RICHARD
But now the blood of twenty thousand men   76
   Did triumph in my face, and they are fled;   77
And till so much blood thither come again,
   Have I not reason to look pale and dead?   79
All souls that will be safe, fly from my side,
For time hath set a blot upon my pride.

AUMERLE
Comfort, my liege. Remember who you are.

KING RICHARD
I had forgot myself. Am I not king?
Awake, thou coward majesty, thou sleepest!
Is not the king's name twenty thousand names?
Arm, arm, my name! A puny subject strikes
At thy great glory. Look not to the ground,
Ye favorites of a king. Are we not high?
High be our thoughts. I know my uncle York
Hath power enough to serve our turn. But who comes
   here?

      Enter Scroop.

SCROOP
More health and happiness betide my liege   91
Than can my care-tuned tongue deliver him!   92

---

65 Discomfort discouragement **72 state** royal power **76 But now** even
now. **twenty** (A seeming discrepancy with *twelve* in l. 70; perhaps the
result of Richard's hyperbole.) **77 triumph** i.e., shine forth **79 pale
and dead** deathly pale **91 More . . . betide** may more health and happiness befall **92 care-tuned** i.e., tuned by care. **deliver** deliver to

KING RICHARD
Mine ear is open and my heart prepared.
The worst is worldly loss thou canst unfold.
Say, is my kingdom lost? Why, 'twas my care,   95
And what loss is it to be rid of care?
Strives Bolingbroke to be as great as we?
Greater he shall not be; if he serve God,
We'll serve Him too, and be his fellow so.   99
Revolt our subjects? That we cannot mend;
They break their faith to God as well as us.
Cry woe, destruction, ruin, and decay;
The worst is death, and death will have his day.
SCROOP
Glad am I that Your Highness is so armed   104
To bear the tidings of calamity.
Like an unseasonable stormy day,
Which makes the silver rivers drown their shores
As if the world were all dissolved to tears,
So high above his limits swells the rage   109
Of Bolingbroke, covering your fearful land   110
With hard bright steel and hearts harder than steel.
Whitebeards have armed their thin and hairless scalps   112
Against Thy Majesty; boys with women's voices
Strive to speak big, and clap their female joints   114
In stiff unwieldy arms against thy crown.   115
Thy very beadsmen learn to bend their bows   116
Of double-fatal yew against thy state;   117
Yea, distaff-women manage rusty bills   118
Against thy seat. Both young and old rebel,   119
And all goes worse than I have power to tell.
KING RICHARD
Too well, too well thou tell'st a tale so ill.

95 care trouble   99 his fellow his (Bolingbroke's) equal   104 armed
prepared   109 his limits its banks   110 fearful full of fears
112 Whitebeards i.e., old men.   thin sparsely haired   114 clap thrust.
female i.e., weak and delicate   115 arms armor   116 beadsmen old
almsmen or pensioners whose duty it was to pray for a benefactor;
here, for the king   117 double-fatal doubly fatal (since the wood of the
yew was used for bows and since its foliage and berries are poisonous)   118–119 distaff-women . . . seat spinning-women wield rusty pikes
(long-handled axes) against your throne

Where is the Earl of Wiltshire? Where is Bagot?   122
What is become of Bushy? Where is Green,
That they have let the dangerous enemy
Measure our confines with such peaceful steps?   125
If we prevail, their heads shall pay for it.
I warrant they have made peace with Bolingbroke.
SCROOP
Peace have they made with him indeed, my lord.
KING RICHARD
O villains, vipers, damned without redemption!
Dogs easily won to fawn on any man!
Snakes in my heart-blood warmed, that sting my heart!
Three Judases, each one thrice worse than Judas!
Would they make peace? Terrible hell
Make war upon their spotted souls for this!   134
SCROOP
Sweet love, I see, changing his property,   135
Turns to the sourest and most deadly hate.
Again uncurse their souls. Their peace is made
With heads and not with hands. Those whom you curse
Have felt the worst of death's destroying wound
And lie full low, graved in the hollow ground.   140
AUMERLE
Is Bushy, Green, and the Earl of Wiltshire dead?
SCROOP
Ay, all of them at Bristol lost their heads.
AUMERLE
Where is the Duke my father with his power?
KING RICHARD
No matter where. Of comfort no man speak!
Let's talk of graves, of worms, and epitaphs,
Make dust our paper, and with rainy eyes
Write sorrow on the bosom of the earth.
Let's choose executors and talk of wills.
And yet not so, for what can we bequeath

122 Bagot (Although the King names Bagot here, he mentions only *three Judases* in l. 132 and Aumerle does not ask about Bagot in l. 141; in 3.4 we learn that Bagot is not executed along with the other three but reappears instead in 4.1.)   **125 Measure our confines** travel over my kingdom.   **peaceful** unopposed   **134 spotted** stained with treason
135 his property its distinctive quality   **140 graved** buried

Save our deposèd bodies to the ground?   150
Our lands, our lives, and all are Bolingbroke's,
And nothing can we call our own but death
And that small model of the barren earth   153
Which serves as paste and cover to our bones.   154
For God's sake, let us sit upon the ground
And tell sad stories of the death of kings!
How some have been deposed, some slain in war,
Some haunted by the ghosts they have deposed,   158
Some poisoned by their wives, some sleeping killed—
All murdered; for within the hollow crown
That rounds the mortal temples of a king   161
Keeps Death his court, and there the antic sits,   162
Scoffing his state and grinning at his pomp,   163
Allowing him a breath, a little scene,   164
To monarchize, be feared, and kill with looks,   165
Infusing him with self and vain conceit,   166
As if this flesh which walls about our life
Were brass impregnable; and humored thus,   168
Comes at the last and with a little pin
Bores through his castle wall, and—farewell, king!
Cover your heads, and mock not flesh and blood   171
With solemn reverence. Throw away respect,
Tradition, form, and ceremonious duty,
For you have but mistook me all this while.
I live with bread like you, feel want,
Taste grief, need friends. Subjected thus,   176
How can you say to me I am a king?
CARLISLE
My lord, wise men ne'er sit and wail their woes,

150 **deposèd** (1) dethroned, as in 4.1 (2) deprived of those functions
carried out by the body in this transitory life (3) deposited   **153 model**
mold, i.e., the body   **154 paste** pastry, pie crust   **158 ghosts** i.e., ghosts
of kings   **161 rounds** circles   **162 antic** grotesque figure, jester
163 Scoffing his state scoffing at the king's regality.   **pomp** ceremony,
splendor   **164 breath** breathing space, moment   **165 monarchize** play
the monarch.   **kill with looks** i.e., order someone's death with a mere
glance   **166 self and vain conceit** vain conceit of himself   **168 humored
thus** having satisfied his humor or whim (referring to Death); or, having
thus indulged the king, having led him on in this humor   **171 Cover
your heads** replace your hats (which have been removed out of respect
for the king)   **176 Subjected** made subject to grief, want, etc. (with pun
on "being treated like a subject")

But presently prevent the ways to wail.   179
To fear the foe, since fear oppresseth strength,   180
Gives in your weakness strength unto your foe,   181
And so your follies fight against yourself.
Fear, and be slain. No worse can come to fight;   183
And fight and die is death destroying death,   184
Where fearing dying pays death servile breath.   185

AUMERLE
My father hath a power. Inquire of him,   186
And learn to make a body of a limb.   187

KING RICHARD
Thou chid'st me well. Proud Bolingbroke, I come
To change blows with thee for our day of doom.   189
This ague fit of fear is overblown;   190
An easy task it is to win our own.   191
Say, Scroop, where lies our uncle with his power?
Speak sweetly, man, although thy looks be sour.

SCROOP
Men judge by the complexion of the sky   194
    The state and inclination of the day.   195
So may you by my dull and heavy eye;
    My tongue hath but a heavier tale to say.
I play the torturer, by small and small   198
To lengthen out the worst that must be spoken:
Your uncle York is joined with Bolingbroke,
And all your northern castles yielded up,
And all your southern gentlemen in arms
Upon his party.
KING RICHARD   Thou hast said enough.   203

179 **presently** immediately.   **prevent . . . wail** block off the paths leading
to grief   **180–181 To fear . . . foe** i.e., to be afraid of the foe is merely a
weakness that, by oppressing your own resolve, gives advantage to the
foe   **183 Fear . . . fight** i.e., if you fear you are sure to be slain, and no
worse fate can come to you if you fight   **184–185 fight . . . breath** to die
fighting is to conquer death in the very act of dying, whereas to die
fearfully pays to death the tribute of servility   **186 power** army (as also
in l. 192).   **of** about   **187 learn . . . limb** i.e., discover how to make a
partial force substitute for a complete one   **189 change** exchange.   **for
. . . doom** i.e., in order to settle our fates, which of us is to die now
190 ague fit paroxysm of shivering. (As with a malarial fever.)   **is overblown** has blown over   **191 our own** i.e., my own kingdom   **194 complexion** appearance   **195 inclination** tendency   **198 by small and small**
little by little   **203 Upon his party** on his side

[*To Aumerle.*] Beshrew thee, cousin, which didst lead me
    forth   204
Of that sweet way I was in to despair!
What say you now? What comfort have we now?
By heaven, I'll hate him everlastingly
That bids me be of comfort any more.
Go to Flint Castle. There I'll pine away;   209
A king, woe's slave, shall kingly woe obey.
That power I have, discharge, and let them go
To ear the land that hath some hope to grow,   212
For I have none. Let no man speak again
To alter this, for counsel is but vain.

AUMERLE
My liege, one word.

KING RICHARD   He does me double wrong   215
That wounds me with the flatteries of his tongue.
Discharge my followers. Let them hence away,
From Richard's night to Bolingbroke's fair day.

                                     [Exeunt.]

❖

3.3   *Enter [with drum and colors] Bolingbroke,
York, Northumberland, [attendants, and forces].*

BOLINGBROKE
So that by this intelligence we learn   1
The Welshmen are dispersed, and Salisbury
Is gone to meet the King, who lately landed
With some few private friends upon this coast.

NORTHUMBERLAND
The news is very fair and good, my lord:
Richard not far from hence hath hid his head.

YORK
It would beseem the Lord Northumberland   7

204 Beshrew confound. (Literally, *curse.*)   **forth** out   **209 Flint Castle**
(Near Chester.)   **212 ear** plow   **215 double wrong** i.e., in deceiving me
and in again leading me into false hope

3.3. Location: Wales. Before Flint Castle.
1 intelligence information   **7 beseem** be appropriate for, be seemly
behavior in

To say "King Richard." Alack the heavy day
When such a sacred king should hide his head!

NORTHUMBERLAND
Your Grace mistakes. Only to be brief
Left I his title out.

YORK   The time hath been,
Would you have been so brief with him, he would
Have been so brief with you to shorten you,   13
For taking so the head, your whole head's length.   14

BOLINGBROKE
Mistake not, uncle, further than you should.

YORK
Take not, good cousin, further than you should,
Lest you mistake the heavens are over our heads.   17

BOLINGBROKE
I know it, uncle, and oppose not myself
Against their will. But who comes here?

Enter Percy.

Welcome, Harry. What, will not this castle yield?

PERCY
The castle royally is manned, my lord,
Against thy entrance.

BOLINGBROKE
Royally? Why, it contains no king?

PERCY   Yes, my good lord,
It doth contain a king. King Richard lies   25
Within the limits of yon lime and stone,
And with him are the Lord Aumerle, Lord Salisbury,
Sir Stephen Scroop, besides a clergyman
Of holy reverence—who, I cannot learn.

NORTHUMBERLAND
O, belike it is the Bishop of Carlisle.   30

BOLINGBROKE   Noble lord,   31
Go to the rude ribs of that ancient castle;   32
Through brazen trumpet send the breath of parley   33

---

13 to as to   **14 taking so the head** i.e., presumptuously omitting thus
his title   **17 mistake** fail to perceive that. (Plays on Bolingbroke's use of
mistake, just as York has punned on *brief* and *head*.)   **25 lies** resides
30 belike probably   **31 lord** i.e., Northumberland   **32 rude ribs** i.e.,
rugged walls   **33 brazen** (1) brass (2) bold.   **breath of parley** i.e., call for
a conference

Into his ruined ears, and thus deliver: 34
Henry Bolingbroke
On both his knees doth kiss King Richard's hand
And sends allegiance and true faith of heart
To his most royal person, hither come
Even at his feet to lay my arms and power,
Provided that my banishment repealed   40
And lands restored again be freely granted.
If not, I'll use the advantage of my power,   42
And lay the summer's dust with showers of blood
Rained from the wounds of slaughtered Englishmen—
The which how far off from the mind of Bolingbroke
It is such crimson tempest should bedrench   46
The fresh green lap of fair King Richard's land,
My stooping duty tenderly shall show.   48
Go signify as much while here we march
Upon the grassy carpet of this plain.
                    [*Northumberland and attendants*
                                        advance to the castle.]
Let's march without the noise of threatening drum,
That from this castle's tattered battlements   52
Our fair appointments may be well perused.   53
Methinks King Richard and myself should meet
With no less terror than the elements
Of fire and water, when their thundering shock   56
At meeting tears the cloudy cheeks of heaven.
Be he the fire, I'll be the yielding water;
The rage be his, whilst on the earth I rain   59
My waters—on the earth, and not on him.   60
March on, and mark King Richard how he looks.   61

The trumpets sound [a parley without and
answer within, then a flourish. King] Richard
appeareth on the walls [with the Bishop of
Carlisle, Aumerle, Scroop, and Salisbury].

34 his ruined ears i.e., its (the castle's) ancient and battered loopholes
40 my banishment repealed i.e., the revocation of my banishment
42 advantage of my power superiority of my army   **46 is** is that
48 stooping duty submissive kneeling   **52 tattered** saw-toothed
53 appointments equipment   **56 fire and water** i.e., lightning and rain
59–60 rain . . . earth i.e., weep contritely as I kneel   **61 s.d. parley**
trumpet summons to a negotiation.   **on the walls** i.e., in the gallery of
the tiring house, above, to the rear of the stage

See, see, King Richard doth himself appear,
As doth the blushing discontented sun 63
From out the fiery portal of the east,
When he perceives the envious clouds are bent 65
To dim his glory and to stain the track
Of his bright passage to the occident.

YORK

Yet looks he like a king. Behold, his eye, 68
As bright as is the eagle's, lightens forth 69
Controlling majesty. Alack, alack, for woe,
That any harm should stain so fair a show!

KING RICHARD [*To Northumberland*]

We are amazed; and thus long have we stood
To watch the fearful bending of thy knee, 73
Because we thought ourself thy lawful king.
And if we be, how dare thy joints forget
To pay their awful duty to our presence? 76
If we be not, show us the hand of God 77
That hath dismissed us from our stewardship;
For well we know, no hand of blood and bone
Can grip the sacred handle of our scepter,
Unless he do profane, steal, or usurp.
And though you think that all, as you have done,
Have torn their souls by turning them from us, 83
And we are barren and bereft of friends, 84
Yet know, my master, God omnipotent, 85
Is mustering in his clouds on our behalf
Armies of pestilence; and they shall strike
Your children yet unborn and unbegot,
That lift your vassal hands against my head 89
And threat the glory of my precious crown. 90
Tell Bolingbroke—for yon methinks he stands—
That every stride he makes upon my land
Is dangerous treason. He is come to open 93
The purple testament of bleeding war; 94

63 blushing i.e., turning red with anger   **65 he** i.e., the sun.   **envious** hostile   **68 Yet** still.   **he** i.e., King Richard   **69 lightens forth** flashes out, like lightning   **73 watch** wait for   **76 awful** reverential, full of awe   **77 hand** signature   **83 torn . . . us** i.e., turned traitor to Richard at peril to their souls   **84 And** and that   **85 know** know that   **89 That** of you that.   **vassal** subject   **90 threat** threaten   **93–94 open . . . testament** begin to carry out a bequest of blood to England. (Blood was often said to be purple.)

But, ere the crown he looks for live in peace,
Ten thousand bloody crowns of mothers' sons   96
Shall ill become the flower of England's face,   97
Change the complexion of her maid-pale peace   98
To scarlet indignation, and bedew
Her pastures' grass with faithful English blood.

NORTHUMBERLAND
The King of Heaven forbid our lord the King
Should so with civil and uncivil arms   102
Be rushed upon! Thy thrice-noble cousin
Harry Bolingbroke doth humbly kiss thy hand;
And by the honorable tomb he swears
That stands upon your royal grandsire's bones,
And by the royalties of both your bloods,   107
Currents that spring from one most gracious head,
And by the buried hand of warlike Gaunt,
And by the worth and honor of himself,
Comprising all that may be sworn or said,
His coming hither hath no further scope   112
Than for his lineal royalties, and to beg   113
Enfranchisement immediate on his knees;   114
Which on thy royal party granted once,   115
His glittering arms he will commend to rust,   116
His barbèd steeds to stables, and his heart   117
To faithful service of Your Majesty.
This swears he, as he is a prince and just,
And as I am a gentleman I credit him.

KING RICHARD
Northumberland, say thus the King returns: 121
His noble cousin is right welcome hither,
And all the number of his fair demands
Shall be accomplished without contradiction.   124
With all the gracious utterance thou hast

96 crowns heads (playing on *crown* in l. 95)   **97 flower . . . face** bloom-
ing face of England   **98 maid-pale** i.e., pale like the complexion of a
young English maid   **102 civil** used in civil strife.   **uncivil** barbarous,
violent   **107 royalties** royal status   **112 scope** purpose, aim   **113 lineal
royalties** hereditary rights as one of royal blood   **114 Enfranchisement**
freedom (from banishment)   **115 party** part   **116 commend** give over
117 barbèd armored   **121 returns** answers   **124 accomplished** fulfilled

Speak to his gentle hearing kind commends.   126
            [*Northumberland retires to Bolingbroke
                                        and York.*]
[*To Aumerle.*] We do debase ourselves, cousin, do we not,
To look so poorly and to speak so fair?   128
Shall we call back Northumberland, and send
Defiance to the traitor, and so die?

AUMERLE
No, good my lord. Let's fight with gentle words
Till time lend friends, and friends their helpful swords.

KING RICHARD
O God, O God, that e'er this tongue of mine,
That laid the sentence of dread banishment
On yon proud man, should take it off again
With words of sooth! O, that I were as great   136
As is my grief, or lesser than my name!
Or that I could forget what I have been,
Or not remember what I must be now!
Swell'st thou, proud heart? I'll give thee scope to beat, 140
Since foes have scope to beat both thee and me.   141
            [*Northumberland returns to the castle.*]

AUMERLE
Northumberland comes back from Bolingbroke.

KING RICHARD
What must the King do now? Must he submit?
The King shall do it. Must he be deposed?
The King shall be contented. Must he lose
The name of king? I' God's name, let it go.
I'll give my jewels for a set of beads,   147
My gorgeous palace for a hermitage,
My gay apparel for an almsman's gown,   149
My figured goblets for a dish of wood,   150
My scepter for a palmer's walking-staff,   151
My subjects for a pair of carvèd saints,
And my large kingdom for a little grave,
A little little grave, an obscure grave;

126 **commends** regards 128 **poorly** abject. **fair** courteously
136 **sooth** cajolery, flattery 140 **scope** freedom 141 **scope** capacity
147 **set of beads** rosary 149 **almsman's** one who lives on alms or
charity 150 **figured** ornamented, embossed 151 **palmer's** pilgrim's

Or I'll be buried in the King's highway,
Some way of common trade, where subjects' feet   156
May hourly trample on their sovereign's head;
For on my heart they tread now whilst I live,
And, buried once, why not upon my head?   159
Aumerle, thou weep'st, my tenderhearted cousin!
We'll make foul weather with despisèd tears;
Our sighs and they shall lodge the summer corn   162
And make a dearth in this revolting land.   163
Or shall we play the wantons with our woes   164
And make some pretty match with shedding tears?   165
As thus, to drop them still upon one place,   166
Till they have fretted us a pair of graves   167
Within the earth; and, therein laid—there lies
Two kinsmen digged their graves with weeping eyes.   169
Would not this ill do well? Well, well, I see
I talk but idly, and you laugh at me.—
Most mighty prince, my lord Northumberland,
What says King Bolingbroke? Will His Majesty
Give Richard leave to live till Richard die?
You make a leg, and Bolingbroke says ay.   175

NORTHUMBERLAND
My lord, in the base court he doth attend   176
To speak with you. May it please you to come down.   177

KING RICHARD
Down, down I come, like glistering Phaëthon,   178
Wanting the manage of unruly jades.   179
In the base court? Base court, where kings grow base,
To come at traitors' calls and do them grace.   181
In the base court? Come down? Down, court! Down,
  king!

156 **trade** passage   159 **buried once** once I am buried   162 **lodge** beat
down. **corn** grain   163 **revolting** rebelling   164 **play the wantons**
sport, frolic   165 **match** game, contest   166 **still** continually
167 **fretted us** eaten away for us, worn (with a play on "complained")
169 **digged** who dug   175 **a leg** an obeisance   176 **base court** outer or
lower court of a castle   177 **May it please you** if you please   178 **glistering** glistening, glittering. **Phaëthon** son of the sun-god, whose
chariot he attempted to steer across the sky; unable to control the
horses of the sun, he was hurled from the chariot by Jupiter   179 **Wanting . . . jades** lacking the skill in horsemanship to control unruly nags
181 **do them grace** (1) bow to them (2) treat them graciously

For night owls shriek where mounting larks should
  sing.   [*Exeunt from above.*]
BOLINGBROKE
What says His Majesty?
NORTHUMBERLAND   Sorrow and grief of heart
Makes him speak fondly, like a frantic man.   185
Yet he is come.

[*Enter King Richard and his attendants below.*]

BOLINGBROKE Stand all apart,   187
And show fair duty to His Majesty.   *He kneels down.* 188
My gracious lord!
KING RICHARD
Fair cousin, you debase your princely knee   190
To make the base earth proud with kissing it.   191
Me rather had my heart might feel your love   192
Than my unpleased eye see your courtesy.
Up, cousin, up; your heart is up, I know,
Thus high at least [*Touching his crown*], although your
  knee be low.
BOLINGBROKE [*Rising*]
My gracious lord, I come but for mine own.
KING RICHARD
Your own is yours, and I am yours, and all.
BOLINGBROKE
So far be mine, my most redoubted lord,   198
As my true service shall deserve your love.
KING RICHARD
Well you deserve. They well deserve to have
That know the strong'st and surest way to get.
[*To York, who weeps.*] Uncle, give me your hands. Nay,
  dry your eyes;
Tears show their love, but want their remedies.   203
[*To Bolingbroke.*] Cousin, I am too young to be your
  father,   204
Though you are old enough to be my heir.

185 fondly foolishly. **frantic** mad   **187 apart** aside   **188 fair duty**
respect   **190–191 debase . . . base** (Continues the word-play on *base* in
l. 180.)   **192 Me rather had** I had rather   **198 redoubted** dread   **203 want
their remedies** lack remedies for what caused them   **204 too young**
(Historically Richard and Bolingbroke were both thirty-three.)

What you will have, I'll give, and willing too,
For do we must what force will have us do.
Set on towards London, cousin, is it so?
BOLINGBROKE
Yea, my good lord.
KING RICHARD   Then I must not say no.
                                        [*Flourish. Exeunt.*]

❖

3.4   *Enter the Queen with* [*two Ladies,*] *her
        attendants.*

QUEEN
What sport shall we devise here in this garden,
To drive away the heavy thought of care?
LADY   Madam, we'll play at bowls.   3
QUEEN
'Twill make me think the world is full of rubs,   4
And that my fortune runs against the bias.   5
LADY   Madam, we'll dance.
QUEEN
My legs can keep no measure in delight   7
When my poor heart no measure keeps in grief.   8
Therefore, no dancing, girl; some other sport.
LADY   Madam, we'll tell tales.
QUEEN
Of sorrow or of joy?
LADY   Of either, madam.
QUEEN   Of neither, girl;
For if of joy, being altogether wanting,   13
It doth remember me the more of sorrow;   14
Or if of grief, being altogether had,
It adds more sorrow to my want of joy.
For what I have I need not to repeat,
And what I want it boots not to complain.   18

3.4. **Location: The Duke of York's garden.**
3 bowls i.e., lawn bowling, a common Elizabethan game **4 rubs** imped-
iments (in the game of bowls) **5 against the bias** i.e., contrary, athwart.
(Literally, not following the naturally curved path of a bowl.) **7 measure** a stately slow dance **8 measure** moderation **13 wanting** lacking **14 remember** remind **18 boots** helps

LADY
  Madam, I'll sing.
QUEEN   'Tis well that thou hast cause,
  But thou shouldst please me better wouldst thou weep.   20
LADY
  I could weep, madam, would it do you good.
QUEEN
  And I could sing, would weeping do me good,   22
  And never borrow any tear of thee.

  Enter Gardeners [a Master and two Men].

  But stay, here come the gardeners.
  Let's step into the shadow of these trees.
  My wretchedness unto a row of pins,   26
  They will talk of state, for everyone doth so   27
  Against a change; woe is forerun with woe.   28
            [The Queen and Ladies stand apart.]
GARDENER *[To one Man]*
  Go bind thou up young dangling apricots
  Which, like unruly children, make their sire
  Stoop with oppression of their prodigal weight.   31
  Give some supportance to the bending twigs.
  [To the other.] Go thou, and like an executioner
  Cut off the heads of too-fast-growing sprays
  That look too lofty in our commonwealth.
  All must be even in our government.   36
  You thus employed, I will go root away
  The noisome weeds which without profit suck   38
  The soil's fertility from wholesome flowers.
MAN
  Why should we in the compass of a pale   40
  Keep law and form and due proportion,
  Showing as in a model our firm estate,   42
  When our sea-wallèd garden, the whole land,
  Is full of weeds, her fairest flowers choked up,
  Her fruit trees all unpruned, her hedges ruined,

---

20 wouldst thou if you would   **22 would . . . good** i.e., if my troubles
were merely the kind that could be helped by weeping   **26 My . . . unto**
i.e., I'll wager my wretchedness against   **27 state** statecraft, politics
28 Against anticipating.   **forerun with** heralded by   **31 prodigal** excessive   **36 even** equal   **38 noisome** harmful   **40 pale** enclosure, enclosed
garden   **42 firm** stable

Her knots disordered, and her wholesome herbs   46
Swarming with caterpillars?
GARDENER   Hold thy peace.
He that hath suffered this disordered spring   48
Hath now himself met with the fall of leaf.   49
The weeds which his broad-spreading leaves did shelter,
That seemed in eating him to hold him up,
Are plucked up root and all by Bolingbroke:
I mean the Earl of Wiltshire, Bushy, Green.

MAN
What, are they dead?
GARDENER   They are; and Bolingbroke
Hath seized the wasteful King. O, what pity is it
That he had not so trimmed and dressed his land
As we this garden! We at time of year   57
Do wound the bark, the skin of our fruit trees,
Lest being overproud in sap and blood
With too much riches it confound itself;
Had he done so to great and growing men,
They might have lived to bear and he to taste
Their fruits of duty. Superfluous branches
We lop away, that bearing boughs may live;   64
Had he done so, himself had borne the crown
Which waste of idle hours hath quite thrown down.

MAN
What, think you the King shall be deposed?
GARDENER
Depressed he is already, and deposed   68
'Tis doubt he will be. Letters came last night   69
To a dear friend of the good Duke of York's,
That tell black tidings.
QUEEN [*Coming forward*] O, I am pressed to death   71
Through want of speaking! Thou, old Adam's likeness, 72
Set to dress this garden, how dares   73

---

46 knots flower beds laid out in patterns **48 suffered** allowed **49 fall
of leaf** i.e., autumn **57 at . . . year** in the appropriate season **64 bearing** fruit-bearing **68 Depressed** brought low **69 'Tis doubt** there is
fear **71 pressed to death** (Allusion to the *peine forte et dure*, inflicted
by pressure of heavy weights upon the chests of indicted persons who
refused to plead and remained silent.) **72 old Adam** (In his role as the
first gardener.) **73 dress** cultivate

Thy harsh rude tongue sound this unpleasing news?
What Eve, what serpent, hath suggested thee   75
To make a second fall of cursèd man?
Why dost thou say King Richard is deposed?
Dar'st thou, thou little better thing than earth,
Divine his downfall? Say, where, when, and how   79
Cam'st thou by this ill tidings? Speak, thou wretch.

GARDENER
Pardon me, madam. Little joy have I
To breathe this news, yet what I say is true.
King Richard, he is in the mighty hold
Of Bolingbroke. Their fortunes both are weighed.
In your lord's scale is nothing but himself
And some few vanities that make him light;
But in the balance of great Bolingbroke,
Besides himself, are all the English peers,
And with that odds he weighs King Richard down.
Post you to London and you will find it so;   90
I speak no more than everyone doth know.

QUEEN
Nimble mischance, that art so light of foot,
Doth not thy embassage belong to me,   93
And am I last that knows it? O, thou thinkest
To serve me last that I may longest keep
Thy sorrow in my breast. Come, ladies, go   96
To meet at London London's king in woe.
What, was I born to this, that my sad look
Should grace the triumph of great Bolingbroke?   99
Gard'ner, for telling me these news of woe,
Pray God the plants thou graft'st may never grow.
                                        Exit [with Ladies].

GARDENER
Poor queen! So that thy state might be no worse,   102
I would my skill were subject to thy curse.
Here did she fall a tear; here in this place   104

75 suggested tempted   **79 Divine** prophesy   **90 Post** hasten. (See note at
1.1.56.)   **93 embassage** message.   **belong to** i.e., concern   **96 Thy
sorrow** the sorrow that you (mischance) report   **99 triumph** triumphal
procession.   **Bolingbroke** (The original spelling, *Bullingbrooke*, indicates the rhyme with *look* in the previous line, pronounced something
like *bruke* and *luke*.)   **102 So that** provided   **104 fall** let fall

I'll set a bank of rue, sour herb of grace.   105
Rue even for ruth here shortly shall be seen,   106
In the remembrance of a weeping queen.   *Exeunt.*

❖

105 rue "herb of grace," a plant symbolical of repentance, ruth, or
sorrow for another's misery   **106 ruth** pity

4.1   *Enter Bolingbroke with the Lords [Aumerle,*
Northumberland, Harry Percy, Fitzwater,
Surrey, the Bishop of Carlisle, the Abbot of
Westminster, and another Lord, Herald,
officers] to Parliament. [The throne is provided
onstage.]

BOLINGBROKE   Call forth Bagot.

   Enter [officers with] Bagot.

   Now, Bagot, freely speak thy mind
   What thou dost know of noble Gloucester's death,
   Who wrought it with the King, and who performed   4
   The bloody office of his timeless end.   5

BAGOT
   Then set before my face the lord Aumerle.

BOLINGBROKE
   Cousin, stand forth, and look upon that man.
                           [Aumerle comes forward.]

BAGOT
   My lord Aumerle, I know your daring tongue
   Scorns to unsay what once it hath delivered.   9
   In that dead time when Gloucester's death was plotted, 10
   I heard you say, "Is not my arm of length,   11
   That reacheth from the restful English court   12
   As far as Calais, to mine uncle's head?"
   Amongst much other talk that very time   14
   I heard you say that you had rather refuse
   The offer of an hundred thousand crowns
   Than Bolingbroke's return to England—   17
   Adding withal how blest this land would be   18
   In this your cousin's death.

AUMERLE   Princes and noble lords,
   What answer shall I make to this base man?

4.1. Location: Westminster Hall.
4 Who . . . King who prevailed upon the King to have the murder performed   **5 office** function.   **timeless** untimely   **9 unsay** deny, take
back   **10 dead** (1) deadly (2) dark, silent   **11 of length** long   **12 restful**
i.e., untroubled by Gloucester   **14 that very time** (An inconsistency;
Gloucester's death occurred before Bolingbroke left England.)   **17 Than**
. . . return than have Bolingbroke return   **18 withal** in addition

Shall I so much dishonor my fair stars   22
On equal terms to give him chastisement?   23
Either I must, or have mine honor soiled
With the attainder of his slanderous lips.   25
              [*He throws down his gage.*]
There is my gage, the manual seal of death,   26
That marks thee out for hell. I say thou liest,
And will maintain what thou hast said is false
In thy heart-blood, though being all too base
To stain the temper of my knightly sword.

BOLINGBROKE
Bagot, forbear. Thou shalt not take it up.

AUMERLE
Excepting one, I would he were the best   32
In all this presence that hath moved me so.

FITZWATER [*Throwing down a gage*]
If that thy valor stand on sympathy,   34
There is my gage, Aumerle, in gage to thine.
By that fair sun which shows me where thou stand'st,
I heard thee say, and vauntingly thou spak'st it,   37
That thou wert cause of noble Gloucester's death.
If thou deniest it twenty times, thou liest,
And I will turn thy falsehood to thy heart,
Where it was forgèd, with my rapier's point.

AUMERLE [*Taking up the gage*]
Thou dar'st not, coward, live to see that day.

FITZWATER
Now, by my soul, I would it were this hour.

AUMERLE
Fitzwater, thou art damned to hell for this.

PERCY
Aumerle, thou liest. His honor is as true
In this appeal as thou art all unjust;   46
And that thou art so, there I throw my gage
              [*Throwing down a gage*]

---

22 stars i.e., sphere, fortune, rank   **23 On . . . chastisement** as to challenge him as my equal   **25 attainder** dishonoring accusation
26 manual . . . death death warrant sealed by my hand   **32 one** i.e., Bolingbroke.   **best** highest in rank   **34 stand on sympathy** i.e., requires correspondence of rank in your opponent   **37 vauntingly** boastfully
46 appeal accusation (as also in l. 80).   **all unjust** totally false

To prove it on thee to the extremest point
Of mortal breathing. Seize it if thou dar'st.
AUMERLE [*Taking up the gage*]
  An if I do not, may my hands rot off   50
  And never brandish more revengeful steel   51
  Over the glittering helmet of my foe!
ANOTHER LORD [*Throwing down a gage*]
  I task the earth to the like, forsworn Aumerle,   53
  And spur thee on with full as many lies   54
  As may be holloed in thy treacherous ear
  From sun to sun. There is my honor's pawn;   56
  Engage it to the trial, if thou darest.   57
AUMERLE [*Taking up the gage*]
  Who sets me else? By heaven, I'll throw at all!   58
  I have a thousand spirits in one breast
  To answer twenty thousand such as you.
SURREY
  My lord Fitzwater, I do remember well
  The very time Aumerle and you did talk.
FITZWATER
  'Tis very true. You were in presence then,   63
  And you can witness with me this is true.
SURREY
  As false, by heaven, as heaven itself is true.
FITZWATER
  Surrey, thou liest.
SURREY   Dishonorable boy!
  That lie shall lie so heavy on my sword
  That it shall render vengeance and revenge,
  Till thou the lie-giver and that lie do lie
  In earth as quiet as thy father's skull.
  In proof whereof, there is my honor's pawn.
               [*He throws down a gage.*]
  Engage it to the trial if thou dar'st.

---

50 An if if   **51 more** any more, again   **53 I . . . like** i.e., I burden the
ground with another gage   **54 lies** accusations of lying; challenges to
combat   **56 sun to sun** sunrise to sunset   **57 Engage . . . trial** take it up
as a pledge to combat   **58 sets me** puts up stakes against me, i.e.,
challenges me to a game.   **throw** (1) throw dice (2) throw down gages
63 in presence i.e., present at court

FITZWATER [*Taking up the gage*]
How fondly dost thou spur a forward horse!   73
If I dare eat, or drink, or breathe, or live,
I dare meet Surrey in a wilderness   75
And spit upon him whilst I say he lies,
And lies, and lies. There is my bond of faith,
To tie thee to my strong correction.
                           [*He throws down a gage.*]
As I intend to thrive in this new world,   79
Aumerle is guilty of my true appeal.
Besides, I heard the banished Norfolk say
That thou, Aumerle, didst send two of thy men
To execute the noble Duke at Calais.

AUMERLE
Some honest Christian trust me with a gage
That Norfolk lies. [*He borrows a gage, and throws it
   down.*] Here do I throw down this,
If he may be repealed to try his honor.   86

BOLINGBROKE
These differences shall all rest under gage   87
Till Norfolk be repealed. Repealed he shall be,
And, though mine enemy, restored again
To all his lands and signories. When he is returned,
Against Aumerle we will enforce his trial.

CARLISLE
That honorable day shall never be seen.
Many a time hath banished Norfolk fought
For Jesu Christ in glorious Christian field,
Streaming the ensign of the Christian cross   95
Against black pagans, Turks, and Saracens;
And, toiled with works of war, retired himself   97
To Italy, and there at Venice gave
His body to that pleasant country's earth
And his pure soul unto his captain, Christ,
Under whose colors he had fought so long.

BOLINGBROKE   Why, Bishop, is Norfolk dead?
CARLISLE   As surely as I live, my lord.

---

73 fondly foolishly.   **forward** willing   **75 in a wilderness** i.e., where
fighting might go on uninterrupted to the death   **79 in . . . world** i.e.,
under the new king   **86 repealed** recalled from exile.   **try** test
87 under gage as challenges   **95 Streaming** flying   **97 toiled** wearied

BOLINGBROKE
Sweet peace conduct his sweet soul to the bosom 104
Of good old Abraham! Lords appellants, 105
Your differences shall all rest under gage
Till we assign you to your days of trial. 107

Enter York.

YORK
Great Duke of Lancaster, I come to thee
From plume-plucked Richard, who with willing soul
Adopts thee heir, and his high scepter yields
To the possession of thy royal hand.
Ascend his throne, descending now from him,
And long live Henry, fourth of that name!
BOLINGBROKE
In God's name, I'll ascend the regal throne.
CARLISLE Marry, God forbid!
Worst in this royal presence may I speak, 116
Yet best beseeming me to speak the truth. 117
Would God that any in this noble presence
Were enough noble to be upright judge
Of noble Richard! Then true noblesse would 120
Learn him forbearance from so foul a wrong. 121
What subject can give sentence on his king?
And who least sits here that is not Richard's subject?
Thieves are not judged but they are by to hear, 124
Although apparent guilt be seen in them; 125
And shall the figure of God's majesty,
His captain, steward, deputy elect,
Anointed, crownèd, planted many years,
Be judged by subject and inferior breath,
And he himself not present? O, forfend it God 130

104–105 bosom . . . Abraham i.e., heaven. (See Luke 16:22.) **105 Lords appellants** lords who appear as formal accusers **107 s.d. Enter York** (Some editors suggest that Richard's scepter, etc., are brought in at l. 162, but York here invites Bolingbroke to ascend the throne with the surrendered scepter, and so perhaps the regalia are brought on here.) **116 Worst** least in rank **117 best beseeming me** i.e., most befitting to me as a clergyman **120 noblesse** nobleness **121 Learn him forbearance** teach him to forbear **124 judged . . . by** condemned unless they are present **125 apparent** manifest **130 forfend** forbid

That in a Christian climate souls refined 131
Should show so heinous, black, obscene a deed! 132
I speak to subjects, and a subject speaks,
Stirred up by God thus boldly for his king.
My lord of Hereford here, whom you call king,
Is a foul traitor to proud Hereford's king.
And if you crown him, let me prophesy:
The blood of English shall manure the ground
And future ages groan for this foul act;
Peace shall go sleep with Turks and infidels,
And in this seat of peace tumultuous wars
Shall kin with kin and kind with kind confound; 142
Disorder, horror, fear, and mutiny
Shall here inhabit, and this land be called
The field of Golgotha and dead men's skulls. 145
O, if you raise this house against this house, 146
It will the woefullest division prove
That ever fell upon this cursèd earth.
Prevent it, resist it, let it not be so,
Lest child, child's children, cry against you woe!

NORTHUMBERLAND
Well have you argued, sir, and for your pains
Of capital treason we arrest you here. 152
My lord of Westminster, be it your charge
To keep him safely till his day of trial.
                    [*Carlisle is taken into custody.*]
May it please you, lords, to grant the commons' suit. 155

BOLINGBROKE
Fetch hither Richard, that in common view
He may surrender; so we shall proceed 157
Without suspicion.

YORK   I will be his conduct. *Exit.* 158

131 **souls refined** civilized people   132 **obscene** odious, repulsive
142 **Shall . . . confound** shall destroy kinsmen by means of kinsmen and
fellow-countrymen by means of fellow-countrymen   145 **Golgotha**
Calvary, the hill outside of Jerusalem called "the place of dead men's
skulls" (see Mark 15:22 and John 19:17) where Jesus was crucified
146 **this house . . . this house** i.e., Lancaster against York. (See Mark
3:25.)   152 **Of** on a charge of   155 **the commons' suit** request of the
commons (i.e., that Richard be formally tried and the causes of his
deposition made public. This line begins the abdication passage omitted
in early quartos of the play.)   157 **surrender** i.e., surrender the crown,
abdicate   158 **conduct** escort

BOLINGBROKE

Lords, you that here are under our arrest,
Procure your sureties for your days of answer.   160
Little are we beholding to your love,   161
And little looked for at your helping hands.   162

Enter Richard and York.

KING RICHARD

Alack, why am I sent for to a king,
Before I have shook off the regal thoughts
Wherewith I reigned? I hardly yet have learned
To insinuate, flatter, bow, and bend my knee.
Give sorrow leave awhile to tutor me
To this submission. Yet I well remember
The favors of these men. Were they not mine?   169
Did they not sometime cry, "All hail!" to me?
So Judas did to Christ. But he, in twelve,
Found truth in all but one; I, in twelve thousand, none.
God save the King! Will no man say amen?
Am I both priest and clerk? Well then, amen.   174
God save the King, although I be not he;
And yet, amen, if heaven do think him me.
To do what service am I sent for hither?

YORK

To do that office of thine own good will
Which tired majesty did make thee offer:
The resignation of thy state and crown
To Henry Bolingbroke.

KING RICHARD

Give me the crown. [*He takes the crown.*] Here, cousin,
    seize the crown.
Here, cousin,
On this side my hand, and on that side thine.
Now is this golden crown like a deep well
That owes two buckets, filling one another,   186
The emptier ever dancing in the air,
The other down, unseen, and full of water.

160 sureties persons who will guarantee your appearance. **your days of answer** the time when you must appear to stand trial **161 beholding** beholden, indebted **162 looked for** expected **169 favors** (1) faces (2) benefits **174 priest and clerk** (In religious services, the clerk or assistant would say "Amen" to the priest's prayers.) **186 owes** owns, has

That bucket down and full of tears am I,
Drinking my griefs, whilst you mount up on high.

BOLINGBROKE
I thought you had been willing to resign.

KING RICHARD
My crown I am, but still my griefs are mine.
You may my glories and my state depose,
But not my griefs; still am I king of those.

BOLINGBROKE
Part of your cares you give me with your crown.

KING RICHARD
Your cares set up do not pluck my cares down.   196
My care is loss of care, by old care done;   197
Your care is gain of care, by new care won.   198
The cares I give I have, though given away;   199
They 'tend the crown, yet still with me they stay.   200

BOLINGBROKE
Are you contented to resign the crown?

KING RICHARD
Ay, no; no, ay; for I must nothing be;   202
Therefore no no, for I resign to thee.   203
Now mark me how I will undo myself: 204
                  [*He yields his crown and scepter.*]
I give this heavy weight from off my head
And this unwieldy scepter from my hand,
The pride of kingly sway from out my heart;
With mine own tears I wash away my balm,
With mine own hands I give away my crown,
With mine own tongue deny my sacred state,
With mine own breath release all duteous oaths.   211
All pomp and majesty I do forswear;
My manors, rents, revenues I forgo;
My acts, decrees, and statutes I deny.

196–200 Your . . . stay i.e., Your assuming the cares of office does not
assuage my griefs. My grief is loss of kingly responsibility, destroyed by
a failure in diligence; your concern is gaining of kingly responsibility,
won by zealous effort. The anxieties I transfer to you I also keep for
myself, despite my giving them to you; they accompany the crown, and
yet still remain with me.   **202 Ay** (1) yes (2) I. (But, says Richard, I am
nothing, and therefore "Ay" is "I" or "nothing," that is, "no.")   **203 no
no . . . thee** (Richard plays on the logic that a double negative equals a
positive.)   **204 undo** (1) undress (2) unmake   **211 release . . . oaths**
release my subjects from their oaths of duty

God pardon all oaths that are broke to me!
God keep all vows unbroke are made to thee!   216
Make me, that nothing have, with nothing grieved,
And thou with all pleased, that hast all achieved!
Long mayst thou live in Richard's seat to sit,
And soon lie Richard in an earthy pit!
God save King Henry, unkinged Richard says,
And send him many years of sunshine days!—
What more remains?

NORTHUMBERLAND [*Presenting a paper*]
                            No more but that you read   223
These accusations and these grievous crimes
Committed by your person and your followers
Against the state and profit of this land;   226
That, by confessing them, the souls of men
May deem that you are worthily deposed.

KING RICHARD
Must I do so? And must I ravel out   229
My weaved-up follies? Gentle Northumberland,
If thy offenses were upon record,
Would it not shame thee in so fair a troop   232
To read a lecture of them? If thou wouldst,   233
There shouldst thou find one heinous article,
Containing the deposing of a king
And cracking the strong warrant of an oath,
Marked with a blot, damned in the book of heaven.
Nay, all of you that stand and look upon me,
Whilst that my wretchedness doth bait myself,   239
Though some of you, with Pilate, wash your hands,   240
Showing an outward pity, yet you Pilates
Have here delivered me to my sour cross,   242
And water cannot wash away your sin.

NORTHUMBERLAND
My lord, dispatch. Read o'er these articles.   244

KING RICHARD
Mine eyes are full of tears; I cannot see.

216 **are** that are   223 **read** i.e., read aloud   226 **state and profit** ordered
prosperity   229 **ravel out** unravel   232 **troop** company   233 **read a
lecture of** speak admonishingly about   239 **bait** torment, harass (as in
bearbaiting)   240 **wash your hands** (See Matthew 27:24. Richard persist-
ently compares himself to Christ; see also 3.2.132; 4.1.171.)   242 **sour**
bitter   244 **dispatch** conclude, be done

And yet salt water blinds them not so much
But they can see a sort of traitors here.   247
Nay, if I turn mine eyes upon myself,
I find myself a traitor with the rest;
For I have given here my soul's consent
T' undeck the pompous body of a king,   251
Made glory base and sovereignty a slave,
Proud majesty a subject, state a peasant.   253
NORTHUMBERLAND   My lord—
KING RICHARD
No lord of thine, thou haught insulting man,   255
Nor no man's lord. I have no name, no title,
No, not that name was given me at the font,
But 'tis usurped. Alack the heavy day,
That I have worn so many winters out
And know not now what name to call myself!
O, that I were a mockery king of snow,
Standing before the sun of Bolingbroke,
To melt myself away in water drops!
Good king, great king, and yet not greatly good,
An if my word be sterling yet in England,   265
Let it command a mirror hither straight,   266
That it may show me what a face I have,
Since it is bankrupt of his majesty.   268
BOLINGBROKE
Go some of you and fetch a looking glass.
                              [*Exit an Attendant.*]
NORTHUMBERLAND
Read o'er this paper while the glass doth come.
KING RICHARD
Fiend, thou torments me ere I come to hell!
BOLINGBROKE
Urge it no more, my lord Northumberland.
NORTHUMBERLAND
The commons will not then be satisfied.
KING RICHARD
They shall be satisfied. I'll read enough

---

247 sort gang   **251 pompous** stately, splendid   **253 state** royalty
255 haught haughty   **265 An if** if.   **sterling** valid currency   **266 straight**
immediately   **268 his** its

When I do see the very book indeed
Where all my sins are writ, and that's myself.   276

    Enter one with a glass.

Give me that glass, and therein will I read.
                    [*He takes the mirror.*]
No deeper wrinkles yet? Hath sorrow struck
So many blows upon this face of mine,
And made no deeper wounds? O flattering glass,
Like to my followers in prosperity,   281
Thou dost beguile me! Was this face the face   282
That every day under his household roof
Did keep ten thousand men? Was this the face
That, like the sun, did make beholders wink?   285
Is this the face which faced so many follies,   286
That was at last outfaced by Bolingbroke?   287
A brittle glory shineth in this face—
As brittle as the glory is the face,
            [*He throws down the mirror*]
For there it is, cracked in an hundred shivers.
Mark, silent king, the moral of this sport:
How soon my sorrow hath destroyed my face.

BOLINGBROKE
The shadow of your sorrow hath destroyed   293
The shadow of your face.
KING RICHARD   Say that again.   294
The shadow of my sorrow? Ha! Let's see.
'Tis very true, my grief lies all within;
And these external manners of laments   297
Are merely shadows to the unseen grief   298
That swells with silence in the tortured soul.
There lies the substance; and I thank thee, King,   300
For thy great bounty, that not only giv'st   301
Me cause to wail, but teachest me the way

---

276 s.d. glass mirror   **281 in prosperity** i.e., in my prosperity   **282 Was this face** (An echo of Marlowe's *Doctor Faustus,* in which the protagonist addresses Helen of Troy.)   **285 wink** close the eyes, blink **286 faced** countenanced   **287 outfaced** defied   **293 shadow** outward show; or, overshadowing nature   **294 shadow** reflection (in the mirror)   **297 manners** forms   **298 shadows to** physical (and therefore imperfect) manifestations of   **300 There** i.e., in the soul   **301 that** who

How to lament the cause. I'll beg one boon,   303
And then be gone and trouble you no more.
Shall I obtain it?
BOLINGBROKE   Name it, fair cousin.
KING RICHARD
"Fair cousin"? I am greater than a king.
For when I was a king, my flatterers
Were then but subjects; being now a subject,
I have a king here to my flatterer.   309
Being so great, I have no need to beg.
BOLINGBROKE Yet ask.
KING RICHARD And shall I have?
BOLINGBROKE You shall.
KING RICHARD Then give me leave to go.
BOLINGBROKE Whither?
KING RICHARD
Whither you will, so I were from your sights.
BOLINGBROKE
Go some of you, convey him to the Tower.   317
KING RICHARD
O, good! "Convey"? Conveyers are you all,   318
That rise thus nimbly by a true king's fall.
                    [*Exeunt King Richard, some lords,*
                              and a guard.]
BOLINGBROKE
On Wednesday next we solemnly proclaim
Our coronation. Lords, be ready all.   321
          Exeunt. Manent [*the Abbot of*] *Westminster,*
                    [*the Bishop of*] *Carlisle, Aumerle.*
ABBOT
A woeful pageant have we here beheld.
CARLISLE
The woe's to come, the children yet unborn,
Shall feel this day as sharp to them as thorn.   324
AUMERLE
You holy clergymen, is there no plot
To rid the realm of this pernicious blot?
ABBOT My lord,
Before I freely speak my mind herein,

303 boon favor   **309 to** as   **317 convey** escort   **318 Convey** steal
321 s.d. Manent they remain onstage   **324 Shall** who shall

You shall not only take the Sacrament
To bury mine intents, but also to effect   330
Whatever I shall happen to devise.
I see your brows are full of discontent,
Your hearts of sorrow, and your eyes of tears.
Come home with me to supper; I'll lay
A plot shall show us all a merry day.   *Exeunt.* 335

❖

330 To . . . intents to conceal my plans   **335 shall** that shall

5.1 *Enter the Queen with [Ladies,] her attendants.*

QUEEN

This way the King will come. This is the way
To Julius Caesar's ill-erected tower, 2
To whose flint bosom my condemnèd lord
Is doomed a prisoner by proud Bolingbroke.
Here let us rest, if this rebellious earth
Have any resting for her true king's queen.

Enter Richard [and guard].

But soft, but see, or rather do not see
My fair rose wither. Yet look up, behold,
That you in pity may dissolve to dew,
And wash him fresh again with true-love tears.
Ah, thou, the model where old Troy did stand, 11
Thou map of honor, thou King Richard's tomb, 12
And not King Richard! Thou most beauteous inn, 13
Why should hard-favored grief be lodged in thee 14
When triumph is become an alehouse guest? 15

KING RICHARD

Join not with grief, fair woman, do not so,
To make my end too sudden. Learn, good soul,
To think our former state a happy dream,
From which awaked, the truth of what we are
Shows us but this. I am sworn brother, sweet,
To grim Necessity, and he and I
Will keep a league till death. Hie thee to France, 22
And cloister thee in some religious house. 23
Our holy lives must win a new world's crown, 24
Which our profane hours here have thrown down.

QUEEN

What, is my Richard both in shape and mind

5.1. Location: London. A street leading to the Tower.
2 Julius . . . tower (The Tower of London, ascribed by tradition to Julius
Caesar, was built by William the Conqueror to hold the city in subordi-
nation.) ill-erected erected for evil ends, or with evil results 11 thou
. . . stand i.e., you ruined majesty, pattern of fallen greatness like the
desolate waste where Troy once stood 12 map of honor i.e., the mere
outline of a once-glorious honor 13 inn residence, house 14 hard-
favored unpleasant-looking 15 is . . . guest i.e., lodges in such a lowly
tavern (i.e., in Bolingbroke) 22 Hie hasten 23 religious house convent 24 new world's heaven's

Transformed and weakened? Hath Bolingbroke
Deposed thine intellect? Hath he been in thy heart?
The lion dying thrusteth forth his paw
And wounds the earth, if nothing else, with rage
To be o'erpowered; and wilt thou, pupil-like,   31
Take the correction, mildly kiss the rod,
And fawn on rage with base humility,
Which art a lion and the king of beasts?

KING RICHARD
A king of beasts, indeed! If aught but beasts,   35
I had been still a happy king of men.
Good sometime queen, prepare thee hence for France.   37
Think I am dead and that even here thou takest,
As from my deathbed, thy last living leave.
In winter's tedious nights sit by the fire
With good old folks, and let them tell thee tales
Of woeful ages long ago betid;   42
And ere thou bid good night, to quite their griefs   43
Tell thou the lamentable tale of me
And send the hearers weeping to their beds.
Forwhy, the senseless brands will sympathize   46
The heavy accent of thy moving tongue,   47
And in compassion weep the fire out;
And some will mourn in ashes, some coal-black,   49
For the deposing of a rightful king.

        Enter Northumberland [and others].

NORTHUMBERLAND
My lord, the mind of Bolingbroke is changed;
You must to Pomfret, not unto the Tower.   52
And, madam, there is order ta'en for you: 53
With all swift speed you must away to France.

KING RICHARD
Northumberland, thou ladder wherewithal
The mounting Bolingbroke ascends my throne,
The time shall not be many hours of age

31 To be at being   **35 king of beasts** (1) lion (2) ruler over beastly men
37 sometime former   **42 Of . . . betid** of woe that happened ages ago
43 quite their griefs requite their tales of woe   **46 Forwhy** because.
senseless inanimate, without feeling.   **brands** firebrands.   **sympathize**
respond to   **47 moving** affecting, exciting sympathy   **49 some** (of the
brands)   **52 Pomfret** Pontefract Castle in Yorkshire   **53 order ta'en** arrangement made

More than it is ere foul sin, gathering head,   58
Shall break into corruption. Thou shalt think,   59
Though he divide the realm and give thee half,
It is too little, helping him to all;   61
He shall think that thou, which knowest the way
To plant unrightful kings, wilt know again,
Being ne'er so little urged, another way
To pluck him headlong from the usurpèd throne.   65
The love of wicked men converts to fear,   66
That fear to hate, and hate turns one or both   67
To worthy danger and deservèd death.   68

NORTHUMBERLAND
My guilt be on my head, and there an end.
Take leave and part, for you must part forthwith.   70

KING RICHARD
Doubly divorced! Bad men, you violate
A twofold marriage, twixt my crown and me,
And then betwixt me and my married wife.
[*To Queen.*] Let me unkiss the oath twixt thee and me;   74
And yet not so, for with a kiss 'twas made.—
Part us, Northumberland: I towards the north,
Where shivering cold and sickness pines the clime;   77
My wife to France, from whence, set forth in pomp,
She came adornèd hither like sweet May,
Sent back like Hallowmas or short'st of day.   80

QUEEN
And must we be divided? Must we part?

KING RICHARD
Ay, hand from hand, my love, and heart from heart.

QUEEN [*To Northumberland*]
Banish us both and send the King with me.

NORTHUMBERLAND
That were some love, but little policy.   84

---

58 gathering head gathering to a head   **59 corruption** putrid matter,
pus   **61 helping** since you helped   **65 To** how to   **66 converts**
changes   **67 That fear** i.e., that fear changes.   **one or both** i.e., the new
king or his partner, or both   **68 worthy** well-merited   **70 part . . . part**
separate . . . depart   **74 unkiss** annul with a kiss (regarded as the seal
of a ceremonial bond)   **77 pines** afflicts, distresse⌐   **clime** region
80 Hallowmas All Saints' Day (November 1), rega. aed as the beginning
of winter.   **short'st of day** the winter solstice   **84 policy** political
practicality

QUEEN
Then whither he goes, thither let me go.
KING RICHARD
So two, together weeping, make one woe.
Weep thou for me in France, I for thee here;
Better far off than, near, be ne'er the near.   88
Go count thy way with sighs, I mine with groans.
QUEEN
So longest way shall have the longest moans.
KING RICHARD
Twice for one step I'll groan, the way being short,
And piece the way out with a heavy heart.   92
Come, come, in wooing sorrow let's be brief,
Since, wedding it, there is such length in grief.
One kiss shall stop our mouths, and dumbly part;   95
Thus give I mine, and thus take I thy heart.
                                    [*They kiss.*]
QUEEN
Give me mine own again. 'Twere no good part   97
To take on me to keep and kill thy heart.   [*They kiss.*]   98
So, now I have mine own again, begone,
That I may strive to kill it with a groan.
KING RICHARD
We make woe wanton with this fond delay.   101
Once more, adieu! The rest let sorrow say.   *Exeunt.*

❧

5.2   *Enter Duke of York and the Duchess.*

DUCHESS
My lord, you told me you would tell the rest,
When weeping made you break the story off,
Of our two cousins coming into London.   3
YORK
Where did I leave?   4

88 Better . . . the near i.e., better to be far apart than near and yet
unable to meet. (The second *near* means "nearer.")   **92 piece . . . out**
lengthen the journey   **95 dumbly** silently   **97-98 'Twere . . . me** it
would not be wise of me to take it upon myself   **101 We . . . wanton** we
sport with our grief.   **fond** (1) loving (2) pointless, foolish

5.2. Location: The Duke of York's house.
3 cousins kinsmen, i.e., nephews (Richard and Bolingbroke)   **4 leave**
leave off

DUCHESS   At that sad stop, my lord,   4
Where rude misgoverned hands from windows' tops   5
Threw dust and rubbish on King Richard's head.

YORK
Then, as I said, the Duke, great Bolingbroke,
Mounted upon a hot and fiery steed
Which his aspiring rider seemed to know,   9
With slow but stately pace kept on his course,
Whilst all tongues cried, "God save thee, Bolingbroke!"
You would have thought the very windows spake,
So many greedy looks of young and old
Through casements darted their desiring eyes
Upon his visage, and that all the walls
With painted imagery had said at once,   16
"Jesu preserve thee! Welcome, Bolingbroke!"
Whilst he, from the one side to the other turning,
Bareheaded, lower than his proud steed's neck,   19
Bespake them thus: "I thank you, countrymen."   20
And thus still doing, thus he passed along.   21

DUCHESS
Alack, poor Richard! Where rode he the whilst?

YORK
As in a theater the eyes of men,
After a well-graced actor leaves the stage,
Are idly bent on him that enters next,   25
Thinking his prattle to be tedious,
Even so, or with much more contempt, men's eyes
Did scowl on gentle Richard. No man cried, "God save
    him!"
No joyful tongue gave him his welcome home,
But dust was thrown upon his sacred head—
Which with such gentle sorrow he shook off,
His face still combating with tears and smiles,
The badges of his grief and patience,   33
That had not God for some strong purpose steeled
The hearts of men, they must perforce have melted,   35

5 misgoverned unruly. windows' tops upper windows 9 Which . . .
know which seemed to know its ambitious rider 16 With painted
imagery i.e., painted with crowds of people, as on a tapestry depicting a
procession. at once all together 19 lower bowing lower 20 Bespake
addressed 21 still continually 25 idly indifferently 33 badges insignia, outward signs 35 perforce necessarily

And barbarism itself have pitied him.
But heaven hath a hand in these events,
To whose high will we bound our calm contents.   38
To Bolingbroke are we sworn subjects now,
Whose state and honor I for aye allow.   40

[*Enter Aumerle.*]

DUCHESS
Here comes my son Aumerle.
YORK   Aumerle that was;   41
But that is lost for being Richard's friend,
And, madam, you must call him Rutland now.
I am in Parliament pledge for his truth   44
And lasting fealty to the new-made king.
DUCHESS
Welcome, my son. Who are the violets now   46
That strew the green lap of the new-come spring?   47
AUMERLE
Madam, I know not, nor I greatly care not.
God knows I had as lief be none as one.   49
YORK
Well, bear you well in this new spring of time,   50
Lest you be cropped before you come to prime.   51
What news from Oxford? Do those jousts and triumphs
hold?   52
AUMERLE   For aught I know, my lord, they do.
YORK   You will be there, I know.
AUMERLE
If God prevent not, I purpose so.
YORK
What seal is that, that hangs without thy bosom?   56
Yea, look'st thou pale? Let me see the writing.

38 **we . . . contents** i.e., we bind ourselves to be calmly content   40 **state**
i.e., royal title.   **allow** acknowledge   41 **Aumerle that was** (Aumerle, as
a member of Richard's party, lost his dukedom, though he remained
Earl of Rutland.)   44 **pledge** the guarantor.   **truth** loyalty   46–47 **Who
. . . spring** i.e., who are the favorites of the new king   49 **lief** happily
50 **bear you** bear yourself   51 **cropped** cut   52 **Do . . . hold** are those
tourneys and pageants going forward. (According to Holinshed, these
tourneys at Oxford were part of a conspiracy against Bolingbroke by the
Abbot of Westminster and others; the new king was to be invited to
attend, and there be assassinated.)   56 **seal** i.e., seal attached to the
border of a document

AUMERLE
My lord, 'tis nothing.

YORK   No matter, then, who see it.
I will be satisfied. Let me see the writing.

AUMERLE
I do beseech Your Grace to pardon me.
It is a matter of small consequence,
Which for some reasons I would not have seen.   62

YORK
Which for some reasons, sir, I mean to see.
I fear, I fear—

DUCHESS   What should you fear?
'Tis nothing but some bond that he is entered into
For gay apparel 'gainst the triumph day.   66

YORK
Bound to himself? What doth he with a bond   67
That he is bound to? Wife, thou art a fool.   68
Boy, let me see the writing.

AUMERLE
I do beseech you pardon me. I may not show it.

YORK
I will be satisfied. Let me see it, I say.
          He plucks it out of his bosom and reads it.
Treason! Foul treason! Villain! Traitor! Slave!

DUCHESS   What is the matter, my lord?

YORK [*Calling offstage*]
Ho! Who is within there? Saddle my horse!—
God for his mercy, what treachery is here?   75

DUCHESS   Why, what is it, my lord?

YORK [*Calling offstage*]
Give me my boots, I say! Saddle my horse!—
Now, by mine honor, by my life, by my troth,   78
I will appeach the villain.

DUCHESS   What is the matter?   79

YORK   Peace, foolish woman.

DUCHESS
I will not peace. What is the matter, Aumerle?

---

62 have seen allow to be seen   **66 'gainst** in anticipation of
67–68 What . . . bound to i.e., why should *he* have the bond instead of
the creditor to whom the debt is owed?   **75 God** i.e., I pray God
78 troth faith, allegiance   **79 appeach** inform against, publicly accuse

AUMERLE
Good Mother, be content. It is no more
Than my poor life must answer.
DUCHESS   Thy life answer?
YORK
Bring me my boots! I will unto the King.

His Man enters with his boots.

DUCHESS
Strike him, Aumerle. Poor boy, thou art amazed.   85
[*To York's Man.*] Hence, villain! Never more come in my
   sight.
YORK   Give me my boots, I say.
        [*His Man helps him on with his boots, and exit.*]
DUCHESS   Why, York, what wilt thou do?
Wilt thou not hide the trespass of thine own?
Have we more sons? Or are we like to have?   90
Is not my teeming date drunk up with time?   91
And wilt thou pluck my fair son from mine age
And rob me of a happy mother's name?
Is he not like thee? Is he not thine own?
YORK   Thou fond mad woman,   95
Wilt thou conceal this dark conspiracy?
A dozen of them here have ta'en the Sacrament,   97
And interchangeably set down their hands,   98
To kill the King at Oxford.
DUCHESS   He shall be none;   99
We'll keep him here. Then what is that to him?   100
YORK
Away, fond woman! Were he twenty times my son
.   I would appeach him.
DUCHESS   Hadst thou groaned for him 102
As I have done, thou wouldst be more pitiful.   103
But now I know thy mind. Thou dost suspect

---

85 Strike him i.e., strike the servant.   **amazed** confused, bewildered
90 Have we more sons (Historically, this Duchess of York was the
Duke's second wife and was not Aumerle's mother.)   **91 teeming date**
period of childbearing   **95 fond** foolish   **97–99 A dozen . . . Oxford**
("Hereupon was an indenture sextipartite made, sealed with their seals
and signed with their hands, in the which each stood bound to other, to
do their whole endeavor for the accomplishing of their purposed exploit." [Holinshed])   **100 that** i.e., the plot   **102 groaned for** i.e., given
birth to (but see note, l. 90)   **103 pitiful** pitying

That I have been disloyal to thy bed,
And that he is a bastard, not thy son.
Sweet York, sweet husband, be not of that mind!
He is as like thee as a man may be,
Not like to me, or any of my kin,
And yet I love him.

YORK   Make way, unruly woman!   *Exit.*

DUCHESS
After, Aumerle! Mount thee upon his horse,   111
Spur post, and get before him to the King,   112
And beg thy pardon ere he do accuse thee.
I'll not be long behind. Though I be old,
I doubt not but to ride as fast as York.   115
And never will I rise up from the ground
Till Bolingbroke have pardoned thee. Away, begone!
                                        [*Exeunt.*]

❖

5.3   *Enter [Bolingbroke, now] King [Henry], with
his nobles [Harry Percy and others].*

KING HENRY
Can no man tell me of my unthrifty son?   1
'Tis full three months since I did see him last.
If any plague hang over us, 'tis he.
I would to God, my lords, he might be found.
Inquire at London, 'mongst the taverns there,
For there, they say, he daily doth frequent,
With unrestrainèd loose companions,
Even such, they say, as stand in narrow lanes
And beat our watch, and rob our passengers—   9
While he, young wanton and effeminate boy,   10
Takes on the point of honor to support   11
So dissolute a crew.

111 **After** go after him.   **his horse** i.e., one of York's horses   **112 Spur
post** ride as fast as possible   **115 I doubt not but** i.e., I am sure I am
able

5.3. Location: The court (i.e., Windsor Castle).
1 unthrifty profligate   **9 watch** night watchmen.   **passengers** passers-
by, wayfarers   **10 wanton** spoiled, pampered.   **effeminate** self-
indulgent   **11 Takes on the** i.e., makes it a

PERCY
My lord, some two days since I saw the Prince,
And told him of those triumphs held at Oxford.   14
KING HENRY   And what said the gallant?
PERCY
His answer was, he would unto the stews,   16
And from the common'st creature pluck a glove,
And wear it as a favor, and with that
He would unhorse the lustiest challenger.   19
KING HENRY
As dissolute as desperate! Yet through both
I see some sparks of better hope, which elder years
May happily bring forth. But who comes here?   22

Enter Aumerle, amazed.

AUMERLE   Where is the King?
KING HENRY
What means our cousin, that he stares and looks
So wildly?
AUMERLE
God save Your Grace! I do beseech Your Majesty
To have some conference with Your Grace alone.
KING HENRY
Withdraw yourselves, and leave us here alone.
                    [*Exeunt Percy and Lords.*]
What is the matter with our cousin now?
AUMERLE [*Kneeling*]
Forever may my knees grow to the earth,
My tongue cleave to my roof within my mouth,   31
Unless a pardon ere I rise or speak.
KING HENRY
Intended or committed was this fault?
If on the first, how heinous e'er it be,   34
To win thy after-love I pardon thee.
AUMERLE
Then give me leave that I may turn the key,
That no man enter till my tale be done.

14 held i.e., to be held   16 stews brothels   19 lustiest most vigorous
and brave   22 happily with good fortune   s.d. amazed stunned,
bewildered   31 My . . . mouth (See Psalm 137:6: "If I do not remember
thee, let my tongue cleave to the roof of my mouth.")   34 If on the first
i.e., if intended only

KING HENRY   Have thy desire.
          [*Aumerle locks the door.*] *The Duke of York*
                    knocks at the door and crieth.
YORK [*Within*]
   My liege, beware! Look to thyself.
   Thou hast a traitor in thy presence there.
KING HENRY [*Drawing*]   Villain, I'll make thee safe.   41
AUMERLE
   Stay thy revengeful hand. Thou hast no cause to fear.
YORK [*Within*]
   Open the door, secure, foolhardy King!   43
   Shall I for love speak treason to thy face?   44
   Open the door, or I will break it open.
                    [*King Henry unlocks the door.*]

          [*Enter York.*]

KING HENRY
   What is the matter, uncle? Speak.
   Recover breath; tell us how near is danger,
   That we may arm us to encounter it.
YORK [*Giving letter*]
   Peruse this writing here, and thou shalt know
   The treason that my haste forbids me show.   50
AUMERLE
   Remember, as thou read'st, thy promise passed.
   I do repent me. Read not my name there;
   My heart is not confederate with my hand.
YORK
   It was, villain, ere thy hand did set it down.
   I tore it from the traitor's bosom, King;
   Fear, and not love, begets his penitence.
   Forget to pity him, lest thy pity prove
   A serpent that will sting thee to the heart.
KING HENRY
   O heinous, strong, and bold conspiracy!
   O loyal father of a treacherous son,
   Thou sheer, immaculate, and silver fountain,   61
   From whence this stream through muddy passages

41 safe harmless   **43 secure** unsuspecting, heedless   **44 speak . . . face**
i.e., speak so disrespectfully as to call you *secure* and *foolhardy*
50 haste . . . show i.e., breathlessness prevents me from revealing
61 sheer clear, pure

Hath held his current and defiled himself,
Thy overflow of good converts to bad,   64
And thy abundant goodness shall excuse
This deadly blot in thy digressing son.   66

YORK
So shall my virtue be his vice's bawd,
And he shall spend mine honor with his shame,
As thriftless sons their scraping fathers' gold.   69
Mine honor lives when his dishonor dies,
Or my shamed life in his dishonor lies.
Thou kill'st me in his life; giving him breath,
The traitor lives, the true man's put to death.

DUCHESS [Within]
What ho, my liege! For God's sake, let me in.

KING HENRY
What shrill-voiced suppliant makes this eager cry?

DUCHESS [Within]
A woman, and thy aunt, great King. 'Tis I.
Speak with me, pity me, open the door!
A beggar begs that never begged before.

KING HENRY
Our scene is altered from a serious thing,
And now changed to "The Beggar and the King."   80
My dangerous cousin, let your mother in.
I know she is come to pray for your foul sin.

> [Aumerle opens the door. Enter Duchess. She
> kneels.]

YORK
If thou do pardon whosoever pray,
More sins for this forgiveness prosper may.   84
This festered joint cut off, the rest rest sound;
This let alone will all the rest confound.   86

DUCHESS
O King, believe not this hardhearted man!
Love loving not itself, none other can.   88

64 converts changes   **66 digressing** transgressing   **69 scraping** parsimo-
nious   **80 The Beggar ... King** (Probably one of Shakespeare's many
allusions to the ballad of King Cophetua and the Beggar Maid.)   **84 for**
because of   **86 alone** untreated.   **confound** ruin   **88 Love ... can** i.e.,
he who does not love his own kin can love no one else, not even the
King

YORK
Thou frantic woman, what dost thou make here?   89
Shall thy old dugs once more a traitor rear?   90
DUCHESS
Sweet York, be patient. Hear me, gentle liege.
KING HENRY
Rise up, good aunt.
DUCHESS   Not yet, I thee beseech.
Forever will I walk upon my knees,
And never see day that the happy sees,   94
Till thou give joy, until thou bid me joy,
By pardoning Rutland, my transgressing boy.
AUMERLE [*Kneeling*]
Unto my mother's prayers I bend my knee.   97
YORK [*Kneeling*]
Against them both my true joints bended be.
Ill mayst thou thrive, if thou grant any grace!
DUCHESS
Pleads he in earnest? Look upon his face.
His eyes do drop no tears, his prayers are in jest;
His words come from his mouth, ours from our breast.
He prays but faintly and would be denied;
We pray with heart and soul and all beside.   104
His weary joints would gladly rise, I know;
Our knees still kneel till to the ground they grow.   106
His prayers are full of false hypocrisy,
Ours of true zeal and deep integrity.
Our prayers do outpray his; then let them have
That mercy which true prayer ought to have.
KING HENRY
Good aunt, stand up.
DUCHESS   Nay, do not say "stand up."
Say "pardon" first, and afterwards "stand up."
An if I were thy nurse, thy tongue to teach,   113
"Pardon" should be the first word of thy speech.
I never longed to hear a word till now;
Say "pardon," King; let pity teach thee how.

---

89 make do   **90 once . . . rear** (by now redeeming Aumerle from
death)   **94 never . . . sees** i.e., never partakes of life's pleasures that
happy people enjoy   **97 Unto** in support of   **104 beside** besides
106 still continually   **113 An if** if

The word is short, but not so short as sweet;
No word like "pardon" for kings' mouths so meet.
YORK
Speak it in French, King: say "pardonne moy."   119
DUCHESS
Dost thou teach pardon pardon to destroy?
Ah, my sour husband, my hardhearted lord,
That sets the word itself against the word!
Speak "pardon" as 'tis current in our land;
The chopping French we do not understand.   124
Thine eye begins to speak; set thy tongue there,
Or in thy piteous heart plant thou thine ear,
That hearing how our plaints and prayers do pierce,
Pity may move thee "pardon" to rehearse.   128
KING HENRY
Good aunt, stand up.
DUCHESS   I do not sue to stand.
Pardon is all the suit I have in hand.
KING HENRY
I pardon him, as God shall pardon me.
DUCHESS
O happy vantage of a kneeling knee!   132
Yet am I sick for fear. Speak it again;   133
Twice saying "pardon" doth not pardon twain
But makes one pardon strong.
KING HENRY   With all my heart
I pardon him.
DUCHESS   A god on earth thou art.   [*All rise.*]
KING HENRY
But for our trusty brother-in-law and the Abbot,   137
With all the rest of that consorted crew,   138
Destruction straight shall dog them at the heels.
Good uncle, help to order several powers   140
To Oxford, or where'er these traitors are.
They shall not live within this world, I swear,
But I will have them, if I once know where.

119 **pardonne moy** pardonnez-moi, excuse me. (An affectedly polite
refusal.)   124 **chopping** logic chopping, changing the sense
128 **rehearse** repeat   132 **happy vantage** fortunate gain   133 **Yet** still
137 **But for** but as for.   **brother-in-law** i.e., the Duke of Exeter, who had
married Bolingbroke's sister   138 **consorted** conspiring, confederate
140 **powers** forces

Uncle, farewell, and, cousin, adieu.
Your mother well hath prayed, and prove you true.   145
DUCHESS
Come, my old son. I pray God make thee new.
                                        Exeunt.

❖

5.4   *Enter Sir Pierce [of] Exton [and his Men].*

EXTON
Didst thou not mark the King, what words he spake,
"Have I no friend will rid me of this living fear?"   2
Was it not so?
FIRST MAN   These were his very words.
EXTON
"Have I no friend?" quoth he. He spake it twice,
And urged it twice together, did he not?
FIRST MAN   He did.
EXTON
And speaking it, he wishtly looked on me,   7
As who should say, "I would thou wert the man
That would divorce this terror from my heart"—
Meaning the King at Pomfret. Come, let's go.
I am the King's friend, and will rid his foe.   11
                                   [Exeunt.]

❖

5.5   *Enter Richard alone.*

KING RICHARD
I have been studying how I may compare
This prison where I live unto the world;
And, for because the world is populous,   3

145 **prove you true** may you prove loyal

**5.4. Location: The court. The opening stage direction in the Quarto
reads** *Manet Sir Pierce Exton, etc.,* **suggesting continuity of action with
the preceding scene.**
2 **will** who will   7 **wishtly** intently   11 **rid** rid him of

5.5. Location: Pomfret Castle. A dungeon.
3 **for because** because

And here is not a creature but myself,
I cannot do it. Yet I'll hammer it out.   5
My brain I'll prove the female to my soul,
My soul the father, and these two beget
A generation of still-breeding thoughts;   8
And these same thoughts people this little world,
In humors like the people of this world,   10
For no thought is contented. The better sort,
As thoughts of things divine, are intermixed
With scruples and do set the word itself   13
Against the word, as thus, "Come, little ones,"   14
And then again,   15
"It is as hard to come as for a camel   16
To thread the postern of a small needle's eye."   17
Thoughts tending to ambition, they do plot
Unlikely wonders—how these vain weak nails
May tear a passage through the flinty ribs
Of this hard world, my ragged prison walls,   21
And, for they cannot, die in their own pride.   22
Thoughts tending to content flatter themselves
That they are not the first of fortune's slaves,
Nor shall not be the last—like seely beggars   25
Who, sitting in the stocks, refuge their shame   26
That many have and others must sit there;
And in this thought they find a kind of ease,
Bearing their own misfortunes on the back
Of such as have before endured the like.
Thus play I in one person many people,
And none contented. Sometimes am I king;
Then treasons make me wish myself a beggar,
And so I am. Then crushing penury   34
Persuades me I was better when a king;
Then am I kinged again, and by and by
Think that I am unkinged by Bolingbroke,
And straight am nothing. But whate'er I be,

---

5 hammer i.e., work, puzzle   **8 still-breeding** constantly breeding
10 humors temperaments, peculiar fancies   **13 scruples** doubts
13–14 do set . . . word i.e., oppose one scriptural passage against its
apparent opposite   **14–17 Come . . . eye** (See Matthew 19:14, 24.)
17 postern narrow gate   **21 ragged** rugged   **22 for** because.   **pride**
prime   **25 seely** simpleminded   **26 refuge their shame** i.e., rationalize
their disgrace by reflecting   **34 penury** poverty

Nor I nor any man that but man is   39
With nothing shall be pleased till he be eased
With being nothing. (*The music plays*.) Music do I hear?   41
Ha, ha, keep time! How sour sweet music is,
When time is broke and no proportion kept!
So is it in the music of men's lives.
And here have I the daintiness of ear
To check time broke in a disordered string;   46
But for the concord of my state and time
Had not an ear to hear my true time broke.
I wasted time, and now doth time waste me;
For now hath Time made me his numbering clock.   50
My thoughts are minutes, and with sighs they jar   51
Their watches on unto mine eyes, the outward watch,   52
Whereto my finger, like a dial's point,   53
Is pointing still, in cleansing them from tears.
Now sir, the sound that tells what hour it is
Are clamorous groans which strike upon my heart,
Which is the bell. So sighs and tears and groans
Show minutes, times, and hours. But my time   58
Runs posting on in Bolingbroke's proud joy,   59
While I stand fooling here, his jack of the clock.   60
This music mads me. Let it sound no more,   61
For though it have holp madmen to their wits,   62
In me it seems it will make wise men mad.
Yet blessing on his heart that gives it me!
For 'tis a sign of love; and love to Richard
Is a strange brooch in this all-hating world.   66

Enter a Groom of the stable.

GROOM
   Hail, royal prince!
KING RICHARD   Thanks, noble peer!

39 Nor neither   **41 being nothing** i.e., being dead   **46 check** rebuke
50 numbering clock i.e., a clock that numbers hours and minutes
(not an hourglass)   **51–52 with . . . watch** i.e., by means of sighs, occurring as regularly as the swinging of a clock's pendulum, my thoughts
tick away, marking periods of time and transferring these manifestations to my eyes, which are like the face of the clock   **53 dial's point**
clock hand   **58 times** quarters and halves   **59 posting** hastening
60 jack of the clock manikin that struck the bell on a clock   **61 mads**
maddens   **62 holp** helped   **66 strange brooch** rare ornament

The cheapest of us is ten groats too dear.   68
What art thou, and how comest thou hither,
Where no man never comes but that sad dog
That brings me food to make misfortune live?

GROOM
I was a poor groom of thy stable, King,
When thou wert king; who, traveling towards York,
With much ado at length have gotten leave
To look upon my sometime royal master's face.   75
O, how it earned my heart when I beheld   76
In London streets, that coronation day,
When Bolingbroke rode on roan Barbary,
That horse that thou so often hast bestrid,
That horse that I so carefully have dressed!   80

KING RICHARD
Rode he on Barbary? Tell me, gentle friend,
How went he under him?

GROOM
So proudly as if he disdained the ground.

KING RICHARD
So proud that Bolingbroke was on his back!
That jade hath eat bread from my royal hand;   85
This hand hath made him proud with clapping him.   86
Would he not stumble? Would he not fall down,
Since pride must have a fall, and break the neck
Of that proud man that did usurp his back?
Forgiveness, horse! Why do I rail on thee,
Since thou, created to be awed by man,
Wast born to bear? I was not made a horse,
And yet I bear a burden like an ass,
Spurred, galled, and tired by jauncing Bolingbroke. 94

Enter one [a Keeper] to Richard with meat.

KEEPER [*To Groom*]
Fellow, give place. Here is no longer stay.

68 ten groats too dear (There is a pun on *royal* and *noble* in the preceding lines. A royal [10 shillings] is worth 10 groats [ten times 4 pence]
more than a noble [6 shillings, 8 pence] is; hence, Richard is saying that
he, "the cheapest of us" because he is a prisoner, is worth no more than
the groom, whom he greets as "noble.")   **75 sometime** former
76 earned grieved   **80 dressed** tended, groomed   **85 eat** eaten. (Pronounced "et.")   **86 clapping** patting, stroking   **94 galled** made sore.
jauncing making the horse prance up and down   **s.d. meat** food

KING RICHARD [*To Groom*]
If thou love me, 'tis time thou wert away.
GROOM
What my tongue dares not, that my heart shall say.
                                        Exit Groom.
KEEPER   My lord, will 't please you to fall to?
KING RICHARD
Taste of it first, as thou art wont to do.   99
KEEPER
My lord, I dare not. Sir Pierce of Exton, who
Lately came from the King, commands the contrary.
KING RICHARD
The devil take Henry of Lancaster and thee!
Patience is stale, and I am weary of it.
                              [*He beats the Keeper.*]
KEEPER   Help, help, help!
         The murderers [*Exton and his men*] *rush in.*
KING RICHARD
How now, what means death in this rude assault?
Villain, thy own hand yields thy death's instrument.
     [*He snatches a weapon from a man and kills him.*]
Go thou, and fill another room in hell.   107
     [*He kills another.*] *Here Exton strikes him down.*
That hand shall burn in never-quenching fire
That staggers thus my person. Exton, thy fierce hand   109
Hath with the King's blood stained the King's own land.
Mount, mount, my soul! Thy seat is up on high,
Whilst my gross flesh sinks downward, here to die.
                                        [*He dies.*]

EXTON
As full of valor as of royal blood!
Both have I spilled. O, would the deed were good!
For now the devil, that told me I did well,
Says that this deed is chronicled in hell.
This dead king to the living king I'll bear.
Take hence the rest, and give them burial here.
                          [*Exeunt, with the bodies.*]

❖

99 **Taste . . . first** i.e., to ensure that it isn't poisoned   **107 room** place
109 staggers causes to stagger

5.6 [*Flourish.*] *Enter Bolingbroke [as King], with the Duke of York, [other lords, and attendants].*

KING HENRY
Kind uncle York, the latest news we hear
Is that the rebels have consumed with fire
Our town of Ciceter in Gloucestershire,　　　3
But whether they be ta'en or slain we hear not.

　　Enter Northumberland.

Welcome, my lord. What is the news?
NORTHUMBERLAND
First, to thy sacred state wish I all happiness.
The next news is, I have to London sent
The heads of Salisbury, Spencer, Blunt, and Kent.
The manner of their taking may appear　　　9
At large discoursèd in this paper here.　　　10
　　　　　　　　　　[*He gives a paper.*]

KING HENRY
We thank thee, gentle Percy, for thy pains,
And to thy worth will add right worthy gains.　　　12

　　Enter Lord Fitzwater.

FITZWATER
My lord, I have from Oxford sent to London
The heads of Brocas and Sir Bennet Seely,
Two of the dangerous consorted traitors　　　15
That sought at Oxford thy dire overthrow.
KING HENRY
Thy pains, Fitzwater, shall not be forgot;
Right noble is thy merit, well I wot.　　　18

　　*Enter Henry Percy [with the Bishop of Carlisle,
　　guarded].*

PERCY
The grand conspirator, Abbot of Westminster,
With clog of conscience and sour melancholy　　　20

5.6. Location: The court.
3 Ciceter i.e., Cirencester　**9 taking** capture　**10 At large discoursèd**
related in full　**12 worth** (1) deserving (2) present worth　**15 consorted**
conspiring　**18 wot** know　**20 clog** burden

Hath yielded up his body to the grave;
But here is Carlisle living, to abide   22
Thy kingly doom and sentence of his pride.   23
KING HENRY   Carlisle, this is your doom:
Choose out some secret place, some reverend room,   25
More than thou hast, and with it joy thy life.   26
So as thou liv'st in peace, die free from strife;
For though mine enemy thou hast ever been,
High sparks of honor in thee have I seen.

Enter Exton, with [attendants bearing] the coffin.

EXTON
Great King, within this coffin I present
Thy buried fear. Herein all breathless lies
The mightiest of thy greatest enemies,
Richard of Bordeaux, by me hither brought.
KING HENRY
Exton, I thank thee not, for thou hast wrought
A deed of slander with thy fatal hand   35
Upon my head and all this famous land.
EXTON
From your own mouth, my lord, did I this deed.
KING HENRY
They love not poison that do poison need,
Nor do I thee. Though I did wish him dead,
I hate the murderer, love him murderèd.
The guilt of conscience take thou for thy labor,
But neither my good word nor princely favor.
With Cain go wander thorough shades of night,   43
And never show thy head by day nor light.
Lords, I protest, my soul is full of woe,
That blood should sprinkle me to make me grow.
Come, mourn with me for what I do lament,
And put on sullen black incontinent.   48
I'll make a voyage to the Holy Land,

22 abide await   **23 doom** judgment   **25 reverend room** place suitable to
religious retirement   **26 More than thou hast** i.e., larger than your
present cell, or more worthy of reverence.   **joy** gladden, enjoy   **35 deed
of slander** i.e., a deed sure to arouse slanderous talk about the new king
43 Cain murderer of his brother Abel; see 1.1.104.   **thorough** through
48 incontinent immediately

To wash this blood off from my guilty hand.
March sadly after. Grace my mournings here,   51
In weeping after this untimely bier.
            [*Exeunt in procession, following the coffin.*]

51 Grace dignify

Date and Text

On August 29, 1597, "The Tragedye of Richard the Second" was entered in the Stationers' Register, the official record book of the London Company of Stationers (booksellers and printers), by Andrew Wise, and was published by him later that same year:

> THE Tragedie of King Richard the second. *As it hath beene publikely acted by the right Honourable the Lorde Chamberlaine his Seruants.* LONDON Printed by Valentine Simmes for Androw Wise, and are to be sold at his shop in Paules church yard at the signe of the Angel. 1597.

This is a good text, printed evidently from the author's papers or a nontheatrical transcript of them. Wise issued two more quartos of this popular play in 1598, each set from the previous quarto, and then in 1603 transferred his rights to the play to Matthew Law. This publisher issued in 1608 a fourth quarto "With new additions of the Parliament Sceane, and the deposing of King Richard" (according to the title page in some copies). The deposition scene had indeed been omitted from the earlier quartos, probably through censorship. A fifth quarto appeared in 1615, based on the fourth. All the quartos after the first attribute the play to Shakespeare. The added deposition scene in quartos four and five seems to have been memorially reconstructed. The First Folio text of 1623 gives a better version of the deposition scene, seemingly because the printers of the Folio had access to the manuscript promptbook for this portion of the text. (Some scholars maintain that the Folio text was derived from an earlier quarto or quartos that had been used as a promptbook, but that case has been weakened by recent research.) Most of the Folio was probably set from quarto three, and perhaps from the final two leaves of quarto five, so that the most authoritative text for all but the deposition scene is the first quarto; nevertheless, some other parts of the Folio text show signs of having made reference to the promptbook, so that its readings, especially in these areas, deserve serious attention. The Folio's stage directions are often illuminating about staging.

Francis Meres mentions the play in 1598 in his *Palladis*

Tamia: Wit's Treasury (a slender volume on contemporary literature and art; valuable because it lists most of the plays of Shakespeare's that existed at that time). Clearly it had been written and performed prior to the Stationers' Register entry in August of 1597. Its earliest probable date is 1595, since the play is seemingly indebted to Samuel Daniel's poem *The First Four Books of the Civil Wars*, published in that year. Shakespeare follows Daniel, for example, in increasing the Queen's age from eleven (according to the chronicles) to maturity, and in other significant details. On December 9, 1595, Sir Edward Hoby invited Sir Robert Cecil to his house in Cannon Row "where as late as it shall please you a gate for your supper shall be open, and King Richard present himself to your view." Although it is by no means certain that this passage refers to a private performance of Shakespeare's play, stylistic considerations favor a date around 1595 rather than 1597. If, as some scholars contend, Daniel's *Civil Wars* was written after Shakespeare's play rather than before it, the date of *Richard II* might be as early as 1594.

Textual Notes

These textual notes are not a historical collation, either of the early quartos and the early folios or of more recent editions; they are simply a record of departures in this edition from the copy text. The reading adopted in this edition appears in boldface, followed by the rejected reading from the copy text, i.e., the quarto of 1597. Only major alterations in punctuation are noted. Changes in lineation are not indicated, nor are some minor and obvious typographical errors.

Abbreviations used:
F the First Folio
Q quarto
s.d. stage direction
s.p. speech prefix

Copy text: the first quarto of 1597 as press-corrected in all four extant copies [Q1]; and, for the deposition scene, 4.1.155–321, the First Folio.

1.1. 118 by my [F] by   **139 But** Ah but   **152 gentlemen** [F] gentleman
163 Obedience bids obedience bids. Obedience bids   **176 gage. My** gage, my

1.2. 25 him. Thou him, thou   **47 sit** [F] set   **48 butcher** butchers   **58 it**
[Q2–5, F] is   **60 begun** begone

1.3. 15 thee the   **33 comest** [Q5] comes   **58 thee** the   **104 s.p. First Herald**
Herald   **172 then but** [F] but   **180 you owe** [F] y'owe   **193 far** fare
222 night [Q4–5, F] nightes   **239 had it** had't

1.4. s.d. Bagot [F] Bushie   **20 our cousin** [F] our Coosens   **23 Bagot here,
and Green** [Q6; not in Q1]   **52 s.d. Enter Bushy** [F] Enter Bushie with news
53 Bushy, what news [F; not in Q1]   **65 s.p. All** [not in Q1]

2.1. 15 life's liues   **18 fond** found   **48 as a** [Q4–5, F] as   **68 s.d.** [at l. 70 in Q1]
70 reined ragde   **102 encagèd** [F] inraged   **113 not** not, not   **124 brother**
brothers   **177 the** [F] a   **209 seize** cease   **257 King's** [Q3–5, F] King
277 Blanc Blan   **284 Coint** Coines

2.2. 31 though [Q2–5, F] thought   **53 Harry** H.

2.3. 30 lordship Lo: **36 Hereford** [Q3–5, F] Herefords   **99 the lord** [F] Lord

2.4. 1 s.p. Welsh Captain Welsh (also at l. 7)

3.2. 32 succor succors   **40 boldly** bouldy   **72 O'erthrows** [F] Ouerthrowes
170 through [Q2–5, F] thorough

3.3. 13 brief with you [F] briefe   **31 lord** [F] Lords   **60 waters—on** water's
on   **100 pastures'** pastors   **119 prince and** princesse

3.4. 11 joy griefe   **26 pins** [F] pines   **27 state, for** state for   **28 change; woe**
change woe   **34 too** [F] two   **55 seized** ceasde   **57 We at** at   **80 Cam'st**
[Q2–5, F] Canst

4.1. 23 him [Q3–5, F] them   **44 Fitzwater** [F] Fitzwaters   **55 As** As it   **56 sun
to sun** sinne to sinne   **77 my bond** [Q3–5, F] bond   **110 thee** [Q2–5, F] the

146 you yon **155–321** [This deposition scene is based on the First Folio text; Q1 has only: "Let it be so, and loe on wednesday next, / We solemnly pro-claime our Coronation, / Lords be ready all." Unless otherwise indicated all the new readings in ll. 115–321 are taken from Q4.] **184 and on** on **252 and** a **256 Nor** No, nor **297 manners** manner

5.1. 41 thee [Q2–5, F] the **84 s.p. Northumberland** [F] King

5.2. 2 off [F] of **11 thee** [F] the [also at ll. 17 and 94] **116 And** An

5.3. s.d. King the King **10 While** Which **36 I may** [Q2–5, F] May **68 And** An **75 shrill-voiced** shril voice **111 s.p. King Henry** yorke **135–136 With . . . him** I pardon him with al my heart

5.4. s.d. Enter [F] Manet **3 s.p. First Man** Man [F; also at l. 6]

5.5. 20 through [F] thorow **22 cannot, die** cannot die **27 sit** [Q3–5, F] set

5.6. 8 Salisbury, Spencer [F] Oxford, Salisbury **12 s.d. Fitzwater** Fitzwaters **43 thorough** through

Shakespeare's Sources

Shakespeare's primary source for *Richard II* was the 1587 edition of Raphael Holinshed's *Chronicles* covering the years 1398 to 1400. As in his earlier *Henry VI* plays and *Richard III*, Shakespeare departs from historical accuracy in the interests of artistic design. Queen Isabel's part is almost wholly invented, for historically she was a child of eleven at the time the events in this play occurred. Her "Garden Scene" (3.4) is a fine piece of invention, bringing together images of order and disorder that are found in the rest of the play. The Duchess of York's role is entirely original; Holinshed reports the scene in which York's son Aumerle (the Earl of Rutland) rides to the new King and begs for mercy while his father simultaneously denounces him as a traitor, but the Duchess is never mentioned. Shakespeare has added the poignant conflict between husband and wife. Northumberland's role as conspirator against Richard and as hatchet man for Bolingbroke is greatly enlarged; for example, Holinshed never names the persons who engage in the original plotting against Richard. Yet Shakespeare's Bolingbroke returns to England on his own initiative, whereas in Holinshed he does so at the barons' invitation, a change that accentuates the puzzle of Bolingbroke's motive. Another invention is the meeting between John of Gaunt and the Duchess of Gloucester (1.2). In fact, most of Gaunt's character and behavior have no basis in Holinshed at all. Shakespeare creates him to fill the role of thoughtfully conservative statesman, agonized by his son's banishment but doggedly obedient to his monarch. Finally, and most important, Shakespeare has greatly enlarged the role and the poetic nature of King Richard, especially in the final two acts.

Many of these alterations are Shakespeare's own; others derive from his reading in other sources. Samuel Daniel's *The First Four Books of the Civil Wars* (1595) may have had an important influence. Although we cannot discount the possibility that Shakespeare's play may have been written first, the consensus today is that he knew Daniel's poem. It gave him the idea of the Queen's maturity and grief (although not the Garden Scene) and the final meeting of King and Queen. Daniel's Hotspur is unhistorically a young man, as in Act 2, scene 3, of Shakespeare's play. Like Shakespeare, Daniel sees York as a man of "a mild temperateness." Daniel's Richard and Bolingbroke ride together into London, not separately as in Holinshed. In Daniel's poem, Bolingbroke's indirect manner of insinuating his desire for Richard's death ("And wished that some would so his life esteem / As rid him of these fears wherein he stood") is verbally close to Shakespeare's depiction of this scene. Richard's final soliloquies in these two works show an unmistakable similarity to one another.

Richard II's reign was a controversial subject in the 1590s and produced other plays of varying political coloration that Shakespeare must have known. *The Life and Death of Jack Straw* (anonymous, 1590–1593) distorts history in its friendly portrayal of Richard's role in the Peasants' Revolt of 1381, and whitewashes governmental policy. In contrast, the anonymous play *Thomas of Woodstock*, sometimes known as *1 Richard II* (1591–1595), is almost a call for open rebellion against tyranny. Many verbal similarities link this latter play with Shakespeare's *Richard II*, and although scholars have difficulty in determining which was written first, the wary consensus is that Shakespeare borrowed from *Woodstock*. Such a hypothesis would explain some of the mysterious references to Woodstock's death in the first act of *Richard II*, since the anonymous play deals with historical events preceding those of Shakespeare's play. Shakespeare's debt to *Jack Straw*, on the other hand, is slight, even though he probably knew the play. Christopher Marlowe's *Edward II* (c. 1592), although dealing with another reign, probably taught Shakespeare much about constructing a play in which a weak king gains sympathy in his suffering, while his successor becomes morally tainted by the act of deposition.

Other sources have been proposed, so many in fact that Shakespeare's task of writing the play has been compared to that of a historical researcher. More probably he assimilated his wide and varied reading without any formal program of study. He had certainly read Edward Hall's *Union of the Two Noble Families of Lancaster and York* (1542), a chief source for his earlier history plays, but in *Richard II* he seems to have recalled little more than its overall thematic pattern. Shakespeare must have known the Complaints of Mowbray and Richard in *A Mirror for Magistrates*, but the verbal echoes are slight in this case. The same is essentially true of *The Chronicles of England* by Jean Froissart, translated by Lord Berners (1525), and two French eyewitness accounts available to Shakespeare only in manuscript: the anonymous *Chronique de la Traïson et Mort de Richard Deux Roi d'Angleterre* and Jean Créton's *Histoire du Roi d'Angleterre Richard*. The Froissart *Chronicles* perhaps gave some hints for Gaunt's refusal to avenge Gloucester's death, for Richard's insensitivity at Gaunt's death, and for Northumberland's role as conspirator. The *Traïson* is notably sympathetic to Richard in his decline, although Shakespeare might also have found this sympathy in Daniel's *Civil Wars*.

Shakespeare's second series of English history plays (*Richard II, 1* and *2 Henry IV, Henry V*) is freer of the Tudor providential view of history than was once supposed. The second series does not lead forward by any direct link to the reign of the Tudors, as does the first. Henry A. Kelly has shown (*Divine Providence in the England of Shakespeare's Histories*, 1970), that Shakespeare does not follow a single "Tudor myth" but allows spokesmen for both Richard II and his opponents to repeat arguments found in the various chronicles. This practice is especially evident in *Richard II*, in which some spokesmen eloquently warn of the disasters that will follow Bolingbroke's assumption of the throne, while other spokesmen are sympathetic to Bolingbroke's takeover as a political necessity.

The Third Volume of Chronicles (1587 edition)
Compiled by Raphael Holinshed

RICHARD THE SECOND

[Holinshed relates the events leading up to the confrontation of Henry, Duke of Hereford, and Thomas Mowbray, Duke of Norfolk, before King Richard in 1398: Richard's coming to the throne at the age of eleven in 1377, popular restiveness over taxes and confused administration, the quarrel between Richard and his uncle the Duke of Gloucester (Thomas of Woodstock), Gloucester's plot to imprison and kill King Richard along with the Dukes of York and Lancaster, the revelation of the plot to Richard by the Duke of Norfolk, Richard's ordering Norfolk to kill Gloucester in secret, Norfolk's reluctantly doing so, popular outcry at the death of Gloucester, and uncertainty among Gloucester's brothers as to how to avenge his death.]

It fell out that, in this Parliament holden at Shrewsbury, Henry, Duke of Hereford, accused Thomas Mowbray, Duke of Norfolk, of certain words which he should utter[1] in talk had betwixt them as they rode together lately before[2] betwixt London and Brentford, sounding highly to the King's dishonor. And for further proof thereof he presented a supplication to the King wherein he appealed the Duke of Norfolk in field of battle[3] for a traitor, false and disloyal to the King and enemy unto the realm. This supplication was read before both the Dukes in presence of the King; which done, the Duke of Norfolk took upon him to answer it, declaring that, whatsoever the Duke of Hereford had said against him other than well, he lied falsely like an untrue knight as he was. And when the King asked of the Duke of Hereford what he said to it, he, taking his hood off his head, said: "My sovereign lord, even as the supplication which I took[4] you im-

---

1 **should utter** was alleged to have uttered   2 **lately before** recently
3 **appealed . . . battle** i.e., brought an accusation against the Duke of Norfolk to be tried by combat   4 **took** gave

porteth, right so I say for truth, that Thomas Mowbray, Duke of Norfolk, is a traitor, false and disloyal to your royal majesty, your crown, and to all the states[5] of your realm."

Then the Duke of Norfolk, being asked what he said to this, he answered: "Right dear lord, with your favor that I make answer unto your cousin here, I say (your reverence saved)[6] that Henry of Lancaster, Duke of Hereford, like a false and disloyal traitor as he is, doth lie in that he hath or shall say of me otherwise than well." "No more," said the King, "we have heard enough"; and herewith commanded the Duke of Surrey, for that turn[7] Marshal of England, to arrest in his name the two Dukes. The Duke of Lancaster (father to the Duke of Hereford), the Duke of York, the Duke of Aumerle (Constable of England), and the Duke of Surrey (Marshal of the realm) undertook as pledges, body for body, for the Duke of Hereford; but the Duke of Norfolk was not suffered to put in pledges and so, under arrest, was led unto Windsor Castle and there guarded with keepers that were appointed to see him safely kept.

Now, after the dissolving of the Parliament at Shrewsbury, there was a day appointed about six weeks after for the King to come unto Windsor to hear and to take some order[8] betwixt the two Dukes which had thus appealed each other. There was a great scaffold erected within the castle of Windsor for the King to sit with the lords and prelates of his realm; and so, at the day appointed, he with the said lords and prelates being come thither and set in their places, the Duke of Hereford, appellant, and the Duke of Norfolk, defendant, were sent for to come and appear before the King, sitting there in his seat of justice. And then began Sir John Bushy to speak for the King, declaring to the lords how they should understand that where[9] the Duke of Hereford had presented a supplication to the King, who was there set to minister justice to all men that would demand the same, as appertained to his royal majesty, he therefore would now hear what the parties could say one against another; and withal[10] the King commanded the Dukes of

---

5 states estates, members of a rank or class of society   **6 your reverence saved** saving your reverence. (An apologetic phrase introducing something that might offend the hearer.)   **7 turn** term, time   **8 take some order** i.e., adjudicate the dispute   **9 where** whereas   **10 withal** in addition

Aumerle and Surrey, the one being Constable and the other Marshal, to go unto the two Dukes, appellant and defendant, requiring them on his behalf to grow to some agreement; and for his part he would be ready to pardon all that had been said or done amiss betwixt them touching any harm or dishonor to him or his realm. But they answered both assuredly that it was not possible to have any peace or agreement made betwixt them.

When he heard what they had answered, he commanded that they should be brought forthwith before his presence to hear what they would say. Herewith an herald in the King's name, with loud voice, commanded the Dukes to come before the King, either[11] of them to show his reason or else to make peace together without more delay. When they were come before the King and lords, the King spake himself to them, willing them to agree and make peace together. "For it is," said he, "the best way ye can take." The Duke of Norfolk, with due reverence, hereunto answered it could not be so brought to pass, his honor saved. Then the King asked of the Duke of Hereford what it was that he demanded of the Duke of Norfolk, "and what is the matter that ye cannot make peace together and become friends?"

Then stood forth a knight who, asking and obtaining license to speak for the Duke of Hereford, said: "Right dear and sovereign lord, here is Henry of Lancaster, Duke of Hereford and Earl of Derby, who saith, and I for him likewise say, that Thomas Mowbray, Duke of Norfolk, is a false and disloyal traitor to you and your royal majesty and to your whole realm; and likewise the Duke of Hereford saith, and I for him, that Thomas Mowbray, Duke of Norfolk, hath received eight thousand nobles to pay the soldiers that keep your town of Calais, which he hath not done as he ought; and furthermore, the said Duke of Norfolk hath been the occasion of all the treason that hath been contrived in your realm for the space of these eighteen years, and by his false suggestions and malicious counsel he hath caused to die and to be murdered your right dear uncle, the Duke of Gloucester, son to King Edward. Moreover, the Duke of Hereford saith, and I for him, that he will prove this with his body against the body of the said Duke of Norfolk within

11 **either** each

lists."[12] The King herewith waxed angry and asked the Duke of Hereford if these were his words, who answered, "Right dear lord, they are my words, and hereof I require right, and the battle against him."

There was a knight also that asked license to speak for the Duke of Norfolk and, obtaining it, began to answer thus: "Right dear sovereign lord, here is Thomas Mowbray, Duke of Norfolk, who answereth and saith, and I for him, that all which Henry of Lancaster hath said and declared, saving the reverence due to the King and his Council, is a lie; and the said Henry of Lancaster hath falsely and wickedly lied as a false and disloyal knight, and both hath been and is a traitor against you, your crown, royal majesty, and realm. This will I prove and defend, as becometh a loyal knight, to do with my body against his. Right dear lord, I beseech you therefore, and your Council, that it may please you in your royal discretion to consider and mark what Henry of Lancaster, Duke of Hereford, such a one as he is, hath said."

The King then demanded of the Duke of Norfolk if these were his words and whether he had any more to say. The Duke of Norfolk then answered for himself: "Right dear sir, true it is that I have received so much gold to pay your people[13] of the town of Calais, which I have done; and I do avouch that your town of Calais is as well kept at your commandment as ever it was at any time before, and that there never hath been by any of Calais any complaint made unto you of me. Right dear and my sovereign lord, for the voyage that I made into France about your marriage, I never received either gold or silver of you, nor yet for the voyage that the Duke of Aumerle and I made into Almaine,[14] where we spent great treasure. Marry, true it is that once I laid an ambush to have slain the Duke of Lancaster that there sitteth; but nevertheless he hath pardoned me thereof and there was good peace made betwixt us, for the which I yield him hearty thanks. This is that which I have to answer, and I am ready to defend myself against mine adversary. I beseech you therefore of right, and to have the battle against him in upright judgment."

After this, when the King had communed with his Coun-

---

12 within lists in the place of combat. (The *King Edward* mentioned here is Edward III.)   **13 people** soldiers   **14 Almaine** Germany

cil a little, he commanded the two Dukes to stand forth that their answers might be heard. The King then caused them once again to be asked if they would agree and make peace together, but they both flatly answered that they would not; and withal the Duke of Hereford cast down his gage and the Duke of Norfolk took it up. The King, perceiving this demeanor betwixt them, sware by Saint John Baptist that he would never seek to make peace betwixt them again. And therefore Sir John Bushy, in name of the King and his Council, declared that the King and his Council had commanded and ordained that they should have a day of battle appointed them at Coventry. Here writers disagree about the day that was appointed, for some say it was upon a Monday in August, other upon Saint Lambert's Day being the seventeenth of September, other on the eleventh of September; but true it is that the King assigned them not only the day but also appointed them lists and place for the combat, and thereupon great preparation was made as to such a matter appertained.

At the time appointed the King came to Coventry, where the two Dukes were ready according to the order prescribed therein, coming thither in great array accompanied with the lords and gentlemen of their lineages.[15] The King caused a sumptuous scaffold or theater and royal lists there to be erected and prepared. The Sunday before they should fight, after dinner, the Duke of Hereford came to the King (being lodged about a quarter of a mile without the town in a tower that belonged to Sir William Bagot) to take his leave of him. The morrow after, being the day appointed for the combat, about the spring of the day[16] came the Duke of Norfolk to the court to take leave likewise of the King. The Duke of Hereford armed him in his tent, that was set up near to the lists, and the Duke of Norfolk put on his armor betwixt the gate and the barrier of the town, in a beautiful house having a fair parclose[17] of wood towards the gate that none might see what was done within the house.

The Duke of Aumerle, that day being High Constable of England, and the Duke of Surrey, Marshal, placed themselves betwixt them, well armed and appointed; and when they saw their time, they first entered into the lists with a great company of men appareled in silk sendal[18] embroidered with silver both richly and curiously,[19] every man having a tipped staff to keep the field in order. About the hour of prime[20] came to the barriers of the lists the Duke of Hereford, mounted on a white courser barded[21] with green and blue velvet embroidered sumptuously with swans and antelopes of goldsmith's work, armed at all points. The Constable and Marshal came to the barriers, demanding of him what he was. He answered: "I am Henry of Lancaster, Duke of Hereford, which am come hither to do mine endeavor against Thomas Mowbray, Duke of Norfolk, as a traitor untrue to God, the King, his realm, and me." Then incontinently[22] he sware upon the holy evangelists that his quarrel was true and just, and upon that point he required[23] to enter the lists. Then he put up his sword, which before he held naked in his hand, and, putting down his visor, made a cross on his horse, and with spear in hand entered into the lists and descended from his horse and set him down in a chair of green velvet at the one end of the lists and there reposed himself, abiding the coming of his adversary.

Soon after him entered into the field with great triumph King Richard, accompanied with all the peers of the realm; and in his company was the Earl of Saint-Pol, which was come out of France in post[24] to see this challenge performed. The King had there above ten thousand men in armor, lest some fray or tumult might rise amongst his nobles by quarreling or partaking.[25] When the King was set in his seat, which was richly hanged and adorned, a king at arms[26] made open proclamation prohibiting all men, in the name of the King and of the High Constable and Marshal, to enterprise or attempt to approach or touch any part of the lists upon pain of death, except such as were appointed to order or marshal the field. The proclamation ended, another herald cried: "Behold here Henry of Lancaster, Duke of Hereford, appellant, which is entered into the lists royal to do his devoir[27] against Thomas Mowbray, Duke of Nor-

18 **sendal** a thin, rich material   19 **curiously** delicately   20 **prime** 9 A.M.
21 **barded** caparisoned, richly covered   22 **incontinently** immediately
23 **required** asked permission   24 **in post** in haste   25 **partaking** taking
sides   26 **king at arms** chief herald   27 **devoir** appointed task, utmost

folk, defendant, upon pain to be found false and recreant!"

The Duke of Norfolk hovered on horseback at the entry of the lists, his horse being barded with crimson velvet embroidered richly with lions of silver and mulberry trees; and when he had made his oath before the Constable and Marshal that his quarrel was just and true, he entered the field manfully, saying aloud, "God aid him that hath the right!"; and then he departed from his horse and sat him down in his chair, which was of crimson velvet curtained about with white and red damask. The Lord Marshal viewed their spears to see that they were of equal length and delivered the one spear himself to the Duke of Hereford and sent the other unto the Duke of Norfolk by a knight. Then the herald proclaimed that the traverses[28] and chairs of the champions should be removed, commanding them on the King's behalf to mount on horseback and address themselves to the battle and combat.

The Duke of Hereford was quickly horsed, and closed his beaver and cast his spear into the rest,[29] and when the trumpet sounded set forward courageously towards his enemy six or seven paces. The Duke of Norfolk was not fully set forward when the King cast down his warder[30] and the heralds cried, "Ho, ho!" Then the King caused their spears to be taken from them and commanded them to repair again to their chairs, where they remained two long hours while the King and his Council deliberately consulted what order was best to be had in so weighty a cause. Finally, after they had devised and fully determined what should be done therein, the heralds cried silence, and Sir John Bushy, the King's secretary, read the sentence and determination of the King and his Council in a long roll, the effect whereof was that Henry, Duke of Hereford, should within fifteen days depart out of the realm and not to return before the term of ten years were expired except[31] by the King he should be repealed[32] again, and this upon pain of death; and that Thomas Mowbray, Duke of Norfolk, because he had sown sedition in the realm by his words, should likewise avoid the realm and never to return again into England nor

---

28 traverses curtained compartments   **29 rest** resting place for the base of the spear   **30 warder** baton   **31 except** unless   **32 repealed** recalled

approach the borders or confines thereof upon pain of death; and that the King would stay[33] the profits of his[34] lands till he had levied thereof such sums of money as the Duke had taken up of the King's treasurer for the wages of the garrison of Calais which were still unpaid. When these judgments were once read, the King called before him both the parties and made them to swear that the one should never come in place where the other was, willingly, nor keep any company together in any foreign region; which oath they both received humbly and so went their ways. The Duke of Norfolk departed sorrowfully out of the realm into Almaine and at the last came to Venice, where he for thought[35] and melancholy deceased; for he was in hope (as writers record) that he should have been borne out[36] in the matter by the King, which when it fell out otherwise it grieved him not a little. The Duke of Hereford took his leave of the King at Eltham, who there released four years of his banishment; so he took his journey over into Calais and from thence went into France, where he remained. A wonder it was to see what number of people ran after him in every town and street where he came before he took the sea, lamenting and bewailing his departure, as who would say[37] that when he departed, the only shield, defense, and comfort of the commonwealth was vaded[38] and gone.

[The Duke of Hereford is well received by the French King Charles the Sixth, who proposes a marriage treaty until the matter is blocked by King Richard's ambassadors.]

But yet, to content the King's[39] mind, many blank charters[40] were devised and brought into the City,[41] which many of the substantial and wealthy citizens were fain[42] to seal, to their great charge,[43] as in the end appeared. And the like

---

33 **stay** detain, hold back   34 **his** i.e., Mowbray's   35 **thought** sorrow
36 **borne out** backed, supported   37 **as who would say** as one might say
38 **vaded** departed   39 **the King's** i.e., Richard's   40 **blank charters**
writs authorizing the collection of revenues or forced loans to the
crown, with blank spaces being left for the collectors to fill in the
name of the payer and the amount he must pay; see *Richard II*,
1.4.48   41 **the City** i.e., London   42 **fain** obliged   43 **charge** expense

charters were sent abroad into all shires within the realm, whereby great grudge and murmuring arose among the people; for when they were so sealed, the King's officers wrote in the same what liked them,[44] as well for charging the parties with payment of money as otherwise.

In this meantime the Duke of Lancaster[45] departed out of this life at the Bishop of Ely's place in Holborn and lieth buried in the cathedral church of Saint Paul in London, on the north side of the high altar, by the Lady Blanche his first wife. The death of this Duke gave occasion of increasing more hatred in the people of this realm toward the King, for he seized into his hands all the goods that belonged to him and also received all the rents and revenues of his lands which ought to have descended unto the Duke of Hereford by lawful inheritance, in revoking his letters patents,[46] which he had granted to him before, by virtue whereof he might make his attorneys general to sue livery[47] for him, of any manner of inheritances or possessions that might from thenceforth fall unto him, and that his homage might be respited with making reasonable fine.[48] Whereby it was evident that the King meant his utter undoing.

This hard dealing was much misliked of[49] all the nobility and cried out against of the meaner sort;[50] but namely[51] the Duke of York was therewith sore moved, who, before this time, had borne things with so patient a mind as he could, though the same touched him very near, as[52] the death of his brother the Duke of Gloucester, the banishment of his nephew the said Duke of Hereford, and other more injuries in great number which, for[53] the slippery youth of the King, he passed over for the time and did forget as well as he might. But now, perceiving that neither law, justice, nor equity could take place where the King's willful will was bent

---

44 liked them they pleased   **45 the Duke of Lancaster** John of Gaunt, who died in February 1399   **46 letters patents** royal grant giving the privilege to sue through one's attorneys for possession of one's inheritance; see *Richard II*, 2.1.202   **47 sue livery** sue for possession of hereditary rights; see previous note and *Richard II*, 2.3.129   **48 that . . . fine** that the formal acknowledgment of allegiance under the feudal system which was incumbent upon him might be postponed by means of his paying a reasonable fine   **49 misliked of** disliked by   **50 of the meaner sort** by those of lower station   **51 namely** especially   **52 as** such as   **53 for** taking into account

upon any wrongful purpose, he considered that the glory of the public wealth[54] of his country must needs decay by reason of the King his[55] lack of wit and want of such as would without flattery admonish him of his duty; and therefore he thought it the part of a wise man to get him in time to a resting place and to leave the following of such an unadvised captain[56] as with a leaden sword would cut his own throat.

Hereupon he, with the Duke of Aumerle his son, went to his house at Langley, rejoicing that nothing had mishappened in the commonwealth through his device or consent. The common bruit[57] ran that the King had set to farm the realm of England unto Sir William Scroop, Earl of Wiltshire and then Treasurer of England, to Sir John Bushy, Sir John Bagot, and Sir Henry Green, knights. About the same time, the Earl of Arundel's son, named Thomas, which was kept in the Duke of Exeter's house, escaped out of the realm by means of one William Scott, mercer, and went to his uncle, Thomas Arundel, late Archbishop of Canterbury, as then sojourning at Cologne.

King Richard, being destitute of treasure to furnish such a princely port as he maintained, borrowed great sums of money of many of the great lords and peers of his realm, both spiritual and temporal, and likewise of other mean persons, promising them in good earnest by delivering to them his letters patents for assurance that he would repay the money so borrowed at a day appointed, which notwithstanding he never paid. . . .

In this year, in a manner throughout all the realm of England, old bay trees withered and afterwards, contrary to all men's thinking, grew green again—a strange sight and supposed to import some unknown event. In this meantime the King, being advertised that the wild Irish daily wasted and destroyed the towns and villages within the English Pale[58] and had slain many of the soldiers which lay there in garrison for defense of that country, determined to make eftsoons[59] a voyage thither and prepared all things neces-

---

54 public wealth common welfare   **55 King his** King's   **56 unadvised captain** ill-advised ruler   **57 bruit** rumor   **58 the English Pale** the area under English jurisdiction. (The year is 1399.)   **59 eftsoons** again

sary for his passage now against the spring.[60] A little before his setting forth, he caused a jousts to be holden at Windsor of forty knights and forty esquires against all comers, and they to be appareled in green, with a white falcon, and the Queen[61] to be there well accompanied with ladies and damsels. When these jousts were finished, the King departed toward Bristol, from thence to pass into Ireland, leaving the Queen with her train still at Windsor. He appointed for his lieutenant general in his absence his uncle the Duke of York. And so, in the month of April, as divers authors write, he set forward from Windsor and finally took shipping at Milford, and from thence with two hundred ships and a puissant power of men-of-arms and archers he sailed into Ireland. . . .

Now whilst he was thus occupied in devising how to reduce them[62] into subjection, and taking orders for the good stay and quiet government of the country, divers of the nobility, as well prelates as other, and likewise many of the magistrates and rulers of the cities, towns, and commonalty here in England, perceiving daily how the realm drew to utter ruin, not like[63] to be recovered to the former state of wealth whilst King Richard lived and reigned (as they took it), devised with great deliberation and considerate advice, to send and signify by letters unto Duke Henry, whom they now called (as he was indeed) Duke of Lancaster and Hereford, requiring him with all convenient speed to convey himself into England, promising him all their aid, power, and assistance if he, expelling King Richard as a man not meet for the office he bare, would take upon him the scepter, rule, and diadem of his native land and region.

[Duke Henry readies a fleet at Le Port Blanc in Brittany and sails for England in the company of Thomas Arundel, Archbishop of Canterbury, and others.]

When the Lord Governor, Edmund, Duke of York, was advertised[64] that the Duke of Lancaster kept still the sea and was ready to arrive (but where he meant first to set foot on

---

60 against the spring in anticipation of the coming of spring   **61 the Queen** i.e., Isabella (then aged twelve), Richard's second wife   **62 them** i.e., the Irish   **63 like** likely   **64 advertised** advised, informed

land there was not any that understood the certainty), he sent for the Lord Chancellor, Edmund Stafford, Bishop of Exeter, and for the Lord Treasurer, William Scroop, Earl of Wiltshire, and other of the King's Privy Council, as John Bushy, William Bagot, Henry Green, and John Russell, knights. Of these he required to know what they thought good to be done in this matter concerning the Duke of Lancaster being on the seas. Their advice was to depart from London unto Saint Albans and there to gather an army to resist the Duke in his landing; but to how small purpose their counsel served, the conclusion thereof plainly declared. For the most part that[65] were called, when they came thither, boldly protested that they would not fight against the Duke of Lancaster, whom they knew to be evil dealt withal.

The Lord Treasurer, Bushy, Bagot, and Green, perceiving that the commons would cleave unto and take part with the Duke, slipped away, leaving the Lord Governor of the realm and the Lord Chancellor to make what shift they could for themselves. Bagot got him to Chester and so escaped into Ireland; the other fled to the castle of Bristol in hope there to be in safety. The Duke of Lancaster, after that he had coasted alongst the shore a certain time and had got some intelligence how the people's minds were affected towards him, landed about the beginning of July[66] in Yorkshire, at a place sometime[67] called Ravenspur, betwixt Hull and Bridlington, and with him not past threescore persons, as some write; but he was so joyfully received of the lords, knights, and gentlemen of those parts that he found means (by their help) forthwith to assemble a great number of people that were willing to take his part. The first that came to him were the Lords of Lincolnshire and other countries adjoining, as the Lords Willoughby, Ross, Darcy, and Beaumont.

At his coming unto Doncaster, the Earl of Northumberland and his son Sir Henry Percy, Wardens of the Marches against Scotland, with the Earl of Westmorland, came unto him, where he sware unto those lords that he would demand no more but the lands that were to him descended by inheritance from his father and in right of his wife. More-

---

65 the most part that most of those who   **66 July** i.e., in 1399
67 sometime formerly

over, he undertook to cause the payment of taxes and tallages[68] to be laid down, and to bring the King to good government, and to remove from him the Cheshire men, which were envied of[69] many; for that the King esteemed of them more than of any other, haply because they were more faithful to him than other, ready in all respects to obey his commandments and pleasure. From Doncaster, having now got a mighty army about him, he marched forth with all speed through the countries, coming by Evesham unto Berkeley. Within the space of three days all the King's castles in those parts were surrendered unto him.

[The Duke of York, unable to resist, goes over to Duke Henry's side. Sir Henry Green, Sir John Bushy, and the Lord William Scroop, Earl of Wiltshire, are taken and executed. Richard is delayed in returning from Ireland by contrary winds. He arrives at last near Barkloughly Castle in Wales, only to learn that the Welsh have already given up his cause, that his trusty counselors have been executed, and that most of the nation is against him. "He became so greatly discomforted that, sorrowfully lamenting his miserable state, he utterly despaired of his own safety and, calling his army together, which was not small, licensed every man to depart to his home." Sir Thomas Percy, Earl of Worcester, Lord Steward of the King's household, breaks his staff of office and joins Duke Henry. Richard takes refuge in Flint Castle, where he agrees to a parley with Duke Henry and his allies, is ambushed by the Earl of Northumberland and his men, and at last confronts his challenger.]

The King, that was walking aloft on the brayes[70] of the walls to behold the coming of the Duke[71] afar off, might see that the Archbishop[72] and the other were come and, as he took it, to talk with him. Whereupon he forthwith came down unto them, and beholding that they did their due reverence to him on their knees, he took them up and, drawing the Archbishop aside from the residue, talked with him a good while; and as it was reported, the Archbishop willed

---

68 tallages levies, taxes   **69 envied of** resented by   **70 brayes** parapets
71 the Duke i.e., the Duke of Hereford (Bolingbroke)   **72 the Archbishop** i.e., the Archbishop of Canterbury

him to be of good comfort, for he should be assured not to have any hurt as touching his person; but he prophesied not as a prelate but as a Pilate.[73] For was it no hurt, think you, to his person to be spoiled of his royalty, to be deposed from his crown, to be translated from principality to prison, and to fall from honor into horror? All which befell him to his extreme heart grief, no doubt, which to increase, means alas there were many, but to diminish, helps, God wot, but a few. . . .

After that the Archbishop had now here at Flint communed with the King, he departed and, taking his horse again, rode back to meet the Duke, who began at that present[74] to approach the castle and compassed it round about, even down to the sea, with his people, ranged in good and seemly order at the foot of the mountains. And then the Earl of Northumberland, passing forth of the castle to the Duke, talked with him awhile in sight of the King, being again got up to the walls to take better view of the army, being now advanced within two bowshots of the castle, to the small rejoicing (ye may be sure) of the sorrowful King. The Earl of Northumberland, returning to the castle, appointed the King to be set to dinner (for he was fasting till then); and after he had dined, the Duke came down to the castle himself and entered the same all armed, his basinet[75] only excepted; and being within the first gate, he stayed there till the King came forth of the inner part of the castle unto him.

The King, accompanied with the Bishop of Carlisle, the Earl of Salisbury, and Sir Stephen Scroop, knight, who bare the sword before him, and a few other, came forth into the utter ward[76] and sat down in a place prepared for him. Forthwith, as the Duke got sight of the King, he showed a reverent duty as became him in bowing his knee, and coming forward did so likewise the second and third time, till the King took him by the hand and lift him up, saying, "Dear cousin, ye are welcome." The Duke, humbly thanking him, said: "My sovereign lord and king, the cause of my

73 Pilate i.e., one washing his hands of the business (as Pontius Pilate attempted to do with the crucifixion of Christ) **74 at that present** at that time **75 basinet** steel headpiece **76 utter ward** outer circuit of the walls of the castle

coming at this present is (your honor saved) to have again restitution of my person, my lands, and heritage through your favorable license." The King hereunto answered: "Dear cousin, I am ready to accomplish your will so that ye may enjoy all that is yours without exception."

Meeting thus together, they came forth of the castle and the King there called for wine; and after they had drunk they mounted on horseback and rode that night to Flint, and so the next day unto Chester . . . and so came to London. Neither was the King permitted all this while to change his apparel, but rode still through all these towns simply clothed in one suit of raiment, and yet he was in his time exceeding sumptuous in apparel, insomuch as he had one coat which he caused to be made for him of gold and stone valued at 30,000 marks. And so he was brought the next way to Westminster.

As for the Duke, he was received with all the joy and pomp that might be of the Londoners and was lodged in the Bishop's palace by Paul's Church. It was a wonder to see what great concourse of people and what number of horses came to him on the way as he thus passed the countries, till his coming to London, where, upon his approach to the city, the Mayor rode forth to receive him, and a great number of other citizens. Also the clergy met him with procession; and such joy appeared in the countenances of the people, uttering the same also with words, as the like not lightly been seen.[77] For in every town and village where he passed children rejoiced, women clapped their hands, and men cried out for joy. But to speak of the great numbers of people that flocked together in the fields and streets of London at his coming I here omit; neither will I speak of the presents, welcomings, lauds, and gratifications made to him by the citizens and commonalty.

But now to the purpose. The next day after his coming to London, the King from Westminster was had to the Tower and there committed to safe custody. Many evil-disposed persons, assembling themselves together in great numbers, intended to have met with him and to have taken him from such as had the conveying of him, that they might have slain him. But the Mayor and aldermen gathered to them the

77 as . . . seen such as had not commonly been seen

worshipful commoners and grave citizens, by whose policy, and not without much ado, the other were revoked from their evil purpose. . . .

After this was a Parliament called by the Duke of Lancaster, using the name of King Richard in the writs directed forth to the lords and other states for their summons. This Parliament began the thirteenth day of September, in the which many heinous points of misgovernance and injurious dealings in the administration of his kingly office were laid to the charge of this noble prince, King Richard.

[Thirty-three articles are brought against Richard, detailing the reasons for which he is accounted worthy to be deposed. The delicate matter of persuading Richard to agree to the deposition is entrusted to certain followers of his who have access to his person. They exhort him to save his life by thus agreeing.]

And first they advised him willingly to suffer himself to be deposed and to resign his right of his own accord, so that the Duke of Lancaster might without murder or battle obtain the scepter and diadem, after which, they well perceived, he gaped; by means whereof they thought he[78] might be in perfect assurance of his life long to continue. Whether this their persuasion proceeded by the suborning of the Duke of Lancaster and his favorers, or of a sincere affection which they bare to the King as supposing it most sure in such an extremity, it is uncertain; but yet the effect followed not,[79] howsoever their meaning was. Notwithstanding, the King, being now in the hands of his enemies and utterly despairing of all comfort, was easily persuaded to renounce his crown and princely preeminence, so that, in hope of life only, he agreed to all things that were of him demanded. And so (as it should seem by the copy of an instrument hereafter following) he renounced and voluntarily was deposed from his royal crown and kingly dignity, the Monday being the nine-and-twentieth day of September and feast of Saint Michael the Archangel, in the year of our Lord 1399 and in the three-and-twentieth year of his reign. The copy of which instrument here ensueth.

78 he i.e., Richard. (The date is September 1399.)   **79 the effect followed not** i.e., Richard's life was not saved by this means

[Holinshed here prints "a copy of the instrument touching the declaration of the commissioners sent from the states in Parliament unto King Richard," followed by "the tenor of the instrument whereby King Richard resigneth the crown to the Duke of Lancaster:]

"In the name of God, amen. I, Richard, by the grace of God King of England and of France, etc., Lord of Ireland, acquit and assoil[80] all archbishops, bishops, and other prelates, secular or religious, of what dignity, degree, state, or condition soever they be, and also all dukes, marquesses, earls, barons, lords, and all my liege men, both spiritual and secular, of what manner or degree they be, from their oath of fealty and homage and all other deeds and privileges made unto me, and from all manner bonds of allegiance, regality, and lordship in which they were or be bounden to me or any otherwise constrained; and them, their heirs, and successors forevermore from the same bonds and oaths I release, deliver, and acquit and set them for free, dissolved and acquit, and to be harmless, forasmuch as longeth[81] to my person by any manner way or title of right that to me might follow of the foresaid things, or any of them. And also I resign all my kingly dignity, majesty, and crown, with all the lordships, power, and privileges to the foresaid kingly dignity and crown belonging, and all other lordships and possessions to me in any manner of wise pertaining, of what name, title, quality, or condition soever they be, except the lands and possessions for me and mine obits[82] purchased and bought. And I renounce all right and all manner of title of possession which I ever had or have in the same lordships and possessions, or any of them, with any manner of rights belonging or appertaining unto any part of them. . . ."

[The King, in the presence of the commissioners, subscribes to this document and delivers it to the Archbishop of Canterbury,]

saying that, if it were in his power or at his assignment, he

---

80 assoil absolve   **81 longeth** belongs   **82 obits** ceremonies performed in behalf of the soul of the deceased

would that the Duke of Lancaster there present should be his successor and king after him. And in token hereof he took a ring of gold from his finger, being his signet, and put it upon the said Duke's finger, desiring and requiring the Archbishop of York and the Bishop of Hereford to show and make report unto the lords of the Parliament of his voluntary resignation and also of his intent and good mind that he bare towards his cousin the Duke of Lancaster to have him his successor and their king after him. All this done, every man took their leave and returned to their own.

Upon the morrow after, being Tuesday and the last day of September, all the lords spiritual and temporal with the commons of the said Parliament assembled at Westminster where, in the presence of them, the Archbishop of York and the Bishop of Hereford, according to the King's request, showed unto them the voluntary renouncing of the King with the favor also which he bare to his cousin of Lancaster to have him his successor; and moreover showed them the schedule or bill of renouncement signed with King Richard's own hand, which they caused to be read first in Latin, as it was written, and after in English. This done, the question was first asked of the lords if they would admit and allow that renouncement; the which, when it was of them granted and confirmed, the like question was asked of the commons and of them in like manner confirmed. After this, it was then declared that notwithstanding the foresaid renouncing, so by the lords and commons admitted and confirmed, it were necessary, in avoiding of all suspicions and surmises of evil-disposed persons, to have in writing and registered the manifold crimes and defaults before done by King Richard to the end that they might first be openly declared to the people and after to remain of record amongst other of the King's records forever.

All thus was done accordingly, for the articles which before ye have heard were drawn and engrossed up and there were ready to be read; but for other causes more needful as then to be preferred, the reading of those articles at that season was deferred. Then, forsomuch as the lords of the Parliament had well considered the voluntary resignation of King Richard and that it was behooveful and, as they thought, necessary for the weal of the realm to proceed unto the sentence of his deposing, there were appointed, by the authority of all the estates there in Parliament assembled, the Bishop of Saint Asaph, the Abbot of Glastonbury, the Earl of Gloucester, the Lord Berkeley, William Thirning, Justice, and Thomas Erpingham with Thomas Grey, knights, that they should give and pronounce the open sentence of the deposing of King Richard.

[Holinshed here prints "the publication of King Richard's deposing," in which the commissioners declare their purpose to deprive Richard "of all kingly dignity and worship and of any kingly worship in himself. And we depose him by our sentence definitive," expressly forbidding all prelates, nobles, and commoners of the realm to offer Richard any obedience.]

Immediately as the sentence was in this wise passed, and that by reason thereof the realm stood void without head or governor for the time, the Duke of Lancaster, rising from the place where before he sat and standing where all those in the house might behold him, in reverent manner made a sign of the cross on his forehead and likewise on his breast and, after silence by an officer commanded, said unto the people there being present these words following:
"In the name of the Father, and of the Son, and of the Holy Ghost, I, Henry of Lancaster, claim the realm of England and the crown, with all the appurtenances, as I that am descended by right line of the blood coming from that good Lord King Henry the Third, and through the right that God of His grace hath sent me, with the help of my kin and of my friends, to recover the same, which was in point to be undone for default of good governance and due justice."
After these words thus by him uttered, he returned and sat him down in the place where before he had sitten. Then the lords, having heard and well perceived this claim thus made by this nobleman, each of them asked of other what they thought therein. At length, after a little pausing or stay made, the Archbishop of Canterbury, having notice of the minds of the lords, stood up and asked the commons if they would assent to the lords, which in their minds thought the claim of the Duke made to be rightful and necessary for the wealth of the realm and them all; whereto the commons with one voice cried, "Yea, yea, yea!" After which answer

the said Archbishop, going to the Duke and kneeling down before him on his knee, addressed to him all his purpose in few words. The which when he had ended, he rose and, taking the Duke by the right hand, led him unto the King's seat, the Archbishop of York assisting him, and with great reverence set him therein, after that the Duke had first upon his knees made his prayer in devout manner unto almighty God.

[The Archbishop of Canterbury delivers a sermon in honor of Henry IV's accession, to which the King replies. October 13 is proclaimed as the solemn day of King Henry's coronation.]

Thus was King Richard deprived of all kingly honor and princely dignity, by reason he was so given to follow evil counsel, and used such inconvenient[83] ways and means, through insolent misgovernance and youthful outrage, though otherwise a right noble and worthy prince. He reigned two-and-twenty years, three months, and eight days. He delivered to King Henry, now that he was thus deposed, all the goods that he had, to the sum of three hundred thousand pounds in coin, besides plate and jewels, as a pledge and satisfaction of the injuries by him committed and done, in hope to be in more surety of life for the delivery thereof. But, whatsoever was promised, he was deceived therein. For shortly after his resignation he was conveyed to the castle of Leeds in Kent, and from thence to Pomfret, where he departed out of this miserable life, as after you shall hear. He was seemly of shape and favor, and of nature good enough if the wickedness and naughty demeanor of such as were about him had not altered it.

His chance[84] verily was greatly infortunate, which fell into such calamity that he took it for the best way he could devise to renounce his kingdom, for the which mortal men are accustomed to hazard all they have to attain thereunto. But such misfortune (or the like) oftentimes falleth unto those princes which, when they are aloft, cast no doubt[85]

---

83 inconvenient improper **84 chance** fortune **85 aloft, cast no doubt**
i.e., prosperous and high on Fortune's wheel, show no concern, make no provision

for perils that may follow. He was prodigal, ambitious, and much given to the pleasure of the body. He kept the greatest port[86] and maintained the most plentiful house that ever any king in England did either before his time or since. For there resorted daily to his court above ten thousand persons that had meat and drink there allowed them. In his kitchen there were three hundred servitors, and every other office was furnished after the like rate. Of ladies, chamberers, and launderers, there were above three hundred at the least. And in gorgeous and costly apparel they exceeded all measure, not one of them that kept within the bounds of his degree. Yeomen and grooms were clothed in silks, with cloth of grain[87] and scarlet, oversumptuous ye may be sure for their estates. And this vanity was not only used in the court in those days but also other people abroad in the towns and countries had their garments cut far otherwise than had been accustomed before his days, with embroideries, rich furs, and goldsmith's work, and every day there was devising of new fashions, to the great hindrance and decay of the commonwealth.

Moreover, such were preferred to bishoprics and other ecclesiastical livings as neither could teach nor preach nor knew anything of the scripture of God but only to call for their tithes and duties; so that they were most unworthy the name of bishops, being lewd[88] and most vain persons disguised in bishops' apparel. Furthermore, there reigned abundantly the filthy sin of lechery and fornication, with abominable adultery, specially in the King but most chiefly in the prelacy, whereby the whole realm by such their evil example was so infected that the wrath of God was daily provoked to vengeance for the sins of the prince and his people. . . .

Thus have ye heard what writers do report touching the state of the time and doings of this King. But if I may boldly say what I think, he was a prince the most unthankfully used of his subjects of any one of whom ye shall lightly read. For although, through the frailty of youth, he demeaned himself more dissolutely than seemed convenient for his royal estate and made choice of such councillors as were not favored by the people, whereby he was the less fa-

86 port style of living   **87 grain** purple   **88 lewd** ignorant

vored himself, yet in no king's days were the commons in greater wealth, if they could have perceived their happy state, neither in any other time were the nobles and gentlemen more cherished, nor churchmen less wronged. But such was their ingratitude towards their bountiful and loving sovereign that those whom he had chiefly advanced were readiest to control him; for that they might not rule all things at their will, and remove from him such as they misliked, and place in their rooms whom they thought good, and that rather by strong hand than by gentle and courteous means, which stirred such malice betwixt him and them, till at length it could not be assuaged without peril of destruction to them both.

[Accusations are brought against those thought to be guilty of the Duke of Gloucester's death and especially against the Duke of Aumerle. Many throw down their gages against him. News arrives of the deaths of the Duke of Norfolk in Venice and of the Duchess of Gloucester. The Abbot of Westminster is involved in a conspiracy against King Henry IV, and the Duke of York rides hastily to Windsor to accuse his own son the Earl of Rutland (i.e., Aumerle) of plotting against the throne. The Abbot of Westminster commits suicide; the Bishop of Carlisle is pardoned.]

And immediately after, King Henry, to rid himself of any suchlike danger to be attempted against him thereafter, caused King Richard to die of a violent death, that no man should afterward feign himself to represent his person, though some have said he was not privy to that wicked offense.

[Various reports attribute Richard's death to forced starvation or to voluntary pining away.]

One writer,[89] which seemeth to have great knowledge of King Richard's doings, saith that King Henry, sitting on a day at his table, sore sighing, said: "Have I no faithful friend which will deliver me of him whose life will be my death and whose death will be the preservation of my life?"

89 **One writer** i.e., Thomas of Walsingham

This saying was much noted of them which were present and especially of one called Sir Piers of Exton. This knight incontinently[90] departed from the court with eight strong persons in his company and came to Pomfret, commanding the esquire that was accustomed to sew[91] and take the assay[92] before King Richard to do so no more, saying, "Let him eat now, for he shall not long eat." King Richard sat down to dinner and was served without courtesy or assay, whereupon, much marveling at the sudden change, he demanded of the esquire why he did not his duty. "Sir," said he, "I am otherwise commanded by Sir Piers of Exton, which is newly come from King Henry." When King Richard heard that word, he took the carving knife in his hand and strake[93] the esquire on the head, saying, "The devil take Henry of Lancaster and thee together!" And with that word Sir Piers entered the chamber, well armed, with eight tall[94] men likewise armed, every of them having a bill[95] in his hand.

King Richard, perceiving this, put the table from him and, stepping to the foremost man, wrung the bill out of his hands and so valiantly defended himself that he slew four of those that thus came to assail him. Sir Piers, being half dismayed herewith, leaped into the chair where King Richard was wont to sit, while the other four persons fought with him and chased him about the chamber. And in conclusion, as King Richard traversed his ground from one side of the chamber to another, and coming by the chair where Sir Piers stood, he was felled with a stroke of a poleax which Sir Piers gave him upon the head, and therewith rid him out of life without giving him respite once to call to God for mercy of his past offenses. It is said that Sir Piers of Exton, after he had thus slain him, wept right bitterly, as one stricken with the prick of a guilty conscience, for murdering him whom he had so long time obeyed as king. After he was thus dead, his body was embalmed and cered[96] and covered with lead, all save the face, to the intent that all men might see him and perceive that he was departed this life;

---

90 incontinently immediately. (The date is February 1400.) **91 sew** serve food **92 take the assay** i.e., taste the food before the King eats **93 strake** struck **94 tall** bold, doughty **95 bill** long-handled, axlike weapon; halberd **96 cered** wrapped in a cerecloth or waxed winding-sheet

for as the corpse was conveyed from Pomfret to London, in all the towns and places where those that had the conveyance of it did stay with it all night, they caused dirige[97] to be sung in the evening and mass of requiem in the morning; and as well after the one service as the other, his face discovered was showed to all that coveted to behold it.

Thus was the corpse first brought to the Tower and, after, through the City to the cathedral church of Saint Paul, barefaced, where it lay three days together that all men might behold it. There was a solemn obsequy done for him, both at Paul's and after at Westminster, at which time, both at dirige overnight and in the morning at the mass of requiem, the King and the citizens of London were present. When the same was ended, the corpse was commanded to be had unto Langley, there to be buried in the church of the Friars Preachers. . . . He was after by King Henry the Fifth removed to Westminster and there honorably entombed with Queen Anne his wife.[98]

The second edition of Raphael Holinshed's *Chronicles* was published in 1587. These selections are based on that edition, Volume 3, folios 493–517.

97 **dirige** (The Office of the Dead in the Roman Catholic Church, based on Psalm 5.)   98 **Anne** Anne of Bohemia, Richard's first wife

Further Reading

Barkan, Leonard. "The Theatrical Consistency of *Richard II*." *Shakespeare Quarterly* 29 (1978): 5–19. Barkan examines the "emotional texture" of the play, finding that the "suppressed passion" of the first half is "balanced and resolved" in the fourth and fifth acts by "a series of explosive releases." With Richard's removal from power, the passionate energies, no longer contained, transform England and the play itself from worlds of ritual to worlds where violence is real.

Berger, Harry, Jr. "Textual Dramaturgy: Representing the Limits of Theatre in *Richard II*." *Theatre Journal* 39 (1987): 135–155. Berger explores the self-conscious theatricality of the characters as it is used as a strategy of "repression and displacement." Focusing especially on the episode of Aumerle and York as a caricature of the relationship of Bolingbroke and Gaunt, Berger finds it emblematic of a play that reveals public display as an effort of misdirection, deflecting attention from the real issues of the "psychopolitical drama."

Brooke, Nicholas. "*Richard II*." *Shakespeare's Early Tragedies*. London: Methuen, 1968. Attending to the play's rhythm and rhetoric, Brooke identifies a pattern of engagement and detachment that generates both a sympathy for Richard and an awareness of the necessity of Bolingbroke's rule.

————, ed. *Shakespeare, "Richard II": A Casebook*. London: Macmillan, 1973. Brooke's casebook presents a number of useful studies of the play including critical essays by E. M. W. Tillyard, Ernst H. Kantorowicz, and M. M. Mahood (see below), as well as an actor's view by John Gielgud.

Campbell, Lily B. "An Introduction into the Division Between Lancaster and York." *Shakespeare's "Histories": Mirrors of Elizabethan Policy*. San Marino, Calif.: Huntington Library, 1947. Using Elizabethan chronicles, political pamphlets, and other sixteenth-century texts, Campbell establishes the relationship between the historical events depicted in *Richard II* and the political concerns of Elizabethan England.

Coleridge, Samuel Taylor. *"Richard II." Coleridge's Writings on Shakespeare,* ed. Terence Hawkes. New York: G. P. Putnam's Sons, 1959. *Richard II,* the most "purely historical" of Shakespeare's plays, is seen by Coleridge as exploring "the vast importance of the personal character of the sovereign." Richard is seen to be "weak, variable, and womanish," sheltering himself from reality "by a cloud of his own thoughts." Bolingbroke is a man of ambition, encouraged by his grievances and those of his country, but "at the same time scarcely daring to look at his own views, or to acknowledge them as designs."

Dorius, R. J. "A Little More than a Little." *Shakespeare Quarterly* 11 (1960): 13–26. Rpt. in *Shakespeare, the Histories: A Collection of Critical Essays,* ed. Eugene M. Waith. Englewood Cliffs, N.J.: Prentice-Hall, 1965. Dorius traces the play's emphasis upon excess, negligence, and waste. Richard's inability to be either politically prudent or economically responsible is revealed by the political action and in the play's iterative imagery of gardens, sickness, and time.

Hawkes, Terence. *"Richard II:* The Word Against the Word." *Shakespeare's Talking Animals.* Totowa, N.J.: Rowman and Littlefield, 1974. For Hawkes, the conflict between Richard and Bolingbroke emerges as a conflict between two opposed views of language. Not only do the antagonists use language differently, but each conceives of language in a fundamentally different way: Richard, as a means of changing reality; Bolingbroke, as an arbitrary symbol system expressing merely provisional conceptions of reality.

Humphreys, A. R. *Shakespeare: "Richard II."* London: Edward Arnold, 1967. Humphreys's sensible introduction to *Richard II* discusses its sources and reputation, and provides an analysis of the play's structure, tone, and contrasting themes.

Kantorowicz, Ernst H. "Shakespeare: *King Richard II."* *The King's Two Bodies: A Study in Medieval Political Theology.* Princeton, N.J.: Princeton Univ. Press, 1957. For Kantorowicz, the play dramatically explores the notion of "the King's two bodies": the belief that the king ruled both in his own person and as a representative of an enduring sacred authority. *Richard II,* he finds, traces the dissolution of the double body: Bolingbroke's ascension to the throne violates the sacramental order and fractures Richard's "twin-born being" as both divine agent and flawed mortal.

Kernan, Alvin B. "The Henriad: Shakespeare's Major History Plays." In *Modern Shakespearean Criticism: Essays on Style, Dramaturgy, and the Major Plays,* ed. Alvin B. Kernan. New York: Harcourt, Brace, and World, 1970. Kernan traces the movement of the second tetralogy from a providential view of history in *Richard II* to a pragmatic one in *Henry V,* in which kingship is understood not as a sacramental identity but as a political role. In *Richard II,* as Richard moves from naive confidence in his divine authority to a terrifying awareness of the ambiguity of his position, the play enacts the transition of world views in political and psychological terms.

Mahood, M. M. *"Richard the Second." Shakespeare's Wordplay.* London: Methuen, 1957. For Mahood, *Richard II* is a play that tests the power and efficacy of language. It contrasts the poetic Richard and his faith in words with the politician, Bolingbroke, for whom words have instrumental rather than intrinsic power.

Ornstein, Robert. *"Richard II." A Kingdom for a Stage: The Achievement of Shakespeare's History Plays.* Cambridge: Harvard Univ. Press, 1972. Ornstein focuses on the play's revelation of Richard's self-absorption so that Richard's fall comes to seem both inevitable and appropriate. The play thus raises disturbing questions about political loyalty that are explored dramatically rather than solved ideologically.

Rabkin, Norman. "The Polity." *Shakespeare and the Common Understanding.* New York: Macmillan, Free Press, 1967. Rabkin sees a delicate balance of sympathies as the primary achievement of *Richard II.* Despite the inevitability of Richard's fall from power, our sympathy for him increases with his defeat; and, though Bolingbroke's victory seems politically desirable, we are made fully aware of the moral costs of political success.

Ribner, Irving. *The English History Play in the Age of Shakespeare,* 1957. Rev. ed., enl., New York: Barnes and Noble,

1965, pp. 151–168. For Ribner, *Richard II* is Shakespeare's first great tragedy of character as well as his first great history play. Richard's weaknesses disqualify him for rule, and in Bolingbroke Shakespeare presents an effective if unlawful king to fill the void. England is perhaps better served by Henry than by Richard, but the play measures the sense of human loss in his victory.

Saccio, Peter. "Richard II: The Fall of the King." *Shakespeare's English Kings: History, Chronicle, and Drama.* New York: Oxford Univ. Press, 1977. Using the chronicle accounts of Richard's reign and the research of modern historians to illuminate the background of *Richard II,* Saccio measures the distance between historical fact and Shakespeare's dramatic fiction.

Sanders, Wilbur. "Shakespeare's Political Agnosticism: *Richard II.*" *The Dramatist and the Received Idea: Studies in the Plays of Marlowe and Shakespeare.* Cambridge: Cambridge Univ. Press, 1968. Sanders finds that the play deliberately obscures its moral focus and sympathy. In different ways, Bolingbroke, Richard, and York all fail to discover a course of action that might redeem the chaos of history. For Sanders, however, the play's refusal to indicate moral and political norms is not artistic failure but evidence of Shakespeare's refusal to accept the moral simplifications of the source material and the orthodox Tudor ideas of history.

Schoenbaum, S[amuel]. "*Richard II* and the Realities of Power." *Shakespeare Survey* 28 (1975): 1–13. Schoenbaum uses the probable fact of the play's performance on the eve of the Essex Rebellion to explore Shakespeare's own political vision. Shakespeare, he finds, is neither a "seditious playwright" nor the "darling of the court"; rather, he is a "political realist" who unsentimentally understands the realities of power.

Tillyard, E. M. W. "The Second Tetralogy." *Shakespeare's History Plays,* 1944. Rpt., New York: Barnes and Noble, 1964. *Richard II,* in Tillyard's view, is built on the contrast not merely between two characters but between two ways of life: one ceremonial and essentially medieval; the other more vigorous, that of Elizabethan England. Richard, the last king to rule with the full authority of medieval kingship, gives way to Henry, the first to rule outside the sanctions of an authentic succession.

Trousdale, Marion. "The Example of *Richard II.*" *Shakspeare and the Rhetoricians.* Chapel Hill, N.C.: Univ. of North Carolina Press, 1982. Considering *Richard II* in the context of Elizabethan rhetorical theory and models, Trousdale finds that the coherence of the play comes not from causal connections between events but from the verbal and structural patterns imposed upon them. Her analysis suggests that the recording of history is less significant than the exploration of the differing ways in which acts and even words may be understood.

Yeats, William Butler. "At Stratford-upon-Avon." *Essays and Introductions.* New York: Macmillan, 1961. Rpt. in part as "Richard II and Henry V" in *Discussions of Shakespeare's Histories: "Richard II" to "Henry V,"* ed. R. J. Dorius. Boston: D. C. Heath, 1964. In response to nineteenth-century condemnation of Richard as sentimental and weak, Yeats argues for Shakespeare's sympathy for him and his poetic nature. In Yeats's view, "Shakespeare cared little for the State," and so Richard's lack of political skill or energy is less telling than his contemplative virtues and the "lyricism which rose out of Richard's mind like the jet of a fountain."

From the 1972 New York Shakespeare Festival production of *Much Ado about Nothing*, with Kathleen Widdoes as Beatrice and Sam Waterston as Benedick, directed by A. J. Antoon at the Delacorte Theater in Central Park and later that season at the Winter Garden Theater on Broadway.

MUCH ADO
—— ABOUT ——
NOTHING

MUCH ADO
ABOUT NOTHING

Introductory Material
Foreword by Joseph Papp
Introduction
Much Ado about Nothing
in Performance

THE PLAY

Supplementary Material
Date and Text
Textual Notes
Shakespeare's Sources
Further Reading

Foreword

Much Ado about Nothing is a perennial delight onstage. In the first place, there's the wonderful relationship between Beatrice and Benedick, two people who are pretending they don't care for each other while they're actually falling in love. Once they're tricked into thinking that each loves the other, they suddenly change their minds and decide that it's destiny. Both of them reflect on this emotional about-face in wonderfully witty soliloquies. I especially like the way Benedick, the confirmed-bachelor-turned-lover, converts his logic to justify his newfound love for Beatrice: he says with a shrug, "the world must be peopled."

This movement from the resistance to the acceptance of love is a marvelous device in the play. It's just plain fun to watch and listen to Benedick and Beatrice, for "They never meet but there's a skirmish of wit between them." And yet I think Shakespeare is making a more profound point at the same time—that extreme emotion of one kind can also contain the opposite extreme: the initial dislike of Benedick for Beatrice and Beatrice for Benedick also holds within it the seeds of love.

The liveliness of this pair sometimes spills over into the other plot of the play, the more somber story of Hero and her fiance, Claudio, who rejects her at the altar because he thinks she's been unfaithful. It's not exactly a comic story, but into the midst of it skip Benedick and Beatrice with lines that, as I recall from the production I directed one summer, brought the house down every night. Beatrice has finally gotten Benedick to the point where he'll do anything to prove that he loves her: "Come, bid me do anything for thee," he begs her. Her two-word answer, straight to the point, is *"Kill Claudio."* The theater goes wild with laughter as the audience watches Benedick's ardor turn to dismay at the prospect of having to make good on a commitment to kill his best friend.

And finally, there is Dogberry, who can't use a word correctly to save his soul but is blissfully unaware of this disability. The way he pronounces grand-sounding words pompously—and incorrectly—is so funny that I can't help laughing out loud even when I'm sitting in a room by myself reading his speeches.

The scene where he is giving instructions to the officers

of the watch (3.3) is one of the funniest scenes ever written. He tells one fellow, "You are thought here to be the most *senseless* and fit man for the constable of the watch," and then addresses the group, "You shall also make no noise in the streets; for, for the watch to babble and to talk is most *tolerable* and not to be endured." Bidding them good night, he says "Adieu. Be *vigitant*, I beseech you." And in his last scene, instead of *begging* Leonato's permission to depart, he says, "I humbly *give you leave* to depart; and if a merry meeting may be wished, God *prohibit* it!"

Dogberry is such a delightful character, in a play full of delightful characters, that he never fails to amuse me. In fact, I could probably go on quoting his lines for the next ten pages, especially that wonderful scene with the watchmen. "First," he says, "who think you the most—" but perhaps I'll let you discover him for yourself.

JOSEPH PAPP

JOSEPH PAPP GRATEFULLY ACKNOWLEDGES THE HELP OF ELIZABETH KIRKLAND IN PREPARING THIS FOREWORD.

Introduction

Much Ado about Nothing belongs to a group of Shakespeare's most mature romantic comedies, linked by similar titles, that also includes *As You Like It* and *Twelfth Night*. All date from the period 1598 to 1600. These plays are the culmination of Shakespeare's exuberant, philosophical, and festive vein in comedy, with only an occasional anticipation of the darker problem comedies of the early 1600s. They also parallel the culmination of Shakespeare's writing of history plays, in *Henry IV* and *V*.

Much Ado excels in combative wit and in swift, colloquial prose. It differs too from several other comedies (including *A Midsummer Night's Dream* and *The Merchant of Venice*) in that it features no journey of the lovers, no heroine disguised as a man, no envious court or city contrasted with an idealized landscape of the artist's imagination. Instead, the prevailing motif is that of the mask. Prominent scenes include a masked ball (2.1), a charade offstage in which the villainous Borachio misrepresents himself as the lover of Hero (actually Margaret in disguise), and a marriage ceremony with the supposedly dead bride masking as her own cousin (5.3). The word *Nothing* in the play's title, pronounced rather like *noting* in Elizabethan English, suggests a pun on the idea of overhearing as well as that of musical notation. Overhearings are constant and are essential to the process of both misunderstanding (as in the false rumor of Don Pedro's wooing Hero for himself) and clarification (as in the discovery by the night watch of the slander done to Hero's reputation, or in the revelation to Beatrice and Benedick of each other's true state of mind). The masks, or roles, that the characters incessantly assume are for the most part defensive and inimical to mutual understanding. How can they be dispelled? It is the search for candor and self-awareness in relationships with others, the quest for honesty and respect beneath conventional outward appearances, that provides the journey in this play.

Structurally the play contrasts two pairs of lovers. The young ladies, Beatrice and Hero, are cousins and close friends. The gentlemen, Benedick and Claudio, Italian gentlemen and fellow officers under the command of Don Pedro, have returned from the war in which they have fought bravely. These similarities chiefly serve, however, to accentuate the differences between the two couples. Hero is modest, retiring, usually silent, and obedient to her father's will. Claudio appears ideally suited to her, since he is also respectful and decorous. They are conventional lovers in the roles of romantic hero and ingenue heroine. Beatrice and Benedick, on the other hand, are renowned for "a kind of merry war" between them. Although obviously destined to come together, they are seemingly too independent and skeptical of convention to be tolerant and accepting in love. They scoff so at romantic sentimentality that they cannot permit themselves to drop their satirical masks. Yet paradoxically their relationship is the more surefooted because it is relentlessly probing and candid.

As in some of his other comic double plots (*The Taming of the Shrew*, for example), Shakespeare has linked together two stories of diverse origins and contrasting tones in order to set off one against the other. The Hero-Claudio plot is Italianate in flavor and origin, sensational, melodramatic, potentially tragic. In fact the often-told story of the maiden falsely slandered did frequently end in disaster—as, for example, in Edmund Spenser's *Faerie Queene*, 2.4 (1590). Spenser was apparently indebted to Ariosto's *Orlando Furioso* (translated into English by Sir John Harington, 1591), as were Peter Beverly in *The History of Ariodanto and Genevra* (1566) and Richard Mulcaster in his play *Ariodante and Genevora* (1583). Shakespeare seems to have relied more on the Italian version by Matteo Bandello (Lucca, 1554) and its French translation by Belleforest, *Histoires Tragiques* (1569). Still other versions have been discovered, both nondramatic and dramatic, although it cannot be established that Shakespeare was reworking an old play. Various factual inconsistencies in Shakespeare's text (such as Leonato's wife, Imogen, and a "kinsman" who are named briefly in both quarto and Folio but have no roles in the play) can perhaps be explained by Shakespeare's having worked quickly from more than one source.

Shakespeare's other plot, of Benedick and Beatrice, is much more English and his own. The battle of the sexes is a staple of English medieval humor (Chaucer's Wife of Bath, the Wakefield play of *Noah*) and of Shakespeare's own early comedy: Berowne and Rosaline in *Love's Labor's Lost*, Petruchio and Katharine in *The Taming of the Shrew*. The merry war of Benedick and Beatrice is Shakespeare's finest achievement in this vein, and was to become a rich legacy in the later English comedy of William Congreve, Oscar Wilde, and George Bernard Shaw. The tone is lighthearted, bantering, and reassuring, in contrast with the Italianate mood of vengeance and duplicity. No less English are the clownish antics of Dogberry and his crew, representing still another group of characters although not a separate plot. Like Constable Dull in *Love's Labor's Lost* or the tradesmen of *A Midsummer Night's Dream*, the buffoons of *Much Ado* function in a nominally Mediterranean setting, but are nonetheless recognizable London types. Their preposterous antics not only puncture the ominous mood threatening our enjoyment of the main plot but, absurdly enough, even help to abort a potential crime. When Dogberry comes, laughter cannot be far behind.

The two plots provide contrasting perspectives on the nature of love. Because it is sensational and melodramatic, the Claudio-Hero plot stresses situation at the expense of character. The conspiracy that nearly overwhelms the lovers is an engrossing story, but they themselves remain one-dimensional. They interest us more as conventional types, and hence as foils to Benedick and Beatrice, than as lovers in their own right. Benedick and Beatrice, on the other hand, are psychologically complex. Clearly they are fascinated with each other. Beatrice's questions in the first scene, although abusive in tone, betray her concern for Benedick's welfare. Has he safely returned from the wars? How did he bear himself in battle? Who are his companions? She tests his moral character by high standards, suspecting that he will fail because she demands so much. We are not surprised when she lectures her docile cousin, Hero, on the folly of submitting to parental choice in marriage: "It is my cousin's duty to make curtsy and say, 'Father, as it please you.' But yet for all that, cousin, let him be a handsome fellow, or else make another curtsy and say, 'Father, as it please me'" (2.1.49–52). Beatrice remains single not from love of spinsterhood but from insistence on a nearly perfect mate. Paradoxically, she who is the inveter-

ate scoffer is the true idealist. And we know from her unceasing fascination with Benedick that he, of all the men in
her acquaintance, comes closest to her mark. The only fear
preventing the revelation of her love—a not unnatural fear,
in view of the insults she and Benedick exchange—is that he
will prove faithless and jest at her weakness.

Benedick is similarly hemmed in by his posturing as "a
professed tyrant to their sex" (1.1.161–162). Despite his reputation as a perennial bachelor, and his wry amusement at
Claudio's newfound passion, Benedick confesses in soliloquy (2.3.7–33) that he could be won to affection by the ideal
woman. Again his criteria are chiefly those of temperament
and moral character, although he by no means spurns
wealth, beauty, and social position; the happiest couples
are those well-matched in fortune's gifts. "Rich she shall
be, that's certain; wise, or I'll none; virtuous, or I'll never
cheapen her; fair, or I'll never look on her; mild, or come
not near me; noble, or not I for an angel; of good discourse,
an excellent musician, and her hair shall be of what color it
please God." This last self-mocking concession indicates
that Benedick is aware of how impossibly much he is asking. Still, there is one woman, Beatrice, who may well possess all of these qualities except mildness. Even her sharp
wit is part of her admirable intelligence. She is a match for
Benedick, and he is a man who would never tolerate the
submissive conventionality of someone like Hero. All that
appears to be lacking, in fact, is any sign of fondness on
Beatrice's part. For him to make overtures would be to invite her withering scorn—not to mention the I-told-you-so
mockery of his friends.

Benedick and Beatrice have been playing the game of verbal abuse for so long they scarcely remember how it
started—perhaps as a squaring-off between the only two in-
telligences worthy of contending with each other, perhaps
as a more profoundly defensive reaction of two sensitive
persons not willing to part lightly with their independence.
They seem to have had a prior relationship with each other
that ended unhappily. They know that true involvement
with others is a complex matter, one that can cause heartache. Yet the masks they wear with each other are scarcely
satisfactory. At the masked ball (2.1), we see how hurtful the
"merry war" has become. Benedick, attempting to pass

himself off as a stranger in a mask, abuses Beatrice by telling her of her reputation for disdain; but she, perceiving who he is, retaliates by telling him as a purported stranger what she "really" thinks of Benedick. These devices cut deeply, and confirm the worst fears of each. Ironically, these fears can be dispelled only by the virtuous deceptions practiced on them by their friends. Once Benedick is assured that Beatrice secretly loves him, masking her affection with scorn, he acquires the confidence he needs to make a commitment, and vice versa in her case. The beauty of the virtuous deceptions, moreover, is that they are so plausible—because, indeed, they are essentially true. Benedick overhears himself described as a person so satirical that Beatrice dare not reveal her affection, for fear of being repulsed (2.3). Beatrice learns that she is indeed called disdainful by her friends (3.1). Both lovers respond nobly to these revelations, accepting the accusations as richly deserved and placing no blame on the other. As Beatrice proclaims to herself, "Contempt, farewell, and maiden pride, adieu!" (l. 109). The relief afforded by this honesty is genuine and lasting.

Because Claudio knows so little about Hero, and is content with superficial expectations, he is vulnerable to a far more ugly sort of deception. Claudio's first questions about Hero betray his romantically stereotyped attitudes and his willingness to let Don Pedro and Hero's father, Leonato, arrange a financially advantageous match. Claudio treasures Hero's outward reputation for modesty, an appearance easily besmirched. When a false rumor suggests that Don Pedro is wooing the lady for himself, Claudio's response is predictably cliché-ridden: all's fair in love and war, you can't trust friends in an affair of the heart, and so farewell, Hero. The rumor has a superficial plausibility about it, especially when the villainous Don John steps into the situation. Motivated in part by pure malice and the sport of ruining others' happiness, John speaks to the masked Claudio at the ball (2.1) as though he were speaking to Benedick, and in this guise pretends to reveal the secret "fact" of Don Pedro's duplicity in love. (The device is precisely that used by Beatrice to put down Benedick in the same scene.) With this specious confirmation, Claudio leaps to a wrong conclusion, thereby judging both his friend and mistress to be false. He gives them no chance to speak in their own defense. To be sure, Hero's father and uncle have also believed in the false report and have welcomed the prospect of the wealthy Don Pedro as Hero's husband. The lady herself raises no objection to marriage with the older man. Still, Claudio has revealed a lack of faith resulting from his slender knowledge of Hero, and of himself.

The nearly tragic "demonstration" of Hero's infidelity follows the same course, because Claudio has not learned from his first experience. Once again the diabolical Don John first implants the insidious suggestion in Claudio's mind, then creates an illusion entirely plausible to the senses, and finally confirms it with Borachio's testimony. What Claudio and Don Pedro have actually seen is Margaret wooed at Hero's window, shrouded in the dark of night and seen from "afar off in the orchard." The power of suggestion is enough to do the rest. John's method, and his pleasure in evil, are much like those of his later counterparts, Iago in *Othello* and Edmund in *King Lear*. Indeed, John is compared with the devil, who has power over men's frail senses but must rely on their complicity and acquiescence in evil. Claudio is once again led to denounce faithlessly the virtuous woman whose loyalty he no longer deserves. Yet his fault is typically human, and is shared by Don Pedro. Providence gives him a second chance, through the ludicrous and bumbling intervention of Dogberry's night watch. These men overhear the plot of Don John as soon as it is announced to us, so that we know justice will eventually prevail even though it will also be farcically delayed. Once again, misunderstanding has become "much ado about nothing," an escalating of recriminations based on a purely chimerical assumption that must eventually be deflated. The painful experience is not without value, for it tests people's spiritual worth in a crisis. Beatrice, like Friar Francis, shows herself to be a person of unshakable faith in goodness. Benedick, though puzzled and torn in his loyalties, also passes the test and proves himself worthy of Beatrice. Claudio is found wanting, but Hero forgives and accepts him anyway. In her role as the granter of a merciful second chance, she foreshadows the beatifically symbolic nature of many of Shakespeare's later heroines.

Much Ado about Nothing comes closer perhaps to potentially tragic action than Shakespeare's other festive comedies. Virtually all the characters are affected by misunderstanding, resort to deception, or take refuge in protective masks. Candor and straightforwardness are ideals more easily praised than achieved. Even Benedick and Beatrice, marvelous though they may be, are far from perfect. Beatrice almost provokes Benedick into a vindictive and unnecessary murder. Despite their self-awareness, these lovers must be rescued from their isolation by a trick that ironically resembles the villainous practices of Don John. In this important sense, Benedick and Beatrice are not wholly unlike Claudio and Hero after all. Both pairs of lovers are saved from their own worst selves by a harmonizing force that works its will through strange and improbable means—even through Constable Dogberry and his watch.

Much Ado about Nothing
in Performance

Much Ado about Nothing has been popular onstage throughout virtually all of its history. According to the quarto of 1600 it was "sundry times publicly acted" by the Lord Chamberlain's men, and the play was performed at court in 1613 for the Princess Elizabeth and Frederick, Elector Palatine. Contemporary allusions in Shakespeare's day indicate that it was more highly regarded than Ben Jonson's writing in a similar vein, that is, in the social comedy of satirical wit. Leonard Digges, for example, while praising Jonson's sophisticated playwriting, admits Shakespeare's greater popularity: "let but Beatrice / And Benedick be seen; lo, in a trice, / The cockpit, galleries, boxes, all are full."

Restoration and eighteenth-century audiences, who tended to prefer comedy of manners to romance, felt comfortable with Shakespeare's play. *Much Ado* in fact became, more so than any other play Shakespeare wrote, a model for later English comedy: the agreeably sharp battle of the sexes between Benedick and Beatrice reemerges in William Congreve's *The Way of the World* (1700), Richard Sheridan's *The Rivals* (1775), Oscar Wilde's *The Importance of Being Earnest* (1895), George Bernard Shaw's *Man and Superman* (1905), and others.

Restoration and eighteenth-century dramatists did undertake to adapt the play, to be sure. William Davenant's *The Law Against Lovers*, at the theater in Lincoln's Inn Fields, London, in 1662, combined *Much Ado* with *Measure for Measure* by making Beatrice a ward of Lord Angelo and Benedick his brother. In this extraordinary situation, the two lovers are soon required to abandon their contest of wits and conspire instead to free Claudio (the Claudio of *Measure for Measure*) and his beloved Juliet, here Beatrice's cousin, from jail. Diarist Samuel Pepys saw the play and especially liked the dancing of the little girl, that is, Beatrice's younger sister Viola (from *Twelfth Night*), who sang a song written by Benedick and danced a saraband with castanets. In 1721 John Rich restored Shakespeare's text for a production at Lincoln's Inn Fields, but the newly restored text did not capture the stage. Charles Johnson's *Love in a Forest*, at the Theatre Royal, Drury Lane, in 1723, included parts of *Much Ado* (especially Benedick's role) in a version of *As You Like It*, and the Reverend James Miller's *The Universal Passion* (Drury Lane, 1737) combined *Much Ado* with Molière's *La Princesse d'Elide*.

Still, Shakespeare's own play (or something considerably closer to it), as interpreted by David Garrick and Hannah Pritchard, did become very popular at Drury Lane in 1748 and in subsequent years, so much so that Garrick chose the play for his great Shakespeare pageant at Drury Lane in 1769, following his Stratford-upon-Avon Jubilee. "Every scene between them," wrote a contemporary observer of Garrick and Pritchard, "was a continual struggle for superiority; nor could the spectators determine to which of them the preference was due." Garrick played Benedick for the last time in May of 1776 during his final year on the stage.

Actor-manager John Philip Kemble followed Garrick in a succession of memorable Benedicks. In April of 1788 at Drury Lane he played opposite Elizabeth Farren's Beatrice in a benefit performance for his wife Priscilla (who played Hero). Kemble continued to have great success with the play, which he regularly revived throughout his stay at Drury Lane. With his move to Covent Garden in 1803 his brother Charles became the principal actor playing Benedick, beginning with a production in John Philip Kemble's inaugural year of management. In 1836 Charles played the role opposite the nineteen-year-old Helen Faucit, in what was billed as his farewell performance on the stage. (In fact, he revived the role one more time, returning to the stage for four performances in 1840 at the request of Queen Victoria.) Faucit and then Ellen Terry starred as Beatrice, rescuing her from the shrewish interpretation common before that time; Faucit and Terry both favored a warmer, more animated, more buoyant mirth. Faucit played the role for a final time opposite Barry Sullivan at Stratford-upon-Avon in 1879 at the opening of the Shakespeare Memorial Theatre. Terry was paired with a deliberate and polished Henry Irving at the Lyceum Theatre in 1882 and subsequently at the Imperial Theatre in Westminster (1903) with Oscar Asche, in a production designed and directed by her son, Edward Gordon Craig. Beatrice was, along with Portia in *The Merchant of Venice*, the role for which Ellen Terry was best known and admired. Nineteenth-century productions of *Much Ado* tended to be lavish. A contemporary account describes the stunning visual impression achieved by Charles Kean at the Princess's Theatre in 1838: "The opening view, the harbor of Messina, was quite a pictorial gem. The gradual illumination of the lighthouse and various mansions, in almost every window, the moon slowly rising and throwing silver light upon the deep blue waters of the Mediterranean, were managed with imposing reality. Then followed the masquerade, with its variegated lamps, bridge, gardens, and lake, seen through the arches of the palace." Henry Irving, in 1882, undertook to go even further. His scene opened on a classical structure of columns and yellow marble steps; the ballroom in Act 2 was done up in crimson and gold, with tapestries; the church scene had an ornamented canopied roof supported by massive pillars, iron gates, stained glass windows, a sumptuous altar, carved oak benches, hanging golden lamps, and statues of saints. Herbert Beerbohm Tree, at His Majesty's Theatre in 1905, provided Sicilian landscapes and Italian gardens to set off a dazzling orchestration of dances and masquerades.

Until the twentieth century, then, a common feature of production was the attempt to entertain through spectacle while focusing the comedy on the combat of wits between Benedick and Beatrice. Whether shrewish or good-natured in their badinage, these lovers were the center of the dramatic interest. More recent productions have tended to try something new by providing an entirely different setting for the action and by looking afresh at the lovers in the context of the whole play. Renaissance decor has not disappeared, of course, as in the influential production directed by John Gielgud at Stratford-upon-Avon in 1949, later with Gielgud himself and Peggy Ashcroft in the chief roles during a revival in 1950. Other directors, however, have chosen for their locations the American Southwest of fast guns and frontier justice with Dogberry as a bumbling sheriff (directed by John Houseman and Jack Landau at Stratford, Connecticut, in 1957), the early Victorian era of crinolines, parasols, and tight lacing (directed by Douglas Seale, Stratford-upon-Avon in 1958), the Regency England of Wellington uniforms (Michael Langham, Stratford-upon-Avon, 1961), the turn-of-the-century Sicily of broiling sun and hot temperament (Franco Zeffirelli, National Theatre, 1965), the Edwardian England of bicycle-riding New Women (William Hutt, Stratford, Canada, 1971), and the small-town America of the post-Spanish-American War era of Teddy Roosevelt, gramophones, brass bands, high wing collars, and Keystone cops (A. J. Antoon, Delacorte Theater, New York, 1972). (Antoon's production, when it was shown subsequently on commercial television, landed at the bottom of the weekly Nielsen ratings and yet was seen on that occasion by more people than in all the play's previous theatrical history.) In 1976 at Stratford-upon-Avon, John Barton set the play in the Victorian India of the British Raj. Six years later Terry Hands, again at Stratford, returned the play close to its original setting by locating it in Caroline England.

By relocating the play, twentieth-century directors have uncovered darker and more complex issues than those generally confronted by eighteenth- and nineteenth-century productions. Zeffirelli sought to illuminate Hero's plight in the milieu of the Sicilian code of machismo and its fierce demands for female chastity. The British Raj in India provided Barton a world of class-conscious privilege and imperialist mentality in the context of which Claudio's self-centered caddishness and Don John's wanton cruelty seemed plausible and even predictable. Small-town America gave Antoon a more genial, if parochial, perspective on the lovers' tribulations, and the Keystone cops, with their frantic slapstick chases in the idiom of silent film, were ultimately as ineffectual as the melodramatic Don John, whom they almost unintentionally managed to bring to ground. Regency England established a mood of carefree affluence that gave credibility to the plots and machinations of bored aristocrats. Hands's Caroline setting provided a world of aristocratic privilege where feeling was easily sacrificed to fashion; the superficial values of Messinan society were literally reflected in the mirrored floor and Plexiglas panels of Ralph Koltai's set. Occasionally these productions strained their audiences' credulity by making nonsense of the play's ceremonial language—what is one to make of "Your Grace" and "my lord" in frontier Texas?—and thus prompted arguments about the virtues and defects of "relevance" in the theater. But at their best such recent productions have done much to explore what is genuinely timeless in *Much Ado* and to discover the balance among its various parts, which earlier productions generally had ignored in favor of the star system of casting.

Staging requirements in the text itself call not only for balance but for juxtaposition. Overheard conversations are frequent, inviting the director to see a resemblance between innocent and vicious modes of deception. Because there is so much playacting and deception, the play calls attention to its own devices of illusion. (This must have been especially true on the Elizabethan stage where, in the absence of scenery, the actors suggested concealment by hiding behind onstage pillars and the like; possibly Beatrice hid herself in her "pleachèd bower" in Act 3, scene 1, by means of a curtained wall, or discovery space, that is, a recessed area, at the rear of the stage.) Characters in the play are incessantly stage-managing scenes of mistaken impressions: Benedick's friends devise a conversation for him to overhear, and Beatrice's friends do the same for her, while Don John improvises a trap for Claudio at the masked ball and then stages a scene of infidelity at Beatrice's window. Masking is not only a device of plot; in the theater it is also a visual metaphor of the roles that characters adopt toward one another. The masked ball is more than a merry occasion; it becomes a pattern for the dancing partners that expresses through their movements the intricate and dangerous rituals of courtship. Dogberry and his watch are funny in part because they are so apart from this courtly world of dance and wit combat, inferior in intelligence and social grace and yet, paradoxically, able to offer the kind of humorous corrective that simplicity and artlessness alone can provide.

MUCH ADO
—ABOUT—
NOTHING

[*Dramatis Personae*

DON PEDRO, *Prince of Aragon*
LEONATO, *Governor of Messina*
ANTONIO, *his brother*

BENEDICK, *a young lord of Padua*
BEATRICE, *Leonato's niece*
CLAUDIO, *a young lord of Florence*
HERO, *Leonato's daughter*
MARGARET,
URSULA, } *gentlewomen attending Hero*

DON JOHN, *Don Pedro's bastard brother*
BORACHIO,
CONRADE, } *followers of Don John*

DOGBERRY, *Constable in charge of the Watch*
VERGES, *the Headborough, or parish constable, Dogberry's partner*
A SEXTON
FIRST WATCHMAN
SECOND WATCHMAN (GEORGE SEACOAL)

BALTHASAR, *a singer attending Don Pedro*
FRIAR FRANCIS
A BOY
MESSENGER *to Leonato*
Another MESSENGER

Attendants, Musicians, Members of the Watch, Antonio's Son and other Kinsmen

SCENE: *Messina*]

1.1   *Enter Leonato, Governor of Messina, Hero his*
daughter, and Beatrice his niece, with a
Messenger.

LEONATO [*Holding a letter*]   I learn in this letter that Don
   Pedro of Aragon comes this night to Messina.
MESSENGER   He is very near by this. He was not three
   leagues off when I left him.
LEONATO   How many gentlemen have you lost in this
   action?   6
MESSENGER   But few of any sort and none of name.   7
LEONATO   A victory is twice itself when the achiever
   brings home full numbers. I find here that Don Pedro
   hath bestowed much honor on a young Florentine
   called Claudio.
MESSENGER   Much deserved on his part and equally re- 12
   membered by Don Pedro. He hath borne himself be- 13
   yond the promise of his age, doing, in the figure of a
   lamb, the feats of a lion. He hath indeed better bettered 15
   expectation than you must expect of me to tell you
   how.
LEONATO   He hath an uncle here in Messina will be very 18
   much glad of it.
MESSENGER   I have already delivered him letters, and
   there appears much joy in him, even so much that joy
   could not show itself modest enough without a badge 22
   of bitterness.   23
LEONATO   Did he break out into tears?
MESSENGER   In great measure.
LEONATO   A kind overflow of kindness. There are no 26
   faces truer than those that are so washed. How much
   better is it to weep at joy than to joy at weeping!
BEATRICE   I pray you, is Signor Mountanto returned 29
   from the wars or no?
MESSENGER   I know none of that name, lady. There was
   none such in the army of any sort.

1.1. Location: Messina. Before Leonato's house.
6 action battle   **7 sort** rank.   **name** reputation, or noble name
12–13 remembered rewarded   **15 bettered** surpassed   **18 will** who
will   **22 modest** moderate   **22–23 badge of bitterness** sign of sorrow,
i.e., tears   **26 kind** natural   **29 Mountanto** montanto, an upward blow
or thrust in fencing

LEONATO What is he that you ask for, niece?

HERO My cousin means Signor Benedick of Padua.

MESSENGER O, he's returned, and as pleasant as ever he 35
was.

BEATRICE He set up his bills here in Messina and chal- 37
lenged Cupid at the flight; and my uncle's fool, reading 38
the challenge, subscribed for Cupid and challenged 39
him at the bird-bolt. I pray you, how many hath he 40
killed and eaten in these wars? But how many hath he
killed? For indeed I promised to eat all of his killing.

LEONATO Faith, niece, you tax Signor Benedick too 43
much, but he'll be meet with you, I doubt it not. 44

MESSENGER He hath done good service, lady, in these
wars.

BEATRICE You had musty victual, and he hath holp to 47
eat it. He is a very valiant trencherman; he hath an 48
excellent stomach. 49

MESSENGER And a good soldier too, lady.

BEATRICE And a good soldier to a lady, but what is he
to a lord? 52

MESSENGER A lord to a lord, a man to a man, stuffed
with all honorable virtues.

BEATRICE It is so indeed; he is no less than a stuffed 55
man. But for the stuffing—well, we are all mortal. 56

LEONATO You must not, sir, mistake my niece. There is
a kind of merry war betwixt Signor Benedick and her.
They never meet but there's a skirmish of wit between
them.

BEATRICE Alas! He gets nothing by that. In our last conflict, four of his five wits went halting off, and now is 62

35 pleasant jocular   37 bills placards, advertisements   37–38 challenged . . . flight undertook to rival Cupid as an archer   38 my uncle's
fool (Perhaps a professional fool in her uncle's service; possibly Beatrice means herself, recalling an earlier flirtation with Benedick.)
39 subscribed for accepted on behalf of   40 bird-bolt a blunt-headed
arrow used for fowling (sometimes used by children because of its
relative harmlessness and thus conventionally appropriate to Cupid)
43 tax disparage   44 meet even, quits   47 musty victual stale food.
holp helped   48 valiant trencherman great eater   49 stomach appetite   52 to compared to   55–56 stuffed man i.e., a figure stuffed to
resemble a man   56 the stuffing i.e., what he's truly made of. well . . .
mortal i.e., well, we all have our faults   62 five wits i.e., not the five
senses, but the five faculties: memory, imagination, judgment, fantasy,
common wit. halting limping

the whole man governed with one; so that if he have
wit enough to keep himself warm, let him bear it for
a difference between himself and his horse, for it is all 65
the wealth that he hath left to be known a reasonable 66
creature. Who is his companion now? He hath every
month a new sworn brother.   68

MESSENGER   Is 't possible?

BEATRICE   Very easily possible. He wears his faith but 70
as the fashion of his hat; it ever changes with the next
block.   72

MESSENGER   I see, lady, the gentleman is not in your 73
books.   74

BEATRICE   No; an he were, I would burn my study. But 75
I pray you, who is his companion? Is there no young
squarer now that will make a voyage with him to the 77
devil?

MESSENGER   He is most in the company of the right noble Claudio.

BEATRICE   O Lord, he will hang upon him like a disease! 81
He is sooner caught than the pestilence, and the taker
runs presently mad. God help the noble Claudio! If he 83
have caught the Benedick, it will cost him a thousand 84
pound ere 'a be cured.   85

MESSENGER   I will hold friends with you, lady.   86

BEATRICE   Do, good friend.

LEONATO   You will never run mad, niece.   88

BEATRICE   No, not till a hot January.

MESSENGER   Don Pedro is approached.

*Enter Don Pedro, Claudio, Benedick, Balthasar,
and [Don] John the Bastard.*

DON PEDRO   Good Signor Leonato, are you come to

---

65 difference heraldic distinguishing feature (with a play on the usual
sense). **is** i.e., takes   **66 to be known** i.e., in order that he may be
recognized as   **68 sworn brother** brother in arms. (*Frater juratus*, an
allusion to the ancient practice of swearing brotherhood.)   **70 faith**
allegiance, or fidelity   **72 block** mold for shaping hats   **73–74 in your
books** i.e., in favor with you, in your account books for credit   **75 an** if
(also in l. 131)   **77 squarer** quarreler   **81 he** i.e., Benedick   **83 presently**
immediately   **84 the Benedick** i.e., as if he were a disease   **85 'a** he
86 hold friends keep on friendly terms (so as not to earn your enmity)
88 run mad i.e., "catch the Benedick"

meet your trouble? The fashion of the world is to avoid 92
cost, and you encounter it.   93
LEONATO Never came trouble to my house in the likeness of Your Grace. For trouble being gone, comfort
should remain; but when you depart from me, sorrow
abides and happiness takes his leave.
DON PEDRO You embrace your charge too willingly.—I 98
think this is your daughter.
                        [*Presenting himself to Hero.*]
LEONATO Her mother hath many times told me so.
BENEDICK Were you in doubt, sir, that you asked her?
LEONATO Signor Benedick, no; for then were you a
child.
DON PEDRO You have it full, Benedick. We may guess 104
by this what you are, being a man. Truly, the lady
fathers herself. Be happy, lady, for you are like an hon- 106
orable father.
BENEDICK If Signor Leonato be her father, she would
not have his head on her shoulders for all Messina, as 109
like him as she is.
                  [*Don Pedro and Leonato talk aside.*]
BEATRICE I wonder that you will still be talking, Signor
Benedick. Nobody marks you.
BENEDICK What, my dear Lady Disdain! Are you yet
living?
BEATRICE Is it possible disdain should die while she
hath such meet food to feed it as Signor Benedick? 116
Courtesy itself must convert to disdain, if you come in 117
her presence.
BENEDICK Then is courtesy a turncoat. But it is certain
I am loved of all ladies, only you excepted; and I would
I could find in my heart that I had not a hard heart, for
truly I love none.
BEATRICE A dear happiness to women! They would 123
else have been troubled with a pernicious suitor. I

92 your trouble i.e., the expense of entertaining me and my retinue
93 encounter go to meet   **98 embrace your charge** greet your burden
104 have it full are well answered   **106 fathers herself** shows by appearance who her father is   **109 his head** i.e., with Leonato's white beard
and signs of age   **116 meet** suitable (with a pun on *meat*)   **117 convert**
change   **123 dear happiness** precious good luck

thank God and my cold blood I am of your humor for 125
that. I had rather hear my dog bark at a crow than a 126
man swear he loves me.

BENEDICK   God keep your ladyship still in that mind! So
some gentleman or other shall scape a predestinate 129
scratched face.

BEATRICE   Scratching could not make it worse, an 'twere
such a face as yours were.   132

BENEDICK   Well, you are a rare parrot-teacher.   133

BEATRICE   A bird of my tongue is better than a beast of 134
yours.   135

BENEDICK   I would my horse had the speed of your
tongue and so good a continuer. But keep your way, 137
i' God's name; I have done.

BEATRICE   You always end with a jade's trick. I know 139
you of old.

DON PEDRO   That is the sum of all, Leonato. Signor 141
Claudio and Signor Benedick, my dear friend Leonato
hath invited you all. I tell him we shall stay here at the
least a month, and he heartily prays some occasion
may detain us longer. I dare swear he is no hypocrite
but prays from his heart.

LEONATO   If you swear, my lord, you shall not be forsworn. [To Don John.] Let me bid you welcome, my
lord, being reconciled to the Prince your brother. I owe 149
you all duty.

DON JOHN   I thank you. I am not of many words, but I
thank you.

LEONATO   Please it Your Grace lead on?

DON PEDRO   Your hand, Leonato. We will go together.   154
                    Exeunt. Manent Benedick and Claudio.

125–126 I am . . . that I am of the same disposition in that matter, i.e., of
loving no one   **129 scape** escape.   **predestinate** inevitable (for any man
who should woo Beatrice)   **132 were** i.e., is   **133 rare** outstanding.
parrot-teacher i.e., one who would teach a parrot well, because you say
the same things over and over   **134 of my tongue** taught to speak like me,
i.e., incessantly   **134–135 of yours** taught to speak like you   **137 a continuer** i.e., in staying power   **139 a jade's trick** i.e., an ill-tempered horse's
habit of slipping its head out of the collar (as Benedick does in this race
of wits)   **141 sum of all** (Don Pedro and Leonato have been conversing
apart on other matters.)   **149 being** since you are   **154 go together** i.e.,
arm in arm (thus avoiding the question of precedence in order of leaving)

CLAUDIO Benedick, didst thou note the daughter of Signor Leonato?

BENEDICK I noted her not, but I looked on her.   157

CLAUDIO Is she not a modest young lady?

BENEDICK Do you question me as an honest man should do, for my simple true judgment? Or would you have me speak after my custom, as being a professed tyrant to their sex?   162

CLAUDIO No, I pray thee, speak in sober judgment.

BENEDICK Why, i' faith, methinks she's too low for a 164 high praise, too brown for a fair praise, and too little for a great praise. Only this commendation I can afford her, that were she other than she is, she were unhandsome, and being no other but as she is, I do not like her.

CLAUDIO Thou thinkest I am in sport. I pray thee, tell me truly how thou lik'st her.

BENEDICK Would you buy her, that you inquire after her?

CLAUDIO Can the world buy such a jewel?

BENEDICK Yea, and a case to put it into. But speak you 175 this with a sad brow? Or do you play the flouting Jack, 176 to tell us Cupid is a good hare-finder and Vulcan a rare 177 carpenter? Come, in what key shall a man take you, to 178 go in the song?   179

CLAUDIO In mine eye she is the sweetest lady that ever I looked on.

BENEDICK I can see yet without spectacles, and I see no such matter. There's her cousin, an she were not possessed with a fury, exceeds her as much in beauty as the first of May doth the last of December. But I hope you have no intent to turn husband, have you?

CLAUDIO I would scarce trust myself, though I had sworn the contrary, if Hero would be my wife.

BENEDICK Is 't come to this? In faith, hath not the world

---

157 noted her not gave her no special attention   **162 tyrant** one cruel or pitiless in attitude   **164 low** short   **175 case** (1) jewel case (2) clothing, outer garments. (There is also a bawdy play on the meaning "female pudenda.")   **176 sad** serious.   **flouting Jack** i.e., mocking rascal
177–178 to tell . . . carpenter i.e., are you mocking us with nonsense? (Cupid was blind, not sharp-eyed like a hunter, and Vulcan was a blacksmith, not a carpenter.)   **179 go in** join in, harmonize with

one man but he will wear his cap with suspicion? Shall 190
I never see a bachelor of threescore again? Go to,
i' faith; an thou wilt needs thrust thy neck into a yoke,
wear the print of it and sigh away Sundays. Look, Don 193
Pedro is returned to seek you.

Enter Don Pedro.

DON PEDRO   What secret hath held you here, that you
followed not to Leonato's?

BENEDICK   I would Your Grace would constrain me to 197
tell.

DON PEDRO   I charge thee on thy allegiance.

BENEDICK   You hear, Count Claudio. I can be secret as
a dumb man—I would have you think so—but on
my allegiance, mark you this, on my allegiance! He is
in love. With who? Now that is Your Grace's part. 203
Mark how short his answer is: with Hero, Leonato's
short daughter.

CLAUDIO   If this were so, so were it uttered. 206

BENEDICK   Like the old tale, my lord: "It is not so, nor 207
'twas not so, but indeed, God forbid it should be so."

CLAUDIO   If my passion change not shortly, God forbid
it should be otherwise.

DON PEDRO   Amen, if you love her, for the lady is very
well worthy.

CLAUDIO   You speak this to fetch me in, my lord. 213

DON PEDRO   By my troth, I speak my thought.

CLAUDIO   And in faith, my lord, I spoke mine.

BENEDICK   And by my two faiths and troths, my lord,
I spoke mine.

---

190 wear . . . suspicion i.e., marry and thus be suspected of wearing his
cap to hide his cuckold's horns, signs of his wife's infidelity   **193 print**
imprint.   **Sundays** i.e., when, owing to the domesticity of the day, you
cannot escape from your yokefellow   **197 constrain** order   **203 part**
speaking part (i.e., to say, "With who?")   **206 If this . . . uttered** i.e., if I
really were in love with Hero and told Benedick, he would blab the
secret this way   **207 old tale** (In the English fairy tale known as "Mr.
Fox," a murderous wooer, discovered in his crimes by the lady he seeks
to marry and victimize, repeatedly disclaims her recital of what she has
seen by the refrain here set in quotations. The story is a variant of the
theme known as "the Robber Bridegroom." Benedick uses it mockingly
here to characterize Claudio's reluctance to admit his "crime" of falling
in love.)   **213 fetch me in** get me to confess

CLAUDIO That I love her, I feel.

DON PEDRO That she is worthy, I know.

BENEDICK That I neither feel how she should be loved
nor know how she should be worthy is the opinion
that fire cannot melt out of me. I will die in it at the
stake.

DON PEDRO Thou wast ever an obstinate heretic in the
despite of beauty.   225

CLAUDIO And never could maintain his part but in the
force of his will.   227

BENEDICK That a woman conceived me, I thank her; that
she brought me up, I likewise give her most humble
thanks. But that I will have a recheat winded in my   230
forehead or hang my bugle in an invisible baldrick,   231
all women shall pardon me. Because I will not do them
the wrong to mistrust any, I will do myself the right to
trust none; and the fine is, for the which I may go the 234
finer, I will live a bachelor.   235

DON PEDRO I shall see thee, ere I die, look pale with
love.

BENEDICK With anger, with sickness, or with hunger,
my lord, not with love. Prove that ever I lose more   239
blood with love than I will get again with drinking,   240
pick out mine eyes with a ballad-maker's pen and   241
hang me up at the door of a brothel house for the sign 242
of blind Cupid.

DON PEDRO Well, if ever thou dost fall from this faith,
thou wilt prove a notable argument.   245

BENEDICK If I do, hang me in a bottle like a cat and   246

---

225 despite contempt **227 force of his will** i.e., refusing to be guided by
reason (which, as defined by the Schoolmen, was the state of the heretic) **230–232 But that . . . me** i.e., women must pardon me for refusing to
have my horn placed on my head (like a cuckold) **230 recheat** hunting
call sounded (*winded*) on a horn to assemble the hounds **231 baldrick**
strap that supports the horn (here invisible because the horn is the
metaphorical one of cuckoldry) **234 fine** end **234–235 go the finer** be
more finely dressed (since without a wife I will have more money to
spend on clothing) **239 Prove** if you can prove **239–240 lose . . . drinking** (According to Elizabethan theory, each sigh cost the heart a drop of
blood, whereas blood was replenished by wine.) **241 ballad-maker's pen**
i.e., such as would be used to write love ballads or satires **242 sign** a
painted sign, such as hung over inns and shops **245 notable argument**
notorious subject for conversation, example **246 bottle** wicker or leather
basket (to hold the cat sometimes used as an archery target)

shoot at me, and he that hits me, let him be clapped on
the shoulder and called Adam. 248

DON PEDRO   Well, as time shall try:
"In time the savage bull doth bear the yoke." 250

BENEDICK   The savage bull may; but if ever the sensible
Benedick bear it, pluck off the bull's horns and set
them in my forehead, and let me be vilely painted,
and in such great letters as they write, "Here is good
horse to hire," let them signify under my sign, "Here
you may see Benedick the married man."

CLAUDIO   If this should ever happen, thou wouldst be
horn-mad. 258

DON PEDRO   Nay, if Cupid have not spent all his quiver
in Venice, thou wilt quake for this shortly. 260

BENEDICK   I look for an earthquake too, then. 261

DON PEDRO   Well, you will temporize with the hours. In 262
the meantime, good Signor Benedick, repair to Leonato's. Commend me to him, and tell him I will not fail
him at supper, for indeed he hath made great preparation.

BENEDICK   I have almost matter enough in me for such 267
an embassage; and so I commit you— 268

CLAUDIO   To the tuition of God. From my house, if I had 269
it—

DON PEDRO   The sixth of July. Your loving friend, Benedick.

BENEDICK   Nay, mock not, mock not. The body of your
discourse is sometimes guarded with fragments, and 274
the guards are but slightly basted on neither. Ere you 275

---

248 **Adam** (Probably refers to Adam Bell, archer outlaw of the ballads.)   250 **In . . . yoke** (Proverbial; also appearing in a varied form in
Kyd's *The Spanish Tragedy*, 2.1.)   258 **horn-mad** stark mad. (From the
fury of horned beasts; with allusion to cuckoldry.)   260 **Venice** (A city
noted for licentiousness.)   **quake** (with a pun on *quiver* in the previous
line)   261 **I . . . then** i.e., my falling in love will be at least as rare as an
earthquake   262 **temporize . . . hours** come to terms, or become milder,
in time (with perhaps a bawdy pun on *hours, whores;* pronounced
something like "hoors")   267 **matter** wit, intelligence   268 **embassage**
mission.   **and so . . . you** (A conventional close, which Claudio and Don
Pedro mockingly play with as though it were the complimentary close
of a letter.)   269 **tuition** protection   274 **guarded** ornamented,
trimmed   275 **guards . . . neither** trimmings are tenuously stitched on
at best, have only the flimsiest connection

flout old ends any further, examine your conscience. 276
And so I leave you.   *Exit.*

CLAUDIO
My liege, Your Highness now may do me good.   278

DON PEDRO
My love is thine to teach. Teach it but how,
And thou shalt see how apt it is to learn
Any hard lesson that may do thee good.

CLAUDIO
Hath Leonato any son, my lord?

DON PEDRO
No child but Hero; she's his only heir.
Dost thou affect her, Claudio?

CLAUDIO   O my lord,   284
When you went onward on this ended action,   285
I looked upon her with a soldier's eye,
That liked, but had a rougher task in hand
Than to drive liking to the name of love.
But now I am returned and that war thoughts   289
Have left their places vacant, in their rooms
Come thronging soft and delicate desires,
All prompting me how fair young Hero is,
Saying I liked her ere I went to wars.

DON PEDRO
Thou wilt be like a lover presently
And tire the hearer with a book of words.
If thou dost love fair Hero, cherish it,
And I will break with her and with her father,   297
And thou shalt have her. Was 't not to this end
That thou began'st to twist so fine a story?   299

CLAUDIO
How sweetly you do minister to love,
That know love's grief by his complexion!   301
But lest my liking might too sudden seem,
I would have salved it with a longer treatise.   303

276 flout old ends quote or recite mockingly proverbial tags of wisdom
(as well as the *ends* of letters that Claudio and Don Pedro have been
parodying). **examine your conscience** look to your own behavior or
speech **278 do me good** do me some good, help me **284 affect** love
285 ended action military action now ended **289 now** now that
297 break open the subject (as also in l. 314) **299 twist** draw out the
thread of **301 his complexion** its outward appearance **303 salved** i.e.,
accounted for, explained

DON PEDRO
What need the bridge much broader than the flood?   304
The fairest grant is the necessity.   305
Look what will serve is fit. 'Tis once, thou lovest,   306
And I will fit thee with the remedy.
I know we shall have reveling tonight;
I will assume thy part in some disguise
And tell fair Hero I am Claudio,
And in her bosom I'll unclasp my heart
And take her hearing prisoner with the force   312
And strong encounter of my amorous tale.
Then after to her father will I break,
And the conclusion is, she shall be thine.
In practice let us put it presently.   *Exeunt.*

❖

1.2   *Enter Leonato and an old man [Antonio],*
brother to Leonato, [meeting].

LEONATO   How now, brother! Where is my cousin,   1
your son? Hath he provided this music?
ANTONIO   He is very busy about it. But brother, I can
tell you strange news that you yet dreamt not of.
LEONATO   Are they good?   5
ANTONIO   As the event stamps them, but they have a   6
good cover; they show well outward. The Prince and   7
Count Claudio, walking in a thick-pleached alley in   8
mine orchard, were thus much overheard by a man of   9
mine: the Prince discovered to Claudio that he loved   10
my niece your daughter and meant to acknowledge it

304 **What need** why need be. **flood** river   305 **The . . . necessity** the
best gift is one that is really needed   306 **Look what** whatever. **'Tis
once** in short, the fact is. (This speech of Don Pedro's is overheard by a
servant of Antonio's, as we learn in the next scene.)   312 **take . . .
prisoner** i.e., command her attention and assent

1.2. Location: Leonato's house.
1 **cousin** kinsman   5 **they** i.e., the news (often treated as a plural noun,
as at 2.1.167)   6 **event** outcome   6–7 **stamps . . . cover** (The image is of
news that is printed and bound in a book; Antonio means that things
look promising at the moment and will be good indeed if they turn out
so.)   8 **thick-pleached alley** walk lined with dense hedges of intertwined
shrubs   9 **orchard** garden   10 **discovered** disclosed

this night in a dance, and if he found her accordant, 12
he meant to take the present time by the top and in- 13
stantly break with you of it.

LEONATO Hath the fellow any wit that told you this? 15

ANTONIO A good sharp fellow. I will send for him, and
question him yourself.

LEONATO No, no; we will hold it as a dream till it ap- 18
pear itself. But I will acquaint my daughter withal, that 19
she may be the better prepared for an answer, if per- 20
adventure this be true. Go you and tell her of it. [*Enter* 21
Antonio's Son, with a Musician, and Others.] Cousins,
you know what you have to do.—O, I cry you mercy, 23
friend; go you with me, and I will use your skill.— 24
Good cousin, have a care this busy time.   *Exeunt.* 25

❖

1.3   *Enter Sir [Don] John the Bastard and Conrade,
his companion.*

CONRADE What the goodyear, my lord! Why are you 1
thus out of measure sad?   2

DON JOHN There is no measure in the occasion that
breeds; therefore the sadness is without limit.   4

CONRADE You should hear reason.   5

DON JOHN And when I have heard it, what blessing
brings it?

CONRADE If not a present remedy, at least a patient suf- 8
ferance.   9

DON JOHN I wonder that thou, being, as thou sayst

12 accordant agreeing, consenting **13 take . . . top** i.e., seize the opportunity. (Proverbially, Time was imagined bald in the back of the head
but with a forelock of hair in the front that opportunistically could be
grabbed.) **15 wit** sense, intelligence **18–19 till . . . itself** till it mani-
fests itself **20–21 peradventure** by chance **23 cry you mercy** beg your
pardon **24 friend** (Addressed perhaps to the musician.) **25 have . . .
time** i.e., take care of yourself

1.3. Location: Leonato's house.
1 What the goodyear (An unexplained expletive, perhaps suggesting
disgust, like "What the deuce.") **2 out of measure** immoderately
4 breeds causes (it) **5 hear** listen to **8–9 sufferance** endurance

thou art, born under Saturn, goest about to apply a 11
moral medicine to a mortifying mischief. I cannot hide 12
what I am: I must be sad when I have cause and smile
at no man's jests, eat when I have stomach and wait 14
for no man's leisure, sleep when I am drowsy and tend 15
on no man's business, laugh when I am merry and 16
claw no man in his humor. 17

CONRADE   Yea, but you must not make the full show of
this till you may do it without controlment. You have 19
of late stood out against your brother, and he hath 20
ta'en you newly into his grace, where it is impossible 21
you should take true root but by the fair weather that
you make yourself. It is needful that you frame the 23
season for your own harvest.

DON JOHN   I had rather be a canker in a hedge than a 25
rose in his grace, and it better fits my blood to be dis- 26
dained of all than to fashion a carriage to rob love from 27
any. In this, though I cannot be said to be a flattering
honest man, it must not be denied but I am a plain-
dealing villain. I am trusted with a muzzle and enfran- 30
chised with a clog; therefore I have decreed not to sing 31
in my cage. If I had my mouth, I would bite; if I had
my liberty, I would do my liking. In the meantime let
me be that I am, and seek not to alter me.

CONRADE   Can you make no use of your discontent?

DON JOHN   I make all use of it, for I use it only. Who 36
comes here?

Enter Borachio.

What news, Borachio?

BORACHIO   I came yonder from a great supper. The

---

11 under Saturn (hence, of a morose disposition)   **11-12 goest ...**
mischief endeavor to cure with moral commonplaces a deadly disease
14 stomach appetite   **15-16 tend on** attend to   **17 claw** flatter.   **humor**
whim   **19 controlment** restraint   **20 stood out** rebelled   **21 grace**
favor   **23 frame** create   **25 canker** dog rose, one that grows wild rather
than being cultivated in formal gardens   **26 blood** mood, disposition
27 fashion a carriage counterfeit a behavior.   **rob love** gain undeserved
affection   **30 trusted ... muzzle** i.e., trusted only as far as one trusts a
muzzled animal   **30-31 enfranchised ... clog** allowed freedom only to
the extent of being hampered by a heavy wooden block   **31 decreed**
determined   **36 for ... only** it is my only resource

Prince your brother is royally entertained by Leonato,
and I can give you intelligence of an intended mar- 41
riage.

DON JOHN   Will it serve for any model to build mischief 43
on? What is he for a fool that betroths himself to un- 44
quietness?

BORACHIO   Marry, it is your brother's right hand.   46

DON JOHN   Who, the most exquisite Claudio?

BORACHIO   Even he.

DON JOHN   A proper squire! And who, and who? 49
Which way looks he?

BORACHIO   Marry, on Hero, the daughter and heir of
Leonato.

DON JOHN   A very forward March chick! How came you 53
to this?

BORACHIO   Being entertained for a perfumer, as I was 55
smoking a musty room, comes me the Prince and 56
Claudio, hand in hand, in sad conference. I whipped 57
me behind the arras, and there heard it agreed upon 58
that the Prince should woo Hero for himself, and having obtained her, give her to Count Claudio.

DON JOHN   Come, come, let us thither. This may prove
food to my displeasure. That young start-up hath all 62
the glory of my overthrow. If I can cross him any way, 63
I bless myself every way. You are both sure, and will 64
assist me?

CONRADE   To the death, my lord.

DON JOHN   Let us to the great supper. Their cheer is the
greater that I am subdued. Would the cook were o' my 68
mind! Shall we go prove what's to be done?   69

BORACHIO   We'll wait upon your lordship.   *Exeunt.*

41 **intelligence** information   43 **model** design, ground plan   44 **What
. . . fool** what kind of fool is he   46 **Marry** by the Virgin Mary, i.e.,
indeed   49 **proper squire** handsome young man. (Said contemptuously.)   53 **forward March chick** precocious young thing (like a chick
hatched prematurely)   55 **entertained for** hired as   56 **smoking** sweet-
ening the air of (with aromatic smoke).   **comes me** comes. (*Me* is used
colloquially.)   57 **sad** serious   58 **arras** tapestry, hanging   62 **start-up**
upstart   63 **cross** thwart (with allusion, in *bless myself*, to making the
sign of the cross)   64 **sure** trustworthy   68–69 **Would . . . mind** i.e.,
would the cook were of a mind to poison the food   69 **prove** try out

2.1   *Enter Leonato, his brother [Antonio], Hero his*
           daughter, and Beatrice his niece [with Margaret
           and Ursula].

LEONATO   Was not Count John here at supper?
ANTONIO   I saw him not.
BEATRICE   How tartly that gentleman looks! I never can 3
  see him but I am heartburned an hour after.   4
HERO   He is of a very melancholy disposition.
BEATRICE   He were an excellent man that were made 6
  just in the midway between him and Benedick. The
  one is too like an image and says nothing, and the 8
  other too like my lady's eldest son, evermore tattling. 9
LEONATO   Then half Signor Benedick's tongue in Count
  John's mouth, and half Count John's melancholy in
  Signor Benedick's face—
BEATRICE   With a good leg and a good foot, uncle, and
  money enough in his purse, such a man would win
  any woman in the world, if 'a could get her good will. 15
LEONATO   By my troth, niece, thou wilt never get thee a
  husband, if thou be so shrewd of thy tongue.   17
ANTONIO   In faith, she's too curst.   18
BEATRICE   Too curst is more than curst. I shall lessen
  God's sending that way; for it is said, "God sends a 20
  curst cow short horns," but to a cow too curst he sends 21
  none.
LEONATO   So, by being too curst, God will send you no
  horns.
BEATRICE   Just, if he send me no husband, for the which 25
  blessing I am at him upon my knees every morning
  and evening. Lord, I could not endure a husband with
  a beard on his face! I had rather lie in the woolen.   28
LEONATO   You may light on a husband that hath no
  beard.

2.1. Location: Leonato's house.
3 tartly sour of disposition   **4 heartburned** afflicted with heartburn or
indigestion   **6 He were** a man would be   **8 image** statue   **9 my . . . son**
i.e., a spoiled child   **15 'a** he   **17 shrewd** sharp   **18 curst** shrewish
20 that way in that respect   **21 curst** i.e., savage, vicious   **25 Just** right,
exactly so   **28 in the woolen** between blankets, without sheets

BEATRICE What should I do with him? Dress him in my
apparel and make him my waiting-gentlewoman? He
that hath a beard is more than a youth, and he that
hath no beard is less than a man; and he that is more
than a youth is not for me, and he that is less than a
man, I am not for him. Therefore I will even take sixpence in earnest of the bearward and lead his apes into 37
hell.   38

LEONATO Well, then, go you into hell?

BEATRICE No, but to the gate; and there will the devil
meet me, like an old cuckold, with horns on his head,
and say, "Get you to heaven, Beatrice, get you to
heaven, here's no place for you maids." So deliver I up
my apes, and away to Saint Peter, for the heavens; he 44
shows me where the bachelors sit, and there live we   45
as merry as the day is long.

ANTONIO [*To Hero*] Well, niece, I trust you will be ruled
by your father.

BEATRICE Yes, faith, it is my cousin's duty to make
curtsy and say, "Father, as it please you." But yet for
all that, cousin, let him be a handsome fellow, or else
make another curtsy and say, "Father, as it please me."

LEONATO Well, niece, I hope to see you one day fitted
with a husband.

BEATRICE Not till God make men of some other metal   55
than earth. Would it not grieve a woman to be over-
mastered with a piece of valiant dust? To make an account of her life to a clod of wayward marl? No, uncle, 58
I'll none. Adam's sons are my brethren, and truly I
hold it a sin to match in my kindred.   60

LEONATO [*To Hero*] Daughter, remember what I told
you. If the Prince do solicit you in that kind, you know 62
your answer.

BEATRICE The fault will be in the music, cousin, if you

---

37 in earnest in advance payment for. **bearward** one who keeps and
exhibits a bear (and sometimes apes) **37–38 lead . . . hell** (An ancient
proverb says, "Such as die maids do all lead apes in hell.") **44 for the
heavens** (A common interjection, like "By God," but here also carrying
its literal meaning, i.e., bound for heaven.) **45 bachelors** unmarried
persons of either sex **55 metal** substance (with a play on *mettle*)
58 marl clay, earth **60 match . . . kindred** i.e., marry incestuously
62 in that kind to that effect (i.e., to marriage)

be not wooed in good time. If the Prince be too impor- 65
tant, tell him there is measure in everything, and so 66
dance out the answer. For, hear me, Hero: wooing,
wedding, and repenting is as a Scotch jig, a measure, 68
and a cinquepace. The first suit is hot and hasty, like 69
a Scotch jig, and full as fantastical; the wedding, man-
nerly-modest, as a measure, full of state and ancientry; 71
and then comes Repentance, and with his bad legs
falls into the cinquepace faster and faster, till he sink
into his grave.
LEONATO Cousin, you apprehend passing shrewdly.   75
BEATRICE I have a good eye, uncle; I can see a church
by daylight.
LEONATO The revelers are entering, brother. Make good
room.   [*The men put on their masks.*]

Enter [as maskers] Prince [Don] Pedro, Claudio,
and Benedick, and Balthasar, [Borachio,] and
Don John.

DON PEDRO Lady, will you walk a bout with your 80
friend?   [*The couples pair off for the dance.*] 81
HERO So you walk softly and look sweetly and say
nothing, I am yours for the walk, and especially when
I walk away.
DON PEDRO With me in your company?
HERO I may say so, when I please.
DON PEDRO And when please you to say so?
HERO When I like your favor, for God defend the lute 88
should be like the case!   89
DON PEDRO My visor is Philemon's roof; within the 90
house is Jove.

65 in good time (1) soon (2) in time to the music, rhythmically
65–66 important importunate, urgent   **66 measure** (1) moderation
(2) rhythm, dance   **68 a measure** a formal dance   **69 clinquepace** five-step
lively dance, galliard   **71 state and ancientry** dignity and traditional
stateliness   **75 apprehend passing shrewdly** understand with unusual
perspicacity   **80 walk a bout** take a turn, join in a section of a dance
(here probably a slow, stately pavane)   **81 friend** lover of either sex
88 favor face   **88–89 God . . . case** i.e., God forbid the face within
should be as unhandsome as its cover, your visor   **90 Philemon's roof**
i.e., the humble cottage in which the peasants Philemon and Baucis
entertained Jove, or Jupiter, unawares. (See Ovid, *Metamorphoses*, 8.)

HERO Why then your visor should be thatched.   92
DON PEDRO Speak low, if you speak love.
                              [*They step aside.*]
BALTHASAR Well, I would you did like me.   94
MARGARET So would not I for your own sake, for I
have many ill qualities.
BALTHASAR Which is one?
MARGARET I say my prayers aloud.
BALTHASAR I love you the better. The hearers may cry
Amen.
MARGARET God match me with a good dancer!
BALTHASAR Amen.
MARGARET And God keep him out of my sight when
the dance is done! Answer, clerk.   104
BALTHASAR No more words. The clerk is answered.   105
                              [*They step aside.*]
URSULA I know you well enough. You are Signor An-
tonio.
ANTONIO At a word, I am not.   108
URSULA I know you by the waggling of your head.
ANTONIO To tell you true, I counterfeit him.
URSULA You could never do him so ill-well unless you 111
were the very man. Here's his dry hand up and down. 112
You are he, you are he.
ANTONIO At a word, I am not.
URSULA Come, come, do you think I do not know you
by your excellent wit? Can virtue hide itself? Go to,
mum, you are he. Graces will appear, and there's an 117
end.   [*They step aside.*] 118
BEATRICE Will you not tell me who told you so?
BENEDICK No, you shall pardon me.
BEATRICE Nor will you not tell me who you are?
BENEDICK Not now.
BEATRICE That I was disdainful and that I had my good

---

92 visor mask. **thatched** i.e., whiskered, to resemble the thatch of a
humble cottage **94–105 Balthasar** (The speech prefixes in the quarto
text for Balthasar's lines read *Bene.* and *Balth.*; some editors speculate
that *Borachio* is intended.) **104 clerk** (So addressed because of Balthasar's repeatedly answering "Amen" like the parish clerk saying the
responses.) **108 At a word** in short **111 do . . . ill-well** imitate his
imperfections so perfectly **112 dry hand** (A sign of age.) **up and down**
exactly **117 mum** be silent **117–118 an end** no more to be said

wit out of the *Hundred Merry Tales*—well, this was   124
Signor Benedick that said so.

BENEDICK   What's he?

BEATRICE   I am sure you know him well enough.

BENEDICK   Not I, believe me.

BEATRICE   Did he never make you laugh?

BENEDICK   I pray you, what is he?

BEATRICE   Why, he is the Prince's jester, a very dull fool.
Only his gift is in devising impossible slanders. None   132
but libertines delight in him, and the commendation   133
is not in his wit but in his villainy, for he both pleases   134
men and angers them, and then they laugh at him and
beat him. I am sure he is in the fleet. I would he had   136
boarded me.   137

BENEDICK   When I know the gentleman, I'll tell him   138
what you say.

BEATRICE   Do, do. He'll but break a comparison or two   140
on me, which peradventure not marked or not laughed   141
at strikes him into melancholy; and then there's a par-
tridge wing saved, for the fool will eat no supper that
night. [*Music.*] We must follow the leaders.   144

BENEDICK   In every good thing.

BEATRICE   Nay, if they lead to any ill, I will leave them
at the next turning.

> *Dance. Exeunt [all except Don John,*
> *Borachio, and Claudio. Don John*
> *and Borachio are unmasked.]*

DON JOHN [*To Borachio*]   Sure my brother is amorous on   148
Hero and hath withdrawn her father to break with
him about it. The ladies follow her, and but one visor
remains.

BORACHIO   And that is Claudio. I know him by his
bearing.

---

124 Hundred Merry Tales (A popular collection of anecdotes first
published by Rastell in 1526.)   **132 Only his gift** his only talent.
impossible incredible   **133 libertines** i.e., those who disregard conventional moral laws   **134 villainy** i.e., mocking, raillery; also,
clownishness   **136 fleet** i.e., crowd, company   **137 boarded** i.e., ac-
costed (continuing the nautical metaphor begun in *fleet*)   **138 know**
become acquainted with   **140 break a comparison** make a scornful
simile or innuendo   **141 peradventure** if it is   **144 leaders** i.e., of the
dance   **148 amorous on** i.e., courting

DON JOHN [*Advancing to Claudio*] Are not you Signor
Benedick?

CLAUDIO You know me well. I am he.

DON JOHN Signor, you are very near my brother in his 157
love. He is enamored on Hero. I pray you, dissuade 158
him from her; she is no equal for his birth. You may
do the part of an honest man in it.

CLAUDIO How know you he loves her?

DON JOHN I heard him swear his affection.

BORACHIO So did I too, and he swore he would marry
her tonight.

DON JOHN Come, let us to the banquet.   165

Exeunt. Manet Claudio.

CLAUDIO
Thus answer I in name of Benedick,
But hear these ill news with the ears of Claudio.
'Tis certain so. The Prince woos for himself.
Friendship is constant in all other things
Save in the office and affairs of love;
Therefore all hearts in love use their own tongues. 171
Let every eye negotiate for itself
And trust no agent; for beauty is a witch
Against whose charms faith melteth into blood. 174
This is an accident of hourly proof, 175
Which I mistrusted not. Farewell therefore Hero! 176

Enter Benedick [*unmasked.*]

BENEDICK Count Claudio?

CLAUDIO Yea, the same.

BENEDICK Come, will you go with me?

CLAUDIO Whither?

BENEDICK Even to the next willow, about your own 181
business, County. What fashion will you wear the gar- 182
land of? About your neck, like an usurer's chain? Or 183
under your arm, like a lieutenant's scarf? You must 184
wear it one way, for the Prince hath got your Hero. 185

157–158 near . . . love close to my brother **165 banquet** light repast of
fruit, wine, and dessert. **s.d. Manet** he remains onstage **171 all** i.e., let
all **174 faith . . . blood** honor gives way to passion **175 accident** occurrence **176 mistrusted** suspected **181 willow** (An emblem of disappointed
love.) **182 County** count **182–183 garland** i.e., of willow **184 lieutenant's
scarf** sash worn as a badge of rank **185 one way** one way or the other

CLAUDIO   I wish him joy of her.

BENEDICK   Why, that's spoken like an honest drovier; so   187
they sell bullocks. But did you think the Prince would   188
have served you thus?

CLAUDIO   I pray you, leave me.

BENEDICK   Ho, now you strike like the blind man. 'Twas   191
the boy that stole your meat, and you'll beat the post.   192

CLAUDIO   If it will not be, I'll leave you.   *Exit.*   193

BENEDICK   Alas, poor hurt fowl! Now will he creep into   194
sedges. But that my Lady Beatrice should know me,   195
and not know me! The Prince's fool! Ha? It may be I
go under that title because I am merry. Yea, but so I
am apt to do myself wrong. I am not so reputed. It is   198
the base, though bitter, disposition of Beatrice that   199
puts the world into her person and so gives me out.   200
Well, I'll be revenged as I may.

Enter the Prince [Don Pedro], Hero, Leonato.
[All are unmasked.]

DON PEDRO   Now, signor, where's the Count? Did you
see him?

BENEDICK   Troth, my lord, I have played the part of Lady   204
Fame. I found him here as melancholy as a lodge in a   205
warren. I told him, and I think I told him true, that   206
Your Grace had got the good will of this young lady,
and I offered him my company to a willow tree, either   208
to make him a garland, as being forsaken, or to bind   209
him up a rod, as being worthy to be whipped.   210

DON PEDRO   To be whipped! What's his fault?

BENEDICK   The flat transgression of a schoolboy, who,   212

187 **drovier** cattle dealer   188 **bullocks** oxen   191 **like the blind man**
(An unidentified allusion to some proverbial story. Cf. the romance
Lazarillo de Tormes, in which the hero steals his master's meat and
revenges himself for the beating he receives by causing the blind man to
jump against a stone pillar.)   192 **post** (1) pillar (2) bearer of news
193 **If . . . be** i.e., if you won't leave me as I asked   194–195 **creep into
sedges** i.e., hide himself away, as wounded fowl creep into rushes along
the river   198–200 **It is . . . out** it is Beatrice's low and harsh disposition that causes her to attribute to the world her own attitudes and to
represent me accordingly   204 **Troth** by my faith   204–205 **Lady Fame**
Dame Rumor   205–206 **lodge in a warren** isolated gamekeeper's hut in
an enclosure for breeding animals   208 **offered . . . to** offered to accompany him to   209–210 **bind . . . rod** tie several willow switches into a
scourge   212 **flat** plain

being overjoyed with finding a bird's nest, shows it
his companion, and he steals it.

DON PEDRO   Wilt thou make a trust a transgression? The   215
transgression is in the stealer.

BENEDICK   Yet it had not been amiss the rod had been
made, and the garland too; for the garland he might
have worn himself, and the rod he might have bestowed on you, who, as I take it, have stolen his bird's
nest.

DON PEDRO   I will but teach them to sing and restore   222
them to the owner.

BENEDICK   If their singing answer your saying, by my   224
faith, you say honestly.

DON PEDRO   The Lady Beatrice hath a quarrel to you.   226
The gentleman that danced with her told her she is
much wronged by you.

BENEDICK   O, she misused me past the endurance of a   229
block! An oak but with one green leaf on it would   230
have answered her. My very visor began to assume life
and scold with her. She told me, not thinking I had
been myself, that I was the Prince's jester, that I was
duller than a great thaw; huddling jest upon jest with   234
such impossible conveyance upon me that I stood like   235
a man at a mark, with a whole army shooting at me.   236
She speaks poniards, and every word stabs. If her   237
breath were as terrible as her terminations, there were   238
no living near her; she would infect to the North Star.   239
I would not marry her, though she were endowed with
all that Adam had left him before he transgressed. She   241
would have made Hercules have turned spit, yea, and   242
have cleft his club to make the fire too. Come, talk not   243
of her. You shall find her the infernal Ate in good ap-   244

---

215 a trust the act of trusting someone   **222 them** i.e., the young birds in
the nest   **224 answer your saying** correspond to what you say   **226 to**
with   **229 misused** abused   **230 block** (of wood)   **234 great thaw** i.e.,
time when roads are muddy and impassable, obliging one to stay dully at
home.   **huddling** piling, heaping up   **235 impossible conveyance** incredible dexterity   **236 at a mark** at the target   **237 poniards** daggers
238 terminations terms, expressions   **239 North Star** (Supposed the most
remote of stars.)   **241 all . . . him** i.e., Paradise before the fall of man
242 Hercules . . . spit (The Amazon Omphale forced the captive Hercules
to wear women's clothing and spin; turning the spit would be an even
more menial kitchen duty.)   **243 cleft** split   **244 Ate** goddess of discord

parel. I would to God some scholar would conjure her, 245
for certainly, while she is here, a man may live as quiet 246
in hell as in a sanctuary, and people sin upon purpose
because they would go thither; so indeed all disquiet,
horror, and perturbation follows her.

Enter Claudio and Beatrice.

DON PEDRO   Look, here she comes.

BENEDICK   Will Your Grace command me any service to
the world's end? I will go on the slightest errand now
to the Antipodes that you can devise to send me on; I 253
will fetch you a toothpicker now from the furthest inch 254
of Asia, bring you the length of Prester John's foot, 255
fetch you a hair off the great Cham's beard, do you 256
any embassage to the Pygmies, rather than hold three 257
words' conference with this harpy. You have no em- 258
ployment for me?

DON PEDRO   None but to desire your good company.

BENEDICK   O God, sir, here's a dish I love not! I cannot
endure my Lady Tongue.   *Exit.*

DON PEDRO   Come, lady, come, you have lost the heart
of Signor Benedick.

BEATRICE   Indeed, my lord, he lent it me awhile, and I
gave him use for it, a double heart for his single one. 266
Marry, once before he won it of me with false dice;
therefore Your Grace may well say I have lost it.

DON PEDRO   You have put him down, lady, you have 269
put him down.

BEATRICE   So I would not he should do me, my lord, lest
I should prove the mother of fools. I have brought
Count Claudio, whom you sent me to seek.

DON PEDRO   Why, how now, Count? Wherefore are
you sad?

245 scholar . . . conjure (Scholars were supposed to be able to conjure
evil spirits back into hell by addressing them in Latin.)   **246 here** i.e., on
earth   **253 Antipodes** people and region on the opposite side of the
earth   **254 toothpicker** toothpick   **255 Prester John** a legendary Christian king of the Far East   **256 great Cham** the Khan of Tartary, ruler of
the Mongols   **257 Pygmies** legendary small race thought to live in
India   **258 harpy** legendary creature with a woman's face and body and
a bird's wings and claws   **266 use** usury, interest.   **double** deceitful (?)
269 put him down got the better of him. (But Beatrice plays with
the phrase in its literal sense.)

CLAUDIO Not sad, my lord.

DON PEDRO How then? Sick?

CLAUDIO Neither, my lord.

BEATRICE The Count is neither sad, nor sick, nor merry,
nor well; but civil count, civil as an orange, and some- 280
thing of that jealous complexion. 281

DON PEDRO I' faith, lady, I think your blazon to be true, 282
though I'll be sworn, if he be so, his conceit is false. 283
Here, Claudio, I have wooed in thy name, and fair
Hero is won. I have broke with her father and his 285
good will obtained. Name the day of marriage, and
God give thee joy!

LEONATO Count, take of me my daughter and with her
my fortunes. His Grace hath made the match, and all 289
grace say Amen to it. 290

BEATRICE Speak, Count, 'tis your cue.

CLAUDIO Silence is the perfectest herald of joy. I were
but little happy if I could say how much! Lady, as you
are mine, I am yours. I give away myself for you and
dote upon the exchange.

BEATRICE Speak, cousin, or if you cannot, stop his
mouth with a kiss, and let not him speak neither.

                    [Claudio and Hero kiss.]

DON PEDRO In faith, lady, you have a merry heart.

BEATRICE Yea, my lord; I thank it, poor fool, it keeps on
the windy side of care. My cousin tells him in his ear 300
that he is in her heart.

CLAUDIO And so she doth, cousin.

BEATRICE Good Lord, for alliance! Thus goes everyone 303
to the world but I, and I am sunburnt. I may sit in a 304
corner and cry, "Heigh-ho for a husband!" 305

DON PEDRO Lady Beatrice, I will get you one.

---

280 civil serious, grave (punning on *Seville* for the city in Spain whence
came bitter-tasting oranges) **280–281 something** somewhat **281 jealous
complexion** i.e., yellow, associated with melancholy and symbolic of jealousy **282 blazon** description. (A heraldic term.) **283 conceit** (1) notion,
idea (2) heraldic device (continuing the metaphor of *blazon*) **285 broke**
spoken **289–290 all grace** i.e., the source of grace, God **300 windy** wind-
ward, safe **303 alliance** relationship by marriage. (Claudio has just called
her "cousin.") **303–304 goes . . . world** i.e., everyone gets married
304 sunburnt (The Renaissance considered dark complexions unattractive.) **305 Heigh-ho . . . husband** (The title of a ballad.)

BEATRICE   I would rather have one of your father's get- 307
ting. Hath Your Grace ne'er a brother like you? Your 308
father got excellent husbands, if a maid could come by
them.
DON PEDRO   Will you have me, lady?
BEATRICE   No, my lord, unless I might have another for
working days. Your Grace is too costly to wear every
day. But I beseech Your Grace, pardon me. I was born
to speak all mirth and no matter.   315
DON PEDRO   Your silence most offends me, and to be
merry best becomes you, for out o' question you
were born in a merry hour.
BEATRICE   No, sure, my lord, my mother cried; but then
there was a star danced, and under that was I born.
Cousins, God give you joy!
LEONATO   Niece, will you look to those things I told
you of?
BEATRICE   I cry you mercy, uncle. [To Don Pedro.] 324
By Your Grace's pardon.   Exit Beatrice.
DON PEDRO   By my troth, a pleasant-spirited lady.
LEONATO   There's little of the melancholy element in 327
her, my lord. She is never sad but when she sleeps,
and not ever sad then; for I have heard my daughter 329
say, she hath often dreamt of unhappiness and waked
herself with laughing.
DON PEDRO   She cannot endure to hear tell of a husband.
LEONATO   O, by no means. She mocks all her wooers
out of suit.   334
DON PEDRO   She were an excellent wife for Benedick.
LEONATO   O Lord, my lord, if they were but a week
married, they would talk themselves mad.
DON PEDRO   County Claudio, when mean you to go to
church?
CLAUDIO   Tomorrow, my lord. Time goes on crutches
till Love have all his rites.
LEONATO   Not till Monday, my dear son, which is hence

307–308 getting begetting (playing on get, "procure," in the previous
speech)   315 matter substance   324 cry you mercy beg your pardon
(for not having obeyed earlier)   327 melancholy element i.e., earth,
associated with the humor of melancholy in the old physiology
329 ever always   334 out of suit out of being wooers to her

a just sevennight and a time too brief, too, to have all 343
things answer my mind. 344

DON PEDRO Come, you shake the head at so long a
breathing, but I warrant thee, Claudio, the time shall 346
not go dully by us. I will in the interim undertake one
of Hercules' labors, which is to bring Signor Benedick and the Lady Beatrice into a mountain of affection
th' one with th' other. I would fain have it a match,
and I doubt not but to fashion it, if you three will but
minister such assistance as I shall give you direction. 352

LEONATO My lord, I am for you, though it cost me ten
nights' watchings. 354

CLAUDIO And I, my lord.

DON PEDRO And you too, gentle Hero?

HERO I will do any modest office, my lord, to help my 357
cousin to a good husband.

DON PEDRO And Benedick is not the unhopefullest hus- 359
band that I know. Thus far can I praise him: he is of a
noble strain, of approved valor, and confirmed honesty. 361
I will teach you how to humor your cousin, that she
shall fall in love with Benedick; and I, with your two
helps, will so practice on Benedick that, in despite of
his quick wit and his queasy stomach, he shall fall in 365
love with Beatrice. If we can do this, Cupid is no
longer an archer; his glory shall be ours, for we are the
only love gods. Go in with me, and I will tell you my
drift.   *Exeunt.* 369

❖

2.2   *Enter [Don] John and Borachio.*

DON JOHN It is so. The Count Claudio shall marry the 1
daughter of Leonato.

BORACHIO Yea, my lord, but I can cross it. 3

---

343 a just sevennight exactly a week   **344 answer my mind** suit my
wishes   **346 breathing** pause, interval   **352 minister** furnish, supply
354 watchings staying awake   **357 do . . . office** play any seemly role
359 unhopefullest most unpromising   **361 strain** ancestry.   **approved**
tested.   **honesty** honor   **365 queasy** squeamish, delicate (about marriage)   **369 drift** purpose

2.2. Location: Leonato's house.
1 shall is going to   **3 cross** thwart (also in l. 7)

DON JOHN   Any bar, any cross, any impediment will be 4
medicinable to me. I am sick in displeasure to him, 5
and whatsoever comes athwart his affection ranges 6
evenly with mine. How canst thou cross this mar- 7
riage?

BORACHIO   Not honestly, my lord, but so covertly that
no dishonesty shall appear in me.

DON JOHN   Show me briefly how.

BORACHIO   I think I told your lordship, a year since,
how much I am in the favor of Margaret, the waiting-
gentlewoman to Hero.

DON JOHN   I remember.

BORACHIO   I can, at any unseasonable instant of the 16
night, appoint her to look out at her lady's chamber
window.

DON JOHN   What life is in that, to be the death of this
marriage?

BORACHIO   The poison of that lies in you to temper. Go 21
you to the Prince your brother; spare not to tell him
that he hath wronged his honor in marrying the renowned Claudio—whose estimation do you mightily 24
hold up—to a contaminated stale, such a one as Hero. 25

DON JOHN   What proof shall I make of that?

BORACHIO   Proof enough to misuse the Prince, to vex 27
Claudio, to undo Hero, and kill Leonato. Look you for
any other issue?

DON JOHN   Only to despite them I will endeavor any- 30
thing.

BORACHIO   Go, then, find me a meet hour to draw Don 32
Pedro and the Count Claudio alone. Tell them that you
know that Hero loves me; intend a kind of zeal both 34
to the Prince and Claudio, as—in love of your 35
brother's honor, who hath made this match, and his
friend's reputation, who is thus like to be cozened with 37

---

4 bar obstacle   **5 medicinable** medicinal.   **displeasure to** dislike of
6–7 whatsoever . . . mine whatever crosses his inclination runs parallel
with mine   **16 unseasonable** unsuitable, unseemly   **21 lies in** rests
with.   **temper** mix, compound   **24 estimation** worth   **25 stale** prostitute   **27 misuse** abuse, deceive   **30 despite** torment   **32 meet** suitable   **34 intend** pretend   **35 as** i.e., saying as follows. (The words
between the dashes are to be understood as instructions to Don John as
to what he is to say.)   **37 like** likely.   **cozened** deceived, cheated

the semblance of a maid—that you have discovered 38
thus. They will scarcely believe this without trial. Offer
them instances, which shall bear no less likelihood 40
than to see me at her chamber window, hear me call
Margaret Hero, hear Margaret term me Claudio; and 42
bring them to see this the very night before the intended wedding—for in the meantime I will so fashion the matter that Hero shall be absent—and there
shall appear such seeming truth of Hero's disloyalty
that jealousy shall be called assurance and all the prep- 47
aration overthrown.   48

DON JOHN Grow this to what adverse issue it can, I will
put it in practice. Be cunning in the working this, and
thy fee is a thousand ducats.   51

BORACHIO Be you constant in the accusation, and my
cunning shall not shame me.

DON JOHN I will presently go learn their day of mar- 54
riage.   *Exit [with Borachio].*

❖

2.3 *Enter Benedick alone.*

BENEDICK Boy!

[*Enter Boy.*]

BOY Signor?

BENEDICK In my chamber window lies a book. Bring it
hither to me in the orchard.   4

BOY I am here already, sir.   5

BENEDICK I know that, but I would have thee hence
and here again. *Exit [Boy].* I do much wonder that one
man, seeing how much another man is a fool when he
dedicates his behaviors to love, will, after he hath

---

38 semblance semblance only, outward appearance.   **discovered** revealed   **40 instances** proofs   **42 hear . . . Claudio** (Many editors read
Borachio for *Claudio*. The present reading may be defended if one
imagines that, by arrangement with Margaret, Borachio is playing the
part of Claudio, but the reading may also be an inconsistency.)
47 jealousy suspicion.   **assurance** certainty   **47–48 preparation** i.e., for
marriage   **51 ducats** gold coins   **54 presently** immediately

2.3. Location: Leonato's garden.
4 orchard garden   **5 I . . . already** i.e., I will be so quick as to use no
time at all. (But Benedick quibbles on the literal sense.)

laughed at such shallow follies in others, become the
argument of his own scorn by falling in love; and such 11
a man is Claudio. I have known when there was no 12
music with him but the drum and the fife, and now 13
had he rather hear the tabor and the pipe. I have 14
known when he would have walked ten mile afoot to
see a good armor, and now will he lie ten nights 16
awake carving the fashion of a new doublet. He was 17
wont to speak plain and to the purpose, like an honest
man and a soldier, and now is he turned orthogra- 19
phy—his words are a very fantastical banquet, just so 20
many strange dishes. May I be so converted and see
with these eyes? I cannot tell; I think not. I will not be
sworn but Love may transform me to an oyster, but I'll
take my oath on it, till he have made an oyster of me,
he shall never make me such a fool. One woman is
fair, yet I am well; another is wise, yet I am well; another virtuous, yet I am well; but till all graces be in
one woman, one woman shall not come in my grace.
Rich she shall be, that's certain; wise, or I'll none; vir- 29
tuous, or I'll never cheapen her; fair, or I'll never look 30
on her; mild, or come not near me; noble, or not I for 31
an angel; of good discourse, an excellent musician, 32
and her hair shall be of what color it please God.
Ha! The Prince and Monsieur Love! I will hide me in
the arbor.   [*He withdraws*.]

Enter Prince [*Don Pedro*], *Leonato, Claudio*.

DON PEDRO   Come, shall we hear this music?
CLAUDIO
   Yea, my good lord. How still the evening is,
   As hushed on purpose to grace harmony!   38
DON PEDRO [*Aside to them*]
   See you where Benedick hath hid himself?

---

11 argument subject   **12–13 there was . . . fife** i.e., his only commitment
was to soldiering   **14 tabor . . . pipe** (Symbols of peaceful merriment.)
16 armor suit of armor   **17 carving** planning.   **doublet** jacket
19–20 turned orthography become fastidious and fashionable in his
choice of language   **29 I'll none** I'll have none of her   **30 cheapen** ask
the price of, bid for   **31, 32 noble, angel** (Each of these words involves a
pun on the meaning "a coin," a noble being worth 6 shillings 8 pence
and an angel 10 shillings.)   **38 grace harmony** do honor to music

CLAUDIO [*Aside in reply*]
   O, very well, my lord. The music ended,   40
   We'll fit the kid-fox with a pennyworth.   41

   Enter Balthasar with Music.

DON PEDRO
   Come, Balthasar, we'll hear that song again.
BALTHASAR
   O good my lord, tax not so bad a voice
   To slander music any more than once.
DON PEDRO
   It is the witness still of excellency   45
   To put a strange face on his own perfection.   46
   I pray thee, sing, and let me woo no more.   47
BALTHASAR
   Because you talk of wooing, I will sing,
   Since many a wooer doth commence his suit
   To her he thinks not worthy, yet he woos,
   Yet will he swear he loves.
DON PEDRO   Nay, pray thee, come,
   Or if thou wilt hold longer argument,
   Do it in notes.
BALTHASAR   Note this before my notes: 53
   There's not a note of mine that's worth the noting.
DON PEDRO
   Why, these are very crotchets that he speaks!   55
   Note, notes, forsooth, and nothing.   [*Music.*]   56
BENEDICK   Now, divine air! Now is his soul ravished! Is   57
   it not strange that sheeps' guts should hale souls out of   58
   men's bodies? Well, a horn for my money, when all's   59
   done.

---

40 The music ended when the music is over **41 We'll . . . pennyworth**
i.e., we'll give our sly victim more than he bargained for. (Benedick is
called *kid-fox*, a term from beast fable, because he is sly like a fox and
is being duped in their game like a kid.) **45–46 It . . . perfection** it is
always characteristic of excellence to pretend not to know its own
skill **47 woo** entreat **53 notes** music **55 crotchets** (1) whim, fancy
(2) musical notes of brief duration **56 nothing** (With a pun on *noting;* the
two words were pronounced alike. Cf. the same pun in the title of the
play, where *Nothing* suggests "noting," or eavesdropping.) **57 air**
melody **58 sheeps' guts** strings on musical instruments. **hale** draw
59 a horn a hunting horn, a more masculine instrument than a fiddle.
(But with a perhaps unconscious allusion to a cuckold's horns.)

The Song.

BALTHASAR
    Sigh no more, ladies, sigh no more,
      Men were deceivers ever,
    One foot in sea and one on shore,
      To one thing constant never.
    Then sigh not so, but let them go,
      And be you blithe and bonny,   66
    Converting all your sounds of woe
      Into Hey nonny, nonny.   68

    Sing no more ditties, sing no moe,   69
      Of dumps so dull and heavy;   70
    The fraud of men was ever so,
      Since summer first was leavy.   72
    Then sigh not so, but let them go,
      And be you blithe and bonny,
    Converting all your sounds of woe
      Into Hey nonny, nonny.

DON PEDRO By my troth, a good song.

BALTHASAR And an ill singer, my lord.

DON PEDRO Ha, no, no, faith, thou sing'st well enough
for a shift.   80

BENEDICK [*Aside*] An he had been a dog that should 81
have howled thus, they would have hanged him, and
I pray God his bad voice bode no mischief. I had as
lief have heard the night raven, come what plague 84
could have come after it.

DON PEDRO Yea, marry, dost thou hear, Balthasar? I 86
pray thee, get us some excellent music, for tomorrow
night we would have it at the Lady Hero's chamber
window.

BALTHASAR The best I can, my lord.

---

66 blithe and bonny cheerful and joyful **68 Hey nonny, nonny** (A
nonsense refrain.) **69 moe** more **70 dumps** mournful songs; also,
dances **72 leavy** leafy **80 for a shift** in a pinch **81 An** if (also in
l. 161) **84 lief** willingly. **night raven** some bird of night, portending
disaster **86 Yea, marry** (A continuation of Don Pedro's speech preceding Benedick's aside.)

DON PEDRO Do so. Farewell. (*Exit Balthasar.*) Come hither, Leonato. What was it you told me of today, that your niece Beatrice was in love with Signor Benedick?

CLAUDIO O, ay! [*Aside to Pedro.*] Stalk on, stalk on; the 95 fowl sits.—I did never think that lady would have 96 loved any man.

LEONATO No, nor I neither, but most wonderful that she should so dote on Signor Benedick, whom she hath in all outward behaviors seemed ever to abhor.

BENEDICK [*Aside*] Is 't possible? Sits the wind in that 101 corner? 102

LEONATO By my troth, my lord, I cannot tell what to think of it but that she loves him with an enraged af- 104 fection; it is past the infinite of thought. 105

DON PEDRO Maybe she doth but counterfeit.

CLAUDIO Faith, like enough. 107

LEONATO O God, counterfeit? There was never counterfeit of passion came so near the life of passion as she discovers it. 110

DON PEDRO Why, what effects of passion shows she?

CLAUDIO [*Aside to them*] Bait the hook well; this fish will bite.

LEONATO What effects, my lord? She will sit you—you 114 heard my daughter tell you how.

CLAUDIO She did indeed.

DON PEDRO How, how, I pray you? You amaze me. I would have thought her spirit had been invincible against all assaults of affection.

LEONATO I would have sworn it had, my lord—especially against Benedick.

BENEDICK [*Aside*] I should think this a gull but that the 122 white-bearded fellow speaks it. Knavery cannot, sure, hide himself in such reverence.

CLAUDIO [*Aside to them*] He hath ta'en th' infection. Hold it up. 126

95–96 Stalk . . . sits i.e., proceed stealthily; the hunted bird is hiding in the bush   **101–102 Sits . . . corner** is that the way the wind is blowing? (i.e., is that how things are?)   **104 enraged** maddened with passion   **105 infinite** farthest reach   **107 like** likely   **110 discovers** betrays   **114 sit you** i.e., sit. (*You* is used idiomatically.)   **122 gull** trick, deception.   **but** except for the fact   **126 Hold it up** keep up the jest

DON PEDRO   Hath she made her affection known to Benedick?

LEONATO   No, and swears she never will. That's her torment.

CLAUDIO   'Tis true, indeed. So your daughter says. "Shall I," says she, "that have so oft encountered him 132 with scorn, write to him that I love him?"

LEONATO   This says she now when she is beginning to write to him, for she'll be up twenty times a night, and there will she sit in her smock till she have writ a sheet 136 of paper. My daughter tells us all.

CLAUDIO   Now you talk of a sheet of paper, I remember a pretty jest your daughter told us of.

LEONATO   O, when she had writ it and was reading it over, she found "Benedick" and "Beatrice" between the sheet?

CLAUDIO   That.   143

LEONATO   O, she tore the letter into a thousand half- 144 pence; railed at herself, that she should be so immodest 145 to write to one that she knew would flout her. "I mea- 146 sure him," says she, "by my own spirit, for I should flout him, if he writ to me. Yea, though I love him, I should."

CLAUDIO   Then down upon her knees she falls, weeps, sobs, beats her heart, tears her hair, prays, curses: "O sweet Benedick! God give me patience!"

LEONATO   She doth indeed; my daughter says so. And the ecstasy hath so much overborne her that my 154 daughter is sometimes afeard she will do a desperate outrage to herself. It is very true.

DON PEDRO   It were good that Benedick knew of it by some other, if she will not discover it.   158

CLAUDIO   To what end? He would make but a sport of it and torment the poor lady worse.

DON PEDRO   An he should, it were an alms to hang him. 161 She's an excellent sweet lady, and, out of all suspicion, 162 she is virtuous.

CLAUDIO   And she is exceeding wise.

---

132 **she** i.e., Beatrice   136 **smock** chemise   143 **That** i.e., that's it
144–145 **halfpence** i.e., small pieces   146 **flout** mock   154 **overborne** overwhelmed   158 **discover** reveal   161 **alms** good deed   162 **out of** beyond

DON PEDRO   In everything but in loving Benedick.

LEONATO   O my lord, wisdom and blood combating in 166
so tender a body, we have ten proofs to one that blood
hath the victory. I am sorry for her, as I have just
cause, being her uncle and her guardian.

DON PEDRO   I would she had bestowed this dotage on 170
me. I would have doffed all other respects and made 171
her half myself. I pray you, tell Benedick of it, and hear 172
what 'a will say.

LEONATO   Were it good, think you?

CLAUDIO   Hero thinks surely she will die; for she says
she will die if he love her not, and she will die ere she
make her love known, and she will die if he woo her,
rather than she will bate one breath of her accustomed 178
crossness. 179

DON PEDRO   She doth well. If she should make tender of 180
her love, 'tis very possible he'll scorn it; for the man,
as you know all, hath a contemptible spirit. 182

CLAUDIO   He is a very proper man. 183

DON PEDRO   He hath indeed a good outward happiness. 184

CLAUDIO   Before God, and in my mind, very wise.

DON PEDRO   He doth indeed show some sparks that are
like wit.

CLAUDIO   And I take him to be valiant.

DON PEDRO   As Hector, I assure you; and in the man- 189
aging of quarrels you may say he is wise, for either he
avoids them with great discretion or undertakes them
with a most Christian-like fear.

LEONATO   If he do fear God, 'a must necessarily keep
peace. If he break the peace, he ought to enter into a
quarrel with fear and trembling.

DON PEDRO   And so will he do, for the man doth fear
God, howsoever it seems not in him by some large 197
jests he will make. Well, I am sorry for your niece.
Shall we go seek Benedick, and tell him of her love?

166 blood natural feeling   **170 dotage** doting affection   **171 doffed** put
or turned aside.   **respects** considerations   **172 half myself** i.e., my
wife   **178 bate** abate   **179 crossness** perversity, contrariety   **180 tender**
offer   **182 contemptible** contemptuous   **183 proper** handsome
184 outward happiness fortune in his good looks   **189 Hector** the
mightiest of the Trojans   **197 by** to judge by.   **large** broad, indelicate

CLAUDIO Never tell him, my lord. Let her wear it out 200
with good counsel.   201
LEONATO Nay, that's impossible. She may wear her
heart out first.
DON PEDRO Well, we will hear further of it by your
daughter. Let it cool the while. I love Benedick well,
and I could wish he would modestly examine himself,
to see how much he is unworthy so good a lady.
LEONATO My lord, will you walk? Dinner is ready.
                            [*They walk aside.*]
CLAUDIO If he do not dote on her upon this, I will never
trust my expectation.
DON PEDRO Let there be the same net spread for her,
and that must your daughter and her gentlewomen
carry. The sport will be when they hold one an opin- 213
ion of another's dotage, and no such matter; that's the 214
scene that I would see, which will be merely a dumb 215
show. Let us send her to call him in to dinner.   216
      [*Exeunt Don Pedro, Claudio, and Leonato.*]
BENEDICK [*Coming forward*] This can be no trick. The
conference was sadly borne. They have the truth of 218
this from Hero. They seem to pity the lady. It seems
her affections have their full bent. Love me? Why, it 220
must be requited. I hear how I am censured. They say
I will bear myself proudly, if I perceive the love come
from her; they say too that she will rather die than give
any sign of affection. I did never think to marry. I must
not seem proud; happy are they that hear their detrac- 225
tions and can put them to mending. They say the lady 226
is fair; 'tis a truth, I can bear them witness; and virtuous; 'tis so, I cannot reprove it; and wise but for 228
loving me; by my troth, it is no addition to her wit,
nor no great argument of her folly, for I will be horribly
in love with her. I may chance have some odd quirks 231

---

200 **wear it out** eradicate it   201 **counsel** reflection, deliberation
213–214 **they . . . dotage** each believes the other to be in love   214 **no
such matter** the reality is quite otherwise   215–216 **dumb show** panto-
mime (lacking their usual banter)   218 **sadly borne** soberly conducted
220 **have . . . bent** i.e., are fully engaged. (The image is of a bow pulled
taut.)   225–226 **their detractions** criticisms of themselves   226 **put . . .
mending** undertake to remedy the defect   228 **reprove** refute   231
quirks witty conceits or jokes

and remnants of wit broken on me, because I have railed so long against marriage. But doth not the appetite alter? A man loves the meat in his youth that he cannot endure in his age. Shall quips and sentences 235 and these paper bullets of the brain awe a man from 236 the career of his humor? No, the world must be peo- 237 pled. When I said I would die a bachelor, I did not think I should live till I were married. Here comes Beatrice. By this day, she's a fair lady! I do spy some marks of love in her.

Enter Beatrice.

BEATRICE Against my will I am sent to bid you come in to dinner.

BENEDICK Fair Beatrice, I thank you for your pains.

BEATRICE I took no more pains for those thanks than you take pains to thank me. If it had been painful, I would not have come.

BENEDICK You take pleasure then in the message?

BEATRICE Yea, just so much as you may take upon a 249 knife's point and choke a daw withal. You have no 250 stomach, signor. Fare you well.   *Exit.* 251

BENEDICK Ha! "Against my will I am sent to bid you come in to dinner." There's a double meaning in that. "I took no more pains for those thanks than you took pains to thank me." That's as much as to say, "Any pains that I take for you is as easy as thanks." If I do not take pity of her, I am a villain; if I do not love her, I am a Jew. I will go get her picture.   *Exit.*

❖

---

235 quips sharp or sarcastic remarks. **sentences** saws, maxims **236 paper bullets** i.e., words **237 career of his humor** pursuit of his inclination **249-250 just . . . withal** i.e., very little. (A daw or jackdaw is a common blackbird, smaller than a crow.) **251 stomach** appetite

3.1 *Enter Hero and two gentlewomen, Margaret and Ursula.*

HERO
Good Margaret, run thee to the parlor.
There shalt thou find my cousin Beatrice
Proposing with the Prince and Claudio.   3
Whisper her ear and tell her I and Ursley   4
Walk in the orchard, and our whole discourse
Is all of her. Say that thou overheardst us,
And bid her steal into the pleachèd bower   7
Where honeysuckles, ripened by the sun,
Forbid the sun to enter—like favorites
Made proud by princes, that advance their pride   10
Against that power that bred it. There will she hide her   11
To listen our propose. This is thy office.   12
Bear thee well in it and leave us alone.   13

MARGARET
I'll make her come, I warrant you, presently.   [*Exit.*]   14

HERO
Now, Ursula, when Beatrice doth come,
As we do trace this alley up and down   16
Our talk must only be of Benedick.
When I do name him, let it be thy part
To praise him more than ever man did merit.
My talk to thee must be how Benedick
Is sick in love with Beatrice. Of this matter
Is little Cupid's crafty arrow made,
That only wounds by hearsay.

Enter Beatrice [behind].

                                Now begin,   23
For look where Beatrice, like a lapwing, runs   24
Close by the ground to hear our conference.

3.1. Location: Leonato's garden.
3 Proposing conversing   **4 Ursley** (A nickname for *Ursula*.)   **7 pleachèd**
formed by densely interwoven branches   **10–11 that ... it** i.e., who dare
set themselves up against the very princes who advanced them   **12 listen our propose** listen to our conversation.   **office** responsibility
13 leave us alone leave the rest to us   **14 presently** immediately
16 trace walk   **23 only ... hearsay** wounds by mere report   **24 lapwing**
bird of the plover family

URSULA [*Aside to Hero*]
  The pleasant'st angling is to see the fish
  Cut with her golden oars the silver stream   27
  And greedily devour the treacherous bait.
  So angle we for Beatrice, who even now
  Is couchèd in the woodbine coverture.   30
  Fear you not my part of the dialogue.
HERO [*Aside to Ursula*]
  Then go we near her, that her ear lose nothing
  Of the false sweet bait that we lay for it.
                           [*They approach the bower.*]
  No, truly, Ursula, she is too disdainful;
  I know her spirits are as coy and wild   35
  As haggards of the rock.
URSULA   But are you sure   36
  That Benedick loves Beatrice so entirely?
HERO
  So says the Prince and my new-trothèd lord.
URSULA
  And did they bid you tell her of it, madam?
HERO
  They did entreat me to acquaint her of it;
  But I persuaded them, if they loved Benedick,
  To wish him wrestle with affection
  And never to let Beatrice know of it.
URSULA
  Why did you so? Doth not the gentleman
  Deserve as full as fortunate a bed   45
  As ever Beatrice shall couch upon?   46
HERO
  O god of love! I know he doth deserve
  As much as may be yielded to a man;
  But Nature never framed a woman's heart
  Of prouder stuff than that of Beatrice.
  Disdain and scorn ride sparkling in her eyes,
  Misprizing what they look on, and her wit   52

27 oars i.e., fins   **30 woodbine coverture** bower, or arbor, of honeysuckle   **35 coy** disdainful   **36 haggards** untamed female hawks.   **rock**
i.e., mountainous terrain   **45–46 as full . . . upon** i.e., as good a wife as
Beatrice   **52 Misprizing** undervaluing

Values itself so highly that to her
All matter else seems weak. She cannot love,   54
Nor take no shape nor project of affection,   55
She is so self-endearèd.
URSULA   Sure I think so,   56
And therefore certainly it were not good
She knew his love, lest she'll make sport at it.
HERO
Why, you speak truth. I never yet saw man,
How wise, how noble, young, how rarely featured,   60
But she would spell him backward. If fair-faced,   61
She would swear the gentleman should be her sister;
If black, why, Nature, drawing of an antic,   63
Made a foul blot; if tall, a lance ill-headed;
If low, an agate very vilely cut;   65
If speaking, why, a vane·blown with all winds;
If silent, why, a block movèd with none.
So turns she every man the wrong side out
And never gives to truth and virtue that
Which simpleness and merit purchaseth.   70
URSULA
Sure, sure, such carping is not commendable.
HERO
No, not to be so odd and from all fashions   72
As Beatrice is cannot be commendable.
But who dare tell her so? If I should speak,
She would mock me into air; O, she would laugh me
Out of myself, press me to death with wit.   76
Therefore let Benedick, like covered fire,
Consume away in sighs, waste inwardly.   78
It were a better death than die with mocks,
Which is as bad as die with tickling.

54 weak unimportant   **55 project** conception, idea   **56 self-endearèd** full
of self-love   **60 How** however.   **rarely** excellently   **61 spell him backward**
i.e., speak contrarily of him by characterizing his virtues as vices
63 black dark.   **antic** buffoon, grotesque figure   **65 agate** i.e., diminutive
person (alluding to the small figures cut in agate for rings)   **70 simpleness**
integrity, plainness   **72 from** contrary to   **76 press me to death** (Pressing
to death with weights was the usual punishment for those accused of
crimes who refused to plead either guilty or not guilty.)   **78 Consume . . .**
sighs (An allusion to the belief that each sigh cost the heart a drop of
blood.)

URSULA
  Yet tell her of it. Hear what she will say.
HERO
  No, rather I will go to Benedick
  And counsel him to fight against his passion.
  And truly, I'll devise some honest slanders   84
  To stain my cousin with. One doth not know
  How much an ill word may empoison liking.
URSULA
  O, do not do your cousin such a wrong!
  She cannot be so much without true judgment—
  Having so swift and excellent a wit
  As she is prized to have—as to refuse   90
  So rare a gentleman as Signor Benedick.
HERO
  He is the only man of Italy,
  Always excepted my dear Claudio.
URSULA
  I pray you, be not angry with me, madam,
  Speaking my fancy: Signor Benedick,
  For shape, for bearing, argument, and valor,   96
  Goes foremost in report through Italy.
HERO
  Indeed, he hath an excellent good name.
URSULA
  His excellence did earn it, ere he had it.
  When are you married, madam?
HERO
  Why, every day, tomorrow. Come, go in.   101
  I'll show thee some attires and have thy counsel
  Which is the best to furnish me tomorrow.
                              [They walk away.]
URSULA [Aside to Hero]
  She's limed, I warrant you. We have caught her, madam.   104
HERO [Aside to Ursula]
  If it prove so, then loving goes by haps;   105

---

84 honest slanders i.e., slanders that do not involve her virtue
90 prized esteemed   **96 argument** skill in discourse   **101 every day,
tomorrow** tomorrow and every day thereafter   **104 limed** caught, like a
bird in birdlime, a sticky substance spread on branches to trap the
birds that perch on them   **105 by haps** by chance

Some Cupid kills with arrows, some with traps.
                              [*Exeunt Hero and Ursula.*]
BEATRICE [*Coming forward*]
    What fire is in mine ears? Can this be true?   107
    Stand I condemned for pride and scorn so much?
    Contempt, farewell, and maiden pride, adieu!
    No glory lives behind the back of such.   110
    And Benedick, love on; I will requite thee,
    Taming my wild heart to thy loving hand.   112
    If thou dost love, my kindness shall incite thee
    To bind our loves up in a holy band;   114
    For others say thou dost deserve, and I
    Believe it better than reportingly.   *Exit.*   116

                            ❖

3.2   *Enter Prince [Don Pedro], Claudio, Benedick,*
          and Leonato.

DON PEDRO   I do but stay till your marriage be consum-   1
    mate, and then go I toward Aragon.   2
CLAUDIO   I'll bring you thither, my lord, if you'll vouch- 3
    safe me.   4
DON PEDRO   Nay, that would be as great a soil in the   5
    new gloss of your marriage as to show a child his new
    coat and forbid him to wear it. I will only be bold with 7
    Benedick for his company, for from the crown of his
    head to the sole of his foot he is all mirth. He hath
    twice or thrice cut Cupid's bowstring, and the little
    hangman dare not shoot at him. He hath a heart as   11
    sound as a bell, and his tongue is the clapper, for what
    his heart thinks his tongue speaks.

---

107 What . . . ears (An allusion to the old saying that a person's ears
burn when one is being discussed in one's absence.)   **110 No . . . such**
no good is spoken of such persons when their backs are turned
112 Taming . . . hand (A figure derived from the taming of the hawk by
the hand of the falconer.)   **114 band** bond   **116 better than reportingly**
on better evidence than mere report

3.2. Location: Leonato's house.
1–2 consummate consummated   **3 bring** escort   **3–4 vouchsafe** allow
5 soil stain   **7 be bold with** ask   **11 hangman** executioner; rogue.
(Playfully applied to Cupid.)

BENEDICK Gallants, I am not as I have been.
LEONATO So say I. Methinks you are sadder.   15
CLAUDIO I hope he be in love.
DON PEDRO Hang him, truant! There's no true drop of
blood in him, to be truly touched with love. If he be
sad, he wants money.
BENEDICK I have the toothache.   20
DON PEDRO Draw it.   21
BENEDICK Hang it!   22
CLAUDIO You must hang it first and draw it after-
wards.
DON PEDRO What, sigh for the toothache?
LEONATO Where is but a humor or a worm.   26
BENEDICK Well, everyone can master a grief but he that   27
has it.
CLAUDIO Yet say I, he is in love.
DON PEDRO There is no appearance of fancy in him, un-   30
less it be a fancy that he hath to strange disguises; as, 31
to be a Dutchman today, a Frenchman tomorrow, or
in the shape of two countries at once, as, a German
from the waist downward, all slops, and a Spaniard   34
from the hip upward, no doublet. Unless he have a   35
fancy to this foolery, as it appears he hath, he is no
fool for fancy, as you would have it appear he is.   37
CLAUDIO If he be not in love with some woman, there
is no believing old signs. 'A brushes his hat o' morn-
ings. What should that bode?
DON PEDRO Hath any man seen him at the barber's?
CLAUDIO No, but the barber's man hath been seen with
him, and the old ornament of his cheek hath already   43
stuffed tennis balls.   44

15 sadder more serious   **20 toothache** (Thought to be a common ailment of lovers.)   **21 Draw** extract. (But Claudio jokes on the method of
executing traitors, who were hanged first and then cut down alive and
drawn, i.e., disemboweled, and finally quartered.)   **22 Hang it** confound
it   **26 Where** where there.   **humor or a worm** (Toothache was ascribed
to "humors," or unhealthy secretions, and to actual worms in the
teeth.)   **27 but** except   **30–31 fancy . . . fancy** love . . . whim, liking
34 slops loose breeches   **35 no doublet** i.e., with a hip-length cloak in
place of the close-fitting doublet   **37 fool for fancy** i.e., lover   **43–44 old
. . . tennis balls** i.e., Benedick's beard has gone to stuff tennis balls. (He
appears onstage beardless in this scene for the first time.)

LEONATO   Indeed he looks younger than he did, by the loss of a beard.

DON PEDRO   Nay, 'a rubs himself with civet. Can you 47 smell him out by that?

CLAUDIO   That's as much as to say, the sweet youth's in love.

DON PEDRO   The greatest note of it is his melancholy.   51

CLAUDIO   And when was he wont to wash his face?   52

DON PEDRO   Yea, or to paint himself? For the which I hear what they say of him.

CLAUDIO   Nay, but his jesting spirit, which is now crept into a lute string and now governed by stops.   56

DON PEDRO   Indeed, that tells a heavy tale for him. Conclude, conclude he is in love.

CLAUDIO   Nay, but I know who loves him.

DON PEDRO   That would I know too. I warrant, one that knows him not.

CLAUDIO   Yes, and his ill conditions; and, in despite of 62 all, dies for him.

DON PEDRO   She shall be buried with her face upwards.   64

BENEDICK   Yet is this no charm for the toothache. Old signor, walk aside with me. I have studied eight or nine wise words to speak to you, which these hobby- 67 horses must not hear. [*Exeunt Benedick and Leonato.*] 68

DON PEDRO   For my life, to break with him about Be- 69 atrice.

CLAUDIO   'Tis even so. Hero and Margaret have by this 71 played their parts with Beatrice, and then the two bears will not bite one another when they meet.

Enter [Don] John the Bastard.

DON JOHN   My lord and brother, God save you!

---

47 civet perfume derived from the civet cat   **51 note** mark   **52 wash** i.e., with cosmetics; similarly with *paint* in the next line   **56 stops** (1) frets on the fingerboard (2) restraints   **62 ill conditions** bad qualities **64 buried . . . upwards** i.e., as the faithful, not as a suicide, who were sometimes buried face downwards (?). (Probably there is also a ribald suggestion, continuing the joke on *dies for him* meaning to make love.)   **67–68 hobbyhorses** i.e., buffoons. (Originally figures in a morris dance made to resemble a horse and rider.)   **69 For** upon.   **break** speak   **71 Margaret** (Ursula joined Hero in playing the trick on Beatrice, but Margaret has been in on it.)

DON PEDRO   Good e'en, brother.   75

DON JOHN   If your leisure served, I would speak with you.

DON PEDRO   In private?

DON JOHN   If it please you. Yet Count Claudio may hear, for what I would speak of concerns him.

DON PEDRO   What's the matter?

DON JOHN   [*To Claudio*]   Means your lordship to be married tomorrow?

DON PEDRO   You know he does.

DON JOHN   I know not that, when he knows what I know.

CLAUDIO   If there be any impediment, I pray you dis-   87
cover it.   88

DON JOHN   You may think I love you not. Let that appear hereafter, and aim better at me by that I now will   90
manifest. For my brother, I think he holds you well   91
and in dearness of heart hath holp to effect your en-   92
suing marriage—surely suit ill spent and labor ill bestowed.

DON PEDRO   Why, what's the matter?

DON JOHN   I came hither to tell you, and, circumstances   96
shortened, for she has been too long a-talking of, the   97
lady is disloyal.

CLAUDIO   Who, Hero?

DON JOHN   Even she—Leonato's Hero, your Hero, every man's Hero.

CLAUDIO   Disloyal?

DON JOHN   The word is too good to paint out her   103
wickedness. I could say she were worse; think you of
a worse title, and I will fit her to it. Wonder not till   105
further warrant. Go but with me tonight, you shall see   106
her chamber window entered, even the night before
her wedding day. If you love her then, tomorrow wed
her; but it would better fit your honor to change your
mind.

CLAUDIO   May this be so?

---

75 **e'en** evening, i.e., afternoon   **87–88 discover** reveal   **90 aim better at**
judge better of.   **that** that which   **91 holds you well** thinks well of
you   **92 holp** helped   **96–97 circumstances shortened** without unnecessary details   **97 a-talking of** under discussion (by us)   **103 paint out**
portray in full   **105–106 till further warrant** till further proof appears

DON PEDRO   I will not think it.

DON JOHN   If you dare not trust that you see, confess not 113
that you know. If you will follow me, I will show you 114
enough; and when you have seen more and heard
more, proceed accordingly.

CLAUDIO   If I see anything tonight why I should not
marry her, tomorrow in the congregation, where I
should wed, there will I shame her.

DON PEDRO   And, as I wooed for thee to obtain her, I will
join with thee to disgrace her.

DON JOHN   I will disparage her no farther till you are my
witnesses. Bear it coldly but till midnight, and let the 123
issue show itself.

DON PEDRO   O day untowardly turned!   125

CLAUDIO   O mischief strangely thwarting!

DON JOHN   O plague right well prevented! So will you
say when you have seen the sequel.   [*Exeunt.*]

❖

3.3   *Enter Dogberry and his compartner [Verges]*
with the Watch.

DOGBERRY   Are you good men and true?

VERGES   Yea, or else it were pity but they should suffer
salvation, body and soul.   3

DOGBERRY   Nay, that were a punishment too good for
them, if they should have any allegiance in them, 5
being chosen for the Prince's watch.

VERGES   Well, give them their charge, neighbor Dog- 7
berry.

DOGBERRY   First, who think you the most desartless 9
man to be constable?

FIRST WATCH   Hugh Oatcake, sir, or George Seacoal, for
they can write and read.

DOGBERRY　Come hither, neighbor Seacoal. [*Seacoal, or Second Watch, steps forward.*] God hath blessed you with a good name. To be a well-favored man is the gift 15 of fortune, but to write and read comes by nature.

SEACOAL　Both which, Master Constable—

DOGBERRY　You have. I knew it would be your answer. Well, for your favor, sir, why, give God thanks, and make no boast of it; and for your writing and reading, let that appear when there is no need of such vanity. You are thought here to be the most senseless and fit 22 man for the constable of the watch; therefore bear you the lantern. This is your charge: you shall comprehend 24 all vagrom men; you are to bid any man stand, in the 25 Prince's name.

SEACOAL　How if 'a will not stand?

DOGBERRY　Why, then, take no note of him, but let him go, and presently call the rest of the watch together and thank God you are rid of a knave.

VERGES　If he will not stand when he is bidden, he is none of the Prince's subjects.

DOGBERRY　True, and they are to meddle with none but the Prince's subjects. You shall also make no noise in the streets; for, for the watch to babble and to talk is most tolerable and not to be endured. 36

WATCH　We will rather sleep than talk. We know what 37 belongs to a watch. 38

DOGBERRY　Why, you speak like an ancient and most quiet watchman, for I cannot see how sleeping should offend. Only have a care that your bills be not stolen. 41 Well, you are to call at all the alehouses and bid those that are drunk get them to bed.

WATCH　How if they will not?

DOGBERRY　Why, then, let them alone till they are sober.

---

15 a good name (Sea coal was high-grade coal shipped from Newcastle, not the charcoal usually sold by London colliers.)　**well-favored** good-looking　**22 senseless** (For *sensible*.)　**24 comprehend** (For *apprehend*.)　**25 vagrom** vagrant.　**stand** stand still, stop　**36 tolerable** (For *intolerable*.)　**37 s.p. Watch** (Here and at ll. 44, 48, 53, and 66 Shakespeare's text does not specify which watchman speaks. These lines are sometimes assigned to the Second Watch, Seacoal, but could be spoken by others of the watch.)　**38 belongs to** are the duties of　**41 bills** pikes, with axes fixed to long poles

If they make you not then the better answer, you may
say they are not the men you took them for.

WATCH Well, sir.

DOGBERRY If you meet a thief, you may suspect him,
by virtue of your office, to be no true man; and for 50
such kind of men, the less you meddle or make with 51
them, why, the more is for your honesty. 52

WATCH If we know him to be a thief, shall we not lay
hands on him?

DOGBERRY Truly, by your office you may, but I think
they that touch pitch will be defiled. The most peace- 56
able way for you, if you do take a thief, is to let him
show himself what he is and steal out of your company.

VERGES You have been always called a merciful man,
partner.

DOGBERRY Truly, I would not hang a dog by my will,
much more a man who hath any honesty in him.

VERGES If you hear a child cry in the night, you must
call to the nurse and bid her still it.

WATCH How if the nurse be asleep and will not hear
us?

DOGBERRY Why then depart in peace, and let the child
wake her with crying, for the ewe that will not hear
her lamb when it baas will never answer a calf when
he bleats.

VERGES 'Tis very true.

DOGBERRY This is the end of the charge: you, Constable,
are to present the Prince's own person. If you meet the 74
Prince in the night, you may stay him.

VERGES Nay, by 'r Lady, that I think 'a cannot. 76

DOGBERRY Five shillings to one on 't, with any man that
knows the statutes, he may stay him; marry, not without the Prince be willing, for indeed the watch ought
to offend no man, and it is an offense to stay a man
against his will.

VERGES By 'r Lady, I think it be so.

DOGBERRY Ha, ah ha! Well, masters, good night. An

---

50 true honest **51 meddle or make** have to do **52 is** it is **56 they . . .
defiled** (A commonplace derived from Ecclesiasticus 13:1.) **74 present**
represent **76 by 'r Lady** i.e., by Our Lady. (A mild oath.)

there be any matter of weight chances, call up me.
Keep your fellows' counsels and your own, and good
night. Come, neighbor. [*He starts to leave with Verges.*]
SEACOAL Well, masters, we hear our charge. Let us go
sit here upon the church bench till two, and then all
to bed.
DOGBERRY One word more, honest neighbors. I pray
you, watch about Signor Leonato's door, for the wedding being there tomorrow, there is a great coil to- 92
night. Adieu. Be vigitant, I beseech you. 93

              Exeunt [Dogberry and Verges].

    Enter Borachio and Conrade.

BORACHIO What, Conrade!
SEACOAL [*Aside*] Peace! Stir not.
BORACHIO Conrade, I say!
CONRADE Here, man. I am at thy elbow.
BORACHIO Mass, and my elbow itched; I thought there 98
would a scab follow. 99
CONRADE I will owe thee an answer for that; and now 100
forward with thy tale.
BORACHIO Stand thee close, then, under this pent- 102
house, for it drizzles rain, and I will, like a true drunk- 103
ard, utter all to thee. 104
SEACOAL [*Aside*] Some treason, masters. Yet stand 105
close. 106
BORACHIO Therefore know I have earned of Don John a
thousand ducats.
CONRADE Is it possible that any villainy should be so
dear? 110
BORACHIO Thou shouldst rather ask if it were possible
any villainy should be so rich; for when rich villains 112
have need of poor ones, poor ones may make what
price they will.

---

92 coil to-do **93 vigitant** (For *vigilant*.) **98 Mass** i.e., by the Mass. **my
elbow itched** (Proverbially a warning against questionable compan-
ions.) **99 scab** i.e., scoundrel (with play on literal meaning) **100 owe
thee an answer** answer later **102–103 penthouse** overhanging structure **103–104 true drunkard** (Alludes to the commonplace that the
drunkard tells all; Borachio's name in Spanish means "drunkard.")
105–106 stand close stay hidden **110 dear** expensive **112 villainy** i.e.,
instigator of villainy

CONRADE I wonder at it.

BORACHIO That shows thou art unconfirmed. Thou 116
knowest that the fashion of a doublet, or a hat, or a
cloak, is nothing to a man.   118

CONRADE Yes, it is apparel.

BORACHIO I mean, the fashion.

CONRADE Yes, the fashion is the fashion.

BORACHIO Tush, I may as well say the fool's the fool.
But seest thou not what a deformed thief this fashion 123
is?

SEACOAL [Aside] I know that Deformed. 'A has been a
vile thief this seven year; 'a goes up and down like a 126
gentleman. I remember his name.

BORACHIO Didst thou not hear somebody?

CONRADE No, 'twas the vane on the house.

BORACHIO Seest thou not, I say, what a deformed thief
this fashion is, how giddily 'a turns about all the hot
bloods between fourteen and five-and-thirty, sometimes fashioning them like Pharaoh's soldiers in the
reechy painting, sometimes like god Bel's priests in the 134
old church-window, sometimes like the shaven Her- 135
cules in the smirched worm-eaten tapestry, where his 136
codpiece seems as massy as his club?   137

CONRADE All this I see, and I see that the fashion wears 138
out more apparel than the man. But art not thou thy- 139
self giddy with the fashion too, that thou hast shifted
out of thy tale into telling me of the fashion?

BORACHIO Not so, neither. But know that I have tonight
wooed Margaret, the Lady Hero's gentlewoman, by

---

116 unconfirmed inexperienced **118 is . . . man** does not make the man.
(But Conrade plays on the phrase in its usual sense.) **123 deformed thief**
i.e., so called because fashion takes such varied and extreme shapes and
because it impoverishes those who follow fashion **126 up and down**
about, here and there **134 reechy** dirty, grimy. (Perhaps this painting is of
the Israelites passing through the Red Sea.) **god Bel's priests** (Probably
alludes to the story of Bel and the Dragon, from the apocryphal Book of
Daniel, depicted in a stained-glass window.) **135–136 shaven Hercules** (A
reference either to Hercules in the service of Omphale—see 2.1.242, note—
or, confusedly, to the story of Samson.) **137 codpiece** decorative pouch at
the front of a man's breeches (indelicately conspicuous in this tapestry)
138–139 fashion . . . man i.e., fashion prompts the discarding of clothes
faster than honest use

the name of Hero. She leans me out at her mistress' 144
chamber window, bids me a thousand times good
night—I tell this tale vilely; I should first tell thee how
the Prince, Claudio, and my master, planted and
placed and possessed by my master Don John, saw afar 148
off in the orchard this amiable encounter. 149

CONRADE And thought they Margaret was Hero?

BORACHIO Two of them did, the Prince and Claudio,
but the devil my master knew she was Margaret; and
partly by his oaths, which first possessed them, partly
by the dark night, which did deceive them, but chiefly
by my villainy, which did confirm any slander that
Don John had made, away went Claudio enraged;
swore he would meet her, as he was appointed, next
morning at the temple, and there, before the whole
congregation, shame her with what he saw o'ernight
and send her home again without a husband.

SEACOAL We charge you, in the Prince's name, stand!

FIRST WATCH Call up the right Master Constable. We 162
have here recovered the most dangerous piece of lech- 163
ery that ever was known in the commonwealth. 164

SEACOAL And one Deformed is one of them. I know
him; 'a wears a lock. 166

CONRADE Masters, masters—

FIRST WATCH You'll be made bring Deformed forth, I
warrant you.

CONRADE Masters—

SEACOAL Never speak, we charge you. Let us obey you 171
to go with us. 172

BORACHIO We are like to prove a goodly commodity, 173
being taken up of these men's bills. 174

CONRADE A commodity in question, I warrant you. 175
Come, we'll obey you.   *Exeunt.*

❖

144 leans me leans. (*Me* is an emphatic marker.)   **148 possessed** (mis-
leadingly) informed; also, perhaps, possessed as by the devil
149 amiable amorous   **162 right Master Constable** (A comic title on the
pattern of "Right Worshipful," etc.)   **163 recovered** (For *discovered.*)
163–164 lechery (For *treachery.*)   **166 lock** lock of hair hanging down on
the left shoulder; the lovelock   **171–172 Let . . . to** (A blunder for *obey
us and.*)   **173 commodity** goods acquired   **174 taken up** (1) arrested
(2) obtained on credit.   **bills** (1) pikes (2) bonds given as security   **175 in
question** (1) subject to judicial examination (2) of doubtful value

3.4   *Enter Hero, and Margaret and Ursula.*

HERO   Good Ursula, wake my cousin Beatrice and desire her to rise.
URSULA   I will, lady.
HERO   And bid her come hither.
URSULA   Well.   [*Exit.*] 5
MARGARET   Troth, I think your other rabato were better. 6
HERO   No, pray thee, good Meg, I'll wear this.
MARGARET   By my troth, 's not so good, and I warrant 8
your cousin will say so.
HERO   My cousin's a fool, and thou art another. I'll wear
none but this.
MARGARET   I like the new tire within excellently, if the 12
hair were a thought browner; and your gown's a most 13
rare fashion, i' faith. I saw the Duchess of Milan's
gown that they praise so.
HERO   O, that exceeds, they say.   16
MARGARET   By my troth, 's but a nightgown in respect 17
of yours: cloth o' gold, and cuts, and laced with silver, 18
set with pearls, down sleeves, side sleeves, and skirts, 19
round underborne with a bluish tinsel. But for a fine, 20
quaint, graceful, and excellent fashion, yours is worth 21
ten on 't.
HERO   God give me joy to wear it! For my heart is exceeding heavy.
MARGARET   'Twill be heavier soon by the weight of
a man.
HERO   Fie upon thee! Art not ashamed?
MARGARET   Of what, lady? Of speaking honorably? Is
not marriage honorable in a beggar? Is not your lord 29

3.4. Location: Leonato's house.
5 Well very well, as you wish   **6 rabato** tall collar supporting a ruff,
stiffened with wire or starch   **8 troth, 's** faith, it is   **12 tire within**
headdress in the inner room   **13 hair** hairpiece attached to the *tire*
(l. 12)   **16 exceeds** i.e., exceeds comparison   **17 nightgown** dressing
gown   **17–18 in respect of** compared to   **18 cuts** slashes in a garment
revealing the underlying fabric.   **laced** trimmed.   **silver** i.e., silver
thread   **19 down sleeves** tight-fitting sleeves to the wrist.   **side sleeves**
secondary ornamental sleeves hanging from the shoulder   **20 round
underborne** with a lining around the edge of the skirt.   **tinsel** cloth,
usually silk, interwoven with threads of silver or gold   **21 quaint** elegant   **29 in** even in

honorable without marriage? I think you would have
me say, "saving your reverence, a husband." An bad 31
thinking do not wrest true speaking, I'll offend no- 32
body. Is there any harm in "the heavier for a husband"? None, I think, an it be the right husband and
the right wife; otherwise 'tis light, and not heavy. Ask 35
my Lady Beatrice else. Here she comes.

Enter Beatrice.

HERO   Good morrow, coz.
BEATRICE   Good morrow, sweet Hero.
HERO   Why, how now? Do you speak in the sick tune? 39
BEATRICE   I am out of all other tune, methinks.
MARGARET   Clap 's into "Light o' love." That goes with- 41
out a burden; do you sing it, and I'll dance it.   42
BEATRICE   Ye light o' love with your heels! Then, if your 43
husband have stables enough, you'll see he shall lack
no barns.   45
MARGARET   O illegitimate construction! I scorn that with 46
my heels.   47
BEATRICE   'Tis almost five o'clock, cousin; 'tis time you
were ready. By my troth, I am exceeding ill. Heigh-ho!
MARGARET   For a hawk, a horse, or a husband?
BEATRICE   For the letter that begins them all, H.   51
MARGARET   Well, an you be not turned Turk, there's no 52
more sailing by the star.   53
BEATRICE   What means the fool, trow?   54
MARGARET   Nothing I; but God send everyone their
heart's desire!

31 saving . . . husband (By this apologetic formula, Margaret suggests
that Hero is too prudish even to hear the word *husband* mentioned.)
An bad if bawdy **32 wrest** misinterpret **35 light** (with a play on the
meaning "wanton") **39 tune** i.e., mood **41 Clap 's** let's shift. **Light o'
love** (A popular song.) **42 burden** bass accompaniment (with play on
the idea of "a weight of a man") **43 Ye . . . heels** i.e., you're light-
heeled, wanton **45 barns** (with pun on *bairns,* children) **46–47 with
my heels** (A proverbial expression of scorn.) **51 H** (with a pun on *ache,*
pronounced "aitch") **52 turned Turk** i.e., turned apostate to the true
faith (by violating your oath not to become a lover) **52–53 no . . . star**
no more navigating by the North Star, i.e., no certain truth in which to
trust **54 trow** I wonder

HERO   These gloves the Count sent me, they are an excellent perfume.   58
BEATRICE   I am stuffed, cousin; I cannot smell.   59
MARGARET   A maid, and stuffed! There's goodly catch-
ing of cold.
BEATRICE   O, God help me, God help me! How long
have you professed apprehension?   63
MARGARET   Ever since you left it. Doth not my wit be-
come me rarely?
BEATRICE   It is not seen enough; you should wear it in   66
your cap. By my troth, I am sick.   67
MARGARET   Get you some of this distilled *carduus bene-* 68
dictus and lay it to your heart. It is the only thing for 69
a qualm.
HERO   There thou prick'st her with a thistle.
BEATRICE   *Benedictus!* Why *benedictus?* You have some
moral in this *benedictus.*   73
MARGARET   Moral? No, by my troth, I have no moral
meaning, I meant plain holy-thistle. You may think
perchance that I think you are in love. Nay, by 'r Lady,
I am not such a fool to think what I list, nor I list not to
think what I can, nor indeed I cannot think, if I would
think my heart out of thinking, that you are in love or
that you will be in love or that you can be in love. Yet
Benedick was such another, and now is he become a   81
man. He swore he would never marry, and yet now,   82
in despite of his heart, he eats his meat without grudg- 83
ing; and how you may be converted I know not, but   84
methinks you look with your eyes as other women do.
BEATRICE   What pace is this that thy tongue keeps?
MARGARET   Not a false gallop.   87

Enter Ursula.

58 perfume (Gloves were often perfumed.)   59 stuffed i.e., stuffed up
with a cold. (But Margaret takes it in a bawdy sense.)   63 professed
apprehension made claim to be witty   66–67 wear . . . cap i.e., as a fool
does his coxcomb   68–69 carduus benedictus the blessed thistle, noted
for medicinal properties (with a pun on *Benedick*)   73 moral hidden
meaning   81–82 a man i.e., like other men   83–84 eats . . . grudging
i.e., is content to be like other men, to be in love   87 Not . . . gallop not
a forced burst of speed (i.e., I speak the truth)

URSULA Madam, withdraw. The Prince, the Count, Signor Benedick, Don John, and all the gallants of the town are come to fetch you to church.

HERO Help to dress me, good coz, good Meg, good Ursula.   [*Exeunt*.]

❖

3.5 *Enter Leonato and the Constable [Dogberry] and the Headborough [Verges].*

LEONATO What would you with me, honest neighbor?

DOGBERRY Marry, sir, I would have some confidence 2
with you that decerns you nearly.   3

LEONATO Brief, I pray you, for you see it is a busy time with me.

DOGBERRY Marry, this it is, sir.

VERGES Yes, in truth it is, sir.

LEONATO What is it, my good friends?

DOGBERRY Goodman Verges, sir, speaks a little off the 9
matter—an old man, sir, and his wits are not so blunt 10
as, God help, I would desire they were, but, in faith,
honest as the skin between his brows.   12

VERGES Yes, I thank God I am as honest as any man living that is an old man and no honester than I.

DOGBERRY Comparisons are odorous. *Palabras*, neigh- 15
bor Verges.

LEONATO Neighbors, you are tedious.

DOGBERRY It pleases your worship to say so, but we are the poor Duke's officers; but truly, for mine own part, 19
if I were as tedious as a king, I could find in my heart to bestow it all of your worship.   21

LEONATO All thy tediousness on me, ah?

DOGBERRY Yea, an 'twere a thousand pound more than

3.5. Location: Leonato's house.
s.d. Headborough local constable   **2 confidence** (A blunder for *conference*.)   **3 decerns** (For *concerns*.)   **9 Goodman** (Title of persons under the social rank of gentleman.)   **10 blunt** (He means *sharp*.)   **12 honest ... brows** (Proverbial expression of honesty.)   **15 odorous** (For *odious*.)   **Palabras** (For *pocas palabras*, "few words" in Spanish.)   **19 poor Duke's officers** (For *Duke's poor officers*.)   **21 of** on

'tis; for I hear as good exclamation on your worship as 24
of any man in the city, and though I be but a poor
man, I am glad to hear it.

VERGES And so am I.

LEONATO I would fain know what you have to say.

VERGES Marry, sir, our watch tonight, excepting your 29
worship's presence, ha' ta'en a couple of as arrant 30
knaves as any in Messina.

DOGBERRY A good old man, sir; he will be talking. As
they say, "When the age is in, the wit is out." God 33
help us, it is a world to see! Well said, i' faith, neigh- 34
bor Verges. Well, God's a good man. An two men 35
ride of a horse, one must ride behind. An honest soul, 36
i' faith, sir, by my troth he is, as ever broke bread, but
God is to be worshiped, all men are not alike, alas,
good neighbor!

LEONATO Indeed, neighbor, he comes too short of you.

DOGBERRY Gifts that God gives.

LEONATO I must leave you.

DOGBERRY One word, sir. Our watch, sir, have indeed
comprehended two aspicious persons, and we would 44
have them this morning examined before your worship.

LEONATO Take their examination yourself and bring
it me. I am now in great haste, as it may appear
unto you.

DOGBERRY It shall be suffigance.   50

LEONATO Drink some wine ere you go. Fare you well.

[*Enter a Messenger.*]

MESSENGER My lord, they stay for you to give your
daughter to her husband.

LEONATO I'll wait upon them. I am ready.   54

[*Exeunt Leonato and Messenger.*]

---

24 exclamation (Possibly for *acclamation*.) **29 tonight** last night. **except-ing** (For *respecting*.) **30 ha'** have **33 When . . . out** (An adaptation of the proverb, "When ale is in, wit is out.") **34 a world** i.e., wonderful. (Prover-bial.) **35 God 's . . . man** i.e., God is good. (A proverbial saying.) **36 of** on **44 comprehended** (For *apprehended*.) **aspicious** (For *suspicious*.) **50 suffigance** (For *sufficient*.) **54 wait upon** attend

DOGBERRY   Go, good partner, go, get you to Francis Sea- 55
  coal. Bid him bring his pen and inkhorn to the jail. We 56
  are now to examination these men.   57
VERGES   And we must do it wisely.
DOGBERRY   We will spare for no wit, I warrant you.
  Here's that shall drive some of them to a noncome. 60
  Only get the learned writer to set down our excom- 61
  munication, and meet me at the jail.   [*Exeunt.*] 62

❖

55–56 Francis Seacoal i.e., the Sexton of 4.2, not the member of the
watch in 3.3   57 examination (For *examine*.)   60 noncome (Probably a
contraction for *non compos mentis*, "not of sound mind," but Dogberry
may have intended *nonplus*.)   61–62 excommunication (For *examination*
or *communication*.)

4.1   *Enter Prince [Don Pedro], [Don John the]*
Bastard, Leonato, Friar [Francis], Claudio,
Benedick, Hero, and Beatrice [with attendants].

LEONATO   Come, Friar Francis, be brief—only to the
plain form of marriage, and you shall recount their
particular duties afterwards.

FRIAR   You come hither, my lord, to marry this lady?

CLAUDIO   No.

LEONATO   To be married to her. Friar, you come to
marry her.

FRIAR   Lady, you come hither to be married to this
Count?

HERO   I do.

FRIAR   If either of you know any inward impediment   11
why you should not be conjoined, I charge you on
your souls to utter it.

CLAUDIO   Know you any, Hero?

HERO   None, my lord.

FRIAR   Know you any, Count?

LEONATO   I dare make his answer, none.

CLAUDIO   O, what men dare do! What men may do!
What men daily do, not knowing what they do!

BENEDICK   How now? Interjections? Why, then, some   20
be of laughing, as ah, ha, he!   21

CLAUDIO
Stand thee by, Friar. Father, by your leave,   22
Will you with free and unconstrainèd soul
Give me this maid, your daughter?

LEONATO
As freely, son, as God did give her me.

CLAUDIO
And what have I to give you back, whose worth
May counterpoise this rich and precious gift?   27

DON PEDRO
Nothing, unless you render her again.

4.1. Location: A church.
11 inward secret   **20–21 some . . . he** (Benedick quotes from Lilly's
Latin grammar on the subject of interjections; according to Lilly, these
are to be classified as laughing interjections.)   **22 Stand thee by** stand
aside   **27 counterpoise** balance, be equivalent to

CLAUDIO
 Sweet Prince, you learn me noble thankfulness. 29
     [*He hands Hero to Leonato.*]
 There, Leonato, take her back again.
 Give not this rotten orange to your friend;
 She's but the sign and semblance of her honor. 32
 Behold how like a maid she blushes here!
 O, what authority and show of truth 34
 Can cunning sin cover itself withal!
 Comes not that blood as modest evidence 36
 To witness simple virtue? Would you not swear, 37
 All you that see her, that she were a maid,
 By these exterior shows? But she is none:
 She knows the heat of a luxurious bed. 40
 Her blush is guiltiness, not modesty.
LEONATO
 What do you mean, my lord?
CLAUDIO   Not to be married,
 Not to knit my soul to an approvèd wanton. 43
LEONATO
 Dear my lord, if you, in your own proof, 44
 Have vanquished the resistance of her youth,
 And made defeat of her virginity—
CLAUDIO
 I know what you would say: if I have known her,
 You will say she did embrace me as a husband,
 And so extenuate the forehand sin. 49
 No, Leonato,
 I never tempted her with word too large, 51
 But, as a brother to his sister, showed
 Bashful sincerity and comely love.
HERO
 And seemed I ever otherwise to you?
CLAUDIO
 Out on thee, seeming! I will write against it. 55

29 learn teach **32 sign and semblance** pretense and outward show
34 authority assurance **36 blood** i.e., blush. **modest evidence** evidence
of modesty **37 witness** bear witness to **40 luxurious** lascivious,
lustful **43 approvèd** proved **44 in . . . proof** in making trial of her
yourself **49 extenuate** excuse, lessen. **forehand sin** sin of anticipating
(marriage) **51 large** broad, immodest **55 Out . . . seeming** i.e., shame
on you, a mere semblance of good

You seem to me as Dian in her orb,   56
As chaste as is the bud ere it be blown;   57
But you are more intemperate in your blood
Than Venus, or those pampered animals
That rage in savage sensuality.

HERO
Is my lord well, that he doth speak so wide?   61

LEONATO
Sweet Prince, why speak not you?

DON PEDRO   What should I speak?
I stand dishonored, that have gone about   63
To link my dear friend to a common stale.   64

LEONATO
Are these things spoken, or do I but dream?

DON JOHN
Sir, they are spoken, and these things are true.

BENEDICK   This looks not like a nuptial.

HERO   True! O God!   68

CLAUDIO   Leonato, stand I here?
Is this the Prince? Is this the Prince's brother?
Is this face Hero's? Are our eyes our own?

LEONATO
All this is so. But what of this, my lord?

CLAUDIO
Let me but move one question to your daughter,
And by that fatherly and kindly power   74
That you have in her, bid her answer truly.

LEONATO
I charge thee do so, as thou art my child.

HERO
O, God defend me, how am I beset!
What kind of catechizing call you this?   78

CLAUDIO
To make you answer truly to your name.

HERO
Is it not Hero? Who can blot that name
With any just reproach?

56 Dian . . . orb i.e., Diana, goddess of chastity, enthroned in the moon
57 be blown open, flower   **61 wide** wide of the mark   **63 gone about**
undertaken   **64 stale** whore   **68 True** (A reply to Don John's speech.)
74 kindly natural   **78 catechizing** formal questioning used by the
Church to teach the principles of faith

CLAUDIO   Marry, that can Hero!
Hero itself can blot out Hero's virtue.   82
What man was he talked with you yesternight
Out at your window betwixt twelve and one?
Now, if you are a maid, answer to this.

HERO
I talked with no man at that hour, my lord.

DON PEDRO
Why, then are you no maiden. Leonato,
I am sorry you must hear. Upon mine honor,
Myself, my brother, and this grievèd Count   89
Did see her, hear her, at that hour last night
Talk with a ruffian at her chamber window,
Who hath indeed, most like a liberal villain,   92
Confessed the vile encounters they have had
A thousand times in secret.

DON JOHN
Fie, fie, they are not to be named, my lord,
Not to be spoke of!
There is not chastity enough in language
Without offense to utter them. Thus, pretty lady,
I am sorry for thy much misgovernment.   99

CLAUDIO
O Hero, what a Hero hadst thou been,
If half thy outward graces had been placed
About thy thoughts and counsels of thy heart!
But fare thee well, most foul, most fair! Farewell,
Thou pure impiety and impious purity!
For thee I'll lock up all the gates of love,   105
And on my eyelids shall conjecture hang,   106
To turn all beauty into thoughts of harm,
And never shall it more be gracious.   108

LEONATO
Hath no man's dagger here a point for me?
                              [*Hero swoons.*]

82 **Hero itself** the name Hero (which in the story of Hero and Leander became a name for a faithful lover)   89 **grievèd** (1) aggrieved, wronged (2) struck with grief   92 **liberal** licentious   99 **much misgovernment** great misconduct   105 **For thee** because of you   106 **conjecture** evil suspicion   108 **be gracious** seem attractive, graceful

BEATRICE
Why, how now, cousin, wherefore sink you down?
DON JOHN
Come, let us go. These things, come thus to light,
Smother her spirits up.
        [*Exeunt Don Pedro, Don John, and Claudio.*]
BENEDICK
How doth the lady?
BEATRICE   Dead, I think. Help, uncle!
Hero, why, Hero! Uncle! Signor Benedick! Friar!
LEONATO
O Fate, take not away thy heavy hand!
Death is the fairest cover for her shame
That may be wished for.
BEATRICE   How now, cousin Hero?
FRIAR Have comfort, lady.
LEONATO
Dost thou look up?
FRIAR   Yea, wherefore should she not?   119
LEONATO
Wherefore? Why, doth not every earthly thing
Cry shame upon her? Could she here deny
The story that is printed in her blood?   122
Do not live, Hero, do not ope thine eyes;   123
For, did I think thou wouldst not quickly die,
Thought I thy spirits were stronger than thy shames,   125
Myself would, on the rearward of reproaches,   126
Strike at thy life. Grieved I, I had but one?
Chid I for that at frugal nature's frame?   128
O, one too much by thee! Why had I one?
Why ever wast thou lovely in my eyes?
Why had I not with charitable hand
Took up a beggar's issue at my gates,
Who, smirchèd thus and mired with infamy,   133
I might have said, "No part of it is mine;
This shame derives itself from unknown loins"?

---

119 wherefore why **122 blood** i.e., blushes **123 ope** open **125 spirits**
life-giving energies, vital powers **126 on . . . reproaches** following this
public disgrace **128 Chid** chided. **frame** plan, order **133 smirchèd**
defamed. **mired** defiled

But mine, and mine I loved, and mine I praised,
And mine that I was proud on, mine so much
That I myself was to myself not mine,   138
Valuing of her—why, she, O she, is fallen   139
Into a pit of ink, that the wide sea
Hath drops too few to wash her clean again
And salt too little which may season give   142
To her foul-tainted flesh!
BENEDICK   Sir, sir, be patient.
For my part, I am so attired in wonder,   144
I know not what to say.
BEATRICE
O, on my soul, my cousin is belied!
BENEDICK
Lady, were you her bedfellow last night?
BEATRICE
No, truly, not; although, until last night,
I have this twelvemonth been her bedfellow.
LEONATO
Confirmed, confirmed! O, that is stronger made
Which was before barred up with ribs of iron!   151
Would the two princes lie and Claudio lie,
Who loved her so that, speaking of her foulness,
Washed it with tears? Hence from her! Let her die.
FRIAR   Hear me a little;
For I have only been silent so long
And given way unto this course of fortune   157
By noting of the lady. I have marked   158
A thousand blushing apparitions
To start into her face, a thousand innocent shames
In angel whiteness beat away those blushes,
And in her eye there hath appeared a fire
To burn the errors that these princes hold   163
Against her maiden truth. Call me a fool;
Trust not my reading nor my observations,

138–139 That . . . her i.e., that I set no value on myself in caring so
much for her   **142 season** preservative   **144 attired in wonder** i.e., filled
with amazement   **151 before** already   **157 given way unto** i.e., accepted.   **course of fortune** turn of events   **158 By . . . lady** i.e., so that I
might observe, or because I have been observing, Hero's reaction (?)
163 errors (Personified as a heretic burned at the stake.)

Which with experimental seal doth warrant   166
The tenor of my book; trust not my age,   167
My reverence, calling, nor divinity,
If this sweet lady lie not guiltless here
Under some biting error.
LEONATO   Friar, it cannot be.
Thou seest that all the grace that she hath left
Is that she will not add to her damnation
A sin of perjury; she not denies it.
Why seek'st thou then to cover with excuse
That which appears in proper nakedness?   175
FRIAR
Lady, what man is he you are accused of?
HERO
They know that do accuse me; I know none.
If I know more of any man alive
Than that which maiden modesty doth warrant,   179
Let all my sins lack mercy! O my father,
Prove you that any man with me conversed   181
At hours unmeet or that I yesternight   182
Maintained the change of words with any creature, 183
Refuse me, hate me, torture me to death!   184
FRIAR
There is some strange misprision in the princes.   185
BENEDICK
Two of them have the very bent of honor;   186
And if their wisdoms be misled in this,
The practice of it lives in John the Bastard,   188
Whose spirits toil in frame of villainies.   189
LEONATO
I know not. If they speak but truth of her,
These hands shall tear her; if they wrong her honor,
The proudest of them shall well hear of it.
Time hath not yet so dried this blood of mine,

166–167 Which . . . book i.e., by means of which observations and
experience I have confirmed what I learned from books   **175 proper** its
own   **179 warrant** sanction, permit   **181 Prove you** if you prove
182 unmeet improper   **183 Maintained the change** held exchange
184 Refuse disown   **185 misprision** mistake, misunderstanding
186 the very bent of an absolute inclination of the mind toward
188 practice scheming   **189 frame** contriving

Nor age so eat up my invention,   194
Nor fortune made such havoc of my means,
Nor my bad life reft me so much of friends,   196
But they shall find, awaked in such a kind,   197
Both strength of limb and policy of mind,   198
Ability in means, and choice of friends,
To quit me of them throughly.
FRIAR   Pause awhile,   200
And let my counsel sway you in this case.
Your daughter here the princes left for dead.
Let her awhile be secretly kept in,
And publish it that she is dead indeed;
Maintain a mourning ostentation,   205
And on your family's old monument   206
Hang mournful epitaphs, and do all rites
That appertain unto a burial.
LEONATO
What shall become of this? What will this do?   209
FRIAR
Marry, this well carried shall on her behalf   210
Change slander to remorse. That is some good.
But not for that dream I on this strange course,   212
But on this travail look for greater birth.   213
She dying, as it must be so maintained,
Upon the instant that she was accused,
Shall be lamented, pitied, and excused
Of every hearer; for it so falls out
That what we have we prize not to the worth   218
Whiles we enjoy it, but being lacked and lost,
Why then we rack the value, then we find   220
The virtue that possession would not show us
Whiles it was ours. So will it fare with Claudio.
When he shall hear she died upon his words,   223
Th' idea of her life shall sweetly creep

194 eat eaten. (Pronounced "et.")   **invention** power to plan (vengeance)   **196 reft** robbed   **197 kind** manner   **198 policy** shrewdness, contriving   **200 quit . . . throughly** revenge myself on them thoroughly   **205 Maintain . . . ostentation** perform all the outward signs of mourning   **206 monument** burial vault   **209 become of** result from   **210 carried** managed   **212 that** i.e., to "change slander to remorse"   **213 on this travail** (1) as a result of this effort (2) from this labor in childbirth   **218 to the worth** as fully as it deserves   **220 rack** stretch (as on a rack)   **223 upon** in consequence of

Into his study of imagination,   225
And every lovely organ of her life   226
Shall come appareled in more precious habit,   227
More moving, delicate, and full of life,
Into the eye and prospect of his soul,   229
Than when she lived indeed. Then shall he mourn,
If ever love had interest in his liver,   231
And wish he had not so accusèd her,
No, though he thought his accusation true.
Let this be so, and doubt not but success   234
Will fashion the event in better shape   235
Than I can lay it down in likelihood.   236
But if all aim but this be leveled false,   237
The supposition of the lady's death
Will quench the wonder of her infamy.
And if it sort not well, you may conceal her,   240
As best befits her wounded reputation,
In some reclusive and religious life,   242
Out of all eyes, tongues, minds, and injuries.   243
BENEDICK
Signor Leonato, let the Friar advise you;
And though you know my inwardness and love   245
Is very much unto the Prince and Claudio,
Yet, by mine honor, I will deal in this
As secretly and justly as your soul
Should with your body.
LEONATO   Being that I flow in grief,   249
The smallest twine may lead me.
FRIAR
'Tis well consented. Presently away;   251
    For to strange sores strangely they strain the cure.   252
Come, lady, die to live. This wedding day

---

225 **study of imagination** musing, imaginative contemplation
226 **organ . . . life** aspect of her when she was alive   227 **habit** apparel   229 **prospect** range of vision   231 **interest in** claim upon.   **liver**
(The supposed seat of the passion of love.)   234 **success** i.e., what
succeeds or happens in time as my plan unfolds   235 **event** outcome
236 **lay . . . likelihood** anticipate its probable course   237 **if . . . false**
i.e., if every other aim miscarry   240 **sort** turn out   242 **reclusive**
cloistered   243 **injuries** insults   245 **inwardness and love** close friendship   249 **Being that** seeing that, since.   **flow in** overflow with, or am
afloat in   251 **Presently** immediately   252 **For . . . cure** strange diseases
require strange and desperate cures

Perhaps is but prolonged. Have patience and endure. 254
              Exit [with all but Benedick and Beatrice].
BENEDICK Lady Beatrice, have you wept all this while?
BEATRICE Yea, and I will weep a while longer.
BENEDICK I will not desire that.
BEATRICE You have no reason; I do it freely.
BENEDICK Surely I do believe your fair cousin is
wronged.
BEATRICE Ah, how much might the man deserve of me
that would right her!
BENEDICK Is there any way to show such friendship?
BEATRICE A very even way, but no such friend. 264
BENEDICK May a man do it?
BEATRICE It is a man's office, but not yours. 266
BENEDICK I do love nothing in the world so well as you.
Is not that strange?
BEATRICE As strange as the thing I know not. It were as
possible for me to say I loved nothing so well as you.
But believe me not; and yet I lie not. I confess nothing,
nor I deny nothing. I am sorry for my cousin.
BENEDICK By my sword, Beatrice, thou lovest me.
BEATRICE Do not swear and eat it. 274
BENEDICK I will swear by it that you love me, and I will
make him eat it that says I love not you.
BEATRICE Will you not eat your word?
BENEDICK With no sauce that can be devised to it. I pro- 278
test I love thee. 279
BEATRICE Why, then, God forgive me!
BENEDICK What offense, sweet Beatrice?
BEATRICE You have stayed me in a happy hour. I was 282
about to protest I loved you.
BENEDICK And do it with all thy heart.
BEATRICE I love you with so much of my heart that
none is left to protest.
BENEDICK Come, bid me do anything for thee.
BEATRICE Kill Claudio.
BENEDICK Ha! Not for the wide world.
BEATRICE You kill me to deny it. Farewell. *[Going.]* 290

---

254 prolonged deferred, put off **264 even** direct, straightforward
266 office duty **274 eat it** i.e., eat your words **278–279 protest** affirm **282 stayed** stopped. **in . . . hour** at an appropriate moment
290 it i.e., my request

BENEDICK   Tarry, sweet Beatrice.

BEATRICE   I am gone, though I am here. There is no love 292
in you. Nay, I pray you, let me go.

BENEDICK   Beatrice—

BEATRICE   In faith, I will go.

BENEDICK   We'll be friends first.

BEATRICE   You dare easier be friends with me than fight
with mine enemy.

BENEDICK   Is Claudio thine enemy?

BEATRICE   Is 'a not approved in the height a villain, that 300
hath slandered, scorned, dishonored my kinswoman?
O, that I were a man! What, bear her in hand until they 302
come to take hands, and then, with public accusation,
uncovered slander, unmitigated rancor—O God, that 304
I were a man! I would eat his heart in the marketplace.

BENEDICK   Hear me, Beatrice—

BEATRICE   Talk with a man out at a window! A proper
saying!

BENEDICK   Nay, but Beatrice—

BEATRICE   Sweet Hero! She is wronged, she is slandered,
she is undone.

BENEDICK   Beat—

BEATRICE   Princes and counties! Surely, a princely testi- 314
mony, a goodly count, Count Comfect; a sweet gallant, 315
surely! O, that I were a man for his sake! Or that I had
any friend would be a man for my sake! But manhood
is melted into curtsies, valor into compliment, and
men are only turned into tongue, and trim ones too. 319
He is now as valiant as Hercules that only tells a lie 320
and swears it. I cannot be a man with wishing, therefore I will die a woman with grieving.

BENEDICK   Tarry, good Beatrice. By this hand, I love
thee.

BEATRICE   Use it for my love some other way than
swearing by it.

---

292 gone i.e., in spirit   **300 approved** proved.   **height** extreme
302 bear her in hand delude her with false hopes   **304 uncovered**
open, unconcealed   **314 counties** counts   **315 count** (1) the title
(2) declaration of complaint in an indictment.   **Comfect** candy or
sweetmeat   **319 trim** nice, elegant, fine. (Used ironically.)   **320 now**
nowadays considered

BENEDICK Think you in your soul the Count Claudio
hath wronged Hero?

BEATRICE Yea, as sure as I have a thought or a soul.

BENEDICK Enough, I am engaged. I will challenge him.   330
I will kiss your hand, and so I leave you. By this hand,
Claudio shall render me a dear account. As you hear   332
of me, so think of me. Go, comfort your cousin. I must
say she is dead; and so, farewell. [Exeunt separately.]

❖

4.2   *Enter the Constables [Dogberry and Verges]
and the Town Clerk [Sexton] in gowns,
Borachio, [Conrade, and Watch].*

DOGBERRY Is our whole dissembly appeared?   1

VERGES O, a stool and a cushion for the sexton.
[*Stool and cushion are brought. The Sexton sits.*]

SEXTON Which be the malefactors?

DOGBERRY Marry, that am I and my partner.

VERGES Nay, that's certain, we have the exhibition to   5
examine.

SEXTON But which are the offenders that are to be examined? Let them come before Master Constable.

DOGBERRY Yea, marry, let them come before me. [*The
prisoners are brought forward.*] What is your name,
friend?

BORACHIO Borachio.

DOGBERRY Pray, write down Borachio. Yours, sirrah?   13

CONRADE I am a gentleman, sir, and my name is Conrade.

DOGBERRY Write down Master Gentleman Conrade.
Masters, do you serve God?

CONRADE, BORACHIO Yea, sir, we hope.

DOGBERRY Write down that they hope they serve God;
and write God first, for God defend but God should   20
go before such villains! Masters, it is proved already

---

330 **I am engaged** I pledge myself   332 **dear** costly

4.2. Location: The jail.
1 **dissembly** (A blunder for *assembly.*)   5 **exhibition** (Possibly for *commission.*)   13 **sirrah** (Used to address inferiors; Conrade objects.)
20 **defend** forbid

that you are little better than false knaves, and it will
go near to be thought so shortly. How answer you for
yourselves?

CONRADE Marry, sir, we say we are none.

DOGBERRY A marvelous witty fellow, I assure you, but 26
I will go about with him. [*To Borachio.*] Come you 27
hither, sirrah, a word in your ear. Sir, I say to you, it
is thought you are false knaves.

BORACHIO Sir, I say to you we are none.

DOGBERRY Well, stand aside. 'Fore God, they are both
in a tale. Have you writ down that they are none? 32

SEXTON Master Constable, you go not the way to examine. You must call forth the watch that are their accusers.

DOGBERRY Yea, marry, that's the eftest way. Let the 36
watch come forth. Masters, I charge you in the
Prince's name accuse these men.

SEACOAL This man said, sir, that Don John, the Prince's
brother, was a villain.

DOGBERRY Write down Prince John a villain. Why, this
is flat perjury, to call a prince's brother villain.

BORACHIO Master Constable—

DOGBERRY Pray thee, fellow, peace. I do not like thy
look, I promise thee.

SEXTON What heard you him say else?

FIRST WATCH Marry, that he had received a thousand
ducats of Don John for accusing the Lady Hero wrongfully.

DOGBERRY Flat burglary as ever was committed.

VERGES Yea, by Mass, that it is. 51

SEXTON What else, fellow?

SEACOAL And that Count Claudio did mean, upon his
words, to disgrace Hero before the whole assembly,
and not marry her.

DOGBERRY O villain! Thou wilt be condemned into everlasting redemption for this. 57

SEXTON What else?

WATCH This is all. 59

---

26 **witty** clever, cunning 27 **go about with** get the better of 32 **in a
tale** in agreement 36 **eftest** (Some sort of blunder for *easiest* or *deft-
est.*) 51 **by mass** by the Mass 57 **redemption** (Dogberry means *damnation.*) 59 **s.p. Watch** (Perhaps both Seacoal and his partner speak.)

SEXTON   And this is more, masters, than you can deny.
Prince John is this morning secretly stolen away. Hero
was in this manner accused, in this very manner
refused, and upon the grief of this suddenly died. Mas-
ter Constable, let these men be bound and brought to
Leonato's. I will go before and show him their exami-
nation.   [*Exit.*]
DOGBERRY   Come, let them be opinioned.   67
VERGES   Let them be in the hands—
CONRADE   Off, coxcomb!
DOGBERRY   God's my life, where's the sexton? Let him   70
write down the Prince's officer coxcomb. Come, bind
them. Thou naughty varlet!   72
CONRADE   Away! You are an ass, you are an ass.
DOGBERRY   Dost thou not suspect my place? Dost thou   74
not suspect my years? O, that he were here to write me
down an ass! But masters, remember that I am an ass;
though it be not written down, yet forget not that I am
an ass. No, thou villain, thou art full of piety, as shall   78
be proved upon thee by good witness. I am a wise
fellow, and, which is more, an officer, and, which is
more, a householder, and, which is more, as pretty a
piece of flesh as any is in Messina, and one that knows
the law, go to, and a rich fellow enough, go to, and a
fellow that hath had losses, and one that hath two
gowns and everything handsome about him. Bring
him away. O, that I had been writ down an ass!

                                              Exeunt.

❖

---

67 opinioned (For *pinioned.*)   **70 God's** may God save   **72 naughty**
wicked   **74 suspect** (For *respect.*)   **78 piety** (For *impiety.*)

5.1 *Enter Leonato and his brother [Antonio].*

ANTONIO
If you go on thus, you will kill yourself;
And 'tis not wisdom thus to second grief   2
Against yourself.
LEONATO   I pray thee, cease thy counsel,
Which falls into mine ears as profitless
As water in a sieve. Give not me counsel,
Nor let no comforter delight mine ear
But such a one whose wrongs do suit with mine.   7
Bring me a father that so loved his child,
Whose joy of her is overwhelmed like mine,
And bid him speak of patience;
Measure his woe the length and breadth of mine,   11
And let it answer every strain for strain,   12
As thus for thus, and such a grief for such,
In every lineament, branch, shape, and form;
If such a one will smile and stroke his beard,
Bid sorrow wag, cry "hem!" when he should groan,   16
Patch grief with proverbs, make misfortune drunk   17
With candle wasters, bring him yet to me   18
And I of him will gather patience.
But there is no such man. For, brother, men
Can counsel and speak comfort to that grief
Which they themselves not feel; but tasting it,
Their counsel turns to passion, which before
Would give preceptial medicine to rage,   24
Fetter strong madness in a silken thread,
Charm ache with air and agony with words.   26
No, no, 'tis all men's office to speak patience   27
To those that wring under the load of sorrow,   28
But no man's virtue nor sufficiency   29
To be so moral when he shall endure   30

5.1. Location: Near Leonato's house.
2 second assist, encourage   7 suit with match   11 Measure his woe let his
woe equal in scope   12 strain strong impulse of the mind   16 wag be off.
cry "hem" i.e., clear the throat as before some wordy speech   17 drunk
i.e., insensible to pain   18 candle wasters those who waste candles by late
study, bookworms, moral philosophers   24 preceptial consisting of pre-
cepts   26 air mere breath, words   27 office duty   28 wring writhe
29 sufficiency ability, power   30 moral prone to moralizing

The like himself. Therefore give me no counsel.
My griefs cry louder than advertisement.   32

ANTONIO
Therein do men from children nothing differ.

LEONATO
I pray thee, peace. I will be flesh and blood;
For there was never yet philosopher
That could endure the toothache patiently,
However they have writ the style of gods   37
And made a push at chance and sufferance.   38

ANTONIO
Yet bend not all the harm upon yourself.
Make those that do offend you suffer too.

LEONATO
There thou speak'st reason. Nay, I will do so.
My soul doth tell me Hero is belied,
And that shall Claudio know; so shall the Prince
And all of them that thus dishonor her.

          Enter Prince [Don Pedro] and Claudio.

ANTONIO
Here comes the Prince and Claudio hastily.

DON PEDRO
Good e'en, good e'en.

CLAUDIO   Good day to both of you.

LEONATO
Hear you, my lords—

DON PEDRO   We have some haste, Leonato.

LEONATO
Some haste, my lord! Well, fare you well, my lord.
Are you so hasty now? Well, all is one.   49

DON PEDRO
Nay, do not quarrel with us, good old man.

ANTONIO
If he could right himself with quarreling,
Some of us would lie low.

CLAUDIO   Who wrongs him?   52

___

32 advertisement advice, counsel   **37 writ the style of** written in language worthy of   **38 push at** defiance of.   **sufferance** suffering   **49 all is one** it makes no difference   **52 Some of us** i.e., Don Pedro and Claudio

LEONATO
Marry, thou dost wrong me, thou dissembler, thou!   53
Nay, never lay thy hand upon thy sword;
I fear thee not.
CLAUDIO   Marry, beshrew my hand   55
If it should give your age such cause of fear.
In faith, my hand meant nothing to my sword.   57
LEONATO
Tush, tush, man, never fleer and jest at me.   58
I speak not like a dotard nor a fool,
As under privilege of age to brag
What I have done being young or what would do
Were I not old. Know, Claudio, to thy head,   62
Thou hast so wronged mine innocent child and me
That I am forced to lay my reverence by,   64
And with gray hairs and bruise of many days
Do challenge thee to trial of a man.   66
I say thou hast belied mine innocent child.
Thy slander hath gone through and through her heart,
And she lies buried with her ancestors—
O, in a tomb where never scandal slept,
Save this of hers, framed by thy villainy!   71
CLAUDIO
My villainy?
LEONATO   Thine, Claudio, thine, I say.
DON PEDRO
You say not right, old man.
LEONATO   My lord, my lord,
I'll prove it on his body if he dare,
Despite his nice fence and his active practice,   75
His May of youth and bloom of lustihood.   76
CLAUDIO
Away! I will not have to do with you.
LEONATO
Canst thou so daff me? Thou hast killed my child.   78
If thou kill'st me, boy, thou shalt kill a man.

53 thou (Used contemptuously instead of the more polite *you*.)
55 beshrew curse   **57 my . . . sword** I had no intention of using my
sword   **58 fleer** sneer, jeer   **62 head** i.e., face   **64 my reverence** i.e., the
reverence due old age   **66 trial of a man** manly contest, i.e., duel
71 framed devised   **75 nice fence** dexterous swordsmanship. (Said contemptuously.)   **76 lustihood** bodily vigor   **78 daff** doff, put or turn aside

ANTONIO
He shall kill two of us, and men indeed.
But that's no matter; let him kill one first.
Win me and wear me! Let him answer me.   82
Come follow me, boy. Come, sir boy, come follow me,
Sir boy, I'll whip you from your foining fence!   84
Nay, as I am a gentleman, I will.
LEONATO   Brother—
ANTONIO
Content yourself. God knows I loved my niece,   87
And she is dead, slandered to death by villains,
That dare as well answer a man indeed
As I dare take a serpent by the tongue.
Boys, apes, braggarts, Jacks, milksops!
LEONATO   Brother Antony—
ANTONIO
Hold you content. What, man! I know them, yea,
And what they weigh, even to the utmost scruple—   94
Scambling, outfacing, fashionmonging boys,   95
That lie and cog and flout, deprave and slander,   96
Go anticly, show outward hideousness,   97
And speak off half a dozen dangerous words   98
How they might hurt their enemies, if they durst,
And this is all.
LEONATO
But, brother Antony—
ANTONIO   Come, 'tis no matter.
Do not you meddle; let me deal in this.
DON PEDRO
Gentlemen both, we will not wake your patience.   103
My heart is sorry for your daughter's death;
But, on my honor, she was charged with nothing
But what was true and very full of proof.
LEONATO   My lord, my lord—
DON PEDRO   I will not hear you.

82 Win . . . me (A proverbial expression, used as a challenge, meaning
he'll have to overcome me before he can claim me as a prize.)   **answer
me** i.e., in a duel   **84 foining** thrusting   **87 Content yourself** i.e., don't
try to stop me   **94 scruple** small measure of weight   **95 Scambling . . .
boys** contentious, swaggering, dandified boys   **96 cog** cheat.   **deprave**
defame, traduce   **97 anticly** fantastically dressed.   **hideousness** frightening appearance   **98 dangerous** threatening, haughty   **103 wake your
patience** put your patience to any further test

LEONATO
No? Come, brother, away! I will be heard.

ANTONIO
And shall, or some of us will smart for it.   110
              Exeunt ambo [Leonato and Antonio].

Enter Benedick.

DON PEDRO
See, see, here comes the man we went to seek.

CLAUDIO   Now, signor, what news?

BENEDICK   Good day, my lord.

DON PEDRO   Welcome, signor. You are almost come to
part almost a fray.

CLAUDIO   We had like to have had our two noses 116
snapped off with two old men without teeth.

DON PEDRO   Leonato and his brother. What think'st
thou? Had we fought, I doubt we should have been 119
too young for them.

BENEDICK   In a false quarrel there is no true valor. I came
to seek you both.

CLAUDIO   We have been up and down to seek thee, for
we are high-proof melancholy and would fain have it 124
beaten away. Wilt thou use thy wit?

BENEDICK   It is in my scabbard. Shall I draw it?

DON PEDRO   Dost thou wear thy wit by thy side?

CLAUDIO   Never any did so, though very many have
been beside their wit. I will bid thee draw, as we do 129
the minstrels, draw to pleasure us.   130

DON PEDRO   As I am an honest man, he looks pale. Art
thou sick, or angry?

CLAUDIO   What, courage, man! What though care killed
a cat, thou hast mettle enough in thee to kill care.

BENEDICK   Sir, I shall meet your wit in the career, an you 135
charge it against me. I pray you, choose another sub- 136
ject.

---

110 s.d. ambo both   **116 We had . . . had** we almost had   **119 doubt**
fear, suspect   **124 high-proof** to the highest degree.   **fain** gladly
129 beside their wit out of their wits (playing on *by thy side* in l. 127)
130 draw (1) draw your weapon (2) draw a bow across a musical instrument   **135 career** short gallop at full speed (as in a tourney)
136 charge level (as a weapon)

CLAUDIO Nay, then, give him another staff. This last 138
was broke 'cross. 139

DON PEDRO By this light, he changes more and more. I
think he be angry indeed.

CLAUDIO If he be, he knows how to turn his girdle. 142

BENEDICK Shall I speak a word in your ear?

CLAUDIO God bless me from a challenge!

BENEDICK [*Aside to Claudio*] You are a villain. I jest not;
I will make it good how you dare, with what you dare,
and when you dare. Do me right, or I will protest your 147
cowardice. You have killed a sweet lady, and her death
shall fall heavy on you. Let me hear from you.

CLAUDIO Well, I will meet you, so I may have good
cheer.

DON PEDRO What, a feast, a feast?

CLAUDIO I' faith, I thank him, he hath bid me to a calf's 153
head and a capon, the which if I do not carve most 154
curiously, say my knife's naught. Shall I not find a 155
woodcock too? 156

BENEDICK Sir, your wit ambles well; it goes easily. 157

DON PEDRO I'll tell thee how Beatrice praised thy wit the
other day. I said thou hadst a fine wit. "True," said
she, "a fine little one." "No," said I, "a great wit."
"Right," says she, "a great gross one." "Nay," said I,
"a good wit." "Just," said she, "it hurts nobody."
"Nay," said I, "the gentleman is wise." "Certain," said
she, "a wise gentleman." "Nay," said I, "he hath the 164
tongues." "That I believe," said she, "for he swore a 165
thing to me on Monday night which he forswore on
Tuesday morning. There's a double tongue; there's
two tongues." Thus did she, an hour together, trans- 168
shape thy particular virtues. Yet at last she concluded 169
with a sigh, thou wast the proper'st man in Italy. 170

---

138 staff spear shaft **139 broke 'cross** i.e., broken by clumsily allowing the
spear to break crosswise against his opponent's shield. (In other words,
Claudio accuses Benedick of having failed in his sally of wit.) **142 turn his
girdle** i.e., find harmless outlet for his anger (? A proverbial expression of
uncertain meaning.) **147 Do me right** give me satisfaction. **protest** proclaim before witnesses **153–156 calf's head, capon, woodcock** (Used as
types of stupidity.) **155 curiously** daintily. **naught** good for nothing
157 ambles i.e., it does not gallop **164 a wise gentleman** i.e., an old fool
164–165 hath the tongues masters several languages **168–169 trans-
shape** distort, turn the wrong side out **170 proper'st** handsomest

CLAUDIO For the which she wept heartily and said she
cared not.

DON PEDRO Yea, that she did, but yet for all that, an if
she did not hate him deadly, she would love him
dearly. The old man's daughter told us all.

CLAUDIO All, all. And, moreover, God saw him when 176
he was hid in the garden.   177

DON PEDRO But when shall we set the savage bull's
horns on the sensible Benedick's head?

CLAUDIO Yea, and text underneath, "Here dwells Ben- 180
edick the married man"?

BENEDICK Fare you well, boy. You know my mind. I
will leave you now to your gossiplike humor. You
break jests as braggarts do their blades, which, God 184
be thanked, hurt not.—My lord, for your many courtesies I thank you. I must discontinue your company.
Your brother the bastard is fled from Messina. You
have among you killed a sweet and innocent lady. For
my Lord Lackbeard there, he and I shall meet, and till
then peace be with him.   [*Exit.*]

DON PEDRO He is in earnest.

CLAUDIO In most profound earnest, and, I'll warrant
you, for the love of Beatrice.

DON PEDRO And hath challenged thee?

CLAUDIO Most sincerely.

DON PEDRO What a pretty thing man is when he goes 196
in his doublet and hose and leaves off his wit!   197

CLAUDIO He is then a giant to an ape; but then is an 198
ape a doctor to such a man.   199

DON PEDRO But, soft you, let me be. Pluck up, my heart, 200
and be sad. Did he not say my brother was fled?   201

*Enter Constables, [Dogberry and Verges, and the
Watch, with] Conrade and Borachio.*

176–177 God . . . garden (Alluding to the trick played on Benedick to love
Beatrice, and also to Genesis 3:8.)   **180 text** (In 1.1.251–256, Benedick
vowed that if he were ever to fall in love, his friends might set a bull's
horns on his head and label him "Benedick the married man.")   **184 as
. . . blades** i.e., as braggarts furtively damage their blades to make it
appear they have been fighting fiercely   **196–197 goes . . . wit** goes about
fully dressed but forgets to equip himself with good sense   **198–199 He
. . . man** he is superior to an ape in stature, but an ape is superior to him
in wisdom. (A doctor is a scholar.)   **200 soft you** wait a minute, not so
fast   **200–201 Pluck . . . sad** collect yourself, my mind, and be serious

DOGBERRY Come you, sir. If Justice cannot tame you,
she shall ne'er weigh more reasons in her balance. 203
Nay, an you be a cursing hypocrite once, you must be
looked to.

DON PEDRO How now, two of my brother's men
bound? Borachio one!

CLAUDIO Hearken after their offense, my lord.   208

DON PEDRO Officers, what offense have these men
done?

DOGBERRY Marry, sir, they have committed false report;
moreover, they have spoken untruths; secondarily,
they are slanders; sixth and lastly, they have belied a 213
lady; thirdly, they have verified unjust things; and to
conclude, they are lying knaves.

DON PEDRO First, I ask thee what they have done;
thirdly, I ask thee what's their offense; sixth and lastly,
why they are committed; and to conclude, what you
lay to their charge.

CLAUDIO Rightly reasoned, and in his own division;
and, by my troth, there's one meaning well suited.   221

DON PEDRO Who have you offended, masters, that you
are thus bound to your answer? This learned constable 223
is too cunning to be understood. What's your offense?

BORACHIO Sweet Prince, let me go no farther to mine
answer. Do you hear me, and let this count kill me. I
have deceived even your very eyes. What your wisdoms could not discover, these shallow fools have
brought to light, who in the night overheard me confessing to this man how Don John your brother in- 230
censed me to slander the Lady Hero, how you were 231
brought into the orchard and saw me court Margaret
in Hero's garments, how you disgraced her when you
should marry her. My villainy they have upon record,
which I had rather seal with my death than repeat over
to my shame. The lady is dead upon mine and my 236

---

203 ne'er . . . balance never again weigh arguments of reason in her
scales. (But the pronunciation of *reason* as "raisin" invokes the comic
image of a shopkeeper weighing produce.) **208 Hearken after** inquire
into **213 slanders** (For *slanderers*.) **221 well suited** put into many
different dresses **223 bound** (playing on the meanings "pinioned" and
"headed for a destination"). **answer** trial, account **230–231 incensed**
incited **236 upon** in consequence of

master's false accusation; and, briefly, I desire nothing
but the reward of a villain.

DON PEDRO [*To Claudio*]
Runs not this speech like iron through your blood?

CLAUDIO
I have drunk poison whiles he uttered it.

DON PEDRO
But did my brother set thee on to this?

BORACHIO   Yea, and paid me richly for the practice of it.   242

DON PEDRO
He is composed and framed of treachery,
And fled he is upon this villainy.

CLAUDIO
Sweet Hero! Now thy image doth appear
In the rare semblance that I loved it first.   246

DOGBERRY   Come, bring away the plaintiffs. By this   247
time our sexton hath reformed Signor Leonato of the   248
matter. And, masters, do not forget to specify, when   249
time and place shall serve, that I am an ass.

VERGES   Here, here comes Master Signor Leonato, and
the sexton too.

> *Enter Leonato, his brother [Antonio], and the
> Sexton.*

LEONATO
Which is the villain? Let me see his eyes,
That when I note another man like him
I may avoid him. Which of these is he?

BORACHIO
If you would know your wronger, look on me.

LEONATO
Art thou the slave that with thy breath hast killed
Mine innocent child?

BORACHIO   Yea, even I alone.

LEONATO
No, not so, villain, thou beliest thyself.
Here stand a pair of honorable men—   260
A third is fled—that had a hand in it.

---

242 **practice** execution   246 **rare semblance** splendid likeness   247 **plaintiffs** (For *defendants*.)   248 **reformed** (For *informed*.)   249 **specify** (For *testify?*)   260 **honorable men** i.e., Don Pedro and Claudio, men of rank

I thank you, princes, for my daughter's death.
Record it with your high and worthy deeds.
'Twas bravely done, if you bethink you of it.
CLAUDIO
I know not how to pray your patience,
Yet I must speak. Choose your revenge yourself;
Impose me to what penance your invention   267
Can lay upon my sin. Yet sinned I not
But in mistaking.
DON PEDRO   By my soul, nor I.
And yet, to satisfy this good old man,
I would bend under any heavy weight
That he'll enjoin me to.
LEONATO
I cannot bid you bid my daughter live—
That were impossible—but, I pray you both,
Possess the people in Messina here   275
How innocent she died; and if your love
Can labor aught in sad invention,   277
Hang her an epitaph upon her tomb
And sing it to her bones—sing it tonight.
Tomorrow morning come you to my house,
And since you could not be my son-in-law,
Be yet my nephew. My brother hath a daughter,
Almost the copy of my child that's dead,
And she alone is heir to both of us.   284
Give her the right you should have given her cousin,   285
And so dies my revenge.
CLAUDIO   O noble sir,
Your overkindness doth wring tears from me!
I do embrace your offer; and dispose   288
For henceforth of poor Claudio.   289
LEONATO
Tomorrow then I will expect your coming;
Tonight I take my leave. This naughty man   291
Shall face to face be brought to Margaret,

267 Impose me to impose on me   **275 Possess** inform   **277 aught** to any
extent   **284 heir to both** (He overlooks Antonio's son mentioned in
1.2.2.)   **285 right** equitable treatment (quibbling on *rite*, "ceremony")
288 dispose you may dispose   **289 For henceforth** for the future
291 naughty wicked

Who I believe was packed in all this wrong,   293
Hired to it by your brother.
BORACHIO   No, by my soul, she was not,
Nor knew not what she did when she spoke to me,
But always hath been just and virtuous
In anything that I do know by her.   298
DOGBERRY Moreover, sir, which indeed is not under 299
white and black, this plaintiff here, the offender, did 300
call me ass. I beseech you, let it be remembered in his
punishment. And also, the watch heard them talk of
one Deformed. They say he wears a key in his ear and 303
a lock hanging by it and borrows money in God's 304
name, the which he hath used so long and never paid 305
that now men grow hardhearted and will lend nothing for God's sake. Pray you, examine him upon that
point.
LEONATO   I thank thee for thy care and honest pains.
DOGBERRY Your worship speaks like a most thankful
and reverend youth, and I praise God for you.
LEONATO   There's for thy pains.   [He gives money.]
DOGBERRY God save the foundation!   313
LEONATO   Go, I discharge thee of thy prisoner, and I
thank thee.
DOGBERRY I leave an arrant knave with your worship,
which I beseech your worship to correct yourself, for
the example of others. God keep your worship! I wish
your worship well. God restore you to health! I hum-
bly give you leave to depart; and if a merry meeting 320
may be wished, God prohibit it! Come, neighbor.   321
               [Exeunt Dogberry and Verges.]
LEONATO
Until tomorrow morning, lords, farewell.
ANTONIO
Farewell, my lords. We look for you tomorrow.

---

293 packed involved as an accomplice   298 by concerning
299-300 under . . . black written down in black and white   303-304 key
. . . by it (This is what Dogberry has made out of the lovelock mentioned
in 3.3.167.)   304-305 in God's name (A phrase of the professional
beggar.)   313 God . . . foundation (A formula of those who received alms
at religious houses or charitable foundations.)   320 give you leave (For
ask your leave.)   321 prohibit (For permit.)

DON PEDRO
We will not fail.

CLAUDIO   Tonight I'll mourn with Hero.

LEONATO [*To the Watch*]
Bring you these fellows on.—We'll talk with Margaret,
How her acquaintance grew with this lewd fellow.   326
Exeunt [*separately*].

✛

5.2   *Enter Benedick and Margaret,* [*meeting*].

BENEDICK Pray thee, sweet Mistress Margaret, deserve well at my hands by helping me to the speech of
Beatrice.

MARGARET Will you then write me a sonnet in praise of
my beauty?

BENEDICK In so high a style, Margaret, that no man liv- 6
ing shall come over it, for in most comely truth thou 7
deservest it.

MARGARET To have no man come over me! Why, shall
I always keep below stairs?   10

BENEDICK Thy wit is as quick as the greyhound's
mouth; it catches.

MARGARET And yours as blunt as the fencer's foils,
which hit but hurt not.

BENEDICK A most manly wit, Margaret; it will not hurt
a woman. And so, I pray thee, call Beatrice. I give thee 16
the bucklers.   17

MARGARET Give us the swords; we have bucklers of
our own.

BENEDICK If you use them, Margaret, you must put in

---

326 lewd wicked, worthless

**5.2. Location: Leonato's garden (?) (At the scene's end, Leonato's house
is some distance away.)**
6 style (1) poetic style (2) stile, stairs over a fence   **7 come over** (1) excel
beyond (2) traverse, as one would cross a stile (3) in Margaret's next
speech, the phrase is taken to mean "mount sexually."   **comely** good
(with an allusion to Margaret's beauty)   **10 keep below stairs** dwell in
the servants' quarters   **16–17 I . . . bucklers** i.e., I acknowledge myself
beaten (in repartee). (Bucklers are shields with spikes [pikes] in their
centers; Margaret uses the word in a bawdy sense in her reply.)

the pikes with a vice, and they are dangerous weapons 21
for maids.

MARGARET Well, I will call Beatrice to you, who I think
hath legs.   *Exit Margaret.*

BENEDICK And therefore will come.

[*Sings.*]   "The god of love,   26
          That sits above,
     And knows me, and knows me,
        How pitiful I deserve—"   29

I mean in singing; but in loving, Leander the good 30
swimmer, Troilus the first employer of panders, and a 31
whole bookful of these quondam carpetmongers, 32
whose names yet run smoothly in the even road of a
blank verse, why, they were never so truly turned over 34
and over as my poor self in love. Marry, I cannot show 35
it in rhyme; I have tried. I can find out no rhyme to
"lady" but "baby," an innocent rhyme; for "scorn," 37
"horn," a hard rhyme; for "school," "fool," a babbling 38
rhyme; very ominous endings. No, I was not born under a rhyming planet, nor I cannot woo in festival 40
terms.   41

     Enter Beatrice.

Sweet Beatrice, wouldst thou come when I called thee?

BEATRICE Yea, signor, and depart when you bid me.

BENEDICK O, stay but till then!

BEATRICE "Then" is spoken; fare you well now. And
yet, ere I go, let me go with that I came, which is, with 46
knowing what hath passed between you and Claudio.

BENEDICK Only foul words; and thereupon I will kiss
thee.

---

21 pikes spikes in the center of a shield. **vice** screw   **26–29 The god
. . . deserve** (The beginning of an old song by William Elderton.)
29 How . . . deserve how I deserve pity. (But Benedick uses the phrase
to mean "how little I deserve.") **30 Leander** lover of Hero of Sestos; he
swam the Hellespont nightly to see her until he drowned   **31 Troilus**
lover of Cressida, whose affair was assisted by her uncle Pandarus
32 quondam former, old-time. **carpetmongers** (A scornful term for
"ladies' men," derived from their presence in the carpeted boudoirs of
their lovers.) **34–35 over and over** i.e., head over heels   **37 innocent**
childish **38 hard** (1) exact (2) unpleasant, because of the association
with cuckold's horns **40–41 festival terms** elevated language   **46 that I
came** what I came for

BEATRICE Foul words is but foul wind, and foul wind is
but foul breath, and foul breath is noisome; therefore 51
I will depart unkissed.

BENEDICK Thou hast frighted the word out of his right 53
sense, so forcible is thy wit. But I must tell thee
plainly, Claudio undergoes my challenge; and either I 55
must shortly hear from him, or I will subscribe him a 56
coward. And I pray thee now tell me, for which of my
bad parts didst thou first fall in love with me?

BEATRICE For them all together, which maintained so
politic a state of evil that they will not admit any good 60
part to intermingle with them. But for which of my
good parts did you first suffer love for me? 62

BENEDICK Suffer love! A good epithet! I do suffer love 63
indeed, for I love thee against my will.

BEATRICE In spite of your heart, I think. Alas, poor
heart, if you spite it for my sake, I will spite it for
yours, for I will never love that which my friend hates.

BENEDICK Thou and I are too wise to woo peaceably.

BEATRICE It appears not in this confession. There's not 69
one wise man among twenty that will praise himself.

BENEDICK An old, an old instance, Beatrice, that lived in 71
the time of good neighbors. If a man do not erect in 72
this age his own tomb ere he dies, he shall live no 73
longer in monument than the bell rings and the 74
widow weeps. 75

BEATRICE And how long is that, think you?

BENEDICK Question: why, an hour in clamor and a 77
quarter in rheum. Therefore is it most expedient for 78
the wise, if Don Worm, his conscience, find no im- 79
pediment to the contrary, to be the trumpet of his own

---

51 noisome noxious **53 his** its **55 undergoes** bears **56 subscribe**
formally proclaim in writing **60 politic** prudently governed **62 suffer**
(1) experience (2) feel the pain of **63 epithet** expression **69 It . . .
confession** i.e., you don't show your wisdom in praising yourself for
being wise **71 instance** proverb **72 time . . . neighbors** good old times
(when one's neighbors spoke well of one) **73–75 he shall . . . weeps** i.e.,
he will be memorialized only during the (brief) time of the funeral
service and the official mourning **77 Question** i.e., an easy question,
which I will answer as follows. **clamor** noise (of the bell) **78 rheum**
tears (of the widow) **79 Don . . . conscience** (The action of the conscience was traditionally described as the gnawing of a worm; cf. Mark
9:48.)

virtues, as I am to myself. So much for praising myself,
who, I myself will bear witness, is praiseworthy. And
now tell me, how doth your cousin?

BEATRICE   Very ill.

BENEDICK   And how do you?

BEATRICE   Very ill too.

BENEDICK   Serve God, love me, and mend. There will I
leave you too, for here comes one in haste.

Enter Ursula.

URSULA   Madam, you must come to your uncle. Yonder's old coil at home. It is proved my Lady Hero hath 90
been falsely accused, the Prince and Claudio mightily
abused, and Don John is the author of all, who is fled 92
and gone. Will you come presently?   93

BEATRICE   Will you go hear this news, signor?

BENEDICK   I will live in thy heart, die in thy lap, and be 95
buried in thy eyes; and moreover I will go with thee
to thy uncle's.   *Exeunt.*

❖

5.3   *Enter Claudio, Prince [Don Pedro, Balthasar],
         and three or four with tapers.*

CLAUDIO   Is this the monument of Leonato?

A LORD   It is, my lord.

CLAUDIO [*Reading from a scroll*]

Epitaph.

"Done to death by slanderous tongues
    Was the Hero that here lies.
Death, in guerdon of her wrongs,   5
    Gives her fame which never dies.
So the life that died with shame
    Lives in death with glorious fame."

90 old coil great confusion   **92 abused** deceived   **93 presently** immediately   **95 die** (with the common connotation of "experience sexual climax")

5.3. Location: A churchyard.
5 guerdon recompense

Hang thou there upon the tomb,
Praising her when I am dumb.

[He hangs up the scroll.]

Now, music, sound, and sing your solemn hymn.

Song.

BALTHASAR

    Pardon, goddess of the night,   12
    Those that slew thy virgin knight;
    For the which, with songs of woe,
    Round about her tomb they go.
    Midnight, assist our moan;
    Help us to sigh and groan,
      Heavily, heavily.
    Graves, yawn and yield your dead,
    Till death be uttered,   20
      Heavily, heavily.

CLAUDIO

Now, unto thy bones good night!
Yearly will I do this rite.

DON PEDRO

Good morrow, masters. Put your torches out.
  The wolves have preyed; and look, the gentle day,   25
Before the wheels of Phoebus, round about   26
  Dapples the drowsy east with spots of gray.
Thanks to you all, and leave us. Fare you well.

CLAUDIO

Good morrow, masters. Each his several way.

DON PEDRO

Come, let us hence, and put on other weeds,   30
And then to Leonato's we will go.

CLAUDIO

And Hymen now with luckier issue speed 's   32
Than this for whom we rendered up this woe.

Exeunt.

❖

12 goddess of the night i.e., Diana, moon goddess, patroness of chastity   **20 uttered** fully expressed   **25 have preyed** i.e., have ceased preying   **26 wheels of Phoebus** i.e., chariot of the sun god   **30 weeds** garments   **32 Hymen** god of marriage.   **speed 's** favor or speed us

5.4   *Enter Leonato, Benedick, [Beatrice], Margaret,*
Ursula, Old Man [Antonio], Friar [Francis],
Hero.

FRIAR
  Did I not tell you she was innocent?

LEONATO
  So are the Prince and Claudio, who accused her
  Upon the error that you heard debated.   3
  But Margaret was in some fault for this,
  Although against her will, as it appears   5
  In the true course of all the question.   6

ANTONIO
  Well, I am glad that all things sorts so well.   7

BENEDICK
  And so am I, being else by faith enforced   8
  To call young Claudio to a reckoning for it.

LEONATO
  Well, daughter, and you gentlewomen all,
  Withdraw into a chamber by yourselves,
  And when I send for you, come hither masked.
  The Prince and Claudio promised by this hour
  To visit me. You know your office, brother: 14
  You must be father to your brother's daughter,
  And give her to young Claudio.   *Exeunt Ladies.*

ANTONIO
  Which I will do with confirmed countenance.   17

BENEDICK
  Friar, I must entreat your pains, I think.   18
FRIAR   To do what, signor?

BENEDICK
  To bind me or undo me—one of them.   20
  Signor Leonato, truth it is, good signor,
  Your niece regards me with an eye of favor.

LEONATO
  That eye my daughter lent her. 'Tis most true.   23

5.4. Location: Leonato's house.
3 Upon because of   **5 against her will** unintentionally   **6 question**
investigation   **7 sorts** turn out   **8 being else** since otherwise I would
be.   **by faith** i.e., by my promise to Beatrice   **14 office** duty   **17 con-**
firmed countenance confident bearing   **18 entreat your pains** i.e.,
impose on you   **20 undo** (1) ruin (2) untie, unbind   **23 That . . . her**
(Alludes to Hero's role in coaxing Beatrice to love Benedick.)

BENEDICK
  And I do with an eye of love requite her.
LEONATO
  The sight whereof I think you had from me,   25
  From Claudio, and the Prince. But what's your will?   26
BENEDICK
  Your answer, sir, is enigmatical.
  But, for my will, my will is your good will   28
  May stand with ours, this day to be conjoined
  In the state of honorable marriage,
  In which, good Friar, I shall desire your help.
LEONATO
  My heart is with your liking.
FRIAR   And my help.
  Here comes the Prince and Claudio.

    Enter Prince [Don Pedro] and Claudio, and two
    or three other.

DON PEDRO
  Good morrow to this fair assembly.
LEONATO
  Good morrow, Prince; good morrow, Claudio.
  We here attend you. Are you yet determined   35
  Today to marry with my brother's daughter?
CLAUDIO
  I'll hold my mind, were she an Ethiope.
LEONATO
  Call her forth, brother. Here's the Friar ready.
                              [*Exit Antonio.*]
DON PEDRO
  Good morrow, Benedick. Why, what's the matter,
  That you have such a February face,
  So full of frost, of storm, and cloudiness?
CLAUDIO
  I think he thinks upon the savage bull.   42
  Tush, fear not, man! We'll tip thy horns with gold,
  And all Europa shall rejoice at thee,   44

25–26 The sight . . . Prince (Alludes to their role in coaxing Benedick to love Beatrice.) **28 is** is that **35 yet** still **42 I . . . bull** (A jocular reminiscence of the conversation in 1.1.250 ff.) **44 Europa** Europe

As once Europa did at lusty Jove   45
When he would play the noble beast in love.

BENEDICK
Bull Jove, sir, had an amiable low,
And some such strange bull leapt your father's cow
And got a calf in that same noble feat
Much like to you, for you have just his bleat.

    Enter [Leonato's] brother [Antonio], Hero,
    Beatrice, Margaret, Ursula, [the ladies masked].

CLAUDIO
For this I owe you. Here comes other reckonings.   51
Which is the lady I must seize upon?

ANTONIO
This same is she, and I do give you her.

CLAUDIO
Why, then she's mine. Sweet, let me see your face.

LEONATO
No, that you shall not, till you take her hand
Before this friar and swear to marry her.

CLAUDIO
Give me your hand before this holy friar.
I am your husband, if you like of me.   58

HERO [*Unmasking*]
And when I lived, I was your other wife;
And when you loved, you were my other husband.

CLAUDIO
Another Hero!

HERO   Nothing certainer.
One Hero died defiled, but I do live,
And surely as I live, I am a maid.

DON PEDRO
The former Hero! Hero that is dead!

LEONATO
She died, my lord, but whiles her slander lived.   65

FRIAR
All this amazement can I qualify,   66

---

45 Europa a princess whom Jove approached in the form of a white bull
and bore on his back through the sea to Crete   **51 I owe you** i.e., I'll pay
you back later (for calling me a calf and a bastard child of Jove).   **other
reckonings** i.e., other matters to be settled first   **58 like of** care for
65 but whiles only while   **66 qualify** moderate

When, after that the holy rites are ended,
I'll tell you largely of fair Hero's death.   68
Meantime let wonder seem familiar,   69
And to the chapel let us presently.   70
BENEDICK
Soft and fair, Friar. Which is Beatrice?
BEATRICE [*Unmasking*]
I answer to that name. What is your will?
BENEDICK
Do not you love me?
BEATRICE   Why, no, no more than reason.
BENEDICK
Why, then your uncle and the Prince and Claudio
Have been deceived. They swore you did.
BEATRICE
Do not you love me?
BENEDICK   Troth, no, no more than reason.
BEATRICE
Why, then my cousin Margaret and Ursula
Are much deceived, for they did swear you did.
BENEDICK
They swore that you were almost sick for me.
BEATRICE
They swore that you were well-nigh dead for me.
BENEDICK
'Tis no such matter. Then you do not love me?
BEATRICE
No, truly, but in friendly recompense.
LEONATO
Come, cousin, I am sure you love the gentleman.
CLAUDIO
And I'll be sworn upon 't that he loves her;
For here's a paper written in his hand,
A halting sonnet of his own pure brain,   86
Fashioned to Beatrice.   [*He shows a paper.*]
HERO   And here's another
Writ in my cousin's hand, stol'n from her pocket,

68 largely at large, in full   **69 let . . . familiar** treat these marvels as
ordinary matters   **70 let us presently** let us go at once   **86 his own
pure** purely his own

Containing her affection unto Benedick.

                      [She shows another paper.]

BENEDICK   A miracle! Here's our own hands against our 90
hearts. Come, I will have thee, but by this light I take 91
thee for pity.

BEATRICE   I would not deny you, but by this good day,
I yield upon great persuasion, and partly to save your
life, for I was told you were in a consumption.

BENEDICK   Peace! I will stop your mouth. *[He kisses her.]*

DON PEDRO   How dost thou, Benedick, the married
man?

BENEDICK   I'll tell thee what, Prince: a college of wit- 99
crackers cannot flout me out of my humor. Dost thou
think I care for a satire or an epigram? No. If a man 101
will be beaten with brains, 'a shall wear nothing hand- 102
some about him. In brief, since I do purpose to marry, 103
I will think nothing to any purpose that the world can
say against it; and therefore never flout at me for what
I have said against it; for man is a giddy thing, and
this is my conclusion. For thy part, Claudio, I did
think to have beaten thee, but in that thou art like to
be my kinsman, live unbruised, and love my cousin.

CLAUDIO   I had well hoped thou wouldst have denied
Beatrice, that I might have cudgeled thee out of thy
single life, to make thee a double-dealer, which out of 112
question thou wilt be, if my cousin do not look ex- 113
ceeding narrowly to thee. 114

BENEDICK   Come, come, we are friends. Let's have a
dance ere we are married, that we may lighten our
own hearts and our wives' heels.

LEONATO   We'll have dancing afterward.

BENEDICK   First, of my word! Therefore play, music. 119
Prince, thou art sad. Get thee a wife, get thee a wife.
There is no staff more reverend than one tipped with 121
horn. 122

90–91 against our hearts i.e., to prove our hearts guilty as charged   **99 college** assembly   **101–103 If . . . him** i.e., if a man allows himself to be cowed by ridicule, he'll never dare dress handsomely or do anything conspicuous that will draw attention   **112 a double-dealer** (1) a married man (2) a deceiver, adulterer   **113–114 look . . . narrowly** pay close attention   **119 of** on   **121–122 tipped with horn** (Alludes to the usual joke about cuckolds.)

Enter Messenger.

MESSENGER
My lord, your brother John is ta'en in flight
And brought with armèd men back to Messina.
BENEDICK   Think not on him till tomorrow. I'll devise
thee brave punishments for him. Strike up, pipers.   126
Dance. [*Exeunt.*]

❖

126 **brave** fine

Date and Text

"The Commedie of muche A doo about nothing a booke" was entered in the Stationers' Register, the official record book of the London Company of Stationers (booksellers and printers), on August 4, 1600, along with *As You Like It*, *Henry V*, and Ben Jonson's *Every Man in His Humor*, all marked as plays of "My lord chamberlens men" (Shakespeare's acting company) and all "to be staied"—that is, not published without further permission. Earlier in the same memorandum, written on a spare page in the Register, occurs the name of the printer James Roberts, whose registration of *The Merchant of Venice* in 1598 was similarly stayed pending further permission to publish. Evidently the Chamberlain's men were attempting to prevent unauthorized publication of these very popular plays. They were too late to forestall the appearance of a bad quarto of *Henry V* in August of 1600, but they did manage to control release of the others. *Much Ado about Nothing* appeared later that same year in a seemingly authorized version:

> Much adoe about Nothing. *As it hath been sundrie times publikely* acted by the right honourable, the Lord Chamberlaine his seruants. *Written by William Shakespeare.* LONDON Printed by V. S. [Valentine Sims] for Andrew Wise, and William Aspley. 1600.

Once thought to have been set up from a theatrical prompt-book and then used itself in the theater as a promptbook before serving as copy for the First Folio of 1623, this 1600 quarto text is now generally regarded as having been set from Shakespeare's own manuscript. The names of the actors Will Kempe and Richard Cowley appear among the speech prefixes in 4.2, indicating that an actual stage production was very close at hand, but other irregularities in speech prefixes and scene headings read more like a manuscript in the last stages of revision than a promptbook for a finished production. The Folio text was based on this 1600 quarto, lightly annotated with reference to the promptbook but providing little in the way of new readings other than the correction of obvious error.

Francis Meres does not mention the play in September of 1598 in his *Palladis Tamia: Wit's Treasury* (a slender volume on contemporary literature and art; valuable because it lists most of Shakespeare's plays that existed at that time), unless (and this seems unlikely) it is his *"Loue labours wonne."* Will Kempe, who played Dogberry, left the Chamberlain's men in 1599. The likeliest date, then, is the winter of 1598–1599, though publication was not until 1600.

Textual Notes

These textual notes are not a historical collation, either of the early quarto and the early folios or of more recent editions; they are simply a record of departures in this edition from the copy text. The reading adopted in this edition appears in boldface, followed by the rejected reading from the copy text, i.e., the quarto of 1600. Only a few major alterations in punctuation are noted. Changes in lineation are not indicated, nor are some minor and obvious typographical errors.

Abbreviations used:
Q the quarto of 1600
s.d. stage direction
s.p. speech prefix

Copy text: the quarto of 1600.

1.1. s.d. Messina Messina, Innogen, his wife   **2 Pedro** Peter [also in l. 9]   **194 s.d. Pedro** Pedro, Iohn the bastard

1.2. 3 s.p. [and elsewhere] Antonio Old   **6 event** euents   **24 skill** shill

1.3. 51 on one   **70 s.d. Exeunt** exit

2.1 s.d. Hero his wife, Hero   **Ursula** [Q adds "and a kinsman"]   **2 s.p. [and elsewhere] Antonio** brother   **37 bearward** Berrord   **44 Peter, for the heavens;** Peter: for the heauens,   **67 hear** here   **79 s.d. and Don** or dumb   **80 a bout** about   **94 s.p. Balthasar** Bene [also at ll. 97 and 99]   **201 s.d. Leonato** Leonato, Iohn and Borachio, and Conrade   **311 s.p. [and elsewhere] Don Pedro** Prince   **369 s.d. Exeunt** exit

2.3. 7 s.d. [at l. 5 in Q]   **24 an** and   **35 s.d. Claudio** Claudio, Musicke   **61 s.p. Balthasar** [not in Q]   **139 us of** of vs

3.1. s.d. Ursula Vrsley   **23 s.d.** [at l. 25 in Q]

3.2. 27 can cannot   **51 s.p. Don Pedro** Bene   **74 s.p. [and elsewhere] Don John** Bastard

3.3. 17 s.p. Seacoal Watch 2 [also at l. 27]   **87 s.p. Seacoal** Watch [also at ll. 95, 105, 125]   **161 s.p. Seacoal** Watch 1 [also at l. 165]   **162 s.p. First Watch** Watch 2 [also at l. 169]   **171 s.p. Seacoal** [missing in Q]

3.4. 17 in it

3.5. 2 s.p. [and elsewhere] Dogberry Const. Dog   **7 s.p. [and elsewhere] Verges** Headb   **9 off** of   **50** [Q provides an "Exit" at this point]

4.1. 4 s.p. Friar Fran   **202 princes** princesse

4.2. s.d. [Q reads "Enter the Constables, Borachio, and the Towne clearke in gownes."]   **1 s.p. Dogberry** Keeper   **2 s.p. [and elsewhere in this scene] Verges** Cowley   **4 s.p. Dogberry** Andrew   **9 s.p. [and elsewhere in this scene] Dogberry** Kemp   **18 s.p. Conrade, Borachio** Both   **39 Seacoal** Watch 1 [also at l. 53]   **47 First Watch** Watch 2   **51 s.p. Verges** Const   **67 s.p. [and elsewhere] Dogberry** Constable   **69 s.p. Conrade** [missing in Q]   **69 Off** of   **73 s.p. Conrade** Couley   **86 s.d. Exeunt** exit

5.1. 16 Bid And   **97 anticly** antiquely, and   **98 off** of   **179 on** one
201 s.d. [at l. 197 in Q]   **251 s.p. Verges** Con. 2

5.2. 41 s.d. [at l. 42 in Q]   **81 myself. So** my self so   **97 s.d. Exeunt** exit

5.3. 2 s.p. A Lord Lord   **3 s.p. Claudio** [missing in Q]   **10 dumb** dead
12 s.p. Balthasar [missing in Q]   **22 s.p. Claudio** Lo

5.4. 53 s.p. Antonio Leo   **96 s.p. Benedick** Leon

Shakespeare's Sources

Shakespeare's probable chief source for the Hero-Claudio plot of *Much Ado* was the twenty-second story from the *Novelle* of Matteo Bandello (Lucca, 1554). A French translation by François de Belleforest, in his *Histoires Tragiques* (1569 edition) was available to Shakespeare, as was the Italian original. The story of the maiden falsely accused was, however, much older than the story by Bandello. Perhaps the earliest version that has been found is the Greek romance *Chaereas and Callirrhoe*, fourth or fifth century A.D., in which the hero Chaereas, warned by envious rivals of his wife's purported infidelity, watches at dusk while an elegantly attired stranger is admitted by the maid to the house where Callirrhoe lives. Chaereas rushes in and strikes mistakenly at his wife in the dark, but is acquitted of murder when the maid confesses her part in a conspiracy to delude Chaereas. Callirrhoe is buried in a deathlike trance but awakens in time to be carried off by pirates. The story reappears in a fifteenth-century Spanish romance, *Tirante el Blanco*, in which the princess Blanche is courted seemingly by a repulsive black man. This Spanish version probably inspired the account in Canto 5 of Ludovico Ariosto's *Orlando Furioso* (1516), to which all subsequent Renaissance versions are ultimately indebted.

In Ariosto's account, as translated into English by Sir John Harington (1591), the narrator is Dalinda, maid to the virtuous Scottish princess Genevra. Dalinda tells how she has fallen guiltily in love with Polynesso, Duke of Albany, an evil man who often makes love to Dalinda in her mistress' rooms but who longs to marry Genevra himself. Consequently, Polynesso arranges for Genevra's noble Italian suitor, Ariodante, and Ariodante's brother Lurcanio, to witness the Duke's ascent to Genevra's window by a rope ladder. The woman who admits the Duke is of course not Genevra but Dalinda disguised as her mistress, having been duped into believing that the Duke merely wishes to satisfy his craving for Genevra by making love to her image. Lurcanio publicly accuses the innocent Genevra and offers to fight anyone who defends her cause (compare Claudio's quarrel with Leonato).

The evil Duke tries to get rid of Dalinda, but all is finally put to rights by Rinaldo (the hero of *Orlando Furioso*) and Ariodante. This account gives an unusually vivid motivation for the maid and the villain—a clearer motivation than in Shakespeare's play. A lost dramatic version, *Ariodante and Genevora*, was performed at the English court in 1583.

Shakespeare probably consulted not only Ariosto but also Edmund Spenser's *The Faerie Queene* (2.4), based on Ariosto. Spenser's emphasis is on the blind rage of Phedon, a young squire in love with Claribell. Phedon is tricked by his erstwhile friend Philemon and by Claribell's maid Pryene into believing Claribell false. Pryene's motive in dressing up as Claribell is to prove she is as beautiful as her mistress. When, after having slain Claribell for her supposed perfidy, Phedon learns the truth, he poisons Philemon and furiously pursues Pryene until he is utterly possessed by a mad frenzy.

Shakespeare's greatest debt is, however, to Bandello's story. Its text follows, somewhat excerpted, in a new translation. In a number of details the story is closer to Shakespeare's play than are those already discussed. Several names are substantially as in Shakespeare: the location is Messina, the father of the slandered bride is Lionato di' Lionati (compare Shakespeare's Leonato), and her lover is in the service of King Piero of Aragon (compare Don Pedro of Aragon). As in Shakespeare, a young knight (named Sir Timbreo) seeks the hand in marriage of his beloved (Fenicia) through the matchmaking offices of a noble emissary. The complication of this wooing is somewhat different in that Timbreo's friend Girondo also falls in love with Fenicia, but Girondo does then plot with a mischief-loving courtier (resembling Shakespeare's Don John) to poison Timbreo's mind against Fenicia, and Girondo thereupon escorts Timbreo to a garden where they see Girondo's servant, elegantly dressed, enter Fenicia's window. No maid takes part in the ruse, however, nor indeed is any woman seen at the window. When Fenicia is wrongly accused, she falls into a deathlike trance and is pronounced dead by a doctor, but is revived. Her father, believing in her innocence, sends her off to a country retreat and circulates the report that she is in fact dead. Soon both Timbreo and Girondo are stricken with remorse, Timbreo magnanimously spares his friend's life, and both confess the truth to Fenicia's family. A year later, Timbreo marries a wife chosen for him by Lionato, who turns out of course to be Fenicia. Girondo marries her sister Belfiore. This account does not provide any equivalent for Beatrice and Benedick. Shakespeare enhances the Friar's role, and provides a brother for Leonato. Claudio and Leonato are of comparable social station in Shakespeare, whereas Bandello makes a point of a difference in social class.

A lost play, *Panecia* (1574–1575), may have been based on Bandello's work. One other version Shakespeare may have known is George Whetstone's *The Rock of Regard* (1576), based on Ariosto and Bandello. It contains a suggestive parallel to Claudio's rejection of Hero in church. Various Italian plays in the tradition of Luigi Pasqualigo's *Il Fedele* (1579), and also a version perhaps by Anthony Munday, *Fedele and Fortunio* (published 1585), are analogous in situation, though Shakespeare need not have known any of them.

For the Beatrice-Benedick plot no source has been discovered, apart from Shakespeare's own earlier fascination with wit combat and candid wooing in *Love's Labor's Lost* and *The Taming of the Shrew*. Nor has a plausible source been found for Dogberry and the watch.

Novelle
Part One
By Matteo Bandello
Translated by David Bevington and Kate Bevington

NOVELLA TWENTY-TWO:
TIMBREO AND FENICIA

During the year of our salvation 1283, the people of Sicily, no longer willing to put up with the domination of their French overlords, massacred all of them on the island one day at the hour of vespers, with unheard-of cruelty; thus was the treachery ordered and carried out throughout the island. They killed not only women and men of the French nation but all Sicilian women who could be suspected of being made pregnant by the French; on one and the same day they cut the French throats, and then if any woman was found pregnant by the French, she was killed without remorse. From this was born the despicable name of "Sicilian Vespers."

When King Piero of Aragon heard of this, he came at once with his army and took charge of the island, as Pope Nicholas III had urged him, declaring that the island belonged to him as husband of Constanza, daughter of King Manfred. King Piero held regal and magnificent court in Palermo several days, celebrating with great festivity his taking of the island. Then, hearing that King Carlo II, son of King Carlo I and possessor of the kingdom of Naples, was approaching by sea with a great army to chase him out of Sicily, he set out against him with the armed force of ships and galleys under his command. When they came together in combat, there was a great fray and cruel slaughter of many men. But in the end King Piero routed the army of King Carlo and took him prisoner. And the better to attend to military matters, he withdrew with all the court to Messina, since in that city one was closest to Italy and most quickly able to cross over into Calabria.

While he was there magnificently holding court, and all was joyful in honor of the victory he had won, and everyone was passing the time in feats of arms and in dancing, one of his knights, a baron, greatly esteemed and especially so by King Piero because he was so brave and had conducted himself so valiantly in the recent fighting, fell head over heels in love with a young lady, the daughter of Master Lionato de' Lionati, gentleman of Messina. She, more than any other lady in the whole country, was of gentle condition, attractive, and beautiful, and little by little the knight was so inflamed with desire of her that without the sweet sight of her he didn't even know how he could live. Now, the baron was called Timbreo di Cardona, and the young woman, Fenicia. He, because he had served King Piero by land and by sea since his youngest days, had been richly rewarded in many ways. Besides the countless gifts that were his, the King had recently given him the county of Colisano along with other lands, so that his income, over and above the allowance the King had already provided, came to more than twelve thousand ducats.

Signor Timbreo now began to pass daily in front of the young lady's house, thinking the day a blessed one whenever he saw her. Fenicia, being clever and sagacious for her age, soon guessed the motive of the knight's strolls. Now, it was well known that Signor Timbreo was one of the King's favorites and that few were valued in the court more highly than he, for which reason he was honored by one and all. Fenicia too, seeing in addition to all she had heard of him that he was well dressed in the courtly fashion, descended from a noble family, handsome, and well-mannered in appearance, began for her part to pay attention to him in an agreeable manner and salute him discreetly. The knight's ardor grew day by day, and the more he gazed on her, the more he felt love's flame; so greatly did this new fire increase in his heart that he felt himself consumed with love for this beautiful young woman, and he decided that he must have her by whatever means possible.

All he did was in vain, however, for to whatever letters he wrote, to whatever messages he sent, she gave no other reply than that she would keep inviolate her chastity, intending it for the man who would be given to her as her husband. At this the poor lover found himself in a most unhappy state, all the more because he was unable to prevail upon her to keep his letters or his gifts. All the same he was determined to have her, and seeing that her constancy was such that if he wanted to possess her he would have to take her as his wife, he concluded after much inner debate to ask her father for her hand in marriage. And although it seemed to him he was demeaning himself considerably in this, still, knowing that she came of ancient and noble blood, he decided not to put matters off any longer, so great was the love he bore this young woman.

Having thus made up his mind, he sought out a gentleman of Messina with whom he was on familiar terms and related what he had decided, telling him what he wanted him to discuss with Master Lionato. The gentleman went and did as the knight had commissioned him. Master Lionato, when he heard this good news, and knowing well enough the influence and worth of Signor Timbreo, without even seeking further advice from relatives or friends, showed by his gracious reply how pleased he was that the knight deigned to ally himself by marriage with their family. And as soon as he was home he told his wife and Fenicia about the promise he had given to Signor Timbreo. The thing greatly pleased

Fenicia, and with devout heart she thanked our lord God for giving her such a glorious end to her chaste love, and her happiness showed in her face.

But fortune, which never ceases to hinder human happiness in other ways, found a novel way of hindering this marriage so much desired by both parties. Listen and you shall hear how.

Soon it was known all over Messina how in a few days' time Signor Timbreo Cardona was to marry Fenicia, the daughter of Master Lionato. This news generally pleased all the people of Messina, since Master Lionato was a gentleman who made himself much loved—he tried to harm no one and to help everyone as much as he could—so that everyone expressed great happiness at the forthcoming alliance. Now, there was in Messina another young knight of a noble family called Signor Girondo Olerio Valenziano, who had shown himself to be very brave in the war just ended and was moreover one of the most magnificent and bountiful members of the court. This man, hearing the news, was plunged into endless despair, because he had just fallen in love with Fenicia's beauty, and so fiercely did the flames of love lodge in his breast that he firmly believed he would die if he could not have Fenicia for his wife. And having determined to ask her father for her hand in marriage, he thought he would suffer every agony of sorrow when he heard the promise that had been made to Signor Timbreo. When he could find no solace of any kind for his grief, he raved like a madman: conquered by passionate desire and losing all sense of reason, he allowed himself to be carried away into doing a thing unworthy not only of a knight and gentleman but, indeed, of anyone.

Almost always, in all their military undertakings, Signor Girondo had been a companion to Signor Timbreo; between them was a fraternal bond. Concerning this love business, however, for whatever cause, they had hid their feelings from one another. Signor Girondo now hit on the idea of sowing discord between Signor Timbreo and his beloved so that the marriage contract would be broken off. And in this event he himself would ask for her hand in marriage from her father, hoping to have her for the asking. He did not hesitate to put this mad idea into effect. Finding a man

suited to his unbridled and blind appetite, he carefully
informed him of his scheme. The man whom Signor
Girondo had taken to be his confidant and assistant in his
crime was a young courtier, a man of poor understanding,
better pleased with evil than with good, who, when he had
been fully instructed in the plot he was to weave, went the
following morning to seek out Signor Timbreo. He found
the knight still at home, relaxing all alone in the garden of
the inn. As he entered there and was seen approaching, the
young man was courteously greeted by Signor Timbreo.
After they had exchanged greetings, the young man spoke to
Signor Timbreo as follows:

"Signor, I have come at this hour to speak with you on
matters of the greatest importance, matters that touch your
honor and profit. And since I may speak of certain things
that could perhaps offend you, I beg you to pardon me; excuse me for my faithful service, and consider that I do this
for a good reason. This much I know: if you are still the
noble knight that you have always been, what I am now going to tell you will be of great benefit to you. To come to the
point: I must tell you that yesterday I heard how you had
met with Master Lionato de' Lionati in order to marry his
daughter Fenicia. Beware, signor, what you do, and look to
your honor. I say this because a gentleman friend of mine
goes almost two or three times a week to lie with her and
enjoy her in love; in fact he is going there as usual this evening, and I am going with him as I have on other occasions.
If you will give me your word and swear not to vex me or my
friend, I will arrange it so that you can see the place and
everything else. And, let me add, it's been many months
that this friend of mine has been enjoying her. The regard I
have for you, and the many favors that you out of your goodness, have done for me, prompt me to make this known to
you. Now you must do as seems best to you. To me it is
enough to have done my duty in this matter, which my obligation to you required."

At this speech Signor Timbreo was dumbfounded and beside himself, almost indeed out of his senses with emotion.
But when he had stood there a good while, a thousand
thoughts revolving in his head until bitter and (so it seemed
to him) just anger overcame the fervent and loyal love he

held for the beautiful Fenicia, he sighed and answered the young man as follows:

"My friend, I can only be eternally obliged to you, seeing how lovingly you care for me and my honor. One day I will show with concrete results how much I am in your debt. For now, I give you all thanks possible. And since you willingly offer to arrange for me to see what I never could have imagined, I pray you, by the love that impelled you to warn me of this fact, go unhesitatingly with your friend. I promise you, on my faith as a true knight, to do no harm to you or him, and to keep this thing a secret always so that your friend can go on enjoying his love in peace. I ought to have been better advised from the first and to have kept my eyes open, inquiring more diligently and minutely into the whole affair."

"Signor," said the young man finally to Signor Timbreo, "this very night, at the third hour, go to the house of Master Lionato, and from those ruined buildings facing out on his garden you will be able to keep watch."

Opposite this hiding place stood the facade of the palazzo of Signor Lionato containing a room of some antiquity at whose windows (open day and night) Fenicia used now and then to appear, because from that side the beauty of the garden might best be enjoyed. Master Lionato and his family, on the other hand, lived in another part of the house, for this palazzo was old and large and roomy enough not only for the household of a gentleman but for the court of a prince.

Now, when everything had been settled on, the deceitful young man went on his way to find the treacherous Girondo, to whom he told all that had been agreed upon with Signor Timbreo Cardona. Signor Girondo was greatly pleased by this, since it seemed to him that his plan was a masterpiece. When the appointed hour arrived, the disloyal Girondo arrayed a servant of his, one whom he had already instructed in what he was to do, in gentlemanly fashion and perfumed him with the sweetest of scents. Then this perfumed servant accompanied the young man who had spoken with Signor Timbreo, while close behind them followed still another man with a ladder on his shoulder.

Who, now, could fully describe Signor Timbreo's state of mind or tell how numerous and how varied were the thoughts that passed through his mind all that day? For my part, I know that I should wear myself out, and all in vain. This overcredulous and unhappy nobleman, blinded with the veil of jealousy, ate next to nothing that day, and anyone who took a look at him would have thought he seemed more dead than alive. Half an hour before the time agreed upon, still thinking it impossible that Fenicia would have given herself as prey to another, he went and hid himself among the ruins in such a way that he could easily see anyone passing by. Then he reflected that young women are fickle, frivolous, giddy, disdainful, and ever hungry for new things. So, damning her one moment and excusing her the next, he waited for any sign of movement.

The night was not very dark, but it was very quiet. Soon he began to be aware of approaching footsteps and some indistinct conversation. Then he saw three men passing by and recognized clearly the young man who had warned him that morning, but the other two he was unable to identify. As the three passed before him he heard what the perfumed man, dressed like a lover, was saying to the one carrying the ladder: "See that you place the ladder carefully at the window without making any noise, because, when we were last here, the Signorina Fenicia told me that you had leaned it there too noisily. Do everything neatly and quietly."

Signor Timbreo heard clearly these words that were as sharp and piercing as kitchen spits in his heart. And although he was alone and had no weapon but his sword— whereas the passers-by were armed with lances in addition to their swords and probably wore armor to boot—so great and so pungent was the jealousy gnawing at his heart and so intense the wrath that inflamed him that he was close to rushing out of his hiding place and making a deadly assault, intending either to kill the one whom he judged to be the lover of Fenicia or else, by being slain, to end right then and there the heartache and excessive grief that he wretchedly suffered. But remembering the promise he had given, and believing that it would be extremely craven and villainous to attack those to whom he had given his word, filled with anger and vexation and wrath and fury, champing at the bit, he waited to see how it would come out.

The three men, arriving below the window of Master Lionato's house on that side we spoke of before, leaned the ladder very gently against the balcony, and the one who took the part of the lover climbed up and went into the house, as though he had an assignation within. When the disconsolate Signor Timbreo saw this, believing firmly that he who had climbed up had gone in to lie with Fenicia, he was assailed with the most intense grief imaginable and thought he was going to faint away. But so powerfully did his just anger (as it seemed to him) work in him that it chased away all jealousy. The fervent and sincere love he bore for Fenicia not only froze completely but turned into cruel hate. And so, not wanting to wait until his rival came out of the house, he left from the place where he had been hiding and went back to his inn.

The young man, who had seen him leave and who clearly recognized him, rightly guessed what the effect on him had been. And so, not long afterward he made a signal, and the servant who had climbed up came back down, and they went together to the house of Signor Girondo and told him the whole thing. He rejoiced at this and already began to think of himself as the possessor of the beautiful Fenicia.

Signor Timbreo, having slept little for the rest of the night, got up early and summoned the Messinese citizen who had served as his intermediary in seeking the hand in marriage of Fenicia from her father, and told him what he wanted him to do. The Messinese citizen, fully informed of the mind and will of Signor Timbreo, went at dinnertime to find Master Lionato, whom he found pacing up and down in the dining room waiting for dinner to be served, while Fenicia, also there, embroidered some work of silk in the company of her two younger sisters and her mother. When the Messinese citizen had arrived and had been graciously welcomed by Master Lionato, he said as follows: "Master Lionato, I have a message for you, and your wife and Fenicia as well, from Signor Timbreo." "You are welcome," replied Master Lionato. "What is it? Wife, and you, too, Fenicia, come hear with me what Signor Timbreo has to say to us." The emissary spoke in this manner: "It is often said that an envoy relating merely what is imposed on him ought not to suffer any penalty for doing so. I come to you sent by another person, and it grieves me infinitely to bring you news that must annoy you. Signor Timbreo di Cardona sends word to you, Master Lionato, and to your wife, that you should provide yourselves with another son-in-law, because he does not intend to have you for his in-laws—certainly not through any failing on the part of yourselves, whom he believes in and considers to be loyal and good, but because he has seen with his own eyes something in Fenicia that he would never have believed otherwise. And so he leaves it to you to provide for your own affairs as you wish. Now, to you, Fenicia, he says that the love he bore you ought never to have received the reward you have given him, and that you ought to provide yourself another husband in just the same way that you have taken another lover. You ought in fact to take the very man to whom you have given your virginity. He, Signor Timbreo, intends to have nothing further to do with you as one who will surely cuckold her husband."

Fenicia, hearing this bitter and vituperative message, was stricken as though dead. So were Master Lionato and his wife. Nevertheless, when he had regained life and breath, which almost failed him in his astonishment, Master Lionato spoke to the emissary as follows: "My friend, I always feared, from the very first time you spoke to me of this marriage, that Signor Timbreo would not hold steady in his request, since I knew then as I know now that I am a poor gentleman and not his social equal. Even so, it seems to me that, if he was having second thoughts about taking her as his wife, it would have been enough for him to say he didn't want her any more, rather than inflicting such a vindictive stain on her with this label of whore. True enough, anything is possible, but I know how my daughter has been brought up and what her habits are. Someday, I firmly believe, God in his great justice will cause the truth to be known."

When this answer had been given, the Messinese citizen went on his way. Master Lionato continued to hold to the opinion that Signor Timbreo had changed his mind about the marital alliance because he was debasing himself too much and falling off from his ancestors. The lineage of Master Lionato was in fact venerable and noble and highly regarded in Messina, but his wealth was only that of a private gentleman, even though ancient records proved that his forefathers had owned much land and many castles with wide-ranging jurisdiction. But through vicissitudes in the island's history and through civil war their seigniories had decayed, as one sees in other families as well. And so now the good father, never having discovered the least behavior in his daughter that was not chaste, concluded simply that the knight disdained their poverty and present lack of good fortune.

For her part, Fenicia, to whom any mishaps brought extreme sorrow and faintness of heart, hearing herself accused of a such a terrible wrong and being a tender and delicate young woman not accustomed to the blows of hostile fortune, abandoned herself to despair, wishing more for death than for life. And so, afflicted by the most profound and penetrating of sorrows, she sank down as though dead and, suddenly losing all the color in her complexion, resembled more a marble statue than a living creature. She was picked up and carried to bed, where, with warm clothes and other remedies, her fallen spirits were recalled to her in short order. And when they sent for the doctor, the news spread through all Messina that Fenicia, the daughter of Master Lionato, was so gravely ill that her life was in danger. When they heard this news, many gentle ladies, relatives and friends, came to visit the disconsolate Fenicia, and when they understood the occasion of her sickness, they busied themselves as best they could to comfort her. And as usually happens when lots of ladies are involved, they said different things about this piteous affair but generally agreed in rebuking Signor Timbreo with bitter censure.

The greater part of them were around the bed of the sick young lady when Fenicia, having perfectly understood what they had been saying, caught her breath as best she could and, seeing that for pity of her nearly all of them were in tears, in a weak voice begged them all to be silent. Then she faintly spoke as follows:

[Fenicia urges them to accept God's will, complaining not against the fact of her repudiation but rather the manner in which it was done, and asserting the dignity of her family. She wonders if perhaps God has done this to spare her the pride and arrogance that might have come through her elevation to such a high social station through the marriage. She prays that God may open Signor Timbreo's eyes, not so that she can marry him but so that her reputation can be cleared. She knows that she is innocent in the eyes of God, to whom she commends her soul. Thereupon Fenicia is so stricken that her doctors give her up for lost and she is mourned by her distraught family.]

Five or six hours passed by, and the order was given for Fenicia's burial on the following day. When the throng of ladies had left, her mother, more dead than alive, kept a relative with her—the wife of a brother of Master Lionato— and the two of them together, not wanting to have anyone else with them, ordered water to be put on the fire and shut themselves up in the room, where, undressing Fenicia, they began to wash her with warm water. The bewildered vital spirits of Fenicia, having taken a walk for some seven hours or so, returned to their proper function when her cold limbs were being washed. Giving manifest signs that she was alive, the young woman began to open her eyes a little. The mother and her sister-in-law nearly cried out in astonishment. But taking courage they put their hands against her heart and felt it give some movement. At this they were firmly convinced that the young woman was alive. And so, with warm clothes and other inducements, without making any noise, they brought Fenicia to the point of being almost completely herself again. Opening her eyes, she said with a deep sigh, "Alas, where am I?" "Don't you see," said her mother, "that you are here with me and your aunt? Such a deep swoon came upon you that we thought you were dead, but, God be praised, you are alive." "Ah, how much better it would be," answered Fenicia, "if I were dead indeed and free of my worries!" "My daughter," said her mother and her aunt, "you must live, since it pleases God, and he will provide a remedy for all things."

At this the mother, hiding the joy she felt, opened a door of the room a little and sent for Master Lionato, who came right away. There is no need to ask if he was happy when he saw his daughter restored to herself. Turning over many things in his mind, he decided first of all that no one should know of this matter, choosing instead to send the young woman out of Messina to the villa of the very brother whose wife was then with them. And so, when they had restored the young woman with delicacies to eat and costly wine, and when she had gotten back her former beauty and strength, he sent for his brother and instructed him fully in what he wanted him to do. The arrangement they made was as follows: Master Girolamo (such was the name of the brother of Master Lionato) was to conduct Fenicia on the following night to his own house and there keep her in secrecy in the company of his wife. And then, when he had provided what was necessary in his villa, early one morning Master Girolamo sent his wife there with Fenicia, along with one of his own daughters and one of Fenicia's sisters, she being thirteen or fourteen years old, whereas Fenicia was sixteen. He did this so that when Fenicia had grown older and had changed in appearance, as happens with maturation, he might then in two or three years marry her off under another name.

[Master Lionato orders a funeral suited to his daughter's rank, buries her coffin with ceremony, and emblazons on her stone monument an epitaph lamenting her cruel fate and protesting her innocence. Signor Timbreo soon begins to have second thoughts, wondering if the man he witnessed might have entered the window to see some other lover. Signor Girondo too is smitten in conscience. Asking Signor Timbreo to come with him to the church where Fenicia's tomb is placed, Signor Girondo admits what he has done and begs to be killed for his crimes. His confession elicits instead a tearful pardon from Signor Timbreo and a request for assistance in doing everything possible to restore Fenicia's good name. The remorse of the two knights in the presence of Master Lionato wins his pardon in turn, and he requests that Signor Timbreo agree to marry a lady of Master Lionato's choosing so long as she is pleasing to Signor Timbreo. Fenicia, still in concealment, is glad to learn of this agreement and of her recovered reputation.

Even though all seems well now, a year or more is allowed to pass, during which time Fenicia grows more and more beautiful. Her sister Belfiore also flowers into womanhood. Escorted at last to the country villa by Master Lionato, the two knights are struck by the young ladies' beauty. Signor Timbreo does not recognize Fenicia, who is presented to him by the name of Lucilla, though a vague stirring in his heart reminds him of Fenicia and increases his love for this lady. He marries her, and at the wedding feast expresses once more his remorse and sense of loss for what he has done. The revelation of Fenicia's identity is the reward for his constancy and devotion. Signor Girondo begs forgiveness anew, is welcomed into the happy group, and successfully pleads for the hand of Belfiore. A double wedding ensues in which Signor Timbreo, having wedded "Lucilla," is now bound in matrimony to his Fenicia. They all prepare to return to Messina, where they are honored by the court of King Piero and his queen and are given a handsome settlement. Master Lionato profits, too, from the royal bounty.]

La Prima Parte de le Novelle del Bandello was first published in Lucca in 1554. This new translation is based on that edition.

Further Reading

Berger, Harry, Jr. "Against the Sink-a-Pace: Sexual and Family Politics in *Much Ado About Nothing.*" *Shakespeare Quarterly* 33 (1982): 302–313. Berger explores the social values and practices that generate both Hero's near-tragedy and Beatrice's wariness of marriage. Males in the play are unable to free themselves of the patriarchal and mysogynist "assumptions of their community," and, accordingly, the comic resolution is unable to resolve convincingly the social tensions and contradictions that have become articulate.

Berry, Ralph. "Problems of Knowing." *Shakespeare's Comedies: Explorations in Form*. Princeton, N.J.: Princeton Univ. Press, 1972. Berry finds a unifying principle for the play's three plots in their common concern with "the limits and methods of knowledge." The verb "to know" occurs with striking frequency in the play, and its action and emotion emerge from the fact that characters are denied reliable means of knowing, depending rather upon the unreliable evidence of eye and ear.

Cook, Carol. " 'The Sign and Semblance of Her Honor': Reading Gender Difference in *Much Ado About Nothing.*" *PMLA* 101 (1986): 186–202. Reading the "merry war" between Beatrice and Benedick as a symptom of the sexual conflicts of Messina, Cook finds that the play's ending in multiple marriages leaves conspicuously unresolved the social and psychological tensions that are revealed by the anxious joking about cuckoldry and indeed in the very plot of a young man too easily persuaded that his lady is unfaithful to him and who can be regenerated and forgiven only after he thinks that he has caused her death.

Evans, Bertrand. *Shakespeare's Comedies*, pp. 68–87. Oxford: Clarendon Press, 1960. Evans patiently traces the play's witty exploitation of the different levels of awareness among characters and the audience. The play is structured around eight "practices," or plots, which are designed to lead characters into error but which finally are resolved in the play's "joyful close."

Fergusson, Francis. *"The Comedy of Errors* and *Much Ado*

About Nothing." Sewanee Review 62 (1954): 24–37. Rpt. in *The Human Image in Dramatic Literature.* Garden City, N.Y.: Doubleday, 1957; Gloucester, Mass.: P. Smith, 1969. Rpt. also in *Shakespeare's Comedies: An Anthology of Modern Criticism,* ed. Laurence Lerner. Harmondsworth and Baltimore: Penguin, 1967; and in *Discussions of Shakespeare's Romantic Comedy,* ed. Herbert Weil, Jr. Boston: D. C. Heath, 1966. Fergusson uses *Much Ado* to explore the nature of laughter and comedy itself. He compares the play to the farce of *The Comedy of Errors,* and finds that *Much Ado* extends and deepens the comedy of mistaken identities of the earlier play through its richer poetic texture and festive form.

Hays, Janice. "Those 'Soft and Delicate Desires': *Much Ado* and the Distrust of Women." In *The Woman's Part: Feminist Criticism of Shakespeare,* ed. Carolyn Ruth Swift Lenz, Gayle Greene, and Carol Thomas Neely. Urbana, Ill.: Univ. of Illinois Press, 1980. For Hays, the Hero-Claudio plot is a "ritual action" in which male fear and distrust of women is articulated and purged. Claudio must learn to move beyond his anxieties to trust and to be trustworthy, and the action works to develop his willingness to open up to emotional possibilities that his self-centeredness has denied him.

Hunter, Robert Grams. *"Much Ado About Nothing." Shakespeare and the Comedy of Forgiveness.* New York and London: Columbia Univ. Press, 1965. For Hunter, *Much Ado* is the first of Shakespeare's comedies of forgiveness, revealing the paradigmatic Christian pattern of sin/contrition/forgiveness. Claudio's sin is the failure to "trust love absolutely." He comes, however, to recognize his error, and the play allows an audience, like Messinan society, to forgive him, seeing him as "an image of its own frailty."

Jorgensen, Paul A. "Much Ado About *Nothing." Redeeming Shakespeare's Words.* Berkeley and Los Angeles: Univ. of California Press, 1962. In an essay exploring the rich significations of the word "nothing" available to Elizabethans, Jorgensen examines a number of Shakespearean uses of the word, including its appearance in the play's title.

Kirsch, Arthur. *"Much Ado About Nothing." Shakespeare*

and the Experience of Love. Cambridge: Cambridge Univ. Press, 1981. Kirsch uses the insights of Freudian psychology and Christian theology to explore the comedy's presentation of the "problems of narcissism." Its three plots, linked, he sees, by "analogies of action and language," demonstrate the possibilities of transcending shallow egotism in a comic triumph of humor, faith, and love.

Leggatt, Alexander. *"Much Ado About Nothing." Shakespeare's Comedy of Love.* London: Methuen; New York: Barnes and Noble, 1974. In the "interplay of formality and naturalism," Leggatt discovers a unity in the play's two romantic plots that serves to complicate the easy antithesis between them that many have seen. The Hero-Claudio plot in its very conventionality is rooted in the "familiar rhythms of life"; the Beatrice-Benedick plot, for all its richly individualized character, is finally seen "as a matter of convention."

Levin, Richard A. "Crime and Cover-up in Messina." *Love and Society in Shakespearean Comedy: A Study of Dramatic Form and Content.* Newark, Del.: Univ. of Delaware Press, 1985. Finding the play's comic action darkened by the unacknowledged anxieties and insecurities of characters in the romantic plots, Levin focuses on the social tensions and contradictions revealed within the world of Messina. The comedy's happy end is achieved only by attributing all malice to Don John and by a too-eager acceptance of the characters' perfunctory repentance.

Nevo, Ruth. "Better than Reportingly." *Comic Transformations in Shakespeare.* London: Methuen, 1980. Nevo examines the "equilibrium" established between the play's two romantic plots. In each, deception works to make manifest what has been "latent," and each transforms its participants to meet the demands of the conventions of both comedy and marriage.

Ormerod, David. "Faith and Fashion in *Much Ado About Nothing.*" *Shakespeare Survey* 25 (1972): 93–105. Ormerod structures his reading of the play around the opposition of "faith" and "fashion." Faith, identified with the mythological figure of Hercules, is the emotional and spiritual condition that resists appearances and makes love possible, but fashion, identified with the blind Cupid, is the commitment to the world of deceptive senses that destroys and "deforms."

Ornstein, Robert. *"Much Ado About Nothing." Shakespeare's Comedies: From Roman Farce to Romantic Mystery.* Newark, Del.: Univ. of Delaware Press, 1986. Ornstein finds in the interrelatedness of its two plots that the play asserts the moral primacy of an "unassuming decency" over the "moral superiority that leads to contempt." The comic ending celebrates the triumph of trust over faithlessness, but "nothing that is painful is forgotten": the wedding scene necessarily reminds us of the agonies of the aborted wedding earlier.

Prouty, Charles Tyler. *The Sources of "Much Ado About Nothing."* New Haven, Conn.: Yale Univ. Press, 1950. Examining the source material and its relation to Shakespeare's play, Prouty traces the connections between the two romantic plots and considers the nature of the main plot, especially the character of Claudio. In addition, he provides a text of Peter Beverley's *History of Ariodanto and Genevra* (1566), an English adaptation of the story from Ariosto's *Orlando Furioso,* which serves as the ultimate source of the Hero-Claudio plot.

Rossiter, A. P. *"Much Ado About Nothing."* In *Angel with Horns and Other Shakespeare Lectures,* ed. Graham Storey. London: Longmans, Green, 1961. Rpt. in *Shakespeare, The Comedies: A Collection of Critical Essays,* ed. Kenneth Muir. Englewood Cliffs, N.J.: Prentice-Hall, 1965. Rossiter attempts to account for the highly wrought wit of *Much Ado,* which he finds as much in the interrelatedness of the plots as in the inventiveness of the language. Language and structure emerge from the play's concern with misapprehension and misprision; the play is a comedy of mistaken identities in which, above all, characters mistake their own natures and needs.

Siegel, Paul N. "The Turns of the Dance: An Essay on *Much Ado About Nothing." Shakespeare in His Time and Ours.* Notre Dame, Ind.: Univ. of Notre Dame Press, 1968. Siegel traces the parallels between and the patterning of the two romantic plots. Beatrice and Benedick repeat with significant variations the actions of Hero and Claudio; the couples are united only at the end in the dance that confirms and celebrates the comic ending.

WILLIAM SHAKESPEARE was born in Stratford-upon-Avon in April, 1564, and his birth is traditionally celebrated on April 23. The facts of his life, known from surviving documents, are sparse. He was one of eight children born to John Shakespeare, a merchant of some standing in his community. William probably went to the King's New School in Stratford, but he had no university education. In November 1582, at the age of eighteen, he married Anne Hathaway, eight years his senior, who was pregnant with their first child, Susanna. She was born on May 26, 1583. Twins, a boy, Hamnet (who would die at age eleven), and a girl, Judith, were born in 1585. By 1592 Shakespeare had gone to London, working as an actor and already known as a playwright. A rival dramatist, Robert Greene, referred to him as "an upstart crow, beautified with our feathers." Shakespeare became a principal shareholder and playwright of the successful acting troupe the Lord Chamberlain's men (later, under James I, called the King's men). In 1599 the Lord Chamberlain's men built and occupied the Globe Theatre in Southwark near the Thames River. Here many of Shakespeare's plays were performed by the most famous actors of his time, including Richard Burbage, Will Kempe, and Robert Armin. In addition to his 37 plays, Shakespeare had a hand in others, including *Sir Thomas More* and *The Two Noble Kinsmen*, and he wrote poems, including *Venus and Adonis* and *The Rape of Lucrece*. His 154 sonnets were published, probably without his authorization, in 1609. In 1611 or 1612 he gave up his lodgings in London and devoted more and more of his time to retirement in Stratford, though he continued writing such plays as *The Tempest* and *Henry VIII* until about 1613. He died on April 23, 1616, and was buried in Holy Trinity Church, Stratford. No collected edition of his plays was published during his lifetime, but in 1623 two members of his acting company, John Heminges and Henry Condell, published the great collection now called the First Folio.

Contributors

DAVID BEVINGTON, Phyllis Fay Horton Professor of Humanities at the University of Chicago, is editor of *The Complete Works of Shakespeare* (Scott, Foresman, 1980) and of *Medieval Drama* (Houghton Mifflin, 1975). His latest critical study is *Action Is Eloquence: Shakespeare's Language of Gesture* (Harvard University Press, 1984).

DAVID SCOTT KASTAN, Professor of English and Comparative Literature at Columbia University, is the author of *Shakespeare and the Shapes of Time* (University Press of New England, 1982).

JAMES HAMMERSMITH, Associate Professor of English at Auburn University, has published essays on various facets of Renaissance drama, including literary criticism, textual criticism, and printing history.

ROBERT KEAN TURNER, Professor of English at the University of Wisconsin–Milwaukee, is a general editor of the New Variorum Shakespeare (Modern Language Association of America) and a contributing editor to *The Dramatic Works in the Beaumont and Fletcher Canon* (Cambridge University Press, 1966–).

JAMES SHAPIRO, who coedited the bibliographies with David Scott Kastan, is Assistant Professor of English at Columbia University.

❖

JOSEPH PAPP, one of the most important forces in theater today, is the founder and producer of the New York Shakespeare Festival, America's largest and most prolific theatrical institution. Since 1954 Mr. Papp has produced or directed all but one of Shakespeare's plays—in Central Park, in schools, off and on Broadway, and at the Festival's permanent home, The Public Theater. He has also produced such award-winning plays and musical works as *Hair*, *A Chorus Line*, *Plenty*, and *The Mystery of Edwin Drood*, among many others.

THE
COMPLETE WORKS OF
WILLIAM SHAKESPEARE